John Locke
A Descriptive Bibliography

THOEMMES

JOHN LOCKE
A DESCRIPTIVE BIBLIOGRAPHY

JEAN S. YOLTON

THOEMMES PRESS

Published by Thoemmes Press, 1998

Thoemmes Press
11 Great George Street
Bristol BS1 5RR, England

US office: Distribution and Marketing
22883 Quicksilver Drive
Dulles, Virginia 20166, USA

ISBN 1 85506 449 9

© Jean S. Yolton, 1998

All rights reserved. No part of this publication may be
reproduced, stored in a retrieval system, or transmitted in
any way or by any means, electronic, mechanical, photocopying,
recording or otherwise, without the written permission of
the copyright holder. Enquiries to the publisher.

British Library Cataloguing-in-Publication Data
A CIP record of this set is available from the British Library.

Title-page illustration
by Joseph-Marie Vien (*c.*1770), engraved by — François

Typeset at MS Typesetting, Cambridge.
Printed in the UK by Creative Print and Design Group Ltd.

This book is printed on acid-free paper, sewn, and
cased in a durable buckram cloth.

CONTENTS

Introduction, Chronology, Location Symbols, Finding List of
Bibliographical Materials — vii

Chapter
I. Letters on Toleration (nos. 1–28) — 1
II. Two Treatises of Government (nos. 29–60) — 29
III. An Essay concerning Human Understanding (nos. 61–154) — 67
   Translations 120   Abridgements and Abstracts 155
IV. Papers on Money (nos. 155–164) — 191
V. Some Thoughts concerning Education (nos. 165–228) — 209
VI. The Reasonableness of Christianity, and its 'Vindications' (nos. 229–247) — 271
VII. Letters to Edward Stillingfleet (nos. 248–250) — 295
VIII. Occasional Contributions to Other Works
   A: Poems (nos. 251–257) — 305
   B: Contributions to Learned Journals, etc. (nos. 258–276) — 313
IX. Posthumous Publications from Manuscripts (nos. 277–345) — 329
X. Correspondence (nos. 346–362) — 385
XI. Works, Collected and Selected (nos. 363–373) — 399
XII. Doubtful and Spurious Works — 431
XIII. Contemporary Criticism (to 1800) — 439

Special Indexes — 469
General Index — 505
Illustrations — 515

JOHN LOCKE: A DESCRIPTIVE BIBLIOGRAPHY

INTRODUCTION

Interest in the life and writings of John Locke, which was so strong in the eighteenth century, has undergone a significant growth period in this, the twentieth, especially since the Lovelace Collection of Locke manuscripts came to the Bodleian Library, Oxford. In 1942 the collection was deposited in the Bodleian Library for safe-keeping during the war. It was finally purchased from the Earl of Lovelace in 1947, with the help of the Pilgrim Trust and of the Delegates of the Clarendon Press.[1] In his last will and testament, Locke bequeathed all his manuscripts and all interleaved books to his cousin Peter King, later first Baron King. Aside from a few bequests (to Anthony Collins and Lady Masham) his library of over three thousand items was divided between King and Francis Cudworth Masham, the son of Sir Francis Masham and his second wife Damaris Cudworth, daughter of the Cambridge Platonist Ralph Cudworth.[2] Although the Masham moiety was largely dispersed in the late eighteenth century, some items have occasionally surfaced. Of the King moiety, some 60 per cent are intact, chiefly in the Mellon collection of approximately 850 volumes which Paul Mellon purchased from the Earl of Lovelace in 1960 and presented to the Bodleian in 1977. Mellon made further donations of Locke manuscripts in 1960 and 1963. Dr. E. S. de Beer, Mellon and the Pilgrim Trust have enabled the library to purchase other Locke manuscripts, also books formerly owned by Locke, some from the Masham moiety.[3]

These two acquisitions and their subsequent availability to scholars have given renewed life to Locke scholarship. In fact in the five years following 1948, over one hundred studies, books and journal articles appeared; in the five-year period of 1966 to 1970 over 240 studies appeared, more than in all

[1] P. A. Long, *A Summary Catalogue of the Lovelace Collection of the Papers of John Locke in the Bodleian Library* (Oxford: Printed for the Library at the University Press, 1959), p. *vii*. Most students of manuscript material in the Lovelace Collection must use microfilm copies, to avoid wear and tear. Copies of the microfilms are available in some U. S. libraries, e.g. at Yale University.

[2] See John Harrison and Peter Laslett's *The Library of John Locke*, Second edition (Oxford: Clarendon Press, 1971), pp. 8-9, 54-61. Hereafter cited as L.L.

[3] See the *Bodleian Library Record* 7 no. 4 (1964) for P. Long's detailing an additional donation of manuscripts by Mellon, and a Bodleian ms. purchase. Further records of acquisitions of books from Locke's library are found in the *Record*, 10 no. 6 (May 1982): 376-82; 11 no. 2 (May 1983): 121-5; 11 no. 3 (Nov. 1983): 191-2; 11 no. 4 (May 1984): 247-51. A note about the establishment of the Locke Room in the Bodleian to house the collection is found in the *Record* 10 no. 1 (Dec. 1975): 4-5.

the years from 1900 to 1933. This increase in the number of studies appears likely to continue, or at least the quantity is holding steady.

The inception of the Clarendon Edition of the Works of John Locke revealed how little bibliographical information about Locke's own publications was available. H. O. Christophersen's *Bibliographical Introduction to the Study of John Locke* (1930) has been the chief resource about early editions and criticism. Now that authoritative texts are being prepared for the Clarendon Edition, the need for a bibliographic analysis of his works and their printing history has become urgent. A history of his publications will, I hope, be of great use to historians of philosophy, politics, economics and religion.

Filling this need is the main purpose of this bibliography. In fact, I have two aims in mind. My first is fully to describe each published printing or translation of his writings, noting the improvements and changes he made to them in his lifetime, and to point out where later printings made changes, usually without authorial sanction. This bibliography will therefore attempt to supply editors with sufficient information to prepare authoritative editions of his writings. I have included posthumous publications, even when they were published after 1800.

A second purpose, and I hope reward, is that this work will show the dissemination and therefore the influence of Locke's writings throughout Europe, not just in the English-speaking world. The range of languages in which translations were made, and the frequency of such translations is significant.

Locke was deeply concerned to see his books accurately printed, a concern often thwarted. Though he contributed a few poems to some collections published in 1654 and 1662, to two editions of a work by Sydenham published in 1668 and 1676 (no. 256–7), and transmitted a brief note for publication in the *Philosophical Transactions* of the Royal Society in 1697 (no. 260), he published nothing else until he was fifty-four years old, and then not separately. His first important work was 'Méthode nouvelle de dresser des recueuils' (no. 266) printed in Le Clerc's *Bibliothèque universelle et historique* in 1686. This work was followed by an abstract of his forthcoming *Essay concerning Human Understanding* for the same journal in 1688 (no. 273).

He himself wrote of his reluctantance to publish: in the 'Epistle to the Reader', he says his *Essay concerning Human Understanding* 'was not meant for those, that had already mastered this Subject [human understanding] . . . but for my own Information, and the Satisfaction of a few Friends . . .' He there speaks of those who '*advised* me to publish it as it is, and since I have been *brought* to let it go abroad . . .' (my italics). 'I have so little affection to be in print that, if I were not flattered this Essay might be of some use to others, . . . I should have confined it to the view of some Friends, who gave the first occasion to it.' His work on education was not published when written; he stated in the dedication that, because he felt his abilities did not match his words, he 'needed Exhortations or Importunities from others' to do so.

When Locke decided to see his works printed, there followed a spate of publications based on the material he had assembled over previous years, some (in his lifetime at least) published anonymously, such as the letters on toleration, the *Two Treatises of Government*, *The Reasonableness of Christianity* and its two *Vindications*. In the catalogue of his library, 'the most remarkable thing about the way Locke chose to enter up his holdings is that he succeeded in concealing the fact that he himself had written any Books other than the *Essay concerning Humane Understanding*, the work on *Education*, and the works on *Money*. *The Reasonableness of Christianity* and its two *Vindications*, the *Letters on Toleration* and, above all, the *Two Treatises of Government* were treated in his catalogues as if he no more knew who wrote them than he did most of the authors of other anonymous works which he possessed . . . he seems [in the case of his *Epistola de Tolerantia*] to be betraying an anxiety to keep the facts about the books he published not simply from his critics or his friends, but even from himself.'[4]

In the Lovelace Collection of manuscripts already referred to, there are lists of persons to whom Locke gave, or considered giving, copies of those publications whose authorship he acknowledged in his lifetime. Such lists are to be found in Bodleian Library MS Locke f. 29, pp. 33, 144 and 158; and c.25, ff. 50–55. Where such lists exist, they are transcribed and recipients identified in the notes to the appropriate entry. There are no lists for the anonymous works.

Locke also kept many papers relating to his contracts to publish his works. Where these exist (in the Lovelace Collection), they are mentioned under the individual editions. Locke was also concerned about authors' and booksellers' rights. Among his papers (Bodleian MS Locke b.4 fols. 75–78) are materials relating to the termination of the printing Licensing Act of 1695: extracts from 'An Act for preventing abuses in printing seditious treasonable and unlicensed books and pamphlets and for regulating printing and printing presses' (14 Car. II, c.33), with his observations on them; a copy of a bill in the hand of John Freke 'for better regulating of printing and printing presses' with Locke's notes on some passages in it; and a copy of the eighteen 'Reason [sic] of the Commons ag<ains>t Reviveing the Printing act <16>95.' These papers are printed as an Appendix in *Corr.* v. 785–96. They are chiefly of interest in showing Locke's concern about the ownership of copyright.

Dr. John Hudson, Bodley's Librarian, wrote to Locke on February 6, 1703, asking if he would give copies of his works to the library (*Corr.* 3248; vii.743–4). Locke answered affirmatively on March 4th (ibid. 3261; vii. 755), and requested his publishers the Churchills to send the *Essay*, the *Letter to Bishop Stillingfleet* and the succeeding '*Replies*', as well as the papers on money and *Some Thoughts concerning Education*. In his acknowledgement (ibid. 3270; vii.764) Dr. Hudson wrote 'I shall not presume to enquire, whether these be all you intended us', probably implying he would like the

---

[4] L.L., p. 43.

library to receive any works published anonymously. In a codicil to his will written in September 1704 (see Chap. XIII, C1714–1) he gave 'to the public library of the University of Oxford' the three letters on toleration, to be bound together with Proast's *The Argument of the Letter concerning Toleration Briefly Consider'd and Answer'd* and Proast's *Third Letter concerning Toleration* (cf. Chap. XIII). He further gave a copy of the *Two Treatises of Government* and *The Reasonableness* and its *Vindications*. In the same codicil he requested that the next (fifth, 1706) edition of the *Essay* 'well-bound' and the third and fourth volumes of the Churchills' *Collection of Voyages* be presented to the Bodleian by the executor of his will.

The codicil is the first evidence we have that Locke was the author of these works. There are other publications falsely attributed to him, especially *A Commonplace Book to the Holy Bible* and *An Account of Mr. Lock's Religion*, an anonymous publication now known to be written by John Milner (cf. Chap. XII).

It is unfortunate that no copy-texts of Locke's publications as printed survive. There are three drafts of the *Essay* and two drafts of the *Education*, none of them printer's copy. There is an abstract of the *Essay* in the hand of Locke's amanuensis Sylvester Brounower in the Lovelace Collection (MS Locke c.28 fols. 52–82) dated 1687, but it is not the original text of the 'Extrait' published in Le Clerc's journal, the *Bibliothèque universelle*. Since the Churchills would have recognised Locke's handwriting, I assume that the copy for those works whose authorship he concealed were all in the hand of an amanuensis (in most cases presumably Brounower).

Whenever the stock of Locke's booksellers, chiefly Awnsham and John Churchill, appeared to be low, they would write to Locke to see if he wished to make corrections or additions before proceeding with a new 'printing' (or as we would now say, a new edition). Locke usually sent additions or corrections. In order to establish Locke's ultimate intentions therefore, the later editions to which he contributed must be considered along with Locke's original text. New errors in typesetting would arise; some old errors never were corrected. For example, in the *Education* in the section on geography (1693 ed., §168) Locke wrote: 'I now live in the House with a Child, whom his Mother has so well instructed this way in geography, that he . . . could readily point being asked, to any County upon the Globe, or any country in the Map of England . . .' In the fourth (1699) and even the fifth (1705) editions the word 'County' has been corrected to 'Country' but the 'Country in the Map of England' remains 'Country', and so remains in later editions.

There are scattered references in his correspondence to his dissatisfaction with the accuracy of the printing. The first recorded comment is to Edward Clarke on November 2, 1692 (*Corr.* 1557; iv. 564) showing Locke's wish to proofread the sheets before the Churchills publish his *Third Letter for Toleration*. Clarke had acted as an intermediary with the publishers, presumably to keep Locke's authorship a secret. Later, on March 12, 1694 (ibid. 1719; v. 30) Locke again wrote to Clarke: 'I had taken some pains to ctifie the faults yet remaining in the book [*Two Treatises of Government*] ou sent me, And to make the edition as good as may be: But there is noe contesting with ever lasting unalterable neglect. . . . Its fate is it seems to be the worst printed that ever booke was, and tis in vain for any one to labour against it.' Again to Clarke on March 19, 1694 (*Corr.* 1723; v. 35): 'But truly I am mightily discouraged from doing any thing more [in supplying corrections] where I meet with nothing but repeated negligence . . . And pray rub up his [Churchill's] carelessness a little. And let him know you find, as far as you have had time to look into it, this second ten times worse than the first edition' [of *Two Treatises*]. But his most scathing comments on the book trade in general are found in a letter to Anthony Collins of June 9, 1704 (*Corr.* 3556; viii. 314-5). The catalyst for these remarks was a poorly executed binding of a Greek Testament, a chore the arrangement of which Collins had undertaken. Locke writes: 'Books seem to me to be pestilent things, and infect all that trade in them, i e all but one sort of men, with something very perverse and brutal. Printers, Binders, Sellers and others that make a trade and gain out of them have universally so odde a turne and corruption of mind that they have a way of dealeing peculiar to them selves, and not conformed to the good of society, and that general fairness that cements man kind. Whether it be that these instruments of truth and knowledg will not bear being subjected to any thing but those noble ends, without revengeing them selves on those who medle with them to any other purpose, and prostitute to mean and misbecomeing designes I will not enquire. The matter of fact I think you will find true, and there we will leave it, to those who sully them selves with printers ink. till they wholly expunge all the candor that nature gives, and become the worst sort of Black cattle.'

* * * * * *

This bibliography covers all editions and translations of Locke's publications to 1801. Because his first separately published work was in Latin, and because he himself is thought to have supervised others' translations into French (especially) or Latin, I have included a record of all known translations of each work in this order: original and English translation OR first English edition, followed by translations in alphabetical order of the language.

The first seven chapters are assigned to works separately published in Locke's lifetime, arranged in chronological order of their initial appearance. Chapter VIII covers occasional poems, and contributions to works by others including journals. Chapter IX covers all posthumous publications from Locke's manuscripts whenever published. The tenth chapter is devoted to collections of correspondence. Chapter XI covers collected works. Chapter XII examines spurious works and doubtful attributions. A final chapter provides a chronological listing of all known criticism to 1800.

Numeration. Each separately published edition in the first eleven chapters ha[s] been numbered consecutively by chronological date of imprint. For edition[s] coming late to my attention, I have used decimal increments, e.g. 147.1, 223.1. *Asterisks* have been used following a number to designate editions whose existence has been attested in a reliable source but either (a) I have not been able to examine one, or (b) there is no surviving copy: some may not have been published at all. The letters A, B, etc., have been used to distinguish issues and states. In the heading it is assumed that, unless otherwise stated, London is the place of publication.

Titles. The titles of all items separately published before 1801 are transcribed in quasi-facsimile. The titles of many editions were printed within a rule, usually a double rule; these are given in terms of inner vertical by horizontal, followed by outer measurements in millimeters, e.g. 'inner 146 × 83 mm, outer 154 × 91 mm'. The term **Oxford rule** (also **parallel** rule) is used to designate a bar or thick rule above a line or thin rule; sometimes these are noted as inverted (also called **total** rule). **French rule** (also called **swell** rule) is used to indicate a rule that thickens into a diamond shape in the center, a diamond elongated left and right into a line.

Collation. The format (folio, quarto, etc.) is followed by the size of the key copy in millimeters, untrimmed or uncut copy if I have found one. Significant size variations are noticed under '*Copies examined*'. The formula in terms of signatures precedes the pagination, with unnumbered pages indicated by italicization. Small brackets ([,]) especially in the collation are used when square brackets occur in the actual work. Here and elsewhere I use normal brackets ([,]) for editorial insertions.

Contents. The contents are given by signature and page number.

Illustrations. Description, size and placement; if on engraved plate, the size of the illustration and the size of the plate is indicated.

Text. Under this heading is given the technical information: usual number of lines to a page, the size of the text (or print block) area, with the space needed for the skeleton frame (headlines, marginal notes and direction lines) supplied within parentheses. The type of paper and kind of watermark, if any. Here are noted printers' ornaments when few in number. A separate paragraph, headed '*Ornaments*' is given when there are substantial numbers of them.

Half-titles. Half-titles are transcribed in quasi-facsimile, like titles.

HT = Head (caption, or drophead) title, from the first page of text, in quasi-facsimile.

Headlines or ***Running titles*** are transcribed, the latter in terms of verso-to-recto wording.

CW = Catchwords. A few selected catchwords are given for most printings, especially when they vary from a previous, page-for-page printing. As a novice bibliographer I examined some editions early in the history of this project without recording catchwords. Some of these, located solely in distant places, I have not been able to re-examine; in a few entries therefore catchwords are not noted. I have recorded the position of signatures occasionally in place of omitted CW. I have found them invaluable in distinguishing variant pages in Locke's *Further Considerations*, no. 160–162 (*pace* Gaskell's *New Introduction to Bibliography*, 1972, p. 333).

Signature positions. The position of signatures relative to the words in the lines immediately above them is given when it is helpful to identify line-by-line resetting of pages. They are also occasionally given for early editions (in place of catchwords) or when there are no CW (or none recorded) and are especially helpful when a title-leaf has been lost or mutilated.

Press figures. Many eighteenth-century English and American books (but rarely Irish or Scottish) have arabic figures, letters, asterisks or obelisks employed by the printers. They seldom occur before 1701. Obeluses and asterisks were frequently a mark of paper quality. Their presence in what may be an otherwise un-noteworthy reprint, has been recorded, chiefly by page numbers and signatures. In the case of some *Works* editions where there are two press figures per gathering (e.g., 300 figures for each 600-page volume in a 4-vol. quarto set), only the frequency and range of figures is given. In a few descriptions I have added a table of figures in terms of inner and outer sides of a forme (cf. no. 33, e.g.), but the figures are so randomly placed in most editions, that it seems of little use.

Notes. General discussion of printing circumstances and peculiarities of the specific item is given, together with any other relevant information, e.g. persons to whom Locke presented copies, how the text varies from a previous edition, etc. Any information relating to date of publication and price of a copy, when found, is included. Quotations from manuscripts follow the methods of transcription found in *Drafts for the Essay* . . . (ed. by P. H. Nidditch and G. A. J. Rogers, Oxford, 1990), pp. xx–xxvi.

References. Citations chiefly in terms of the most accessible sources, using the abbreviations cited below (pp. xxiii–xxix).

Notices. Announcements of the publication, sometimes with summaries of the content, are found in early scholarly journals, and are briefly listed if not included in *Notes*. *The London Gazette* is the chief source of publication date for many early editions, although one or two were advertised in *The Post-Boy*. 'Advertisements' found in the final column(s) of *The London Gazette*, a one-page sheet (two columns to a page) include brief notices of a few books published; for example, issue 2886 for 6-10 July 1693 includes 'Some Thoughts concerning Education. Printed for A. and J. Churchill, at the Black Swan in Pater-noster Row' (cf. no. 165). These brief announcements are mixed in with notices to creditors, offers of rewards for anyone returning runaway servants or deserters, stolen horses, and lost property notices. None of the advertisements for Locke's publications includes any further information, a price or even a 'Just Published' statement. Critical writings, other than 'notices' are listed in Chap. XIII.

Copies examined. Under this heading are the symbols for libraries owning copies that I have examined. It is not a full calendar of known locations; nor, though it is fairly exhaustive of those libraries, does it necessarily cover their complete holdings of Locke materials. Where information has been acquired by correspondence, square brackets have been used. For library symbols, see pp. xx–xxii below. The library owning the key copy examined, that which has served as a model, is recorded first, with its shelfmark. Many descriptions are based on books in the (John and Jean) Yolton collection.[5]

* * * * * *

It would be useful to include a separate chapter for a list of works dedicated to Locke. Fulton's bibliography of Robert Boyle lists forty-eight works dedicated to Boyle, published from 1651-1930. And one of Boyle's own works, *Memoirs for the Natural History of Human Blood* (1683/4; Fulton 146) was dedicated to 'The very Ingenious and Learned Doctor J.L.', probably meaning Locke (Locke's copy is not listed in his library catalogue). Such a chapter would be very short, since the only other dedications to him that I have found are these: Richard Burthogge's *An Essay upon Reason* (1694; L.L. 538); John Wynne's abridgement of the *Essay*. Burthogge's *Of the Soul of the World, and of Particular Souls, in a Letter to Mr. Lock* . . . (1699; L.L. 541) was addressed to Locke, but that is not a dedication. William Molyneux's *Dioptrica Nova* (1692) begins with a dedicatory letter to members of the Royal Society, which includes a passage warmly commending John Locke's *Essay concerning Human Understanding*. Jean Le Clerc dedicated vol. 1 of his *Logica* to Boyle; vol. 2, entitled 'Ontologia' was dedicated to Locke (1692; L.L. 762-3, 763 is a presentation copy). John Dunton's *The New Practice of Piety* (London, 1704), an enlarged edition of his *Religio bibliopolae*, is also dedicated to Locke. The anonymous *An Essay on Capacity and Genius*, attributed to William Andrew Mitchell (London, [1820?]) was dedicated 'To

---

[5] To be permanently housed in York University Library, North York, Ontario.

the Immortal Memory of John Locke.' There may be others, but I have not found them.

* * * * * *

I should like to thank Desmond Neill, Librarian Emeritus of Massey College, University of Toronto, for his helpful discussions about matters bibliographical. The late Robert Shackleton helped me greatly with his fund of knowledge, bibliographical insights and 'table-talk'. Richard Landon and Luba Hussel, Librarians of the Thomas Fisher Rare Books Library of the University of Toronto, not only opened the resources of that collection to me, but generously provided useful information whenever I asked for help. J. S. G. Simmons, Emeritus Fellow of All Souls College, Oxford, has been of tremendous help in connection with Russian materials. John Stephens, of Robin Waterfield, Ltd., Oxford, has assisted me in many ways, including imparting numerous informational ana. University-Professor Dr. Bernhard Fabian of the University in Münster has provided me with much useful information about books in the German language and/or printed in Germany. I should also like to express my gratitude to Prof. Gary W. Shanafelt, of McMurry University, Abilene, Texas, for supplying fraktur fonts, and helping with their installation, while I was working on the compilation of this manuscript.

I sincerely appreciate the award of a research grant from the Canada Council (now the Social Sciences and Humanities Research Council of Canada) in 1975, which enabled me to begin this bibliography. I must acknowledge the great debt I owe to many librarians for access to and use of their collections, especially the Oxford college libraries, the National Library of Scotland, the British Library, the Folger Shakespeare Library and, more important of all, that of Locke's own university, the Bodleian Library, Oxford.

I reserve my deepest gratitude to John Yolton, not only for the usual encouragement and helpful judgments of a husband, but for having chosen excellent places to teach, to spend sabbatical leaves, and for having been invited to so many universities to read papers and partake in conferences, most of them locations of the greatest libraries in Europe and North America.

September 1995
Piscataway, New Jersey

CHRONOLOGY

This table is planned to provide dates that should be serviceable for the publishing history of Locke's writings. It is not a chronological framework for a life of Locke, although significant biographical dates are included. The dates are given in Old-Style (or Julian) calendar, except that I have taken the year to begin January 1st (not March 25).

For many incidents in his life or publications precise dates do not exist. In the dates, a. (for *ante*) is to be taken to imply shortly before. In the dates for books, a precise date is to be taken as the earliest notice that the book had been, was, or was about to be published, and not necessarily as the day of publication.

This note and most of the information has been supplied from E. S. de Beer's edition of *The Correspondence of John Locke* (1976-89; no. 362).

1632	29 August. Locke born at Wrington, Somerset, near Bristol.
1646?	Admitted to Westminster School.
1652-67	Student of Christ Church, Oxford; usually resident in Oxford.
1656	14 February. Graduates B.A.
1658	29 June. Graduates M.A.
1660	11 December. Writes first treatise on the civil magistrate (published 1967 in *Two Tracts on Government*; no. 342).
	24 December. Elected lecturer in Greek at Christ Church.
1661 or 2	Composed second treatise on the civil magistrate (included in *Two Tracts on Government*).
1667	Spring? Joins Lord Ashley's household in London. Until November 1675 usually resides in London. Composed 'An Essay concerning Toleration' (cf. no. 330).
1668	23 November. Elected Fellow of the Royal Society.
1670	1 March. The Fundamental Constitutions of Carolina sealed (see no. 316, *Notes*).
1671	First drafts of the *Essay concerning Human Understanding* (called A and B).
1672	October-November. Visits Paris.
1673	15 October-21 December 1674. Locke secretary to the Council of Trade and Foreign Plantations.
1675	6 February. Locke graduates Bachelor of Medicine.
	12 November-March 1677. Locke travelling in France; resides usually in Montpellier 25 December to 15 March 1677.
1676	Autumn? Translates Nicole's three essays (cf. no. 313)

1677	April. Travelling; some time in Toulouse.
1677	23 May–29 June 1678. Usually resident in Paris.
1678	29 June–18 Nov. Second tour of France.
	18 Nov.–22 April 1679. Resides in Paris.
1679	30 April. Returns to London. Goes to Oxford in December.
1679–82?	Writes his *Two Treatises of Government*. Locke and James Tyrrell write in defence of toleration against Stillingfleet.
1683	21 January. Shaftesbury dies in Amsterdam.
	7 September. Locke in Rotterdam.
	9 September–5 August 1684. Locke resides in Amsterdam. Now writing a consecutive version of the *Essay*.
1684	9 July. First of letters to Edward Clarke on the education of his son (these became the basis for his *Some Thoughts concerning Education*).
	13 September–10 February 1689. Locke in the Netherlands, on tour, in Utrecht, Amsterdam, Cleves, etc.
	15 November. Deprived of his studentship at Christ Church, Oxford.
1685	Draft C of the *Essay*.
	13 May. Goes into hiding in Amsterdam.
1686	a.24 April. Locke sends Clarke transcripts of part of the *Essay*.
	Early September? His 'Méthode nouvelle de dresser des recueuils' published (no. 266).
1688	c. 27 January. The 'Extrait' of the *Essay* printed (no. 273). The *Abrégé* (no. 274) published probably about April.
1689	10 February. Leaves Holland.
	12 February. Locke returns to London. Resides there until July 1690, when he goes to Oates, the home of Sir Francis and Lady Masham.
1689	April. The *Epistola de tolerantia* published at Gouda.
	3 October. *A Letter concerning Toleration* licensed for publication.
	18 November. *Two Treatises of Government* advertised.
	Mid-December. The *Essay* published.
1690	24 June. *A Second Letter concerning Toleration* licensed for publication.
	Autumn. Several trips between his London lodgings and Oates; from about this time Oates is to be regarded as his home.
1691	27 November. *Some Considerations of the Consequences of the Lowering of Interest and Raising the Value of Money* licensed for publication
1692	20 June. *Third Letter for Toleration* licensed.
	23 November? *A Third Letter for Toleration* published.
1693	10 July. *Some Thoughts concerning Education* advertised.
	31 August. *Some Thoughts* licensed for publication.

	...ring? The second edition of *Two Treatises* published (*Corr.* says 30 March)
	March. One half share in *Essay concerning Human Understanding* assigned by T. Dring to the Churchills.
	c. 26 May. The second edition of the *Essay* published.
1695	*c.* 25 February. *Short Observations on a Printed Paper* published.
	26 April. 'A Letter in 3 partes concerning Tolera[ti]on' entered in the *Transcript*.
	Late June? The third edition of *Some Thoughts concerning Education* published ('now out', 2 July 1695).
	12 August. *The Reasonableness of Christianity* advertised.
	Autumn? The third edition of the *Essay* published (in press, 2 July)
	c. October. *A Vindication of the Reasonableness of Christianity* published.
	31 December. *Further Considerations concerning Raising the Value of Money* advertised.
1696	15 May. The Commission for Trade and Plantations (the Board of Trade) established; Locke appointed a commissioner.
1697	*a.* 17 March. *A Letter* (to Bishop Stillingfleet) published. *A Second Vindication of the Reasonableness of Christianity* published.
	a. 10 April. Writing 'The Conduct of the Understanding' for inclusion in the *Essay*.
	Early August. Pierre Coste joins the Masham household at Oates.
	Early September. *Mr. Locke's Reply* [to Stillingfleet's] *Answer to His Letter* published.
1698	2 July. Copy of *Mr. Locke's Reply* and 'Second Reply' by Stillingfleet entered in *Transcript* of Stationers Company Register.
	c. November. *Mr. Locke's Reply* [to Stillingfleet's] *Answer to His Second Letter* published. The fourth edition of *Some Thoughts concerning Education* published.
1699	11 December. The fourth edition of the *Essay* advertised.
1700	Late May? Coste's French translation of the *Essay* published.
1701	Late May. Burridge's Latin translation of the *Essay* published.
1702	5–6 May. Locke's last recorded visit to London.
1703	4 May. Locke's first extant letter to Anthony Collins.
1704	17 August. The first proofs of Locke's *Paraphrase and Notes on the Epistle to the Galatians*.
	28 October. Locke dies.

LOCATION SYMBOLS

For facilitating reference, the symbols for libraries given below are those used in two main sources. North American libraries are cited by the symbols used in common by the American Union List of Serials, the National Union Catalog of Pre-1956 Imprints, and the O.C.L.C. data base, with one exception: 'OC' for the Cincinnati and Hamilton County Public Library is too easily confused with 'Oc', the library of Christ Church, Oxford. The former has therefore been changed to 'OCin'. Symbols for United Kingdom and continental libraries are those used in the ESTC data base. For the few continental libraries I have visited which are not in the ESTC list, I have supplied brief citations, e.g. Han, Utr, etc. Symbols for those known only through correspondence are given within square brackets.

ABu	Aberdeen University Library
AMu	Amsterdam University Library
[BBR]	Bibliothèque royale Albert Ier, Brussels (by correspondence)
[Berlin]	or [Berlin (Potsd.S.)][6]
BRu	Bristol University Library
C	Cambridge University Library
	C (Keynes) indicates the Geoffrey Keynes Collection, now at the University Library.
CaBVaU	University of British Columbia Library
CaNSHDa	Dalhousie University Library, Nova Scotia
CaOHM	McMaster University Library, Hamilton, Ont.
CaOLW	University of Western Ontario Library
CaOTU	Thomas Fisher Rare Books Library, University of Toronto
CaQMM	McGill University Library
CaQMMO	Osler Library at McGill University
CaQQL	Laval University Library, Quebec
Cch	Library of Christ's College, Cambridge
Ck	King's College Library, Cambridge
	Ck (Keynes) indicates John Maynard Keynes Collection, now at King's College
CLaslett	Private collection of Peter Laslett, Cambridge

[6] Information from the union list at the Staatsbibliothek zu Berlin, supplied by Annette Wehmeyer. Libraries covered are Humboldt University in Berlin, the Berlin City Library; state libraries in Dresden, Jena and Gotha; and the University Library in Tübingen. Material at the Staatsbibliothek in Berlin is partly housed in the Unter den Linden building, and partly in another building on Potsdamer Strasse (indicated by '[Berlin (Potsd.S.)]'.

CLU-C	William Andrews Clark Library, University of California at Los Angeles
Ct	Trinity College, Cambridge
CtY	Yale University Library
DFo	Folger Shakespeare Library
DLC	Library of Congress
Dm	Marsh's Library, Dublin
[Dresden]	State Library at Dresden[6]
Dt	Trinity College, Dublin
E	National Library of Scotland
Eu	Edinburgh University Library
EXu	Exeter University Library (includes Crediton Parish Library)
GEU	Emory University Library, Atlanta
[GhU]	Ghent University Library (by correspondence only)
[GOT]	Niedersächsische Staats-und Universitätsbibliothek, Göttingen (information from ESTC and Jefcoate)
[Gotha]	State Library at Gotha[6]
Gu	Glasgow University Library
Han	Niedersachsische Landesbibliothek, Hannover
[Hum]	Humboldt University Library, Berlin[6]
InNd	University of Notre Dame Library (Indiana)
L	British Library
MB	Boston (Mass.) Public Library
MH	Harvard College Library (including the Houghton Library)
MH-AH	Andover-Harvard Theological Library
Mun	Bavarian State Library, Munich
MWA	American Antiquarian Society Library, Worcester, Mass.
NjP	Princeton University Library (New Jersey)
NjR	Rutgers University Library, New Brunswick, N.J.
NN	New York Public Library
NNPM	Pierpont Morgan Library, New York
NRU	Rochester University Library (New York)
O	Bodleian Library, Oxford
Oa	All Souls College, Oxford
Ob	Balliol College, Oxford
Obr	Brasenose College, Oxford
Oc	Christ Church, Oxford
Occ	Corpus Christi College, Oxford
OCin	Cincinnati and Hamilton County Public Library
OCU	University of Cincinnati Library
Oh	Hertford College, Oxford
Oj	Jesus College, Oxford
Om	Merton College, Oxford
Oman	Mansfield College, Oxford
Omc	Manchester College, Oxford

Oo	Oriel College, Oxford
Op	Pembroke College, Oxford
Oq	Queen's College, Oxford
Osj	St. John's College, Oxford
P	Bibliothèque nationale, Paris
PP	Free Library of Philadelphia
PPH	Historical Society of Pennsylvania (Philadelphia)
PPL	Library Company of Philadelphia
PU	Van Pelt Library, University of Pennsylvania
SAN	St. Andrew's University Library
Thoemmes	Thoemmes Antiquarian Books, Bristol
[Tüb]	University Library at Tübingen[6]
TxDaMP	Bridwell Library, Southern Methodist University, Dallas
TxHR	Rice University Library, Houston, Texas
Utr	Utrecht University Library
Vat	Biblioteca Vaticana
ViU	University of Virginia Library
ViW	Williamsburg (Virginia) Foundation Library
WaU	University of Washington Library, Seattle
Wol	Herzog August Bibliothek, Wolfenbüttel
Y	Private collection of John and Jean Yolton
Yu	University of York Library (Heslington, Yorks.)

Other libraries or collections have been examined for this study, frequently to look at one or two editions only. They are the late Esmond de Beer's collection (now at the University of Otago, New Zealand), Exeter Cathedral Library, the German Society of Pennsylvania (in Philadelphia); Leiden University Library (Netherlands); the Petty Library in Skipton, Yorks.; and Winchester Cathedral Library.

FINDING LIST OF BIBLIOGRAPHICAL MATERIALS[7]

Aaron, R. I.: *John Locke*. Third Edition. Oxford: Clarendon Press, 1971.
   This edition includes a bibliographic note by Charlotte Johnston; see below.
Abkoude, Johannes van: *Naamregister van de bekendste en meest in gebruik zynde Nederduitsche boeken* . . . Rotterdam: G.A. Arrenberg, 1788. 2 vols.
Ackers = Ross, J. C.: *Charles Ackers' Ornament Usage*. Oxford Bibliographical Society Occasional Publication no. 21, 1990.
Alden, John Eliot, note, *Publications of the Bibliographical Society of America*, 35 (1943): 309.
Alston, R. C.: *A Bibliography of the English Language from the Invention of Printing to the Year 1800*. Leeds, Bradford, etc.: Printed for the Author by E. J. Arnold [and others] 1965–date.
   Vol. 7 covers 'Logic, Philology, Epistemology, Universal Language'; v. 10, Education, Teaching of Languages'.
Ashcraft, Richard: *Revolutionary Politics & Locke's* Two Treatises of Government. Princeton University Press, 1986.
Attig, John C.: *The Works of John Locke: a Comprehensive Bibliography*. Westport, Conn.: Greenwood Press, 1985.
Axtell = Locke, John: *The Educational Writings of John Locke: a Critical Edition*, edited by James Axtell. Cambridge: University Press, 1968.
   Checklist of all known printings, including translations of *Some Thoughts concerning Education*: pp. 98–104.
Axtell, J.: 'Locke, Newton, and the Elements of Natural Philosophy', *Paedagogica Europea*, 1 (1965): 235–45.
Axtell, J.: 'Locke's Review of the *Principia*', *Notes and Records of the Royal Society* 20 no. 2 (Dec. 1965): 152–61.
Ayers, Michael: 'Locke's Translations from Nicole's Essais: the Real First Edition', *The Locke Newsletter* 11 (1980): 101–3.
Barbier, A. A.: *Dictionnaire des oeuvrages anonymes*. 3. éd., revue et augmentée par MM. Olivier Barbier [et al.] Paris: P. Daffis, 1872–79. 8 parts.
Biographia Britannica, or The Lives of the Most Eminent Persons who have flourished in Great Britain and Ireland. London: Printed for W. Innys, W. Meadows [et al.], 1747–66. 7 vols. folio.
   An incomplete second edition 'with corrections, enlargements and the

---

[7] Abbreviations for items briefly cited in the bibliographical descriptions precede an equals sign ('=').

addition of new lives' by Andrew Kippis, was published in 5 vols. folio, 1778-93.

Bibliotheca annua, or The Annual Catalogue for the Year 1699 [-1703] Facsim. reprint of the 1700-1704 ed. London: Gregg Press, 1964. 2 vols.

Birch, Thomas: *The History of the Royal Society of London for Improving of Natural Knowledge* . . . London: A. Millar, 1756-57. 4 vols.

 Facsim. reprints by G. Olms Verlag and Johnson Reprint Corp. in 1968.

Blackburne, Francis: *Memoirs of Thomas Hollis, Esq;.* London, 1780. 2 vols. folio.

Bond, W. H.: *Thomas Hollis of Lincoln's Inn.* The Sandars Lectures in Bibliography. Cambridge: University Press, 1991.

Bowers, Fredson: *Principles of Bibliographical Description.* Princeton University Press, 1949.

Bowers, Fredson, Johan Gerritsen and Peter Laslett: 'Further Observations on Locke's *Two Treatises of Government*: Three Contributions', *Transactions of the Cambridge Bibliographical Society*, 2 pt. 1 (1954): 63-87.

 For earlier 'Observations' see under Laslett, Peter.

The Bowyer Ledgers. Edited by Keith Maslen and John Lancaster. London: Bibliographical Society; New York: Bibliographical Society of America, 1991.

 Accompanied by microfiches of the manuscript printing accounts.

Bowyer Orn. = Maslen, K.D.: *The Bowyer Ornament Stock.* Oxford Bibliographical Society Occasional Publication no. 8, 1973.

Boyle, Robert: *Works.* New edition [ed. by Thomas Birch]. London: J. and F. Rivington [et al.] 1772. 6 vols.

Christophersen, H.O.: *A Bibliographical Introduction to the Study of John Locke.* Skrifter utg. av det Norske Videnskaps-Akademi i Oslo, III; Hist.-filos. Klasse, no. 8. Oslo: I Kommisjon hos J. Dybwad, 1930.

 Reprint by B. Franklin, New York, 1968.

Cioranescu, A.: *Bibliographie de la littérature française du 17. siècle* (Paris: Editions du C.N.R.S., 1965. 3 vols.) OR *Bibliographie de la littérature française du 18. siècle* (ibid., 1969. 3 vols.)

 Reference is made to these works by respective date of publication.

Colie, Rosalie L.: 'John Locke in the Republic of Letters', in *Britain and the Netherlands, Papers delivered to the Oxford-Netherlands Historical Conference, 1959*, ed. by J. S. Bromley and E. H. Kossman . . . (London: Chatto & Windus, 1960), pp. 111-29.

Corr. = Locke, John: *The Correspondence.* Edited by E. S. de Beer. Clarendon Edition of the Works of John Locke. Oxford: Clarendon Press, 1976-89. 8 vols.

Cranston, Maurice: *John Locke, a Biography.* London: Macmillan, 1957.

 Reprinted by Oxford University Press, 1985.

De Beer, E. S.: 'Bishop Law's List of Books Attributed to Locke', *The Locke Newsletter* 7 (1976): 47-54.

Dictionnaire de biographie française (1929-date).

Dictionnaire des journalistes (1600-1788). Edited by Jean Sgard. Grenoble: Presse universitaire de Grenoble, 1976.

DNB = *Dictionary of National Biography*.

EEB = *Early English Books, 1641-1700: Selected from Donald Wing's Short Title Catalogue*. Ann Arbor, Mich.: University Microfilms, 1961-date. Microfilm collection.

The Eighteenth Century: a microfilm collection based on the ESTC. Woodbridge, Conn.: Research Publications, 1983-date.

ESTC: *An Eighteenth Century Short Title Catalog*. Stanford, Calif.: Research Libraries Group, 1982-date.
 Bibliographic record available through the RLIN online computer network.

Evans, Charles: *American Bibliography*. Chicago: Evans, 1903-59. 14 vols.
 Facsim. of the works listed are available, by citation number, on micro-opaque cards, published by Readex Microprint.

Fabian, Bernhard: *The English Book in Eighteenth-Century Germany*. The Panizzi Lectures, 1991. London: British Library, 1992.

Feather, John: *A Dictionary of Book History*. London: Croom Helm, 1986. Also published in New York by Oxford University Press, 1986.

Feather, John: *The Provincial Book Trade in Eighteenth-Century England*. Cambridge: University Press, 1985.

Fulton, John F.: *A Bibliography of Robert Boyle*. Second Edition. Oxford: Clarendon Press, 1961.

Gaskell, Philip: *A Bibliography of the Foulis Press*. Second Edition. Winchester: St. Paul's Bibliographies, 1986.

Gaskell, Philip: *A New Introduction to Bibliography*. Oxford: Clarendon Press, 1972.

Gibson, W. T.: Biographical note on John Wynne, *Oxoniensia*, 52 (1987): 204-8.

Goldsmiths' Lib. = *Catalogue of the Goldsmiths' Library of Economic Literature*. Compiled by M. Canney and D. Knott. Vol.1: Printed Books to 1800. London: Cambridge University Press, 1970.
 A microfilm copy of books in this collection, arranged by its citation numbers, is in the set, *Goldsmiths'-Kress Library of Economic Literature*, 1st segment (Woodbridge, Conn.: Research Publications, 1983.)

GV = *Gesamtverzeichnis des deutschsprachigen Schrifttums (GV), 1700-1910*. Munich: Saur, 1979-87. 160 vols.

Heawood = Heawood, Edward: *Watermarks, Mainly of the 17th and 18th Centuries*. Monumenta charta papyracea historiam illustrantia, 1. Hilversum: Paper Publications Society, 1950.

Hodgson, Norma and Cyprian Blagden: *The Notebook of Thomas Bennet and Henry Clements (1686-1719), with Some Aspects of Book Trade Practice*. Publications of the Oxford Bibliographical Society, new series vol. 6, 1956.

Horwitz, Robert H. and Judith B. Finn: 'Locke's Aesop's Fables', *The Locke Newsletter* 6 (1975): 71-88.

The House of Commons, 1660–1690, edited by B. D. Henning. London: History of Parliament Trust, 1983.

Israel, Jonathan I.: *The Dutch Republic: Its Rise, Greatness, and Fall, 1477–1806.* Oxford: Clarendon Press, 1995.

Jefcoate, G. and K. Kloth, compilers: *A Catalogue of English Books Printed before 1801 Held by the University Library at Göttingen.* Edited for the [Niedersächsische Staats- und Universitätsbibliothek] by Bernhard Fabian. Hildesheim: Olms-Weidmann, 1987–88. 7 vols. in 2 parts. Part 1 works published before 1701; part 2, between 1701 and 1800.

Johnston, Charlotte S. [née Ware]: 'A Bibliography of John Locke.' Unpublished D. Phil. (Oxon.) thesis, 1956. (Shelfmark M.S. D. Phil. d.1638.)

Available only for consultation at the Bodleian Library, Oxford. It contains an introduction, description of manuscripts and English-language printed works; it covers most editions of the 'toleration letters' (no. 1–15), *Two Treatises* (no. 16–31), the *Essay* (32–84), the 'Conduct of the Understanding' (no. 85–106), and editions of the collected works (no. 107–23), all chiefly in Oxford locations.[8]

Johnston, Charlotte S.: 'The Printing History of the First Four Editions of the *Essay concerning Human Understanding*', in Aaron, R. I.: *John Locke*. Third Edition (Oxford: Clarendon Press, 1971), pp.313–30 (Appendix II).

Jones, G. P.: 'The Political Reform Movement in Sheffield', *Transactions of the Hunter Archaeological Society*, 4 (1937): 57–68.

Kelly, Patrick Hyde: 'A Note on Locke's Pamphlets on Money', *Transactions of the Cambridge Bibliographical Society*, 5 (1969): 61–73.

Kenyon, Sir Frederic G.: Letter, *Times Literary Supplement*, no. 1629 (20 April 1933).

Kleerkooper, M. M.: *De boekhandel te Amsterdam voornamelijk in de 17e eeuw: biographische en geschiedkundige aanteekeningen verzameld . . .* Bijdragen tot de geschiedenis van den Nederlandschen boekhandel, uitg. door de Vereeniging ter bevordering van de belangen des boekhandels, X. The Hague: M. Nijhoff, 1914–16. 2 vols.

L.L. = *The Library of John Locke*, by John Harrison and Peter Laslett. Second Edition. Oxford: Clarendon Press, 1971.

First published in 1965 as Oxford Bibliographical Society Publication, new series vol. 13.

Landmarks of Science: a Comprehensive Collection of the Source Materials in the History of Science. New York: Readex Microprint Corp., 1966–70.

Microprint cards arranged alphabetically by main entry.

Laslett = Locke, John: *Two Treatises of Government*: a Critical Edition . . . by Peter Laslett. Third Edition. Cambridge: University Press, 1989.

Checklist of all known printings: pp. 121–129.

Laslett, Peter: 'The 1690 Editions of Locke's *Two Treatises of Government*:

---

[8] Mrs. Johnston has requested that I not cite this work.

Two States', *Transactions of the Cambridge Bibliographical Society*, 1 pt.4 (1952): 341-7.
   For further details, see under Bowers, F.
Lewine, J.: *Bibliography of Eighteenth-Century Art and Illustrated Books*. London, 1898.
Li, Ming Hsun: *The Great Recoinage of 1695-6*. London: Weidenfeld & Nicholson, 1963.
Locke, John: *An Essay concerning Human Understanding*. Edited ... by Peter H. Nidditch. Clarendon Edition of the Works of John Locke. Oxford: Clarendon Press, 1975.
Locke, John: *Drafts for the* Essay concerning Human Understanding *and Other Philosophical Writings*. Edited ... by Peter H. Nidditch and G. A. J. Rogers. Clarendon Edition of the Works of John Locke. Oxford: Clarendon Press, 1990-date. 3 vols. (in progress).
The Locke Newsletter. Edited by Roland Hall (at the Dept. of Philosophy). Heslington, York: University of York, Autumn 1970-date.
Long, P.: *A Summary Catalogue of the Lovelace Collection of the Papers of John Locke in the Bodleian Library*. Oxford: Printed for the Library at the University Press, 1959. Issued also as Oxford Bibliographical Society Publication, new series no. 8.
Milton, J. R.: 'John Locke and the Fundamental Constitutions of Carolina', *The Locke Newsletter* 21 (1990): 111-133.
Montuori, Mario: *John Locke on Toleration and the Unity of God*. Amsterdam: J. C. Gieben, 1983.
Neustroev, A. N.: *Ukazatel' k russkim povremennym izdaniiam i sbornikam za 1703-1802 gg*. [Index to Russian periodicals ... 1703-1802.] Vaduz: Kraus Reprint, 1963.
   Facsim. reprint of the St. Petersburg (1898) edition.
The New Palgrave Dictionary of Money & Finance. Edited by Peter Newman, Murray Milgate, John Eatwell. London: Macmillan; New York: Stockton Press, 1992. 3 vols.
Nichols, John: *Literary Anecdotes of the Eighteenth Century*. London: Printed for the Author by Nichols, Son and Bentley, 1812-16. 9 vols.
   Reprinted by AMS Press, New York, 1966.
Nidditch, Peter H.: *A Bibliographical and Text-Historical Study of the Early Printings of* Some Thoughts concerning Education. Sheffield, 1973.
Oldenburg, Henry: *Correspondence*. Edited and translated by A. Rupert Hall and Marie Boas Hall. Madison: University of Wisconsin Press, 1965-86. 13 vols.; vols. 10-11 published by Mansell, London; 12-13 by Taylor & Francis, London.
Plomer, Henry R. and others: *Dictionaries of the Printers and Booksellers Who Were at Work in England, Scotland and Ireland, 1557-1775*. London: Bibliographical Society, 1977.
   Reprint in compact one-vol. form of the dictionaries covering 1557-1640, 1641-1667, 1668-1725 and 1726-1775, first published separately

1910-32. Reference is made to the revelant vol. according to the date of printing.

Porter, Noah: 'Marginalia *Locke*-a-na', *The New Englander and Yale Review*, new ser. 11 (July 1887): 33-49.

Rhodes, Dennis E.: 'Two Editions of Alexander Pope in Italian Translation', *The Library*, 6th ser., 14 no. 2 (June 1992): 140-43; and 'A Further Note . . .', ibid., 6th ser., 15 no. 3 (Sept. 1993): 226.

Rochedieu, C. A.: *Bibliography of French Translations of English Works, 1700-1800*. Chicago: University of Chicago Press, 1948.

Rogers, G.A.J., editor: *Locke's Philosophy: Content and Context*. Oxford: Clarendon Press, 1994. Papers from the Clarendon Locke Conference at Christ Church, Oxford, 1990.

Rosicka, Janina: 'Locke and the Polish Enlightenment', in *Locke's Philosophy: Content and Context*, edited by G. A. J. Rogers (Oxford: Clarendon Press, 1994), pp. 237-52.

Sauvy, Anne: *Livres saisis à Paris entre 1689 et 1801*. La Haye: M. Nijhoff, 1972.

Sayce, R.A.: *Compositorial Practices and the Localization of Printed Books, 1530-1800*. Reprinted with Additions and Corrections. Occasional Publications of the Oxford Bibliographical Society, no. 13 (1979).

Schankula, H. A. S.: 'A Summary Catalogue of the Philosophical Manuscript Papers of John Locke', *Bodleian Library Record*, 9 (1973): 24-35; 'Additions and Corrections', ibid., pp. 81-82.

Schøsler, Jørn: *Bibliographie des éditions et des traductions d'ouvrages philosophiques français et particulièrement des écrivains obscurs, 1680-1800*. Etudes romanes de l'Université d'Odense, vol. 22. Odense: University Press, 1986.

Schøsler, Jørn: 'Les éditions de la traduction française par Pierre Coste de l'Essay concerning Human Understanding de Locke', in *Actes du VIIIe Congrès des romanistes scandinaves* (Odense: University Press, 1983), pp. 315-24.

Svodnyi kat. = *Svodnyi katalog russkoi knigi grazhdanskoi pechati XVIII veka, 1725-1800*. [Union catalogue of Russian civil-type books of the 18th century, 1725-1800. Edited by I.P. Kondakov, under the auspices of the RSFSR's Ministry of Culture.] Moscow, 1962-67. 5 vols.

T.C. = *The Term Catalogues, 1668-1709 A.D.* [Compiled and edited] by Edward Arber. London: Privately Printed, 1903-06. 3 vols.

Transcript = *A Transcript of the Registers of the Worshipful Company of Stationers from 1640-1708 A.D.* London: Printed for the Roxburghe Club, 1913-14. 3 vols.

Unspeakable Curll = Straus, Ralph: *The Unspeakable Curll, being Some Account of Edmund Curll, Bookseller; to which is added a full list of his books*. London: Chapman & Hall, 1928.

Weller, E.O.: *Die falschen und fingirten Druckorte* . . . Hildesheim: G. Olms, 1960. 2 vols.

First published in 1864. Vol. 2 covers French imprints.

Wing² = Wing, D. G. *Short-title Catalogue of Books Printed in England, Scotland, Ireland, Wales and British America, and of English Books Printed in Other Countries, 1641–1700.* Second Edition, Revised and Enlarged. New York: Modern Language Association of America, 1972–88. 3 vols.

Wolf, Edwin, 2d: 'A Parcel of Books for the Province', *Pennsylvania Magazine of History and Biography*, 89 (1965): 428–46.

Woodfall = Goulden, R. J.: *The Ornament Stock of Henry Woodfall, 1719–1747: a Preliminary Inventory Illustrated.* Occasional Papers of the Bibliographical Society (London), no. 3, 1988.

Yolton, Jean S.: 'The First Editions of John Locke's *Some Thoughts concerning Education*', *Papers of the Bibliographical Society of America*, 75 no. 3 (1981): 315–21.

Yolton, Jean S., editor: *A Locke Miscellany.* Bristol: Thoemmes, 1990.

Yolton, Jean S.: 'A Note on the Manuscript of Locke's Translation of Nicole's *Essais de morale*', *The Locke Newsletter* 11 (1980): 104–7.

Yolton, Jean S. and John W. Yolton: *John Locke: a Reference Guide.* Boston, Mass.: G. K. Hall & Co., 1985.

Yolton, John W.: 'Locke's Unpublished Marginal Replies to John Sergeant', *Journal of the History of Ideas*, 12 (Oct. 1951): 528–59.

CHAPTER I
Letters on Toleration (nos. 1–28)

Locke's *Epistola de tolerantia* was written in the winter of 1685–86, probably just after the revocation of the Edict of Nantes, 18 October 1685. It was dedicated (or addressed) to Philipp van Limborch, a Remonstrant theologian living in Amsterdam, who had become one of Locke's principal friends. '[What was] relevant was the treatment to which divines who uttered Socinian and other heretical views were liable to be subjected by orthodox Calvinists. Locke had good reason to write the *Epistola de Tolerantia* for him [Limborch]' (De Beer, *Corr.* ii.651).

The work was quickly translated into English by a Unitarian merchant, William Popple, with the title, *A Letter concerning Toleration* (1689). The translator also added the heading 'Postscript' to the final eleven paragraphs following 'Vale' ('Farewell') where Locke adds 'a few words about heresy and schism.'

In his preface 'To the Reader' to his translation (no. 3 et seq.), Popple states that it 'has already been translated both into Dutch and French', but the French translation was not published at that time. In a letter to Locke dated 18 July 1689, Limborch stated 'it has been done into French by Mr. de Cene', presumably Charles Le Cène (*Corr.* 1158; iii. 647, de Beer's translation). Limborch added, 'people will now soon be able to read it in four languages', Latin, English, Dutch and French. The project to publish Le Cène's translation appears to have been abandoned, for unknown reasons. The first French translation to appear was in the *Oeuvres diverses* of 1710 (no. 372).

A French-language summary notice of the Latin edition appearing in Le Clerc's *Bibliothèque universelle*, 15 (1689) has been taken by some, erroneously, to be the French appearance of the work mentioned by Popple.

The very first attack or criticism was on the English translation. It was written by the Rev. Thomas Long, who in 1689 published *The Letter for Toleration Decipher'd* . . . (cf. Chap. XIII, C1689-1). But the Rev. Jonas Proast, of Queen's College, Oxford, sometime archdeacon, anonymously attacked the anonymous 'letter' in his *The Argument of the Letter concerning Toleration Briefly Consider'd and Answer'd* (1690; C1690-3).

Proast's attack was answered by Locke's anonymous *Second Letter concerning Toleration* (1690; no. 25). Proast's reply, *A Third Letter concerning Toleration* (1691; C1691-1) drew forth Locke's *Third Letter for Toleration* (1692; no. 27).

After a hiatus, the controversy was revived by Proast's publishing *A Second Letter to the Author of the Three Letters for Toleration* (1704; C1704-1), intended as a reply to Locke's *Third Letter*. In a postscript, Proast also referred to the anonymous *Rights of Protestant Dissenters* (1704; C1704-2), attributed to John Shute, Lord Barrington, claiming that its author was a disciple of Locke. A 'fourth letter for toleration', written in answer to these two works, was found in Locke's papers by his nephew Peter King, and published in Locke's *Posthumous Works* (1706; no. 299). The three English 'toleration' letters, and the fourth as published in the *Posthumous Works* are reprinted in all *Works* editions (no. 363 et seq.).

The authorship of these 'letters' was kept secret during Locke's lifetime and revealed in the codicil to his will (cf. C1714-1). Many people, besides Limborch, knew or guessed its authorship. Locke's copy-text does not survive for any of the 'letters' but was probably in the recognizable hand of his amanuensis Sylvester Brounower, recognizable at least to the Churchills, who kept his authorship a secret.

1. Epistola de tolerantia (anonymous). 1689. Gouda. long 12°
EPISTOLA [swash P] | de | TOLERANTIA | ad | Clariffimum Virum | T.A.R.P.T.O.L.A. [swash R, P] | Scripta à | P.A.P.O.I.L.A. [swash Ps] | [orn. of printer's flowers, diamond-shaped 21 × 21 mm] | *GOUDÆ*, | Apud JUSTUM [swash J] AB HOEVE. | [rule 40 mm] | cIɔ Iɔc LXXXIX.
Coll: long 12° (138 × 80 mm cut) A–D^{12} [$7 signed]; 48 leaves; pp. *1–2* 3–96. (O copy has fore-edge untrimmed 90 mm wide.)
Contents: A1^r title (verso blank), A2^r–D12^v (3–96) text.
Text (C3^r): 24 lines (D10^r [91] has 25 with CW in 25th line); 100 (108) × 58 mm; 83 R. Poor-quality laid paper without watermarks; with vertical chainlines. Page no. at external ends of headlines.
HT: EPISTOLA | de | TOLERANTIA.
RT, A2^v–D12^r: EPISTOLA | DE TOLERANTIA. D12^v has headline: EPISTOLA DE TOLERANTIA.
CW: Page. A12^v Chri- [Chriftianus] B9^r injun- [injungere'] C6^r po- [ponitur.] C9^v (im-) mor- [mortalem,] D4^v ho- [hominum]
Notes: Published anonymously. Le Clerc in his 'Eloge de feu Mr. Locke' (*Bibliothèque choisie* 6, 1705; cf. C1705-5) states that it was written during 1686 in Utrecht; Christophersen, that 'it had been written by Locke already early in 1685, during a short stay at Cleve.' According to Le Clerc, the initials stand for 'Theologiae apud Remonstrantes Professorem, tyrannidis osorem, Limburgium Amstelodamsem' and 'pacis amico, persequutionis osore, Joanne Lockio Anglo' (Professor of Theology among the Remonstrants, Enemy of Tyranny, Limborch of Amsterdam. From a Friend of Peace, Enemy of Persecution, John Locke, Englishman). Instead of 'Limburgium Amstelodamensen', part of the dedication means 'Libertatis Amantem' (Lover of Liberty), according to a letter written twenty years after its composition, from

Limborch to Lady Masham (letter of 24 March 1705, as cited by M. Montuori).[1] Whether it was a small book ('libellus') dedicated to Limborch, or a personal letter to him, Limborch persuaded Locke to let it be published (see Montuori, ibid., pp. xxii–xxvii).

'Tergow' (or 'Ter Gouw') cited as the place of publication in the codicil to Locke's will (*Corr.* viii.426) is a variant name of Gouda. The work was published a few days before April 26, 1689 (cf. *Corr.* 1131, letter from Limborch; iii.607) and it was undoubtedly Limborch who saw it through the press: 'the printer had given me a few [copies] because I had supervised the correction' ('typographus mihi pauca [exemplaria] dederat quia correctioni praefueram', Limborch to Locke, 15 April 1690, in *Corr.* 1283, iv. 57–8). *Notices*: *Bibliothèque universelle* 15 (1689): 402–12; *Histoire des ouvrages des savans* 6 (1689–90): 20–26.

References: Attig 41; Christophersen pp. 13–15; L.L. 2941.

Copies examined: O (8° N.67 Th.; fore-edge not trimmed) [Berlin (Potsd.Str.)] C (Keynes) Ck (Keynes) [GOT] L (C.111.b5 (1)) MH (*EC65.L7934 689e, formerly owned by Thomas Hollis) NNPM (gift of Thomas Hollis to Rodolf Valtravers of Berne;[2] then to John Disney the antiquary) Occ (leaf B5 bound after B6)

2. Epistola. Amsterdam, 1705. long 12°
In red & black: [red line:] JOANNIS LOCKII | EPISTOLA | DE | [red:] TOLERANTIA. | Accedit | [red:] SAMUELIS STRIMESII, Pr. Th. | DE PACE | [red:] ECCLESIASTICA | DISSERTATIO. | [orn., small irons 3, 2, 1: 11 × 10 mm] | AMSTELODAMI, | [rule 54 mm] | Apud [red:] JANSSONIO-WAESBERGIOS, | M D C C V.
Coll: long 12° (132 × 72 mm cut) A–D^{12} *^{8} (–*1) ^{2}A–^{2}C^{12} ^{2}D^4 [$ half + 1 (–^{2}A6) signed]; 95 leaves; pp. *1–2* 3–96; *iii–xvi* 1–80 [= 190]
Contents: A1^r title (verso blank), A2^r–D12^v (3–96) Locke's text; *2^r–*6^v (*iii–xii*) pref. to Strimesius, *7^r–*8^r (*xiii–xv*) 'Dissertatio | BREVIARUM' [summary of argument], *8^v blank, ^{2}A1^r–^{2}D4^v (1–80) Strimesius's text.
Text (B3^r): 24 lines; 99 (108) × 57 mm; 83 R. Medium-quality laid paper with vertical chainlines; no visible watermarks. Page no. at external ends of headlines.
HT, A2^r: EPISTOLA | de | TOLERANTIA. *2^r: PRAEFATIO. ^{2}A1^r: SAMUELIS STRIMESII | DISSERTATIO | THEOLOGICA, | DE | PACE ECCLE- | SIASTICA | AD | AUDITORES SUOS, | Theol. Candidatos.

---

[1] Remonstrants' Library MSS. III D.16-54, now in the library of the University of Amsterdam. Quoted by M. Montuori in his *John Locke and the Unity of God*, p. xxi.

[2] For further information about Valtravers (or Giovanni Ridolfo Vautravers), in addition to that in *The Life of Thomas Hollis*, by Francis Blackburne, see two articles by Dennis E. Rhodes, 'Two Editions of Alexander Pope in Italian Translation', *The Library*, 6th ser., 14 no. 2 (June 1992): 140–43; and 'A Further Note . . .', ibid., 6th ser., 15 no. 3 (Sept. 1993): 226.

RT, from verso to recto: A2ᵛ–D12ʳ: *EPISTOLA* | *DE TOLERANTIA* ²Al ᵛ–
²D4ʳ: *De Pace* | *Eccleſiaſticâ*
Headlines, *2ᵛ–*6ᵛ: *PRAEFATIO*. [swash P, R]
CW: Page. A12ᵛ (Chri-) ſtianus B9ʳ injun- [injungere,] C6ʳ po- [ponitur.] C9ᵛ (im-) mor- [mortalem,] D4ᵛ (tyran-) nicis
Notes: Text is chiefly a line-for-line reprint of the first edition (no. 1), the first of any to name Locke as the author. Strimesius's work may have been published separately, and the missing leaf *1 its title-page. Alternatively it may have been a half-title. Raymond Klibansky, in the preface to his edition of the Latin and English texts (Oxford, 1968; p. xxxvii) states 'The inclusion of Strimesius' treatise in the same book strongly indicates that this edition was arranged by Limborch, whose particular interest in Strimesius' work is well attested.' He also records that the only copy he has located is in the Biblioteca Nazionale Vittorio Emanuele in Rome (shelf-mark: Miscell. Valenti 1389).
Reference: Attig 42.
Copies examined: Oc (WF 8.14) Mun.

3. Epistola. English trans. 1689. 4°. (Anonymous)
Within a double rule, inner 167 × 100 mm, outer 178 × 108 mm: A | LETTER | CONCERNING | Toleration: | Humbly Submitted, *&c.* | [rule 97 mm] | LICENSED, *Octob*. 3. 1689. | [double rule 98/95 mm] | LONDON, | Printed for *Awnſham Churchill*, at the *Black* [swash B] | *Swan* at *Amen-Corner*. 1689.
Coll: 4° (205 × 145 mm cut) A⁴ B–I⁴ [$ 2 signed]; 36 leaves; pp. *i–viii* 1–61 62–64 [=72].
Contents: A1ʳ HT, A1ᵛ advt. by Churchill, A2ʳ title, A2ᵛ blank, A3ʳ–A4ᵛ pref., B1ʳ–I3ʳ (1–61) text, I3ᵛ–I4ᵛ (62–64) advt. of '*Books lately Printed for Awnſham Churchil* . . .'
Text (F3ᵛ): 35 lines; 164 (185) × 109 (122) mm; 93R. Pref. set 21 lines, 143 ital. Biblical citations set roman in external margins on, e.g. p. 1, 2, 38. Medium-quality paper with watermark similar to Heawood 737 and 745. Page no. at external ends of headlines. Page 45 (G3ʳ) has 36 lines with text in direction line. Pref. set 21 lines, 145 ital.
Half-title: [rule 108 mm] | A | LETTER | CONCERNING | TOLERATION. | [rule 102 mm]
HT, A3ʳ: TO THE | READER.
B1ʳ: [double rule 108 mm] | A | LETTER | CONCERNING | TOLERATION.
Headlines, A3ᵛ–A4ᵛ: To the Reader.
B1ᵛ–I3ʳ: *A Letter concerning Toleration.*
CW: Page. A4ᵛ A Letter, B2ᵛ Souls, [Souls;] D4ᵛ thus E2ᵛ ſuch [ſuch,] G3ʳ Another
Notes: The translation of Locke's first separately published work was made by William Popple, a Unitarian merchant, possibly with Locke's cooperation. However the phrase frequently attributed to Locke, 'Absolute Liberty, Just

and True Liberty, Equal and Impartial Liberty, is the thing that we stand in need of', is from the preface, and is Popple's own.

Popple has been criticized for slanting his translation to reflect the political situation in England. Where the Latin text, written in a Dutch environment, speaks of equal liberties to be permitted 'Remonstranti, Antiremonstranti, Lutherano, Anabaptistae, Sociniano', Popple has changed the text for an English audience, to read 'Presbyterians, Independents, Anabaptists, Arminians, Quakers, and others'. Further he omits some phrases and adds others: for example, where the Latin reads 'in fidem autem consistit verae et salutiferae religionis vis et efficacia' (translated as 'All the Life and Power of true Religion consists in the inward and full perswasion of the mind') Popple adds 'And faith is not Faith without believing.'

Locke was aware that the 'Epistola' was being translated by Popple almost as soon as the Latin work appeared, for he commented about it in a letter to Limborch dated 6 June 1689 (*Corr.* 1147; iii.633–4). And he seemed to have approved of the translation, for in his *Second Letter concerning Toleration* (1690; no. 25) he writes 'And whatever Absurdities there be in this way of proceeding, there is none in the Author's way of expressing it; as you would more plainly have seen, if you had looked into the Latin Original . . . yet the Translator is not to be blamed, if he chose to express the Sense of the Author, in words that very lively represented the extream Absurdity they are guilty of, who under pretence of Zeal for the Salvation of Souls, proceed to the taking away their Lives' (p.10).

In a codicil to his will (*Corr.* viii. 426; cf. C1714-1) Locke admitted authorship of this and the second and third toleration letters: 'three letters concerning Toleration the first whereof I writt in Latin and was published at Tergow in Holland 1689 under this title Epistola de Tolerantia and afterwards translated into English without my privity . . .' These three he bequeathed (with other works) to the Bodleian Library together with Proast's *Argument* (C1690-3) and his *Third Letter concerning Toleration* (C1691-1): 'Both which Treatises it is my Will should be bound up in one volume with my three letters on the same subject that therein any one who pleaseth may have the convenience to examine what my Opponent and I have sayd in this controversy'.

An entry in the registers of the Stationers' Company reporting the licensing date on the title-leaf was made 26 April 1695 (*Transcript*, p. 457).

Some copies lack half-title (leaf A1).

A microfilm copy is in the EEB collection, reel 540, no. 9.

Notice: *Bibliothèque universelle* 19 (1690): 365–91 (includes no. 23 and C1690-3).

References: Attig 51; Christophersen p.15; ESTC r014566; L.L. 2943; T.C. II. 284; Transcript iii. 457; Wing^2 L2747.

Copies examined (* indicates leaf A1 lacking): O^{1}* (4° S.70 Th; presentation copy; 205 × 145 mm cut) [Berlin] C CaQMMO Cch (16.16 (4)) Ck*(Keynes) CLU-C (189 × 149 mm cut) CtY (K8.L79/bbg689) DFo (acc.13001)   DLC   Eu   L (698.i.2 (11))   MH (*EC65.L7934B691t; gift of T. Hollis)   NjP (Ex.6106.32.8)   O² (Pamph.195 (10); A1 bound after A4)   O³ (Gough Pamph.769 (3); 204 × 155 mm cut)   O⁴ (Firth e.32 (1); closely cut to 180 × 145 mm)   Oa   Oc*   Occ   Oq*   P (D².1537)   SAN   TxDaMP

4. Epistola. English trans. 2d ed., 1690. 12°. (Anonymous)
Within a double rule, inner 117 × 60 mm, outer 124 × 67 mm: A | LETTER | Concerning | TOLERATION. | [rule 56 mm] | LICENSED, *Octob.* 3. 1689. | [rule 57 mm] | *The Second Edition Corrected.* | [rule 56 mm] | LONDON, Printed for *Awnſham Churchill* | at the *Black* [swash k] *Swan* in *Ave-Mary Lane.* | MDCXC.
Coll: long 12° (138 × 73 mm cut) A–D¹² [$5 (–B5) signed]; 48 leaves; pp. *i–iv* 1–87 88–92 [= 96].
Contents: A1ʳ title (verso blank), A2ʳ,ᵛ pref., A3ʳ–D10ʳ line 4 (1–87) text, D10ʳ rest–D12ᵛ (87–92) advt. 'Books printed for Awnſham Churchil.'
Text (C3ʳ): 33 lines in sheets A–C, 32 lines in D; 110 (118) × 58 mm; 66 R. Pref. set 66 ital. Biblical citations set roman within outer edge of text in a 2-, 3-, or 4-line block space, 13 mm wide. Part of text in direction line, p. 50 (C3ᵛ). Poor-quality laid paper with watermark similar to Heawood 749 and initials CB. Page no. at external ends of headlines.
HT, A2ʳ: [double rule 55 mm] | TO THE | READER.
A3r: [double rule 57 mm] | A | LETTER | CONCERNING | TOLERATION.
D7r: [double rule 56 mm] | POSTSCRIPT. [swash Ps, R]
Headlines, A3ʳ–D10ʳ: *A Letter concerning Toleration.* [swash T]
CW: Page. A3ʳ never [inever] ('i' from 'if', 1st word in 2nd line of text A2ᵛ (p. 2) has moved to line 1; in some copies lost altogether) A12ᵛ Go- [Government] B12ᵛ God, C8ʳ never- [neverthelefs] D3ʳ That D11v Dr. [Memorials]
Notes: A slightly revised text, with some typographical errors. Headline on A11ᵛ (p. 18) reads '*Lttter*'; the '8' in page number 84 fails to print. Final line of p. 74 reading 'are justified by daily experience, and', has letters 'ce' turned south vertically. A microfilm copy of this edition is in the EEB collection, reel 767, no. 42.
References: Attig 52; Christophersen p.15; ESTC r021477; L.L. 2942; T.C. II. 305; Wing² L2748.
Copies examined: Y   C   CaOTU (Locke L63.E74E6 1690)   C(Keynes)   Ck¹(Keynes A12.1)   Ck²(Keynes A12.28)   CLaslett   DFo (acc.142764)   EXu   Han   L   (4103.a.2)   MH   (*EC65.L7934B692t)   NjP (Ex.6106.332.8.11)   O   Oc   Occ   PPL (Wing L2748/63035.D)

5. Epistola. English. *s.l.*, 1740. 8° in 4s
A | LETTER | CONCERNING | TOLERATION. | [rule 80 mm] | Written by MR. LOCKE. | [rule 82 mm] | LICENSED, *October* 3d, 1689.

| [rule 81 mm] | [orn. 12 × 11 mm] | [rule 81 mm] | Printed in the Year M.DCC.XL.

Coll: 8° in 4s (173 × 112 mm cut) A–F⁴ [$1 (+ A2 & 3, B2 & 3) signed]; 24 leaves; pp. *i–ii* iii 4–48.

Contents: A1ʳ title (verso blank), A2ʳ–A3ᵛ (iii–4) 'To the Reader', A4ʳ–F4ᵛ (5–48) text.

Text (C1ʳ): 45 lines; 146 (158) × 81 (94) mm; 67 R. Medium-quality laid paper with vertical chainlines, fleur-de-lys watermark. Biblical citations in external margins. Page no. within square brackets as headlines.

HT A2ʳ: [double rule 80/82 mm] | TO THE | READER.
   A3ʳ: [double rule 80/79 mm] | A | LETTER | CONCERNING | TOLERATION.

Headlines, A2ᵛ: To the READER.
   A3ᵛ–F3ʳ: *A Letter concerning Toleration.* [swash T]
   F4ʳ,ᵛ *POSTSCRIPT.* [swash Ts]

CW: Page. C3ᵛ Judg- [Judgment] D4ᵛ Exe- [Execution.] E2ᵛ (Com-) mon- [mon-wealth]

Press figures: none.

Note: Reprint of the 1690 edition, probably printed in London.

References: Attig 53; ESTC t178061.

Copies examined: O (Vet.A4 e.2336) Ct

6. Epistola. English trans. Boston, Mass., 1743. long 12° in 6s
A | LETTER | Concerning | TOLERATION. | [rule 76 mm] | by *John* [swash J] *Locke*, Gent. | [rule 76 mm] | The THIRD EDITION. | [rule 76 mm] | [orn., rosettes in rows of 3, 4, 3; 17 × 23 mm] | [double rule 76 mm] | BOSTON, Printed and Sold by ROGERS and | FOWLE in Queen- ſtreet, next to the Priſon. | [rule 17 mm] | 1743.

Coll: long 12° in 6s (190 × 117 mm uncut) A–F⁶ G⁴ [$3 (–A2, G3) signed]; 40 leaves; pp. *1-7* 8-13 41 15-72 73 74-77 *78-80*. Page 14 called '41'.

Contents: A1ʳ half-title (verso blank), A2ʳ title (verso blank), A3ʳ,ᵛ pref., A4ʳ–G3 (7–77) text, G3ᵛ–G4 blank.

Text (E2ʳ): 35 lines; 144 (151) × 76 mm; 82 R. Heavy laid-paper with watermark 'VII'. Page no. centered in square brackets at head of page. Blank G4 often wanting.

Half-title: [double row of roll orn. 4 × 74 mm] | Mr. LOCKE | ON | TOLERATION. | [double row of roll orn. 4 × 74 mm]

HT A3ʳ: [double row of roll orn. 4 × 74 mm] | TO THE | READER.
   A4ʳ: [double row of roll orn. 4 × 74 mm] | A | LETTER | CONCERNING | TOLERATION.
   G1ʳ: [double row of roll orn. 4 × 74 mm] | *POSTSCRIPT.* [swash Ts]

CW: Page. B2ᵛ (as E3ʳ Under- [Underſtanding] E6ᵛ Excom- [munication *sic*] F6ʳ wondred [wondered] Note: C3ᵛ (30) has no CW; F6ᵛ (72) instead of CW ends with 'Farewel.'

Notes: Reprint of the 1690 edition (no. 4). Facsim. in Evans microcard set.

References: Attig 54; ESTC w019884; Evans 5227.
Copies examined: DLC (AC901.M5 no. 331.1; lacks A2 and G4) MH (Eg689 *lc*; 183 × 98 mm cut) MWA (183 × 97 mm cut) NN (185 × 98 mm cut) O (Vet. K4.e.7; trimmed to 177 × 94 mm) PPL (Am1743 Loc/66714.D)

7. Epistola. English. Glasgow, 1757. 12° in 6s.
A | LETTER | CONCERNING | TOLERATION. | By *JOHN* [swash J] LOCKE, Efq; | A NEW EDITION. | GLASGOW: | Printed by R. URIE, M.DCC.LVII.
Coll: 12° in 6s (178 × 100 mm cut) π²A-R⁶ S² [$ half signed]; 106 leaves; pp. *i–v* vi–ix *10–11* 12–212.
Contents: π1ʳ half-title (verso blank), π2ʳ title (verso blank), A1ʳ–A3ʳ (*v–ix*) pref., A3ᵛ (*x*) blank, A4ʳ–S2ᵛ (*11–212*) text.
Text (E1ʳ): 18 lines; 99 (111) × 90 (73) mm; 110 R with 1 mm leading between lines. Medium-quality paper with fleur-de-lys watermark. Page no. external ends of headlines.
Half-title: A | LETTER | CONCERNING | TOLERATION.
HT A1ʳ: TO THE | READER.
A4ʳ: A | LETTER | CONCERNING | TOLERATION.
R2ᵛ: [200] | POSTSCRIPT.
RT A4ᵛ–R2ʳ: A LETTER | concerning TOLERATION.
Headline R3ʳ–S2ᵛ: POSTSCRIPT.
CW: none.
Notes: Reprint of the 1690 edition (no. 4). Infrequent biblical citations in the margins. No headlines in pref. A microfilm copy of this edition is in the collection, *The Eighteenth Century*, reel 351, no. 12.
References: Attig 55; Christophersen, pp. 15, 99; ESTC t109472.
Copies examined: O (Vet.A5 f.2174) L (8405.de.22) NjR (F-3 #39577)

8. Epistola. English trans. 1762. 12° in 6s
A | LETTER | CONCERNING | *TOLERATION*. [swash Ts] | [rule 77 mm] | By JOHN [swash J] LOCKE, Efq; | [rule 76 mm] | *The Twelfth* [swash Ts] *Edition Corre*ɕ*t*ed. | [rule 77 mm] | [orn. 11 × 12 mm] | [rule 81 mm] | LONDON: | Printed for R. RICHARDS, in *Holbourn*. | MDCCLXII.
Coll: 12° in 6s (170 × 96 mm cut) A–F⁶ (–F6) [$ half (–C3, F3) signed; B3 signed 'B5')]; 35 leaves; pp. *1–5* 6–70.
Contents: A1ʳ (*1*) title (verso blank), A2ʳ,ᵛ (*3–4*) pref., A3ʳ–F5ᵛ (*5–70*) text.
Text (D4ᵛ): 32 lines (some 33 or 34); 130 (140) × 78 mm; 77 R. Medium-quality laid paper with fleur-de-lys watermark and initials IA. Horizontal chainlines. Page no. at external ends of headlines. RTs with many errors.
HT: [double rule 77 mm | A | LETTER | CONCERNING | TOLERATION.

RT: *A Letter | concerning Toleration*. Errors as follows: A3^v tolerrtion
B2^v, C5^v, D4^v, E1^v, F5^v Tolerrtion
B5^r, C6^r, D5$_r$, E4^r, F3^r coecerning
B5^v, C4^v, D5^v, E5^v, F4^v concerniag
D6^v *A Le tter*
CW: Page. B2^v But D1^v Amongſt E6^v that F1^v Common- [Commonwealth]
Press figures: none.
Notes: Standard reprint of text, with many typographical errors. A fairly scarce printing: I have only been able to find one, Peter Laslett's copy.
Reference: Attig 56.
Copy examined: CLaslett

9. Epistola. English trans. Wilmington, Del., 1764. 8°
A | LETTER | Concerning | TOLERATION. | [rule 66 mm] | By *JOHN* [swash J] *LOCKE*, Gent. | [rule 66 mm] | The FOURTH EDITION. | [rule 66 mm] | [triangular orn. of rosettes in rows of 8, 6, 4, 2, 1, 16 × 27 mm] | [double rule 66 mm] | *WILMINGTON*, [swash T] | Printed and Sold by JAMES ADAMS, in *Market- | ſtreet*, 1764.
Coll: 8° (164 × 106 mm uncut; 155 × 92 cut) A–E^8 [$ half (–A2, A4, E3) signed]; 40 leaves; pp. *i–iv* v–vii 8–77 78–80.
Contents: A1^r half-title (verso blank), A2^r title (verso blank), A3^{r,v} pref., A4^r–E7^r (vii 8–77) text, E7^v–E8^v (78–80) blank.
Text (A8^r): 35 lines; 116 (124) × 67 mm; 66 R. Pref. set 66 ital. Fair-quality laid paper with hollow letter L as watermark. Page no. within parentheses as headlines. All rules on title made from 5 barely touching segments.
Half-title: [framed orn. rule of rosettes 6 × 65 mm] | Mr. *LOCKE* | ON | TOLERATION. | [orn. rule 6 × 65 mm]
HT A3^r [orn. rule 6 × 65 mm] | TO THE | READER.
  A4^r [orn. rule 6 × 65 mm] | A | LETTER | CONCERNING | TOLERATION.
  E5^v [orn. rule 6 × 65 mm] | POSTSCRIPT.
Headline A3^v To the READER.
CW: Page. A8^r (as D3^r Under- [Underſtanding] D6^v Excom- [Excommunication] D7^v (Impu-) ni [nity] ('ty' of CW fallen off?) E4^r wondered
  Note: Text in direction line p. 30 (B7^v). 'Farewel.' is last text word on p. 72 (E4^v).
Notes: Line-by-line reprint of no. 6, even to CW. The place of publication is in what is now the state of Delaware. A facsim. reprint is in the Evans microcard set.
References: Attig 57; ESTC w013421; Evans 9712.
Copies examined: PP (A172.3/L79; lacks E8) MWA PPH (Ud*89/vol.3; inscribed 'David Cooper's Book) PPL (Am 1764/53068.O.1; trimmed to 160 × 91 mm; lacks Al, E8)

10. Epistola. English trans. 'New ed.', 1784. 12° in 12s and 6s
A | LETTER | CONCERNING | TOLERATION. [swash Ts, A] | [rule 63 mm] | By JOHN [swash J] LOCKE, Eſq. | [rule 59 mm] | *A NEW EDITION.* [swash T] | [rule 63 mm] | PUBLISHED FOR THE BENEFIT OF | MANKIND. | [French rule 53 mm] | LONDON: | Printed for J. OSBORNE and T. GRIFFIN, | in St. Paul's Church-Yard, and | J. MOZLEY, *Gainſbrough.* | MDCCLXXXIV.
Coll: 12° in 12s and 6s (136 × 87 mm cut; uncut width 92 mm) A^{12} B^6 C^{12} D^6 E^{12} F^6 [$ half (–A6) signed]; 54 leaves; pp. *i–iii* iv–vi 7 8–106 *107–108*.
Contents: A1^r title (verso blank), A2^r–A3^v (*iii*–vi) pref., A4^r–F5^v (7–106) text, F6 (*107–8*) blank.
Text (A7^r): 27 lines; 105 (114) × 64 mm; 77 R. Poor-quality laid paper without watermark, with vertical chainlines. Page no. at external end of headlines. Footnote citations at bottom of page, e.g. '* Deut. ii.' Postscript (pp. 99–106) set 23 lines with whole line spacing between paragraphs, and 1.5 mm leading between lines.
HT, A4^r: [thick double rule 62 mm] | A | LETTER | CONCERNING | TOLERATION.
Headlines: Of TOLERATION. (A5^r has headline ending in a dash, not a period; E11^r lacks period.)
CW: Page. B6^r abſo- [abſolutely] E8^r Govern- [Governments]
Press figures: none.
Note: Standard reprint, based on 1740 ed. (no. 5).
References: Attig 58; ESTC t155050.
Copies examined: O (Vet. A5 f.1287)   C

11. Epistola. English. York, 1788. 12° in 6s
A | LETTER | CONCERNING | TOLERATION. | BY JOHN LOCKE, ESQ. [swash Q] | [rule 64 mm] | A NEW EDITION, WITH ALTERATIONS. | [rule 64 mm] | [French rule 32 mm] | YORK: | PRINTED BY WILSON, SPENCE, AND MAWMAN; | FOR T. WILSON and R. SPENCE, *High-Ouſegate.* | *Anno* 1788.
Coll: 12° in 6s (142 × 86 mm cut) A^4 B–R^6 S^2 [$ half signed]; 102 leaves; pp. *i–iii* vi–ix x 13 14–205 *206–208* [= 204]. Page no. iv–v and 11–12 omitted.
Contents: A1^r title (verso blank), A2^r–A4^r (*iii*–ix) pref., B1^r–S1^r (*13–205*) text, S1^v–S2 (*206–208*) blank.
Text (K1^r): 18 lines; 103 (114) × 60 mm; 114 R with 1.5 mm leading between lines. Fair-quality laid paper without watermark. Vertical chainlines. Page no. at external end of headlines. No marginal notes.
HT A2^r: PREFACE | TO THE | FIRST ENGLISH EDITION.
   B1^r: A | LETTER | CONCERNING | TOLERATION.
   Q6^v: POSTSCRIPT.
Headlines: A2^v–A4^r PREFACE.
   R1^r–S1^r POSTSCRIPT.

Headlines, verso to recto: B1ᵛ–Q6ʳ: A LETTER | CONCERNING TOLERATION.
CW: none.
Press figures: none.
Notes: Reprint of the 1740 edition (no. 5). A microfilm copy is to be found in the collection, *The Eighteenth Century*, reel 320, no. 11.
References: Attig 59; Christophersen p. 99; ESTC t108178.
Copies examined: Y C L (8403.b.9) O (Douce L.30)

12. Epistola. English trans. '4th ed.', Windsor, Vt., 1788. 8° in 4s.
A | LETTER | CONCERNING | TOLERATION. | [rule 81 mm] | By JOHN [swash J] LOCKE, Gent. | [rule 83 mm] | The FOURTH EDITION. | [rule 86 mm] | Civil Governors go miſerabl[y] out of their Province, | whenever they take upon them the Care of Truth. | If it wants ſuch aid, it cannot be of GOD. | DOCTOR PRICE. | [orn. rule 85 mm] | WINDSOR: | Printed by ALDEN SPOONER, for JOSEPH THOMSON. | M,DCC,LXXXVIII.
Coll: 8° in 4s (183 × 120 mm uncut) A⁴ B–I⁴ [$1 signed]; 36 leaves; pp. *i–ii* iii–iv 5–7 8–66 67 68–71 72.
Contents: A1ʳ title (verso blank), A2ʳ,ᵛ (iii–iv) dedication, A3ʳ,ᵛ (5–6) pref., A4ʳ–I4ʳ (7–71) text, I4ᵛ (72) blank.
Text (B4ʳ): 32 lines; 134 (145) × 86 mm; 84 R. Poor-quality laid paper with vertical chainlines, without watermarks. No headlines or RTs; page no. centered within square brackets as headlines.
HT A2ʳ [double orn. rule of rosettes 81 mm] | To his Excellency THOMAS | CHITTENDEN, Eſq.
A3ʳ [orn. rule 81 mm] | TO THE | READER.
A4ʳ [orn. rule 81 mm] | A | LETTER.
I2ʳ [orn. rule 81 mm] | POSTSCRIPT. [swash Ts]
Headlines: A2ᵛ DEDICATION.
A3ᵛ To the READER.
CW: Page. A4 by D2 (chriſ-) tianity. E2ᵛ granted [granted,] I1ᵛ POSTSCRIPT. [swash Ts]
Notes: Standard reprint of text, with dedication signed (p. iv): 'THE EDITOR. Windſor, October 24th, 1788.' Popple's pref. signed 'The TRANSLATOR.' The place of publication is in the state of Vermont. All copies I have seen appear to have lost the 'y' of 'miserably' in the tenth line of the title.

The quotation in the title is 'in fact an amalgam of two bits of the section "Of Liberty of Discussion" from [Richard] Price's *Observations on the Importance of the American Revolution* ([London] 1784).' In the 1784 Boston reprint, the first part of the quotation (p. 21) reads: 'But in reality, civil power has nothing to do with any such matters: and civil governors go miserably out of their proper province, whenever they take upon them the care of truth, or the support of any doctrinal points'. 'The second part comes

in a discussion of Christians using the civil power to defend their religion: "If it wants such aid it cannot be of God" (page 26).' I am indebted to John Stephens for this information. A facsim. reprint is in the Evans microcard set.
References: Attig 60; Christophersen p. 99; ESTC w0011365, t006142 (briefer); Evans 21207.
Copies examined: L (8463 cc.2 (2)) MWA

13*. Epistola. English trans. Stockbridge, Mass. 1790.
'A Letter concerning Toleration. By John Locke, Gent. Stockbridge [Massachusetts] Printed by Loring Andrews, 1790.'
Title taken from citation in Evans (22622). No known surviving copy. Attig. (*61, p. 15) cites a solicitation for subscriptions for this edition in *The Western Star* for April 27, 1790.

14. Epistola. English trans. Huddersfield, 1796. 12° in 6s. Two issues.
14A (first issue): A | LETTER | CONCERNING | [outline type:] TOLERATION. | [double rule 43 mm] | BY JOHN LOCKE, ESQ. | [double rule 43 mm] | [orn., swagged vase 16 × 26 mm] | [Oxford rule 46 mm] | [script type:] *Huddersfield:* | PRINTED FOR THE EDITOR, BY J. BROOK. | 1796.
14B (second issue): . . . [as in 1st issue, until penultimate line:] PRINTED AND SOLD BY J. BROOK, BOOKSELLER. | 1796.
Coll: 12° in 6s (170 × 104 mm) A^3 (−A3 in 2d issue) B−F^6 G^4 (−G4 in 1st issue) [$ half signed]; 36 leaves; pp. *1−4* + 1 leaf + *5* 6−70 + 1 leaf (*71−72*) [= 72]. Second issue without A3 but has advt. leaf (G4) at end.
Contents: A1^r title (verso blank), A2^{r,v} (*3−4*) pref., A3^{r,v} editor's pref. (in 1st issue), B1^r−G3^v (*5−70*) text, G4^r (*71*) advt. by Brook, G4^v (*72*) blank.
Text (D6r): 36 lines; 127 (138) × 72 mm; 70 R. Gatherings A and G were one sheet. Medium-quality wove paper without watermark. Page no. at external end of headlines.
HT: A2^r: [double rule 70 mm] | TO THE READER. | [French rule 13 mm] A3^r: [double rule 70 mm] | THE EDITOR'S ADDRESS. | [French rule 13 mm]
B1^r: [double rule 70 mm] | A | LETTER | CONCERNING | TOLERATION. | [French rule 20 mm]
G2^v: [double rule 69 mm] | POSTSCRIPT. | [French rule 12 mm]
Headlines: *A Letter concerning Toleration.*
CW: Page. B1^r The ['The] D2^v But [But,] E6^v public
Press figures: none.
Notes: The 'Editor's Address' (lacking in the second issue) is signed: 'Halifax, | June 2, 1796. | J. COCKIN.' I have been unable to determine any textual changes made to the text from previous printings. The advt. on the last leaf (lacking in the first issues I have seen) is headed: 'Lately publiſhed, and Sold by J. BROOK, Huddersfield, . . .' The text follows that of the 1784 ed.

(no. 10). A microfilm copy of the second issue is to be found in the collection, *The Eighteenth Century*, reel 3262, no. 11.
References: Attig 62; Christophersen p.99; ESTC 1st issue: t155049; 2nd issue: t108834.
Copies examined: First issue: NjP (6106.332.5; lacks G4 at end) O (24821.f.1)
  Second issue: L (8410 bbb.16; trimmed to 162 × 98 mm) Gu

15. Epistola. English. 1800. 8o
A | LETTER | CONCERNING | TOLERATION. | [French rule 20 mm] | By JOHN [swash J] LOCKE, Eſq. | [French rule 20 mm] | A NEW EDITION. | [orn. French rule 33 mm] | LONDON: | Printed by J. CROWDER, Warwick-Square, | FOR J. JOHNSON, IN ST. PAUL'S CHURCH-YARD. | [rule 11 mm] | 1800.
Colophon, K2^r: Printed by J. Crowder, Warwick-ſquare.
Coll: 8° (173 × 107 mm uncut) A^4 χ^2 B–I^8 K^2 [$ half signed; χ1 signed 'A4']; 72 leaves; pp. *i–iii* iv–v *vi–ix* x–xii *1* 2–131 *132* [= 144]. (Leaves A2 and 3 are conjugate in my copy, as are A1 with χ2; perhaps A4 was to have been detached and mounted before A1.)
Contents: A1^r title (verso blank), A2^r–A3^r (*iii–v*) 'ADVERTISEMENT.' (dated June 1800), A3^v (*vi*) blank, A4^r (*vii*) half title, A4^v (*viii*) blank, χ1^r ('A4')–χ2^v (*ix*–xii) pref., B1^r–K2^r (*1*–131) text, K2^v (*132*) blank.
Text (C1^v): 23 lines; 118 (126) × 67 mm; 102 R with 1 mm leading. Good-quality laid paper with pro patria watermark. In my copy, the top of watermark shows at inner margin, top edge of leaves A1–4, χ1–2; bottom of mark at inner margin head of leaves K1–2; leaves K1–2 could be part of A1 & 4, A2 & 3, or χ1–2; but in view of the watermark, A1–4 are not part of the *same* sheet. Page no. for the body of the text at external ends of headlines. 'Advertisement' and pref. without headlines; page no. within parentheses centered at head instead.
Half-title, A4^r: A | LETTER | CONCERNING | TOLERATION.
HT, A2^r: [Oxford rule 71 mm] | *ADVERTISEMENT.*
  χ1^r: [Oxford rule 69 mm] | THE TRANSLATOR | TO | THE READER.
  B1^r: [Oxford rule 68 mm] | A | LETTER | CONCERNING | TOLERATION.
RT: A LETTER | CONCERNING TOLERATION.
CW: none.
Press figures: iv (A2^v)–4 xi (χ2^r)–3 6 (B3^v)–3 18 (C1^v)–2 29 (C7^r)–3 38 (D3^v)–3 54 (E3^v)–2 66 (F1^v)–2 77 (F7^r)–1 94 (G7^r)–1 102 (H3^v)–2 108 (H6^v)–4 118 (I3^v)–5 Note: Outer formes are signed 4 times, inner 8; only 3 sheets have figures on both inner and outer formes (C, F and H; also possibly A, χ and K if originally one sheet).
Notes: Appears to be a standard reprint but with changes in paragraphing and capitalization. The 'postscript' section (I6^r et seq.) is not so headed or

marked. A microfilm copy is in the collection, *The Eighteenth Century*, reel 3091, no. 20.
References: Attig 63; Christophersen p. 99; ESTC t103884.
Copies examined: Y L (4374.a.36) O (Vet.A5 f.1193) Oman (lacks A1) P (R.42171)

16*. Epistola. Dutch. 1689?
A summary review of item no. 1 (the first Latin edition) appeared in Jean Le Clerc's journal, *Bibliothèque universelle et historique*, t.15 for 1689, pp. 402–12. The final paragraph indicates that 'on l'a traduit d'abord en Anglois, & en Flamand. Il est deja imprimé en ceux Langues, & peut-être qu'on le verra encore en François.' No Flemish (or Dutch) translation is elsewhere recorded, nor have I found any surviving copies. But there undoubtedly was a Dutch translation, for in a letter dated 6 September 1689 Limborch informs Locke 'The French translation has not appeared so far, nor do I know whether it will; but the Dutch is on sale in our shops and is being read by many people with great approval.' (De Beer's translation, *Corr*. 1178; iii, 681–2.) In an earlier letter of 8 July 1689 (*Corr*. 1158; iii. 647) Limborch had recorded that it had been translated into Dutch, and would soon be published. I have found no record of any locations of this edition.

17*. Epistola. Dutch trans. Harlingen, 1730. 8°
J. Abkoude, in his *Naamregister* (1788) lists a Dutch translation with title: Brief over verdraagszaamheit, and imprint: Harlingen: Folkert van der Plaats, 1730; in octavo priced at 11 st[uivers].
No Dutch libraries recorded in the Centrale Catalogus Boeken (at the Royal Library in the Hague) have submitted a record of this edition. Nor have I found any surviving copies elsewhere. Attig (*70) records this same entry from Abkoude.

18. Epistola. Dutch trans. (anon.) 2d ed. Amsterdam, 1734. 8°
Section title: EEN | BRIEF | Aangaande de | VERDRAAGZAAMHET. | GESCHREVEN | DOOR | JOANNES [swash J] LOCKE. | *Uit het Latyn Vertaalt*. | TWEDE DRUK.
In: VERZAMELING | Van eenige | VERHANDELINGEN | Over de | VERDRAAGZAAMHEID | En | VRYHEID VAN GODSDIENST. | [orn., vase with birds above scrolls, 26 × 46 mm] | TE AMSTERDAM, | By { JACOB TER BEEK En ISAAK TIRION, } Boekverkoopers. | MDCCXXXIV.
Collation of the whole: 8° (156 × 97 mm cut) *^{8} A–E^8 ^{2}A–^{2}C^8 ^{2}D^6 ^{3}A–^{3}E^8 ^{3}F^2 ^{4}A–^{4}D^8 ^{4}E^2 [$ half signed]; pp. *i–xvi* 1–2 3–80; *1–2 3–*60; 1–2 3–83 84; *1–2 3–24 25–26 27–*68. Locke's text on first set (A–E^8 ; *1–*80 pp.).

Contents: *1ʳ title (verso blank), *2ʳ 'ORDER | DER | VERHANDELINGEN.', *2ᵛ 'DRUK-FOUTEN' [errata], *3ʳ-*8ᵛ 'BERIGT aan den | LEZER.', A1ʳ (1) section title (verso blank), A2ʳ-E8ᵛ (3–80) Locke's text in Dutch; ²A1ʳ section title (verso blank), ²A2ʳ-²D6ᵛ (3–80) 'De Godsdienst vry van Heerschappy, door G. Noodt'; ³A1ʳ section title (verso blank), ³A2ʳ-³F2ʳ (3–83) 'Aanmerkingen over de Verdraagzaamheid van J. Barbeyrac', ³F2ᵛ blank; ⁴A1ʳ section title (verso blank), ⁴A2-⁴B4ᵛ (3–24) 'Predakaatsi over de Natuur van Christus Koninkryk, door B. Hoadly', ⁴B5ʳ section title (verso blank), ⁴B6ʳ-⁴E2ᵛ (27–68) 'Predikaatsi over het Gedrag van Paulus tegen de Christenen voor zyne Bekeering, door J. Drieberge'.

Text (B3ʳ): 36 lines; 127 (135) × 67 mm; 71 R. Medium-quality laid paper with coat-of-arms watermark. RTs match titles of individual works, with page no. at external ends. Each separate work preceded by a section-title (verso blank); first page of each text called 'Pag. 3.'

RT, pp. 4–79 (first set): Een Brief aangraande de | VERDRAAGZAAMHEIT.

CW: Page.

Notes: A collection of five works: by Locke, G. Noodt, Barbeyrac, B. Hoadley, and J. Drieberge, each separately paged. The translators are anonymous. Noodt was a professor of law at Leiden and 'argued strongly for toleration in a famous address, in Latin, delivered at Leiden in February 1706 . . .'[3] His published speech was abstracted in the *Bibliothèque choisie*, 11 (1707): 231–259; within two years it was fully translated into French and English, subsequently in German. His 'was the culminating Dutch defence [of toleration] in secular, natural right terms, rather than theological principles.' (Ibid.)

Barbeyrac was a journalist and translator of Pufendorf, Grotius and Cumberland on natural law. For more information see the *Dictionnaire des journalistes, 1600–1789*, ed. Jean Sgard (Grenoble, 1976), pp. 20–21.

That Locke's work is called the second printing attests to an earlier edition, probably that of 1730.

Reference: Attig 72.

Copy examined: Leiden Univ. Lib. (597.G15 (2))

19. Epistola. Dutch trans. (anon.) 3d ed. Amsterdam, 1774. 8° Includes Dutch trans. of *Second Letter concerning Toleration*.

Section title: EERSTE | BRIEF | OVER DE | VERDRAAGZAAMHEID. | GESCHREVEN | DOOR | JOANNES [swash J] LOCKE. | *Uit het Latyn Vertaald.* | Derde Druk.

In: DE | VRYHEID | VAN | GODSDIENST | IN DE | BURGERLYKE MAATSCHAPPY | BETOOGD en VERDEEDIGD, | *Uit het Regt der*

---

[3] Jonathan Israel: *The Dutch Republic: Its Rise, Greatness, and Fall, 1477–1806* (Oxford, 1995), p. 674; he discusses the 'later stages of the toleration debate'.

Nature en der Volken, en uit de | *Nature van den Kristelyken Godsdienst,* | DOOR DE ZEER VERMAARDE MANNEN | LOCKE, | NOODT, | BARBEYRAC, | HOADLY EN DRIEBERGE. | Voor welker Verhandelingen geplaatst is een | *VERTOOG ter INLEIDINGE,* | Waarin zo de Grondbegin els van die Vryheid, en van het | Regt der Overheid omtrent haare zorge voor den Gods- | dienst, als de Oorſprong der Dwalingen wegens de | Heerſchappy over denzelven worden aangeweezen, | DOOR DEN HEER | R. D. B. G. D. I. H. M. V. | [Oxford rule 54 mm] | *Te AMSTERDAM,* | By *JAN* [swash J] *DÓLL,* | MDCCLXXIV.

Collation of the whole: 8° (203 × 125 mm cut) †⁶ *-4*⁸ 5*⁴ (−5*4) A–2E⁸ 2F² [$ half signed]; 267 leaves; pp. *i–xii* I–LXIX *LXX* 1-2 3-82 *83-84* 85-224 *225-226* 227-298 *299-300* 301-382 *383-384* 385-408 *409-410* 411-452 [= 534].

Contents: †1 blank, †2ʳ (*iii*) title, †2ᵛ blank, †3ʳ-†5ᵛ (*v–x*) 'BERICHT van den UITGEVER' (signed V. D. V.), †6ʳ (*xi*) contents, †6ᵛ (*xii*) blank, *1ʳ-5*3ʳ (I–LXIX) 'Vertoog ter Inleidinge', A1ʳ (*1*) section title, A1ᵛ blank, A2ʳ–F1ᵛ (*3–82*) text of first 'toleration' letter, F2ʳ (*83*) section title, F2ᵛ blank, F3ʳ–O8ᵛ (*85–224*) text of second 'toleration' letter, P1ʳ–T5ᵛ (*225–298*) 'Redenvoering over den Godsdienst vry van Heerschappy' by G. Noodt, T6ʳ–2A7ᵛ (*299–382*) 'Aanmerkingen over de Verdraagzaamheid' by J. Barbeyrac, 2A8ʳ–2C4ᵛ (*383–408*) 'Predikatie over de Natuur van Kristus Koningryk' by B. Hoadly, 2C5ʳ–2F2ᵛ (*409–452*) 'Predikatie over het Gedrag van Paulus tegens de Christenen voor zyne Bekeering' by J. Drieberge.

Text (A2ᵛ): 30 lines; 138 (150) × 81 mm; 93 R. Translator's note set 27 lines, 107 ital. with 1.5 mm leading. Excellent-quality laid paper without watermark. Page no. at external ends of headlines, with RTs matching individual works.

HT, †6ʳ: ORDER | DER | VERHANDELINGEN.
 A2ʳ: EERSTE | BRIEF | OVER DE | VERDRAAGZAAMHEID.
 F3ʳ: TWEEDE | BRIEF | OVER DE | VERDRAAGZAAMHEID.

Section title, F2ʳ: TWEEDE | BRIEF | OVER DE | VERDRAAGZAAMHEID. | GESCHREVEN | DOOR | JOANNES LOCKE.

Headline, †3ʳ-†5ᵛ: BERIGT van den UITGEVER.

RT A2ʳ–F1ʳ (4–81): *Eerſte Brief over de* | VERDRAAGZAAMHEID.
 F5ᵛ–O8ʳ: *Tweede Brief over de* | VERDRAAGZAAMHEID.

CW: Page. A2ʳ maar

Notes: A reprint of the 1734 edition, but with Locke's *Second Letter concerning Toleration*, in Dutch, added. Each work preceded by a section title (verso blank); first text page of each also called, e.g., 'Pag. 85.'

Reference: Attig 72 n. (omits mention of 2d 'Letter')

Copy examined: AMu (291.F24)

20. Epistola. French trans. (anon.) [s.l.] 1764. 12° in 6s
Caption title: [Oxford rule 62 mm] | LETTRE | *De* JEAN LOCKE *ſur la tolerance.*
In: TRAITÉ | *SUR LA* | TOLERANCE, | *AUGMENTÉ* | D'UNE LETTRE | DE JEAN LOCKE | *SUR LE MEME SUJET.* [swash Us, J] | [Oxford rule, thick/thin, 62 mm] | M. DCC. LXIV.
Collation of the whole: 12° in 6s (168 × 97 mm cut) A–2C⁶ [$ half signed]; 156 leaves; pp. *i–iii* iv–vi 7–204 105–107 *208* 209–309 *310–312*. Pages 205–7 called '105–7'.
Contents: A1ʳ title (verso blank), A2ʳ–A3ᵛ (*iii–vi*) 'Avertissement', A4ʳ–S2ʳ (7–107 rectē 207) Voltaire's text, S2ᵛ blank, S3ʳ–2C5ʳ (209–309) Locke's text, 2C5ᵛ–2C6ʳ contents, 2C6ᵛ blank.
Text (T3ʳ): 29 lines; 121 (131) × 66 mm; 84 R. 'Avertissement' set 24 lines 99 ital. Medium-quality laid paper without watermark. Page no. centered at head of page within parentheses as headlines.
CW: Gathering (on 6ᵛ). B autre S (l'ambi-) tion T (Egli-) fe. V eux- [eux-mêmes] X que Y (man-) ger Z du 2A aucun 2B de
Notes: Voltaire's work was first published anonymously in Geneva in 1763. The text of Locke '*est extraite d'un volume des oeuvres diverses de Locke ...*', wherein are also to be found 'On the Conduct of the Understanding' and the discourse on miracles (*Avertissement*, p. vi), probably that published in 1710 (no. 372). Not mentioned in Rochedieu. Cioranescu gives no imprint for this 1764 edition. A. A. Barbier (in *Oeuvres anonymes*) lists Voltaire as the author of the first work.
The inspiration for the anonymously published work by Voltaire was 'l'affaire Calas', a controversy about a Protestant merchant of Toulouse who was executed in 1762 for murdering his son; it was more likely he had covered up his son's suicide. Through Voltaire's interference, especially by this work, Calas was posthumously pardoned in 1765. Cf. *Dictionnaire de biographie française*, entry under Calas (7: 882–3).
References: Attig 73; Cioranescu 64854.
Copies examined: O (Vet.E5 f.292)   CtY (Hfd3/767)

21. Epistola. German trans. (Olearius). [s.l.], 1710. 8°
Herrn | Johann Lodens | Vormahlig = Königl. Engelländi = | ſchen Staats = Bebientens | Sendſchreiben [ornamental S] | von der | TOLERANZ, | Oder von der | Religions- und Gewiſſens = | Freyheit. | Aus dem Lateiniſchen Exemplar überſetzt/ | und mit einigen nützlichen Anmerckungen | erläutert. | [orn. rule: 9 suns, colon, 10 suns, 75 × 4 mm] | Gedruckt im Jahr Chriſti 1710.
Coll: 8° (156 × 95 mm) 𝔄–H⁸ J⁴ [$ 5 (–C5, I3,4) signed]; 68 leaves; pp. i–*xii* 1–124 [= 136].
Contents: A1ʳ title, A1ᵛ Biblical quotations from John 19.15, Luc. 19.15, 2 Chron. 12.8, Apoc. 17.16 and Ezech. 43.7-8, A2ʳ–A6ᵛ (*iii–xii*) translator's pref., A7ʳ–I1ʳ (1–117) text, I1ᵛ–I4ᵛ (118–124) 'Zum Beschluss' (Postscriptum).

Text (B4ᵛ): 32 lines; 136 (143) × 78 mm; 84 fraktur, except I1ᵛ–I4 (118-24) set 28 lines, 95 fraktur. Footnotes set 70 fraktur. Laid paper, with small posthorn watermark. No running titles. Page numbers, 1-124, centered at top of page within 6 orn. (sun, colon, right paren., number, left paren., colon, sun); in the prelim. pages the same ornaments surround a small 'o'.
CW: Page. B6ʳ Ver = [Verſtand] C5ʳ Nach = [Nachdem] E4ᵛ Obrig = [Obrigkeit] G1ᵛ Men = [Menſchen] H4ᵛ ih = [ihnen]
Notes: Anonymous translation of the first or second Latin edition (1689 or 1705; no. 1 or 2) but with some help from Popple (no. 3). The translator follows the Latin text in the list of sects to be permitted equal liberties (Remonstrants, Antiremonstrants, Lutherans, Anabaptists and Socinians) but (*pace* Popple) adds Quakers and other parties. He does not add Popple's 'Faith is not faith without believing' to *his* translation of the original 'in fidem autem consistit verae et salutiferae religionis vis et efficacia' (Cf. no.3, *Notes*). The pref. is dated 6 Jan. 1710., and signed 'Der Uberſetzer.' Last page of text has tailpiece of flowers, 42 × 50 mm. Christophersen attributes this translation to Gottfried Olearius, who includes 80 numbered explicatory footnotes of his own.
References: Attig 75; Christophersen p. 100.
Copies examined: MH-AH [Berlin] [GOT] Thoemmes (in stock 1991)

22. Epistola. German trans. (Olearius). [s.l.], 1714. 8°
In fraktur and roman: Herrn | < Johann Lodens > / | Vormah < li > g = Königl. En < gel > ländi = | ſchen Staats = Bedientens/ | Sendſchreiben [orn. S] | von der | TOLERANZ, | ... [&c. as in no. 21, until orn. rule: 19 suns, 73 × 4 mm] | Aufs neue gedruckt im Jahr Chriſti | M DCC XIV.
Coll: 8° (165 × 94 mm cut) A–H⁸ I⁴ [$ half + 1 (–C5) signed]; 68 leaves; pp. i–xii 1-124 [= 136].
Contents and Text: as no. 21, but on poorer quality laid paper, without watermark.
CW: Page. A2ᵛ nüſſen/ B5ᵛ (ſeligma =) chenden B6ʳ Ver = [Verſtand] C5ʳ Nach = [Nachdem] E4ᵛ Obrig = [Obrigkeit] F2ᵛ gewiſſe G1ᵛ Men = [Menſchen] H4ᵛ ih = [ihnen] H7ʳ welche J1ᵛ im
Pages 92 and 116 (G4ᵛ, H8ᵛ) have CW on same line as text.
Notes: Line-by-line reprint of no. 21, even to the omission of a signature on C5, and the identical flower orn. on p.124 (42 × 50 mm). The translator's pref. is dated 6 Jan. 1710., and signed 'Der Uberſetzer.' A close examination of the lines indicates it has been newly typeset. My copy (the only one I have found) has a mutilated title leaf, indicated by the angle brackets in the title transcription. Dr. Bernhard Fabian knows of no other copies.
Copy examined: Y (formerly in Philosophisches Seminar, Heidelberg)

22.1. Epistola. German trans. (Olearius). [s.l.], 1724. 8°
Herrn | Johann Lodens | Vormahlig = Königl. Engelländi = | ſchen Staats = Bedientens | Sendſchreiben [ornamental S] | von der | TOLERANZ, |

Ober von der | Religions- und Gewissens = | Freyheit. | Aus dem Lateinischen Exemplar überseßt/ | und mit einigen nüßlichen Anmerdungen | erläutert. | [orn. rule: 12 suns, colon, 13 suns, 75 × 3 mm] | Aufs neue gedruckt im Jahr Christi | M DCC XXIV.
Coll: 8° (165 × 100 mm cut) A-H⁸ J⁴ [$ half + 1 (-C5) signed]; 68 leaves; pp. i–xii 1–124 [= 136].
Contents: as no. 21.
Text (D4ᵛ): 32 lines; 132 (141) × 75 mm; 83 fraktur except I1ᵛ–I4 (118–124) set 28 lines 95 fraktur. Footnotes set 69 fraktur. Fair-quality laid paper, small part of an unidentifiable watermark at top inner edge of first (or 8th) leaf of each gathering. Same flower ornament on p. 124 (42 × 50 mm). Page no. within ornaments centered at head of page, followed by 75 mm rule, e.g. [acorn orn.]): 109 :([acorn orn.].
CW: Page. A2ᵛ nüſ- [nüſſen/] B5ᵛ (ſeligma =) chen = [chenden] B6ʳ Ver = [Verſtand] C5ʳ Nach = [Nachdem] E4ᵛ Obrig = [Obrigkeit] F2ᵛ ge = [gewiſſe] G1ᵛ Men = [Menſchen] H4ᵛ ih = [ihnen] H7ʳ wel = [welche] J1ᵛ im
Page 92 (G4ᵛ) has CW on same line as text.
Notes: A line-for-line and, except for pages 118–24, page-for-page reprint of no. 21 or 22. Only on those last seven pages ('Zum Beschluss') do the pages end differently, because this edition puts a full line space between paragraphs.
 I have not found a reference to or record of any other owners of this edition. My copy was recently acquired from Thoemmes Antiquarian Books, Bristol.
Copy examined: Y

23. Epistola. German trans. (Olearius). Hamburg and Leipzig, 1728. 8°
Section title: Herrn | Johann Lodens, [orn. J, L] | Vormahlig = Königl. Engelländi = | ſchen Staats-Bedientens / | Sendschreiben [orn. S] | von der | TOLERANZ, | Oder von der | Religions- und Gewiſſens = | Freyheit. | Aus dem Engliſchen ins Teutſche | überſeßt. | [2 acorn orns.]
In (in fraktur & roman): Die | Rechtmäßigkeit, Nothwendigkeit | und Nußbarkeit | Der | TOLERANZ | und | Gewiſſens = Freyheit, [orn. G, F] | Klärlich und kräfftig aus unterſchiedenen | über dieſe Materie verfertigten Schrifften | erwieſen, und zum gemeinen Beſten auffs | Neue zuſamen gedruckt, | Nebſt einer Vorrede | Von dem | Eyfer [orn. E] in und über die Religion, [orn. R] | und | Anmerckungen [orn.A] | über | des gelehrten Halleſiſchen JCti und Profeſſoris, | Herrn Böhmers, anno 1726. gehaltene Diſſertation | von der | TOLERANZ. | [rule 89 mm] | 2. Theſſ .I. v.6. | Es iſt recht bey GOtt, Trübſal zu vergelten denen, die an = | dern (um der Religion willen) Trübſal anthun. | [rule 87 mm] | Hamburg und Leipzig, | Bey Jonas Korten, anno 1728.
Collation of the whole: 8° (161 × 94 mm cut) πA-D⁸ πE⁴ A-E⁸ F-2H⁸ [$5 (-πE3, πE4, S2) signed]; 284 leaves; pp. 1–3 4–8 9 10–69 61 71–72 1 2–188 189 190–274 275 276–384 385–386 387–456 457 458–496 [= 568]. (Prelim. p. 70, at inner margin, called 61; the 4 of p. 476 is inverted.)

Contents: ᵖA1ʳ title (verso blank), ᵖA2ʳ–A4ᵛ (3–8) 'Ordnung der Tractate in diesem Wercke.', ᵖA5ʳ–C1ᵛ (9–34, 61) 'Vorrede' subscribed 'Geschrieben in Amsterdam, von Johann Christian Seitz, den 27. Julii 1727.', ᵖC2ʳ–E3ᵛ (35–69, 61) 'Anmerckungen', ᵖE4ʳ·ᵛ (71–72) errata ('Zu corrigiren.', 27 lines on recto and 7 on verso), A1ʳ–M6ᵛ (1–188) 'Abdruck eines Christlichen Bedenckens ...' by Seitz, M7ʳ section title for Noodt, M7ᵛ–S1ᵛ (190–274) 'Rede von der Freiheit des Gewissens ...' by Gerard Noodt, S2ʳ section title for Locke, S2ᵛ–2A8ᵛ (276–384) Locke's text, 2B1ʳ section title, 2B1ᵛ biblical quotation from 1 Kings 12–13, 2B2ʳ–2F4ᵛ (387–456) 'Kurtze und deutliche- in Natürlich- und Göttl. Rechten gegründete Vorstellung ... von Johann Christian Seiz', 2F5ʳ section title, 2F5ᵛ–2H8ᵛ (458–496) 'Vernünfftige und Schrifftmäßige Untersuchung ...', translated from the English (anon.)

Text (S5ʳ): 29 lines; 124 (135) × 74 mm; 85 fraktur. Umlauts were printed as superscript fraktur e's throughout. Text includes quotations from Latin texts set 85 R, and from German-language texts set in Schwabacher (a bolder, simpler fraktur). Coarse-textured paper without watermarks. Each text page has as heading, centered ornaments: flower pointing left + (o) + flower pointing right, above broken rule, 73 mm. Page no. at upper external corners except prelim. p. '61' (rectē 70), and 351, both of which are set at upper inner corners.

Head title, ᵖC2ʳ: [rule 71 mm] | Einige Anmerckungen | über | Des gelehrten Hallenſiſchen JCti und | Profeſſoris, Herrn Böhmers, anno 1726. | gehaltene Diſſertation, | von der | TOLERANZ, | Worinnen die Unzulänglichkeit ſeiner Lehr = | Sätze in dieſem wichtigen Stück be = | ſcheidentlich gezeiget wird. | Anno 1727.

Section titles, A1ʳ: Abdruck [ornamental A] | eines Chriſtlichen | Bedenckens, [orn. B] | So | über die Fragen: | *I.* Was eine Obrigkeit zu Rettung | ihres Gewiſſens bey ihren Unter = | thanen, ſo anderer Religion ſind, | zu thun habe? | *II.* Ob in Religions = Sachen einige | Gewalt gebraucht, und die Frey = | heit der Gewiſſen gekräncket wer = | den dörffte? | *III.* Ob die in ſolchen Sachen auffge = | richtete Verträge, Zuſagungen und | Endſchwüre verbündlich ſeyn? | Auß dem heiligen Wort Gottes / der | Catholiſchen Kirchen älteſten Vätern Zeug = | nüß und geſunden Vernunfft = Gründen | an eine | Hohe Standes = Perſon [ornamental H, S, P] | auff begehren geſtellet, | und mit dero Zulaſſung aus Licht gegeben worden.

M7ʳ: Des | berühmten | GERHARDI | NOODTS | Profeſſoris zu Leiden [orn.L] | in Holland, | gelehrte | Rede / [orn. R] | von der | Freiheit des Gewiſſens, [orn. F, G] | Wie ſelbige in dem | Natur = und Völcker = Recht, [orn. N, V, R] | gegründet iſt. | Nach dem Lateiniſchen *Original* in das | Teutſche überſetzet. | [2 acorn orns.]

S2ʳ: section title for Locke's text, as transcribed above.

2B1ʳ: Kurtze und deutliche = | In Natürlich = und Göttl. Rechten | gegründete | Vorſtellung [orn. V] | Von dem | Recht und Macht Weltlich = und | Chriſtlicher Obrigkeit | In | Religions = [orn. R] | und Kirchen = Dingen, [orn. K, D] | Worinnen mit vielen unwiderſprechlichen | Beweißthůmern dargethan wird, welch eine | abſurde, unvernůnfftige, ungerechte, Antichriſtiſche, allen | Fluch Gottes nach ſich ziehende Sache das Zwingen, | Straffen und Verfolgen in = und ůber Religions = | Kirchen und Gewiſſens = Dingen ſey? | Allen Verfolgern und Verfolgten zur dienlichen | Nachricht aus Licht gegeben | Von | JOHANN CHRISTIAN SEIZ. | Gebet dem Kayſer, was des Kayſers iſt, und | GOtt was Gottes iſt! Einem jeden Reſpect, Furcht | und Gehorſam, wo, worinnen und ſo weit | es ſich gebůhret.

2F5^r: Vernůnfftige und Schrifftmåßige | Unterſuchung, [orn. U] | Wie nőthig und heylſam einer die | allgemeine Ruhe liebenden Obrigkeit | die Bůrgerliche Tolerantz in | Religions = Sachen, | Hingegen | Wie gefåhrlich und ſchådlich dem | gemeinen Weſen das Straffen / Zwin = | gen und Verfolgen wegen der | Religion ſeye. | Erſt in Engliſcher, und her = | nach in Frantzőſiſcher Sprache gedruckt / | und aus dieſerwegen ſeiner Vortreflichkeit zu | dieſer Zeit, da die Obrigkeit von denen Geiſtli = | chen an vielen Orten zum Straffen, Zwingen | und Verfolgen, wegen der Religion bereits | verleitet worden, und noch ferner will verleitet | werden, ins Hochteutſche überſetzet, und | zum Druck befőrdert.

CW: Page (in fraktur). A7^r Tha- [Thaten] C4^r beför = [befördern] ^{2}C4^r Natur S2^v war = [warhaffig] T6^r meh = [mehreres] U3^v GOtt X8^v Men = [Menſchen] Y5^r haben = [habendes] Z3^v Gott- [Gottheit] 2A8^r der = [derjenigen] 2G7^r [roman:] Ultrà [*Ultrà,*]

Notes. A reprint of the 1710 or 1714 editions of the German translation (no. 21 or 22), but without the footnotes, despite the claim that it is translated from the English language. The lists of sects to be permitted equal liberties follows the Latin list, and as in the earlier editions includes Quakers. None of Popple's other insertions appear here either. Seitz's *Anmerckungen* and the Abdruck were written in answer to an inaugural dissertation, entitled 'De tolerantiae religiosae affectibus civilibus', presented at Halle in 1726, where Justus (Jobst) Henning Boehmer (1674–1749) was *praeses*, and Karl Heinrich Fuhrmann *respondens*. Noodt's discourse on liberty of conscience was originally written in Latin, and was also translated into French, and into Dutch (see no. 18-19). The penultimate piece in the vol., Seitz's *Vorstellung*, was first published in 1712. Dr. Bernhard Fabian informs me the final piece is a translation of *The Reasonableness of Toleration, and the Unreasonableness of Penal Laws and Tests; Wherein is prov'd by Scripture, reason and antiquity, that liberty of conscience is the undoubted right of every man, and tends to the flourishing of kingdoms and commonwealths; and that persecution for meer religion is unwarrantable, unjust, and destructive to humane society* ..., a 40-page pamphlet attributed to William Penn (London, 1687; Wing^2 P1352; ESTC r023116). There is another copy of this 5-part publication in the University Library of Halle in Saxony.

Reference: GV under Seitz: 'Nutzbarkeit der Toleranz u. Gewissensfreyh. 8. Hamburg. 728.'

Copy examined: Y

24. Epistola. German trans. (anon.). Leipzig, 1796. 8°
In fraktur: J. Locke | über Dulbung, | eine Epistel, | aus dem Englischen, | den | Herren Oberconsistorialräthen, | Hermes, Hilmer und Woltersdorf | gewidmet | von | dem Uebersetzer. | [French rule 19 mm] | [French rule 67 mm] | Leipzig, | in der Pottischen Buchhandlung. | 1796.
Coll: 8° (168 × 97 mm cut))(^{8} (–)(1.8 = I^2) A–H^8 I^2 [$ 2 (–I2) signed]; 72 leaves; pp. *I–III IV–XII 1* 2–131 *132* [= 144].
Contents:)(1^r title (verso blank),)(2^r–)(6^v (*III*–XII) translator's introduction, A1^r–I2^r (*1*–131) text, I2^v blank.
Text (B2^r): 22 lines; 109 (114) × 62 mm; 100 fraktur with 1 mm leading between lines. Medium-quality laid paper with coat-of-arms (?-illegible) watermark. Page no. in upper external corners as headlines. Gathering)(is 2d to 7th leaves of I gathering, I1 and 2 being 1st and 8th leaves, as seen by watermark.
CW: Page.
Notes: A new German translation by an unidentified hand.
References: Attig *76 ('unverified'); Christophersen p. 100; GV 89: 366.
Copy examined: Mun (Polem. 3113^i)

25. Second Letter concerning Toleration. 1690. 4° (Anonymous).
Within a double rule, inner 176 × 105 mm, outer 187 × 114 mm: A | SECOND | LETTER | CONCERNING | TOLERATION. | [rule 101 mm] | LICENSED, | *June* 24. 1690. | LONDON: [swash D, N] | Printed for *Awnſham* and *John* [swash J] *Churchill*, at the | *Black* [swash B] *Swan* in *Ave-Mary=Lane*, near *Pater-* [swash P] | *Noſter=Row*. [swash N, R] M DC XC.
Coll: 4° (217 × 160 mm uncut) A^4 (–A2.3 = K^2) B–I^4 K^2 [$ half signed]; 36 leaves; pp. *i–iv* 1–68 [= 72].
Contents: A1^r half-title, A1^v advt. by A. Churchill (50 lines), A2^r title (verso blank), B1^r–K2^v (1–68) text, signed 'PHILANTHROPUS.' and dated 'May 27, 1690.'
Text (G3^v): 40 lines (D3^v has 37 lines; the rest of E, leaves of D and F, and K2^r = p. 67 have 39); 162 (175) × 102 (122) mm; 80 R. Medium-quality laid paper with watermark Heawood 749. Page no. at external ends of headlines. Page references to the Bible or Proast's *Argument* set roman in external margins.
Half-title: [rule 101 mm] | A | SECOND LETTER | CONCERNING | TOLERATION. | [rule 101 mm]
HT: [double rule 104/102 mm] | TO THE | AUTHOR | OF THE | Argument of the Letter concerning Tolera- | ration, [sic] briefly conſidered and anſwered.
Headlines: A Second Letter concerning Toleration. (The 'A' is frequently a swash sort throughout, e.g. on D1^v, D2^r and D4^r; G1^v, H1^{r,v}); 'A' is lacking on K2^r (p. 67).

CW: Page. B4ᵛ your C4ʳ Con- [Confequences;] F1ᵛ Some- [Sometimes] H4ʳ (which [(which *i.e. ital. paren.*] I1ʳ SUB- [SUBJECTS;]
Notes: Published anonymously. Written in answer to the anonymous attack by Jonas Proast: *The Argument of the Letter concerning Toleration Consider'd and Answer'd* (1690; no. C1690-3). Text has frequent marginal citations to the Bible or his critic. There are frequent misprints, e.g. B1ʳ, line 6: 'yeilded'. A record of the licensing date on the title was made in the registers of the Stationers' Company on 26 April 1695. A microfilm copy of this edition is in EEB, reel 540, no. 10.
Notice: Bibliothèque universelle 19 (1690): 365-91 (covers also no. 3 and C1690-3).
References: Attig 87; Christophersen p. 17; ESTC r005485; L.L. 2945; T.C. II. 323; Transcript iii.457; Wing² L2755.
Copies examined: Y (205 × 144 mm cut) C CaOTU (Locke L63.E74E6 1690 (2)) C (Keynes) CaQMMO (trimmed to 205 × 150 mm) Ck Ck(Keynes) CLU-C CtY (K8.L79/bc690) DFo (acc.133525; uncut) Dm Dt Eu Gu L (698.i.2 (12)) MH (*EC65.L7934.B692t) NjP (Ex.6106.332.8) O¹ (4° S.70 Th) O² (4° D.14 Art B.S.; lacks A1; trimmed to 182 × 131 mm) O³ (Pamph. 201 (43); lacks A1; trimmed to 190 × 150 mm) Oa Oc Occ (lacks A1) Oq (trimmed to 190 × 145 mm) P (D².1538 (2))

26. Second Letter concerning Toleration. Dutch trans. 1774. *See* no. 19.

27. Third Letter for Toleration. 1692. 4° (anonymous)
Within a double rule, inner 154 × 104 mm, outer 164 × 114 mm: A | THIRD LETTER | FOR | TOLERATION, | TO THE | AUTHOR | OF THE | THIRD LETTER | CONCERNING | Toleration. | [double rule 100 mm] | LONDON, | Printed for *Awnſham* and *John* [swash J] *Churchill*, at the *Black* | *Swan* in *Pater-Noſter-Row*. MDCXCII.
Coll: 4° (201 × 142 mm cut) A² B-2Y⁴ [$ half signed]; 178 leaves; pp. *i-iv* 1-350 351-352 [=356].
Contents: A1ʳ half-title (verso blank), A2ʳ title, A2ᵛ note explaining textual abbrevs. (4 items), B1ʳ-2Y3ᵛ (1-350) text, 2Y4ʳ errata in 2 cols. (36 and 35 lines), 2Y4ᵛ advt. in 2 cols. (33 lines each) by Churchills.
Text: (F3ʳ): 40 lines (pp. 224, 241, 263, 340-2, and 348-9 have 39); 162 (173) × 102 (116) mm; 82 R. Medium-quality laid paper, mixed, with watermarks similar to Heawood 753 and 726. Page no. at external ends of headlines. Text in direction line on H1ʳ 49, Z1ʳ (169) and 2X4ᵛ (344).
Half-title: [rule 104 mm] | A | THIRD LETTER | FOR | TOLERATION. | [rule 104 mm]
HT: A Third LETTER *for Toleration.* [swash Ts] | [rule 100 mm]
Headlines: A Third *Letter for Toleration.* (Heading on verso of 4th leaf of gatherings 2D-2K, and on verso of 2d leaf of all other gatherings lacks tail of letter *f* in 'for'.)

CW: Page. B4ʳ (5) *Prin-* [*Principles*]   2C1ʳ (193) *where-* [*whereas,*]
           K3ʳ (69) *con-* [*conform*]   2E3ᵛ (214) *Pe-* [*Penalties*]
           R1ᵛ (122) *mode-* [*moderate*]   2K2ᵛ (252) *Pul-* [*Pulpit,*]
           2A2ᵛ (180) *Penal-* [*Penalties*] 2N2ᵛ (276) *Expe-* [*Experiment*]

Notes: Proast's reply to Locke's second 'letter' preempted Locke's title style; this 'third letter' is in answer to Proast's *A Third Letter concerning Toleration*, also published anonymously in 1691 (cf. C1691-1). Here the text concludes: 'Your most Humble Servant, PHILANTHROPUS. June 20, 1692.' License recorded in the registers of the Stationers' Company, along with the first two 'parts' on 26 April 1695. The text of this 'letter' is divided into ten chapters, all with titles except the first; chapter numbers are printed at the head of external margins, with page references to Proast's 'third letter' elsewhere in the margins. Some pages are in double cols. of varying widths, where Locke is quoting his own earlier 'letters' or Proast (i.e. pp. 35, 40-42, 66-7, 175-9, 190-92, 250-52). A microfilm copy is in EEB, reel 540, no. 11.

Notice: *Histoire des ouvrages des savans* 10 (1693-94): 24-39 (also covers C1691-1)

References: Attig 89; Christophersen pp. 18-19; ESTC r005673; L.L. 2947; T.C. II.423; Transcript iii.457; Wing² L2765.

Copies examined: Y   C   CaOTU (Locke L63.E74E6 1690 (3))   C(Keynes)   CaQMMO   Ck(Keynes)   CtY (K8.L79/bc690)   DFo (acc.141334)   Eu   Gu   L (1113.h.2)   MH (*EC65.L7934.692t, gift of Thomas Hollis)   O¹ (C.3.10 Linc.; A2 bd. before A1; trimmed to 192 × 142 mm)   O² (4° S.70 Th. (5))   Occ (lacks A1)   P (D².1538 (3))

28. Letters concerning Toleration. 1765. 4°
LETTERS CONCERNING TOLERATION | BY IOHN LOCKE | LONDON, PRINTED FOR A. MILLAR, H. WOOD- | FALL, I. WHISTON AND B. WHITE, I. RIVINGTON, | L. DAVIS AND C. REYMERS, R. BALDWIN, HAWES | CLARKE AND COLLINS, W. IOHNSTON, W. OWEN, | S. CROWDER, T. LONGMAN, B. LAW, C. RIVINGTON, | E. DILLY, R. WITHY, C. AND R. WARE, S. BAKER, | T. PAYNE, A. SHUCKBURGH, M. RICHARDSON | MDCCLXV | - FOR ON EARTH, | WHO AGAINST FAITH AND CONSCIENCE CAN BE HEARD | INFALLIBLE? YET MANY WILL PRESUME: | WHENCE HEAVIE PERSECUTION -

Coll: 4° (288 × 218 mm cut) A⁴ B-3E⁴ [$ half (-B1, K2) signed]; 204 leaves; pp. *i-viii* 1-3 *4-28* 29-33 *34-66* 67-69 *70-116* 117-119 *120-379* 380-383 *384-399* 400 [= 408].

Contents: A1ʳ title (verso blank), A2ʳ-A3ᵛ pref.to this ed., A4ʳ contents, A4ᵛ blank,
  Epistola de tolerantia: B1ʳ section title (verso blank), B2ʳ-E2ᵛ (*3-28*) text.
  A Letter concerning Toleration: E3ʳ section title (verso blank), E4ʳ Popple's pref., E4ᵛ blank, F1ʳ-K1ᵛ (*33-66*) text.
  A Second Letter . . .: K2ʳ section title (verso blank), K3ʳ-Q2ᵛ (69-116) text.

A Third Letter . . .: Q3^r section title (verso blank), Q4^r–3C2^r (119–379) text, 3C2^v blank.

A Fourth Letter . . .: 3C3^r section title (verso blank), 3C4^r–3E4^r (383–399) text, 3E4^v blank.

Illustration: Leaf preceding title has engraved portrait of Locke after Kneller, by F. B. Cipriani, in oval frame with a liberty cap, subscribed 'IOHN LOCKE', 115 × 96 mm; plate measures 200 × 120 mm.

Text (T3^v): 46 lines; 214 (228) × 141 (159) mm; 93 R. Good-quality laid paper with fleur-de-lys watermark, similar to Heawood 71-73 and initials IW. Marginal page citations set roman. Page no. at external ends of headlines.

HT A2^r: PREFACE TO THIS EDITION

  B2^r: EPISTOLA DE TOLERANTIA

  E4^r: TO THE READER

  F1^r: A LETTER CONCERNING TOLERATION

  K3^r: A SECOND LETTER CONCERNING TOLERATION | TO THE AUTHOR OF THE ARGUMENT OF THE | LETTER CONCERNING TOLERATION BRIEFLY | CONSIDERED AND ANSWERED

  Q1^r: A THIRD LETTER FOR TOLERATION | TO THE AUTHOR OF THE THIRD LETTER | CONCERNING TOLERATION

  3C4^r: A FOURTH LETTER FOR TOLERATION

Headlines: For A2^v–Q2^v, same as HTs.

  Q4^v–3C2^r: A THIRD LETTER FOR TOLERATION

  3C4^v–3E4^r: A FOURTH LETTER FOR TOLERATION

CW: Page. B4^r vel G2^r (re-) ceived N1^r guilty; S2^r there, [there] 2A3^v im- [impracticable] 2P2^r (in-) trenching 3B1^r religion, Note: Each of the final pages of the 'Epistola' and of the four 'letters' has no CW.

Press figures: B4^r (7)–I C3^r (13)–I D1^v (18)–I (2 on inner forme, 1 on outer)

Notes: Thomas 'Hollis prepared for a new editon of Mr. Locke's Letters on Toleration; and for that purpose engaged Mr. [Richard] Baron to correct the press; . . . having fixed upon the younger [William] Strahan for the printer . . . at the same time [Hollis] prevailed with Mr. Millar, the chief proprietor, to have the letters printed on royal quarto paper . . . Mr. Hollis gave Baron twenty guineas, which he had promised him, for correcting the press for the new edition of Locke's 'Letters concerning Toleration.'[4] Aside from the title being all in capital letters and the use of the letter I (instead of J), beneath the facing portrait there is a liberty cap; another liberty cap is at the foot of the last text page: these occurrences are typical of Hollis editions. Copies presented by Hollis also have a liberty figure with liberty cap and a rod, surmounted by a star on an extra leaf bound at the end, supplied by a metal stamp or 'smoke print' (according to W. H. Bond). Hollis's presentation copies usually also are bound in red morocco, with gold tooling from special stamps. Further details on Hollis editions

---

[4] Blackburne, *Memoirs of Thomas Hollis*, i.224, 254.

can be found in Prof. Bond's *Thomas Hollis of Lincoln's Inn* (Cambridge University Press, 1991).

This is the first time since 1705 that the Latin text was printed. The 'fourth' letter with its two missing pages was first published in the *Posthumous Works* of 1706 (no. 299). A draft version of those pages can be found in Lord King's *Life of John Locke* (1829), pp. 360–61 (cf. no. 299). All four English letters are included in editions of collected works beginning with that of 1714 (no. 363–71).

The quotation on the title-leaf is from Milton's *Paradise Lost*, Book 12, lines 528–31.

There was a brief advertisement of this edition in the *London Chronicle*, 22–24 January 1765, as a new edition in 'Royal 4to . . . 12 s. 6 d.' The advertisement was repeated in the following 24–26 January issue (information supplied by John Stephens).

A microfilm copy of this work is in *The Eighteenth Century*, reel 3154, no.10.

References: Attig 93; Christophersen p. 99; ESTC t114245.

Copies examined: Y   [Berlin]   C (Acton b.48.73; lacks port., A1–2)   C (Keynes; presentation copy, with bookplate of Joseph Smith, British consul at Venice)   CaOTU (Locke L63.L48 1765)   CtY (K8.L79/ + bf765)   [GhU]   L (696.m.16)   MH^1 (TP2115.70.5, presentation copy to Harvard College)   MH^2 (X27.20.12, presentation copy to Joseph Mitchell)   NjP (Ex.6106.1765q)   O (Radcliffe d.98, presentation copy to 'Radcliffe Library, Oxford')   ViW

After 1800 the collected letters on toleration were largely ignored in the English-speaking world until an edition was published in Bombay in 1867, and another by A. Murray in 1870, reprinted in 1876 in Ward Lock's Library of Standard Books. The first English 'letter' was printed in the journal, *The Millenial Harbinger*, in 1844; other reprints appeared in 1851, 1950, 1955 and 1983.

A critical edition of the Latin and English texts of the first 'letter', edited by Mario Montuori appeared in 1963. It was reprinted with other papers in Montuori's *John Locke on Toleration and the Unity of God* in 1983. Under the auspices of Unesco new bilingual editions of the Latin text with facing translations, in the series 'Philosophy and World Community' and under the general editorship of Raymond Klibansky, were published in French (1964), Hungarian (1973; reissued in 1982), Italian (1961), Japanese (1970), Polish (1963) and Spanish (1962). The Italian translation without the accompanying Latin was also separately reprinted in 1963. A Hebrew translation was published in 1990.

The Latin text of the first letter, edited and with preface by Klibansky, was newly translated by J. W. Gough and published in 1968 (Oxford University

Press). Gough's translation is more literal and faithful than Popple's; it is especially to be esteemed for its 'Notes' (pp. 156–63) where Gough signals his variations from Popple's version.

The French translation of the first 'letter' reprinting the text from the *Oeuvres philosophiques* of 1821–25 (see ch. XI, End note) was reissued in facsimile in 1980. A new German translation appeared in 1827; another with Popple's English translation facing, in 1957. A new Italian translation was published in 1920. A reprint of that translation was included in C. A. Viano's edition of Locke's *Scritti editi e inediti sulla tolleranza* (1961; no. 341).

A Spanish translation, preceded by a translation of the 'Conduct of the Understanding', was published in 1827 under the misleading title: *Del Gobierno Civil*. A new Spanish translation appeared in 1966.

A critical edition of the four 'letters' is to appear in the Clarendon Edition of the Works of John Locke.

CHAPTER II
Two Treatises of Government (nos. 29–60)

The composition and structure of Locke's anonymously published *Two Treatises of Government* has been dealt with in great detail in Peter Laslett's introduction to his modern edition of that work (Cambridge, 1960, pp. 3–15; 2nd edition, *ibid*. 1967. Herein cited as 'Laslett'). He there offers arguments for believing that the second 'treatise' was written before the first, in the period 1679 to 1683; it is generally agreed that the first was written before 1683. There are insertions in the first, especially a reference to Judge Jeffreys in section 129, that have to have been made in 1689, but this and others are merely updating insertions. Chronologically both treatises cannot be a justification of the 'Glorious Revolution of 1689' (*ibid*. p. 48 et seq.). The first treatise was 'intended as a complete refutation of Filmer['s] Patriarcha' published in 1680, though there is material contradicting Filmer in the second treatise as well. Richard Ashcraft in his recent work, *Locke's Two Treatises of Government* (London, 1987) states his reasons for believing that the first treatise was written before the second, that the first belongs to the period 1680–81 because of the political debate of determining the succession and 'the relative authority of the king or Parliament to render a binding decision' thereon. The political arguments in the second treatise appear 'to establish the case for its having been written in 1681–2 *after* Locke had essentially completed the *First Treatise*.' (Ashcraft, Appendix, pp. 286–97).

In the 'References' section given for each edition, the numbers cited under 'Laslett' are those found in his Appendix A: Check-list of Printings, 1689–1956 (pp. 121–9).

It is surprising to be able to note that all translations of this work up to 1800 were only of the second treatise, although a German translation of the complete work was said to appear in 1716 (cf. no. 57). Even up to the present time there has never been a French translation of the first treatise against Filmer.

29. Two Treatises. 1690. 8°. Two states. Anonymous.
Within a double rule, inner 147 × 78 mm, outer 155 × 86 mm: TWO | TREATISES | OF | 𝕲obernment: | In the former, | The *falſe Principles*, [swash P] and *Foundation* | OF | Sir *ROBERT FILMER*, [swash Rs, B] | And his FOLLOWERS, | ARE | 𝔇etected and 𝔒berthrown. | The latter is an | ESSAY | CONCERNING THE | True Original, Extent, and End | OF | Civil Government. | [double rule 72 mm] |

LONDON, | Printed for *Awnſham Churchill*, at the *Black* [swash k] | *Swan* in *Ave-Mary-Lane*, by *Amen-* | *Corner*, 1690.

Coll: 8° (172 × 102 mm cut) A⁸ (±A2; –2 leaves = 2H²) B–P⁸ Q⁸ (±Q⁸) R–2G⁸ 2H² 2I1 [$ half (–P4; –Q4 in 1R issue) signed]; 240 leaves (241 if 2I1 present); pp. *i–xii* 1–213 *214–216* 217–334 345 336–464 269–271 [i.e. 465–467] 468 + 1 leaf (469–470) [= 480 or 482]. Page 335 numbered '345'.

Contents: A1ʳ blank, A1ᵛ licensing note, A2ʳ title (verso blank), A3ʳ–A5ᵛ pref., A6ʳ,ᵛ contents, B1ʳ–P3ʳ (1–213) text of first treatise, P3ᵛ blank, P4ʳ section title, P4ᵛ blank, P5ʳ–2H2ʳ (217–271, *recte* 467) text of second treatise, ending '*FINIS.*', 2I1ʳ (469) 22.5-line errata, 2I1ᵛ blank.

Text: (G4ʳ) 31 lines (except G1–2ʳ, H2, Q); 145 (156) × 77 mm; 94 R. Leaves G1 and H2, and recto of G2 have 32 lines. Sheet S has blank lines between paragraphs. For peculiarities of Q, see *States* below. The preface is set 117 R, 25 lines. Page no. centered within parentheses as headlines. Text frequently in the direction line, e.g. on Z2ᵛ, 2A6ᵛ, 2B3ᵛ, 2D2ᵛ and 2G1ᵛ. Watermark similar to Heawood 2722; but sheet Q in 1X state has posthorn watermark in some copies. Although watermarks are indecisive, it appears 2H was imposed with sheet A.

HT, A3ʳ: [double rule 75 mm] | THE | PREFACE.

B1ʳ: [double rule 77 mm] | BOOK I.

P5ʳ: [double rule 76/75 mm] | BOOK II.

Headline, A3ᵛ–A5ᵛ: The PREFACE. [swash P, R]

Section title to second treatise: AN | ESSAY | Concerning the | True Oringinal, [sic] Extent and End | OF | CIVIL GOVERNMENT.

CW: Page. B3ʳ deveſt [veſted (*sic*)] C4ᵛ A– [our A–] D6ʳ 35. But [35. But] H7ᵛ Tha [That] I6ʳ 97. As [97. From] M1ᵛ (Obe-) dience [bedience] N4ʳ 144. Fo [144. For] N5ʳ (of ones own) *and* [Brain (recte '*and* Brain'] S4ᵛ Com- [Commoners] 2Cʳ Prero- [Prerogative]

Catchwords in sheet Q:

	1X	1R
Q1ʳ	9. I	[same]
Q1ᵛ	10. Beſides	(con-) fiſts
Q2ʳ	hath	(Ex-) ecution [falling 'n']
Q2ᵛ	Mankind,	(de-) ſtroyed
Q3ʳ	Nature	yet,
Q3ᵛ	And	(Go-) vernment
Q4ʳ	with- [without]	14. 'Tis [in text line 32]
Q4ᵛ	may	15. To
Q5ʳ	*naturally*	CHAP.
Q5ᵛ	CHAP.	treated
Q6ʳ	Fun- [Fundamental]	thing
Q6ᵛ	Deſign	ſome
Q7ʳ	State,	be

Q7ᵛ	19. And	(ima-) gin	
Q8ʳ	not	of	
Q8ᵛ	CHAP.	[same]	

States: This first edition exists in two states, being two different settings of sheet Q, which Peter Laslett in his edition designates 1X and 1R (for *wrong* and *right?*); some copies have a cancellans title leaf, identical to conjugate title leaf (at Yale, Geoffrey Keynes copy now in Cambridge University Library, and a copy at the Royal Library at the Hague). Laslett suggests the title leaf may have been spoilt. There are no political implications indicated by the omission of some of the text from the earlier 1X state, because 'the new passage [in 1R] is of such a content that its cancellation would have served no apparent purpose whatsoever.' The passage in question occurs in Chapter III of the second treatise, part of § 20 and 21. That 1X is the earlier is indicated also by the fact that the contents leaf (A6) indicates chapter III begins on p. 235 (Q6ʳ) as it does in 1X, but in 1R that chapter begins on p. 234 (Q5ᵛ). Locke's preface tells us that some of his original text was lost: 'what Fate has otherwise disposed of the Papers that should have filled up the Middle, and were more than all the rest, 'tis not worth while to tell thee . . . there will be no great miss of those which are lost . . .' Presumably he himself made good the omission by rewriting material for inclusion in 1R. 'Whether this was new, originally overlooked in error, or a return of matter originally excised for some reason is a moot point.'[1] Since copies of both 1X and 1R survive in approximately equal numbers, it is fair to assume that many copies of sheet Q were printed before the omission was noticed. The second state of sheet Q is a cancellans for the first, 1X, state. The chief differences are tabled below. There are other differences between 1X and 1R in other sheets and other copies. Details of these are carefully delineated in Laslett's article and in that by Fredson Bowers, J. Gerritsen and Laslett.[2]

State 1X

1. Q1ʳ, Q2ᵛ, Q4ʳ,ᵛ, (225, 228, 231-3) set 30 lines; Q1ᵛ, Q2ʳ, Q3ʳ,ᵛ, Q5ʳ and Q8ᵛ set 29 lines
2. Q2ʳ (228) ll.22-3: 'mude- | rer'
3. Q4ʳ (231) signed
4. 231 line 13: 'eafiy' [for 'eafily']
5. Q6ʳ has chap. heading and 17 lines, Q6ᵛ-7ʳ (236-7) has 24 lines 117R

State 1R

225-31 set 31 or 32 lines; 232 in 28 lines

228.19-20: 'mude- | rer'
No signature on 231
231 line 5: 'eafie'
235-7 set 94R, 31 lines

---

[1] P. Laslett, 'The 1690 Edition of Locke's *Two Treatises of Government*: Two States', *Transactions of the Cambridge Bibliographical Society* 1 (1952): 341-47.

[2] 'Further Observations on Locke's *Two Treatises of Government*: Three Contributions' by Fredson Bowers, Johann Gerritsen and Peter Laslett, *Transactions of the Cambridge Bibliographical Society* 2 pt.1 (1954): 63-87.

6. Letter 'W' for pp. 235–7   'VV' frequently for 'W', pp. 235–7
7. Q7ᵛ (238) set 30 lines   238 set 31 lines
8. Q8ʳ (239) set 31 lines   239 set 31 lines
9. §21 omitted (from p. 240 = Q8ᵛ)   § 21 begins p. 239 line 15 (Q8ʳ)
10. Lacks errata slip on 2I1ʳ   Usually have errata slip.

There are many other differences. In state 1X Chap. III ('*Of the State of War.*') begins on p. 235; in 1R, on p. 234. Most notably the text for the second 'Treatise', §14 (on p. 233 lines 4–5) in 1X reads: 'the two Men, in *Soldania*, in or between, a *Swiss* and an *Indian*', but in 1R (p. 232 lines 23–6) reads 'the two Men, in the Desert Island mentioned by *Garcilasso De la Vega*, in his History of *Peru*, or between a *Swiss* and an *Indian*'.

Notes: Laslett states that Locke decided to publish his *Two Treatises of Government* in the summer of 1689. The licensing note reads: [rule 75 mm] | LICENSED. | *Aug.* 23. | 1689. | J. *Fraſer.* | [rule 75 mm]. It was advertised in *The London Gazette*, no. 2505, the issue for 14–18 November 1689. Laslett and Gerritsen estimate 'probably not over 1000 copies' were printed.

There are other variants: A5ʳ line 1 ends '*cno-*' (*cerning*) in 1X, '*con-*' in 1R; but some copies (L, MH and O) of 1R and Laslett's own copy of 1X both have '*cno-*'. Page 306 (X1ᵛ) line 16 reads 'Judge' in most copies of 1X (and in 1R at L, O), but has been corrected to 'judge' in other copies. Harvard's copy of 1R has erratic pagination for sheet P: instead of the expected 209–224, the page numbers are 209, 211, 212-3, 214-6, 217, 216-217, 220-221, 220-221, 224. This error must have been caught early on. The text was divided between two printers, called press I and II. Press I 'actually printed fifteen sheets (B–Q) and press II fifteen sheets (T–2G, then R, S, and A + 2H)', in that order, an 'equal assignment of work' (Bowers, *loc. cit.*). The parentheses used to encircle the page numbers as headlines are different for the two printers, as are the ligatured letters 'ct' and '*is*'. Press I set sheet Q in the 1X state. When it was corrected and enlarged, some of the lines set by press I were used but moved (see 'muderer', item 2 in the two *States*), but the variation in the shape and form of the parentheses surrounding the page numbers match those by press II in the headlines for sheets R–2H. Hence the certainty that the later 1R version of sheet Q was printed by press II. That printer also ran out of Ws and had to use 'VV' in nine places. Though watermarks are indecisive, sheet 2H was part of sheet A.

A microfilm copy of this edition, state 1X (from the copy at Union Theological Seminary, New York) is in EEB, reel 388, no. 24.

References: Attig 100; Christophersen p.19; ESTC r002930; L.L. 1293; Laslett British 1; T.C. II.292; Wing² L2766.

Notice: *Bibliothèque universelle* 19 (1690): 559–91 (with summaries).

Copies of 1X examined: O¹ (Don. e. 253) C (Keynes; with canc. title) CaOTU (Locke L63.T86 1690; lacks A1) CaQMMO (lacks A1) Ck(Keynes A11.14)¹ CLaslett CLU-C¹ CtY (Ocg45/L793/690; with canc. title) DFo (acc.153337; lacks A3-4) Du (Press L.5.18) O² (Vet.A3 e.1239, lacks A1) OCin (lacks A1) Oq

Copies of 1R examined: O³ (Vet.A3 e.844) C (without errata slip) Ck (Keynes A11.15)² CLU-C² (*PR3541.L57T9 1690) DLC (JC153.L8 1690; without errata slip) L (C.107.e.89; with canc. A2; formerly 1472.*aaa*.3) MH (*EC65.L7934.690ta, with cancellans A2) Occ (f.7.75)

30. 2T. 2d ed., 1694. 8° Anonymous.
Within a double rule, inner 142×79 mm, outer 149×85 mm: TWO | TREATISES | OF | Government: | In the former, | *The falſe Principles and Foundation* | OF | Sir *ROBERT FILMER*, | And his FOLLOWERS, | ARE | 𝕯𝖊𝖙𝖊𝖈𝖙𝖊𝖉 𝖆𝖓𝖉 𝕺𝖇𝖊𝖗𝖙𝖍𝖗𝖔𝖜𝖓. | The latter is an | ESSAY | CONCERNING | The True Original, Extent, and End | OF | Civil-Government. | [rule 71 mm] | 𝕿𝖍𝖊 𝕾𝖊𝖈𝖔𝖓𝖉 𝕰𝖉𝖎𝖙𝖎𝖔𝖓 𝕮𝖔𝖗𝖗𝖊𝖈𝖙𝖊𝖉. | [rule 71 mm] | *LONDON*, Printed for *Awnſham* and *John* [swash J] *Churchill* at | the *Black Swan* in *Pater-noſter-Row*, 1694.

Coll: 8° (174 × 104 mm cut) A⁴ B–Z⁸ 2A⁴ (± several leaves; see Notes) [$ half (+ A3) signed; B4 signed '*B*4'; O3 signed 'O5')]; 184 leaves; pp. *i–viii*, 1–161 *162 163 164* 165–358 *359–360* [= 368].

Contents: A1ʳ title (verso blank), A2ʳ–A3ᵛ pref. (A3ᵛ with 5 lines of text, followed by 40.5 lines of errata), A4ʳ,ᵛ contents, B1ʳ–M1ʳ (1–161) text of first treatise, M1ᵛ blank, M2ʳ section title (verso blank), M3ʳ–2A3ᵛ (165–358) text of second treatise, 2A4ʳ,ᵛ advt.: 'Books Printed for, and Sold by A. *and* J. Churchill . . .'

Text (Q4ᵃ): 35 lines; 142 (153)×77 mm; 81R. Page no. centered within parentheses as headlines. Very poor quality paper, with no visible watermarks; sheets U and Z on different quality paper, also 2A in O copy.

Section title to second treatise, M2ʳ (p. 163): [rule 72 mm] | AN | ESSAY | Concerning the | *True Original, Extent, and End* | OF | Civil Government. | [rule 69 mm]

HT, A2ʳ: [double rule 74/72 mm] | THE | PREFACE.
  B1r: [double rule 78/77 mm] | BOOK I.
  M3r: [double rule 76/75 mm] | BOOK II.

RT, A2ᵛ–A3ᵛ: *The PREFACE*

CW: Page. B3ʳ an [and,] E3ᵛ con- [contrary] G7ᵛ Pri- [Primogeniture] M1ʳ AN O2ʳ 41. there [41. There] S7ʳ *a* U4ʳ judg- [judging] 2A1ᵛ *forced*

Notes: The text is that of the first edition; some passages were rewritten, especially §§105 and 106 in the first treatise, and in §§50 and 83 of the second. 'It had over 150 alterations of sense or extensions, but the final text was worse than ever, so bad Locke felt like abandoning the whole book.' (Laslett, p. 9) Some of the leaves are cancellantia, not found in all copies: G6 (91-2), G8 (95-6), H2 (99-100), H3 (101-2), H7 (109-10), I1-3 (113-18),

I5 (121-2), K5 (137-8), K7-8 (141-4) and L1-3 (145-50). I have not recorded cancellantia in all copies I examined. It was 'a cheap and nasty little book, price sixpence' (Laslett ed., p. 9). It was published in the spring of 1694 (*Corr.* v.viii).

A microfilm copy of this edition is in EEB, reel 793, no. 25.

References: Attig 101; Christophersen p.19; ESTC r000867; L.L. 1293a; Laslett British 2; T.C. II. 541; Wing² L2767.

Copies examined: Y (G6, H3, H7, I1, I5, K5, K7-8 & L3 cancellantia) CaOTU (Locke L63.T86 1694; G6, G8, H3, H7, I1-3, I5, K5, K7-8, L1-3 cancellantia)   Ck (Keynes A11.16)   CLaslett   CtY (Ocg45/L793/690B; G6, H2, H7, I2-3, I5, K5, K7, L1-2 cancel.)   Dm   Gu (Bi.2k-y; lacks 2A4)   L (523 b.11; G6, G8, H2, H7, I1-3, I5 and K8 cancel.)   MH (*EC65.L7934 690tb)   O (Godw. Subt. 289; G6, 8; H3, H7, I1-3, I5, K5, K7-8 and L1-3 cancel.)   Oc¹ (a.3.151; G6, 8; H3, 7; I1-3, K5, 8 cancel.)   Oc² (B.196; G6, 8, H3, 7; L1-3; O1-3, 5 cancel.)   Occ (ST320.1 Lo)   OCin (RA320.1/L81td 1695)   Om (C4.36)   ViU   York Minster (2.O.11)

31. 2T. [3rd ed.] 1698. 8° Anonymous.

Within a double rule, inner 153 × 84 mm, 161 × 93 mm outer: TWO | TREATISES | OF | Government: | In the Former, | *The Falſe Principles* [swash P] *and Foundation* | OF | Sir *Robert Filmer*, [swash R, F] | And His FOLLOWERS, | ARE | Detected and Overthrown. | The Latter is an | ESSAY | CONCERNING | The True Original, Extent, and End | OF | Civil-Government. | [rule 80 mm] | LONDON: Printed for *Awnſham* and *John* [swash J] *Churchill*, at the | *Black* [swash k] *Swan* in *Pater-Noſter-Row*. 1698.

Coll: 8° (207 × 135 mm uncut) A⁴ (−A4 = D4 cancellans) B-C⁸ D⁸ (±D4) E-K⁸ L⁸ (±L6) M-Z⁸ 2A⁴ [$ half signed]; 183 leaves; pp. *i-vi* 1-94 55 96-161 *162 163 164* 165-358 *359-360* [= 366]. Page 95 called in error '55'.

Contents: A1ʳ title (verso blank), A2ʳ-A3ʳ pref. (last page with 13 lines of text, rule, 'ERRATA.', and 33 lines of errata), A3ᵛ contents, B1ʳ-M1ʳ (1-161) text of 1st treatise, M1ᵛ blank, M2ʳ (163) section title, M2ᵛ blank, M3ʳ-2A3ᵛ (165-358) text of 2nd treatise, 2A4 blank.

Text (C4ᵛ): 35 lines; 167 (175) × 91 mm; 95R. Poor-quality laid paper without watermark. No headlines or RTs; page no. centered at head of page within parentheses as headlines. Page 315 has lost its right end paren. ('(315'). Pref. set 66R and ital. mixed.

Section title, M3ʳ (p. 163): [rule 91 mm] | AN | ESSAY | Concerning the | True Original, Extent, and End | OF | 𝕮𝖎𝖛𝖎𝖑 𝕲𝖔𝖇𝖊𝖗𝖓𝖒𝖊𝖓𝖙. | [rule 91 mm]

HT, A2ʳ: The PREFACE.

   B1ʳ: [double rule 89/88 mm] | BOOK I. | [rule 90 mm]

   M3ʳ: [double rule 90 mm] | BOOK II. | [rule 90 mm]

Headlines: A2ᵛ: The PREFACE.

   A3r: The PEEFACE. [sic]

Two Treatises of Government 35

A3v: The CONTETNS [sic] of BOOK I.

CW: Page. B3ʳ and, D4ᵛ (re-) quires E3ᵛ con- [contrary] G7ᵛ Pri- [Primogeniture] L6ʳ Grant L6ᵛ Power M1ʳ AN O2ʳ 41. There U4ʳ Judg- [judging] 2A1ᵛ *forced*

Press figures: † on versos of leaves only: 14 (B7) 16 (B8) 32 (C8) 46 (D7) 64 (E8) 78 (F7) 94 () 110 (H7) 112 (H8) 126 (I7) 142 (K7) 174 (M7) 176 (M8) 190 (N7) 206 (O7) 208 (O8) 222 (P7) 224 (P8) 238 (Q7) 240 (Q8) 272 (S8) 288 (T8) 302 (U7) 304 (U8) 350 (Z7) 352 (Z8)

Table	(i)	(o)
Sig.	7ᵛ	8ᵛ
A		
B	†	†
C		†
D	†	
E		
F	†	
G	†	
H	†	†
I	†	
K	†	
L		
M	†	†
N	†	
O	†	†
P	†	†
Q	†	†
R		
S		†
T		†
U	†	†
X	†	
Y		
Z	†	†
2A		

Notes: Substantially a line-for-line reprint of the 1694 edition, with 'very minor alterations' (Laslett, p. 9) and considered the third edition, though it lacks an edition statement.

Leaves D4 (pp. 39/40) and L6 (pp. 155/6) are cancellantia in most copies. A Harvard copy has the cancellandum D4 in place and the D4 cancellans as the fourth leaf of gathering A. There are several spelling and punctuation changes between them, e.g. 'Surpluſſage' in §42 (cancellans reads

'Surpluſage'); 'so much out of anothers Plenty: For as will keep' (ibid. cancellans: . . . 'another's Plenty, as will keep'. A notable wording change in the D4 cancellans is in the second sentence at the beginning of §41: the original reads 'And how will it appear, that *Propriety* in Land gives a Man Power over the Life of another?' The cancellans changed '*Propriety*' to '*Property*', following the wording of the first and second editions.

The original L6 (found in the Folger copy and elsewhere), following the wording of the 1st and 2d editions, has the last clause in §162 reading: 'this Dominion was to belong all to one of his Issue exclusive of all others.' The only change in the L6 cancellans is to omit the first 'all', this clause then reads: 'this Dominion was to belong to one of his Issue, exclusive of all others.' Later editions follow the reading from a hypothetical second master copy: '. . . belong in peculiar to one of his Issue, exclusive of all others.' The manuscript correction in Christ's College copy reads: 'belong "in peculiar" to one of his *Issue* exclusive of all others.'

In his *Memoirs of Thomas Hollis, Esq.*, Francis Blackburne tells us that 'Mr Hollis had the good fortune to recover this copy [that is, one of this edition] with Mr. Locke's own corrections, and there is reason to believe, that he collated the three editions of these tracts himself, with no little labour [for his edition of 1764, no. 35] before he sent the book to Christ's College', Cambridge (i. 223-4). An unsigned letter (by Hollis) mounted inside the front cover is dated April 20, 1764; it offers this copy to the master of the college, Dr. Thomas. It is an uncut copy with frequent corrections, additions (often a single word), underlinings for emphasis, and alterations, mostly in the outer and bottom margins, chiefly in Locke's hand. There are a few notes, chiefly on the end flyleaf, in Coste's hand. The blank leaf facing the title has in Locke's hand the quotation from Livy Book IX, ch. 1 ('Quod si nihil . . . praebuerimus.') that appears on the title in the fourth and later editions. Peter Laslett used this copy for his definitive edition in 1960, wherein he makes it clear that the fourth edition 'was not necessarily (or exclusively) based on the Christ's copy' (Edit. note, p. 148).

Unusually for this early a publication, there are press figures (listed above). A copy cost 3 s. 6 d. per copy in 1700, according to Edwin Wolf 2d, in his article, 'A Parcel of Books for the Province in 1700' (*The Pennsylvania Magazine of History and Biography* 89 (1965): 428-46).

A microfilm copy is in EEB, reel 793, no. 26. Another microfilm copy is in the Goldsmiths'-Kress Library of Economic Literature, no. 3546 (showing D4 and L6 are cancellantia).

References: Attig 102; Christophersen p. 19; ESTC r000868; L.L. 1294; Laslett British 3; T.C. III.57 and III.114 (Feb. 1699); Wing^2 L2768.

Copies examined: O (8° Q.15 Th.; presentation copy) BRu C CaOTU (Locke L63.T86 1698; leaf D4 and L6 cancellantia; no figure on p. 224) Cch (BB3.7a, uncut; Hollis binding in red morocco; without fig. on P8v) Ck(Keynes) CLaslett (lacks leaf 2A4, without press figure on P8v) CLU-C CtY (Ocg45/L793/690c; D4 canc.) DFo (acc. 138212, lacks 2A4;

only D4 canc.) [GOT] Han (lacks 2A4) L (522.d.39) MH¹ (*EC65.L7934 690tc (A)) MH² (*EC65.L7934 690tc (B), with D4 and D4 cancel.) NjP (Ex.7507.592.13) NjR (X JC153.L8 1698) Oc (a.1.110) Oo (2Hf.11, without figures on P8^v, Q7^v) TxDaMP (lacks 2A4; leaf D4 not canc.) ViU

32. 2T. 4th ed., 1713. 12°
Within a double rule, inner 140 × 72 mm, outer 148 × 79 mm: TWO | TREATISES | OF | GOVERNMENT: | In the Former, | The falſe Principles and Foundation of | Sir ROBERT FILMER, | And his FOLLOWERS | Are Detected and Overthrown. | The Latter, is an | ESSAY | Concerning the | True Original, Extent, and End of | CIVIL-GOVERNMENT. | [rule 69 mm] | By JOHN [swash J] LOCKE, Eſq; | [rule 69 mm] | 𝕿𝖍𝖊 𝕱𝖔𝖚𝖗𝖙𝖍 𝕰𝖉𝖎𝖙𝖎𝖔𝖓. | [rule 68 mm] | Quod ſi nihil cum potentiore juris humani relinquitur | inopi, at ego ad deos vindices humanæ ſuperbiæ | confugiam: Et precabor ut iras ſuas vertant in | eos, quibus non ſuæ res, non alienæ ſatis ſint: quo- | rum ſævitiam non mors noxiorum exſatiet: Pla- | cari nequeant, niſi hauriendum ſanguinem lani- | andaq; viſcera noſtra præbuerimus. Liv. 1. 9. c. I. | [rule 79 mm] | LONDON: Printed for John [swash J] Churchill at the | Black Swan in Pater-noſter-row. 1713.
Coll: 12° (174 × 93 mm cut) A¹² (± A1) B–Q¹² [$6 (–H5) signed]; 192 leaves; pp. 1–6 7–175 176–8 168 190–379 380–384. Page 189 called '168'.
Contents: A1^r title (verso blank), A2^r–A3^v (3–6) pref., A4^r–H4^r (7–175) text of 1st treatise, H4^v blank, H5^r (177) section title, H5^v blank, H6^r–Q10^r (179–379) text of 2d treatise, Q10^v–Q11^r (380–381) contents, Q11^v–Q12^v (382–384) advt. of books printed for J. Churchill.
Text (C5^v): 35 lines; 142 (152) × 77 mm; 81R. Bottom of hollow letter 'ID' as watermark at fore-edge.
HT, A4^r: [orn rect. floral rule 12 × 76 mm] | OF | GOVERNMENT. | [rule 76 mm]
H6^r: [orn. rule of angle and curve symbols 12 × 70 mm] | OF | CIVIL-GOVERNMENT. | [rule 76 mm]
Headlines, A4^v–H4^r (8–175): Of Government.
H6^v–Q10^r (180–379): Of Civil-Government.
Section title, H5^r: [rule 74 mm] | AN | ESSAY | Concerning the | True Original, Extent, and End | OF | CIVIL-GOVERNMENT. | [rule 75 mm]
CW: Page. A8^r time [time,] D6^r Heir [Heir,] G5^v acknow- [acknowledg'd] A8^r ey [they (DFo has CW 'they')] M7^v their P6^v 210. Put [210. But]
Press figures: none.
Notes: This edition has a cancellans title leaf. It 'reproduc[es] Locke's text for posterity, possibly from the hypothetical second master copy' (Laslett, p. 147). The only known master copy is that of the 1698 edition, with manuscript corrections in Locke's and Coste's hands (now at Christ's College, Cambridge; cf. no. 31). There are still minor typographical errors in this

edition. Nichols (i.67) says this edition was printed by William Bowyer. *The Bowyer Ledgers* (entry 154) notes it was 'printed by Bowyer at Norton's and Rawlins's' in 1713, during the period when his own premises could not be used because of a disastrous fire.

The Latin quotation appears on the title page for the first time. (Translation: 'But if in dealing with the mighty, the weak are left no human rights, yet will I seek the protection of the gods, who visit retribution on intolerable pride; and I will beseech them that they turn their anger on those who are not content with their own possessions or with heaping up that of others; whose rage is not sated with the death of the guilty: these things they deny being content with, unless we yield them our blood to drink and our flesh to feast on.' The Latin text in the Loeb Classical Library edition (IX.i. 8-9) varies slightly: Quod si nihil . . . non suae redditae res, non alienae accumulatae satis sint; quorum saevitiam non mors noxiorum, non deditio exanimatorum corporum, non bona sequentia domini deditionem exsatient, nisi hauriendum . . . praebuerimus. ('But if in dealing with the mighty . . . those who are not content with the restitution of their own possessions, nor the heaping up in addition of other men's; whose rage is not sated with the death of the guilty, nor with the surrender of their lifeless bodies; nor with the master's goods going with that surrender, unless we yield them . . .')

References: Attig 103; Christophersen p. 100; ESTC t112896; Laslett British 4.
Copies examined: O (Vet.A4 e.974) C Ck(Keynes) CLaslett DFo (JC153.L8 1713) L (521.c.25) NjP (Wit.7507.592.12; ex libris John Witherspoon) PPL (Ii Lock/64209.D)

33. 2T. 5th ed., 1728. 8° Three states

33A (First state). Within a double rule, inner 159 × 80 mm, outer 166 × 84 mm: TWO | TREATISES | OF | GOVERNMENT: | In the Former, | The falſe Principles and Foundation of | Sir *ROBERT FILMER*, | And his FOLLOWERS, | Are *Detected* and *Overthrown*. | The Latter, is an | ESSAY | Concerning the | True Original, Extent, and End of | CIVIL GOVERNMENT. | [rule 77 mm] | The FIFTH EDITION. | [rule 77 mm] | *Quod* [swash Q] *ſi nihil cum potentiore juris humani relinquitur inopi,* | *at ego ad deos vindices humanæ ſuperbiæ confugiam: Et* | *precabor ut iras ſuas vertant in eos, quibus non ſuæ res,* | *non alienæ ſatis ſint: quorum ſævitiam non mors noxiorum* | *exſatiet: Placari nequeant, niſi hauriendum ſanguinem* | *laniandaque viſcera noſtra præbuerimus.* Liv. l. 9. c. I. | [rule 78 mm] | LONDON: | Printed for A. BETTESWORTH in *Pater-Noſter-Row*, | J. PEMBERTON in *Fleetſtreet*, and E. SYMON in | *Cornhill*. M.DCC.XXVIII.

33B (Second state). TWO | TREATISES | . . . [&c. as in 1st state until 14th line:] CIVIL GOVERNMENT. | [rule 77 mm] | By *JOHN* | [swash J] *LOCKE* Eſq; | [rule 77 mm] | The FIFTH EDITION. | . . . [&c. as in first state]

33C (Third state), as 2d state except Bettesworth's address reads: in *Pater-Noſter-Row*. [full-stop after '*Row*']

Coll: 8° (198 × 125 mm) A⁸ (−A3–6 [= X⁴]; ±A1) B–U⁸ X⁴ [$ half signed]; 160 leaves; pp. *i–viii* 1–140 *141–142* 143–308 *309–312* [= 320].
Both states II and III may have A1 cancellans.
Contents: A1ʳ (*i*) title (verso blank), A2ʳ–A4ᵛ (*iii–viii*) pref., B1ʳ–K6ᵛ (1–140) text of first treatise, K7ʳ (*141*) section title of second treatise, K7ᵛ blank, K8ʳ–X2ᵛ (143–308) text of second treatise, X3ʳ (*309*) contents of Book I, X3ᵛ (*310*) contents of Book II, X4ʳ,ᵛ (*311–312*) advt. for booksellers Bettesworth, Pemberton, and Symon.
Text (B7ᵛ): 38 lines; 157 (169) × 86 mm; 83R. Bottom of outline 'E' as watermark. Good quality laid paper. Page numbers in upper external corners of headlines. Tailpiece on A4ᵛ: vase of fruit on sconce between peacocks, 35 × 57 mm (same as found in *Works*, 1727, vol. 3; no. 365).
Section title, K7ʳ: [rule 85 mm] | AN | ESSAY | Concerning the | *True Original, Extent and End* | OF CIVIL GOVERNMENT. | [rule 85 mm]
HT, A2ʳ: [double rule 85/84 mm] | THE | PREFACE.
B1ʳ: [triple rule of fleurons, 19 × 86 mm] | THE | FIRST TREATISE | CONCERNING | GOVERNMENT. | [rule 85 mm]
K8ʳ: [triple rule of fleurons, 19 × 83 mm] | OF | CIVIL | GOVERNMENT. | [rule 86 mm] | BOOK II. | [rule 86 mm]
Headlines, B1ᵛ–K6ʳ, K8ᵛ–X1ʳ (from verso to recto): *The Firſt* [*Second*] *Treatiſe* | *concerning Government.* (Verso page also indicates chapter numbers, e.g. Chap. IV.)
A2ᵛ–A4ᵛ: *The PREFACE.* [swash P]
K6ᵛ: *The Firſt Treatiſe.*
X2ᵛ: *The Second Treatiſe.*
States: There are three states of this edition: the first state lacks the author statement. The second uses the same relative spacing between words, but the lines have been moved more closely together to insert the author statement (by a stop-press correction). States I and II have a comma following '*Row*', and the 9th line is indented below the 8th. The third state is identified by a full stop following '*Row*' in Bettesworth's address; also the word 'Are' in the 9th line of the title is directly under the 'And' of the line above. In some copies the title leaf of States II and III are cancellantia, but from the same typesetting as the cancellandum. All states of the title-page are of the same setting of lines, but in State III they are differently spaced to the left and right; the double rules are slightly differently set. I suspect a few sheets of the first state were printed off before the omission of the author's name was noticed (as in the PPL copy), and the title corrected before the end of the print run.³ Those already incorrectly printed received a cancellans title leaf.
CW: Page. B5ʳ that F1ʳ all I2ᵛ Patriarchal [patriarchal] O1ᵛ la- [laborious] Q3ʳ Com- [Community] T4ᵛ dif- [difference]

---

3 I would like to think this edition was printed by Samuel Palmer, It might explain how Ben Franklin (who worked for Palmer around this time) got his hands on a copy before the omission of the author's name was noticed.

Press figures: iv (A2ᵛ)-2   vi (A3ᵛ)-4   13 (B7ʳ)-2   15 (B8ʳ)-4   26 (C5ᵛ)-2   29 (C7ʳ)-3   45 (D7ʳ)-1   47 (D8ʳ)-3   61 (E7ʳ)-2   62 (E7ᵛ)-4   75 (F6ʳ)-3   80 (F8ᵛ)-4   91 (G6ʳ)-2   96 (G8ᵛ)-2   104 (H4ᵛ)-3   107 (H6ʳ)-1   125 (I7ʳ)-3   126 (I7ᵛ)-4   132 (K2ᵛ)-4   143 (K8ʳ)-4   157 (L7ʳ)-2   159 (L8ʳ)-4   171 (M6ʳ)-2   176 (M8ᵛ)-4   189 (N7ʳ)-4   191 (N8ʳ)-2   208 (O8ᵛ)-3   212 (P2ᵛ)-3   237 (Q7ʳ)-2   238 (Q7ᵛ)-1   243 (R2ʳ)-3   266 (S5ᵛ)-1   272 (S8ᵛ)-4   286 (T7ʳ)-4   288 (T8ᵛ)-4   302 (U7ᵛ)-3

Table

Sig.	(i)						(o)			
	2ʳ	3ᵛ	5ᵛ	6ʳ	7ᵛ	8ʳ	2ᵛ	4ᵛ	7ʳ	8ᵛ
A	–	4					2	–		
B	–	–	–	–	–	4	–	–	2	–
C	–	–	2	–	–	–	–	–	3	–
D	–	–	–	–	–	3	–	–	1	–
E	–	–	–	–	4	–	–	–	2	–
F	–	–	–	3	–	–	–	–	–	4
G	–	–	–	2	–	–	–	–	–	2
H	–	–	–	1	–	–	–	3	–	–
I	–	–	–	–	4	–	–	–	3	–
K	–	–	–	–	–	4	4	–	–	–
L	–	–	–	–	4		–	–	2	–
M	–	–	–	2	–	–	–	–	–	4
N	–	–	–	–	–	2	–	4	–	–
O	–	–	–	–	–	–	–	–	–	3
P	–	–	–	–	–	–	3	–	–	–
Q	–	–	–	–	1	–	–	–	2	–
R	3	–	–	–	–	–	–	–	–	–
S	–	–	1	–	–	–	–	–	–	4
T	–	–	–	–	4	–	–	–	–	4
U	–	–	–	–	3	–	–	–	–	–
X	–	–								

Notes: The text is a reprint of the fourth (1713) edition, and the first to be printed after the death of Awnsham Churchill in 1728. Presumably the booksellers were asserting their ownership of the copy, which they had bought from the heirs of Awnsham Churchill. According to Francis Blackburne (*Memoirs of Thomas Hollis, Esq.*, i. 223-4) this edition, 'printed in 1728, for Bettesworth, Pemberton, and Symon, besides innumerable faults peculiar to itself, had copied the very errors of the first edition pointed out in the list of the errata.' In the first treatise, §41 here reads '*Propriety* in Land', and the last clause in §162 reads 'belong in peculiar to one of his *Issue* . . .' (Cf. no. 32, Notes.)

Princeton University Library's copy (7507.592.12) was unavailable.

A microfilm copy of the British Library's copy of the third state of this edition is to be found in the collection, *The Eighteenth Century*, reel 3370, no. 3.

References: Attig 104; Christophersen p. 100; ESTC 1st state n062053, 2d t060917; Laslett British 8.

Copies examined. State I: PPL (Ii.Lock/393.O, gift of Benj. Franklin; mutilated: top of title leaf, including first 3 lines of title, torn away)
  State II: Y (A1 cancellans) CaOTU (Locke L63.T86 1728; A1 cancellans; '2' on p. 171) CLaslett (A1 cancellans; without fig. on p.171) MH (*EC65.L7934.690th) O (Vet.A4 e.834; A1 cancellans) ViW (320.1/L79t/1728/5)
  State III: Osj (A.6.20) CtY (Ocg45/L793/690cd; A1 cancellans) InNd (A1 cancellans) L (1489.ff.14; A1 cancellans)

34. T2 only. 1753. 8° in 4s
OF | CIVIL | POLITY | [double rule 77 mm] | [double rule 77/76 mm] | LONDON: | Printed M.DCC.LIII.

Coll: 8° in 4s (205 × 108 mm cut) B⁴ ²B⁶ C–E⁴ F² [$2 signed]; 24 leaves; pp. 1–2 i–vi 1–10 7–36 [=48].

Contents: B1ʳ title (verso blank), B2ʳ–B4ᵛ (i–vi) 'ADVERTISEMENT.', ²B1ʳ–²B5ᵛ (1–10) text headed 'SECT. I–III,' ²B6ʳ–C1ʳ (7–9) text 'SECT. III.', C1ᵛ–F2ᵛ (10–36) text 'SECT. IV [–X].'

Text (C3ʳ): 28 lines leaded by 1 mm spacing; 150 (161) × 88 mm; 117R. Good-quality laid paper with vertical chainlines. Top edges show part of fleur-de-lys watermark. Page no. centered within parentheses as headlines.

HT, ²B1ʳ: [double rule 85 mm] | OF | CIVIL POLITY.

CW: Page. ²B2ʳ pro- [produces] C4ᵛ (van-) "quiſh'd E2ʳ (In-) "ſtru- ["ſtruments,] No CW on p. 20 (D2ᵛ).

Press figure: ²B4ʳ (7)–*

Notes: Text is '*extracted from* Mr. Locke's *Essay* on Civil Government, *with some Alterations and Additions*,' followed by suggested further reading (pp. i–vi). Contents of the section are headed as follows:
  Sect. I: *Of the Social Nature of Man.* (pp. 1–2)
  II: *Of a State of Nature, and the Introduction of Property.* (pp. 2–6)
  III: *Of Conjugal Society, and Succession to Property.* (pp. 7–10)
  III bis: *Of the Subjection of Children to Parents.* (2d 7–9)
  IV. *The End and Design of Civil Union.* (2d 10, 11–12)
  V. *Of the Requisites to Make a Man a Member of Civil Society.* (12–13)
  VI. *Of the Origin of Civil Government.* (14–18)
  VII. *Of the Forms of Civil Government.* (18–20)

VIII. *Of the several Powers belonging to Sovereignty.* (21–28)
IX. *Of the Establishment of RELIGION.* (28–32)
X. *General Reflections.* (32–36, ending 'Finis.')

References: Attig 140; ESTC t185105 ('An adaptation of' the 2nd treatise); Laslett British 11.

Copies examined: O (Vet.A5 e.1335 (1)) CLaslett CLU-C Ct

35.2T. '6th printing', 1764 (Hollis's ed.) 8°
TWO TREATISES OF GOVERNMENT | BY IOHN LOCKE | SALUS POPULI SUPREMA LEX ESTO | LONDON PRINTED MDCLXXXVIIII | REPRINTED, THE SIXTH TIME, BY A. MILLAR, H. | WOODFALL, I. WHISTON AND B. WHITE, I. RI- | VINGTON, L. DAVIS AND C. REYMERS, R. BALD- | WIN, HAWES CLARKE AND COLLINS; W. IOHN- | STON, W. OWEN, I. RICHARDSON, S. CROWDER, | T. LONGMAN, B. LAW, C. RIVINGTON, E. | DILLY, R. WITHY, C. AND R. WARE, S. BAKER, | T. PAYNE, A. SHUCKBURGH, I. HINXMAN | MDCCLXIIII

Coll: 8° (207×124 mm cut) A^6 $B-N^8$ O^8 ($\pm$O7) $P-2D^8$ [$4 signed]; 214 leaves; pp. *i–xii* 1 2–56 5 58–1$\overset{.}{9}$1 192–193 194–416 [= 428]. The '7' of page no. 57 frequently fails to print.

Contents: A1^r (*i*) note on edition (verso blank), A2^r (*iii*) half-title (verso blank), A3^r (*v*) title (verso blank), A4^r (*vii*) contents of Book I, A4^v (*viii*) contents of Book II, A5^r–A6^v (*ix–xii*) preface, B1^r–N8^r (*1–191*) text of first treatise, N8^v blank, O1^r–2D8^v (*193–416*) text of second treatise.

Illustrations: 1. Frontispiece, usually facing half-title, an oval portrait of Locke after Kneller, engraved by Cipriani, with a liberty cap at bottom of oval and subscribed 'IOHN LOCKE', 146×101 mm on plate 195×111 mm.
2. Presentation copies also have an extra leaf bound at end with a 'smoke print' of a seated liberty figure (cf. no. 28).

Text (G4^r): 32 lines; 149 (159)×84 mm; 93R. Fair-quality laid paper (usually browning) without watermarks. Page no. at external ends of headlines.

Half-title: TWO TREATISES OF GOVERNMENT. | IN THE FORMER THE FALSE PRIN- | CIPLES AND FOUNDATION OF SIR | ROBERT FILMER AND HIS FOL- | LOWERS ARE DETECTED AND | OVERTHROWN. | THE LATTER IS AN ESSAY CON- | CERNING THE TRUE ORIGINAL | EXTENT AND END OF CIVIL | GOVERNMENT.

HT, B1^r: [leaf orn. 7×11 mm] | OF GOVERNMENT | BOOK I
O1^r: [leaf orn. 7×11 mm] | OF CIVIL-GOVERNMENT | BOOK II
Headlines, B1^v–N8^r: OF GOVERNMENT.
O1^v–2D8^v: OF CIVIL-GOVERNMENT.

CW: Page. D1^r singly H5^r inheritance K3^r portion, [portion;] O3^v done S3^r p [put ('ut' of CW lost in some copies)] U7^v (re-) gulating Z3^v go- [government] 2C1^r con- [*conſtitution*]

Press figures: ix (A5ʳ)-1 9 (B5ʳ)-4 11 (B6ʳ)-1 24 (C4ᵛ)-3 43 (D6ʳ)-3 44 (D6ᵛ)-2 60 (E6ᵛ)-1 76 (F6ᵛ)-3 79 (F8ʳ)-1 90 (G5ᵛ)-3 108 (H6ᵛ)-5 123 (I6ʳ)-5 134 (K3ᵛ)-5 144 (K8ᵛ)-1 156 (L6ᵛ)-1 159 (L8ʳ)-2 172 (M6ᵛ)-5 174 (M7ᵛ)-3 190 (N7ᵛ)-4 198 (O3ᵛ)-4 212 (P2ᵛ)-4 223 (P8ʳ)-5 234 (Q5ᵛ)-1 255 (R8ʳ)-3 265 (S5ʳ)-4 267 (S6ʳ)-5 276 (T2ᵛ)-3 303 (U8ʳ)-3 318 (X7ᵛ)-4 320 (X8ᵛ)-5 331 (Y6ʳ)-3 332 (Y6ᵛ)-4 342 (Z3ᵛ)-5 349 (Z7ʳ)-4 365 (2A7ʳ)-2 379 (2B6ʳ)-4 393 (2C5ʳ)-4 411 (2D6ʳ)-1

Table

Sig.	(i)					(o)					
	3ᵛ	5ᵛ	6ʳ	7ᵛ	8ʳ	2ᵛ	4ᵛ	5ʳ	6ᵛ	7ʳ	8ᵛ
A	–	–	–	–	–	–	–	1	–	–	–
B	–	–	1	–	–	–	–	4	–	–	–
C	–	–	–	–	–	–	3	–	–	–	–
D	–	–	3	–	–	–	–	–	2	–	–
E	–	–	–	–	–	–	–	–	1	–	–
F	–	–	–	–	1	–	–	–	3	–	–
G	–	3	–	–	–	–	–	–	–	–	–
H	–	–	–	–	–	–	–	–	5	–	–
I	–	–	5	–	–	–	–	–	–	–	–
K	5	–	–	–	–	–	–	–	–	–	1
L	–	–	–	–	2	–	–	–	1	–	–
M	–	–	–	3	–	–	–	–	5	–	–
N	–	–	–	4	–	–	–	–	–	–	–
O	4	–	–	–	–	–	–	–	–	–	–
P	4	–	–	–	5	–	–	–	–	–	–
Q	–	1	–	–	–	–	–	–	–	–	–
R	–	–	–	–	3	–	–	–	–	–	–
S	–	–	5	–	–	–	–	4	–	–	–
T	–	–	–	–	–	3	–	–	–	–	–
U	–	–	–	–	3	–	–	–	–	–	–
X	–	–	–	4	–	–	–	–	–	–	5
Y	–	–	3	–	–	–	–	–	4	–	–
Z	5	–	–	–	–	–	–	–	–	4	–
2A	–	–	–	–	–	–	–	–	–	2	–
2B	–	–	4	–	–	–	–	–	–	–	–
2C	–	–	–	–	–	–	–	4	–	–	–
2D	–	–	1	–	–	–	–	–	–	–	–

Notes: One of the editions edited by Thomas Hollis, with the usual 'liberty' cap beneath the portrait of Locke engraved by Cipriani as frontispiece.[4] The editorial note on A1ʳ states: 'The present Edition of this Book has not only been collated with the first three Editions, which were published during the Author's Life, but also has the Advantage of his last Corrections and Improvements, from a Copy delivered by him to Mr. Peter Coste, communicated to the Editor, and now lodged in Christ College, Cambridge.' 'The *Treatises on Government* [were] advertised and published in June 1764' (Blackburne, *Memoirs of Thomas Hollis, Esq.*, index in vol.1). It was re-advertised briefly in the *London Chronicle* for January 24–26, 1765 as '8vo bound 5/-.', along with the Hollis edition of the *Letters on Toleration* (1765; no. 25), as I have learned from John Stephens.

Some copies have O7 cancellans.

References: Attig 105; Christophersen p.100; ESTC t147646; Laslett British 13.

Copies examined: Y (O7 cancellans; lacks front. & A1) O^1 (Radcliffe e.271; gathering A leaves bound in order 3 1 2 5 6 4; Hollis presentation copy) C CaOHM (lacks A1-2) CaOTU (Locke L63.T86 1764; O7 cancellans) Cch (BB3.7; §A bd. as O^1) CLaslett (lacks front.) CtY (Ocg45/L793/690d; O7 cancel.) L^1 (521.i.15) L^2 (C.66.e.9) NjP (7507.592) NNPM (Hollis binding) O^2 (24817.e.60; A3-4 bound before A1) P (*E.2008; Hollis binding; O7 canc.) PPL (Ii Lock/Log1457.O Mackenzie)

36. 2T. Dublin, 1766. 12°
TWO | TREATISES | OF | GOVERNMENT. | IN THE FORMER | The Falſe Principles and Foundation of Sir | ROBERT FILMER and his Followers | are detected and overthrown. | THE LATTER IS | AN ESSAY | CONCERNING | The TRUE ORIGINAL EXTENT and END | of CIVIL GOVERNMENT. | By JOHN [swash J] LOCKE. | *Salus populi ſuprema lex eſto.* | DUBLIN: | Printed by and for SARAH COTTER; and J. SHEPPARD, | Bookſellers, in *Skinner-Row*, | M DCC LXVI.

Coll: 12° (168 × 95 mm cut) A⁴ B-D¹² P¹² (-P.2.11 = A2.3; see *Notes* below) [$5 (-A2, -A3) signed]; 170 leaves; pp. *1-2* [i]-[iii] *iv-vi* 1 2-331 332 [= 340].

Contents: A1ʳ (*1*) title, A1ᵛ (*2*) note on edition, A2ʳ-A3ʳ ([i]-[iii]) pref., A3ᵛ (*iv*) blank, A4ʳ,ᵛ (*v-vi*) contents, B1ʳ-H4ᵛ (*1-152*) text of first book, H5ʳ-P10ʳ (*153-331*) text of second book, P10ᵛ (*332*) blank.

Text (D5ʳ): 37 lines; 135 (144) × 72 mm; 73R. Chainlines horizontal. Watermark is stylised flower and letters 'F E BARBOUIN'.

HT, B1ʳ: [double rule 70/71 mm] | OF | GOVERNMENT. | [rule 71 mm] H5ʳ: [double rule 69/70 mm] | OF | CIVIL-GOVERNMENT. | [rule 71 mm]

---

[4] Information about the bindings and special decorative tools adorning volumes presented by Hollis are given in W.H. Bond's *Thomas Hollis of Lincoln's Inn* (1991).

Headlines, B1ᵛ–H4ᵛ: OF GOVERNMENT.
H5ᵛ–P10ʳ: OF CIVIL-GOVERNMENT.
CW: Page. B3ᵛ diſ- [diſagreeing] C8ʳ will [will,] D12ᵛ (va-) niſhed [niſhes] E9ᵛ (im-) poſſible [Poſſible] L1ʳ incon- [inconveniences] M12ʳ (*exc*-) *cutive* N9ʳ a common- [a common-wealth] O4ʳ (be-) for [fore] P7ᵛ (*re-*) *corded*

Notes: Text is a reprint of the 1764 Hollis edition, with his editorial note on A1ᵛ. Bodleian Library's and Peter Laslett's copies have leaves in sheet P bound in the order: P1 A2 P3 P2 P5 P4 P7 P6 P9 P8 A3 P10 (pp. 313–4 {i–ii} 317–8 315–6 321–2 319–20 325–6 323–4 329–30 327–8 [iii]–*iv* 331–2). Leaves A1 and 4 comprised a separate sheet, and A2 and 3 were detached from P; the rest of the sheet was folded normally. Abnormal folding was needed to give the correct sequence of leaves. The outer forme in the diagram below shows the usual imposition for a common duodecimo in italics; the imposition needed for this copy is shown in roman.

A1ʳ	A12ᵛ	A11ʳ	A2ᵛ
P1ʳ	P10ᵛ	P3ʳ	P2ᵛ
P4ᵛ	P7ʳ	P6ᵛ	P5ʳ
A4ᵛ	A9ʳ	A10ᵛ	A3ʳ
P2ᵛ	P9ʳ	P8ᵛ	P3ʳ
A6ᵛ	A7ʳ	A8ᵛ	A5ʳ

< cut

References: Attig *106; ESTC t175280; Laslett British 14.
Copies examined: O (Vet.A5.f.3707) CLaslett Dm L¹ (1509/2578) L² (521.*l*.15)

37. 2T. '7th' printing, 1772. 8°
TWO | TREATISES OF GOVERNMENT | BY JOHN LOCKE | SALUS POPULI SUPREMA LEX ESTO | LONDON PRINTED MDCLXXXVIIII | REPRINTED THE SEVENTH TIME BY J. WHISTON, | W. STRAHAN, J. AND F. RIVINGTON, L. DAVIS, | W. OWEN, HAWES, CLARKE AND COLLINS, W. JOHN- | STON, B. WHITE, T. CASLON, S. CROWDER, T. LONG- | MAN, B. LAW, C. RIVINGTON, E. AND C. DILLY, | J. WILKIE, T. CADELL, S. BAKER, T. PAYNE, | T. DAVIES, G. ROBINSON, T. BECKET, AND J. ROB- | SON. | M D CC LXXII.

Coll: 8° (230×140 mm uncut) A⁴ a² B–2A⁸ 2B⁴ [$ half signed; Y4 signed 'E4']; 194 leaves; pp. *i–vi* vii–x *xi–xii 1* 2–173 *174–175* 176–312 31 314–376 [= 388]. Page 313 called '31'.

Contents: A1ʳ (*i*) title (verso blank), A2ʳ (*iii*) 'ADVERTISEMENT | To the fixth Edition in 1764.' (as in no. 35), A2ᵛ blank, A3ʳ (*v*) half title, A3ᵛ blank, A4ʳ–a1ᵛ (vii–x) pref., a2ʳ,ᵛ contents, B1ʳ–M7ʳ (*1–173*) text of first book, M7ᵛ blank, M8ʳ–2B4ᵛ (*175–376*) text of second book.

Text (F3ʳ): 32 lines; 150 (159)×84 mm; 93 R. Fleur-de-lys watermark on good-quality laid paper. Page no. at external ends of headlines.

Half-title, A3ʳ: identical with 1764 ed. (no. 35).

Table of press figures

Sig.	(i)						(o)					
	1ᵛ	3ᵛ	5ᵛ	6ʳ	7ᵛ	8ʳ	2ᵛ	4ᵛ	5ʳ	6ᵛ	7ʳ	8ᵛ
A	–						2	–				
B	–	–	–	–	–	–	2	–	–	–	–	–
C	–	–	–	4	–	–	–	–	–	–	–	–
D	–	–	–	–	5	–	–	–	–	–	4	–
E	2	–	–	–	–	–	–	5	–	–	–	–
F	–	5	–	–	–	–	–	–	–	–	–	–
G	–	–	–	3	–	–	–	–	–	–	–	–
H	–	–	3	–	–	–	–	–	–	–	–	4
I	–	4	–	–	–	–	–	–	–	–	–	–
K	–	–	–	4	–	–	–	–	–	–	–	–
L	–	5	–	–	–	–	4	–	–	–	–	–
M	–	–	–	4	–	–	–	–	–	5	–	–
N	–	–	–	–	–	–	–	–	–	–	6	–
O	–	5	–	–	–	–	–	–	–	–	–	–
P	–	–	–	–	–	–	4	–	–	–	–	–
Q	–	–	–	–	–	I	–	–	–	6	–	–
R	–	–	–	5	–	–	–	–	–	–	6	–
S	–	–	–	–	2	–	–	6	–	–	–	–
T	5	–	–	–	–	–	3	–	–	–	–	–
U	–	6	–	–	–	–	–	–	–	–	–	–
X	–	–	–	5	–	–	–	–	4	–	–	–
Y	–	–	–	6	–	–	3	–	–	–	–	–
Z	5	–	–	–	–	–	–	–	–	–	–	–
2A	–	–	–	–	–	–	–	–	–	4	–	–
2B	4	–					5	–				

HT, A4^r: PREFACE
B1^r: OF GOVERNMENT | BOOK I
M8^r: OF CIVIL GOVERNMENT | BOOK II
Headlines, B1^v–M7^r: OF GOVERNMENT
M8^v–2B4^v: OF CIVIL GOVERNMENT
CW: D1^r (be-) cauſe H5^r gives K7^v heir N4^v incon- [inconveniencies] O3^v *richly*, S2^v form S3^r the U7^v benefit X2^v govern- [government] 2B2^v diſtinction
Press figures: *xii* (a2^v)-2   4 (B2^v)-2   27 (C6^r)-4   45 (D7^r)-4   46 (D7^v)-5   50 (E1^v)-2   56 (E4^v)-5   70 (F3^v)-5   91 (G6^r)-3   106 (H5^v)-3   112 (H8^v)-4   118 (I3^v)-4   139 (K6^r)-4   148 (L2^v)-4   150 (L3^v)-5   171 (M6^r)-4   172 (M6^v)-5   189 (N7^r)-6   198 (O3^v)-5   212 (P2^v)-4   236 (Q6^v)-6   239 (Q8^r)-1   251 (R6^r)-5   253 (R7^r)-6   264 (S4^v)-6   270 (S7^v)-2   274 (T1^v)-5   276 (T2^v)-3   294 (U3^v)-6   313 (X5^r)-4   315 (X6^v)-5   324 (Y2^v)-3   331 (Y6^r)-6   338 (Z1^v)-5   364 (2A6^v)-4   370 (2B1^v)-4   372 (2B2^v)-5
Notes: Text is a reprint of 1764 edition, without portrait frontispiece. A microfilm copy is in the collection, *The Eighteenth Century*, reel 3438, no. 2.
References: Attig 107; Christophersen p. 100; ESTC t110391; Laslett British 16.
Copies examined: O (Vet.A5.e.1238)   [Berlin]   CaOTU (Locke L63.T86 1772; uncut)   CLaslett   CtY (Ocg45/L793/690e)   L (1509/2012)   MH (KE6255)   PPL (Am 1772.Loc/Aqi8.L793)

38. Second Treatise. Boston, Mass., 1773. 4°
AN | ESSAY | CONCERNING | THE | TRUE ORIGINAL EXTENT | AND END | OF | CIVIL GOVERNMENT. | BY | THE LATE LEARNED | JOHN [swash J] LOCKE, Esq. | [rule 80 mm] | BOSTON: [swash T] | Re-Printed andSold [no space] by Edes and Gill, in | Queen-Street, 1773.
Coll: 4° (198 × 124 mm cut) A^4 B–Q^4 R^2 (-R2) [$2 signed]; 65 leaves; pp. *1–3* 4–129 *130*.
Contents: A1^r (*i*) title (verso blank), A2^r–R1^r (3–129) text, R1^v blank.
Text (E2^r): 44 lines; 151 (163) × 82 mm; 68 R. Fair-quality laid paper, with horizontal chainlines. No visible watermarks.
HT A2^r: [double rule 81 mm] | AN ESSAY | CONCERNING THE TRUE | ORIGINAL EXTENT AND END | OF CIVIL-GOVERNMENT. | [rule 81 mm]
Headlines: *Of Civil-Government.*
CW: Page. B2^v where G2^r continue M4^v done Q4^r (au-) thority
Notes: Text is a reprint of the second 'treatise' from Hollis's edition (1764, or 1766) omitting the editorial note and first chapter. There are no paragraph or chapter numbers; but chapters, often starting in mid-page, indicated by a rule and italic titles, e.g. [rule 80 mm] | '*Of PROPERTY.*' Page no. in upper external ends of headlines. I have not found any copies with leaf R2, which was presumably blank.

A microfilm copy of this edition is available in the collection *The Eighteenth Century*, reel 414, no. 1; another is available in the Evans microcard set.

References: Attig 120; Christophersen p. 100; ESTC w031951; Evans 12834; Laslett American 1.

Copies examined: DLC (JC153.L85; flyleaf inscribed 'John Pierce ^Jun^ | His Book 1773') CtY (Ocg45/L793/773) L (8005.bb.32) MWA PPL (Am Lock/67121.O) PU (*EC65.L7933/D773e 1773)

39. 2T. Dublin, 1779. 12°

TWO | TREATISES | OF | GOVERNMENT. | IN THE FORMER | The Falſe Principles and Foundation of Sir | ROBERT FILMER and his Followers | are detected and overthrown. | THE LATTER IS | AN ESSAY | CONCERNING | The TRUE ORIGINAL EXTENT and END | of CIVIL GOVERNMENT. | By JOHN [swash J] LOCKE. | *Salus populi ſuprema lex eſto.* | DUBLIN: | Printed for J. SHEPPARD and G. NUGENT, | Bookſellers, in *Anne-Street, Stephen's-Green.* | M,DCC,LXXIX.

Coll: 12° (168 × 97 mm cut) A⁴ (A1 + 2 leaves from P + A4) B–O¹² P¹² (–2 leaves; see *Notes*) [$5 (–A3, –A4) signed]; 170 leaves; pp. *I–II* i–iii *iv–vi* 1 2–331 *332* [= 340].

Contents: A1ʳ (*I*) title, A1ᵛ (*II*) edition note (from Hollis ed., no. 35), A2ʳ–A3ʳ (i–iii) pref., A3ᵛ blank, A4ʳ·ᵛ (*v–vi*) contents, B1ʳ–H4ᵛ (*1–152*) text of first treatise, H5ʳ–P10ʳ (*153–331*) text of second treatise, P10ᵛ blank.

Text (C3ᵛ): 37 lines; 134 (143) × 72 mm; 73R. Watermark similar to Heawood 2396: bunch of grapes, and 'D ANGOUMOIS'. Page no. at external ends of headlines. Preliminary pagination set within square brackets.

HT, A2ʳ: [Oxford rule 68 mm] | PREFACE.
  B1ʳ: [Oxford rule 68 mm] | OF | GOVERNMENT. | [rule 70 mm]
  H5ʳ: [Oxford rule 68 mm] | OF | CIVIL-GOVERNMENT. | [rule 69 mm]

Headlines: B1ᵛ–H4ᵛ: OF GOVERNMENT.
  H5ᵛ–P10ʳ: OF CIVIL-GOVERNMENT.

CW: Page. B5ᵛ argu- [argument] C7ᵛ pre- [preferred] G2ᵛ plea- [pleaſant] I11ʳ run- [running] M4ᵛ *le-* [*legiſlative*] O2ʳ pow- [power]

Notes: Reprint of Dublin edition of 1766 (no. 36). Laslett's and CaOTU copies have leaves A2 and 3 bound between P5 and the resultant P6 (pp. 322 & 323). A microfilm copy is in the collection, *The Eighteenth Century*, reel 3295, no. 2.

References: Attig 108; ESTC t062033; Laslett British 18.

Copies examined: O (Vet.A5 f.1560) C CaOTU (Locke L63.T86 1779) CLaslett CtY (Ocg45/L793/690f) Dm Dt L (1488.bb.6) ViU

40. 2T. Dublin, 1794. 8°
TWO | TREATISES | OF | GOVERNMENT. | IN THE FORMER | The Falfe Principles and Foundation of Sir ROBERT FILMER | and his Followers are detected and overthrown. | THE LATTER IS | AN ESSAY | CONCERNING | The TRUE ORIGINAL EXTENT and END of | CIVIL GOVERNMENT. | [orn. rule of leaves 46 mm] | By JOHN [swash J] LOCKE. | [orn. rule of leaves 49 mm] | *Salus populi fuprema lex efto.* | [orn. rule of leaves 63 mm] | DUBLIN: | Printed by WILLIAM M'KENZIE, No. 33, | COLLEGE-GREEN. | [Oxford rule 7 mm] | 1794

Coll: 8° (209 × 122 mm cut) A^4 $B-U^8$ [$2 signed]; 156 leaves; pp. *i–iii* iv–vi vii–viii 1 2–141 *142* 143–304 [= 312].

Contents: A1^r title, A1^v edition note as in no. 35, A2^r–A3^v (*iii*–vi) pref., A4^{r,v} contents, B1^r–K7^r (*1–141*) text of first treatise, K7^v–U8^v (*142–304*) text of second treatise.

Text (F1^r): 37 lines; 155 (167) × 88 mm; 84 R. Wove paper, without watermarks. Pref. set 31 lines, 95 R. Chapter titles set ital., frequently in mid-page, e.g. 'CHAP. IX. | *Of Monarchy, by Inheritance from Adam.*'

HT, B1^r: OF | GOVERNMENT.

K7^v: OF | CIVIL-GOVERNMENT. | [French rule 61 mm]

Headlines, B1^v–K7^r, K8^r (2–141, 143 [!]): OF GOVERNMENT.

K8^v–U8^v (144–304): OF CIVIL-GOVERNMENT.

CW: Page. C7^v *given*, F7^r §.90: [§.90.] G2^v alien H1^r xxv [xxv,] N4^v *honour* S3^r concurred U1^r revolutions

The following lack catchwords: E5^r, G1^v, G7^v, G8^v, K6^v, L3^v, L8^v, M7^v, N5^v, O5^r, P3^v, P4^r, P5^r, Q3^r, Q4^r, Q7^r and U1^v–8^r.

Note: Text is a reprint of the Dublin ed. of 1779 (no. 39).

References: Attig 109; ESTC n022259; Laslett British 20.

Copies examined: CaOTU (Locke L63.T86 1794) CLaslett Dm Dt

41. Second Treatise. Selections. Sheffield (1794?) 12° in 6s
THE | *SPIRIT* [swash T] | OF | JOHN LOCKE | ON | CIVIL GOVERNMENT, | *REVIVED BY* | THE CONSTITUTIONAL SOCIETY | OF | *SHEFFIELD.* | [French rule 24 mm] | SHEFFIELD: | PRINTED FOR THE SOCIETY, BY J. GALES, | AND SOLD, BY SYMONDS AND RIDGEWAY, D.I. EATON, LONDON, | AND ALL THE BOOKSELLERS.

Coll: 12° in 6s (175 × 96 mm) π^6 (–π6) D^3 [$3 (–D3); C2 signed 'B2']; 26 leaves; pp. *I–II i–iii* iv–viii 1 2–42 [= 52].

Contents: π1^r (*I*) half-title (verso blank), π2^r (*i*) title (verso blank), π3^r–5^v (*iii–viii*) pref.: 'To the People', A1^r–D3^v (*1–42*) text.

Text (C3^r): 38 lines; 138 × 79 mm; 73R. Dedicatory pref. is set 42 lines, 65R. Page no. centered within parentheses as headlines. Medium-quality laid paper without visible watermarks.

Half title: [double rule 78 mm] | THE SPIRIT | OF | *JOHN* [swash J] *LOCKE.* | [double rule 78 mm]

50   *John Locke: A Descriptive Bibliography*

HT: THE SPIRIT | OF | JOHN [swash J] LOCKE.
CW: Page. A2ʳ (go-) vernment, B6ᵛ (cer-) tain B7ʳ beſt, C8ᵛ force, D1ᵛ deſtructive
Press figures: none.
Notes: Text consists of selections from 8 chapters (herein renumbered) of the second Treatise beginning with Chap. VIII ('Of the Beginning of Political Societies') and concluding with Chap. XIX ('Of the Dissolution of Governments'). The preface begins: 'Fellow Citizens, In conformity to the promise made at our Public Meeting on the 7th of April 1794, we present you' [with Locke's second treatise]. New chapters begin, often in mid-page, with heading, e.g., 'CHAPTER VII. | OF TYRANNY.'

The text was edited by Henry Yorke (Attig, based upon G. P. Jones's article, 'The Political Reform Movement in Sheffield', *Transactions of the Hunter Archaeological Society*, 4 (1937): 57–68).

Judging by ESTC records, many copies lack half-title; the British Library copy lacks title leaf and preface. There is also a copy in the Public Record Office (shelfmark KB.33/6/5). A microfilm of their copy is in *The Eighteenth Century*, reel 258, no. 1. Another microfilm copy is in the Goldsmiths'-Kress Library of Economic Literature, no. 16136.

References: Attig 141; Christophersen p. 100 n.4; ESTC n038468; Laslett British 21 (in error: collation as 78 pp.)
Copies examined: DLC (AC901.B3 vol. 8:1; lacks half-title) CtY (Oca10/1/1808L; lacks half-title) L (8464 a.2l; lacks π2–5) PPL (11056.D.2)

42. 2T. Glasgow, 1796. 12° in 6s.
TWO | TREATISES | OF | GOVERNMENT: | In the Former, | The Falſe Principles and Foundation of | SIR ROBERT FILMER, | AND HIS FOLLOWERS, | are *Detected* and *Overthrown*. | The Latter is an | ESSAY | Concerning the True Original, Extent, and End of | CIVIL-GOVERNMENT. | BY JOHN [swash J] LOCKE, ESQ; | [rule 74 mm] | *The Sixth Edition.* | [rule 75 mm] | *Quod ſi nihil cum potentiore juris humani relinquitur inopi, at ego ad | deos vindices humanæ ſuperbiæ confugiam: Et precabor ut iras ſuas | vertant in eos, quibus non ſuæ res, non alienæ ſatis ſint; quorum ſœ- | vitiam non mors noxiorum exſatiet: Placari nequeant, niſi hauriendum | ſanguinem laniandaq; viſcera noſtra præbuerimus.* | LIV. 1.9. c.1. | [French rule 14 mm] | GLASGOW, | PRINTED BY W. PATON, | FOR R. SMITH, BOOKSELLER, PAISLEY, | AND D. BOAG, THE PUBLISHER. | [Oxford rule 14 mm] | 1796.
Coll: 12° in 6s (165 × 99 mm cut) A⁶ B–X⁶ 2A–2P⁶ Q³ [$ half signed; C2 and C3 both signed 'C3')]; 219 leaves; pp. *1–3* 4–6 *7* 8–205 206–207 208–431 432–438.
Contents: A1ʳ title (verso blank), A2ʳ–A3ᵛ (*3–6*) pref., A4ʳ–S1ʳ (7–205) text of first treatise, S1ᵛ blank, S2ʳ–2P6ʳ (207–431) text of second treatise, 2P6ᵛ contents, Q1ʳ–Q3ʳ 'SUBSCRIBERS NAMES.', Q3ᵛ blank.

Text (C3ʳ): 31 lines; 130 (141)×75 mm; 84 R. Poor quality paper, with vertical chainlines, watermarked '1795'. Page no. at external ends of headlines.
HT, A4ʳ: OF | GOVERNMENT. | [French rule 24 mm]
  S2ʳ: AN | ESSAY | CONCERNING THE | *True Original, Extent and End* | OF | CIVIL-GOVERNMENT. | [French rule 27 mm]
Headlines, A4ᵛ–S1ʳ (8–205): Of Government.
  S2ᵛ–2P6ʳ: Of Civil-Government.
CW: Page. D2ʳ 'through F2ᵛ (o-) 'ver N1ʳ 'Moreover, ['Moreover] R3ᵛ (fuc-) ceed- [ceeded] X5ᵛ proportions 2C6ᵛ ap- [appeal] 2K1ʳ hands. [hands,] 2M3ᵛ 102. Where- [202. Wherever]
No CW when the end of a section coincides with the end of a page, e.g. B1ᵛ, L6ᵛ.
Notes: Text is that of sixth (1764) edition, according to Laslett, but the title-page follows that of 1713 or 1728 (no. 32 or 33).
References: Attig 110; ESTC t175281; Laslett British 22.
Copies examined: O (Vet.A5 f.2884)   E   MH (KD43258; lacks Q³; grangerised)

43. Second Treatise. Dublin, 1798. long 12°
AN | ESSAY | CONCERNING THE | TRUE ORIGINAL EXTENT AND END | OF | CIVIL GOVERNMENT. | *BY JOHN* [swash J] *LOCKE*. | *Salus populi ſuprema lex eſto*. | WITH NOTES. | [French rule 38 mm] | Τοῖς γαρ ἀνίσοις, τὰ ἴσα ἀνισα γίγνοιτ ἀν', ἐι μὴ τυγχάνοι | τοῦ μετροu. | Plato de leg. l. 6. | [French rule 38 mm] | *DUBLIN:* | GEORGE BONHAM. | [broken double rule 9 mm] | 1798.
Coll: long 12° (192×114 mm uncut) A–I¹² [$5 signed]; 108 leaves; pp. *i–ii* iii–vi 1–210 [=216].
Contents: A1ʳ title (verso blank), A2ʳ–A3ᵛ (iii–vi) 'ADVERTISEMENT.' (editor's preface), A4ʳ–I12ᵛ (1–210) text of second treatise.
Text (C3ʳ): 36 lines; 131 (141)×72 mm; 73 R. Wove paper, no watermarks. Page no. in external corners of headlines. Pref. has page no. centered within parentheses. Notes at foot of pages set 62 R; where continued to a following page, also have own catchwords.
HT, A2ʳ: [Oxford rule 69 mm] | ADVERTISEMENT. | [French rule 48 mm]
  A4ʳ: [Oxford rule 70 mm] | OF | CIVIL GOVERNMENT. | [French rule 38 mm]
Headlines: OF CIVIL GOVERNMENT.
CW: Page. A6ʳ has A12ᵛ denied D9ᵛ number (for footnotes: 'imperfections') H12ᵛ for I7ᵛ reverence
Notes: Reprint of the text of the Hollis edition (no. 35), with notes and annotations by the Rev. Thomas Elrington (identified in no. 44), placed beneath the direction line. Elrington was an active member of various literary and scientific societies; at his death in 1835 he had been Bishop of Leighlin

and Ferns (Church of Ireland) for some twelve years (cf. DNB). The Greek quotation is translated as 'For when equality is given to unequal things, the resultant will be unequal, unless due measure is applied.'

I am grateful to Mike Gollop of the Brotherton Library at the University of Leeds for supplying details of this edition.

A microfilm copy of the Henry E. Huntington Library's uncut copy is in *The Eighteenth Century*, reel 2502, no. 50.

References: Attig 121; ESTC n017504; Laslett British 23.

Copy examined: LEu (by corresp.)

44. Second Treatise. '2d' Elrington ed. Dublin, 1798. long 12°
AN | ESSAY | CONCERNING THE | TRUE ORIGINAL EXTENT AND END | OF | CIVIL GOVERNMENT. | *BY JOHN* [swash J] LOCKE. | *Salus populi ſuprema lex eſto.* | WITH NOTES, | BY THE REV. THOMAS ELRINGTON, | S.F.T.C.D. AND M.R.I.A. | [French rule 38 mm] | Τοῖς γαρ ἀνίσοις, τὰ ισα ανισα γίγνοιτ' ἀν, ἐι μη τυγχάνοι | τοῦ μετρου. | Plato de leg. 1. 6. | [Oxford rule 42 mm] | SECOND EDITION. | [Oxford rule inverted, 42 mm] | *DUBLIN:* | GEORGE BONHAM. | [double rule 14 mm] | 1798.

Coll: long 12° (192 × 114 mm uncut) A^{12} (±A1) $B-I^{12}$ [$5 signed]; 108 leaves; pp. *i–ii* iii–vi 1–210 [= 216].

Contents, *Text*, *HTs* and headlines identical with 1798 edition (no. 43).

Notes: A reissue of no. 43, with cancellans title leaf (and its varying or lacking accents), identifying the author of the notes. All other features are identical with no. 43.

References: Attig 121 n.; ESTC t182847.

Copies examined: O (Vet.A5 e.5060, uncut) Dt

45*. Second Treatise. Dutch trans. Groningen, 1728. 12°
Johannes van Abkoude, in *Naamregister van de bekendste en meest in gebruik zynde Nederduitsche Boeken . . . 1600 tot het jaar 1761* (Rotterdam, 1773) lists a translation of Locke's second treatise, in duodecimo, priced at 11 stuivers, as follows:

> Over de Burgerlyke Regering / 1728. Groning[en]. Sipkes Cost en Bandsma, 12 [i.e. 12°]. 11 st.

Not listed in Attig or Laslett.
I have been unable to find a record of anyone's owning this edition.

46. Second Treatise. French trans. (Mazel). Amsterdam, 1691. 12°
DU | GOUVERNMENT | CIVIL, | Où l'on traitte de l'Origine, des | Fondemens, de la Nature, | du Pouvoir, & des Fins | des Sociétez Poli- | tiques. | *Traduit de l'Anglois.* | [orn. vignette, wolf upright against a tree, with scroll at left: 'QUERENDO' 34 × 45 mm] | A AMSTERDAM, | Chez ABRAHAM WOLFGANG, | prés de la Bourſe. | MDCXCI.

Coll: 12° (136 × 74 mm cut) *⁶ A–N¹² O⁶ [$ half + 1 (–*4) signed]; 168 leaves; pp. *i–xii* 1–321 322–324 [= 336].
Contents: *1ʳ title (verso blank), *2ʳ–*5ᵛ 'AVERTISSEMENT.', *6ʳ,ᵛ 'TABLE DES CHAPITRES.', A1ʳ–O5ʳ (1–321) text of second treatise, O5ᵛ–O⁶ (322–324) blank.
Text (A12ʳ): 31 lines; 109 (117) × 53 mm; 70 R. Introductory 'Avertissement' set 24 lines, 94 R. Medium-quality paper with chainlines horizontal. Watermark similar to Heawood 305. Page no. at outer corners of headlines. Since preliminary sheets were usually the last to be printed, I think * and O made up one sheet.
HT, A1ʳ: LE | GOUVERNEMENT | CIVIL. | De ſa véritable Origine, de ſon | Etenduë, & de ſa Fin.
Headlines: *Le Gouvernement Civil.*
CW: Page. A1ʳ juriſ- [juriſdiction] C1ᵛ pro- [proviſions] E4ᵛ ſor- [ſorte] H9ᵛ natu- [naturel,] K2ᵛ Gou- [Gouvernement,] L10ᵛ con- [connoiſſe]
Notes: Locke's anonymous text is here an anonymous translation, traditionally attributed to David Mazel, 'one of Huguenot pastors living in Holland' (Laslett, p. 12), of the second treatise in its 1R version (no. 29) with the first chapter omitted. The text is divided into 18 chapters (omitting Locke's section numbers), each chapter with sections numbered from one. Laslett's listing of 'French 1' is of the summary review of the first English edition of 1690 that appeared in the *Bibliothèque universelle*, 19 (cf. no. 29, *References*).
Notices: *Bibliothèque universelle*, 20 (1691): 263–5; *Histoire des ouvrages des savans* 7 (1690–91): 457–65.
References: Attig 166; Christophersen p.101; L.L.1291 (under 'Government'); Laslett French 2.
Copies examined: O (Vet.B3 f.178) BBR [Berlin] C [GhU] Wol

47. Second Treatise. French trans. (Mazel) 'New ed.' Geneva, 1724. 12°
DU | GOUVERNEMENT | CIVIL, | *OU L'ON TRAITE DE L'ORIGINE* | *DES FONDEMENS, DE LA NATURE,* | *DU POUVOIR, ET DES FINS DES* | *SOCIETEZ POLITIQUES.* [4th–7th lines, all swash Ns, Qs, Rs] | Traduit de l'Anglois. | *NOUVELLE EDITION.* [swash Ns] | [orn., woven strap 26 × 38 mm] | A GENEVE, | Chez DU VILLARD & JAQUIER. [swash Q] | [rule 44 mm] | MDCCXXIV.
Coll: 12° (166 × 96 mm cut) A–P¹² Q⁶ [$ half (–Q3) signed]; 186 leaves; pp. *i–viii* 1–115 126–127 118–328 335–365 366–370 [= 372]. Page 116–17 called 126–27; 329–334 omitted.
Contents: A1ʳ title (verso blank), A2ʳ–A4ᵛ 'Avertissement', A5ʳ–Q4ʳ (1–365) text of second treatise, Q4ʳ–Q5ʳ (366–367) contents for 18 chapters, Q5ᵛ–Q6 (368–370) blank.
Text (F4ʳ): 28 lines; 116 (125) × 62 mm; 83 R. Introduction set 24 lines 107 R. Fair-quality laid paper.
CW: Page.

Signature positions: A5 état D2 alors on G obligé I3 force N6 par là Q2 les hommes
Note: Text is straight reprint of 1691 (no. 46).
References: Attig 167; Christophersen p. 101; Laslett French 3; Rochedieu p. 194.
Copies examined: P (*E.2010)   Vat

48. Second Treatise. French trans. (Mazel) 'New ed.' Brussels (Paris?) 1749. 12°
DU | GOUVERNEMENT | CIVIL, | *Où l'on traite* | *DE L'ORIGINE, DES FONDEMENS,* | *DE LA NATURE,* | *DU POUVOIR, ET DES FINS* | *DES SOCIETE'S POLITIQUES.* [swash Q] | *Traduit de l'Anglois* de Mr. LOCKE. | [rule 58 mm] | NOUVELLE EDITION, | *Revue & corrigée.* | [rule 60 mm] | [woodcut orn., helmet & scrolls 27 × 46 mm] | A BRUXELLES. | [triple rule, thin/thick/thin 34 mm] | M.DCC.XLIX.
Coll: 12° (164 × 99 mm cut) *⁶ A-P¹² [$ half signed; P4 signed 'M4']; 186 leaves; pp. *I-II* III-XII 1-358 *359-360* [= 372].
Contents: *1ʳ (*I*) title (verso blank), *2ʳ-*4ᵛ (III-VIII) introductory note, *5ʳ-*6ᵛ (IX-XII) supplementary introd., A1ʳ-P11ᵛ (1-358) text of second treatise, P12ʳ,ᵛ (*359-360*) 'TABLE DES CHAPITRES.'
Text (F2ᵛ): 27 lines; 111 (121) × 61 mm; 83 R. Pref. set 24 lines, 96 R. Good-quality laid paper, with watermark: a bunch of grapes, similar to Heawood 2372. Chainlines horizontal. Final text page has a woodcut ornament of a vase with fruit, 26 × 27 mm.
HT, A1ʳ: LE | GOUVERNEMENT | CIVIL. | De ſa véritable Origine, de ſon | Etendue, & de ſa Fin.
*2ʳ [triple rule 61 mm] | AVERTISSEMENT | *De l'Edition de* 1724.
*5ʳ: [triple rule 60 mm] | SUPPLEMENT | *à l'Avertiſſement précédent.*
Headlines: *2ᵛ-*4ᵛ: AVERTISSEMENT.
A1ᵛ-P11ᵛ: *Le Gouvernement Civil.*
CW: Gathering. C12ᵛ tous E12ᵛ ſoi- [ſoi-même:] H12ᵛ met- [mettent] O12ᵛ plus
Notes: Text is a reprint of the 1724 edition, 'not much amended' (Laslett), in 18 chapters. Supplement to the pref. is selected quotations from the *Bibliothèque universelle*, v. 19 (the summary of the first English edition), and from the *Bibliothèque choisie*, v. 6 (Locke's 'Eloge', both articles by Jean Le Clerc). Weller (1749: II.113) says this 'new' ed. really printed in Paris.
References: Attig 168; Laslett French 4; Rochedieu p. 194.
Copies examined: O (Vet.B4 f.323)   [GOT]   P (*E.2011)

49. Second Treatise. French trans. (Mazel) 'New ed.' Brussels (Paris?), 1754. 12°
DU | GOUVERNEMENT | CIVIL, | *Où l'on traite* | *DE L'ORIGINE, DES FONDEMENS,* | *DE LA NATURE,* | *DU POUVOIR, ET DES*

FINS | DES SOCIETE'S POLITIQUES. | *Traduit de l'Anglois de M. LOCKE.* | [rule 59 mm] | *NOUVELLE EDITION,* | *Revue & corrigée.* | [rule 59 mm] | [diamond-shaped pr. orn. 25 × 25 mm] | A BRUXELLES. | [Oxford rule 43 mm] | M.DCC.LIV.

Coll: 12° (165 × 100 mm cut) *6 (± *1) A–P12 [$ half signed; P4 signed 'M4']; 186 leaves; pp. *I–II* III–XII 1–358 359–360 [= 372].

Contents, Text, HT and *Headlines*, and *Signature positions*: identical with 1749 (no. 48).

Note: Title leaf is a cancellans; all other details, including signature on p. 343, indicate it is the same printing as no. 48. Chainlines are horizontal on the same kind of paper as no. 48, except for title leaf, where they are vertical. Again Weller (1754: II.138) says published in Paris; but GV 1700–1910 (vol. 89, p. 633) has an entry giving 'Lips. 754.' as imprint for this French edition. Perhaps it was really printed in Leipzig.

References: Attig *169; Laslett French 5; Rochedieu p. 194.

Copies examined: P (*E.2012)   AMu (1304.E 9)   [BBR]   Vat

50. Second Treatise. French trans. (Mazel/Rousset) '5th ed.' Amsterdam, 1755. 12°

In red & black: DU | [red line:] GOUVERNEMENT | CIVIL, | [red:] PAR MR. LOCKE. | TRADUIT DE L'ANGLOIS | *Cinquieme Edition éxactement revûë & corrigée ſur* | *la 5. Edition de Londres & augmentée de* | *quelques Notes,* | [red:] Par L.C.R.D.M.A.D.P. | [engr. orn., vignette of seated Neptune, 44 × 56 mm, subscribed 'L.F.D.B. del. F.M. la Cavé Sculp.'] | [red:] A AMSTERDAM, | *Chez J.* [swash J] SCHREUDER | & *PIERRE MORTIER* le Jeune. | [red:] M. DCC. LV.

Coll: 12° (180 × 110 mm uncut) *12 (– 2 leaves = P2?) A–N12 O6 P2 [$ half + 1 (–P2) signed]; 174 leaves; pp. *I–V VI–X XI XII–XIV XV XVI–XVIII XIX–XX* 1 2–328 [= 348].

Contents: *1r (*I*) half-title (verso blank), *2r (*III*) title (verso blank), *3r–*5v (*V–X*) introductory note, *6r–*7v (*XI–XIV*) supplementary introd., *8r–*9v (*XV–XVIII*) 'AVERTISSEMENT | Sur cette cinquiéme Edition', *10r,v (*XIX–XX*) contents by chap., A1r–P2v (*1–328*) text of second treatise.

Text (E7r): 29 lines; 118 (128) × 69 mm; 82 R. Pref.: 25 lines, 95 R. Chainlines horizontal. No visible watermarks. Preliminary gathering * and gathering P were one sheet.

Half-title, *1r: DU | GOUVERNMENT | CIVIL.

HT, *3r: [framed headpiece, leaves & vase on pedestal 21 × 69 mm] | AVERTISSEMENT | *de l'Edition de* 1724.

*6r: [headpiece, scrollwork leaves 22 × 69 mm] | SUPLÉMENT | *à l'Avertiſſement précédent.*

*8r: [headpiece, 3 bouquets 21 × 67 mm] | AVERTISSEMENT | Sur cette cinquiéme Edition.

A1r: [headpiece as on *8r] | TRAITÉ | DU | GOUVERNEMENT | CIVIL. | De ſa véritable Origine, de ſon | Etenduë, & de ſa Fin.

Headlines, *3ᵛ–*9ᵛ: AVERTISSEMENT.
A1ᵛ–P2ᵛ: LE GOUVERNEMENT CIVIL.
CW: Page. A6ʳ Prin- [Principes] C10ᵛ pla- [place] E1ʳ obli- [obliger] H6ᵛ Su- [Suprême] L3ʳ quoi- [quoiqu'il] N3ᵛ mû- [mûrement]
Footnotes which continue to another page also have their own CW.
Notes: Reprint of the 1724 edition, 'very little modified, but with an extra advertisement and 25 notes: editor unidentified.' – Laslett. In his *The Dutch Republic*, Jonathan I. Israel identifies the editor as Jean Rousset de Missy, a Huguenot radical and a leading journalist at the Hague and in Amsterdam, 'the foremost popularizer of John Locke's radical political ideas in the Republic . . . His 1755 French version of Locke's *Two Treatises* became one of the most widely used editions of the eighteenth century' (pp. 1048–9). His evidence is a letter from Rousset to Willem Bentinck van Rhoon (a representative of the Prince of Orange at the Hague) dated 26 June 1748, wherein he presses for 'the immediate reprinting of a French edition' (ibid. p. 1074). The letter is now British Library MS. Egerton 1745 fo. 486. Other information about Rousset is in the *Dictionnaire des journalistes* (1976).
    Sections numbered with arabic numerals. The initials of the engraver stand for F. Morellon la Cavé.
References: Attig 170; Christophersen p.101; Laslett French 6; Rochedieu p. 194.
Copies examined: CLaslett (uncut) [Berlin (Potsd.S.)] [GhU (acc.23386)] [GOT] L (8012.a.53) MH (Gov522.15.14) NjP (7507.592.161) O (Vet.B5 f.98; lacks *1) Wol

51. Second Treatise. French trans. (Mazel/Rousset) '6th ed.', Amsterdam, 1780. 12°
In red & black: DU | [red line:] GOUVERNEMENT | CIVIL, | [red:] PAR MR. LOCKE. | TRADUIT DE L'ANGLOIS. | [red:] SIXIEME EDITION. | *Exactement Revue & Corrigée fur la derniere* | *Edition de Londres & augmentée de* | *quelques Notes,* | [red:] Par L.C.R.D.M.A.D.P. | [orn. of mixed irons 32 × 30 mm] | [red:] A AMSTERDAM, | Chez BARTHELEMI VLAM. | [red:] MDCCLXXX.
Coll: 12° (193 × 115 mm uncut) *10 A–N12 O8 [$ half + 1 (–O5) signed; F7 signed 'E7']; 174 leaves; pp. *I–V* VI–X *XI* XII–XIV *XV* XVI–XVIII *XIX–XX* 1 2–328 [= 348].
Contents: *1ʳ (*I*) half-title (verso blank) *2ʳ (*III*) title (verso blank), *3ʳ–*5ᵛ (*V–X*) introductory note to the '*Edition de* 1724', *6ʳ–*7ᵛ (*XI–XIV*) supplementary note, *8ʳ–*9ᵛ (*XV–XVIII*) note on 'cette 5. Edition', *10ʳ,ᵛ (*XIX–XX*) chapter contents, A1ʳ–O8ᵛ (*1–328*) text of second treatise.
Text (D7ʳ): 29 (or 30) lines; 117 (126) × 70 mm; 81 R. Chainlines horizontal. No watermarks. First (*) gathering appears to be an octavo with a bifolium sheet (leaves 5 and 6) inserted in the middle. Page no. at outer ends of headlines.
Half-title, *1ʳ: DU | GOUVERNEMENT | CIVIL.

HT: [rect. ornament 16 × 69 mm] | TRAITÉ | DU | GOUVERNEMENT | CIVIL. | De ſa véritable Origine, de ſon | Etendue, & de ſa Fin. | [orn. rule of suns 70 mm]

Headlines: LE GOUVERNEMENT CIVIL. Errors on p. 11 (A6r): 'GOUVRNEMENT'; 71 (C12r) and 89 (D9r): 'GOUVERNEMENE'; and 150 (G3v): 'GOUEVRNEMENT'.

CW: Gathering (chiefly). Gathering in sheets *, A–F and I–N, also on verso of 4th leaf. Gathering, and additional ones in §§ B, F and G randomly placed (all random ones listed here). Page CW in sheet H.
*4^v où *10^v TRAI- [TRAITÉ] A4^v (s'a-) ban- [bandonner] A12^v com- [comme] B1^v IV. B4^v (au-) tre B12^v (travail-) ler; C4^v gens [gens-là] D4^v arri- [arriver] E4^v CHA- [CHAPITRE] F4^v eut F8^r V. F12^v (com-) men- [mencement.] G5^r XVII. G6^v *nés* G10^r XXV. [with 30th line of text] H1^v quel- [quelque] H2^r pour I4^v *vie* K4^v les K12^v ils L4^v j'ai M4^v du M12^v (ren-) dent- [dent-ils] N4^v de

Note: Page-for-page reprint of no. 50. Anti-Orangist feelings and a sympathy with the American Revolution were probably the incentive to reprint Rousset's edition of 1755. The political unrest at this time is described in Jonathan Israel's *The Dutch Republic*, pp. 1090–1112. Vlam now owned the Wetstein firm's copy or license to print.

References: Attig 171; Christophersen p. 101; Laslett French 7; Rochedieu p. 194.

Copies examined: Y   O (Vet.B5 e.95, uncut)   MH (Gov522.15.15)

52. Second Treatise. French trans. (Mazel) 'Rev. ed.', Paris, 1783. 12°
DU | GOUVERNEMENT | CIVIL, | PAR M. LOCKE, | TRADUIT DE L'ANGLOIS; | ÉDITION EXACTEMENT REVUE | *& corrigée ſur la dernière de Londres,* | *augmentée d'un Précis Hiſtorique de la Vie* | *de l'Auteur, & ornée de ſon Portrait.* | [orn., sunburst within diamond-shaped leaf border 30 × 43 mm] | A LONDRES; | *Et ſe trouve à* PARIS, | Chez SERVIERE, Libraire, rue Saint- | Jean-de-Beauvais. | [Oxford rule 52 mm] | M. DCC. LXXXIII.

Coll: 12° (182 × 112 mm uncut) a^{12} A–Q^{12} [$6 signed (a3–6 signed iij–vj)]; 204 leaves; pp. j–*iv* v–xxiv 1 2–384 [= 408].

Contents: ai^r (*j*) half-title (verso blank), aii^r (*iij*) title (verso blank), aiij^r–av^v (v–x) 'AVERTISSEMENT.', avj^r–a11^v (xj–xxij) biog. sketch of Locke from Le Clerc's 'Eloge', a12^{r,v} (xxiij–xxiv) contents of chapters, A1^r–Q12^v (1–384) text of second treatise.

Illustration: engr. plate bound facing title, portrait of Locke after Kneller 121 × 74 mm, on plate 149 × 86 mm. Port. in oval frame, above pedestal subscribed 'JEAN LOCKE | *Né en Aout 1632, et Mort* [swash N, M] | *en Octobre 1704.*' Plate signed 'C.ƒ.M.s.'

Text (B7^r): 25 lines with 1 mm leading; 125 (136) × 67 mm; 99 R. Chainlines horizontal. Fair-quality laid paper with bunch of grapes as watermark.

Half-title: DU | GOUVERNEMENT | CIVIL.

Headlines, aiij^v-av^v: *AVERTISSEMENT*.
    a12^v: TABLE.
RT, avj^v-a11^r: PRÉCIS HISTORIQUE | DE LA VIE DE M. LOCKE. (a11^v: PRÉCIS HISTORIQUE, &c.)
    A1^v-Q12^r: DU GOUVERNEMENT CIVIL, | PAR M. LOCKE. (Q12^v: DU GOUVERNEMENT CIVIL, &c.)
CW: Gathering. A12^v de B12^v ſe I12^v ſociété N12^v que P12^v chapitre
Notes: There is no indication of the copy used for this edition, probably it was Rousset's 1780 (no. 51), but it omits Rousset's supplementary notice. The sketch of Locke's life is condensed from Le Clerc's 'Eloge' in the *Bibliothèque choisie* 6 (1705; no. C1705-5). The 'Avertissement' is that of the 1724 ed. (no. 47), though not so noted.
References: Attig 172; Christophersen p. 101; ESTC t192655; Laslett French 8; Rochedieu p. 194.
Copies examined: O (Vet.E5 e.118, uncut) [BBR] CLaslett Y

53. Second Treatise. French trans. (Mazel) 1790. Selections
Caption title: *Du Gouvernement Civil, de ſa véritable | origine, de ſon étendue & de ſa fin, | par Locke.*
IN: BIBLIOTHEQUE | DE | L'HOMME PUBLIC; | OU | ANALYSE RAISONÉE | DES PRINCIPAUX OUVRAGES | FRANÇOIS ET ÉTRANGERS, | *Sur la Politique en general, la Légiſlation, les | Finances, la Police, l'Agriculture, & le Com- | merce en particulier, & ſur le Droit naturel & | public.* | PAR M. le Marquis DE CONDORCET, Secrétaire | perpetuel de l'Académie des Sciences, l'un des | Quarante de l'Académie Françoiſe, de la Société | Royale de Londres; M. DE PEYSONEL, | ancien Conſul-général de France à Smirne, &c.; | M. LE CHAPELIER, Député de l'Aſſemblée | Nationale, & autres Gens de Lettres. | [double rule 56 mm] | TOME SECOND. | [double rule 56 mm] | [orn., vase with swags, 8 × 38 mm] | *A PARIS,* | Chez BUISSON, Libraire, Hotel de Coetloſquet, | rue Haute-Feuille, N°. 20. | [French rule 34 mm] | 1790.
Collation of the whole: 8° (199 × 120 mm cut) A-O^8 P^2 [$ half signed; A3 signed 'A', A4 signed 'Aiv')]; 114 leaves; pp. *1-2* 3-228.
Locke's text: pp. 135-211 (K2^r-N6^r). Brief introd. (by Condorcet?) on pp. 135-6. Text divided in 19 parts, indicated by marginal headings, e.g. 'Des propriétés.', 'De l'eſclavage.'
Text: 28 lines; 143 (155) × 78 mm; 101 R with 1.4 mm spacing between lines. Fine laid paper without watermarks. Page no. at upper external corners.
RT: GOUVERNEMENT CIVIL, | DE LOCKE.
CW: Gathering.
Notes: The verso of the title leaf of the first vol. for 1790 (beginning vol.) states the intention to publish a vol. each month, at the cost of 3 vols. for 9 livres, 6 for 17, or 12 for 32, to be sent by post. That first vol. contained selections from Aristotle's Politics, the *Republic* of Jean Bodin, a discourse

from Machiavelli on the first decade of Livy, and a brief extract from the memoirs of the Duc de Sully. The second vol. also contains (pp. 5-135) extracts from Hume's 'Essais moraux et politiques', the Amsterdam 1764 ed. There is no indication from which edition Locke's work was selected, but it is probably from the 1783 ed. (no. 52).
References: Attig 179; Laslett French 9.
Copy examined: L (271.f.6 (2))

54. Second Treatise. French trans. 'Rev. ed.', Paris, [1795] Two impressions: 8° and 4°
TRAITÉ | DU | GOUVERNEMENT | CIVIL, | PAR M. LOCKE, | TRADUIT DE L'ANGLAIS; | *Revue et corrigée exactement, sur la* | *dernière Édition de Londres.* | [orn., cushion with hatchet, sword & leaves 20 × 28 mm] | A PARIS, | De l'Imprimerie de Desveux, rue des | Ménestriers, n°. 607, | Et chez Royez, Libraire, rue J. - J. | Rousseau, maison Bullion. | [French rule 64 mm] | *L'An III de la République française.* [i.e. 1795]
54A: First issue, octavo on laid paper:
   Coll: 8° (202 × 120 mm cut) a^8 B-Z^8 [$4 signed; F3 signed 'F5']; 184 leaves; pp. *j-iv* v-xxx *31* 32-312 213 314-365 *366* 367-368. Gathering a signed in small roman: iij, iv. Page 313 called '213'.
54B: Second issue, quarto on wove or laid paper:
   Coll: 4° (260 × 200 mm cut) A^4 B-2Z^4 [$2 signed; B2 and C2 both signed 'B2', 2G2 and 2G3 both signed 'Gg3']; 184 leaves; pp. *j-iv* v-xxx *31* 32-365 *366* 367-368. Page 313 correctly numbered.
54A *Contents*: a1^r (*j*) half-title, a1^v (*ij*) publisher's note (with 19 lines of text), a2^r (*iij*) title (verso blank), a3^r-a6^r (*v-xj*) 'AVERTISSEMENT.' (as in 1724 ed.), a6^r bottom third- a7^v (xj-xiv) supplementary note, a8^r-B7^v (xv-xxx) biographical sketch of Locke, B8^r-Z7^r (*31-365*) text of second treatise, Z7^v-Z8^{r,v} (*366-68*) chapter contents.
54B *Contents*: A1^r (*j*) half-title (verso blank), A2^r (*iij*) title, A2^v (*iv*) publisher's note, A3^r-B2^r (v-xj) 'AVERTISSEMENT.' (as in 1724 ed.), B2^r bottom third-B3^v (xj-xiv) supplementary note, B4^r-D3^v (xv-xxx) biographical sketch of Locke, D4^r-2Z3^r (*31-365*) text of second treatise, 2Z3^v-2Z4^{r,v} (*366-388*) chapter contents.
Text (p. 42): 28 lines; 144 (155) × 79 mm; 103 R, including 1.5 mm leading. No visible watermarks. Page 31 has engr. headpiece: plowman with 2-horse team, rising sun behind hills at right, 25 × 75 mm. 'Avertissement' set 20 lines 139R with 3 mm leading between lines. Page no. at outer corners of headlines.
Half-title: DU GOUVERNEMENT CIVIL.
HT, aiij^r *or* A3^r (p. v): [segmented orn. rule 78 mm] | AVERTISSEMENT. a8^r *or* B4^r (p. 15): [Oxford rule 77 mm] | VIE | DE | JOHN LOCKE. | *Depuis l'année* 1632, *jusqu'à l'année* 1704. | Traduit du Plutarche Anglais.

B8ʳ *or* D4ʳ (p. *31*): [headpiece, horses, framed 25×75 mm] | DU | GOUVERNEMENT | CIVIL, | DE sa véritable origine, de son | étendue et de sa fin. | [Oxford rule 78 mm]
Headlines, a1ᵛ or A2ᵛ: [Oxford rule 74 mm] | *AVIS DES ÉDITEURS.*
  pp. xvj–xxx: VIE DE JOHN LOCKE.
RT, pp. 32–365: DU GOUVERNEMENT CIVIL, | PAR M. LOCKE.
CW: Gathering (by page no.) 64: qui 144 (com-) bien 192: en 240: tems 296: I [Il] 336: bien
Signature positions.

	First issue:	Second issue:
	aiv (vii) ce*u*x˄ *q*ui	B (ix) au*t*re
	C3 (37) da*n*s le	H (57) l'é*g*ard
	G (97) po*i*nt	N (97) po*i*nt
	K3 (149) po*i*nt	R2 (131) so*n* f˄ils
	N2 (195) po*i*nt	Bb2 (195) n'˄est˄ poi*n*t
	Q (241) *q*ui	Hh (241) peuple, q˄ui
	T (289) *n*e sauroit	Oo (289) n*e* sauroit
	Y (337) autori*s*é,	Vv (337) autoris˄é˄

Notes: This is the first French edition to use 'Traité' in its title. The two issues use the same setting of type; however the large paper issue seems to have a cleaner, clearer impression, possibly because of better quality paper. The editor's note (found on the verso of the half- title in 54A, on the verso of the title in 54B) is worth quoting as much for its political content as for its bibliographic information: 'La nouvelle Édition des OEuvres de LOCKE est desirée depuis long-tems; il n'en existe aucune uniforme, belle et complète de toutes ses OEuvres; le Gouvernement despotique avoit empêché qu'on ne connût beaucoup son TRAITÉ DU GOUVERNEMENT CIVIL, et on ne peut choisir un moment plus favorable pour en publier une Édition correcte et plus belle que toutes celles qui ont paru, que celui où l'on sent en France la nécessité urgente d'un bon Gouvernement: Nous publierons à *la suite*, *format* in-8°, L'ENTENDEMENT HUMAIN [unknown], L'ÉDUCATION DES ENFANS [unknown] et les OEUVRES PHILOSOPHIQUES [unknown] du même Auteur, qui sont à peine connus en français.

'On peut s'incrire chez les Libraires désignés, parce qu'on n'en tire qu'un nombre d'Exemplaires borné, à cause de la cherté du papier.

'Les mêmes Libraires ont également sous presse la même Édition format *in*-12, même papier et même caractère que le *format* in-8°.'

The text is undoubtedly a reprint of the 1749 or 1754 'Bruxelles' editions (no. 48 or 49), with a slightly differing introduction, rather than of the more recent Amsterdam one; it is not based on the 1783 Paris edition, which lacks the supplementary note. The later, large-paper issue has the page no. corrected, but has made new errors in signatures.

References: Attig 173 as 12° ('Also issued in 8° and 8° large-paper editions.'); Christophersen p. 101; Laslett French 10 b-c; Rochedieu p. 194 ('In-4; *also* in-8.')

Copies examined: A (first issue, 8°): O (Vet.E5.e.119; laid paper)
  B (second issue, 4°): O (Vet.E5.d.40; wove paper) P (*E.419; 255 × 194 mm cut; laid paper)

55. Second Treatise. French trans. (Mazel) 'Rev. ed.', Paris, [1795] 12°

TRAITÉ | DU | GOUVERNEMENT | CIVIL, | PAR M. LOCKE, | TRADUIT DE L'ANGLAIS; | R*EVUE et corrigée exactement, sur* | *la dernière Edition de Londres.* | [orn., platter with fruit, 13 × 23 mm] | A Paris, | De l'Imprimerie de DESVEUX, rue des | Ménestriers, n°. 607, | Et chez ROYEZ, Libraire, rue J. J. | Rousseau, maison Bullion. | [French rule 51 mm] | L'AN III *de la République française.* [1795]

Coll: 12° (166 × 98 mm cut) *¹² a¹² (-a1, -a2) B-V¹² X4 [$ half signed; sheet a signed in roman iij, iv, v; sheet * signed '2*', '3*', '4*', '5*' and '6*']; 254 leaves; pp. *I-XXIV* v-xvj 17 18-482 *483* 484-486 *487-488* [= 508]. Leaves a1 and 2 (pp. *j* ij-iv) lacking: torn out (see *Notes* below).

Contents: *1ʳ (*I*) title (verso blank), *2ʳ-*12ᵛ (*III-XXIV*) 'Vie de John Locke' (from Le Clerc's 'Eloge'), a3ʳ-a6ᵛ (v-xij) 'Avertissement', a6ᵛ-a8ᵛ (xij last 5 lines-xvj) 'Supplément À l'Avertissement précedent', a9ʳ-X1ᵛ (*17-482*) text, X2ʳ-X3ᵛ (*483-486*) 'Table des Chapitres.', X4 blank.

Text: 24 lines; 122 (133) × 67 mm; 101R with 1.5 mm leading. 'Vie de John Locke' set 18 lines, 138R with 2.5 mm leading. Poor quality laid paper with horizontal chainlines, except sheet X has vertical chainlines. No watermarks. Page no. at outer ends of headlines. Text in modernized spelling.

HT, a4ʳ: [framed headpiece, leaves about a pedestal, with wreaths, 19 × 65 mm, signed 'N'] | DU | GOUVERNEMENT | CIVIL, | DE sa *véritable origine, de* | *son étendue et de sa fin.* | [Oxford rule 66 mm]

RTs (from verso to recto) pp. *III-XXIII*: VIE | DE JOHN LOCKE. (Pp. *VII-XII*: 'JONH'.) Page *XXIV*: VIE DE JONH LOCKE.
  pp. 18-481: DU GOUVERNEMENT CIVIL, | PAR M. LOCKE.

CW: Gathering (on leaf 12ᵛ): * Avertissement B *lui-* [*lui-même*] D (supputa-) tion H seulement N *forces* P droits T (dé-) pendre V auxquels

Notes: Another edition following the text of the octavo and quarto editions issued in the same year (no. 54A and B). The material has been rearranged. The only copy I have located (in the British Library) has leaves a1-2 torn out; I suspect they might have contained the editor's note found in no. 54 (see its *Notes*).

References: Attig 173 (coll.: [12], v-xvj, [1], 18-486p. 12°.); Laslett French 10 (coll: 12mo, [22] + v-xvi + 17-481 pp.)

Copy examined: L (523.c.16)

56. Second Treatise. French trans. (Mazel/Rousset) '7th ed.', Paris, 1795. 12°

DU | GOUVERNEMENT | CIVIL, | PAR M. LOCKE, | TRADUIT DE L'ANGLAIS. | SEPTIÈME ÉDITION, | Exactement revue et corrigée sur la dernière | Edition de Londres, et augmentée de | quelques Notes. | PAR L.C.R.D.M.A.D.P. | [woodcut orn., vase of flowers 21 × 42 mm] | A PARIS, | Chez ANDRÉ, Imprimeur-Libraire, rue de | la Harpe, au ci-devant Collège de Bayeux, | N°. 477. | [French rule 40 mm] | AN III. (1795.)

Coll: long 12° (160 × 100 mm cut) a^8 A–O^{12} P^4 [\$ half signed; a3–5 signed 'a3', 'a3' and 'a4' respectively, L4 signed 'L2')]; 180 leaves; pp. *i–iii* iv–vii *ix* x–xij *xiii* xiv–xvj *1* 2–342 *343–344* [= 360].

Contents: a1^r (*i*) title (verso blank), a2^r–a3 [i.e. a4]^v (*iii–viij*) note on 1724 edition, a4 [i.e. a5]^r–a6^v (*ix–xij*) supplementary note, a7^r–a8^v (*xiii–xvj*) note on the 5th [!] edition, A1^r–P3^v (*1–342*) text of second treatise, P4^{r,v} (*343–44*) chapter contents.

Text (M3^r): 30 lines; 127 (134) × 71 mm; 84 R. Very poor-quality laid paper, with horizontal chainlines. No watermarks. Page no. at outer ends of headlines.

HT, a2^r: AVERTISSEMENT | DE L'EDITION DE 1724.

 a4 [i.e. a5]^r: SUPPLÉMENT | A l'Avertissement précédent.

 a7^r: AVERTISSEMENT | *sur la cinquième edition.*

 A1^r: [woodcut vignette, ship in harbour, leafy frame 28 × 67 mm] | TRAITÉ | DU | GOUVERNEMENT | CIVIL; | De sa véritable origine, de son étendüe, et | de sa fin. | [Oxford rule 69 mm]

 P4^r: TABLE | DES CHAPITRES.

RT: LE GOUVERNEMENT | CIVIL.

CW: Gathering (on leaf 12^v) A tout [from footnotes] C (aug-) mente F de I (pré-) sent L gouvernement, O (For-) tescue,

 Note: CWs taken from last line of page, whether it is text or footnote, e.g. A12^v.

Notes: An unaltered reprint of 1780 edition (no. 51).

References: Attig 174; Laslett French 11; Rochedieu p. 194.

Copies examined: O (Vet.E5 f.185) CLaslett InNd (JC153.L7930F3 1795; 161 × 94 mm cut) P (*E.324)

57*. Two Treatises. German trans. Jena, 1716.

' "Two treatises of Government", London 1619 [sic] – Dasselbe in deutscher Uebersetzung, Jena 1716'.

The above citation is from GV: *Gesamtverzeichnis 1700–1910*, vol. 89, p. 366. I have been unable to locate any copy of this edition. Not listed in Attig or Laslett. Dr. B: Fabian knows of no copies.

58. Second Treatise. German trans. (Mazel/anon.) Frankfurt, 1718. small 12°

In fraktur and roman: LE | GOUVERNEMENT | CIVIL, | Oder | Die Kunst | Wohl zu Regieren / | Durch den berühmten Engelländer | JEAN LOCK | Beschrieben / | Nunmehro aber | Wegen der sonderbahren darin= | nen enthaltenen und zum Theil auf den Engli= | schen Staat gerichteten Reflexionen / | aus der | Englischen und Frantzös. Sprache in die | Hochteutsche übersetzet von | G. | [rule 64 mm] | Frandfurth und Leipzig. 1718. | Bey Johann Bernhardt Hartung.

Coll: small 12° (132 × 88 mm closely trimmed) a⁶ χ1 A-X¹² Y⁶ (-Y6 [= χ1?]) [$ half + 1 (+ a5) signed]; 264 leaves; pp. *i-xiv* 1 2-22 32 24-386 87 388-513 *514* [= 528]. Page 23 called '32'; 387 has lost its '3'.

Contents: a1ʳ (*i*) title (verso blank), a2ʳ-a6ᵛ (*iii-xii*) Locke's pref., χ1ʳ·ᵛ (*xiii-xiv*) contents of 18 chapters, A1ʳ-Y5ʳ (*1-513*) text, Y5ᵛ blank.

Text (B12ᵛ): 26 lines; 111 (119) × 65 mm; 85 fraktur. Poor-quality laid paper without watermarks, chainlines horizontal. Page no. in outer corners of headlines.

Headlines are by chapter no. and brief title, with chap. no. on versos, and chap. titles on rectos, e.g. 'Das XVII. Cap. | Von der Thranney.'

CW: Page.

Notes: German translation based on Mazel's French translation of 1691 (no. 46). The only copy I have seen has the contents leaf (χ1) bound after the preface; perhaps it was the original Y6. The use of a fraktur e superscript as an umlaut was usual in the eighteenth century.

References: Attig 182; Christophersen p. 101; GV ('–die Kunst wohl zu regieren. 12. Frankfurt. Hartung, 718.')

Copies examined: Wol (Sf 136; lacks Y6)   [Berlin (Potsd.S.)]

59. Second Treatise. Italian trans. (Mazel/anon.) 'Amsterdam' (Italy?), 1773. 8°

[Outline type:] IL | GOVERNO CIVILE | [outline type:] *DI Mʳ. LOCKE.* | *TRADOTTO* | NELL'ITALIANO IDIOMA | E DEDICATO | [script type:] *A Sua Eccessenza il Sig.* | GIROLAMO DURAZZO | DELL'ECCELLENTISSIMO MARCELLO. | [orn., garlanded shell 24 × 45 mm] | AMSTERDAM | [Oxford rule 76 mm] | *MDCCLXXIII.*

Coll: 8° (185 × 120 mm cut) a⁴ A-S⁸ [$ half signed; A4 signed 'A7']; 148 leaves; pp. *i-ii* iii-vii *viii* 1-288 [= 296].

Contents: a1ʳ (*i*) title (verso blank), a2ʳ-a4ʳ (*iii-vii*) dedication, a4ᵛ (*viii*) contents of chapters, A1ʳ-S8ᵛ (*1-288*) text.

Text (F3ʳ): 30 lines; 126 (138) × 76 mm; 92 R. Mixed paper, sheets A-N watermarked with 3 fleur-de-lys in a circle and initials BB; sheets a and O-S with a shield and initials FS within. Pref. set 27 lines 95 ital.; footnotes set 66 roman. Page no. at external ends of headlines, indented 6 mm; catchwords also slightly indented from right margin. Each section within a chapter numbered from I in roman numerals; no catchwords when a

section ends at the bottom of a page. Chapters may begin mid-page; if so, preceded by a 3-bar rule (thick over 2 thins), 73 mm.
HT a2ʳ: ECCELLENZA.
    a4ʳ: [headpiece of of suns & small floral irons 20 × 76 mm] | TRATTATO | DEL | [outline type:] GOVERNO CIVILE | Della ſua vera Origine, della ſua | Eſtenſione, e del ſuo Fine. | [Oxford rule 33 mm]
Headlines: DEL GOVERNO CIVILE (on versos); CAPITOLO XVIII. (e.g., on rectos)
CW: Page. A2ʳ ama- ["amato] B7ʳ Gover- [Governo] E7ʳ e pro- [e propor] H8ʳ So- [Società] L4ᵛ ogget- [oggetto] P5ʳ inco- [incoronazione.] R7ʳ Priu- [Principi] S4ʳ (aperta-) "mente
Notes: An anonymous translation from the French text of David Mazel, probably the 1755 ed. (no. 50). The British Library Catalogue states: 'The place of publication is probably fictitious.' I would suggest, from the typeface style, that the edition was printed in Italy.
References: Attig 188; Laslett Italian 1.
Copies examined: Y C(Keynes) CLaslett L (1568/5024) O (Vet.B5 f.38) P (*E.2013)

60. Second Treatise. Swedish trans. (Mazel?/Harmens). Stockholm, 1726. 8°
In red and black, Swedish fraktur and roman: [red line:] JOHAN LOCKEs | Oförgripelige | Tankar | Om | [red:] Werldſlig [ornamental W] | [red:] Regerings [orn. R] | Rätta | [red:] Urſprung/ Gräntſor | [red:] och Ändamål; | Öfwerſatte ifrån Engelſtan | Af | [red:] HANS HARMENS | [red:] Translat. Regni. | Med Kongl. Maj:ts alranådigaſte Privilegio. | [thick rule 68 mm] | [rule 54 mm] | [red:] STOCKHOLM, | Uti det Kongl. Tryderiet/ | Åhr 1726.
Coll: 8° (163 × 108 mm cut))(⁴ A–2A⁸ [$ half + 1 (–B3, B5, C5, E4, H3, M5, N4, Z5, 2A4)]; 196 leaves; pp. i–viii 1 2–382 383–384 [= 392].
    Note: PPL copy has inner forme of sheet S inverted, resulting in a page sequence: 273 278 279 276 277 274 275 280 281 286 287 284 285 282 283 288.
Contents:)(1ʳ (i) title (verso blank),)(2ʳ–)(4ᵛ (iii–viii) translator's pref., A1ʳ– 2A7ᵛ (1–382) text of second treatise, 2A8ʳ,ᵛ (383–384) contents of 18 chapters.
Text (R3ʳ): 27 lines; 129 (141) × 75 mm; 95 fraktur. Bolder fraktur, similar to Schwabacher, used for emphasis. The umlauts above vowels, here shown conventionally, were printed as superscript fraktur e's, as in German language publications generally in the eighteenth century. Pref. set 21 lines, 120 fraktur, beginning with orn. D4. Footnotes set 86 fraktur; where continue on to the next page, they have their own catchwords also. Watermark: double-ringed shield with lyre as center. Text on A1ʳ begins with ornamental E6. Each following chapter begins with a 3-line orn.

letter. Text ends (2A7ʳ) with tailpiece 46 × 50 (face surrounded by wreath & scrolls). Page no. at outer ends of headlines.
HT,)(2ʳ: Företal. [orn. F]
A1ʳ: [woodcut block of leaves & flowers in a bowl 30 × 75 mm] | Det Första Capitlet.
2A8ʳ: Förtekning | På Capitlen / såsom de hwaran = | nan i ordning fölia.
Headlines or *RTs* are chapter titles set Swedish fraktur above a segmented 74 mm rule, on rectos and versos where short, from verso to recto otherwise, e.g., 'Om Ofwerhetens | Förmån.'
CW: Page (in fraktur). A3ʳ an = [annan] F6ʳ fri = [frihet] K4ᵛ hwar = [hwarken] P5ʳ alle = [allenast] X2ʳ under = [underhanden /]
Notes: Text based on David Mazel's French translation (no. 46 or 47).
References: Attig 216; Christophersen p. 101; Laslett Swedish 1.
Copies examined: Y (163 × 108 mm cut) CaOTU (Locke L63.T86S9 1726; 161 × 106 mm cut) Mun (Pol.g.1153*m*, 166 × 105 mm cut; blank sheet & 2A8 bound after title leaf) O (Vet.C4 e.19; 167 × 102 mm cut) PPL (Ii Locke, 150 × 102 mm cut; inner forme of sheet S inverted; see above)

Since 1800 there have been fairly frequent reprints of the complete work: twice in 1821; 1824; 1884, 1887 (in Morley's Universal Library); in 1903, 1924, 1947, 1949 and 1953. The first English edition to receive any editorial attention since Thomas Hollis (1764; no.35) was a critical edition, with extensive introductory material, by Peter Laslett in 1960 (2nd ed., 1967), frequently reprinted.

A Czech translation of Laslett's edition appeared in 1965. A German translation of the second treatise based on Laslett's edition appeared in 1966. Other complete editions were published in German (1906 and 1967), and a critical edition in Italian in 1948 and 1960.

Most reprints and translations are of the second treatise alone: in English in 1814, 1889, 1901, 1905 (in Cassell's National Library), 1937, 1939, 1946, 1947, 1953, 1955, 1956, 1966, 1980 and 1982; in French in 1802, 1953 ad 1967; in German in 1906 and 1967. Other translations have appeared in Hebrew (1959), Hindi (1960), Italian (1925, 1956 and 1974), Japanese (1947), Korean (1970), Norwegian (1947), Portuguese (1833 and 1963), Russian (1902), and Spanish (1821, 1941, 1966 and 1969).

Selections from the complete work, and especially from the second treatise, and unremarkable abridgments have appeared frequently in English and in many other languages. As early as September or October 1690 random sentences were plagiarised from *Two Treatises* and from works by Robert Ferguson, Gilbert Burnet and others in a 31-page pamphlet entitled *Political Aphorisms* (1691; ESTC r216382), sometimes attributed to its publisher Thomas Harrison (Wing² H917C). Aside from reprint editions it appeared greatly revised under the title *Vox Populi, Vox Dei* in 1709 (ESTC n052631) and frequently thereafter. For precise details see 'Locke's Revolution Principles and the Formation of Whig Ideology' by Richard Ashcraft and M. M. Goldsmith, *The Historical Journal* 26 (1983): 773–800.

CHAPTER III
Essay concerning Human Understanding (nos. 61–154)

Locke had worked on what became the *Essay concerning Human Understanding* since 1671, the date of the earliest existing draft (now called Draft A; see no. 331–5). He himself tells us in the 'Epistle to the Reader': "Were it fit to trouble thee with the History of this Essay, I should tell thee that five or six Friends meeting at my Chambers, and discoursing on a Subject very remote from this, found themselves quickly at a stand, by the Difficulties that rose on every side. . . .[I]t was necessary to examine our own Abilities, and see, what Objects our Understandings were, or were not fitted to deal with . . . Some hasty and undigested Thoughts, on a Subject I had never before considered, which I set down against our next meeting, gave the first entrance into this Discourse, which having been thus begun by Chance, was continued by Intreaty; written by incoherent parcels; and, after long intervals of neglect, resum'd again, as my Humour or Occasions permitted; and at last . . . it was brought into that order, thou now seest it" (Nidditch ed., p. 7). According to Jean Le Clerc (no. C1706-3, p. 8) the friends included James Tyrrell and Dr. David Thomas (cf. *Corr.* i.495 n. and i.293 n. respectively).

The sixth edition (1710; no. 66) and all subsequent editions follow the text of the fifth edition, not without occasional typographical errors. Those editions printed in the *Works* (Chapter XI) follow the same text, but omit the long footnotes from Locke's 'Letters' to Bishop Stillingfleet, since the 'Letters' themselves are included in the *Works* in full. This most popular and enduring of all Locke's writings had been issued in fifty-six different editions and translations by 1800, not counting abstracts and abridgements.

Further detailed information about this work is to be found in Peter Nidditch's definitive edition (Oxford: Clarendon Press, 1975), pp. xii–xxxvii.

61. Essay concerning Human Understanding. 1st edition. 1690. 2° in 4s. Two issues.

61A. First issue. Within a double rule, inner 261 × 138 mm, outer 270 × 147 mm: AN | ESSAY | CONCERNING | 𝔥umane 𝔘nderſtanding. | [rule 133 mm] | In Four BOOKS. | [rule 133 mm] | *Quam* [swash Q] *bellum eſt velle confiteri potius neſcire quod neſ-* | *cias, quam iſta effutientem nauſeare, atque ipſum ſibi* | *diſplicere!* Cic. de Natur. Deor. *l.* I. | [double rule 132 mm] | [small pr. flower orn. 6 in row, 5 rows, 3d & 4th inverted, 36 × 32 mm] | [double rule 134/130 mm] | *LONDON:* [swash D] | Printed by *Eliz. Holt,* for **Thomas Baſſet,** at the | *George* in *Fleetſtreet,* near St. *Dunſtan*'s [swash D] | Church. MDCXC.

    Coll: folio in 4s (310–330 × 195 mm cut) A⁴ [a]₂ B–3C⁴ [$ first half]; 198 leaves; pp. *i–xii* 1–183 *184* 185–286 269 288–295 294 297–302 230 304–362 *363–384* [= 396]. Page 287 called '269', 296 called '294', 303 called '230'.

61B. Second issue, with cancellans t. p., within a double rule, inner 268 × 134 mm, outer 278 × 146 mm: AN | ESSAY [Ss inverted] | CONCERNING | [. . . &c. as in first issue except:] . . . [smaller orns. in rows of 4, 5, 5, 5 and 4, 2d–5th inverted 24 × 18 mm] | [double rule 131 mm] | *LONDON:* [swash D, roman colon] | Printed for *Tho. Baſſet,* [swash T, B] and ſold by *Edw. Mory* | at the Sign of the *Three Bibles* in St. *Paul*'s [swash T, B, P] | Church-Yard. MDCXC.

    Coll: as for first issue, except A⁴ (±A1).

Contents: A1ʳ (*i*) title (verso blank), A2ʳ–A3ᵛ (*iii–vi*) dedication to Thomas Herbert, Earl of Pembroke, signed 'JOHN LOCKE.', A4ʳ–[a2]ʳ (*vii–xi*) pref. to the reader, [a2]ᵛ (*xii*) errata in 3 columns of 53, 53 & 48 lines, B1ʳ (*1–36*) text of Book I, F3ʳ–2A4ʳ (*37–183*) text of Book II, 2A4ᵛ (*184*) blank, 2B1ʳ–2L2ᵛ (*185–260*) text of Book III, 2L3ʳ–3A1ᵛ (*261–362*) text of Book IV, 3A2ʳ·ᵛ (*363–364*) contents by book & chapter, 3A3ʳ–3C4ᵛ (*365–384*) contents by book, chapter & section.

Text (C2ʳ): 54 lines; 250 (269) × 128 (146) mm; 92 R. Cut page size varies. Headlines extend 18 mm in outer margins beyond text. Dedication set 145 R, 34 lines. Epistle to reader set 43 lines, 117 ital. Contents set in 2 columns, 93 ital. Most sheets have watermark similar to Heawood 387, with 'R RONDEL' in a cartouche; 2E–2X have watermark similar to Heawood 2077 with initials 'MC'. Chainlines vertical.

HT, A2ʳ: [double rule 146 mm] | TO THE | RIGHT HONOURABLE | THOMAS | EARL OF | **Pembroke** and **Montgomery,** | *Baron* Herbert *of* Cardiff, *&c.* | *Lord-Lieutenant of the County of* Wilts, *and One of* | *Their Majeſties moſt Honourable Privy Council.*

A4ʳ: [double rule 148 mm] | THE | EPISTLE | TO THE | READER.

B1ʳ: [double rule 148 mm] | OF | **Humane Underſtanding.** | [rule 130 mm]

Headlines, set ital. within double rules, with book no. set roman in inner corner of versos; chap. number, roman in inner corners on rectos. Longer chapter titles set as running titles.

Examples: '*Simple Ideas.* Book II. | Chap. VIII. *Simple Ideas.*'

'*Remedies of the Imperfection* Book III. | Chap. XI. *and Abuſe of Words.*'

CW: Page. B3ᵛ this. [this] H3ᵛ perceive, [perceive] N1ᵛ need [needful,] R4ʳ will, [will:] Z3ʳ Gold, [Gold;] 2F4ᵛ (Un-) derſtan- [derſtanding,] 2K2ᵛ Under- [Underſtandings] 2N2ᵛ (Uni-) verſe, [verſe] 2T3ʳ which [which,] 3C3ᵛ (more) their [more their]

Notes: Although the title-page omits Locke's name, and thus the work may appear to have been anonymously published, the dedication to Thomas

Herbert, the eighth Earl of Pembroke, is signed 'JOHN LOCKE.' The date, 24th of May 1689, and the address 'Dorset Court' were not appended to the dedication until the fourth edition of 1700 (no. 64). Dorset Court, Westminster, was the address of Locke's lodgings at the house of Mrs. Rabsy Smithsby, to which he had moved on 18 March 1689 (cf. *Corr.* iii. 596, n. 5). We can infer that Locke had requested permission of Pembroke to dedicate the work to him by Pembroke's letter of 25 November 1687 (*Corr.* 982; iii.306). That letter accompanied one from Dr. David Thomas (ibid. 306-7) wherein Thomas states "you will find his approbation to the printing both the shorter and larger treatice and though he seemes not fond of a dedication yet I find it will very well please". The 'shorter' was the French 'Abregé' reprinted from the *Bibliothèque universelle* (no. 271), with a dedication to Pembroke added; the 'Extrait' (no. 270) itself in that journal carried no dedication. De Beer notes (*Corr.* ibid.) that "This is the earliest notice to show that Locke intended to print the *Essay*."

The first edition of the *Essay* was ready for distribution in late November 1689; Locke received bound copies on December 3, 1689 (Bodleian Lib. MS Locke f. 29, p. 36). Following the usual practice at that time, the title-page bears the date 1690. The bookseller Thomas Basset had signed a contract with Locke on May 24, 1689 (MS Locke b.1, f. 109) in which he engaged to pay Locke ten shillings per printed sheet, and provide him with 25 copies. A notation at the bottom of the contract states Locke received £29.[1] We do not know what size sheet was involved, but this first edition contains 99 folio sheets (of which 90½ are text, the rest ancillary matter), or 49½ if a quarto sheet is intended (the work is a small folio arranged as a quarto). Peter Nidditch defines[2] "a sheet for this financial purpose as being the equivalent of so much as was contained in a sheet of Milton's *History of England* in octavo" and agrees with Charlotte S. Johnston[3] that there were 58 'sheets', though he elsewhere (op. cit., p. xv) states there was a total of about 100 sheets. There were 57 sheets for the revised, second edition.

It is generally assumed that the Holt issue is the earlier because the title-page of the other, Mory, issue is a cancellans. I would assume that after all pages of the text had been printed, Basset came to some financial arrangement with Edward Mory to help sell it. Johnston has stated (op. cit.): "It is probable that Mory acquired his rights in the book only shortly before the advertisement in the *London Gazette* of 29 May 1690 which gives his name as publisher." We do not know the number of copies printed; Peter Nidditch (op. cit.) has estimated about 900 copies were published, chiefly of the Holt

---

[1] See 'A Note on Locke and Copyright', p. 262, in the article by Peter Lindenbaum: 'Authors and Publishers in the Late Seventeenth Century: New Evidence on Their Relations', *The Library*, 6th ser., v. 17 no. 2 (Sept. 1995): 250-269.

[2] *An Essay concerning Human Understanding*. Edited with an introd., critical apparatus and glossary by Peter H. Nidditch. Clarendon Edition of the Works of John Locke (Oxford, 1975), p. xviii. (A detailed history of the text, its genesis, development and of early additions is found in the introd., pp. ix-xxxvii.)

[3] 'Appendix II: The printing history of the first four editions of the *Essay concerning Human Understanding*.' In: Aaron, R.I.: *John Locke* (Third ed., Oxford, 1971), pp. 313-320.

issue. But it is possible there were as few as 500. We do not know the price, although it was perhaps the same as or a bit less than that charged for the fourth edition, which sold for fourteen shillings in 1700.[4]

The Latin quotation on the title is from Cicero's *De rerum natura*, Book I, 84, but is slightly changed from the text in the Oxford Classical Texts edition, where it begins "Quam bellum erat, Vellei, [the addressee Velleius, the Epicurean speaker] confiteri potius nescire quod nescires. . ." (How delightful it would be, Velleius, if when you did not know a thing, you would admit your ignorance, instead of uttering this nonsense, which must make even your own gorge rise in disgust!).

Most copies of the first issue I have seen have manuscript corrections on A3^v and A4^r: only Balliol's and Queen's College, Oxford copies lack them. A3^v, line 6 corrects 'certain', in the phrase ". . . if I were not [certain]ly sensible of them, . . ." to 'extream' (occasionally 'extreme' or 'extrem'). A4^r *l*. 21 has the insertion 'some' at the end of the line in the phrase, "Every step the mind takes in its Progress towards Knowledge, makes | Discovery . . ." None of the second issues I have seen has these corrections. James Tyrrell's copy of the first issue (now in the British Library) has these corrections in Locke's hand, as well as an insertion on A2^r, *l*. 9 of the text, of 'in' in the phrase "are to be found `in' it." The changes and additions Locke made for the second edition (no. 62) are interleaved and bound in where substantial, written in Tyrrell's hand where brief. A copy formerly belonging to Lady Mary Calverley, which the National Library of Scotland acquired in 1938, has the title-page inscribed at the upper right corner (presumably by the recipient) "M. Calverley | ye gift of ye Author". Locke has written his initials "JL" over the double rule preceding the imprint; he has also made the corrections on A3-4, but the first is 'HIGH' (rather than 'extream'). Her copy is bound in dark red morocco (i.e. 'turkey'), gold tooled on spine and sides, gilded edges.

Many copies of both issues, indiscriminately, have other pagination errors (in addition to 287, 296 and 303 cited in the collation): (1) 76 is called '50'; (2) 77 called '55'; (3) 85 called '83'. Further errors are (4) p. 55, last line: 'Underwandings' for 'Understandings'; (5) p. 90: § 24 omitted from the numbering in Book II, Chap. 14; (6) p. 57, RT for Book II, Chap. VIII reads 'Chap. V.'; (7) p. 263, RT for Book IV, Chap. I reads 'Chap. XI.' Finally the book and chapter contents on 3A2^r omits Book III, Chap. VII ('Of Particles') and lists titles of chapters VIII-XI as belonging to Chap. VII-X. This error is not corrected until the 17th edition of 1775 (no. 81). There are many additional typographical errors, most of them detailed by Nidditch in his edition.

The list of intended recipients of presentation copies of the Essay (Bodleian MS Locke c.25 f.50) is headed 'Copys 90', without a title. The list provides

---

[4] See Edwin Wolf 2nd, "A Parcel of Books for the Province in 1700", *The Pennsylvania Magazine of History and Biography*, 89 (1965), 428-46. Books shipped by the Churchills to James Logan in Philadelphia included 6 copies of Locke's *Essay* as £4. 4 s. 0 d. (or 14 s each), 6 copies of *Some Thoughts concerning Education* and 6 copies of *Two Treatises of Government*, each lot at £1. 1 s. 0 d.

for 48 copies. On 3 and 9 December 1689 Locke sent his binder John Graves to the printer for copies. In the list ten names are underlined with a row of dots; thirty-four are underlined normally; four are not underlined. E.S. de Beer suggests the markings are probably to distinguish different kinds of bindings: 8 in turkey (morocco) at 6 s. each (two of them were extra, according to Graves' bill of 9 January 1690), 32 had gilt backs at 2 s. each; one in parchment at 1 s. 2 d. (The bills are MS Locke b.1, ff. 122, 143, 145). On July 4, 1690, Graves charged Locke for two further copies, by their price with gilt spines; in November there was a further copy in turkey. As the ten persons distinguished by dotted underlines include Pembroke (the dedicatee) and Queen Mary, it is reasonable to assume that they were to receive the copies bound in turkey; those with normal underlining would receive those with gilt spines. Thomas Sydenham is an early name on the list, but since he died on 29 December 1689, his name has been deleted. Of the four names at the end of the list, that of Christ Church is a late addition; a second, Sibelius, may also be a late addition (cf. *Corr.* 1352, 1489; iv.186-7, 440-1). The other two names are Grigg and Guise. Locke first wrote the column of capital letters, in nine or ten cases continuing with a name or names; later he added further names. The list is as follows:

Ashley Atwood
Boyle Bellamont Bridges
Clarke le Clerc Carbury Calverly Charleton Chichley Christchurch
Duke Dalone Daranda
Ely B\p
Freke Furly Facio Forfar Fermin
Grig Goodall Guenellon Guise
Hamden. Huygens. Helmont Mrs Hunt Hutton
J Johnson
K
L Mrs Lockart
Monmouth. Masham
Newton
O
Pembroke. Pople. Ed Pocock
Queen
R
Somers. Syl. C:Shaftesbury Sibelius [also 'Sydenham' deleted]
Tilotson. Tyrrell. Thomas
U
W walls
X
Yonge

The recipients can be identified as follows: 'Ashley' is Anthony Ashley Cooper, later third Earl of Shaftesbury; 'Atwood' possibly William Atwood (cf. DNB); Richard Coote, Earl of Bellomont (DNB: 'Bellamont'); the Hon. Robert Boyle; Brook Bridges, a financial genius and officer of the Bank of England; 'Syl' is Locke's servant Sylvester Brounower; Mary, Lady Calverley; William Charleton, truly Wm. Courten; John Vaughan, third Earl of Carbery; 'Chichley' is possibly Sir John Chicheley; Christ Church, Oxford; Edward Clarke, dedicatee of *Some Thoughts concerning Education*; 'Dalone' is Abel Tassin d'Allonne, private secretary to Queen Mary; Paul D'Aranda, an Amsterdam merchant, later in England; Mrs. Isabella Duke, sister of Sir Walter Yonge; 'Facio' is Nicolas Faccio (or Fatio) de Duillier; Thomas Firmin; Robina Douglas, Countess of Forfar; 'Freke' is probably John Freke, a correspondent and friend known as 'the bachelor', "alternatively M might be for John Freke the stock-jobber or for Thomas Freke" (*Corr.* viii.456); Benjamin Furly, the Quaker (cf. *Corr.* iii.39 n.); Dr. Charles Goodall; Mrs. Anne Grigg (cf. *Corr.* i.334 n.2); Dr. Peter Guenellon, Amsterdam physician; 'Guise' is Lady (Elizabeth) or Sir John Guise; Richard or John Hampden; Baron F.M. van Helmont; 'Mrs. Hunt' is possibly Frances, wife of Rowland Hunt, a friend of Mrs. Duke; Dr. John Hutton, a Scottish physician; 'Huygens', Christian Huygens van Zuylichem, or Konstantijn Huygens the younger; James Johnstoun; Jean Le Clerc; Martha Lockhart, great niece of Cromwell; Queen Mary; Damaris, née Cudworth, Lady Masham; Isaac Newton; Thomas Herbert, Earl of Pembroke; Charles Mordaunt, Earl of Monmouth, later third Earl of Peterborough; Edward Pococke, junior, son of the orientalist; William Popple, translator of *Epistola de tolerantia*; Margaret Cooper, Countess of Shaftesbury; Dr. Caspar Sibelius, a Dutch physician, for a time in Ireland; John Somers, Baron Somers; Dr. David Thomas, physican at Salisbury; Dr. John Tillotson, Archbishop of Canterbury; Dr. Francis Turner, Bishop of Ely; James Tyrrell; Dr. George Walls of Worcester, a friend from Westminster School and Christ Church, Oxford, onetime chaplain at Hamburg;[5] and Sir Walter Yonge.

As noted in 'Copies examined' below, Guenellon and Tyrrell's copies are now located at the New York Public Library and the British Library respectively. William Molyneux's copy is in the Bodleian Library; it must have been a later gift, since his name is not on this list. Mrs. Duke's copy has been offered for sale at an auction by Christie's, New York, on November 11, 1994, as lot no. 49; its provenance includes Mortimer L. Schiff and, by descent John M. Schiff. Mr. Karl Schick (of Sunderland, Mass.) has recently acquired a copy once in the possession of Philip Yorke, the first Earl of Hardwicke, which I feel strongly is Lord Somers' copy, passed on through Mary (née Cocks), Somers' granddaughter and Hardwicke's wife (cf. DNB, under Somers, Yorke).

---

[5] Not to be confused with George Wall, who was a pupil of Locke at Christ Church and his companion in France later. Cf. John Milton's article, 'John Locke, George Wall and George Walls', *The Locke Newsletter*, 22 (1991): 81–91.

A notice of publication and summary of the principal contents appeared in Le Clerc's journal, *Bibliothèque universelle et historique* 17 (May 1690): 388–427, as 'Notice V'. Also a brief record appeared in the *Acta eruditorum* for 1691, pp. 501–5.

A microfilm copy of both issues (from the Huntington Library, San Marino, Calif.) is in EEB, 361 no. 2 for the first issue; 639 no. 21 for the second.

Cambridge University Library's copy (Syn.3.69.2) of the first issue was used by Scolar Press in 1970 for their facsimile reprint of this edition. As an appendix they reprinted the title-page and the major expansion of the text from that library's copy of the second edition: part of 1.4 (pp. 34–6), 2.21 (pp. 132–52) and the new 2.27 (pp. 178–90).

References: Alston 7:75–6; Attig 228; Christophersen p. 26; ESTC r022993 for 61A, r009934 for 61B; Johnston pp. 313–16; L.L. 1781; T.C. II. 302; Wing^2 L2738–9 (both issues).

Copies examined: First issue: O^1†† (Don. c.77; err. 1–3 corrected) C^1 (Syn.3.69.2 (err. 1–3 corr.) CaNSHDa Ck(Keynes)^1 CLU-C^1 (err. 1–3 corrected) CtY^1† (K8.L79/ + f690b; inscribed 'R Spry' and 'Ex li: Dan: MacEune pret: 7 solidor') DFo (L2736; err.3 corr.) DLC (err. 1–3 corr.) Dm Dt E L^1† (C.122 f.14; James Tyrrell's copy, with notes) MH (*fEC65.L7934.689e2; err. 1–3 corr.) NjP (2 private collection copies: WHS and RHT) NN (P. Guenellon's copy) O^2† (LL.24 Sheld.; Wm. Molyneux's copy; err. 3 corr.) Oa (err. 4 corrected) OCin Oman Oq Osj PPL (*Wing L2738/6037.F; err. 1–3 corr.) PU (B1290 1690) TxHR (err. 3 corr.) ViU (err.3 corr.) Yu

Second issue: O^3 (Vet.A3 c.78) C^2 (Hunter a.69.1) Ck(Keynes)^2 CLU-C^2 CtY^2 (K8.L79/ + F690A) Han (Leib.Marg.38; Leibniz's copy, with some pencilled corrections, chiefly of typographical errors) L^2 (C.122 f.13) MH (*fEC65.L7934.689e2a; err.1–3 corr.) NjP (Ex.6106.333.12q) NNPM O^3 (Vet.A3 c.78) Oo TxDaMP (err.1–3 corr.) Vat (Ferraioli II.225) ViU (lacks leaves A3-4; err. 1–3 corr.)

† Has 31 leaves of 2d ed. additions mounted & bd. in appropriate places.
†† Has 31 leaves of 2d ed. addition bound tog. at end of vol.

62. Essay. 2nd ed., 1694. 2° in 4s. Two issues; two states of first issue.

62A1: First issue, first state. Within a double rule, inner 260 × 133 mm, outer 269 × 143 mm]: AN | ESSAY | [&c. as in 1st edition, except] . . . In Four BOOKS. | [rule 130 mm] | Writtten [sic] by *JOHN* [swash J] *LOCKE*, Gent. | [rule 128 mm] | *The Second Edition, with large Additions.* | [rule 128 mm] | . . . [&c. as in 1st ed., except: rule 127 mm] | LONDON, | Printed for **Thomas Dring** at the *Harrow*, over = againſt | the *Inner-Temple Gate* [swash G] in *Fleet-ſtreet*; and **Samuel** | **Manſhip**, at the *Black Bull* [2d B swash] in *Cornhill*, near the | *Royal Exchange*, M DC XCIV.

62A2: First issue, second state. As in first state, except: **Manſhip**, at the *Ship* in *Cornhill*, near the | *Royal Exchange*, M DC XCIV.

Coll: 2° in 4s (328 × 215 mm cut) A² [b]⁶ a–c⁴ B–3F⁴ 3G–3I² [$ half signed]; 230 leaves; pp. *i–xl 1–39 40 41–90 93–96 95–219 220 221–299 300 301–396 997 398–407 408–420* [= 460]. Pages 91–4 called '93–6'; 397 called '997'.

62B: Second issue. As in first issue with a double rule, inner 258 × 133 mm, outer 268 × 142 mm, except: LONDON, | Printed for 𝔄wn𝔱𝔥am and 𝔍o𝔥n 𝔚𝔥urc𝔥il, at the *Black* [swash B] | *Swan* in *Pater-Nofter-Row*, [swash P, N, R] and 𝔖amuel 𝔐an𝔰𝔥ip at the | *Ship* in *Cornhill*, near the *Royal Exchange*, M DC XCIV.

Coll: as first issue, both states, except A² (± A1).

Contents: A1ʳ (*i*) title (verso blank), A2ʳ–[b]1ʳ (*iii–vi*) dedication, [b]2ʳ–6ʳ (*vii–xv*) 'Epistle to the Reader', [b]6ᵛ (*xvi*) errata in 2 cols. (32 & 31 lines), a1ʳ,ᵛ (*xvii–xviii*) contents by book & chap., a2ʳ–c4ʳ (*xix–xxxix*) contents by book, chap. & section, c4ᵛ (*xl*) blank, B1ʳ–F4ʳ (*1–39*) text of Book I, F4ᵛ (*40*) blank, G1ʳ–2F2ʳ (*41–219*) text of Book II, 2F2ᵛ (*220*) blank, 2F3ʳ–2Q2ʳ (*221–299*) text of Book III, 2Q2ᵛ (*300*) blank, 2Q3ʳ–3F4ʳ (*301–407*) text of Book IV, 3F4ᵛ (*408*) blank, 3G1ʳ–3I2ʳ (*409–419*) index in double cols.), 3I2ᵛ (*420*) blank.

Illustration: portrait of Locke as frontispiece, facing title, within a wreath above a pedestal, subscribed 'Mʳ. *John Locke*.' and '*Sylvester Brounower ad vivum delin: P Vanderbanck sculp*.' 239 × 159 mm on plate 245 × 165 mm.

Text (T3ʳ): 54 lines; 252 (269) × 127 (147) mm; 93 R. Marginal notes set 68 ital. Watermark: fool's cap and initials 'MC'. Text occasionally in the direction line (i.e. pp. 32, 74, 102, 306, 313). Scattered pages have only 53 lines with a blank line preceding the next numbered section (e.g. 3, 17, 28, 53, 62–3, 314, etc.).

HTs for pref. to reader ([b2]ʳ), contents (a1ʳ), and text (B1ʳ) same as those for 1st edition. The dedication heading (A2ʳ) has been expanded: [double rule 145 mm] | TO THE | RIGHT HONOURABLE | THOMAS | EARL OF | 𝔓embro𝔨e and 𝔐ontgomer𝔶, | *Baron Herbert of* Cardiff, *Lord* Rofs *of* Kendal, | *Par, Marmion, St. Quintin and* Shurland; | *Lord Privy-Seal, Lord Lieutenant of the County of* | Wilts, *and of* South-Wales; *and one of Their* | *Majefties moft Honourable Privy-Council.*

This edition, the first to have an index, has HT: [double rule 148 mm] | INDEX.

Headlines or RTs are italicised chapter titles or title summaries within rules, as in first edition (no. 61).

CW: Page. H1ʳ Impreffions [Impreffions;] N4ᵛ §.24. The [§.25. The] S3ᵛ Action [action] T4ʳ be- [becaufe] 2A1ᵛ a con- [a contradiction] 2G2ʳ compre- [comprehenfive] 2S1ʳ §.17. 2Z4ʳ limitted 3E2ʳ §.9. The [§.9. Firft,]

Notes: The first issue of this edition exists in two states, the second state reflecting Manship's relocation from the Black Bull, across the street to the Ship. The second issue has a cancellans title leaf largely printed from the same setting as the first issue, attested to by relative word spacing and the continued use of 'Writtten' in the eighth line. De Beer estimates it was published c. 26 May 1694 (*Corr.* v.vii). *The London Gazette*, issue 2980 for 31 May–4 June 1694 carried the advertisement: "An Essay concerning Humane Understanding, in Four Books. Written by John Locke, Gent. The Second Edition with Large Additions. Printed for A. & J. Churchil, at the Black Swan in Pater-noster Row, and S. Manship at the Ship in Cornhill."

Although the agreement to publish a second edition was made with Thomas Basset, by the time the work appeared, Basset had "disposed of the Copy to me [Manship] and one more" (*Corr.* 1718; v.29), probably because of insolvency. The 'one more' is undoubtedly Thomas Dring. Dring in turn quite soon after sold his share to the Churchills.

An entry in the registers of the Stationers' Company, dated 29 April 1695, records a transaction whereby Thomas Dring sold his half share in the rights to Locke's *Essay* to Awnsham Churchill, reflecting the transition from the first to the second issue of this second edition. The entry reads as follows: "Entred . . . booke or coppy by virtue of an assignem^t beareing date the 5th of March *Anno* Dom. 1693 [Old style], under the hand and seale of THOMAS DRING and by virtue of the above menc̄oned order entituled the moiety or one halfe parte of *An Essay concerning humane learninge understanding*, under the hand and seale of THOMAS DRING and by virtue of the above menc̄oned order entituled the moiety or one halfe parte of *An Essay concerning humane learninge understanding*, by **John Lock**, Gent^l with large addicons, now a reprinting in folio . . . vj^{d}". (*Transcript*, iii.462.)

When Thomas Basset was running out of copies of the first edition in February 1693 O.S. (*Corr.* 1607; iv.645–6), he signed a contract with Locke, dated 10 March 1693 (now Locke MS.b.1, f. 168) to pay him ten shillings per sheet for additional materials for a new printing. These additions included an expansion of Book I, Chap. IV; the chapter on power (2.21) was almost entirely new; a new chapter, 'Of Identity and Diversity', was inserted as 2.27, making chapters 27–31 be renumbered as 2.28–32; and a discussion was added to 2.9.8. A section numbered 23 was still omitted from Book II, chap. XIV. Other numerous additions were made throughout, sectional summaries added in the margins, and an analytical index supplied. Locke further had an engraving made from his portrait done by his amanuensis Sylvester Brounower (only after vainly trying to reclaim possession of one by John Greenhill in the possession of Thomas Stringer and his wife). Brounower's portrait, engraved by P. Vanderbanck, served also as the frontispiece to the third and fourth editions.

Locke also had the corrections and new material (comprising 31 leaves) printed up separately for his friends to insert in their copies of the first edition. These additions survive as a block of pages in some copies, are clipped and inserted into the binding of others (See *Copies*, no. 61). As a block these sheets have the collation: $\dagger^2 + 17$ leaves $+ (a)^4 (b)^4 (-(b)4) + 5$ leaves. An entry in Locke's notebooks (MS Locke f. 29 p. 83) has a presentation list in 2 columns, one headed 'Copia A' (I would guess, the set of 31 leaves to insert in their first edition copies) and the other headed 'T' (for *text* of complete copy of the second edition, again a guess). The names in the 'A' list are as follows: 'Burlington' (Richard Boyle, first Earl of), 'Ashley' (Anthony Ashley Cooper, third Earl of Shaftesbury), 'Ashurst' (probably one of the sons of Henry Ashurst who was one of the trustees for the Boyle Lectures; William was a baronet and became Lord Mayor of London in 1693), 'Warr' (short form possibly for Henry Booth, Baron Delame, Earl of Warrington, a supporter of William III), 'Clarke' (Edward Clarke a friend, for whom *Some Thoughts concerning Education* was written), 'Molineux' (William Molyneux, friend, scientist, Irish MP, and a member of the Royal Society), 'Pople' (William Popple, London merchant, translator of *Epistola de tolerantia*), 'Newton' (Sir Isaac Newton), 'Masham' (Sir Francis Masham, or more probably his wife, Damaris Cudworth, Lady Masham, the friend with whom Locke lodged in the 1690s until his death), 'Tyrrell' (James Tyrrell, the historian and political writer; a friend), 'Wallis' (Dr. George Walls of Worcester, from Christ Church, Oxford, chaplain at Hamburg), 'Clerc' (Jean Le Clerc, friend at Amsterdam, theologian and biblical scholar, editor of the *Bibliothèque universelle*, etc.), 'Guenelon' (Dr. Peter Guenellon, medical graduate living in Amsterdam), 'Gresham Colledg' (first home of the Royal Society), 'Dr. Fr. Bernard' (physician and friend Locke knew in Paris; a Gassendist); 'Dr. Cox' (Daniel Coxe, F.R.S.; he had been entrusted with Robert Boyle's papers after Boyle's death), 'Dr. Dickinson p[e]r Guenellon' (Dr. Edmund Dickinson, an Oxford physician and Locke correspondent). The names in the 'T' list repeat some of those in the 'A' list, and are as follows: 'Ashley', 'Newton', 'Clarke', 'Somers' (also known as the Lord Keeper, Sir John Somers of Evesham), 'Pople', 'Treb' (Sir George Treby, Chief Justice of Common Pleas from 1692), 'Clerc', 'Furly' (Benjamin Furley, a Quaker and friend), 'Wright' (possibly Alderman William Wright, a leading Whig in Oxford city politics and a friend of Shaftesbury, the first Earl), 'Freke' (John Freke, a barrister and a member of the Middle Temple), 'Firmin' (Thomas Firmin, a Socinian, and friend of John Tillotson).

Another list in the Lovelace Collection of the Bodleian Library (MS Locke c.25, f. 51) is headed 'Copys 94, with the words 'of understanding' inserted. It provides for 24 copies. The names are in two columns, the first of 15 names numbered 2–16, the first name 'Ashley' being marked for two copies. The second column contains eight names, in roughly alphabetical order. All the names are crossed through except Clarke, Clericus (Le Clerc, i.e.), Furly, Glanville, Guenelon, Montague, and Slone. All are followed by crosses except Clarke, Clericus, Furly, Molesworth, Sommers, Glanville, Guenelon, Pepys, and Slone. Since both Tyrrell's and Molyneux's copies of the first edition have been bound with second edition inserts, the significance of the crossings-through and the crosses is impossible to determine. The list is as follows:

2 ~~Ashley~~ 2×
3 ~~Canterbury~~ ×   ~~Bridges~~ ×
4 Clarke
5 Clericus
6 ~~Freke~~ ×   ~~Fletcher~~ ×
7 Furly   Glanville
8 ~~Johnson~~ ×   Guenelon
9 ~~Masham~~ ×   ~~Kidder~~ ×
10 ~~Molyneux~~ ×   Montague ×
11 ~~Molesworth~~
12 ~~Pembroke~~ ×
13 ~~Popple~~ ×   ~~Pepys~~
14 ~~Somers~~   Slone
15 ~~Treby~~ ×
16 ~~Trombal~~ ×

Those persons not recipients of the first edition (no. 61) can be identified as follows: 'Canterbury' is again the Archbishop John Tillotson; 'Trombal' is Sir William Trumbull; Andrew Fletcher, of Saltoun; William Glanville, brother-in-law of John Evelyn; Richard Kidder, bishop of Bath and Wells; Charles Montague, later Earl of Halifax; Samuel Pepys; Dr. (later Sir) Hans Sloane.

Peter Nidditch, in his edition of this work, estimates 700 copies were printed. A microfilm of the first issue, second state is in the EEB, reel 2033, no. 19: of the second issue on reel 767, no. 40.

References: Alston 7:78, 77; Attig 229; Christophersen 26–7; ESTC r218621 for 62A2, r021459 for 62B; L.L. 1782; T.C. II. 541; Wing^2 L2740A for 62A (states not noted); L2740 for 62B.

Copies examined. 62A1: CaOTU   CtY (Franklin collection 421.1690b)   MH (*fEC65.L7934.689e2ba)   PPL (Wing L2740.1/6208.F)
62A2: O^1 (Vet.A3 c.128)   Dm   WaU (192.2/Es7 1694)
62B: Y   [BBR]   C   C(Keynes)   CaOHM   CLU-C   CtY^{2,3} (K8.L79/+f694; 2 copies)   DLC   Dt   L (528.m.6)   NjP (Ex.6106.333q)   O^2 (Vet.A3 c.140)   O^3 (4 Delta.312)   Oc   TxDaMP   TxHR   ViU

63. *Essay.* 3rd ed., 1695. 2° in 4s.
Within a double rule, inner 259×135 mm, outer 268×143 mm: AN | ESSAY | ... [&c. as in 1st–2nd ed., except:] Written by *JOHN* [swash J] *LOCKE*, Gent. | [rule 129 mm] | *The Third* [swash Ts] EDITION. | [rule 130 mm] | ... [&c., quotation, as in 1st & 2nd ed.] | [rule 129 mm] | *LONDON*: [roman colon] | Printed for 𝔄𝔴𝔫𝔰𝔥𝔞𝔪 and 𝔍𝔬𝔥𝔫 𝔆𝔥𝔲𝔯𝔠𝔥𝔦𝔩 at the *Black* [swash k] | *Swan* in *Pater-Noster-Row*, and 𝔖𝔞𝔪𝔲𝔢𝔩 𝔐𝔞𝔫𝔰𝔥𝔦𝔭, at the | *Ship* in *Cornhill*, near the *Royal Exchange*, 1695.
Coll: 2° in 4s (318×200 mm cut) A^2 [b]^6 a–c^4 B–3F^4 3G–3I^2 [$ half signed; R1 signed 'K']; 230 leaves; pp. *i–xl* 1–39 40 41–90 93–96 95–120 123 122–219 220 221–299 300 301–407 408–420 [=460]. Page 91–94 called '93–6'; 121 called '123'.

Contents: A1ʳ (*i*) title (verso blank), A2ʳ–[b]1ᵛ (*iii–vi*) dedication, [b2]ʳ–6ᵛ (*vii–xvi*) epistle to reader, a1ʳ·ᵛ (*xvii–xviii*) contents of book and chaps., a2ʳ–c4ʳ (*xix–xxxix*) contents of book, chap. and sections, c4ᵛ (*xl*) blank, B1ʳ–3F4ʳ (1–407) text (as in 2nd ed., no. 62), 3F4ᵛ blank, 3G1ʳ–3I1ʳ (*409–419*) index in double cols., 3I1ᵛ (*420*) advt. by Churchills (30 items, 64 lines).

Illustration: port. of Locke by Vanderbanck, after Brounower, as in 2nd ed. (no. 62).

Text (D2ᵛ): 54 lines; 252 (269) × 127 (147) mm; 93 R. Marginal notes set 68 ital. Dedication set 34 lines, 145 ital; readers' epistle set 44 lines, 117 R. Watermark fool's cap and initials 'DH' (occasionally 'CM'). Scattered pages with 53 lines, some with text in direction line, as in 2nd ed. (but p. 313 = 2S1ʳ reset).

*HT*s, headlines or running titles same as 2nd ed. (no. 62).

CW: Page. H1ʳ Impreſſions [Impreſſions;] N4ᵛ §.24. The [§.25. The] S3ᵛ voluntary T4ʳ be- [becauſe] 2A1ᵛ a con- [a contradiction] 2G2ʳ com- [comprehenſive] 2S1ʳ acquain- [acquaintance] 2Z4ʳ limited 3E2ʳ §.9. Firſt,

For the 'large additions'. Pages 221–5: χ1ʳ always   χ1ᵛ that   χ2ᵛ §.18. Some   Pages 423–8: †1ʳ is   †1ᵛ §8. Though   †2ʳ Belief,

Notes: Published in the autumn of 1695 (*Corr.* v.vii), text is a line-by-line reprint of 2d ed. (no. 62) with minor adjustments (except pp. 313–314, which have been respaced) and the errata of the 2d ed. corrected, but also with many misprints.

In the British Library copy "are inserted printed slips, containing proofs of the 'large additions' incorporated in the next [fourth] edition: including two entire chapters, one in book II. [ch.33] 'Of the Association of Ideas,' the other in book IV. [ch.19] 'Of Enthusiasm'." (British Lib. *Catalogue of Printed Books*). Many variants from the 3d ed. are inscribed in the margin by a contemporary hand, e.g. at 1.3.1–7, 9–10, etc. There are slips (versos blank) inserted at 1.4.8, 1.8.5, 2.12.1; new sections 1.8.9–10 inserted, with the old 1.8.9 lined out. There are large insertions printed on both sides of leaves (their size about 2.5 mm. smaller at outer edges (text measuring 128 (147) × 248 (265) mm, 54 lines 92R) for 4.8.11 (p. 345.4), 4.17.4 (p. 386.44), 4.17 before last para. of four (p. 387.6). Whole pages numbered 221–5 inserted to follow p. 219 as Book 2, Ch. 33, 'Of the Association of Ideas.' Book 4 Ch.19, '*Of Enthusiasm*.' has been inserted to follow p. 407, numbered pp. 423–9, p. 423 signed †. Additionally there is much underlining throughout. This only known copy of the additional material printed to bring owners of the 3d ed. up to date was presumably printed as a group of sheets, and the owners thereof added the changes to their copies.

Locke's record of presentation copies for this edition (probably copied out in 1700, Bodleian Lib. MS Locke c.25 f.53ᵛ) lists 'Monsʳ Coste' (Pierre Coste, came to England through friendship with Jean Le Clerc, as tutor to the Masham's son Francis Cudworth Masham, and to translate the *Essay* into

French under Locke's supervision), 'Sʳ Fl Shepheard' (Sir Fleetwood Sheppard, the poet and courtier, a fellow Student of Locke's at Christ Church, Oxford, in the 1650s), and 'Boulton' (Richard Boulton, physician educated at Brasenose College, who corresponded with Locke in 1698; see *Corr.* vi. 375-6).

Peter Nidditch, in his edition of this work, estimates 800 copies were printed. This third edition was sold out by January 1699 (*Corr.* 2359; vi.552-3, letter to Thomas Molyneux, dated 25 January 1698/9). A microfilm copy is in EEB, reel 767, no. 41.

References: Alston 7:79; Attig 230; Christophersen p. 27; ESTC r020221; Johnston p. 319; L.L. 1783; Wing² L2741.

Copies examined: Y C Ck(Keynes) CLU-C CtY (K8.L79/ + f695; ex lib. Thomas Carlyle, gift of Rev. T. Arnold) DFo (S.P. Lamprecht's copy) EXc L (527.n.13; bound with 'large additions' made for 4th ed., no.64; lacks front.; inscribed 'Francis Turnour') MH (*fEC65.L7934.689e2c; closely trimmed 290 × 180 mm) NjP (Ex.6106.333.11q) NN NRU O (4 Delta.301) Oc PPL (Wing L2741/7818.F) WaU (B1290.1695) Yu

64. *Essay.* 4th ed., 1700. 2° in 4s.

Within a double rule, inner 260 × 131 mm, outer 269 × 141 mm: AN | ESSAY | CONCERNING | 𝔥umane 𝔘nderſtanding. | [rule 125 mm] | In Four BOOKS. | [rule 126 mm] | *Written by JOHN* [swash J] *LOCKE, Gent.* | [rule 125 mm] | *The Fourth Edition, with large Additions.* | [rule 127 mm] | Eccles. XI. 5. | *As thou knoweſt not what is the way of the Spirit, nor how the bones* | *do grow in the Womb of her that is with Child: even ſo thou* | *knoweſt not the works of God, who maketh all things.* | [rule 127 mm] | *Quam* [swash Q] *bellum eſt velle confiteri potius neſcire quod neſcias, quam* | *iſta effutientem nauſeare, atque ipſum ſibi diſplicere!* | Cic. de | Natur. Deor. *l.* I. | [rule 128 mm] | LONDON: | Printed for *Awnſham* and *John* [swash J] *Churchil*, at the *Black-Swan* in | *Pater-Noſter-Row*; and *Samuel Manſhip*, at the *Ship* in | *Cornhill*, near the *Royal-Exchange*, MDCC.

Coll: folio in 4s (316 × 210 mm cut) A² [b]⁶ a–c⁴ B–2F⁴ 2G² (–2G2) 2H–3K⁴ 3L–3M² 3N² (–3N2) [$ half (+ A2) signed]; 242 leaves; pp. *i–xl* 1–39 40 41–90 93–96 95–226 233–311 *312* 313–370 317 372–379 390–391 382–438 *439–450* [= 484]. Pages 91–4 called '93–6', 371 called '317', 380–81 called '390–91'. Page numbers 227–32 omitted.

Contents: A1ʳ (*i*) title (verso blank), A2ʳ–[b]1ᵛ (*iii–vi*) dedication, [b]2ʳ–6ᵛ (*vii–xvi*) reader's epistle, a1ʳ·ᵛ (*xvii–xviii*) contents by book and chap., a2ʳ–c4ʳ (*xix–xxxix*) contents by book, chap. and sections, c4ᵛ (*xl*) blank, B1ʳ–F4ʳ (*1–39*) text of Book I, F4ᵛ (*40*) blank, G1ʳ–2G1ʳ (*41–226*) text of Book II, 2H1ʳ–2R4ʳ (*233–311*) text of Book III, 2R4ᵛ (*312*) blank, 2S1ʳ–3K3ᵛ (*313–436*) text of Book IV, 3K4ʳ–3N1ʳ (*439–449*) index, 3N1ᵛ (*450*) errata in 2 cols. (26 & 24 lines).

Illustration: portrait of Locke as frontispiece, as in 2d and 3d editions (no. 62–3), by Vanderbanck after Brounower.

Text (2D2ᵛ): 54 lines; 249 (267) × 129 (148) mm; 94 R. Dedication set 34 lines, 145 R; reader's epistle set 43 lines, 116 ital; index set 67 R. Fair-quality laid paper, mixed, watermarked with fool's cap and initials KIS or SG.

HT A2ʳ: [double rule 142/144 mm] | TO THE | RIGHT HONOURABLE | THOMAS | EARL OF | Pembroke and Montgomery, | *Baron Herbert of* Cardiff, *Lord* Rofs *of* Kendal, | Par, Fitzhugh, Marmion, *St. Quintin, and* Shur- | land; *Lord Prefident of his Majefties moft Honour-* | *able Privy-Council, and Lord Lieutenant of the* | *County of* Wilts, *and of* South Wales.

HTs for reader's epistle ([b]2ʳ, contents (a1ʳ), text (B1ʳ), the following books and index (3K4ʳ) same as in 1st–3d editions (no. 61–3).

Headlines or RTs are ital. chapter titles within rules as in 1st–3d editions.

CW: Page. H1ʳ Impreffions M4ᵛ §.25. If X3ʳ Apprehen- [Apprehenfions,] 2E1ᵛ §.5. There- [§.5. Therefore] 2G1ʳ Champions 2P2ʳ § 7. This 3A1ᵛ Stan- [Standards] 3E3ᵛ ad- [advantage]

Press figures: None.

Notes: In a letter to Dr. Thomas Molyneux in January 1699 (*Corr.* 2539; vi.552–3) Locke stated the last edition of the *Essay* 'is now out of print'. A new agreement with Manship and the Churchills relating to further additions of the *Essay* (Bodleian Lib. MS Locke b. 1, f.218) offered Locke ten shillings per sheet of additions to be made. The additions and alterations for the 4th ed. included many minor improvements in italicisation and punctuation and the occasional addition or revision of a few words. Major changes were a new chapter (2.23) entitled 'Of the Association of Ideas', another (4.19), 'Of Enthusiasm'. Locke had these two chapters and other 'large additions' printed 'by themselves' for the use of friends who owned an earlier edition, just as he had done for the second edition. These additions can be seen in the British Library's copy of the third edition (no. 63). The sheets were not ready until after mid–April 1700 (letter from A. Churchill, *Corr.* 2718; vii.69).

The quotation from *Ecclesiastes* appears on the title for the first time. The subscription, '*Dorfet-Court* 24th | of *May.* 1689.' in the dedication also occurs for the first time. Some sentences were added in the reader's epistle. This edition was advertised in *The London Gazette*, no. 3556, for 7–11 December 1699 (cf. *Corr.* vi.vii) but bore the imprint date of the following year. Its projected appearance was announced in the *History of the Works of the Learned*, 1 no. 10 (Oct. 1699, p. 639), in the 'State of Learning' section, subheaded 'LONDON.': "A Fourth Edition of Mr. *Lock*'s *Essay on Humane Understanding* is in the Press, and will soon be Publish'd with very large and considerable Additions, and particularly a Chapter concerning *Enthusiasm*." Otherwise the text follows that of the 2d (not 3d) edition.

The typesetting was divided between two, possibly three printers, the first two books to one and Books III and IV to the other(s): witness the omission of pages 227–232 in the numbering, and the lack of leaf 2G2. The printer of the first half used the letter 'U' as signature (pp. 145 and 147); of the second half, 'Vv' (pp. 329 & 331). There is also a different style of type for the section sign (§): in sheets 2H–2Z (pp. 233–352) it measures 4 × 2.2 mm and is in a fatter style from that used in sheets A–2G (pp. 1–226), where it measures 4 × 1.3 mm; it is different again in sheets 3A–3K, measuring 3.3 × 1.8 mm. The second printer omits a period after the section sign. There again were many typographical errors, most noticeably in the running titles, e.g. 209: '*Adequate and Inadeqeuate Ideas.*'; 391 and 393 (rectē 381 and 383, 3C3^r and 3C4^r): '*Knowledge of Existence of othe* [sic] *Things.*'; 423: '*Euthusiasm.*' Pages 428–36 (3I2^v–3K2^{r,v}) have varying headlines: pp. 428–9, 434: '*Wrong Assent or Errour.*'; 430–31: '*Wrong Assent, or Error.*'; 432–3, 435–6: '*Wrong Assent, or Errour.*'

Locke's agreement with the booksellers entitled him to six bound copies. His notebook (Bodleian Lib. MS Locke f.29, p. 158) lists 5 recipients: 'E Pembroke' (the dedicatee), 'Dr South' (Robert South, the divine, a fellow student at Westminster School and Christ Church, Oxford), 'Mr. Bold' (Samuel Bold, Rector of Steeple in Dorset, who published works in defence of Locke), 'Le Cler' (Jean LeClerc, a recipient of the 3rd ed.), and 'Dr Molyneux' (William Molyneux's brother, Thomas, MD from Dublin, later FRS).

Another distribution list occurs in MS Locke c.25 f.54, headed 'Humane Understanding 1700', and contains thirteen names, not numbered. Four names are marked 'gt', that is, for gilt bindings. "It is perhaps a preparatory list rather than a copy of the operative list." (E.S. de Beer, private papers).

That list is as follows:

E Pembroke gt
Ld Chancellor gt
Dr South
M^r Le Clerc
Mr Bold
Dr Molyneux
Dr Sloan
Col: Cothrington gt
Mr Cunningham
Ld Masham gt [a probable slip for 'Lady']
Mr Coste
Mr Freke
Cos King

Pembroke, the Lord Chancellor John Somers, Le Clerc and Freke were recipients of the first and second editions (no. 61–62); Hans Sloane of the second; and Pierre Coste of the third (no. 63). The new names can be identified as Dr. Robert South; Samuel Bold; Dr. Thomas Molyneux, brother of William; 'Cothrington' as Col. Christopher Codrington; Alexander Cunningham; and Peter King, later first Baron King, Locke's cousin and executor.

This edition was entered by Bennet and Clements in their 'conger' books by "A. Churchill ½ from T. Dring". The 'conger' purchased 440 copies of this edition from the printers for 7/6 and 7/9 on November 15, 1699 and sold copies to other booksellers at 12/- (a profit of 35 to 37.5 per cent.)[6] This is the edition sold to James Logan in Philadelphia for 14 shillings. (See *Notes* to the first edition, no. 61).

Nidditch estimates 800 copies were printed.

References: Alston 7:80; Attig 231 Christophersen p. 27; ESTC r039072; Johnston pp. 319-20; L.L. 1783a; T.C. III.176; Wing² L2742.

Copies examined: Y   C   CaQMMO   Ck(Keynes)   CLU-C   Ct   CtY (1971.1)   DFo (S.P. Lamprecht's copy)   EXu   L (527.n.10)   MH (*fEC65.L7934.689e2d)   NjP (Ex.6106.333.13q)   NRU   O (F1.4 Art; presentation copy from Locke)   Oa (Chr. Codrington's copy)   Oc   Oq   PPL¹ (Wing L2742/Log409.F)   PPL² (1105.F)   PPL³ (9182.F)   Yu (BIH 1700)

65. *Essay*. 5th ed., 1706. 2° in 4s.

Within a double rule, inner 268 × 133 mm, outer 278 × 138 mm: AN | ESSAY | . . . [&c. as in 4th ed., except:] *The Fifth Edition, with large Additions.* | [rule 131 mm] | ECCLES. XI. 5. | *As thou knoweſt not what is the Way of the Spirit, nor how the* | *Bones do grow in the Womb of her that is with Child: Even* | *ſo thou knoweſt not the Works of God, who maketh all things.* | [rule 131 mm] | Quam [swash Q] *bellum eſt velle confiteri potius neſcire quod neſcias, quam* | *iſta effutientem nauſeare, atque ipſum ſibi diſplicere!* Cic. de | Natur. Deor. 1. I. | [rule 131 mm] | LONDON: | Printed for *Awnſham* and *John* [swash J] *Churchill,* at the *Black Swan* in | *Pater-Noſter-Row*; and *Samuel Manſhip*, at the *Ship* in *Corn-* | *hill*, near the *Royal Exchange*, M DCC VI.

Coll: 2° in 4s (356 × 225 mm cut) A^2 [b]-[i]² (-[i]2 = 4H1) B-2N⁴ 2O² 2Y-4G⁴ 4H² (-4H2) [*]² [**]² [$ half signed]; 292 leaves; pp. *i-xxxiv* 1-210 203 212-232 225 234-258 260-261 255 263 263bis 264-284 345-422 425-464 467-604 605-614 [= 584]. Page 211 called '203'; 233 called '225'; 259-262 called '260', '261', '255', '263' respectively. Page no. 285-344, 423-4 and 465-6 omitted.

Contents: A1^r (*i*) title (verso blank), A2^r-[b]1^v (*iii-vi*) dedication, [b]2^r-[d]1^r (*vii-xiii*) reader's epistle, [d]1v-[d]2r (xiv-xv) contents by book and chapter, [d]2^v-[i]1^v (*xvi-xxxiv*) contents by book, chap. & sections, B1^r-H1^v (1-50) text of Book I, H2^r-2O2^v (51-284) text of Book II, 2Y1^r-3K3^v (345-440) text of Book III, 3K4^r-4G4^v (441-604) text of Book IV, 4H1^r-[**]2^r (605-613) index, [**]2^v (*614*) errata (in 2 cols., 43 & 42 lines).

Text, sheets B-2O (X3^r): 49 lines, 285 (304) × 147 (162) mm, 117 R; sheets 2Y-4G (3A2^v): 49 lines, 286 (305) × 145 (160) mm, 117 R. Sheets B-2O

---

[6] See *The Notebook of Thomas Bennet and Henry Clements (1686-1719)*, edited by N. Hodgson and Cyprian Blagden (*Oxford Bibliographical Society Publications*, n.s. 6, Oxford 1956), p. 206.

good quality laid paper, with watermark Heawood 458; remaining sheets, Heawood 2723 and initials 'RH'. Dedication set 39 lines, 143 roman; reader's epistle, 39 lines, 116 ital; footnotes set 81 R. Some copies lack watermarks entirely, or in sheets 2Y–4G only.

HT, A2^r: [double rule 157/158 mm] | TO THE | RIGHT HONOUR-ABLE | THOMAS EARL OF | 𝔓𝔢𝔪𝔟𝔯𝔬𝔨𝔢 and 𝔐𝔬𝔫𝔱𝔤𝔬𝔪𝔢𝔯𝔶, | *Baron* Herbert *of* Cardiff, *Lord* Rofs *of* Kendal, | Par, Fitzhugh, Marmion, *St.* Quintin, *and* Shur- | land; *Lord Prefident of his Majefty's moft Ho-* | *nourable Privy-Council, and Lord Lieutenant of* | *the County of* Wilts, *and of* South Wales.

Head titles for the reader's epistle ([b]2^r), contents ([d]1^v and [d]2^v), the beginning of Book I (B1^r) and the index (4H1^r) same as in 1st–4th editions.

Headlines and running titles as in 1st–4th editions (no. 61-4).

CW: Page H1^r Teachers, M4^v ad- [advantage] U3^r (3. The) Perception [3. The Perception] 2C4^v §.15. Befides, [§.15. Befides] 2O1^v §.15. 3A2^v Me-[Memory,] 3H4^v § 27. Se- [§ 27. Secondly,]

Press figures: None.

Notes: The first posthumous edition incorporates very few revisions of changes in the text, chiefly an expansion of 2.21 (8 lines omitted from § 23; new §§ 48, 56, 71). A notable feature is the inclusion as footnotes of excerpts from Locke's *Letter* to Bishop Edward Stillingfleet, his *Reply* and his second *Reply* (1697-99; no. 246-48), with brief quotations from the bishop. These are inserted at (1) 1.1.8, (2) 1.4.8, (3) 2.2.2, (4) 2.23.1), (5) 2.23.2, (6) 2.27.29, (7) 3.3.11, (8) 4.1.2, and (9) 4.3.6. These insertions are included in all future separately published English editions of the *Essay*, but are not found in editions reissued from a *Works* edition, that is the 1793 and 1795 editions (no. 87-9), and later such, post-1800 editions.

There is no frontispiece (portrait of Locke) in this edition.

In a codicil to his will Locke anticipates the textual changes (*Corr.* viii.426). Nidditch concludes that the inclusion of the excerpts "must have been approved by Peter King (1669-1734) Locke's relation and executor" (Nidditch ed., p. xxxii). He also estimates that 900 copies were printed. The 'conger' (cf. no. 63, *Notes*) purchased 300 copies on 19 November 1705 and retailed them to members of the trade at 14/-.

The text was again divided between two printers: not only are page numbers 285-344 omitted, but text for the first two books employs more squat capital letters (measuring 3.2 mm tall) than those used in Books III–IV (where they measure 4 mm in height). The letters B, H, Q, U and W are from a noticeably different font, as is the style of the section sign (§). The printer of 2Y-4G also omits a period after it (e.g., '§ 27.', *not* '§.27.')

In some copies the index is bound following p. *xxxiv*, indicating the 4H1 was originally part of [i] (pp. *605-6*).

This edition received an extensive summary, particularly of Book I, in Le Clerc's *Bibliothèque choisie*, 12 (1707): 80-123. This summary is used as an abridgement of Book I in Bosset's French translation of Wynne's abridgement (no. 133-41).

A microfilm copy is in the collection, *The Eighteenth Century*, reel 357, no. 2.

References: Alston 7:81; Attig 232; Christophersen pp. 22, 92; ESTC t033271.

Copies examined: Y* C Ck(Keynes) CLU-C CtY (Mia6/ + Ed971.Z937; ex lib. Jonathan Edwards) DFo Dt* L (8406.h.13) MH (*fEC65.L7934.689e2e) O¹ (Vet.A4 b.63; 380 × 240 mm cut) O²* (Vet. A4 c.68) Oc Osj PPL (*Ia Lock/6314.F) PU (fEC65.L7933.690e) ViU*

* Index bound at front, after [i]1.

66. *Essay*. 6th ed., 1710. 2 vols. in 8°. Two issues.

66A (1). First issue. Vol. 1, within a double rule, inner 164 × 88 mm, outer 171 × 95 mm: AN | ESSAY | CONCERNING | Human Underſtanding. | [rule 83 mm] | In Four BOOKS. | [rule 83 mm] | Written by *JOHN* [swash J] *LOCKE*, Gent. [rule 81 mm] | *The Sixth Edition, with large Additions.* | [rule 83 mm] | VOLUME I. | [rule 83 mm] | ECCLES. XI. 5. | *As thou ... Spirit,* | *nor ... of her* | *that is ... knoweſt not* | *the Works of God, who maketh all things.* | [rule 80 mm] | *Quam* [swash Q] *bellum eſt velle confiteri potius neſcire quod* | *neſcias, quam iſta effutientem nauſeare, atque* | *ipſum ſibi diſplicere!* Cic. de Natur. Deor. l. I. | [rule 86 mm] | LONDON: | Printed and Sold by *H. Hills*, and the Bookſellers | of *London* and *Weſtminſter*. 1710.

66A (2) Vol.2: AN | ESSAY | CONCERNING | HUMANE UNDERSTANDING. | [rule 91 mm] | By | *JOHN* [swash J] *LOCKE*, Gent. | [rule 90 mm] | VOLUME II. | [rule 89 mm] | [orn. small irons in rows of 3, 4 and 3, 18 × 24 mm] | [rule 88 mm] | LONDON: | Printed in the Year MDCCX.

Coll: 8° (193 × 123 mm cut). Vol. 1: *⁸ **⁸ A-Z⁸ 2A² [$ half signed]; 202 leaves; pp. *i-xxxii* 1-157 258 159-371 372 [= 404]. Page 158 called '258'.

Vol. 2: A⁶ B-Y⁸ Z⁴ a-c⁴ d² [$ half signed; I4 signed 'L4']; 192 leaves; pp. *i-xvi* 1-340 341-368 [= 384]. First page of each gathering B-D also signed 'Vol.II.'; E-O signed 'Voll.II.'; remaining sheets (P-d) omit vol. designation in direction line. Page 9 has its numeral inverted.

66B (1). Second issue. Vol. 1, within a double rule, inner 167 × 83 mm, outer 174 × 91 mm: AN | ESSAY | CONCERNING | *Humane Underſtanding*. | [rule 79 mm] | In FOUr BOOKS. | [rule 79 mm] | Written by *JOHN* [swash J] *LOCKE*, Gent. | [rule 80 mm] | **The Sixth Edition, with large Additions.** | rule 79 mm] | VOLUME I. | [rule 79 mm] | ECCLES. xi. 5. | *As thou knoweſt ... Spirit,* | *nor how ... of her* | *that ... knoweſt not* | *the Works ... things.* | [rule 79 mm] | *Quam* [swash Q] *bellum e· ... quod* | *neſcias, ... atque ip-* | *ſum ſibi diſplicere!* Cic.

de Natur. Deor. l. I. | [rule 78 mm] | LONDON: | Printed for A. and J. CHURCHILL, at the | Black Swan in Pater-noſter-Row; and SAMUEL | MANSHIP, at the Ship in Cornhill. 1710.

66B (2) Vol. 2, within a double rule, inner 166 × 83 mm, outer 175 × 92 mm: AN | ESSAY | CONCERNING | Humane Underſtanding. | [rule 80 mm] | BY | JOHN [swash J] LOCKE, Gent. | [rule 79 mm] | VOLUME II. | [rule 77 mm] | [diamond shaped orn. of small fleurons, 1, 2, 3; inverted 3, 2, 1 in 6 rows, 24 × 12 mm] | [rule 89 mm] | [4 lines of imprint, as in vol. 1]

Coll: as first issue, except vol. 1: *^{8} (±*1); vol. 2: A^6 (±A1).

Contents. Vol. 1: *1^r (*i*) title (verso blank), *2^r-*3^v (*iii–vi*) dedication, *4^r-**1^v (*vii–xviii*) reader's epistle, **2^r (*xix*) contents of Books I–II by book & chap., **2^v-**8^v (*xx–xxxii*) contents of Books I–II by book, chap. & sections, A1^r-E2^r top half (1–67.5) text of Book I, E2^r lower half-2A2^r (67.–25–371) text of Book II, 2A2^v (*372*) blank.

Vol. 2: A1^r (*i*) title (verso blank), A2^r (*iii*) contents of Books III–IV by book & chap., A2^v-B2^v (*iv–xvi*) contents of Books III–IV by book, chap. & sections, B3^r-I6^v (1–120) text of Book III, I7^r-Z4^v (121–340) text of Book IV, a1^r-d2^r (*341–367*) index to complete work, d2^v (*368*) blank.

Illustration: frontispiece is engraved port. of Locke by Brounower facing right, in an oval frame similar to that in 4th ed. (no. 64) with a coat of arms at bottom of frame (3 doves in alternate blocks of a 6-part quartering), subscribed 'S. *Brounower ad vivum delin*. T.*Nutting Sculpsit*' measuring 168 × 97 mm, the inscription 'M^r. *John Locke*.' below; the plate measures 185 × 104 mm.

Text: Vol. l (B1^r): 43 lines, 158 (167) × 95 mm, 74 R; v.2 (B5^v): 43 lines, 157 (166) × 94 mm, 73 R. Fair-quality laid paper, without watermarks. Dedication set 32 lines 97R; reader's epistle set 34 lines 93 ital. Footnotes set 67 R. Page no. at outer ends of headlines.

HT, v.1 and 2: [double rule 93 mm] | OF | Humane Underſtanding. | [rule 93 mm]

Dedication, v. l: *2^r [double rule 93 mm] | TO THE | RIGHT HONOURABLE | THOMAS | EARL OF | *PEMBROKE* AND *MONTGOMERY*, | *Baron* Herbert *of* Cardiff, *Lord* Roſs *of* | Kendal . . . [&c.]

Headlines or RTs in italics, with roman for emphasis, are shortened chapter titles, omitting book and chap. numbers.

CW: Page. Vol. 1: B3^r Propo- [Propoſitions,] B7^r Thoughts. E7^r con- [contemplation,] K7^v (*Compo-*) ſition; [ſition*;] R2^r con- [conſidered] Y5^r Repreſen- [Repreſentation] No CW on v.l, p. 14 (B7v).

Vol.2: C7^r Signifi- [Signification] C7^v by H8^v convincing N1^v *i.e.* S1^v when S2^v (Co-) lours

Press figures: None.

Notes: Reprint of the 5th edition, the first to appear in a smaller (octavo) format, and the first whose title reads 'Human' (not 'Humane') 'Understanding'.

The phrase in the imprint, 'Booksellers of London. . .' is frequently an indication of a pirate's work; the title leaves for the authorised booksellers are cancellans. Henry Hills, jun. "became notorious for pirating every good poem or sermon that was published" (Plomer, p. 155). One can only speculate that the Churchills and Manship caught up with Hills, seized his stock and pasted on their own title leaves. Entry 23 in the *Bowyer Ledgers* indicates Bowyer finished printing this edition 7 September 1710: "LEDGER A3. Sare, Locke's titles reptd, 800", that is 800 copies printed. Richard Sare was a bookseller to whom Bowyer frequently supplied stock. There are no ornaments; text of each book begins with a plain 4-line initial, of each chapter with a 3-line initial.

A microfilm copy of the second issue is in the collection, *The Eighteenth Century*, reel 7423 no. 2.

References: Alston 7:83; Attig 233; Christophersen p. 92 (2d issue only); ESTC 1st issue: n009328; 2d issue: t063925.

Copies examined:
  First issue: Y CaOTU (Locke L63.E82 1710) Cch (I.15.14-15) NjP (Ex.6106.333.14) O (Vet. A4. e. 1300-1)
  Second issue: O (Vet. A4. e. 867-8) L (1476.aaa.30) Osj

67. *Essay*. 7th ed., 1716, 1715. 2 vols. in 8°

Vol. 1, within a double rule, inner 163 × 90 mm, outer 169 × 98 mm: AN | ESSAY | CONCERNING | Human Underſtanding. | . . . [&c. as in 6th ed., first issue, except:] *The Seventh* [swash v] *Edition, with large Additions.* | [rule 87 mm] | VOLUME I. | [rule 86 mm] | ECCLES. XI. 5. | As thou knoweſt . . . Spirit, | nor . . . of her | that . . . knoweſt not | the . . . things. | [rule 86 mm] | *Quam* [swash Q] . . . *quod* | *neſcias* . . . *atque* | *ipſum ſibi diſplicere!* Cic. de Natur. Deor. l. I. | [rule 86 mm] | LONDON: | Printed for *J.* [swash J] *Churchill*, at the *Black-Swan* in *Pater-* | *Noſter-Row*; and *Samuel Manſhip*, at the *Ship* in | *Cornhill*. 1716.

Vol. 2: AN | ESSAY | CONCERNING | HUMANE UNDERSTANDING. | [rule 92 mm] | BY | *JOHN* [swash J] *LOCKE*, Gent. | [rule 92 mm] | [orn., vase of flowers 23 × 40 mm] | [rule 92 mm] | LONDON: [roman colon] | Printed for A. and J. CHURCHILL, at the *Black-Swan* | in *Pater-noſter-row*, and S. MANSHIP, at the *Ship* | againſt the *Royal-Exchange* in *Cornhill*, 1715.

Coll: 8° (198 × 122 mm cut). Vol. 1: *⁸ **⁸ A–Z⁸ 2A² [$ half signed]; 202 leaves; pp. i–xxxii 1–371 372 [=404].

Vol. 2: A⁶ B–Y⁸ Z⁴ a–c⁴ d² [$ half signed]; 192 leaves; pp. *i* xvi 1–340 341–368 [=384]. First page of each sheet in vol. 2 also signed 'Vol. II.' in direction line.

Contents and *Illustration* (front. by Brounower, facing right) same as 6th ed. (no. 66).

Text (v.2, E3ʳ; same for both vols.): 43 lines; 154 (164) × 92 mm; 71 R. Good-quality laid paper with no visible watermarks. Headlines or RTs are chapter titles in italics. Page no. at outer corners of headlines. Marginal notes or topics set ital. within the page block, in varying widths and heights. Headline for Book I, ch. III (pp. 29-47), '*No Innate Practical Principles.*', in error continues (onto pp. 47-8) as headline; ch. IV (occupying pp. 47-67) otherwise correctly headed '*No Innate Principles.*'

HT, v. 1, *2^r: [double rule 92 mm] | TO THE | RIGHT HONOURABLE | THOMAS | EARL OF | PEMBROKE *and* MONTGOMERY, | *Baron* Herbert *of* Cardiff, *Lord* Rofs *of* Kendal, | . . . [&c., as in no. 66]

v. 1, A1^r: [double rule 93 mm] | OF | Humane Underftanding. | [rule 93 mm]

v. 2, B3^r: [double rule 92 mm] | OF | *Humane Underftanding.* | [rule 93 mm]

CW: Page. Vol. 1: B3^r Propo- [Propofitions,] B7^v may E7^r con- [contemplation,] R2^r con- [confidered] Y5^r Reprefen- [Reprefentation] Vol.2: C7^v qua- [*quatenus*] H8^v con- [convincing] Nl^v re- [reprefented] S1^v when S2^v (Co-) lorus [lours]

Press figures: None.

Notes: Text is a line-by-line reprint of the 6th ed. and follows its text (as based on the 5th ed.; no. 65). Vol. 1, p. 158 and v. 2, p. 9 have correct page numbers. The type fonts, including §s, are different in vol. 2 from vol. 1. Sewing of first gathering in vol. 2 is seen to be between leaves A4 and A5. Vol. 1 title-page reads 'Human', vol. 2 'Humane Understanding.' A microfilm copy is in the collection, *The Eighteenth Century*, reel 353, no. 1.

References: Alston 7:84; Attig 234; Christophersen p. 92; ESTC t065491.

Copies examined: O (Vet.A4 e.862-3) CaOTU (Locke L63.E82 1716) CLU-C L (8405.f.23) NjP (Ex.6106.333.15) PU (B1290 1716)

68. *Essay.* 8th ed., 1721. 2 vols. 8°

Vol. 1, within a double rule, inner 162 × 90 mm, outer 168 × 98 mm: AN | ESSAY | . . . [&c. as in 7th ed., except:] 𝕿𝖍𝖊 𝕰𝖎𝖌𝖍𝖙𝖍 𝕰𝖉𝖎𝖙𝖎𝖔𝖓, 𝖜𝖎𝖙𝖍 𝖑𝖆𝖗𝖌𝖊 𝕬𝖉𝖉𝖎𝖙𝖎𝖔𝖓𝖘. | .. [&c. as in 6th ed., 1st issue and 7th ed. until 14th line:] ECCLES. XI. 5. | As . . . nor | how . . . that is | with Child: . . . of | God, . . . Things. [swash T] | [rule 88 mm] | *Quam* [swash Q] . . . *nefcias,* | *quam ifta effutientem naufeare, atque ipfum fibi defpli-* [sic] | *cere!* Cic. de Natur. Deor. l. I. | [rule 87 mm] | LONDON: | Printed for A. CHURCHILL and A. MANSHIP; | and Sold by W. TAYLOR, at the Ship and Black | Swan in *Pater-nofter-Row*. 1721.

Vol. 2: AN | ESSAY | CONCERNING | HUMAN UNDERSTANDING. | [rule 89 mm] | BY | *JOHN* [swash J] *LOCKE*, Gent. | [rule 88 mm] | VOLUME II. | [rule 87 mm] | [orn., vase of flowers, 23 × 40 mm] | [rule 87 mm] | *LONDON*: [roman colon] | Printed for A. CHURCHILL, at the *Black-Swan* in | *Pater-nofter-Row*, and A. MANSHIP, at the *Ship* | againft the *Royal-Exchange* in *Cornhill*, 1721.

Coll: 8° (195 × 130 mm cut). Vol. 1: a⁸ (±a1) *a⁸ A–Z⁸ 2A² [$ half signed]; 202 leaves; pp. *I–II i* ij–iv *v–xxx* 1–240 141 242–372 [= 404]. Page 241 called '141'.

Vol. 2: A⁸ (–2 leaves = d²) B–Y⁸ Z⁴ a–c⁴ d² [$ half signed]; 192 leaves; pp. *i–xvi* 1–340 *341–368* [= 384].

Contents. Vol. 1: a1ʳ (*I*) title (verso blank), a2ʳ–a3ᵛ (*j–iv*) dedication, a4ʳ–*a1ʳ (*v–xv*) reader's epistle, *a1ᵛ (*xvi*) chap. contents of Books I–II, *2aʳ–*a8ᵛ (*xvii–xxx*) contents by book, chap. and sections of Books I–II, A1ʳ–E2ʳ (1–67 line 5) text of Book I, E2ʳ–2A2ᵛ (67, bottom 25 lines–372) text of Book II.

Vol. 2: A1ʳ (*i*) title (verso blank), A2ʳ (*iii*) contents of Book III–IV by book and chap., A2ᵛ–B2ᵛ (*iv–xvi*) contents by book, chap. and sections, B3ʳ–I6ᵛ (1–120) text of Book III, I7ʳ–Z4ᵛ (121–340) text of Book IV, a1ʳ–d2ʳ (*341–367*) index in double cols., d2ᵛ (*368*) blank.

Illustration: engraved portrait as frontispiece to vol. 1, subscribed 'G. Kneller pin. Vertue sculp.', with subcaption '*Johannes Locke*.' The engraving measures 159 × 96 mm on plate 178 × 102 mm.

Text (v. 1, C3ᵛ; same for both vols.): 48 lines; 155 (166) × 93 mm; 65 R. Good-quality laid paper without watermarks. Page no. at external ends of headlines. Dedication set 33 lines ital., begins with orn. 6-line initial T ('THIS'); reader's epistle set 34 lines roman. Topical contents of sections set within page block in italics.

HT, v.1, a2ʳ: [floral headpiece, with bird in flight left, dog at right, pedestal bowl of fruit center, 9 × 87 mm] | To the Right Honourable | THOMAS | Earl of *Pembroke* [swash k] and *Montgomery*, | Baron [swash B] Herbert *of* Cardiff, *Lord* Roſs *of* Ken- | dal, . . . [&c., as in no. 66]

v.1, A1ʳ: [double rule 89 mm] | OF | Humane Underſtanding. | [rule 88 mm]

v.2, B3ʳ: [double rule 89 mm] | OF | *Humane Underſtanding*. | [rule 89 mm]

Headlines or RTs are chapter titles in italics, with upper- and lower-case roman for emphasis.

CW: Page. Vol.1: C7ᵛ this E8ʳ con- [Contemplation] R2ʳ con- [conſidered] Y5ʳ the

Vol.2: C7ᵛ qua- [quatenus] H8ᵛ con- [convincing] N1ᵛ re- [repreſented] P1ʳ (Bo-) dies, R1ʳ Fal- [Falſhood] S1ᵛ when S2ᵛ (Co-) lours T3ʳ Diſ- [Diſagreement]

Press figures. Vol. 1: *xii* (a6ᵛ)-2   *xiv* (a7ᵛ)-I   *xviii* (*a1ᵛ)-I   3 (A2ʳ)-I   8 (A4ᵛ)-2   31 (B8ʳ)-2   46 (C7ʳ)-3   48 (C8ᵛ)-3   63 (D8ʳ)-2   78 (E7ᵛ)-2   89 (F5ʳ)-3   109 (G7ʳ)-2   116 (H2ᵛ)-2   132 (I2ᵛ)-3   143 (I8ʳ)-2   157 (K7ʳ)-2   158 (K7ᵛ)-2   162 (L1ᵛ)-2   180 (M2ᵛ)-2   191 (M8ʳ)-2   208 (N8ʳ)-2   212 (O2ᵛ)-2   223 (O8ʳ)-2   237 (P7ʳ)-2   253 (Q7ʳ)-2   254 (Q7ᵛ)-2   269 (R7ʳ)-2   271 (R8ʳ)-2   287 (S8ʳ)-2   303 (T8ʳ)-2   320 (U8ᵛ)-2   331 (X6ʳ)-2   336 (X8ᵛ)-I or 2   349 (Y7ʳ)-I   355 (Z2ʳ)-2   364 (Z6ᵛ)-I   369 (2A2ʳ)-I

Note: CaOTU copy has '1' on p. 336; O² has '2', neither found elsewhere. The figures (chiefly 2 and 3) occur randomly throughout, chiefly on 7ᵛ and 8ʳ on the inner forme and on 2ᵛ and 7ʳ on the outer. Eleven of the 26 sheets are signed on both formes.

Vol.2: none.

Notes: Text is a reprint of the 7th ed. (no. 67) following the text of the 5th ed. (no. 65), and the layout of the 6th. Title leaf of vol. 1 is a cancellans. A microfilm copy is in the collection, *The Eighteenth Century*, reel 3195, no. 27, continued onto 3196, no. 1.

References: Alston 7:85; Attig 235; Christophersen p. 92; ESTC t063926.

Copies examined: O¹ (Godw. 463-4)   CaOTU (Locke L63.E82 1721)   O² (Vet.A4 e.1412-13; with figure on v.1, p. 336)   L (1487 fff.26; no figure on v.1, p. 364)   OCU (B1290/1692, v.2 only)   PU (B1290 1721)   Vat

69. *Essay*. 9th ed., 1726. 2 vols., 8°. Two states of vol. 1.

69A (1). Vol. 1. First state. Within a double rule, inner 164 × 91 mm, outer 171 × 97 mm: AN | ESSAY | CONCERNING | Human Underſtanding. | [rule 85 mm] | In Four BOOKS. | [rule 85 mm] | Witten [sic] by *JOHN* [swash J] *LOCKE*, Gent. | [rule 87 mm] | 𝕿𝔥𝔢 𝕹𝔦𝔫𝔱𝔥 𝕰𝔡𝔦𝔱𝔦𝔬𝔫, 𝔴𝔦𝔱𝔥 𝔩𝔞𝔯𝔤𝔢 𝕬𝔡𝔡𝔦𝔱𝔦𝔬𝔫𝔰. | [rule 84 mm] | VOLUME I. | [rule 85 mm] | ECCLES. XI. 5. | As thou . . . nor | how . . . that is | with Child: . . . of | God, who maketh all Things. [swash T] | [rule 85 mm] | Quam [swash Q] bellum eſt velle confiteri potius neſcire quod neſcias, | quam iſta effutientem nauſeare, atque ipſum ſibi diſplicere! | Cic. de Natur. Deor. l. I. | [rule 84 mm] | LONDON, Printed by T. W. [swash T] for A. CHURCHILL; | And | EDM. PARKER, at the *Bible* and *Crown* in | *Lombardſtreet*. M.DCC.XXVI.

69B (1). Vol. 1, second state: as above except 'Written by *JOHN* [swash J] LOCKE, Gent.'

69 (2). Vol. 2, within a double rule, inner 161 × 89 mm, outer 164 × 92 mm: AN | ESSAY | CONCERNING | Human Underſtanding. | [rule 83 mm] | BY | *JOHN* [swash J] *LOCKE*, Gent. | [rule 82 mm] | VOLUME II. | [rule 83 mm] | [orn. vase with face below, between birds 23 × 30 mm] | [rule 83 mm] | LONDON, Printed by *M.J.* [swash M] for A [bold font, no period] CHURCHILL; | And | EDM. PARKER, at the *Bible* and *Crown* in | *Lombard-Street*. M.DCC.XXVI.

Coll: 8° (193 × 124 mm cut). Vol. 1: a⁸ *a⁸ A-Z⁸ 2A² [$ half signed; O3 and O4 both signed 'O3']; 202 leaves; pp. I-II i ij-iij iv-xxx 1-372 [= 404]. Vol. 2: A⁴ a⁴ B-Y⁸ Z-2C⁴ [$ half signed 192 leaves; pp. *i-xvi* 1-340 341-368 [= 384]. First page of each sheet also signed 'Vol.II.' in direction line.

Contents. Vol. 1: a1ʳ title (verso blank) a2ʳ-a3ᵛ (*i-iv*) dedication, a4ʳ-*a1ʳ (*v-xv*) reader's epistle, *a1ᵛ (*xvi*) contents by book and chap., *a2ʳ-*a8ᵛ (*xvii-xxx*) contents by book, chap. and sections, A1ʳ-E2ʳ (1-67) text of Book I, E2ʳ-2A2ᵛ (67 bottom-372) text of Book II.

Vol. 2: A1ʳ (*i*) title (verso blank), A2ʳ (*iii*) contents by book & chap. of Books III–IV, A2ᵛ–a4ᵛ (*iv–xvi*) contents of Books III–IV by book, chap. & sections, B1ʳ–I4ᵛ (1–120) text of Book III, I5ʳ–Z2ᵛ (121–340) text of Book IV, Z3ʳ–2C4ʳ (*341–367*) index, 2C4ᵛ (*368*) blank.

Illustration: v. 1 has front. portrait of Locke, facing right, by Vertue after Kneller, as in 8th ed. (no. 68), subcaptioned '*Johannes Locke.*'

Text: 44 lines. Vol. 1 (C8ʳ): 161 (169) × 92 mm; 74 R. Vol. 2 (E8ᵛ): 160 (169) × 91 mm; 73 R. Watermark similar to Heawood 2804. Notes set 66 R.

HT, v. 1: [double rule 82 mm] | OF | Humane Underſtanding. | [rule 82 mm]

v. 2: [double rule 84 mm] | OF | *Humane Underſtanding.* | [rule 83 mm]

*RT*s or headlines are brief versions of chapter titles in italics.

CW: Page. Vol. 1: C7ᵛ this E8ʳ Objects R2ʳ(Bo-) dies Y5ʳ *Courage*,
 Vol. 2: C7ᵛ (miſ-) apply H8ᵛ both I1ᵛ Mora- [Morality] Nlᵛ are Q7ʳ acci-[accidental] S1ʳ (Agree-) men [ment] S2ᵛ whether

Press figures. Vol. 1: 13 (A7ʳ)–1 18 (B1ᵛ)–1 43 (C6ʳ)–1 57 (D5ʳ)–2 62 (D7ᵛ)–1 70 (E3ᵛ)–2 86 (F3ᵛ)–2 106 (G5ᵛ)–2 118 (H3ᵛ)–1 148 (K2ᵛ)–2 171 (L6ʳ)–1 203 (N6ʳ)–1 230 (P3ᵛ)–1 265 (R5ʳ)–1 280 (S4ᵛ)–1 292 (T2ᵛ)–2 317 (U7ʳ)–2 331 (X6ʳ)–1

Vol. 2: none.
 Note: The figures in vol. 1 occur in a random pattern, on either inner or outer forme (except K, where they are on both; no figures occur on sheets a, *a, I, M, O, Q, Y–2A.

Notes: Basically a reprint of the 8th ed. (1721), following the text of the 5th ed. (no. 65), with same frontispiece. Book III, chap. 7 still omitted from contents in vol. 2, p. *iii* (see *Notes*, no. 61). A microfilm of the British Library copy, with 'Witten' in the 8th line of the title is in the collection, *The Eighteenth Century*, reel 3363, no. 2. It is corrected to 'Written' in most other copies I have seen, a stop-press correction (thereby achieving a second state).

References: Alston 7:86; Attig 236; Christophersen p. 92; ESTC t063946 (1st state).

Copies examined. State I: CaOTU (Locke L63.E82 1726; 2 cops.) [GOT] L (8475.e.28)

State II: O¹ (Vet.A4 e.1288–9, lacks front.; has 2 leaves bd. at end of vol.2 with advt. of books sold by Parker) C CaOTU³ (Locke L63.E82 1726a) CtY (K8.L79/f726) [GOT] MH (Phil.2114.20; vol.2 lacks title leaf) O² (Vet. A4 c.2041) Oj Osj (L10:27) PPL (Ia Lock/67823.O)

70. Essay. 10th ed., 1731. 2 vols. in 8°. Two issues, 2 states of 2d issue.

70A (1). First issue. Vol. 1, within a double rule, inner 155 × 89 mm, outer 161 × 94 mm: AN | ESSAY | . . . [&c. as in 9th ed. until 6th line:] In FOUR BOOKS. | [rule 88 mm] | Written by *JOHN* [swash J] *LOCKE*, Gent. | [rule 80 mm] | 𝕿𝖍𝖊 𝕿𝖊𝖓𝖙𝖍 𝕰𝖉𝖎𝖙𝖎𝖔𝖓, 𝖜𝖎𝖙𝖍 𝖑𝖆𝖗𝖌𝖊 𝕬𝖉𝖉𝖎𝖙𝖎𝖔𝖓𝖘. | . . .

[&c. as in 9th ed., until:] *Quam . . . quam | iſta . . . diſplicere!* | Cic. de Natur. Deor. l. I. | [rule 80 mm] | LONDON: | Printed for ARTHUR BETTESWORTH and CHARLES HITCH, at the | *Red Lion* in *Pater-noſter-Row*; EDMUND PARKER, at the *Bible and* | *Crown* in *Lombard-ſtreet*; JOHN PEMBERTON, at the *Buck* againſt | *St. Dunſtan's Church*, in *Fleet-ſtreet*; and EDWARD SYMON, | againſt the *Royal Exchange*, in *Cornhill*. M.DCC.XXXI.

70A (2). Vol. 2, within a double rule, inner 157 × 85 mm, outer 163 × 91 mm: AN | ESSAY | [&c. as in 9th ed., v. 2, except:] . . . [orn. vase of flowers 25 × 39 mm] | [rule 81 mm] | LONDON: | Printed for ARTHUR BETTESWORTH and CHARLES | HITCH, at the *Red Lion* in *Pater-noſter-Row*; | EDMUND PARKER, at the *Bible* and *Crown* in | *Lombard Street*; JOHN PEMBERTON, at the *Buck* | againſt *St. Dunſtan's Church* in *Fleet-Street*; and | EDWARD SYMON, againſt the *Royal Exchange* in | *Cornhill*. M.DCC.XXXI.

Coll: 8° (193 × 120 mm cut). Vol. 1: $^\pi$A^8 *a^8 A–Z^8 2A^2 [$ half signed; $^\pi$A4 signed 'a4']; 202 leaves; pp. *I–II i* ii–iv *v–xxx* 1–372 [= 404]. Vol. 2: A^4 a^4 B–Y^8 Z^4–2C^4 [$ half signed]; 192 leaves; pp. *i–xvi* 1–340 *341–368* [= 384]. First page of each sheet also signed 'Vol.II.'

70B.1 (1). Second issue, first state. Vol. 1 as first issue, except: . . . *Quam . . . quod* | *neſcias . . . ipſum* | *ſibi diſplicere!* | Cic. de Natur. Deor. 1. I. | [rule 86 mm] | LONDON: | Printed for EDMUND PARKER, at the *Bible* and | *Crown* over againſt the New Church in *Lombard-* | *Street*. M.DCC.XXXI.

70B.1 (2). Vol. 2 as second issue, first state, but with imprint: LONDON: | Printed for EDMUND PARKER, at the *Bible* | and *Crown*, over againſt the New Church | in *Lombard-Street*. M.DCC.XXXI.

70B.2 (1). Second issue, second state. Vol.1, as first state, except: LONDON: | Printed for EDWARD SYMON, over againſt the | *Royal Exchange* in *Cornhill*. M.DCC.XXXI.

70B.2 (2). Vol. 2, as second issue, first state, but with imprint: . . . LONDON: | Printed for EDWARD SYMON, over | againſt the *Royal Exchange* in *Cornhill*. | M.DCC.XXXI.

Coll: Vol. 1 as first issue, except $^\pi$A^8 (± $^\pi$A1); vol. 2, as first issue, except A^4 (± A1).

Contents. Vol. 1: $^\pi$A1^r (*I*) title (verso blank; in second issue, first state, verso has advt. for works of John Norris, sold by E. Parker), $^\pi$A2^r–A3^v (*i–iv*) dedication, $^\pi$A4^r–*a1^r (*v–xv*) reader's epistle, *a1^v (*xvi*) contents by book & chap., *a2^r–*a8^v (*xvii–xxx*) contents by book, chap. and sections, A1^r–E2^r (*1–67.5*) text of Book I, E2^r–2A2^v (*67 bottom 25 lines–372*) text of Book II.

Vol. 2: A1^r (*i*) title (verso blank), A2^r (*iii*) contents by book & chap., A2^v–a4^v (*iv–xvi*) contents by book, chap. and sections, B1^r–I4^v (*1–120*) text of Book III, I5^r–Z2^v (*121–340*) text of Book IV, Z3^r–2C4^r (*341–367*) index, 2C4^v blank.

Illustration: v. 1 has front. port. of Locke, by Vertue after Kneller, as in 8th ed. (no. 68).

Text (v.1, G4ᵛ; for both vols.): 44 lines; 154 (162)×87 mm; 69 R. Dedication set roman, 33 lines; reader's epistle in ital., 38 lines. Medium-quality laid paper watermarked with design of a bird on a perch.

HT, v.1, ᵖA2ʳ: [orn.rectangle, with eagle centered, 10×85 mm] | To the Right Honourable | THOMAS | Earl of *Pembroke* and *Montgomery*, | . . . [&c.]

 v.1, A1ʳ: [double rule 85 mm] | OF | Human Underſtanding. | [rule 84 mm]

 v.2, B1ʳ: [double rule 85 mm] | OF | *Humane Underſtanding.* | [rule 85 mm]

Headlines or RTs are italic chapter title summaries.

CW: Page. Vol. 1: A2ʳ De- [Demonſtration,] C7ᵛ this E8ʳ Objects R1ᵛ §.15. Be- [§.15. Beſides] R2ʳ think, Y5ʳ Reſemblances

 Vol. 2: C7ᵛ (miſ-) apply I1ᵛ Mora- [Morality] Q7ʳ acci- [accidental] S1ʳ (Agree-) ment S2ᵛ whether

Press figures. Vol. 1: x (ᵖA6ʳ)-2   xxv (*a6ʳ)-1   2 (A1ᵛ)-3   12 (A6ᵛ)-3   24 (B4ᵛ)-1   31 (B8ʳ)-1   34 (C1ᵛ)-1   41 (C5ʳ)-1   50 (D1ᵛ)-3   61 (D7ʳ)-3   76 (E6ᵛ)-1   78 (E7ᵛ)-1   86 (F3ᵛ)-3   96 (F8ᵛ)-3   98 (G1ᵛ)-2   114 (H1ᵛ)-3   116 (H2ᵛ)-1   142 (I7ᵛ)-1   155 (K6ʳ)-1   173 (L7ʳ)-2

Vol.2: none.

 Note: Figures in vol. 1 occur randomly only through sheet L, eleven on inner and eight on outer formes; only sheets A, B–F and H have figures on both formes.

Notes: A reprint based on the 9th ed. (1726; no. 69), following the text of the 5th ed. (no. 65), and the layout of the 6th. Title leaves of the second issue, both states, are cancellantia. I cannot determine any priority between the two states of the second issue. Watermarks and press figures are same in all issues. All have the first leaf ᵖA4 of vol. 1 signed 'a4' in error. Microfilm copies of the first issue and second issue, 2d state, are in the collection, *The Eighteenth Century*, reel 3363 no. 3 and reel 3364 no. 1 respectively.

References: Alston 7:87–9; Attig 237; Christophersen p. 92; ESTC (in order of issues and states) t063937, t187748, t063936.

Copies examined. First issue: O¹ (Vet.A4 e. 1510-1)   CaOTU (Locke L63.E82 1731a)   L (8475 e.10)

 Second issue, 1st state: O² (Vet.A4 e.788-9)   L (1608/23)   PPL (Ia Lock/70010.O)

 Second issue, 2nd state: O³ (Vet.A4 e.2125-6)   Ct   L (8405 e.35)

71. *Essay*. 11th ed., 1735. 2 vols. in 8°. Two issues.

71A (1). First issue. Vol. 1, within a double rule, inner 158×89 mm, outer 165×95 mm: AN | ESSAY | CONCERNING | Human Underſtanding. | . . . [&c. as in 10th ed., first issue, until:] THE ELEVENTH EDITION. | [rule 87 mm] | VOLUME I. | [rule 87 mm] | ECCLES. XI. 5 | *As thou*

... Spirit, nor | how ... with | Child: Even ... God, | who maketh all Things. [swash T] | [rule 86 mm] | Quam [swash Q] ... neſcias, | quam ... ſibi diſ- | plicere! | Cic. de Natur. Deor. l. I. | [rule 84 mm] | LONDON: | Printed for A. BETTESWORTH and C. HITCH at the *Red* | *Lion* in *Pater-Noſter-Row*; E. PARKER at the *Bible* and | *Crown* in *Lombard-Street*; J. and J. PEMBERTON at the | *Golden Buck* in *Fleetſtreet*; and E. SYMON againſt the *Royal-* | *Exchange* in *Cornhill*. MDCCXXXV.

71A (2) Vol. 2, within a double rule, inner 159 × 89 mm, outer 166 × 95 mm: AN | ESSAY | CONCERNING | Human Underſtanding. | [rule 86 mm] | BY | JOHN [swash J] LOCKE, Gent. | [rule 87 mm] | VOLUME II. | [rule 86 mm] | [orn., cornucopias surrounding basket of fruit, a cherub beneath, 29 × 35 mm] | [rule 85 mm] | LONDON: | ... [imprint as in vol. 1]

Coll: 8° (202 × 124 mm). Vol. 1: $^{\pi}A^8$ *a^8 A–Z^8 2A^2 [$ half signed]; 202 leaves; pp. *I–II i ii–iv v–xxx* 1–62 62 64–329 130 331–372 [= 404]. Page no. 62 repeated, 63 omitted.

Vol. 2: A–2A^8 [$ half signed]; 192 leaves; pp. *i–xvi* 1–229 232 231–233 134 235–334 535 336–340 *341–368* [= 384]. Vol. 2, pp. 230, 234 and 335 called '232', '134' and '535' respectively. First leaf of each sheet also signed 'Vol. II.'

71B (1). Second issue. Volume 1, as first issue, within a double rule, inner 170 × 89 mm, outer 174 × 94 mm, except: As ... nor | how ... is | with ... Works of | God ... Things. [swash T] | [rule 87 mm] | Quam [swash Q] ... quod | neſcias ... ipſum | ſibi diſplicere! | Cic. de Natur. Deor. l. I. | [rule 87 mm] | LONDON: | Printed for EDMUND PARKER, at the *Bible* and | *Crown* over-againſt the New Church in *Lombard-* | *Street*. M.DCC.XXXV.

71B (2). Vol. 2. As 10th ed. 1st issue (70A), within a double rule, 169 × 90 mm, outer 174 × 94 mm, except orn. is basket of leaves on pedestal upheld by cherubs, leaves & Chinese bell, 37 × 52 mm, and imprint reads: LONDON: | Printed for EDMUND PARKER, at the *Bible* | and *Crown*, over-againſt the New Church | in *Lombard-Street*. M.DCC.XXXV.

Coll: vol. 1 as first issue, except $^{\pi}A^8$ (±$^{\pi}$A1); vol. 2: π^2 A^8 (–A1) B–2A^8; 193 leaves, where the verso of π1 carries an advt., 'A Catalogue of the Works of the Rev. John Norris ...' sold by Edmund Parker.

Illustration, in v. 1: front. portrait of Locke by Vertue after Kneller, as in 8th ed. (no. 68), 159 × 95 mm on plate 176 × 100 mm. Likeness and quality deteriorating.

Contents. Vol. 1: $^{\pi}$A1^r (*I*) title (verso blank), $^{\pi}$A2^r–$^{\pi}$A3^v (*i–iv*) dedication, $^{\pi}$A4^r–*a1^r (*v–xv*) reader's epistle, *a1^v (*xvi*) contents of Books I–II by book & chap., *a2^r–*a8^v (*xvii–xxx*) contents by book, chap. & sections, A1^r–E2^r (1–67 line 5) text of Book I, E2^r–2A2^v (67 bottom 25 lines–372) text of Book II.

Vol. 2: A1ʳ (1st issue) or ᵗ2ʳ (2d issue) = (*i*) title (verso blank), A2ʳ (*iii*) contents by book & chap. A2ᵛ–A8ᵛ (*iv–xvi*) contents of Books III–IV by book, chap. & sections, B1ʳ–I4ᵛ (1–120) text of Book III, I5ʳ–Z2ᵛ (121–340) text of Book IV, Z3ʳ–2A8ʳ (*341–367*) index, 2A8ᵛ (*368*) blank.

Text (v.1, I4ʳ; same for both vols.): 44 lines; 163 (173) × 89 mm; 74 R. Dedication set 93R, 33 lines; reader's epistle, 37 lines 83 ital.; footnotes set 62 R. Medium-quality laid paper watermarked with a horn. RTs are brief chapter titles in italic.

HT, v.1, ᵗA2ʳ: [framed headpiece, fan shell on pedestal with birds & flowers, 23 × 86 mm] | To the Right Honourable | THOMAS | Earl of *Pembroke* and *Montgomery*, | . . . [&c., as in 1731 ed., no. 70]
v. l, A1ʳ: [double rule 87 mm] | OF | Human Underſtanding. | [rule 88 mm]
v. 2, B1ʳ: [double rule 92 mm] | OF | *Humane Underſtanding.* | [rule 91 mm]

CW: Page. Vol. 1: A2ʳ De- [Demonſtration,] G8ʳ §.3. *Attention* L2ʳ Ap- [Application.] N2ʳ (A-) gents, [gent,] S2ᵛ §.2. Ha- [§.2. Having] U4ʳ prov [proves (fallen type?)]
Vol. 2: D6ᵛ Conſtitution H1ʳ Re- [Reverend] L4ᵛ *Matter* [*Matter*,] Q2ᵛ Pro- [Propoſitions,] S8ᵛ Things [Things,]

Press figures. Vol. 1: *vi* (ᵗA4ᵛ)-2   *viii* (ᵗA5ᵛ)-1   *xxii* (*a4ᵛ)-1   *xxiv* (*a5ᵛ)-1   6 (A3ᵛ)-1   8 (A4ᵛ)-1   29 (B7ʳ)-2   31 (B8ʳ)-2   36 (C2ᵛ)-1   47 (C8ʳ)-1   50 (D1ᵛ)-1   52 (D2ᵛ)-1   78 (E7ᵛ)-1 OR 79 (E8ʳ)-2   93 (F7ʳ)-1   95 (F8ʳ)-1   98 (G1ᵛ)1   100 (G2ᵛ)-1   127 (H8ʳ)-2   128 (H8ᵛ)-2   140 (I6ᵛ)-1   142 (I7ᵛ)-1   150 (K3ᵛ)-1   152 (K4ᵛ)-1   166 (L3ᵛ)-1   168 (L4ᵛ)-1
Vol. 2: *vi* (A3ᵛ)-1   207 (O8ʳ)-2   208 (O8ᵛ)-1   212 (P1ᵛ)-2   216 (P4ᵛ)-2   232 (Q3ᵛ)-1   246 (R3ᵛ)-1   262 (S3ᵛ)-1   276 (T2ᵛ)-1   294 (U3ᵛ)-1   306 (X1ᵛ)-1   '535' (Y8ʳ)-3   336 (Y8ᵛ)-3   342 (Z3ᵛ)-1   365 (2A7ʳ)-3   366 (2A7ᵛ)-3

Note: Press figures in vol. 1 again occur randomly only through sheet L on both inner and outer formes. In vol. 2 again randomly only on sheets A and O–2A, in either forme of sheets, except O–P, Y and 2A where they occur in both.

Notes: Text is a reprint of the 10th ed. (no. 70), following the text of the 5th ed. (no. 65), and the layout of the 9th. The second issue has cancellans title leaves. Vol. 2 of the second issue has a leaf bound before the title whose verso contains an advertisement for works of John Norris sold by Parker. Page no. for v. 1, p. 356 has wrong font '3'. Vol. 2 has text in direction line on p. 115 (I2ʳ). A microfilm copy of the first issue is in the collection, *The Eighteenth Century*, reel 3364 no. 2.

References: Alston 7:90–1; Attig 238; Christophersen p. 92; ESTC 1st issue: t063935; 2d issue: t143487.

Copies examined: **First issue**: Y (with fig. on v.1, p. 79; lacks index)   O (Vet. A4 e.1180, 1179; with fig. on v.1, p. 78)   CLU-C   L (08463.e.74; with fig. on v. 1, p. 79)

Second issue: O (Vet. A4 e.1314–15; with fig. on v.1, p. 79)

72. *Essay*. 12th ed., 1741. 2 vols 8°. Two issues

72 A (1). First issue. Vol. 1, within a double rule, inner 161 × 85 mm, outer 169 × 92 mm: AN | ESSAY | CONCERNING | Human Underſtanding. | [rule 82 mm] | In FOUR BOOKS. | [rule 83 mm] | Written by *JOHN* [swash J] *LOCKE*, Gent. | [rule 81 mm] | The TWELFTH EDITION. | [rule 81 mm] | VOLUME I. | [rule 80 mm] | ECCLES. XI. 5. | As thou . . . Spirit, nor | how the . . . that is | with Child: . . . Works of | God who maketh all Things. [swash T] | [rule 82 mm] | *Quam bellum . . . quod* | *neſcias, . . . ipſum* | *ſibi diſplicere!* | Cic. de Natur. Deor. l. I. | [rule 80 mm] | LONDON: | Printed for C. HITCH in *Pater-noſter-Row*; | J. PEMBERTON in *Fleetſtreet*; J. BEECROFT in | *Lombard-Street*; and S. SYMON in *Cornhill*. | [rule 19 mm] | M DCC XLI.

72 A (2). Vol. 2, within a double rule, inner 163 × 88 mm, outer 168 × 92 mm: AN | ESSAY | CONCERNING | Human Underſtanding. | [rule 85 mm] | BY | *JOHN* [swash J] *LOCKE*, Gent. | [rule 86 mm] | The TWELFTH EDITION. | [rule 84 mm] | VOLUME II. | [rule 84 mm] | LONDON: | Printed for C. HITCH in *Pater-Noſter-Row*; | J. PEMBERTON in *Fleet-ſtreet*: J. BEECROFT | in *Lombard-Street*; and S. SYMON in *Cornhill*. | [rule 18 mm] | M DCC XLI.

Coll: 8° (220 × 124 mm cut). Vol. 1: $^{\pi}A^8$ *a^8 A–Z^8 2A^2 [$ half signed]; 202 leaves; pp. *I–II i ij–iv v–xxx 1 2–372* [=404].

Vol. 2: A–2A^8 [$ half signed]; 192 leaves; pp. *i–xvi 1–340 341–368* [=384]. First leaf of each sheet also signed 'VOL.II.'

72 B (1). Second issue. Vol. 1, within a double rule, inner 163 × 88 mm, outer 168 × 93 mm, as 1st issue, until 20th line:] *Quam bellum . . . quod ne-* | *ſcias, ipſum ſibi* | *diſplicere!* | Cic. de Nat. Deor. l. I. | [rule 84 mm] | LONDON: | Printed for JOHN BEECROFT, at the *Bible* and | *Crown*, over-againſt the New Church in *Lombard-* | *Street*. M DCC XLI.

72 B (2). Vol. 2, within a double rule, as 1st issue; with imprint as 2d issue, vol. 1.

Coll: vol. 1 as first issue, except $^{\pi}A^8$ (±$^{\pi}A1$); vol. 2 as first issue, except π^2 A^8 (–A1).

Contents: same as 11th ed. (1735, no. 71), except 2d issue, π1^r in vol. 2 is blank, π1^v has advt. for Works by John Norris for sale by Beecroft.

Illustration: frontispiece in vol. 1, same as in 8th ed. (no. 68).

Text: Vol. 1 (D7^r): 43 lines; 159 (169) × 89 mm. 74 R. Vol. 2 (G4^v): 44 lines; 163 (173) × 89 mm; 74 R. Dedication set 33 lines roman; reader's epistle, 38 lines ital. Footnotes set 50 lines (when occupy a whole page), 65 R. Both vols. on medium quality paper with fleur-de-lys watermark. Text in direction line, v.2 I2^r (p. 115).

HT, v. 1, $^{\pi}A2^r$: [rect. framed headpiece of seated lion surrounded by peacocks & leaves, 25 × 88 mm] | To the Right Honourable | THOMAS | Earl of *Pembroke* and *Montgomery*, | . . . [&c. as in 1731 ed., no. 71]

v.1, A2^r: [double rule 88 mm] | OF | Human Underſtanding. | [rule 89 mm] v.2, B1^r: [double rule 89 mm] | OF | *Humane Underſtanding.* | [rule 89 mm]

Headlines or RTs are chap. title summaries in italics, with page no. in outer corners.

CW: Page. Vol. 1: ^{2}A2^r De- [Demonſtration,] G8^r §.3. *Attention* L2^r Ap- [Application] R2^r think, Y5^r (Reſem-) blances

Vol. 2: C7^v (miſ-) apply H8^v both I1^v Morality N1^v are Q7^r acci- [accidental] S1^r (Agree-) ment

Press figures. Vol. 1: 18 (B1^v)-1 or 3   34 (C1^v)-1   48 (C8^v)-3   50 (D1^v)-1   61 (D7^r)-3   68 (E2^v)-1   74 (E5^v)-1 or 3   96 (F8^v)-3   108 (G6^v)-3   111 (G8^v)-1   125 (H7^v)-3   134 (I3^v)-1   141 (I7^r)-3   146 (K1^v)-1   156 (K6^v)-3   176 (L8^v)-3   189 (M7^r)-1   191 (M8^r)-1   205 (N7^r)-3   207 (N8^r)-1   221 (O7^r)-1   223 (O8^r)-1   228 (P2^v)-1   239 (P8^r)-3   244 (Q2^v)-3   272 (R8^v)-3   274 (S1^v)-1 [lst issue only]   276 (S2^v)-1, 3 or none   290 (T1^v)-1   324 (X2^v)-1   335 (X8^r)-3   354 (Z1^v)-3

Vol.2: none.

   Note: Vol. 1 has 21 sheets with figures I or 3 (none on §§ $^\pi$A, a, A, U or Y) of which 12 sheets have figures on inner and outer formes, randomly on the outer, and chiefly on 1^v or 8^r on the inner.

Notes: Reprint of the 11th ed. (1735; no. 71), following the text of the 5th ed. (no. 65), and the layout of the 9th (no. 69). It is the first to give the edition statement on the second volume. Second issue has cancellans title leaves. Some copies have no figure on p. 276; my copy has none on p. 354. Signature I2 of vol. 2 on same line with direction line. A microfilm copy of the first issue is in the collection, *The Eighteenth Century*, reel 3262 no. 29.

References: Alston 7:92-3; Attig 239; Christophersen p. 92; ESTC first issue: t063934, 2d: t165603.

Copies examined. First issue: Y (has figure 3 on p. 18, 3 on p. 74, 1 on 276, none on 354)   O^1 (Vet.A4 c.1368-9; has figure 1 on p. 18, 1 on 74 and 1 on 276, none on 48)   L (8464 bbb.34; has 3 on p. 18, 3 on 74, and none on 276)   MH-AH (has figure 1 on 18, 1 on 74, and 1 on 276)

   Second issue: O^2 (26782 e.27-8; has figure 3 on p. 74, 1 on 274 and 3 on 276)   PPL (Ia Lock/67283.O; has figure 1 on 18, and 3 on 276)

73. *Essay.* 13th ed., 1748. 2 vols. in 8°

Vol 1, within a double rule, inner 160 × 84 mm, outer 167 × 90 mm: AN | ESSAY | CONCERNING | Human Underſtanding. | . . . [&c. as in 12th ed., until 10th line:] The THIRTEENTH EDITION. | [rule 79 mm] | VOLUME I. | [rule 79 mm] | ECCLES. XI. 5. | As . . . nor how | the bones . . . with child: | Even ſo . . . maketh | all things. | [rule 80 mm] | Quam . . . quod neſcias, | quam . . . diſplicere! | CIC. *de Nat. Deor. l.* I. | [rule 78 mm] | LONDON: | Printed for S. BIRT, D. BROWNE, C. HITCH, J. HODGES, | J. OSWALD, J. SHUCKBURGH, A. MILLAR, J. BEE- | CROFT, J. WARD, M. COOPER, and the Executors of | H. PEMBERTON. M DCC XLVIII.

Vol. 2, within a double rule, inner 159 × 86 mm, outer 167 × 93 mm, as in 10th ed. of 1741 until the 9th line: The THIRTEENTH EDITION. | [rule 84 mm] | VOLUME II. | [rule 84 mm] | *LONDON:* | Printed for S. BIRT, D. BROWNE, C. HITCH, J. HODGES, | J. OSWALD, J. SHUCKBURGH, A. MILLAR, J. | BEECROFT, J. WARD, M. COOPER, and the Exe- | cutors of H. PEMBERTON. M.DCC.XLVIII.

Coll: 8° (195 × 123 mm cut). Vol. 1: $^\pi A^8$ $^*a^8$ A–Z^8 2A^2 [$ half signed]; 202 leaves; pp. *i* ii–iv *v–xxx 1* 2–372 [= 404].

Vol. 2: A–2A^8 [$ half signed]; 192 leaves; pp. *i–xvi* 1–169 172 171–263 164 265–340 *341–368* [= 384]. Page 170 called '172'; 264 called '164'. First page of each sheet also signed 'VOL. II.' in direction line.

Contents: Same as 11th ed. (1735), except vol. 2, p. *368* (2A8^v) has advt., 'A Catalogue of the Works' of John Norris, sold by Beecroft (similar to that in 1735 ed., 2d issue; no. 71B).

Illustration: frontispiece in vol. 1, same as 8th ed., 1721 (no. 68).

Text: Vol. 1 (D3^v): 44 lines; 162 (171) × 89 mm; 74 R. Vol. 2 (R4^r); 43 lines; 158 (168) × 90 mm; 74 R (p. 117 = I3^r has 45 lines, 160 (170) × 90 mm). Medium-quality laid paper without watermarks.

Headlines or RTs are chapter title summaries in large & small caps where brief, in italics when longer, or a mixture, e.g. '*Complex* IDEAS.' (v.1, pp. 123–6). Page no. at outer corners of headlines.

HT, v.1, $^\pi A2^r$: [framed headpiece, vase between peacocks & seated cupids, 28 × 88 mm] | To the Right Honourable | THOMAS | Earl of *Pembroke* and *Montgomery,* | . . . [&c.]

v.1, A1^r: [orn. rule of flowers & bird, 8 × 88 mm] | OF | Human Underſtanding.

v.2, B1^r: [double rule 88 mm] | OF | *Human Underſtanding.* | [rule 87 mm]

CW: Page. Vol. 1: ^{2}A2^r propoſed G8^r §.3. Attention N2^r (A-) gents, S2^v §.2. Having U4^r proves

Vol. 2: D6^v Conſtitution H1^r Reverend L4^v only Q2^v Pro- [Propoſitions,] S8^v Things T8^v Know- [Knowledge:]

Press figures. Vol.1: none.

Vol. 2: *v* (A3^r)-1   *xiv* (A7^v)-2   12 (B6^v)-1   110 (H7^v)-2   112 (H8^v)-1   152 (M1^v)-2 or none   173 (M7^r)-2   189 (N7^r)-1   191 (N8^r)-3   202 (O5^v)-1   214 (P3^v)-2   220 (P6^v)-1   229 (Q2^v)-1   234 (Q5^v)-3   253 (R7^r)-1   255 (R8^r)-1   265 (S5^r)-3   266 (S5^v)-1 or none   274 (T1^v)-3   281 (T5^r)-2   301 (U7^r)-3   303 (U8^r)-3   335 (Y8^r)-3   351 (Z8^r)-2   352 (Z8^v)-3   362 (2A5^v)-2

Note: Vol. 2 has randomly scattered figures about equally occurring on inner or outer formes, on both formes in §§ A, H, M–N, P–U and Z; no figures in §§ C–G, I–K and X.

Notes: Line-by-line reprint of 12th ed. (1741; no. 72) with text following that of 5th ed. (no. 65), and the layout of the 9th (no. 69). A microfilm copy of this edition is in the collection, *The Eighteenth Century,* reel 3364, no. 3.

References: Alston 7:84; Attig 240; Christophersen p. 92; ESTC t063944.

Copies examined: O¹ (Vet. A4 e.1414-15; lacks portrait & figure on 266) O² (Vet. A4 e. 1166; lacks figure on p. *xiv*) EXu L (8405 h.25) MH-AH PPL (Ia Lock/67345.O)

74. *Essay.* 14th ed., 1753. 2 vols. in 8°

Vol. 1, within a double rule, inner 160 × 81 mm, outer 167 × 88 mm: AN | ESSAY | CONCERNING | Human Underſtanding. | [rule 75 mm] | In FOUR BOOKS. | [rule 75 mm] | Written by *JOHN* [swash J] *LOCKE*, Gent. | [rule 74 mm] | The FOURTEENTH EDITION. | [rule 74 mm] | VOLUME I. | [rule 77 mm] | ECCLES. XI. 5 | As ... how | the ... child: | Even ... maketh | all things. | [rule 76 mm] | Quam ... neſcias, | quam ... diſplicere! | CIC. *de Nat. Deor. l.* I. | [rule 78 mm] | LONDON: | Printed for S. BIRT, D. BROWNE, T. and T. LONGMAN, J. | SHUCKBURGH, C. HITCH and L. HAWES, J. HODGES, | J. OSWALD, A. MILLAR, J. BEECROFT, J. and J. | RIVINGTON, J. WARD, and M. COOPER. 1753.

Vol. 2, within a double rule, inner 162 × 88 mm, outer 172 × 92 mm, as vol. 2 of 1748, except: BY | *JOHN* [swash J] *LOCKE*, Gent. | [rule 85 mm] | The FOURTEENTH EDITION. | [rule 85 mm] | VOLUME II. | [rule 86 mm] | *LONDON*: | Printed for S. BIRT ... LONGMAN, | J. SHUCKBURGH ... J. | HODGES ... BEECROFT, | J. and J. ... COOPER. | [rule 20 mm] | M.DCC.LIII.

Coll: 8° (200 × 124 mm trimmed). Vol. 1: ᵖA⁸ *a⁸ A–Z⁸ 2A² [$ half signed]; 202 leaves; pp. *I–II i* ii–iv *v–xxx 1* 2–372 [=404].

Vol. 2: A–2A⁸ [$ half signed]; 192 leaves; pp. *i–xvi 1*–340 *341*–368 [=384].

Contents: same as 11th–13th eds. (1735, 1741 and 1748; no. 71–73) except vol. 2, p. *368* (2A8ᵛ) has advt. for books sold by Beecroft.

Illustration: Vol. 1 has frontispiece of engr. port. of Locke, facing right, by Vertue after Kneller, as in 8th ed. (no. 68), subcaptioned '*Johannes Locke.*'

Text (v.2, E1ᵛ; same for both vols.): 44 lines; 158 (169) × 90 mm; 73 R. Medium-quality laid paper, with fleur-de-lys watermark. Page no. at outer ends of headlines.

HT, v. 1 A1ʳ: [framed headpiece of leaves & flowers 8 × 87 mm] | OF | Human Underſtanding. | [rule 88 mm]

Headlines or RTs: Chapter titles in italic, large & small capitals, or mixed, e.g. '*Of* POWER.'

CW: Page. Vol. 1: A2ʳ (pro-) cure ²A2ʳ propoſed G8ʳ §.3. N2ʳ (A-) gents, S2ʳ §.11. Having U4ʳ proves

Vol. 2: B3ʳ Propo- [Propoſitions,] D6ᵛ prove H1ʳ *Ideas*, L4ᵛ that Q2ᵛ Experience. S8ᵛ (an-) ſwer, T8ᵛ But

Press figures. Vol. 1: 52 (D2ᵛ)-2   63 (D8ʳ)-1   66 (E1ᵛ)-1   84 (F2ᵛ)-2   107 (G6ʳ)-2   112 (G8ᵛ)-1   122 (H5ᵛ)-1   136 (I4ᵛ)-2   142 (I7ᵛ)-1   159 (K8ʳ)-1   170 (L5ᵛ)-1

Vol. 2: none.

Notes: Reprint of no. 71 (1748), following the text of the 5th ed. (no. 65), and the layout of the 9th.

References: Alston 7:95; Attig 241; Christophersen p. 92; ESTC n006218.
Copies examined: O (Vet. A5 e. 2456-57) CaOTU (Locke L63.E82 1753) CtY (K8.L79/F753) L (1509/1505) MH (Phil.2115.31) PPL (Ia Lock/13.O, vol. 2 only)

75. *Essay*. 15th ed., 1753. 2 vols. 8° in 4s. Three issues (Berwick & s.l.)
75A (1). First issue. Vol. 1: AN | ESSAY | CONCERNING | HUMAN UNDERSTANDING. | IN FOUR BOOKS. | WRITTEN BY | JOHN [swash J] *LOCKE*, Gent. | The Fifteenth Edition. | VOLUME I. | ECCLES. XI. 5. | AS THOU KNOWEST NOT WHAT IS THE WAY OF THE SPIRIT, | NOR HOW THE BONES DO GROW IN THE WOMB OF HER THAT | IS WITH CHILD: EVEN SO THOU KNOWEST NOT THE WORKS | OF GOD, WHO MAKETH ALL THINGS. | Quam bellum eſt velle confiteri potius neſcire quod neſcias, quam iſta | effutientem nauſeare, atque ipſum ſibi diſplicere! | CIC. *de Nat. Deor. l.* I. | BERWICK: | PRINTED BY *ROBERT TAYLOR*. | [rule 20 mm] | M.DCC.LIII.
75A (2). Vol. 2: AN | ESSAY | CONCERNING | HUMAN UNDERSTANDING. | BY | JOHN [swash J] *LOCKE*, Gent. | The Fifteenth Edition. | VOLUME II. | Printed in the Year M.DCC.LIII.
Coll: 8° in 4s (219 × 122 mm cut). Vol. 1: π¹ a–c⁴ A–3G⁴ [$1 signed]; 225 leaves; pp. *I–II i* ii–iv *v–xxviii* 1 2–419 *420* [= 450]. First page of each sheet also signed 'VOL.I.' in direction line.
Vol. 2: π¹ a–b⁴ A–3E⁴ [$1 signed]; 213 leaves; pp. *i–xviii* 1 2–384 *385–408* [= 426]. First page of each gathering also signed 'VOL. II.'
75 B (1). Second issue. Vol. 1 as 1st issue, but lines 4, 6, & 8 in red (i.e. 'HUMAN UNDERSTANDING.' 'JOHN LOCKE, Gent.', and 'VOLUME I.') and imprint reads: Printed in the Year M. DCC. LIII.
75 B (2). Vol. 2 as 1st issue of vol. 2 but lines 4, 6, & 8 in red; same imprint.
Coll: as lst issue except v.1: π¹ (± π1); v.2, π¹ (± π1).
75 C. Same as 2d issue but titles in black ink.
Contents: Vol. 1: π1ʳ (*I*) title (verso blank), a1ʳ–a2ᵛ (*i–iv*) dedication, a3ʳ–b3ʳ (*v–xiii*) epistle to reader, b3ᵛ–A2ᵛ (*xiv–xxviii*) contents of Books I-II by book, chap. & sections, A3ʳ–K4ʳ (*1–75 line 12*) text of Book I, K4ʳ–3G4ʳ (75 bottom 12 lines–419) text of Book II, 3G4ᵛ blank.
Vol. 2: π1ʳ (*i*) title (verso blank), a1ʳ–b4ᵛ (*iii–xviii*) contents of Books III-IV by book, chap. & sections, A1ʳ–S2ʳ (*1–139*) text of Books III, S2ᵛ–3B4ᵛ (140–384) text of Book IV, 3C1ʳ–3E4ᵛ (*385–408*) index.
Illustration: poor-quality engr. port. of Locke by T. Phinn after Kneller, subscribed '*Johannes Locke.*' as frontispiece, 135 × 87 mm., on plate 156 × 100 mm.
Text (v.1, V4ʳ; same for both vols.) 38 lines; 160 (170) × 90 mm; 85 R with 1 mm leading; some pages with 37 lines. Good-quality laid paper, with vertical chainlines, no watermarks. Dedication set 30 lines, 107 R. Reader's epistle set 39 lines, 85 ital. Notes set 66 R. Contents and index set in double cols. divided by series of diamonds as rule.

HT, v.1 a1ʳ: To the RIGHT HONOURABLE | THOMAS | Earl of *Pembroke* and *Montgomery,* | *Baron* Herbert *of* Cardiff, *Lord* Roſs *of* Kendal, | ... [&c.]

v.1 A3ʳ: OF | HUMAN UNDERSTANDING.

Headlines or running titles have brief chapter titles in italic, with 'BOOK I.', e.g., (sheets C–G have 'B. I.') at inner margin on versos, 'Chap. IV.', e.g., at inner margins on rectos, with page no. at outer ends of headlines.

CW: Page. Vol. l: E4ᵛ §.7. FOR, R1ᵛ (ve-) ry 2M1ʳ new 3A4ʳ (Collecti-) on Vol. 2: A1ʳ Improvement, I4ᵛ §.37. I DO 2B1ʳ Con- [Connexion] 2Q4ʳ demon- [demonſtrated,]

Notes: The text is a reprint from a recent edition, probably the 10th or 11th (1731 or 1735), legally printed for Scotland in Berwick-upon-Tweed. The second issue, with cancellans title leaves, is of the same printing "possibly for illegal import into England." For a discussion of the legality of "printing in Scotland, Ireland, and the British possessions overseas, books which were copywrit in England and Wales" see John Feather's *The Provincial Book Trade in Eighteenth-Century England* (Cambridge, 1985), especially p. 142, n. 29, where this edition is described as "The only such book known to me with a deliberately falsified imprint".

It is a completely newly arranged typesetting, and does not follow the usual page-for-page reprints commonly found.

A microfilm copy of the first (Berwick) issue is in T*he Eighteenth Century* collection, reel 5327, no. 12.

References: Alston 7:96 (B issue, "12°"); Attig 242 (A issue); ESTC 1st issue: t121093, 2d issue n009329 (imprint: 'London?')

Copies examined: A issue: L (1609/500)
B: O (Vet.A5 e. 5278-79)
C: Y

76. *Essay*. New ed., 1759. Glasgow. 3 vols., 12° in 6s

AN | ESSAY | CONCERNING | HUMAN UNDERSTANDING. | IN FOUR BOOKS. | WRITTEN BY | JOHN [swash J] LOCKE, ESQ. | IN THREE VOLUMES. | VOLUME THE FIRST. | ['SECOND.', 'THIRD.'] | A NEW EDITION CORRECTED. | *As thou knoweſt not what is the way of the ſpirit,* | *nor how the bones do grow in the womb of her that* | *is with child: even ſo thou knoweſt not the works* | *of* GOD, *who maketh all things.* ECCL. xi. 5. | *Quam* [swash Q] *bellum eſt velle confiteri potius neſcire quod ne-* | *ſcias, quam iſta effutientem nauſeare, atque ipſum* | *ſibi diſplicere!* CIC. de Nat. Deor. l. 1. | GLASGOW: | Printed by ROBERT URIE. | MDCCLIX.

Coll: 12° in 6s (164 × 90 mm cut). Vol. 1: A–2K⁶ [$ half signed]; 198 leaves; pp. *i–iii* iv– xxxiii *xxiv* xxv–xli *xlii* 43–395 *396*.

Vol. 2: A–2L⁶ 2M² [$ half signed]; 206 leaves; pp. *i–ii* iii–xx 21–410 *411–412*.

Vol. 3: A–2H⁶ 2I² [$ half signed]; 188 leaves; pp. *i–ii* iii–xviii 19–376.

Contents. Vol. 1: A1ʳ (*i*) title (verso blank), A2ʳ–A4ᵛ (*iii*–viii) dedication, A5ʳ–B6ʳ (ix–xxiii) reader's epistle, B6ᵛ blank, C1ʳ (xxv) 'THE PARTICULAR CONTENTS.' by book & chap., C1ᵛ–D3ʳ (xxvi–xli) 'GENERAL' contents by book, chap. & sections, D3ᵛ blank, D4ʳ–M6ʳ (43–143) text of Book I, M6ᵛ–2K6ʳ (144–395) Book II, ch. 1–21, 2K6ᵛ blank.
Vol. 2: A1ʳ (*i*) title (verso blank), A2ʳ (iii) 'THE GENERAL CONTENTS.', A2ᵛ–B4ᵛ (iv–xx) 'THE PARTICULAR CONTENTS.', B5ʳ–T6ᵛ (21–228) text of Book II, ch. 22–3, U1ʳ–2M1ʳ (229–410) text of Book III, 2M2ʳ,ᵛ blank.
Vol. 3: A1ʳ (*i*) title (verso blank), A2ʳ (iii) 'THE GENERAL CONTENTS.', A2ᵛ–B3ᵛ (iv–xviii) 'THE PARTICULAR CONTENTS.', B4ʳ–2F6ᵛ (19–348) text of Book IV, 2G1ʳ–2I2ᵛ (349–376) 'THE INDEX.'
Text (v.3, Z3ʳ; same for all vols.): 36 lines; 131 (140) × 69 mm; 73 R. Chainlines horizontal, with part of a star as watermark (bottom of a foolscap?) at top of 6th leaf. Page no. at external ends of headlines. Dedication set 28 lines roman; reader's epistle 30 lines ital.
HT, v. 1, A2ʳ: To the RIGHT HONOURABLE | THOMAS | EARL OF | Pembroke and Montgomery, | Baron HERBERT of Cardiff, Lord | ROSS of Kendal, Par, Fitzhugh, Mar- | mion, St. Quintin, and Shurland; | Lord Lieutenant of the county of Wilts, | and of South-Wales.
v.1 D4ʳ, v. 2 B5ʳ and v.3 B4ʳ: OF | HUMAN UNDERSTANDING.
RT, with book numbers on versos, and chap. no. on rectos at inner margin, e.g. 'AN ESSAY ON Book III. | Ch. 33 HUMAN UNDERSTANDING.'
Catchwords: none.
Notes: Reprint edition. Text follows that of 9th ed., 1726 (no. 69). Vol. 2's 'general contents' (by book & chapter) is correct in listing eleven chapters of Book III (p. iii = A2ʳ). All previous editions have an incorrect listing. I have found no copies with a frontispiece portrait. The blank leaf at end of vol. 2 usually wanting. A microfilm copy of this edition is in the collection, *The Eighteenth Century*, reel 3121 no. 8.
References: Alston 7:97; Attig 243; ESTC t101518.
Copies examined: O (Vet.A5 f.1844–46) C CaOTU (Locke L63.E82 1759) L (1607/4943) MH (KPC948) Private owner (v.2–3 only) ViU (v.3 only)

77. *Essay.* 15th ed., 1760. 2 vols. 8°
Vol. 1: AN | ESSAY | CONCERNING | Human Underſtanding. | In FOUR BOOKS. | Written by JOHN [swash J] LOCKE, Gent. | The FIFTEENTH EDITION. | VOLUME I. | ECCLES. XI. 5. | *As thou knoweſt not what is the way of the Spirit, nor how the bones do* | *grow in the womb of her that is with child: Even ſo thou knoweſt not* | *the works of God, who maketh all things.* | Quam [swash Q] bellum eſt velle confiteri potius neſcire quod neſcias, quam | iſta effutientem nauſeare, atque ipſum ſibi diſplicere! | CIC. *de Nat. Deor. l.* I. | LONDON: | Printed for D. BROWNE, C. HITCH and L. HAWES, J. SHUCKBURGH, | A. MILLAR,

J. BEECROFT, J. RIVINGTON, J. WHISTON, S. | BAKER, T. PAYNE, J. WARD, R. BALDWIN, W. JOHNSTON, | W. OWEN, J. RICHARDSON, S. CROWDER, P. DAVEY and B. | LAW, T. LONGMAN, L. DAVIS, E. DILLY, R. WITHY, and M. COOPER. | [rule 26 mm] | M.DCC.LX.

Vol. 2: AN | ESSAY | CONCERNING | Human Underſtanding. | BY | JOHN [swash J] LOCKE, Gent. | The FIFTEENTH EDITION. | VOLUME II. | LONDON: | . . . [&c., as in vol. 1, except 4th-5th lines of imprint:] P. DAVEY and | B. LAW . . .

Coll: 8° (205 × 116 mm cut). Vol. 1: $^{\pi}A^8$ $^*a^8$ A–Z^8 2A^2 [$ half signed]; 202 leaves; pp. *I–II i* ii–iv *v–xxx* 1 2–372 [= 404]. First leaf of each sheet also signed 'VOL. I.' in direction line.

Vol. 2: A–2A^8 [$ half signed]; 192 leaves; pp. *i–xvi* 1 2–340 341–368 [= 384]. First leaf of each sheet also signed 'VOL.II.' in direction line.

Contents: Same as 11th–12th eds., 1735 and 1741 (no.71–72), including the advertisement for books sold by Beecroft, as in no. 72, at the end of vol.2 (2A8^v = p. 368).

Illustration: vol. 1 frontispiece: portrait of Locke by Vertue after Kneller, subscribed '*Johannes Locke*.' as in 8th ed. (no. 68).

Text (v.1 K3^r; same for both vols.): 44 lines; 160 (172) × 91 mm. 73 R. Poor-quality laid paper, without watermarks. Dedication set 38 lines roman; reader's epistle, 40 lines roman. Final page of index (v.2, 2A8^r) has engr. vignette of a putto seated within a shell, surrounded by birds & leaves, on a pedestal, 42 × 62 mm.

HT, v.1 $^{\pi}A2^r$: [orn., angel between birds, with scrolls, 28 × 82 mm] | To the RIGHT HONOURABLE | THOMAS | Earl of *Pembroke* and *Montgomery*, | *Baron* Herbert *of* Cardiff, . . . [&c. as in previous eds.]

v.1 A1^r: [orn. rule, book between angels, with leaves & flowers, 10 × 88 mm] | OF | Human Underſtanding. | [flower rule 90 mm]

v.2 B1^r: [orn. rule, sun with birds & leaves, 12 × 85 mm] | OF | Human Underſtanding. | [flower rule 86 mm]

Headlines or RTs are chapter titles in large & small caps if brief; in italics if long, e.g. '*Of the Modes of Thinking.*', 'INFINITY.'

CW: Page. Vol.1: A5^r (*them*-) ſelves, [*themſelves*] K6^v Place [Place.] P2^r diſ- [diſpleaſed] T2^v Con- [Conſciouſneſs] Y2^r diſ- [diſcerned]

Vol.2: B6^r Art [Art,] E2^r Exami- [Examination,] H4^v v. [*v.g.*] N7^r *Tra*- [*Trapezium*] T8^v Know- [Knowledge:] Z4^v De- [Deſcribed]

Press figures: None.

Notes: Reprint of the 13th ed., 1748 (no. 73), following the text of the 5th (1706) ed. and the layout of the 9th (no.69). A microfilm copy of this edition is in the collection, *The Eighteenth Century*, reel 3231 no. 1.

References: Alston 7:98; Attig 244; Christophersen p. 92; ESTC t063927.

Copies examined: L (528.i.20–21; with ms. notes by J.Horne Tooke) CtY (K8.L79/f690) MH (KE39995) O Oo (2 Td.2-3)

78. *Essay.* 'New ed.', 1765. Edinburgh. 3 vols. in-12°. Four isues.

78A. First issue: AN | ESSAY | CONCERNING | HUMAN UNDERSTANDING. | IN FOUR BOOKS. | WRITTEN BY | JOHN [swash J] LOCKE, GENT. | IN THREE VOLUMES. | VOLUME THE FIRST. | ['SECOND.', 'THIRD.'] | A NEW EDITION CORRECTED. | *As thou . . . nor how* | *the bones . . . child:* | *even . . .* GOD, *who ma-* | *keth all things.* ECCL. xi. 5. | *Quam* [swash Q] *. . . neſcias,* | *quam . . . diſpli-* | *cere!* CIC. de Nat. Deor. l. I. | EDINBURGH: | Printed by A. DONALDSON and J. REID, | For WILLIAM COKE. | MDCCLXV.

78B. Variant state, as first state except: ⟨Pr⟩inted by A. DONALDSON and J. REID. | For A. DONALDSON, and ſold at his ſhops | in *London* and *Edinburgh.* | MDCCLXV.

78C.1. Variant state of vol.1 only, same as 78B except: Printed by A. DONALDSON and J. REID. | For A. DONALDSON, and ſold at his ſhops in *London* | and *Edinburgh.* | MDCCLXV.

78D. Variant state, as first state of vols. 1–3 except: Printed by A. DONALDSON and J. REID. | For WILLIAM COKE, and FRANCIS SHAND. | MDCCLXV.

Coll: 12° in 6s (170 × 97 mm cut). Vol. 1: a–b⁶ c⁴ A–2B⁶ 2C⁴ [$ half signed]; 170 leaves; pp. *i–iii* iv–vii *viii* ix–xviii *xix–xx* xxi–xxxii *1* 2–306 *307–308* [= 340].

Vol. 2: a⁶ b³ A–2D⁶ 2E³ [$ half (+ Ee2) signed]; 174 leaves; pp. *i–iv* v–xviii *1* 2–329 *330* [= 348].

Vol. 3: a⁶ b³ (–b3 [= 2B1]) A–2A⁶ 2B¹ [$ half signed]; 153 leaves; pp. *i–iv* v–xvi *1* 2–273 *274* 275–290 [= 306].

First page of each sheet in each vol. also signed in direction line, respectively, 'VOL. I.', 'VOL. II.', 'VOL. III.'

Contents. Vol. 1: a1ʳ (*i*) title (verso blank), a2ʳ–a4ʳ (*iii*–vii) dedication, a4ᵛ–b3ᵛ (*viii*–xviii) epistle to reader, b5ʳ (*xix*) vol. 1 contents by book & chap., b5ᵛ–c4ᵛ (*xx*–xxxii) contents by book, chap. & sections, A1ʳ–C3ᵛ (*1*–306) text of Books 1–2.21, C4 blank.

Vol. 2: a1ʳ (*i*) title (verso blank), a2ʳ (*iii*) vol. 2 contents by book & chap., a2ᵛ–b3ᵛ (*iv*–xviii) contents by book, chap. & sections, A1ʳ–2E3ʳ (*1*–329) text of Books 2.22–3, 2E3ᵛ blank.

Vol. 3: a1ʳ (*i*) title (verso blank), a2ʳ (*iii*) vol. 3 contents by book & chap., a2ᵛ–b2ᵛ (*iv*–xvi) contents by book, chap. & sections, A1ʳ–Z5ʳ (*1*–273) text of Book 4, Z5ᵛ–2B1ʳ (*274*–290) index of all vols., 2B1ᵛ blank.

Text (v.3 P3ʳ; same for all vols.): 39 lines; 141 (150) × 76 mm; 72 R. Dedication set 32 lines 83R; reader's epistle, 39 lines 71 ital; footnotes and index set 54 R. Medium- quality laid paper with horizontal chainlines. First issue (78A) has paper watermarked with a fleur-de-lys. Page no. at external ends of headlines.

HT, v.1 a2ʳ To the RIGHT HONOURABLE | THOMAS | EARL OF | Pembroke and Montgomery, | Baron HERBERT of Cardiff, Lord ROSS | . . . [&c.]

v.1–3 (A1ʳ): OF | HUMAN UNDERSTANDING.

*RT*s or *Headlines* are chapter titles or title summaries set ital., with book number at inner margin of verso page, chap. numbers at inner margin of rectos, e.g.: *Of the degrees of aſſent*. Book IV. | Chap. 16. *Of the degrees of aſſent*.

CW: Page. Vol. 1: B12ᵛ propoſitions. H2ᵛ Theſe, Sl ᵛ (ex-) iſtence
  Vol. 2: D3ʳ (be-) ginning M3ʳ idea); U5ᵛ (dif-) ferent,
  Vol. 3: B2ᵛ immediate I1ʳ co- [co-exiſtence] R5ᵛ weakens

Press figures. These marks *appear* to be press figures: in most cases daggers are placed immediately before the first signature of each gathering. The first issue (78A) has an obelus (†) in vol. 2 only preceding signature b (p. xiii). Other issues (78B–D) have an obelus before the vol. 1 signatures a3, b3 and before the signatures of the first recto of each sheet A–X, A and 2A, and a double dagger (‡) before Y1r. Vol. 3 has an obelus before signatures b and A–2B. A note inserted (perhaps in Desmond Neill's handwriting) in the Bodleian Library's copy of the first issue (Vet.A5 f.1992-94) reads: "These three vols. [f.1992-4] are with, I think, one exception without the obelus mark which generally precedes $1 in Vet [f.1042] The exception is the 1/4 sheet b in volume II for there both copies ha[ve] † on $1. The obelus has been found to be the indication of the use of different paper in Foulis Press books, and it seems probable that the same convention is in use here. For the new set [f.1992] has a fleur-de-lys watermark which I have not found in the Vet. [f.1042-4] set."

Notes: Text is a reprint of 1759 ed. (no.76A). In most copies of the variant state (78B) the 'Pr' in 'Printed' on the title of vol. 1 fails to print. 78C is a variant state with imprint lines rearranged, found in vol. 1 of the Bodleian's 3rd set (Vet.A5 f.2132-4) only. The only priority between states I can determine is on the 'nothing-before-something' principle: that sheets without a dagger (or obelus) were printed before the other states with daggers. The titles with variant imprints were printed on a 'stop-press' basis, and are not cancellans. No frontispiece portrait included here.

References: Alston 7:99–100 (78A & B respectively); ESTC t168732 (78A); t184752 (78B); n006225 (78D).

Copies examined. 78A: O¹ (Vet.A5 f. 1992-94) C (7180 d.112-4) L (1509/2357) PPL (Ia Locke/3567.D (Mackenzie))
  78B: O² (Vet.A5 f. 1042-44) O³ v.2-3 (Vet.A5 f.2133-4)
  78C: O³ v.1 (Vet.A5 f.2132)
  78D: CaQMM (Cutter BG.79 1765; vol.1 only) CaOTU (Locke L63.E82 1765)

79. *Essay*. 16th ed., 1768. 2 vols. 8°
Vol. 1: AN | ESSAY | CONCERNING | Human Underſtanding. | . . . [&c. as in no. 77 (1760), except:] The SIXTEENTH EDITION. | . . . [&c. until 10th line:] As . . . the bones | do grow . . . thou | knoweſt . . .

things. | Quam [swash Q] . . . quam | iſta . . . diſplicere! | CIC. *de Nat. Deor. l.* I. | LONDON: | Printed for H. WOODFALL, A. MILLAR, J. BEECROFT, | J. and F. RIVINGTON, J. WHISTON, S. BAKER, T. PAYNE, | L. DAVIS and Co. R. BALDWIN, HAWES, CLARKE and | COLLINS, B. WHITE, W. JOHNSTON, W. OWEN, T. CASLON, | S. CROWDER, T. LONGMAN, B. LAW, C. RIVINGTON, | E. and C. DILLY, T. DAVIES, ROBINSON and ROBERTS, | A. and J. SHUCKBURGH, and T. CADELL. | [rule 25 mm] | M.DCC.LXVIII.

Vol. 2: AN | ESSAY | CONCERNING | Human Underſtanding. | BY JOHN [swash J] LOCKE, Gent. | The SIXTEENTH EDITION. | VOLUME II. | LONDON: | . . . [&c. as in vol. 1 except 'E. and C. DILLY.', that is, a period instead of a comma].

Coll: 8° (210 × 133 mm cut). Signatures and pagination as in no. 77 (1760). First leaf of each sheet signed, respectively, 'VOL.I.', 'VOL.II.'

Contents: Same as no. 77 (1760), following the pattern in the 11th–12th ed. (no. 71–72), including the advt. by Beecroft at the end of v. 2, p. 368 (2A8ᵛ).

Illustration: vol. 1 has engr. front. portrait of Locke, subscribed '*Johannes Locke.*' as in 8th ed.

Text (v.1 B3ʳ; same for both vols.): 44 lines; 162 (173) × 93 mm; 73 R. Medium-quality laid paper without watermarks. Page no. at external ends of headlines. Dedication set 34 lines roman; reader's epistle, 40 lines roman.

HT: v.1 ᵖA2ʳ: [framed headpiece of vase of flowers on pedestal surrounded by leaves and fruit, 27 × 84 mm] | To the RIGHT HONOURABLE | THOMAS | Earl of *Pembroke* and *Montgomery*, | . . . [&c.]

v.1 A1ʳ: [framed headpiece, flowers, 7 × 98 mm] | OF | Human Underſtanding. | [row of 5-starred rosettes 2 × 99 mm]

v.2 B1ʳ: [framed headpiece, angel face between open books, surrounded by leafy scrolls 11 × 89 mm] | OF | Human Underſtanding. | [orn. rule 2 × 92 mm]

RTs or headlines are chapter titles or title summaries in vol. 1, in large and small caps. (e.g. 'PERCEPTION.') or in italics or a mixture of both; in vol. 2, italics only.

CW: Page. Vol. 1: A2ʳ propoſed K1ʳ §.17. Having K6ᵛ Place. O4ʳ Priſon- [Priſon-Doors] P2ʳ diſpleaſed T2ᵛ Conſciouſneſs, Y2ʳ diſcerned

Vol. 2: B6ʳ Art [Art,] E2ʳ Exami- [Examination,] H4ᵛ v. [v.g.] N7ʳ Tra- [Trapezium] T8ᵛ Know- [Knowledge:] Z4ᵛ De- [Deſcribed,]

Press figures. Vol. 1: *ix* (ᵖA6ʳ)–2   *xxv* (*a6ʳ)–I   *xxx* (*a8ᵛ)–3   14 (A7ᵛ)–I   18 (B1ᵛ)–3   43 (C6ʳ)–I   45 (C7ʳ)–I   60 (D6ᵛ)–2   72 (E4ʳ)–I   74 (E5ᵛ)–3   96 (F8ᵛ)–I   111 (G8ʳ)–I   127 (H8ʳ)–I   139 (I6ʳ)–I   159 (K8ʳ)–I   162 (L1ᵛ)–I   190 (M7ᵛ)–I   196 (N2ᵛ)–I   203 (N6ᵛ)–I   209 (O6ʳ)–I   239 (P5ᵛ)–2   251 (Q6ʳ)–2   270 (R7ᵛ)–2   287 (S8ʳ)–2   294 (T3ᵛ)–I   315 (U6ʳ)–I   334 (X7ᵛ)–I   344 (Y4ᵛ)–3   350 (Y7ᵛ)–I   358 (Z3ᵛ)–I   365 (Z7ʳ)–3   370 (2A1ᵛ)–3

Vol. 2: *iii* (A2ʳ)–4   *xiii* (A7ʳ)–5   4 (B2ᵛ)–I   10 (B5ᵛ)–I   22 (C3ᵛ)–5   29

(C7ʳ)-5 34 (D1ᵛ)-5 40 (D4ᵛ)-3 50 (E1ᵛ)-1 52 (E2ᵛ)-1 68 (F2ᵛ)-5 70 (F3ᵛ)-5 82 (G1ᵛ)-5 84 (G2ᵛ)-2 98 (H1ᵛ)-1 105 (H5ʳ)-1 120 (I4ᵛ)-1 127 (I8ʳ)-3 132 (K2ᵛ)-4 142 (K7ᵛ)-2 153 (L5ʳ)-4 155 (L6ʳ)-4 168 (M4ᵛ)-4 170 (M5ᵛ)-4 184 (N4ᵛ)-1 190 (N7ᵛ)-5 200 (O4ᵛ)-4 203 (O6ʳ)-2 210 (P1ᵛ)-2 212 (P2ᵛ)-5 226 (Q1ᵛ)-2 228 (Q2ᵛ)-5 248 (R4ᵛ)-4 254 (R7ᵛ)-5 268 (S6ᵛ)-5 271 (S8ʳ)-4 281 (T5ʳ)-4 282 (T5ᵛ)-4 296 (U4ᵛ)-5 302 (U7ᵛ)-4 308 (X2ᵛ)-5 318 (X7ᵛ)-5 322 (Y1ᵛ)-2 333 (Y7ʳ)-2 338 (Z1ᵛ)-3 349 (Z7ʳ)-2 364 (2A6ᵛ)-4 366 (2A7ᵛ)-4

   Note: In vol. 1 all sheets have figures, randomly placed, on either inner or outer forme, but not on a page with a signature nor on 5ʳ; only sheets *a, C, E, N, Y and Z signed on both formes. In vol. 2 all sheets have figures on both inner and outer formes, and not on signed pages.

Notes: Reprint of no. 77, following text of 5th ed. (1706; no. 65), and the layout of the 9th (no. 69). It was advertised for sale in the *London Chronicle* for May 16/19, 1772 at 9/- bound. A microfilm copy of this edition is in the collection, *The Eighteenth Century*, reel 3231 no. 2.

References: Alston 7:101; Attig 246; Christophersen p. 92; ESTC t063928.

Copies examined: Y CtY (K8.L79/f768) [GOT] L (528 i.22-3) MH (*AC85.H7375Zz768*l*; O.W. Holmes family copy) O (Vet.A5 e.1832-3) Oc PPL (Ia Lock/66363.O; ex lib. Benjamin & Richard Rush)

80. *Essay*. 17th ed., 1772. Dublin. Vol.1. only found. 8°

Vol. 1: AN | ESSAY | CONCERNING | Human Underſtanding. | In FOUR BOOKS. | Written by JOHN [swash J] LOCKE, Gent. | The SEVENTEENTH EDITION. | VOLUME I. | ECCLES. XI. 5. | As . . . bones | do . . . child: Even ſo thou | knoweſt . . . things. | Quam . . . quam | iſta . . . diſplicere! | CIC. de Nat. Deor. 1. I. | DUBILN: [sic] | Printed by and for HENRY SAUNDERS, in CASTLE-STREET. | [rule 25 mm] | M,DCC,LXXII.

Collation of vol. 1: 8° (206 × 120 mm cut) π1 A–Z⁸ 2A² [$ 2 signed (-2A2)]; 187 leaves; pp. *i–ii* 1 2–372 [= 374]. First page of each gathering also signed 'VOL. I.' Untrimmed edge on one leaf measures 220 × 138 mm.

Contents of vol. 1: π1ʳ (*i*) title (verso blank), A1ʳ–2A2ᵛ (1–372) text of Books I–II.

Text (A4ᵛ): 44 lines; 161 (170) × 91 mm; 73 R. Fair-quality laid paper without watermarks.

HT, vol.1 [framed headpiece, basket of flowers, centered 10 × 88 mm] OF | Human Underſtanding. | [orn. rule 90 mm]

*RT*s or headlines are brief chap. titles in italics.

CW: Page. Vol. 1 : A5ʳ (*them-*) *ſelves* K1ʳ *heavenly* K6ʳ *Place*. O4ʳ *Priſon-* [*Priſon-Doors*] P2ʳ *diſpleaſed* T2ᵛ *Conſciouſneſs*, Y2ʳ *diſcerned*

Notes: This appears to be a reprint of the 16th (1768) London edition. But the only copy I have been able to locate is defective: not only is vol. 2 lacking, but vol. 1 lacks quires B–E and G, and repeats L (i.e. lacks pp. 17–80 and

97–112; 161–176 repeated). The preliminary sheets of vol. 1 probably contained dedication, contents and reader's epistle but are lacking. If a perfect copy is ever located, I expect the 1777 Dublin edition (no. 82) to be a re-issue of this one: the typesetting of vol. 1 here and of the 1777 edition is identical. The title-page in the 1777 edition could incorporate stop-press corrections in the 'volume' line and in the imprint. I suspect the project of publishing this edition was suspended, and not resumed until the 1777 edition. Not listed in ESTC.
Reference: Attig 247.
Copy examined: O (Vet.A5 e.4625)

81. *Essay*. 17th ed., 1775. 2 vols.in 8°
Vol. 1: AN | ESSAY | CONCERNING | Human Underſtanding. | IN FOUR BOOKS. | Written by JOHN [swash J] LOCKE, Gent. | The SEVENTEENTH EDITION. | VOLUME I. | ECCLES. xi. 5. | As thou . . . *the bones* | *do grow* . . . *thou* | *knoweſt* . . . *all things*. | Quam [swash Q] . . . quam | iſta . . . diſplicere! | CIC. *de. Nat. Deor. l.* I. | [double rule 91 mm] | LONDON: | Printed for JOHN BEECROFT, N°.23, Pater-noſter-Row; | W. STRAHAN, J. and F. RIVINGTON, J. WHISTON, S. BAKER, | T. PAYNE, L. DAVIS; HAWES, CLARKE and COLLINS; | B. WHITE, W. OWEN, T. CASLON, S. CROWDER, | T. LONGMAN, B. LAW, C. RIVINGTON, J. WILKIE, | E. and C. DILLY, T. DAVIES, J. ROBSON, T. BECKET, | G. ROBINSON, T. CADELL, W. RICHARDSON, T. EVANS, | and E. JOHNSTON. | [rule 24 mm] | M DCC LXXV.
Vol. 2: AN | ESSAY | CONCERNING | Human Underſtanding. | BY | JOHN [swash J] LOCKE, gent. | The SEVENTEENTH EDITION. | VOLUME II. | [double rule 90 mm] | . . . [imprint as in vol. 1]
Coll: 8° (220 × 115 mm cut). Vol. 1: $^{\pi}A^8$ $^*a^8$ A–Z^8 2A^2 [$ half signed]; 202 leaves; pp. *I–II i* ii–iv *v–xxx* 1 2–372 [= 404].
Vol. 2: A–2A^8 [$ half signed]; 192 leaves; pp. *i–xvi* 1 2–340 *341–368* [= 384].
Contents: same as first issue of 1741 ed. (no. 72), following the text of the 5th ed. (no. 65), and the layout of the 9th. Vol. 2, p. 368 (2A8^v) has advt. of books sold by Beecroft. Bodleian Library's copy of vol. 1 has an extra leaf at end (χ1) with advt. for books sold by Donaldson (cf. no. 78).
Illustration: vol. 1 has engr. front., portrait of Locke by Vertue after Kneller, as in previous editions, subcaptioned: '*Johannes Locke*.'
Text (v.1 K3^r; same for both vols.): 44 lines; 160 (171) × 92 mm; 73 R. Medium-quality laid paper, without watermark. Dedication set 34 lines roman; reader's epistle, 40 lines roman. Notes set 66 R; when they occupy a full page they are 60 lines.
HT, v.1 $^{\pi}$A2^r: [headpiece of mixed rules of flowers and crosses 27 × 80 mm] | To the RIGHT HONOURABLE | THOMAS | Earl of *Pembroke* and *Montgomery*, | . . . [&c.]
v.1 A1^r: [orn. rule of flowers and crosses 8 × 90 mm] | OF | Human Underſtanding. | [orn. rule 90 mm]

v.2 B1ʳ: [triple row of rules of flowers, 10 × 92 mm] | OF | Human Underſtanding. | [orn. rule 92 mm]

Headlines or RTs are brief chapter titles in italics.

CW: Page. Vol. 1: A5ʳ (*them-*) *ſelves*, [*ſelves and*] K1ᵛ *heavenly* K6ᵛ *Place.* O4ʳ *Priſon-* [Priſon-Doors] P2ʳ *diſ-* [diſpleaſed] T2ᵛ *Conſciouſneſs,* Y2ʳ *diſ-* [diſcerned]

Vol. 2: B6ʳ *Art*, E2ʳ *Exami-* [Examination,] H4ᵛ *v.g.* N7ʳ *Trapezium* T8ᵛ *Know-* [Knowledge:] Z4ᵛ *Propo-* [Propoſitions]

Press figures. Vol. 1: *viii* (ᵖA5ᵛ)–I *xi* (ᵖA7ʳ)–7 *xxx* (*a8ᵛ)–7 14 (A7ᵛ)–5 16 (A8ᵛ)–3 18 (B1ᵛ)–5 29 (B7ʳ)–3 43 (C6ʳ)–3 45 (C7ʳ)–3 59 (D5ᵛ)–3 60 (D6ᵛ)–3 73 (E5ʳ)–3 74 (E5ᵛ)–5 86 (F3ᵛ)–5 96 (F8ᵛ)–3 98 (G1ᵛ)–3 109 (G7ʳ)–5 120 (H4ᵛ)–7 122 (H5ᵛ)–7 143 (I8ʳ)–I 144 (I8ᵛ)–I 146 (K1ᵛ)–7 156 (K6ᵛ)–7 170 (L5ᵛ)–I 172 (L6ᵛ)–I 188 (M6ᵛ)–I 191 (M8ʳ)–I 201 (N5ʳ)–7 206 (N7ᵛ)–I 222 (O7ᵛ)–I 224 (O8ᵛ)–7 237 (P7ʳ)–7 238 (P7ᵛ)–I 253 (Q7ʳ)–7 255 (Q8ʳ)–7 260 (R2ᵛ)–I 267 (R6ʳ)–7 274 (S1ʳ)–7 285 (S7ʳ)–7 297 (T5ʳ)–7 308 (U2ᵛ)–7 318 (U7ᵛ)–7 332 (X6ᵛ)–I 334 (X7ᵛ)–7 340 (Y2ᵛ)–I 342 (Y3ᵛ)–7 358 (Z3ᵛ)–7 360 (Z4ᵛ)–7 372 (2A2ᵛ)–I

Vol. 2: *viii* (A4ᵛ)–3 *xi* (A6ᵛ)–3 2 (B1ᵛ)–I 16 (B8ᵛ)–7 26 (C5ᵛ)–7 32 (C8ᵛ)–I 41 (D5ʳ)–7 47 (D8ʳ)–I 52 (E2ᵛ)–I 63 (E8ʳ)–I 78 (F7ᵛ)–I 80 (F8ᵛ)–3 91 (G6ᵛ)–7 96 (G8ᵛ)–7 102 (H3ᵛ)–7 109 (H7ʳ)–I 121 (I5ʳ)–7 132 (K2ᵛ)–3 139 (K6ᵛ)–5 148 (L2ᵛ)–3 155 (L6ᵛ)–5 162 (M1ᵛ)–3 164 (M2ᵛ)–I 190 (N7ᵛ)–5 192 (N8ᵛ)–3 196 (O2ᵛ)–5 206 (O7ᵛ)–5 219 (P6ʳ)–3 220 (P6ᵛ)–3 232 (Q4ᵛ)–5 235 (Q6ᵛ)–5 246 (R3ᵛ)–5 253 (R7ʳ)–3 269 (S7ʳ)–5 270 (S7ᵛ)–5 274 (T1ᵛ)–7 288 (T8ᵛ)–7 299 (U6ʳ)–3 301 (U7ʳ)–5 310 (X3ᵛ)–I 317 (X7ʳ)–7 326 (Y3ᵛ)–7 336 (Y8ᵛ)–7 348 (Z6ᵛ)–7 351 (Z8ʳ)–5 360 (2A4ᵛ)–7 366 (2A7ᵛ)–5

Note: Vol. 1 has each sheet figured on both inner and outer formes, except sheets *a, T and 2A, randomly, but not on a page carrying a signature. Vol. 2 has figures similarly placed to vol. 1, and only § I lacks a figures on both formes.

Notes: Text is a line-by-line reprint of the 1768 edition (no. 77), following the text of the 5th ed., and the layout of the 9th (no. 69), with minor changes. For the very first time in a London edition, the book and chapter contents for Book III correctly lists all eleven chapter titles (see no. 61, *Notes*). A microfilm copy of this edition is in the collection, *The Eighteenth Century*, reel 3233, no. 4.

References: Alston 7:102; Attig 248; Christophersen p. 92; ESTC t110403.

Copies examined: O (Vet.A5 e.2233, 2232; with χ1 leaf) Ck (Keynes) L (1609/3730) PU (B1290 1775)

82. *Essay*. '18th ed.', Dublin, 1777. 2 vols. 8°

Vol. 1: AN | ESSAY | CONCERNING | Human Underſtanding. | IN FOUR BOOKS. | Written by JOHN [swash J] LOCKE, Gent. | The EIGHTEENTH EDITION. | VOLUME I. | ... [&c., as in no. 78, with

quotations from Eccles. & Cicero, until imprint:] DUBLIN: | Printed by and for H. SAUNDERS, W. SLEATER, | D. CHAMBERLAINE, and J. POTTS. | [rule 24 mm] | M,DCC,LXXVII.
Vol. 2: AN | ESSAY | CONCERNING | Human Underftanding. | BY | JOHN [swash J] LOCKE, Gent. | The EIGHTEENTH EDITION. | VOLUME II. | DUBLIN: | . . . [imprint as vol. l until last line:] M DCC LXXVII.

Coll: 8° (205 × 126 mm cut). Vol. 1: $^{\pi}A^8$ *$^{*}a^8$ A-Z^8 $2A^2$ [$ 2 signed (-2A2)]; 202 leaves; pp. *I-II i-iii* iv *v-xxx* 1 2-372 [= 404]. First page of each sheet also signed 'VOL. I.' in direction line.

Vol. 2: A-Z^8 $2A^8$ [$ 2 signed, sheets A-K; $ half signed, L-2A]; 192 leaves; pp. *i-xvi* 1 2-340 *341-368* [= 384]. Also signed 'VOL. II.' in direction line of 1st page of each sheet.

Contents. Vol. 1: $^{\pi}A1^r$ (*1*) title (verso blank), $^{\pi}A2^r$-$^{\pi}A3^v$ (*i-iv*) dedication, $^{\pi}A4^r$-*$^{*}a1^r$ (*v-xv*) reader's epistle, *$^{*}a1^v$ (*xvi*) contents by book & chap., *$^{*}a2^r$-*$^{*}a8^v$ (*xvii-xxx*) contents by book, chap. & sections, $A1^r$-$2A2^v$ (*1-372*) text of Books I-II.

Vol. 2: $A1^r$ (*i*) title (verso blank), $A2^r$-$A8^v$ (*iii-xvi*) contents by book, chap. & sections, $B1^r$-$Z2^v$ (*1-340*) text of Books III-IV, $Z3^r$-$2A8^r$ (*341-367*) index, $2A8^v$ blank.

Text: 44 lines; 162 (171) × 92 mm; 74 R. Good-quality laid paper, without watermarks. Page no. at outer ends of headlines.

HT, v.1: as 1777 ed. (no. 80)
  v.2: [framed headpiece, 2 flowers centered, with crossed stems 10 × 86 mm] | OF | Human Underftanding. | [orn. rule 88 mm]

Headlines are chapter title summaries in italics.

CW: Page. Vol. 1: $A5^r$ (*them-*) *felves* $K1^r$ §.17. Having $K6^r$ Beings, $O4^r$ Prifon- [Prifon-Doors] $P2^r$ difpleafed $T2^v$ *Confcioufnefs*, $Y2^r$ difcerned
  Vol. 2: $B6^r$ Art, $E2^r$ Exami- [Examination,] $H4^v$ *v.g.* $N7^r$ *Trapezium* $T8^v$ Know- [Knowledge:] $Z4^v$ De- [Defcribed]

Notes: A reissue of the 1772 edition (no. 80), almost line-for-line, with a note at end of 'Epistle to the Reader' still stating "In the 6th [1710] edition there is very little added or altered . . ." The book and chap. contents for Book III again lists only ten chapters, following the pattern set by all previous London editions until the 17th (no. 81).

References: Alston 7:103; Attig 250; ESTC t185902.

Copies examined: O^1 (Vet.A5 e.2027-28)   L (1560/3083) O^2 (Vet. A5 e.4626: vol. 2 only; lacks sheet 2A)

83. *Essay*. 'New ed.', 1777. Edinburgh. 3 vols. 12° in 6s
AN | ESSAY | CONCERNING | HUMAN UNDERSTANDING. | IN FOUR BOOKS. | WRITTEN BY | JOHN [swash J] LOCKE, ESQ. | IN THREE VOLUMES. | VOLUME THE FIRST. | ['SECOND.', 'THIRD.'] | A NEW EDITION CORRECTED. | *As thou . . . nor how* | *the bones . . . with child:* | *even fo . . . the works of* GOD, *who maketh all* | *things.*

Eccl. xi. 5. | *Quam* [swash Q] *bellum . . . nefcias,* | *quam . . . difplicere!* | Cic. de Nat. Deor. l. i. | EDINBURGH: | Printed for J. Dickson and C. Elliot. | [rule 26 mm] | M,DCC,LXXVII.
Coll: 12° in 6s (174 × 100 mm cut). Vol. 1: A–2K⁶ [$ half signed]; 198 leaves; pp. *i–iii* iv–xxiii *xxiv* xv–xli *xlii* 43–395 396. First page of each sheet also signed 'Vol.I.' in direction line.
Vol. 2: A–2L⁶ 2M³ [$ half signed]; 207 leaves; pp. *i–ii* iii–xx 21 410 *411–414*. Also 'Vol.II.'
Vol. 3: A–2H⁶ 2I³ [$ half signed]; 189 leaves; pp. *i–ii* iii–xviii 19–376 *377–378*. Also 'Vol.III.'
Contents. Vol. 1: A1ʳ (*i*) title (verso blank), A2ʳ–A4ᵛ (iii–viii) dedication, A5ʳ–B6ʳ (ix–xxiii) 'Epistle to the Reader', B6ᵛ blank, C1ʳ (xxv) contents by book, chap. & sections, C1ᵛ–D3ʳ (xxvi–xli) contents by book, chap. and sections, D3ᵛ blank, D4ʳ–M6ʳ (43–143) text of Book 1, M6ᵛ–2K6ʳ (144–395), text of Book 2, ch.1–21, 2K6ᵛ blank.
Vol. 2: A1ʳ (*i*) title (verso blank), A2ʳ (iii) contents by book, chap. and sections, A2ᵛ–B4ᵛ (iv–xx) contents by book, chap. & sections, B5ʳ–2M1ʳ (21–410) text of Book 2, chap. 22–Book 3, 2M2–3 blank.
Vol. 3: A1ʳ (*i*) title (verso blank), A2ʳ (iii) contents by book & chap., A2ᵛ–B3ᵛ (iv–xviii) contents by book. chap. & sections, B4ʳ–2F6ᵛ (19–348) text of Book 4, 2G1ʳ–2I2ᵛ (349–376) index, 2I3 blank.
Text (v.1 H3ʳ, same for all vols.): 36 lines; 131 (139) × 73 mm; 73 R. Vol. 1 dedication set 27 lines, 94 R with .9 mm leading between lines; reader's epistle set 30 lines, 85 ital. with .9 mm leading between lines. Medium-quality paper with fleur-de-lys watermark. Page no. at outer corners of headlines.
HT, v.1, A2ʳ: To The RIGHT HONOURABLE | THOMAS | EARL OF | PEMBROKE and MONTGOMERY, | Baron Herbert of Cardiff, Lord | Ross OF Kendal, Par, Fitzhugh, | . . . [&c.]
v.1 D4ʳ, v.2 B5ʳ and v.3 B4ʳ: OF | HUMAN UNDERSTANDING.
*RT*s with book and chap. no. at inner margins, e.g. 'An Essay On Book II. | Ch. 28. Human Understanding.'
Catchwords: none.
Notes: Reprint of no. 78 (1765), again without a portrait (frontispiece) of Locke.
References: Alston 7:104; Attig 249; ESTC n006222
Copies examined: Y L (1568/4546) O (Vet. A5 e.4878–80)

84. *Essay.* 17th ed., 1786. 2 vols. 8°
Vol. 1: AN | ESSAY | CONCERNING | Human Underftanding. | In Four Books. | Written by JOHN [swash J] LOCKE, Gent. | The Seventeenth Edition. | VOLUME I. | Eccles. xi. 5. | *As thou . . . the bones* | *do grow . . . thou* | *knowe*ſ*t . . . God, who maketh all things.* | Quam [swash Q] bellum . . . quam | ifta . . . difplicere! [wrong font !] | Cic. de Nat. Deor. l. i. | LONDON: | Printed for H.

Woodfall, A. Millar, J. Beecroft, | J. and F. Rivington, J. Whiston, S [full stop faint or wanting] Baker, T. Payne, | L. Davis and Co. R. Baldwin, Hawes, Clarke and | Collins, B. White, W. Johnston, W. Owen, T. Caslon, | S. Crowder, T. Longman, B. Law, C. Rivington, | E. and C. Dilly, T. Davies, Robinson and Roberts, | A. and J. Shuckburgh, and T. Cadell. | [rule 26 mm] | M.DCC.LXXXVI.

Vol. 2: as vol. 1, omitting quotations from Eccles. and Cicero, except: 'VOLUME II.' and 'S. BAKER.'

Coll: 8° (205 × 107 mm). Vol. 1: $^\pi$A^8 *$^\pi$a^8 A–Z^8 2A^2 [\$ 2 (–2A2) signed]; 202 leaves; pp. *i–xxxii 1* 2–372 [= 404]. 'VOL.I.' on \$ 1 of each sheet.

Vol. 2: A^4 B^4 ^{2}B8 C–2A^8 [\$ 2 signed]; 192 leaves; pp. *i–xvi 1* 2–340 *341–368* [= 384]. First page of each gathering also signed 'VOL.II.' in direction line.

Contents. Vol. 1: $^\pi$A1^r (*i*) title (verso blank), $^\pi$A2^r–$^\pi$A3^v (*iii–vi*) dedication, $^\pi$A4^r–*a1^r (*vii–xvii*) reader's epistle, *a1^v (*xviii*) contents by book and chap., *a2^r–*a8^v (*xix–xxxii*) contents by book, chap. and section, A1^r–E2^r (*1–67.5*) text of Book I, E2^v–2A2^v (*67.–25–372*) text of Book II.

Vol. 2: A1^r (*i*) title (verso blank), A2^r (*iii*) contents by book & chap., A2^v–B4^v (*iv–xvi*) contents by book, chap. and sections, ^{2}B1^r–I4^v (*1–120*) text of Book III, I5^r–Z2^v (*121– 340*) text of Book IV, Z3^r–2A8^r (*341–367*) index, 2A8^v blank.

Illustration: front. is engr. portrait of Locke by Vertue after Kneller, subscribed '*Johannes Locke*.' as in previous editions.

Text (v. 1 H3^v; same for both vols.): 44 lines; 161 (171) × 93 mm; 74 R. Medium-quality laid paper, without watermark.

Headlines or running titles are brief chapter titles set in large & small capitals, italics, or mixed, as in 1768 ed. (no. 79) with page no. at outer ends of headlines.

CW: Page. Vol. 1: A5^r *Praiſe* D1^r and K1^v thoſe K8^v other [other,] P2^r diſpleaſed S8^v (an-) ſwer Y2^r diſcerned

Vol. 2: B6^r Art, D1^r were E2^r Exami- [Examination,] H4^v *v.g.* N7^r *Trapezium* T1^r (A-) greement T8^v Know- [Knowledge:] Z4^v (Propo-) ſitions

Press figures: None.

Notes: Text is a reprint of the 1768 or 1775 edition (no. 79, 81). It is curious that the names of the booksellers as printed match the imprint of the 1768 edition line for line and word for word, given the frequency with which the names change from edition to edition.

References: Alston 7:106; Attig 251; ESTC n009330 ('1768' in error in imprint).

Copy examined: CtY (K8.L79/f786; front. port. present earlier, missing in 1995)

85. *Essay*. '19th' ed., Dublin, 1786. 2 vols.in 8°

Vol. 1: AN | ESSAY | CONCERNING | Human Underſtanding. | . . . [&c. as in no. 82, except:] The Nineteenth Edition. | . . . [&c. with

quotations from Eccles. and Cicero, as in no. 80, with imprint:] DUBLIN: | Printed by and for W. SLEATER, H. CHAMBERLAINE, | and J. POTTS. | [rule 27 mm] | M,DCC,LXXXVI.
Vol. 2: AN | ESSAY | CONCERNING | Human Underſtanding. | BY | JOHN LOCKE, Gent. | The NINETEENTH EDITION. | VOLUME II. | DUBLIN: | . . . [&c. as in vol. 1]
Coll: 8° (206 × 125 mm cut). Vol. 1: $^\pi$A^8 *a^8 A–Z^8 2A^2 [$2 signed]; 202 leaves; pp. *i–xxxii 1* 1–372 [=404]. First page of each gathering also signed 'VOL.I.'
Vol.2: A–Z^8 2A^8 [$2 signed]; 192 leaves; pp. *i–xvi 1* 2–340 *341–368* [=384]. First page of each gathering also signed 'VOL.II.'
Contents. Vol. 1: $^\pi$A1^r title (verso blank), $^\pi$A2^r–$^\pi$A3^v dedication, $^\pi$A4^r–*a1^r reader's epistle, *1^v book and chap. contents, *a2^r–*a8^v book, chap. & section contents, A1^r–E2^r (*1–67*.5) text of Book I, E2^r–2A2^v (p. 67, line 25–p. 372) text of Book II.
Vol. 2: same as 1777 ed. (no. 82).
Text: 44 lines; 162 (169; varies) × 91 mm; 73 R. Good-quality laid paper with an illegible watermark and lettering 'EAUJ^{EUN}'. Footnotes set 66 R. At head of each chapter is an Oxford rule. Topical headings to text inset with the text block in italics. Again, the contents of Book III and its chapters lists only ten chapters, an error that was finally corrected in the 17th London ed. of 1775 (see no. 61, 81, *Notes*).
HT, v.1 $^\pi$A2^r: [Oxford rule 86 mm] | To the RIGHT HONOURABLE | THOMAS | Earl of *Pembroke* and *Montgomery*, | *Baron* Herbert *of* Cardiff, *Lord* Roſs *of* Kendal, | . . . [&c.]
v.1 A1^r: [Oxford rule 85 mm] | OF | Human Underſtanding. | [French rule 50 mm]
Catchwords: Page. Vol. l: A5^r *Praiſe* K1^v thoſe L2^r Ap- [Application:] P2^r diſpleased T2^v have Y2^r diſcerned
Vol. 2: B6^r Art, E2^r Exami- [Examination,] H4^v *v.g.* N7^r *Trapezium* T8^v Know- [Knowledge:] Z4^v De- [Deſcribed,]
Note: Line-by-line reprint of the Dublin edition of 1777 (no. 82).
References: Alston 7:105; Attig 252; ESTC t185514.
Copy examined: O (Vet A5. e.2474–5)

86. *Essay*. 18th ed., 1788. 2 vols. in 8°.
AN | ESSAY | CONCERNING | Human Underſtanding. | IN FOUR BOOKS. | Written by JOHN [swash J] LOCKE, Gent. | THE EIGHTEENTH EDITION. | VOLUME I. ['II.'] | ECCLES. xi. 5. | As . . . bones | do . . . thou | knoweſt . . . things. | Quam [swash Q] . . . quam | iſta . . . diſplicere! | CIC. de Nat. Deor. *l*. I. | [Oxford rule 89 mm] | LONDON: | Printed for J. F. and C. RIVINGTON, T. and T. PAYNE, L. DAVIS, | B. and B. WHITE, S. CROWDER, T. LONGMAN, B. LAW, C. | RIVINGTON, J. ROBSON, J. JOHNSON, C. DILLY, N. CO- | NANT, G. G. J. and J. ROBINSON, T. CADELL, J. NICHOLS, | W.

RICHARDSON, W. OTRIDGE, J. SEWELL, W. GOLDSMITH, | S. HAYES, LEIGH and SOTHERBY, [sic] W. LOWNDES, G. and T. | WILKIE, SCATCHERD and WHITAKER, and R. RYAN. | [rule 28 mm] | MDCCLXXXVIII.

Coll: 8° (210 × 125 mm cut). Vol. 1: A^8 *a^8 B–2F^8 2G^2 [$ half signed]; 242 leaves; pp. *i–xxxii* 1 2–32 30 34–452 [= 484]. First page of each gathering also signed 'VOL.I.' in direction line. Page 33 called '30'.

Vol. 2: A–2E^8 2F^2 [$ half signed]; 226 leaves; pp. *i–xvi* 1 2–410 411–436 [= 452]. Leaf D3 signed 'D'; 2D6 signed 'Z3'. First page of each gathering also signed 'VOL.II.'

Contents: Vol. 1: A1^r (*i*) title (verso blank), A2^r–A3^v (*iii–vi*) dedication, A4^r–*a1^r (*vii–xvii*) reader's epistle, *a1^v (*xviii*) contents by book & chap., *a2^r–*a8^v (*xix–xxxii*) contents by book, chap. & sections, B1^r–2G2^v (*1–452*) text of Books 1–2.

Vol. 2: A1^r (*i*) title (verso blank), A2^r (*iii*) contents by book & chap., A2^v–A8^v (*iv–xvi*) contents by book, chap. & sections, B1^r–L3^v (*1–150.27*) text of Book 3, L3^v–2D5^v (*150.-4–4l0*) text of Book 4, 2D6^r–2F2^v (*411–436*) index.

Text: 39 lines; 163 (173) × 91 mm; 84 R. Medium-quality laid paper, watermarked with 2 small circles. Page no. at outer corners of headlines. Topical headings set roman within page block at outer margins.

HT, v.1 and 2 B1^r [Oxford rule 91 mm] | OF | Human Underſtanding. | [rule 90 mm]

Headlines or RTs: Summarised chapter titles set in large and small roman or in italics, or a mixture of both.

CW: Page. Vol. 1: D1^r know- [knowledge?] O1^v (*com-*) *poſition*; [*poſition**;] P7^r com- [complex] S7^v Whe- [Whether] Y1^r cohe- [coheſion,] 2D5^r unde- [undetermined,]

Vol. 2: B6^r and, E2^r §.4. H4^v was N7^r believe T2^r demon- [demonſtrated] 2D2^r incoherent.

Note: No CW on Y1^v.

Press figures. Vol.1: *x* (A5^v)–2   *xx* (*a2^v)–5   *xxvii* (*a6^r)–6   6 (B3^v)–4   18 (C1^v)–2   '30' (D1^v)–8   50 (E1^v)–6   70 (F3^v)–4   94 (G7^v)–4   106 (H5^v)–I   112 (H8^v)–5   118 (I3^v)–4   125 (I7^r)–5   130 (K1^v)–5   132 (K2^v)–I   146 (L1^v)–8   152 (L4^v)–2   166 (M3^v)–6   172 (M6^v)–8   180 (N2^v)–7   186 (N5^v)–4   207 (O8^r)–2   208 (O8^v)–6   214 (P3^v)–3   234 (Q5^v)–3   242 (R1^v)–8   266 (S5^v)–3   287 (T8^r)–3   294 (U3^v)–8   301 (U7^r)–6   319 (X8^v)–6   333 (Y7^v)–2   349 (Z7^r)–2   366 (2A7^v)–4   368 (2A8^v)–8   382 (2B7^v)–3   392 (2C4^v)–2   399 (2C8^r)–I   400 (2C8^v)–2   402 (2D1^v)–4   431 (2E8^r)–4   446 (2F7^v)–8   450 (2G1^v)–3

Note: Unusually there are 2 figures on the outer forme and 1 on the inner of § 2C.

Vol. 2: *x* (A5^v)–3   6 (B3^v)–4   22 (C3^v)–3   24 (C4^v)–8   36 (D2^v)–7   46 (D7^v)–2   56 (E4^v)–7   58 (E5^v)–2   66 (F1^v)–3   82 (G1^v)–4   100 (H2^v)–3   106 (H5^v)–5   114 (I1^v)–3   128 (I8^v)–4   143 (K8^r)–3   148 (L2^v)–2   162 (M1^v)–2   180 (N2^v)–8   205 (O7^r)–2   210 (P1^v)–2   240 (Q8^v)–3   244

(R2ᵛ)–1   246 (R3ᵛ)–8   266 (S5ᵛ)–8   268 (S6ᵛ)–3   287 (T8ʳ)–4   292 (U2ᵛ)–8   299 (U6ʳ)–3   318 (X7ᵛ)–8   333 (Y7ʳ)–4   351 (Z8ʳ)–4   352 (Z8ᵛ)–2   358 (2A3ᵛ)–5   376 (2B4ᵛ)–5   390 (2C3ᵛ)–7   392 (2C4ᵛ)–8   404 (2D2ᵛ)–2
Notes: For first time in London editions, title-pages of both vols. are the same, including the quotations. Text is a reprint of the 6th edition (1710, no. 66) following the edition of 1786 (no. 84) but not line-by-line. There is no frontispiece portrait.
References: Alston 7:107; Attig 253; ESTC t110610.
Copies examined: O (Vet.A5 e.2957–8)   CaQMM (BG.L79.1788: vol. 1 only)   L (1560/740)

87. *Essay*. 19th ed., 1793. 2 vols. in 8°. With 'Conduct', 'Reading and Study', &c.
AN | ESSAY | CONCERNING | Human Underſtanding. | Written by JOHN [swash J] LOCKE, Gent. | THE NINETEENTH EDITION. | TO WHICH ARE NOW FIRST ADDED, | I. An Analyſis of Mr. Locke's Doctrine of Ideas, on a large Sheet. | II. A Defence of Mr. Locke's Opinion concerning Perſonal Identity, | with an Appendix. | III. A Treatiſe on the Conduct of the Underſtanding. | IV. Some Thoughts concerning Reading and Study for a Gentleman. | V. Elements of Natural Philoſophy. | VI. A New Method of a Common-Place Book. | EXTRACTED FROM THE AUTHOR'S WORKS. | [French rule 51 mm] | VOLUME I. [II.] | [French rule 50 mm] | LONDON: | Printed for T. Longman, B. Law and Son, J. Johnſon, C. Dilly, | G.G.J. and J. Robinſon, T. Cadell, W. Richardſon, W. Otridge, | J. Sewell, F. and C. Rivington, W. Goldſmith, S. Hayes, Leigh and | Sotheby, T. Payne, W. Lowndes, R. Faulder, B. and J. White, | G. and T. Wilkie, Scatcherd and Whitaker, R. Ryan, and E. Jeffereſy. | 1793.
Coll: 8° (211 × 129 mm cut). Vol. 1: A⁸ a⁸ B–2K⁸ [$ half signed]; 272 leaves; pp. *i–xxxii* 1 2–510 *511–512* [= 544]. Direction line on first page of each $ also signed 'Vol.I.'
Vol. 2: a⁸ (–a1) B–2G⁸ 2H–2K⁴ [$ half (–a2) signed]; 251 leaves; pp. *i–xiv* 1 2–298 *299–300* 301–320 *321–322* 323–401 *402–404* 405–412 *413–414* 415–440 *441* 442–459 *460–488* [= 502]. First page of each sheet also signed 'Vol.II.'
Illustration: Vol. 1 has table inserted after p. *xxxii* measuring 412 × 515 mm, mentioned as item I on the title-page, recto headed 'An ANALYSIS of Mr. LOCKE's Doctrine of IDEAS in his ESSAY on HUMAN UNDERSTANDING.'
Contents. Vol. 1: A1ʳ (*i*) title (verso blank), A2ʳ–A3ᵛ (*iii–vi*) dedication, A4ʳ–a1ʳ (*vii–xvii*) reader's epistle, a1ᵛ–a8ᵛ (*xviii–xxxii*) contents by book, chap. & sect., B1ʳ–F6ᵛ (*1–76*) text of *Essay*, Book I, F7ʳ–2E6ʳ (*77–427* line 10) text of Book II, 2E6ʳ–2K7ᵛ (*427* bottom 21 lines–*510*) text of Book III, chap. 1–6, 2K8ʳ,ᵛ blank.
Vol. 2: a2ʳ (*i*) title (verso blank), a3ʳ (*iii*) contents of this vol, a3ᵛ blank,

a4ʳ–a8ᵛ (*v–xiv*) contents of the *Essay* by book, chap. & sections, B1ʳ–U5ᵛ (*1–298* text of *Essay* Book III ch. 7–Book IV, U6ʳ (*299*) section title (verso blank), U7ʳ–X8ᵛ (301–320) Law's 'Defence', Y1ʳ (*321*) section title (verso blank), Y2ʳ–2D1ʳ (323–401) text of 'Conduct', 2D1ᵛ blank, 2D2ʳ (*403*) section title (verso blank), 2D3ʳ–2D6ᵛ (405–412) text of 'Reading & Study', 2D7ʳ (*413*) section title (verso blank), 2D8ʳ–2F4ᵛ (415–440) text of 'Elements', 2F5ʳ (*441*) section title (verso blank), 2F5ᵛ–2F6ʳ (442–443) diagram for index to a 'Common-place book', 2F6ᵛ–2G6ʳ (444–459) text of 'Method' for a commonplace book, 2G6ᵛ blank, 2G7ʳ–2K1ᵛ (461–482) alphabetical index to *Essay*, 2K2ʳ–2K3ᵛ (*483–486*) 'Index to the additional pieces in the second volume', 2K4 blank.

Text (v.1 K1ᵛ; same for both vols.): 41 lines; 172 (183) × 96 mm; 80 R. Wove paper without visible watermarks. Page no. in outer corners of headlines. Dedication set roman 36 lines; reader's epistle 41 lines roman. Notes to text set 62R within page block.

HT, v.1 A2ʳ (Dedication): [double rule 96 mm] | TO THE RIGHT HONOURABLE | THOMAS, | Earl of *Pembroke* and *Montgomery*, | Baron Herbert *of* Cardiff, . . . [&c.]

v.1 B1ʳ and v.2 B1ʳ: [double rule 96 mm] | OF | Human Underſtanding.

Section titles, v. 2 U6ʳ: A | DEFENCE | OF | MR. LOCKE'S OPINION | CONCERNING | PERSONAL IDENTITY.
v.2 Y1ʳ: OF THE | CONDUCT | OF THE | UNDERSTANDING.
v.2 2D2ʳ: SOME THOUGHTS | CONCERNING | READING AND STUDY | FOR A | GENTLEMAN.
v.2 2D7ʳ: ELEMENTS | OF | NATURAL PHILOSOPHY.
v.2 2F5ʳ: A NEW | METHOD | OF A | COMMON-PLACE-BOOK. | TRANSLATED OUT OF THE FRENCH FROM THE SECOND | VOLUME OF THE BIBLIOTHEQUE UNIVERSELLE.

Headlines or RTs are abbreviated chapter titles in italics, with (e.g.) 'Book 4.' at inner end of headlines on versos, and 'Ch.17.' at inner end on rectos.

CW: Page. Vol. 1: C4ᵛ propo- [propoſition] K1ʳ charac- [characters] Q2ʳ ſwift- [ſwiftneſs] Y5ᵛ philo- [philoſophize,] 2E2ᵛ under- [underſtanding] 2I7ʳ com- [comprehended]
Vol. 2: E2ʳ ſigni- [ſignification] I4ᵛ pro- [production.] M7ʳ ſtand- [ſtanding] U3ʳ whe- [whether] Z1ᵛ under- [underſtandings] 2D6ʳ fur- [furniſhed]

Press figures. Vol. 1: *xiv* (A7ᵛ)–6 *xviii* (a1ᵛ)–6 2 (B1ᵛ)–5 16 (B8ᵛ)–7 31 (C8ʳ)–6 47 (D8ʳ)–5 50 (E1ᵛ)–7 68 (F2ᵛ)–8 78 (F7ᵛ)–6 96 (G8ᵛ)–5 100 (H2ᵛ)–9 106 (H5ᵛ)–2 114 (I1ᵛ)–4 128 (I8ᵛ)–6 142 (K7ᵛ)–I 148 (L2ᵛ)–4 175 (M8ʳ)–8 191 (N8ʳ)–8 192 (N8ᵛ)–I 203 (O6ʳ)–3 205 (O7ʳ)–4 210 (P1ᵛ)–3 224 (P8ᵛ)–6 240 (Q8ᵛ)–6 253 (R7ᵛ)–2 262 (S3ᵛ)–6 281 (T5ʳ)–4 294 (U3ᵛ)–5 306 (X1ᵛ)–9 324 (Y2ᵛ)–5 335 (Y8ʳ)–8 338 (Z1ᵛ)–5 345 (Z5ʳ)–3 354 (2A1ᵛ)–9 368 (2A8ᵛ)–6 374 (2B3ᵛ)–5 380 (2B6ᵛ)–9 386 (2C1ᵛ)–6 400 (2C8ᵛ)–2 414 (2D7ᵛ)–I 422 (2E3ᵛ)–I 432 (2E8ᵛ)–6 436 (2F2ᵛ)–I 463 (2G8ʳ)–4 479 (2H8ʳ)–2 496 (2I8ᵛ)–I 500 (2K2ᵛ)–I 502 (2K3ᵛ)–6

Vol. 2: *viii* (a5ᵛ)–I 15 (B8ʳ)–I 16 (B8ᵛ)–4 28 (C6ᵛ)–2 30 (C7ᵛ)–5 36 (D2ᵛ)–9 57 (E5ʳ)–5 58 (E5ᵛ)–2 68 (F2ᵛ)–9 79 (F8ʳ)–5 96 (G8ᵛ)–6 111 (H8ʳ)–4 116 (I2ᵛ)–9 126 (I7ᵛ)–5 130 (K1ᵛ)–8 141 (K7ʳ)–5 159 (L8ʳ)–9 160 (L8ᵛ)–6 171 (M6ʳ)–6 190 (N7ᵛ)–I 194 (O1ᵛ)–9 205 (O7ʳ)–I 221 (P7ᵛ)–4 223 (P8ʳ)–I 232 (Q4ᵛ)–5 235 (Q6ʳ)–4 246 (R3ᵛ)–4 249 (R5ʳ)–2 258 (S1ᵛ)–2 264 (S4ᵛ)–6 285 (T7ʳ)–9 287 (T8ʳ)–2 303 (U8ʳ)–6 308 (X2ᵛ)–5 318 (X7ᵛ)–6 328 (Y4ᵛ)–8 350 (Y7ᵛ)–6 365 (2A7ʳ)–4 366 (2A7ᵛ)–8 381 (2B7ʳ)–2 383 (2B8ʳ)–8 386 (2C1ᵛ)–2 415 (2D8ʳ)–6 429 (2E7ᵛ)–6 431 (2E8ʳ)–8 446 (2F7ᵛ)–6 448 (2F8ᵛ)–8 450 (2G1ᵛ)–9 471 (2H4ʳ)–5 476 (2I2ᵛ)–6 484 (2K2ᵛ)–6

Notes: Text of the *Essay* is a reprint of the 1788 ed. (no. 86) with additional material as indicated in the title. Item I was first published as a broadside in 1766 (no. C1766-1) and was included by Bishop Edmund Law in his 1777 edition of the *Works* (no. 370). Item II is a reprint of Law's *Defence of Mr. Locke's Opinion*, first published separately in 1769 (no. C1769-1), and also included in the 1777 *Works*.

These 2 vols., with a collective t.p. (vol. 2's a1 leaf, lacking here) are the first two vols. of the *Works* ed. of 1794 (no. 371). The text of the *Essay* does not include excerpts from Locke's exchange with Stillingfleet, since the *Letters to Stillingfleet* are printed in the *Works* edition. A microfilm copy of this edition is in the collection, *The Eighteenth Century*, reel 3231, no. 3.

References: Alston 7:108; Attig 255; Christophersen p. 92-3; ESTC t063929.

Copies examined: O¹ (Vet. A5 e. 4921) C L (526 i.30-31) O² (26782 e. 62-63; vol. 1 lacks fold. plate) WaU (192.2/Es7)

88. *Essay*, 1795. 3 vols. in 12°, *with* 'Conduct'. Two states.

88 A. First state: AN | ESSAY | CONCERNING | Human Underſtanding; | WITH | *Thoughts* [swash T] *on the Conduct of the Underſtanding.* | BY JOHN [swash J] LOCKE, ESQ. [swash Q] | COLLATED WITH DESMAIZEAUX'S EDITION. | To which is prefixed, | THE LIFE OF THE AUTHOR. [swash Ts] | IN THREE VOLUMES. | [double rule 22 mm] | VOL. I. ['II.', 'III.'] | [double rule 21 mm] | LONDON: | PRINTED FOR C. BATHURST, C. NOURSE, T. CARNAN, F. NEW- | BERY, R. CATER, R. BROTHERTON, W. JOHNSTONE, [sic] | P. VALLIANT, N. CONANT, T. DAVIES, L. DA- | VIES, A. MILLAR, R. TONSON, G. KEITH, | W. OWEN, AND | L. HAWIS. [sic] | [rule 10 mm] | 1795.

Coll: 12° (188 × 114 mm uncut). Vol. 1: a¹² (±a1) b¹² C² d² (–d2) A-L¹² M⁶ (–M6 = d1?) [$ half signed]; 164 leaves; pp. *i-iii* iv-xv *xvi-xvii* xviii-xix xx-xxi xxii-xxiv *xxv* xxvi-xxx *xxxi* xxxii-liii *liv* 1 2-271 272-274 [= 328]. First page of each gathering also signed 'VOL.I.' in direction line. Vol. 1 p. xiv printed 'vix'; xli inverted; xlvi as 'xliv' (D. Neill informs me in his copy, p. xlviii "the x has slipped and the 'l' is missing" and that p. 154 reads '5 4'; in MH copy the 'xl' for p. xlviii has risen 2 mm above the rest of the line.)

Vol. 2: a⁶ b² A-L¹² [$ half signed]; 140 leaves; pp. *i–iii* iv–xvi *1* 2–264 [= 280]. First page of each gathering also signed 'VOL.II.' in direction line.
Vol. 3: a⁶ b² (-b2) A-M¹² ²M¹⁰ [$ half signed)]; 161 leaves; pp. *i–iii* iv–xiv *1* 2–225 226–227 228–308 [= 322]. First page of each gathering also signed 'VOL.III.' in direction line.

88 B (Second state): As first state until imprint: LONDON: | PRINTED FOR ALLEN & WEST, PATER NOSTER ROW, J. MUNDELL | AND Co. EDINBURGH, MOZLEY & Co. GAINSBOROUGH, | AND J. & A. DUNCAN, GLASGOW. | [rule 10 mm] | 1795.

Coll: Vol. 1 as first issue except a¹² (± a1).
Vol. 2–3 as first issue except a⁶ (± a1).

Contents. Vol. 1: a1ʳ (*i*) title (verso blank), a2ʳ–a8ʳ (*iii*–xv) contents of vol., a8ᵛ blank, a9ʳ–a10ʳ (*xvii*–xix) dedication, a10ᵛ blank, a11ʳ–b3ᵛ (*xxi*–xxx) reader's epistle, b4ʳ–d1ʳ (*xxxi*–liii) life of author (from Le Clerc), d1ᵛ blank, A1ʳ–D11ᵛ (*1*–70 line 22) text of Book I, D11ᵛ–M4ʳ (70 bottom 8 lines–271) text of Book II, ch. 1–21, M4ᵛ–M5ᵛ (272–74) blank.

Vol. 2: a1ʳ (*i*) title (verso blank), a2ʳ–a8ᵛ (*iii*–xvi) contents of vol., A1ʳ–F4ᵛ (*1*–128) text of Book II, ch.22–33, F5ʳ–L12ᵛ (129–264) text of Book III.

Vol. 3: a1ʳ (*i*) title (verso blank), a2ʳ–b1ᵛ (*iii*–xiv) contents of vol., A1ʳ–K5ʳ (*1*–225) text of Book IV, K5ᵛ blank, K6ʳ–N10ᵛ (227–308) text 'Of the Conduct of the Understanding.'.

Text (v.1 C5ʳ; same for all vols.): 40 lines; 145 (153) × 80 mm; 72 R. Wove paper watermarked '1794'. Page no. at outer ends of headlines. Book no. at inner margin of headlines on versos, e.g. 'Book. IV.'; chap. no. at inner margins on rectos, e.g. 'Chap. 3.'

HT, v.1 a9ʳ: [double rule 70 mm] | TO THE RIGHT HONOURABLE | THOMAS, | EARL OF PEMBROKE AND MONTGOMERY, | Baron HERBERT of Cardiff, Lord ROSS of Kendal, . . . [&c.]

v.1–3 A1ʳ: [double rule 70 mm] | OF | HUMAN UNDERSTANDING. | [double rule 70 mm]

v.3 K6ʳ [double rule 69 mm] | OF THE | CONDUCT OF THE UNDERSTANDING. | [rule 70 mm] | *Quid* [swash Q] *tam temerarium tamque indignum sapientis gravi-* | *tate atque constantia, quam aut falsum sentire, aut quod non* | *satis explorate perceptum sit et cognitum sine ulla dubitatione* | *defendere?* CIC. de Natura Deorum, lib. I. | [rule 70 mm]

CW: none.

Press figures. Vol. 1: x (a5ᵛ)-3   *xxi* (a11ʳ)-5   lii (c2ᵛ)-3   10 (A5ᵛ)-I   16 (A8ᵛ)-6   46 (B11ᵛ)-4   48 (B12ᵛ)-4   64 (C8ᵛ)-4   70 (C11ᵛ)-6   93 (D11ʳ)-7   95 (D12ʳ)-6   119 (E11ʳ)-4   141 (F11ʳ)-7   143 (F12ʳ)-3   152 (G4ᵛ)-4   167 (G12ʳ)-5   183 (H8ʳ)-6   191 (H12ᵛ)-I   194 (I1ᵛ)-5   196 (I2ᵛ)-4   239 (K12ʳ)-4   240 (K12ᵛ)-6   250 (L5ᵛ)-7   264 (L12ᵛ)-I

Vol. 2: viii (a4ᵛ)-6   xiv (b1ᵛ)-6   19 (A10ʳ)-3   20 (A10ᵛ)-6   39 (B8ʳ)-6   40 (B8ᵛ)-3   62 (C7ᵛ)-3   72 (C12ᵛ)-5   82 (D5ᵛ)-6   93 (D11ʳ)-I   109 (E7ʳ)-3   118 (E11ᵛ)-4   122 (F1ᵛ)-3   124 (F2ᵛ)-7   158 (G7ᵛ)-I   165 (G11ʳ)-6

172 (H2ᵛ)-7   191 (H12ʳ)-3   213 (I11ʳ)-7   214 (I11ᵛ)-6   222 (K3ᵛ)-3   224 (K4ᵛ)-4   244 (L2ᵛ)-6   250 (L5ᵛ)-5

Vol. 3: vi (a3ᵛ)-6   xiii (b1ʳ)-4   21 (A11ʳ)-6   22 (A11ᵛ)-I   26 (B1ᵛ)-5   28 (B2ᵛ)-4   70 (C11ᵛ)-I   72 (C12ᵛ)-4   74 (D1ᵛ)-7   98 (E1ᵛ)-3   120 (E12ᵛ)-6   124 (F2ᵛ)-I   142 (F11ᵛ)-4   167 (G12ʳ)-6   168 (G12ᵛ)-7   190 (H11ᵛ)-6   192 (H12ᵛ)-7   208 (I8ᵛ)-4   215 (I12ᵛ)-3   239 (K12ʳ)-I   250 (L5ᵛ)-3   264 (L12ᵛ)-I   277 (M7ʳ)-3   278 (M7ᵛ)-I   290 (²M1ᵛ)-I

Notes: Title leaves for vol. 1 of first state and for all vols. of the second state are cancellans. In both states some letters and punctuation after booksellers' names are faint or fail to print. Text is probably a reprint of the 1777 Edinburgh edition (no. 83) but without that edition's index, and conflated with Le Clerc's 'Life' following the 19th edition of 1793 (no. 87), and with the 'Conduct'. Like that edition, the exchange with Bishop Edward Stillingfleet, first incorporated as notes in the 5th edition of the *Essay*, is not included here, because it is included in the *Works* edition. Presumably the Bathurst et al. consortium were the authorised printers, but individual books were no longer a monopoly after 1774, except for the Bible and the Prayer Book. Perhaps the Bathurst consortium, Allen & West, and Mundell shared the publishing.

The quotation at the head of the text of the 'Conduct' is from Book I, §1: 'What is so ill-considered or so unworthy of the dignity of a philosopher as to hold an opinion that is not true, or to maintain with unhesitating certainty a proposition not based on adequate examination, comprehension and knowledge?' (Loeb Classical Library ed., 1933, pp. 2-3).

A microfilm copy of this edition (from the Harvard College Library copy) is in the collection, *The Eighteenth Century*, reel 1261 no. 15.

References: Alston 7:109 (1st issue only); Attig 256, 256.1; Christophersen p. 93; ESTC t063943, n009331.

Copies examined: 1st issue: L (8409 bbb.21; 172 × 99 mm cut)   [D. Neill (uncut copy)] O (Vet A5 e. 2490-92; vol.3 misbound: a4 before a3, e.g. pp. iv, vii-viii, v-vi, x-xiv)

2d issue: MH (Phil.2115.32.3; 2 copies of vol.1)

89. *Essay.* 20th ed., 1796. 2 vols. in 8°. With 'Conduct', &c.

AN | ESSAY | CONCERNING | Human Underſtanding. | . . . [&c. as in 19th ed. of 1793 no. 87, except:] | THE TWENTIETH EDITION. | TO WHICH ARE NOW ADDED, | I. Analyſis . . . [&c.] | LONDON: | Printed for T. Longman, B. Law and Son, J. Johnſon, C. Dilly, | G.G.J. and J. Robinſon, T. Cadell, W. Richardſon, W. Otridge, | J. Sewell, F. and C. Rivington, Ogilvy and Speare, S. Hayes, Leigh | and Sotheby, T. Payne, W. Lowndes, R. Faulder, B. and J. White, | Vernor and Hood, G. and T. Wilkie, Scatcherd and Whittaker, E. Jefferey, | and Cadell and Davies. | 1796.

Coll: 8° (211 × 129 mm cut). Signatures and pagination identical with 1793 ed. (no. 87), including the folded plate (here on laid paper, watermarked with a fleur-de-lys, 'MIEL' and '9641'), 416 × 540 mm folded to 205 × 112 mm.

Contents, Text: Same as no. 87, printed on medium-quality wove paper, without watermarks. Vol. 2 here, similarly, lacks first leaf (a1) the collective title for the *Works*.

CW: none.

Press figures. Vol. 1: *xi* (A6^r)–3   *xiii* (A7^r)–I   *xxii* (A3^v)–9   8 (B4^v)–9   15 (B8^r)–3   30 (C7^r)–5   47 (D8^r)–6   50 (E1^v)–6   77 (F7^r)–6   79 (F8^r)–3   84 (G2^v)–I   100 (H2^v)–6   116 (I2^v)–4   122 (I5^v)–6   141 (K7^r)–5   143 (K8^r)–3   157 (L7^r)–9   171 (M6^r)–2   176 (M8^v)–5   182 (N3^v)–I   192 (N8^v)–2   203 (O6^r)–5   208 (O8^v)–9   210 (P1^v)–3   224 (P8^v)–I   236 (Q6^v)–I   244 (R2^v)–2   251 (R6^r)–3   269 (S7^r)–2   270 (S7^v)–3   282 (T5^v)–9   299 (U6^v)–6   301 (U7^r)–3   306 (X1^v)–6   334 (Y7^v)–8   345 (Z5^r)–8   351 (Z8^r)–9   368 (2A8^v)–3   372 (2B2^v)–2   378 (2B5^v)–3   399 (2C8^r)–6   400 (2C8^v)–5   416 (2D8^v)–5   420 (2E2^v)–5   440 (2F4^v)–8   457 (2G5^r)–6   475 (2H6^r)–I   480 (2H8^v)–7   482 (2I1^v)–2   492 (2I6^v)–7   498 (2K1^v)–8   504 (2K4^v)–6

Vol. 2: *vii* (a5^r)–9   *xiii* (a8^r)–I   10 (B5^r)–I   22 (C3^v)–3   29 (C7^r)–4   34 (D1^v)–5   50 (E1^v)–2   52 (E2^v)–I   66 (F1^v)–5   72 (F4^v)–3   82 (G1^v)–6   98 (H1^v)–6   109 (H7^r)–2   114 (I1^v)–3   130 (K1^v)–5   146 (L1^v)–8   148 (L2^v)–3   162 (M1^v)–7   172 (M6^v)–9   191 (N8^r)–6   206 (O7^v)–9   208 (O8^v)–I   210 (P1^v)–3   212 (P2^v)–I   230 (Q3^v)–I   240 (Q8^v)–6   250 (R5^v)–3   256 (R8^v)–5   258 (S1^v)–5   269 (S7^r)–I   280 (T4^v)–8   282 (T5^v)–9   301 (U7^r)–6   303 (U8^r)–9   308 (X2^v)–I   314 (X5^v)–9   326 (Y3^v)–2   332 (Y6^v)–5   350 (Z7^v)–9   352 (Z8^v)–6   361 (2A5^r)–7   370 (2B1^v)–3   386 (2C1^v)–8   388 (2C2^v)–2   408 (2D4^v)–6   410 (2D5^v)–2   420 (2E2^v)–5   426 (2E5^v)–I   444 (2F6^v)–9   450 (2G1^v)–3   464 (2G8^v)–2   468 (2H2^v)–6   474 (2I1^v)–9   485 (2K3^r)–6

Note: A new printing of no. 87, with different press figures. Extracted from the 1794 edition of the *Works* (no. 371). The excerpts of the exchange with Bishop Stillingfleet therefore again are not included.

References: Alston 7:110; Attig 255.1; Christophersen p. 93; ESTC n006228.

Copies examined: O (2672 e.13-14)   Ck (Keynes)   L (1509/2363; without figure in v.1 p. 269)   NjP (6106.333.17)

90. *Essay*. 1798. Edinburgh & Glasgow. 3 vols. in 12°. *With* Conduct.

AN | ESSAY | CONCERNING | Human Underſtanding; | . . . [&c. as in 1795 edition, second issue, no. 88B except:] EDINBURGH: | PRINTED FOR MUNDELL & SON; AND J. MUNDELL, | COLLEGE, GLASGOW. | [rule 11 mm] | 1798.

Coll: 12° (176 × 97 mm cut). Vol. 1: a–b^{12} c^2 d^2 (–d2) A–L^{12} M^6 (–M6 = d1?) [$ half signed]; 164 leaves; pp. *i–iii* iv–xv xvi–xvii xviii–xix xx–xxi xxii–xxx *xxxi* xxiii–liii *liv* 1 2–271 *272–274* [= 328]. First page of each gathering also signed 'VOL.I.'

Vol. 2: a^6 b^2 A–L^{12} [$ half signed]; 140 leaves; pp. *i–iii* iv–xvi 1 2–264 [= 280]. First page of each gathering also signed 'VOL.II.' in direction line.

Vol. 3: a^6 b^2 (–b2) A–M^{12} N^{12} (–N12 = b1?) [$ half (–N6) signed]; 162 leaves; pp. *i–iii* iv–xiv 1 2–225 *226–227* 228–291 192 293–308 *309–310*

[= 324]. Page 291 called '192'. First page of each gathering also signed 'VOL.III.' in direction line.

Text: 40 lines; 143 (153) × 80 mm; 72 R. Medium-quality wove paper is not watermarked.

Contents: same as no. 88, except vol.3's gathering for pp. 289–310 are correctly signed 'N'.

Headlines or RTs are chapter titles in italics, with book no. at inner margin on versos, e.g. 'Book IV.', and chap. numbers on rectos, e.g. 'Chap. 3.'

CW: none.

Press figures. Vol. 1: xxii (a11^v)-3 xxiv (a12^v)-2 xxxiv (b5^v)-2 xlviii (b12^v)-3 23 (A12^r)-3 24 (A12^v)-4 46 (B11^v)-4 48 (B12^v)-2 52 (C2^v)-2 70 (C11^v)-3 94 (D11^v)-3 96 (D12^v)-4 98 (E1^v)-2 100 (E2^v)-4 141 (F11^r)-3 143 (F12^r)-4 167 (G12^r)-2 168 (G12^v)-4 172 (H2^v)- 2 190 (H11^v)-3 194 (I1^v)-3 205 (I7^r)-4 237 (K11^r)-4 239 (K12^r)-3 261 (L11^r)-3 262 (L11^v)-2 266 (M1^v)-2

Vol. 2: xi (a6^r)-4 12 (A6^v)-3 15 (A8^r)-2 34 (B5^v)-3 48 (B12^v)-4 69 (C11^r)-2 70 (C11^v)-4 76 (D2^v)-3 82 (D5^v)-2 111 (E8^r)-4 120 (E12^v)-3 126 (F3^v)-2 141 (F11^r)-3 159 (G8^r)-2 168 (G12^v)-3 170 (H1^v)-2 189 (H11^r)-4 196 (I2^v)-2 214 (I11^v)-4 220 (K2^v)-3 239 (K12^r)-4 244 (L2^v)-4 263 (L12^r)-3

Vol. 3: xii (a6^v)-3 14 (A7^v)-4 24 (Al2^v)-2 28 (B2^v)-3 46 (B11^v)-4 70 (C11^v)-3 72 (C12^v)-2 87 (D8^r)-3 93 (D11^r)-2 98 (E1^v)-2 117 (E11^r)-3 143 (F12^r)-2 144 (F12^v)-4 158 (G7v)-2 165 (G11^r)-4 170 (H1^v)-3 192 (H12^v)-4 214 (I11^v)-4 216 (I12^v)-3 237 (K11^r)-4 238 (K11^v)-3 263 (L12^r)-3 264 (L12^v)-4 278 (M7^v)-2 288 (M12^v)-4 290 (N1^v)-4 301 (N7^r)-2

Notes: Line-for-line reprint of no. 88, probably printed in England, but with different press figures. A microfilm copy of this edition is in the collection, *The Eighteenth Century*, reel 3437, no. 2.

References: Alston 7:111; Attig 256.2; Christophersen p. 93; ESTC t063939.

Copies examined: O^1 (Vet.A5 e.2154-6; contents for v.3 bound in front of that of v.2) C (C.151.E3; lacks vol. 3) L (8470 cc.21) MH (Phil.2115.32.5) O^2 (Vet.A5 e.5555; lacks vol.2)

91. *Essay*. French trans. (Coste) Amsterdam, 1700. 4°
ESSAI PHILOSOPHIQUE | CONCERNANT | L'ENTENDEMENT | HUMAIN, | OU L'ON MONTRE QUELLE EST L'ETENDUE DE NOS | CONNOISSANCES CERTAINES, ET LA MANIÈRE | DONT NOUS Y PARVENONS. | *Traduit de l'Anglois de Mr.* [swash A, M] LOCKE, | Par PIERRE COSTE, | Sur la Quatriéme Edition, revûë, corrigée, & augmentée par l'Auteur. | *Quàm bellum eſt velle confiteri potius neſcire quod neſcias, quàm* | *iſta effutientem nauſeare, atque ipſum ſibi displicere!* | Cic. de Nat. Deor. Lib. I. | [orn.: wolf leaning against tree, with scroll 'QVÆRENDO', 32 x 43 mm] | A

AMSTERDAM, | Chez HENRI SCHELTE. | [rule 47 mm] | M. DCC. | Avec Privilége de Noſſeigneurs les Etats de Hollande & de Weſt-Friſe.
Coll: 4° (250 x 195 mm cut) π¹ *² 2*–7*⁴ 8*² (–8*2) A–2Q⁴ 2R⁴ (±2R4) 2S–6E⁴ [$ half + 1 (–*2, –6E3) signed]; *1 signed '*3']; 508 leaves; pp. i–lvi 1–936 937–960 [= 1016].
Contents: π1ʳ (i) title (verso blank), *1ʳ ('*3')–2ᵛ (iii–vi) Locke's dedication to Pembroke, 2*1ʳ–2*4ᵛ (vii–xiv) 'Avertissement du traducteur', 3*1ʳ (xv) 'Monsieur Locke au Libraire', 3*1ᵛ–4*3ᵛ (xvi–xxviii) author's preface (includes material added to pref. of 2nd & 3rd English eds.), 4*4ʳ–8*1ᵛ (xxix–lvi) contents by book, chap. & sections, 8*1ᵛ (lower 2/3ds) errata in 2 cols. of 30 lines each, A1ʳ–4ᵛ (1–8) 'Avant-propos: Dessein de l'auteur dans cet ouvrage' (trans. of Book I Chap. I), B1ʳ–M2ᵛ (9–92) text of 'Livre Premier' (in 3 chap., equivalent to Book I Chap. II–IV), M3ʳ–3Q4ʳ (93–495) 'Livre Second' (Book II text), 3Q4ᵛ–4O4ᵛ (496–664) text of Book III, 4P1ʳ–6B4ᵛ (665–936) text of Book IV, 6C1ʳ–6E3ʳ (937–957) index, 6E3ᵛ (958) 'Privilegie' (permission to print granted at the Hague, 15 May 1700), 6E4ʳ,ᵛ blank.
Illustration: frontispiece is engraved portrait of Locke in oval frame (with oval coat-of-arms quartered in 6 parts, 3 doves alternating with 3 stipled blocks) by 'P. a Gunst' after Greenhill, 211 x 159 mm, on plate 221 x 169 mm; subscribed 'JEAN LOCKE', and a description of Locke (4 lines in Latin) ascribed to Jean Le Clerc (cf. Corr. viii.445).
Text (O3ᵛ): 37 lines; 175 (185) x 108 (128) mm; 94 R. Dedication set 31 lines, 118 ital. Contents and index set in double columns. Medium-quality laid paper in body of vol.; title leaf and gathering * on heavier weight paper with sewing between the two leaves of gathering *. Watermark: horse within a circle; except prelim. sheets (*s), leaf 2R4, sheets 40–4P and 6A–6E have armorial mark; 5V–5Z have bunch of grapes. End of Books II–IV have tailpiece of a bear seated on leafy pedestal (42 x 79 mm). Page no. at outer corners of headlines. The number for the first page of the 'Avant-propos' and for each book preceded by 'Pag.', e.g. 'Pag. 496'. Contents for each section or part of section has marginal summary set roman.
HT *2ʳ: A MONSEIGNEUR | LE COMTE | DE | PEMBROKE ET MONTGOMERY, | Baron Herbert de Cardiff, Seigneur Roſs de Kendal, Par, | Fitzhugh, Marmion, St. Quintin, & Shurland; Préſident | du Conſeil Privé de ſa Majeſté, & Lieutenant de Roy | dans le Comté de Wilts & de la Province de | Galles Meridionale.
A1ʳ: [framed headpiece of berries & leaves about a heart 23 x 124 mm] | ESSAI PHILOSOPHIQUE | CONCERNANT | L'ENTENDEMENT HUMAIN. | [rule 101 mm]
B1ʳ, M3ʳ, 3Q4ᵛ, and 4P1ʳ: framed headpiece of two angels upholding framed picture of castle 25 x 108 mm] | ESSAI . . . [&c. as on A1ʳ] | [fillet of printer's flowers 104 mm] | LIVRE PREMIER. ['SECOND.', 'TROISIÉME.', 'QUATRIÉME.']

Headlines or RTs are chapter title summaries in italics, with chapter numbers in capital letters in external margins on line with first line of text. Headline on each recto page also indicates book no., e.g. 'LIV. II.' Headline on 2R1-3 reads: '*De la Puiſſance.*'; on 2R4: '*De la Puißance.*'

CW: Page. *3ᵛ (*rai-*) *ſon* 3*1ᵛ qui- [quiconque] A3ʳ par H4ʳ à [à porter] 2E4ᵛ ſervent 2S1ᵛ (appa-) rences 3N4ʳ Idées 4O3ᵛ (tra-) ceroit 5F1ᵛ ver- [verbale,] 5Z1ᵛ (a-) voient 6C2ʳ Cel- [Celle]

Notes: Locke was very interested in having his *Essay* available to a wider audience than might be reached by the English editions. Jean Le Clerc (in his 'Eloge', *Bibliotheque universelle* 6 (1705): 379-90) tells us that "Mr. Coste, qui demeuroit alors, dans la même maison que l'Auteur, le traduisit avec beaucoup de soin, de fidelité & netteté, sous ses yeux, & cette version est très-estimée. Elle a fait connoître ses sentimens deçà la mer, avec plus d'étendue que l'Abregé, qui avoit paru en 1688, ne pouvoit le faire. Comme l'Auteur étoit présent, il corrigea divers endroits de l'Original, pour les rendre plus clairs & plus faciles à traduire, & revit la Version avec soin; ce qui fait qu'elle n'est guere inferieure à l'Anglois, & qu'elle est souvent plus claire."

Coste began translating the third edition of 1695 (no. 63) in July or August 1696. In August 1697 he moved to Oates, where Locke was residing, as tutor to the Masham's son, and there continued to work on the translation. The title-page here indicates he has translated from the (not yet published) 1700 (4th, no. 64) edition, but "his version did include most (though not all) of the changes from earlier Editions that Locke made for incorporation in the Fourth Edition . . . Coste chiefly relied [on] the Third Edition." (*Essay*, ed. Nidditch, 1975, p. xxxv). In this as in all subsequent editions of the French translation, Coste changed the first chapter of Book I into the introduction ('Avant-propos') and consequently renumbered the second to fourth chapters as Chapter 1-3. His rearrangement was unfortunately followed by A.C. Fraser in his 1894 edition (Oxford University Press; 2 vols.). The footnotes supplied by Coste deal exclusively with linguistic matters, explicating terms where the English original was difficult to turn into French.

The note, 'Monsieur Locke au Libraire', is obviously part of a letter sent to Henri Schelte in answer to a query about the quality of Coste's translation, for Locke replies that "the clarity of thought and knowledge of the French language, for which the public has already received such visible proofs that they furnished you with a sufficient guarantee of the excellence of his work on my *Essay*, without your having to ask me for my opinion . . . his nicety of mind and suppleness of pen let him find ways of correcting all those faults I discovered as he read me what he had translated. Thus I can tell the reader I presume he will find in this work all the qualities one might wish in a good translation". (My translation; letters to and from Schelte not in *Corr.*)

The text of the 4th English ed. included a new chapter, 'On the Association of Ideas' (2.33) and one on enthusiasm (4.19). Both these chapters are included in this first French edition.

Leaf 2R4 (pp. 319-20) is a cancellans, as can be seen from the different style of italicizing the double s in the headline noted above. An accident in the press in typesetting, rather than textual content, is the probable explanation.

The 'Avant-propos' and each book begin with a 6 or 7-line woodcut decorated initial.

Recently Jørn Schøsler has looked at the vocabulary of Coste's translation, especially as modifications progress from this first through his fourth edition (no. 91, 94-6), and the changing tenour of his notes, "exprimant le scepticisme du traducteur, notamment par rapport aux raisonnements de Locke sur la nature de l'âme."[6]

Notices: *Histoire des ouvrages des savans*, 16 (1700): 291-308. *Mémoires pour l'histoire des sciences et des beaux arts* (known as '*Journal de Trévoux*') Jan./Feb. 1701: 116-31. *Nouvelles de la république des lettres*, Aug. 1700: 123-54.

References: Attig 349; Christophersen p.27; L.L. 1802; Rochedieu p. 192.

Copies examined: (all with 2R4 cancellans): Y   C (7180 c.16)   Ck(Keynes)   CLaslett   DFo   (B1293.F7   1700)   Dt   (Fag.N.5.10)   [GOT]   Han (Leib.Marg.39; Leibniz's copy, with random pencilled underlining)   L (8408 h.18)   O (Vet.B4 d.25)   P (R.4994)   Utr (Y.Qu.85) [Wellesley College Lib. (q192.2/O13)]   Wol (Vb 4° 3)

92. *Essay*. French trans. (Coste) The Hague, 1714. 4°
ESSAI PHILOSOPHIQUE | CONCERNANT | L'ENTENDEMENT HUMAIN, | ... [&c. as in no. 91, except printer's orn. is tree with man's body as trunk, above a lion in profile, 44 × 34 mm] | A LA HAYE, | Chez PIERRE HUSSON. | [rule 53 mm] | M. DCC. XIV. | *Avec Priviléges de Nosseigneurs les Etats de Holland & de West-Frise.*

Coll: 4° (245 × 195 mm cut) π^1 *^{2} 2*-7*^{4} 8*^{2} (-8*2) A-2R^4 (± 2R4) 2S-6E^4 [$ half + 1 (-*2,-6E3) signed; *1 signed '*3']; 508 leaves; pp. *i–lvi* 1-936 937-960 [= 1016].

Contents: $\pi 1^r$ title (verso blank), '*3'(= *1)^r-*2^v dedication, 2*1^r-6E4^v identical with no. 91 (1700).

Illustration: engr. plate as frontispiece, identical with that in no. 91.

Text, headlines, &c., identical with 1700 edition (no. 91), except for first three leaves.

Notes: A reissue of the sheets of no. 91 with the first (title) leaf as a cancellans, on heavier paper, chainlines 23 mm apart; sheet * on lighter paper with a fleur-de-lys watermark centered in inner gutters and chainlines 28 mm apart. Paper in the body of the printing is with 26 mm chainlines, with same watermarks as no. 91. The sewing for leaves *1.2 is seen to be between them. Page 958 (6E^v) includes same Dutch privilege granted to H. Schelte.

I doubt if this is a piracy. It seems more likely that Pierre Husson had shares in this work (as he is known to have had in others) and decided to issue it

---

[6] 'Les Editions de la traduction française par Pierre Coste de l'Essay concerning Human Understanding de Locke', *Actes du VIIIe Congrès des romanistes scandinaves* (Odense University Press, 1983): pp. 315-24.

under his own imprint. The Schelte firm could have transferred some unsold sheets to him; Schelte was still in business in 1714; his widow, Susanna Pelt, requested consent from the Burgermaster of Amsterdam on 19 February 1717 to act as a bookseller and sell books from her deceased husband's stock (Kleerkooper, M. M.: *De boekhandel te Amsterdam* (1914), pp. 675-6; cf. p. 954, where in June 1721 Pierre Husson had a 2/12 share in a work to be published by Rudolph and Gerald Wetstein and others).
Reference: Attig 350.
Copies examined: Y Dt (Gall.00.11.2) MH (Phil.2114.48.5)

93. *Essay.* French trans. (Coste) 1723. 'Amsterdam' [Basel?] 4°. Piracy.
ESSAI PHILOSOPHIQUE | CONCERNANT | L'ENTENDEMENT | HUMAIN, | Où l'on montre quelle eſt l'Etendue de nos Connoiſſan- | ces certaines, & la Maniere dont nous y parvenons. | *Traduit* [swash T] *de l'Anglois de Mr.* [swash M] LOCKE, | Par PIERRE COSTE, | Nouvelle Edition, revûë, corrigée, & augmentée par l'Auteur. | *Quàm* [swash Q] . . . *quàm* | *iſta . . . diſplicere!* | Cic. de Nat. Deor. Lib. I. | [ornament: open book, globe, dividers, palette, seated figure, etc. enframed in leafy border 43 × 56 mm] | *Suivant la Copie imprimée* | A AMSTERDAM, | [rule 110 mm] | Chez HENRI SCHELTE. | [rule 70 mm] | M DCC XXIII.
Coll: 4° (200 × 155 mm cut) *⁴ (-*4) b-g⁴ h² A-6E⁴ [$ 3 (-*3, -h2, -I3, -6C3) signed]; 509 leaves; pp. *i-lviii* 1-370 373 372-715 816 717-936 937-960 [=1018]. Page 371 called '373' with second '3' inverted; 716 called '816'. An untrimmed lower corner of one page (in my copy) shows the paper to measure 209 × 162 mm uncut.
Contents: *1ʳ title (verso blank), *2ʳ-*3ᵛ (*iii-vi*) dedication to Earl of Pembroke, b1ʳ-b4ᵛ (*vii-xiv*) 'Avertissement du traducteur', c1ʳ (*xv*) 'Monsieur Locke au Libraire', c1ᵛ-e1ʳ (*xvi-xxxi*) author's pref., e1ᵛ-h2ᵛ (*xxxii-lviii*) contents by book, chap. & sections, A1ʳ-M2ᵛ (1-92) text of first book, M3ʳ-3Q4ʳ (93-495) text of second book, 4Q4ᵛ-4O4ᵛ (496-664) text of third book, 4P1ʳ-6B4ᵛ (665-936) text of fourth book, 6C1ʳ-6E3ᵛ (937-958) index, 6E4 blank.
Illustration: engraved plate of Locke's portrait by 'P. Fehr' after Greenhill, as in no. 91-2. Plate has been recut; also in all copies it has been closely trimmed at the outer side and at bottom, beneath the inscription 'JEAN LOCKE', thus measuring 181 × 143 mm.
Text (3H3ʳ): 36 lines; 152 (162) × 92 (114) mm; 84 R. Poor-quality laid paper, watermarked with armorial shield, 3 arrows within. Page no. in outer corners of headlines. Dedication set 118 ital. on *2ʳ, rest 94 ital.
HT *a2ⁱ: same as in 1700 and 1714 editions (no. 91-2), except 4th line reads: 'PEMBROKE ET MONTGOMERY.'
A1ʳ, B1ʳ, M3ʳ, 3Q4ᵛ and 4P1ʳ: [unframed headpiece, triple vase with flowers 35 × 93 mm] | ESSAI PHILOSOPHIQUE [swash Q] | CONCERNANT | L'ENTENDEMENT HUMAIN. | [rule 94 mm on A1r and B1r; orn. row of suns 93 mm elsewhere]

Headlines or RTs are chap. titles in italics followed by book no. on recto pages in large and small capitals, e.g. 'LIV.II.' Chap. no. in upper external margins level with first line of text, set in capitals, e.g. 'CHAP.III.'
CW: Page. *2ᵛ *être* c1ᵛ ſont A3ʳ pa [par] H4ʳ à porter 2E4ᵛ (ſer-) vent [ſervent] 2S1ᵛ (apparen-) ces [rences] 3N4ʳ idées 3O1ᵛ Objets 4O3ᵛ des 5Zᵛ (verba-) le, 5Z1ᵛ (a-) voyent [voient] 6Cʳ Nôtre
Notes: This edition is a piracy, probably printed at Basel, according to Weller.[7] (See also no. 92, *Notes*). I think this is the edition Dr. Bernhard Fabian of the University of Münster says was printed in Basel by Brandmüller; further that it was listed in the Leipzig Fair Catalogue in 1725. The author's pref. and the contents have been completely rearranged, reprinting the text of no. 91-2. The dedication, Locke's note and the text are line-by-line, page-by-page reprint of no. 91-2. Unframed headpiece of 2 griffins (14 × 93 mm) at head of 'Avertissement du traducteur'; of a bowl containing musical instruments, with scrolls, (35 × 92 mm) before author's pref. End of reader's epistle and final page of text have tailpiece of 2 hearts surrounded by leaves (40 × 84 mm). Page 958 (6E3ᵛ) has tailpiece of vase of flowers, 37 × 63 mm. Each chap. begins with 4-line initial. Marginal contents of sections set 84 ital. The errata listed in no. 91-2 have been corrected in this edition.
References: Attig 351; Christophersen p.97; Rochedieu p. 192.
Copies examined: Y CaOTU (Locke L63.F7 1723) Ck (Keynes) CLaslett CtY (K8.L79/fh723) [GOT] O (Vet.D4 e.108; formerly Vet. B4 e.68) P (R.4995)

94. *Essay.* French trans. (Coste) 2nd ed., Amsterdam, 1729. 4°
In red & black: [red line:] ESSAI PHILOSOPHIQUE | CONCERNANT | [red:] L'ENTENDEMENT | HUMAIN, | OU L'ON MONTRE QUELLE EST L'ETENDUE DE NOS | CONNOISSANCES CERTAINES, ET LA MANIERE | DONT NOUS Y PARVENONS. | [red:] *PAR M. LOCKE.* | Traduit de l'Anglois | [red:] *PAR M. COSTE.* | Seconde Edition, revûë, corrigée, & augmentée de quelques Additions | importantes de l'Auteur qui n'ont paru qu'après ſa mort, & de quelques | Remarques du Traducteur. | *Quàm* [swash Q] *bellum eſt velle confiteri potius neſcire quod neſcias, quàm* | *iſta effutientem nauſeare, atque ipſum ſibi diſplicere!* Cic. de Nat. Deor. Lib. I. | [engr. plate of seated Minerva, with books, cherubs, &c., with cartouche at base: "VIVITUR INGENIO, | CETERA MORTIS | ERUNT." and '*B. Picart fecit 1728.*' 69 × 98 mm on plate 71 × 106 mm] | A AMSTERDAM, | [red:] Chez *PIERRE MORTIER.* | M. DCC. XXIX.
Coll: 4° (255 × 195 mm cut) π¹ *² 2*-5*⁴ 6*⁴ (-6*4) A-4G⁴ 4H² [$ half + 1 (-4H2) signed; *1.2 signed '*2' and '*3' respectively]; 328 leaves; pp. *i-ix* XII-XX *XXI* XXII *XXIII* XXIV-XXXI *XXXII* XXXIII-XLI *XLII* XLIII-XLVI *1* 2-6 1 8-595 596-612 [= 656]. Page 7 called 'Pag.1.'

---

[7] Weller, E. O. *Die falschen und fingirten Druckorte*, 2. Aufl. (Leipzig, 1864), II. 91: under 1729. He confuses this piracy with the authorised 2nd French edition.

Contents: π1ʳ (*i*) title (verso blank), *1ʳ ("*2')–2*1ᵛ (*iii–viii*) Coste's dedication to Edmund Sheffield, Duke of Buckinghamshire (dated 10 Mai 1729.), 2*2ʳ–3*2ᵛ (*ix* XII–XX) 'Avertissement du traducteur', 3*3ʳ·ᵛ (*XXI–XXII*) 'Avis sur la seconde edition', 3*4ʳ–4*4ʳ (*XXIII–XXXI*) 'Eloge de M. Locke' (reprint of Coste's obituary note from the *Nouvelles de la république des lettres*, Feb. 1705), 4*4ᵛ–6*1ʳ (*XXXII–XLI*) Locke's pref., 6*1ᵛ (*XLII* upper half) 'Monsieur Locke au Libraire', 6*1ᵛ–6*3ʳ (*XLII* lower half–XLV top third) 'Additions et corrections' (in 2 cols., 64 R), 6*3ʳ·ᵛ (XLV lower part–XLVI) contents by books & chapters, A1ʳ–A3ᵛ (*1–6*) 'Avant-propos' (Book I, Ch. 1), A4ʳ–4F2ʳ ('I'–595) text of Book I chap. 2 through Book IV, 4F2ᵛ–4H2ʳ (*595–611*) index: 'Table des principales matieres', 4H2ᵛ blank.

Illustrations: frontispiece is engraved port. of Locke, by Pieter van Gunst after Noah Greenhill, same as that in 1700 and 1714 printings (no. 91-2). The dedication to the Duke of Buckinghamshire (*1ʳ) is headed by an engraved framed headpiece of a seated male figure left, Minerva at right, and two boars supporting the Buckinghamshire coat-of-arms, with inscription 'CO⟨M⟩MITER SED FORTITER' (the 1st M obscured by a club held by left figure), 88 × 124 mm on plate 99 × 137 mm.

Text (T2ʳ): 46 lines; 192 (203) × 124 (146) mm; 83 R. Gathering * on heavy laid paper with armorial watermark; rest of vol. on poor-quality laid paper with no visible watermark. Dedication set 20 lines with 2 mm leading, 177 R. Translator's note set 27 lines, 138 R. "Avis sur cette édition" set 40 lines 95 ital; Locke's pref. set 46 lines, 83 ital. Coste's 'Eloge' set same as main text. The 'Avant-propos' and Books I–II begin with 8-line woodcut floral initials, Books III–IV with 5-line floral woodcut initials; all have ornamental head & tailpieces.

HT, *2ʳ [headpiece, as in *Illustrations*, above] | A MONSEIGNEUR | MONSEIGNEUR | EDMUND SHEFFIELD | DUC DE | BUCKINGHAMSHIRE & NORMANBY, | MARQUIS DE NORMANBY, COMTE DE | MULGRAVE, BARON DE BUTTERWICK, | &c.

A1ʳ: [triple orn. fillet 21 × 128 mm] | ESSAI PHILOSOPHIQUE | CONCERNANT | L'ENTENDEMENT HUMAIN. | [orn. floral fillet 2 × 123 mm]

A4ʳ, H2ʳ: [double orn. fillet 14 × 127 mm] | ESSAI . . . [&c. as on A1ʳ]

2R3ʳ: [unframed headpiece of vase centered with leaves & flowers 32 × 122 mm] | ESSAI . . . [&c. as on A1ʳ]

3G3ᵛ: [headpiece as on 2R3ʳ] | ESSAI PHIOSOPHIQUE [sic] | CONCERNANT | L'ENTENDEMENT HUMAIN. | [orn. floral fillet 2 × 123 mm]

CW: Page. *3ᵛ (culti-) ver, 3*1ᵛ pu- [pureté] 5*1ʳ *met- [mettre]* A3ʳ occu- [occupe] H4ʳ §.9. Du 2E1ʳ (permet-) te 2S1ᵛ CHA- [CHAPITRE] 3L4ʳ tou- [toutes] 3X2ʳ com- [complet] 4D2ᵛ cet- [cette]

Notes: This second French edition incorporates some of the changes Locke made for the 1706 English edition (no. 65): lines added to 2.21.48, 2.21.56, and 2.21.71 (all to the chapter on power). In a letter dated 12 August 1701 to Philippus van Limborch (*Corr.* 2979; vii.401-14) Locke included a transcription of Coste's translation of the addition to 2.21.71, which does not appear in the 1714 printing or the 1723 piracy. This letter, with the addition, first appeared in *Some Familiar Letters* (1708; no. 346) pp. 490-504.

Edmund Sheffield, the second Duke of Buckinghamshire, to whom Coste dedicates this edition of his translation, was the surviving son of John Sheffield, the first Duke; he died unmarried in 1735, "when all his titles became extinct" (DNB). I can only assume he was one of the "several young noblemen and gentlemen" to whom Coste acted as tutor after Locke's death (*ibid.*)

The fifth English edition (1706) also included nine selections from the Locke-Stillingfleet debate (no. 248-50) added as extensive footnotes. Of these, only the note to 4.3.6, after the sentence, "We have the *Ideas* of *Matter* and *Thinking*", is included in this edition. On the other hand Coste supplies many notes on his own, either in explanation or in citing other authors: Montaigne, Samuel Clarke, Terence, Vergil, Pascal, Malebranche, Barbeyrac, etc. According to Schøsler (see no. 91, *Notes*) not only did Coste change the person to whom the work was dedicated, he also added or expanded several of his notes, both linguistic and explicative, frequently disagreeing with Locke, and citing Montaigne in his own support.

Bernard Picart (1673-1733), the engraver of the vignette on the title-page, was a Freemason, Huguenot, known chiefly for his engravings in *Cérémonies et coutumes religieuses de tous les peuples du monde*, chiefly written by Jean-Frédéric Bernard and published at Amsterdam in 13 vols. in 1723. Bernard was the publisher of Locke's *Oeuvres diverses* (no. 372-3; cf. Jonathan Israel's *The Dutch Republic*, pp. 1040, 1048). The 'Avis' to this edition (p. XXII) concludes with the statement that this second edition is "fort au dessus de la Prémiére, & par consequent, de la *Réimpression* qui en a été faite en 1723, en quelque Ville de Suisse qu'on n'a pas voulu nommer dans le Titre" [i.e. the piracy of 1723, no. 93].

References: Attig 352; Christophersen p. 97; Rochedieu p. 192.

Copies examined: Y CaOTU (Locke L63.E82F7 1729) Ck (Keynes) CtY (K8.L79/fh729) [GOT] [GhU] L (8408 h.17) O (Art.CC.74) P (4° R.2474)

95. *Essay.* French trans. (Coste) 3d ed., Amsterdam, 1735. 4°
In red & black: [red line:] ESSAI | PHILOSOPHIQUE | CONCERNANT | [red:] L'ENTENDEMENT | HUMAIN, | OU L'ON MONTRE QUELLE EST L'ETENDUE DE NOS [swash Ts, Q] | CONNOISSANCES CERTAINES, ET LA MANIERE [swash Ts] | DONT NOUS Y PARVENONS. [swash T] | [red:] PAR M. LOCKE, | TRADUIT DE L'ANGLOIS | [red:] PAR M. COSTE. | Troifiéme Edition, revûë, corrigée, & augmentée de quelques Additions | importantes de l'Auteur qui n'ont paru qu'après fa mort, & de quelques | Remarques du

Traducteur. | *Quam* [swash Q] *bellum . . . quàm* | *ifta . . . difplicere!* | Cic. de Nat. Deor. Lib. I. | [engr. plate as in no. 94, 69 × 105 mm] | A AMSTERDAM, | [red:] Chez *PIERRE MORTIER.* | M. DCC. XXXV.

Coll: 4° (251 × 198 mm cut) *-5*⁴ 6*² (-6*2 = *I*1) A-4H⁴ *I*¹ [$3 signed]; 330 leaves; pp. *I-IX* X-XXIX *XXX* XXXI-XXXIX *XL-XLI* XLII *1* 2-59 *60* 61-601 *602-618* [= 660].

Contents: *1ʳ (*I*) title (verso blank), *2ʳ-*4ᵛ (*III-VIII*) dedication to Duke of Buckingham, 2*1ʳ-3*1ᵛ (*IX-XVIII*) 'AVERTISSEMENT DU TRADUCTEUR.', 3*2ʳ,ᵛ (*XIX-XX*) 'Avis sur cette troisieme edition', 3*3ʳ-4*3ʳ (*XXI-XXIX*) Coste's 'Eloge' (from *Nouvelles de la république des lettres*), 4*3ᵛ-5*4ʳ (*XXX-XXXIX*) Locke's pref., 5*4ᵛ (*XL*) 'Monsieur Locke au Libraire', 6*1ʳ,ᵛ (*XLI*-XLII) contents by book & chap., A1ʳ-A3ᵛ (*1-6*) 'Avant-propos' (text of Book I ch. 1, A4ʳ-H2ʳ, 'Livre I' (translation of Book I ch. 2-4, called 'Chap.I'-'III') H2ᵛ-2S1ʳ (60-321) text of Book II, 2S1ᵛ-3H1ᵛ (322-426) text of Book III, 3H2ʳ-4G1ʳ (427-601) text of Book IV, 4G1ᵛ-*I*1ʳ (602-617) index, *I*1ᵛ (*618*) errata in 2 cols., subscribed: "Achevé d'imprimer le 30. Novembre 1734."

Illustration: engr. framed headpiece preceding dedication, as in 1729 edition (no. 94). Published without the portrait of Locke as frontispiece.

Text (2A3ʳ): 46 lines; 189 (201) × 123 (146) mm; 84 R. Dedication set 20 lines, 167 R; translator's note set 27 lines, 133 R. Good paper without visible watermarks. Ornamental head and tailpieces. Page no. at outer ends of headlines.

HT *2ʳ: same as in 1729 ed. (no. 94).

A1ʳ, A4ʳ, H2ᵛ, 2S1ᵛ and 3H2ʳ: ESSAI | PHILOSOPHIQUE | CONCERNANT | L'ENTENDEMENT HUMAIN. | [orn. fillet 4 × 121 mm]

Headlines are chap. titles in italics, followed by book no. in large & small caps., e.g. '*De la Puiffance*. LIV. II.'

CW: Page. 2*1ᵛ pu- [pureté] 4*4ʳ *met*- [*mettre*] A3ʳ pro- [propre] C3ᵛ pei- [peine] H4ʳ §.9. Du L1ʳ (mouve-) ment [ment:] 2B4ᵛ (re-) cher- [ehercher. sic] 2E1ʳ le 2S1ᵛ §.3. Mais 3F3ʳ ri- [ridicule] 3M2ᵛ tou- [toutes] 3Q3ʳ (fon-) de- [demens] 3X2ʳ (par-) ticu- [ticulier] 4E4ʳ pro- [propre]

Notes: Text is a reprint of no. 94 (1729) with correction of minor errors. But Coste has added at least a dozen new notes, chiefly to Book II; he has also expanded others. According to Schøsler (see *Notes* to no. 91), the most striking is Coste's examination of Locke's refutation of the Cartesian notion of the soul.

References: Attig 353; Christophersen p. 97; Rochedieu p. 192.

Copies examined: Y   MH (Phil.2115.48.7)   NjP (B1293.F7xC6 1735 (Ex))   P (R.4996)   Vat   WaU (192.2 Es7Fc3; lacks front.; cut 253 × 192 mm)

96. *Essay*. French trans. (Coste). 4th ed., Amsterdam, 1742. 4°

In red & black: [red line:] ESSAI | PHILOSOPHIQUE | *CONCERNANT* | [red:] L'ENTENDEMENT | HUMAIN, | . . . [&c. as in no. 95, until

12th line:] Quatrième Edition, revûe, corrigée, & augmentée de quelques Additions im- | portantes de l'Auteur qui n'ont paru qu'après fa mort, & de plufieurs Re- | marques du Traducteur, dont quelques-unes paroiffent pour la premiére | fois dans cette Edition. | *Quam* [swash Q] . . . *quàm* | *ifta . . . difplicere!* | Cic. de Nat. Deor. Lib. I. | [engr. vignette as in no. 94] | A AMSTERDAM, | [red:] Chez PIERRE MORTIER. | M. DCC. XLII.

Coll: 4° (247 × 192 mm cut) *-5*⁴ 6*² (-6*2) A-4I⁴ (-4I4) [$ half + 1 signed]; 332 leaves; pp. *I-VIII* X-XVIII *XIX* XX *XXI* XXII-XXIX *XXX* XXXI-XXXIX *XL-XLI* XLII *1* 2-6 *7* 8-59 *60* 61-603 *604-622* [= 664].

Contents: *1ʳ (*I*) title (verso blank), *2ʳ-*4ᵛ (*III-VIII*) dedication to Duke of Buckinghamshire, 2*ʳ-3*1ᵛ (*IX-XVIII*) translator's note, 3*2ʳ,ᵛ (*XIX-XX*) 'Avis sur cette 4. éd.', 3*3ʳ-4*3ʳ (*XXI-XXIX*) Coste's 'Eloge' of Locke, 4*3ᵛ-5*4ʳ (*XXX-XXXIX*) Locke's pref., 5*4ᵛ (*XL*) 'M. Locke au Libraire', 6*1ʳ,ᵛ (*XLI-XLII*), contents by books & chap., A1ʳ-A3ᵛ (*1-6*) 'Avant-Propos', A4ʳ-H2ʳ (*7-59*) text of Book I Chap. 'I'-'III', H2ᵛ-4G2ʳ (*60-603*) text of Books II-IV, 4G2ᵛ-4I3ʳ (*604-621*) index, subscribed 'Achevé d'imprimer le 19. d'Août 1741.', 4I3ᵛ blank.

Illustrations: engr. plate as frontispiece, portrait of the older Locke, facing right, by F. Morellon la Cave, after Kneller, dated 1734, 216 × 158 mm on plate 226 × 168 mm.

Text (H3ᵛ): 45 lines; 188 (201) × 122 (144) mm; 83 R. Good laid paper, with no visible watermarks. Marginal subject contents of sections set 52 R. Translator's note set 27 lines 138 ital; Coste's 'Eloge' set 46 lines 83 R; Locke's pref. 46 lines 82 ital. Footnotes set 66 R. Page no. at external ends of headlines.

HT A1ʳ, A4ʳ, 2S1ᵛ and 3H2ʳ: ESSAI | PHILOSOPHIQUE | CONCERNANT | L'ENTENDEMENT HUMAIN. | [orn. fillet 4 × 121 mm]

Headlines or RTs (where long) are italic chapter titles or title summaries in italics, followed by book number in large & small capitals, e.g. 'LIV. IV.' Chapter no. in large & small caps in margin at outer ends of first line of text, e.g 'CHAP. XI.'

CW: Page. *3ʳ Vous- [Vous-même] 4*1ʳ fu- [fujet] A2ʳ nature, B3ʳ dé- [déployer] P4ᵛ (em-) pêche- [pêchement] 2E3ʳ hom- [hommes] 2N2ʳ *Meur*- [*Meurtre.*] 3D2ᵛ (difficul-) tez, 3P3ᵛ (re-) gar- [gardent] 3Z1ʳ Droits, 4F4ʳ Con- [Connoiffance]

Notes: This is the last edition revised by Coste, who died in 1747. The text reprints line-by-line that of 1735 (no. 95), with minor corrections. However Coste again adds more notes and expands others, chiefly to express his own scepticism, returning to the question of the soul of animals.

References: Attig 354; Christophersen p. 97; Rochedieu p. 192.

Copies examined: Y   CaOTU (Locke L63.E82F7 1742)   CaQQL (B1293.F814 l742)   MH (Phil.2115.48.11)   NjP (6106.333.6.11)   NRU   P (R.4997)

97. *Essay.* French trans. (Coste) '4th ed.', 1750. Amsterdam (Paris?). 4 vols. in 12°

ESSAI | PHILOSOPHIQUE [swash Q] | CONCERNANT | L'ENTENDEMENT | HUMAIN, | *Où l'on montre quelle eſt l'etenduë de nos connoiſſances* | *certaines, & la maniere dont nous y parvenons.* | PAR M. LOCKE. | Traduit de l'Anglois | *PAR M. COSTE,* | Quatriéme Edition, revuë, corrigée & augmentée de quelques | Additions importantes de l'Auteur qui n'ont paru qu'après ſa | mort, & de pluſieurs Remarques du Traducteur, dont quel- | ques-unes paroiſſent pour la premiere fois dans cette Edition. | *Quam . . . quàm iſta | effutientem . . . diſplicere*! Cic. de Nat. | Deor. Lib. I. | TOME PREMIER. ['SECOND.', 'TROISIÉME.', 'QUATRIÉME.'] | [orn. star on roundel 8 × 8 mm] | A AMSTERDAM. | Chez *PIERRE MORTIER.* | [rule 54 mm] | M.DCC.L.

Coll: 12° (165 × 97 mm cut). Vol. 1: π^2 *-3^{*12} 4^{*2} (-4*2) $\tilde{a}^2$ (-$\tilde{a}$2) A-Q^{12} R^2 [$ half signed]; 234 leaves; pp. *i–iv I* II–XV *XVI* XVII–XX *XXI* XXII–XLV *XLVI* XLVII–LXXIV *LXXV–LXXVI 1* 2–15 *16–17* 18–172 *173* 174–385 *386–388* [= 468].

Vol. 2: π^2 $\tilde{a}^2$ (-$\tilde{a}$2) A-X^{12} Y^8 [$ half (+Y5) signed]; 263 leaves; pp. *i–vi 1* 2–518 *519–520* [= 526].

Vol. 3: π^2 $\tilde{a}^2$ (-$\tilde{a}^2$) A-T^{12} V^4 (-V4) [$ half (-T6, -V2) signed]; 234 leaves; pp. *i–vi 1* 2–46 *47* 48–293 *284* 295–356 *357* 358–443 *404* 445–462 [= 468]. Page 294 called '284'; 444 called '404'.

Vol. 4: π^2 $\tilde{a}^2$ (-$\tilde{a}$2) A-R^{12} S^4 (-S4) T-Y^6 Z^3 [$ half (+Z2) signed]; 237 leaves; pp. *i–vi 1* 2–413 *414–468* [= 474].

First page of each sheet in vols. 1–3 also signed in direction line, e.g. 'Tome II.' In vol. 4 only sheets ã and T–Z show vol. indication: 'Tome IV.' on first page of sheet ã; and sheets T–Z read '*Tom.IV.*'

Contents: Vol. 1: $\pi1^r$ (*i*) half-title (verso blank), $\pi2^r$ (*iii*) title (verso blank), *1^r–*8^r (*I–XV*) translator's note, *8^v–*10^v (*XVI–XX*) 'Avis sur cette edition', *11^r–2*11^r (*XXI–XLV*) Coste's 'Eloge', 2*11^v–4*1^r (*XLVI–LXXIII* top 1/3) Locke's pref., 4*1^r–4*1^v (*LXXIII* lower 2/3–*LXXIV*) 'Monsieur Locke au Libraire', ã$1^{r,v}$ (*LXXV–LXXVI*) contents by book & chap., A1^r–A8^r (*1–15*) 'Avant-propos' (text of 1.1), A8^v (*16*) quotation from Cicero repeated from title, A9^r–H2^v (*17–172*) 'Livre I, ch. 1–3' (text of 1.2–4), H3^r–R1^r (*173–385*) text of 2.1–13, R1^v–R2 blank.

Vol. 2: $\pi1^r$ (*i*) half-title (verso blank), $\pi2^r$ (*iii*) title (verso blank), ã$1^{r,v}$ (*v–vi*) contents of vol. by book & chap., a1^v blank, A1^r–Y7^v (*1–518*) text of 2.14–31, Y8 blank.

Vol. 3: $\pi1^r$ (*i*) half-title (verso blank), $\pi2^r$ (*iii*) title (verso blank), ã$1^{r,v}$ (*v–vi*) contents by book & chap., A1^r–B11^v (*1–46*) text of 2.32–33, B12^r–P10^v (*47–356*) text of Book III, P11^r–T12^v (*357–462*) text of 4.1–3.

Vol. 4: $\pi1^r$ (*i*) half-title (verso blank), $\pi2^r$ (*iii*) title (verso blank), ã$1^{r,v}$ (*v–vi*) contents by book & chap., A1^r–S3^r (*1–413*) text of 4.4–21, S3^v blank, T1^r–Z3^v (*415–462*) 'Table des principales matières' (index).

Text (v. 1 F1ʳ): 30 lines; 127 (136) × 60 (76) mm; 84 R. Fair laid paper, watermarked with bunch of grapes, and word 'VAUD'; § ã watermarked '+ AUVERRUNE 794'. Topical headings of sections set roman in outer margins. Page no. in outer corners of headlines.
Half-title: ESSAI | PHILOSOPHIQUE [swash Q] | CONCERNANT | L'ENTENDEMENT | HUMAIN. | [Oxford rule 70 mm] | TOME PREMIER. ['SECOND.', 'TROISIEME.'] (Vol. 4 has triple rule, thin/thick/thin, 74 mm, before '*TOME QUATRIEME.*')
Headlines or RTs are chapter titles in italics, followed by book no. in large & small caps., e.g. '*Qu'il n'y point | de Principes innés.* LIV. I.' with page no. at outer ends of headlines.
CW: Page. Vol. 1: *5ʳ (repré-) ſenrer [ſenter] B6ʳ s'ap- [s'appercevoir (*sic*)] H1ᵛ (fonde-) mens, K12ᵛ (re-) cevons Q4ᵛ (Philo-) ſophie
  Vol. 2: A12ᵛ (certai-) ne- [tainement,] G4ʳ quoi- [quoique] T12ʳ tres
  Vol. 3: A1ᵛ (menta-) le G3ᵛ (don-) ner P6ᵛ (quel-) le
  Vol. 4: B11ʳ (dan-) gereux G9ʳ (par-) ties O5ʳ com- [comparées] S1ʳ conſ- [conſtitutions,]
    Footnotes that continue on the following page have catchwords also. Vol. 3 without CW on p. 346 (P5ᵛ). Vol. 4 without CW on I11ᵛ (p. 214), K12ʳ (239), L4ᵛ (248), S3ʳ (p. 413); and on inner forme of sheet V (V3ᵛ, 4ʳ, 5ᵛ, and 6ʳ).
Notes: Reprint of the 4th ed. of 1742 (no. 96), omitting Coste's dedication to Edmund Sheffield, Duke of Buckingham & Normanby, and Locke's portrait as frontispiece. The note, 'Avis sur cette nouvelle edition' in no. 98 (1755) implies this edition is a piracy and was actually printed in France. (See no. 98, *Notes*.) I am indebted to B. Blasselle of the Bibliothèque nationale (Paris) for his help with some of the details of this edition.
References: Attig 355; Christophersen p. 97; Rochedieu p. 192.
Copies examined: P (R.12150–53) L (528.d.18–21; v.1 has ã1 bd. before *1)

98. *Essay*. French trans. (Coste). 5th ed., Amsterdam & Leipzig, 1755. 4°
In red & black: ESSAI | [red line:] PHILOSOPHIQUE | CONCERNANT | [red:] L'ENTENDEMENT | HUMAIN, . . . [&c. as in no. 96, until 10th line:] TRADUIT DE L'ANGLOIS PAR M. COSTE. | [red:] CINQUIEME EDITION REVUE ET CORRIGE'E. | *Quam . . . quàm | iſta . . . diſplicere!* | CIC. de Nat. Deor. Lib. I. | [orn. engr. plate with 2 putti strolling near shipwreck, overhead a scroll reading 'NIL DESPERANDUM AUSPICIBUS PALLADE ET MERCURIO', subscribed *S. Fokke indel. ft.*, 67 × 101 mm on plate 71 × 109 mm] | *A AMSTERDAM ET A LEIPZIG,* | [red:] Chez J. SCHREUDER & PIERRE MORTIER le Jeune. | MDCCLV.
Coll: 4° (249 × 194 mm cut) π² *-5*⁴ A-4I4 (-4I4) [$ half + 1 (-4I3) signed]; 333 leaves; pp. *i–iv I–VII VIII–XVI XVII XVIII XIX XX–XXVII XXVIII XXIX–XXXVII XXXVIII–XL* 1 2–6 7 8–59 60 61–321 322 323–426 427 428–603 604–622 [= 666].

Contents: π1ʳ half-title (verso blank), π2ʳ title (verso blank), *1ʳ-*3ᵛ (*I–VI*) Coste's dedication to Edmund Sheffield, Duke of Bucks. and Normanby, *4ʳ-2*4ᵛ (*VII–XVI*) 'AVERTISSEMENT DU TRADUCTEUR.', 3*1ʳ˒ᵛ (*XVII–XVIII*) 'AVIS SUR LA QUATRIEME EDITION, Publiée en 1742', 3*2ʳ (*XIX*) 'AVIS SUR CETTE NOUVELLE ÉDITION.', 3*2ᵛ-4*2ʳ (*XX–XXVII*) Coste's 'ELOGE DE MR. LOCKE' (cf. C1705-3), 4*2ᵛ-5*3ʳ (*XXVIII–XXXVII*) 'PREFACE DE L'AUTEUR.', 5*3ᵛ (*XXXVIII*) 'MONSIEUR LOCKE AU LIBRAIRE.', 5*4ʳ˒ᵛ (*XXXIX–XL*) contents by book & chap., A1ʳ-A3ᵛ (*1-6*) 'Avant-propos', A4ʳ-H2ʳ (*7-59*) text of 'Livre I', H2ᵛ-2S1ʳ (*60-321*) text of Book II, 2S1ᵛ-3H1ᵛ *322-426*) text of Book III, 3H2ʳ-4G2ʳ (*427-603*) text of Book IV, 4G2ᵛ-4I3ʳ (*604-621*) index, 4I3ᵛ (*622*) blank.

Illustration: engr. portrait of the older Locke, facing left, signed 'G. Kneller Eques pinxit 1697. P. Tanjé ſculp. 1754.', within oval frame lettered 'JEAN LOCKE NÉ EN AOUT M.D.C.XXXII MORT LE XXVIII. OCTOBRE. M.D.C.C.IV.' on a pedestal with 6-part heraldic shield and 4 italic lines in Latin, '*Adſcribebat JOANNES CLERICUS.*' Here the portrait faces three-quarters to the viewer's left, and within the same frame (with same inscription) is a mirror image of the portrait in the 1742 edition. All portraits by Greenhill in earlier English and French editions face right. Engraving measures 215 × 157 mm on plate 226 × 164 mm.

Text (D1ᵛ): 46 lines; 189 (201) × 119 (141) mm; 83 R. Prelim. gathering on heavy laid paper; body of vol. on good laid paper, without watermarks. Page no. at external ends of headlines; chap. no. in external margins on line with first line of text. Translator's note set 27 lines 138 R; Coste's 'Eloge' set 46 lines set 83 R; Locke's pref. set 46 lines 82 ital.

Half-title: ESSAI | PHILOSOPHIQUE [swash Q] | CONCERNANT | L'ENTENDEMENT | HUMAIN.

HT, A1ʳ, A4ʳ, H2ᵛ, 2S1ᵛ and 3H2ʳ: ESSAI | PHILOSOPHIQUE | CONCERNANT | L'ENTENDEMENT HUMAIN. | [orn. fillet as rule 115 mm]

Headlines or RTs are chapter title summaries in italics, followed by book no. in large & small caps, e.g '*Des Degrés d'Aſſentiment.* LIV. IV.'

CW: Page. *3ʳ deſ- [deſſein,] 3*3ʳ Cette 4*1ʳ preuve A2ʳ pour- [pourvu] B3ʳ (dé-) plo- [ployer] P4ᵛ (em-) pêche- [pêchement] 2E3ʳ Hom- [Hommes] 2N2ʳ Meur- [*Meurtre*.] 3D2ᵛ (difficul-) tés, 3P3ᵛ (re-) gar- [gardent] 3Z1ʳ droits, 4F4ʳ con- [connoiſſance]

Notes: Preliminary matter has been reworded and reset. The text and the index are a line-for-line reprint of 1742 ed. (no. 96) with very little change. There is a note on p. *XIX* stating "On en a fait aussi une [édition] en *France* [no. 97, 1750] quoique le Titre porte Amsterdam, en quatre Volumes *in*-12, dont on peut dire que ni le Papier, ni le Caractére, ni le Format, ne répondent à l'importance de l'Ouvrage" as found in the five true Holland editions; however the note states the booksellers made use of some of the corrections and capitalisations here where they were judged good or necessary. The final 14 lines from the translator's note in earlier editions are also omitted.

J. Lewine, in his *Bibliography of Eighteenth-Century Art and Illustrated Books* (London, 1898) says the portrait after Kneller is by Fokke, although it is not signed (p. 321). He appears to have confused it with the engraved title vignette.

References: Attig 356; Rochedieu p. 192.
Copies examined: Y CaOTU (Locke Coll.L63.E82F7 1755) Ct [GhU (136K20)] MH (Phil.2115.48.12) Utr (179.A.24)

Dr. B. Fabian reports a copy of this edition at the University of Münster.

99. *Essay*. French trans. (Coste) 'New' ed., 1758. 'Amsterdam' (Paris?). 4 vols. in-12°
ESSAI | PHILOSOPHIQUE [swash Q] | CONCERNANT | L'ENTENDEMENT | HUMAIN, | OÙ L'ON MONTRE | *Quelle eſt l'étendue de nos connoiſſances certaines,* | *& la maniere dont nous y parvenons.* | PAR M. LOCKE. | *Traduit de l'Anglois par M.* COSTE. | NOUVELLE EDITION, | Revue, ... de | l'Auteur ... Remarques | du ... dont | quelques-unes paroiſſent pour la premiere | fois dans cette Edition. | *Quam* [swash Q] ... *iſta* | *effutientem* ... *diſplicere!* Cic. de Nat. | Deor. Lib. I. | TOME PREMIER. ['SECOND.' 'TROISIEME.', 'QUATRIEME.'] | [orn. star on roundel 8 × 8 mm] | A AMSTERDAM, | AUX DÉPENS DE LA COMPAGNIE. | [Oxford rule 54 mm] | M. DCC. LVIII.
Colophon, v.1, π1^v: *Ce Livre ſe trouve* | A PARIS, | Chez DE HANSY, le jeune, | Libraire, rue Saint-Jacques, | près les Mathurins. | [orn. rule 67 mm]
Coll: 12° (165 × 97 mm cut). Vol. 1: π^4 *-3*^{12} 4*^{2} (-4*2) a^2 (-a2) A-Q^{12} R^2 (-R2) [$ half signed]; 235 leaves; pp. *1-8 I II-XV XVI XVII-XX XXI XXII-XLV XLVI XLVII-LXXIV LXXV-LXXVI 1 2-15 16-17 18-172 173 174-385 386* [=470].

Vols. 2–4: same as 1750 edition (no. 97). First page of each gathering in all vols. signed in the direction line, e.g. '*Tome IV.*'
Contents: Vol. 1: π1^r blank, π1^v (2) bookseller's note, π2^r (3) half-title (verso blank), π3^r blank, π3^v (6) portrait of Locke, π4^r (7) title (verso blank), *1^r–R1^v (*I-LXXVI 1-386*) identical with 1750 edition (no. 97).

Vols. 2–4: contents identical with 1750 edition (no. 97).
Illustration: vol. 1 has frontispiece portrait of Locke by C. Duflos after Kneller, 134 × 83 mm on plate 145 × 89 mm.
Half-title, all vols.: ESSAI | PHILOSOPHIQUE | CONCERNANT | L'ENTENDEMENT | HUMAIN. | TOME Ier. ['TOME II.', 'III.', 'IV.']
Text: Same as no. 97 except for first four leaves of vol. 1: their chainlines are vertical; as are first 2 leaves of each vol. 2–4. Chainlines in rest of all vols. are horizontal, with a bunch of grapes as watermark.
Notes: A reissue of the same sheets used in no. 97 except for the first 4 leaves of vol. 1, and first 2 leaves of v. 2–4, as indicated by identical signature

positions. Thus they form a cancellans gathering for gathering π^2 in all vols. of that edition. Indicating the vol. numbers in the direction line for each gathering in vol. 4 seems to be a stop-press correction. I again assume this is a piracy, the phrase 'At the Expense of the Company' of booksellers frequently denotes an unauthorised publication.
References: Attig 357; Christophersen p. 97; Rochedieu p. 192.
Copies examined: P (D.12154–57) [BBR] CaOTU (Locke L63.E82F7 1758; vol.1 lacks π1 (bookseller's note) and π3 (front. port.))

100 and 101. *Essay*. French trans. (Coste) 'New ed.', 1774. Amsterdam. 4 vols. in-12°

These two editions are very similar in imprint, size and use of hollow type on the title page. They both have as imprint 'Aux Dépens de la Compagnie', often an indication of an unauthorised printing. They both use roman numerals for the imprint date, though one has those numerals italicized; in the other, roman font. The preliminary pages of the edition with italicized imprint date are numbered in upper-case roman numerals, the other has lower-case. Further the volumes have different numbers of pages, neither edition patterned after earlier 4-vol. duodecimo pagination (cf. no. 97, 99). In one edition, the gatherings are half signed in arabic numerals throughout; the other, also half signed, but vols. 1 and 3 signed French style in roman (e.g. ij, iij, iv, v, vj). I suspect that the edition with non-italicized imprint date (and gatherings signed French style) was really printed in France. I can find no explanation for two very similar editions being printed in the same year. (Attig only notices the French-style edition; Rochedieu does not distinguish the two.)

100. *Essay*. French trans. (Coste) Amsterdam, 1774. With italicized imprint date (in roman numerals). Two issues.

101A (First issue). Vols.1–4: [hollow type:] ESSAI | [hollow type:] PHILOSOPHIQUE | *CONCERNANT* | [decorative hollow type:] L'ENTENDEMENT | HUMAIN, | OU L'ON MONTRE | *Quelle eſt l'étendue de nos connoiſſances certai-* | *nes, & la maniere dont nous y parvenons.* | PAR M. LOCKE. | *Traduit de l'Anglois par M. COSTE.* | NOUVELLE ÉDITION, | Revue, corrigée & augmentée de quelques Additions | importantes de l'Auteur, qui n'ont paru qu'après ſa | mort, & de pluſieurs Remarques du Traducteur, dont | quelques-unes paroiſſent pour la premiere fois dans | cette Édition. | *Quàm...neſ-* | *cias,... ſibi* | *diſplicere!* Cic. de Nat. Deor. Lib. I. | TOME PREMIER. ['SECOND.', 'TROISIEME.', 'QUATRIEME.'] | [orn., radiant sun, 8 × 8 mm] | *A* AMSTERDAM, | Aux Dépens de la Compagnie. | [orn. double rule with scrolls 56 mm] | *M. DCC. LXXIV.*

101B (Second issue) Vols. 1–3 as first issue. Vol. 4: as v.1–3 except 'PHILOSOPHIQUE' and 'L'ENTENDEMENT' not in hollow type, and line 20 reads 'TOME QUATRIEME.'; orn. rule at bottom is segmented,

52 mm, and imprint date reads: 'M, DCC, LXXIV.' (i.e. commas, not full stops).

Coll: 12° (183 × 105 mm uncut). Vol. 1: a–c^{12} A–N^{12} O^3 [$ half (–a2) signed; N4 signed 'M4']; 195 leaves; pp. *I–V* VI–XVI *XVII* XVIII–XX *XXI* XXII–XL *XLI* XLII–LXXII *1* 2–12 *13–15* 16–140 *141* 142–316 *317–318* [=390]. First page of sheets a–c signed also 'Tome I.' in direction line; sheets A–O signed '*Tome I*.'

Vol. 2: π^2 A–R^{12} S^6 [$ half signed]; 212 leaves; pp. *i–iv 1* 2–417 *418–420* [=424].

Vol. 3: π^2 A–P^{12} Q^{10} [$ half signed]; 192 leaves; pp. *i–iv 1* 2–36 *37* 38–290 *291* 292–378 *379–380* [=384].

Vol. 4: π^2 χ^1 A–Q^{12} R^2 [$ half (+R2) signed]; 197 leaves; pp. *i–vi 1* 2–388 [=394].

First page of each sheet in vols. 2–4 also signed '*Tome II*.', '*III*.', '*IV*.' respectively.

Contents: Vol. 1: a1^r (*I*) half-title (verso blank), a2^r (*III*) title (verso blank), a3^{r}a8^v (*V–XVI*) 'Avertissement du traducteur', a9^r–a10^v (*XVII–XX*) 'Avis sur cette 4. édition.', a11^r–b8^v (*XXI–XL*) Coste's 'Eloge', b9^v–c11^v (*XLI–LXX*) Locke's pref., c12^{r,v} (*LXXI–LXXII*) 'M. Locke au Libraire', A1^r–A6^v (*1–12*) 'Avant-propos' (1.1 of *Essay*), A7^r blank, A7^v (*14*) repeat of quotation from Cicero as on title, A8^r–F10^v (*15–140*) text of 1.2–4 (called 1.1–3), F11^r–O2^v (*141–316*) text of 2.1–13, O3^{r,v} (*317–18*) contents of vol. 1 by book & chapter.

Vol. 2: π1^r (*i*) half-title (verso blank), π2^r (*iii*) title (verso blank), A1^r–S5^r (*1–417*) text 2.14–31, S5^v–S6^r (*418–19*) contents of vol., S6^v blank.

Vol. 3: π1^r (*i*) half-title (verso blank), π2^r (*iii*) title (verso blank), A1^r–B6^v (*1–36*) text of 2.32–33, B7^r–N1^v (*37–290*) text of Book 3, N2^r–Q9^v (*291–378*) text of 4.1–3, Q10^{r,v} (*379–80*) contents of vol.

Vol. 4: π1^r (*i*) half-title (verso blank), π2^r (*iii*) title (verso blank), χ1^{r,v} (*v–vi*) contents of vol., A1^r–O10^v (*1–332*) text of 4.4–21, O11^r–R2^v (*333–388*) index.

Text (v.3 L12^v; same for all vols.): 33 lines; 124 (133) × 62 (78) mm; 76 R. Good laid paper watermarked with bunch of grapes, 'ROBAILLIOT' and 'FIN'. Page no. at outer ends of headlines level with text block. Section summaries set roman in margin. Footnotes set 55 R. Chapter no. in external margins beneath an Oxford rule, level with 1st line of text, e.g. 'CHAP.IV.'

Half-titles, v.1–4: [1st 4 lines as title, both issues] | HUMAIN. | *TOME PREMIER*. ['*SECOND*.'; '*TROISIEME*.'; '*QUATRIEME*.' swash Q].

HT, v.1 A1^r: [orn. rule 8 × 57 mm] | ESSAI | [hollow type:] PHILOSOPHIQUE | CONCERNANT | L'ENTENDEMENT HUMAIN. | [Oxford rule 61 mm] | AVANT-PROPOS. | [rule 61 mm]
v.1 A8^r: [framed headpiece with chalice 21 × 67 mm] | ESSAI | [. . . next 4 lines as on A1^r] | *LIVRE PREMIER*. | DES NOTIONS INNÉES. | [rule 61 mm]

v.1 F11^r: [framed headpiece with cherubs 24 × 68 mm] | . . . [next 5 lines as on A1^r] | *LIVRE SECOND.* | [rule 61 mm]
v.2 A1^r: [framed headpiece of flowers 22 × 73 mm] | . . . [next 4 lines as in v.1] | [orn. Oxford rule 62 mm] | *SUITE DU LIVRE II.* | [rule 60 mm]
v.3 A1^r: [framed headpiece of small fleurons 18 × 62 mm] | ESSAI | [hollow type:] PHILOSOPHIQUE | CONCERNANT | L'ENTENDEMENT HUMAIN. | [orn. Oxford rule 62 mm] | *SUITE DU LIVRE II.*
v.3 B7^r: [headpiece & 6 lines as on v.3 A1^r] | *LIVRE TROISIEME.* | DES MOTS. | [rule 61 mm]
v.3 N2^r: [headpiece & 6 lines as on v.3 A1^r] | *LIVRE QUATRIEME.* | DE LA CONNOISSANCE. | [rule 60 mm]
v.4 A1^r: [orn. & 5 lines as on v.3 A1^r] | *SUITE DU LIVRE IV.* | [orn. Oxford rule 61 mm]

Headlines or RTs are chapter title summaries in italics, followed by book no. in roman, e.g. 'De l'Exiſtence | de Dieu. Liv. IV.'

CW: Gathering. v.1: A12^v (propo-) ſition K12^v comme
v.2: B12^v (mo-) ment L12^v (l'eſ-) prit;
v.3: B12^v (habi-) tude N12^v (enſem-) ble
v.4: D12^v telle L12^v (l'eſ-) prit

Notes: Reprint of the text of the 4th ed. of 1742 (no. 96). In vol. 3 possibly § π formed the 2 center leaves of § Q, but this is difficult to tell. In the second issue, the first 2 leaves in vol. 4 printed on heavier paper, 163 × 100 mm cut, with vertical chainlines; they were not part of § R. In my copy the marginal notes on v.3 p. 2 except for the last 3 letters in each line do not print. The British Lib. copy has blank leaves tipped onto the outer edge of each textual leaf, with ms. notes on several tippings at the beginning of vol. 1; resulting pages measure 205 to 215 mm in width.

Thoemmes, catalogue 62 (1993) has another copy, recently sold to the University of California at Los Angeles; Brown University, Providence, R.I., also reports a copy.

Reference: Rochedieu p. 193.
Copy examined. First issue: L (8466.e.1, uncut; 4 vols. bd. in 2)
Second issue: Y

101. *Essay.* French trans. 1774. Amsterdam. With roman imprint date (in roman numerals)

Vols. 1 and 3: [ornate hollow type:] ESSAI | PHILOSOPHIQUE | CONCERNANT | [ornate hollow type:] L'ENTENDEMENT | [hollow type:] HUMAIN, | OU L'ON MONTRE | *Quelle eſt l'étendue de nos connoiſſances certai-* | *nes, & la maniere dont nous y parvenons.* | PAR M. LOCKE. | *Traduit de l'Anglois par M.* COSTE. | NOUVELLE ÉDITION | Revue, corrigée & augmentée de quelques aditions [sic] | importantes de l'Auteur, qui n'ont paru qu'après | ſa mort, & de pluſieurs remarques du Traducteur, [1st 'u' in 'Traducteur' faint or missing] | dont quelques-unes paroiſſent pour la premiere | fois dans cette Edition. |

Quam bellum . . . *quod* | *neſcias, quàm* . . . *ipſum* | *ſibi diſplicere*! [roman !] Cic. de Nat. Deor. Lib. I. | TOME PREMIER. ['TROISIEME.'] | [orn.: roundel bisected by lines into eighths, 8 × 8 mm] | A AMSTERDAM, | AUX DÉPENS DE LA COMPAGNIE. | [orn. Oxford rule 53 mm] | M. DCC. LXXIV.

Vols. 2 & 4: *ESSAI* | [ornate hollow type:] PHILOSOPHIQUE | CONCERNANT | L'ENTENDEMENT | HUMAIN, | Où L'ON MONTRE *quelle eſt l'étendue de nos* | *connoiſſances certaines, & la maniere dont* | *nous y parvenons.* | PAR M. LOCKE. | *Traduit de l'Anglois par M.* COSTE. | NOUVELLE ÉDITION, | Revue, corrigée & augmentée de quelques additions importantes de | l'Auteur . . . Remar- | ques . . . la pre- | miere fois dans cette Edition. | *Quam* . . . *quod neſcias,* | *quàm* . . . *diſplicere!* | Cic. de Nat. Deor. Lib. I. | TOME SECOND. ['QUATRIEME.'] | [2 facing fleurons as orn. 7 × 20 mm] | A AMSTERDAM, | AUX DÉPENS DE LA COMPAGNIE. | [Oxford rule 50 mm] | M. DCC. LXXIV.

Coll: 12° (170 × 97 mm cut). Vol. 1: a–c^{12} d^6 A–M^{12} N^8 [$ half (–aij) signed in roman numerals]; 194 leaves; pp. *j–v* vj–xvj *xvij* xviij–xxj *xxij* xxiij–xlvj *xlvij* xlviij–lxxix *lxxx* lxxxj *lxxxij–lxxxiv 1* 2–132 *133* 134–304 [= 388].

Vol. 2: π^2 χ^1 A–Q^{12} R^{12} (–R12 = χ1?) [$ half signed]; 206 leaves; pp. *j–vj 1* 2–192 173–191 182 193–386 [= 412]. Page no. 172–92 repeated, second 192 called '182'.

Vol. 3: π^2 χ^1 A–O^{12} P^8 [$ half (+ Pv, Pvj) signed in roman]; 179 leaves; pp. *j–vj 1* 2–34 *35* 36–267 *268* 269–352 [= 358].

Vol. 4: π^2 χ^1 A–Q^{12} R^4 [$ half signed)]; 199 leaves; pp. *j–vj 1* 2–391 *392* [= 398].

First leaf of each gathering also signed, e.g., '*Tome I.*'

Contents: Vol. 1: a1^r (*j*) half-title (verso blank), a2^r (*iij*) title (verso blank), a3^r–a8^v (*v*–xvj) 'Avertissement du traducteur', a9^r–a11^r (*xvij*–xxj) 'Avis sur cette 4. éd.', a11^v–b11^v (*xxij*–xlvj) Coste's 'Eloge', b12^r–d4^v (*xlvij*–lxxix) Locke's pref., d4^v–d5^r (*lxxx*–lxxxj) 'Monsieur Locke au Libraire', d5^v–d6^v (*lxxxij*–lxxxiv) contents of vol. 1 by book & chap., A1^r–F6^v (*1*–132) text of Book 1, F7^r–N8^v (*133*–304) text of 2.1–13.

Vol. 2: π1^r (*j*) half-title (verso blank), π2^r (*iij*) title (verso blank), π3^r–χ1^v (*iv*–*vj*) contents of vol. 2, A1^r–R11^v (*1*–386) text of 2.14–31.

Vol. 3: π1^r (*j*) half-title (verso blank), π2^r (*iij*) title (verso blank), χ1^{r,v} (*v*–*vj*) contents of vol. 3, A1^r–B5^v (*1*–34) text of 2.32–33, B6^r–M2^r (*35*–267) text of Book 3, M2^v–P8^v (*268*–352) text of 4.1–3.

Vol. 4: π1^r (*i*) half-title (verso blank), π2^r (*iii*) title (verso blank), χ1^{r,v} (*v*–*vi*) contents of vol. 4, A1^r–O9^v (*1*–330) text of 4.4–21, O10^r–R4^r (331–391) index, R4^v (*392*) blank.

Text (v.2 H3^r; same for all vols.): 35 lines; 118 (126) × 60 (74) mm; 67 R. Section content notes in outer margins. Page no. in outer external corners of headlines. Chapter no. at corners level with first line of text, e.g. 'CHAP. X.' or 'CHAP. | XXXI.' Good laid paper, not watermarked.

Half-titles of vols. 1 and 3 repeat first 4 lines of title, followed by: [hollow type:] HUMAIN. | [orn. rule as on title] | TOME PREMIER. ['TROISIEME.'] | [orn. rule]. Vols. 2 and 4 read: ESSAI | PHILOSOPHIQUE | CONCERNANT | L'ENTENDEMENT | HUMAIN. | TOME II. ['IV.']

Headlines or *RTs* are chap. title summaries and book numbers in italics. Chap. no. in outer margins on 2 lines, just below 1st line of text, e.g. 'CHAP. | XXI.'

Catchwords: Gathering (leaf 12ᵛ). Vol. 1: A (con-) noiſſance C ame K peut
  Vol. 2: B dans D (ex-) trêmement L a
  Vol. 3: B que C latin, N ſ.12.
  Vol. 4: D le H CHA- [CHAPITRE] L foi,

Notes: Reprint of the text of the 4th ed. of 1742 (no. 96). Dedication to Edmund Sheffield, as usual, omitted. With the differing style of vols. 1 and 3, as against that in vols. 2 and 4, I think two different printers produced this edition.

References: Attig 358; Rochedieu p. 193.

Copies examined: CaOTU (Locke L63.E82F7 1774)   CtY (K8.L79/fh774)   [GhU]   P (R.12150-53)

102. *Essay*. French trans. (Coste) '4th ed.', Paris, 1786-87. Paris. 4 vols.in 12°. Two issues.

102A.1-2. First issue. Vol. 1 & 2: ESSAI | PHILOSOPHIQUE | CONCERNANT | L'ENTENDEMENT | HUMAIN, | *Où l'on montre quelle eſt l'étendue de nos* | *connoiſſances certaines, & la maniere* | *dont nous y parvenons.* | PAR M. LOCKE. | *Traduit de l'Anglois par M.* COSTE. | Quatrieme Édition, revue, corrigée & augmentée de | quelques additions importantes de l'Auteur, qui | n'ont paru qu'après ſa mort, & de pluſieurs remar- | ques du Traducteur, dont quelques-unes paroiſſent | pour la premiere fois dans cette Edition. | *Quàm* [swash Q] . . . *neſcias,* | *quàm . . . diſpli-* | *cere!* Cic. de Nat. Deor. Lib. I. | TOME PREMIER. ['SECOND.'] | [double rule 33 mm] | A PARIS, | Chez SERVIERE, Libraire, rue St. Jean-de- | Beauvais. | [rule 19 mm] | 1786.

102A.3-4 and 102B. Second issue of vols. 1-2 and only issue of vols. 3-4 same as first issue except 'TOME TROISIEME.' and 'QUATRIEME.' but with imprint: A PARIS. |

Chez { SAVOYE, Libraire, rue Saint-Jac- ques.
       SERVIERE, Libraire, rue Saint- Jean-de-Beauvais.

| [rule 19 mm] | 1787.

Coll: 12° (167 × 96 mm cut). Vol. 1: A-Y¹² [$ half (-A2) signed]; 264 leaves; pp. *1-5* 6-111 *112-113* 114-282 *283* 284-525 *526-528*.
  Vol. 2: A-2B¹² [$ half (-A2, -V6, -2B5) signed; X5 signed 'S5']; 300 leaves; pp. *1-5* 6-595 *596-600*.

Vol. 3: A-Y^{12} Z^6 [$ half (-A2) signed]; 270 leaves; pp. *1-5* 6-58 *59* 60-416 *417* 418-540.

Vol. 4: π^2 A-Z^{12} Aa^4 [$ half (-A2) signed]; 282 leaves; pp. *1-5* 6-562 *563-564*.

Direction line on first page of each sheet also signed, e.g. 'TOME IV.'

Contents: Vol. 1: A1^r (*1*) half-title, A1^v (*2*) advt. for French editions of Locke's *Education* and 2nd *Treatise*, A2^r (*3*) title (verso blank), A3^r-A9^v (*5-18*) 'Avertissement du traducteur', A10^r-A12^v (*19-24*) 'Avis sur cette 4. éd.', B1^r-C1^v (*25-50*) Coste's 'Eloge', C2^r-D9^r (*51-89*) Locke's pref., D9^v-E8^r (*90-91*) 'M. Locke au Libraire', D10^v-E8^r (*92-111*) 'Avant-propos' (translation of 1.1), E8^v (*112*) repeat of quot. from Cicero as on title, E9^r-M9^v (*113-282*) text of 'Livre I' (tr. of 1.2-4), M10^r-Y9^v (*283-522*) text of 2.1-13, Y10^r-Y11^r (*523-525*) vol. 1 chapter contents, Y11^v-Y12 blank.

Vol. 2: A1^r (*1*) half-title (verso blank), A2^r (*3*) title (verso blank), A3^r-2B8^v (*5-592*) text of 2.14-31, 2B9^r-2B10^r (*593-595*) contents of vol. 2, 2B10^v-2B12 blank.

Vol. 3: A1^r (*1*) half-title (verso blank), A2^r (*3*) title (verso blank), A3^r-C5^v (*5-58*) text of 2.32-33, C6^r-S4^v (*59-416*) text of Book III, S5^r-Z5^v (*417-538*) text of 4.1-3, Z6^{r,v} (*539-540*) contents of vol. 3.

Vol. 4: π1^r (*1*) half-title (verso blank), π2^r (*3*) title (verso blank), A1^r-X1^r (*5-485*) text of 4.4-21, X1^v-X2^v (*486-488*) contents of vol. 4, X3^r-2A3^v (*489-562*) index, 2A4 blank.

Text (v.1 O5^r; same for all vols.): 29 lines; 121 (130) × 65 mm; 84 R. Good laid paper watermarked in a cartouche CAUVELIVRE. Page no. at outer ends of headlines.

Half titles: first 4 lines as on t.p., followed by: HUMAIN. | TOME PREMIER. ['SECOND.', &c.]

Headlines or RTs are chapter title summaries in italics between book and chapter no., e.g. 'LIV. I. *Qu'il n'a point* | *de principes innés*. CHAP. III.'

CW: Gathering.

Notes: Text is reprinted from the 4th ed. (1742, no. 96) following the 1774 text (no. 100), though not page-by-page. The change in imprint of the first two (or 3?) vols. of second issue are of a 'stop-press' nature; the rest of the title has not been reset. (I cannot tell about the third vol. since the only copy I found, at the Vatican Library, lacks vol. 3.

References: Attig 359 (for 2d issue only); Rochedieu p.193 (2d issue only).

Copies examined: First issue: Vat (Racc. Gen. Filosofia V186; v.3 wanting) Second issue: P (Z. Renan 4963)

103. *Essay*. French trans. (Coste) 'New ed.', Amsterdam, 1791. 4 vols. in 12°

Vol. 1: [hollow type:] ESSAI | [hollow type:] PHILOSOPHIQUE | CONCERNANT | [decorative hollow type:] L'ENTENDEMENT | HUMAIN, | OU L'ON MONTRE | *Quelle* [swash Q] . . . *certaines,* | *& la maniere . . . parvenons.* | PAR M. LOCKE. | *Traduit de l'Anglois par M.* COSTE. | NOUVELLE ÉDITION, | Revue, corrigée &

augmentée de quelques Additions | importantes de l'Auteur, qui n'ont paru qu'après fa | mort, & de plufieurs Remarques du Traducteur dont | quelques-unes paroiffent pour la premiere fois dans | cette Édition. | *Quàm* [swash Q] . . . *potiùs quod* | *nefcias, quàm . . . ipfum* | *fibi difplicere!* | CIC. de Nat. Deor. Lib. I. | TOME PREMIER. | [orn.: sunburst bisected by lines into eights, 8 × 8 mm] | *A AMSTERDAM,* | AUX DÉPENS DE LA COMPAGNIE. | [Oxford rule 45 mm] | M. DCC. LXXXXI.

Vols. 2-4 as vol. 1 except: TOME SECOND. ['TROISIEME.', 'QUATRIEME.'] and orn. before imprint varies: v.2 orn. is radiant face 8 × 9 mm; v.3 orn. is leafy scroll with finial 10 × 19 mm; v.4 orn. is small flower 9 × 11 mm.

Coll: 12°(162 × 97 mm cut). Vol. 1: a–c^{12} A–M^{12} N^4 [$ half signed]; 184 leaves; pp. *I-V* V–XVI *XVII* XVIII–XX *XXI* XXII–XXX *XLI* XLII–LXXII *1* 2–130 *131* 132–294 *295-296* [= 368].

Vol. 2: π^2 A–Q^{12} R^2 [$ half signed]; 196 leaves; pp. *i–iv 1* 2–387 *388* [= 392].

Vol. 3: A–O^{12} P^{10} [$ half (–A2) signed]; 178 leaves; pp. *1-5* 6–38 *39* 40–356.

Vol. 4: π^2 A–P^{12} Q^4 [$ half (+Q3) signed]; 186 leaves; pp. *i–iv 1* 2–366 *367-368* [= 372].

First page of each sheet also signed in direction line '*Tome I.*' ['*II.*', &c.]

*Contents:*Vol. 1: $a1^r$ (*I*) half-title (verso blank), $a2^r$ (*III*) title (verso blank), $a3^r$–$a8^v$ (*V–XVI*) 'Avertissement du traducteur', $a9^r$–$a10^v$ (*XVII–XX*) 'Avis sur cette quatrieme édition', $a11^r$–$b8^v$ (*XXI–XXXX*) Coste's 'Eloge', $b9^r$–$c11^v$ (*XLI–LXX*) Locke's pref., $c12^{r,v}$ (*LXXI–LXXII*) 'M. Locke au Libraire', A1^r–B7^r (*1–13*) 'Avant-propos', B7^v (*14*) quotation from Cicero, book I, B8^r–F5^v *15–130*) 'Livre I', F6^r–N2^v (*131–292*) text of 2.1–13, N3^{r,v} (*293–294*) vol. contents by chap., N4 (*295–296*) blank.

Vol. 2: $\pi1^r$ (*i*) half-title (verso blank), $\pi2^r$ (*iii*) title (verso blank), A1^r–R1^r (*1–385*) text of 2.14–31, R1^v–R2^r (*386–387*) vol. contents by chap., R2^v (*388*) blank.

Vol. 3: A1^r (*i*) half-title (verso blank), A2^r (*iii*) title (verso blank), A3^r–B7^v (*1–38*) text of 2.32–33, B8^r–M4^r (*39–271*) text of Book 3, M4^v–P9^v (*272–354*) text of 4.1–3, P10^{r,v} (*355–356*) vol. contents by chap.

Vol. 4: $\pi1^r$ (*i*) half-title (verso blank), $\pi2^r$ (*iii*) title (verso blank), A1^r–N10^v (*1–309*) text of 4.4–21, N11^{r,v} (*309–310*) vol. contents by chap., N12^r–Q4^v (*311–366*) index.

Text (v.1 E3^r; same for all vols.): 36 lines; 123 (130) × 69 (78) mm; 68 R. Good laid paper watermarked with bunch of grapes and '1790'. Page no. in outer ends of headlines, within margin of outer edges of text.

Half-titles, vols. 1–4: same as 1st 4 lines of title, followed by: HUMAIN. | TOME PREMIER. ['SECOND.', 'TROISIEME.', 'QUATRIEME.'] Bottom of vol. 3 A1^r also signed '*Tome III.* A' [= signature].

HT, v.1 A1ʳ: [orn. fillet 5 × 60 mm] | ESSAI | [hollow type:] PHILOSOPHIQUE | CONCERNANT | L'ENTENDEMENT | HUMAIN. | [Oxford rule 61 mm] | AVANT-PROPOS.
v.1 A8ʳ: [headpiece of musical horns and branches within a curving leafy frame, 26 × 74 mm] | . . . [5 lines as on A1ʳ] | *LIVRE PREMIER.*
v.1 F6ʳ: [framed headpiece of knot between flowers 25 × 65 mm] | . . . [4 lines as on v.1 A1ʳ] | [Oxford rule 59 mm] | *LIVRE SECOND.*
v.2 A1ʳ: [framed headpiece of blindfolded cupid with quiver 23 × 69 mm] | . . . [5 lines as in v. 1 A1ʳ] | *SUITE DU LIVRE II.*
v.3 A3ʳ: [framed headpiece of landscape scene with church tower, shed & house, 23 × 65 mm] | . . . [4 lines as in vol. 1 A1ʳ] | [Oxford rule 62 mm] | *SUITE DU LIVRE II.*
v.3 B8ʳ: [unframed headpiece of shell with scrolls, 23 × 67 mm] | . . . [4 lines as in vol. 1 A1ʳ] | [Oxford rule 59 mm] | *LIVRE TROISIEME.*
v.3 M4ᵛ: [framed headpiece of Roman landscape 28 × 69 mm] | [4 lines as on v.1 A1ʳ] | [Oxford rule 59 mm] | *LIVRE QUATRIEME.*
v.4 A1ʳ: [framed headpiece of bowl of fruit, with leaves, 20 × 65 mm] 5 lines as in vol. 1 A1ʳ] | *SUITE DU LIVRE IV.*
Headlines or RTs are chapter title summaries in italics followed by book no. in large and small caps., e.g. '*Des degrés | d'aſſentiment.* LIV. IV.' Chapter no. in external margins, beneath short Oxford rule aligned with 1st line of text, e.g. 'CHAP. III.'
CW: Gathering (on leaf 12ᵛ). v. 1: *a* & C nos H (cer-) tain
v.2: B d'un F aſſuré, K qui O certains
v.3: C (ma-) tiere: G approprié L mais O attendre,
v.4: A quelques D (cer-) tain, L avec O Idées
Notes: Reprint of text of the 4th ed. of 1742 (no. 94), probably as reprinted in the 1774 editions (no. 100 or 101).
Reference: Attig 360.
Copies examined: Y   O (Vet. B5 f.34–37)

104. *Essay.* French trans. (Coste) 'New ed.', Paris, 1795. 4 vols. in 12°
ESSAI | PHILOSOPHIQUE | CONCERNING | L'ENTENDEMENT HUMAIN, | Où l'on montre quelle est l'étendue de nos | connaissances certaines, et la manière | dont nous y parvenons. | PAR M. LOCKE. | *Traduit de l'Anglais par M.* COSTE. | Nouvelle Édition, revue, corrigée et augmentée de | quelques additions importantes de l'Auteur, qui n'ont | parus qu'après sa mort, et de plusieurs remarques du | Traducteur, dont quelques-unes paraissent dans cette | Édition. | *Quam bellum est velle confiteri potius nescire quod nescias, | quàm ista effucientem* [sic] *nauseare, atque ipsum sibi displicere!* | Cic. de Nat. Deor. Lib. I. | [rule 76 mm] | TOME PREMIER. ['SECOND.', 'TROISIÈME.', 'QUATRIÈME.'] | [rule 76 mm] | A PARIS, | Chez LETELLIER, Libraire, rue Hautefeuille, n°. 34 | [French rule, vol.1 35 mm; v.2, rule 29 mm; v.3–4, bold rule 31, 26 mm] | 1795.

Coll: 12° (167 × 98 mm cut). Vol. 1: π² A–R¹² [$ half signed; R5 and R6 both signed 'R6']; 206 leaves; pp. *i–iv 1* 2–9 *10* 11–13 *14* 15–34 *35* 36–60 *61 62 63* 64–75 *76–77* 78–191 *92* 192–214 *215* 216–227 *28* 229–253 *254 255– 259 260* 261–263 *64* 265–284 *285* 286–338 *339* 340–406 *407–408* [= 412]. Page no. 192, 228 and 264 have lost digits.

Vol. 2: π² A–T¹² V² [$ half signed]; 232 leaves; pp. *i–iv 1* 2–66 *67* 68–98 *99* 100–105 *106* 107–121 *122* 123–307 *308* 309–322 *323* 324–331 *332* 333– 341 *442* 343 *348* 345–347 *344 353* 350–352 *349* 354–409 *410* 411–445 *444* 447–460 [= 464]. Page no. 342 called '442'; the '3' in 364 inverted; 446 omitted, replaced by repetition of 444. On the outer form of sheet P (pp. 337–360) the 8th page was transposed with the 12th (P4ᵛ with P6ᵛ) and the 13th page with the 17th (P7ʳ with P9ʳ), while the text follows the page numbers.

Vol. 3: π² A–R¹² S⁴ [$ half signed]; 210 leaves; pp. *i–iv 1* 2–42 *43* 44–57 *58* 59–101 *102* 103–129 *30* 131–205 *206* 207–209 *210* 211–242 *243* 244– 320 *321* 322–416 [= 420]. First digit of page no. 130 lost; the '9' in no. 229 almost lost.

Vol. 4: π² A–P¹² Q⁴ [$ half (–Q2) signed]; 186 leaves; pp. *i–iv 1* 2–19 *0* 21– 27 *28* 29–35 *38–39* 38–39 *40* 41–67 *68* 69–128 *129* 130–160 *161* 162– 204 *205* 206–213 *214* 215–221 *222* 223–246 *247* 248–274 *27* 276–360 *361* 362–366 *367–368* [= 372]. Page no. 36–37 omitted, 38–39 repeated; first digit of no. 20 lost, and last digit of 275.

Contents: Vol. 1: π1ʳ (*i*) half-title (verso blank), π2ʳ (*iii*) title (verso blank), A1ᵣ–A5ᵣ (*1–9*) 'Avertissement du traducteur', A5ᵛ–A7ᵛ (*10–13*) 'Avis sur cette 4. éd.', A7ᵛ–B5ᵛ (*14–34*) Coste's 'Eloge', B6ʳ–C6ᵛ (*35–60*) Locke's pref., C7ʳ·ᵛ (*61–62*) 'M. Locke au Libraire', C8ʳ–D2ʳ (*63–75*) 'Avant-propos' (translation of 1.1), D2ᵛ (*76*) repeat of quot. from Cicero's *De nat. deor.*, D3ʳ–I11ᵛ (*77–214*) text of 'Livre I' (tr. of 1.2–4), I12ʳ–R11ᵛ (*215– 406*) text of 2.1–13, R12ʳ·ᵛ (*407–408*) contents of vol. by chapters.

Vol. 2: π1ʳ (*i*) half-title (verso blank), π2ʳ (*iii*) title (verso blank), A1ʳ–V2ʳ (*1–459* line 3) text of 2.14–31, V2ʳ·ᵛ (*459* line *4–460*) contents of vol.

Vol. 3: π1ʳ (*i*) half-title (verso blank), π2ʳ (*iii*) title (verso blank), A1ʳ–B3ᵛ (*1– 42*) text of 2.32–33, B4ʳ–O4ʳ (*43–320*) text of Book 3, O5ʳ–S4ʳ (*321–415* line 18) text of 4.1–3, S4ʳ·ᵛ (*415* line *19–416*) contents of vol.

Vol. 4: π1ʳ (*i*) half-title (verso blank), π2ʳ (*iii*) title (verso blank), A1ʳ–Q2ᵛ (*1–364*) text of 4.4–19, Q3ʳ·ᵛ (*365–366*) contents of vol., Q4 blank.

Text: 28 lines; 126 (134) × 77 mm; 89 R with 1 mm leading. Poor-quality thin browning laid paper with no visible watermark; horizontal chainlines. Page no. at external corners of headlines. Section summaries in italics precede each section. Direction line on first page of each gathering also indicates vol. no., '*Tome I.*' e.g. When the beginning of a chapter occurs on a new page, page no. is omitted.

Half-title: ESSAI | PHILOSOPHIQUE | CONCERNANT | L'ENTENDEMENT HUMAIN. | [rule 75 mm] | TOME PREMIER. ['SECOND.', &c.] | [rule 75 mm]

HT, v.1 D3ʳ (p. 77): framed headpiece of flowers and leaves, 22 × 76 mm + 4 lines as on half-title + Oxford rule 77 mm.
  v.2 A1ʳ: framed headpiece of footed vase with flowers set in a landscape 19 × 80 mm + 4 lines as on half-title + Oxford rule 77 mm.
  v.3 A1ʳ: framed headpiece of woman seated washing at stream bank, lambs left, building right, 27 × 78 mm + 4 lines as on half-title + Oxford rule 77 mm.
  v.3 B10ʳ (p. *43*) and O5ʳ (p. *321*): triple rule, thin/thick/thin 77 mm + 4 lines as on half-title + Oxford rule 77 mm.
  v.4 A1ʳ: same as v.1 D3ʳ (above).
Headlines or *RTs* are brief chapter titles in italics, with book no. on versos and chap. no. on rectos in large and small caps., e.g. 'LIV.II. *De la perception.* | *De la perception.* CHAP. IX.', 'LIV. I. *Que nuls principes* | *de pratique ne sont innés.* CHAP. II.' Headlines in vol. 1 sheet K versos (pp. 216-40) read in error 'LIV. I', as does P1ᵛ (p. 338).
CW: Gathering (on leaf 12ᵛ). Vol. 1: B (bon-) heur F que O de
  v.2: B idée M surfaces S (appa-) rences
  v.3: C Et G si M lui-même
  v.4: A bien H (coexis-) tent O §.4.
Notes: Standard reprint, probably following no. 102 (1786-87) but without index. The first edition to use modern spelling ('paraissent' instead of 'paroissent', 'connaissance', etc.) and to use a short 's' (instead of the long s: 'ſ'). Not listed in Rochedieu.
References: Attig 361 ('unverified', with inaccurate title); Christophersen p. 97 n.3.
Copy examined: Y

105. *Essay.* French trans. (Coste) '5th ed.', Paris, 'An VII' (1799). 4 vols. 12° in 8s & 4s
ESSAI | PHILOSOPHIQUE | CONCERNANT | L'ENTENDEMENT | HUMAIN, | *Où l'on montre quelle est l'étendue de nos* | *connoissances certaines, et la manière dont* | *nous y parvenons.* | Par LOCKE. | *Traduit de l'Anglois par* COSTE. | Cinquième Édition, revue, corrigée et augmentée de | quelques additions importantes de l'Auteur, qui n'ont | paru qu'après sa mort, et de plusieurs remarques du | Traducteur. | [rule 60 mm] | TOME PREMIER. ['SECOND.', 'TROISIÈME.', 'QUATRIÈME.'] | [rule 60 mm] | [French rule 34 mm] | A PARIS, | Chez BOSSANGE, MASSON et BESSON. | [rule 41 mm] | AN VII.
Coll: 12° in 8s and 4s (169 × 96 mm cut). Vol. 1: a⁸ b⁴ c⁸ d⁴ e⁸ f⁴ A⁸ B⁴ → X⁸ Y⁴ [$ half (–a2) signed]; 168 leaves; pp. *j–v vj–lxxij 1* 2-261 *262* 263-264 [= 336]. Prelim. sheets signed in italics.
  Vol. 2: π² A⁸ B⁴ → 2F⁸ 2G⁴ 2H⁶ [$ half signed]; 188 leaves; pp. *j–iv 1* 2-370 *371-372* [= 376].
  Vol. 3: π² A⁸ B⁴ → 2D⁸ 2E⁴ 2F² [$ half signed]; 172 leaves; pp. *j–iv 1* 2-337 *338* 339-340 [= 344].

Vol. 4: π² A⁸ B⁴ → 2D⁸ 2E⁴ 2F⁴ [$ half signed]; 174 leaves; pp. *j–iv 1* 2–291 292 *293–342 343–344* [= 348].

First page of each gathering signed, e.g., '*Tome* I.' in direction line.

Contents: Vol. 1: *a*1ʳ (*j*) half-title, *a*1ᵛ (*ij*) advt., *a*2ʳ (*iij*) title, *a*2ᵛ (*iv*) 'Quam bellum' quotation from Cicero, *a*3ʳ–*a*8ʳ (*v*–xv) 'Avertissement du traducteur', *a*8ᵛ–*b*2ᵛ (xvj–xx) 'Avis sur cette Edition', *b*3ʳ–*c*6ᵛ (xxj–xxxvj) 'Eloge de Locke' from Coste, *c*7ʳ–*e*6ʳ (xxxvij–lix) author's pref., *e*6ʳ–*e*6ᵛ (lix lower half–lx) 'Auteur au libraire', *e*7ʳ–*f*4ᵛ (lxj–lxxij) 'Avant-propos', A1ʳ–I6ᵛ (*1–108*) text of 'Livre I' (1.2–4), I7ʳ–YS3ʳ (*109–261*) text of 2.1–13, Y3ᵛ (*262*) blank, Y4ʳ,ᵛ (*263–264*) contents by chapters.

Vol. 2: π1ʳ (*j*) half-title, π1ᵛ (*ij*) advt., π2ʳ (*iij*) title, π2ᵛ (*iv*) Cicero quotation, A1ʳ–2H4ᵛ (*1–368*) text of 2.14–21, 2H5ʳ,ᵛ (*369–370*) contents of vol., 2H6 blank.

Vol. 3: π1–2 same as vol. 2, A1ʳ–C5ᵛ (*1–34*) text of 2.32–33, C6ʳ–Y1ᵛ (*35–258*) text of Book 3, Y2ʳ–2F1ᵛ (*259–338*) text of 4.1–3, 2F2ʳ,ᵛ (*339–340*) contents of vol.

Vol. 4: π1–2 same as vols. 2–3, A1ʳ–2B3ʳ (*1–293*) text of 4.4–21, 2B3ᵛ (*294*) blank, 2B4ʳ,ᵛ (*295–296*) chapter contents, 2B5ʳ–2F3ᵛ (*297–342*) alphabetical index, 2F4 blank.

Text (v.1 C8ᵛ; same for all vols.): 37 lines; 127 (135)×68 mm; 68 R. Watermark: 'DEU--I' and '---MIN-' in cartouches (dashes denote illegible letters).

Half titles: ESSAI | PHILOSOPHIQUE | CONCERNANT | L'ENTENDEMENT | HUMAIN. | [rule 68 mm] | TOME PREMIER. ['SECOND.', 'TROISIÈME.', 'QUATRIÈME.'] | [rule 68 mm].

*R T*s or headlines are chap. titles in italics with book no. at outer ends of versos, and chap. no. on rectos, e.g. 'LIV. IV. *De la foi, etc.* | *De la foi, etc.* CHAP. XVIII.' Longer titles split between verso and recto page. Page no. at outer ends of headlines.

CW: Gathering. Vol.1: B4ᵛ (ma-) nière P8ᵛ les
 v.2: C8ᵛ veux [quantité] M4ᵛ (hom-) mes 2B9ᵛ (sup-) posons
 v.3: E8ᵛ (pro-) pre S4ᵛ sert 2C4ᵛ connoissances
 v.4: A8ᵛ doivent M4ᵛ que 2C4ᵛ d'où [D'où]

Notes: Reprint following the text and style of the 1786–87 edition (no. 102). The advertisement in vol. 1, leaf *a*1ᵛ (p. *ij*) is for Locke's *De l'education des enfans* (1783); no. 210) and for *Du gouvernement civil*, probably the 1783 edition (no. 52) since it states it is 'augmentée d'un Précis historique de la Vie de l'Auteur. 1 vol. *in*–12.' Note the omission of 'Monsieur' before the author's and translator's names, in this revolutionary period.

Reference: Attig 362.

Copies examined: MH (Phil.2115.48.14) O¹ (Vet. E5 f.175–178) O² (Vet. E5 f.142–145; vol. 3 lacks leaf 2F1 (pp. *337–338*))

106*. *Essay*. French translation. Bern, 1800. 4 vols. in 8°.
  This edition is listed in the *Gesamtverzeichnis*, 1700-1910. If it was published no copies survive in German libraries, in Britain, France or North America. Neither Attig nor Rochedieu mention it. Dr. B. Fabian reports he was unable to locate any copy.

107*. *Essay*. German translation. Königsberg, 1755. Ghost.
  "The first German translation [of the *Essay*] appeared at Königsberg in 1755" reported H. R. Fox Bourne in his *The Life of John Locke*, vol. 2 (London, 1876), p. 441 n.2. Christophersen (p. 97) reports Bourne's information but states "I have never come across a copy of this edition." Neither have John Attig nor I. I feel fairly sure Bourne was confusing the German translation of the *Conduct of the Understanding* with that of the *Essay*. Entitled *Johann Lockens Anleitung des menschlichen Verstandes zur Erkäntniss der Wahrheit*, that work *was* published in Königsberg in 1755 (see no. 309). Dr. Marie-Louise Spieckermann, of the Englisches Seminar at the University of Münster confirms it is a ghost.

108. *Essay*. First German trans. (Poleyen) 1757. Altenburg. 4° Four states.
  Herrn Johann Lockens | Versuch | vom | Menschlichen Verstande. [ornamental M, V] | Aus dem Englischen übersetzt | und | mit Anmerkungen versehen | von | Heinrich Engelhard Poleyen, | Professor der Philosophie und Mathematik zu Weißenfels. | [engr. orn. (tailpiece) of seated astronomer with telescope, 77 × 90 mm] | [rule 163 mm] | Altenburg, in der Richterischen Buchhandlung. 1757.
Coll: 4° (245 × 181 mm cut): π^5 ($\pi 2 + \chi 1$) *^{4} a-e^4 A-5G^4 [$3 signed]; 425 leaves; pp. *i-lviii* 1 2-9 10 11-75 76 77-415 416 417-555 556 557-768 769-792 [= 850].
Contents: $\pi 1^r$ (*i*) title (verso blank), $\pi 2^r$ (*iii*) ornamental dedication to Friedrich Christian, Prince of Saxony (verso blank), $\pi 3^r(\chi 1^r)$–$\pi 5^v$ (*v-x*) text of dedication (set 18 lines, 104 fraktur), *1^r*–*4^v* (*xi-xviii*) translator's pref., a1^r-b2^v (*xix-xxx*) Coste's biography, concluding with 'Lobschrift' (copy of epitaph), b3^r-c2^v (*xxxi-xxxviii*) Locke's pref., c3^r-e4^v (*xxxix-lviii*) Gilbert's abstract (cf. no. 147 et seq.), A1^r-B1^r (*1-9*) 'Einleitung' (Book I ch. 1 as introd.), B1^v-K2^r (*10-75*) 1. Buch, 1.-3. Hauptstück (trans. of 1.2-4), K2^v-3F4^r (*76-415*) German text of Book 2, 3F4^v-4A2^r (*416-555*) text of Book 3, 4A2^v-5D4^v (*556-768*) text of Book 4, 5E1^r-5G4^r (*769-791*) 'Register' (alphabetical index), 5G4^v (*792*) errata.
States: 108A (*First state*): p. 792 errata with a heading and 6 lines.
  108B (*Second state*): p. 792 errata of 28 lines, including headings, citing 17 corrections to the body of the text.
  108C (*Third state*): p. 792 errata of 36 lines: 3-line note, followed by 3 subheadings (2 corrections to the Foreword, 1 to the 'Auszuge', and 24 corrections (in 26 lines) to the body of the text.

108D (*Fourth state*): p. 792 errata of 41 lines, with 3 lines of headings, citing 35 corrections to the body of the text.
Illustration: frontispiece is engraved portrait of Locke in oval frame on armorial pedestal, whose base shows 4-line quotation from Le Clerc, with subscripts: 'G. Kneller Eques pinxit. 1697.' and 'I.C. Sysang ſc.', 206 × 140 mm on plates 216 × 148 mm.
Text (3F3^v): 45 lines; 191 (204) × 134 (144) mm; 81 fraktur. Watermark: fleur-de-lys, with initials 'CC'. Page no. at outer end of headlines. Topical headings of sections set in outer margins, 57 fraktur. Translator's note set 70 fraktur. Headpieces on *1^r; tailpieces on pp. *xviii, lviii*, 9, 415, 768 and 791 (*4^v, e4^v, B1^r, 3F4^r, 5D4^v and 5G4^r).
HT: [unframed headpiece of torch in swagged frame 63 × 125 mm] | Verſuch | vom menſchlichen Verſtande. | [thick rule 106 mm] | [rule 88 mm]
RTs or headlines are summaries of chap. titles, followed by book and chap. no.; if long, they continue from verso to recto page, e.g. "Noch andere Betrachtungen | von einfachen Begriffen. 2. B. 8. H." RTs for Book 2, ch. 1 (pp. 78-98 = K3^v-N1^v) have RT beginning on recto page and ending on verso: "und deren Urſprung. 2. B. 1. H. | Von Begriffen überhaupt".
CW: Page (in fraktur). b4^v (ſchlech-) te- [teſten] D1^v begreift [begreift,] 2C3^v Ma- [Materie] 3E1^v Ge- [Gewebe] 3S4^r Zwey- [Zweytens,] 4O4^v blind- [blindlings] 5C3^r in- [inſonderheit]
Notes: The translator says he based his translation on the text in the *Works* (1727, no. 365), but his arrangement of Book I follows Coste, and some notes incorporate matter from Coste. But the 170 explanatory notes chiefly refer to contemporary German authors.
References: Attig 378; Christophersen p. 97.
Copies examined: First state: L (1248.*l*.1)   Thoemmes (as of 3.95)
  Second state: O (Vet.D5 d.76)   Wol (Vb.386)
  Third state: CaOTU (Locke L63.E82G4 1757)   MH (Phil.2115.49.5*)
  Fourth state: Y (lacks front.)

109. *Essay*. German trans. (Tennemann) Jena; Leipzig, 1795-97. 3 vols. in-8°
Vol.1: Locke's | Verſuch | über den | menſchlichen Verſtand | [French rule 23 mm] | aus dem Engliſchen überſetzt | mit einigen Anmerkungen und einer Abhandlung: | über | den Empirismus in der Philoſophie | von | D. Wilhelm Gottlieb Tennemann. | Erſter Theil. | [French rule 67 mm] | Iena, | im Verlag des akademiſchen Leſeinſtituts. | 1795.
Vol. 2: as v. 1, except ſt in 'Verſtand' is ligatured, until 5th line: [French rule 37 mm] | . . . | [&c. until 12rh line:] Zweiter Theil. | [rule 72 mm] | Leipzig, | bey Iohann Ambroſius Barth, 1797.
Vol. 3: as v. 2 until 10th line: von | Wilhelm Gottlieb Tennemann | Doctor der Philoſophie, Mitglied der Churfürſtlichen | Akademie nützlicher Wiſſenſchaften zu Erfurt und | Ehrenmitglied der lateiniſchen Geſell- | ſchaft zu Jena. | Dritter Theil. | [rule 72 mm] | Leipzig, | bey Iohann Ambroſius Barth, 1797.

Coll: 8o (167 × 98 mm cut). Vol. 1: *–3*⁸ A–2K⁸ 2L⁴ [$ half + 1 signed]; 292 leaves; pp. *I–III* IV–XVI *XVII* XVIII–XLVIII *1* 2–536 [= 584].
Vol. 2: π² A–2K⁸ 2L⁴ [$ half + 1 signed]; 268 leaves; pp. *i–iv 1* 2–238 *329* 330–531 *532* [= 536].
Vol. 3: *⁴ A–2G⁸ 2H⁴ [$ half + 1 signed]; 248 leaves; pp. *I–III* IV–VI *VII–VIII 1* 2–420 *421–423* 424–470 *471* 472–488 [= 496].

Contents: Vol. 1: *1ʳ (*I*) title (verso blank), *2ʳ–*8ᵛ (*III–XVI*) 'Vorrede des Uebersetzers', 2*1ʳ–3*7ᵛ (*XVII–XLVI*) 'Vorrede des Verfassers', 3*8ʳ,ᵛ (*XLVII–XLVIII*) vol. contents by book & chap. A1ʳ–M4ʳ (*1–185*) text of Book 1, M4ᵛ–2L4ᵛ (*186–536*) Book 2.1–20.
Vol. 2: π1ʳ (*i*) title (verso blank), π2ʳ,ᵛ (*iii–iv*) vol. contents by book and chap., A1ʳ–X4ᵛ (*1–328*) Book 2.21–33, X5r–2L4r (*329–531*) Book 3, 2L4ᵛ blank.
Vol. 3: *1ʳ (*I*) title (verso blank), *2ʳ–*3ᵛ (*III–VI*) 'Vorrede' explaining publication move to Leipzig, *4ʳ,ᵛ (*VII–VIII*) vol. contents by book & chap., A1ʳ–2D2ᵛ (*1–420*) Book 4, 2D3ʳ (*421*) section title (verso blank), 2D4ʳ–2G3ᵛ (*423–470*) text of Tennemann's 'Abhandlung', 2G4ʳ–2H4ᵛ (*471–488*) alphabetical index to all vols.

Text. Vol. 1: 26 lines; 121 (133) × 68 mm; 93 R with 1.5 mm leading; watermark 'F'. Text of vol. 1 has very few ligatured letters: an occasional 'ſt', and always 'ſs' and 'ſſ'. Vols. 2–3 additionally have ligatured 'fi'. Text of vols. 2–3: 30 lines; 129 (141) × 71 mm; 86 R with 1 mm leading; no watermarks. First page of each gathering of vols. 2–3 only also signed in direction line, e.g. 'Locke's. II. ['III.'] Theil.' All vols. have page no. at outer ends of headlines.

HT v.1 A1ʳ: [French rule 66 mm] | Locke's | Verſuch | über den | menſchlichen Verſtand. [No ligatures.]
v.2 A1ʳ: [rule 69 mm] | Locke's | Verſuch über den | menſchlichen Verſtand. | [French rule 34 mm]
v.3 A1ʳ: [rule 66 mm] | Viertes Buch. | Von der Erkenntniſs | und | der Meinung.

Section title, vol. 3, p. *421* (2D3ʳ): 'Abhandlung | über den | Empirismus in der Philoſophie | vorzüglich | den Lockiſchen.'

Headlines on verso pages indicate book no., e.g. 'Zweites Buch.'; rectos indicate chapters, e.g. 'Neuntes Kapitel.'

CW: Page. Vol. 1: I7ʳ Got- [Gottes,] T5ᵛ Ein- [Eindruck] 2G2ʳ benen- [benennen,]
Vol. 2: A3ʳ (Be-) we- [wegung] L7ʳ zwei- [zweite] 2C2ᵛ Wahr- [Wahrheit]
Vol. 3: B7ᵛ (un-) deut- [deutlich] L1ᵛ Evi- [Evidenz] Z3ᵛ Win- [Winkel]

Notes: A new translation by Tennemann. It does not follow Coste's arrangement of treating the first chapter of the first book as an introduction. In the 'Vorrede' to vol. 3 the translator apologizes for the delay in the appearance of vols. 2 and 3, because of an accident at the press. The delay has been to the benefit of readers, because it has allowed him to revise his translation. The statement therefore implies that the first vol. printed in Jena

is part of the set with those vols. printed in Leipzig, that they are not two different editions. Tennemann's 'Abhandlung' at the end of vol. 3 is his own study of empiricism, with reference to Locke's views.
References: Attig 379 (ignores Leipzig imprints); Christophersen p. 98.
Copies examined: O (Vet. D5 f.48–50) L (8463.bbb.25) MH (Phil.2115.49.10) Mun (Ph.Sp.499; vol. 1 only) (A copy reported at MH-AH was missing in 1992)

110. *Essay*. Latin trans. (Burridge). 1701. folio
Within a double rule, inner 254 × 135 mm, outer 265 × 146 mm: DE | INTELLECTU | HUMANO. | [broken rule 129 mm] | In Quatuor [swash Q] Libris. | [rule 132 mm] | Authore *JOHANNE LOCKIO* [swash J] Armigero. | [rule 131 mm] | Editio Quarta Aucta & Emendata, & nunc primum | Latine reddita. | [broken rule 131 mm] | ECCLES. XI. 5. | *Quemadmodum ignoras quæ fit via venti, ut ignoras quæ via offium* | *in utero gravidæ: ita ignoras opus ipfius Dei, qua via faciat* | *hæa omnia.* | [rule 133 mm] | Cicero de Natur. Deor. lib. I. | *Quam* [swash Q] *bellum est confiteri potius nefcire quod nefcias, quàm ifta effutientem* | *naufeare, atque ipfum fibi difplicere!* | [broken rule 131 mm] | *LONDINI:* | Impenfis Aunfhami & Johan. Churchil, [swash J] ad Infigne Nigri Cyoni, in vico | vulgò dicto 𝕻ater = 𝕹ofter = 𝕽ow. MDCCI.
Coll: folio (320 × 205 mm) π¹ a–f² A² C–2V² 3A–4N² (–4N2) [$1 signed]; 168 leaves; pp. *i–xxvi* 1–68 65–164 177–231 223 233–317 *318* [= 336]. Page no. 65–68 repeated; 165–172 omitted; 232 called '223'.
Contents: π1ʳ (*i*) title (verso blank), a1ʳ–a2ʳ (*iii–v*) dedication, a2ᵛ blank, b1ʳ–b2ᵛ (*vii–x*) 'Epistola ad lectorem' (reader's epistle), c1ʳ–f2ᵛ (*xi–xxvi*) contents by book, chap. & section, A1ʳ–I1ᵛ (1–30 line 35) text of Book 1, I1ᵛ–2V2ᵛ (30 lower half–164) Book 2, 3A1ʳ–3P1ʳ (177–233) Book 3, 3P1ᵛ–4N1r (234–317) Book 4, 4N1ᵛ blank.
Illustration: frontispiece is portrait of Locke by Vanderbanck after Brounower, as in 3d ed. of the *Essay* (no. 63).
Text (H2ᵛ): 63 lines; 263 (277) × 131 (150) mm; 84R. Medium-quality paper with foolscap watermark. Gatherings 4L–4N on poorer quality, browning paper. Printed by at least two different printers, witness the number jump between pp. 164 and 177 (sheets 2V and 3A). Sheets A–2V use a more angular section sign, without points, e.g. '§ 19.' The printer of the rest of the volume uses a rounder § sign, and more points, e.g. '§. 23.' Dedication set 143 ital.; reader's epistle set 84 R. Page no. at outer ends of headlines. Topical contents of sections and the few footnotes set in smaller roman type at outer margins.
HT A1ʳ: [rule 150 mm] | [rule 152 mm] | COGITATA QUAEDAM | DE | Intellectu Humano. | [rule 132 mm]
Dedication, a1ʳ: [rule 153 mm] | [rule 151 mm] | ILLUSTRISSIMO VIRO | THOMÆ | Comiti PEMBROKIÆ | ET | MONTGOMERIÆ, |

Baroni Herbert de Cardiff, Domino Rofs de | Kendal, Par, Fitzhugh, Marmion, St. Quin- | tin, & Shurland; Sanctioris Concilii Sere- | niffimi Regis noftri Præfidi, atque Comita- | tus Wiltoniæ, & Cambriæ Auftralis Domi- | no Præfecto.

Headlines are chapter title summaries set within rules in upper and lower case italics, with roman-font book numbers at inner margin on versos, chap. numbers on rectos, e.g. 'Duratio & Simplices iftius modi. Lib. II. | Cap. XIV. Duratio & Simplices iftius modi.' Pages 2-3 (A1ᵛ-A2ʳ) read: 'INTRODUCTIO. [swash U] Lib. I. | Cap. I. INTRODUCTIO. [swash U]'. Book no. in headlines for pp. 234-256 (3P1ᵛ-3U2ᵛ) read in error 'Lib. III.' (rectē 'Lib. IV.').

CW: Page. E1ʳ (ratio-) nem 2K1ᵛ à [quam] (3d line of text on following page begins 'à') 3D2ᵛ §.13. Hinc 3T2ʳ (di-) cendum 4C2ʳ (ma-) jor 4M2ʳ §.17. Quar- [§.17. Quartò]

Press figures: none.

Notes: Locke was interested in having the *Essay* translated into Latin, and sought the help of Le Clerc and William Molyneux to locate a willing, competent translator (cf. *Corr.* 1857; v.286-87), Ezekiel Burridge, an acquaintance of Molyneux's, laboured slowly to complete the task. The text is translated from the 4th ed. of 1700 (no. 64) with its very few footnotes, and has no index. The 'Epistle to the Reader' stops after the sixth paragraph (Nidditch ed., p. 10 line 26); a brief note then follows stating that the author devoted the rest of his epistle to giving details about previous editions. The text of the reader's epistle in all subsequent Latin editions matches this one. This edition is listed in the *Bibliotheca annua* for 1701 (p. 78, item no. 50) without a price.

A microfilm of the British Library's copy of this edition is in the collection, *The Eighteenth Century*, reel 358, no. 1.

References: Attig 421; Christophersen p. 28; ESTC t063933; L.L. 1800.
Notice: *Acta eruditorum*, 1702: 357-62.
Copies examined: Y [BBR] CLU-C Ct CtY (K8.L79/ + f701b) [GhU] [GOT] L (8406 i.11) MH (Phil.2115.29.125F) O (4. Delta 263) P (R.458) Wol (Vb. 4° 6)

111. *Essay*. Latin trans. (Burridge/anon.). New ed., Leipzig, 1709. 8°
JOHANNIS LOCKII, | Armigeri | LIBRI IV | DE | INTELLECTU | HUMANO. | Ecclef. XI. 5. | *Quemadmodum* [swash Q] . . . *ut ignoras,* | *quæ via* . . . *gravidæ: ita ignoras* | *opus* . . . *hæc* | *omnia.* | Cicero de Nat. Deor. L. I. | *Quam* [swash Q] . . . *nefcias* | *quam* . . . *ipfsum* | *fibi difpicere!* [sic] | Noviffima editio juxta Exemplar Londini Anno | 1701. in fol. editum,expreffa,fummoque [without spaces] ftudio | a vitiis typographicis in illo occurren- | tibus purgata. | [orn. monogram TG, upright T with branches, surmounted by G-shaped snake, 41 × 34 mm] | LIPSIÆ, | Sumptibus THEOPHILI GEORGI, | 1709.

Coll: small 8° (169 × 100 mm cut):)(⁸ (-)(8) 2)(-4)(⁸ A-3N⁸ [$ half + 1 signed; 2)(4 signed 'b4'; 3N3 and 3N5 both signed 'Nnn3']; 503 leaves; pp. i–lxii 1 2–943 944 [= 1006]. O copy has lost '3' from page no. 273.

Contents:)(1^r (*i*) title (verso blank),)(2^r–)(7^r (*iii–xiii*) 'Epistola ad lectorem',)(7^v–4)(7^r *(xiv–lx)* 'Elenchus Capitum' (book, chap, & section contents, in double cols.), 4)(8 (*lxi–lxii*) blank, A1^r–F7^r (*1–93* line 6) text of Book 1, F7^r–2I5^r (93 lower half–*505*) Book 2, 2I5^v–2U6^v (*506–684*) Book 3, 2U7^r–3N8^r (*685–943*) Book 4, 3N8^v blank.

Illustration: frontispiece is engraved portrait of Locke, unsigned, after Greenhill's, in oval frame above pedestal, with armorial shield in six parts (3 with doves in flight), subscribed '*Mr. John Locke.*', 145 × 85 mm on plate 150 × 87 mm.

Text (U5^r): 32 lines; 136 (146) × 79 mm; 85 R. Fair-quality paper without visible watermarks. Page no. at outer ends of headlines.

HT A1^r: [unframed headpiece of crowned palm tree surrounded by leaves, 23 × 80 mm] | COGITATA QUÆDAM | DE | INTELLECTU HU- | MANO.

Headlines or RTs are summarized chapter titles in italics, with book no. at inner margin on versos, chap. no. on rectos. If long the headline is spread from verso to recto, e.g. '*De aliis* Lib. II. | Cap. XVIII. *Modis Simplicibus.*'

CW: Page. A4^r (ne-) quit [quit,] M3^v maxi- [maxime] 2C7^v mem- [membra,] 2T5^v (conven-) niunt. [niunt,] 3M8^v homi- [hominum]

Notes: As stated in title, a reprint of Burridge's translation, with corrections, probably by Thiele who admits revising the 1741 ed. (no. 112). Locke's preface stops after the first six paragraphs, as in the 1701 Latin edition. The few footnotes include those to the travel writers in 1.4.8 and the definition of a 'gry' in 4.10.10, as in Burridge's translation (no. 110); there is no dedication, nor any kind of alphabetical index. Topical headings of sections are printed ital. inset within the page block. Leaf 2X2^v (p. 682) for '*Lib. IV.*' reads '*Lib. III.*' in headline.

References: Attig 422; Christophersen p. 97.

Copies examined: Y [BBR] CaOTU (Locke L63.E82L3 1709) [GhU] [GOT] MH (Phil.2115.49.20) L (8403 f.29) O (Vet. D4 f.50) PU (B1290.A8 1709)
  Note: All copies except CaOTU lack leaf 4)(8 (pp. *lxi–lxii*).

112. *Essay*. Latin trans. (Burridge/Thiele). Leipzig, 1741. 8°
IOHANNIS LOCKII | *ARMIGERI* | LIBRI IV. | DE | INTELLECTV | HVMANO, | DENVO EX NOVISSIMA EDI- | TIONE IDIOMATIS ANGLICANI, | LONGE ACCVRATIORI IN PVRIOREM | STYLVM LATINVM TRANSLATI. | PRAEFIXAE SVNT HVIC EDITIONI | AVCTORIS SCRIPTA ET VITA, NEC | NON ELENCHVS CAPITVM. | CURA | M. GOTTHELFF HENR. THIELE, | RECTORIS SCHOLAE LVBENENSIS. | [monogram-like ornament, letter T with snake-shaped G intertwined, 43 × 37 mm] |

[rule 78 mm] | *LIPSIAE,* | APVD THEOPHILVM GEORGI. | CIƆ IƆCC XXXXI.

Coll: small 8° (172 × 100 mm cut):):(⁸ (-):(8) (a)-(h)⁸ A-3Q⁸ 3R⁴ [$ half + 1 (-(a)1) signed]; 571 leaves; pp. *i-xiv 1-2 3-36 3 38-79 80-128 1 2-15 6 17-42 4 44-54 5 56-110 111 112-400 40 402-935 36 937-966 96 968-1000* [= 1142]. (O copy has lost '7' from page no. 37; '1' from second '16'; '5' from 55; '3' from 403; '9' from 936; and no. 111 is completely missing. My copy has lost '4' from no. 43; all of '55'; no. 111 is very faint; all other numbers are present.)

Contents:):(1ʳ (*i*) title (verso blank),):(2ʳ-):(7ᵛ (*iii-xiv*) 'Epistola ad lectorem' (abridged as in 1709 ed.), (a)1ʳ (*1*) section title to Le Clerc's 'Eloge' (verso blank), (a)2ʳ-(a)3ʳ (*3-5*) translator's '*Præloquium*.' subscribed '*Scripſi in Muſaeo die* 1 *Januarii anni MDCCXI*.', (a)3ᵛ-(e)8ʳ (*6-79*) text of Le Clerc's 'Eloge', (e)8ᵛ-(h)7ᵛ (*80-126*) contents by book, chap. & sections by page no., (h)8 (*127-128*) blank, A1ʳ-F8ʳ (*1-95* line 12) text of Book 1, F8ʳ-2L1ᵛ (*95 lower half-530*) Book 2, 2L2ʳ-2Y6ᵛ (*531-716* line 17) Book 3, 2Y6ᵛ-3R4ᵛ (*716 lower half-1000*) Book 4.

Illustration: frontispiece is engraved portrait of Locke, as in 1709 edition (no. 111).

Text (T4ᵛ): 32 lines; 138 (150) × 81 mm; 87R. Fair-quality laid paper with no visible watermarks. Topical contents of sections set ital. within page block. Page no. at outer ends of headlines. Judging by the size of the page numbers, sheets (a)-(h), A-H, R-2H, 2R-2Z and 3I-3R were set by a different printer; the printer of A-H et al. used smaller-font page numbers than the other.

HT A1ʳ: [unframed headpiece of leaves & branches 35 × 90 mm] | COGITATA QUÆDAM [swash Q] | DE | INTELLECTU HUMANO.

Headlines and RTs are chapter titles in ital., with book no. in inner margins of verso pages, chap. no. on rectos, e.g. '*Nulla principia ingenita. Lib. I.* | *Cap. IV. Nulla principia ingenita.*' If longer titles, they spread from verso to recto.

Section title (a)1ʳ: p. 1: ACVTISSIMI & DOCTISSIMI | VIRI | DOMINI | IOHANNIS LOCKII | ANGLI | VITA & SCRIPTA | EX GALLICO *IOHANNIS CLERICI* | ELOGIO TOMO VI BIBLIOTHECAE | SELECTAE EXTANTE, LATIO | DONATA VARIISQVE ACCES- | SIONIBVS AVCTA.

CW: Page.):(7ᵛ ACUTISSIMI [ACVTISSIMI] A4ʳ que A4ᵛ idcir- [idcirco] M3ᵛ (di-) citur 2C7ᵛ fit, 2C8ʳ pictu- [picturâ] 2T5ᵛ ſatis 2T5ʳ negle- [neglectus] 2T6ʳ (*mo-*) rem 3M8ᵛ pro- [probabilem]

Notes: A reprint of the anonymous emendation of Burridge (no. 111) with Thiele's translation of Le Clerc's 'Eloge', augmented ('from another source') by Locke's epitaph. Again there are very few footnotes (as in no. 110-111), no dedication, and no index.

References: Attig 424; Christophersen p. 97.

Copies examined: Y CaOTU (Locke L63.E82L3 1741; sheets (a)-(h) bound after sheet 3R) CtY (K8.L79/ff741) MH (Phil.2115.49.25)

NjP (Ex.6106.333.59.1741)   NjR (X B1292 1741)   O (Vet. D4 e.99)
Wol
    Note: All copies seen, except CaOTU, lack leaf (h)8 (pp. *127–8*).

113. *Essay.* Latin trans. (Burridge/Thiele). Leipzig, 1758. 2 vols. in-8°
Vol. 1, in red & black: JOHANNIS | [red line:] LOCKII | ARMIGERI | LIBRI IV. | [red:] DE INTELLECTU | HUMANO, | [red:] DENUO EX NOVISSIMA EDITIONE | idiomatis Anglicani, longe accuratiori in puriorem | Stylum translati, & nuper aliquot Notis Criticis | illuſtrati. | [red:] TOMUS I. | *Cui præfixa ſunt ſcripta & Vita, & Elenchus Capitum* | CURA | [red:] M. GOTTHELFF HENRICI THIELE, | Rectoris Scholæ LUBENENSIS. | [tailpiece of heart pierced by arrows, with swagged scrolls 36 × 41 mm] | [red:] LIPSIÆ, | Apud THEOPHILUM GEORGI. | [red rule 65 mm] | MDCCLVIII.
Vol. 2, as vol. 1 but black ink only and 'TOMUS II.'
Coll: 8° (192 × 122 mm). Vol. 1: a–c⁸ d⁴ A–Y⁸ Z⁴ [$ half (–a2) signed]; 208 leaves; pp. *i–iv* v–lvj *1*–214 217 216–265 66 267–331 432 333–360 [=416]. Page 215 called '217'; 332 called '432'; 266 lost its '2'.
Vol. 2: A–T⁸ [$ half (–T3) signed]; 152 leaves; pp. *1–2* 3–13 15 14 16–304. Page no. 14 and 15 interchanged.
    First page of each gathering also signed in direction line, e. g., 'Lockii. Tomo I.'
Illustration: anon. portrait of Locke facing left, after Verelst, signed 'Antonio Baratti scul.', 145 × 87 mm on plate 155 × 95 mm.
Contents: Vol. 1: a1ʳ blank, a1ᵛ (*ii*) anon. port. of Locke (as above), a2ʳ (*iii*) title (verso blank), a3ʳ–a5ᵛ (v–x) 'Epistola *ad* lectorem', a6ʳ,ᵛ (xj–xij) 'Praeloquium' by Thiele, a7ʳ–d4ᵛ (xiij–lvj) Le Clerc's 'Eloge', A1ʳ–D7ʳ (1–61) text of Book I, D7ᵛ–Y6ᵛ (62–348) text of Book II, Y7ʳ–Z4ᵛ (349–360) 'Elenchus Capitum' (contents by book, chap. and §§, in double cols.).
    Vol. 2: A1ʳ (*1*) title (verso blank), A2ʳ–H3ʳ (3–117) text of Book III, H3ᵛ–T3ʳ (118–293) text of Book IV, T3ᵛ–T8ᵛ (394–304) 'Elenchus Capitum' (contents, in double cols.).
Text (v.1 G7ᵛ; v.2 same): 47 lines; 156 (163) × 90 mm; 66 R. Page no. at outer corners of headlines. Fair-quality laid paper with foolscap watermarks at top edge of 5th and 8th leaves. Many footnotes, set 58 R, sometimes set in double columns. The front. portrait is printed on the same paper as the body of the text. Unframed floral headpiece, 17 × 82 mm on vol.1 a3ʳ, A1ᵣ and v.2 A2ʳ; floral tailpiece with birds, 31 × 40 mm, in v.1 a5ᵛ; floral tailpiece, 18 × 29 mm on v.1 a6ᵛ, and floral tailpiece, inverted-triange shape, 40 × 50 mm on v.1 d3ᵛ.
Headlines or RTs are chap. titles in italics, with italic book and chap. no. in inner margins respectively. For example: 'De Profecto *noſtro* Lib.IV. | Cap.XII. *in rerum* Cognitione.'
Headline, a6ᵛ (p.xij): PRÆLOQUIUM.

RT, from verso to recto: a7ᵛ-d4ᵛ (xiv-lvj): *JOHANNIS LOCKII | SCRIPTA ET VITA*. (except b1ʳ and d3ʳ in error read '*JOHANNIS LOCKII*')
CW: Page. Vol. 1: a6ʳ acutiffi- [acutiffimo] A4ʳ (con-) tra- [traria] M3ᵛ rela- [relationes] Q6ᵛ (ge-) nus X1ᵛ uni- [uniforme,] Y1ʳ (tan-) tum
Vol. 2: B2ʳ rum- [rumpi] E8ᵛ com- [communi] L3ᵛ (cogni-) tio; Q4ᵛ (contami-) nata [nata,]
Notes: Reprint of Thiele's emendation of Burridge, following no. 109, with Thiele's translation of Le Clerc's 'Eloge'. Contents combine book, chapter, and section topics in one list. There is no general index.
Reference: Attig 425.
Copies examined: DFo (187 × 120 mm cut; acc. no. 196280; vol. 1 inscribed on flyleaf 'Ex libris Chʳ. Blêmi Rosano | anno 1791.') Mun (Ph.Sp.497; 2 vols. in 1)

114. *Essay*. Latin trans. (Burridge et al.; notes Marugi). Naples, 1788-91. 5 vols. in-8°
Vol. 1: JOHANNIS | LOCKII | ARMIGERI | *LIBRI IV.* | DE INTELLECTU | HUMANO | Denuo ex noviffima editione idiomatis Anglicani, | longe accuratiori in puriorem ftylum translati: | notis criticis DOMINI GOTTELFF HENRICI THIELE, | DOMINI COSTE, ac FRANCISCI SOAVE illuftrati; | accedunt nonnullæ meditationes Doct. JOHANNIS | LEONARDI MARUGJ ad textum illuftrationefque | accomodatæ. | TOMUS I. | *Cui præfixa funt fcripta, vita, & Elenchus* | *Capitum.* | [scroll orn. 24 × 38 mm] | NEAPOLI | Ex officina VINCENTII MANFREDII | *SUPERIORUM FACULTATE.* | [Oxford rule 65 mm] | MDCCLXXXVIII.
Vols. 2-4 as vol. 1 until line 14: TOMUS II. ['III.', 'IV.'] | *Apponitur Elenchus Capitum.* | [scroll orn. 24 × 38 mm] | NEAPOLI | . . . [&c. as in vol. 1] | MDCCLXXXIX.
Vol. 5 as vols. 2-4 until line 14: TOMUS V. | . . . [&c. as vols. 2-4 until last line:] MDCCXCI.
Coll: 8° (200 × 120 mm cut). Vol. 1: A-Y⁸ [$ half signed]; 176 leaves; pp. *1- 2* 3-253 *4* 255-352. Page 254 called '4'.
Vol. 2: A-S⁸ T¹⁰ (T4 + χ1.2) [$ half signed]; 154 leaves; pp. *1-2* 3-308.
Vol. 3: A-V⁸ X⁴ [$ half signed]; 164 leaves; pp. *1-2* 3-328.
Vol. 4: A-T⁸ V¹⁰ (V4 + χ1.2) [$ half signed]; 162 leaves; pp. *1-2* 3-312 133 314-324. Page 313 called '133'.
Vol. 5: A-R⁸ S⁴ T² [$ half signed]; 142 leaves; pp. *1-2* 3-281 282-284.
Contents: Vol. 1: A1ʳ (*1*) title (verso blank), A2ʳ-A3ᵛ (3-6) Marugi's dedicatory letter to the reader, A4ʳ-A7ʳ (7-13) Locke's epistle to the reader (1st 6 paragraphs as in previous Latin eds.), A7ᵛ-E3ᵛ (14-70) Le Clerc's 'Eloge', E4ʳ,ᵛ (71-72) Locke's epitaph, E5ʳ-F2ᵛ (73-84 line 7) introduction (trans. of 1.1), F2ᵛ-Q6ᵛ (84 lower half-252) translation of 1.2-4 (called Book I), Q7ʳ-Y2ʳ (253-339 line 7) text of Books 2.1-8. Y2ʳ (339 lines 8- 37) errata, Y2ᵛ-Y5ʳ (340-345) 'Index rerum praecipuarum' (contents by

book, chap. & §§), Y5ᵛ–Y7ʳ (346–349) contents of Marugi's 'Meditations', Y7ᵛ–Y8ᵛ (350–352) imprimatur (a series of answers to successive requests for permission to print, finally granted).

Vol. 2: A1ʳ (1) title (verso blank), A2ʳ–T1ᵛ (3–290) text of Book 2.9–2.20, T2ʳ–T5ᵛ (291–298) Soave's 'Analysis affectum' (of Locke's text 2.20), T6ʳ (299) errata, T6ᵛ–T9ᵛ (300–306) contents of Locke's text by chap. no. and sections, T10ʳ,ᵛ (307–308) contents of Marugi's 'Meditations'.

Vol. 3: A1ʳ (1) title, A1ᵛ (2) 'MONITUM' (note re numbering error in v.2), A2ʳ–V7ʳ (3–317) text of Book 2.21–2.33, V7ᵛ–X4ᵛ (318–328) contents of text by book, chap. & sections.

Vol. 4: A1ʳ (1) title (verso blank), A2ʳ–O8ᵛ (3–224) text of Book 3, P1ʳ–V7ᵛ (225–318) text of 4.1–3, V8ʳ–V10ʳ (319–23) contents of text by book, chap. and sections, V10ᵛ (324) errata.

Vol. 5: A1ʳ (1) title (verso blank), A2ʳ–R8ᵛ (3–272) text of 4.4–21, S1ʳ–S3ᵛ (273–278) appendix (Soave's criticism and confutation of Leibniz's system), S4ʳ,ᵛ (279–80) vol. contents of Locke's text, T1ʳ (281) errata, T1ᵛ–T2ʳ,ᵛ (282–284) blank.

Text: 37 or 38 lines; 141 (151) × 85 mm; 75 R, with notes set 62 R. Marugi's letter set 122 roman with 1.5 mm leading; Locke's 'epistle' set 74 ital. Good laid paper with decorated orb as watermark. Page no. in outer corners of headlines. First page of text in each vol., following HT, begins with a 7-line factotum.

HT v.1, E6ʳ; v.2–5, A2ʳ: [ornamental triple rule 10 × 82 mm] | TENTAMEN | PHILOSOPHICUM | DE | INTELLECTU HUMANO. | [rule 81 mm]

*RT*s and headlines are title summaries set in italics, with book no. at inner margin on versos, chap. numbers on rectos, e.g. 'Nulla principia ingenita. Lib. I. | Cap. III. Nulla principia ingenita.', 'De idearum Lib. II. | Cap. I. noſtrarum origine.'

CW: Page. v. 1: D7ᵛ (di-) vinæ H3ʳ ad- [adhuc] L7ᵛ noti- [notitia] R1ᵛ juſmo- [juſmodi]

v.2: C1ᵛ po- [potentia] M2ᵛ lan- [lantibus]

v.3: A3ᵛ (pau-) cio- [ciora] H6ʳ ſuc- [ſuccorum] R1ᵛ ho- [hominis]

v.4: B6ʳ con- [conjugentes] G1ʳ tan- [tanquam] M9ᵛ lon- [longe]

v.5: A5ᵛ en- [entium] G7ʳ ma- [materia,] P4ᵛ (per-) cipi- [cipimus]

Notes: Text is basically a reprint of Thiele's emendation of Burridge (no. 111–113), with Latin notes from Coste's French edition (no. 91 et seq.), notes from Soave (see Italian abridgement, no. 144) and 'meditations' from Marugi interspersed in Books 1 and 2 as long footnotes. Vol. 3 pp. 237–52 has a separate chapter of Marugi's 'Meditations'; vol. 4, pp. 255–66 include a long footnote from Coste's 'Reflexiones' (extracts of letter to Le Clerc as editor of the *Nouvelles de la république des lettres*; see C1705-3).

Reference: Attig 426.

Copy examined: O (Vet. F5 e.168)

114.1*. *Essay.* Polish trans. (Cyankiewicz) Cracow, 1784.
"Logika czyli myśli z Lokko o rozumie ludzkim wyjęte" [Logic, or Thoughts about Human Reason from Locke]. Cracow, 1784.

Notes: This information comes from Janina Rosicka's essay, 'Locke and the Polish Enlightenment', in *Locke's Philosophy: Content and Context*, edited by G. A. J. Rogers (1994), p. 249, and footnote: "Andrzej Cyankiewicz [1740?-1803?] was the translator. It is impossible to show which French edn. was the basis of this translation." Elsewhere the author states "The translator . . . was a poet, lecturer at the Jagiellonian University, and Catholic priest. The *Essay* appeared in 1784 in Cracow, the translation probably having been commission[ed] by Hugo Kołłątaj. It was a detached and rather literal translation of selected parts of the *Essay*. The *Letter to the Reader* and some unimportant fragments of the *First* and the *Third Books* were omitted. The *Second* and the *Fourth Books* were translated almost complete. It is likely that Kołłątaj was responsible for this appropriate selection." (*ibid.*, p. 246, fn. 23.) Other details about Kołłątaj are contained in Rosicka's essay.

115. *Essay.* Abridgement (Wynne). 1696. 8°
Within a double rule, inner 133 × 76 mm, outer 139 × 84 mm, left inner vertical broken: AN | ABRIDGMENT | OF | M^r. *Locke's Eſſay* | CONCERNING | Humane Underſtanding. | [double rule 71 mm) | LONDON, | Printed for A. and J. [swash J] *Churchill* at the *Black* | *Swan* in *Pater-noſter-Row*, and *Edw. Caſtle* | next *Scotland-Yard-Gate*, [swash Y] near *Whiiehall*, [sic] 1696.
Coll: 8° (178 × 115 mm cut) A^4 B-X^8 [$ half (+ A3) signed]; 164 leaves; pp. *i-viii* 1-310 *311-320* [= 328].
Contents: A1^r (*i*) title (verso blank), A2^r-A4^r (*iii-vii*) Wynne's dedication to Locke signed 'Oxon, Ap. 17. | 1695. . . . JOHN WYNNE.', A4^v (*viii*) errata (20.7 lines), B1^r-B3^v (1-6) 'Introduction' (summary of Book I), B4^r-I4^v (7-120) abridgement of Book 2, I5^r-N2^r (121-179) of Book 3, N2^v-X3^v (180-310) of Book 4, X4^r-X8^r (*311-319*) book and chap. contents, X8^v (*320*) advt. of books sold by Churchills.
Text (E7^v): 29 lines; 136 (147) × 73 mm; 93R. Fair-quality laid paper, watermarked with letters similar to Heawood 3020 and 2078. Wynne's dedication is set 21 line 117 ital.; the introduction is set 29 lines 92 ital. Text in direction line on p. 73 (F5^r).
Headlines are page no. within parentheses.
CW: Page. B8^v *Hard-* [*Hardneſs,*] F2^r (pow-) er I5^v (Appre-) hend, O5^v Signi- [Signification;] S2^r (Axi-) om, V3^r (con-) veyed
Press figures: none.
Notes: The abridgement was Wynne's own idea and is based on the 2nd and 3rd editions (textually the same). Locke is said to have approved an abridgement in principle. This is one of the very few books dedicated to Locke (curiously). Wynne was a member of Jesus College, Oxford, and became Principal in

1712. He was later made Bishop of St. Asaph, and then translated to Bath and Wells. A biographical note by W. T. Gibson is to be found in *Oxoniensia*, 52 (1987): 204-8. The abridgement is notable for its exclusion of most of Book I. The 'Introduction' consists of truncated sentences from Chapter I, §§ 1-7 only, as follows: §1, first sentence; §2, revision of first sentence; §3, 2d and 3d paragraphs and first sentence of 4th paragraph; §5, entire; §6, omitting 2 sentences in middle; §7, entire. Rather than rephrasing, Wynne's abridgement was accomplished by making strategic deletions in each chapter, sometimes adding transitional phrases, and keeping to Locke's own words.

This work was advertised in *The London Gazette*, no. 3164, the issue for 5-9 March 1696; it was therefore available by 9 March 1696.

A microfilm copy is in the collection EEB, reel 606, no. 7.

References: Alston 7:121; Attig 267; Christophersen p. 28; ESTC r023044; L.L. 179l; T.C.II.571 and III.6 (Hilary Term 1697); Wing^2 L-2735.

Copies examined: O (8° U.107 Art; gift of J. Wynne) C CaOTU (Locke L63.A27 1696) C(Keynes) Ck(Keynes) CLU-C CtY (K8.L79/g696) DFo (acc.175678) Dt (Fag. K.l4.77) L (8404 bb.2l) MH (*EC65.L7934.D696a) NjP (6106.333.129) Oa (k.10.17) Oc OCU (B1292.1696) Oj Oo PPL (Wing L2735/67747.O)

116. *Essay*. Abridgement (Wynne). 2d ed., 1700. 8°

Within a double rule, inner 141×79, outer 149×88 mm: AN | ABRIDGMENT | OF | *Mr*. Locke's *Eſſay* | CONCERNING | Humane Underſtanding. | [rule 75 mm] | The Second Edition, Corrected and | Enlarged. | [rule 75 mm] | *LONDON*, | Printed for *A*. and *J*. *Churchil*, [swash J] at the *Black* | *Swan* in *Pater-Noſter-Row*. 1700.

Coll: 8° (183 × 120 mm cut) A^4 B-V^8 X^4 [$ half signed]; 160 leaves; pp. *i–viii* 1-308 *309-312* [= 320]. Gathering V signed on outer forme 'U' and 'U4', on inner 'V2' and 'V3'.

Contents: A1^r (*i*) title (verso blank), A2^r-A4^r (*iii–vii*) Wynne's dedication to Locke (reprinted from 1st ed.), A4^v (*viii*) errata (10.5 lines), B1^r-B3^v (1-6) introd., B4^r-I4^r (7-119) abridged text of Book 2, I4^v-M7^v (120-174) of Book 3, M8^r-X2^v (175-308) of Book 4, X3^r-X4^v (*309-312*) contents by book and chapters.

Text (E7^v): 30 lines; 139 (151)×75 mm; 93R. Fair-quality laid paper, without watermarks. Dedication set 23 lines 115 ital; introd. 30 lines, 93 ital. Last line of p. 266 reprinted as 1st line of 267. Pages 85, 89 and 109 (G3^r, G5^r and H7^r) have text in direction line. Each chap. whether at top or mid-page, headed with a rule (70 to 76 mm).

Headlines for body of text are page no. set within parentheses. Headlines for A2^v-A4^r are 'The Dedication.'; for B1^v-B3^v, 'The Introduction.', both with page no. at external corners.

CW: Page. B3^r Re- [Refolution] C4^v where- [wherein] F2^v *Second-* [*Secondly,*] I8^r (enlar-) ges L2^r (ve-) ry Q6^r Tri- [Triangle] T8^v de- [degrees] U7^r (Con-) dition [dition,]

Press figures: none.
Notes: The first edition of the abridgement is here expanded by summaries of 2.33, the chapter 'On the Association of Ideas' and of 4.19, 'Of Enthusiasm', both chapters Locke added to the 4th edition of the *Essay*. Signed at the end of the dedication: OXON. Ap. 17. 1695. | Honoured SIR, | Your very Humble | and Oblig'd Servant, | JOHN WYNNE.

A microfilm copy of this edition is in the collection EEB, reel 767, no. 39.
References: Alston 7.122; Attig 268; Christophersen p. 29; ESTC r020235; Wing² L-2736.
Copies examined: Y   C   Ck(Keynes)   CLU-C   CtY (K8.L79/g700)   DFo   L (8405 cc.14)   MH (*EC65.L7934.D696ab)   NjP (6106.333.128)   Occ (VI.82)   PPL (Wing L2736/68117.O)

117. *Essay*. Abridgement (Wynne). 3d ed., 1721. 12°
Within a double rule, inner 135 × 64 mm, outer 142 × 70 mm: AN | ABRIDGMENT | OF | Mr. *LOCKE*'s | ESSAY | Concerning | *Humane Underſtanding.* | [rule 60 mm] | The Third Edition, Corrected. | [rule 60 mm] | *LONDON:* | Printed for A. CHURCHILL, and | ſold by W. TAYLOR at the *Ship* | and *Black Swan* in *Pater-noſter-* | *Row.* 1721.
Coll: 12° (172 × 100 mm cut) A¹² (±A1) B-Q¹² [$ half signed; A9 signed 'B4']; 192 leaves; pp. *i-viii* 1 2-371 *372-376* [=384].
Contents: A1ʳ (*i*) title (verso blank), A2ʳ-A4ᵛ (*iii-viii*) Wynne's dedication dated 'Ap. 17. 1695.', A5ʳ-A8ᵛ (*1-8*) introduction, A9ʳ-G5ʳ (*9-145*) text of Book 2, G5ᵛ-K1ᵛ (*146-210*) of Book 3, K2ʳ-Q10ʳ (*211-371*) of Book 4, Q10ᵛ-Q12ᵛ (*372-376*) contents of text by book and chap.
Text (C6ʳ): 28 lines; 129 (142) × 70 mm; 93R. Good unwatermarked laid paper; cancellans title leaf has a fleur-de-lys watermark. The dedication is headed by a framed rectangular ornament, *Bowyer Orn.* 27, and begins with 4-line initial *Bowyer Orn.* 187I. The introduction ends with *Bowyer Orn.* tailpiece 163; Book 2 concludes with tailpiece 154.
HT, A2ʳ: [headpiece, *Bowyer Orn.* 27] | To the much Eſteemed | Mr. *JOHN* [swash J] *LOCKE*.
A5ʳ [headpiece, *Bowyer Orn.* 47] | THE | INTRODUCTION.
Headlines, except for the introduction, are page no. within parentheses. A1ᵛ-A4ᵛ have headline, '*The Dedication.*'; A5ᵛ-A8ᵛ: 'The Introduction.', with page no. at upper outer corners. The beginning of each chap. headed by a rule, e.g. [rule 70 mm] | CHAP. IX. | *Of Perception.*
CW: Page. B2ʳ approaching C6ʳ (be-) yond D4ᵛ (*for-*) row E5ʳ Con- [*Concubine*] L3ʳ *Fuſi-* [*Fuſibility,*] P5ʳ (dou-) ble, P12ʳ (Pro-) poſition,
Press figures: Page. (An asterisk following the figure indicates it is located beneath the CW.) 13 (A11ʳ)-2*   14 (A11ᵛ)-2   28 (B6ᵛ)-2   31 (B8ʳ)-6   77 (D7ʳ)-6   86 (D11ᵛ)-6   97 (E5ʳ)-5   98 (E5ᵛ)-5   122 (F5ᵛ)-5   133 (F11ʳ)-5   146 (G5ʳ)-5   160 (G12ᵛ)-2   176 (H8ᵛ)-5   182 (H11ᵛ)-2   207 (I12ʳ)-I*   208 (I12ᵛ)-I   213 (K3ʳ)-5*   OR   230 (K11ᵛ)-2   229 (K11ʳ)-I*   244 (L6ᵛ)-6   254 (L11ᵛ)-2   268 (M6ᵛ)-5   278 (M11ᵛ)-2

292 (N6ᵛ)-5   295 (N8ʳ)-5*   317 (O7ʳ)-5*   327 (O12ʳ)-3*   338 (P5ᵛ)-6
352 (P12ᵛ)-6   368 (Q8ᵛ)-6   375 (Q12ʳ)-I

Notes: Text is a reprint of the 2nd (1700) edition, printed by William Bowyer, with his ornaments (*Bowyer Ledgers*, no. 667); the charge to the Churchills for printing 1000 copies in 16 sheets was entered 13 May 1720, an indication printing was completed. The same day one copy was delivered; the remaining 999 copies were delivered 14 October 1720; does a 5-month gap indicate dissatisfaction or a change of booksellers? does it account for the cancellans title leaf? The account was paid 10 February 1721.

A microfilm copy of this edition is to be found in the collection, *The Eighteenth Century*, reel 2111, no. 3.

References: Alston 7:123; Attig 269; ESTC t063930.

Copies examined: Y (without fig.on p. 213, 230)   O (Vet. A4 f.525)   C (VIII.22.42)   L (1486 de.6; has fig. on p. 213; without fig. on p. 375)   Obr (Yarb.L.38)   Om (F1.6; has fig. on p. 230)   PPH (Dj.97)

118*. *Essay*. Abridgement (Wynne) "4th ed.", 1728. Dublin. 8°

"An abridgment of Mr. Locke's essay concerning humane understanding... Fourth edition,... Dublin, J. Hyde and E. Dobson, 1728."

Coll: 8°: [6], 176 [pp.]

Note: I have been unable to locate copies of this edition. Alston in his *Bibliography of the English Language*..., from which the above information comes, says copies are to be found in the Glasgow Public Library and the National Library of Ireland, Dublin (shelfmark: Dublin 1728 (26)). Not listed in Attig. The 1734 Dublin printing appears to be a reprint of this edition. The ESTC's record states the format is a duodecimo, as reported by the National Library of Ireland, and that there is an 'unverified' copy at the University of Ulster in Londonderry.

References: Alston 7:124; ESTC t163342.

119. *Essay*. Abridgement (Wynne). 4th ed., 1731. 12°

Within a double rule, inner 128 × 67 mm, outer 133 × 73 mm: AN | ABRIDGMENT | OF | Mr. *LOCKE*'s | ESSAY | Concerning | Human Underſtanding. | [rule 64 mm] | The Fourth Edition, Corrected. | [rule 65 mm] | LONDON: [swash D] | Printed for J. and J. KNAPTON, at the *Crown* | in St. *Paul's Church-Yard*; [swash P, Y] A. BETTES- | WORTH and C. HITCH, at the *Red-Lion* | in *Pater-Noſter-Row*; J. PEMBERTON, | at the *Golden-Buck* in *Fleet-Street*; and T. ASTLEY, at the *Roſe* in St. *Paul's* | *Church-Yard*. [swash Y] M.DCC.XXXI.

Coll: 12° (162 × 100 mm cut) A–Q¹² [$ half (–B6, –C6, –D6) signed]; 192 leaves; pp. *i–iii* iv–viii 9 10–96 197 98–285 288 286–87 289–379 380–384.

Contents: A1ʳ (*i*) title (verso blank), A2ʳ–A4ᵛ (*iii*–viii) Wynne's dedication, A5ʳ–A8ᵛ (9–16) introd. (set 93 ital.), A9ʳ–G5ʳ (17–153) abridged text of

Book 2, G5ᵛ–K1ᵛ (154–218) of Book 3, K2ʳ–Q10ʳ (219–379) of Book 4, Q10ᵛ–Q12ᵛ (*380–384*) contents of book and chapters.

Text (L4ᵛ): 28 lines; 130 (141)×71 mm; 93R. Laid paper with horizontal chainlines. Watermark (on C11–12) is crowned fleur-de-lys; otherwise no visible watermarks. The first chapter of each book, including the 'Introduction', begins with a 3-line initial; following chapters with a 2-line initial. The dedication is headed with an unframed leafy headpiece of a woman seated on either side of a pedestal vase surmounting a lion's head, 22 × 72 mm; the first line of text is a 4-line ornamental initial I. The introduction (A5ʳ) starts with an unframed headpiece of a bowl of flowers, with rampant dogs, 22 ×72 mm; it closes with a leafy scroll tailpiece of a seated Britannia, 34 × 43 mm; Book 2 with a dove against a sunburst, above a sconce with scrolls, 33 × 44 mm.

HT, A5ʳ: [unframed headpiece of bowl of flowers between facing rampant dogs, 22 × 72 mm] | THE | INTRODUCTION.

Headlines are page no. centered within parentheses, except pp. iv–viii, where they read '*The Dedication.*' and pp. *1–8* ('The Introduction.') with page no. at the outer corners.

CW: Page. B11ʳ Appli- [Application] E2ʳ (con-) fider [confider] G1ʳ (confi-) dered [dered,] G11ʳ *Genus*; [*Genus*,] M4ʳ (connec-) tion [tion,] O2ʳ that' [that] O8ʳ themfelves. [themfelves:] P6ᵛ (Rea-) *fon*; [*fon*;] P12ʳ (Pro-) pofition, [pofition?]

Press figures: Variations have been found in the Bodleian Library and British Library copies, Desmond Neill's, Thoemmes and my own, as follows.

	L	O	DN	Thoem.	Y
87 (D8ʳ)	C	w	C	C	C
106 (E5ᵛ)	C	C	w	C	C
108 (E6ᵛ)	–	–	–	C	–
156 (G6ᵛ)	C	C	C	C	C
178 (H5ᵛ)	–	w	w	–	w
204 (I6ᵛ)	C	C	C	C	C
250 (L5ᵛ)	C	C	C	C	C
274 (M5ᵛ)	w	w	C	–	w
300 (N6ᵛ)	C	C	C	C	C
322 (O5ᵛ)	C	C	C	C	C
324 (O6ᵛ)	C	w	C	w	w

Note: C printed in italics in text. Straight reprint of 3d ed. (1721). The first ed. of abridgement to spell 'human' rather than 'humane' in title. Dedication is subscribed '*Oxon.* | *Ap.* | *1695.*' Bodleian Library's copy has an extra gathering A (pp. 1–16, with page no. within square brackets as headlines) bound at end, in octavo format with vertical chainlines. The gathering, not found in other copies, is a description of recent publications and an alphabetical list of 'PLAYS Sold by T. ASTLEY.'

A facsimile reprint of this edition, with an introduction by G. A. J. Rogers, was published by Thoemmes, Bristol, in 1990. Unfortunately the re-printer rearranged the last four pages of sheet M so that page no. 285–288 are in numerical sequence; but despite the numbering error, the textual sequence of the original printing was correct (as can be quickly determined by the catchwords).
References: Alston 7:125; Attig 270; Christophersen p. 95; ESTC t063941.
Copies examined: Y   O (Vet.A4 f.683)   C (7180 d.92)   CLU-C (*PR3541.L57E75w 1721)   L (8406 bb.21)

120. *Essay*. Abridgement (Wynne) "5th ed.", Dublin, 1734. 12°
Within a double rule: AN | ABRIDGMENT | OF | Mr. *LOCKE*'s | ESSAY | CONCERNING | Humane Understanding. | [rule 67 mm] | The Fifth Edition, Corrected. | [double rule 69 mm] | *DUBLIN:* | Printed by and for S. HYDE, Bookſeller | in *Dame-Street*, M,DCC,XXXIV.
Coll: 12° (163 × 97 mm cut) A–G^{12} H^8 [$5 (–H4, –H5) signed]; 92 leaves; pp. i–vi 1 2–167 165 169–176 *177–178* [= 184]. Page 168 incorrectly repeats number '165'.
Contents: A1^r (*i*) title (verso blank), A2^r–A3^v (*iii–vi*) Wynne's dedication, A3^r–A6^v (*1–6*) introduction, A7^r–H7^v (*7–176*) text, H8^{r,v} (*177–178*) contents by book & chap. of Books II–IV.
Text (B11^r): 42 lines (sometimes 41); 136 (140) × 75 mm; 65R. Laid paper with letter 'L' as watermark. Dedication and introd. have headlines: '*The Dedication.*' and '*The Introduction.*' respectively. Body of text has page no. within parentheses centered at head of page. Ornamental headpiece on A3^r (p. *1*); lion's head tailpiece with floral swags on H7^v (p. *176*). Not octavo, as stated by Alston.
CW: Page.
Note: Standard reprint using Dublin text of 1728 (no. 118).
References: Alston 7:126; Attig 271; ESTC t150434 (also records copy at National Library of Ireland).
Copy examined: C (Hib.8.734.2)

121. *Essay*. Abridgement (Wynne) 5th ed., 1737. 12°
AN | ABRIDGMENT | . . . [etc., as in no. 119 until 8th line: rule 72 mm] | The FIFTH EDITION Corrected. | [rule 71 mm] | *LONDON:* | Printed for A. BETTESWORTH and C. HITCH, at the | *Red-Lion* in *Pater-Noſter-Row*; J. and J. PEMBER- | TON, at the *Golden-Buck* in *Fleet-Street*; J. and P. | KNAPTON, at the *Crown* in *Ludgate Street*; and | T. ASTLEY, at the *Roſe* in *St. Paul's Church-Yard*. [swash Y] | M DCC XXXVII.
Coll: 12° (160 × 100 mm cut) A–Q^{12} [$ 6 (–B6, –C6, –D6) signed; E5–6 both signed 'E5', P4–5 both signed 'P5']; 192 leaves; pp. i–iii iv–viii 9 10–45 36–37 48–379 *380–384* [= 384]. Pages 46–47 (B11^v–B12^r) misnumbered 36–37.

Contents: A1^r (*i*) title (verso blank), A2^r–A4^v (*iii–viii*) dedication, A5^r–A8^v (*9–16*) introduction, A9^r–Q10^r (*17–379*) text, Q10^v–Q12^v (*380–384*) contents.

Text (E12^v): 28 lines; 130 (140) × 71 mm; 93R. Laid paper with fleur-de-lys watermark, chainlines horizontal. Foredges of leaves K12, L12, M8 and P8 in my copy show possible letters I and V as additional watermarks. Page no. as headlines centered at head of page within parentheses. Introd. set ital. 27 or 28 lines, 94 ital. Headpieces are rectangular orn. of a chalice surrounded by doves, 23 × 79 mm on A2^r; 2 facing squirrels surrounded by scrolls, 8 × 73 mm on A5^r. Tailpiece on A8^v, bowls of flowers surrounded by cupids, 32 × 44 mm (similar to Woodfall 219[8]), repeated on p. 153 (G5^r). The dedication on p. iii begins with a 4-line framed factotum I, similar to Woodfall 337, but inverted, with a dove at top.

CW: Page. A11^v (toge-) ther, C6^r (be-) yond D11^v (eafi-) ly H12^v (oc-) cafion M4^r (Connec-) tion O2^r that O8^r themfelves, [themfelves:] P6^v (*Rea-*) *fon* P12^r (Pro-) pofition?

Press figures: 21 (A11^r)-4 22 (A11^v)-1 96 (D12^v)-1 102 (E3^v)-1 120 (E12^v)-4 142 (F11^v)-4 144 (F12^v)-1 166 (G11^v)-4 168 (G12^v)-4 182 (H7^v)-1 185 (H9^r)-1 205 (I7^r)-1 214 (I11^v)-4 232 (K8^v)-1 238 (K11^v)-1 261 (L11^r)-4 286 (M11^v)-4 288 (M12^v)-1 310 (N11^v)-4 334 (O11^v)-1 *381* (Q11^r)-4 *382* (Q11^v)-1

Note: Reprint of the 4th ed. of 1731 (no. 119).

References: Alston 7:127; Attig 272; Christophersen p. 95; ESTC n028282

Copies examined: O (Vet.4 f.447) CtY (K8.L79/g737) NjP (6106.333.126) Oj (inscribed 'J Wynne St. John's | April 1796')

122. *Essay.* Abridgement (Wynne). 6th ed., Glasgow (Foulis), 1744. 8° in 4s
AN | ABRIDGMENT | OF | Mr. *LOCKE's* | ESSAY | Concerning | HUMAN UNDERSTANDING. | The Sixth EDITION Corrected. | GLASGOW: | Printed and fold by ROBERT FOULIS | M, DCC, XLIV.

Coll: 8° in 4s (170 × 110 mm cut) π^2 A–2D^4 2E^2 [$ half signed]; 112 leaves; pp. *i–iv* 1-48 48-79 81-217 *218-220* [=224]. Page no. 48 repeated, 80 omitted.

Contents: π1^r (*i*) title (verso blank), π2^{r,v} (*iii–iv*) Wynne's dedication, A1^r–A2^v (*1-4*) introduction, A3^r–2E1^r (*5-217*) text, 2E1^v–2E2^r (*218-219*) contents by book & chap., 2E2^v (*220*) advt. by Foulis (26 numbered items; set 56R).

Text (B1^v): 35 lines; 48 (152) × 83 mm; 84R. Dedication set 67 R. Medium-quality laid paper, with vertical chainlines. Body of text has page no. centered at head of page within parentheses as headlines.

Headlines, pp. 1-4: *The Introduction*.

CW: Page. D4^v ap- [appearance] G1^v there- [thereupon] L3^v where- [wherein] 2B3^r Senfation

---

[8] R. J. Goulden: *The Ornament Stock of Henry Woodfall*, Occasional Papers of the Bibliographical Society, no. 3 (1988). Cited as Woodfall.

Notes: A standard reprint. Gaskell reports two settings of the title-page, reading the same, set on two different quality papers, 'medium-good quality; thin marks 6/?HR, 6/1'; "TYPE: RPI, RLP Case, RB I"; and "Issue on inferior paper, [? Small Crown] . . . Poor quality; no marks. 8°" The page numbering error causes the recto pages 48–78 to be evenly numbered and the versos in odd numbers.

References: Alston 7:128; Attig 273; Gaskell 53; ESTC t150433 ('pending': questions re 2 settings of title)

Copies examined: O (Vet.A4 e.2411)   MH (Phil.2115.45.5)

123. *Essay.* Abridgement (Wynne) "6th ed.", Dublin, 1751. 12°

AN | ABRIDGMENT | OF | Mr. *LOCKE*'s | ESSAY | CONCERNING | HUMANE UNDERSTANDING. | [rule 69 mm] | The SIXTH EDITION, Corrected. | [double rule 70 mm] | *DUBLIN*: | Printed for J. EXSHAW, at the *Bible* on *Cork-Hill*, | M,DCC,LI.

Coll: 12° (168 × 98 mm cut) A–H^{12} [$5 signed]; 96 leaves; pp. *1–6 i* ii–v iv 7–42 49–190 *191–192* [= 192]. Page vi called 'iv'; no. 43–48 omitted.

Contents: A1^r *(1)* title (verso blank), A2^r–A3^v *(3–6)* Wynne's dedication, A4^r–A6^v *(i–v, 'iv')* introduction, A7^r–D4^r *(7–49)* text of Book 2, D4^v–E8^v *(80–112)* of Book 3, E9^r–H11^v *(112–190)* text of Book 4, H12^{r,v} *(191–192)* contents by book & chapter.

Text (B11^v): 41 lines; 135 (144) × 71 mm; 66R. Fair laid paper with watermark 'Macdonald'. Text of introduction set 30 lines, 94R (141 (151 × 73 mm). Body of text has page no. at head centered within parentheses as headlines. Decorative tailpiece on p. 112 (E8^v), 32 × 49 mm.

Headlines, A2^v–A3^v: *DEDICATION.*

A4^v–A6^v: [rule 73 mm] | [rule 72 mm] | *The INTRODUCTION.*

CW: Page.

Signature positions: A5 w$_\wedge$ell $_\wedge$as B Op$_\wedge$eration C3 eno$_\wedge$ugh D *really* D5 *others*$_\wedge$, E whe*n* F4 *their*$_\wedge$ Operations G4 perſwad$_\wedge$e H2 make uſe

Note: A standard reprint. Not listed in Alston or Attig.

Reference: ESTC t150435 (Dt only location)

Copy examined: Dt (120. ss.21)

124. *Essay.* Abridgement (Wynne). 7th ed., Glasgow, 1752. Two issues (8° and 12°)

AN | ABRIDGMENT | OF | Mr. *LOCKE*'s | ESSAY | CONCERNING | HUMAN UNDERSTANDING. | THE SEVENTH EDITION. | GLASGOW, | PRINTED AND SOLD BY ROBERT AND ANDREW FOULIS | M DCC LII.

Coll: 8° in 4s (160 × 95 mm cut): A–2L^4 [$ half signed];
variant issue: 12° in 6s (143 × 85 mm cut): A–Z^6 [$ half signed; Z5–6 advts.].

Pagination both: pp. *1–6* 7–270 *271–272* (additionally *273–276* in variant).

Contents: A1ʳ (*1*) title (verso blank), A2ʳ-A4ʳ (*3-5*) Wynne's dedication, A4ᵛ blank, A4ʳ-B2ʳ {variant A5ʳ-A6ʳ} (*7-11*) introduction, B2ᵛ-2L3ᵛ {variant A6ᵛ-Z3ᵛ} (*12-270*) text of Books 2-4, 2L4ʳ,ᵛ {variant Z4ʳ,ᵛ} (*271-272*) contents by book & chap., {variant Z5ʳ-Z6ᵛ} (*273-276*) Foulis's advertisements.

Text (I1ᵛ): 29 lines; 113 (121) × 63 mm; 77 R. Octavo issue has medium-good quality laid paper, foolscap, with "marks 5/ii; size of sheet 17 × 13 in." according to Gaskell. Duodecimo issue is "medium-poor quality; thin; no marks" (Gaskell). Page no. centered within parentheses as headlines in body of text.

Headlines, A2ᵛ-A3ʳ: DEDICATION.

CW: none.

Notes: Reprint of the 1744 Foulis edition. According to Gaskell, "published by 4 December 1752 (GC.) *Price*: Retail: 8°, 2*s*. 6*d*. (CP 9)." The CaOTU copy of the 12° issue has 2 leaves of § Z bound between pp. 268 and 269, that is, Z3.4 should have been removed and inserted after Z6 (§ Z sequence should be bound: 1 2 5 6 3.4). A microfilm copy of this edition is in the collection, *The Eighteenth Century*, reel 3293, no. 3.

References: Alston 7:129 (12° issue only); Attig 274 (12° issue only); Christophersen p. 95; ESTC t063940; Gaskell 233.

Copies examined: 8° issue: Y C (7180 e.20) O (Vet.A5 f.1793)
  12° issue: CaOTU (Locke L63.A27 1752; § Z misbound, leaves in order 1 2 5 6 3 4) L (8409.aaa.7)

125. *Essay*. Abridgement (Wynne). 'New ed.', Edinburgh, 1767. 12° in 6s
AN | ABRIDGMENT | OF | MR. *LOCKE*'s | ESSAY | CONCERNING | HUMAN UNDERSTANDING. [rule 74 mm] | A NEW EDITION, with ADDITIONS. | [rule 74 mm] | CAREFULLY REVISED and CORRECTED. | [Oxford rule 73 mm] | EDINBURGH: | Printed by A. DONALDSON, and fold at his Shops | in London and Edinburgh. | [Oxford rule 27 mm] | M DCC LXVII.

Coll: 12° in 6s (172 × 100 mm cut) A-Y⁶ Z⁴ [$ half signed]; 136 leaves; pp. *1-2* 3 iv-v 6 *7-10* 11 *12-252* 253 *254-271* 272.

Contents: A1ʳ (*1*) title (verso blank), A2ʳ-A3ʳ (*3-v*) Wynne's dedication, A3ᵛ-A5ᵛ (*6-10*) Introduction, A6ʳ-I5ᵛ (*11-106*) text of Book 2, I6ʳ-N2ʳ (*107-147*) of Book 3, N2ᵛ-X6ᵛ (*148-252*) text of Book 4, Y1ʳ-Z4ʳ (*253-271*) contents by book, chap. & sections, Z4ᵛ (*272*) errata note (2 lines).

Text (K3ʳ): 33 lines; 136 (146) × 75 mm; 83 R. Medium-quality paper watermarked with 'S' and fleur-de-lys; horizontal chainlines. Page no. in outer corners of headlines.

HT: LOCKE's ESSAY | CONCERNING | HUMAN UNDERSTANDING. | [rule 74 mm]

RTs, from verso to recto; at inner margin print book and chap. no., e.g.: LOCKE's ESSAY ON Book III. | Ch. 9. HUMAN UNDERSTANDING.

CW: Page. B1ʳ 'to, C6ᵛ Ab- [Abſtraction] D2ʳ them- [themſelves;] K1ᵛ *a con-*
[*a connexion*] N6ᵛ Per- [Perception] S3ᵛ ſome- [ſometimes]
No CW on I1ᵛ.
Notes: A reprint of the Foulis edition of 1752 (no. 124). The errata call for correcting 'dono- | minate' to 'denominate' on p. 29 lines 9–10; and for adding § 6. to 17th line on p. 92. A microfilm copy is in the collection, *The Eighteenth Century*, reel 3293, no. 4.
References: Alston 7:130; Attig 275; Christophersen p. 95; ESTC t063945.
Copies examined: Y   C (Hunter d.76.9)   L (8475 a.20)   O (Vet.A6 e.2142)

126. *Essay*. Abridgement (Wynne). '7th ed.', Dublin, 1769. 12°
AN | ABRIDGMENT | OF | Mr. *LOCKE*'s | ESSAY | CONCERNING | HUMAN UNDERSTANDING. | [engr. port., oval 55 × 52 mm on plaque 62 × 58 mm] | [rule 70 mm] | The Seventh Edition, Corrected. | [double rule 70 mm] | *DUBLIN:* | Printed by JOHN [swash J] EXSHAW, in Dame-ſtreet. | [orn. rule of circles 0.8 × 24 mm] | M,DCC,LXIX.
Coll: 12° (175 × 100 mm cut) A⁸ (±A1) B–O¹² P⁴ [$ 5 signed (–A5, –P3 & P4)]; 168 leaves; pp. *1–10 i* ii–vi *1* 2–318 *319–320* [= 336].
Contents: A1ʳ (*1*) title (verso blank), A2ʳ–A3ᵛ (*3–6*) contents by book & chapter, A4ʳ–A5ᵛ (*7–10*) Wynne's dedication, A6ʳ–A8ᵛ (*i*–vi) introduction, B1ʳ–P3ᵛ (*1–318*) text. P4 blank.
Text (H5ʳ): 36 lines; 130 (139) × 80 mm; 72 R. Fair quality paper with horizontal chainlines, except the title leaf, where they are vertical. No visible watermarks.
CW: Page. A8ʳ (Under-) ſtand- [ſtandings;] C6ʳ (With-) out E11ᵛ (ſe-) cret H12ᵛ (ap-) ply M6ᵛ Wa. [Way.] O8ʳ (confident-) ly
Notes: A standard reprint. Title-page is a cancellans, with vertical chainlines, probably to cope with the engraved portrait of Locke (of poor quality) thereon; the impression of the plate's edge touches the bottom of the letters of the title's 7th line.
References: Alston 7:131; Attig 276; ESTC t185683.
Copies examined: O (Vet.A5 e.3982)   Dt (OLS B-1-968)

127. *Essay*. Abridgement (Wynne). "New ed.", Edinburgh, 1770. 12° in 6s.
AN | ABRIDGMENT | OF | Mr. *LOCKE*'s | ESSAY | CONCERNING | HUMAN UNDERSTANDING. | [rule 73 mm] | A New Edition, with Additions. | [rule 76 mm] | Carefully revised and corrected. | [double rule 76 mm] | EDINBURGH: | Printed by A. Donaldson, and ſold at his Shops | in London and Edinburgh. | [Oxford rule, broken, 29 mm] | M.DCC.LXX.
Coll: 12° in 6s (175 × 100 mm cut) A–Y⁶ Z⁴ [$ half signed; D2 and D3 both signed 'D3']; 136 leaves; pp. *i–ii* 3 iv–v *6* 7–10 *11* 12–252 *253* 254–271 *272*.
Contents: A1ʳ title (verso blank), A2ʳ–A3ʳ (*3*–v) dedication, A3ᵛ–A5ᵛ (*6–10*) introduction, A6ʳ–I5ᵛ (*11–106*) text of Book 2, I6ʳ–N2ʳ (*107–147*) of Book

3, N2ᵛ–X6ᵛ (148–252) of Book 4, Y1ʳ–Z4ʳ (*253–271*) contents by book, chapter & section, Z4ᵛ blank.
Text (E1ᵛ): 33 lines; 136 (146) × 75 mm; 83 R. Medium-quality paper with fleur-de-lys watermark within armorial shield at foredge of 4th leaf of some gatherings. Page no. at outer corners of headlines.
HT: [double rule 73 mm] | AN ABRIDGMENT | OF | LOCKE's ESSAY. | [rule 75 mm]
RT, e.g.: AN ABRIDGMENT OF Book II. | Ch.17. LOCKE's ESSAY. (Pages 145 and 147 read 'Ch.2.' in headline (rectē Ch. 11.)
CW: Page. B1ʳ to, C6ᵛ *Ab-* [*Abſtraction*] D2ʳ them- [themſelves;] I1ᵛ they K1ᵛ *a con-* [*a connexion*] N6ᵛ Per- [Perception] S3ʳ (exa-) mine) S3ᵛ great
Press figures: 12 (A6ᵛ)–1   24 (B6ᵛ)–1   35 (C6ʳ)–1   48 (D6ᵛ)–2   60 (E6ᵛ)–2   72 (F6ᵛ)–1   84 (G6ᵛ)–1   96 (H6ᵛ)–1   108 (I6ᵛ)–1   120 (K6ᵛ)–O   144 (M6ᵛ)–1   264 (Y6ᵛ)–1   270 (Z3ᵛ)–1 (Marks on pp. 144 et seq. are of smaller font.)
Notes: A line-by-line reprint of the 1767 edition (no. 125), but not always page for page, and lacking errata. However, the first correction for p. 29 ('denominate') has been made, but the § 6. was not added to p. 92.
A microfilm copy of this edition is in *The Eighteenth Century*, reel 5568, no.2.
References: Alston 7:132; Attig 277; Christophersen p. 95; ESTC t063932.
Copies examined: Y (flyleaf inscribed 'H I Yeatman | Ball Coll Scho | 1773') CaOTU (Locke L63.A27 1770)   L¹ (8473 a.12)   L² (1133 b.16)   NjP (6106.333.127)

128. *Essay.* Abridgement (Wynne). '11th ed.', 1774. 12°
AN | ABRIDGMENT | OF | Mr. LOCKE's | ESSAY | CONCERNING | HUMAN UNDERSTANDING. | [engr. port. of Locke in circle 53 mm diameter, on plaque 59 × 59 mm] | [rule 69 mm] | The ELEVENTH EDITION, Corrected. | [double rule 67 mm] | *LONDON:* | PRINTED FOR S. HOOPER. | [rule 24 mm] | MDCCLXXIV.
Coll: 12° (172 × 98 mm cut) A⁶ B–E¹² F–S⁶ [3d leaf only of sheet A signed 'A5'; B–E $5 signed; F–S $3 signed; I3 not signed, I4 signed 'I3']; 132 leaves; pp. *1–8 i* ii–iii v *1* 2–81 *82* 83–136 *137* 138–250 *251–252* [= 264]. Page iv misnumbered 'v'.
Contents: A1ʳ (*1*) title (verso blank), A2ʳ,ᵛ (*3–4*) contents by book & chap., A3ʳ–A4ᵛ (*5–8*) Wynne's dedication, A5ʳ–A6ᵛ (*i–'v'*) Introduction, B1ʳ–E5ʳ (*1–81*) text of Book 2, E5ᵛ–I2ᵛ (*82–136*) of Book 3, I3ʳ–S5ᵛ (*137–250*) of Book 4, S6 blank.
Text (G2ᵛ): 39–40 lines approx., with half-line space between paragraphs; 133 (141 to 144) × 70 mm; 65R. Mixed medium-quality laid paper, with various watermarks, 'L. BRUN', 'DUCOMUCOIX' (?), 'P. TOIL' (?). There is no HT but each of Books 2–4 begins with, e.g. [2 double rules 69 mm] | BOOK III. | [rule 68 mm]
RTs from verso to recto: AN ESSAY ON THE | HUMAN UNDERSTANDING.

CW: Page. B1ᵛ (con-) verſant C6ᵛ ſame D7ᵛ Liberty [Liberty,] G2ʳ (Know-) ledge [ledge,] I3ʳ (cer-) tain L1ʳ (Confi-) deration R2ʳ (over-) turning
Press figures: none.
Note: A standard reprint in the pattern of the 1767 ed. (no. 125)
References: Alston 7:133; Attig 278; ESTC n029121.
Copies examined: Y   CaOTU (Locke L63.A27 1774)   L (1560/3543; lacks S6)   O (Vet.A5.f.2825)

129. *Essay*. Abridgement (Wynne). 'New ed.', Edinburgh & London, 1778. 12° in 6s
AN | ABRIDGMENT | OF | MR. *LOCKE*'s | ESSAY | CONCERNING | HUMAN UNDERSTANDING. | [rule 75 mm] | A NEW EDITION, with ADDITIONS. | [rule 75 mm] | CAREFULLY REVISED and CORRECTED. | [Oxford rule 76 mm] | EDINBURGH: | Printed for ALEXANDER DONALDSON; | And ſold at his Shop, No. 48. St. Paul's Church-yard, | LONDON; and at Edinburgh. | [rule 26 mm] | M,DCC,LXXVIII.
Coll: 12° in 6s (175 × 104 mm cut) A-Y⁶ Z⁴ [$ half signed]; 136 leaves; pp. *i-ii* iii-v 6 7-10 *11* 12-271 *272*.
Contents: A1ʳ (*i*) title (verso blank), A2ʳ-A3ʳ (iii-v) Wynne's dedication, A3ᵛ-A5ᵛ (6-10) introduction, A6ʳ-X6ᵛ (*11-252*) abridgment of Books 2-4, Y1ʳ-Z4ʳ (253-271) contents by book, chap. & section, Z4ᵛ blank.
Text (K1ᵛ): 32 lines; 133 (148) × 77 mm; 86 R with 1 mm leading between lines. Laid paper, fleur-de-lys watermark.
RTs between 75 mm rules, with book and page shown in inner corners, e.g.: [rule] | AN ABRIDGMENT OF Book III. | Ch. 5. LOCKE's ESSAY. | [rule]
CW: Page. D2ʳ them- [themſelves;] I2ᵛ Neither K1ᵛ imagination S3ᵛ great
Press figures: 12 (A6ᵛ)-2   24 (B6ᵛ)-1   36 (C6ᵛ)-1   48 (D6ᵛ)-1   60 (E6ᵛ)-2   72 (F6ᵛ)-1   84 (G6ᵛ)-1   96 (H6ᵛ)-1   108 (I6ᵛ)-2   120 (K6ᵛ)-2   132 (L6ᵛ)-1   144 (M6ᵛ)-2   156 (N6ᵛ)-2   168 (O6ᵛ)-1   180 (P6ᵛ)-1   192 (Q6ᵛ)-1   204 (R6ᵛ)-1   228 (T6ᵛ)-2   240 (U6ᵛ)-1   251 (X6ʳ)-1   264 (Y6ᵛ)-1
Notes: A reissue of no. 127, with different press figures. Perhaps printed in England.
References: Alston 7:124; Attig 279; ESTC t185309.
Copies examined: O¹ (Vet.A5 e.3702)   Ck (Keynes)   O² (Vet.A5 e.5626)

130. *Essay*. Abridgement (Wynne). 'New ed.', 1779. 12° in 4s
AN | ABRIDGMENT | OF | MR. LOCKE's | ESSAY | CONCERNING | HUMAN UNDERSTANDING. | [rule 74 mm] | A NEW EDITION, with ADDITIONS. | [rule 74 mm] | CAREFULLY REVISED and CORRECTED. | [double rule 74 over 65 mm] | LONDON: | Printed for and Sold by *J*. [swash J] *Nicholſon, Cambridge.* | [rule 32 mm] | M.DCC.LXXIX.
Coll: 12° in 4s (186 × 112 mm cut) A-2S⁴ ²2s² (=2T²) [$ half signed]; 166 leaves; pp. *1-2* 3 iv-v 6 7-10 *11* 12-301 *302* 303-330 *331-332*. § 2S signed 'Ss', ²2S signed 'Sſ'.

Contents: A1ʳ (*1*) title (verso blank), A2ʳ–A3ʳ (*3–v*) Wynne's dedication, A3ᵛ–B1ᵛ (*6–10*) introduction, B2ʳ–Q3ᵛ (*11–126.5*) text of Book 2, Q3ᵛ–Z²r (*126 rest–179.17*) of Book 2, Z2ʳ–2P4ʳ (*179 rest–301*) of Book 4, 2P4ᵛ–2T1ᵛ (*302–330*) contents by book, chap. & section, 2T2 blank.

Text (L2ʳ): 26 lines with 2 mm leading between; 131 (144) × 76 mm; 100 R (65 R sized type). Medium-quality laid paper, without watermarks. Chainlines horizontal except final leaf ²2S [= 2T] which has vertical chainlines. Page no. at outer ends of headlines.

R Ts from versos to rectos with book and chap. no. at inner margins, e.g.: AN ABRIDGMENT OF Book II. | Ch.23. LOCKE's ESSAY.

C W: C1ᵛ difor- [difordered] G2ʳ (an-) nual M3ʳ (con-) tinue T3ᵛ (intelli-) gent 2C4ʳ (de-) monftration 2I3ᵛ (*Judg-*) *ment*, 2P2ᵛ (Confidera-) tion

Press figures: none.

Note: Standard reprint. Not noticed by Alston or Attig.

Reference: ESTC n043107 (CaQMM only loc.)

Copy examined: CaQMM (inscribed to 'The Rt. Hon Lord Mapʳ ... Trumpington St | Cambridge')

131. *Essay*. Abridgement (Wynne). 'New ed.', 1782. 12° in 4s.
AN | ABRIDGMENT | OF | Mr. *LOCKE*'s | ESSAY | CONCERNING | HUMAN UNDERSTANDING. | [rule 71 mm] | A NEW EDITION, with ADDITIONS. | [rule 72 mm] | CAREFULLY REVISED and CORRECTED. | [rule 70 mm] | [rule 64 mm] | *LONDON:* | Printed for & Sold by *J.* [swash J] *Nicholfon, Cambridge.* | M. DCC. LXXXII.

Coll: 12° in 4s (180 × 107 mm cut) A⁴ (±A1) B–2S⁴ ²2S [= 2T²] [$ half signed; 2S signed 'Ss'; ²2S signed 'Sf']; 165 leaves; pp. *1–2* iv–v 6 7–10 *11* 12–301 *302* 303–330 *331–332*.

Contents, *Text*, *R Ts*, and catchwords identical with no. 130 (1779).

Press figures: none.

Notes: Reissue of no. 130 with cancellans title leaf. Here A1 and ²2S have vertical chainlines. Not listed in Alston, Attig or ESTC. I have found no libraries recording a copy of this printing.

Copy examined: Y

131.1. *Essay*. 'Abridged'. 'New ed.', Dresden, 1791. 8°
JOHN *LOCKE's Efq*. | [orn. type:] ESSAY | CONCERNING | HUMAN UNDERSTANDING, | ABRIDGED. | [segmented rule 65 mm] | A NEW EDITION, with ADDITIONS. | [segmented rule 65 mm] | CAREFULLY REVISED and CORRECTED. | [segmented double rule 64 mm] | DRESDEN, | Printed for C. and F. WALTHER. | M.DCC.XCI.

Coll: 8° (170 × 96 mm) A⁸ (–A8) B–Y⁸ Z² [$5 (–A3, –Z2) signed]; 177 leaves; pp. *1–3* 4–5 6 7–11 *12* 13–316 *317* 318–354.

Contents: A1ʳ title (verso blank), A2ʳ–A3ʳ (*3–5*) Wynne's dedication, A3ᵛ–A6ʳ (*6–11*) 'Introduction' (summary of 1.1.1–4), A6ᵛ–U7ᵛ (*12–316*) text of abridgement of Books II–IV, U8ʳ–Z2ᵛ (*317–354*) contents by book and section.

Illustration: frontispiece is poorly done portrait of Locke (facing left) in oval frame with wreath at left, above rectangular pedestal inscribed in outline type 'JOHN LOKE.', 132 × 86 mm. Headlines include 'DEDICATION.', 'INTRODUCTION.'

Text (A5^v): 33 lines; 116 × 64 mm; 70 R. Page no. at outer ends of headlines. Half- or full-line space between most sections throughout.

HT (A6^v): [unframed headpiece, 9 × 63 mm] | AN ABRIDGMENT | OF | LOCKE's ESSAY. | [rule 63 mm]

Headlines, verso to recto, A7^v–U7^r: 'AN ABRIDGMENT OF | LOCKE's ESSAY.', with book no. at inner gutter of verso leaf, chap. no. on rectos, e.g. 'AN ABRIDGMENT OF BOOK IV. | Ch. 21 LOCKE's ESSAY.' (A7^r: 'AN ABRIDGMENT OF &c.'; U7^v 'AN ABRIDGMENT &c.') U8^v–Z2^v: CONTENTS OF BOOK II. ['III.', 'IV.']

CW: Page. B7^r beco- [become] E6^r (Re-) flecting H1^r (weak-) nefs L7^v Second- [*Secondly:*] N3^v ,without ['without'] P2^v know- ['knowledge] S4^v (di-) vine U6^r appea- [appearances] X2^r 8Sub- [8 Subftance]

Notes: Information from a microfilm copy supplied by the Sächsische Landesbibliothek, Dresden (shelfmark: Phil. B.372). This is the only copy known in Germany (or elsewhere, to my knowledge). I received a clipping from an unidentifiable British bookseller's catalogue listing it as lot 61 (at £90), and including a lot 60 (Locke's *Essay*, 1694, at £300), from which price I assume this was a recent listing. The measurements above are within 2 per cent. accuracy.

References: none.

132. *Essay*. Abridgement (Wynne). Boston, Mass., 1794. 12° in 6s
AN | ABRIDGMENT | OF | MR. LOCKE's | ESSAY | CONCERNING | HUMAN UNDERSTANDING. | [Oxford rule 75 mm] | BOSTON: | PRINTED by MANNING & LORING, | For J. WHITE, THOMAS & ANDREWS, D. WEST, | E. LARKIN, J. WEST and the PROPRIETOR of | the Bofton Bookftore. | [Oxford rule 14 mm] | 1794.

Coll: 12° in 6s (174 × 110 mm cut) A–V^6 W^6 [$2 on 1st & 3d leaf (–N1) signed]; 126 leaves; pp. *i–iii* iv–v *vi* vii–viii 9 10–12 *13* 14–90 *91* 92–250 *251–252*.

Contents: A1^r (*1*) title (verso blank), A2^r–A3^r (*iii–v*) 'Contents', A3^v–A4^v (*vi–viii*) Wynne's dedication, A5^r–A6^v (9–12) 'INTRODUCTION', B1^r–H2^v (*13*–90) text of Book 2, H3^r–M6^r (*91*–143) of Book 3, M6^v–W5^v (143–250) of Book 4, W6 blank.

Text (L2^r): 37 lines; 125 (134) × 75 mm; 68 R. Medium-quality paper with horizontal chainlines (28 mm wide), no visible watermarks. Page no. at outer ends of headlines. Page *13* (B1^r) headed by 3-line ornamental fillet; p. 91 (H3^r) by double rule 74 mm. Each chap. with 2-line heading in large & small caps, e.g. 'CHAP. XVI. | OF THE DEGREES OF ASSENT.'

RTs from verso to recto: AN ESSAY ON THE | HUMAN UNDERSTANDING.

CW: Page. B3ᵛ (pleaſ-) ure H1ᵛ (ſim-) ple N1ᵛ (intu-) ition Q2ʳ (affirm-) ed W2ᵛ error
Note: First American edition; standard reprint. According to ESTC, the bookstore proprietor was William Pynson Blake. A facsimile is in the Evans microcard set.
References: Alston 7:135; Attig 280; Evans 27227; ESTC w023203
Copies examined: OCin   DLC (B1292.1794)   MB (*XH.794.L79A)   MH (*EC65.L7934.D696ag)   MWA (DB)   NN (KGD)   PPL (Am1794Loc/63775.D)   TxHR (*B1290.1794)   Vat

133. Essay. Abridgement. French trans. (Bosset). 1720. 8°
ABREGE | DE | L'ESSAY | De Mr. LOCKE. | SUR | L'Entendement Humain, [comma] | [rule 90 mm] | *Traduit de l'Anglois* | Par Monſieur BOSSET. | [rule 88 mm] | A *LONDRES*, | Chez JEAN WATTS. M DCC XX.
Coll: 8° (195 × 123 mm cut) A⁴ B-R⁸ S⁴ T⁸ U⁴ [$ half signed]; 148 leaves; pp. i–viii 1 2–4 *5* 6–104 *105* 106–144 *145* 146–243 *244* 245–264 *265* 266–286 *287–288* [= 296].
Contents: A1ʳ (*i*) title (verso blank), A2r,v (*iii–iv*) Bosset's dedication to John Wynne, Bishop of St. Asaph (signed 'J.P. Bosset.' from London 7 Oct. 1719), A3ʳ–A4ᵛ (*v–viii*) Bosset's preface, B1ʳ–B2ᵛ (*1–4*) 'Avant-propos' (translation of Wynne's 'introduction' or summary of 1.1.1), B3ʳ–R2ʳ (*5–243*) trans. of Wynne's abridgement of Books 2–4, R2ᵛ–S4ᵛ (*244–264*) Le Clerc's review (from *Bibliothèque universelle*), T1ʳ–U3ᵛ (*265–286*) 'Nouveau sisteme sur les idées' (by Bosset?), U4ʳ,ᵛ (*287–288*) contents by book & chapters.
Text (E7ᵛ): 35 lines; 143 (154) × 80 mm; 82 R. Mixed paper, some very poor, without watermarks. Page no. in outer corners of headlines.
HT, A2ʳ: [framed headpiece, fountain scene with cupids 26 × 72 mm] | A | MYLORD | Evêque de St. ASAPH, | [text follows.]
A3ʳ: [framed headpiece of ships lying off a port, 26 × 72 mm] | PRÉFACE.
B1ʳ: [framed headpiece of artist sketching architectural ruins] | AVANT-PROPOS.
T1ʳ: [framed headpiece of portrait with leaves 20 × 72 mm] | NOUVEAU SISTEME | SUR | LES IDEES. | – E Cœlo deſcendit, γνῶθι σεαυτόν. | JUVEN:
RTs or headlines are chapter titles in italics.
Press figures: none.
CW: Page. A4ᵛ *Frag-* [*Fragment*] E8ᵛ l'ex- [l'expérience,] L2ᵛ *im-* [*immédiate*] Q6ᵛ verſio [verſion]
Notes: A translation of Wynne's abridgement, followed by 'Extrait Fait par l'Illustre Mr. Le Clerc du Premier Livre de Mr. Locke sur l'Entendement Humain' reprinted from *Bibliothèque universelle & historique* for 1690 (t. 17, pp. 399–426), omitting the first four sentences from Le Clerc's summary review, chiefly of Book I (see no. 61, Notes).

170   *John Locke: A Descriptive Bibliography*

The 'Nouveau sisteme' in 4 chapters that follows the extract was probably written by Bosset: by content it is not by Locke, Le Clerc or Pierre Coste. Its chapter titles, as translated, are (1) Of ideas in general; (2) Which ideas can be defined; (3) The origin of our ideas; and (4) Of complete and incomplete, clear and obscure ideas. There is no entry for Bosset in Cioranescu (17th or 18th century volumes).

John Watts (1707?-1763) had one of the most important printing houses in London. Cf. Plomer, p. 304.

References: Attig 365; Christopersen p. 98; ESTC n029118; Rochedieu p. 193 ('12°').

Copies examined: Y (ex lib.Schönborn-Buchheim) L (CUP.407.kk.34; 193 × 115 mm cut) O (Vet.A4 e.1340) PPL (Ia Loc/Log.3347.D)

134. *Essay*. Abridgment, French (Bosset). New ed., Geneva, 1738. 8°
In red & black: [red line:] ABREGÉ | DE | [red:] L'ESSAI | DE MONSIEUR | [red:] LOCKE | SUR | [red:] L'ENTENDEMENT | HUMAIN, | *Traduit de l'Anglois* | Par Mr. [red:] BOSSET. | NOUVELLE EDITION. | [scroll ornament 28 × 50 mm] | [red:] A GENEVE, | Chez PELLISSARI & COMP. | [red rule 62 mm] | MDCCXXXVIII.

Coll: 8° (213 × 138 mm uncut) †⁴ 2†² A-R⁸ S⁴ T² [$ half (-A1) signed]; 148 leaves; pp. *I-III* IV-XII *1* 2-280 *281-284* [= 296].

Contents: †1ʳ (*I*) title (verso blank), †2ʳ,ᵛ (*III-IV*) dedication to Wynne, †3ʳ-†4ᵛ (V-VIII) Bosset's preface, 2†1ʳ-2†2ᵛ (IX-XII) 'Avant-propos' (trans. of Wynne's 'introduction'), A1ʳ-B2ᵛ (*1-20*) 'Extrait fait par Mr. Le Clerc', B3ʳ-R1ᵛ (21-258) trans. of Wynne's abridgement of Books 2-4, R2ʳ-S4ᵛ (259-280) 'Nouveau systeme sur les idées', T1ʳ-T2ᵛ (*281-284*) 'Table des matières' (contents).

Text (G4ʳ): 36 lines; 154 (163) × 79 mm; 85 R. Dedication set 136 R. Mixture of excellent heavy & thin paper watermarked with an oval & letters C & O. Page no. in outer corners of headlines. Ornamental headpiece on †3ʳ, B3ʳ, H5ʳ, L1ʳ and R2ʳ: framed rectangle of painter's pallettes and a mask, 27 × 82 mm, almost identical with *Bowyer Ornaments*, no. 59 (said to measure 24 × 74 mm), except background has horizontal shading. Ornamental tailpiece on K12ᵛ: a heart with scrolls 28 × 38 mm; scroll orn. from title repeated as tailpiece on H4ᵛ and S4ᵛ.

HT, †2ʳ: [framed rect. headpiece: helmet with draped flags, 34 × 80 mm] | A MYLORD | Evêque de St. Asaph.

A1ʳ: [headpiece as on †2ʳ] | ABREGÉ | DE | L'ESSAI | DE Mr. LOCKE | SUR | L'Entendement Humain. | [double rule 78 mm]

Headlines or RTs are chap. title summaries in italics, with chap. no. at inner margins.

CW: Page. C4ᵛ tou- [toujours,] H2ᵛ vien- [viennent] O3ʳ ab- [abſtraites]

Notes: Reprint of the 1720 edition (no. 133) rearranged to put Le Clerc's review (from the *Bibliothèque universelle*) first, since Wynne omitted most of

Book 1 from his abridgement. I have no explanation for the presence of the Bowyer-type ornament used here (see *Text*); however they were frequently copied for use by other printers.

References: Attig 366; Christophersen p. 98; Rochedieu p. 193.

Copies examined: CaOTU (Locke L63.A27F7 1738) L (8471.bbb.54; heavy paper in A–F, K–N) O (Vet.D4.e.101; uncut, heavy paper throughout)

135. *Essay*. Abridgement, French (Bosset). 'New ed., London' (Paris?) 1741. 12°

In red & black: [red line:] ABREGÉ | DE | [red:] L'ESSAY | DE MONSIEUR | [red:] LOCKE, | SUR | [red:] L'ENTENDEMENT | HUMAIN, | *Traduit de l'Anglois* | *Par* MR. [red:] BOSSET. | NOUVELLE EDITION. | [pedestal as orn. 17×35 mm] | [red:] A LONDRES, | Chez JEAN NOURSE. | [red rule 41 mm] | M. DCC. XLI.

Coll: 12° (170×96 mm cut) †^{8} A–Q^{12} [$ half (–B3) signed in arabic no., except A5 & 6 signed Av, Avj; B5 & 6 signed Bv–vj; C5 signed Cv]; 200 leaves; pp. *I–III* IV V VI–XVI *1* 2–28 *29* 30–161 *162* 163–213 *214* 215–347 *348* 349–376 *377–384* [=400].

Contents: †1^r (*I*) title (verso blank), †2^{r,v}(*III–IV*) Bosset's dedication to Wynne, †3^r–†5^r (*V–IX*) Bosset's preface, †5^v (*X*) rest of pref. & Wynne's 'imprimatur' of translation, †6^r–†8^v (*XI–XVI*) 'Avant-propos' (Wynne's introduction), A1^r–B2^v (*1–28*) Le Clerc's 'extrait', B3^r–P6^r (*29–347*) trans. of Books 2–4, P6^v–Q8^v (*348–376*) 'Nouveau système des ideés', Q9^r–Q11^r (*377–381*) contents, Q11^v–Q12 blank.

Illustration: frontispiece is oval portrait of Locke after Kneller signed '*Cl. Duflos sculp.*' within rectangular frame 133×81 mm, on plate 144×92 mm. Oval frame has inscription: "JEAN LOCKE NÉ LE ... AOUT M.D.C.XXXII MORT LE XXVIII. OCTOBRE M.D.CC.IV." A 4-line subscription below the portrait reads: "*Par l'art délicat du Graveur* | *Tu vois ici de LOCKE la veritable Image;* | *Et par les soins du Traducteur* | *Les plus beaux traits de son Ouvrage.*"

Text (L4^r): 30 lines; 128 (138)×63 mm; 85 R. Good-quality paper with tail of foolscap (?) watermark at foredge of 8th leaf. Page no. in outer corners of headlines. Decorative headpiece on †2^r, †3^r, †6^r, A1^r, B3^r, G9^v, I11^v and P6^v: framed orn. of vase with leaves, 19×65 mm. Ornamental tailpieces of fruit & flowers (27×39 mm) on †8^v; pedestal orn. from title repeated on G9^r.

HT, A1^r: [framed headpiece, vase with leaves 19×65 mm] | ABREGÉ | DE L'ESSAY | DE MR. LOCKE | SUR | L'ENTENDEMENT HUMAIN. | [orn. fillet of rosettes 62 mm]

Headlines or RTs are chapter title summaries in italics, with book no. on recto page in large & small caps. Longer titles run from verso to recto, e.g. '*Des Idées en général,* | *& de leur Origine.* LIV. II.' Le Clerc's 'extrait' is headed '*Extrait du premier Livre* | *de Mr.* LOCKE.'

CW: Page. †5ᵛ AVANTPROPOS †6ᵛ (nous) ſont A2ᵛ Raiſon; A3ʳ s'augmen- [s'augmentent] D5ʳ CHAPI- [CHAPITRE] H1ʳ (circonſ-) tances L6ʳ CHAPI- [CHAPITRE] N11ᵛ CHAPITRE P6ʳ NOUVEAU P12ᵛ (ex-) preſſion (No CW on A1ʳ.)
Press figures: none.
Note: Reprint following the format adopted in the Geneva 1738 printing (no. 134), but using the spelling 'Essay' of the 1720 London edition (Geneva editions use 'Essai'). John Nourse specialized in French literature, especially scientific works (cf. Plomer). This edition was probably printed in Paris.
References: Attig 367; ESTC t186227; Rochedieu p. 193.
Copies examined: Y [BBR] CaOTU (Locke L63.A27F7 1741) O (Vet.A4 f.972)

136. *Essay.* Abridgement, French (Bosset). 3d ed., Geneva, 1741. 8°.
In red & black: [red line:] ABREGÉ | DE | [red:] L'ESSAI | DE MONSIEUR | [red:] LOCKE, | SUR | [red:] L'ENTENDEMENT | HUMAIN, | *Traduit de l'Anglois* | Par [red:] J. P. BOSSET. | *Troiſiéme Edition plus exacte que les précédentes.* | [tailpiece-like orn. of crossed club, cadduceus & sceptre cap above, cloud below 41 × 45 mm] | [red:] A GENEVE, | Chez HENRI-ALBERT GOSSE & COMP. | [red rule 60 mm] | MDCCXLI.
Coll: 8° (197 × 122 mm cut) †⁸ ††⁴ A–R⁸ S–T⁴ [$ half (+ ††3, + S3, + T3) signed]; 156 leaves; pp. *I–II* III–XXIV *1* 2–279 *280* 281–283 *284–288* [= 312].
Contents: †1ʳ (I) title (verso blank), †2ʳ,ᵛ (III–IV) translator's preface, †3ʳ–†5ᵛ (V–X) '*Avant-propos*' (Wynne's introduction), †6ʳ–††4ᵛ (XI–XXIV) 'Analyse de l'ouvrage suivant', A1ʳ–B3ᵛ (*1–22*) Le Clerc's 'extrait' of Book I, B4ʳ–S4ʳ (*23–279*) Wynne's abridgement of Books 2–4, S4ᵛ (*280*) ornamental tailpiece (50 × 66 mm), T1ʳ–T2ʳ (*281–283*) trans. of 'Rules of a society . . . for the promoting of truth and Christian charity' (first pub. in no. 316), T2ᵛ (*284*) 25-line errata (14 items), T3ʳ–T4ᵛ (*285–288*) contents of abridgement by book & chap.
Text (L1ᵛ): 33 lines; 139 (148) × 79 mm; 84 R. Excellent-quality laid paper without watermarks. Page no. in outer corners of headlines. Ornamental fillets before each internal chapter. Additional ornaments (to those noted) are framed headpieces of mask with scrolls & flowers, 27 × 82 mm on †1ʳ, B4ʳ, I2ʳ and L8ʳ, (same as Bowyer-type orn. in no. 134, q.v.). Finely scrolled tailpiece on †2ᵛ and B3ᵛ 28 × 50 mm; bolder scrolled tailpiece (28 × 50 mm) on H8ᵛ and I1ᵛ
HT, A1ʳ: [framed rectangle with helmet, draped flags & scrolls 34 × 81 mm] | ABREGÉ | DE | L'ESSAI | DE MR. LOCKE | SUR | L'Entendement Humain. | [broken double rule 78 mm]
T1ʳ: [headpiece of repeated fleurons & small irons, 21 × 77 mm] | LOIX | *Pour une Societé qui s'aſſemble une fois la* | *ſemaine, dont les Membres*

ont pour uni- | que deſſein d'augmenter leurs connoiſſances | utiles, & de propager la vérité & la | charité Chrêtienne.

Headlines are italicized chap. title summaries, if long extending from verso to recto page.

CW: Page. C4^v (rentre-) ront H2^v cepen- [cependant] O2^v (con-) noiffe, S1^r (con-) duite

Notes: An unknown editor has put together this edition reprinting Bosset's preface and the translation of Wynne's abridgement, with Le Clerc's summary review from the *Bibliothèque universelle*, but omitting Bosset's dedication to Wynne and his 'Nouveau systeme'. The 'analyse' is similar to but not a translation of Gilbert's *Abstract* (no. 147 et seq.); it contains careful citations to books and chapters of the *Essay* for each of its points. The 'Rules of a society' was first published in Desmaizeaux's *Collection of Several Pieces* (1720); it is not by Locke and was sent to him by Richard King (cf. no. 316, *Notes*); nor was it previously translated.

References: Attig 368; Christophersen p. 98; Rochedieu p. 193.

Copies examined: Y [BBR]   CtY (K8.L79/gh741)   MH (Phil.2115.48.10)   O (Vet.D4 e.88)

137. *Essay*. Abridgement, French (Bosset). 'New ed., London' (Paris?) 1746. 12°

In red & black: [red line:] ABRÉGÉ | DE | [red:] L'ESSAY | . . . [&c. as in no.135, until last 2 lines: [red Oxford rule, 57 mm] | M. DCC. XLVI.

Coll: 12° (167 × 99 mm) †^{8} A–Q^{12} [$ half (–B3) signed; L5 and 6 both signed 'L5']; 200 leaves; pp. *I–III* IV V *VI–XVI 1* 2–28 *29* 30–161 *162* 163–213 *214* 215–347 *348* 349–376 *377–384* [= 400].

Contents, and *Illustration* identical with no. 135.

Text (L4^r): 30 lines; 127 (137) × 64 mm. Medium-quality paper, with watermark 'WOVEN OF P DIR' (?) at foredge of 8th leaf. Page no. at outer corners of headlines. Headpiece on †2^r, B3^r is framed rectangle of vases with flowers, 19 × 64 mm; on G9^v and P6^v is framed rectangle of a basket, 18 × 64 mm. Ornament on head title same as on A1^r in no. 135.

HT, A1^r: same as in no. 135.

Headlines or *RTs*: same as in no. 135.

CW: Page. A3^r s'augmen- [s'augmentent] D5^r CHAPI- [CHAPITRE] H1^r (circonſ-) tances L6^r CHA- [CHAPITRE] N11^v CHAPITRE P6^r NOU- [NOUVEAU]

Press figures: none.

Notes: This is a fairly close reprint of the 1741 'London' edition, line-for-line.

References: Attig 369; ESTC t186245; Rochedieu p. 193.

Copy examined: O (Vet.A4 f.898)

138. *Essay.* Abridgement, French (Bosset). 'New ed., London' (Paris?). 1751. 12°

ABBRÉGÉ [sic] | DE | L'ESSAY | DE MONSIEUR | LOCKE, | SUR | L'ENTENDEMENT | HUMAIN, | *Traduit de l'Anglois* | *Par* MR. BOSSET, | *NOUVELLE EDITION.* [swash T] | [orn., small iron 8 × 11 mm] | A LONDRES, | Chez JEAN NOURSE. | [Oxford rule 58 mm] | M. DCC LI.

Coll: 12° (163 × 95 mm) †⁸ A-Q¹² [$ half signed]; 200 leaves; pp. *I-III* IV V VI-X *XI* XII-XVI *1* 2-28 *29* 30-161 *162* 163-213 *214* 215-347 *348* 349-376 *377-382 383-384* [= 400].

Contents: †1ʳ (*I*) title (verso blank), †2ʳ,ᵛ (III-IV) dedication to Wynne, †3ʳ–†5ᵛ (*V-X*) Bosset's preface, †6ʳ–†8ᵛ (*XI-XVI*) 'Avant-propos' (Wynne's 'introduction'), A1ʳ-B2ᵛ (*1-28*) Le Clerc's extract, B3ʳ-P6ʳ (*29-347*) translation of Wynne's abridgement of Books 2-4, P6ᵛ-Q8ᵛ (*348-376*) 'Nouveau système sur les idées', Q9ʳ-Q11ʳ (*377-381*) contents, Q11ᵛ-Q12 blank.

Illustration: Deteriorating-quality portrait of Locke by Duflos after Kneller, as in no. 135, plate worn.

Text (C9ᵛ): 30 lines; 126 (135) × 65 mm; 83 R. Medium-quality laid paper watermarked with a bunch of grapes. Page no. in outer corners of headlines. Framed headpiece of lyre with tree branches, 21 × 69 mm on †2ʳ; of bowl of flowers with leaves (as in no. 137) on †3ʳ and I11ᵛ; of vase with leaves on †6ʳ; of leaning tower with baskets & scrolls (19 × 74 mm) on B3ʳ and P6ᵛ; G9ᵛ has same headpiece as on HT. Ornamental tailpiece of leaves (23 × 48 mm) on †5ʳ, †8ᵛ and G9ʳ. Oxford rule or triple rule (thin/thick/thin) at beginning of each chapter.

HT, A1ʳ: [framed headpiece of standing globe, with leaves & drapery 21 × 70 mm] | ABBRÉGÉ | DE L'ESSAY | DE MR. LOCKE. | SUR | L'ENTENDEMENT HUMAIN. | [triple rule, thin/thick/thin 62 mm]

Headlines or RTs are chapter title summaries in italics, with book no. on recto page in large & small caps; if long, RTs extend from verso to recto, e.g. 'Des vrayes | & des fauſſes idées. LIV. II.' If headlines are very brief, book no. are printed after chapter titles on recto *and* verso pages.

Press figures: none.

CW: Page. †5ᵛ AVANT-PROPOS †6ᵛ (*nous* ſont) des A1ʳ (Prin-) cipes, A2ᵛ raiſon; D5ʳ CHAPI- [CHAPITRE] H1ʳ (circonſ-) tances L6ʳ CHA- [CHAPITRE] N11ᵛ CHAPITRE P12ᵛ (ex-) preſſion

Notes: Reprint of no. 137, probably also printed in Paris. Signature errors have here been corrected, but occasional errors occur in headlines, chiefly book numbers, e.g. p. 217 (K1ʳ) includes 'LIV. V.'; p. 261: 'LIV. VI.' Not listed in Rochedieu.

References: Attig 370; Christophersen p. 98; ESTC t063931.

Copies examined: Y [GhU (Ph.562)] L (1472.aa.45) O¹ (Vet.E5.f.174) O² (Vet.E5.e.221) Vat

139. *Essay.* Abridgement, French (Bosset). 4th ed., Geneva, 1788. 8°
ABRÉGÉ | DE | L'ESSAI | DE MONSIEUR | LOCKE, | SUR | L'ENTENDEMENT | HUMAIN, | *Traduit de l'Anglois* | Par J. P. BOSSET. | *Quatrième Edition plus exacte que les précédentes.* | [rectangular orn. 6 × 16 mm] | *A GENEVE.* | [rule 45 mm] | 1788.
Coll: 8° (186 × 125 mm uncut) A–P⁸ Q⁴ R² [$ half signed 'ij, iij, iv']; 126 leaves; pp. *I–II* III–XXI *XXII* 1 2–228 229–230 [= 252].
Contents: A1ʳ (*I*) title (verso blank), A2ʳ,ᵛ (III–IV) editor's preface, A3ʳ–A5ᵛ (V–X) 'Avant-propos' (Wynne's introduction), A6ʳ–B3ʳ (XI–XXI) 'Analyse de l'oeuvre suivant' (after Gilbert), B3ᵛ blank, B4ʳ–C4ᵛ (1–18) 'Livre premier, Extrait fait par M. Le Clerc', C5ʳ–Q3ʳ (19–223) Bosset's trans. of Wynne's abridgement of Books 2–4, Q3ᵛ–Q4ʳ (224–5) trans. of 'Rules of a Society' (cf. no. 136), Q4ᵛ–R1ᵛ (226–228) contents of vol., R2 blank.
Text (L2ʳ): 36 lines; 135 (142) × 78 mm; 75 R. Good-quality laid paper with fleur-de-lys watermark. Page no. at outer ends of headlines. There are several framed headpieces: B4ʳ (*p. 1*) has vignette of seated scholar, 24 × 76 mm; B6ʳ (*p. 5*) has flowers with wheat sheaves, 23 × 99 mm; H8ʳ (*p. 105*), urn on a pedestal, 23 × 65 mm; and L1ᵛ (*p. 140*) has landscape view of a farm with stream, and distant village, 33 × 79 mm. Ornamental tailpieces on A2ᵛ (*p. IV*): cherub with books, 23 × 47 mm; A5ᵛ (*p. X*), bouquet in sconce-like vase, 32 × 36 mm; B3ʳ (*p. XXI*), fruit & vegetables on a platter, 10 × 28 mm; H7ᵛ (*p. 104*), vase with scrolls on a pedestal, 28 × 35 mm; L1ʳ, cornucopia with swags & leaves, 19 × 37 mm; and Q3ʳ vase on a pedestal, 19 × 12 mm.
Headlines or RTs are chapter title summaries in italics; when long, split between verso and recto pages, e.g. '*De l'affociation des idees, & des habitudes* | *corporelles & fpirituelles.*'
CW: Gathering (on leaf 8ᵛ). B (en-) fui [fuit] G Nos
      No CW in sheets M, O and P.
Notes: Reprint of the Geneva edition of 1741 (no. 136), with its different spelling of the title.
References: Attig 371; Rochedieu p. 193.
Copies examined: O¹ (Vet.D5 e.426, uncut, in blue wrapper) O² (Vet.D5 e.419)

140*. *Essay.* Abridgement, French. Dresden, 1788. 8°
"abrégé de l'Essai sur l'entendement hum. trad. de l'Anglois. gr. 8. Dresd. Walther. 788."

The above citation is from *GV 1700–1910*, the fourth item listed under 'Locke, John' (vol. 89, pp. 366–67).
  Rochedieu (p.193) after listing 6 French abridgements he knew about, then lists "Essai sur l'entendement humain, traduit par Walther. Dresden: Walther, 1788."

I am assuming both these citations refer to the same item. There is no such edition listed in the *National Union Catalog of pre-1956 imprints* or its supplement, nor in any of the British and Irish libraries I have consulted. Nor is it found in any continental libraries I have used; it does not appear in the Dutch union catalogue at the Hague. It is not noticed in Attig. Beginning with no. 134, all Geneva editions spell Locke's title as 'Essai', whereas the French editions from London stick to 'Essay'. Perhaps Dresden was the true place of printing at least of the 1788 edition of the abridgement, instead of Geneva (no. 139).

141. *Essay.* Abridgement, French (Bosset). Uppsala, 1792. 8°
ABBRÉGÉ | [script type:] *DE L'ESSAY* | *DE MONSIEUR* [hollow script:] LOCKE, | SUR | [script:] *L'ENTENDEMENT* | [script:] *HUMAIN.* | [orn. rule, 4 small pairs of leaves, 45 mm] | *Traduit de l'Anglois* PAR MONSIEUR BOSSET. | [rule 28 cm] | [engr. oval-framed port. of Locke within rectangular frame, 67 × 55 mm on plaque 73 × 62 mm] | [orn. rule 74 mm] | *Aux Dépens de Jean Fr. Edman.* [swash J]
Colophon (on T4^v): A UPSAL, | CHEZ LA VEUVE DU DIRECT. JEAN EDMAN. | MDCCXCII.
Coll: 8° (182 × 110 mm cut) π^2 (-π2) A-S^8 T^4 [$5 (-S5; -T2, +T3-4) signed; B4 and B5 both signed 'B5']; 149 leaves; pp. *I–III* IV–VI *VII* VIII–X *1* 2–21 *22* 23–123 *124* 125–163 *164* 165–263 *264* 265–284 *285–288* [=298]. Leaf A1 also signed 'N:o 5' in direction line.
Contents: $\pi1^r$ (*I*) title (verso blank), A1^r–A2^v (*III–VI*) Bosset's preface, A3^r–A4^v (*VII–X*) 'Avant-propos' (Wynne's 'Introduction'), A5^r–B7^r (*1–21*) Le Clerc's extract, B7^v–R1^r (*22–263*) Wynne's abridgement of Books 2–4, R1^v–T2^v (*264–284*) 'Nouveau systeme sur les idées', T3^r–T4^v (*285–288*) contents (p. *288* has remainder of contents and colophon).
Text (N5^r): 37 lines; 113 (141) × 76 mm; 71 R. Type is of nineteenth-century style. Line spaces between paragraphs. Good laid paper, watermarked 'II'. Ornamental rules between chapters. Page no. at external ends of headlines. Occassional double Ss in text chiefly of unusual type, e.g. 'Fauſſes', 'asſez', 'grosſeurs', 'puisſans'. etc. Frequent ornaments (tailpieces), e.g. on A1^r: spray of flowers, 23 × 64 mm; A3^r: feathers and an arrow, 27 × 49 mm; A5^r: star with sunburst, 53 × 66 mm.
HT: [orn. (tailpiece), sunburst, 53 × 65 mm] | [hollow type:] ABBRÉGÉ | [decorative hollow type:] DE L'ESSAY | DE MR. LOCKE | SUR | L'ENTENDEMENT HUMAIN. | [orn. rule 36 mm] | LIVRE PREMIER. | EXTRAIT FAIT PAR | MR. [script type:] LE CLERC.
Headlines or RTs for body of text are chap. title summaries in italics, followed by book no. in large & small caps, e.g. '*De la Verité en général.* LIV. IV.' If long, titles run from verso to recto headline. Page *IV–VI, VIII–X* have ornamental double rule with garland wrapped about it as headline, 4 × 31 mm.
CW: Page. A2^v Frag- [Fragment] C3^v croy- [croyant] G2^v mani- [maniere] L3^r Lan- [Langue] N4^v diſ- [diſcourir (*sic*)] R1^v (mon-) tre

Note: Standard reprint, following the title's spelling and the content of the London 1751 ed. (no. 138).
Reference: Attig 372.
Copies examined: Y CaOTU (Locke L63.A27F7 1792) O (Vet. C5 e.20)

142. Essay. Abridgement. German trans. (Tittel). Mannheim, 1791. 8°
Locke | von | menschlichen Verstande | [French rule 48 mm] | zu leichtem und fruchtbarem Gebrauch zergliedert | und geordnet | [French rule 40 mm] | von | Gottlob August Tittel | Marggräfl. Badenschen wirkl. Kirchenrath, der akademischen | Fürstenschule Ephorus und der Philosophie ordentl. | Professor zu Karlsruh. | [orn., 2 seated cherubs 30 × 41 mm] | [orn. double rule 85 mm] | Mannheim, | in der Hofbuchhandlung bei Schwann und Götz | [French rule 28 mm] | 1791.
Coll: 8° (196 × 122 mm) *⁸ **⁸ A–2M⁸ [$5 signed]; 296 leaves; pp. I–III IV–XII XIII XIV–XX XXI XXII–XXXII 1–3 4–557 558–560 [= 592].
Contents: *1^r (I) title (verso blank), *2^r–*6^v (III–XII) translator's introduction, *7^r–**2^v (XIII–XX) "Locke an den Leser" (Locke's introduction), **3^r–**6^v (XXI–XXVIII) "Kurze Nachricht von Locke's Leben und Schriften" (summary of Le Clerc's 'Eloge' from the Bibliothèque choisie, t.6), **7^r–**8^v (XXIX–XXXII) "Skiagraphie, oder Verzeichniss aller im gegenwartigen Werk abgehandelten Momente", A1^r (1) half-title, A1^v (2) Latin with German trans. of quotation from Seneca (4 lines), A2^r–2M6^r (3–555) text, 2M6^v–2M7^r (556–557) "Allgemeine Abtheilung der Wissenschaften," 2M7^v (558) errata (15 lines), 2M8 (559–560) blank.
Text (C4^v): 29 lines; 151 (163) × 85 mm; 103 fraktur with 1 mm leading. Fair paper without watermarks; chainlines vertical. Page no. in outer corners of headlines. An Oxford rule (11 mm) centered as headlines. Divided into topics, with each topic headed by a framed scroll ornament, 17 × 81 mm.
Half-title: Locke's | Versuch | vom | menschlichen Verstande. | [French rule 40 mm]
CW: Gathering (in fraktur, on leaf 8^v). B (Ge-) rech- [rechligkeit,] H 3. Rela- [3. Relationsbegriffe] 2B Ter- [Terminus]
Notes: The translator's own abridgement, with the text organized under various topics.
References: Attig 384; GV 89: 367 col.1, no.1; Christophersen p. 99.
Copies examined: L (8463 ccc.8) Mun (Ph.sp. 498; lacks 2M8) O (Vet.D5 e.351; lacks 2M8)

143. Essay. Abridgement, Greek trans. (Wynne-Soave/anon.). Venice, 1796. 8°
In red & black Greek type: [red line:] ΕΓΧΕΙΡΙΔΙΟΝ | ΜΕΤΑΦΥΣΙΚΟ-ΔΙΑΛΕΚΤΙΚΟΝ | [red:] Η | [red:] ΕΠΙΤΟΜΗ ΑΚΡΙΒΕΣΤΑΤΗ | ΤΟΥ | [red:] ΔΕΙΓΜΑΤΟΣ | ΤΟΥ ΚΥΡΙΟΥ | [red:] ΛΟΚΚΙΟΥ | [red] Περιβοήτου Φιλοσόφου | ΠΕΡΙ ΤΗΣ ΑΝΘΡΩΠΙΝΗΣ | [red:] ΔΙΑ-ΝΟΙΑΣ. | Μεταφραθεῖσα ἐκ τῆς Ἀ'γγλικῆς Διαλέκτου | [woodcut

device of a bee and initials N Γ within double frame, 24 × 36 mm] |
͵αψ ϠϚ'. [red word:] ΕΝΕΤΙΗΣΙΝ, 1796. | [orn. rule 94 mm] | Παρὰ
Νικολάῳ Γλυκεῖ τῷ ἐξ Ἰωαννίνων. | [red:] CON LICENZA DE'
SUPERIORI.
Coll: 8° (190 × 121 mm cut) a⁸ A-T⁸ V⁸ (-2 leaves = V4.5?) [$ half signed];
166 leaves; pp. α'-β' γ'-ιε' ιϚ' [= *i*-*ii* iii-xv *xvi*] 1-316 [= 332]. First recto
of sheets A-V and V3 recto also signed 'Saggio Lock.' in direction line.
Contents: a1ʳ title (verso blank), a2ʳ-a5ᵛ (γ'-ι') 'Prolegomena' (introd.), a6ʳ-
a8ʳ (ια'-ιε') contents, a8ᵛ (ιϚ') licence to print by Inquisitor General of the
Holy Office of Venice (in Italian) to Nicolò Glichi, printer in Venice, dated
14 April 1796 (on condition he present copies to public libraries in Venice
and Padua), A1ʳ-T6ʳ (1-299) text of Greek trans. of Wynne's abridgement
(from Soave's translation), T6ᵛ-V5ᵛ (300-314) "Ἀνάλυσις τοῦ Συγ-
γράμματος" (outline of *Essay*, books II-IV), V6ʳ,ᵛ (315-16) errata.
Text (F1ʳ): 30 or 31 lines; 144 (158) × 95 or 96 mm; 96 Greek. Introd. set 20
lines, 150 Greek with 2 mm. leading, in a more upright type; paged in
Greek numerals at outer ends of top lines, without headlines. Body of the
text paged in arabic numbers at outer ends of headlines. Frequently brief
topics in Italian as footnotes. Medium-quality laid paper (very thin and
white) without watermarks. Ornamental 5-line initials begin each book (I
on p. 1, II on p. 25, III on p. 139, and IV on p. 196). Ornamental rule
before each chapter.
At head of title, p. 1: [framed headpiece of flower & leaves 26 × 89 mm] |
ΒΙΒΛΙ'ΟΝ ΠΡΩ˜ΤΟΝ | ΠΕΡΙˋ ΤΩ˜Ν Α'ΡΧΩ˜Ν ΤΩ˜Ν
ΛΕΓΟΜΕ'ΝΩΝ | Ε'ΜΦΥ'ΤΩΝ.
Headlines or RTs are chap. titles in upper & lower case Greek, with chap.
no. at inner margins, e.g. "Περὶ τῆς Ἀντιλήψεως. Κεφ. Θ.' Where long
they extend from verso to recto pages.
CW: Page. a3ᵛ EI- [EI'NAI] B1ᵛ σιν E3ʳ (θέ-) λει G7ʳ ὁδ ὧν K5ʳ Ἀλλὰ O4ᵛ
ἡμεῖς R1ʳ KE- [ΚΕΦΑ'ΛΑΙΟΝ] T2ᵛ deci- [decisive] V4ʳ (κα-) θολι-
[θολικὰς]
Notes: A Greek translation of one of Soave's translations (no. 144-6) of
Wynne's abridgement. The place of publication is a variant of 'Venetia'
(Βενετία). The text uses old-style Greek type with many ligatures; the
foonotes are in Italian. Page 314 (V5ᵛ) has a tailpiece of flowers in a wall
sconce, 50 × 53 mm.
Reference: Attig 387.
Copy examined: O (Vet. F5 e.144)

144. *Essay*. Abridgement, Italian trans. (Wynne/Soave) Milan, 1775. 3 vols.
in 8°
SAGGIO | FILOSOFICO | [ornate hollow type:] DI GIO. LOCKE | SU
L'UMANO INTELLETTO | COMPENDIATO | DAL Dr. WYNNE |
Tradotto, e commentato | DA FRANCESCO SOAVE C. R. S. | *Prof. di
Filoſ. Mor. nel R. Ginnaſio di Brera.* | [rule 76 mm] | VOLUME

PRIMO. ['SECONDO.', 'TERZO.'] | [rule 77 mm] | [orn.: open book with pen, scrolls 15 × 49 mm] | IN MILANO. | [Oxford rule 75 mm] | Per GAETANO MOTTA. | *Con Licenza de' Superiori.* | MDCCLXXV.

Coll: 8° (202 × 133 mm uncut). Vol. 1: *⁸ A–L⁸ M⁴ [$ half (–*2, –*3); signed; *4.5 signed '*3', '*4' respectively]; 100 leaves; pp. *i–xvi* 1–182 *183–184* [= 200]. First recto pages of sheets B–M signed in direction line '*Vol. I.*'

Vol. 2: A–M⁸ N⁴ [$ half (–A2) signed]; 100 leaves; pp. *1–4* 5–195 *96* *197–200*. First recto page of B–N also signed '*Vol. II.*' Page 196 has lost its first digit.

Vol. 3: A–M⁸ [$ half (–A2) signed]; 96 leaves; pp. *1–4* 5–187 *188–192*. First recto page of sheets B–E, G–M also signed '*Vol. III.*'

Contents: Vol. 1: *1ʳ (*i*) half title (verso blank), *2ʳ (*iii*) title (verso blank), *3ʳ (*v*) salutatory dedication to Count Carlo Firmian (verso blank), *4ʳ,ᵛ (*vii–viii*) text of dedication, *5ʳ–*7ᵛ (*ix–xiv*) Soave's preface, *8ʳ,ᵛ (*xv–xvi*) vol. contents, A1ʳ–A3ᵛ (*1–6*) introduction (summary of 1.1.1), A4ᵛ–B3ᵛ (*7–38*) trans. of Le Clerc's 'extrait' (from *Bibliothèque universelle*), C4ʳ–G2ʳ (*39–99 line 9*) Soave's 'Analisi dell' umano intelletto', G2ʳ–M3ᵛ (*99 rest–182*) abridgement of 2.1–12, M4 blank.

Vol. 2: A1ʳ (*1*) half title (verso blank), A2ʳ (*3*) title (verso blank), A5ʳ–N2ᵛ (*5–196*) abridgement of 2.13–3.8, N3ʳ–N4ʳ (*197–199*) vol. contents, N4ᵛ blank.

Vol. 3: A1ʳ (*1*) half title (verso blank), A2ʳ (*3*) title (verso blank), A3ʳ–L7ʳ (*5–173*) abridgement of 3.9–4.19, L7ᵛ–M6ʳ (*174–187*) 'Appendice', M6ᵛ–M7ᵛ (*188–190*) vol. contents, M8ʳ (*191*) advt. by Motta for Italian trans. of Locke's *Conduct* (priced at 'tre Paoli Romani.'), M8ᵛ blank.

Text (v.1 E4ʳ; same for all vols.): 28 lines; 128 (137) × 76 mm; 92 R. Analyses and appendices set 30 to 31 lines, 85 R; footnotes 80 R. Dedication set 112 ital. with 1 mm leading. Excellent heavy laid paper, crowned coat-of-arms watermark. Page no. in headlines at outer corners. Vol. 1 has tailpieces: on *7ᵛ is an arrow case with leaves and flowers, 13 × 47 mm; on A3ᵛ fruit with flowers, 15 × 50 mm; on M3ᵛ a vase of flowers with scrolls, 21 × 33 mm. Vol. 2 N2ᵛ has a tailpiece of leaves and flowers, 23 × 39 mm.

Half-titles: [ornamental hollow type:] COMPENDIO | DI | [hollow type:] LOCKE.

HT, v.1–3: [headpiece, stars surrounding double roll of leaves, 15 × 68 mm] | [ornamental hollow type:] COMPENDIO | *DEL SAGGIO FILOSOFICO* | DI GIO. LOCKE | SOPRA | ALL' UMANO INTELLETTO. | [thick rule 73 mm] | [rule 69 mm].

v.3 L7ᵛ: [Oxford rule, 74/71 mm] | [decorative hollow type:] APPENDICE. | Cʀɪᴛɪᴄᴀ ᴅɪ LEIBNITZ | ᴀʟ Sᴀɢɢɪᴏ ᴅɪ LOCKE. | Sɪsᴛᴇᴍᴀ ᴅɪ LEIBNITZ | Cᴏɴꜰᴜᴛᴀᴢɪᴏɴᴇ ᴅᴇʟ Mᴇᴅᴇsɪᴍᴏ.

Headlines are book no. on versos, chap. no. on rectos in large & small caps, e.g. 'Lɪʙʀᴏ II.', 'Cᴀᴘᴏ VI.'

CW: none.
Notes: Text is a translation of Wynne's abridgement from Bosset's French translations thereof (cf. no. 133 et seq.), greatly expanded by interspersed appendices, 'Analisi delle Passioni', 'Riflessioni intorno ai *Sogni*, a' fenomeni de' *Sonniloqui* e de' *Sonnamboli*, e al *Delirio*, e alla *Pazzia*.', etc.

The first two pages of the appendix contain Leibnitz's introductory statement of his intentions translated from his *Nouveaux Essais* (22 lines, taken from his *Oeuvres philosophiques. . .*, 1765). The remainder is a summary of selected material from Condillac's criticism of Leibnitz, taken from his *Traité des systèmes*.
References: Attig 393.
Copies examined: Y (uncut)   CaOTU (Locke L63.E82I7 1775, vols.1-2 only)   CtY (Mudd: WA27950)

145*. *Essay.* Abridgement, Italian trans. (Wynne/Soave). Venice, 1790. 3 vols. in 12°. With *Conduct*.
"Saggio filosofico di Gio: Locke su l'umano intelletto. Compendiato dal Dr. Winne. Tradotto, e commentato da Francesco Soave . . . Seconda edizione veneta. In Venezia, nella Stamperia Baglioni, 1790."
Coll: 3 v. 12°
Note: The above information from Attig 394. I have been unable to see a copy, but the University of Chicago and the University of California (at Berkeley) libraries are reported in the *N.U.C.* to own them. I presume the arrangement and contents are the same as in the 1794 edition (no. 146). Attig adds a note: "Includes as v.3 Guida dell'intelletto nella ricerca della verità. Opera postuma di Gio: Locke. Tradotta e commentata da Francesco Soave . . . Seconda edizione veneta. In Venezia, nella Stamperia Baglioni. 1790."

146. *Essay.* Abridgement, Italian trans.(Wynne/Soave) Venice, 1794. 3 vols. in 12°. With *Conduct*
Vols. 1-2: SAGGIO | FILOSOFICO | DI GIO: LOCKE | SU L'UMANO INTELLETTO | *COMPENDIATO* | DAL D^r. WINNE | Tradotto, e Commentato | DA FRANCESCO SOAVE C.R.S. | *Prof di Fil. Mor. nel R. Ginnafio de Brera.* | [Oxford rule, tapered 46/40 mm] | TERZA EDIZIONE VENETA. | TOMO PRIMO. ['SECONDO.'] | [ornament (tailpiece) of double-headed eagle, 28×36 mm]. | VENEZIA, MDCCXCIV. | Nella Stamperia Baglioni. | *Con Licenza de' Superiori, e Privilegio.*
Vol. 3: GUIDA | DELL' | INTELLETTO | NELLA RICERCA | DELLA VERITA' | Opera Postuma | DI GIO: LOCKE | Tradotto . . . [&c. as in vol. 1-2, except 'TOMO TERZO.']
Coll: 12° (159 × 88 mm cut). Vol. 1: a^6 A-K^{12} [$ half signed]; 126 leaves; pp. *I-II* III-XII 1-238 *239-240* [=252].
Vol. 2: A-G^{12} [$ half signed]; 84 leaves; pp. *1-2* 3-168.

Vol. 3: A–F^{12} G^6 [$ half (–F6) signed; G2 signed 'C2']; 78 leaves; pp. *1–2* 3–156.

First recto page of each sheet A–K in vol. 1 also signed in direction line, '*Locke*, [swash k] Tom. I.'; vol.2 sheets B–G: '. . . Tom. II.'; vol.3 sheets B–G: '. . . Tom. III.'

Contents: Vol. 1: a1^r (*I*) title (verso blank), a2^r–a4^v (III–VIII) translator's preface, a5^r–a6^v (IX–XII) contents, A1^r–A2^v (1–4) Wynne's 'introduction', A3^r–B1^r (5–25) Le Clerc's extract, B1^v–K11^r (26–237) abridgement of Book 2, K11^v (238) printing license dated 29 Nov. 1793, K12 blank.

Vol. 2: A1^r (*1*) title (verso blank), A2^r–G11^v (3–166) abridgement of Books 3–4, G12^{r,v} (167–168) contents.

Vol. 3: A1^r (*1*) title (verso blank), A2^r–F9^r (3–137) trans. of the *Conduct of the Understanding*, F9^v–G3^v (138–150) "Appendice: Del metodo che dee tenersi per trovare la verità, e per insegnarda ad altri", G4^r–G6^r (151–155) contents, G6^v (156) license to print.

Text (v.1 E3^v; same all vols.): 28 lines; 127 (134) × 66 mm; 68 R. Good quality laid paper, without watermarks. Page no. at outer ends of headlines.

Head title, vols. 1–2: COMPENDIO | DEL | SAGGIO FILOSOFICO | DI GIOVANNI LOCKE | SOPRA [S ital] | L'UMANO INTELLETTO.

Vol. 3: GUIDA | DELL'INTELLETTO | NELLA RICERCA | DELLA VERITA'. | [rule 65 mm]

Headlines, v.1–2, are book no. on versos, chapter no. on rectos in large and small caps, e.g. 'L<small>IBRO</small> S<small>ECONDO</small>', 'C<small>APO</small> D<small>UODECIMO</small>.' For vol. 3, title is on versos, article (or section) no. on rectos: 'G<small>UIDA DELL</small>' I<small>NTELLETTO</small>. | A<small>RTICOLO</small> IV.'

CW: Page. Vol. l: A2^r pro- [produrre] D12^v a ſe- [portarle (2d line of text on E1^r begins 'a ſeguir)] I5^v (ec-) ma

Vol. 2: A6^v vole- [*volere,*] D11^r ſpe- [ſpecie]

Vol. 3: A5^r ſe- [ſecondo.] E1^v men- [mente]

Note: Translation of Wynne's abridgement, following the pattern of the French (Bosset) abridgement, with notes and 'appendici' by Soave interspersed. This is also the second appearance of 'Of the Conduct of the Understanding' in Italian (cf. no.145, above).

Reference: Attig 395.

Copies examined: O (Vet. F5 f.11–12)   Vat (RG filosof. v–682)

147. *Essay*. Abstract (Gilbert). 1709. 8°

Within a double rule, inner 149 × 80 mm, outer 155 × 87 mm: AN | ABSTRACT | OF THE | ESSAY | OF | *Human Underſtanding*. | [rule 76 mm] | [double row of small fleurons, 2d row inverted, 19 × 26 mm] | [rule 77 mm] | *LONDON,* | Printed in the Year M.DCC.IX.

Coll: 8° (186 × 120 mm) A^8 B^4 [$ half signed]; 12 leaves; pp. *1–2* 3–24.

Contents: A1^r (*1*) title (verso blank), A2^r–B4^v (3–24) text.

Text (A4^r): 38 lines; 155 (164) × 80 mm; 82 R. Medium-quality laid paper without visible watermarks.

Headlines are page no. centered within parentheses.

CW: Page. A2^r (3.) Simple A7^v (con-) fifts B2^r be B4^r 3ly. If

Press figures: none.

Note: Sir Geoffrey Gilbert, a judge and chief baron of the Irish Exchequer, made this brief outline of the *Essay*. The design of the small fleurons (4 per row, 2d row inverted) are very similar to those on the title of Locke's *Education* (no. 165–6). A microfilm copy of this abstract is in the collection, *The Eighteenth Century*, reel 258, no. 17.

References: Alston 7 p.27n.; Attig 282; Christophersen p. 95; ESTC t060819.

Copies examined: O (Vet.A4 e.1512) C Dt L (8466 aa.30)

147.1. *Essay*. Abstract (Gilbert), 1728: In *The Present State of the Republick of Letters*.

Caption title: [headpiece of leaves, 8 × 77 mm] | ARTICLE XXIV. | An ABSTRACT of the Eſſay of Human | Underſtanding.

IN: The Preſent State | OF THE | REPUBLICK | OF | LETTERS. | For May 1728. | VOL. I. | *Fungar vice cotis, acutum* | *Reddere quæ ferrum valet, ex fors ipſa ſecandi.* | Horat. | LONDON: | Printed for WILLIAM INNYS, at the Weſt | End of St. Paul's. M DCC XXVIII. | Price One Shilling.

Collation of the whole: 8° (198 × 120 mm cut) π² A⁴ B–2K⁸ 2L⁸ (–2 leaves = π) [$ half signed]; pp. I–IV *i* ij–v viij 1 2–500 *i* ij–xij. Gathering 2L (*i*–xij pp. at end) is an index to the vol. Numerous errors in pagination, some page no. omitted. First page of each monthly issue also signed in direction line: 'FEBRUARY 1728.', for example.

Gilbert's text: 2C1^r–2D3^v (pp. 373–394).

Text 2C2^v): 37 lines; 152 (161) × 81 mm; 84 R. Some pages with 38 lines: 160 (170) × 81 mm. Page no. at outer corner of headlines. There are headpieces at the start of each article in this journal, none of which I have been able to identify.

Headlines, from verso to recto, with article no. at inner margins, e.g.: The Preſent State of Art. 24. | Art. 24. the Republick of Letters.

CW: Page. 2C1^r (Sen-) ſation 2C5^r 3dly, [3dly.] 2D2^r (experi-) ence

Press figures: chiefly 2, occasional 4, one per gathering. 376 (2C2^v)–4 382 (2C5^v)–2

Notes: The text of Gilbert's abstract is preceded by a note: *It would be ſuperfluous to add any thing to | recommend the following Abſtract of | Mr.* LOCKE'*s celebrated Eſſay on Hu- | man Underſtanding, after I have aſſured | my Readers, that it was drawn up by no | leſs a Man than the late Lord Chief Ba- | ron* GILBERT.

Gilbert's 'Abstract' is in the May issue of the first vol. of a monthly journal, the sucessor to the *Memoirs* (later, '*New Memoirs*) *of Literature*. The journal was absorbed in *The Literary Magazine* in 1737. A microfilm of the whole is

in the *English Literary Periodicals* set (available through University Microfilms, Ann Arbor, Mich.)
I have found no bibliographic reference to this printing.
Copy examined: Y

148. *Essay*. Abstract (Gilbert). Dublin, 1728. 8°
AN | ABSTRACT | OF THE | ESSAY | OF | Human Underſtanding. | [rule 72 mm] | By Mr. *LOCKE*. [swash K] | [rule 72 mm] | Abridg'd by the Late Lord Chief | Baron *GILBERT*. [swash B] | [rule 72 mm] | *LONDON*: [swash D, roman colon] | Printed, and *Dublin* Re-printed, and Sold | by *George Faulkner*, and *James Hoey*, [swash J] in | *Chriſt-Church-Yard*, [swash Y] 1728.
Coll: 8° (154 × 90 mm cut) A–C⁸ [$ 2 signed]; 24 leaves; pp. *1-3* 4-47 *48*.
Contents: A1ʳ *(1)* title (verso blank), A1ᵛ *(2)* note on compiler of abstract, A2ʳ–C8ʳ *(3-47)* text, C8ᵛ *(48)* printer's advt. (for 5 items, including *Ocean*, by Edward Young, and Pope's *Dunciad*).
Text: 22 lines; 122 (130) × 72 mm; 110 R with 1 mm leading. Medium-quality paper without watermarks.
Headlines are page no. centered within parentheses.
HT A2ʳ: [triple orn. rule 9 × 72 mm] | AN | ABSTRACT | OF THE | Eſſay of Human Underſtanding.
CW: Page. A2ʳ (precep-) tion A8ᵛ (pro-) duce B4ʳ (particu-) lari- [larity] C7ʳ (ordina-) ry
Note: The statement in the imprint, 'London Printed, Dublin Reprinted' attests to the existence of no. 147.1, of which this a newly set reprint. There is the same note on the verso of the title, "It would be superfluous . . . *drawn up by no less a Man than the late Lord Chief Baron* GILBERT." A microfilm copy is in the collection, *The Eighteenth Century*, reel 4045, no. 10.
References: Alston 7 p. 27n.; Attig 283; Christophersen p. 95; ESTC n015861.
Copies examined: O (Godw. Pamph.2753 (2))   CLU-C (*PR3541.L57E75g 1728; disbound)

149. *Essay*. Abstract (Gilbert). Dublin, 1735. 8° in 4s
AN | ABSTRACT | OF THE | ESSAY | OF | Human Underſtanding. | [rule 72 mm] | *By the late Lord Chief Baron* GILBERT. | [rule 72 mm] | [printer's orn., vase surmounted by Mercury with bow, 24 × 39 mm] | [rule 70 mm] | *DUBLIN*: | Printed by JAMES HOEY, at the Sign of *Mercury* in | *Skinner-Row*, next Door to the *Tholſel*, 1735.
Coll: 8° in 4s (162 × 95 mm cut) A⁴ B–D⁴ [$ half (-D2) signed]; 16 leaves; pp. *1-3* 4-30 *31-32*.
Contents: A1ʳ *(1)* title (verso blank), A2ʳ–D3ᵛ *(3-30)* text, D4ʳ,ᵛ *(31-32)* advts. by printer.
Text (B3ʳ): 31 lines; 128 (139) × 75 mm; 82R. Page no. at outer ends of headlines.

Headlines: LOCKE's E*ſſ*ay.
CW: Page. A2ᵛ 2 [2.] C1ᵛ I By [I. By]
Note: Reprint of 1728 edition (no. 148). Fair-quality laid paper, not watermarked.
References: Alston 7 p.27 n.; Attig 284; ESTC n015862.
Copies examined: Dt   PU (B1291.G5 1735)

150. *Essay*. Abstract (Gilbert). 1751. *In* Synopsis compendiaria.
Section title: AN | ABSTRACT | OF | Mr. LOCKE's *Eſſay* | ON | Human Underſtanding, | Drawn up by the late | Lord Chief Baron GILBERT.
In: *Synopſis Compendiaria* | LIBRORUM | HUGONIS GROTII | DE | *Jure Belli et Pacis*, | SAMUELIS CLARKII | DE | *Dei Exiſtentiâ et Attributis*, | ET | JOANNIS LOCKII | DE | *Intellectu Humano*. | [double rule 81 mm] | CANTABRIGIÆ: | TYPIS ACADEMICIS EXCUDIT J. BENTHAM. | Sumptibus GUL. THURLBOURN et THO. MERRILL, | ibidem Bibliopolarum. Proſtant venales apud B. DOD, Londini; | J. FLETCHER, Oxonii; J. BARRY, Glaſguæ; et A. KINCAID, | Edinburgi. | [rule 26 mm] | M.DCC.LI.
Collation of the whole: 8° (192 × 126 mm cut) a^4 b^2 A–M^8 [$ half (–L2, –L3) signed]; 102 leaves; pp. *i–vi* '(1)'–'(4)' *I–II* 1 2–152 153–154 155–163 164–167 168–192 [= 204].
Text: approx. 33 lines; 151 (162) × 81 mm; 93R. Good-quality laid paper, without watermarks.
Contents of the whole: a1ʳ (*i*) title (verso blank), a2ʳ (*iii*) dedication to Edmund Keene, S.T.P. (verso blank), a3ʳ (*v*) section title to Grotius (verso blank), a4ʳ–b1ᵛ {(1)–(4)} contents of Grotius by book & chap., b2ʳ (*I*) advt. by Thurlbourn, b2ᵛ (*II*) advt. by Merrill, A1ʳ–K4ᵛ (*1–152*) Grotius's text in Latin, K5ʳ (*153*) section title to Clarke (verso blank), K6ʳ–L2ʳ (*155–163*) text of Clarke in Latin, L2ᵛ blank, L3ʳ (*165*) section title to Locke, L4ʳ–M8ᵛ (*167–192*) text of Gilbert's 'abstract' in English.
Note: Clarke's text is a Latin translation of *A Demonstration of the Being and Attributes of God* (1706), being the Boyle lectures for 1704. This whole collection was edited and abridged by William Dodd. Gilbert's text is reprinted from no. 148 or 149.
References: Attig 285; Christophersen p.99; ESTC t150355.
Copies examined: O (Vet.A5 e.2488)   C (Cam.d. 751.5)

151. *Essay*. Abstract (Gilbert). London and York, 1752. 8° in 4s
AN | ABSTRACT | OF | Mr. *LOCKE*'s ESSAY | ON | Human *Underſtanding*. | [rule 78 mm] | *By the Rt. Hon. Sir* JEFFREY [swash J] GILBERT, *Knt*. | *Late Lord Chief Baron of his Majeſty's Court of Exchequer in* | Ireland, *and afterwards of that in* England. | [rule 76 mm] | [scroll orn. 15 × 35 mm] | [double rule 77 mm] | *DUBLIN* Printed: | *London*, Reprinted for WILLIAM SANDBY, at the *Ship* | over-

againſt St. *Dunſtan's* Church, in *Fleetſtreet*; and ſold | by JOHN HILDYARD, in *York*. [swash Y] MDCCLII. | [Price ONE SHILLING.]
Coll: 8° in 4s (215 × 125 mm cut) π¹ A–F⁴ G⁴ (–G4 = π1) [$ half (–G2) signed]; 28 leaves; pp. *1–3* 4–55 *56*.
Contents: π1ʳ (*1*) title, π1ᵛ (*2*) 'ADVERTISEMENT TO THE DUBLIN Edition', A1ʳ–G3ʳ (*3–55*) text, G3ᵛ (*56*) advt. by Sandby & Hildyard for 8 vols. 8° of *Parliamentary or Constitutional History of England* (coverage to 1640; price 2 guineas in half-binding).
Text (F1ʳ): 22 lines, with 1 mm leading; 145 (160) × 76 mm; 131 R. Medium-quality laid paper without watermarks. There is an ornamental tailpiece of basket of fruit above a framed sun, 20 × 23 mm, on G3ʳ.
HT: [unframed headpiece of a naked figure supporting basket of fruit, leaves & flowers, 25 × 75 mm] | ABSTRACT | OF | *Mr.* LOCKE's *Eſſay on* | *Human Underſtanding*.
Headlines are page no. centered within parentheses.
CW: Page. A2ʳ *2*. The B3ᵛ (Per-) ception, C2ᵛ per- [perfectly] E3ᵛ (Diſagree-) ment G1ʳ I. Ori- [I. Original]
Press figures: none.
Notes: Standard reprint from the 1728 edition (no. 147.1 or 148). Note on p. 2 is copied from the 1728 abstract (no. 147.1). A microfilm copy of this printing is in the collection, *The Eighteenth Century*, reel 258, no. 10.
References: Alston 7 p. 27 n.; Attig 286; Christophersen p. 95; ESTC t063942.
Copies examined: Y   CtY (K8.L79/g752)   L (8465.c.33)   MH (*EC65.H7267Zz725m; ex libris Thomas Hollis) O¹ (26782 e.4) O² (Godw.Pamph. 1859 (17))

152. *Essay*. Abstract (Gilbert). 1791. 8°. In Gilbert's *Law of evidence*.
Section title: ABSTRACT | OF | MR. *LOCKE's* ESSAY | ON | HUMAN UNDERSTANDING. | [French rule 24 mm] | [rule 11 mm] "Ne te quæſiveris extra; | Eque ſuis latebris demerſum protrahe VERUM."
In: THE | LAW | OF | EVIDENCE, | BY | LORD CHIEF BARON GILBERT. | [French rule 47 mm] | CONSIDERABLY ENLARGED | By CAPEL LOFFT, | BARRISTER AT LAW. | [French rule 48 mm] | TO WHICH IS PREFIXED, | Some ACCOUNT of the AUTHOR; his Abſtract of LOCKE's Eſſay; | and his ARGUMENT in a Caſe of HOMICIDE in IRELAND. | VOL. I. | [Oxford rule 100 mm] | LONDON: | PRINTED BY A. STRAHAN AND W. WOODFALL, | LAW-PRINTERS TO THE KING'S MOST EXCELLENT MAJESTY, | FOR J. F. & C. RIVINGTON, T. LONGMAN, C. DILLY, | W. CLARKE & SON, & W. OTRIDGE. | 1791.
Coll. of vol. 1: 8° (230 × 114 mm cut) A⁴ a–g⁸ h⁴ χ² B–4I⁸ 4K⁴ [$ half (+ A3) signed]; 686 leaves; pp. *i–ii* iii–iv *v* vi–viii i–xli *xlii* xliii–xlv *xlvi* 1–2 3–31 *32* 1–2 3–42 43–46 *1* 2–1240 [= 1372].
Illustrations: The four engraved illustrations are a front. portrait of Judge

Gilbert by T. Holloway after Dahl; 2 plates inserted between c5 and c6, the first an engraving, on the verso of a blank page, of epitaph-like biographical details including positions and honours; the second leaf, on the recto, a copy of his church monument. A large folded plate, following χ^2 and preceding p. 1 is an outline chart headed "Analysis of the Law of Evidence" (3.5 pages deep by 4 pages wide).

Gilbert's 'Abstract' of Locke's Essay, in the 4th set of preliminary pagination: e8^r–h4^v (1–42).

Contents of vol. 1: A1^r title (verso blank), A2^{r,v} (iii–iv) 'Advertisement', A3^r–A4^v (v–viii) "Aphabetical Index of Cases Contained in First Volume", a1^r–c5^r (i–xli) preface, c5^v (*xlii*) 'Additional Notice', c6^r–c7^r (xliii–xlv) Gilbert's will, c7^v blank, c8^r (*1*) section title for Gilbert's 'Argument on the distinction between manslaughter and murther' (verso blank), d1^{r,v} (3–4) pref. to 4th ed. of the 'Argument', d2^r–e7^r (5–31) text of the 'Argument', e7^v blank, e8^r (*1*) section title to 'Abstract' of Locke's *Essay*, e8^v (*2*) advertisement for Dublin ed. of Gilbert's 'Law of Evidence', f1^r–h4^v (3–42) text of 'Abstract', χ1^r (*43*) errata for vol. (verso blank), χ2^r (*45*) section title for 'Law of Evidence' (verso blank), B1^r–4K4^v (1–1240) vol. 1 of *Law of Evidence*.

Text: 31 lines with 2 mm. leading; 182 (194) × 90 (111) mm; 115 R. Medium-quality laid paper, without watermark. No headlines for Locke's text. Headlines for the main text are page topics in large and small caps, with subordinate words or phrases in italics (different on most pages).

HT, f1^r: ABSTRACT [swash Ts] | OF | MR. *LOCKE*'s ESSAY | ON | HUMAN UNDERSTANDING.

CW: Page. f4^r *of* f7^r FOURTHLY, [4thly,] g6^r I. Fir*ſ*t: [Fir*ſ*t:] h3^r (con-) joined (When footnotes carry over to next page, they have own CW.)

Press figures: 6 (f2^v)–2 29 (g6^r)–2

Note: Gilbert's 'Abstract' is part of the prefatory matter in this fifth edition of Gilbert's work. Gilbert's *Law of Evidence* was first published anonymously in Dublin in 1754; here it is a reprint with Lofft's revisions and additions, complete in 4-vols. octavo, published 1791–96. This is the first edition to include Gilbert's 'abstract'; given the four sets of preliminary paging, it seems that adding Gilbert's 'Abstract' of Locke's *Essay* was a late thought, especially since the earlier editions of Gilbert's *Law of Evidence* do not include it. A microfilm copy of the set is in the collection, *The Eighteenth Century*, reel 1205, no. 6.

References: Alston 7 p. 27n. (Dublin ed., 1795–97 cited); Attig 287; Christophersen p. 95; ESTC t095571 (for set).

Copies examined: O (8° A.12.8 Jur.) L^1 (6281.ff.7) L^2 (708.g.9)

153. *Essay*. Extract (4.10). Russian trans. (Antonskiĭ). In: *Vecherniâiâ zariâ* (Moscow, 1782).

Caption title in old Russian: О ПОЗНАНІИ | Божія Бытія. (*) | . . . [first 3 lines of text, followed by footnote:] (*) Разсужденіе г. Локка, Извѣсшнаго славнаго | Аглинскаго Писашеля.

In: ВЕЧЕРНЯЯ ЗАРЯ (Moscow) ch. 3 (October 1782): pp. 18–42.

Title romanized: O poznanii, Bozhiya bytiya ('On the consciousness of the nature of God.') The footnote states: 'Reasoning of Mr. Locke, famous writer of the English language.' In the periodical: *'Twilight, a monthly publication'*.

Collation of October issue: 8° (193 × 112 mm cut) π² А-Д⁸ Е² [$5 signed]; 44 leaves; pp. *i–iv 1* 2–83 *84* [= 88]. Locke's text on pp. 18–42 (Б1ᵛ–Б5ᵛ).

Contents: π1ʳ title, π1ᵛ censor's note approving publication, signed by Anton Barsov, π2ʳ contents of the issue (verso blank), А1ʳ–4Б1ᵛ (1–18) 'Razsuzhdenie o bytii Boga', 4Б1ᵛ–Б5ᵛ (18–42) Russian translation of Essay 4.10, Б6ʳ–Е2ʳ (43–83) text of articles 3–15 of this issue, Е2ᵛ blank.

Text: 31 lines; 143 (157) × 85 mm; 93 old-style Cyrillic. Fair-quality paper, without watermarks. First page of each gathering also signed '1782. Chast' Ш. Sentiab.' in the direction line.

CW: Page. А3ᵛ не- [неизслѣдимою] Б5ʳ ни- [ничего]

Notes: A translation of the Essay, Book IV, Chap. 10. The text is in old Russian (pre-reform) orthography, and keeps exactly to the italics, where they occur, of Locke's text. An italicized note at the end of the article informs us it was a report to the Latin philologists at the Imperial Moscow University Student Seminar by Mikhail Antonskiĭ.

This is the second article in this monthly issue; the first, 'Argument for the existence of God derived from consideration of nature', is cited also in Neustroev as if it were *about* Locke, but is more likely to be copied from any of the 17th or 18th century divines. The title of the periodical includes a statement that it was published 'for the benefit of the schools named after Catherine and Alexander, which have been established in St. Petersburg, including the best passages from ancient and modern writers revealing to mankind the way to the knowledge of God, of himself and of his duties, presented both in moral homilies and in the above-mentioned examples, that is, in short stories, novellas, humorous stories and other works in verse and prose; serving as a continuation of *Morning Light*' (romanized: '*Utrenniago svieta*'). Complete details as to this periodical, '*Vechernyaya zarya*', concerning editors, publishers, objectives, and history, can be found in *Svodnyĭ katalog Russkoi knigi grazhdanskoi pechati XVIII veka, 1725–1800*, vol. 4 (Moscow: 'Kniga', 1966), no. 138.

The censor's approval for publication states: 'At the instance of the Curators of the Imperial Moscow University, I have read the book entitled: TWILIGHT, Part II [July–Dec. vol.], and have found in it nothing contravening the instructions given me concerning the consideration of books printed at the University Press; wherefore the said book may be printed. ANTON BARSOV, Collegial Counsellor, Professor of Rhetoric and Censor of books printed at the University Press.'[9]

---

[9] I am indebted to J. S. G. Simmons for drawing my attention to the Russian material, and to Marcus C. C. Wheeler for translations.

Reference: Neustroev p. 349.
Copy examined: NN (Slavonic Reserve)

154. *Essay*. 'Syllabus'. Cambridge, 1796. 12° in 6s.
A | *SYLLABUS* [swash Y] | OF | [outline type:] LOCKE'S ESSAY | ON THE | HUMAN UNDERSTANDING. | [orn. French rule 46 mm] | Non fumum ex fulgore, ſed ex fumo dare lucem | Cogitat, ut ſpecioſa dehinc miracula promat. | [French rule 12 mm] | Not ſmoke from fire, but from a cloud of ſmoke, | His fire quick lighten'd, and his wonders broke. | HORACE. | [orn. French rule 46 mm] | 𝕮𝖆𝖒𝖇𝖗𝖎𝖉𝖌𝖊; [sic] | PRINTED BY BENJAMIN FLOWER: [swash J] | FOR W. H. LUNN, AND J. DEIGHTON; AND SOLD BY | [all following Js swash:] J. MARCH, NORWICH; J. ABEL, NORTHAMP- | TON; G. G. AND J. ROBINSONS [sic], AND | T. CONDER, LONDON. | [French rule 13 mm] | M DCC XC VI.
Coll: 12° in 6s (160 × 100 mm cut) π¹ A–C⁶ D² (–D2 = π1) [$ half signed]; 20 leaves; pp. *i–ii* 1–3 4–38 [= 40].
Contents: π1ʳ (*i*) half-title (verso blank), A1ʳ (*1*) title (verso blank), A2ʳ–D1ᵛ (*3–38*) text.
Half-title: [orn. rule 59 mm] | A | SYLLABUS | OF | [hollow type:] LOCKE'S ESSAY | ON THE | HUMAN UNDERSTANDING. | [French rule 20 mm] | (Price One Shilling.) | [orn. rule 59 mm]
HT: [double rule 74 mm] | A SYLLABUS, &c. | [French rule 20 mm]
Text (B3ʳ): 38 lines slightly leaded; 125 (135) × 74 mm; 66 R. Medium-quality wove paper not watermarked. Page no. centered at head of page within parentheses as headlines.
CW: Page. A2ʳ Brutes B2ᵛ Voluntary C5ᵛ (exa-) amine [mine]
Press figures: none.
Note: Text consists of very brief, one-sentence summaries of each section, in order.
References: Alston 7 p. 27n.; Attig 288; Christophersen pp. 95–6; ESTC t063938.
Copies examined: C (Cam.d.796.7; lacks π1)   L (8407.aa.36 (1))   O (Vet.A5.e.4775)

The *Essay* was frequently reprinted after 1800, chiefly from sheets of the *Works* editions (chap. XI) with cancellans title-pages, or in stereotyped editions. Reprints were issued in London in 1805, 1812, 1817, 1819, 1823, 1824, 1825, 1828, 1829, 1832, 1836, 1838, 1841, 1846, 1853, 1860, 1864, 1869, 1875, 1877, 1879, 1880, 1881, 1891, 1905, 1909, 1910, and in Ward Lock's 'World Library' printing in the 1880s (frequently reprinted); in Edinburgh in 1801, 1815 and 1819; and in Dublin in 1816. American reprints were published in New York and Boston in 1803, 1806, 1813, 1824, 1825, 1908, and in Philadelphia in 1844, 1846, 1847, 1849, 1850, 1852, 1853, 1854, 1856, 1860 and 1864.

The first notable edition exhibiting editorial attention (before 1975) was that of Alexander Campbell Fraser published by the Clarendon Press, Oxford, in 1894. In two octavo volumes, it treats Book I, Chap. I (all 8 sections) as 'Introduction' (following Coste's French translations); Chapters II–IV were consequently renumbered as I–III. This edition was reprinted in facsimile in 1959.

John Yolton edited a line-by-line reprint of the 5th edition (1706; no. 63) correcting typographical errors, modernizing punctuation, and omitting the quotations from the Locke-Stillingfleet controversy, for Everyman's Library in 1961 (frequently reprinted).

In 1975 Peter H. Nidditch edited a critical edition with extensive introduction, critical apparatus and glossary for the Clarendon Edition of the Works of John Locke.

Abridgements of the *Essay* have been issued many times, sometimes called *Contraction* (1819), *Epitome* (1823), *Catechetical Compendium* (1823), *Analysis* (1873), and *Analytical Abstract* (1808). Wynne's abridgement was reprinted in 1822. Other abridgements have been compiled by Louisa Capper (1811), Denis McCarthy (1823), A. J. Valpy (1831), John Murray (1852 and 1857), Robert Cleary (1873), Mary Whiton Calkins (1905; reprinted 1906, 1912, 1920, 1927, 1933, 1939 and 1949), Andrew Seth Pringle-Pattison (1924; reprinted 1928, 1947, 1950 and 1960), Raymond Wilburn (1947), A. J. Ayer (1952), A. D. Woozley (1964), Maurice Cranston (1965), and John Yolton (1965 and 1977; reprinted 1985, 1990; revised 1993). The 'Syllabus' (no. 154) was reprinted in 1802, 1807, 1809, 1812, 1820, 1824, 1828 and 1829.

Besides these abridgements, there have been many selections, too numerous and unimportant to record.

As to translations, a revision of Coste's French edition (no. 91 et seq.) made by Emilienne Naert appeared in 1972. German translations appeared in 1868, 1872–73, 1894, 1897, 1898, 1962, and a German translation of Fraser's edition in 1911–13. There have been Hungarian translations (1964), Polish (1955), Russian (1960), Serbian (1962), Spanish (1956, 1980 and 1982).

Abridgements in translation include one in French (by Paul Lemaire) in 1925, in Hebrew (1935), Italian (1924, 1925, 1926, 1935, 1940, 1942 and 1962). Soave's Italian translation of Wynne was reprinted in 1801, 1807 and 1815, and a revision in 1943.

An interesting Portuguese abridgement written in the 1750s but not permitted to be published in the eighteenth century is that relying on Le Clerc's summary of Book I (included in no. 133 et seq.) and a French translation of Wynne's abridgement of Book II. Edited with an extensive introduction by Joaquim de Carvalho, it was published in 1951 in the *Boletim* of the University of Coimbra Library.

CHAPTER IV
Papers on Money (nos. 155–164)

'The Great Recoinage' controversy of the 1690s was the impetus for Locke's writings on mercantile and monetary theory. In the 1660s Sir Josiah Child had argued that the legal rate of interest should be lowered. It was still a topic for political discussion in the early 1690s: Child was still pressing the argument, and was supported by London merchants. Locke however defended a legal rate of interest but refused to fix it below the current rates. This was the occasion for his publishing *Some Considerations of the Consequences of the Lowering of Interest and Raising the Value of Money* in 1692.

When William Lowndes, Secretary of the Treasury, proposed in 1695 to raise the nominal value of coins, Locke slightly revised *Some Considerations* and also published two further pamphlets, *Short Considerations*, and *Further Considerations*. At that time gold and silver coins had a value equivalent to their metal content, representing nothing but their silver or gold quantity. Locke rejected devaluation, basing his argument on this 'commodity theory' of money. He considered 'raising of the denomination or the increase of alloy' to be debasement and fraud.

There already was debasement, since coins were punched or hammered, and were easily reduced in metal content by chipping off bits, or 'clipping'. New milled silver coins were coming into use by 1695.

Further details of the rate of interest and coinage controversies can be found in (1) *The Great Recoinage of 1695–6*, by Ming Hsun Li (London: Weidenfeld & Nicholson, 1963); (2) *The New Palgrave: A Dictionary of Political Economy* (4 vols., London: Macmillan Press, 1987), iii.229–30; and (3) Maurice Cranston's biography, *John Locke* (London: Macmillan, 1957), pp. 350–51.

The first editions of *Some Considerations* and *Short Observations* appeared anonymously; consequently there are no lists of recipients of presentation copies. But *Further Considerations* and the collective *Several Papers* were issued under the author's name. For these therefore there are lists of names, which I have included in the bibliographical descriptions following.

Detailed bibliographical information on these money pamphlets has been published by Patrick Hyde Kelly: "A Note on Locke's Pamphlets on Money", *Transactions of the Cambridge Bibliographical Society*, 5 (1969): 61–73, cited in this chapter as 'Kelly'.

155. Some Considerations. 1692. 8° Three states. Anonymous.

Within a double rule, inner 133 × 69 mm, outer 139 × 75 mm: Some Confiderations | OF THE | CONSEQUENCES | OF THE | *Lowering of Intereft,* | AND | Raifing the Value | OF | MONEY. [large 3 mm period] | [rule 64 mm] | *In a Letter to a Member of Parliament.* | [rule 65 mm] | LONDON, | Printed for *Awnfham* and *John* [swash J] | *Churchill,* at the *Black-Swan* in | *Pater-Nofter-Row.* 1692.

Coll: 8° (155 × 92 mm cut) A⁴ B–N⁸ + χ1 [$ half signed]; 100 (or 101) leaves; pp. *i–iv* [1]–[4] 1–192 (+ *193-194*) [= 200 or 202].

Contents: A1ʳ (*i*) blank, A1ᵛ (*ii*) licence note, A2ʳ (*iii*) title (verso blank), A3ʳ–A4ᵛ ([1]–[4]) prefatory letter dated 'Nov. 7. 1691.', B1ʳ–I8ᵛ (1–128 text), K1ʳ–K2ᵛ (129-132) criticism of *A Letter to a Friend concerning Usury*, K3ʳ–N8ʳ (133–191) text 'Of Raising Our Coin', N8ʳ,ᵛ (191 bottom–192) postscript, χ1ʳ (*193*) (when present) errata (verso blank).

Text (C4ʳ): 31 lines; 126 (136) × 66 mm; 81 R. Poor-quality laid paper, with foolscap watermark. Pref. has page no. centered within square brackets as headlines; in body of text they are within parentheses. There is no drophead title.

States: There are 3 states depending on the presence of χ1 and whether it contains an errata of 11.2 lines or 19.3 lines. Patrick Kelly in his "Note on Locke's Pamphlets on Money" posits a 4th state, the 4th having the 19.3 line errata bound at the end of *Short Observations*, but the single-leaf errata's positioning in the Goldsmiths' Library copy (no. 3130; cf. no. 158 below) is merely a vagary of the binder.

Thus, state A: no errata.

B: 11.2 line errata on p. *193*

C: 19.3 line errata on p. *193*

Many copies have the errata clipped and mounted elsewhere, e.g. on p. *iv* or [4].

Caption title, K3ʳ: *Of Raifing our* Coin

CW: Page. B2ʳ Pre- [Pretences] B5ʳ Now D2ʳ For- [Forbearance] F3ʳ (Con-)fumption. G2ᵛ made H3ʳ 2. That L4ᵛ Nor [Nor,] N8ʳ Trea_ [Treated (CW has hyphen on line)]

*Signature position*s:

B Conve˰ying	L3 and ˰ melt
D2 *impofes*	N *the*
G *the* ballance	N2 give ˰ Order
H4 hap*pen* ˰ to	N3 is C˰oin'd
I People	N4 much ˰ as ˰ the

Notes: The work was licensed for printing on November 27, 1691 (as noted in *Transcript* iii, p.435). It was available by December 7, since a letter to Edward Clarke from Locke dated 4 December 1691 supplies an erratum (*Corr.* 1435; iv. 337-9). An earlier letter to Clarke dated December 4, 1691 may "perhaps refer to *Some Considerations*" (E. S. de Beer, *Corr.* iv.337 n.5). The license on A1ᵛ reads: [rule 63mm] | LICENSED, | *Novemb.* 27. 1691.

Papers on Money 193

Ja. Frafer. | [rule 63 mm]. The Lovelace Collection in the Bodleian Library (MS Locke b.1 fol. 161) contains a declaration by Awnsham and John Churchill, dated 3 March 1692 N.S., that "the sole right of and in the copy or book" of this work "remains in the hands of Mr. John Locke". The publication was anonymous, p. 192 being signed 'Your moft humble Servant.' [S inverted]. It was also full of numerous errors and shows signs of being 'brought out in haste'. *A Letter to a Friend concerning Usury*, by R.C., criticised here, was published in 1690 (L.L. 3030; Wing² C106).

A microfilm copy of this edition, state C, is in the EEB collection, reel 606 no. 9; there is no indication which copy was used for filming. Another microfilm copy is in the Goldsmiths'-Kress Library of Economic Literature, no. 2941 (state A: no errata).

References: Attig 494; Christophersen p. 23; ESTC r023025; Kelly 1a–c (for these 3 issues); L.L. 1787, 1790; T.C.II.413; Wing² L2760.

Copies examined: First state (A): O¹ (80 G.160 (2) Art.) CaOTU (Locke L63.S63 1692aa) CtY¹ (NZ/Z692L) DFo¹ (L2760; ex lib. Claud. Gilbon; Cashel Lib. copy)

Second state (B): Ck¹ (Keynes A.12.2; err. mounted on A4ᵛ) Ck² (Keynes A.12.3; err. mounted on p. 192) CtY² (Nga49/692L; err. mounted on A4ᵛ) DFo² (L2760; err. mounted on A4ᵛ) MH (Nor.3104) NjP (ExW: HG937.L79; err. mounted on p. 192) Oc (a.3.147; err. mounted on A4ᵛ)

Third state: (C): C(Syn.8.69.30 (3)) CaQMMO (1039) Ck³ (Keynes A.12.4; err. mounted on p. 192) Ct (NQ16.159) L (1139 c.4; errata bd.after A4) NjP (HG937.L79 ExW) NN (TF; missing 9.91) O² (Vet.A3 f.659; err. bd. after *Short Obs.*, no. 158) Oa (k.6.26; err. mounted. between A4 and B1)

156. Some Considerations. 2d ed., 1696. 8° Issued in *Several Papers*.
Within a double rule, inner 139×72 mm, outer 144×78 mm: Some Confiderations | OF THE | CONSEQUENCES | OF THE | *Lowering of Intereft,* | AND | *Raifing the Value* | OF | MONEY. [3 mm period] | [rule 68 mm] | *In a Letter fent to a Member of Par-* | *liament,* 1691. | [rule 68 mm] | 𝕿𝖍𝖊 𝕾𝖊𝖈𝖔𝖓𝖉 𝕰𝖉𝖎𝖙𝖎𝖔𝖓 𝕮𝖔𝖗𝖗𝖊𝖈𝖙𝖊𝖉. | [rule 67 mm] | LONDON, | Printed for *Awnfham* and *John Churchil,* [swash J] at | the *Black-Swan* [swash k] in *Pater-Nofter-Row.* 1696.

Coll: 8° (158 × 95 mm cut) A⁴ (± A1) B–N⁸ [$ half signed]; 100 leaves; pp. *i*–*iv* [1]–[4] 1–192 [= 200].

Contents: A1ʳ (*i*) title-page to *Several Papers* (no. 163), A1ᵛ (*ii*) license note, A2ʳ (*iii*) title (verso blank), A3ʳ–A4ᵛ ([1]–[4]) prefatory letter, B1ʳ–K1ʳ (1–129) text, K1ᵛ–K3ʳ (130–133) criticism of *A Letter to a Friend concerning Usury*, K3ᵛ–N8ᵛ (134–192 line 15) text 'Of Raising our Coin', N8ᵛ (192 last 16 lines) italic postscript signed '*John Lock.*'

Text: Same as no. 155, but poor-quality laid paper watermarked with letter 'O'. There are usually offprint traces mutually between the licensing note and the title (A1ᵛ and A2ʳ), but not on CLU-C, DFo or Goldsmith's Library copy. The title leaf for the second issue of *Several Papers* (no. 163) is a cancellans. Text is in the direction line on N6^v.

CW: Page. B5^r (Mo-) ney D2^r (ha-) ving G1^r (Pro-) hibiting H3^v (fet-) led I1^r (lef-) fen'd, L4^v fup- [fuppos'd] L5^v (light-) er [er,] N8^r over- [overplus]

Signature positions:

B Conveying
D2 the ˄ Clothier
F3 the ˄ f me ['a' lost from 'same']
G ground, ˄ perhaps
H4 conftant

I as
L3 you ˄ fpe˄nd
N *our*
N2 gre*at* Value

Notes: Listed in the Term Catalogue for Hilary 1695, this is a corrected reprint of the first edition. No longer anonymous, p. 192 is additionally signed: '*John Lock.*' It appears only to have been issued with 2d editions of *Short Observations* (no. 159) and *Further Considerations* (no. 161-2): details in no. 163. A microfilm copy of this edition is in the EEB collection, reel 570, no. 6 (part of *Several Papers*, Cambridge Univ. Lib. copy). Two other copies in microfilm (also as part of *Several Papers*) are to be found in the Goldsmiths'-Kress Library of Economic Literature, no.3314 and 3315. A facsim. reprint of the set of *Several Papers*, including this edition, was published by A.M. Kelley, New York, in 1968.

References: Attig 495; Christophersen p. 23; Kelly 1e; T.C.II.540; Wing^2 L2761.

Copies examined: O^1 (Vet.A3 f.260; no errata)   C (Syn.7.69.19)   Ck (Keynes A.12.6; lacks A1)   CLU-C (lacks A1)   Ct (S.15.63)   CtY (Ngc95/G5.696*l*)   DFo (L2757; lacks A1)   DLC (HG937.L74)   Han (presentation copy from Locke to Leibniz)   L (1391 a.5)   NjP (HG937.L79 Ex)   NjR (X HC246.L814S; lacks leaf A2)   NN (TF)   O^2 (80 P.211 Art.; 'Ex dono Auctoris')   O^3 (Vet.A3 f.803)   O^4 (Locke coll.7/208)   Oq (GG.b.85)   Osj (HB3/G5)   PPL (Wing L2757/ Log51.D.1)   Utr (I.oct.424)

157. Some Considerations. Selection. 1718. 8° in 4s.

A | TREATISE | OF | Raising [S inverted] *our COIN*, | Taken out of a | Book written by Mr. *J. Lock*, [swash J] | ENTITULED, | *Some Confiderations of the Confe-* | *quences of Lowering of Inte-* | *reft, and Raifing the Value* | *of Money.* [swash f's] | Printed in the Second Volume of his | Works, in *Folio*. | [double rule 5 mm apart, 81mm] | LONDON: | Printed for *William Churchill* at the *Black* | *Swan*, in *Pater-Nofter-Row*. 1718. | [Price Six-pence.]

Coll: 8° (180 × 111 mm cut) A-F^4 [$ half signed]; 24 leaves; pp. 1-3 4-47 48.

Contents: A1^r (*1*) title (verso blank), A2^r-F4^r (*3-47*) text, F4^v blank.

Text (C2^r): 37 lines; 152 (163) × 84 mm; 82 R. Very poor quality laid paper, without watermarks. Tailpiece on p.47 (45 × 52 mm): profiled emperor within garlanded circle on pedestal, with 2 cherubs. Page no. centered at head of page within square brackets as headlines.

HT A2^r: OF | RAISING *our* COIN.
CW: Page. A3^r (quan-) tity B1^r Con- [Contracts,] D1^r (car-) ried F3^v *That*
Press figures: none.
Notes: The text is reprinted from Locke's *Works* (1714), vol. 2, pp. 39 line 48 to p.55, the last third of *Some Considerations*, beginning with a subsection heading '*Of Raising our Coin.*' to the end. The publisher was a nephew of A. and J. Churchill.

It has been reproduced from the British Library copy in the microfilm set, *The Eighteenth Century*, reel 265, no. 30. Another microfilm copy is in the collection, Goldsmiths'-Kress Library of Economic Literature, no. 5485.
References: Attig 497; ESTC t106906.
Copies examined: O (G. Pamph. 1149 (6)) CLU-C (*PR3541.L57S47 1718) CtY (By50/A2) [GOT] L (8225 c.61) PU (HG937.L74)

158. Short Observations. 1st ed., 1695. 8°
Caption title: (1) | SHORT | 𝔒𝔟𝔰𝔢𝔯𝔳𝔞𝔱𝔦𝔬𝔫𝔰 | ON A | Printed PAPER, | Intituled, | *For encouraging the Coining Silver* [swash v] | *Money in England, and after* | *for keeping it here.* [swash fs] | [rule 65 mm] | LONDON, Printed for *A. and J. Churchill*, [swash J] at | the *Black Swan* in *Pater-Noſter-Row.* 1695. | [rule 65 mm]
Coll: 8° (150 × 90 mm cut) A^8 B^4 [$ half signed]; 12 leaves; pp. 1–24.
Contents: A1^r (1) caption title and 10 lines of text, A2^v (2–24) rest of text ending 'FINIS. | [rule 65 mm] | ADVERTISEMENT.' followed by 4 lines of advt. for *Some Considerations*.
Text (A2^v): 31 lines; 129 (140) × 67 mm; 83 R, but p. 24 set 71 R with 34 lines of text preceding 'FINIS.'. Medium-quality paper watermarked with foolscap. Page no. within parentheses as headlines.
CW: Page. A1^r plain A6^r (Pro-) jects B1^r their B1^v The
Signature positions:

A B$_\wedge$ut   B before, $_\wedge$ and
A2 conſum$_\wedge$able   B2 that $_\wedge$ by $_\wedge$ this
A3 re$_\wedge$quiſite
A4 Bul$_\wedge$lion

Notes: Published anonymously. Listed in Term Catalogues for Hilary (February) 1695. A microfilm copy of this edition is in the EEB collection, reel 767, no. 43. Another copy is in the microfilm collection, Goldsmiths'-Kress Library of Economic Literature, no. 3130, with the 19.3 line errata leaf for *Some Considerations* (1692) bound after B4; see *Notes* to no. 155.
References: Attig 501; Christophersen p. 24; ESTC r020204; Kelly 2a; L.L. 1788; T.C. II.540; Wing^2 L2758.
Copies examined: CaOTU (Locke L63.S63 1692aa (2)) C (Keynes) Ck^1 (Keynes A.12.4 (2)) Ck^2 (Keynes A.12.5; disbound) Ct^1 (NQ16.159 (2)) Ct^2 (Y9.36 (2)) CtY (NZ/Z692L (2)) DFo (acc.165876) L (1139 c.4 (22)) NjP (ExW HG937.L79 (2)) O^1 (Vet.A3 f.659 (2)) Oa^1 (k 6.26 (2)) Oa^2 (xxi.9.2) Oc (a.3.124)

159. Short Observations. [2d ed., 1696] 8° Issued in *Several Papers*.
Caption title: (1) | SHORT | **Obſervations** | . . . [&c. as in no. 158, until 7th line:] For [roman F] *encouraging the Coining Silver* | *Money in* England, *and after* | *for keeping* [swash k] *it here.* [swash f's throughout]
Coll: 8° (160 × 95 mm cut) A⁸ B⁴ [$ half signed]; 12 leaves; pp. 1–24.
Contents: A1ʳ (1) caption title and 15 lines of text, A2ᵛ–B4ᵛ (2–24) rest of text, ending '*FINIS.*'
Text (A2ᵛ): 31 lines; 129 (140) × 68 mm; 83 R. Medium-quality paper with foolscap watermark. Page no. centered within parentheses as headlines. Text in direction line on p. 5, 22 (A3ʳ and B3ᵛ).
CW: Page. A1ʳ (im-) poſſible A6ʳ Crown- [Crown-piece] B1ᵛ Mo- [Money]
Signature positions:

A that ⁁ I	B and ⁁ not
A2 *tha*⁁t	B2 Bill, ⁁ that
A3 aga⁁in ⁁ bring	
A4 paſſ⁁es ⁁ as	

Note: Issued as part of *Several Papers* (no. 163), the text reset, some textual changes, but lacking imprint in head title and lacking advertisement on p. 24. Usually found as second item in no. 163, but in Locke's presentation copy at the Bodelian Library it is bound as the third item. A copy of this edition is in the EEB microfilm collection, reel 570, no. 6 (part of *Several Papers*, Cambridge Univ. Lib. copy). Two other copies (as part of *Several Papers*) are in the microfilm collection, Goldsmiths'-Kress Library of Economic Literature, no. 3314 and 3315. A facsimile reprint is included in the set of *Several Papers*, published by A.M. Kelley, New York, in 1968.
References: Attig 501 n.; Kelly 2b; Wing² L2759.
Copies examined: C (Syn.7.69.19 (2)) CaOTU (Locke L63.S49 1696 (2)) Ck (Keynes A.12.6 (2)) Ct (Y.36.1) CtY (Ngc95/G5.696*l* (2)) DFo (L2757 (2)) DLC (HG937.L74 (2) Han L (1391 a.5 (2)) NjP (HG937.L79 Ex (2)) NjR (HC246.L814S (2)) NN (TF (2)) O¹ (8° P.211 Art. (3) 'Ex Dono Auctoris') O² (Vet.A3 f.260 (2)) O³ (Vet. A3 f.803 (2)) O⁴ (Locke coll. 7/208 (2)) Oc (4.B.210 (2)) Oq (GG.b.85 (2)) Osj (HB3/G5 (2)) Utr (I.oct.424 (2)

160. Further Considerations. [1st ed.] 1695. 8°. Two states.
Within a double rule, inner 136 × 69 mm; outer 144 × 78 mm: FURTHER | **Conſiderations** | Concerning | *Raiſing the Value* | OF | MONEY. [period above line] | WHEREIN | Mr. *Lowndes*'s Arguments for it | in his late Report concerning | *An Eſſay for the Amendment of* | *the Silver Coins*, are particu- | larly Examined. | [rule 66 mm] | LONDON, | Printed for *A.* and *J. Churchil* [swash J] at the *Black* [swash k] | *Swan* in *Pater-Noſter-Row*, MDCXCV.
Coll: 8° (170 × 95 mm cut) A–H⁸ [$ half (–A4 in some copies) signed]; 64 leaves; pp. *i–xvi* 1–111 *112* [=128].

Contents: A1^r title (verso blank), A2^r–A4^v (*iii–viii*) dedication, headed "TO THE | Right Honorable | Sr *John Sommers*, Kt. | Lord Keeper of the Great | Seal of *England*, and | one of His Majefties | moft Honorable Privy | Council." (signed at end: "Your Lordfhips moft humble | and moft Obedient Servant | JOHN LOCKE.", A5^r–A7^r (*ix–xiii*) pref. ending in 6 lines of text followed by rule & advt. for books sold by Churchills (3 lines of heading & 18 lines of advt.), A7^v–A8^v (*xiv–xvi*) rest of advt., B1^r–H8^r (1–111) text (111 has 26 lines), H8^v (*112*) errata.

States. A (First state) has 6.2 lines of errata on p. *112*, and leaf A4 frequently not signed.

B (Second state) has 7.8 lines of errata on p. *112*.

Patrick Kelly (in his 'Note on Mr. Locke's Pamphlets') reports as an additional state what must be a mixed-sheet copy at Goldsmiths' Library, which has sheets H and I1 from the *Second Edition*, first state (no. 161) with H8^v containing the 'ADVERTISEMENT' of 9 lines. The errata on I1^r is printed on the upper half and repeated on the lower half of the page. I have only seen a microfilm copy in the collection Goldsmiths'-Kress Library of Economic Literature, no. 3127 (with 'Cuontry.' and 'pulick'; A4 not signed).

Text (F3^r): 31 lines; 129 (140) × 67 mm; 83R. Fair-quality paper with posthorn watermark & initials 'ND'. Dedication set roman; pref. set 93 ital., 27 lines. Black letter and italics used for emphasis throughout. Page no. as headlines, set within parentheses.

HT, B1^r: [double rule 65/66 mm] | FURTHER | 𝕮𝖔𝖓𝖋𝖎𝖉𝖊𝖗𝖆𝖙𝖎𝖔𝖓𝖘 | Concerning | *Raifing the Value* | OF | MONEY.

CW: Page. A4^r the A8^r Him- [Himfelf.] D1^v on; [on:] D6^r you D6^v found: E2^r (Bul-) lion, E2^v but F3^v deno- [denomination] G1^r Re- [Refpect,] G3^r This G5^r (ac-) quained [quainted] H3^r 6 Whe- [5. Whether] H5^v I can- [I cannot]

Signature positions:

A2 Lords ˏ Juftices
A3 iˏn Nature
A4 will ˏ thˏereby
B Men ˏ give
B2 is ˏ to ˏ Wheat
B3 the 𝕾𝖙𝖆𝖓𝖉𝖆𝖗𝖉
B4 gˏreaˏt
C Exchan*g*e
C2 whom ˏ I
C3 price. ˏ For
C4 *are* ˏ but
D *the*
D2 buy ˏ Bu*l*lion
D3 Eˏxp*o*rtation
D4 Mr. *Low*ndes

E lig*h*ter
E2 more ˏ to *u*s
E3 the ˏ cheap
E4 Shillinˏgs ˏ and
F Money,
F2 us, Credit
F3 *Englan*d, ˏ as
F4 denominatˏion,
G no*t*
G2 Part ˏ of ˏ the
G3 *Denom*inations
G4 make juft
H clip'd
H2 Univerfal, *a*nd
H3 *of* Silver
H4 *a* grˏeat

Notes: This work was advertised for sale in the 28-31 December 1695 issue of the *Post-Boy* (just a bare listing of the title and bookseller). In a letter from John Freke and Edward Clarke dated 17 December 1695 Locke was informed that "Mr Churchill promises me the whole shall be printed by the end of this week" (*Corr.* 1981; v. 486). The text ends: "*to the publick Services | FINIS.*", that is, the final sentence is without a full stop. In some (early?) copies of the first state, A3ʳ line 10, in the 'Dedication' has the misprint 'Cuontry.' for 'Country.'; also leaf A4 is not signed; line 19 recto of that leaf reads 'pulick' (for 'publick'): resetting of the page is not involved, rather they are stop-press corrections, since the lines are otherwise from the same typesetting and are identical in spacing. Those reading 'pulick' with A4 not signed are thus earlier printings of sheet A (Kelly's 3d).

There are two lists of people to whom Locke gave copies of this edition. The first list (without a heading) is in the handwriting of Lady Masham (Bodleian Library's MS Locke c.25 fo.52ʳ). The list "provides for thirty-six persons by their proper names and for six by their official designations (the three commissioners of the Treasury collectively)" (*Corr.* viii. 452). The names are not in any order, and all but the last five (Furly, Johnstoun, Eyre, William Molyneux, and Child) are preceded by an 'x', of indeterminable significance. The second list, in Locke's hand, is found in a folio-sized sheet of paper, MS Locke c.25 fo.53, which has been folded so as to make four columns on each side. The list for *Further Considerations* is in the first column of the recto and is probably his more permanent record of forty-eight numbered copies. The recipients' names are again not in order; some are listed by official titles, e.g. 'L<or>ds Justices'. The list is headed "Further consider | ations concerning | the raising the | value of Money 1695 | 1 Edit". Lady Masham's name was last but has been deleted, and Cornelius Lyde entered beneath hers. Many otherwise unidentified recipients were Locke's correspondents. The recipients from both lists, in alphabetical order, are identified as follows:

Lord Ashley (Anthony Ashley Cooper, third Earl of Shaftesbury)
Mr. Ashley (? Maurice Ashley Cooper)
William Blathwaite (member of the Council of Trade)
John Egerton, Earl of Bridgewater (member of the Council of Trade)
James Chadwick[1] (a Commissioner for Customs from 1694)
Mr.Chamberlain (? Dr. Hugh Chamberlen, physician, author of a land-bank scheme)
Sir Josiah Child (author of *A Discourse about Trade*, 1690)
Edward Clarke
Samuel Clarke (commissioner of Customs)
Mr. Conyers (? John Conyers, MP; 2d cousin of Sir Frank Masham)

---

[1] Chadwick (c.1660-1697), an MP, in 1682 had married Mary, the daughter of John Tillotson, then Dean of Canterbury (later Archbishop). See *The House of Commons, 1660-1690*, ed. B. D. Henning (History of Parliament Trust, 1983), ii: 40.

William Cavendish, Duke of Devonshire (a 'Lord Justice')
Charles Sackville, Earl of Dorset (as Lord Chamberlain)
Sir Samuel Eyre (Lady Masham: 'Judg Ayres')
Dr. Edward Fowler, Bishop of Gloucester
Sir Stephen Fox (a Lord Commissioner of the Treasury)
John Freke, 'the Bachelor'
Benjamin Furly
Sidney Godolphin, Earl of Godolphin (a 'Lord Justice')
Sir Edward Harley (MP; father of Robert Harley, first Earl of Oxford)
Sir John Holt (Lord Chief Justice)
James Johnstoun
Christopher Leijoncrona ('Monsr Leencrun'; Lady Masham: 'Raincrowne'; Swedish representative in London, 1691–1710)
Robert Liddell (helped prepare bylaws for the Bank of England)
William Lowndes (author of *A Report containing an Essay for the Amendment of the Silver Coins*, 1695)
Cornelius Lyde
Sir Francis Masham
Sir Philip Meadows (member of the Council of Trade)
Robert Molesworth (later Viscount Molesworth; 2 copies)
William Molyneux
Charles Montagu (later Earl of Halifax; a Lord Commissioner of the Treasury)
Charles Mordaunt, Earl of Monmouth (from 1697 third Earl of Peterborough)
Colonel Lewis Mordaunt
Thomas Herbert, Earl of Pembroke (a 'Lord Justice')
John Pollexfen (member of the Council of Trade)
William Popple (translator of *Epistola de tolerantia*)
Sir Fleetwood Sheppard (poet, courtier; fellow student in the 1650s at Christ Church, Oxford)
Charles Talbot, Duke of Shrewsbury (a 'Lord Justice')
John Smith (commissioner of the Treasury)
John Somers, Baron Somers ('Lord Keeper', Lord Chief Justice; 2 copies)
Charles Spencer, Lord Spencer (later third Earl of Sunderland)
Thomas Grey, Earl of Stamford (member of the Council of Trade)
Dr. Thomas Tenison, Archbishop of Canterbury (a 'Lord Justice'; 2 copies)
Sir John Treby (Lord Chief Justice)
Sir Thomas Trevor (Attorney General; later Baron Trevor)
Sir William Trumbull (Secretary of State)
—— Vernon (probably James Vernon, an under-secretary in Shrewsbury's office)
—— Yard (probably Robert Yard, also an under-secretary in Shrewsbury's office)
Sir Walter Yonge

A copy of this edition, second state, is in the EEB microfilm collection, 606 no. 8.

References: Attig 502; Christophersen p. 23; ESTC r023043; Kelly 3a–d; L.L. 1789; T.C. II.571 (Hilary 1696); Wing² L2745.

Copies examined: A (First state): CLU-C Ct¹ (S.15.61 (3)) DFo¹ (191615) DFo² (L2760; with no. 155) O¹ (Vet.A3 e.1072) Oa¹ (XXI.15 (8)) Oc (a.3.148; A4 not signed) Oj (M16.15 (3); A4 not signed) Oq (GG.b.1)
 B (Second state): CaQMMO (1040; trimmmed to 153 × 91 mm) Ck (Keynes A.12.4(3)) Ct² (Y.9.36 (3)) CtY (NZ/Z695k; A4 not signed) L¹ (1027 a.2) L² (1139 d.6 (1)) L³ (104 k.11) MH (ECon.205.1*) NjP (ExW HG937.L79 (3)) O² (8o B.218 (2) Linc.) O³ (Godw. Pamph. 1413 (3)) Oa² (k.10.12) Oa³ (XXI.9)

161. Further Considerations. 'Second' ed., 1695. 8°. Two issues.

Within a double rule, inner 136 × 71 mm, outer 144 × 79 mm : FURTHER | 𝕮𝖔𝖓𝖘𝖎𝖉𝖊𝖗𝖆𝖙𝖎𝖔𝖓𝖘 | Concerning | *Raiſing the Value* | OF | MONEY. [period above line] | WHEREIN | Mr. *Lowndes*'s Arguments for it | in his late Report concerning | An *Eſſay for the Amendment of* [swash ſs] | *the Silver Coins*, are particu- | larly Examined. | [rule 68 mm] | *The Second Edition Correɑed.* | [rule 68 mm] | LONDON, | Printed for *A.* and *J. Churchil* [swash J] at the *Black* [swash k] | *Swan* in *Pater-Noſter-Row*, MDCXCV.

Coll: 8° (170 × 95 mm cut) A–C⁸ D⁸ (±D6) E⁸ (±E2) F⁸ G⁸ (±G3) H⁸ (±H5) + I1 (when present) [$ half signed]; 64 or 65 leaves; pp. *i–xvi* 1–111 112 + 113–114 [= 128 or 130]. An uncut corner in the NN copy shows uncut page size was about 180 × 100 mm.

Contents: A1ʳ (*i*) title (verso blank), A2ʳ–A4ᵛ (*iii–viii*) dedication signed 'JOHN LOCKE.', A5ʳ–A7ʳ (*ix–xiii*) pref. ending after 6 lines, followed by rule 65 mm, with advt. for books sold by Churchills, A7ᵛ–A8ᵛ (*xiv–xvi*) rest of advt., B1ʳ–H8ʳ (*1–111*) text ending 'FINIS.', H8ᵛ (*112*) advt., I1ʳ (*113*) errata (verso blank).

Text (B5ᵛ): 30 or 31 lines; 127 (138) × 70 mm; 82 R, with italic and black letter for emphasis. Sheets B–G lack watermarks (except where 1st ed. setting). Page no. within parentheses as headlines.

Issues: There are two issues of this edition; both use sheets A and H of the first edition. (There is a third issue, with different, changed sheets A, F and H, with an edition statement in black letter, and with 112 pages: this is treated as a true third edition. See no.162.)

The *first* issue has a new setting of sheets B–E and G, and of F shared in both issues (see *Signature Positions* below). Some copies have the first edition of gathering G; some have D6 as cancellans.

The *second* issue has sheets B–E and G again newly set, and any of D6, E2 or G3 may be cancellantia; H5 is almost always a cancellans.

There are also two different errata slips, usually bound as pp. *113–114*. The earlier has heading 'ERRATA.', 3 italic subheadings and 11.7-lines of errata (16 lines in all). The later 'ERRATA', between rules (66 and 68 mm) has 12.7 lines of corrections, as one solid paragraph without subheadings; it is usually trimmed to a half-sheet and/or mounted elsewhere. Since the errata sheet was an extra slip (not integral to a gathering) it is sometimes lacking.

Cancellanda and cancellantia. (Third ed. for comparison)

	First Issue	*2nd Issue* (cancellans)	*Third Edition* (no. 162)
D6 (43/44)			
43.61	1/5	1/5	line 4: one fifth
.18	fhou'd	fhould	fhould
.29	Cacao	Cacaco	Cacaco
44.9	1200 for the 1500	240 for the 300	240 for the 300
.11	2/3	line 10: 2/3	lines 10/11: two | thirds
E2 (51/52)*	Pages set 31 lines	Set 32 lines	Set 32 lines
51.6	twenty *per Cent.* I am . . .	lines 6–9: 20 *per* | *Cent.* And yet . . . are | grown dearer. I am . . .	lines 6–10: Twen- | ty *per Cent.* And yet . . . grown | dearer. I am . . .
G3 (85/86)	G3^r set 31 lines	G3^r set 30 lines	G3^r set 31 lines
785.4	coined	coined	Coin'd
.20	notto	not to	not to
86.22–30	First column of table reads: 1 2 3 4 1 3 5 7	1 1 3 2 5 3 7 4	1 1 3 2 5 3 7 4
H5 (105/106)	Pages set 31 lines	H5^r set 33 lines H5^v set 36 **	Pages set 31 lines
105.26	by | *particular men:* And	by *particular men:* | And	lines 26/27: by | *particular men:* And

* E2^r (51) cancellans has new sentence added in line 6 (reset in 3d ed.): "And yet at the fame | time he tells them in the paffage above ci- | ted out of *p.* 115. that all other things are | grown dearer."

** H5^r has last 10 lines set 72R; H5^v, also 72R, has 3 sentences added, beginning at line 16: "I am not for hindring thofe who have clip'd money | from any recompence which can be provided and | made them. The queftion here, is not whether | the honeft Country Man fhall bear the lofs of his | clip'd Money without any more ado, or pay a | Tax to recompence himfelf. That which I hum- | bly conceive the Nation is moft concerned in, is, | that Clipping fhould be finally ftopp'd, and that | the Money which remains fhould go according to | its true Value, for the carrying on of Commerce, | and the prefent fupply of Peoples Exigences, till | that part of it which is defac'd, can by the Mint | be brought to its legal and due Form."

CW: Page. D6ʳ you [cancellans: same] D6ᵛ found [cancellans: same] E2ʳ (Bul-) lion, E2ʳ cancellans: but E2ᵛ is [cancellans: same] G3ʳ This [cancellans: same] G3ᵛ The [cancellans: same] G4ʳ (feven-) teen H5ʳ men, H5ʳ cancellans: greater H5ᵛ I can- [I cannot]

Signature Positions. Sheets A and H as no. 160; both issues of sheet F are the same.

FIRST ISSUE	SECOND ISSUE	FIRST ISSUE	SECOND ISSUE
B give	giv‿e	E ⅕	O‿ne
B2 to Wheat	to meaſure	E2 theirs to	t h e y a‿r e (cancellans: more ‿ to ‿ us)
B3 𝕾𝖙𝖆𝖓𝖉𝖆𝖗𝖉	𝕾𝖙𝖆‿𝖓𝖉𝖆𝖗𝖉	E3 cheap	the ‿ cheap
B4 charge	a ‿ gre‿at	E4 Shillings ‿ and	Shillings ‿ and
C Exchange	receive	F Money	
C2 whom ‿ I	De‿bt	F2 us, Credit	
C3 price. ‿ For	un‿der	F3 England, as	
C4 but P‿rojects	Riches	F4 denomination	
D juſt ‿ the	the	G we	not
D2 Bul‿lion	Bulli‿on	G2 Part ‿ of ‿ the	the Money
D3 Exportat‿ion	Exportation	G3 Den‿ominations	Den‿ominations
D4 p. 72‿.	M‿r. ‿ Lowndes	G4 make juſt	make juſt

Notes: This second edition is frequently found as part of *Several Papers* (no. 163), bound with no. 156 and 159. A notice of publication in the *Post-Boy* for 9-11 January 1695/6 would indicate that this edition appeared very soon after the first. The title-page is that of the first-edition setting with the lines spaced more closely together to permit the insertion of the italic edition statement. There are numerous typographical errors, although corrections of those in the errata lists to the first edition have been made. Most of the cancellantia occur through correcting the mathematics involved in dealing with interest and the intrinsic value of money. The advertisement on p. *112* is for *Some Considerations* (4 lines) and *Short Observations* (5 lines), with a final line: 'Both Written by Mr. *Locke*.' A microfilm copy of the second issue is in the Goldsmiths'-Kress Library of Economic Literature, no. 3128: it has the G3 cancellans, with corrections made to the recto, but the verso is the first edition setting. Another copy of the second issue is in Goldsmiths' 3314, as part of *Several Papers* (no. 163B).

References: Attig 503; Christophersen p.23; ESTC r201949; Kelly 3e-h; Wing² L2746.

Copies examined (all part of *Several Papers*, except CtY and Oc):
A: First issue. C (Keynes B3.46; D6 canc.; 12.7-line err.)
CaOTU (Locke L63.F87 1695; lacks err.)
Ct¹ (S.15.63 (3); A1 bd. after A2; D6 canc.; lacks err.)
CtY¹ (NZ/Z692l; bd. with no. 155 & 158; lacks err.; has all cancellantia)
NjP¹ (ExW HG937.L79 (3); 12.7-l. err.)

NN (TF (3); 12.7-l. err.)
O¹ (Locke coll. 7/208 (3); D6, E2, H5 canc.; §G is 1st ed.; 12.7-l. err.)
Oc (4.B.210 (4); §G 1st ed.; 16-l. err.)
Occ (LG1.21 (4); §G 1st ed.; 16-l. err.)
Oj (P.12.Gall.(3); gift of Jonathan Edwards, 1712; 16-l. err.)
Oq (GG.b.85 (3); 12.7-l. err.)
B: Second issue (all with H5 canc. except CtY²):
  Ct² (NQ16.159; D6, E2 canc.; 12.7-l. err.; Newton's copy)
  CtY² (Ngc95/G5/696*l* (3); 12.7-l. err.; sheet H from no. 162)
  DFo (L2757 (3); sheets D E G are 3d ed.; H5 canc.; lacks A1; 12.7-l. err.)
  DLC (G3 canc.; lacks A1 and err.)
  L (1391 a.5; lacks A1 and err.)
  NjP² (HG937.L79 Ex (3); lacks A2; G3 canc.; 12.7-l. err.)
  O² (8° P.211.Art. (2); D6 canc.; lacks err.)
  O³ (Vet.A3 f.803 (3); D6 canc.; 12.7-l. err.)
  O⁴ (Locke 7/208 (3); §G is 1st ed.; D6 canc.)
  Osj (HB31.G5 (3); 12.7-l. err.)
  Utr (I.oct. 424 (3); lacks A1; 12.7-l. err.)

162. Further Considerations. '𝔖𝔢𝔠𝔬𝔫𝔡' [i.e. 3d] ed., 1696. 8°
Within a double rule, inner 138 × 72 mm, outer 144 × 78 mm: FURTHER | 𝕮𝖔𝖓𝖋𝖎𝖉𝖊𝖗𝖆𝖙𝖎𝖔𝖓𝖘 | ... [&c. as in no. 161, until line 13:] 𝕿𝖍𝖊 𝕾𝖊𝖈𝖔𝖓𝖉 𝕰𝖉𝖎𝖙𝖎𝖔𝖓 𝕮𝖔𝖗𝖗𝖊𝖈𝖙𝖊𝖉. | [rule 68 mm] | LONDON, | Printed for *Awnſham* and *John Churchil*, [swash J] at | the *Black-Swan* [swash k] in *Pater-Noſter-Row*. 1696.
Coll: 8° (165 × 95 mm cut) A–H⁸ [$ half signed]; 64 leaves; pp.*i–xvi* 1–112 [=128].
Contents: A (*i–xvi*) same as no. 161, B1ʳ–H8ᵛ (1–112) text.
Text: as no. 161; but paper watermarked with letter O.
CW: Page. A4ʳ the A8ʳ Him- [Himſelf] D6ʳ you D6ᵛ found: [found:] D8ʳ (re-)ceive E2ʳ are E2ᵛ Pence E8ᵛ number [of Inches (CW part of text)] F3ᵛ deno- [denomination] G3ʳ This G3ᵛ The H3ʳ 5. Whe- [5. Whether] H3ᵛ car- [carrying] H5ᵛ go
Signature positions (B–E and G as in no. 160, except E2 and G3):

  A2 Juſtices   F4 denomi˄nation
  A3 *in* Nature   G3 Deno˄mi*n*ations
  A4 wil*l* th˄ereby   H *c*lip'd
  E2 they *a*re   H2 Univerſal, and
  F Mo*n*ey   H3 *the* ˄ uſes
  F2 u˄s, ˄ Credit   H4 Money, a ˄ great
  F3 Eng˄*l*and,

Notes: This printing becomes the true third edition, since sheets A, F and H have been reset from earlier printings, that is all sheets are now newly set. Sheets B–E and G are those of the 2d ed., 2d issue. The title-page setting for the first 12 lines follows no. 161, even including the large (3 mm) point after

'MONEY.' There are no cancellantia: the textual changes by cancellantia in no. 161 are repeated here, their text follows that of the 2d ed., 2d issue. Sheet H has been completely reset to accomodate the expansion from p. 105 of the 2d issue, thus permitting the text to expand onto p. 112. There is no errata slip; no advt. on p. 112. Attig (504 n.) does not distinguish this ed. from no. 161.

The second copy at Trinity College, Cambridge (S.15.63 (3)) and the copy in the EEB microfilm set have sheet E of *Some Considerations* (no. 156) bound in place of this work's sheet E.

I have only found this edition as part of *Several Papers* (no. 163). As part of no. 163, a copy was printed in facsimile by A.M. Kelley, New York, in 1968. Another copy is in the EEB microfilm collection, reel 570, no. 6. (as part of *Several Papers*); another copy ibid., reel 870, no. 9 alone (from Huntington Library at San Marino, Calif.). It is also included in the microfilm set, Goldsmiths'-Kress Library of Economic Literature, no. 3315 (part of 163B).
References: Attig 504 n.; ESTC r023372; T.C. II.571; Wing^2 L2746A.
Copies examined: C (Syn.7.69.19 (3))   CaOTU^1 (Locke L63.S49 1696 (3))   CaOTU^2 (Locke L63.F87 1695)   Ck (Keynes A.12.6 (3))   Ct^1 (NQ16.159)   Ct^2 (S.15.63 (3))   Han   NjP (HG937.L79 Ex (3))   NjR (HC246.L815S (3))   O (Vet.A3 f.260 (3))   Utr (I.oct.424)

163. Several Papers. 1696. 8° Two issues
A (First issue). Within a double rule, inner 131 × 72 mm, outer 138 × 79 mm: SEVERAL | PAPERS | Relating to | *Money,* | *Intereſt* and | *Trade,* &c. | Writ upon ſeveral Occaſions, and | Publiſhed at different Times. | [rule 67 mm] | By *JOHN LOCKE,* [swash J] Eſq; | [rule 67 mm] | LONDON: | Printed for *A.* and *J. Churchill,* [swash J] at the | *Black-Swan* [swash k] in *Pater-Noſter-Row,* 1696.
B (Second issue). Within a double rule, inner 131 × 72 mm, outer 136 × 79 mm, same as first issue until 10th line: By Mr. *JOHN LOCKE,* [swash J] | [rule 67 mm] | LONDON: . . . | [&c. as in 1st issue]
Coll: 8° (160 × 95 mm cut) A1 leaf from no. 156 (±A1).
Text: Leaf A1 in the cancellans has the watermark of a rampant lion within a shield.
Note: The closest estimate to a date of publication is November 1696 (cf. *Corr.* viii. 452). This work consists of a collective title leaf for no. 156, 159 and no. 161 or 162. In the second issue the title leaf is a cancellans, but all lines are of the same typesetting (some slightly moved), with the author statement rephrased as a stop-press correction. The verso, containing the licence statement for no. 156, in many copies has an offset impression of the title of no. 156.

This collective work was presented to James Chadwick, Leibniz and Lady Masham, following the list in the Bodleian Library's MS Locke c.25, fo. 53^r, second column. Chadwick was a Commissioner for Customs (see no. 160). In a list of recipients of copies of Locke's *Reply to the . . . Bishop of Worcester's*

Answer to His Letter (no. 249), a note at the end reads 'Money Mr Stepney', perhaps naming a fourth recipient, George Stepney (MS Locke c.25 fo. 55^r). Stepney became a member of the Council of Trade in June 1697.

Several libraries own the set of pamphlets (no. 156, 159 and 161 or 162) bound together, but lack the title leaf which constitutes this edition, for example, CLU-C, DFo, PU and Utr. There is little or no correlation between the two issues and the inclusion of 161 or 162, though more copies survive with no. 162. In 1968 the reprint house Augustus M. Kelley, in New York, published a facsimile of the set, *Several Papers*, in their series: Library of Money and Banking History, using no. 156, 159, and 162, with 163B title page, with all signatures removed; it was re-reprinted in 1989. A microfilm copy in the EEB microfilm collection, reel 570, no. 6. Another copy with a second issue title-page is found on the microfilm set 'Goldsmiths'-Kress Library of Economic Literature', no. 3314-5 (2 copies).

References: Attig 504 (B issue); ESTC r019558 (B issue); Kelly 4a-b; L.L. 1792; T.C. II.596 and III.6 (Hilary Term 1697: 'by Mr. John Locke').

Copies examined: A (First issue): O^1(Vet.A3 f.260; with no. 162) O^2 (Vet A3 f.803; with 161B) NjP^1 (HG937.L79 ExW; with 161A) NN (TF; with 161A) Oq (GG.b.85; with 161A)

B (Second issue): O^3 (8° P.211 Art; 'Ex dono Auctoris'; with 161B) C (Syn.7.69.9; with 162) CaOTU (Locke L63.S49 1696; with 162) Ck (Keynes A.12.6; with 162) Ct (S.15.63; with 161A) CtY^1 (Ngc95/G5.Z696*l*; with 161B title, sheets are no. 162) Han (presentation copy to Leibniz; with 162) L (1391 a.5; with 161B) NjP^2 (HG937.L79 Ex, with 162) NjR (X HC246.L814S; with 162) O^4 (Locke 7/208; with 161B) Osj (HB3/G5; with 161B) PPL (Wing L2757/Log51.D; with 162)

164. Several Papers. Italian trans. Florence, 1751. 4° in 8s.

In red and black. Vol. 1: [red line:] RAGIONAMENTI | *SOPRA* | [red:] LA MONETA L'INTERESSE DEL DANARO | [red:] LE FINANZE E IL COMMERCIO | SCRITTI E PUBBLICATI IN DIVERSE OCCASIONI | *DAL SIGNOR* | [red:] GIOVANNI LOCKE | TRADOTTI LA PRIMA VOLTA DALL'INGLESE | [red:] CON VARIE ANNOTAZIONI. | *TOMO PRIMO.* | [orn.: framed engr. headpiece of 'DENARIVS FAMILIÆ CARISIÆ', obverse & reverse, in frame 62 × 95 mm, on plate 69 × 102 mm subscribed '*A.Sveicart fecit.*'] | [red:] IN FIRENZE MDCCLI. | Appreſſo ANDREA BONDUCCI. | [rule 109 mm] | [red:] *CON LICENZA DE' SUPERIORI.*

Vol. 2: RAGIONAMENTI | . . . [&c. as in vol. 1, until 8th line:] TRADOTTI | LA PRIMA VOLTA DALL'INGLESE | CON VARIE ANNOTAZIONI E CON UN DISCORSO | *SOPRA* | [red:] IL GIUSTO PREGIO DELLE COSE | [red:] E DELLA MONETA | E | [red:] IL COMMERCIO DE' ROMANI. | *TOMO SECONDO.* | [red rule 50 mm] | [rule 42 mm] | [red rule, broken, 36 mm] | [red:] IN

FIRENZE, MDCCLI. | Appreſſo ANDRE BONDUCCI. | rule 105 mm] | [red:] *CON LICENZA DE' SUPERIORI*.

Coll: 4° in 8s (265 × 194 mm uncut). Vol. 1: §⁸ (-§8) χ1 §§⁸ A-M⁸ [$ half (-§4) signed]; 113 leaves; pp. *I-II* III-VII *VIII* IX-XXXIII *XXXIV* 1-176 175-189 *190* [= 226]. Mispaginated: no. 175-6 repeated.

Vol. 2: §⁸ §§⁴ A-V⁸ ²A-F⁸ ²G¹⁰ [$ half (-§2; + ²G5) signed]; 230 leaves; pp. *I-IV* V-XI *XII* XIII-XXIII *XXIV* 1-186 *187-188* 189-303 204 305-316 *317-320* 1-2 3-116 [= 460]. Page 304 called '204'.

Contents. Vol. 1: §1ʳ (*I*) title (verso blank), §2ʳ-4ʳ (*III-VII*) dedication to Emanuele di Richecourt signed: "Firenze, li 25 Novembre 1750. S.C. | . . . | GIO. FRANCESCO PAGNINI. | ANGELO TAVANTI.", §4ᵛ blank, §5ʳ-§§4ᵛ (*IX-XXVI*) 'AVVISO DEI TRADUTTORI AL LETTORE.', §§5ʳ-§§6ᵛ (*XXVII-XXX*) contents, §§7ʳ-§§8ʳ (*XXXI-XXXIII*) Locke's dedication to 'Giovanni Sommer' [sic], §§8ᵛ blank, A1ʳ-M8ʳ (1-189) Italian trans. of the part of *Some Considerations* relating to interest (divided into 32 sections), M8ᵛ blank.

Vol. 2: §1ʳ (*I*) title (verso blank), §2ʳ (*III*) 3-line quotation from Dante's *Paradiso* (Canto 19, verse 120), §2ᵛ blank, §3ʳ-§6ʳ (*V-XI*) contents, §6ᵛ blank, §7ʳ-§§1ᵛ (*XIII-XVIII*) Locke's dedication, §§2ʳ-§§4ʳ (*XIX-XXIII*) preface, §§4ᵛ blank, A1ʳ-M5ᵛ (1-186) "Nuove considerazioni sull' augumentare la valuta della moneta" (trans. of *Further Considerations*, divided into articles, each in several sections), M6ʳ section title (verso blank), M7ʳ-S7ᵛ (189-286) trans. of *Some Considerations* relating to coinage (called 'Parte Seconda', divided into articles and sections), S8ʳ-V6ᵛ (287-316) "Breve osservazioni . . ." (trans. of *Short Observations*), V7ʳ (*317*) monetary table from 1696 ed. of *Further Observations* (50 × 69 mm, reprinted from 1740 *Works* ed.), V7ᵛ blank, V8 blank (stub used to mount folded table, 'Illustration' below), ²A1ʳ section title (verso blank), ²A2ʳ-²G10ᵛ (3-116) text of Pagnini's 'Saggio'.

Illustration: Stub in vol. 2 after p. *316* is mounting for folded table (sheet 440 × 594 mm) headed "TAVOLA DELLA BONTÀ PESO E VALVTA.", credited to Isaac Newton.

Text (F3ʳ): 29 lines; 172 (184) × 108 mm; 118 R. Excellent-quality paper, watermarked at gutters of 1st & 4th leaves with a sphere surmounted by double cross, quartered with letters A C G and L. Dedication set 35 lines, 100 R; translators' introduction set 29 lines 118 ital. Footnotes set in double columns 81 ital. Page no. centered at top of page as headlines for v.2, pp. 287-316 ('Breve osservazioni'); for pp. 3-116 (Pagnini's 'Saggio') at top outer corners (no headlines). Vol. 1 p. 189 ends with a tailpiece of a face framed above a shell, with swags, 37 × 39 mm, repeated in v.2 p. 237; v.2 p. 316 (V6ᵛ) has a framed diapered block as tailpiece, 40 × 48 mm.

Dedication, v.1 §2ʳ: A Sua ECCELLENZA | *IL SIGNOR CONTE:* | EMMANUELLE | DI RICHECOURT.

HT v.1 A1ʳ: CONSIDERAZIONI | SULLA RIDUZIONE DEGLI' INTERESSI | DELLA | MONETA. | [rule 105 mm]

v.2 A1^r: NUOVE CONSIDERAZIONI | SULL' AUGUMENTARE LA VALUTA | DELLA MONETA. | [rule 105 mm]
v.2 S8^r: BREVI OSSERVAZIONI | SOPRA DI UN FOGLIO STAMPATO | CHE HA PER TITOLO | *Per animare la gente a battere la Moneta di* | *Argento in Inghilterra; e dei modi per dopo* | *conſervarvela.*
v.2 ^{2}A2^r: SAGGIO. | *PARTE PRIMA.* | [rule 102 mm]
v.2 ^{2}C6^r: *PARTE SECONDA* [sic]
Section titles. Vol. 2 p. 187 (M6^r): PARTE SECONDA | DELLA LETTERA | SULLE CONSEGUENZE DELLO SBASSARE | GL'INTERESSI DEL DANARO | CHE CONCERNE L'AUGMENTO DELLA VALUTA | DELLA MONETA.
Vol.2 ^{2}A1^r: SAGGIO | SOPRA IL GIUSTO PREGIO DELLE COSE | LA GIUSTA VALUTA | DELLA MONETA | E SOPRA IL COMMERCIO DEI ROMANI.
RT v.1 pp. 2–189 (A1^v–M8^r) from verso to recto: CONSIDERAZIONI | SOPRA GL' INTERESSI. (With page no. at outer ends of headlines.)
Vol. 2 pp. 2–186 (A1^v–M5^v) from verso to recto, e,g,: ARTICOLO I. | SEZIONE I.
Vol. 2 pp. 190–286 (M7^v–S7^v) from verso to recto, e.g.: ARTICOLO II. | SEZIONE IV.
Vol. 2 'Saggio' ^{2}A2^r–^{2}C5^v from verso to recto, e. g.: PARTE I. | SEZIONE I. [–II.]
Vol. 2 ^{2}C6^v–^{2}G5^v: PARTE II. | SEZIONE I. [–IX.]
CW: Page. Vol. 1: A1^v (e-) vitarne A2^r traffi- [traffico,] D4^v (comune-)mente E3^r (prov-) vedere E7^v cam- [cambiandoſi] F8^v (l'an-) no K4^v (l'ac-) creſci- [creſcimento] M2^r (prez-) zo
Vol. 2: §5^r *Bre-* [*Brevi*] A7^v (to-) ſe B3^r (Mo-) ne- [neta] E4^r (con-) ſeguen- [ſeguenza] F3^r Mone- [Moneta] K2^v (ſpe-) cie L6^r ſola- [ſolamente] M7^v (Mo-) ne- [neta] P1^v Mone- [Moneta] Q5^v all'al- [all'altra,] S5^v (guadagne-) rebbe- [rebbero] T7^v gra- [gravezze] ^{2}C7^v (an-) che ^{2}G5^r (ſupe-) riore
Notes: Translation by Giovanni Francesco Pagnini and Angelo Tavanti, based on the 1740 folio *Works* edition (no. 366). Vol. 1 leaf following §7 is an insertion (repairing an accident at the press?). The text of *Some Considerations* is divided into two parts, with text of *Further Considerations* (divided into 2 parts, first into 6 articles, 2d into 2, each with sections) coming between (see *Contents* above). The answer to *A Letter to a Friend concerning Usury*, in *Some Considerations* pp. 129–32 (Kelly's ed., pp. 301–3) is omitted. The 'Saggio' at the end of vol. 2 is the work of Pagnini; it is without headlines, but has page no. at top of page in outer corners. Kelly's 'Checklist of Printings' (his edition, pp. 161–62), though otherwise quite accurate, calls Pagnini's 'Saggio' "Uno Discorso sopra il Giusto Pregio . . ." (from the title page?) and gives its pagination as vol. l, pp. 190–298. No such copies can be found.

A microfilm copy of this work can be found in the Goldsmiths'-Kress Library of Economic Literature, no. 8635 (with Pagnini's 'Saggio' bound at end of vol. 1).

References: Attig 507; Kelly Italian 1.
Copies examined: Vat (Mai XI. K.IV. 41–42, uncut) [BBR] CaOTU (Locke L63.S49I8 1751; 'TAVOLA' bound at end of vol.1) DLC (HG937.S745 1751) O (Vet.F5.d.64–65; vol.2 lacks leaf V8 and 116 pp. 'Saggio', at end)

Aside from the usual inclusion of these pamphlets on money in *Works* editions (Chapter XII, below), there was a selection published at the end of J. R. McCulloch's *The Principles of Political Economy* (1870; reprinted in 1878). The three pamphlets were reprinted from the 9th edition of the *Works* (together with *Some Thoughts concerning Education*) by Ward Locke in 1883. But there has been no editorial attention given to them since 1751, until recently. The definitive edition of these three pamphlets, together with ancillary manuscript material, has been edited by Kelly and published in the Clarendon Edition of the Works of John Locke under the title *Locke on Money* (Oxford: Clarendon Press, 1991; 664 pp. in 2 vols.).

An Italian translation of *Some Considerations* was edited and translated by Francesco Fagiani and published in Bologna in 1978.

CHAPTER V

Some Thoughts concerning Education (nos. 165–228)

The impetus for writing *Some Thoughts concerning Education* grew out of a request from Locke's friends, Edward Clarke and his wife Mary (née Jepp) of Chipley, near Wellington in Somerset, for some instructions in educating their son Edward "and more generally of their other children". Locke's counsels were embodied in a series of letters dating from July 1684 through March 1691. The letters are no. 782, 799, 893, 807, 822, 829, 844, 845, 929, 999, 1098 and 1370 in E.S. de Beer's edition of the *Correspondence*. Letter 809, dated 7 February 1685 NS, concerns bringing up girls, and was not included in the published *Thoughts*.

There is no printers' copy of the text surviving. Locke kept copies of his letters, some of which we only know through surviving drafts (included in *Corr.*). He presumably kept a draft or copy of these instructions, for in a letter to Clarke in May 1686 (no. 849; iii.1-4) he wrote: "For I doubt not but when I revise the foul copy, which I keep by me on purpose, I shall myself find occasion for additions or alterations." In November 1684 he composed a long list of instructions for the Clarkes, copied by his secretary Sylvester Brounower (sent with *Corr.* 791; ii.648). Presumably this copy, headed 'Of Education', went astray, for the instructions were again copied by Brounower and sent in January 1685. This latter draft, now at the British Library (as Add. MS. 38771) is slightly longer than the first, and therefore later, since it includes what became §§ 23-8 in the two earliest editions, matter on 'costiveness', not mentioned in the November 1684 draft. This earlier draft, known as the Nynehead version, after various travels, has at last found a home at Harvard College Library (as MS. Eng. 860), the gift of Lady Eccles (formerly Mrs. Mary Hyde). The British Library draft is that transcribed by Sir Frederic G. Kenyon and published by the Roxburghe Club in 1933 with the title, *Directions concerning Education* (no. 320).

Fuller details about the differences between the two drafts, the text of the instructions in the *Correspondence*, and the editions published in Locke's lifetime can be found in the critical edition edited by John W. and Jean S. Yolton for the Clarendon Edition of the Works of John Locke, published in 1989.

165–6. Education. [1st and 2d ed.] 1693. 8°. Anonymous.
Within a double rule, inner 142 × 72 mm, outer 149 × 79 mm (2d ed.: inner

143 × 72 mm, outer 150 × 79 mm): SOME | THOUGHTS | CONCERNING | Education. | [10 or 13 mm below, double rule 69 mm] | [3 rows of floral orn. of 4 irons each, 3d row inverted, 17 × 15 mm, skewed left *or* squared] | [double rule 69 mm] | LONDON, | Printed for A. and J. *Churchill,* [swash J] | at the *Black Swan* [swash k] in *Pater-* | *noſter-row,* 1693.

Coll: 8° (180 × 110 mm cut) A⁴ B–R⁸ S⁴ [$ half signed]; 136 leaves; pp. *i–viii* 1–262 263–264 [= 272].

Contents: A1ʳ (*i*) title (verso blank), A2ʳ–A4ʳ (*iii–vii*) dedication: "TO | Edward Clarke | Of *CHIPLEY,* Eſq;" signed: "Your moſt humble | and moſt faithful | Servant.", A4ᵛ blank, B1ʳ–S3ᵛ (1–262) text (in §§ numbered 1–172, 172 *bis*, 173–77, 179–202), S4ʳ·ᵛ (263–264) alphabetical contents of the sections in double cols.

Text (N1ᵛ): 29 lines; 136 (148) × 69 (84) mm; 93R. Medium-quality laid paper, with watermark Heawood 2720. Page no. at outer corners of headlines. Sections have topical headings set ital. in margins.

Editions: The two different editions of this work can be distinguished on the t.p. by whether the first set of rules is 10 or 13 mm below 'Education.' and whether the row of orn. is skewed or squared off, for the 1st or 2d ed. respectively. Other distinctions (1st ed. given first) are whether the verso of leaf A2 has CW 'I my' or 'I'; whether the same page has '*deferr*' or '*defer*' in line 3; and whether A3ᵛ (p. *vi*) has '*Patronnge*' or '*Patronage*' in line 19 (leading to Peter Nidditch's distinction of NN and NA copies; see below). The text in both editions is virtually the same, the 2d being a line-by-line reprint of the first, except for 7 lines that end differently. There are many accidental variants between editions. There are substantive errors in the first (NN) edition, detailed below. The only substantive error in the 2d (NA) edition is the numbering of § 29 as § 22; the substantive errors in the first edition have been corrected, and are the readings followed in the 3d edition. Both editions have many typographical errors, many corrected in the 2d, but the 2d also introduces new ones.

HT: [double rule 68 mm] | SOME | THOUGHTS | CONCERNING | EDUCATION.

Headlines: *Of EDUCATION.* [swash U]

CW: Page. Same in both editions except for these (2d ed. within curved brackets): A2ᵛ I my {I} H3ᵛ Children {Children,} L3ʳ §.122. [2d '2' different font] {§.122. [same fonts]} M4ᵛ Way [way] {Way [Way]}

Notes: The dedication is dated 7 March 1692 (Old Style, that is 1693). The first edition was available certainly by mid-July 1693, for Edward Clarke acknowledges receipt of a copy in a letter dated 22 July 1693 (*Corr.* 1644; iv.701). The work was also advertised in the *London Gazette,* no. 2886 for 6–10 July 1693. Both editions were published anonymously. An entry for this edition was made in the Registers of the Stationers' Company on 21 Sept 1693 (*Transcript,* p. 430). It was licensed for publication on 30 August 1693 and entered for distribution by A. and J. Churchill to the 'conger' during the same year (cf. Hodgson and Blagden: *Notebook of Thomas Bennet and Henry Clements*, p. 205). It was briefly mentioned, with an attribution to Locke, in the *Histoire des ouvrages des savans*, November 1693: 130. Determining how many copies were printed can only be an estimate. A print-run of 200 to 500 copies was not unusual.

The second edition can only have been printed within a short period after the first, while the publisher still had sheets of the first on hand, since Locke's own copy (now in the Bodleian Library) is a mixed-sheet copy: all gatherings except K (pp. 129-144) are of the first edition, K is of the second. This copy unfortunately was the copy used by Scolar Press (Menston, Yorks.) for their facsimile reprint in 1970.

I have not found any other mixed-sheet copies, but to facilitate such determinations, at least one variant per gathering is given below.

Nor do we know the price charged, but it must have been the same as or less than that charged for the 4th ed. of 1699 (no. 167), which was 3 s. 6 d. each.

In the Lovelace Collection of Locke's manuscripts in the Bodleian Library, there are lists of persons to whom Locke presented copies of his acknowledged works (MS Locke f.29 p. 144; and MS Locke c. 25 ff.50-5). Recipients of this work are listed below. Of the 24 or 25 copies presented, there is a known location for two: one in Sheffield University Library is Sir Walter Yonge's; that belonging to William Molyneux was recently offered for sale by W. Thomas Taylor, the Texas bookseller. Both these copies are of the second edition.

Locke was known to be concerned at the quality of the printing of his writings, and to try to read the sheets before they were finally printed, a fact shown in his correspondence (e.g. 1557, iv.564; 1719, v.30). I think the Churchills completed printing the first edition before Locke had made corrections; that he was so incensed by the errors that he insisted the whole first edition be suppressed, and the barely distinguishable second edition be made. That the known presentation copies are of the 2d edition signifies to me that he preferred his friends to have the more correct edition.

Aside from the substantive errors listed below, there were also some 'stop-press' corrections, found in some copies of the 1st edition. Notably these are as follows:
a) 3 line 23: 'not sickly Constitution' corrected to 'nor sickly Constitution'
b) 107.4: 'Founation' to 'Foundation'
c) 111.20: 'familiarity' to 'familiarly'
d) 121.19: 'hearden' to 'harden'
e) 154.24: 'th ing' to 'thing'

These are the salient points of contrast between the two editions. Much discussion and coverage has been given in the following publications.
1) Sir Frederic G. Kenyon, letter, *Times Literary Supplement* no. 1629, 20 April 1933. He appealed for location of copies of the 2d ed.
2) John Eliot Alden, note, *Papers of the Bibliographical Society of America* 37

(1943): 309. He distinguished the two editions from the CW on A2ᵛ as the 'I my' and 'I' editions, and inclined to thinking the 'I' edition later.

3) Peter Nidditch, *A Bibliographical and Text-Historical Study of the Early Printings of John Locke's* Some Thoughts concerning Education (Sheffield, 1973). Written chiefly in criticism of James Axtell's *The Educational Writings of John Locke* (Cambridge University Press, 1968), he also covers in great detail the differences between the 1st and 2d (NN and NA) editions, preferring to consider the NA the earlier, chiefly because the presentation copy at Sheffield is the NA edition.

4) Jean S. Yolton, bibliographic note, *Papers of the Bibliographical Society of America* 75 (1981): 315–321. Detailed comparisons and arguments for considering NN the first edition.

The comparisons and differences between these two editions, even as to frequent italicized colons (in 1st ed.) and different styles of ligatured letters, substantive and accidental variants, are exhaustively given in the Clarendon Edition of the Works of John Locke, edited by John Yolton and me (Oxford University Press, 1989).

Presentation Copies. Following the record made by E.S. de Beer for vol. 8 of the *Correspondence* (pp. 450, 454–8) from Locke MS Locke c.25, to 53, these persons received copies. The first list (MS Locke f.29, p.144) gives 25 names, including 'JL', but omitting 'Mrs Smith' and Francis Limborch. 'JL' is omitted from the second list.

Lord Ashley (Anthony Ashley Cooper, later third Earl of Shaftesbury)
John Bonville
Brook Bridges
Edward Clarke
Paul d'Aranda
Mrs. Isabella Duke
Thomas Firmin
Robina Douglas, Countess of Forfar
John Freke
Benjamin Furly
Dr. Peter Guenellon
Baron F. M. van Helmont
Thomas Herbert, Earl of Pembroke
James Johnstoun
Jean Le Clerc
Francis Limborch
Dr. (later Sir) Thomas Molyneux
William Molyneux
Charles Mordaunt, Earl of Monmouth (from 1697, third Earl of Peterborough)
Robert Pawling
William Popple
Mrs. Smith

John Somers, Baron Somers
Dr. John Tillotson, Archbishop of Canterbury
Sir John Treby, Lord Chief Justice
Sir Walter Yonge

Substantive Variants (2nd ed. reading within parentheses)
p. 66 lines 24–27 (F1^v): "When constant custom has made any one thing easy and natural to them, and they practise it with (without) Reflection . . ."
71.2–4 (F4^r): "To this purpose, their being in their presence, should be made easie to them; they shall (should) be allowed . . ."
76.4 (F6^v): ". . . any of the proudest of your (you) grown Men, . . ."
113.12–15 (I1^4): ". . . Love and Fear, as the great Principle, whereby you will always have hold upon him, to turn his Mind to the ways of Vertue of (and) Honour."
116.3–5 (I2^v): "And if you carefully observe the Characters of this (his) Mind now in the first Scenes of his Life . . ."
179.18–20 (N2^r): "This being a play amongst you, tempt him not to it, least (lest) you make it Business . . ."
192.1–4 (N8^v): ". . . it is better to let him pass them (pass them by) quietly, than to vex him about them to no purpose . . ."
197.14–19 O3^r): "In which abstract Speculations when young Men have had their Heads imploy'd a while without finding the Success and Imployment (Improvement,) or Use of it which they expected, they are apt to have mean Thoughts . . ." ('Improvement' in *Corr.* 844; ii.775)

Variants in other gatherings (than A, F, I, N and O; 2nd ed. reading within parentheses)
B3^v (p.6) lines 26–7: wash- | ed (wa- | shed)
C5^v (26) 5–6: Per- | ristaltick (Pe- | ristaltick)
D2^r (35) 25: why would (should) we think it strange
E6^v (60) 23–4: to | a Degree, (to a | Degree,)
G5^r (89) 14: Carelessness (Carelesness)
H3^r (101) 14–15: Chastisements (Chastisement) carries with it
K4^v (136) 27: are not to be slight; (slightd;)
L5^v (154) 26–7: if he | persists (if | he persists)
M4^v (168) 28: neglect o (of) them
P4^v (216) 5–7: to fix it in his Me- | mory, and to incourage him to go on, | as to set him . . . (to fix it in his | Memory, and to incourage him to | go on, as to set him . . .)
Q4^v (232) 9–10: first Princi- | ples (Prin- | ciples)
R6^r (251) 3: rnns (runs)
S4^r contents: *Governour* 64. (94. rectē)

A microfilm copy of the first edition (NN) from the Union Theological Seminary, New York, is in EEB, reel 845, no. 17; of the second (NA) from the University of Illinois Library is in reel 1797, no. 18.

References: Alston 10:111; Attig 523; Axtell British 1–2 (eds. not distinguished); ESTC 1st r007482, 2d r213714; L.L. 1020 (under

'Education'), 1785 (now in Bodleian Lib.); T.C. II.467; Wing^2 L2762A (1st ed.), L2762 (2d).

Copies examined:
First ed. (NN): Y ABu C (Keynes B.3.44) CaOTU (Locke L63.S66 1693a) CaQMM CaQMMO Ck^1(Keynes A.12.7) Ck^2 (Keynes A.12.8) CLU-C Ct (H24.25) E.S. de Beer^1 DFo (2 cops.) EXu L^1 (8307 bb.29) MH^1 (*EC65.L7934.693sb) O^1 (Locke e.2; Locke's own, mixed sheets) O^2 (*260 g.512) Oq (ZZ k.4) PPL (Wing L2762/66732.O) PU (LB475.L6 1693) SKI (Petyt Lib.) Wol (Pa.232)

Second ed. (NA): Y C (Syn 7.69.46) Cch (D.R.32) Ck^3 (Keynes A.12.9) Ck^4 (Keynes A.12.10) CtY (K8.L79/H693) E.S. de Beer^2 Dt (137.g.227) EXu L^2 (1030 f.1) MH^2 (*EC65.L7934.693s) NjP (Ex.6504.592.14) NN O^3 (Vet.A3 e.653) Occ (W.h.7.2) OCin SAN ViW

Through correspondence with libraries reporting the ownership of a 1693 edition in the *National Union Catalog of pre-1956 Imprints* or in Wing, I have determined that the following own the first ed.:

Countway Library of Medicine, Boston, Mass.
H.E. Huntington Library, San Marino, Calif.
University of Michigan
University of Minnesota
Union Theological Seminary, New York (McAlpin Collection)
Williams College, Williamstown, Mass.

Those reporting the second edition are:
University of California at Berkeley
Medical Center, Duke University, Durham, N.C.
University of Georgia
H.E. Huntington Library, San Marino, Calif.
Lehigh University, Bethlehem, Penn.
University of North Carolina
University of Wisconsin at Madison

167. Education. 3d ed., 1695. 8°

Within a double rule, inner 140 × 76 mm, outer 148 × 85 mm: SOME | THOUGHTS | CONCERNING | Education. | [rule 72 mm] |
   Doctrina vires promovet infitas,
   Rectiq; cultus pectora roborant:
     Utcunq; defecere mores,
       Dedecorant bene nata culpæ.
Hor. L. IV. Od. 4. | [rule 73 mm] | 𝕿𝖍𝖊 𝕿𝖍𝖎𝖗𝖉 𝕰𝖉𝖎𝖙𝖎𝖔𝖓 𝕰𝖓𝖑𝖆𝖗𝖌𝖊𝖉. | double rule 73 mm] | LONDON, | Printed for *A.* and *J. Churchill*, [swash J] at the | *Black Swan* in *Pater-nofter-row*, 1695.

Coll: 8° (170 × 110 mm cut) A^4 B–2A^8 2B^4 [$ half signed]; 192 leaves; pp. *i–viii* 1–374 375–376 [= 384].

Contents: as no. 165-66 until B1ʳ-2B3ᵛ (1-374) text, 2B4ʳ·ᵛ (375-376) alphabetical index to sections in double cols.

Text (H6ᵛ): 29 lines; 136 (147) × 69 (84) mm; 93R. Medium-quality paper watermarked with a crowned horn and '6'. Page no. at outer corners of headlines. Topical headings of sections set ital. in outer margins.

HT: [double rule 68 mm] | SOME | THOUGHTS | CONCERNING | EDUCATION.

Headlines: Of EDUCATION. [swash U]

CW: Page. A2ᵛ *lofs* B1ᵛ there- [therefore] E4ʳ (fa-) miliar, K6ᵛ Rules; [Rules:] O7ᵛ appre- [apprehends,] Y7ᵛ (far-) ther

Notes: No longer anonymous, the dedication is signed and dated: "Your moſt humble and | moſt faithful Servant, *JOHN LOCKE*. 7 March. 1692. [O.S.]" It was published in late June (?) 1695 (cf. *Corr.* v. vii); it was advertised in the *London Gazette* no. 3098 for July 18-22, 1695. As to the number of copies printed, from the fact that a contract with the Churchills survives, we know no more than 1500 were printed. The contract (Bodleian Library MS. Locke b.1, fo. 173) promises to pay Locke "five pounds Sterl upon every Impression wee shall print or cause to be printed of his Booke called some thoughts concerning education, and Ten shillings p sheet printed for all additions that he shall make to the same, the Impressions not to exceed fiveteen hundred Bookes, & to deliver him Twenty five books bound in Calve skin Lettʳᵈ on every Impression . . ." The contract, signed by both Churchills, is dated June 20, 1694.

The quotation from Horace appears for this first time in this edition. It has been translated by Edward Bulwer Lytton, Baron Lytton, as follows:

"Still training speeds the inborn vigour's growth;
"Sound culture is the armour of the breast.
    "Where fails the moral lore,
        "Vice disennobles even the noblest born."[1]

The text has been expanded by adding new §§ 37, 62, 93-4, 98, 117, 176 and 205. Renumbering of sections was necessary because of this new material, but some sections from the 1693 edition were split; § 87 expanded into §§ 88-9, § 143 divided into §§ 150-1, § 157 into §§ 165-6, § 177 into §§ 188-90. But the 1st edition §§ 176-7 are combined into one, an expanded § 178; and there were two §§ 172 in the first edition. The 203 sections of the 1693 editions have become 216 sections here. The last section is numbered 217, but there is no § 213 here or in later English printings.

There are also many minor differences from the 1693 editions: corrections of spelling and punctuation, and some small expansions, often only a sentence or a phrase.

As with the 1693 edition, a list of recipients of copies given by the author survives (Bodley's MS Locke c.25, fo. 53), headed 'Education Copys 95'. Ten

---

[1] *The Odes and Epodes of Horace* (Edinburgh, 1869); reprinted in *The Odes of Horace, in English Verse* (London, 1929), p. 255.

names are the same as the earlier list: Lord Ashley, Bridges, Edward Clarke, Lady Forfar, Furley, Guenellon, William Molyneux, the Earl of Pembroke, and Treby. The new names (as recorded in *Corr.* viii. 454–8) are: Maurice Ashley Cooper; Mr. John Conyers (?); Pierre Coste; Charles Sackville, Earl of Dorset (as Lord Chamberlain); Andrew Fletcher of Saltoun; Robert Harley (later Earl of Oxford); Ecbert Lidell; Mr. Marlow (unindentified); Damaris Cudworth, Lady Masham; Samuel Pepys; Mrs. Pitt (? relative of Moses Pitt); Sir Fleetwood Sheppard; Mr. Teut (Marcus Antonius or Willem); and James Tyrrell.

The list in MS Locke f.29, p. 145 omits Bridges, but includes 'Chicheley' (? Sir John).

A microfilm copy of this edition is in the EEB collection, reel 793, no. 23.

References: Alston 10: 112; Attig 524; Axtell British 3; Christophersen p. 57; ESTC r000816; L.L. 1786; Wing² L2763.

Copies examined: Y   C   CaOTU (Locke L63.S66 1695)   Ck (Keynes A.12.11)   CLU-C   CtY (K8.L79/H695)   Gu (3i.2.ky; lacks t.p.)   Han (P-A 1748)   L   (8309.aa.38)   MH (*EC65.L7934.693sd)   NjP (Ex.6504.592.13)   O   (12.Theta [Θ].956)   PU (LB475.L6 1695)   TxDaM-P

168. Education. 4th ed., 1699. 8°

Within a double rule, inner 136 × 77 mm, outer 145 × 86 mm: SOME | THOUGHTS | CONCERNING | Education. | . . . [&c. as in no. 167, until 12th line:] | 𝕿𝖍𝖊 𝕱𝖔𝖚𝖗𝖙𝖍 𝕰𝖉𝖎𝖙𝖎𝖔𝖓 𝕰𝖓𝖑𝖆𝖗𝖌𝖊𝖉. | [double rule 74 mm] | LONDON, | Printed for A. and J. Churchill, [swash J] at the | Black Swan in Pater-noſter-row, 1699.

Coll: 8° (190 × 116 mm cut) A⁴ B–2B⁸ [$ half signed]; 196 leaves; pp. *i–viii* 1–368 367–380 *381–382* [= 392] Page no. 367–8 repeated.

Contents: as no. 165–7 until B1ʳ–2B7ᵛ (1–380) text, 2B8ʳ,ᵛ (*381–382*) alphabetical index of contents of sections in double cols.

Text (I1ᵛ): 29 lines; 135 (146) × 69 (83) mm; 93 R. Medium-quality paper watermarked with a horn within shield and letter H and D. Topical headings of sections set ital. in outer margins. Page no. at external corners of headlines.

HT: same as no. 167.

Headlines: *Of EDUCATION.* [swash U, C]

CW: Page. A2ᵛ *loſs* B1ᵛ there- [therefore] E4ʳ (Chil-) dren, K7ʳ Rules; [Rules:] O8ᵛ appre- [apprehends,] Y8ᵛ (far-) ther 2A8ᵛ Em- [Employment]

Notes: The edition was published late in November 1698 (Cf. *Corr.* vi.vii), presumably when the Churchills had used up their stock of the 3d ed. The title-page date of 1699 reflects the usual practice of dating works published late in the year with the following year's date. The work is largely a reprint of the third, but with new errors, especially of spelling, introduced. There are a few substantial changes: § 7 is expanded by one page, § 94 by half a page, and §§ 192–3 are slightly rephrased. The only large addition occurs in § 167, the section headed 'Latin', where more details about the skills of a tutor or teacher needed to encourage and instruct his pupil are described.

A very short list of recipents from the author of this edition is found in the Bodleian Library MS Locke c.25, fo. 53ᵛ: Abbé Jean-Baptiste Du Bos, Mr. Crell (? Samuel Crellius), and Dr. (later Sir) Thomas Molyneux (cf. *Corr.* viii.455-7).

We are fortunate to have evidence of the price of this edition. Edwin Wolf 2nd, in his article, "A Parcel of Books for the Province in 1700" (*The Pennsylvania Magazine of History and Biography*, 89, 1965: 428-46) gives details of a transaction entered into by James Logan, a bookseller in Philadelphia, with the Churchills to supply him some 100 volumes of their recent publications. The shipment included 6 copies of this edition at £ 1. 1s. 0d. or 3s. 6d. a copy, 6 copies of *Two Treatises of Government* at the same price, and 6 copies of Locke's *Essay* at £ 4. 4s. 0d. or 14s. each. The 'conger' of booksellers, as reported in *The Notebook of Thomas Bennet and Henry Clements* (ed. Hodgson and Blagdon, 1956, p. 159) pooled 700 copies, '35 drawn', for which they paid 1 s. 8 d. each, and sold to the trade for 2 s. 6 d. A microfilm copy of this edition is in the EEB collection, reel 793, no. 24.

References: Alston 10: 113; Attig 525; Axtell British 4; ESTC r000866; L.L. 1786a; T.C. III.113; Wing² L2764.

Copies examined: Y   C   C (Keynes)   CaOTU (Locke L63.S66 1699) CLU-C   CtY (K8.L79/H699)   Dt   [GOT]   L (8409.b.7)   MH (*EC65.L7934.693se)   O (8° P.210 Art.)   PPL¹ (Wing L2764/ Log3287.D)   PPL² (Log356.O)   PPL³ (8570.O)   ViU   Wol (Pa.233)

169. Education. 5th ed., 1705. 8°
Within a double rule, inner 139 × 74 mm, outer 147 × 82 mm: SOME | THOUGHTS | CONCERNING | Education. | [rule 70 mm] |
Doctrina vires promovet infitas,
Rectique cultus pectora roborant:
   Utcunque defecere mores,
      Dedecorant bene nata culpæ.
Hor. L. IV. Od. 4. | [rule 70 mm] | *By Mr.* JOHN LOCKE. [swash J] | [rule 71 mm] | 𝔗𝔥𝔢 𝔉𝔦𝔣𝔱𝔥 𝔈𝔡𝔦𝔱𝔦𝔬𝔫 𝔈𝔫𝔩𝔞𝔯𝔤𝔢𝔡. | [rule 70 mm] | LONDON, | Printed for A. and J. Churchill, [swash J] at the | *Black Swan* in Pater-no*ft*er-row, 1705.

Coll: 8° (188 × 115 mm cut) A⁴ B-2B⁸ 2C⁴ [$ half (+ Cc3) signed]; 200 leaves; pp. *i-viii* 1-390 391-392 [= 400].

Contents: as no. 165-68 until B1ʳ-2C3ᵛ (1-390) text, 2C4ʳ,ᵛ (391-392) alphabetical index of section topics in double cols. by page no., although the subheading for each column is 'Sect.'

Text (I1ᵛ): 30 lines; 139 (150) × 72 (86) mm; 93R. Medium-quality laid paper, with no visible watermark. Page no. at external ends of headlines.

HT: [double rule 71/69 mm] | SOME | THOUGHTS | CONCERNING | EDUCATION.
Headlines: *Of EDUCATION.* [swash D, U, A, N]
CW: Page. A2^v Cor- [Corruption] B2^r (con-) ſider, D5^r §.34. E4^r Who- [Whoever] K8^r (Wel-) come O8^v rea- [reaſon] U3^v Diffi- [Difficulties] Y7^r (Po-) ets, Z3^r (De *sic*) ſigns
Press figures: none.
Notes: This is the first edition of this work to have Locke's name on the title-page as well as at the end of the dedication, and the first posthumous edition, though Locke must have made substantial changes and expansions. In § 143, on 'breeding', five and a half printed pages have been added concerning 'roughness', 'contempt', 'censoriness', 'railery', 'contradiction', and 'captiousness'. The insertion in § 195 of a long quotation from La Bruyère's *Les Caractères, ou Mœurs de ce siècle*, appended to *Les Caractères de Théophraste* (1696 edition) is presumably Locke's own translation of that material, interrupted halfway by two paragraphs of commentary. There are also minor changes: a sentence added to § 7, a marginal note in § 60, the first sentence of § 93 rephrased, and two sentences added at the end of § 167.

This edition is signed at the end of the dedication, exactly like the first-fourth, but a misprint (one of many) occurs in the dating: '7 March, 1690.' Since this edition is the model for all subsequent English editions, whether issued separately or in a collected 'works', this error (for '1692' Old Style) has been perpetuated into the twentieth century.

The 'conger' of booksellers reported in *The Notebook of Thomas Bennet and Henry Clements* (1956, p. 159) pooled 400 copies in a transaction dated 11 July 1705, from which Bennet and Clements drew 35, paid the 'conger' 1/8 and sold others to the trade at 2 s. 6d, presumably allowing those others a profit of one shilling per copy.

A microfilm copy of this edition is in the collection, *The Eighteenth Century*, reel 1299, no. 5.

References: Alston 10:115; Attig 526; Axtell British 5; Christophersen p. 57 (issued "in the same year" as the 4th); ESTC t069876.
Copies examined: Y C C(Keynes) CtY (Lba14/693loc) L (8313.cc.41) O (Vet.A4 e.890)

170. Education. 6th ed., 1709. 8°
Within a double rule, inner 141 × 73 mm, outer 150 × 83 mm: SOME | THOUGHTS | CONCERNING | Education. | . . . [&c. as in no.169 until 12th line:] *By Mr.* JOHN LOCKE. [swash J] | | [rule 70 mm] | 𝔗𝔥𝔢 𝔖𝔦𝔵𝔱𝔥 𝔈𝔡𝔦𝔱𝔦𝔬𝔫 𝔈𝔫𝔩𝔞𝔯𝔤𝔢𝔡. | LONDON, | Printed for *A.* and *J. Churchill*, [swash J] at the | *Black Swan* in *Pater-noſter-row*, 1709.
Coll: 8° (195 × 120 mm cut) A^4 B–2B^8 2C^4 [$ half signed]; 200 leaves; pp. *i–viii* 1–390 391–392 [= 400].
Contents: as no. 169.

Text (I7ᵛ): 30 lines; 139 (150) × 72 (86) mm; 93 R. Good-quality laid paper, with foolscap (?) watermark. Topical headings set ital. in outer margins. Page no. at outer ends of headlines.

HT: [double rule 71/69 mm] | SOME | THOUGHTS | CONCERNING | EDUCATION.

Headlines: *Of EDUCATION.* [swash D, U, T, N]

CW: Page. Same as no. 169 except the following: D5ʳ §.34. The D5ᵛ §.35. The D8ʳ thought [thoughts,] F6ʳ pre- [prefent;] G1ᵛ (Mi-) ftake [ftake,] L1ʳ love [love,] L4ʳ In- [Inclination] L4ᵛ Tem- [Tempers,] L5ʳ Sea- [Sea-Chart;] Q3ʳ Con- [contrary] X1ʳ Solicifms [folicifms] X2ʳ Part Z3ʳ (De-) figns [Signs *sic*] 2B2ᵛ §. 205. 2B8ᵛ (head-) ftrong [ftrong,]

Press figures: none.

Notes: A line-by-line reprint of 5th ed. (no. 169), including the misdating of the dedication. There is a microfilm copy of this edition in *The Eighteenth Century*, reel 4448, no. 2.

References: Alston 10:116; Attig 527; Axtell British 6; ESTC t069877.

Copies examined: Y   CtY (Lba14/693lcd)   L (1493 r.40; sheet 2B misfolded, leaves in sequence: 2 1 3-6 8 7)   O (Vet.A4 e.873)   Oc (O.s.9.3)   PPL (Ia Lock/677839.O (Wolf))   PU (LB475.L6A3)

171. Education, 1710. 12°. Piracy.

Within a double rule, inner 128 × 68 mm, outer 134 × 75 mm : SOME | THOUGHTS | CONCERNING | EDUCATION. | [rule 65 mm] |
Doctrina vires promovet in fitas,
Rectique cultus pectora roborant:
  Utcunque defecere mores,
    Dedecorant bene nata culpæ.
Hor. L. IV. Od. 4. | [rule 66 mm] | *By Mr.* JOHN LOCKE. [swash J] | [rule 64 mm] | LONDON, | Printed for a Society of Stationers, and | Sold by *J.* Baker [swash J] at the *Black Boy* in Pater- | *Nofter-Row.* 1710.

Coll: 12° (160 × 95 mm cut) A-N¹² O⁶ [$ half (-I6, K6, L6, M6, N6) signed; E2 signed 'C2']; 162 leaves; pp. *i–vi* 1-162 169-322 323-324 [= 324]. Page no. 163-8 omitted.

Contents: A1ʳ (*i*) title (verso blank), A2ʳ-A3ᵛ (*iii–vi*) dedication, A4ʳ-O5ᵛ (1-322) text, O6ʳ,ᵛ (*323-4*) alphabetical index of contents by page no. in double cols.

Text (B7ᵛ): 33 lines; 135 (146) × 72 mm; 83 R. Pages 319-322 set 41 lines, 66 R. Poor-quality paper, without watermarks. Page no. at external ends of headlines. Topical headings set ital. within page text block.

HT: [double rule 70/71 mm] | SOME | THOUHGTS [sic] | Concerning | EDUCATION.

Headlines: *Of EDUCATION.*

CW: Page. A3ʳ (*ver-*) *tuous,* D4ᵛ(In-) convenience G7ᵛ (Com-) men- [mendation] K2ʳ (Bo-) dies, M6ʳ (*Geometry;*) wherein [*metry;* wherein] N10ᵛ (na-) tural O4ʳ Advantages

Press figures: none.
Notes: Reprints the text of no. 170, but without edition statement. A possible piracy, given the ambiguities of copyright law, with the lapse of the Licensing Act in 1695. The Churchills used the sheets of this printing for their 7th ed. (no. 172).
References: Alston 10:116; Attig 528; Axtell British 7; Christophersen p. 101; ESTC t069878.
Copies examined: Y   CLU-C   L (1030 f.2)   O (Vet.A4 f.828)   PPL (Ia Lock/64499.D)

172. Education. 7th ed., 1712. 12°. Two issues.
172A. First issue: Within a double rule, inner 113 × 65 mm, outer 120 × 70 mm: SOME | THOUGHTS | CONCERNING | EDUCATION. | [rule 59 mm] | . . . [&c. as in no. 171, until 10th line:] Hor. *L. IV. Od.* 4. | [rule 59 mm] | *By Mr.* JOHN [swash J] LOCKE. | [broken rule 63 mm] | *The Seventh* Edition. | [rule 62 mm] | LONDON, | Printed for *A.* and *J. Churchill*, [swash J] at the | *Black Swan* in *Pater-Nofter-Row*, 1712.
Coll: 12° (160 × 95 mm cut) A^{12} (±A1) B–N^{12} O^6 [$ half (-I6, K6, L6, M6, N6) signed; E2 signed 'C2')]; 162 leaves; pp. *i–iv* 1–162 169–322 323–324 [=324]. Page no. 163–168 omitted.
172B. Second issue: as above until 13th line, intact rule 60 mm] | *The Seventh* Edition. | [rule 61 mm] | LONDON, | Printed for *A.* and *J. Churchill*, [swash J] and | Sold by *John Kent*, [swash J, K] at the *Black Swan* | and *Bible* in St. *Paul's Church-Yard*, [swash Y] 1712.
Coll: same as first issue except A^{12} (±A1).
Contents, Text, HT and *Headlines* and catchwords identical with no. 171.
Press figures: none.
Notes: Here I assume the Churchills caught up with the pirates, and took over their remaining stock. Only the title leaves of these issues are cancellantia. The same errors in caption and pagination, and lines per page 319–22 occur. Even though the 'Society of Stationers' and J. Baker thought to capitalize on the popularity of this work, the Churchills must have encountered difficulty in selling it, for they brought in John Kent to help move it. Kent is not listed in Plomer.
  In the second issue, in the quotation from Horace, the 't' in *cultus* and (in some copies only) the 'e' in *mores*' have fallen below the line.
References: Alston 10:117 (1st issue only); Attig 529 (2d issue only); Axtell British 8 (2d issue only); ESTC t214442 (1st issue), t069879 (2d issue).
Copies examined:
  172A (1st): EXu   O (2621 f.49)
  172B (2d): Y   L (1485.n.15)   MH (*EC65.L7934.693sh)   Obr (Sigma D.7.15)

173. Education. 1721. 12°.
Within a double rule, inner 131 × 72 mm, outer 139 × 80 mm: SOME | THOUGHTS | CONCERNING | EDUCATION. | [rule 69 mm] | ... [&c. as in no. 171, until 10th line:] HOR. L. IV. Od. 4. | [rule 68 mm] | *By Mr.* JOHN LOCKE. [swash J] | [rule 68 mm] | *LONDON:* | Printed for A. CHURCHILL; and Sold | by W. TAYLOR, at the *Ship* and *Black* | *Swan* in *Pater-Noſter-Row*. M DCC XXI.
Coll: same as no.172, except A^{12} (±A1).
Contents and *Text* identical with no.171-2, with a different cancellans title leaf, on extremely poor quality paper, without watermark.
Press figures: none.
Notes: Though John Churchill has here dropped out of bookselling, Awnsham Churchill is still using up the sheets from the 1710 piracy (no.171). The same pagination, errors, lines per pp. 319-22 and catchwords, and signature positions occur. The title leaf is still a cancellans, without an edition statement.
References: Attig 530; Axtell British 9; ESTC t179629 (O sole loc.)
Copies examined: O (Vet.A4. f. 1548)   NjR (X LB475.L6 1721)

174. Education. 8th ed., 1725. 12°.
Within a double rule, inner 138 × 69 mm, outer 142 × 75 mm: SOME | THOUGHTS | CONCERNING | EDUCATION. | ... [&c. as in no. 171 until 12th line:] By JOHN LOCK, *Eſq*; | [rule 67 mm] | 𝕮𝖍𝖊 𝕮𝖎𝖌𝖍𝖙𝖍 𝕮𝖉𝖎𝖙𝖎𝖔𝖓. | [rule 67 mm] | *LONDON:* [swash D] | Printed by *H. P.* for *A.C.* and Sold by | JOHN OSBORN and THO. LONG- | MAN at the *Ship* and *Black Swan* in | *Pater-Noſter-Row.* | [rule 23 mm] | M.DCC.XXV.
Coll: 12° (165 × 95 mm cut) A^{12} (±A1) B-O^{12} [$ half (-L6, M6, N6, O6) signed; D2-4 signed 'C2', 'D4' and 'D4' respectively; G4 and G5 both signed 'G4']; 168 leaves; pp. *i-vi* 1-162 169-331 332-336 [=336]. Page no. 163-8 omitted.
Contents: A1ʳ (*i*) title (verso blank), A2ʳ-A3ᵛ (*iii-vi*) dedication, signed '*JOHN LOCKE.*' and dated '*March* 7. 1690.'; A4ʳ-O10ʳ (*1-331*) text, O10ᵛ-O11ʳ (*332-333*) contents by page no., O11ᵛ-O12 (*334-336*) blank.
Text (C6ᵛ): 33 lines; 137 (146) × 73 mm; 83R. Medium-quality laid paper, with watermark Heawood 2804. Topical headings for sections in itals. inset within page block. Page no. at outer corners of headlines, except p. 280 has its no. at the inner (right) corner, and p. 285 has it in the upper left. Page 331 has tailpiece of Minerva in wheeled chariot drawn by peacocks, within a cloud, 25 × 44 mm.
HT (A4ʳ): [orn. rule of small irons 5 × 72 mm] | SOME | THOUGHTS | CONCERNING | EDUCATION.
Headlines: *Of* EDUCATION.
CW: Page. C11ᵛ Autho- [Authority] E4ᵛ weigh- [weighing] L3ᵛ Know- [Knowledge.]

Press figures: Page. (Asterisks indicate variants or lacking in some copies. See *Copies examined* below.) 28 (B5ᵛ)-2* 42 (C2ᵛ)-1* 52 (C5ᵛ)-1* 54 (C6ᵛ)-1* 80 (D7ᵛ)-2 90 (D12ᵛ)-1 159 (G11ʳ)-2 161 (G12ʳ)-2 182 (H7ᵛ)-2* 206 (I7ᵛ)-2* 212 (I10ᵛ)-2* 229 (K7ʳ)-1* 231 (K8ʳ)-1* 252 (L6ᵛ)-2* 254 (L7ᵛ)-2* 274 (M5ᵛ)-1 276 (M6ᵛ)-1 300 (N6ᵛ)-1 303 (N8ʳ)-1*

Notes: The title leaf is a cancellans. The text has been newly set, though it closely follows the previous editions (no. 171-3) in making the same pagination error and having the same sixth leaves unsigned. The signature positions are different. The printer is possibly Henry Plowman. I am unsure of the identity of the bookseller 'A.C.' Axtell gives the publisher as Awnsham Churchill: I have found no copies with such an imprint (unless he so identifies 'A.C.').

References: Alston 10:119; Attig 531; Axtell British 10; ESTC t128964.

Copies examined: O¹ (Vet.A4 f.874; lacks figure on p. 303) L (1507/852; has variant press figures: 28-1 52-2 54-2 229-2 231-2 252-1 254-1 and none on pp. 42 & 303) O² (Vet.A4 f.1305; has variant figures on 159-1 161-1 182-1 206-1 212-1 229-2 and 231-2)

175. Education. '9th ed.', Dublin, 1728. 12° in 6s. Two issues

175A. First issue: SOME | THOUGHTS | CONCERNING | EDUCATION. | [rule 70 mm] | . . . [4 lines of verse, as in no. 171, until 9th line: rule 71 mm] | HOR. L. IV. OD. 4. | [rule 71 mm] | By *JOHN LOCKE*, [swash J] Eſq; | [rule 70 mm] | The NINTH EDITION. | [rule 70 mm] | Publiſh'd at the Requeſt of ſeveral of the Nobility of | this KINGDOM. | [rule 67 mm] | *DUBLIN:* | Printed by WILL. FORREST, in *Hoey*'s | Alley, *Warbourgh*'s Street, for BEN. | HICKEY, Bookſeller in *Eſſex* Street, near *Eſſex* Gate, MDCCXXVIII.

Coll: 12° in 6s (165 × 95 mm cut) A⁶ B-2E⁶ [$ half signed]; 168 leaves; pp. i-vi 1-325 326-330 [=336]. With page numbering errors; see *Notes* below.

175B. Second issue, as above but with rules 71, 72, 70, 71 and 72 mm respectively, until imprint: *DUBLIN:* [swash U] | Printed by S. POWELL, | For GEORGE RISK, at *Shakeſpear*'s Head, | GEORGE EWING, at the *Angel* and *Bible*, | And WILLIAM SMITH, at the *Hercules*, | Bookſellers, in *Dame*'s-ſtreet, M DCC XX VIII.

Coll: same as first issue, except A⁶ (±A1) and page numbering errors corrected.

Contents: A1ʳ (i) title (verso blank), A2ʳ-A3ᵛ (iii-vi) dedication, A4ʳ-2E4ʳ (1-325) text, 2E4ᵛ blank, 2E5ʳ-2E6ʳ (327-9) contents by page no., 2E6ᵛ blank.

Illustration: front. is an engraved port. of Locke by P. Simms, badly copied after Kneller, the oval frame within a rectangle 128 × 79 mm, subscribed '*Johannes Locke*', on a plate 141 × 82 mm.

Text (E5ᵛ): 33 lines; 132 (143) × 71 mm; 81R. Some early pages have 34 lines, later ones 32. Poor-quality paper, with illegible watermark (? letter N). Dedication set 33 lines 80 ital. Page no. at external ends of headlines. Topical headings of sections inset in page block in ital.

HT: [framed headpiece of a Minerva seated on a shell in the sea, a horn blower (Pan?) at left, a mermaid right, 25 × 71 mm] | SOME | THOUGHTS | CONCERNING | *EDUCATION*. [swash U, T]
Headlines: *Of* EDUCATION.
CW: Page. A3^r *ha-* [*having*] H6^r Chil- [Children] Q6^v §, 126. [§. 126.] X2^v (Scho-) lars. Z3^v (im-) prints 2D3^r can- [cannot]
Notes: The title leaf in the second issue is a cancellans. My copy of the earlier issue of this edition has incorrect page numbers in sheet Z. The copy reported to the ESTC file (by the University of Liverpool Library) states 'pages 264, 265 misnumbered 304 and 305': perhaps the whole sheet was originally numbered 299–310. Mine has the pages numbered: 259 300–301 262 303 264–265 306 267 308–309 270, that is 264–5 are correct but other pages are incorrect. In the later issue the page numbers have been corrected (and there is a different imprint). My copy of the first issue also has 12 pages at the end (an extra sheet 'a', $1 signed) containing 185 subscribers' names (a1^r–5^r, 5^v blank) and an advt. for "*Books, lately Printed for* Ferdinando Davys, *and fold in* Effex *Street, near* Effex *Gate*." (not found elsewhere, and perhaps not belonging to this work).

A notable, if not ironic misprint starts in this edition: in § 161, captioned '*Drawing*', there is a line reading: "I do not mean that I would have your Son a *perfect Printer* . . ." Ironic because Locke was so outspoken about the character faults of "all those who make a trade and gain out of" books (cf. Introd., pp. ix–xi). Prior to this edition, the words were, correctly typeset, 'a *perfect Painter*.' This error is continued in later editions, including those published in London and Edinburgh; it is not corrected until the 13th London edition of 1764.

The omission of page no. 163–168 from earlier printings is here corrected, though not in the 'contents of the sections': that index is obviously copied from entries no. 171–174.

There is an unframed headpiece on p. *iii* (cornucopia, with cherubs, 12 × 68 mm); a tailpiece on p. 325 (ornamental shield surrounded by lions, 39 × 48 mm), and on p. 329 (wild man with crossed clubs, 18 × 34 mm). The advertisement (sheet a) is headed by a framed headpiece of a landscape scene, a shepherdess with crook at right, 23 × 68 mm.

References: Alston 10:120 (B issue); Attig 532 (B issue); Axtell British 11 (only 'Dublin' given as imprint); ESTC t155625 (A issue; copy also at Liverpool Univ. Lib.: Y72.2.81); ESTC t175208 (B issue).
Copies examined:
A (first issue): Y   D (Dublin 1728 (27); pagination not recorded)
B (2nd issue): C (Hib.7.728.23)   O (Vet.A4 f.700)

176. Education. 9th ed., 1732. 12°
Within a double rule, inner 133 × 72 mm, outer 139 × 78 mm: SOME | THOUGHTS | CONCERNING | EDUCATION. | [rule 67 mm] | . . . [&c. as in no. 171, until 10th line:] HOR. L. IV. *Od.* 4. | [rule 66

mm] | By *JOHN LOCKE*, [swash J] Efq; | [rule 66 mm] | *The* NINTH EDITION. | [rule 67 mm] | *LONDON:* | Printed for A. BETTESWORTH and C. HITCH | in *Pater-Nofter-Row*, J. PEMBERTON in | *Fleetftreet*, and E. SYMON in *Cornhill*. | [rule 22 mm] | M DCC XXXII.
Coll: 12° (165 × 95 mm cut) A–O¹² [$5 signed]; 168 leaves; pp. *i–vi* 1 2–162 169–331 332–336 [= 336]. Page no. 163–8 omitted.
Contents: A1ʳ (*i*) title (verso blank), A2ʳ–A3ᵛ (*iii–vi*) dedication, A4ʳ–O10ʳ (*1–331*) text, O10ᵛ blank, O11ʳ,ᵛ (*333–334*) contents of the sections by page no., O12 (*335–6*) blank.
Text (B8ʳ): 33 lines; 137 (146) × 73 mm; 83R. Medium-quality paper with unicorn watermark (? like Heawood 4010) and letter H; sheet A in O¹ copy has a 'V' within a double circle at upper outer edge of leaves 11–12. Page no. at external end of headlines. Dedication set 33 lines 82 ital. Topical headings of sections set ital. within page block.
HT: [unframed headpiece, lion left, chasing flowers, 9 × 75 mm] | SOME | THOUGHTS | CONCERNING | *EDUCATION*.
Headlines: *Of* EDUCATION.
CW: Page. A2ᵛ (*in-*) *corrigible* B5ᵛ Quali- [Quality;] D11ʳ (Re-) wards H5ʳ (rea-) fon K7ᵛ (play-) ing M4ʳ capa- [capable] O9ʳ Gen- [Gentleman]
Press figures: iv (A2ᵛ)-3 33 (B8ʳ)-2 52 (C5ᵛ)-3 75 (D5ʳ)-2 OR 90 (D12ᵛ)-2 102 (E6ᵛ)-2 104 (E7ᵛ)-3 124 (F5ᵛ)-2 130 (F8ᵛ)-2 153 (G8ᵛ)-2 191 (H12ʳ)-3 203 (I6ʳ)-3 228 (K6ᵛ)-3 255 (L8ʳ)-2 274 (M5ᵛ)-2 280 (M8ᵛ)-3 304 (N8ᵛ)-3 322 (O5ᵛ)-3
Notes: A line-by-line reprint of no. 174, with the same pagination error. Dedication still dated '*March* 7. 1690.' Notice the varying press figures in sheet D. The typographical error noticed in the Dublin edition of 1728 (no.175) also occurs in this and the following London, Dublin and Edinburgh editions (until 1764); it is difficult to think an English printer made the same error as the Dublin one independently (who copied from whom?).
References: Alston 10:121; Attig 533; Axtell British 12; ESTC t069880.
Copies examined: Y (lacks A1; with figure on p. 90) CaOTU (Locke L63.S66 1732; with figure on p. 75) L (08311 h.122; with figure on p. 75) O¹ (Vet.A4 f.1019; with figure on p. 90) O² (Vet.A4 f.725; with figure on p. 75) Occ (370.1 Lo; with figure on p. 90) PPL (Ia Lock/51.D)

177. Education. '10th ed.', Dublin, 1737. 12°. Found with Rollin's *New Thoughts* . . .
SOME | THOUGHTS | CONCERNING | *EDUCATION*. [swash D, T] | [rule 72 mm] | . . . [&c. as in no. 171, until 10th line: HOR. L. IV. OD. 4. | [rule 73 mm] | By *JOHN LOCKE*, [swash J] Efq; | [rule 72 mm] | The TENTH EDITION. | [rule 73 mm] | Publifh'd at the Requeft of feveral of the Nobility | of this KINGDOM. | [rule 73 mm] | *DUBLIN:* | Printed by R. REILLY on *Cork-Hill*; | For GEORGE RISK, GEORGE EWING, and WIL- | LIAM SMITH, Bookfellers, in *Dame's-ftreet*. | [rule 33 mm] | M,DCC,XXXVII.

Coll: 12° (172 × 100 mm cut) A-K¹² [$5 signed]; 120 leaves; pp. *1-6 7-237* 238-240.
Contents: A1ʳ (*1*) title (verso blank), A2ʳ-A3ᵛ (*3-6*) dedication, A4ʳ-K11ʳ (*7-237*) text, K11ᵛ blank, K12ʳ,ᵛ (*239-240*) contents of the sections by page no.
Illustration: front. is port. of Locke (after Kneller) signed 'P. Simms.', same as found in 1728 Dublin ed. (no. 175).
Text (E5ᵛ): 39 lines; 143 (152) × 75 mm; 73R. Some pp. have 38 lines (138 (147) × 74 mm). Medium-quality laid paper watermarked with bunch of grapes. Page no. at external ends of headlines. Topical headings of sections inset in ital. within page block. Framed headpiece on p. 3 is a winged Mercury & trumpets, surrounded by eagles, 24 × 74 mm; on p. 7, a cameo port. within scrollwork, 25 × 76 mm; and a tailpiece on p. 237 of pheasants facing inwards beside an urn surmonted by a head, 39 × 42 mm.
Headlines: Of EDUCATION.
CW: Page. B10ʳ §.52. Beat- [§.52. Beating] C11ᵛ (remem-) ber, E4ᵛ have H4ᵛ would ('f' at left end of line; see *Notes*) K7ᵛ Expences,
Notes: Straightforward reprint, newly set. Last line of p. 126 (in § 115) reads: " uck every Day a new nurse, I make account it", that is, the long S from 'suck' has fallen to the direction line. Further, § 175 (on p. 194) incorrectly numbered '§ 159.' and § 164 called '146'. The error, '*Printer*' (for '*Painter*') still occurs in § 161.

Usually this edition is found bound with Rollin's *New Thoughts* (1738; see no. 179. Cf. Alston).

A microfilm copy is in the collection, *The Eighteenth Century*, reel 3781, no. 1.
References: Alston 10:122; Attig 534; Axtell British 13 (listed with Rollin); ESTC t110612.
Copies examined: O (Vet.A4 f.650; with Rollin) L (1568/1057; with Rollin)

178. Education. 10th ed., 1738. 12°
SOME | THOUGHTS | CONCERNING | EDUCATION. | [rule 71 mm] |
Doctrina vires promovet infitas,
Rectique cultus pectora roborant:
  Utcumque defecere mores,
    Dedecorant bene nata culpæ. |
HOR. lib. IV. od. 4. | [rule 70 mm] | *By* JOHN LOCKE, [swash J] *Efq*. | [rule 70 mm] | The TENTH EDITION. | [rule 71 mm] | *LONDON,* | Printed for A. BETTESWORTH and C. HITCH, | in *Pater-Nofter-Row*; J. and J. PEMBERTON, | in *Fleetftreet*; and E. SYMON, in *Cornhill*. | [rule 28 mm] | M DCC XXXVIII.
Coll., *Text* and *Headlines* same as no. 176, including omission of page no. 163-168. Medium-quality paper without watermarks.

Contents: A1ʳ (*i*) title (verso blank), A2ʳ–A3ᵛ (*iii–vi*) dedication, A4ʳ–O10ʳ (*1–331*) text, O10ᵛ–O11ʳ (*332–333*) contents by page no., O11ᵛ (*334*) advt. for books by Bettesworth and Hitch, O12ʳ (*335*) advt. by J. & J. Pemberton, O12ᵛ (*336*) advt. by E. Symon.
CW: Page. C11ᵛ Autho- [Authority] E4ᵛ weighing L3ᵛ Know- [Knowledge.] O3ʳ can- [cannot]
Press figures: none.
Note: A line-by-line reprint of no.176 (1732).
References: Alston 10:124; Attig 535; Axtell British 14; ESTC t069881.
Copies examined: Y C (7700 d.670) CLU-C (*PR3541.L57L6 1738) CtY (Lba14/693*l*ck; sheets B–O only; sheet A is of 1752 ed., no.181) L (8309 aa.53) O (Vet.A4 f.875) PPL (Ia Lock/Log1632.D (Mackenzie))

179. Education. Dublin, 1738. 12°. With Rollin.
SOME | THOUGHTS | CONCERNING | *EDUCATION*, [swash D, T] | By *JOHN LOCKE*, [swash J] Eſq; | To which are added, | NEW | THOUGHTS | CONCERNING | *EDUCATION*, | By Mr. *ROLLIN*. | [double rule 73 mm] | *DUBLIN:* | Printed by R. REILLY on *Cork-Hill*; | For G. RISK, G. EWING, and W. SMITH, | Bookſellers in *Dame's-Street*. | M,DCC,XXXVIII.
Coll: 12° (172 × 100 mm cut) A¹² (±A1) B–K¹² ²A–²D¹² [$5 signed]; 168 leaves; pp. *1–6 7–237 238–240; i–ii iii–x 1–84 85–86* [= 336].
Contents, Text, Headlines and CW for Locke's text (pp. *1–240*) are identical with no. 177, but title leaf is a cancellans, with new imprint date, to include Rollin's work. There is also a front. port. of Locke by P. Simms, as found in no. 177.
Rollin's title, ²A1ʳ: NEW | THOUGHTS | CONCERNING | *EDUCATION*, [swash D, T] | BY | Mr. *ROLLIN*. | Late Principal of the University of PARIS, | now Profeſſor of Eloquence in the Royal College, | Member of the Royal Academy of Inſcriptions, and | Author of the Method of Teaching and Studying the | BELLES LETTRES. | [rule 72 mm] | Done from the *French*, with Notes. | [rule 73 mm] | *DUBLIN:* | . . . [&c. as on A1ʳ above, until penultimate line:] Bookſellers, in *Dame's-Street*. | M,DCC,XXXVIII.
Contents of Rollin's work: ²A1ʳ (*i*) title (verso blank), ²A2ʳ,ᵛ (*iii–iv*) 'The Preface', ²A3–5ᵛ (*v–x*) translator's pref., ²A6ʳ–²D11ᵛ (*1–84*) text, ²D12 (*85–86*) blank.
Note: A reissue of no. 176, with the same errors on p. 126 and p. 194, but now officially accompanied by Rollin's work. Rollin's text is a translation of Book I of his *De la manière d'enseigner et d'étudier les belles-lettres, par rapport à l'esprit et au coeur*, first published in 4 vols., 1726-28 (cf. Cioranescu 53926). Charles Rollin (1661–1741) was rector of the University of Paris in 1694; he wrote chiefly on ancient history. A critical notice of his historical work, pejoratively speaking, can be found in the *Bibliothèque raisonnée* 26 (1741): 77 et seq. A copy of Rollin's work is in

the microfilm set *The Eighteenth Century*, reel 3781, no. 2 (following film copy of the Dublin 1737 ed., no. 177).

References: Alston 10:123; Attig 536; Axtell British 15; ESTC t155628 (for Rollin: t110613).

Copies examined: O (Vet.A4 f.655) C (Hib.7.738.4; lacks port.) CtY (Lba14/693*l*ch) PPL (Ia Lock 66166.D, lacks port.; ex lib. Wm. Rush)

180. Education. 11th ed., 1745. 12°
SOME | THOUGHTS | CONCERNING | EDUCATION. | . . . [&c. as in no. 178 until 10th line:] HOR. lib. iv. od. 4. | [rule 74 mm] | *By* JOHN LOCKE, [swash J] *Efq*; | [rule 75 mm] | *The* [swash T] ELEVENTH EDITION. | [double rule 74 mm] | *LONDON:* | Printed for A. WARD, S. BIRT, T. OSBORNE, | C. HITCH, J. OSWALD, A. MILLAR, J. HODGES, | H. PEMBERTON, and M. COOPER. | [rule 17 mm] | M DCC XLV.

Coll: 12° (172 × 100 mm cut) A–O^{12} [$5 signed]; 168 leaves; pp. *i–vi 1* 2–305 305 307–325 326–330 [= 336]. Page no. 305 repeated, 306 omitted.

Contents: A1^r (*i*) title (verso blank), A2^r–A3^v (*iii–vi*) dedication, A4^r–O10^r (*1–325*) text, O10^v–O11^r (*326–327*) contents, O11^v–O12^r (*328–329*) advt. by C. Hitch, O12^v (*330*) advt. by S. Birt.

Text (E10^r): 33 lines; 135 (145) × 74 mm; 83R. Some early pages have 32 lines (130 (139) × 74 mm). Good-quality laid paper with fleur-de-lys watermark. Page no. at external ends of headlines. Dedication set 32 lines, 81 ital. Page 325 has orn. tailpiece of vase with fruit and scrollwork, 34 × 44 mm.

HT: [double roll of small crowns, 2d roll inverted, 7 × 74 mm] | SOME | THOUGHTS | CONCERNING | *EDUCATION.*

Headlines: *Of* EDUCATION.

CW: Page. C11^v Autho- [Authority] E4^v weighing L3^v Know- [Knowledge.] O3^r can- [cannot]

Press figures: 15 (A11^r)-3 16 (A11^v)-3 40 (B11^v)-I 55 (C7^r)-I 64 (C11^v)-I 79 (D7^r)-I 81 (D8^r)-I 92 (E1^v)-2 94 (E2^v)-2 118 (F2^v)-3 125 (F6^r)-3 142 (G2^v)-2 184 (G12^v)-3 198 (I6^v)-2 225 (K8^v)-3 234 (K12^v)-3 248 (L7^v)-2 255 (L11^r)-2 280 (M11^v)-I 292 (N5^v)-3 295 (N7^r)-3 317 (O6^r)-I

Notes: A line-by-line reprint of no. 178, but earlier errors in page numbering have here been corrected, and a new one created. There is a microfilm copy in *The Eighteenth Century*, reel 4658, no. 1.

References: Alston 10:125; Attig 537; Axtell British 16; ESTC t069882.

Copies examined: O (Vet A.4 f.1306) C (7240 d.83) CaOTU (Locke L63.S66 1745) CLU-C (*PR3541.L57S6 1745) L (1490.s.22) PPL (Ia Lock/69013.D)

181. Education. 12th ed., 1752. 12°
SOME | THOUGHTS | CONCERNING | EDUCATION. | [rule 72 mm] | . . . [&c. as in no. 178 until 9th line:] *Dedecorant benè nata culpæ.* | HOR. lib. iv. od. 4. | [rule 72 mm] | *By* JOHN LOCKE, [swash J] Efq;

| [rule 72 mm] | The TWELFTH EDITION. | [double rule 72 mm] | LONDON: | Printed for S. BIRT, D. BROWNE, T. LONGMAN, | J. SHUCKBURGH, C. HITCH and L. HAWES, | J. HODGES, J. OSWALD, A. MILLAR, J. and J. | RIVINGTON, J. WARD, and M. COOPER. | [rule 22 mm] | M,DCC,LII.

Coll: 12° (164 × 100 mm) A–O^{12} [$6 signed]; 168 leaves; pp. *i–vi 1* 2–325 *326–330* [= 336]. Leaf I2 signed 'I^2'.

Contents, Text, Headlines and CW same as no.180, with different press figures. Issued without a frontispiece. Medium-quality paper watermarked with a fleur-de-lys and 'VII'.

Press figures: 15 (A11^r)-5 33 (B8^r)-2 56 (C7^v)-2 138 (F12^v)-3 150 (G6^v)-2 172 (H5^v)-3 201 (I8^r)-2 222 (K6^v)-4 246 (L6^v)-2 262 (M2^v)-4 305 (N12^r)-6 306 (N12^v)-6 316 (O5^v)-5 319 (O7^r)-4

Notes: This is a line-by-line reprint of the 1745 edition (no. 180). Yale's copy is a mixed-sheet copy: only sheet A of this edition, sheets B–O are the sheets of the 1738 ed. (no. 178).

References: Alston 10:127; Attig 538; Axtell British 17; Christophersen p. 101; ESTC t069883.

Copies examined: O (Vet.A5 f.654) CtY (sheet A only: Lba14/693lck; trimmed to 162 × 96 mm; see *Notes* above) L (8307.c.21) PPL (Ia Lock/ 268.D) Vat

182. Education. '12th ed.', Edinburgh, 1752. 12°
SOME | THOUGHTS | CONCERNING | EDUCATION. |
  Doctrina [swash D] *vires promovet in ſitas,*
  Rectique cultus pectora roborant:
    Utcumque defecere mores,
      Dedecorant [swash D] *bene nata culpæ.*
| HOR. lib. iv. 4. | By *JOHN LOCKE,* [swash J] Eſq; | *The* [swash T] TWELFTH EDITION. | *EDINBURGH:* | Printed for J. BROWN, and ſold by him at his | Shop in the *Parliament-Cloſe*, and the Book- | ſellers in Town and Country. 1752.

Coll: 12° (165 × 98 mm cut) A–O^{12} [$ half (-A3, -A6, -B6, -C6) signed]; 168 leaves; pp. *i–vi 1* 2–325 *326–330* [= 336].

Contents: A1^r (*i*) title (verso blank), A2^r–A3^v (*iii–vi*) dedication, A4^r–O10^r (*1– 325*) text, O10^v–O11^r (*326–7*) contents by page no., O11^r (*328*) advt. for 4 titles 'JUST PUBLISHED', O12^r (*329*) advt. for 'New Books of Entertainment' (chiefly novels) 'lately published', O12^v blank.

Illustration: front. is oval framed portrait of Locke, facing right, on a pedestal base, signed '*G. Kneller pin^t. T Phinn sculp.*', poorly done, subscribed '*Johannes Locke*', 137 × 84 mm, on plate 154 × 92 mm.

Text (C5^v): 33 lines; 136 (145) × 72 mm; 83R. Good-quality laid paper, chainlines horizontal. Fleur-de-lys watermark, with 'IV' at outer edge of leaves A8 and B11. Unidentified tailpiece on O10^r (p. 325) of a lion's face between monkeys each holding clubs and clutching manes (?) of facing

horses, initial W with small p or d as part of W, 48 × 70 mm. Page no. at outer corners of headlines.
HT: [double roll of crowns, 2d inverted, 7×71 mm] | SOME | THOUGHTS | CONCERNING | *EDUCATION*.
Headlines: Of EDUCATION.
CW: Page. A2ᵛ *after-* [*afterwards*] C11ᵛ Autho- [Authority] E4ʳ not G3ᵛ in- [injure] L3ᵛ Know- [Knowledge.] O3ʳ can- [cannot]
Notes: A line-by-line reprint of the 1745 London edition (no. 180). Sections are numbered 1–215, 217 (instead of the usual omission of § 213). Section 199, in error, called '109'. A microfilm copy of this edition is *The Eighteenth Century*, reel 3687, no. 8.
References: Alston 10:126; Attig 539; Axtell British 18; ESTC t155626.
Copies examined: Y   CaOTU (Locke L63.S66 1752)   CtY (Lba14/693*lcl*)
  L (1578/7083)   O (Vet.A5 f.1295)

183. Education. 13th ed., 1764. 12°
SOME | THOUGHTS | CONCERNING | EDUCATION. | [rule 72 mm] |
Doɛ́trina vires promovet in ſitas,
Reɛ́tique cultus peɛ́tora roborant:
   Utcunque defecere mores,
      Dedecorant bene nata culpæ.
| HOR. L. IV. Od. 4. | [rule 71 mm] | By JOHN LOCKE, [swash J] Eſq; | [rule 72 mm] | THE THIRTEENTH EDITION. | [double rule 72 mm] | *LONDON:* | Printed for A. MILLAR, H. WOODFALL, J. WHISTON and | B. WHITE, J. RIVINGTON, L. DAVIS and C. REYMERS, | R. BALDWIN; HAWES, CLARKE, and COLLINS; W. | JOHNSTON, W. OWEN, J. RICHARDSON, S. CROWDER, | T. LONGMAN, B. LAW, C. RIVINGTON, E. DILLY, R. | WITHY, C. and R. WARE, S. BAKER, T. PAYNE, A. | SHUCKBURGH, and J. HINXMAN. | M DCC LXIV.
Coll: 12° (172 × 100 mm cut) A–O¹² [$5 (+ B6, + E6; -I5) signed; D3 signed 'C3']; 168 leaves; pp. *i–viii 1* 2–148 1 150–325 326–328 [= 336]. Page 149 has lost its '49'.
Contents: A1ʳ (*i*) title (verso blank), A2ʳ–A3ᵛ (*iii–vi*) dedication (dated *March* 7, 1690), A4ʳ,ᵛ (*vii–viii*) contents, A5ʳ–O11ʳ (*1–325*) text, O11ᵛ blank, O12ʳ (*327*) advt.: "*This Day are publiſhed*, NEW EDITIONS OF" (6 items by Locke), O12ᵛ (*328*) advt. for William Dodd's *Commentary on the Old and New Testament*, "in which will be inserted the Manuscript Notes and Collections of John Locke".
Text (C12ᵛ): 32 lines; 134 (143)×74 mm; 84 R. Some pages have 33 lines, 137 (146)×72 mm. Medium-quality laid paper, not watermarked. Topical headings of sections inset in ital. within page block. Dedication set 33 lines, 83 ital. Page no. at external ends of headlines. Orn. tailpiece on p. 325 is a sun face between cornucopias, 20 × 30 mm.
HT: [orn. rectangle of a cherub centered amid scrollwork 8 × 72 mm] | SOME | THOUGHTS | CONCERNING | EDUCATION.

Headlines: Of EDUCATION.
CW: Page. A2ᵛ (*in-*) *corrigible* C12ᵛ Authority D4ʳ (Vene-) ration G4ᵛ in- [injure] L3ᵛ (Scho-) lars. L4ᵛ Know- [Knowledge.] O4ʳ can- [cannot]
Press figures: 4 (A6ᵛ)-5   14 (A11ᵛ)-3   37 (C11ʳ)-5   38 (C11ᵛ)-2   42 (C1ᵛ)-5   74 (D5ᵛ)-3   77 (D7ʳ)-4   92 (E2ᵛ)-3   110 (E10ᵛ)-5   125 (F7ʳ)-5   150 (G7ᵛ)-2   157 (G11ʳ)-3   173 (H7ʳ)-1   182 (H11ᵛ)-3   193 (I5ʳ)-2   206 (I11ᵛ)-3   212 (K2ᵛ)-3   230 (K11ᵛ)-5   248 (L8ᵛ)-2   271 (M8ʳ)-3   277 (M11ʳ)-2   292 (N6ᵛ)-3   317 (O7ʳ)-1   318 (O7ᵛ)-5
Notes: A line-by-line reprint of no. 181. The alphabetical 'contents of the sections' is still following that given in no. 176 and 178, where no. 163–8 are omitted from the pagination, e.g. 'Geography' (the heading on p. 270) is indexed as '276'.

Finally the irritating typographical error occurring in § 161 is here corrected: "a *perfect Painter*" instead of the incorrect 'Printer' (see no. 175).

A microfilm copy is in the collection, *The Eighteenth Century*, reel 3816, no. 11.
References: Alston 10:128; Attig 540; Axtell British 20; ESTC t069884.
Copies examined: Y   CLaslett   CaOTU (Locke L63.S66 1764)   L (8314 a.2)   MWA (G351.L8l4.S764)   O (Vet.A5 e.4401)

184. Education. '13th ed.', 1769. 12° Piracy.
SOME | THOUGHTS | CONCERNING | EDUCATION. | . . . [4 lines of verse, as in no. 182, until 9th line:] HOR. lib. iv. od. 4. | [rule 78 mm] | By *JOHN LOCKE*, [swash J] Eſq; | The THIRTEENTH EDITION. | LONDON: | Printed for J. and R. TONSON in the *Strand*. | [segmented Oxford rule 19 mm] | M DCC LXIX.
Coll: 12° in 6s (172 × 100 mm closely trimmed) a⁴ A–2C⁶ 2D⁴ [$ half signed]; 164 leaves; pp. *i–viii* 1 2–319 320 [= 328].
Contents: a1ʳ (*i*) title (verso blank), a2ʳ–a3ᵛ (*iii–vi*) dedication, a4ʳ,ᵛ (*vii–viii*) contents of the sections by page no., A1ʳ–2D4ʳ (*1–319*) text, 2D4ᵛ blank.
Illustration: front. is port. of Locke by T. Phinn after Kneller.
Text: 31 lines; 147 (156) × 74 mm; 93 R with 1 mm leading. Poor-quality printing on poor-quality laid paper with fleur-de-lys watermark. Page no. at outer ends of headlines.
Headlines: Of EDUCATION.
CW and *Press figures*: none.
Notes: A reprint probably based on the 1764 edition, but without the many rules usually found on the title. The usual omission of § 213 has been corrected by changing §§ 214–7 to number 213–6. John Stephens has said this is almost certainly an Edinburgh piracy. Both Jacob Tonson and his nephew Jacob had died, in 1736 and 1767 respectively. The badly produced portrait (by T. Phinn) matches that in the Edinburgh, 1752 edition (no. 182, itself copied from the Irish editions of 1737 and 1737, no. 177 and 179). A very scarce edition; there are no copies recorded in the British Isles. The only

copies recorded outside Boston, Mass., are those at Oberlin (Ohio) College Library and at the Universities of Illinois and Oregon.
References: Alston 10:129; Attig 541; Axtell British 21; ESTC n023688.
Copy examined: Boston (Mass.) Pub. Lib. (LB475.L6A3 1766 *sic*)

185. Education. 14th ed., 1772. 12°
SOME | THOUGHTS | CONCERNING | EDUCATION. | [rule 72 mm] | . . . [&c. as in no. 183, until 13th line: [rule 73 mm] | THE FOURTEENTH EDITION. | [double rule 72 mm] | *LONDON:* | Printed for J. WHISTON W. STRAHAN, J. and F. RIVINGTON, B. WHITE, L. DAVIS, HAWES, CLARKE | and COLLINS, W. JOHNSTON, W. OWEN, T. CASLON, | S. CROWDER, T. LONGMAN, B. LAW, C. RIVINGTON, | E. DILLY, J. WILKIE, T. CADELL, S. BAKER, | T. PAYNE, T. DAVIES, G. ROBINSON, T. BECKET, | and J. ROBSON. | [rule 18 mm] | MDCCLXXII.
Coll: 12° (172 × 100 mm cut) A–O^{12} [$ half signed]; 168 leaves; pp. *i–viii 1* 2–325 326–328 [= 336].
Contents: A1^r (*i*) title (verso blank), A2^r–A3^v (*iii–vi*) dedication (dated *March* 7, 1690), A4^{r,v} (*vii–viii*) contents by page no., A5^r–O11^r (*1–325*) text, O11^v blank, O12^r (*327*) advt. for Locke's publications ('*Lately Publiſhed*', 6 items as in no.183), O12^v blank.
Text (C12^v): 32 lines; 132 (142) × 73 mm; 83R. Some early pages have 33 lines, 137 (145) × 73 mm. Medium-quality laid paper, not watermarked. Dedication set 33 lines, 83 ital. Page no. at external ends of headlines.
HT: [orn. rectangle of scrolls 5 × 72 mm] | SOME | THOUGHTS | CONCERNING | EDUCATION.
Headlines: Of EDUCATION.
CW: Page. A2^v (*in-*) corrigible B7^r 3. Be- [3. Becauſe,] C12^v Authority D4^r (Vene-) ration E5^v weighing G4^v (injure) their G8^r in- [injured] L3^v (Scho-) lars. L4^v Know- [Knowledge.] M4^r other- [otherwiſe] O4^r can- [cannot] O6^r Mer- [Merchants]
Press figures: 14 (A11^v)-5 16 (A12^v)-3 26 (B5^v)-4 62 (C11^v)-6 77 (D7^r)-6 102 (E7^v)-3 127 (F8^r)-4 149 (G7^r)-3 170 (H5^v)-4 181 (H10^r)-3 199 (I8^r)-4 205 (I11^r)-6 210 (K1^v)-4 212 (K2^v)-3 236 (L2^v)-4 254 (L11^v)-3 271 (M8^r)-6 293 (N7^r)-4 295 (N8^r)-4 306 (O1^v)-4
Notes: A line-by-line reprint of no. 183, with the same errors in the alphabetical 'contents of the sections'. A copy of this edition is in the microfilm collection, *The Eighteenth Century*, reel 5397, no. 5.
References: Alston 10:131; Attig 542; Axtell British 22; Christophersen p. 101; ESTC t069885.
Copies examined: Y C (7240 d.84) CaOTU (Locke L63.S66 1772) L (8307 aaa.8) MH (*AC.A/191.Zz772*l*; lacks O12; Amos Bronson Alcott copy, stamped 'F.ALCOTT PRATT.') O (Vet.A5 e.2646) Vat

186. Education. '14th ed.' (1778). 12° Two issues
186A (First state): SOME | THOUGHTS | CONCERNING | EDUCATION. | [rule 81 mm] |
Doctrina vires promovet infitas,
    Rectique cultus pectora roborant:
Utcunque defecere mores,
    Dedecorant bene nata culpæ.
| HOR. L. IV. Od. 4. | [rule 81 mm] | By JOHN LOCKE, [swash J] Efq; | [rule 81 mm] | THE FOURTEENTH EDITION. | [double rule 81 mm] | LONDON: | Printed and Sold by H. FENWICK, Cheapfide. 1778.
186B (Second state), as 1st state until last line: Printed for a Company of Bookfellers.
Coll: 12° (165 × 102 mm cut) A^4 B–G^{12} H^2 [$5 (+ F6, + G6; –H2) signed]; 78 leaves; pp. *i–viii 1* 2–148 [= 156].
Contents: A1^r (*i*) title (verso blank), A2^r–A3^r (*iii–v*) dedication (dated *March 7, 1690.*), A3^v blank, A4^{r,v} (*vii–viii*) contents by correct page no., B1^r–H2^v (*1*–148) text.
Text (D1^r): 49 lines; 144 (151) × 82 mm; 59 R. Very poor-quality printing. Fair-quality laid paper with large fleur-de-lys watermark. Topical headings in ital. inset within outer edges of text block. Page no. at outer ends of headlines. Tailpiece on p. 148 is a framed face in profile, between leafy scrolls, 28 × 46 mm.
HT: [rectangular orn. of suns, 80 mm] | SOME | THOUGHTS | CONCERNING | EDUCATION.
Headlines: *Of* EDUCATION.
CW: Page. A2^v *But* B1^v care- [carefully] B6^r (ufe-) ful C10^r added {'adde' in 2d issue} [added] D8^r (bet-) ter F7^v Know- [Knowledge,] G5^v (what-) ever H1^v tho'
Press figures: none.
Note: A newly set reprint, following the text and format of no. 177. The second state was achieved by a stop-press correction, and its date of publication is possibly soon after 1778. Alston estimates 1770. I am indebted to Sarah Reed of the University of Birmingham Library for details of the first state, which exactly matches the other state except for the imprint and the presence of the letter 'd' in the catchword on p. 43.

A microfilm copy of the second state is in the collection, *The Eighteenth Century*, reel 3543, no. 1.

Plomer lists Henry Fenwick as a printer in London, 1769–1776; his source is Nichols III.571.

References: Alston 10:130; Attig *543; Axtell British 23; ESTC 1st state t220674, 2d t069886 (Sole locations for each state)

Copies examined. 1st state: Univ. of Birmingham Library (r.LB475.L6; info. by corr.) 2d state: L (1478.aaa.32; 165 × 95 mm cut)

187. Education. '15th ed.', Dublin, 1778. 12°
SOME | THOUGHTS | CONCERNING | EDUCATION. | [rule 68 mm] |
Doctrina vires promovit [sic] infitas,
  Rectique cultus pectora roborant:
    Utcunque defecere mores,
      Dedecorant bene nata culpæ. |
HOR. L. IV. Od. 4. | [rule 68 mm] | By JOHN LOCKE, [swash J] Efq; | [rule 68 mm] | THE FIFTEENTH EDITION. | [double rule 68 mm] | DUBLIN: | PRINTED BY J. KIERNAN, FOR | T. WALKER, No. 79, DAME-STREET. | [rule 22 mm] | M,DCC,LXXVIII.
Coll: 12° (165 × 96 mm cut) A–O^{12} [$5 signed]; 168 leaves; pp. *i–viii 1* 2–325 326–328 [=336].
Contents: A1^r (*i*) title (verso blank), A2^r–A3^v (*iii–vi*) dedication, A4^{r,v} (*vii–viii*) contents, A5^r–O11^r (*1–325*), O11^v–O12 (*326–328*) advt. of 10 titles, with quoted reviews, of books 'published by R. Walker.'
Text (B7^v): 33 lines; 134 (144) × 69 mm; 82 R. Fair-quality laid paper watermarked with a bunch of grapes. Page no. at external ends of headlines. Topical headings of sections inset at outer edge of page block within italics. Sections numbered as in authorized English editions (i.e. omitting 213).
HT: [orn. rectangle, chain-like, 6 × 68 mm] | SOME | THOUGHTS | CONCERNING | EDUCATION.
Headlines: Of EDUCATION.
CW: Page. B7^r 3. Becaufe, E5^v weighing G8^r in- [injured] M4^r other- [otherwife] O6^r Mer- [Merchants]
Notes: A line-by-line reprint of no. 185. Axtell in error gives the publication date as 1777.
References: Alston 10:132; Attig 544; Axtell British 24; ESTC t155627.
Copies examined: O (Vet.A5 f.2972; lacks port.) Dt (25.E.26) NjP (6504.592.11)

188. Education. 'New ed.' (Edinburgh?), 1779. 12°
SOME | THOUGHTS | CONCERNING | EDUCATION. |
Doctrina vires promovet infitas,
Rectique cultus pectora roborant:
  Utcumque defecere mores,
    Dedecorant bene nata culpæ.
HOR. lib. iv. od. 4. | [rule 78 mm] | By JOHN LOCKE, [swash J] Efq; | rule 78 mm] | A NEW EDITION. | [Oxford rule 78 mm] | LONDON: | Sold by J. and R. TONSON in the *Strand*. | [Oxford rule in 7 segments, 26 mm] | M DCC LXXIX.
Coll: 12° (180 × 110 mm cut) A–N^{12} O^6 P^2 [$ half signed]; 164 leaves; pp. *i–viii 1* 2–240 245 242–244 247 246–319 320 [=328]. Page no. 241 called '245', 245 called '247'.

Contents: A1ʳ (*i*) title (verso blank), A2ʳ-A3ᵛ (*iii–vi*) dedication (dated March 7. 1690.), A4ʳ,ᵛ (*vii–viii*) contents of sections by page no., A5ʳ-P2ʳ (*1–319*) text (§§ 1–216), P2ᵛ (*320*) blank.

Text (F5ʳ): 31 lines with 1 mm leading; 147 (160) × 80 mm; 95 R (with leading). Good-quality laid paper, with no visible watermarks. Topical headings of sections set ital. within outer edge of page block. Page no. at outer ends of headlines.

Headlines: *Of* EDUCATION.

CW: Page. A5ʳ (pri-) vilege D4ʳ (conver-) fation G7ᵛ (re-) ceive L9ʳ (gram-) mar N9ʳ (fome-) thing.

Press figures: none.

Notes: A reprint following the edition of 1769 (no. 184), with text corrected to 216 sections. The typographical error, '*Printer*' instead of '*Painter*' in § 161 again rears its ugly head here (cf. no. 175, *Notes*). Desmond Neill is of the opinion this edition was printed in Scotch type; ESTC record states the imprint is false. Sheet L in CaOTU and CtY copies are paged 233–240 245 242–244 247 246–256; text is in correct order, ignoring page numbers.

A microfilm of the British Library copy is in the collection, *The Eighteenth Century*, reel 3435, no. 16 with "poor print and loss of print throughout due to condition of material". A better-quality film of the same copy is in reel 5571, no.5.

References: Alston 10:133; Attig 545; Axtell British 25; Christophersen p. 101; ESTC t155624.

Copies examined: CaOTU (Locke L63.S66 1779) CtY (Lba14/693.lcn) L (1509/2577) O (2621 e.140; flyleaf signed 'Thomas Fretwell | 1797', given by Edward Spencer Dodgson 21 Oct. 1913)

189. Education. 1800. 12° in 6s
SOME | [hollow type:] THOUGHTS | CONCERNING | 𝔈𝔡𝔲𝔠𝔞𝔱𝔦𝔬𝔫. | [double rule 74 mm] |
  Doctrina vires promovet insitas,
  Rectique cultus pectora roborant:
    Utcumque defecere mores,
    Dedecorant bene nata culpæ.
| HOR. lib. iv. od. 4. | [double rule 74 mm] | [Oxford rule 22 mm] | By JOHN LOCKE, [swash J] ESQ. | [Oxford rule, inverted, 22 mm] | [orn. French rule 34 mm] | LONDON: | PRINTED FOR W. BAYNES, PATERNOSTER-ROW, | BY | Hemingway and Crook, Blackburn. | [French rule 13 mm] | 1800.

Colophon, p. 248: [tailpiece of 2 people near a tree, 12 × 22 mm] | Printed by Hemingway and Crook, Blackburn.

Coll: 12° in 6s (188 × 112 mm uncut) A-U⁶ X⁴ [$ half signed; R3 signed '3R']; 124 leaves; pp. *i–iii* iv–vi 7 8–245 246–248.

Contents: A1ʳ (*i*) title (verso blank), A2ʳ-A3ᵛ (*iii*–vi) dedication (dated March 7, 1690.), A4ʳ-X3ʳ (*7–245*) text, X3ᵛ-X4ᵛ (*246–248*) contents by page no.

Illustration: front. port. of Locke after Brounower in oval subscribed "Pub.ᵈ Dec.ʳ 1800.", 66 × 51 mm; beneath in script: "John Locke Esq.'", on plate 105 × 77 mm.
Text (E3ᵛ): 37 lines; 131 (139) × 74 mm; 71 R. Medium-quality wove paper, without watermarks. Page no. at external ends of headlines. Topical headings of sections set small roman with page block. Dedication set 37 lines, 71 R.
HT: [broken Oxford rule 72 mm] | SOME | THOUGHTS | concerning | EDUCATION.
Headlines: OF EDUCATION.
CW: Page. A2ᵛ best C1ʳ (com-) pany F1ᵛ (de-) bauched K5ᵛ (re-) ceived, Q2ᵛ (con-) clude, T6ᵛ § 897. Music [§ 197. Music]
Press figures: none.
Notes: A newly set reprint, probably following the text of no. 185 or 188; sections numbered as usual 1–212, 214–217. The portrait is a very poor likeness. At last, the index has correct citations to the sections. A microfilm copy of this edition is in the collection, *The Eighteenth Century*, reel 3438, no. 1.
References: Alston 10:134; Attig 546; Axtell British 26; Christophersen p. 101; ESTC t069887.
Copies examined: Y (uncut)   CaOTU (Locke L63.S66 1800; cop.1, 169 × 105 mm cut; cop.2 lacks front.)   L (8307 ccc.7)   O¹ (Vet.A5 e.4681)   O² (Vet.A5 e.1243; lacks front.)

190. Education. Dutch trans. (anon.). Rotterdam, 1698. 8°
In red & black: [red line:] VERHANDELING | over de | [red:] OPVOEDING | der | [red:] KINDEREN, | *Behelzende verſcheydene nutte Aenmerkingen* | die de | [red:] OUDERS | Ten opzigt van 't Lichaam, doch voorna- | mentlijk van de Ziel hunner Kinderen in de | Opvoeding hebben waar te nemen. | *Door* | [red:] Dʳ· JOHANNES LOCK. | Na den derden Engelſchen druk vertaalt. | [engr. vignette, forest scene with figures, subscribed on a ribbon: 'So BAARD een BOS zijn beſte Vruchten', 39 × 82 mm] | Te ROTTERDAM, | [rule 70 mm] | By BARENT BOS, ['Barent Bos,' in red] Boek- | verkooper. 1698.
Coll: 8° (157 × 96 mm cut) π1 *⁸ A–Z⁸ [$ 5 signed]; 193 leaves; pp. *i–vi* 1–11 12 1–352 353–368 [= 386].
Contents: π1ʳ blank, π1ᵛ (*ii*) poem of 28 lines ital. headed 'Op de Tytelprint.', *1ʳ (*iii*) engr. half-title (verso blank), *2ʳ (*v*) title (verso blank), *3ʳ–*8ʳ (1–11) Locke's dedication to Clarke headed 'BEMINDE LEZER', *8ʳ (11, bottom 10 lines) 'DRUKFOUTEN aldus te verbeteren.' and 8.5 lines of errata, *8ᵛ (*12*) poem of 14 lines headed 'Op dit | WERKJE | van den | Heer LOK.' signed '*P. Rabus.*', A1ʳ–Y8ᵛ (1–352) Dutch text, Z1ʳ–Z6ᵛ (*353–364*) index of topics: 'BLADWYZER der voornaamſte zaaken.', Z7–8 blank.
Text (Q2ʳ): 29 lines; 117 (128) × 70 mm; 80 R. Good-quality laid paper, with

oval watermark. Page no. at external ends of headlines; A1^r paged 'Fol. I.' Locke's dedication set 25 lines, 94 ital.

Half-title: [engr. headpiece with Roman warrior and other figures near a temple, 127 × 80 mm on plaque 131 × 83 mm with caption below:] D^r. Joannes [swash J] Locks | OPVOEDING DER KINDEREN. | By BARENT BOS. 1697. (Engr. signed 'A. *Schoonebeek fec*.')

HT A1^r: Eenige | BEDENKINGEN | over de | Opvoeding | der | KINDEREN.

Headlines, from verso to recto: *Van de opvoeding* | *der Kinderen*. [swash K]

CW: Page.

Notes: Dutch translation of the third 1695 English edition of 1695 (no. 167). In 217 sections, omitting § 213 as usual in most English-language editions.

References: Attig 574; Axtell Dutch 1; Christophersen p. 97.

Copies examined: AMu (2478.E39)   Utr (333.J63; lacks Z7–8)   ViW (LB475.L6B2 1698; cut to 149x 96 mm; p. 123 has lost its '3'; lacks sheet Z)

191. Education. Dutch trans. (Verwer). Amsterdam, 1753. 8°

J. LOCKE [swash J] | OVER DE | OPVOEDING | DER | KINDEREN; | *Van nieuws uit het Engelſch vertaelt*, | naer den Elfden Druk, | door | PIETER ADRIAEN VERWER: | *Vermeerdert met eenige* AENTEEKENINGEN | *en het* LEVEN VAN DEN SCHRYVER. | [orn. footed vase with swags, 15 × 27 mm] | *Te* AMSTERDAM, | By K. VAN TONGERLO *en* F. HOUTTUIN. | MDCCLIII.

Coll: 8° (160 × 105 mm cut) π^2 *-4*^{8} 5*^{8} (-5*4.5 = π^2) χ1 A–2F^8 [$5 signed; 5*6 signed '*****4']; 273 leaves; pp. *i–iv I–III* IV–VIII IX–XI XII–LXXVI LXXVII–LXXVIII 1 2–452 453–464 [= 546].

Contents: π1^r blank, π1^v (*ii*) 26-line poem headed 'UITLEGGING DER TITELPRINT, AAN DE JEUGD.' & signed 'B. DE BOSCH.', π2^r (*iii*) engr. framed plate of Minerva slaying evil figures, with landscape background & temple (128 × 78 mm, on plate 132 × 84 mm signed 'J.C. Philips del. 1753.'), π2^v (blank), *1^r (*I*) title (verso blank), *2^r–*4^v (*III–VIII*) 'VOORREDEN VAN DEN VERTALER.', *5^r (*IX*) section title (verso blank), *6^r–5*6^v (*XI–LXXVI*) 'HET LEVEN DEN HEERE JOHAN LOCKE.' (trans. of Le Clerc's 'Eloge' from *Bibliothèque choisie*), χ1^r (*LXXVII*) Locke's Latin epitaph (in capital letters), χ1^v (*LXXVIII*) Dutch trans. of epitaph, A1^r–2F2^v (*1–452*) text, 2F3^r–2F7^v (*453–462* top third) alphabetical index of sections by page no., 2F7^v–2F8^v (*462* bottom two-thirds–*464*) advt. by publisher (of 15 other books, with prices).

Text (M4^r): 33 lines; 117 (127) × 63 (74) mm; 71 R. Good-quality laid paper, with coat-of-arms watermark. Page no. at external ends of headlines. Topics of sections set roman at outer margins beyond text block. Translator's foreword set 28 lines 81 ital.; Le Clerc's 'Life' set 29 lines 82 R.

Section title, p. IX: HET | LEVEN | VAN DEN HEERE | JOHAN LOCKE. [swash J]

HT *6ʳ: HET | LEVEN | VAN DEN HEERE | JOHAN LOCKE, [swash J] | GETROKKEN | UIT HET FRANSCH | VAN DEN HEERE | JEAN LE CLERC.
A1ʳ: J. LOCKE [swash J] | OVER DE | OPVOEDING | DER | KINDEREN. | [orn. rule of 2 intertwined ribbons, 61 mm]
Headlines, *6ᵛ–5*6ʳ, from recto to verso: HET LEVEN | VAN J. LOCKE. [swash J]
5*6ᵛ: HET LEVEN VAN J. LOCKE. [swash J]
A1ᵛ–2F2ʳ, from recto to verso: J. LOCKE OVER DE | OPVOEDING DER KINDEREN.
2F2ᵛ: J LOCKE OVER DE OPVOEDING. [No punctuation after 'J']
CW: Page. *2ᵛ on- [onder] 4*4ʳ Vier- [Vierde] C5ᵛ (regel-) ma- [matige] G4ᵛ wor- [worden.] N2ʳ ge- [gezegt] R8ᵛ (ge-) na- [nade] V6ᵛ Ge- [Geluid] Z6ʳ aen- [aengewent] 2E1ᵛ die- [dienen]
Notes: Text is a new translation based on the 11th ed. of 1745 (no. 180). The translator has added voluminous notes relevant to Dutch culture, e.g, to § 70, learning with a tutor; § 147, description of education in Holland. The wording of the Latin epitaph varies slightly from the original and from that in the 1714 *Works*; for example, it reads 'Lockius' rather than 'Locke', 'Siste Viator' is omitted, as is the phrase 'Ut veritate unice litaret'. This edition is listed in Abkoude as published by S.J. Baalde for one guilder, 12 stuivers.
References: Attig 575; Axtell Dutch 2.
Copies examined: Y (lacks χ1)   AMu (673.C1)   Utr (Y.oct.416)

192. Education. French translation (Coste). Amsterdam, 1695. 8°
DE | L'EDUCATION | DES | ENFANS. | Traduit de l'Anglois. | Par P** C**** | [tailpiece-like orn., wolf on hind legs leaning against a tree, with scroll: 'QUÆRENDO', 32 × 44 mm] | A AMSTERDAM, | Chez ANTOINE SCHELTE, Marchand Li- | braire près de la Bourſe. | M.DC.XCV.
Coll: 8° (145 × 95 mm cut) *⁸ **⁴ A–2B⁸ 2C⁶ [$ half + 1 (–*5; –**3) signed; *3 signed '**3']; 218 leaves; pp. *i–xxiv* 1–265 66 267–295 95 296–412 [= 436]. Page no. 266 and 295 have lost their 2s; 43 has 3 inverted.
Contents: *1ʳ (*i*) title (verso blank), *2ʳ–*3ᵛ (*iii–vi*) dedication to Mlle. Anne Wolfgang, *4ʳ–**4ʳ (*vii–xxiii*) 'PREFACE DU TRADUCTEUR.', **4ᵛ (*xxiv*) errata (14.2 lines, 'Fautes à corriger.'), A1ʳ–2C6ᵛ (*1–412*) text.
Text (L5ʳ): 26 lines (pp. *1–409*); 107 (116) × 56 (68) mm; 85 R. Pages 410–12 (2C5ᵛ–2C6ᵛ) are 32 lines, 66 R. Mixed quality laid paper with vertical chainlines, e.g. sheets F–G, Q, T, Z–2C poor quality without watermarks; the rest are fair-quality with small foolscap watermark. The copy at the State Library in Hannover has horizontal chainlines in sheets M and N. First page of text (A1ʳ) reads 'Pag. I.', Dedication set 15 lines 130R. Pref. set 26 lines, 80 R (with internal quotations in italics). Notes in outer margins in smaller roman. Page no. at external ends of headlines.

Headpiece on *4ʳ (pp. *vii*): a cock in a basket with foliage, 14 × 54 mm. Square tailpiece on **4ʳ (p. *xxiii*): flowerpot, 23 × 27 mm.

HT: [headpiece of leaves & flowers, 12 × 54 mm] | DE | L'EDUCATION | DES | ENFANS.

Headlines, from verso to recto: DE L' EDUCATION | DES ENFANS.

CW: Page. *2ʳ Ou- [Ouvrage] 2*2ʳ Mai- [Maiſon] A1ʳ plus A2ᵛ fai- [faire] C7ᵛ (froi-) de, [de] D8ʳ ſe- [ſecretement] H4ᵛ li- [liberté] M1ʳ (tou-) ché P3ᵛ pren- [prendre] S2ᵛ bon- [bonne-Maiſon,] V5ʳ Lo- [Logique] Z8ᵛ §.CLXXXIV. 2B1ᵛ hom- [homme]

Notes: This translation of the 1693 editions (probably from the second) was made by Pierre Coste, 'a student in theology' and a friend of Jean Le Clerc, both translator and author being anonymous. The caption title of the dedication is "A | MADEMOISELLE | ANNE WOLFGANG, | *Femme* | DE MR. PHILIPPE | DE LA FONTAINE.", is addressed to '*Mademoiselle Ma Cousine*', and is signed 'ANTOINE SCHELTE.' The substantive variants of the 1693 editions here follow the 2d (NA: no. 166), e.g. "without Reflection" from § 64 (p. 66), as "sans une reflexion"; § 94 (p. 113) "of Vertue and Honour" as "le chemin de la vertu & de l'honneur." There are 203 numbered sections, thus correcting the repetition of § 172 in the first edition. The translator's pref. incorporates all but the last paragraph of Locke's dedication.

References: Attig 577; Axtell French 1; Christophersen p. 57; L.L. 1784; Rochedieu p. 194.

Notice: *Histoire des ouvrages des savans* 11 (1694/95): 435-42.

Copies examined: O (Vet.B3 f.332) AMu (OK80.179) CaOTU (Locke L63.S66F7 1695) Han L (722 b.32)

193. Education. French trans. (Coste/anon.) [Geneva?] 1699. 12° False imprint

NOUVELLES | INSTRUCTIONS | POUR | L'EDUCATION | DES | ENFANS. | [orn., vase of flowers on platform, 28 × 38 mm] | A AMSTERDAM, | Chez JAQUES [swash J, Q] MENASSION. | [rule 61 mm] | M. DC. XCIX.

Coll: 12° (154 × 80 mm cut) *¹² (-*6.7 = X1.2) A-V¹² X² [$ half (+X2) signed]; 252 leaves; pp. *i-xx* 1 2-484 [= 504].

Contents: *1ʳ (*i*) title (verso blank), *2ʳ,ᵛ (*iii-iv*) publisher's note, *3ʳ-*8ᵛ (*v-xvi*) translator's pref., *9ʳ-*10ᵛ (*xvii-xx*) 'Indice du Contenu des Sections.', A1ʳ-X2ᵛ (*1-484*) text (§§ I-CCXVI.).

Text (G3ᵛ): 29 lines; 121 (130) × 58 (68) mm; 83 R. Poor-quality paper, without watermarks. Topical headings of sections set in outer margins of text block in roman.

HT: [framed flower headpiece 25 × 66 mm] | NOUVELLES | INSTRUCTIONS | POUR | L'EDUCATION | DES | ENFANS.

Headlines, from verso to recto: DE L'EDUCATION | DES ENFANS.

CW: Page. A1ʳ hom- [hommes] D8ʳ J'a- [J'avoue] Q10ᵛ An- [Anglois] No CW on D6ᵛ, D7ʳ.

Notes: This edition is a piracy, actually printed in Geneva (cf. *Corr.* 2601; vi.649–50). Coste's preface to his second edition (no. 194, pp. XXX–XXXII) also comments unfavourably on this edition which has "paru à *Geneve*". Here the publisher explains it has been greatly enriched by "de nouvelles pensées, qui remplissent souvent les douze et les quinze pages tout de suite", implying they are from the third English edition (no. 167), but the text is Coste's translation, expanded by anonymous translations of those sections (e.g. 37, 62, 93–4, 98) by which Locke himself improved the third edition. The translator's pref. also includes an abridgement of Locke's dedication to Clarke, and reveals Locke to be the author; he feels free to reveal that information since it has already been made public in the *Histoire des ouvrages des sçavans*, issue for November 1693. Of course Locke's authorship was revealed in the dedication to the third edition, the one he is claiming to use.

In Coste's letter to Locke (29 June 1699; *Corr.* ibid.) Desmaizeaux is quoted as stating: "Le Traducteur est, dit-on, un homme de peu de jugement, comme il paroit par ces deux beveuës: Dans l'endroit où vous conseillez de faire lire aux Enfans *Raynard the Fox*, il a mis à la marge on peut donner aux Enfans les Fables et les *Contes* de la Fontaine. C'est l'entendre. . . . D'ailleurs ce beau faiseur de Notes écrit fort mal. Il s'est hazardé de faire une Préface qui n'est, dit-on, qu'un continuel galimathias."
References: Attig 578; Axtell French 2.
Copies examined: MH (*EC65.L7934.Eh695cb) O (Vet.B3.f.338)

194. Education. French trans. (Coste). [2d] ed., Amsterdam, 1708. 8°
In red & black: DE | [red line:] L'EDUCATION | DES | [red:] ENFANS; | Traduit de l'Anglois | [red:] DE MR. LOCKE, | *Par PIERRE COSTE.* [swash Ps, T] | Sur la derniére Edition revûe, corrigée, & | augmentée de plus d'un tiers par l'Auteur. | [orn. tree, with scroll 'QUÆRENDO' 33 × 44 mm] | [red:] A AMSTERDAM, | Chez HENRI SCHELTE. | [rule 34 mm] | [red:] MDCCVIII.
Coll: 8° (157 × 99 mm cut) *–2*⁸ A–K⁸ L⁸ (±L7) M–2C⁸ 2D⁸ (–2D3 = L7 cancellans) [$5 signed; 2D4-6 called 'Dd3-5']; 231 leaves; pp. *I–II* III–XXXII 1–421 *422–430* [=462].
Contents: *1ʳ (*I*) title (verso blank), *2ʳ–2*8ᵛ (III–XXXII top half) translator's pref., 2*8ᵛ (XXXII bottom) errata of 9 lines, A1ʳ–'2D3ᵛ' (1–421) text, '2D3ᵛ'–'2D7ᵛ' (*422–430*) 'TABLE DES MATIERES.'
Illustration: front. is engr. portrait of Locke after Kneller, 133 × 81 mm on plates 141 × 90 mm, subscribed '*J. B. Scotin.*'
Text (H4ᵛ): 32 lines; 127 (136) × 65 (80) mm; 80 R. Fair-quality laid paper without watermarks. Page no. at external ends of headlines. First text page called 'Pag. I.' Very infrequent notes occur in outer margins in roman. Translator's preface set 21 lines 117R, except where Coste is quoting part of Locke's dedication: those pages (IV–X) are set 26 lines, 95 ital.
HT: DE | L'EDUCATION | DES | ENFANS.
Headlines, from verso to recto: DE L'EDUCATION | DES ENFANS.

CW: Page. *7ᵛ (Ou-) vra- [vrage] A1ᵛ (pour-) tant D7ʳ (s'op-) po- [poſer]
E6ᵛ mê- [même] L7ʳ dans M4ᵛ (ja-) mais R1ᵛ (croi-) re
X8ᵛ fai- [faire] '2D4'ᵛ inſ- [inſtruiſant.]

Notes: This edition is based on the 5th English ed. (no. 169), but the sections have been split in some cases to result in 223 numbered sections, and the whole further divided into twenty-eight chapters. For example, chapter I, 'De la Santé: Précautions nécessaires pour la conserver aux Enfans', covers English §§ 2–30, numbered 3–31; ch. II, 'Du Soin qu'on doit prendre de l'Ame des Enfans', covers English §§ 31–42, numbered 32–43 in the French translation; the final chapter, XXVIII, 'Conclusion de tout l'ouvrage', is numbered § 223, corresponding to § 217 of the last English edition. This is the pattern followed in all subsequent French editions.

This translation may be presumed to have been supervised by Locke, since Coste was living in the same house (the Masham's) with Locke from 1698, as tutor to Francis Cudworth Masham in order to translate the *Essay concerning Human Understanding* under Locke's supervision. The November 1708 issue of the *Journal de Trévoux* notes its appearance, and states further: "mais M. Coste l'a retouchée: & pour la rendre conforme à la dernière Edition de son original, il a été obligé de la refondre presque entierement" (pp. 1971–2).

A textual comparison of those sections the 'pirate' added to his 1699 edition with those same sections here reveals a completely different turn of phrase. There are also many minor improvements in phraseology over Coste's 1695 edition.

The Bibliothèque nationale's copy of this edition has the original L7 in place, and the cancellans as the third leaf of sheet 2D. The cancellandum has a footnote on p. 174 (from the reference to 'Books' in the penultimate paragraph of § 94 of the English edition) ending "que je viens de dire, qu'un jeune homme seroit en grand danger de se gâter l'Esprit par la lecture de ces sortes de Livres."; cancellans reads: "que je viens de dire, que qui a besoin de consulter ces sortes de Livres n'en fera jamais un fort bon usage, ni pour soi, ni pour autrui." The latter reading is followed in subsequent editions.

References: Attig 579; Axtell French 3; Christophersen p. 102; Rochedieu pp. 193–4.

Copies examined: Y (L7 canc.; lacks front.) [BBR] P (8° R.25183; misbound, sheet 2* bound after H; has L7 & L7 cancel) Wol (Pa.235; 153 × 98 mm cut; L7 canc.)

195. Education. French trans. (Coste). Paris, 1711. 12° in 8s and 4s.
DE | L'EDUCATION | DES | ENFANS; | Traduit de l'Anglois | DE MR. LOCKE, | *Par PIERRE COSTE*. [swash T] | Sur la derniére Edition revûe, corrigée, & | augmentée de plus d'un tiers par l'Auteur. | [orn., standing Minerva, with owl & scroll: 'NE EXTRA ORTAS', 33 × 36 mm] | A PARIS, | Chez JEAN MUSIER, à la deſcente du | Pont-Neuf, à l'Olivier. | [broken rule 37 mm] | M.DCCXI. | *AVEC PRIVILEGE DU ROY*. [swash U, Y]

Coll: 12° in 8s and 4s (160 × 102 mm cut) π1 ã⁸ é⁴ (-é4 = π1) A⁸ B⁴ → 2O⁸ 2P⁴ [$ half signed in roman, (i.e., 'iiij' and 'ij'); A2 and A3 both signed 'Aij']; 240 l*eaves; pp. I–II j–ij* iij–xxij *1–443 444–456* [= 480].

Contents: π1ʳ (*I*) half title (verso with CW only), ã1ʳ (*j*) title (verso blank), ã2ʳ–é3ᵛ (iij–xxij) translator's pref., A1ʳ–2O6ʳ (1–443) text, 2O6ᵛ–2P2ᵛ (*444–452*) 'Table des matieres', ending with 22-line errata, 2P3ʳ–2P4ʳ (*453–55*) statement of privilege, 2P4ᵛ blank.

Text (N4ʳ): 31 lines; 129 (136) × 66 (80) mm; 83 R. Fair-quality laid paper, with horizontal chainlines, no visible watermarks (? lost in trimming). Page no. at external ends of headlines (same as in no. 194). Marginal notes set in smaller roman. Index set 83R. Framed headpiece on A1ʳ: vase on pedestal, with scrolls, 21 × 62 mm.

HT: DE | L'EDUCATION | DES | ENFANS.

CW: Gathering. π1ᵛ (= é4ᵛ) DE B4ᵛ repas C8ᵛ (l'eſto-) mac H4ᵛ (abandon-) née M4ᵛ fortes R8ᵛ (décou-) vrir V4ᵛ (maſ-) ſacres; 2B8ᵛ (d'au-) tres 2H8ᵛ (Bré-) *viarium* 2N4ᵛ petit 2O8ᵛ (u- [set 67R]) niverſelles [set 83R]

Notes: Straightforward reprint of 1708 (no. 194), with 223 sections divided into 28 chapters. The style of signatures to the preliminary matter indicates a Parisian printer, and is probably an unauthorised edition. The Bibliothèque nationale copy has the half title bound after é3; the presence of a catchword on the otherwise blank verso is unusual. The 'privilege' to print is dated May 6, 1711 and signed 'La Marque Tilladet.'

References: Attig 580; Axtell French 4; Rochedieu p. 194.

Copies examined: NjP (Ex.6504.592.1711) P (D². 4697; π1 bd. after é3)

196. Education. French trans. (Coste). '6th ed.', Amsterdam [Berne?] 1715. 8°. Piracy.

In red & black: DE | [red line:] L'EDUCATION | DES | [red:] ENFANS; | Traduit de l'Anglois | [red:] DE MR. LOCKE, | *Par PIERRE COSTE*. | Sixiéme Edition; | Revûe, corrigée, & augmentée. | [orn., monogram-like, 34 × 46 mm] | *Suivant la Copie imprimée* | [red:] A AMSTERDAM. | [rule 60 mm] | [red:] M DCC XV.

Coll: 8° (162 × 95 mm cut) *⁸ **⁴ A–2G8 [$ half signed]; 252 leaves; pp. *1–2 3–24* 'Pag.1', *2–468 469–480* [= 504].

Contents: *1ʳ (*1*) title (verso blank), *2ʳ–**4ᵛ (*3–24*) translator's pref., A1ʳ–2G2ᵛ (*1–468*) text, 2G3ʳ–2ʳ (*469–477*) contents by chap. & §§, 2G7ᵛ–2G8 (*478–80*) blank.

Text (O7ᵛ): 32 lines; 133 (142) × 65 (78) mm; 83 R. Medium-quality paper without watermarks. Pref. has pp. 3–9 line 22 set 28 lines, 94 ital; rest of pref. set 29 lines, 91R. Notes in outer margins set roman. Page no. at external ends of headlines.

HT: DE | L'EDUCATION | DES | ENFANS.

Headlines, from verso to recto: Dᴇ ʟ'Eᴅᴜᴄᴀᴛɪᴏɴ | ᴅᴇs Eɴғᴀɴs.

CW: Page. A5ʳ (cet-) te pra- [te pratique] H1ʳ don- [donner] Y8ᵛ (re-)gar- [gardent]

Notes: A piracy, possibly printed at Geneva, but the Bodleian Lib. catalogue says it originated in Berne. It follows the arrangement of the 1708 edition, with 223 §§ divided into 28 chapters. The pref. is chiefly a translation of Locke's dedication, signed: "A *CHIPLEY* dans la Province de *Som- | erſet* le 2. Avril 1708." There it also states it is based on the French translation published in Geneva, which contained Locke's own additions; only the 1699 piracy (no. 193) was published in Geneva, and this edition seems to follow both: it incorporates all Coste's notes and those from no. 193, with many quotations from Montaigne.
References: Attig 581.
Copies examined: Y   AMu (OK.84.44)   O (Vet.B4 f.302)

197. Education. French trans. (Coste) 3d ed., Amsterdam, 1721. 8°
In red & black: DE | [red line:] L'EDUCATION | DES | [red:] ENFANS; | Traduit de l'Anglois | [red:] DE M. LOCKE, | *Par M.* COSTE. | Sur l'Edition Angloiſe publiée aprés la mort de | l'Auteur, qui l'avoit revûe, corrigée, | & augmentée de plus d'un tiers. | [engr. framed vignette, oxen with cart in a circular frame, ribbon above: 'TRAHITE ÆQUO JUGO.', 45 × 55 mm on plate 47 × 57 mm] | [red:] A AMSTERDAM, | Chez STEENHOUWER & UYTWERF. | [rule 32 mm] | [red:] MDCCXXI.
Colophon, p. 505: *Achevé d'imprimer le 22 Avril* 1721.
Coll: small 8° (162 × 102 mm cut) *⁸ **⁸ ***² (-***2) A–2I⁸ [$ 5 signed]; 273 leaves; pp. *I–III* IV–V *VII* VIII–XIII *XIV* XV–XXXI *XXXII–XXXIV* 1 2–505 506–512 [= 546].
Contents: *1ʳ (*I*) title (verso blank), *2ʳ–*3ᵛ (*III–VI*) Coste's dedication to Monsieur de la Motte signed 'A Londres, ce 4. Avril 1721.', *4ʳ–*7ʳ (*VII–XIII*) 'Avertissement sur cette troisieme edition', *7ᵛ–**8ʳ (*XIV–XXXI*) translator's preface 'sur l'edition de 1708', **8ᵛ (*XXXII*) errata note (37.2 lines), ***1ʳ,ᵛ (*XXXIII–XXXIV*) chapter contents, A1ʳ–2I5ʳ (*1–505*) text, 2I5ᵛ–2I8ᵛ (*506–512*) alphabetical 'table des matieres'.
Illustration: front. is oval port. of Locke, facing right, on a pedestal, with inscription on frame: 'IEAN LOCKE NE LÉ . . . AOUT M.D.C.XXXII. MORT LE XXVIII.OCTOBRE M.D.C.C.IX.'; with 4 line subscription in script type; engr. 132 × 81 mm on plate 139 × 86 mm; subscribed 'G. Kneller Eques Pinxit 1697. B. Picart sculp. 1721.'
Text (G2ᵛ): 30 lines; 124 (134) × 65 (77) mm; 83 R. Good-quality laid paper with foolscap watermark. Page no. at external ends of headlines. Topical section headings set in small roman in outer margins. Dedication set 21 lines 117 ital; 'Avertissement' 27 lines 92R; preface same as body of text. Orn. tailpiece of a crown above garlanded fleur-de-lys 41 × 51 mm on p. XIII; similar tailpiece in outline, 24 × 37 mm, p. 505.
HT: DE | L'EDUCATION | DES | ENFANS.
Headlines, from verso to recto: DE L'EDUCATION | DES ENFANS.
CW: Page. 2*1ʳ le- [lequel] A2ᵛ don- [donné] E7ᵛ au- [autre] K6ᵛ pe- [petits] P5ᵛ tou- [toûjours] V5ᵛ ca- [capable,] 2B8ᵛ l'é- [l'étude] 2I2ʳ (gran-) de

Notes: A slight revision over Coste's 2d ed. of 1708 (no. 194). The translator's preface again includes most of Locke's dedication to Clarke, and a sharp criticism of the 1699 piracy (no. 193). Most of the footnotes are by Coste. Coste's dedication is to a friend (possibly Antoine Houdar de La Motte). In some copies the title vignette is slightly askew. Rochedieu states this translation was also published "in-12" by H. Schelte: I have found no such copies.
References: Attig 582; Axtell French 5; Rochedieu p. 194.
Notice: *Bibliothèque ancienne et moderne* 15 (1721): 449–52.
Copies examined: Y AMu CtY (Lba14/693/hb) Vat (R.Gen.Filos. V391) ViW (LB475.L6D4 1721, trimmed to 154 × 101 mm)

198. Education. French trans. (Coste). Amsterdam [Geneva?] 1727. 8°. Piracy.
DE | L'EDUCATION | DES | ENFANS; | *Traduit de l'Anglois* | *De Mr. LOCKE,* | PAR Mr. COSTE. | *Sur l'Edition Angloiſe publiée* | *après la mort de l'Auteur, qui* | *l'avoit revûë, corrigée, &* | *augmentée.* | [orn., vase of flowers 29 × 39 mm] | Suivant la Copie imprimée | A [swash A] AMSTERDAM. [swash T] | [rule 57 mm] | M DCC XXVII.
Coll: 8° (149 × 92 mm cut))(⁴ (-)(4) *⁸ (-*1) **⁴ A–2G⁸ [$ half + 1 signed]; 254 leaves; pp. *i–vi* ᵗ3–24, 'Pag.I.', 2–468 469–480 [= 508].
Contents:)(1ʳ (*i*) title (verso blank),)(2ʳ–)(3ᵛ (*iii–vi*) dedication to M. de La Motte, *2ʳ–**4ᵛ (ᵗ3–24) translator's preface, A1ʳ–2G2ᵛ (*1–468*) text, 2G3ʳ–2ʳ (*469–477*) contents by chapter and §§, 2G7ᵛ–2G8 (*478–80*) blank.
Illustration: front. is port. of Locke, copied from no. 197, with birth and death details around oval frame, 134 × 82 mm, subscribed: 'Joh. Am̃an. scul Scaphu-' [?].
Text (Y3ʳ): 32 lines; 133 (143) × 66 (79) mm; 83 R. Poor-quality paper without watermarks. Page no. at external ends of headlines. Topical section headings set small roman in margins.
HT: DE | L'EDUCATION | DES | ENFANS.
Headlines same as 1715 piracy (no. 196).
CW: Page. Identical with no. 196.
Notes: Again a piracy, from style of the first signature I would assume printed in Switzerland (Basle or Geneva). Frontispiece and dedication are copied from 1721 edition (no. 197); the rest of the text uses the sheets of the 1715 piracy (no. 196). One should consider the preliminary gathering (')(') as a cancellans for its leaf *1. There appears to be a confusion in Attig: his no. 583 states 'A Amsterdam' imprint date 1727, and is called 'septieme edition'; his no. 584 is dated 1730 but the title and imprint follow this edition.
References: Attig 583–584; Christophersen p. 102
Copy examined: O (Vet.B4 f.304; closely trimmed)

199. Education. French trans. (Coste) 4th ed., Amsterdam, 1733. 12°
In red & black: DE | [red line:] EDUCATION | DES | [red:] ENFANS; | Traduit de l'Anglois de M. LOCKE. | [red:] Par *M. COSTE.* [swash T] |

QUATRIE'ME EDITION. | Sur l'Edition Angloife publiée après la mort de | l'Auteur, qui l'avoit revûe, corrigée, & | augmentée de plus d'un tiers. | [red:] TOME PREMIER. ['SECOND.'] | [engr. headpiece, table with orn. frame showing man with cadduceus, horned man, 2 cherubs & seated women, above banner inscribed 'Non Norunt Haec Monumenta Mori', 45 × 54 mm, on plaque 49 × 61 mm] | [red:] A AMSTERDAM, | Chez *HERMAN UYTWERF*. [swash Y, T] | [red:] MDCCXXXIII.

Coll: 12° (165 × 96 mm cut) *⁸ χ1 **⁸ A-L¹² 2χ1 M-Z¹² [$ half + l signed]; 294 leaves; pp. *I–III* IV–VI *VII* VIII–XIII *XIV* XV–XXXI XXXII–XXXIV 1 2–264 *i–ii* 265 266–542 543–552 [= 588]. First page of each sheet *-M signed in direction line: 'Tom. I.'; L–Z signed 'Tom. II.'

Contents: *1ʳ (*I*) title of v.1 (verso blank), *2ʳ–*3ᵛ (*III–VI*) dedication to M. de la Motte, *4ʳ–*7ʳ (*VII–XIII*) 'Avertissement sur cette edition', *7ᵛ–**7ʳ (*XIV–XXXI* top half) translator's pref., **7ʳ (*XXXI* bottom) errata ('FAUTES A CORRIGER') of 9.1 lines and note ('Achevé d'imprimer le 11. de Novembre 1732.'), **7ᵛ–**8ᵛ (*XXXII–XXXIV*) contents of 28 chap. (called 'Sections'), A1ʳ–L8ᵛ (*1–264*) text of chap. I–XII (§§ 1–112), 2χ1ʳ (*i*) title of vol. 2 (verso blank), M1ʳ–Z7ᵛ (*265–542*) text of chap. XIII–XXVIII (§§ 113–223), Z8ʳ–Z12ᵛ (*543–552*) alphabetical 'table des matieres'.

Illustration: Vol. 1 has front., portrait of Locke by B. Picart after Kneller, same as in 1721 ed. (no. 197), 133 × 82 mm on plate 141 × 88 mm.

Text (G5ʳ): 29 lines; 122 (132) × 62 (75) mm; 83 R. Medium-quality laid paper without visible watermark. Page no. at external ends of headlines. Dedication set 20 lines 116 ital. Topical headings of sections set 73 R in outer margins.

HT: same as no. 197.

Headlines: same as no. 197.

CW: Page.

Notes: The 'Avertissement' says it is a revision of the 2d (1708) and 3d (1721) editions, with more quotations from Montaigne added; it is signed: 'A Oxford ce 6. Septembre 1732.' The text, as usual, is divided into 28 chapters and 223 sections.

References: Attig 585; Axtell French 6; Rochedieu p. 194.

Copies examined: AMu (OK.86.18) [GhU (Ph 648)] Wol (Pa.236)

200. Education. French trans. (Coste). 5th ('Mr COSTE') ed., Amsterdam, 1737. 12°. With 'Traité de bonheur'.

In red & black. Vol. 1: DE | [red line:] L'EDUCATION | DES | [red:] ENFANS | Traduit de l'Anglois de M. LOCKE. | [red:] Par Mr COSTE. | CINQUI'EME EDITION. | Sur l'Edition Angloife publiée après la mort de | l'Auteur, qui l'avoit revûe, corrigée, & | augmentée de plus d'un tiers. | [red:] TOME PREMIER. | [engr. vignette, a man sowing followed by oxen pulling a plough, overhead a scroll reading 'SERERE NE DUBITES', 51 × 65 mm on plaque 64 × 78 mm] | [red:] A

AMSTERDAM, | Chez HERMAN UYTWERF. [swash M, N, U] | [red:] M.DCC.XXXVII.

Vol. 2: as vol. 1 except line 4 reads 'ENFANS,' and line 11 reads 'TOME SECOND.'

Coll: 12° (161 × 95 mm cut) π1 *^{12} A–H^{12} χ1 I–T^{12} V^6 [$ half signed]; 248 leaves; pp. *I–II i–xx xxj–xxiv* 1–191 *192 III–IV* 193–396 *397–400* 401–467 *468* [=496]. First page of sheets *-H also signed in direction line 'Tome I.'; of I–V signed 'Tome II.'

Contents: 'Vol. 1': π1^r (*I*) title of vol. 1 (verso blank), *1^r–*4^r (i–vij) 'Avertissement sur cette 5. edition' (signed '*A Oxford ce 6. Septembre 1732.*'), *4^v–*10^v (viij–xx) translator's pref., *11^{r,v} (*xxj–xxij*) contents of 'Education' by chapters (called 'Sections'), *12^{r,v} (*xxiij–xxiv*) contents of 'Traité du bonheur' (5 parts, each in several chapters), A1^r–H12^r (1–191) French text of *Education* (12 chap., §§ 1–112), χ1^r (*III*) title of 'Tome 2' (verso blank), I1^r–R6^v (193–396) text of chap. 13–28 (§§ 113–223), R7^r (*397*) half-title to 'Traité' (verso blank), R8^{r,v} (*399–400*) 'Avis au lecteur', R9^r–V6^r (401–467) text of 'Traité du bonheur', V6^v blank.

Illustration: Vol. 1 has front., portrait of Locke, facing right, copied from 1721 edition (no.197), subscribed '*J.B. Scotin*', 133 × 82 mm on plates 141 × 88 mm.

Text (B12^v): 36 lines; 122 (129) × 63 (74) mm; 67 R. Medium-quality laid paper, with bunch of grapes watermark. 'Avertissement' set 25 lines 96R; translator's preface set 36 lines 71R. Topical headings of sections set roman in outer margins. Page no. at external ends of headlines. Framed headpieces on p. i (*1^r): a fan within a shaded framed background, with scrolls 21 × 70 mm; *4^v, vase between Chinese hats, with leaves, 24 × 70 mm. Tailpieces on *4^r and R8^v, Chinese hat between lanterns, leaves, 21 × 39 mm; *10^v has framed star above flowers, 34 × 36 mm.

HT, A1^r: [framed headpiece as on *1^r] | DE | L'EDUCATION | DES | ENFANS.

I1^r: [framed headpiece as on *4^r] | DE | L'EDUCATION | DES | ENFANS. | [orn. rule of 8-point stars 60 mm]

R8^r: [framed headpiece of vase on pedestal above a face, with leaves, 21 × 66 mm] | AVIS | AU LECTEUR.

R9^r: [framed rectangle as on *1^v] | TRAITÉ | DU | BONHEUR. | [orn. rule of 8-point stars 67 mm]

Half-title, R7^r: TRAITÉ | DU | BONHEUR | DANS TOUS | LES ETATS | DE LA VIE.

Headlines, pp. 2–191 and 192–395, from verso to recto: D<small>E</small> L'E<small>DUCATION</small> | D<small>ES</small> E<small>NFANS</small>.

p. 396: D<small>E</small> L'E<small>DUCATION</small> D<small>ES</small> E<small>NFANS</small>.

pp. 402–67, from verso to recto: T<small>RAITE</small>' <small>DU</small> B<small>ONHEUR</small>. | *Dans tous les Etats de la Vie.*

CW: Gathering (on leaf 12^v). * L'EDU- [DE L'EDUCATION] A boir^e F (in-)

décences K rien N (méri-) te P eſpé-) rer S adju- [adjugerent] Sheets E and H without CW.

Notes: This edition is barely distinguishable from another typesetting of 1737 (described in no. 201, following), the most notable distinction being that line 6 of the title reads 'M' COSTE.' Also the catchword on p. 432 (S12^v) 'adju-' (for 'adjugerent') in no. 201 incorrectly reads 'aju-' for 'ajugerent'. Both texts have the same pagination and are set 67 R with 36 lines per page (more or less) but the size of the page block as well as most of the ornaments differ. Framed initials: *1^r has V^3; *4^v, E^4; A1^r, L^5; I1^r with L^4; R9^r, I^4.

The prelim. quire is signed with an 8-point star (no.201 has 5-point); p. vij has 12 lines of text (no. 201 has 7). Ornamental rules here are a series of 8-point stars; in the other 1737 edition they are decorative squares. Further, in the 'Avis au lecteur' to the *Traité de bonheur*, there are notable differences on p. 400 lines 5, 8 and 9 (no.201 text given within curved brackets): ceſſe . . . C'eſt . . . preſente . . . voy . . . j'ay . . . {ceße . . . C'est . . . préſente . . . vois . . . j'ai . . .}.

Of the two 1737 editions I think this is the earlier, chiefly because it is more cleanly printed and has less typographical errors. It is possible that very few exemplars of this edition were printed, and that the 'company of booksellers' undertook a hasty reprint. It is possible that they had to run off more copies of this edition, for that reason, but had already broken up the type and therefore had to reset the work completely. It is equally likely that this is the later of the two, for the same reasons. The spelling differences on p. 400, noted above, are in a more modern style in no. 201.

The text of the *Education* is a reprint based on the 1733 edition (itself a reprint of the 1721, no. 197 and 199), with the anonymous 'Traité du bonheur' added. I have not been able to determine its authorship, but suspect it is a partial reprint of the *Traité du bonheur* by M. Formentin (Christian name unknown) published in Paris in 1706 (236 pp.).

References: (without distinction between 200 and 201): Attig 586; Axtell French 7; Christophersen p. 102; Rochedieu p. 194.

Copies examined: P (D2.4698; lacks front.) PU (LB475.L614 1737; 164 × 90 mm cut)

201. Education. French trans. (Coste) 5th ('M. COSTE.') ed., Amsterdam, 1737. 12°. With 'Traité du bonheur'.

In red & black: DE | [red line:] L'EDUCATION | DES | [red:] ENFANS, | Traduit de l'Anglois de M. LOCKE. | [red:] Par M. COSTE. | . . . [&c. as in no 200, until 9th line:] l'Auteur, qui l'avoit revûë, corrigée, & | . . . [&c. until vignette of a seated woman reading, beneath whom are 3 scrolls, 'VIRTUTI. INGENIO. DOCTRINAE.' 36 × 59 mm on plate 62 × 61 mm] | . . . [imprint as in no. 200]

Coll: 12° (164 × 90 mm cut) Same as no. 200.

Contents and *Illustration*: Same as no. 200.

Text (B12^v): 36 lines; 128 (137) × 64 (74) mm; 67R. Medium-quality laid paper without watermark. 'Avertissement' and translator's pref. set same as no. 200. Topical headings of sections set roman in outer margins. Framed headpieces are: on p. i (*1^r) sconce-like vase with leaves 21 × 70 mm; on p.viij (*4^v), oval chalice between scroll-like leaves, 19 × 66 mm. Tailpieces on p.vij (*4^r): shell in oval frame of leaves 29 × 42 mm; on *10^v is 4 fleurons (2 upright, 2 inverted) 11 × 12 mm; and on R9^v (p. *400*): flowers above scrolls, 31 × 35 mm.
HT, A1^r: [framed headpiece of scrolls & leaves, 19 × 71 mm] | DE | L'EDUCATION | DES | ENFANS.
  I1^r: [framed headpiece of Chinese hat between bells, 21 × 65 mm] | DE | L'EDUCATION | DES | ENFANS. | [rule of orn. squares 61 mm]
  R8^r: [framed headpiece as on I1^r] | AVIS | AU LECTEUR.
  R9^r: [framed headpiece, same as in no. 200, on *1^r] | TRAITÉ | DU BONHEUR. | [orn. rule of squares, 68 mm]
Half-title, R7^r: same as in no. 200.
Headlines: Same as no. 200.
CW: Gathering. Same as no. 200, except A12^v: 'boire'; and S12^v 'aju-' for 'ajugerent'.
Note: This is a line-by-line, page-for-page printing of no. 200, though I suspect this is the later printing. The title vignette for vol. 1 in copies at the University of Toronto and Bodleian Libraries, and my own is the same as found in no. 200. The Bibliothèque nationale copy (R.42169) has the vignette of the 'reading woman' on the title of both vols. There are minor title-page differences: (1) a comma after 'ENFANS' in both vols. here, (2) '*M*. [not '*M*'] *COSTE*', and (3) 'revûë' (as against 'revûe') in lines 4, 6 and 9 respectively. For other differences, see *Notes* to no. 200.

The framed headpiece on R9^r (p. 401) in this edition is the same as that found on p. i (*1^r) and R9^r of no. 200. I would therefore assume both 1737 editions were printed by the *same* printer.

The Bibliothèque nationale and Rochedieu both report this edition as being issued as an octavo (shelfmark D^2.4698) and also in a duodecimo (shelfmark R. 42169), but they are both duodecimos. I have found no octavo copies. Perhaps Rochedieu was relying on BN's catalogue.

I am greatly indebted to Ann Thomson of the Université de Caen and to Dan Traister of the Van Pelt Library, University of Pennsylvania, for helping me sort out the details of these two 1737 editions.
References: as in no. 200.
Copies examined: Y CaOTU (Locke L63.S66F7 1737; lacks front. and v.2 title leaf) O (Vet.B4 f.128; lacks front.; cut 160 × 95 mm) P (R.42169; ex lib. Duc de Liancourt)

202. Education. French trans. (Coste). Amsterdam (Vander Kloot), 1743. 12°

DE | L'EDUCATION | DES | ENFANS; | Traduit de l'Anglois. | DE M^R. LOCKE, | *Par PIERRE COSTE*. | Sur la derniere Edition revûë, corrigée, | & augmentée de plus d'un tiers | par l'Auteur. | [orn., vase with scrolls 29 × 43 mm] | A AMSTERDAM, | Chez J. VANDER KLOOT | dans le Kalvers-Stratt. | [rule 43 mm] | M. DCC XLIII.

Coll: 12° (160 × 98 mm cut) ã^{12} A–T^{12} [$ half signed in roman, ij, iij, &c.]; 240 leaves; pp. *j–ij* iij–xxiv *1* 2–440 *441–456* [=480].

Contents: ã1^r (*j*) title (verso blank), ã2^r–ã12^v (iij–xxiv) translator's pref., A1^r–T4^v (*1*–440) text, T5^r–T10^r (*441–451*) contents by chap. and §§, T10^v–T12 (*452–456*) blank.

Text (L4^r): 31 lines; 131 (149) × 66 (77) mm; 84 R. Fair-quality laid paper without visible watermark. Page no. at external end of headlines. Topical headings set roman in outer margins. Notes set 62R.

HT: [tailpiece of wall sconces, 22 × 67 mm] | DE | L'EDUCATION | DES | ENFANS.

Headlines, from verso to recto: DE L'EDUCATION | DES ENFANS.

CW: Gathering (on leaf 12^v). B danger F §.86 [§.86.] L communément

Notes: Reprint of 1733 edition (no. 199) with dedication and 'Avertissement' omitted. Text, as usual, in 223 §§ divided into 28 chapters. I am unsure of the punctuation after 'AMSTERDAM' and 'KLOOT' because the only copy (Bodley's) I was able to locate has a slightly mutilated title-page. I strongly suspect this printing is a piracy, actually printed in Paris, because of the style of the preliminary signatures and the roman signature numerals. The Uytwerf firm was the authorized publisher at this time.

References: Attig 587; Axtell French 8.

Copy examined: O (Vet.B4 f. 332)

203*. Education. French trans. (Coste). '5th ed.', Amsterdam, 1743 (Uytwerf). 12°

"De l'éducation des enfans; traduit de l'anglois. De Mr. Locke, par M. Coste . . . Cinquième édition, revûe & corrigée. A Amsterdam, chez Maynard Uytwerf. 1743. xxxi, [3], 544, [12] p. port. 12°."

This citation is from Attig (588) with an asterisk preceding the entry to indicate he has been unable to see the item but has identified his source, in this case Axtell French 9. I have been unable to locate any copies of this edition. Axtell states it is the 'official 5th Coste edition.' The 1744 Uytwerf edition (no. 204) which follows, Axtell states is the same as his no. 9. This 1743 edition is not found in the Bodleian or Cambridge University libraries or any libraries contributing to the National Union Catalog of pre-1956 imprints, nor in any of the libraries cited in my list of locations.

204. Education. French trans. (Coste). '5th ed.', Amsterdam, 1744. 12°
In red & black: DE | [red line:] L'EDUCATION | DES | [red:] ENFANS; | Traduit de l'Anglois de M. LOCKE, | [red:] *Par M. COSTE*, [swash P, T] | *Membre de la Société Royale de* LONDRES. | CINQUIE'ME EDITION, | Revûe & corrigée. | [red:] *TOME PREMIER.* ['SECOND.'] | [framed engr. headpiece, table with bones in anatomy theatre, with cherubs & Mercury, above cherubs holding scroll: Non Norunt Haec Monumenta Mori, 45 × 54 mm on plate 48 × 62 mm] | [red:] A AMSTERDAM, | Chez *MAYNARD UYTWERF.* | [red:] MDCCXLIV.

Coll: 12° (165 × 95 mm cut) *^{8} χ1 **^{8} A-L^{12} 2χ1 M-Z^{12} 2A^2 [$ half + 1 (-2A2) signed; **5 and **6 both signed '**5']; 296 leaves; pp. *I-II* III-VI VII VIII-XIII *XIV* XV-XXXI *XXXII-XXXIV* 1 2-264 *i-ii* 265 266-544 545-556 [= 592]. Sheets **-L also signed '*Tom. I.*' in direction line of first page; pp. 265-556, sheets M-2A signed '*Tom. II.*'

Contents: *1^r (*I*) title (verso blank), *2^r-*3^v (*III-VI*) dedication to M. de la Motte, *4^r-*7^r (*VII-XIII*) 'Avertissement sur cette 5. edition', *7^v-**7^r (*XIV-XXXI*) translator's pref., **7^v-**8^v (*XXXII-XXXIV*) 'Table des sections' (chapters), A1^r-L12^v (*1-264*) text of ch. 1-12 (§§ 1-112), 2χ1^r (*i*) title of vol. 2 (verso blank), M1^r-Z8^v (*265-544*) text of ch. 13-28 (§§ 113-223), Z9^r-2A2^r (*545-555*) alphabetical 'table des matières', 2A2^v blank.

Illustration: front. is port. of Locke after Kneller by B. Picart, same as in 1733 ed. (no. 199).

Text (K3^r): 29 lines; 118 (127) × 63 (80) mm; 82 R. Very poor-quality laid paper without watermarks. Page no. at outer ends of headlines.

HT: DE | L'EDUCATION | DES | ENFANS.

Headlines, from verso to recto: DE L'EDUCATION | DES ENFANS.

CW: Page. A1^v in- [infenfible] G2^r Lan- [Langues,] M6^r Crain- [Crainte] R2^r qu'el- [qu'elles]

Notes: Though Coste did not die until 1747, I have been unable to determine if he here made any significant changes in this edition over his 4th ed. of 1733 (no. 199).

References: Attig 589; Axtell French 10; Christophersen p. 102.

Copies examined: CaOTU (Locke L63.S66F7 1744; lacks front. and vol.2 title leaf) L (8306 b.5) O (Vet.B4 f.203)

205. Education. French trans. (Coste). '6th ed.', Lausanne, 1746. 12°
In red & black: DE | [red line:] L'EDUCATION | *DES* | [red:] ENFANS, | Traduit de l'Anglois de | [red:] M^R. LOCKE. | *Par Mr.* COSTE, *Membre de la* | *Société Royale de* LONDRES. | [red:] SIXIEME EDITION, | Revûe & corrigée. | [red:] TOME PREMIER. ['SECOND.'] | [orn. subscribed '*Papillon Sculp*', v. 1, of Mercury and a cherub, 22 × 29 mm; vol. 2, of 2 cherubs above pierced hearts, 21 × 30 mm] | [red:] A LAUSANNE, | Chez MARC-MIC. BOUSQUET & Comp. | [red rule 57 mm] | MDCCXLVI.

Coll: 12° (178 × 105 mm uncut) *⁸ χ1 **⁸ A–L¹² 2χ1 M–Z¹² 2A⁴ [$ half (–*3; +*5, +**5) signed]; 298 leaves; pp. *I–III IV–VI VII VIII–XIII XIV* XV–XXXI *XXXII–XXXIV 1* 2–264 *i–ii* 265 266–560 [= 596]. First leaf of each sheet **-L signed in direction line 'Tom. I.'; sheets M–2A signed 'Tom. II.'

Contents: *1ʳ (*I*) title of vol. 1 (verso blank), *2ʳ–*3ᵛ (*III–VI*) dedication to M. de la Motte, *4ʳ–*7ʳ (*VII–XIII*) 'Avertissement sur la 5. édition' (signed: A Londres le 5. Juillet 1743), *7ᵛ–**7ʳ (*XIV–XXXI*) translator's pref., **7ᵛ–**8ᵛ (*XXXII–XXXIV*) chapter contents, A1ʳ–L12ᵛ (*1–264*) text of ch. 1–12 (§§ 1–112), 2χ1ʳ (*i*) title of vol. 2 (verso blank), M1ʳ–Z8ᵛ (*265–544*) text of ch. 13–28 (§§ 112–223), Z9ʳ–2A4ᵛ (*545–560*) 'Table des matières'.

Text (E3ʳ): 29 lines; 121 (129) × 60 (79) mm; 83 R. Dedication set 24 lines, 100 ital; 'Avertissement', 25 lines 99R. Footnotes set 70R; with CW if run on to next page. Medium-quality laid paper without watermark. Cleaner typeface than earlier editions. Page no. at external ends of headlines.

HT: DE | L'EDUCATION | DES | ENFANS.
Headlines, from verso to recto: DE L'EDUCATION | DES ENFANS.
CW: Page. (Vol. 1:) A12ᵛ affuré, B7ᵛ (cô-) té, C12ʳ don- [donnoit] E3ᵛ (qu'el-) les G4ʳ (con-) train- [trainte] I10ᵛ (par-) les K6ᵛ libre- [librement] (Vol.2:) M7ʳ pren- [prendre] O5ʳ (tou-) tes Q1ᵛ ma- [manieres,] S4ᵛ mo- [moment] V9ʳ (con-) tente Z6ᵛ (arri-) ver

Notes: Reprint of 5th French ed. of 1744 (no. 204).
References: Attig 590; Axtell French 11; Rochedieu p. 194 (at Amsterdam!)
Copies examined: O (Vet.D4 e.95–96; bd. in 2 vols., uncut) Han (P-A 985)

206. Education. French trans. (Coste). '8th ed.', Paris, 1747. 2 vols. 12° in 8s and 4s.

EDUCATION | DES | ENFANS. | TRADUCTION ANGLOISE | DE M. LOCKE, | Par M. COSTE, Membre de la Société | Royale de LONDRES. | HUITIEME EDITION, | Revue & corrigée. | TOME PREMIER. ['SECOND.'] | [orn., vase of flowers on pedestal, with scrolls 28 × 48 mm] | A PARIS, | Chez DAVID le jeune, Quai des Auguſtins, | au Saint-Eſprit. | [Oxford rule 57 mm] | M DCC XLVII. | Avec Approbation & Privilege du Roi.

Colophon, last page of both vols.: [Oxford rule 81 mm] | De l'Imprimerie de LE BRETON petit-fils D'HOURY, Imprimeur ordinaire DU ROI.

Coll: 12° in 8s and 4s (164 × 93 mm cut). Vol. 1: a⁸ b⁴ c⁴ A⁸ B⁴ → T⁸ V⁴ X⁸ Y⁴ Z⁶ [$ half signed in lower-case roman ('iiij', 'ij'); c1 signed 'e', B2 signed 'Aij']; 154 leaves; pp. *j–iij* iv–vj *vij* viij–xiij *xiv* xv–xxx *xxxj* xxxij *1* 2–276 [= 308]. First page of sheets *b* and Z signed 'Tom. I.' in direction line; c and A–Y signed 'Tome I.'

Vol. 2: π² A⁸ B⁴ → X⁸ Y⁴ Z⁸ 2A⁴ [$ half signed; L2 signed 'Gij']; 146 leaves; pp. *j–ij* iij–iv *1* 2–288 [= 292]. First page of each sheet A–Z signed 'Tome II.' in direction line, of sheet 2A 'Tom.II.'

Contents: Vol. 1: a1ʳ (j) title (verso blank), a2ʳ-a3ᵛ (*iij*-vi) dedication to M. de la Motte (signed: A Londres ce 4 Avril 1721), a4ʳ-a7ʳ (*vij*-xiij) 'AVERTISSEMENT SUR LA CINQUIEME EDITION' (signed: A Londres le 5 Juillet 1743), a7ᵛ-c3ᵛ (*xiv*-xxx) translator's preface, c4ʳ·ᵛ (xxxj-xxxij) contents of ch. 1-12 (called 'sections'), A1ʳ-Y4ᵛ (*1-264*) text of ch. 1-12 (§§ 1-112), Z1ʳ-Z5ᵛ (265-274) alphabetical index of vol., Z6ʳ·ᵛ (275-276) 'Approbation' dated '8 Fevrier 1746. SOUCHAI' and privilege reaffirmed by Vincent (5 Mai 1746), ending in colophon.
  Vol. 2: π1ʳ (j) title (verso blank), π2ʳ·ᵛ (iij-iv) contents of chapters 13-28, A1ʳ-Z7ᵛ (*1-278*) text of chap. 13-28 (§§ 113-223), Z8ʳ-2A4ᵛ (279-288) alphabetical index of vol.2, ending with colophon (2 lines).
Illustration: front. is oval-framed portrait, facing right, after Kneller, subscribed "JEAN LOCKE | *Né en aoust 1632.* | *Mort le 28 octobre 1704.*", 129 × 79 mm on plate 140 × 87 mm.
Text (v.1 A3ᵛ; same both vols.): 29 lines; 118 (127) × 64 (77) mm; 83 R. Footnotes set 68R; marginal notes in italics. Medium-quality laid paper, watermarked with bunch of grapes within oval, and 'AUVERGNE 1742'. Vertical chainlines. Page no. at outer ends of headlines. Orn. rule, 4 × 62 mm on *a*iij ʳ; tailpieces on c4ᵛ (entwined straplike device with leaves, 39 × 52 mm), and in vol. 2 on π2ᵛ (diamond-shaped face with leaves, 20 × 21 mm).
HT, vol.1: [framed headpiece of flowers surrounded by scales and scrolls, 19 × 71 mm] | DE | L'ÉDUCATION | DES | ENFANS.
  vol.2: [framed headpiece of sun, with small irons, 16 × 62 mm] | DE | L'ÉDUCATION | DES | ENFANS. | [Oxford rule 57 mm]
Headlines, from verso to recto: DE L'ÉDUCATION | DES ENFANS.
CW: Gathering. Vol. 1: A8ᵛ chofe E8ᵛ (di-) rectement M4ᵛ ceux Q4ᵛ Enfans V4ᵛ (d'a-) me,
  Vol. 2: B4ᵛ † F4ᵛ tout G8ᵛ (ordinai-) re L8ᵛ (prompte-) ment Q4ᵛ (Hemif-) phere X8ᵛ (bien-) aifes
Note: Reprint of 5th French ed. of 1744 (no. 204).
References: Attig 591; Axtell French 12.
Copies examined: O (Vet.E4 f.92) CLU-C CtY (Lba14/693*l*hg)

207. Education. French trans. (Coste). '8th ed.', Lausanne, 1760. 12°
In red & black: DE | [red line:] L'EDUCATION | DES | [red:] ENFANS, | *Traduit de l'Anglois de* | [red:] M. JEAN LOCKE. | *Par M.* COSTE, *Membre de la* | Societé Royale de LONDRES. | [red:] HUITIEME EDITION, | *Revuë & corrigée.* | [red:] TOME PREMIER. ['SECOND.'] | [orn., vol. 1: crown 16 × 26 mm; v.2: scrolls 12 × 30 mm] | [red:] A LAUSANNE, | Chez MARC-MICHEL BOUSQUET | & Compagnie. | [red rule 56 mm] | MDCCLX.
Coll: 12° (162 × 96 mm cut) *⁸ χ1 **⁸ A-L¹² 2χ1 M-Z¹² 2A⁴ [$ half (+ *5, + **5) signed]; 298 leaves; pp. *I-III* IV-VI VII VIII-XIII *XIV* XV-XXXI XXXII-XXXIV 1 2-264 *i-ii* 265 266-544 545 546-560 [=596]. First

page of each sheet ** through L signed 'Tom. I.'; sheets M–Z signed 'Tom. II.'

Contents: same as 1746 edition (no. 205).

Text (N4ʳ): 30 lines; 125 (135)×72 mm; 83 R. Medium-quality laid paper without watermark. Page no. at external ends of headlines.

Headlines same as no. 205.

CW: Page. C7ᵛ mai- [maître] G2ʳ Lan- [Langues,] M7ʳ pren- [prendre] T12ᵛ hom- [hommes]

Note: Page-by page reprint of the French (Lausanne) edition of 1746 (no. 205), newly set in type.

References: Attig 592; Axtell French 13; Rochedieu p. 194.

Copies examined: O (Vet.D5 f.60–61) AMu (512.E.23, 24)

208. Education. French trans. (Coste). '7th ed.', Amsterdam, 1776. 12°. With 'Traité du bonheur'.

DE | L'ÉDUCATION | DES | ENFANS, | *Traduit de l'Anglois de M. LOCKE.* | Par M. COSTE. | *SEPTIEME ÉDITION.* | Sur l'Edition Angloiſe publiée après la mort | de l'Auteur, qui l'avoit revue, corrigée, | & augmentée de plus d'un tiers. | [orn., shell on pedestal 30 × 48 mm] | A AMSTERDAM, | Chez *la Veuve MERKUS, Libraire*. | [Oxford rule 54 mm] | M.DCC.LXXVI.

Coll: 12° (170 × 100 mm cut) π1 a¹² (–a12) A–V¹² [$6 (–a2, –A2) signed; a3 signed 'Aiij', a4–6 signed 'ajv, av, avj' respectively]; 252 leaves; pp. *I–II j–ij iij–xx xxj–xxij* 1–397 *398–403* 404–477 *478–480* [= 504].

Contents: π1ʳ (*1*) half title (verso blank), a1ʳ (*j*) title (verso blank), a2ʳ–a3ᵛ (*iij–vj*) 'Avertissement sur cette 7. edition' subscribed 'Oxford, ce 6 Septembre 1732', a4ʳ–a10ᵛ (*vij–xx*) translator's pref., a11ʳ,ᵛ (*xxj–xxij*) contents of chapters ('sections'), A1ʳ–R7ʳ (1–397) text, R7ᵛ blank, R8ʳ (*399*) section title to 'Traité', R8ᵛ blank, R9ʳ,ᵛ (*401–2*) 'Avis au lecteur', R10ʳ–V11ʳ (*403–477*) text of 'Traité du bonheur', V12ʳ,ᵛ (*479–480*) contents of 'Traité'.

Text (I3ʳ): 34 lines; 127 (134)×70 mm; 75 R. Medium-quality laid paper with bunch of grapes watermark. Page no. at external ends of headlines. Footnotes set 56R.

Half title: [framed headpiece of birds centered between arrows and quivers, 24 × 68 mm] | DE | [hollow type:] L'EDUCATION | DES | [decorative hollow type:] ENFANS.

HT: DE | L'EDUCATION | DES | ENFANS.

Headlines, from verso to recto: DE L'EDUCATION | DES ENFANS.

Section title, R8ʳ: TRAITÉ | DU | BONHEUR | *DANS TOUS* | LES ÉTATS | *DE LA VIE*.

CW: Gathering (on leaf 12ᵛ). B d'émulation F d'une N il L12ᵛ without CW.

Notes: Reprint of the French 1737 edition (no. 200), based on the 5th English edition, even to the inclusion of the 'Traité' (by Formentin?). The firm Arkstée & Merkus was responsible for many editions of Rousseau's *Emile*.

References: Attig 593; Axtell French 14.
Copies examined: O (Vet.B5 f.42) Wol (Pa. 237)

209. Education. French trans. (Coste) 'New ed.', Paris, 1783. 2 vols. in-12°. With 'Méthode'.
DE | L'ÉDUCATION | DES | ENFANS, | *Traduit de l'Anglois* | DE M. JEAN LOCKE, | *Par M.* Coste, *Membre de la Société* | *Royale de Londres.* | NOUVELLE ÉDITION, | Ornée du Portrait de l'Auteur, | *A laquelle on a joint la Méthode obſervée pour* | *l'Éducation des* ENFANS DE FRANCE. | [rule 64 mm] | TOME PREMIER. ['SECOND.'] | [rule 64 mm] | [orn. 8 × 19 mm] | A LONDRES; | *Et ſe trouve à* Paris, | Chez Serviere, Libraire, rue Saint- | Jean-de-Beauvais. | [thick rule 58 mm] | [rule 53 mm] | M.DCC.LXXXIII.
Coll: 12° (165 × 100 mm cut). Vol. 1: π^2 A-N^{12} O^{10} (-O10) P^6 [\$ half (-Ovj) signed in roman]; 173 leaves; pp. *i-vi 1* 2-341 342 [= 346]. First page of each gathering signed '*Tome I.*' in direction line.
Vol. 2: π^2 A-N^{12} O^8 (-O8) [\$ half signed in roman]; 166 leaves; pp. *i-iv 1* 2-298 299 300-326 327-328 [= 332]. First page of each gathering signed '*Tome II.*'
Contents: Vol. 1: $\pi1^r$ (*i*) half title, $\pi1^r$ (*ii*) advt. (11 works, chiefly on education), $\pi2^r$ (*iii*) title (verso blank), A1^r-A2^v (*1-4*) dedication to M. de la Motte, A3^r-A6^v (*5-12*) 'Avertissement sur cette Edition', A7^r-B3^v (*13-20*) translator's pref., B4^r-P1^r (*31-331*) text of §§ 1-116 (Chapters 1-13), P1^v-P6^r (*332-341*) contents of chapters and §§ of vol. 1, P6^v blank.
Vol. 2: $\pi1^r$ (*i*) half title (verso blank), $\pi2^r$ (*iii*) title (verso blank), A1^r-N5^v (*1-298*) text of §§ 117-223 (chap. 14-28), N6^r-O2^r (*299-315*) text of 'Méthode', O2^v-O7^v (*316-326*) contents of vol. 2 by chapters and §§, O8 blank or wanting.
Illustration: Vol. 1, as front. has port. of Locke, facing right, after Kneller, not signed, 129 × 78 mm on plate 158 × 94 mm.
Text (vol.1 I3^r; same both vols.): 34 lines; 118 (127) × 62 mm; 81 R. Medium-quality laid paper without watermark. Page no. at external ends of headlines.
Half-title, both vols.: DE | L'ÉDUCATION | DES | ENFANS.
HT, both vols.: [framed headpiece of flowers 19 × 64 mm] | DE | L'ÉDUCATION | *DES ENFANS.*
Headlines, from verso to recto: De l'Education | des Enfans.
CW: Gathering (leaf 12^v). Vol.1: B §.X. H voulez N §.CXI. Sheet O without CW.
Vol.2: B SECTION. G *Angleterre* N régné
Notes: Locke's text follows that of the 1744 (Uytwerf) edition (no. 204). The 'Méthode' is an anonymous work, its authorship not identified in any subsequent (19th or 20th century) editions.
References: Attig 594; Axtell French 15; ESTC t192648; Rochedieu p. 194.

Copies examined: Mun (Paed. Th. 2797^b; lacks port.) O (Vet.E5 f.165–166)

210. Education. French trans. (Coste). 'New ed.', Paris, 1798. 2 vols. in-12°. With 'Méthode'.

DE | L'ÉDUCATION | *DES* | ENFANS, | TRADUIT DE L'ANGLAIS | DE M. JEAN LOCKE, | PAR M. COSTE, | *Membre de la Société* | *Royale de Londres.* | NOUVELLE ÉDITION. | *A laquelle on a joint la Méthode observée en* | *France pour l'Éducation des Enfans.* | [rule 59 mm] | TOME PREMIER. ['SECOND.] | [rule 59 mm] | À PARIS, | Chez MOUTARDIER, Imprimeur- | Libraire, Quai des Augustins, No. 28. | AN VIe. M.DCC.XCVIII.

Coll: 12° (170 × 95 mm cut). Vol. 1: A–M^{12} [$ half signed]; 144 leaves; pp. *1–5* 6–16 *17* 18–34 *35* 36–276 *277* 278–288. First page of each sheet signed '*Tom.I.*' in direction line.

Vol. 2: A–K^{12} L^8 M^{12} [$ half (+L5, +L6) signed; M1 and M^4 both signed 'M'; M7 signed 'M4'; M11 signed 'N']; 140 leaves; pp. *1–5* 6–268 *269* 273–282 [=280]. Page no. 271–2 omitted. First page of each sheet also signed '*Tom.II.*'

Contents: Vol. 1: A1^r (*1*) half title (verso blank), A2^r (*3*) title (verso blank), A3^r–A4^v (*5–8*) dedication to M. de la Motte, A5^r–A8^v (*9–16*) 'Avertissement sur cette édition' dated '5 juillet 1743', A9^r–B5^v (*17–34*) translator's pref., B6^r–M6^v (*35–276*) text of chap. 1–13 (§§ 1–113), M7^r–M12^v (*277–288*) contents of vol. 1 by chap. and §§.

Vol. 2: A1^r (*1*) half title (verso blank), A2^r (*3*) title (verso blank), A3^r–L8^v (*5–256*) text of ch. 14–28 (§§ 117–223), M1^r–M6^v (*257–268*) text of 'Méthode', M7^r–M12^v (*269–280*) contents of vol. 2 by chap. and §§.

Text (vol.1 L5^r; same in both vols.): 34 lines; 119 (127) × 63 mm; 81 R. Fair-quality laid paper, with an illegible name at outer edges of 8th leaf ('LE M | E – M'?). Page no. at external ends of headlines.

HT, both vols.: [framed headpiece of village seen in distance, 14 × 59 mm] | DE L'ÉDUCATION | DES | ENFANS. | [Oxford rule 62 mm]

Headlines, from verso to recto: DE L'EDUCATION | DES ENFANS.

CW: Gathering (on leaf 12^v). Vol. 1: B §.IX. C doucement H peut I nombre, M cas

Vol.2: C SECTION G tems K pas Sheet L has no CW.

Notes: Reprint of 1783 ed. (no. 209) following the text of the 5th French edition, with its inclusion of the anonymous 'Méthode'.

References: Attig 595; Axtell French 16.

Copy examined: O (Vet.E5 e.138–139)

211. Education. German trans. (Starck). Greifswald, 1708. 8°

Des Herrn John Locke [ornamental D, H; swash J] | Gedanken | von | Erziehung [orn. E] | junger Edelleute / [orn. E] | Aus dem Englischen/ und zwar | der vollständigsten Edition überseßt/ | und mit Anmerckungen / zugleich

| auch durchaus mit Titulen be= | rer Materien ver= | sehen | von | Seb. Gottfr. Starck / [orn. S, G, S] | LL. Or. Prof. Publ. | [rule 77 mm] | Greiffswald/ | Bey Johann Wolffgang Fickweiler. | Ao. 1708.
Colophon: Greiffswald/ | Gedruckt bey Georg=Heinrich Adolphi/ | Königl. Univerſ. Buchdr.
Coll: 8° (172×105 mm cut))(^{8} A–2E^8 [$ half + 1 (-)(4) signed]; 232 leaves; pp. *i–xvi* 1 2–262 362 264–353 374–375 356–357 378–379 360–361 382–383 364–365 386–387 368–447 448 [=464]. Page 262 called '362'; inner forme of sheet Z numbered in 370s and 380s, instead of 350s and 360s.
Contents:)(1^r (*i*) title,)(1^v (*ii*) translator's formal dedication,)(2^r–)(4^v (*iii–viii*) text of translator's dedication,)(5^r–)(8^v (*ix–xvi*) Locke's dedication to Clarke, A1^r–2E8^r (*1–447*) text of German trans., 2E8^v (*448*) colophon.
Text (C4^v): 31 lines; 129 (139)×77 mm; 87 fraktur. Fair-quality laid paper without watermark. Page no. centered at top within rosettes above a rule, as headlines. Footnotes set 71 fraktur. Where footnotes continue to next page, both text and notes have CW. Text in direction line, p. 111.
HT: [rectangular headpiece, sunflower with leaves, 24×72 mm] | J. N. J. | Einige Gedancken | von der | Kinder = Erziehung. [orn. Es, G, K]
CW: Page (in fraktur).)(5^v alle= [allewege] A6^v (ge=) meine E7^r fei= [feine] L3^v gu= [guten] P7^r Mit= [Mittel] U7^v auff [auf] Z5^r wer- [werden] 2C2^v neh= [nehmen] 2E6^v (Ge=) wohn= [wohnheit]
Notes: Text based on 3d or 4th English ed. with dedication correctly dated 1692, and 216 sections of text. Frequent footnotes by the translator. Translator's dedication is to Herren Dohm-Vrobst Dechant of the Episcopal Society in Brandenburg. Axtell (German 1 note), following Christophersen, mentions a 1708 edition published in Hamburg, and a 1709 in 'Griefswald'. The GV (*Gesamtverzeichnis*, 1700–1910), does list an octavo published in Hamburg in 1708, with the same title as this Greifswald edition: "Gedanken v. Erziehung jung. Edelleute. 8. Hamburg. 708." This listing is possibly an error for 'Hanover', given the different sources from which GV was compiled. Aside from the Leipzig edition of 1708 (no. 212) I have found no other German editions until that of 1729 (no. 213). Attig further states "Reprinted in 1709 [unverified]".
References: Attig 600; Christophersen p. 103.
Copies examined: Y Han (Bu. 2568) L^1 (1568/1848; closely trimmed) L^2 (1568/9223 (1)) Wol (O 190.ii 8° Helmst.)

212. Education. German trans. (Olearius). Leipzig, 1708. 8°. With Fénelon's '*Education des filles*' (German tr.)
Herrn Johan Locks | Unterricht | von | Erziehung der Kinder / | aus dem Englischen; | Nebst | Herrn von Fenelon | Ertz = Bischoffs von Cammerich | Gedancken | von Erziehung der Töchter / | aus dem Frantzösischen übersetzet. | Mit einigen anmerdungen und einer | vorrede. | [orn. flying horse 49×63 mm] | Leipzig / | bey Thomas Fritschen / | 1708.

Coll: 8° (168 × 100 mm cut) a–b⁸ e⁴ 𝔄–2𝔒⁸ [$ half + 1 signed]; 348 leaves; pp. *1-3* 4-68 *69-72 1* 2-476 *477-479* 480-612 *613-624* [= 696].
Contents: a1ʳ (*1*) title (verso blank), a2ʳ-e2ᵛ (*3-68*) 'Vorrede zu dieser übersetzung', e3ʳ-e4ᵛ (*69-72*) Locke's dedication to Clarke, A1ʳ-2G6ᵛ (*1-476*) text in 217 §§, 2ʳ (*477*) section title to Fénelon (verso blank), 2G8ʳ-2Q2ᵛ (*479-612*) Fénelon's text in 13 chap., 2Q3ʳ (*613*) contents by chap. of Fénelon, 2Q3ᵛ-2Q8ᵛ (*614-624*) alphabetical index to both works.
Text: 30 lines; 120 (138) × 71 mm; 85 fraktur. Fair-quality laid paper without watermark. Page no. at external ends of headlines.
Section title, p. 477: Des | Herrn von Fenelon, | Ertz = Bischoffen von Cammerich / | Gedancken | von | Erziehung der Töchter / | aus dem Frantzösischen übersetzet.
Headlines (from verso to recto), a2ᵛ-e2ʳ (pp. *4-67*): Vorrede | zu dieser übersetzung.
A1ᵛ-2G6ᵛ (pp. *2-476*): Bedencken von erziehung | der kinder. | [rule 70 mm]
CW: Page.
Notes: A new translation attributed to G. Olearius by Christophersen; it is based on the 5th English edition of 1705 (no. 168), with additional notes by the translator. The text is in 213 sections, but the translator has created a §213 by so numbering the last sentence found in §212. Attig and Axtell admit to not verifying or seeing this edition. The translator's preface includes part of Le Clerc's 'Éloge' from the *Bibliothèque choisie*, 6 (1705). Fénelon's *De l'éducation de filles* was first published in Paris in 1687. This edition not in GV.
References (all as published in 1710): Attig 601; Axtell German 1 n.; Christophersen p. 103.
Copy examined: Wol (Pa.234)

213. Education. German trans. (Olearius). Hanover, 1729. 8°. With Fénelon.

Herrn Johann LOCKS | Unterricht | von | Erziehung der Kinder, [orn. R, K] | aus dem Englischen; | Nebst | Herrn von FENELON | Ertz = Bischoffs von Cammerich | Gedancken | von Erziehung der Töchter, [orn. E, T] | aus dem Frantzösischen übersetzt. | Mit einigen Anmerckungen und einer | Vorrede. | [oval engr. vignette of formal garden with shrubs, scroll above: 'DEVS DAT INCREMENTVM', 40 × 72 mm, on plate 42 × 72 mm] | HANOVER | Verlegts Nicolaus Förster und Sohn, 1729.
Coll: 8° (164 × 104 mm cut) a-d⁸ e⁴ A-2Q⁸ [$ half + 1 signed; c3 and e3 both signed 'c3']; 348 leaves; pp. *1-3* 4-68 *69-72 1* 2-476 *477-479* 480-612 *613-624* [= 696].
Contents and headlines for Locke's text same as no. 212.
Text (Z3ʳ): 30 lines; 126 (130) × 70 mm; 84 fraktur. Medium-quality laid paper, without watermark. 'Vorrede' set 37 lines, 70 fraktur. Page no. at outer ends of headlines.
HT: [unframed headpiece of fleurons, arcs & circles, 19 × 70 mm] |

JOHANN LOCKEN | Bedencken | von | Erziehung der Kinder/ | wie dieselbe besser massen gesche = | hen möge.
Headlines, from verso to recto: Bedencken von erziehung | der kinder.
2G8ᵛ–2Q1ʳ: Fenelons gedancken | von erziehung der töchter.
CW: Page. b4ʳ (hin =) ter A1ʳ ge = [gestalt] G5ʳ kind = [kindheit] L5ᵛ er = [erlangen,] O12ᵛ (be =) nennet 2B1ᵛ (sol =) te [te.] 2G4r (ge =) rich = [richtet;] 2M2ᵛ (wer =) den.
Notes: Line-for-line reprint of no. 212.
References: Attig 601 n.; Axtell German 1; Christophersen p. 103; GV v.89 p. 366.
Copies examined: Y L (8307.a.20)

214. Education. German trans. (Schwabe). Leipzig, 1761. 8°
Herrn Johann Lodens | Gedanken | von | Erziehung | der Kinder, | von neuem aus dem Englischen übersetzet, | gegen das | Herrn Costens französischen Uebersetzung, | nach der neuesten pariser Ausgabe von 1747, | verglichen, | und mit dessen Anmerkungen begleitet. | [orn., shell 22 × 36 mm] | Leipzig, | verlegts Johann Paul Krauß, | Buchh. in Wien, 1761.
Coll: 8° (185 × 117 mm cut) a–d⁸ e² A–2B⁸ 2C² [$ half + 1 (–e2) signed]; 236 leaves; pp. *I–III* IV–VIII *IX* X–LXII *LXIII* LXIV–LXVII *LXVIII 1* 2–368 367–368 371–404 [= 472]. Page no. 369–70 omitted, 367-8 repeated.
Contents: a1ʳ (*I*) title (verso blank), a2ʳ–a4ᵛ (*III–VIII*) 'Vorrede' (pref.) dated Easter 1761, a5ʳ–d7ᵛ (*IX–LXII*) Le Clerc's 'Éloge' from *Bibliotheque choisie*, d8ʳ–e2ʳ (*LXIII–LXVII*) Locke's dedication to Clarke (dated 7. Mar. 1690), e2ᵛ (*LXVIII*) contents of 28 chap. (called 'Abschnitt'), A1ʳ–2C2ᵛ (*1*–404) text.
Text (G5ʳ): 33 lines; 145 (157) × 73 (88) mm; 88 fraktur. Medium-quality laid paper, without watermark. Le Clerc's 'Eloge' set same as text; 'Vorrede' set 34 lines, 114 fraktur, with 1 mm leading. First page of each gathering also signed in direction line: 'Locke v. Erzieh. d. K.' (sheets E and H have 'Loke'). Page no. at external ends of headlines. Rectangular headpiece on pp. *III, IX, LXIII*, 25 × 77 mm; tailpiece, bust of helmetted figure with leaves, 36 × 49 mm on p. 404. Topical headings of sections set small fraktur in external margins.
HT: [headpiece of flowers in scrolled frame, 34 × 71 mm] | Gedanken | von | Erziehung der Kinder. | [Oxford rule 37/36 mm]
Headlines, a2ᵛ–a4ᵛ: Vorrede.
RT, from verso to recto, a5ʳ–d8ʳ: Historische Lobschrift | des Herrn Joh. Lodens. d8ᵛ–e2ʳ: Lodens Zuschrift | an Eduard Clarke von Chipley.
Headlines give chap. no. on versos; rectos give brief chap. titles, e.g. 'Der IX Abschnitt. | Nothwendigkeit eines Hofmeisters.'
CW: Page (in fraktur): a2ᵛ gelin = [gelinden] b1ʳ allge = [allgemeinen] A8ᵛ bekom = [bekommen,] E1ᵛ als = [alsdann] K2ʳ meh = [mehrer] P4ʳ anmer = [anmerken,] T5ᵛ 165. §. Z3ʳ (Red =) ner

Notes: A new translation "by Johann Joachim Schwabe (1714–84), follower of Gottsched, a professor in Leipzig and for a long time compiler of the Fair Catalogues" (Fabian, *The English Book in Eighteenth-Century Germany*, p. 55). He was identified as the translator in Friedrich A. Weiz's bibliographical work, *Das gelehrte Sachsen* (Leipzig, 1780), pp. 227–8. He uses the English text found in the third vol. of the 1722 *Works* (no. 364). The translator says he knows of the earlier German translations both first published in 1709 and the reprint of the Leipzig edition in 1729 (no. 211–13), but has found them both unsatisfactory and annoying to read; he found Coste's French translation (using the 1747 edition; no. 207) more fluid and elegant, and has used Coste's chapter divisions and his notes as well as adding some of his own. The text follows Locke's paragraph numbering of 217 sections, but the translator has created a § 213 by so numbering the last sentence found in § 212 (that beginning 'The time therefore I should think the fittest . . .'). He has also greatly expanded Coste's and Locke's own notes, supplying German translations of Montaigne from Gottsched. I am indebted to Dr. Bernhard Fabian for the biographical information. A microfilm copy of this edition is in the collection, *German Baroque Literature* (following the "descriptive catalogue of the collection of Harold Gantz" published in New Haven, by Research Publications, 1974), no. 1631.
References: Attig 602; Axtell German 2 n.; Christophersen p. 103; GV 1700–1910 (dated '1762').
Copies examined: Y Mun (Paed. Th. 2798; 185 × 117 mm cut)

215. Education. German trans. (Rudolphi). Vienna & Wolfenbüttel, 1787. 8°. In: Campe.
Section title: Handbuch | der | Erziehung | aus dem Englischen des John Locke | übersetzt | von | Rudolphi.
Series title: Allgemeine Revision | des gesammten | Schul = und Erziehungswesen | von | einer Gesellschaft | praktischer Erzieher. | [rule 72 mm] | Neunter Theil. | [rule 58 mm] | Herausgegeben | von | J. H. Campe | Hochfürstl. Braunschweig = Lünenburgischen und Anhalts | Dessauischen Schul = und Erziehungsrath, Mitglied der | Erziehungsgesellschaft in Stockholm. | [orn., palms, 24 × 48 mm] | [orn. rule 75 mm] | Wien und Wolfenbüttel, | bey Rudolph Gräßer und Compagnie | und in der Schulbuchhandlung. | 1787.
Coll: 8° (176 × 106 mm cut A⁸ *⁶ (sheet * inserted after A1) B–2P⁸ 2Q²)(⁸ [$ 5 (–*5, –2Q2) signed]; 320 leaves; pp. *1–2 III IV–VIII IX X–XIV 3–5 6–239 244 241–612 613–628 [= 640]. Page no. 240 called '244'. First page of each gathering signed in direction line 'A. Rev. d. E. 9. B.'
Contents: A1ʳ (*1*) series title (verso blank), *1ʳ–3ᵛ (*III–VIII*) Campe's 'Vorrede' signed 'Salzdalen im Julius 1787.', *4ʳ–6ᵛ (*IX–XIV*) 'Inhalt' for text of 24 chapters, A2ʳ (*3*) section title (verso blank), A3ʳ–2Q2ᵛ (*5–612*) text of Locke's *Education*,)(1ʳ (*613*) 'Anzeiger',)(1ᵛ–)(4ʳ (*614–619*) 'Ankündigung der Monatsschrift under dem Titel: Braunschweigisches

Journal' ed. by Ernst Christian Trapp and J.H. Campe (notice & advt.),)(4ᵛ-5ʳ (620-621) 'Preisfrage',)(5ᵛ-6ʳ (622-623) list of books published,)(6ᵛ blank,)(7ʳ·ᵛ (625-626) errata for vols. 6-9 of the series,)(8ʳ·ᵛ (627-628) blank.

Text (U5ʳ): 26 lines; 136 (149)×76 mm; 114 fraktur, with 1 mm leading. Notes set 83 fraktur with leading. Very thin grey-toned paper; possible bunch-of-grapes as watermark at foot of 2d and 7th leaves. Page no. at external end of top lines. Ornamental branch, 5×17 mm, as headlines. Page 612 concludes 'Ende des neunten Theils.' followed by a tailpiece: heartlike shield on rectangular pedestal base above grass, 32×50 mm.

CW: Page. A7ʳ die= [dieses] C8ᵛ (Ma=) gen H5ʳ (schid=) liche P3ʳ beob= [beobachtet] X8ʳ verhin= [verhindert,] 2A8ᵛ (anzuhal=) ten 2F8ᵛ (Bi=) bel, 2M6ʳ Schrit= [Schritten]

Notes: A new translation by L. Rudolphi, divided into 24 chapters after the French and later editions, but combining some shorter chapters, e.g. chap. I covers §§ 1-30, II covers §§ 31-42. The 'Vorrede' by Campe criticizes Ouvrier's translation (no. 216); the body of the text is full of footnotes, chiefly signed by Campe. Yale Univ. Library's copy of the set has a rubber stamp on verso of title of vol.8 reading 'Printed in Austria.'

References: Attig 604; Axtell German 3; Christophersen p. 103.

Copies examined: CtY (Lb13/785c v.9) L (1578/3524, vol.9; lacks sheet)(at end)

216. Education. German trans. (Ouvrier). Leipzig, 1787. 8°
John Locke, Esq. | über die | Erziehung der Jugend | unter den höheren Volksklassen. | [rule 23 mm] | Aus dem Englischen übersezt | und mit | Zusätzen und Anmerkungen versehen | von | Carl Siegmund Ouvrier. | [rule 70 mm] | Mit Churfürstlich=Sächsischer Freiheit. | [rule 69 mm] | Leipzig, 1787. | Bei Siegfried Lebrecht Crusius.

Colophon, p. 491: Dessau, | Gedruckt bey Heinrich Heybruch, Hochfürstl. Hof= und Regierungs=Buchdrucker.

Coll: 8° (166×100 mm cut) a-d⁸ (-d1) e² χ1 A-2G⁸ 2H⁶ [$ half + 1 (+Hh5) signed]; 280 leaves; pp. I-III IV-XLVII LVIII XLIX-LXVI LXVII-LXVIII 1 2-160 159-175 178-239 340 241-251 522 253-337 228 339-352 252 354-381 283 383-491 492 [=560]. Page no. 159-60 repeated, 176-77 omitted; & other misnumbering.

Contents: a1ʳ (I) title (verso blank), a2ʳ-a4ᵛ (III-VIII) Locke's dedication to Clarke, a5ʳ-b4ᵛ (IX-XXIV) translator's & editor's pref., b5ʳ-e2ᵛ (XXV-LXVI) Le Clerc's 'Éloge' (from *Bibliothèque choisie*, with additions from the *British Plutarch 5*, 1776), χ1ʳ (LXVII) half title (verso blank), A1ʳ-2G5ᵛ (1-474) text of 215 §§ (numbering errors corrected) and postscript by Ouvrier ('Zusatz des deutschen Herausgebers. Abriss der Lehrgegenstände.') 2G6ʳ-2H4ʳ (475-487.27) 'Inhalt' (summary of text), 2H4ʳ-2H6ʳ (487.28-491) summary index of translator's notes & colophon, 2H6ᵛ (492) errata (12.3 lines).

Text: 30 lines with 1 mm leading; 128 (140)×71 mm; 85 fraktur. Fair-quality laid paper. Page no. at external ends of headlines.
Half title, p. LXVII: Handbuch | für | Eltern und Erzieher.
HT: Von Erziehung der Kinder. | [orn. Oxford rule 57 mm].
Headlines from chapter divisions identify brief subject, e.g. '24. Abschnitt. Vom Unterricht | in der Logik.'
CW: Page (in fraktur). A1^v I. Ab- [I. Abschnitt.] I2^v Ver- [Verbot] X2^v bei- [beides]
Notes: The translator, Ouvrier, says it is his own work but he has benefitted from Coste's and Campe's work (no. 215). He has followed the French edition of 1747 (no. 207), itself based on the 5th English, dividing the text into 27 'Abschnitt' (215 sections) and conclusion. There are extensive footnotes covering several pages: after 8th section (between §§ 71 & 72: pp. 102–11), after 21st section (between §§ 136 & 137: pp. 234–48), amid 24th section (§§ 155–6 and pp. 169–170, pp. 280–93 and 321–40) and between §§ 194 & 195 (pp. 386–444).
References: Attig 603; Axtell German 2.
Copy examined: O (Vet.D5 f.99)

217. Education. Italian trans. (Coste/Marchini). Lucca, 1735. 12°
L'EDUCAZIONE | DE' FIGLIUOLI | *Tradotta già dall' Ingleſe* | DEL | SIG.^{OR} [very small font 'OR'] LOCKE | *IN LINGUAGGIO FRANCESE* [swash Ns] | E da queſto | TRASPORTATA NELL' | ITALIANO. | [orn. monogram with initials S, G, M, 20×46 mm] | IN LUCCA, MDCCXXXV. | [segmented rule, 62 mm] | Per Salvatore, e Giandomenico Ma- | reſcandoli.)(*Con Lic. de Sup.*
Coll: 12° (148×80 mm cut) §^{12} *^{12} A–V^{12} [$ half signed] 264 leaves; pp. i–xlviii 1–476 477–480 [= 528].
Contents: §1^r (*i*) title (verso blank), §2^r–§7^v (*iii–xiv*) dedication to Signora Chiara Guinigi Parensi, from the translator Fabio Marchini, §8^r–§10^v (*xv–xx*) 'Avvertimento' (Coste's 'Avertissement' to his 4th French edition of 1733), §11^r–*6^r (*xxi–xxxv*) Coste's pref. to his translation, *6^v–*12^v (*xxxvi–xlviii*) table of contents of 28 'Sezzioni' (Chapters) and of the 223 sections, A1^r–V10^v (1–476) Italian translation of Coste's text of 1733, V11–12 blank.
Text (A12^v): 33 lines; 117 (125)×61 mm; 70 R. Dedication set 27 lines in 84 ital. 'Avvertimento' set mixed roman & ital., 32 or 33 lines (varies). Poor-quality laid paper watermarked with fleur-de-lys surmounting cartouche with letter A and P over a bunch of grapes. Page no. at external ends of headlines.
HT: DELLA | EDUCAZIONE | DE' FIGLIUOLI.
RT, from verso to recto: *DELLA EDUCAZIONE* | *DE' FUGLIUOLI.*
CW: Page. A2^r (ne-) ces- [ceſſaria] C1^v eſer- [eſercizj:] C2^r ſe G12^v (l'azio-) ni N2^v (gagliar-) da Q1^v Gram- [Gramatica,] T8^r na- [nazioni,]
Notes: The text closely follows Coste's, including the division into 28

chapters with the resulting increase to 223 sections. The dedicatee was the wife of Giacomo Parensi.

I have found no bibliographic record or location of copies of this edition anywhere. My own copy, fortuituously purchased, is the only one I know of.
Copy examined: Y (bookplate of Angelo Antonelli)

218. Education. Italian trans. (Coste/anon.). Venice, 1735. 2 vols. in 12°
Vol. 1, in red & black: DELLA | [red line:] EDUCAZIONE | DEI | [red:] FANCIULLI | Scritto in Lingua Inglese | DAL SIGNOR | [red:] LOCKE, | Indi Tradotto in Lingua Francese | DAL SIGNOR | [red:] COSTE, | E finalmente Tradotto in Lingua Italiana | dall' Edizione Francefe fatta in | Amfterdam l'anno 1733. | [red:] TOMO PRIMO. | [orn., flowered scroll 18 × 25 mm] | [red:] VENEZIA. | [rule 51 mm] | [red:] Appresso Francesco Pitteri. | In Merceria all'Infegna della Fortuna Trionfante, | [red:] MDCCXXXV. | *Con Licenza de' Superiori, e Privilegio.*
Vol. 2 in black, lines 1–5 as in v. 1, line 6 et seq.: *DAL SIGNOR* | LOCKE, | . . . [&c. until:] TOMO SECONDO. | . . . [&c. as in v. 1]
Coll: 12° (157 × 96 mm cut). Vol. 1: *¹² **¹² (– 6 leaves = N⁶) A–M¹² N⁶ [$ half signed]; 168 leaves; pp. *i–iv* v–xxxvj 1–299 *300* [= 336]. First page of sheets C and F–N also signed 'Tom.I.' in direction line.
 Vol. 2: A⁶ B–P¹² [$ half signed; G2 and G4 both signed 'G2']; 174 leaves; pp. *1–2* 3–334 *135* 336–348. Page no. 335 called '135'. First page of sheets B–P also signed 'Tom.II.'
Contents: Vol. 1: *1 (*i–ii*) blank, *2ʳ (*iii*) title (verso blank), *3ʳ–*4ᵛ (*v–viij*) Coste's dedication ('al Signor della Motta' signed 'Londra 4. Aprile 1721. COSTE.', *5ʳ–*7ᵛ (*ix–xiv*) Coste's 'avvertimento' (pref. to 1733 French edition), *8ʳ–**6ʳ (*xv–xxxv*) Coste's pref. to 1708 French ed. (cf. no. 195), **6ᵛ (*xxxvj*) contents of ch. 1–12 (§§ 1–112), A1ʳ–N6ʳ (1–299) text of ch. 1–12, N6ᵛ (*300*) blank.
 Vol. 2: A1ʳ (*1*) title (verso blank), A2ʳ–P2ᵛ (3–328) text of ch. 13–28 (§§ 113–223), P3ʳ,ᵛ (329–30) chap. contents of vol.2, P4ʳ–P12ʳ (331–347) alphabetical index of topics, P12ᵛ (348) printing permission to Pitteri, dated 27 March 1735.
Illustration: Vol. 1 has as front. engraved oval portrait of Locke after Kneller, facing right, subscribed 'Io. Cattini Fecit., 138 × 82 mm on plate 142 × 88 mm. It was copied from the French editions (cf. no. 198, 200), and has a 4-line verse subscription in Italian: "*Perche del LOCK tu vegga il volto e l'opra,* | *Qui dopppia arte s'adopra,* | *Nè fare il vario dilicato stile,* | *L'opra o il volto potea più al ver simile.*"
Text (D7ᵛ): 26 lines; 125 (134) × 63 (73) mm; 97 R. Footnotes set 54 R; topical headings set 54 R, 9 mm wide, in outer margins. Good-quality laid paper with floral watermark. Preliminary pages without headlines.
HT, both vols.: DELL' EDUCAZIONE | DEI FANCIULLI. | [orn., man's face, with leaves, 17 × 57 mm]

RT, from verso to recto: DELL' EDUCAZIONE | DEI [or 'DE I'] FANCIULLI. (Some headlines lack period after 'FANCIULLI', e.g. 25, 27, 115; pp. 217, 245 and 251 both read 'DE I' and end with a colon [:].)
CW: Page. Vol. 1: A1^r prin- [principal] D12^r trat- [trattamento] N4^v con- [confiderabili;] Vol. 2: B8^v que- [quegli] G9^v ge- [genere] M3^v ori- [origine]
Notes: An anonymous translation based on the 1733 French ed. (no. 200).
References: Attig 611; Axtell Italian 1.
Copy examined: O (Vet.F4 f.19)

219. Education. Selections, Italian trans. (Becelli). Verona, 1736. 8°
ARTE | DELL'EDUCARE | I FANCIULLI | DI GIOVANNI LOCHE | INGLESE | RIDOTTA AD AFORISMI | *CON ALCUNE GIUNTE* | [orn., cup with angels & scroll: 'DELA MIA | MORTE ETERNA VITA | I VIVO | [2d scroll:] SEMPER | EADEM', 53 × 39 mm] | IN VERONA MDCCXXXVI | [broken rule 80 mm] | Per Dionigi Ramanzini Librajo a S. Tomio. | *Con Licenza* [swash z] *de' Superiori.*
Coll: square 8° (197 × 134 mm cut) *^{8} A–G^8 [$ half signed]; 64 leaves; pp. *i*–*xvi* 1–69 70 71–110 *111–112* [=128].
Contents: *1^r (*i*) title (verso blank), *2^r–*4^v (*iii–viii*) dedication by Giulio Cesare Becelli to Antonio Grimani, captain of Verona, *5^r–*8^r (*ix–xv*) 'PROEMIO' (pref.), *8^v (*xvi*) imprimatur dated 21. Agosto 1736, A1^r–G7^v (1–110) text, G8 blank.
Imprimatur, p. *xvi*: NOI REFORMATORI | Dello Studio di Padova. . . . per . . . Approbazione del P. F. Lauro Maria Picinelli, Inquisitore di Verona. 21 Agosto 1736.'
Text (D6^r): 29 lines; 137 (147) × 80 mm; text set 95 R. Dedication set 23 lines 111 ital; pref. 29 lines 94R; 'Giunte' 94 ital. Good-quality laid paper with compass as watermark. Page no. at external ends of headlines.
RT, from verso to recto: 'Arte dell'Educare | I Fanciulli.' Some headlines (pp. 11, 21 and 53) read 'I fanciulli.'; p. 35 reads 'I Fanciulii.'; p. 44: 'Arte dell'Educar'. Final page: 'Arte dell'Educare'.
CW: Page. A3^r (*buo-*) *ni*, B6^r (*fe-*) *gno* D6^v e fchie- [e fchieti] E6^v (lin-) gua G3^v (*me-*) *mo-* [*morie*]
Notes: Text consists of 100 aphorisms or sentences selected & translated from the *Education* numbered in roman numerals & set in roman type, followed by a comment ('Giunta', numbered 1–44 and 'Ultima') from Becelli, set in italic. Quotations from Locke occupy roughly 20 per cent of the total text. Each section headed, e.g., 'LXXI.' for Locke's text, and '*GIUNTA* (31)'.
References: Attig 626; Axtell Italian 2.
Copy examined: O (Vet.F4 e.38)

220. Education. Italian trans. (Coste/Marchini). Lucca, 1750. 8°
L'EDUCAZIONE | DE' FIGLIUOLI | *Tradotta già dall' Inglefe* | DEL | SIG^{OR}. [smaller font 'OR'] LOCKE | *IN LINGUAGGIO FRANCESE* [swash U, Ns] | E da quefto | TRASPORTATA NELL' | ITALIANO.

| [orn., cornucopia with scrolls 40 × 58 mm] | IN LUCCA, MDCCL. | Per Salvatore, Giandomenico Marefcandoli | [broken rule 82 mm] | Con Licenza de' Superiori.

Coll: 8° (174 × 106 mm cut) a–b⁸ A–2B⁸ [$ half signed]; 216 leaves; pp. *i–xxxii 1–367 268 399–428 429–430* [= 432]. Page 368 called '268'; page no. 369–398 omitted.

Contents: a1ʳ (*i*) title (verso blank), a2ʳ–4ʳ (*iii–vii*) translation of 'Avertissement' to French 4th ed. of 1733 (no. 200), a4ᵛ–b2ᵛ (*viii–xx*) trans. of Coste's pref., b3ʳ–b8ᵛ (*xxi–xxxii*) contents by chapters and sections, A1ʳ–2B7ᵛ (*1–428*) trans. of text in 28 'sezzione' and 223 §§, 2B8 (*429–430*) blank.

Text (N8ᵛ): 31 lines; 136 (145) × 82 mm; 88 R. 'Notice' set 31 lines roman; pref., 31 lines roman and ital mixed. Good-quality paper without watermark. Page no. at external end of headlines.

HT: DELLA | EDUCAZIONE | DE' FIGLIUOLI.

RT, from verso to recto: DELLA EDUCAZIONE | DE' FIGIUOLI.

CW: Page. a2ᵛ Fran- [Francia] C2ʳ cor- [correre] A8ᵛ diffi- [difficilmente] 2B1ʳ Gen- [Gentiluomo,]

Notes: A new setting of the 1735 Italian edition published in Lucca (no. 217) with the omission of the dedication by the translator, Fabio Marchini. Since the dedication to the earlier edition carries his name, this edition appears (wrongly) to be an anonymous translation.

References: Attig 612; Axtell Italian 3.

Copy examined: O (Vet.F4 e.39)

221. Education. Italian trans. (anon.) Venice, 1751. 12°

DELLA | EDUCAZIONE | DEI | FANCIULLI | Scritto IN Lingua Inglese | *DAL SIGNOR* | LOCKE. | Indi Tradotto in Lingua Francefe | dal Signor Coste. | E finalmente in Lingua Italiana | dall'Edizione Francefe fatta in | Amfterdam l'anno 1733. | TOMO PRIMO. [- 'SECUNDO.'] | [orn., vase of flowers in sconce 25 × 33 mm] | IN VENEZIA, MDCCLI. | [rule 58 mm] | Presso Francesco Pitteri. | Con Licenza de' Superiori, e Privilegio.

Coll: 12° (150 × 85 mm cut) *¹² **¹² A–V¹² [$ half (–*2, –K5) signed; **6 signed '*6']; 264 leaves; pp. *i–iv v–xlviij 1–224 225–226 227–480* [= 528]. First leaf of sheets A–K signed 'Locke. Tom. I.' in direction line; of L–V also 'Locke. Tom. II.'

Contents: *1 blank, *2ʳ (*iii*) title (verso blank), *3ʳ–*4ᵛ (*v–viij*) dedication to 'Signor della Motta' (Fénelon), *5ʳ–*7ᵛ (*ix–xiv*) trans. of Coste's pref. to 4th ed. of 1733 (no. 200), *8ʳ–**6ʳ (*xv–xxxv*) trans. of Coste's pref. to 1708 French ed., **6ᵛ–**12ʳ (*xxxvi–xlvij*) contents by vol., chap. and sections numbered within each chap., **12ᵛ (*xlviij*) imprimatur (reprinted from no. 218), A1ʳ–K4ᵛ (*1–224*) text of chap. 1–12, K5ʳ (*225*) title of vol. 2 (verso blank), K6ʳ–V5ᵛ (*227–466*) text of chap. 13–28, V6ʳ–V12ᵛ (*467–480*) alphabetical index to topics.

Illustration: engraved front. is Locke's portrait, after Kneller, without subscription of its source, 122 × 62 mm on plate, 127 × 67 mm. It has been copied from the 1735 Italian edition (no. 218), including the 4-line verse subscription.

Text: 34 lines; 118 (125) × 60 mm; 70 R. Medium-quality laid paper, no visible watermarks. Page numbers at outer ends of headlines.

HT, p. 1: [orn. rule of small irons, 6 × 57 mm] | DELLA | EDUCAZIONE | DEI | FANCIULLI. | [rule 59 mm]

RT, from verso to recto: *Dell' Educazione* | *dei Fanciulli.*

CW: Page. A3^r lo- [loro] E4^r mag- [maggior] L10^r van- [vantaggio.] R1^v ap- [appena]

Notes: Reprint of the Venice 1735 Italian edition (no. 218), itself based on the French 1733 edition. Chapter divisions of the French edition retained, section numbering overall replaced by section numbering from one within each chapter.

References: Attig 613; Axtell Italian 4.

Copy examined: O (Vet.F5 f.13)

222. Education. Italian trans. (Coste/anon.). Venice, 1782. 2 vols. in 12°. With Rollin.

EDUCAZIONE | DEI | FANCIULLI | *DEL SIGNOR* | LOCKE | QUINTA EDIZIONE | AGGIUNTOVI | *L'Iſtruzione de' Fanciulli, e Giovanette* | *del Sig. Carlo Rollin.* | TOMO PRIMO. ['SECONDO.'] | [oval tailpiece, 2 doves on nest, 23 × 42 mm] | IN VENEZIA, MDCCLXXXII. ['I's in date fallen below line] | [orn. rule of 10 § laid horizontally, 40 mm] | PRESSO FRANCESCO PITTERI. | *Con Licenza de' Superiori, e Privilegio.*

Coll: 12° (158 × 84 mm cut). Vol. 1: a^{12} b^6 A–L^{12} [$ half signed]; 150 leaves; pp. *i–iv* v–xxxvi 1–262 263–264 [= 300]. First page of each sheet signed '*Locke. Tom.I.*' in direction line.

Vol. 2: a^6 A–L^{12} [$ half signed]; 138 leaves; pp. *i–ii* iii–xii 1–168 *169–170* 171–264 [= 276]. First page of each sheet A–G also signed '*Locke. Tom. II.*' (period after *Locke* sometimes omitted); sheets H–L: '*Rollin Tom. II.*'

Contents: Vol. 1: a1 blank, a2^r (*iii*) title (verso blank), a3^r–a4^r (v–vii) note of Pitteri to the reader, a4^v–a8^r (viii–xv) Coste's 'Avertissement' from 4th French ed. (1733), a8^v–b3^v (xvi–xxx) Italian trans. of Coste's pref. to French 1708 ed. (no. 195), b4^r–b6^v (xxxi–xxxvi) contents of vol. 1 (chap. 1–19), A1^r–L11^v (1–262) text of chap. 1–19, L12 blank.

Vol. 2: a1^r (*i*) title (verso blank), a2^r–a3^v (iii–vi) contents of vol. 2, (ch. 20–28), a4^r–a6^r (vii–xi) contents of Rollin's text, a6^v (xii) imprimatur licensing Pitteri (dated 27. Aprile 1782), A1^r–G12^v (1–168) text of chap. 20–28, H1^r (*169*) section title to Rollin (verso blank), H2^r–L12^v (171–264) Italian trans. of Rollin's *New Thoughts concerning Education*.

Illustration: vol. 1 has poorly engraved portrait of Locke in oval frame as front., unsigned, 123 × 62 mm, on plate 130 × 68 mm, copied from the previous Italian edition (no. 221).

Text: 36 lines; 124 (131)×60 mm; 69 R. Fair-quality laid paper without watermarks, except title leaf (with 'DW'). Page no. at external ends of headlines indented 4 mm.
Section title, v.2, p. 169 (H1ʳ): ISTRUZIONE | PER LA [swash A] | BUONA EDUCAZIONE | DE' FANCIULLI, E DELLE | GIOVANETTE. | DEL SIGNOR | CARLO ROLLIN.
RT, from verso to recto: *Dell' Educazione | dei Fanciulle.*' (varies, without pattern; some read: *Della Educazione | dei Fanciulli.*)
CW: Page. Vol. 1: a3ᵛ (*mon-*) tre a12ᵛ d' [d'ogni] A1ʳ o del- [o della] C11ᵛ (ra-) gio- [gione,] F7ᵛ tut- [tutte] H10ʳ difet- [difetti] L8ᵛ (cor-) po
Vol. 2: A3ʳ (Te-) ne- [nebre] C2ᵛ nel- [nello] E9ᵛ (Ami-) ci G10ʳ (E-) ſtra- [ſtranei,] H5ᵛ (quel-) la L4ᵛ ver- [verſo]
Notes: This edition, like the previous Italian one, omits the section numbers, but retains Coste's textual division of 28 chapters; it appears to be a new (or revised) translation of the previous Italian edition (no. 221), but follows the text of the Dublin 1737 or 1738 edition (no. 177 or 179). The English translation of Rollin's work was first included in the Dublin 1737 edition (no.177).
References: Attig 614; Axtell Italian 5; Christophersen p. 103.
Copy examined: L (8310.a.25)

223. Education. Italian trans. (anon). Venice, 1792. 2 vols.-in 12°. With Rollin.
EDUCAZIONE | DEI | FANCIULLI | DEL SIGNOR | LOCKE | SESTA EDIZIONE | . . . [&c. as in no. 222, until 11th line:] [orn., doves on a nest, 23×42 mm] | IN VENEZIA, MDCCXCII. | [orn. rule of horizontal §§, 38 mm] | PRESSO GIUSEPPE ROSSI QU: BORTOLO. | *Con Licenza de' Superiori, e Privilegio.*
Collation, and *Contents*: same as no. 222, except vol. 2 p. xii (a6ᵛ) gives license to print to Giuseppe Rossi, and is dated 31 Agosto 1790. Paper cut to 158×93 mm.
Illustration: front. same as in no. 222, 123×62 mm on plate 130×68mm.
Text (E4ʳ): 36 lines; 124 (131)×63 mm; 69 R. Fair-quality laid paper without watermarks. Page no. inset 4 mm from external page block in headlines, as in no. 222.
HT, v. 1 and 2: [framed orn. headpiece of chalice and fruit, 24×58 mm] | DELL' | EDUCAZIONE | DEI FANCIULLI. | [rule 59 mm]
Section title, v.2, p. *169*: ISTRUZIONE | PER LA | BUONA EDUCAZIONE | DE' FANCIULLI, E DELLE | GIOVANETTE | DEL SIGNOR | CARLO ROLLIN.
CW: Page. Vol. 1: A1ʳ o del- [o della] C3ᵛ men- [mente] I7ʳ gran- [grande,]
Vol. 2: A1ʳ rar- [rargli] C2ᵛ nel- [nello] F2ᵛ stan- [stanza]
Notes: A new setting, line by line, of 1782 edition (no. 222). Internal sections within the usual 28 chapters numbered from one. The only copy seen has paper trimmed to 158×93 mm.

References: Attig 615; Axtell Italian 6.
Copy examined: O (Vet.F5.f.18)

223.1*. Education. Polish trans. (Truskolawski). 1781.
Książka o edukacji dzieci J. Locke'a [The Book about Child Education by J. Locke]. 1781.

The above information taken from Janina Rosicka's essay, 'Locke and the Polish Enlightenment', in *Locke's Philosophy: Content and Context*, edited by G. A. J. Rogers (Oxford, 1994), p. 249. The footnote (ibid., no. 37) gives contradictory information: "In 1795 the Piarist Edmund Truskolawski translated this work from the French edn. by Coste." Since she writes of a second translation in 1801 and a third in 1959, I can only assume this 1781 translation was done by Truskolawski. Elsewhere (p. 243) Rosicka states that Polish scholars "abstracted from his *Thoughts concerning Education*, adapted it to Polish reality, and 'forgot' about his approval of private education. In the otherwise good translation of his book which appeared in 1781, the translator expunged all passages concerning private education." I have found no further information.

224*. Education. Russian trans. (Popovskii). Moscow, 1759. 2 vols. 8°
О | ВОСПИТАНІИ | ДѢТЕЙ | ГОСПОДИНА ЛОККА | Переведено | сь францусскаго на россійскій | языкь | Императорскаго Московскаго Универси- | тета Профессоромь Николаемь | Поповскимь. | [orn. tailpiece] | [orn. rule of fleurons] | Печатово при Императорскомь Москов- | скомь Университеть, | 1759 года.
Title transliterated: O vospitanīi dieteĭ Gospodina Lokka, Perevedeno s' frantsusskago na rossiĭskiĭ iâzyk Imperatorskago Moskovskago Universiteta Professorom' Nikolaem' Popovskim'. Pechatovo pri Imperatorskom' Moskovskom' Universitet', 1759 goda.
Title translated: On the education of children, by the gentleman Locke. Translated from the French into the Russian language by Imperial Moscow University Professor Nikolai Popovskii. Printed at Imperial Moscow University Press, 1759.
Coll. 8°. Vol. 1: [6], 1–240, 239–248 pp. Page no. 239–40 repeated.
  Vol. 2: [2], 266 pp.
Note: Information from *Svodnyi katalog*, 3720. Title transcribed from photograph, ibid. The letter a in the 6th line printed as small 'A' (not 'a'), the other letters being in lower case. The lower-case Ts in the 8th–9th, 13th–14th lines are printed in old-style 'm'. I have not been able to see a copy.

225*. Education. Russian trans. (Popovskii). Moscow, 1760. 2 vols. 8°
О | ВОСПИТАНІИ | ДѢТЕЙ | ГОСПОДИНА ЛОККА | . . . [&c., same as no. 224, but with imprint date 1760.]
Note: All other details, including pagination error are the same as 1759

edition, but the title leaves are cancellantia. Information from *Svodnyi katalog*, 2d entry under 3720. I have not seen a copy. Attig's source for his reference to this and the following entry is "*Eighteenth-century Russian publications* ; 3720a."
Reference: Attig *634 ('unverified').

226*. Education. Russian trans. (Popovski). 2d ed., Moscow, 1788. 8°
О | ВОСПИТАНІИ | ДѢТЕЙ | ГОСПОДИНА ЛОККА | . . . [&c., same as no. 224, until edition statement:] Изд. 2-е. М., тип. Комп. типографич., 1788.
Transliterated: . . . Izd. 2-e. M., tip. Komp. tipografich., 1788.
Translated: . . . 2d printing. Moscow, Company of Printers, 1788.
Coll. 8°. Vol. 1: pp. I–VIII, 9–323. Vol. 2: pp. 1–331.
Note: Information from *Svodnyi katalog* 3721. I have not seen a copy.
Reference: Attig *634 ('unverified').

227. Education. Swedish trans. (anon). Stockholm, 1709. 8°
In Swedish fraktur and roman, with decorative T, A and U in 2d, 4th and 7th lines: Herr JOHAN LOCKES | Tankar | och | Anmärkningar | angående | Ungdomens | Uppfostring | Först skrefne uti Engelskan/men | nu för deras serdeles wärde och | nyttighet uppå Swenska | öfwersatte. | Doctrina vires promovet infitas, | Rectique cultus pectora roborant: | Utcumque defecere mores, | Dedecorant bene nata culpæ. | *Horat. Lib.* IV. *Od.* 4 [I roman, V ital.] | [orn. rule of small fleurons, 83 mm] | STOCKHOLM / | Tryckt hos JULIUS G. MATTHIÆ Åhr 1709.
Coll.: 8° (162 × 99 mm closely cut))(⁸ A–U⁸ [$5 signed]; 168 leaves; pp. *i–xvi* 1 2–320 [= 336].
Contents:)(1ʳ (¹) title (verso blank),)(2ʳ–)(6ᵛ (*iii–xii*) translator's pref.,)(7ʳ–)(8ᵛ (*xiii–xvi*) translation of Locke's dedication to Clarke, A1ʳ–U8ᵛ (*1–320*) text in 218 §§.
Text (M3ʳ): 34 lines; 140 (149) × 82 mm; 81 Swedish fraktur. Fair-quality paper with coat-of-arms watermark. Page no. in parentheses centered at head of page between orn. suns, with an 80 mm rule beneath. Page *1* has framed headpiece of leaves (25 × 82 mm); pp. *xvi* has rectangular tailpiece of bell and horns, inscribed 'SONO PROBANTVR', 30 × 40 mm; p.320 has tailpiece of shell and flowers, 16 × 41 mm.
CW: Page (in fraktur). A1ʳ (hwil =) ket E4ᵛ (al =) tid K5ʳ bar = [barnets] O1ᵛ (dageli =) gen R8ᵛ (or =) saken
Note: Text is a translation of the 5th English edition of 1705 (no. 169), by an anonymous translator. Dedicatory letter dated '7 Martii 1692.'
References: Attig 638; Axtell Swedish 1.
Copy examined: L (8309.aa.40)

228. Education. Abstract, 1761. In *Essays on Education* . . . 8°

Caption title: | [headpiece, vase with leaves between 2 dogs, 11 × 78 mm] | AN EXTRACT from | Mr. LOCKE's Thoughts Concerning | EDUCATION. | [rule 79 mm]

IN: ESSAYS | ON | EDUCATION | BY | MILTON, LOCKE, | AND THE | AUTHORS of the SPECTATOR, *&c.* | To which are added | Obſervations on the ancient and | modern Languages | By R. WYNNE, A.M. | Rector of *Ayot St. Laurence* in *Hertfordſhire*. | LONDON: | Printed for J. and R. TONSON in the Strand. | [rule 25 mm] | M DCC LXI.

Coll. of the whole: 8° (200 × 125 mm cut) π^2 A^4 $B-S^8$ T^8 (-T4.5 = π^2) [$ half (-T4) signed]; 148 leaves; pp. I–IV i–v vi–viii 1 2–197 *198* 199–255 *256* 257–283 *284* [=296].

Locke's text: pp. 23–122 ($C4^r$–$I5^v$).

Contents: $\pi1^r$ (*I*) half title (verso blank), $\pi2^r$ (*III*) title, $A1^r$–$A2^v$ (*i–v*) Wynne's dedication to the king, $A3^r$–$A4^v$ (*v–viii*) preface, $B1^r$–$C3^v$ (*1–22*) selection from 'Milton's Tractate of Education' (dedicated to Samuel Hartlib), $C4^r$–$I5^v$ (*23–122*) Locke's text, $I6^r$–$O3^r$ (*123–197*) 'Essays on Education by the authors of the *Spectator*, *Tatler*, and *Guardian*', $O3^v$–$T6^r$ (*198–283*) 'Observations on the ancient and modern Languages' (in 13 chapters) by Wynne, $T6^v$ blank.

Illustration: leaf mounted after R8, numbered '256' is a folded table of simple characters, exhibiting the thirty-three sounds of the English language, 263 × 355 mm (with watermark 'IV').

Text ($D4^r$): 32 lines; 149 (160) × 81 mm; 93 R. Medium-quality laid paper with fleur-de-lys watermark. Page no. at outer ends of headlines (beyond page block).

Half title: [orn. rule 3 × 78 mm] | ESSAYS | ON | EDUCATION. | [orn. rule 3 × 79 mm]

Headlines, pp. 1–197: ESSAYS on EDUCATION. p. 199: Obſervations, *&c*.

RT, from verso to recto, pp. 198–283: Obſervations *on the* ancient | *and* modern Languages.

CW: Page. $B3^r$ lan- [languages,] $D1^r$ twenty- [twenty-five] $E3^v$ (ſcho-) lars $E7^r$ them- [themſelves] $G1^v$ Chro- [Chronology;] $H6^r$ (un-) faſhion- [faſhionableneſs] $I2^v$ (cuſ-) tom,

Press figures: 42 ($D5^r$)-5 116 ($H1^v$)-5 132 ($K2^v$)-5 180 ($N2^v$)-5 240 ($Q8^v$)-5

Notes: Locke's text is a selection from §§ 70: 'Of Public and Private Education', 73: 'Of Tasking Children'; 92: 'Of Tutors', etc. These are selections from Locke's sections with introductory phrases rewritten, omissions not noted; sections are not arranged in original numerical order.

References: Attig 566; Axtell British 19; ESTC t130263.

Copies examined: CaOTU (Locke W95.E88 1761) CaQQLa (LB7.W989 1761; lacks fold. plate & pp. 279–284) DFo (195898) L (232.h.34; lacks half title) O (Vet.A5 e.2377) OCin (RA370.10942/W989) PPL (Ia.Milt.69031.0)

In second place in popularity, after the *Essay*, Locke's educational work continued to be frequently printed after 1800: reprints, selections and translations appeared. Some editions also received extensive editorial attention. Reprints were issued in Britain in 1802, 1809, 1836, 1880, 1886, 1902 (under title: *How to Bring up Your Children*, in the series 'A Book for Every Parent'), and in 1964 (an abridgement by F. W. Garforth). Editors giving attention to the text, its variants and notes, were the Rev. Evan Daniel in 1880; Rev. R. H. Quick in 1880 (the best nineteenth-century edition, frequently reprinted through 1934); and J. W. Adamson in 1912 under the title: *The Educational Writings of John Locke*. Adamson included the *Conduct of the Understanding* (revised ed., 1922). James Axtell's edition of 1968 (using Adamson's title) has an extensive introduction, transcripts of Locke's letters to Clarke, 'Thoughts on Reading and Study for a Gentleman' (first published in Desmaizeaux's *Collection of Several Pieces*, 1720) and the notes 'on study' from Locke's journal (Bodleian MS Locke f.2, pp. 86-140), John Yolton and I have published a critical edition for the Clarendon Edition of the Works of John Locke in 1989, which includes 'Thoughts on Reading and Study'.

American reprints were issued in 1830, 1869, 1910 (as part of the *Harvard Classics* set), and an abridgement by Peter Gay was issued in 1964.

There have also been numerous selections, often appearing as part of a large collection of texts, and in journals.

Both French, German and Italian-language editions have continued to be issued, Coste's translation was reprinted in 1821, an abridgement of it in 1882 (reprinted 1886). Gabriel Compayré did a new translation into French in 1882 also, which was reprinted in 1889, 1904, and under the title: *Quelques pensées sur l'éducation*, in 1966. There were new German translations more frequently than simple reprints: one by Moritz Schuster was published in 1869 (reprinted in 1873 and 1881); another by Ernst von Sallwürk in 1883 (revised in 1897 and 1910); another by Ludwig Wattendorf in 1907 (revised 1913). Ouvrier's translation (cf. no. 216) was reprinted in 1920 in the series: Universal-Bibliothek, no. 6147-50. New editors and translators were also Heinz Wohlers in 1962 (reprinted 1970) and Johann Bernhard Deermann, in 1967.

The 1782 Italian edition (no. 222) was reprinted in 1888. New Italian translations appeared in 1922 (by G. Marchesini), in 1923 (by O. Pogliaghi and C. Gualdini, with an introduction by Armando Carlini), in 1927 (by Antonio Marcuzzi), in 1928 (by Mario Barbagallo), in 1932 (by Tullio Marchesi), in 1940 (by S. Drago del Boca), in 1946 (by Fernanda Pivano), in 1950 (by G. Caglioni and P. Montanari) and in 1977 (by A. Gallitto and F. Inzodda). Selections have also appeared in many Italian journals and collections.

Most other languages did not see translations of *Some Thoughts* until well into the nineteenth or even twentieth century. It was first translated into Czech in 1875; into Japanese in 1953, in Rumanian in 1907; a new

Rumanian translation appeared in 1971. There was a new Polish translation by Jan Znosko in 1801; the third and most recent, by F. Wnorowski appeared in 1959. The *Education* was translated into Serbo-Croatian in 1950; and two Spanish translations appeared, the first in 1825 and a new one in 1982.

CHAPTER VI

The Reasonableness of Christianity, and Its Vindications (nos. 229–247)

Despite the harsh treatment Locke received from some religious critics of his *Essay concerning Human Understanding*, many calling him a Socinian, a deist, or a 'Hobbist' (tantamount to 'atheist'), Locke was a very religious person. Indeed, he spent much of his last years writing religious works, *The Reasonableness of Christianity*, and his *Paraphrases* of St. Paul's epistles.

It was his professed desire for truth and his effort to reconcile the divisive controversies amid Christians in England that spurred him to write and publish anonymously the *Reasonableness*. In the winter of 1694/5 he began the reading, note-taking, chiefly of the Scriptures, and writing, in an effort diligently to consider "wherein the Christian faith consists" apart from any "opinions and orthodoxies of sects and systems" (*Corr.* 1901, letter to Philippus van Limborch, 10 May 1695; v. 390, trans.).

The work was published in early August, being advertised for sale in the 8–12 August 1695 issue (no. 3104) of *The London Gazette*. A few months later, in issue 3132 (14–18 November 1695) the anonymous *Vindication* was also advertised. In it Locke stated that the *Reasonableness* had been written "chiefly for those who were not yet thoroughly or firmly Christians . . . that is those who either wholly disbelieved, or doubted the Truth of the Christian Religion" (pp. 6–7, 10). It was more specifically written in reply to an attack by the Rev. John Edwards, in his *Some Thoughts concerning the Several Causes and Occasions of Atheism, Especially in the Present Age; with Some Brief Reflections on Socinianism, and on a Late Book Entituled* The Reasonableness of Christianity . . .' (London, 1695).

Numerous attacks in the late seventeenth century upon deism so called, often equated with Epicureanism and atheism, included the charge that Locke's *Reasonableness* was a deist book. The *Second Vindication*, published in March 1697, again anonymously, was a more detailed answer to Locke's critics. It is also extremely and tediously long.

Locke's authorship of all three of these works was acknowledged in a codicil to his will wherein he listed those works of his own that he wished to present to the Bodleian Library. A copy of his will is to be found in Le Clerc's *Account of the Life . . . of John Locke*, 3d ed. (1714), pp. 29–34 (cf. C1714-1) and in *Corr.* viii.419–27. Since in his lifetime he did not admit to his authorship of *The Reasonableness* and its 'Vindications' even to himself (they are listed in his library catalogue anonymously, under the heading 'Christianity'; cf. L.L. 697-701), we have no record of whom he gave copies to. We do have distribution lists of his acknowledged works. However, his authorship was widely rumoured at the time; John Edwards, in his *Socinian Creed* (1697) confidently names John Locke as the author.

We are fortunate that a contract between Locke and the Churchills for the publication of the *Reasonableness* survives (Bodleian Library MS Locke b.1 f.178). It is dated 12 June 1695 and states they, the Churchills, will pay him ten shillings per sheet "for every Impression wee shall print . . . during [Locke's] life, this first impression not to exceed fiveteen hundred, and no Impression afterwards to be above one thousand books . . ." Since the work as first published required nineteen and a quarter gatherings, Locke must have received slightly less than £10. John C. Higgins-Biddle, in the introduction to his forthcoming edition of the *Reasonableness* (for the Clarendon Edition of the Works of John Locke) states that "Locke had the Churchills add to this contract that they would present him with twenty-five bound copies for every impression. The book . . . seems to have sold for three shillings unbound."

Pierre Coste, at the request of the Wetstein firm in Amsterdam, undertook to translate the *Reasonableness* (no. 240) into French. He later made a summary translation and rearrangement of both *Vindications*, which was published first in 1703. Coste's translations were the basis for other translations, into Dutch and German (cf. no. 239, 242-7). Anne Sauvy, in her *Livres saisis à Paris entre 1678 et 1701* (La Haye: M. Nijhoff, 1972; no. 999) informs us that Coste's translation was put on the 'Index' by decree of the Holy Office on September 25, 1737. Two copies were seized at St. Cloud (part of five packets being shipped to Paris) as attested by the official report of the 'Commissaire de la Marre', dated 23-24 May 1706 (Bibliothèque Nationale MS. français 21743 f.49).

229. Reasonableness. 1695. 8°. Three states. Anonymous
Within a double rule, inner 127 × 71 mm, outer 134 × 78 mm]: THE | REASONABLENESS | OF | 𝕮𝖍𝖗𝖎𝖘𝖙𝖎𝖆𝖓𝖎𝖙𝖞, | As delivered in the | SCRIPTURES. | [double rule 67/66 mm] | *LONDON:* | Printed for *Awnſham* and *John Churchil*, [swash J] | at the *Black Swan* in *Pater-Noſter-* | *Row.* 1695.
Coll: 8° (170 × 110 mm cut) A² B-V⁸ [$ half signed; quire V signed U, V2, V3, V4]; 154 leaves; pp. *i-iv* 1-304 [= 308]. Page no. 196 sometimes prints as '96'.
Contents: A1ʳ (*i*) title (verso blank), A2ʳ·ᵛ (*iii-iv*) preface (16 lines on recto, 12 on verso followed by errata, see *Variants*, below), B1ʳ-V8ᵛ (1-304) text, ending with advertisement by Churchills.
Text (C8ʳ): 29 lines; 137 (148) × 68 (80) mm; 95 R, except p. 304 has 20 lines of text set 73 R plus advertisement. Pref. set 146 ital. Good-quality laid demy paper with a crowned horn watermark. Page no. at external ends of headlines. Text in direction line on pp. 254, 257.

HT: [double rule 66 mm] | The Reaſonableneſs of Chri- | ſtianity as delivered in | the Scriptures.
Headlines, from verso to recto: 'The Reaſonableneſs | of Chriſtianity, &c.'
Page 12 has 'The Reaſonableneß, &c.'
CW: Page. B3ʳ (ne-) ceſſity G1ᵛ Pro- [Prophecy] L2ᵛ (Diſ-) ciples R2ʳ diffe- [rent (CW part of text)] T7ʳ Wit, [Wit] V4ʳ (Chur-) ches [ches,]
Variants: There are three states of this first edition.
  State I: errata of 11.4 lines (ending 'r. life and.')
  State II: errata of 11.7 lines (ending 'r. the Apoſtles.')
  State III: errata of 13 lines (ending 'l. 14 read them,')
Some copies have broken inner rule at bottom lower left on title, in others it is in its aligned place. There are several typographical errors throughout, uncorrected in all states, though noted in the errata. For example, p. 271 line 2 reads 'apohtegms' for 'apophthegms'; p. 295.22 reads 'the A- | ples' for 'the Apo- | ſtles'. There are other differences in sheet V, detailed below, some of which seem by chance to coordinate with the errata. A check by Hinman collator indicates that all these differences are 'stop-press' corrections to a single type-setting. The differences in errata and quire V occur randomly in all copies.

Differences	Type A	Type B
1) 296.28 (V4ᵛ):	Reference	References
2) 297.29 (V5ʳ):	Truthc	Truths
3) ibid. CW:	delivereds	delivered
4) 297.1 (V5ʳ):	regard eth	regard the
5) 304.4 (V8ᵛ):	(ab-) ſtract	ſtra&
6) 304.17:	without	without [i inverted]

States I and II errata have not been corrected in the text of any copies. From the three additional errata of State III some corrections have been made in some copies. Further the difference noted in the 5th item is interesting in that the ligatured 'ct' and '&' are found vertically adjacent in a printer's typecase. Also the type III errata (in lines 12–13) itself contains an error, p. 303 being intended for "p. 203 l. 20 r. Treatise?" All errors in the three different types of errata were corrected in the second edition.

Notes: Dr. John Higgins-Biddle, in his edition of this work (in press) estimates less than fifteen hundred copies were printed, as intimated in the contract (see illustrations). The flyleaf of a copy in St. John's College, Cambridge, gives its price as '3 s.', its probable cost, with a note that it was mentioned in the London Gazette, issue for 8–12 August 1695 (no. 3104). It was listed in the Term Catalogues for Hilary Term 1696 (II. 568) together with its Vindication, as the thirteenth item. It was also listed under 'reprints' for Trinity Term 1696 (II. 596) along with the Vindication, but with no mention of a second edition (which might be implied). It received a summary review in the October 1696 issue of Acta eruditorum, pp. 463–9.

The Harvard interleaved copy, which was Locke's own, bears a purple-ink rubber stamp, 'Library | Ben Damph Forest. | Case C | Shelf I | Number

23' (shelfmark handwritten); it was the gift of Christian A. Zabriskie, in memory of Edward Powis Jones. Another copy (states not noted) is at GOT. A microfilm copy of the third state is in the EEB microfilm collection, reel 216 no. 5.

References: Attig 639; Christophersen p. 35, 58; ESTC r022574; L.L. 697 (under 'Christianity'); T.C. II. 568; Wing^2 L2751.

Copies examined (includes states & differences in sheet V):
C (Syn 7.64.156; III, A1, 5–6, B2–4) C (Peterborough coll.; III, B1–4, A5–6) CaOTU (Locke L63.R43 1695; III; A1–6) CaQMMO (III; A1 5–6, B2–4) Ck^1 (Keynes A.12.17; III; A1–6) Ck^2 (Keynes A.12.16; I; B1–6) Ct (K4.60; I; A1, 4–6, B2–3) DFo (acc. 156765; I; A1, 5–6, B2–4) Dt^1 (Fag.Y.9.7; III; A1, 5–6; B2–4) Dt^2 (GG.ii.41; II; B1–6) Dt^3 (LL.11.56; II; A1–6) Eu (JA 835; II; A 1–6) Exeter Cathedral (III; A1–6) Han (T-A 3723; III; A1, 5–6, B2–4) L (852 b.23; III; A1, 5–6, B2–4) MH^1 (*EC65.L7934.695ra, Locke's interleaved copy; II; B1–6) MH^2 (*EC65.L7934.695raa; III; B1, 5–6, A2–4) MH-AH (II, B1–6) O^1 (Vet.A3 f.937; I; A1–6) O^2 (Vet.A3 f.532; II; A1–6) O^3 (Vet.A3 f.631; III; B1–6) O^4 (Baden Powell 91; I; A1, 5–6, B2–4) Oa (Y.15.3; III; A1–6) Occ (T.7.25; II; A1, B2–6)

230. Reasonableness. 2d ed., 1696. 8° Anonymous.

Within a double rule, inner 124 × 69 mm, outer 131 × 77 mm: THE | REASONABLENESS | OF | 𝕮𝖍𝖗𝖎𝖘𝖙𝖎𝖆𝖓𝖎𝖙𝖞, | As delivered in the | SCRIPTURES. | [rule 67 mm] | 𝕿𝖍𝖊 𝕾𝖊𝖈𝖔𝖓𝖉 𝕰𝖉𝖎𝖙𝖎𝖔𝖓. | [rule 67 mm] | To which is added, | A Vindication of the ſame, from [no space after comma] | Mr. *Edwards*'s Exceptions. | [rule 64 mm] | *LONDON:* | Printed for *Awnſham and John Churchil*, [swash J] | at the *Black Swan* in *Pater-Noſter-* | *Row*. 1696.

Coll: 8° (170 × 110 mm cut) A^2 B–U^8 X^2 [$ half signed; U2 & 4 signed 'V2', 'V4']; 156 leaves & *Vindication* (see no. 231); pp. *i–iv* 1–259 602 261–301 303 302 304–307 308 [=312]. Page no. 260 called '602'; 302 and 303 interchanged; in some copies '5' in '85' fails to print.

Contents: A1^r (*i*) title (verso blank), A2^{r,v} (*iii–iv*) preface, B1^r–X2^r (1–307) text, X2^v (308) advt. of books sold by Churchills. Text (C8^v): 29 lines; 147 (148) × 67 (78) mm; 94 R. Pref. set 142 ital, 14 lines on recto, 15 on verso. Good-quality laid paper with crowned foolscap watermark. Page no. at external ends of headlines, extending 11 mm beyond print block. Text in direction line on p. 257.

HT: [rule 65 mm] | [rule 64 mm] | The Reaſonableneß of Chri- | ſtianity, as delivered in the | Scriptures.

Headlines, from verso to recto: 'The Reaſonableneſs | of Chriſtianity, &c.' The double s in versos of leaves 1–5 & 7 in sheets C–N, U and X, and versos of leaves 1–4 of sheets O–P, R–T and in leaves Q1–4, Q6 and Q8 read 'ß'.

CW: Page. B3^r (ne-) ceſſity G5^v King- [Kingdom] I4^r live; [lieve; (error)] N4^r

(com-) plained R3ᵛ diffe- [rent (CW part of text)] T4ᵛ up [in (CW part of text)] T5ᵛ them [them,] T8ᵛ Wit, [Wit] U6ᵛ delivered U8ᵛ (And) the [And the ('And' repeated)]

Notes: Since the Vindication was also available separately, it has been treated as a separate entry: see the following record. As implied at the head of this chapter, this second edition with its accompanying Vindication was available in late October 1695. The errata of the first edition have here been corrected, but new errors introduced. According to John Higgins-Biddle the only significant addition here is "the addition of three passages which expand on the reconstruction of Jesus's ministry and teaching". Otherwise there are minor changes in phrasing, adding or substituting a word or phrase, and changes in spelling, capitalization, punctuation and italicization.

The Term Catalogues list what is probably this edition with its Vindication under 'reprints' during Trinity Term 1696 (II.596); but it is listed for Hilary 1697 (III.1) as the second edition, with the Vindication.

The Exceptions of Mr. Edwards in his Causes of Atheism was an anonymous pamphlet published in 1695 (cf. ch. XII, no. C1695-2).

A microfilm copy of this edition is in the EEB collection, reel 1263, no. 2.

References: Attig 640; Christophersen p.58; ESTC r025016; L.L. 698; T.C. III.1; Wing² L2752.

Copies examined: Y   C (Peterborough coll. C.2.32)   C (Keynes) CaQMMO   Ck¹ (Keynes A.12.18)   Ck² (Keynes A.12.19; lacks Vindic.) CLU-C CtY (K8.L79/m696)   DFo¹ (acc. 142189)   DFo² (acc.163167) Dt (Fag.Y.9.7) Gu (Bh8. i.19)   Han (T-A3724)   L (700 e.19)   MH-AH (BR120.L6 1696)   O¹ (8° Q.16 Th. 'Ex Dono Joan.Lock Autoris')   O² (8° K31.Th (6))   Oa (y16.9)   Oc (O.I.5.4)   Oj (O4.23.Gall)   PPL (Wing L2752/Log672.O.1)

231. Vindication. 1695. 8° Anonymous. Two issues.
Within a double rule, inner 126×69 mm, outer 131×75 mm: A | VINDICATION | OF THE | REASONABLENESS | OF | Chriſtianity, &c. | From Mr. Edwards's | REFLECTIONS. | [double rule 66/65 mm] | LONDON: | Printed for Awnſham and John Churchil, [swash J] | at the Black-Swan in Pater-Noſter- | Row. 1695.

Issues: A (first) has original leaf A4; B (second) has cancellans A4; see Notes below.

Coll: 8° in 4s (185×120 mm uncut, varies) A⁸ (±A4) B-E⁴ [$ half signed]; 24 leaves; pp. i-iv 1-40 41-44 [=48].

Contents: A1ʳ (i) half title (verso blank), A2ʳ (iii) title (verso blank), A3ʳ-E2ᵛ (1-40) text, E3ʳ-E4ᵛ (41-44) 'Books lately Printed for ... A. & J. Churchill.'

Text (B3ᵛ): 29 lines, but 28 on pp.3, 13 and 31-39; 137 (148) × 67 (80) mm; 101 R. Good-quality laid paper, with crowned foolscap watermark. Footnotes and references set in external margins. Page no. at outer ends of headlines, 11 mm beyond text block.

Half title: [rule 68 mm] | A | VINDICATION | OF THE | REASONABLENESS | OF | Chriſtianity, &c. | [rule 66 mm]
HT: [double rule, 64/65 mm] | A | VINDICATION | OF THE | REASONABLENESS | OF | Chriſtianity, &c.
Headlines, from verso to recto: A Vindication of the | Reaſonableneß of Chriſtianity, &c.
CW: Page. A4ʳ Self- [*Self-conceit*;] C3ʳ (Wri-) tings D1ᵛ belie- [believing,]
Notes: Though this work is usually found attached to the *Reasonableness*, as noted on that work's title-page, it was available separately, a copy in blue wrappers was found at the University of Exeter Library (on deposit from Crediton Parish Library), one of only two copies I have found to have the cancellandum leaf A4 (pp. 3-4). The cancellandum, following upon a point Locke made in his defence against Edwards, "I shall not complain of him, since he joyns me, p. 104. with no worse Company than two Eminently Pious and Learned * Prelates of our Church . . .", has a marginal note identifying those two prelates as "* Bp. *Taylor*, and Bp. *Crofts*." The cancellans sheet (found in almost all copies) reads "Bp. *Taylor*, and the Author of The Naked Truth." In other words, Locke gave away the secret of the authorship of *The Naked Truth*, a controversial work published in 1675 (see the biography of Herbert Croft in the *Biographia Britannica* (1st ed., 1750), iii.1527-31, especially note D).

A microfilm copy of this edition, second issue, is in the EEB collection, reel 501, no. 11.
References: Attig 669; Christophersen p. 59; ESTC r025016; L.L. 699; T.C. II.596 and III.1 (both with 2d ed. of *Reasonableness*); Wing² L2769.
Notice: Acta Eruditorum, July 1698: 341-2.
Copies examined (all except EXu and O² bd. with no.230; for shelfmarks see that entry)
 A (First issue): C (Peterborough C.2.32) EXu (Crediton colln.(2) uncut)
 B (2d issue): Y CaQMMO Ck² CLU-C CtY DFo² Dt Gu Han L MH-AH O¹ O² (8° K.31 Th (6)) Oa Oc Oj PPL

232. Reasonableness & first 'Vindication'. 5th ed., 1731. 8°
THE | REASONABLENESS | OF | CHRISTIANITY, [swash Y] | As delivered in the | SCRIPTURES. | [rule 77 mm] | To which is added, | A Vindication of the ſame, from | Mr. EDWARDS's Exceptions. | [rule 77 mm] | By JOHN [swash J] LOCKE, *Eſq*; | [rule 78 mm] | The FIFTH EDITION. | [rule 78 mm] | LONDON: | Printed for A. BETTESWORTH and C. HITCH, | in *Pater-noſter Row*; J. PEMBERTON, near | St. *Dunſtan*'s Church in *Fleet-ſtreet*, and | E. SYMON, in *Cornhill*. 1731.
Coll: 8° (200 × 122 mm cut) A-S⁸ T² [$ half (+T2) signed; R2 and 3 both signed 'R2']; 146 leaves; pp. *1-5* 6-260 *261* 262-292. Erroneous signing of R3 corrected in O³ copy.
Contents: A1ʳ (*1*) title (verso blank), A2ʳ,ᵛ (*3-4*) preface, A3ʳ-R2ᵛ (*5*-260) text of *Reasonableness*, R3ʳ-T2ᵛ (*261*-292) text of *Vindication*.

Text (E1ᵛ) 32 lines; 151 (161) × 78 mm; 94 R. Medium-quality laid paper without watermarks. Page no. at external end of headlines. Marginal notes have been moved to the foot of the page, below a rule. Some quires (e.g. P or Q) may be on poorer quality paper. Framed headpiece on p. 3 (A2ʳ): cornucopia within circular frame between angels, 26 × 82 mm; p. 261: seated Minerva between lions, 25 × 78 mm. Diamond-shaped tailpiece on p. 260: woman's bust above scrolls, 39 × 42 mm.

HT, p. 5: [framed headpiece of 3 mermaids upholding cornucopias, 28 × 77 mm] | THE | REASONABLENESS | OF | CHRISTIANITY, | As Delivered in the | SCRIPTURES.

Headlines (from verso to recto): pp. 6–259: *The Reaſonableneſs of Chriſtianity,* | *as delivered in the* Scriptures.
p. 260: *The Reaſonableneſs of Chriſtianity, &c.*
pp. 262–92: *A Vindication of the | Reaſonableneſs of Chriſtianity.*
Headline on p. 292 not adjusted for absence of facing recto page.

CW: Page. A3ᵛ where- [wherein] E6ʳ alſo [alſo,] K2ᵛ (be-) lieving O8ᵛ Commu- [Communication] S1ᵛ ne- [neceſſary]

Press figures: 78 (E7ᵛ)-* 80 (E8ᵛ)-*

Notes: No longer anonymous, the text is a reprint of the 2d edition of 1696 (no. 230), including the *Vindication* (no. 231). There is no way to account for this being called the fifth edition, even if those printed in the *Works* in 1714, 1722 and 1727 (no. 363–5) or the French translations were counted. Attig in error records this edition as "The fifteenth [sic] edition."

References: Attig 641; ESTC t168363.

Copies examined: Y L (1568/6799) O¹ (Vet.A4 e.1688) O² (Vet.A4 e.2095) O³ (Vet.A4 e.1325)

233. Second Vindication. 1697. 8o. Anonymous. Two issues.

233A. First issue. Within a double rule, inner 133 × 70 mm, outer 140 × 77 mm: A SECOND | VINDICATION | OF THE | 𝕽eaſonableneſs | OF | Chriſtianity, &c. | [rule 73 mm] | By the Author of the *Reaſonableneſs* | *of Chriſtianity*, &c. | [double rule 73 mm] | LONDON, | Printed for *A.* and *J. Churchill,* [swash J] at the *Black* | *Swan* in *Pater-Noſter-Row*, 1697.
Coll: 8° (170 × 110 mm cut) A⁸ a⁴ A–X⁸ Y⁸ (±Y⁴) Z–2G⁸ [$ half signed]; 252 leaves; pp. *i–xxiv* 1–480 [= 504]. First gathering signed in italics.

233B. Second issue with cancellans title leaf, title within a double rule, inner 140 × 78 mm, outer 147 × 83 mm, as 1st issue until 7th line: [rule 74 mm] | By the Author of the *Reaſonableneſs* | *of Chriſtianity,* &c. | [double rule 72/74 mm] | LONDON, | Printed for *A.* and *J. Churchill,* [swash J] at the *Black* | *Swan* in *Pater-Noſter-Row,* and *Edward* | *Caſtle,* next *Scotland-Yard-Gate,* [swash Y] by | *White-Hall*, 1697.
Coll: same as first issue except A⁸ (±A1), and errata on a4ᵛ.

Contents: A1ʳ (*i*) title (verso blank), A2–a4ᵛ (*iii–xxiv*) 'Preface to the Reader', A1ʳ–2G8ᵛ (1–480) text. First issue has 19 lines of text on a4ᵛ; second issue has 12 lines of text and errata of 17.5 lines.

Text (R3ʳ): 29 lines; 135 (147) × 66 (80) mm; 93R. Pref. set 116 ital, with 23 lines. Medium-quality laid paper with fleur-de-lys watermark (quires U-2D different paper with watermark letter B). External marginal width is to accomodate page no. in headlines.

HT: [double rule 69 mm] | *A Second Vindication of the* | *Reaſonableneſs of Chriſtianity*, &c.

RT, from verso to recto: *A Second Vindication of the* | *Reaſonableneſs of Chriſtianiy*, &c.

CW: Page. A2ʳ (Ex-) cellencies B4ʳ (no-) thing B8ᵛ brings E8ᵛ (King-) dom [dom,] F3ʳ King- [Kingdom;] L2ʳ Faith, L7ᵛ *Un-* [*Unmasker*] M8ᵛ (repen-) tance Q4ʳ (a-) mongſt R4ʳ Accu- [Accuſation] U8ʳ dis- [disbelieved] Y4ʳ (Chri-) ſtians 2A3ʳ when 2B8ᵛ makes 2G4ʳ (far-) ther,

Notes: An anonymous work published in Trinity Term 1697 as a more detailed answer to Edwards' criticism. Locke received a copy from the Churchills on 17 March 1697 (cf. MS Locke f.10 p.343). The preface contains a letter to Samuel Bold signed 'A.B.'; Bold wrote the Churchills on March 26, 1697 that he had received a copy of this 'Second Vindication' last week, but in a letter to 'the author of *The Reasonableness*' on the same day he "had no certain knowledge of the authorship" (*Corr.* 2233, 2232; vi. 65–69).

There were two issues, either because it sold slowly and Castle was brought in to help move it, or he owned a share in the copy. The cancellans title leaf is from the same typesetting as the first issue, with the lower lines moved more closely together. The issues are also distinguished by the inclusion of an errata of 17.5 lines on p. *xxiv*: the earlier issue lacks the errata, or has it mounted on that page or on p.480. Leaves a3 and a4 were reset by moving lines to allow room for the errata: a4ᵛ (p. *xxiv*) originally has 19 lines of text and no errata; reset page has 12 lines of text and a 17.5-line errata. All copies seen have a cancellans leaf Y4 (pp. 343–4), possibly correcting a printing error. A microfilm copy of the second issue is in the EEB collection, reel 1127, no. 16.

Notice: *Acta eruditorum*, 1698: pp. 341–2.

References: Attig 680 (2d issue only); Christophersen pp. 64–5; ESTC r039074 (2d issue); L.L. 700; T.C. III. 23; Wing² 1st issue L2756A, 2d issue L2756.

Copies examined: First issue: C¹ (C.6.1) CLU-C Oj (H.12.12; gift of Jonathan Edwards, 1712) PPL¹ (Wing L2756.1/Log3291.D)
Second issue: C² (Peterborough D.4.26) CaOLW (BR120.L63) CtY (K8.L79/P697) DFo (acc.202733) L (4017 a.5) MH-AH (BR120.L6 1696 (3)) O (8° Q.17 Th; 'Ex Dono Joan. Lock | Auctoris.') Oa (y13.1) Oc (O.I.5.5) PPL² (Wing L2756 (2)/Log672.O) TxDaM-P

234. Reasonableness & Vindications. 6th ed. (& '5th') eds., 1736. 2 vols. in-8°

Vol. 1: THE | REASONABLENESS | OF | *CHRISTIANITY*, [swash Y] | As deliver'd in the | SCRIPTURES. | To which is added, | A FIRST and SECOND | VINDICATION | of the SAME; | FROM SOME |

EXCEPTIONS and REFLECTIONS | in a *Treatiſe* [swash T] by the Rev. Mr. EDWARDS, | Intitled, *Some Thoughts* [swash T] *concerning the ſe-* | *veral Cauſes and Occaſions of* Atheiſm, *eſpe-* | *cially in the preſent Age.* | [rule 85 mm] | *By* JOHN LOCKE, *Eſq*; | [rule 84 mm] | The SIXTH EDITION. | [double rule 84 mm] | LONDON: | Printed for A. BETTESWORTH and C. HITCH, in *Pater-* | *noſter-Row*; J. PEMBERTON, againſt St. *Dunſtan*'s Church | in *Fleet-ſtreet*; and E. SYMON, in *Cornhill*. | M.DCC.XXXVI.

Vol.2: A SECOND | VINDICATION | OF THE | REASONABLENESS | OF | CHRISTIANITY, [swash Y] | As deliver'd in the | SCRIPTURES. | [rule 79 mm] | *By* JOHN LOCKE, *Eſq*; | [rule 79 mm] | The FIFTH EDITION. | [rule 79 mm] | [2 orn., each 11 × 12 mm] | [rule 79 mm] | LONDON: | Printed [swash P] *for* A. BETTESWORTH and C. HITCH, | in *Pater-noſter Row*; [swash P] J. PEMBERTON, a- | gainſt St. *Dunſtan*'s [swash D] Church in *Fleet-ſtreet*; and E. SYMON, in *Cornhill*. 1736.

Coll: 8° (200 × 122 mm cut). Vol. 1: π^2 A^8 (–A1) B–S^8 T^2 [$ half signed; R2 and 3 both signed 'R2']; 147 leaves; pp. *i–ii 1–5* 6–260 *261* 262–292 [= 294].

Vol. 2: A–2B^8 2C^4 [$ half signed]; 204 leaves; pp. *i–iii* iv–xvi *1* 2–392 [= 408]. Bodley's first copy has p. 345 called '343' (Z5^r), but second copy has a stop-press correction.

Contents. Vol. 1: $\pi 1^r$ (*i*) blank, $\pi 1^v$ advt. of '*BOOKS Printed for* E. SYMON . . .' (14 items), $\pi 2^r$ (*1*) title (verso blank), A2^{r,v} (*3–4*) preface, A3^r–R2^v (*5*–260) text of *Reasonableness*, R3^r–T2^v (*261–292*) text of (first) *Vindication*.

Vol. 2: A1^r (*i*) title (verso blank), A2^r–A8^v (*iii*–xvi) 'PREFACE TO THE READER.', B1^r–2C4^v (*1–392*) text of *Second Vindication*.

Text: v. 1: same as 1731 ed. (no. 232); v. 2: 32 lines; 148 (158) × 79 mm; 98 R. Both vols. have medium-quality laid paper watermarked with Letter B. Page no. at external end of headlines.

Headlines, from verso to recto in v.1 same as 1731 ed. (no. 232); v. 2: *A Second* Vindication *of the* | *Reaſonableneſs* of CHRISTIANITY.

CW: Page. Vol. 1 same as 1731 edition (no.232). Vol. 2: B8^v *in* E8^v Covenant L2^r (Mat-) ters M8^v Plea- [Pleaſure] R4^r *This* V8^v ſigni- [ſignify] 2A3^r every 2B8^v *the*

Press figures. Vol. 1 same as 1731 edition. Vol. 2: 4 (B2^v)-2 43 (D6^r)-2 60 (E6^v)-I 74 (F8^r)-I 93 (G7^r)-I 109 (H7^r)-2 118 (I3^v)-2 120 (I4^v)-I 137 (K5^r)-2 152 (L4^v)-2 154 (L5^v)-2 175 (M8^r)-2* 182 (N3^v)-2 198 (O3^v)-2 205 (O7^r)-I 220 (P6^v)-2 222 (P7^v)-I 238 (Q7^v)-2 269 (R7^r)-I 270 (R7^v)-2 285 (T7^r)-2 287 (T8^v)-2 302 (U7^v)-2 315 (X6^r)-I 320 (X8^v)-2 324 (Y2^v)-2 335 (Y8^r)-I 338 (Z1^v)-2 345 (Z5^r)-I** 354 (2A1^v)-I 383 (2B8^r)-2 384 (2B8^v)-I 386 (2C1^v)-2

* O^2 copy has 'I'. ** Found only in O^2 copy.

Notes: Vol. 1 uses the sheets from the 5th (1731) edition of the *Reasonableness* and its *Vindication* (no. 232), with the same signature positions and the two press figures, but with a cancellans title and advertisement leaves.

The Bodleian Library's second copy accompanies vol. 1 of the 1748 printing (no. 235). Vol. 2 here is a new setting of the previous (and only) edition of the *Second Vindication* (no. 233). It might possibly have been issued as a companion vol. to no. 232.

References: Attig 642; ESTC v.1: t180141; v. 2: n034304.

Copies examined: O^1 (Vet.A4 e.2095-6; vol.1 has two title leaves, the 1731 edition one following that for 1736)   O^2 (Vet.A4 e.1325 vol.2 only)

235. Reasonableness & Vindication. '6th ed.' of vol. [1] only, 1748. 8°

THE | REASONABLENESS | OF | CHRISTIANITY, [swash Ts, Y] | As Delivered in the | SCRIPTURES. | [rule 80 mm] | To which is added, | Two Vindications of the ſame, from | Mr. EDWARDS's Exceptions. | [rule 82 mm] | By JOHN LOCKE, Eſq; | [rule 82 mm] | The SIXTH EDITION. | [rule 82 mm] | LONDON: | Printed for J. OSBORN, at the Golden-Ball in | Pater-noſter-Row, 1748.

Coll: 8° (200 × 122 mm cut) A^8 (±A1) B-S^8 T^2 [$ half signed]; 146 leaves; pp. *1-5* 6-260 *261* 262-292.

Contents, *Text*, *HT*, *Headlines* and *Press figures* same as 1731 ed. (no. 232).

Note: This vol. 1 of the set of *Reasonableness* and its *Vindications* uses (again) the sheets of the 1731 ed., with the same paper and signature positions, but with a new, cancellans title leaf. Vol. 2 of the Bodleian Library set is the 2d vol. of the 1736 edition (no. 234), presumably sold together. ESTC reports another copy at Wesley College, Bristol.

References: Attig 643; ESTC t199381.

Copies examined: O (Vet.A4 e.1325 vol. 1)   L (RB.23.a.9631 vol. 1)

236. Reasonableness. 7th ed., 1764. 8°

THE | REASONABLENESS | OF | CHRISTIANITY, | AS DELIVERED IN THE | SCRIPTURES. | [rule 80 mm] | By JOHN [swash J] LOCKE. | [rule 80 mm] | The SEVENTH EDITION. | [triple rule, thin/thick/thin, 82 mm] | LONDON: | Printed for A. MILLAR, H. WOODFALL, J. WHISTON | and B. WHITE, J. RIVINGTON, L. DAVIS and C. | REYMERS. W. OWEN, R. BALDWIN, HAWES, CLARKE | and COLLINS, W. JOHNSTON, S. CROWDER, T. LONG- | MAN, B. LAW, C. RIVINGTON, E. DILLY, R. WITHY, | S. BAKER, T. PAYNE, C. and R. WARE, J. SHUCK- | BURGH, J. HINXMAN, M. RICHARDSON. | M.DCC.LXIV.

Coll: 8° (220 × 125 mm cut) A^2 B-R^8 [$ half (+A2) signed]; 130 leaves; pp. *i-iv 1* 2-251 *253-254* 255-257 [=260]. Page no. 252 omitted.

Contents: A1^r (*i*) title (verso blank), A2^{r,v} (*iii-iv*) 'THE PREFACE.', B1^r-R7^r (*1*-254) text, R7^v blank, R8^r (*256*) advt. for Locke's publications, R8^v blank.

Text (F4^r): 32 lines; 149 (161) × 79 mm; 94 R. Medium-quality laid paper without watermark. Chainlines vertical, 26 mm apart. Orn. tailpiece on p. 254 (face in leafy pyramid, 22 × 28 mm).

The Reasonableness of Christianity 281

Headlines, from verso to recto: The Reaſonableneſs of Chriſtianity, | as delivered in the Scriptures.
CW: Page. C4ᵛ *come* F8ᵛ conſiſted O3ᵛ *ſeek* Q1ʳ (Obli-) gation? R1ᵛ were R6ᵛ Chriſt [*Chriſt*]
Press figures: 15 (B8ʳ)-2 16 (B8ᵛ)-3 25 (C5ʳ)-3 31 (C8ʳ)-4 40 (D4ᵛ)-3 43 (D6ʳ)-3 52 (E2ᵛ)-3 59 (E6ʳ)-3 79 (F8ʳ)-I 80 (F8ᵛ)-I 89 (G5ʳ)-I 95 (G8ʳ)-I 109 (H7ʳ)-I 110 (H7ᵛ)-I 125 (I7ʳ)-I 140 (K6ᵛ)-I 143 (K8ʳ)-3 157 (L7ʳ)-5 159 (L8ʳ)-I 169 (M5ʳ)-3 171 (M6ʳ)-3 191 (N8ʳ)-I 192 (N8ᵛ)-I 196 (O2ᵛ)-I 207 (O8ʳ)-4 221 (P7ʳ)-4 223 (P8ʳ)-4 233 (Q5ʳ)-3 238 (Q7ᵛ)-4 246 (R3ᵛ)-I
Notes: A new setting of the 1731 edition of the *Reasonableness* (no. 232), without the encumbrance of either *Vindication*.
References: Attig 644; ESTC t149957.
Copies examined: O (Vet.A5 e.3248) PPL (A.Lock/745.O)

237. Reasonableness, in Watson's *Tracts*, vol.4, 1785. 8°
Caption title: THE | REASONABLENESS | OF | CHRISTIANITY, | AS DELIVERED IN THE | SCRIPTURES. | [Oxford rule 55 mm]
In: A | COLLECTION | OF | THEOLOGICAL TRACTS, | IN SIX VOLUMES. | By RICHARD WATSON, D.D. F.R.S. | LORD BISHOP of LANDAFF, | AND | REGIUS PROFESSOR *of* DIVINITY *in the* UNIVERSITY *of* | CAMBRIDGE. | [rule 101 mm] | VOL. IV. | [rule 102 mm] | LONDON, | Printed by J. NICHOLS; | for T. EVANS, London; J. & J. MERRILS, [sic] Cambridge; | and J. & J. FLETCHER, Oxford. | [rule 35 mm] | M.DCC.LXXXV.
Collation of the set: 6 vols., 8° (215 × 142 mm cut). Vol. 4 has collation: A⁴ B–2K⁸ 2Y² (-2Y2) [$ half signed]; 261 leaves; pp. *i–iii* iv–vii *viii* 1 2–513 514 [=522].
Locke's text: pp. 1–108 (B1ʳ–H6ᵛ).
Contents: A1ʳ title (verso blank), A2ʳ–A4ᵛ 'CONTENTS.' with 20 or more lines introducing each text, B1ʳ–2Y1ʳ (*1–513*) texts, 2Y1ᵛ blank.
Text (D5ᵛ): 49 lines; 182 (191) × 103 mm; 74 R. Medium-quality laid paper without watermark. Page no. at outer ends of headlines. First leaf of each sheet also signed 'VOL. IV.' in direction line.
Headlines, from verso to recto: THE REASONABLENESS OF CHRISTIANITY, | AS DELIVERED IN THE SCRIPTURES.
CW: Page. B2ʳ (keep-) ing C5ᵛ (un-) der D7ʳ (bap-) tiſm F7ʳ tranſ- [tranſgreſſors] G8ᵛ (rea-) ſon.
Press figures (in Locke's text): 14 (B7ᵛ)-I 30 (D7ᵛ)-4 38 (D3ᵛ)-2 58 (D5ᵛ)-4 66 (F1ᵛ)-I 68 (F2ᵛ)-7 84 (G2ᵛ)-I 90 (G5ᵛ)-4 100 (H2ᵛ)-7 102 (H3ᵛ)-2
Notes: Text is a reprint from the 3d ed. of the *Works* (1727), vol. 2, with an introductory note by Watson on A2ʳ. The title-pages of the set read as vol. 4 above (but vol. 'I.', 'II.', 'III.', 'V.' and 'VI.' respectively) except for the imprint which is the same in vols. 4 and 5. Vols. 1–3 and 6 read: "CAMBRIDGE: | Printed by J. ARCHDEACON, Printer to the UNIVERSITY; | for J. & J.

MERRILL, Cambridge; T. EVANS, London; | and J. & J. FLETCHER, Oxford. | [short rule] | M.DCC.LXXXV."

Other texts in this volume are (1) Samuel Clarke's *Discourse concerning the unchangeable Obligations of Natural Religion* . . .; (2) *A Discourse on Prophecy* by John Smith; (3) *An Essay on the Teaching and Witness of the Holy Spirit* by Lord Barrington; (4) 'An Essay concerning Inspiration' from Dr. Benson's *Paraphrase and Notes on St. Paul's Epistles*, followed by (5) a prefatory 'Essay concerning the Unity of Sense' from the same source. A microfilm copy is in the collection, *The Eighteenth Century*, reel 2700, no. 2.
References: Attig 645; Christophersen p. 104; ESTC t076630 (set).
Copies examined: Y MH–AH (621 Watson) O (1419 e.2459) Omc

238. Reasonableness, in Watson's *Tracts*, vol. 4, 1791. 8°
Caption title: THE | REASONABLENESS | OF | CHRISTIANITY, | . . . [&c. as no.237]
In: A | COLLECTION | OF | THEOLOGICAL TRACTS, | . . . [&c. as in no. 237, until 10th line:] CAMBRIDGE. | [rule 103 mm] | SECOND EDITION. | [rule 102 mm] | VOL. IV. | [rule 103 mm] | LONDON: | Printed for T. EVANS in the Strand, and in the Great Market, Bury St. | Edmund's; J. and J. MERRILL, Cambridge; J. FLETCHER, and PRINCE and | COOKE, Oxford; | P. HILL, Edinburgh; and W. M'KENZIE, Dublin. | [rule 21 mm] | M.DCC.XCI.
Collation of the set: 6 vols., 8° (217 × 132 mm). Collation of vol. 4: A⁴ B–2K⁸ 2Y² (-2Y2); 261 leaves; pp. *i–iii* iv–vii *viii* 1 2–513 514 [= 522].
Locke's text: pp. *1*–108 (B1ʳ–H6ᵛ).
Contents: same as no. 237.
Text (E3ʳ): 49 lines; 177 (186) × 108 mm; 73 R. Medium-quality laid paper without watermark. Page no. at outer ends of headlines. First page of each sheet also signed 'VOL.IV.' in direction line.
Headlines: same as no. 237.
CW: Page. B2ᵛ (fore-) going C5ᵛ (un-) der E1ʳ (Meſ-) fiah; F1ᵛ Meffiah G8ᵛ (rea-) fon. H6ᵛ A DIS- [A DISCOURSE]
Press figures: vi (A3ᵛ)-4 2 (B1ᵛ)-4 27 (C6ʳ)-I 48 (D8ᵛ)-2 50 (E1ᵛ)-2 60 (E6ᵛ)-I 74 (F5ᵛ)-4 91 (G6ʳ)-2
Notes: This set and its arrangements are the same as those of the 1785 edition, only that, judging from the press figures, they have all been reset. ESTC notes another issue with imprint: ". . . Evans, and in the Great Market, . . ."
References: Attig 645 n.; Christophersen p. 104; ESTC n000433 (set).
Copies examined: O (8° S.284.Th) C (1389.10.2) L (495 f.4) NjR (Old Religion)

239. Reasonableness. Dutch trans. (Coste/anon.) Amsterdam, 1729. 8°
DE | SCHRIFTMATIGE | REDELYKHEYT | van 't | CHRISTENDOM. | door | JOHANNES LOCK, | *Uyt het Engels vertaalt.* | *Eph.* 4. *v.* 5. *Een Heere, een Gelove,* | *Eenen Doop. v.* 6. *Een God ende*

Vader | van alle, die daar is boven alle, en- | de door alle, ende in u alle. | [orn., bust on pedestal with cornucopias, 32 × 44 mm] | t' AMSTERDAM, | By EVERT VISSCHER, | Boekverkooper in de Dirk van Haffelt Steeg. 1729.

Coll: 8° (157 × 96 mm cut) *² A–S⁸ T² [$5 (–T2) signed]; 148 leaves; pp. *i–iv* 1–290 291–292 [= 296].

Contents: *1ʳ (*i*) title (verso blank), *2ʳ (*iii*) 'Voorreden van den Overzetter', *2ᵛ (*iv*) 'Voorreden van den Autheur' (18 lines), A1ʳ–T1ᵛ (1–290) text of Dutch trans. of *Reasonableness*, T2ʳ,ᵛ (291–292) chapter contents by page no.

Text: 30 lines (occasionally 29); 123 (132) × 69 mm; 82 R. Good-quality laid paper with foolscap watermark. Page no. at external ends of headlines.

Headlines, from verso to recto: *Schriftmatige Redelykheyt | van 't Chriſtendom.*

CW: Page.

Notes: The anonymous translator has used Pierre Coste's first French translation of 1696 (no. 240), following his division of Locke's text into 15 chapters. But he has identified Locke as the author, and has himself assigned section numbers (§§ 1–241) to the text.

The Biblical quotation on the title-page is from St. Paul's Epistle to the Ephesians: "One Lord, one faith, one baptism, one God and Father of us all, who is above all and through all and in all."

Reference: Attig p. 104 n.
Copy examined: Utr (333 J.63 (2))

240. Reasonableness. French trans. (Coste). Amsterdam, 1696. 8°
Anonymous.

In red & black: QUE | [red line:] LA RELIGION | CHRETIENNE | EST | [red:] TRES-RAISONNABLE, | *Telle qu'elle nous eſt repreſentée dans* | [red:] L'ECRITURE SAINTE. | Traduit de l'Anglois, imprimé à Londres, | chez A. & J. Churchill. | [orn., vase of flowers 36 × 43 mm] | A AMSTERDAM. | [red:] Chez HENRI WETSTEIN. 1696.

Coll: 8° (156 × 98 mm cut) *⁸ (–4 leaves = Z⁴) A–Y⁸ Z⁴ [$ half + 1 (–*4, –Z3) signed]; 184 leaves; pp. *i–viii* 1–356 357–360 [= 368].

Contents: *1ʳ (*i*) title, *1ᵛ (*ii*) Biblical quotation from John 5. 39, *2ʳ–*3ᵛ (*iii–vi*) translator's note, *4ʳ (*vii*) Locke's preface, *4ᵛ blank, A1ʳ–Z2ᵛ (1–356) text of French translation of *Reasonableness*, Z3ʳ–Z4ʳ (357–359) contents of chapters, Z4ᵛ blank.

Text (O1ʳ): 30 lines; 122 (131) × 65 (78) mm; 82R. Trans. preface set 96 R; author's pref. 95 ital. Medium-quality laid paper with illegible watermark. Page no. at external end of headlines.

HT: [headpiece, face between leaves, 11 × 63 mm] | QUE | LA RELIGION | CHRETIENNE | EST | TRES-RAISONNABLE, | *Telle qu'elle nous eſn repreſentée dans* | *l'Ecriture Sainte.*

Headlines, from verso to recto: *Que la Religion* [swash R] *Chretienne | eſt très-Raiſonnable, &c.*

CW: Page. A3ʳ (quelques-) uns C3ʳ (paſ-) ſages F2ʳ com- [combien] G8ʳ (ma-) niére L8ᵛ (ja-) mais O4ᵛ leſ- [leſquels] P7ʳ E- [Evangiles] Q5ᵛ (œu-) vres: S2ʳ (condam-) na- [nation] V1ʳ pra- [pratiquer] Y2ʳ (com-) me

Notes: In October 1695 Jean Le Clerc reported to Locke from Amsterdam that the Wetstein firm was having the *Reasonableness* translated into French (*Corr.* 1958; v.452). In late June or early July 1696 Pierre Coste, in a letter from Amsterdam to the Churchills for forwarding to the author, stated that he had just finished translating that "a little English book entitled *The Reasonableness* . . .", and stated that if the author had not read it in English, he might find pleasure in seeing it in French, rather guilelessly preserving the fiction of Locke's anonymity (*Corr.* 2107, v.660). Coste was the anonymous translator of this first edition in French. His text is fairly faithful to the first English edition of 1695 (no. 227), but he has taken the liberty of dividing the work into fifteen chapters, with chapter titles, "qui est en Anglois un Discours suivi", and he has tried to stick faithfully to the sense of the original "si on excepte quelques courts transitions que la division des Chapitres m'a obligé de faire." (p. *vi*)

References: Attig 658; Christophersen p. 58; L.L. 701; Rochedieu p. 193.

Notices: *Bibliothèque choisie* 2 (1703): 284–305 (covers no. 241 also).
Histoire des ouvrages des savans, Feb. 1703: 79–92

Copies examined: O¹ (Vet.B3 f.380; bd. with no. 241) Ck (Keynes) CtY (Me65/L496/In3) [GOT] L (700 c.20 (1)) O² (Vet.B4 f.227, substitutes title leaf of 2d ed., 1715, for leaf *1; bound with no. 241) P (D.21545) Wol (Te.761; 153 × 95 mm cut; with no. 241)

241. Vindications. French abridgement & trans. (Coste). Amsterdam, 1703. 8° Anonymous.

QUE | LA RELIGION | CHRÉTIENNE | EST | TRES-RAISONNABLE, | *Telle* [swash T] *qu'elle nous eſt repréſentée dans* | L'ECRITURE SAINTE. | SECONDE PARTIE, | Traduite de l'Anglois. | [orn., wolf standing against a tree, with scroll 'QVÆRENDO', 32 × 42 mm] | A AMSTERDAM, | Chez HENRI SCHELTE. | [rule 39 mm] | MDCCIII.

Coll: 8° (160 × 100 mm cut) *² A–V⁸ [$5 signed]; 162 leaves; *i–iv* 1–318 319–320 [= 324]. First page of each sheet signed '*Part. II.*' in direction line.

Contents: *1ʳ (*i*) title (verso blank), *2ʳ·ᵛ (*iii–iv*) 'TABLE DES MATIERES PRINCIPALES', A1ʳ–V7ᵛ (1–318) French text of abridgement of both 'Vindications' (divided into 7 'Objections'), V8 blank.

Text (D5ʳ): 30 lines; 122 (132) × 62 mm; 82 R. Medium-quality laid paper without watermark. Page no. at external end of headlines. Tailpiece (shaped like an inverted triangle) of a face with leaves, 34 × 42 mm, on p. 318.

HT: [headpiece, Indian's head with leaves, 15 × 60 mm] | QUE | LA RELIGION | CHRÉTIENNE | EST | TRES-RAISONNABLE, &c. | [rule 60 mm] | SECONDE PARTIE, | *Contenant un examen plus exaɕt de*

quel- | ques endroits de cet Ouvrage, & des | Reflexions nouvelles qui mettent toute la | matiere dans un plus grand jour.
Headlines, from verso to recto: *Que la Religion Chrêtienne* [swash Q, R] | *est tres-Raisonnable, &c.*
CW: Page. A1ʳ con- [,,connois] C1ᵛ (Chré-) tien? D7ʳ mon- [monde,] I2ᵛ E- [Evangile,] M2ᵛ li- [liberté] P6ᵛ dé- [défendit] S6ʳ l'er- [l'erreur] V7ʳ (écri-) vant,
Notes: Issued as the 2nd vol. to no. 240, this is a translation and abridgement of Locke's two 'Vindications', made by Pierre Coste, anonymously. He has rearranged the contents to become 'I.-VII. Objections' and grouped the material accordingly, without any mention of John Edwards. It is a rather free translation, with Coste's own connecting passages and clarifications where he felt they were needed ('as rarely as possible'), indicated by using double 'guillemets' (old-style quotation marks) at the beginning of each line of his insertions. Locke's authorship is still concealed.
References: Attig 681; Christophersen p. 70; L.L. 702a; Rochedieu p. 193 (with no. 240 as 2 vol. in-12)
Notices: *Bibliothèque choisie*, 2 (1703): 284–305 (with notice of no. 240)
Histoire des ouvrages des savans, Feb. 1703: 79–92 (with notice of no. 240)
Copies examined: O (Vet.B4 f.227 (2)) Ck (Keynes) Wol (Te.761 (2))

242. Reasonableness & Abridged Vindications. French trans. (Coste) 2d ed. Amsterdam, 1715. 2 vols. in 8°. With 'Religion des dames'
In red & black: LE | [red line:] CHRISTIANISME | [red:] RAISONNABLE, | *Tel qu'il nous eſt repreſenté dans* | [red:] L'ECRITURE SAINTE. | Traduit de l'Anglois | [red:] De MR. LOCKE. | Seconde Edition, revûë, corrigée; & augmentée d'une | DISSERTATION où l'on établit le vrai & l'unique | Moyen de réunir tous les Chrétiens malgré la diffe- | rence de leurs ſentimens. On a joint à cette Edi- | tion la RELIGION DES DAMES. | [red:] TOME PREMIER. [-'SECOND.'] | [oval orn., Athenian reading, with cherubs 42 × 50 mm] | [red:] A AMSTERDAM, [swash T] | Chez L'HONORE' et CHATELAIN. | [rule 39 mm] | M DCCXV.
Coll: 8° (165 × 100 mm cut). Vol. 1: *⁸ (-*8) A-2A⁸ [$ half + 1 signed]; 199 leaves; pp. *I–III* IV–XII *XIII–XIV* 1–384 [= 398].
Vol. 2: π² A-V⁸ (-V8) X-Z⁸ 2A⁴ [$ half + 1 (-2A3) signed]; 189 leaves; pp. *i–iv* 1–318 *319–320* 321–370 *371–374* [= 378]. First page of each sheet signed 'Part.II.' in direction line (but X1ʳ signed Part II.).
Contents. Vol. 1: *1ʳ (*I*) title (verso blank), *2ʳ-*5ᵛ (*III-X*) 'AVERTISSE- MENT DU TRADUCTEUR, *sur cette Nouvelle Edition*', *6ʳ,ᵛ (*XI-XII*) author's preface, *7ʳ,ᵛ (*XIII-XIV*) vol. contents by chapters, A1ʳ-Y5ᵛ (1– 346) text of *Reasonableness*, Y6ʳ-2A8ᵛ (347–384) text of 'Dissertation sur la réunion des Chrétiens', ending with 10-line errata.
Vol. 2: π1 blank, π2ʳ (*iii*) title (verso blank), A1ʳ-V7ᵛ (1–318) text of abridgement of 'Vindications', X1ʳ (*319*) section title (verso blank),

X2^r–Y2^v (321–338) Coste's preface to 'Religion des dames', Y3^r–2A2^v (339–370), text of 'Religion des dames', 2A3^{r,v} (371–372) contents of 'Religion' (7 'articles').

Illustration: front. to vol. 1 is engraved port. of Locke facing right (after Kneller, but unsigned) within an oval frame, above a pedestal on which is written 'JEAN LOCKE' and a 4-line Latin subscription quoting 'JOHANNES CLERICUS' (Jean Le Clerc), 134 × 79 mm on plate 143 × 86 mm.

Text: 30 lines; vol. 1 (A8^v): 126 (136) × 69 mm; vol. 2 (A6^v): 124 (133) × 64 (78) mm; 84 R. Footnotes set 66 R; very occasionally they are marginal in the second volume. Good-quality laid paper with fleur-de-lys watermark. Page no. at external end of headlines. Title page of the second volume is the same as for the first except the 'R' in 'Mr. Locke' is smaller and superscript. First pages of both vols. include 'Pag.' (Pag. I, Pag. 339). Vol. 2, p. 318 has orn. triangular tailpiece of leaves and flowers, 34 × 42 mm; and a tailpiece of an angel's head surrounded by flowers on p. 370.

HT, v.1, p.1: [triple orn. rule 8 × 68 mm] | LE | CHRISTIANISME | RAISONNABLE, | Tel qu'il nous eſt repréſenté dans | l'Ecriture Sainte. | [rule 66 mm]

v.1 p. 347: [framed rectangular orn. of vase on pedestal with leafy scrolls 21 × 60 mm] | DISSERTATION | Où ſur les Principes du CHRIS- | TIANISME RAISONNABLE on | établit le vrai & l'unique Moyen | de reünir tous les Chrétiens, mal- | gré la difference de leurs Senti- | mens.

v.2, p.1: same as HT in no. 241.

Section title, v.2, p. 319: LA RELIGION | DES | DAMES | Diſcours où l'on montre que la Reli- | gion eſt & doit être à la portée des | plus ſimples, des femmes & des gens | ſans Lettres. | TRADUIT DE L'ANGLOIS. | Seconde Edition revûe & corrigée.

Headlines, from verso to recto: v.1 pp. 2–345: LE CHRISTIANISME | RAISONNABLE. CHAP I. [-XV.]

v.1, p. 346: LE CHRISTIANISME, &c.

v.1, pp. 348–83: DISSERTATION SUR LA | RÉUNION DES CHRÉTIENS.

v.2, pp. 2–317, same as in no. 241.

v.2, pp. 322–37: *Diſcours ſur la | Religion des Dames.*

v.2, pp. 340–69: LA RELIGION | DES DAMES.

CW: Page. Vol.1: A1^v (atten-) tion, A3^r (Juſ-) tice D2^r s'adon- [s'adonnoient] G8^r occa- [occaſion] H3^v De- [Depuis] K3^v (mira-) cles M4^v 23- [23-26.] O5^r Je [2. Je] P7^r alte- [alterez] R8^v (a-) voir X1^v au- [auroient] Y2^r ac- [accepter] Z2^v (Li-) vre

Vol.2: in sheets A–V same as 1703 vol. (no. 241). X8^v Da- [Dames] Y6^r reme- [remede] 2A2^r puiſ- [puiſſance,]

Notes: The text of the *Reasonableness* has been revised and improved by Coste under Locke's direction; in 1697 he came to England and joined the Masham household at Oates, where Locke was living, as tutor to Francis Cudworth Masham. In his translator's note, he explains he has changed the title to a more suitable one, following Jean Le Clerc, who so called it in his

'Eloge de feu M. Locke' published in the *Bibliothèque choisie* (no.C1705-5). In the 'Avertissement', Coste states that the 'dissertation' (probably written by Coste) would have been published at the beginning of the second part of this work if it had not arrived too late at the hands of the printer (p. IX).

The second vol. uses the sheets of the 1703 pages of the *Vindications*, quires A–V^8 (no. 241), with a 2-leaf preliminary gathering as cancellans for sheet * of that edition. In his 'Discours sur la Religion des dames' (pp. 321–338) Coste tells us that it was written by a theologian of the Anglican Church; in a footnote he identifies him as a Mr. Stephens. The 'Religion des dames' is a translation of *A Lady's Religion, in a Letter to the Honourable My Lady Howard, by a Divine of the Church of England* (1697; Wing^2 L159, ESTC r212982), its dedicatory 'letter' signed 'Adeisidamon' ('not religious' *Anglicē*). A second edition was published in 1704 (ESTC t175237). If Coste is correct, its author is most likely to have been William Stephens (1647?–1718), a divine known for his strong whig principles (DNB) rather than Edward Stephens (d. 1706), a pamphleteer who "published a great number of pamphlets on political and theological subjects" (ibid.). There was an earlier edition of this French translation which I have been unable to locate.

To the prefatory epistle of this French translation Coste adds the identifying footnote and five more paragraphs at the end, reinforcing the author's principles.

This is a fairly scarce edition, no copies being listed in the *National Union Catalog of pre-1956 Imprints* or in the Dutch union catalogue at the Royal Library in the Hague. Of all the libraries I have visited (see Introduction, Library Symbols section) only the Bibliothèque nationale and the Herzog August Bibliothek (in Wolfenbüttel) possess a copy. Brown University Library, Providence, R.I., also reports owning a copy. Despite the Bodleian Library's catalogues, their copy (Vet.B4 f.227) is a copy of no. 240–41, with vol. 1 possessing the title leaf to this 1715 edition as a cancellans.

Notice: Bibliothèque ancienne et moderne 4 (1715): 230–32.
References: Attig 659; Christophersen p. 104; Rochedieu p. 193.
Copies examined: Y P (D^2. 20003) Wol (Te.762)

243*. Reasonableness. French trans. The Hague, 1730. 8°
"Le Christianisme raisonnable . . .
   "La Haye: Gosse et J. Neaulme, 1730. In-8."

Note: The above citation is from Rochedieu, p. 193. I have not been able to verify that this edition exists. It is possible that Gosse and Neaulme were the printers of the third edition, listed below. This edition is not listed in the Dutch union catalogue (at the Royal Library in the Hague) or in the *National Union Catalog of pre-1956 imprints* for North American libraries. Nor have I found it in any British or European libraries (*cf.* Introduction, Library Symbols section).

244. Reasonableness & Abridged Vindications. French trans. (Coste) 3d ed., Amsterdam, 1731. 2 vols. in 8°. With 'Religion des dames'.

In red & black: LE | [red line:] CHRISTIANISME | RAISONNABLE, | *Tel* [swash T] *qu'il nous eſt repreſenté dans* | [red:] L'ECRITURE SAINTE. | Traduit de l'Anglois | [red:] De M. LOCKE. | Troiſiéme Edition, revûë, corrigée & augmentée d'une | DISSERTATION . . . [&c. as in no. 242 until 12th line:] tion la RELIGION DES DAMES. | [red:] TOME PREMIER. ['SECOND.'] | [orn., sun above floating whale, with scrolls 29 × 48 mm] | [red:] *A AMSTERDAM*, [swash T] | Chez ZACHARIE CHATELAIN. | [rule 37 mm] | [red:] M.DCC.XXXI.

Coll: 8° (162 × 100 mm cut). Vol. 1: *⁸ (-*8) A-2A⁸ 2B⁴ [$ half + 1 signed]; 203 leaves; pp. *I-III* IV-X XI-XIV 1 2-351 52 353-389 390-392 [= 406]. The '3' in no. 352 fails to print. Sheets A-L, N-X, Z-2B also signed '*Tom. I*' in direction line; sheet Y signed '*Tome I.*'

Vol. 2: *² A-Y⁸ [$ half + 1 signed; *2 signed '*']; 178 leaves; pp. *i-iv* 1 2-299 300-302 303-350 *351-352* [= 356]. Sheets A and V signed '*Tome II.*' in direction line; B-T and Y signed '*Tom. II.*'

Contents. Vol. 1: *1ʳ (*I*) title (verso blank), *2ʳ-*4ᵛ (*III*-VIII) translator's pref., *5ʳ,ᵛ (IX-X) Locke's preface, *6ʳ,ᵛ (XI-XII) chapter contents, *7ʳ (*XIII*) 'FAUTES A CORRIGER.' (errata of 6.3 lines; verso blank), A1ʳ-Y8ʳ (*1-351*) French trans. of *Reasonableness*, Y8ᵛ-2B3ʳ (*352-389*) 'Dissertation sur la Réunion des Chrétiens' (by Coste), 2B3ʳ-2B4 blank.

Vol. 2: *1ʳ (*i*) title (verso blank), *2ʳ,ᵛ (*iii-iv*) contents of vol., A1ʳ-T6ʳ (*1-299*) Coste's abridgement of *Vindications*, T6ᵛ blank, T7ʳ (*301*) section title (verso blank), T8ʳ-V7ʳ (*303-317*) Coste's 'Discours', V7ᵛ-Y7ᵛ (*318-350*) text of *La Religion des dames*, Y8ʳ,ᵛ (*351-352*) contents of 'La Religion'.

Illustration: front. to vol. 1 is engraved portrait of Locke, same as that found in 1715 ed. (no. 242), with the engraved portrait probably re-incised.

Text (v.1 H5ʳ; same both vols.): 30 lines; 124 (134) × 69 mm; 83 R. Fair-quality laid paper, with illegible watermark. Page no. at external end of headlines.

Head titles and *headlines* throughout are same as found in 2nd edition of 1715. The section title for *La Religion des dames* (v.2 p. *301*) varies slightly: "LA RELIGION | DES | DAMES | Diſcours où l'on montre que la Reli- | gion eſt & doit être à la portée | des plus ſimples, des femmes & | des gens ſans Lettres. | TRADUIT DE L'ANGLOIS. | Troiſiéme Edition revûe & corrigée."

CW: Page. Vol. 1: A1ᵛ (atten-) tion, D2ʳ s'adon- [s'adonnoient] H3ᵛ *plus* K3ᵛ (ma-) ,,niére M2ᵛ (AC-) coû- [coûtumé] O7ʳ Je [2. Je] S1ʳ (com-) me V3ᵛ (com-) ment X1ᵛ ma- [magnifiques,] Z2ʳ (Com-) munions

Vol. 2: A3ᵛ ,,toute C6ᵛ (dif-) pu- [puter] G5ᵛ (pro-) poſer L1ᵛ dans L5ᵛ Chriſ- [Chriſtianisme] N1ʳ (Mon-) de Q5ʳ (Catalo-) gues V7ʳ Lors [Lorſque] X8ʳ ſo- [ſobre] Y6ʳ Paul

Notes: A newly set reprint of the 1715 edition (no. 242), with some new typographical errors. Vol.1, pp. 1–66 (A1^r–E1^v) are a word-for-word reprint of text in 1715 edition, with some very slight changes in phraseology. RLIN reports a copy at Brown University, Providence, R.I.
References: Attig 660; Christophersen p. 104; Rochedieu p. 193.
Copies examined: Y AMu (610.A35) [GhU] O (110 k.155-6) P (D.55116) Wol

245. Reasonableness & Abridged Vindications. French trans. (Coste). 4th ed., Amsterdam, 1740. 2 vols.-in 8°. With 'La Religion des dames'.
In red & black: LE | [red line:] CHRISTIANISME | RAISONNABLE, | *Tel qu'il nous eſt représenté dans* | [red:] L'ECRITURE SAINTE. | Traduit de l'Anglois de M. LOCKE, | [red:] *Par M. COSTE.* | Quatrième Edition, revue, corrigée & augmen- | tée d'une DISSERTATION où l'on établit | le vrai & l'unique Moyen de réunir tous les | Chrétiens malgré la différence de leurs fenti- | mens. On a joint à cette Edition la RELI- | GION DES DAMES. | [red:] TOME PREMIER. ['SECOND.'] | [engr. orn., scroll above: 'LIBERTAS EX FOEDERE ET PACE', below 2 cherubs beside fasces, 37 × 46 mm on plate 39 × 47 mm] | [red:] A AMSTERDAM, | Chez ZACHARIE CHATELAIN. | [red:] M. DCC. XL.
Coll: 8° (164 × 107 mm uncut). Vol. 1: *^{4} χ1 (called '*5') A–Z^8 [$5 signed]; 189 leaves; pp. *I–III* IV–X 1 2–328 *329* 330–364 *365–368* [= 378]. First page of each sheet signed '*Tom. I.*' in direction line.
Vol. 2: *^{2} A–V^8 [$5 signed; *2 signed '*']; 162 leaves; pp. *i–iv* 1 2–274 *275–277* 278–318 *319–320* [= 324]. First page of each sheet signed '*Tome II.*'
Contents. Vol. 1: *1^r (*I*) title (verso blank), *2^r–*4^v (*III–VIII*) translator's preface, *5^{r,v} (*IX–X*) 'PREFACE DE L'AUTEUR', A1^r–X4^v (*1–328*) text of *Reasonableness*, X5^r–Z6^v (*329–364*) text of Coste's 'Dissertation sur la Réunion des Chretiens', Z7^{r,v} (*365–366*) contents of vol., Z8 blank.
Vol. 2: *1^r (*i*) title (verso blank), *2^{r,v} (*iii–iv*) contents ('TABLES DES MATIERES Contenues dans ce Volume'), A1^r–S1^v (*1–274*) text of abridgement of *Vindications*, S2^r (*275*) section title (verso blank), S3^r–S8^v (*277–290*) Coste's pref. ('Discours sur la religion des dames'), T1^r–V7^v (*291–318*) text of 'La Religion des dames', V8^{r,v} (*319–320*) contents by chapters of 'La Religion des dames'.
Illustrations. Vol. 1 has engr. portrait of Locke facing right, after Kneller, poorly done, same as in no. 242. The engraved orn. on the title page of vol. 1 is signed '*B. Picart del. C.d.Putter fec. 1739.*' (not signed in vol.2).
Text (v.1 G3^r; same both vols.): 34 lines; 119 (129) × 64 mm; 70 R. Fair-quality laid paper with watermark of a crowned shield, surmounted by orb & cross. Page no. at external ends of headlines. Translator's pref. set 25 lines 95R; author's pref. 93 ital. Coste's 'Discours' in vol. 2 set 34 lines 70 ital.
HT, v. 1 A1^r: [orn. double rule 11 × 64 mm] | LE | CHRISTIANISME | RAISONNABLE, | Tel qu'il nous eſt repréſenté dans | l'Ecriture Sainte. | [orn. rule 2 × 63 mm]

v.2 A1ʳ: 1st 7 lines same as vol. 1 followed by 'SECONDE PARTIE.'
Section title, vol. 2 p. 275 (S2ʳ): LA RELIGION | DES | DAMES | Diſcours où l'on montre que la Re- | ligion eſt & doit être à la portée | des plus ſimples, des femmes & | des gens ſans Lettres. | TRADUIT DE L'ANGLOIS. | Quatrième [swash Q] Edition revûe & corrigée.
Headlines for vol. 1, pp. 2-327, from verso to recto, include chap. number, e.g.: 'LE CHRISTIANISME | RAISONNABLE. CHAP. XI.'
Vol. 1, p. 328 (X4ᵛ) has headline: LE CHRIST. RAIS. C.XV.
Vol. 1, pp. 330-363: DISSERTATION SUR LA | REUNION DES CHRETIENS.
Vol. 1, p. 364: DISSERTATION SUR, &c.
Vol. 2, pp. 1-274: LE CHRISTIANISME | RAISONNABLE. PART. II.
Vol. 2, pp. 278-289: DISCOURS SUR LA | RELIGION DES DAMES. (p. 290: DISCOURS, &c.)
Vol. 2, pp. 292-317: LA RELIGION | DES DAMES. (p. 318: LA RELIGION DES DAMES.)
CW: Page. Vol.1: A5ʳ (re-) reçoive D3ᵛ Phi- [Philippe] I6ʳ diffé- [différens] dé- [dédaigne] S8ᵛ hom- [hommes.]
Vol. 2: B4ʳ ,,met- [,,mettre] I1ʳ (trou-) ve O2ʳ cro- [croyance] R6ᵛ (Li-) vre
Notes: A newly set reprint with very slight revisions, following text of the previous edition (no. 244).
References: Attig 661; Christophersen p. 104; Rochedieu p. 193.
Copies examined: CaOTU (Locke L63.R43F7 1740; lacks front.) AMu (OK80-344) [BBR] [GhU (VH2170)] NjP (Ex.5707.591.1740) O (Vet.B4 f.134-5; lacks v.1 leaf Z8) P (D.55117) Vat Wol

246. Reasonableness & Abridged Vindications. German trans. (Coste/ Meinigen) Braunschweig, 1733. 2 vols. in 8°
Vol. 1: Johann Locks | gründlicher | Beweiß/ [ornamental B] | Daß die | Chriſtliche Religion/ [orn. C, R] | So wie ſie uns in der Heil. Schrift | vorgeſtellet wird/ | Höchſt billig/ Vernünftig/ und Raiſonable ſey. | Allen Irr = Geiſtern zu deutlicher und genugſamer | Uberzeigung/ überſetzt herausgegeben/ | von | D. Joh. Chriſtoph Meinigen. | [engr. orn., pastoral scene, with man holding small tree, scroll above: 'LABORE ET COELI FAVORE', 44×62 mm] | [thick rule, 80 mm] | [rule 73 mm] | Braunſchweig/ MDCCXXXIII. | Zu finden in der Rengeriſchen Buchhandlung.
Vol. 2, same as vol. 1 through 11th line:] D. Joh. Chriſtoph Meinigen. | [rule 78 mm] | Zweyter Theil. | [thick rule 76 mm] | [rule 68 mm, right end failing to print] | Braunſchweig/ MDCCXXXIII. | . . . [&c. as in vol. 1]
Coll: 8° (172 × 104 mm cut). Vol. 1: a⁸ (-a8) b⁸ A-U⁸ [$5 signed]; 176 leaves; pp. i-xxx 1 2-232 133-136 237-245 146 247-270 171 272-275 176 277-290 191 292-320 [= 350]. Pages 233-6, 246, 271, 276 and 191 incorrectly called 133-6, 146, 171, 176 and 191 respectively.
Vol. 2: A-S⁸ [$5 signed]; 144 leaves; pp. 1-3 4-205 106-107 208-288. Pages 206-7 incorrectly numbered 106-7. First page of each sheet signed 'Locks Relig. II. Th.' in direction line.

Contents. Vol. 1: a1ʳ (*i*) title (verso blank), a2ʳ–a7ᵛ (*iii–xxx*) Meinigen's preface ('Vorrede') subscribed: 'Geschrieben zu Leipzig/ den 7. Febr. 1733.', A1ʳ–U8ᵛ (*1–320*) German text of *Reasonableness* (from Coste's translation).
    Vol. 2: A1ʳ (*1*) title (verso blank), A2ʳ–S8ᵛ (*3–288*) German trans. of Coste's abridgement of the 'Vindications'.
Illustration: Vol. 1 has frontispiece portrait of Locke, facing right, after Kneller, in oval frame, with subscription '*LOCKIUS*', unsigned and poorly done, copying that found in the 1715 French edition (no. 242); without the 4-line subscription from Le Clerc.
Text (v.1 B4ᵛ; same in both vols.): 32 lines; 136 (148) × 81 mm; 85 fraktur. Preface is 29 lines, 93 fraktur, 135 (147) × 71 (86) mm with marginal biblical citations. The body of the text is without footnotes, they are incorporated in the text. Poor-quality laid paper without watermarks. Arabic page no. centered at head of page between parentheses and orn. stars, e.g. " * (307) * ", as headlines. Vol. 1, p. 320, with last line reading '𝕰𝕹𝕯𝕰', followed by tailpiece of a mulberry-like figure, with leaves, 28 × 52 mm.
HT v.1: [framed headpiece of leafy scrolls about '*CVM DEO*', 27 × 78 mm] | Das I. Capitel. | [3 lines of chapter's title]
    v.2: [same headpiece as vol. 1] | Der Andere Theil. | [5.3 lines, explaining contents of second part, trans. from French heading].
CW: Page (in fraktur). Vol. 1: a6ʳ (wol-) ten C7ʳ auge- [angenommen] I5ʳ (un =) fern P1ᵛ Un = [Unfern] T6ᵛ (ei =) nes
    Vol. 2: A2ᵛ dem = [demjenigen] C7ʳ Gleich = [Gleichwie] K2ʳ erin = [erinnere/] O4ʳ (Wahr =) heiten S5ᵛ (Tefta =) mente
Notes: Translation of Coste's French translation of the *Reasonableness* and its 'Vindications', using the 1715 ed. (no. 242). The preface by the translator gives no indication of the source of this material, nor does he include Locke's or Coste's introductory remarks. The text of the *Reasonableness* is divided into fifteen chapters; that of the 'Vindications' into seven objections ('Einwürffen'), both following Coste's arrangements.
    The style of the title-page and the headpiece indicate these two vols. are from the same printer.
    Thoemmes Antiquarian Books of Bristol had a 2-vol. set for sale in 1994.
References: Attig 663 (v.1 only); Christophersen p. 105 (vol.1 only); GV: "2. Thl. 8. Braunschw. Runge. 733."
Copies examined: Y   L (1224 c.19 (1); vol. 1 only)   O (Vet.D4 e.112; v.1 only)   Wol (Vb.462 (2); v.1 only)

247. Reasonableness & Abridged Vindications. German trans. (Coste/ anon.) Berlin & Leipzig, 1758–59. 8°
Vol. 1: Des berühmten Engländers | Johann Loke | Vernunftmäßiges | Christenthum, [ornamental C] | wie es | in der Heiligen Schrift | enthalten ist: | Nebst | einer kurzen Abhandlung | des | Herrn Coste, | worinn | das

einzige wahre Mittel, alle Christen, der Ver= | schiedenheit ihrer Meynungen unerachtet, mit | einander zu vereinigen, | gezeiget wird, | ins Deutsche übersetzt. | [rule 101 mm] | Berlin und Leipzig, | Verlegts Christian Friedrich Günther, | Buchhändler in Glogau, 1758.

Vol. 2: [Lines 1-6 as in v. 1] | enthalten ist. | [orn. of bowl of fruit above swagged pedestal 35 × 52 mm] | Zweyter Theil, [orn. Z, T] | ins Deutsche übersetzt. | [orn. rule 90 mm] | Berlin und Leipzig, | Verlegts Christian Friedrich Günther, | Buchhändler in Glogau, 1759.

Coll: 8° (195 × 115 mm cut). Vol. 1: π² A-R⁸ S⁶ [$ half + 1 (-S4) signed]; 144 leaves; pp. *i-iv 1* 2-280 *281-284* [= 288].

Vol. 2: A-O⁸ P⁴ [$ half + 1 (-P3) signed]; 116 leaves; pp. *1-3* 4-229 *230-232*. First page of sheets C-P signed 'Zweyter Theil.' in direction line.

Contents. Vol. 1: π1ʳ (*i*) title (verso blank), π2ʳ,ᵛ (*iii-iv*) 'Vorrede des Verfassers' (trans. of Coste's preface), A1ʳ-Q6ᵛ (*1-252*) text of *Reasonableness* divided into 15 'Hauptstück', Q7ʳ-R4ᵛ (*253-280*) 'Anhang' (trans. of Coste's 'Dissertation sur la réunion des Chrétiens'), R5ʳ,ᵛ (*281-282*) 'Innhalt' (contents of vol. by chapter), R6 (*283-284*) blank.

Vol. 2: A1ʳ (*1*) title (verso blank), A2ʳ,ᵛ (*3-4*) introduction ('Einleitung'), A3ʳ-P1ʳ (*5-225*) trans. of Coste's condensation of the 'Vindications', P1ᵛ-P3ʳ (*226-229*) 'Beschluss', P3ᵛ-P4ᵛ (*230-232*) blank.

Text: 84 fraktur. Vol. 1: 36 lines; 152 (164) × 87 mm. Vol. 2: 34 lines; 148 (159) × 85 mm. Poor-quality laid paper without watermark. Page no. at external ends of headlines. Framed headpiece on v.1 π2ʳ: framed headpiece of heart, angel above, between shells, 36 × 85 mm. Tailpiece, vol. 1 π2ᵛ: tree, 45 × 81 mm.

HT, v. 1 A1ʳ: [framed headpiece, flowers with scallop shells, 32 × 85 mm] | Das Vernunftmäßige Christenthum, | wie es | in der heiligen Schrift | enthalten ist. | [orn. rule, stars, 2 × 89 mm]

v.1 Q7ʳ: [3 rosettes] | [orn. rule of stars, 2 × 89 mm] | Abhandlungen | worinn | aus den Grundsätzen | des | Vernunftmäßigen Christenthums | das einige wahre Mittel, alle Christen, | der Verschiedenheit in ihren Meynungen un = | erachtet, mit einander zu vereinigen | gezeiget wird.

v.2 A2ʳ: [rectangular headpiece of artist's palette surrounded by vases, 31 × 87 mm] | Erläuterung | des Vernunftmäßigen Christenthums, | wie es | in der Heiligen Schrift enthalten ist. | Worinnen eine genauere Untersuchung eini = | ger in diesem Werk befindlichen Stellen angestellet | wird, nebst einigen neuen, diese ganze Materie | in ein helleres Licht setzenden | Betrachtungen. | [Oxford rule in 4 segments, 74 mm]

Headlines. Vol. 1, pp. 2-252 versos: Das Vernunftmäßige Christenthum.

Vol. 1, pp. 3-251 rectos, e.g.: Das fünfte Haupt.

Vol. 1, pp. 254-79, from verso to recto: Das einige wahre Mittel | des vernunftmäßigen Christenthums. (p. 280: Das einige wahre Mittel, &c.)

Vol. 2, pp. 4-225: Das Vernunftmäßige Christenthum.

Vol. 2, pp. 226-9: Erläuterung | des vernunftmäßigen Christenthums.

CW: Page (in fraktur). Vol.1: A4ʳ menſch = [menſchliche] C7ʳ als I4ᵛ (Aus-) drucks, O8ʳ Schrif = [Schriften] R7ᵛ Hier = [Hierzu]
Vol. 2: (wie =) ,,der [,,derfahren,] C7ᵛ (Chri =) ſten F1ʳ Ueber = [,,Ueberdem] K2ᵛ hal = [haltene] M2ᵛ pre = [predigte] O4ʳ Wei = [Weiſe] P1ᵛ (Soll =) te

Notes: An anonymous translation of Coste's French texts, following Coste very closely. The text of the 'Reasonableness' is divided into 15 chapters, followed by the translation of Coste's 'Dissertation on the reunion of the Christians'. The second vol. contains Coste's rearrangement of the 'Vindications' into seven 'Einwürffen' (objections) and a 'Beschluss' (conclusion).

Dr. Marie-Luise Spieckermann of the Englisches Seminar of the Westfälische Wilhelms- Universitat at Münster has supplied me with details of a copy in the Hessische Landes- und Hochschulbibliothek at Darmstadt (shelfmark Günderrode 308). I am also grateful for further information from Karin Berst at Darmstadt.

Glogau, the location of Guenther's business, is located in what is now Poland.

References: Attig 664 (vol. 1 only); Christophersen p. 105; GV 1700–1910.
Copies examined: German Society of Penn. at Phila. (Ea.10, 1–2) MH–AH

The *Reasonableness* was not the most popular of Locke's publications. The *Second Vindication* was especially verbose and wearisome, rarely reprinted after 1748, except in all *Works* editions (see Chapter XII).

After 1800 the *Reasonableness* is reprinted with Locke's 'An Essay for the Understanding of St. Paul's Epistles' (Chapter IX, no. 277 et seq.) in 1810; alone in 1811 (in Boston, Mass.). A 'new edition' was issued with both 'Vindications' in 1824, with a cancellans title leaf using the *Works* edition of 1824. It was further reprinted in New York in 1835 with the 'Essay for the Understanding of St. Paul's Epistles' and the posthumous 'Discourse of Miracles' (cf. no. 299, 312) in the series, The Christian Library, vol. 6 (itself reprinted in 1835 as vol. 25 of the 'Sacred Classics' series). Other reprints of the *Reasonableness* were issued in 1846, 1850, 1853 (?) and 1914. An edition with annotated text edited by George Ewing was published in Chicago in 1965. Abridgements were published in 1946 (by J.A. Ferris) and in 1958 (compiled by Ian Ramsey).

Post-1800 foreign-language translations of the *Reasonableness* are very few. J.-P. Migne included it in vol. 4 of his *Démonstrations évangeliques de Tertullien* . . . (Paris-Montrouge, 1843). There was a German edition by Carl Winckler in 1914, and an Italian translation by Ida Cappiello in 1976. Mario Sina as compiler and translator of Locke's *Scritti filosofici e religiosi* (Milano, 1979) includes the *Reasonableness* and the first *Vindication*, based on the 1823 edition of the *Works*, 7: 1–158; the Italian texts with prefaces are found on pp. [253]–442 and [443]–476 respectively. The *Reasonableness* was finally translated into Spanish (Madrid, 1977) by L. Gonzalez-Puertas.

The *Reasonableness* and its 'Vindications' are included in every collected *Works* edition (beginning in 1714; Chap.XII). John C. Higgins-Biddle's critical edition of the *Reasonableness* is in the press. It is intended to include both 'Vindications' in the Clarendon Edition of the Works of John Locke.

CHAPTER VII
Letters to Stillingfleet (nos. 248–50)

The controversial nature of the reception of Locke's *Essay* and of the *Reasonableness* has been noted in earlier chapters. The *Essay* itself generated most of the attacks, to which Locke was reluctant to reply: "But yet if any one thinks fit to be angry, and rail at it, he may do it securely: For I shall find some better way of spending my time, than in such kind of Conversation" (*Essay*, ed. P. H. Nidditch, 1975, 'Preface to the Reader', p. 9). Further, ". . . yet this I must own, that I have not had the good luck to receive any light from those Exceptions [of John Edwards and other critics] I have met with in print against any part of my Book . . ." (ibid., p. 11).

John Edwards' 'Exceptions' to the *Reasonableness* (cf. Chap. VI pref.) were bad enough; but Edward Stillingfleet, the then Bishop of Worcester, goaded Locke too far, charging him with unorthodox religious beliefs in his *A Discourse in Vindication of the Doctrine of the Trinity; with an Answer to the late Socinian Objections against It from Scripture, Antiquity and Reason* . . . (London, 1696; no. C1696-6). Locke's self-defence resulted in a spate of pamphlets: his *A Letter to Edward, Lord Bishop of Worcester* (1697); Stillingfleet's *The Bishop of Worcester's Answer to Mr. Locke's* Letter, *concerning Some Passages Relating to his* Essay of Humane Understanding (1697; no. C1697-13); *Mr. Locke's Reply* (1697); Stillingfleet's *The Bishop of Worcester's Answer to Mr. Locke's Second Letter: Wherein His Notion of Ideas is Prov'd to Be Inconsistent with It Self and with the Articles of the Christian Faith* (1698; no. C1698-4); and *Mr. Locke's Reply to . . . the Bishop*['s] *Answer to His Second Letter* (1697).

As noted in the description of the 5th edition of the *Essay* (1706; no.65), selections from Locke's exchange with Bishop Stillingfleet were added as footnotes to that and all subsequent editions, except those editions published late in the eighteenth century that were extracted from *Works* editions.

248. Letter to Stillingfleet. 1697. 8°. Two issues, three states of 2d issue.
248A (First issue). Within a double rule, inner 143 × 77 mm, outer 151 × 84 mm: A | LETTER | TO | Edward L^d Biſhop of Worceſter, | Concerning ſome | PASSAGES | RELATING TO | Mr. LOCKE's Eſſay | OF | Humane Underſtanding: | IN A LATE | Diſcourſe of his Lordſhips, | IN | *Vindication of the Trinity.* [swash T] | [rule 75 mm] | By *JOHN LOCKE,* [swash J, K] Gent. | [rule 75 mm] | LONDON:

Printed for *A.* and *J. Churchill*, [swash J] at | the *Black* [swash k] *Swan* in *Paternoſter-Row.* [swash R] 1697.
Coll: 8° (190 × 115 mm cut) A–O⁸ P⁴ [$ half signed]; 116 leaves; pp. *i–iv* 1–227 228 [= 232].

248B.I (Second issue), State I. Within a double rule, inner 142 × 77 mm, outer 150 × 86 mm: A | LETTER | To the Right Reverend | *Edward* L^d *Biſhop* of *Worceſter,* | . . . [&c. as in 1st issue, until imprint:] *London*: Printed by *H. Clark,* [swash k] for *A.* and *J. Churchill,* [swash J] | at the *Black* [swash k] *Swan* in *Pater-Noſter-Row*; [swash R] and | *Edw. Caſtle,* next *Scotland-yard* by *Whitehall,* 1697.

248B. II (Second issue), State II: as State I until last 2 lines: at the *Black* [swash k] *Swan* in *Pater-noſter-Row*; [swash R] and | *Edw. Caſtle,* next *Scotland-yard* by *Whitehall,* 1697

248.B II (Second issue), State III: as State I and II except '*Pater-Noſter-Row*;' and '*Whitehall.*'

Coll: same as first issue, states I–III, except A⁸ (± A2).

Contents: A1ʳ (*i*) half title (verso blank), A2ʳ (*iii*) title (verso blank), A3ʳ–O8ʳ (1–219) text signed 'John Locke.', O8ᵛ–P4ʳ (220–227) 'POSTSCRIPT.' signed '*Oates, Jan.* 7. | 1696/7.' (+ rule, followed by '*ERRATA.*' of 12.5 lines), P4ᵛ (228) advt. for '*Books Printed for, and ſold by*' the Churchills (14 items).

Text (B4ᵛ): 28 lines; 129 (143) × 62 (78) mm; 93 R. Medium-quality laid paper without watermark. No headlines, but page no. centered within parentheses. External marginal citations to Stillingfleet's text and to Locke's *Essay*.

Half-title: [rule 66 mm] | Mr. Locke's | LETTER | TO THE | Bishop of Worceſter. | [rule 65 mm]

HT: [double rule 65 mm] | A | LETTER | TO THE | Biſhop of Worceſter, &c.

CW: Page. B5ʳ "Think- ["Thinking,] C5ʳ (hav-) ing F3ᵛ (Cer-) tainty I4ʳ whe- [whether] N3ʳ (conſi-) dering P1ᵛ Heats [Heats,]

Notes: In the first issue Locke did not address the bishop with his proper courtesy title. The second issue with its cancellans title remedies that lapse, and also shows the need for another bookseller to help sell the work.

The copy of the second issue, first state, at the University of Utrecht Library has an offset impression of the first issue's title-page on P1ʳ (p. 221). My copy of the second issue has the same offset on the verso of the half-title. It seems about equal numbers of both states I and II of the second issue survive, fewer of the third state. The first state has the cancellans title reading '*Noſter-*' and a comma after '*Whitehall*' in the imprint, although the unaltered lines in some copies seem to use the same typesetting as the first issue. Other copies have '*noſter-*' and a comma after '*Whitehall*'. The third state differs again. Desmond Neill of Massey College Library, Toronto, has privately stated his suspicion that cancellans title leaves were printed 'four up', four to a sheet and then cut apart. Such a procedure would explain these minor variations in the imprint. There is no priority between them.

Locke had finished the composition of this 'Letter' by January 7, 1697; friends John Freke and Edward Clarke gave the manuscript to the Churchills on January 21st, and it was available in print by March 17th (cf. *Corr.* 2179; v.754-5; and 'Principal Dates', v.vii).

James Johnstoun had received his presentation copy by March 20 (*ibid.* 2225; vi.56) A list of persons to whom Locke probably presented copies is in Bodleian Library MS Locke c.25 fo.53^v, 2d column. (The third column, headed '3 Rep<ly> to Bp Worcester | 1698' must refer to Locke's *Second Reply*, no. 250. The only list for Locke's *Reply*, no. 249, is in another notebook.) The list is headed '1697' and contains 42 numbered names in random order, 9 of which are marked with an 'x', probably denoting a special binding. The name of John Toland the deist and controversial writer, originally in this list, has been deleted and the name of Locke's servant Sylvester Brounower inserted. The names are listed as follows, with more information supplied in parentheses.

Bp of Worcester 1 × (Edward Stillingfleet)
Mr Clarke 2 (Edward Clarke, to whom *Education* is dedicated)
Mr Freke 3 (probably John Freke 'the bachelor')
Dr Tindall 4 (Matthew Tindall, deist, author of *Christianity as Old as the Creation*)
Mr Molineux 5 (William Molyneux)
Mr Burridg 6 (Ezechiel Burridge, Latin translator of the *Essay*)
Mr Tyrrell 7 (James Tyrrell)
Mrs Berkeley 8 × (Elizabeth Berkeley; became wife of Gilbert Burnet, Bp. of Salisbury in 1700)
Ld Keeper 9 × (Baron John Somers, Lord Chancellor from 22 April 1697)
—— C.J. Treby 10 × (Lord Chief Justice Sir John Treby)
—— —— Holt 11 × (Lord Chief Justice Sir John Holt)
—— Ashley 12 × (Anthony Ashley Cooper, 3d Earl of Shaftesbury)
Mr Ashley 13 (probably Maurice Ashley, a relative of the above)
Mr Chadwick 14 (James Chadwick, a Commissioner for Customs; see no.160)
Mr. Firmin 15 (Thomas Firmin, a philanthropist and friend; died Dec. 1697)
Ld Privy Seale 16 × (Thomas Herbert, Earl of Pembroke)
Arc: Bp Canterbury 17 × (Dr. Thomas Tenison)
Mr Wynn 18 (John Wynne, abridged Locke's *Essay*; later, Bp. of St. Asaph)
J. Johnston 19 (James Johnstoun, correspondent)
Mr Bentley 20 (Richard Bentley)
Mr Cunninghame 21 (Alexander Cunningham; critic of Bentley; cf. DNB)
Mr Leibnits 22 (Gottfried Wilhelm Leibnitz)
Mr Burthogg 23 (Richard Burthogge)

Mr Furley 24 (Benjamin Furly, friend at Amsterdam)
Mr Le Clerc 25 (Jean Le Clerc)
Dr Guenellon 26 (Pierre Guenellon, physician, friend and correspondent in Holland)
Mr Coste 27 (Pierre Coste, French translator of the *Essay* and other Locke works)
Dr South 28 (Robert South, D.D, noted divine)
Lady Masham 29 (Damaris née Cudworth, wife of Sir Francis Masham)
Mr Fraser 30 (James Fraser, 'covenanting divine' – DNB)
Mr Sec Trumbul 31 (Sir William Trumbull)
Bp: Gloucester 32 (Edward Fowler, Bishop)
Ld Monmouth 33 × (Charles Mordaunt, Earl of Monmouth, 3d Earl of Peterborough)
~~Mr Toland~~ 34 Syl (Sylvester Brounower, Locke's amanuensis)
Sr Littleton Powys 35 (a judge; cf. DNB)
Dr Wall 36 (George Walls; see no. 61, n.4)
Mr Hill 37 (Abraham Hill, 'man of science' – DNB)
Dr Sloan 38 (Hans Sloane)
Mr Newton 39 & ye first letter (Isaac Newton)
Dr Richardson 40 (Thomas Richardson, 'lecturer at Gray's Inn' – *Corr.* viii.457)
Sr Godfry Kneller 41 (the portrait painter)
Mr Crell 42 (probably Samuel Crellius)

* * * * *

If we can identify 'Bp Stillingfleet Letter to' as this work cited in Hodgson and Blagden's edition of *The Notebook of Thomas Bennet and Henry Clements* (1956) on p. 34, the 'Letter' was sold by Bennet to Reinier Leers in Rotterdam on 29 December 1696 at a price below retail, of 1 s. 6 d. (probably at a retail price in England of 1 s. 9 d.).

The first issue is fairly scarce. In addition to the copies I have examined, Wing reports it can be found at 'LLU' (unidentified), and Newberry Library, Chicago.

A microfilm of the Harvard College Library copy of the 1st issue is in the EEB collection, reel 1657 no. 3; of the 2d issue in reel 921, no. 27.

References: Attig 440; Christophersen p. 37; ESTC 1st issue r040014, 2d r008183; L.L. 1793, 1796; T.C. III. 23; Wing^2 1st issue L2748A, 2d L2749.

Notice: Acta eruditorum, 1699: 12–19 (together with Stillingfleet's answer; cf. C1697-13).

Copies examined. 1st issue: Y   Csj (Hh.12.14)   Han (PA1742; 194 × 115 mm)   MH (*EC65.L7934.697)   NR   O^1 (Vet.A3 e.1873)   Winchester Cathedral Lib.

2d issue, state I (No∫ter / Whitehall,): Bristol Univ. (HOd; ex-libris St. George's Chapel, Windsor)   CaQMMO (1045; lacks A1)   Ck^1 (Keynes 13.1)   CLU-C   DFo (acc.144644)   Utr (Y.oct.449)

2d issue, state II (*nofter / Whitehall*,): Y C¹ (Peterborough L.1.10) CaOTU (Locke L63.L47 1697) CaOHM (B14638) Ck² (Keynes A.12.23) Ck³ (Keynes A.12.24) CLaslett (lost?) CtY (K8.L79/q697) EXu L (8464.b.14) NjP (Ex.6106.357) NjR (X B1253.C3EWL) O² (8° P.209 'Ex dono Auctoris') Oo (2Td.5)
2d issue, state III (No*fter / Whitehall.*): C² (Hhh.1020) O³ (Pamph.224 (21)) O⁴ (Vet.A2 e.279 (3)) Oa (y.9.28) PPL (Wing L2749/69134.O)

249. Reply to Stillingfleet. 1697. 8°
Within a double rule, inner 142 × 76 mm, outer 150 × 84 mm: M^r. *Locke*'s [swash L] Reply | To the Right Reverend the | Lord Bifhop of *Worcefter*'s | ANSWER to his LETTER, | Concerning fome | PASSAGES | RELATING TO | M^r. LOCKE's Effay | OF | 𝕳umane 𝖀nderftanding: | IN A LATE | Difcourfe of his Lordfhips, | IN | *Vindication of the Trinity.* [swash T] | [rule 72 mm] | *London:* Printed by *H. Clark,* [swash k] for *A.* and *J.* [swash J] *Churchill,* | at the *Black* [swash k] *Swan* in *Pater-Nofter-Row*; [swash R] and | *E. Caftle,* next *Scotland-yard* by *Whitehall.* 1697.
Coll: 8° (190 × 115 mm cut) A² B–M⁸ N⁴ O² [$ half signed]; 96 leaves; pp. *i–iv 1–174 175–176 1–7 8–12* [= 192].
Contents: A1^r (*i*) half title (verso blank), A2^r (*iii*) title (verso blank), B1^r–M6^v (1–172) text, M7^{r,v} (173–4) 'Poftfcript.', M8^r (*175*) section title (verso blank), N1^r–4^r (1–7) text of 'Remarks', N4^v (*8*) errata covering pp. 18–101 (18 lines), O1^r–2^v (*9–12*) advt. for books printed for and sold by Churchills.
Text (B4^v): 30 lines; 140 (153) × 70 (80) mm; 93 R. Medium-quality laid paper without watermark. No headlines; page no. centered at top within parentheses. The left parenthesis is faulty on pp. 25, 57, 89, 121, 139, 155 and 171 (fol. 5^r of gatherings C, E, G, and I, fol. 6^r of K and L).
Half-title: [rule 68 mm] | M^r. *Locke*'s Reply | TO THE | Bifhop of *Worcefter*'s | ANSWER to his LETTER. | [rule 67 mm]
Head title, M7^r (p. 173): 𝕻oftfcript.
  N1^r (2d set, p.1): [double rule 69/68 mm] | AN | ANSWER | TO | REMARKS | UPON AN | ESSAY | Concerning | Humane Underftanding, *&c.*
Section title, M8^r (p. *175*): [rule 67 mm] | AN | ANSWER | TO | REMARKS | UPON [P larger font] AN | ESSAY | Concerning | Humane Underftanding. | [rule 67 mm]
CW: Page. B8^r (*Cer-*) tainty E5^r (with-) out G8^v (cru-) cified, M2^r (Lord-) fhip
Notes: Written in reply to *The Bishop of Worcefter's Answer to Mr. Locke's Letter* (no.C1697–13), it was finished (and is so dated on p. 172) 'London, 29 Jun. 1697.' It was published in late August or early September 1697, as witnessed by a letter to William Molyneux dated 11 September 1697, where Locke writes: "If you have received my reply to the Bishop before this comes to your hand . . ." (*Corr.* 2310; vi. 189). The 'Answer to

Remarks' (7 pp. at end) is a reply to Thomas Burnet's *Remarks upon 'An Essay concerning Human Understanding': in a Letter Address'd to the Author* (1697; no. C1697-4).

A list of 38 persons to whom Locke presented copies is in Bodleian Library MS Locke c. 25 fo.55^r, headed 'Reply Copys 97'. It is probably a preparatory, not final list, for otherwise it is hard to comprehend the omission of Stillingfleet's name. The names are as follows: Lord Ashley (3d Earl of Shaftesbury), Maurice Ashley, Dr. Richard Bentley, Mrs. Elizabeth Berkeley, Samuel Bold, Ezekiel Burridge, Dr. Richard Burthogge, Lady (Mary) Calverley, Edward Clarke, Thomas Firmin, Mr. Fraser (? James), John Freke, Benjamin Furly, Dr. Peter Guenellon, Abraham Hill, Sir John Holt, James Johnstoun, Peter King (Locke's cousin, later Baron King), Jean Le Clerc, Leibniz, Lady Masham, William Molyneux, Isaac Newton, Earl of Pembroke, Lord Monmouth (3d Earl of Peterborough from 1697), William Popple, Thomas Richardson, Dr. Hans Sloane, Lord John Somers, Dr. Robert South, Lord Spencer (later 3d Earl of Sunderland), Dr. Thomas Tenison, Matthew Tindall, Sir John Treby, Sir William Trumbull, James Tyrrell, Dr. George Walls, and John Wynne. Most of these persons received copies of the *Letter* to Stillingfleet (and are identified above, no. 248). The new names are (1) Samuel Bold, a clergyman who published several defences of Locke; (2) Lady Calverley, who also received a copy of the *Essay* (no.61, q.v.); (3) Peter King; (4) William Popple, a merchant, who translated Locke's *Epistola de tolerantia* into English; and (5) Charles, Lord Spencer, the statesman and friend of Lord Somers (cf. DNB). Some of those receiving the first *Letter* are omitted in this list. Newton's name is followed by "this and my first". The list ends with 'Money Mr Stepney', a reference presumably to *Several Papers* (see no.163).

A microfilm copy is in the EEB collection, reel 921, no. 27, following the first *Letter*.

References: Attig 443; Christophersen p. 40; ESTC r007915; L.L. 1797; T.C. III.51; Wing^2 L2753.

Notice: *Acta eruditorum*, 1699: 19-20 (also covers no. C1698-4).

Copies examined: Y   Bristol Univ. (HOd)   C (Ven.7.69.6)   CaOHM (B14639)   CaQMMO (no. 1046; Osler copy)   CaOTU (Locke L63.M57 1697)   Ck^1 (Keynes A.13.2)   Ck^2 (Keynes A.13.1; lacks A1)   CLU-C   CtY (K8.L79/q697(2))   DFo (acc.141338)   L (528.i.24)   MH (*EC65.L7934.697r; has front. port. by Vertue after Kneller, subscribed 'Johannes Locke.')   NjP (Ex.6106.376)   NjR (X B1253.C3EWL/2)   NR (H.H. Warner copy; lacks sheet O)   O (8° P.209 (2) 'Ex dono Auctoris')   Oa (y.9.29)   Oo (2Td.5 (3))   PPL (Wing 2753/67296.O)   TxDaM-P

250. Second Reply to Stillingfleet. 1699. 8°
Within a double rule, inner 144 × 77 mm, outer 151 × 87 mm: M^r. *Locke*'s [swash L] Reply | To the Right Reverend the | Lord Biſhop of *Worceſter*'s | Anſwer to his Second Letter: | Wherein, beſides other

incident Mat- | ters, what his Lordſhip has ſaid | [turned vertically, reading from bottom to top:] Concerning |
{ Certainty by Reaſon, Certainty by |
Ideas, and Certainty of Faith. |
The Reſurrection of the ſame Body. |
The Immateriality of the Soul. |
The Inconſiſtency of Mr. *Locke*'s | Notions with the Articles of the |
Chriſtian Faith, and their Ten- | dency to *Sceptiſm*, is examined. |
[rule 74 mm] | LONDON: | Printed by H. C. for 𝔄. and 𝔍. 𝔠𝔥𝔲𝔯𝔠𝔥𝔦𝔩𝔩, | at the *Black Swan* in *Pater-noſter-Row*; and | 𝔈. 𝔠𝔞𝔰𝔱𝔩𝔢, next *Scotland-yard* by *Whitehall*, | M DC XCIX.

Coll: 8° (195 × 115 mm cut) A^2 (–A2 = H1) B–2F^8 2G^2 H^1 [$ half signed]; 228 leaves; pp. *i–ii* 1–77 79 78 80–207 206 209–452 453–454 [= 456]. Page no. 78 and 79 interchanged; 208 called '206'. Some copies have A2 bound after A1.

Contents: A1^r (*i*) title (verso blank), B1^r–2G2^v (1–452 text), ending 'Oates, 4 May, | 1698. John Locke.', H1^r (*453*) errata in 2 cols. each of 19 lines, ending '*FINIS*.', H1^v blank.

Text (F4^r): 35 lines; 144 (156) × 72 (86); 83 R. Good-quality laid paper, some sheets (e.g. 2E) with bunch of grapes and 'COMIR' (?) watermark. Headlines are page no. centered within parentheses.

CW: Page. B4^r (Satisfa-) ction, B8^v (Lord-) ſhip E3^v (*de*-) *ſire* H2^r (de-) ſerves M3^r *incon*- [*inconſiſtent*] Q4^r what- [whatever] T1^v How- [However,] X4^v be- [becauſe] 2B7^v (ano-) ther 2D4^v (aſk-) ing, 2F7^v ac- [accuſed]

Notes: Written in reply to Stillingfleet's *The Bishop of Worcester's Answer to Mr. Locke's Second Letter* . . . (no. C1698-4), this third 'letter' is longer than either of its predecessors by far. E. S. de Beer estimates it was published in November 1698 (*Corr*. vi. vii) though the imprint date is given for the following year, a practice usual at the time for books ready in November or December. 'Oates' was the name of the Masham residence in Essex.

A list of persons to whom Locke presented copies survives in the Bodleian Library's MS Lock c.25 fo.53^v, 3d column. The list of 41 persons, not in numerical order, is headed '3 Rep to Bp Worcester | 1698'. I list below the names as they appear, with additional information in parentheses:

Bp Worcester 1
Arch BP 4 (Dr. Thomas Tenison)
Ld Chancellor 2 (Lord John Somers)
  Privy Seale 3
  Peterbourgh 7
  Spencer 19
  C J Treby 5
    Holt 6
Baron Powis 8
Ldy Masham 34 (Damaris Cudworth, wife of Sir Francis Masham)
Mrs Berkley 9

Bp Glocester 23
Sr G: Kneller 18
Mr Freke 10
Dr South 14
Dr Tindal 15
Mr Wynne 20
Secretary Johnstown 11
Dr Bently 17
Mr Coste 35
Mr le Clerc 24
    at Amsterdam
Dr Guenellon 25
Mr Furley 27
Mr Popple 12
Mr King 13
Mr Burridge 21
Dr Sloan 16
Mr Tyrrell 22
Mr Hill 22 (? in error for '26')
Mr Gastrell 28 (Francis Gastrell, later Bishop of Chester)
Mr Bold 29
Ld Carbery 30 (John Vaughan, 3d Earl of Carbery)
Mr Newton 31
Dr Woodward 32 (John Woodward, physician and member of the Royal Society)
Mr Clarke 33
Monsr du Bos 36 (Abbé Jean-Baptiste du Bos)
Dr Covel 37 (John Covel, Master of Trinity College, Cambridge)
Mr Ashley 38
Mrs E: Masham 39 (Esther, daughter of Sir Francis Masham by his first marriage)
Dr Molyneux 40 (Thomas Molyneux, physician, brother of William)
Mr Crell 41

The new names are Gastrell, Carbery, Woodward, du Bos, Esther Masham, Covel, and Thomas Molyneux. The other persons were recipients of Locke's first *Reply* (no. 249).

The printer, 'H.C.' is presumably H. Clark, printer of the earlier 'Letters'. The 'conger' of booksellers, as reported in *The Notebook of Thomas Bennet and Henry Clements* (1956, p. 159) on November 1698 reported a purchase of 500 copies 'pooled', including 25 'returnable drawn' for which they paid 2 s. 4d. each, and sold to the trade at 3 s. 9d, allowing for a gross profit of 1 s. 3d. This 'Second Reply' was listed in the *Bibliotheca-annua* for 1699 (p. 5, no. 68-9) as being priced at five shillings.

A microfilm copy is to be found in the EEB collection reel 1529, no. 24.

References: Attig 445; Christophersen p. 42; ESTC r032483; L.L. 1798; T.C. III.105; Wing^2 L2754.

Notice: 'Article 1: Mr. Locke's Reply to [the Bishop's] Second Letter' is a summary review in the *Nouvelles de la république des lettres*, Oct. 1699: 363–85, and Nov. 1699: 483–513; it also discusses Stillingfleet's 'Answers' (cf. no. C1697-13, C1698-4).

Copies examined: CaOTU (Locke L63.M58 1699; sheet 2E on poor browning paper) CaOHM (B11928) CaQMMO (no.1047) Ck (3 copies: Keynes A13.5; A13.14; A13.3, lacking err.leaf) CLU-C CtY (K8.L79/q697 (3)) DFo^1 (acc. 153338; gift of S.P. Lamprecht, lacks err. leaf) DFo^2 (L-2754; err. bound as leaf A2) DFo^3 (153336; sheet 2G and err. leaf lacking; S.P. Lamprecht's copy) Han (PA1742 (2)) L (699.e.50) MH (*EC65.L7934.699r) NjP (Ex.6106.3761) NjR (X B1253.C3EWR) O (8° P.209 Art. (3) 'Ex dono Auctoris') Oa Oc (O.5.3.5) OCU (B1294.S82) Omc Oo (2Td.6 (2)) PPL (Wing 2754/67982.O) PU (B1294.L7 1699)

None of the pamphlets in this controversy with Stillingfleet generated sufficient interest to be published again until very recently. Some short selections from the *Letter* were published in a collection on and entitled *Jonathan Swift*, edited by C.T. Probyn in 1978. Locke's 'Second Reply' was abstracted in a collection published in 1856 under the title: *The Resurrection of the Same Body Not an Article of the Christian Faith*. J. A. St. John extracted the philosophical arguments of the controversy in his *Philosophical Works of John Locke* (1843; v. 2, pp. 339–411).

Mario Sina in his collection, *Scritti filosofici e religiosi* [di] *John Locke*, has translated the first *Letter* into Italian, using the 1823 *Works* edition, 4: 1–96.

The *Letter* and the two 'Replies' have been included in all *Works* editions (see Chap. XII). Further, a critical edition by M. A. Stewart is to be included in the Clarendon Edition of the Works of John Locke.

CHAPTER VIII
Occasional Contributions to Other Works
A: Poems (nos. 251–57)

The very first material Locke published was two poems, one in Latin, one in English, in an Oxford collection celebrating the successful outcome of the war with Holland during the protectorate of Oliver Cromwell, published in 1654. Eight years later, his next publication was again a poem in a collection celebrating the arrival in England of Catherine of Braganza for her marriage with Charles II.

Later, another poem appeared in 1668 as a dedication to the second edition of his mentor Thomas Sydenham's *Methodus curandi febres*.

Locke's poems from the 1654 collection were included in the continuation of the popular *Poems on Affairs of State*, in 1697. This miscellaneous collection was reprinted many times from 1698 to 1733, with changes to the content, including 16-page or continuously paged 'addenda', a 'second part', second, third, fourth and fifth editions, second, third and fourth volumes, and a piracy. The publication details of this collection are briefly covered in the multi-volume modern edition published since 1963 by Yale University Press.

251. Poems in *Musarum Oxoniensium* (1654)
"PAX regit Augusti. . .": 8-line poem, unrhymed, signed: 'J. LOCKE ex Æd. Chriſti.'
AND
"IF Greece with ſo much mirth . . .", 44-line poem. rhymed (as bb cc, &c.) signed 'J. LOCKE Student of Ch. Ch.'
IN: [orn. rules of repeated fleurons, 5 mm wide, 155 × 100 mm] | MUSARUM [swash Us, R] | OXONIENSIVM | ΕΛΑΙΟΦΟΡΙ'Α. | SIVE, | Ob Fædera, Auſpiciis | SERENISSIMI | OLIVERI | Reipub. Aug. [swash R, A] Scot. & Hiber. | DOMINI PROTECTORIS, | Inter Rempub. Britannicam & Ordines | Fœderatos Belgii Fæliciter | STABILITA, [swash Ts] | Gentis Togatæ ad vada Iſidis | Celuſma Metricum. | [rule 86 mm] | OXONIÆ, Excudebat Leonardus Lichfield Academiæ | Typographus 1654.
Collation of the whole work: 4° (183 × 140 mm cut) A–L⁴ [$2 signed]; 44 leaves; pp. *i–iv* 1–29 50–51 32–33 54–55 36–68 89–104 [=88]. Inner forme of sheet E misnumbered 50–51, 54–55; pages 69–84 in gatherings K–L called 89–104.

Contents of the whole: A1ʳ (*i*) title (verso blank), A2ʳ,ᵛ (*iii–iv*) dedication to Cromwell signed 'Procan: JO: OWEN', A3ʳ–I4ᵛ (1–68) poems in Latin, K1ʳ–L4ᵛ (89–104) poems in English.

Text: approx. 35 lines (varies); 143 (153) × 88 mm; approx. 80 R. Number of lines depends on no. of poems and author statements per page. Watermark is horn and sphere, with grapes. Both poems begin with 2-line initials.

Headlines, from verso to recto: Mu∫arum OXONIENSIUM | ἘΛΑΙΟΦΟΡΙ'Α.

CW: Page. D4ᵛ cu [Cui] F4ᵛ que<m> [Quem ('m' fails to print)] G1ʳ Quid K3ᵛ Shal [Shall] K4ʳ Now

No CW when an author's signature is at end of page, e.g. pp. 25, 26.

Notes: Locke's Latin poem occurs on p. 45 (G1ʳ) and the English on pp. 94–95 (K3ᵛ–K4ʳ). The collection, written on the occasion of a treaty between Great Britain and the Belgian federation, includes poems from Dr. Busby, John Wall, Nathaniel Crewe, Robert South, and others, chiefly Christ Church men; also from the printer subscribed: Esquire Bedle of Divinity.

References: Attig 1; Christophersen p. 8; Wing² O-902 (entire collection)

Copies examined: O1 (B. 13.4 Linc. (10))   CaOTU   O² (Pamph.C.100 (10))   O³ (Wood 484 (4))

252.1. Poems in 'Musarum' reprinted in *Poems on Affairs of State*, 2d vol.: (*State Poems Continued*), 1697.

"Pax regit Augusti . . ."
   AND
"If Greece with so much mirth . . ."

In: State Poems; | CONTINUED | From the time of *O. Cromwel*, to the YEAR 1697. | WRITTEN | By the Greate∫t WITS of the Age, *viz.* |

The Lord Roche∫ter,	Mr. Milton,
The Lord D-----t,	Mr. Prior,
The Lord V-----n,	Mr. Stepney,
The Hon. Mr. M-----ue,	Mr. Ayloffe, *&c.*
Sir F. S---d,	

WITH | Several Poems in Prai∫e of *Oliver Cromwel*, | in *Latin* and *Engli∫h*, by |

D. South,	D. Crew,
D. Locke,	Mr. Busby, *&c.*
Sir W. G----n,	

Also ∫ome Mi∫cellany POEMS by the ∫ame, | never before Printed. | [rule 82 mm] | Now carefully Examined with the Originals, and | Publi∫hed without any Ca∫tration. | [rule 83 mm] | Printed in the year MDCXCVII.

Collation of this (second) *vol.*: 8° (188 × 128 mm cut) A⁴ B–Q⁸ R⁴ [$ half signed]; 128 leaves; pp. *i–viii* 1–248 [=256].

Text: 36 lines; 147 (158) × 85 mm. Poor-quality paper with armorial watermark. Page catchwords.

Headlines, from verso to recto: *POEMS on* | *State Affairs.*
Note: These 'State Poems' constitute the second vol. of a collection, the first vol. of which was published with the title (within a double rule, inner 147 × 86 mm, outer 151 × 90 mm): "POEMS | ON | 𝔄ffairs of 𝔖tate: | FROM | The Time of *Oliver Cromwell*, to the | Abdication of K. *James* the Second. | *Written by the greateſt Wits of the Age.* | VIZ. |

Duke of *Buckingham*,   Mr. *Milton*,
Earl of *Rocheſter*,   Mr. *Dryden*,
Lord *Bu*-------*ſt*,   Mr. *Sprat*,
Sir *John Denham*,   Mr. *Waller*.
Andrew Marvell, Eſq;   Mr. *Ayloffe*, &c.

| [rule 83 mm] | With ſome Miſcellany Poems by the ſame: | Moſt whereof never before Printed. | [rule 83 mm] | *Now carefully examined with the Originals, and* | *Publiſhed without any Caſtration.* | [rule 82 mm] | Printed in the Year 1697." The first vol. collates as 8° A–Q⁸ [$ half signed]; pp. *i–xvi* 1–224 245–260 [= 256]. The Bodleian copy of vol. 1 (Rawl. 521) has a different collation, with a briefer preface: A⁴ B–Q⁸ R⁴; pp. *i–viii* 1–224 245–267 268 [= 256]. In both copies page 260 ends '*FINIS.*', but the Bodley's copy has 'Addenda' on pp. 261–7 (more poems), and p. 268 contains an advertisement for this 2d vol. (34 lines listing the contents of this vol., and the price of 3 s.). Rutgers University Library copy has an 'Addenda' following Q8 (signed A⁸, paged 1–16). The second edition of Wing enters the Bodleian Library copy under the first author listed on the title leaf, Buckingham, as B5316; a retrospective ESTC record is r026563; and a microfilm of this first vol. is in EEB reel 1326 no. 5.

Locke's poems, reprinted in the '*State Poems Continued*' or the second vol., are part of those listed in the contents (called 'Index') as "*Select Poems out of* Muſarum Oxonienſium | in *Oliv.* Protect. *&c.* 1654." They occupy p. 8 (B4ᵛ) and pp. 12–13 (B6ᵛ–B7ʳ). The poem, "Pax regit Augusti . . ." is followed by an anonymous translation, also in 8 lines, beginning "A peaceful Sway the great *Auguſtus* bore" and ending "VVho thus alone two pagan Gods excel." Both poem and translation are signed 'J. Locke, *ex Æde Chriſti.*'

A microfilm of the Union Theological Seminary's copy of vol. 1 is in EEB, reel 1337, no. 42. A different 2d vol. of *Poems on Affairs of State*, with title: *Poems on Affairs of State, The Second Part . . . Written against Popery and Slavery* (London: Printed in the Year 1697.) is found in reel 1428 no. 16 (but thus far, no microfilm copy of the other second vol. containing Locke's poems).
References: Attig 4; CBEL ii. 184 (collection); Christophersen p. 8; ESTC for
    vol. 1: r026892; Wing² P2719–20.
Copy examined: O (Antiq.e.E 80)

252.2. Poems in 'Musarum' reprinted in *Poems on Affairs of State*, 2d vol.,
    1699.
"Pax regit Augusti . . ."
    AND

"If Greece with so much mirth . . ."
IN: State Poems; | CONTINUED | . . . [&c. as in no. 252.1, except 'Mr. Stepney,' until 2d set of names:]

Dr. South,   Dr. Crew,
Dr. Locke,   Mr. Busby, &c.
Sir W. G----n,

| Alfo fome Mifcellany POEMS by the fame, | never before Printed. | [rule 82 mm] | Now carefully Examined with the Originals, and | Publifhed without any Caftration. | [rule 83 mm] | Printed in the Year M DC XC IX.

Collation of this (second) vol.: 8° A⁴ B–Q⁸ R⁴ S⁸ [$ half signed]; 136 leaves; pp. *i–viii* 1–165 182 167–264 [=272]. Page 166 called '182'.

Text: 36 lines; 147 (158) × 85 mm; 81R. Poor-quality laid paper with coat-of-arms watermark.

CW: B4ᵛ Pax B6ᵛ Glory B7ʳ But

Note: Again this is the second volume of a collection, the first vol. of which has an identical title to no. 252.1, in double rules (inner 150 × 83 mm, outer 158 × 87 mm), except 'Mr, *Milton*,' and 'Mr. *Waller*,' until the penultimate text line: | 𝕿𝖍𝖊 𝕿𝖍𝖎𝖗𝖉 𝕰𝖉𝖎𝖙𝖎𝖔𝖓, 𝕮𝖔𝖗𝖗𝖊𝖈𝖙𝖊𝖉 𝖆𝖓𝖉 𝖒𝖚𝖈𝖍 𝕰𝖓𝖑𝖆𝖗𝖌𝖊𝖉. | [rule 77 mm] | Printed in the Year 1699." Its collation is A⁴ B–Q⁸ R⁴; pp. *i–viii* 1–224 245–267 268; p. 268 with an advertisement for the 'State Poems CONTINUED'.

Locke's two poems, with a translation of the first, occupy the same pages 8 and 12–13 (B4ᵛ and B6v–B7ʳ) as in no. 252.1. Page 248 in this second vol. ends with '*FINIS*.', but gathering S (pp. 249–264) is headed '*Additions*.' This vol. is a new typesetting (a line-by-line reprinting) of the 1697 edition.

A copy of both vols. is in EEB, reel 1468 no. 3.

References: ESTC r030534; Wing² P2721.

Copy examined: O (Antiq.e.E 83)

253. Poems in 'Musarum' reprinted 1702.
"Pax regit Augusti . . ."
   AND
"If Greece with so much Mirth . . ."
IN: State Poems; | CONTINUED | . . . [&c. as in no. 252.1 and .2, until 2d set of names:]

Dr. South,   Dr. Crew,
Dr. Locke,   Mr. Busby, &c.
Sir W. G-----n,

Alfo fome Mifcellany POEMS by the fame, | [rule 80 mm] | Now carefully Examined with the Originals, and | Publifhed without any Caftration. | [rule 81 mm] | Printed in the Year MDCCII.

Collation: 8° (184 × 110 mm cut) A⁴ B–Q⁸ R⁴ S⁸ [$ half signed]; 136 leaves; pp. *i–viii* 1–264 [=272].

Text: 36 lines (approx.); 147 (158) × 83 mm; 82 R. Medium-quality laid paper, not watermarked.

CW: Page. B4^r The B4^v Pax B5^r To B6^v Glory B7^r But
Press figures: none.
Note: Again this is the second vol. of a collection, the first vol. of which has a title identical to no. 252.2 (except 'Mr. *Milton*,'), within a double rule (inner 149 × 83 mm, outer 157 × 91 mm), until the 5th last line: [rule 79 mm] | 𝕿𝖍𝖊 𝕱𝖔𝖚𝖗𝖙𝖍 𝕰𝖉𝖎𝖙𝖎𝖔𝖓, 𝕮𝖔𝖗𝖗𝖊𝖈𝖙𝖊𝖉 𝖆𝖓𝖉 𝖒𝖚𝖈𝖍 𝕰𝖓𝖑𝖆𝖗𝖌𝖊𝖉. | [rule 79 mm] | Printed in the Year, 1702.

Locke's poems occupy the same pages 8 and 12–13. The first poem and its translation on p. 8 both signed 'J. Locke, *ex Aede Chiſti*.'; that on p. 13: 'J. Locke, *Student of Ch. Ch.*' The other details are the same as in no. 252.1 and 252.2, though this is a new typesetting. A microfilm copy of the first vol. of this edition is in the collection, *The Eighteenth Century*, reel 3145 no. 6.
References: ESTC t108847, vol.1 only.
Copy examined: O^1 (Douce P.464 (2))
Vol. 1 of the set only also at L (1485.c.27) and O^2 (Harding C.48 (1))

254. Poem in 'Musarum' reprinted 1705.
"If Greece with so much mirth . . ."
IN (title within a double rule, inner 151 × 90 mm, outer 160 × 99 mm): A New | COLLECTION | OF | POEMS | Relating to | 𝕾𝖙𝖆𝖙𝖊 𝕬𝖋𝖋𝖆𝖎𝖗𝖘, | FROM | OLIVER CROMWEL | To this preſent Time: | By the Greateſt | Wits of the Age: | Wherein, not only thoſe that are Contain'd in | the Three Volumes already Publiſhed are | incerted, but alſo large Additions of chiefeſt | Note, never before Publiſhed. | The whole from their reſpective Originals, | without Caſtration. | [double rule 85/84 mm] | *LONDON*, | Printed in the Year, M D CC V.
Collation of the whole: 8° (195 × 115 mm cut) A–2P^8 [$ half signed; A2 signed 'Aa2']; 304 leaves pp. *i–xvi* 1–591 592 [= 608].
Locke's poem: M7^v–M8^r (pp. 174–5).
Contents of the whole: A1^r title (verso blank), A2^r–A3^r preface, A3^v blank, A4r–A8^v contents (by page order), B1^r–2P8^r (1–591) text, 2P8^v blank.
Text: 40 lines approx., 83 R. Fonts vary between pages: sheets K–R use a different font from sheets A–I and S; sheet L and most of M use 'VV' instead of W's. Medium-quality laid paper without watermark. No press figures.
HT: [double rule 86/85 mm] | POEMS | ON | 𝕾𝖙𝖆𝖙𝖊 𝕬𝖋𝖋𝖆𝖎𝖗𝖘. | [rule 84 mm]
Headlines for vol., from verso to recto: *POEMS on* | *State-Affairs.*
Notes: Only one of the poems from 'Musarum Oxoniensium' is printed here. Text, without a heading is printed with 14 lines on p. 174 and 30 on p. 175; poem signed 'J. Locke, Student of *Ch. Ch.*' ESTC states this edition is "A piracy of the first 3 volumes of 'Poems on Affairs of State' (Case)." The record also quotes the Bodleian Library as reporting "2 versions of p. 564. One has catchword 'The', and the other ends 'Finis' (Refs. Case 237)." There is a microfilm copy of both vols. in *The Eighteenth Century*, reel 1277 no. 6.

Reference: ESTC n005917.
Copies examined: O (Antiq.e.E.1705/6) MH (*EC7.A100B705n)

255. Poem in *Domiduca Oxoniensis* (1662). Two issues.
"Crowns, Scepters, Thrones . . ." a 56-line poem.
In (within ornamental rule 155 × 94 mm): DOMIDUCA | OXONIENSIS: | Sive | Muſæ Academicæ | GRATULATIO | Ob Auſpicatiſſimum | Sereniſsimæ Principis | CATHARINÆ | LUSITANÆ, | Regi ſuo Deſponſatæ, | In Angliam appulſum. | [orn., Oxford University seal, 31 × 32 mm] | OXONIÆ, | Excudebant A. & L. Lichfield, Acad. Typogr. | Anno Dom. M. DC. LX. II.
Collation of the whole: 4° (large-paper copy 200 × 145 mm cut; 170 × 115 mm other issue) A–B⁴ a–c⁴ C–M⁴ ²A–C⁴ [$1 (+ A2, C–F2, H–K2) signed]; 72 leaves; pp. *1–144* (unpaged).
Locke's poem, beginning "Crowns, Scepters, Thrones . . ." is found on ²B3ʳ–4ᵛ, signed at the end 'Jo. Locke M. A. and *Student* | of Ch. Ch.' (page no. pencilled in, 134–136).
Contents: A1ʳ title (verso blank), A2ʳ dedication to the king signed 'RICARDUS BAYLIE, *Vice-can. Oxon.*', A2ᵛ poem by Baylie, A3ʳ–M4ᵛ poems chiefly in Latin, ²A1ʳ–²C4ᵛ poems in English.
Text: 22 lines if full page; 98R with 1.5 mm leading between lines. Medium-quality laid paper without watermark.
Headlines: DOMIDUCA OXONIENSIS.
CW: Page. B1ʳ Triſtis ²B2ʳ *Madam*, ²B2ᵛ When ²B3ʳ When
No CW when end of page and poem coincide.
Notes: Locke's poem is in rhyming couplets (aa, bb, cc, dd, etc.). Most of the poems are by persons associated with Christ Church, Oxford, to celebrate the arrival in England of Catherine of Braganza, the future wife of King Charles II, for their marriage on May 21, 1662. In two parts, the first part contains poems in Latin, Greek, Hebrew and Arabic; the second, with a caption title 'Upon the Queens Landing' has poems in English. Both copies I have seen, at the Bodleian Library, have been paginated in pencil. There were two issues, one a large-paper copy.
 A microfilm copy is in the EEB collection, reel 1024, no. 11.
References: Attig 2; Christophersen p. 8; L.L. 2163 (collection); Wing² O-875 (collection).
Copies examined. Large-paper copy: O¹ (Antiq. e. E. 1662 (1))
 Regular issue: O² (4° M16.Art.BS (3))

256. Poem in Sydenham's *Methodus curandi febres* (1668).
Caption title: [orn. rule of fleurons repeated, 8 × 73 mm] | In tractatum de Febribus D.D. Syden- | ham, praxin medicam apud Londi- | nenſes mira ſolertia æque ac | fælicitate exercentis.
IN: THOMÆ SYDENHAM | Med. Doct. | *METHODUS* [swash T, U] | CURANDI [U wrong font] FEBRES | Propriis Obſervationibus |

Superstructa. | [rule 72 mm] | *Editio Secunda*, priori multò auctior ac | emendatior; cui etiam accessit Sectio | Quinta de *Peste* sive *Febre Pestilentiali*. | [rule 73 mm] | *Multa egerunt qui ante nos fuerunt, sed non | peregerunt: multum adhuc restat operæ, | multumque restabit: neque ulli nato post | mille sæcula præcidetur occasio aliquid ad- | huc adjiciendi*. Seneca. | [rule 69 mm] | LONDONI, | Impensis J. Crook, [swash J] apud quem veneunt | in Vico vocato D*uck*-lane propè | Little Brittain, MDCLXVIII.

Coll. of the total work: 8° (155 × 94 mm cut) $A^8 \chi^2$ B–O^8 P^8 (-2 leaves = χ^2) [$ half signed]; 120 leaves; pp. *i–xx* 1–218 *219–220* [= 240].

Locke's poem, of 27 couplets, occupies pp. *xvii–xx* (χ1.2), and is in italic type, with a blank line between couplets.

Contents of the whole: A1^r (*i*) title (verso blank), A2^r–A4^v (*iii–viii*) dedication to Robert Boyle, A5^r–A7^v (*ix–xiv*) preface, A8^r (*xv*) errata of 10.5 lines (verso blank), χ1.2 (*xvii–xx*) Locke's poem, B1^r–P5^v (1–218) Sydenham's text, P6 blank.

Sydenham's text (E4^v): 26 or 27 lines; 126 (139) × 61 mm; 94 R. Locke's poem set ital. in 2-line couplets, with a blank line between (18 lines and 8 blanks), 122 (131) × 75 mm. Medium-quality paper without watermark.

HT: [rule of small irons 8 × 54 mm] | [rule of small irons inverted 8 × 54 mm] | Sectio Prima. | DE | *Febribus Continuis*.

CW: Page. χ1^r Qui χ1^v Quid χ2^r Quis B1^r (sangui-) neæ

Notes: Locke's poem was not part of the first edition of Sydenham's work published in 1666. The poem is signed: 'J. Lock A. M. ex Æde | Christi Oxon.' A microfilm copy of this work is in EEB collection, reel 802, no. 32.

References: Attig 3; Christophersen pp. 8–9; Wing^2 S-6132 (Sydenham's work)

Copies examined: O (Vet. A3 f.528)   L (1166.c.8; Locke's poem bd. at end of vol.)

257. Poem in Sydenham's *De febribus* (1668) reprinted in 1676.

Caption title: AUTHORI [swash U, T, R] | IN | Tractatum ejus de FEBRIBUS.

IN (within a double rule, inner 145 × 82 mm, outer 154 × 89 mm): Observationes Medicæ | CIRCA | MORBORUM | ACUTORUM | HISTORIAM | ET | CURATIONEM. | [rule 79 mm] | Authore | THOMA SYDENHAM M.D. [rule 79 mm] | Cicero de Nat. Deor. | Opinionum *Commenta delet dies*: Naturæ *judicia | confirmat*. | [rule 78 mm] | LONDINI, | Typis *A. C.* Impensis *Gualteri Kettilby*, ad | insigne Capitis Episcopalis in Cœmeterio | D. Pauli. 1676.

Collation of the whole work: 8° (177 × 110 mm) A^8 (a)–(b)^8 (c)^4 B–2H^8 [$ half signed]; 268 leaves; pp. *i–lvi* 1–425 *426–480* [= 536].

Locke's poem: (c)3^r–(c)4^r (pp. *liii–lv*).

Contents of the whole: A1 blank, A2^r (*iii*) title, A2^v (*iv*) imprimatur (signed Roger L'Estrange, 23 Oct. 1675), A3^r–A7^r (*v–xiii*) dedication to John

Mapletoft of Gresham College and the Royal Society, A7ᵛ blank, A8ʳ–(c)2ʳ (*xv–li*) 'Praefatio,' (c)2ᵛ blank, (c)3ʳ–(c)4ʳ (*liii–lv*) poem by Locke, (c)4ᵛ (*lvi*) errata of 22.5 lines, B1ʳ–2E5ʳ (1–425) text, 2E5ᵛ blank, 2E6ʳ–2H8ʳ (427–479) 'Elenchus Rerum', 2H8ᵛ blank.

Illustration: frontispiece portrait of Sydenham by A. Blooteling after Maria Beale.

Sydenham's text (B2ᵛ): 29 lines; 134 (145) × 75 mm; 94 R. Good-quality paper without watermark. Locke's poem set 20 lines ital. per full page, in 10 couplets, 2 mm between couplets (131 (136) × 89 mm).

CW: (c)3ʳ *Fit* (c)3ᵛ *Nec*

Notes: Sydenham's work is a new edition of his *Methodus curandi febres*, with additional material, e.g. on vomiting. Locke's poem, set in italics, is a line-by-line reprint of the poem printed in the earlier edition of Sydenham's work (no. 256), and is signed 'J. Lock A. M. Ex Æede | Chriſti Oxon'. A microfilm copy of the work is in EEB, reel 827, no.5.

References: Attig 3 n.; Christophersen p. 8; T.C. I.238; Wing² S-6134.

Copies examined: O (8° B. 47 Med.) CLU-C L (C.112.aa.11)

CHAPTER VIII

Occasional Contributions to Other Works
B: Contributions to Learned Journals, &c.
(nos. 258–76)

In the spirit of the newly-founded Royal Society, with its emphasis on recording observations of natural phenomena, Locke is thought to have contributed several articles to the society's *Philosophical Transactions*. He was responsible for 'communicating' interesting short pieces by others. Of the five pieces with Locke's name or initials attached to them, only two, his note about "extraordinary large Nails" and his "Register of the Weather for the Year 1692" (no. 260 and 262) are really by Locke. He had a role in getting the other pieces published, chiefly as a transfer agent. All five articles are listed under Locke's name in the *Index* to the first 70 vols. of the *Transactions*, as well as a sixth: "Translation of a letter concerning the books and ancient writings dug out of the ruins of an edifice near the site of the old city of Herculaneum" (in vol. 49, pp. 112 et seq.), published in the late 1740s. This entry is undoubtedly an error for John Locker the antiquary, who indeed travelled on the continent (cf. DNB).

Locke is the editor of Robert *Boyle's General History of the Air*, published posthumously, in which Locke includes his barometric observations in Oxford from June 1666 to June 1683, and a letter dated 5° May 1666 relating to the barometer which he had sent to Boyle (cf. no. 276).

In 1686 in the journal, *Bibliothèque universelle et historique*, Jean Le Clerc published a French translation of Locke's "New Method of Making Common-Place Books" and in 1688 Locke's extract of his *Essay concerning Human Understanding* (no. 266 and 273 respectively). Locke's authorship of other extracts for this journal is a more contentious problem.

In his 'Eloge de feu Mr. Locke' (Article V, *Bibliothèque choisie*, 6 (1705): 342–411) Le Clerc states that Locke "me donna alors *la Nouvelle Méthode de dresser des Recueuils* qui est dans le 2. Tome [1686] de la Bibliotheque Universelle. Il me fit aussi quelques Extraits, comme celui de Mr. *Boyle*, touchant les Remedes Specifiques, qui est dans le meme Tome & quelques autres dans la suite." Rosalie Colie, in her "John Locke in the Republic of Letters" (*Britain and the Netherlands: Papers delivered to the Oxford-Netherlands Historical Conference, 1959*, ed. J. S. Bromley & E. H. Kossmann (London: Chatto & Windus, 1960), pp. 111–29) infers that Locke was the author of the extracts of Newton's *Principia* published in the

Bibliothèque universelle, vol. 8, since a "short Latin summary . . . headed 'Newtons System | Mar 88' . . . coincides, except for the first and last paragraphs, with the [French language] review of the *Principia* . . .", that is the Latin summary in Bodleian Library MS. Locke c. 31 ff. 99-100 (a vol. of miscellaneous papers). Citing Le Clerc's 'Eloge' she states that the possibilities for the other extracts, "to judge by the books he owned at this time, are Ray's *Methodus Plantarum*, Burnet's *Critique de Varillas*, Bayle's *Commentaire Philosophique* and Pufendorf's *De Rebus Suecis* [sic]. Among these the strongest possibilities are the *Commentaire Philosophique*, about which he was at this time in correspondence with Damaris Cudworth, and Ray's *Methodus plantarum*, reviewed in 1688."

The extract of Bayle's pseudonymous commentary (in t.3, pp. 335-60) has the caption title: "Commentaire Philoſophique *sur ces Paroles de* JESUS CHRIST *contrain-les d'entrer . . . Traduit de Anglois du S. Jean Fox de Bruggs par M. J. F.* A Cantorbery, & ſe trouve à Amſterdam chez Wolfgang. I & II Partie. 2 voll. in 12. 1686." (Wing² B1469B) It is certainly possible that Locke wrote the extract, but it was published in the August 1686 issue; Lady Masham's letters to Locke about it are dated October 3 and November 7, 1687, a year later (*Corr.* 967, iii.278, and 975, iii.294 respectively). She was reading the work with admiration at the time and wanted to know the real name of its French author, suggesting Bernier. Locke's replies do not survive, but we can infer from her second letter that he did not know who wrote it, nothing more. He owned the work (L.L. 236).

Attig lists two works by Boyle extracted on consecutive pages in Le Clerc's journal, as if the second were the English-language title of the first (*De speciforum remediorum . . . concordia*, Fulton² 167), the second being *A Free Enquiry into the Vulgarly Receiv'd Notion of Nature* (1686; Fulton² 170; Attig 24). There is no evidence Locke wrote this extract, though he owned the work (L.L. 470). He is unlikely to have written the extracts of Ray's *Historia plantarum*, published in 3 vols. (1686-1704). The extract of vol. 1 appeared in the *Bibliothèque universelle*, 3 (1686): 1-7 (Attig 25); the extract of vol. 2 (confused by Rosalie Colie with Ray's *Methodus plantarum*) appeared in the same journal, vol. 9 (1688): 179-86, stating it represented "le jugement d'un Botaniste, qui demeure à plus de deux cent lieuës de Londres", hardly a description of Locke. Nor did he own Ray's *Historia*; he did own Ray's *Methodus plantarum* published in 1682 (L.L. 2445). That he did not own the *Historia* is no proof that he did not write the extract; he owned *Of Specifick Medicines* by Boyle (L.L. 468) but not its Latin translation, the edition extracted in Le Clerc's journal. He owned Burnet's critique of Varillas (L.L.520; reviewed in t. 3, pp. 130-38), and Bayle's *Commentaire philosophique* (L.L. 236), but not Pufendorf's *De rebus suecicis* (reviewed in t. 3, pp. 424-84).

Locke is more likely to have written the extract of Sydenham's *Schedula Monitoria* (1687) in vol. 6 of the *Bibliothèque universelle*. In a letter to Limborch dated April 10, 1687 (*Corr.* 926; iii.169) Locke writes: "Please remember me to Mr. Le Clerc, and tell him that I have recently received from England a new work of Sydenham's, which I have not yet read; if he would like to have the book itself or an epitome of it I would be glad to send him one or other, whichever he might prefer." (Trans. by E.S. de Beer.)

Unless more evidence is forthcoming, possibly from Locke's journals, I would only attribute the extracts of Boyle's 'Of Specifick Medicines', the Newton, and, with some hesitation, the Sydenham notices to Locke.

258. Article in *Philosophical Transactions* of the Royal Society, 1675 (by R. Lilburne)
Caption title: *An Extract of a Letter, written to the Publisher by Mr. J. L.* | about *poisonous Fish in one of the* Bahama *Islands*.
IN: *Philosophical Transactions of the Royal Society*, 10 no. 114 (May 24, 1675): 312.
Note: The original ms. of the letter dated 2 May 1675 is in the library of the Royal Society: MS. L5-6, no. 90. Addressed to Henry Oldenburg, secretary of the Royal Society from 1662, it is also printed as *Corr*. 299, i. 423; in Oldenburg's *Correspondence* (ed. A.R. and M.B. Hall) no. 2667, xi. 322; and in Desmaizeaux's *Collection of Several Pieces* (1720; no. 316 below), pp. 249-51. Locke used information supplied to him by Richard Lilburne, then in the Bahamas (cf. *Corr*. 290; i. 406-7). A draft of Locke's reply to Lilburne with additional queries is in Bodleian Library's MS Locke d.9, pp. 87 and 236 (reprinted *Corr*. 298A; viii.428-9). Locke owned most of the vols. of the *Philosophical Transactions* (L.L. 2302). This article is cited in Fox Bourne, i. 329 n.2, and in Thomas Birch's *History of the Royal Society* (1756-57), iii.220.
References: Attig 19; Christophersen p. 13.
Copies examined: NjR   O (Per.3974.d.1037)

259. Article in *Philosophical Transactions*, Feb. 1697 (by Thomas Molyneux)
Caption title: II. *Account of a not yet Described* Scolopen- | dra Marina, *by* Thomas Molyneux, M. D. | S. R. S. *Communicated by* Mr. Locke.
IN: *Philosophical Transactions of the Royal Society*, 19 no. 225 (February 1697): 405-12.
Note: In a letter sent from Dublin to Locke, dated 'Januar. 5th. 1696/7,' William Molyneux offers an "inclosd Peice of Natural History [which] I am desired by My Brother [Thomas Molyneux] to present to you . . . If upon perusing it, you think it may deserve it; You may send it by the Penny-post to the Royal Society, to fill up an empty page in the Transactions." (*Corr*. 2170; v.746-7) Thomas Molyneux published a supplementary notice *ibid*. 21 no. 251 (April 1699): 127-9.
Reference: Attig 20; Christophersen p. 13.
Copies examined: NjR   O (Radcliffe AA63-98 Med.)

260. Article in *Philosophical Transactions*, July 1697.
Caption title: I. *An Account of one who had horny excrescen- | cies or extraordinary large Nails on his Fin- | gers and Toes, by Mr.* Locke.
IN: *Philosophical Transactions of the Royal Society*, 19 no. 230 (July 1697): 694 [i.e. 594]–596.
Notes: This letter by Locke is headed 24 May 1678. Its present location is unknown. It is not included in de Beer's edition of the *Correspondence*, but the contents are briefly summarised in letters to Robert Boyle of 27 July l678 and 16 June 1679 (*Corr.* 397, i.599–600, and 478, ii.38–39 respectively). Locke was known to be in Paris from the end of May 1677 until late June 1678. The article includes a footnote defining a 'gry', a term Locke invented (cf. *Essay* 4.10.10). The final five lines of text explain Figures 1–4, which were not printed with the account. This article was cited by Fox Bourne (i. 385, n.1).
Reference: Attig 21; Christophersen p. 13.
Copies examined: NjR O (Radcliffe AA63–98 Med.)

261. Article in *Philosophical Transactions*, July 1701 (by Benjamin Furly)
Caption title: IV. *Part of a Letter giving an Account of a perſon | who can neither Read nor Write, yet will reckon | Summs to great exaɑ̃neſs.* Communicated by Mr Locke.
IN: *Philosophical Transactions of the Royal Society*, 22 no. 272 (July 1701): 893–4.
Note: The letter is headed 'Rotterdam, March 25. 1701.' It is undoubtedly the portion of a letter from Benjamin Furly in Amsterdam to his son Arent, then in England, forwarded by Locke in his letter to Dr. Hans Sloane of 14 July 1701 (*Corr.* 2956; vii. 373–4). He therein states he "put it into your hands to print it or otherwise as you should think fit." The enclosure, a copy written out by Arent Furly, is now Bodleian Library MS. Locke c.9, ff. 13–14.
References: Attig 22; Christophersen p. 13.
Copies examined: NjR O (Radcliffe AA63–98 Med.)

262. Article in *Philosophical Transactions*, April 1705.
Caption title: II. *A Regiſter of the Weather for the year* 1692, *kept | at* Oates *in* Eſſex. *By Mr* John Locke.
IN: *Philosophical Transactions of the Royal Society*, 24 no. 298 (April 1705): 1917–37.
Note: In a letter from Oates dated 21 February 1704, Locke offered Dr. (later Sir) Hans Sloane his 'register of the air', further stating "Mr Churchil printed the former part of it in Mr Boyles general history of the air" (*Corr.* 3466, viii.207–8; cf. no.276). He had hoped this remainder would be published in a second edition, but time was running out and "it will be lost if not published in my lifetime". The Churchills indeed gave permission for Locke to get it published in *The Philosophical Transactions*; they did not publish a second

edition of Boyle's work. Locke's letter of transmittal to Sloane, with comments on the value of such a register, was written 15 March 1704 (*Corr.* 3489; viii. 239-40).
References: Attig 23; Christophersen p. 13.
Copies examined: NjR O (Radcliffe AA63-98 Med.)

263. Review of Boyle, in *Bibliothèque universelle*, 1686.
Caption title: XV. De SPECIFICORUM REMEDIO- | RUM *cum corpuſculari Philoſophia Concor-* | *dia, cui acceſſit Diſſertatio de varia ſim-* | *plicium Medicamentorum utilitate, uſuque.* | *Ex Anglico in Latinum Sermonem traduce-* | *bat D.A. M.D. Auctore* ROBERTO | BOYLEO *nobili Anglo Societatis Regiæ* | *Socio.* Londini 1686. in 12.
IN: *Bibliothèque universelle et historique*, 2 (1686): 263-77.
Notes: Locke's review of the Latin edition of "Of the Reconcileableness of Specifick Medicines to the Corpuscular Philosophy" (1685). The English edition is Fulton 166; Wing² B4013. Fulton was unable to identify 'D.A.' the translator of the Latin edition (Fulton 167). Boyle's work is cited as Wing² B3939. L.L. lists only the English edition: 468.
Reference: Attig 24; Christophersen p. 13.
Copies examined: Y O (Per.3977.f.37)

264. Review of Sydenham, in *Bibliothèque universelle*, 1687.
Caption title: SCHEDULA MONITORIA *De No-* | *væ Febris Ingreſſu per Tho.* SYDEN- | HAM M.D. *Londin.* 1686. p. 115. | & rimprimé A Amſterdam chez | Wetſtein en 1687.
IN: *Bibliothèque universelle & historique*, 6 (1687): 553-9.
Notes: Though Locke claimed to have received the London edition from his bookseller (see Chapter introd.), this extract indicates an Amsterdam printing. The record in his library catalogue however is for the 2nd edition, published in London in 1688 (L.L. 2811). Locke had studied medicine with Sydenham, and esteemed him highly.
Reference: Christophersen p. 13.
Copies examined: Y O (Per.3977.f.37)

265. Review of Newton, in *Bibliothèque universelle*, 1688.
Caption title: 3. PHILOSOPHIÆ NATURALIS PRINCI- | PIA MATHEMATICA. *Auctore* Js. | NEWTON *Trin. Coll. Cantab. Soc.* | *Matheſeos Profeſſore Lucaſiano & So-* | *cietatis Regalis Sodali.* 4. Londini. | *Proſtant ap. Sam. Smith.* 1687. pagg. | 510.
IN: *Bibliothèque universelle & historique*, 8 (Mar. 1688): 436-50.
Notes: See Chapter introd. for presuming Locke to be the author of this extract. Locke's copy (L.L. 2083) survives in the library of Trinity College, Cambridge, with the inscription: "Ex dono Auctissimi Authoris, qui errores propria manu correxit." A discussion by James Axtell of Locke's authorship

of this epitome is in *Notes and Records of the Royal Society*, 20 no.2 (Dec. 1965): 152–61.
Reference: Attig 29.
Copies examined: Y   O (Per.3977.f.37)

266. 'Methode nouvelle', in *Bibliothèque universelle*, 1686.
Section-title: METHODE | NOUVELLE | De dreſſer des | RECUEUILS | Communiqué par | l'Auteur.
Caption title: EPISTOLA. | Lettre de Monſieur J.L. | 2. à Monſieur N. T. contenant une Methode | nouvelle, & facile de dreſſer des Recueuils, | dont on peut faire un Indice exact en deux | pages.
In: *Bibliothèque universelle & historique* 2 (July 1686): 315–340.
Contents: O2^r (*315*) section title, O2^v–O3^r (316-7) diagrammatic table designed for a quick index to a commonplace notebook (described below), O3^v–P2^v (318-40) text, with sample entries.
Illustration: the first two facing pages are each divided by rules into 2 columns vertically (each 28 mm wide), with a short inner column at left for capital letters; the first column for initial letters A B C D E, 2d for F G H I L, 3d for M N O P R, and 4th for S T V X Z and Q. Each letter's area is further subdivided by red lines for the first occurring vowels a e i o and u (to follow the initial capital letter), except Q has only one line, u, as part of vowels assigned to Z. As examples Locke has also entered page numbers: '4' under A | e, '18.24' under C | o, '2.14' under E | i, etc.
Text (O4^v): 33 lines; 108 (117) × 54 mm; 66 R. Good-quality laid paper with fleur-de-lys watermark. Horizontal chainlines. Page no. at outer ends of headlines.
RT, from verso to recto: *Bibliotheque Univerſelle* | *& Hiſtorique de l'Année* 1686.
Notes: 'N.T.' is Nicolas Toinard to whom Locke wrote in February 1685 (chiefly in Latin; *Corr.* 811; ii.691-3), requesting his enclosed 'method' be published in his journal. The letter forms the first part of this article, followed by a sample entry, 'Ebionita' (E | i.14 above), and more details explaining how to make and use this table as an index to one's commonplace book. The work includes other samples, 'Acheron' (A | e.4 above), 'Haeretici' (H | a.16), 'Confessio fidei' (C | o.18), and the continuation of 'Haeretici' (H | a.22). This quick way to index under initial vowels does put words like 'Ebionita', 'Elixir' and 'Erinnys' for example, in the same space (by using first and third letters in the index word, ignoring intervening consonants).

Toinard was presumably associated with Jean Le Clerc in the publication of this *Bibliothèque universelle*. Though Locke's text was in Latin and English, he trusted Toinard to find someone to translate it; the translator was undoubtedly Le Clerc. The Royal Society's *Philosophical Transactions* had just resumed publication after a hiatus of four years, but "No other English journals are known to have appeared in 1685" (*Corr.* ii. 692 n.). Given Locke's reluctance to publish, it is a bit surprising he pressed for the

publication of this, his first significant publication, when he was 53 years old. In a letter to Le Clerc, October 2, 1686 (*Corr*. 866; iii.38-9) Locke asks Le Clerc that any copies "designed for me of our Methodus Adversarium" be sent him in Utrecht. The July and August 1686 issues were combined under one cover, so this 'method of making commonplace books' probably did not appear until September 1686. The original Latin and English manuscript text is now British Library Add. MS 28728, ff. 54-63; once in the library of Jacques-Charles Brunet (to 1868), it was purchased from a Mr. Labussiere on 27 May 1871 by the British Library.
References: Attig 30; Christophersen p. 11.
Copies examined: Y O (Per.3977.f.37)

267. 'Methode nouvelle'. English trans. (anon.) 1706. 8°
Within a double rule, inner 143 × 70 mm, outer 150 × 78 mm: A | NEW METHOD | OF MAKING | Common-Place-Books; | WRITTEN | By the late Learned Mr. *John Lock*, [swash J, k] | Author of the *ESSAY* [swash y] *concerning* | *Humane Underſtanding*. [swash U] | [rule 67 mm] | 𝔗𝔯𝔞𝔫𝔰𝔩𝔞𝔱𝔢𝔡 𝔣𝔯𝔬𝔪 𝔱𝔥𝔢 𝔉𝔯𝔢𝔫𝔠𝔥. | [rule 67 mm] | TO WHICH | Is added Something from Monſieur *Le* | *Clerc*, relating to the ſame Subject. | A TREATISE neceſſary for all Gentle- | men, eſpecially *Students* of *Divinity*, *Phyſick*, | and *Law*. | There are alſo added Two Letters, containing a | moſt Uſeful Method for inſtructing Perſons that | are Deaf and Dumb, or that Labour under any | Impediments of Speech, to ſpeak diſtinctly; writ | by the late Learned Dr. *John Wallis*, [swash J] Geometry | Profeſſ. [sic] *Oxon*, and *F. R. S.* | [rule 66 mm] | *LONDON*: | Printed for *J. Greenwood*, [swash J] Bookſeller, at the | End of *Cornhil*, next *Stocks-Market*, [swash ks] 1706.
Coll: 8° (167 × 107 mm cut) A-I⁴ [$2 signed]; 36 leaves; pp. *I-VI* i-v *vi* 1 2-60 [=72].
Contents: A1⁴ (*I*) title (verso blank), A2ʳ-A3ᵛ (*III-VI*) dedicatory letter to (Sir) Edward Northey, of Hackney, A4ʳ-B2ʳ (i-v) Le Clerc's note, B2ᵛ-B3ʳ (*vi-*1) diagrammatic table (copied from no. 266), B3ᵛ-E2ᵛ (2-24) English trans. of Locke's 'Methode', E3ʳ-G2ᵛ (25-40) '*A Letter of Doctor* John Wallis *to* Robert Boyle, *Esq*;' signed: Oxford, March 14, 1661/2., G3ʳ-G4ʳ (41-43) Oldenburg's account of the Royal Society, G4ᵛ-I4ᵛ (44-60) Wallis's letter to Thomas Beverly "*concerning his Method for instructing Persons* Deaf *and* Dumb."
Text (C4ʳ): 34 lines; 139 (150) × 63 (72) mm; 82 R. No visible watermarks. Page no. centered within parentheses at top of page, except for pages cited below ('Headlines'). Pages 15, 17, 19 & 23 are blank except for page no. Marginal notes in italics; caption headings extend 4 mm beyond text block.
Head title, p. i (A4ʳ): Monſieur *Le Clerc*'s Cha- | racter of Mr. *LOCK*'s | Method, | WITH HIS | ADVICE | About the | USE | OF | Common-Places.

Page 2 (B3ᵛ): *Mr. Lock's Letter to* Monſieur Toi- | nard, *containing a New and Eaſie* | *Method of making* Common-Place | *Books, an exact Index of which may* | *be made in Two Pages.*

Headlines: pp. III–IV: *Epiſtle Dedicatory.*

From recto to verso, pp. ii–v: Mr. *Le Clerc*'s Advice about | the Uſe of *Common-Places.* pp. *vi–1*: The INDEX.

CW: Page. A4ᵛ *Ex-* [*Excellent*] B2ʳ (eſpecial-) ly E4ʳ (Advanta-) geous F4ᵛ (ſup-) ply H2ʳ (Situati-) on

Note: The English translation of no. 266, probably unauthorized or a piracy. It differs slightly from the English text found in Locke's *Posthumous Works* (no. 299). I have found no information about the source of the dedication to Northey or of the Wallis exchange. Northey was attorney general at this time (cf. DNB). Though there was a Greenwood selling books in Leeds in the 1790s, the ESTC record for this 'New Method' provides the only occurrence of J. Greenwood's name. In the bookseller's assembling bits and pieces from various sources, it resembles publications 'the unspeakable' Edmund Curll was known for (cf. C1714-1).

References: Attig 31; Christophersen pp. 11–12; ESTC t113609.

Copies examined: OCin (RA029.4/L814n 1706) C (Adams 7.70.4) CLU-C DFo (acc.156106) O (Vet.A4 e.895)

268. 'Methode nouvelle'. Dutch trans. (anon.) Amsterdam, 1739. 4°
EENE | NIEUWE MANIER | om | VERZAAMELINGEN | OF | AANTEKENINGEN | te maaken, | Opgeſteld en gemeen gemaakt | door | JOHANNES [swash J] LOCKE. | En uit het Franſch (de oorſpronkelyke taal, daar het | in geſchreven, en in de *Bibliotheque Univerſelle,* | tome ſecond, te vinden is) in het Neder- | duitſch overgezet. | En ook tegens de Engelſche Vertaaling, achter | *the Poſthumous Works of Mr. John Locke* ge- | voegd, naagezien. | [orn.: vase of flowers, inverted triangle shape, 16 × 49 mm] | *Te AMSTERDAM,* [swash Ts] | By KORNELIS DE WIT, Boekverkooper op den | Nieuwendyk, tuſſchen de twee Haarlemmer Sluizen, | in den Staaten Bybel. | [rule 49 mm] | MDCCXXXIX.

Coll: 4° (200 × 156 mm cut) A–D⁴ [$ half signed]; 16 leaves; pp. *i–v* 2–4 3–24 25–26 [= 32]. Page no. 1 omitted, 3–4 repeated.

Contents: A1ʳ (*i*) title (verso blank), A2ʳ–A3ʳ (*iii–v*) "VOORBERICHT | AAN DEN | LEEZER.", A3ᵛ–A4ʳ (2–3) diagrammatic table in red & black (same as in no. 266), A4ᵛ–D3ʳ (4, 3–24) text, D3ᵛ blank, D4ʳ (*25*) advt. by de Wit for 3 Locke titles, D4ᵛ blank.

Text (B3ʳ): 29 lines; 138 (154) × 100 (107) mm; 94 R. Paper with watermark similar to Heawood 420. Page no. at outer ends of headlines. Foreword (p. *iii*) preceded by a headpiece of repeated small irons, 7 × 111 mm.

Headlines, from verso to recto: *Nieuwe Manier om Verzaamlingen,* | *of Aanteekeningen te maaken.*

CW: Page. B1ᵛ nodig [noodig] C3ᵛ ſim- [ſimplicitas] D2ᵛ „Lief- [„Liefde]

Notes: A translation of the 'Méthode nouvelle', using the text in *Posthumous Works* (no. 299). The advertisement is for (1) a Dutch edition of Locke's 'Essay for Understanding St. Paul' in 8° for 6 stijvers; (2) for a Dutch edition of his *Paraphrases and Notes on . . . St. Paul to the Romans*, 4° at 1:8; and (3) the Dutch edition of his *Reasonableness of Christianity* at 14 stijvers. No Dutch edition of the first item is known. A Dutch translation of the *Reasonableness* was published for another bookseller in 1729 (cf. no. 239). The only known Dutch edition of any part of the *Paraphrase and Notes* was that to the 'Romans', not published until 1768 (no. 296).
References: Attig 32.
Copies examined: O (Vet. B4 e.74)   AMu (770.A3)

269*. 'Methode nouvelle'. Dutch trans. (anon.) Amsterdam, 1757. 4°
EENE | NIEUWE MANIER | om | VERZAMELINGEN | OF | AANTEEKENINGEN | te maaken, | . . . [&c. as in no. 268, until similar ornament 17 × 43 mm] | *Te AMSTERDAM*, | By KORNELIS DE WIT, Boekverkooper. | MDCCLVII.
Coll: 4° (213 × 155 mm uncut); pp. *i–ii* iii *iv* 1–50.
Text: 139 (151) × 99 (109) mm; 29 lines (varies); 94 R. Page no. at outer ends of headlines.
Headlines, from verso to recto: *Nieuwe Manier om Verzamelingen,* | *of Aanteekeningen te maaken.*
CW: Page.
Notes: Reprint of no. 268, newly typeset. Information from photostats supplied by the Bibliothèque Royale Albert Ier, Brussels. Attig omits this edition but mentions a reprint by S. J. Baalde, Amsterdam, 1769 in 4° (no.32 n.)

270*. 'Methode nouvelle'. Dutch trans. (anon.) 3d printing, Amsterdam, 1762. 4°
EENE | NIEUWE MANIER | om | VERZAMELINGEN | OF | AANTEEKENINGEN | te maaken, | . . . [&c. as no. 268, until 16th line:] *the Poſthumous Works of Mr. John Locke* ge- | voegd, naagezien. | DERDEN DRUK. | [orn.: shield with scrolls, 20 × 33 mm] | *Te AMSTERDAM*, | By KORNELIS DE WIT, Boekverkooper. | MDCCLXII.
Coll: pp. 50. Paper uncut measures 210 × 155 mm and is probably 4°.
Notes: The third printing, newly typeset and presumably a reprint of no. 269. Information from photostat supplied by the library of the University of Ghent (acces. no. 28033).

271*. 'Méthode nouvelle'. Dutch trans. (anon.) Amsterdam, 1769. 4°
'nieuwe manier om aanteekeningen te maken'. Amsterdam: S. J. Baalde, 1769. 4°
Note: This information from Abkoude, p. 320. The work was priced at 11 st[uivers]. I have not found any library possessing this edition; nor is there any

record of it in the union catalogue in the Royal Library at the Hague. Attig (32 n.) gives collation as [6], 50 p.

272. 'Methode nouvelle'. German trans. (anon.) Frankfurt & Leipzig, 1711. 8°

Des berühmten Engelländers / | Herrn JOHANN LOCKS | Neuerfundene Manier / | EXCERPTA | und | LOCOS | COMMUNES | einzurichten. | Nebst allerhand curiöſen | Anmerckungen. | Aus dem Frantzöſiſchen überſetzet. | [floral orn. 30 × 55 mm] | Frandfurt und Leipzig / | Gedruckt und verlegt durch Johan von Wiering. 1711.

Coll: 8° (small; estimation 157 × 86 mm) 𝔄-𝔅⁸ [$ 5 (-A2) signed]; 16 leaves; pp. *i–ii* 1 2–30 [= 32].

Contents: A1ʳ (*i*) title, A1ᵛ–A2ʳ (*ii–1*) diagrammatic table in roman font, A2ᵛ–B8ᵛ (2–30) text.

Text (B8ᵛ only): 32 lines. At head of each page, centered, are 2 facing fleurons, with page no. at outer ends. Text chiefly in fraktur and roman fonts (Latin quotations).

CW: A2ᵛ baren [„baren] A4ʳ modum: [Je (CW part of text)] B3ʳ fol = [folgender] B6ᵛ ocu- [oculus] B7ʳ (lit-) teraturæ [Periculoſum (pp. 27 and 30 interchanged; p. 30 starts 'Periculoſum')]

Notes: Information from a microfilm supplied by the Staatsbibliothek zu Berlin (shelfmark: Bibl. Diez 8° 7742, housed in the Unter den Linden building). Title page bears a circular stamp reading 'Ex Biblioth. Regis Berolinenſi'). This is one of two known surviving copies, another being reported at Bamberg Staats-Bibliothek (shelfmark Alt.308 Beiband 5). The anonymous translation has been made from the original in the *Bibliothèque universelle* (no. 266), with most of its French text here translated into German (fraktur font). Its Latin quotations have been left as is, and only the material headed 'Acheron' (here 'Acherusia') left in French, both in roman font. Some of the original text has been omitted and pp. 27 and 30 transposed (copying printer's errors?). The diagrammatic chart is the same as that found in no. 266, with only the page no. citations changed.

References: none.

273. Extract of the Essay. In *Bibliothèque universelle*, 1688.

Caption title: II. | Extrait d'un Livre Anglois qui n'eſt pas | encore publié, intitulé ESSAI PHI- | LOSOPHIQUE concernant L'EN- | TENDEMENT, où l'on montre quel- | le eſt l'étenduë de nos connoiſſances | certaines, & la maniere dont nous y par- | venons. Communiqué par Monſieur | LOCKE.

In: *Bibliothèque universelle & historique*, 8 (Jan. 1688): 49–142.

Collation of the vol.: 12° (135 × 73 mm cut) *¹² (-6 leaves or half sheet = 2A⁶) A–Z¹² 2A⁶ [$ half + 1 signed]; pp. *i–xii* 1–264 263–468 4 470–538 539–562 [= 574]. Page no. 263–4 repeated; 469 has lost '69'. First page of each sheet also signed '*Tome* VIII.'

Contents of the vol.: *1ʳ (*i*) title, *1ᵛ (*ii*) note from editors J. Le Clerc and J.C.

de la Crose about omissions from previous volume, *2ʳ˒ᵛ (*iii–iv*) errata for t. 7 (? to be detached), *3ʳ–*6ᵛ (*v–xii*) 'Table des Livres', A1ʳ–Z6ᵛ (1–538) text, Z7ʳ–2A5ʳ (*539–560*) 'Indice des Matieres', 2A6ʳ˒ᵛ (*561–562*) errata for t.8.

Locke's text: C1ʳ–F11ᵛ (pp. 49–142).

Text (C1ᵛ): 32 lines; 110 (119) × 53 mm; 69 R. Page no. at outer ends of headlines.

Headlines (for the journal), from verso to recto: *Bibliotheque Univerſelle | & Hiſtorique de l'Année* 1688.

CW: Page. C4ʳ blan- [blancheur] D6ʳ tou- [toutes] E9ᵛ (enco-) re F10ᵛ (don-) ner

Notes: Communicated to the editor Jean Le Clerc, who translated it into French. Locke had some copies run off separately for friends (no. 274). Locke's original manuscript used by Le Clerc does not survive, but an English language copy, in Sylvester Brounower's hand does (cf. no. 275 below). The first book has a one-paragraph summary of 17 lines; the text of Book 2 is divided into XXXI sections, Book 3 in X, and Book 4 in XX. In the '*Table des Livres*' the entry reads: LOCKE Extrait d'un Manuſcrit Anglois, intitulé Eſſai philoſophique, concernant l'entendement.

Signature positions:
C3 ſimpₐles
C4 Ainſi, *j*'appelle
E5 & ₐ ſans
E6 *néa*ₐmoins
F3 qu'ellₐes

References: Attig 38; Christophersen p. 12.
Copies examined: Y O (Per.3977.f.37)

274. Extract of the Essay (Abrégé). Amsterdam, 1688. 12o
ABREGÉ | *D'un Ouvrage intitulé* | ESSAI | PHILOSOPHIQUE | TOUCHANT | L'ENTENDEMENT. | [orn., globe mounted on a pommel, 35 × 25 mm] | A AMSTERDAM | [rule 45 mm] | CIƆ IƆC LXXXVIII.

Coll: 12o (124 × 72 mm cut) π² A–C¹² D¹² (-2 leaves = π²) [$ half signed]; 48 leaves; pp. *i–iv* 1–92 [= 96].

Contents: π1ʳ (*i*) title (verso blank), π2ʳ˒ᵛ (*iii–iv*) dedication to Lord Pembroke, signed 'J. LOCKE.', A1ʳ–D10ᵛ (1–92) text.

Text: 32 lines; 110 (119) × 53 mm; 68 R. Very poor quality paper, not watermarked. Page no. at outer ends of headlines.

HT: ABREGÉ | *d'un Livre intitulé* | ESSAI PHILOSOPHIQUE [swash Q] | *touchant* | L'ENTENDEMENT.

Dedication headed: [rule 60 mm] | A MONSEIGNEUR | LE COMTE | DE PEMBROKE | ET MONTGOMERY &c.

Headlines, from verso to recto: *Abregé d'un Eſſai | touchant l'Entendement*.

CW: Page. A4ʳ blan- [blancheur] B6ʳ tou- [toutes] C9ᵛ (enco-) re D10v (don-) ner

Notes: Locke's first separately published work, it is a reprint, with title-page and dedication added (and new skeleton formes for the body of the text) of the 'extract' or epitome first published in the *Bibliothèque universelle et historique de l'année* 1688, t. 8, pp. 49–142 (no. 273). De Beer thinks it was "published probably about April" (1688; cf. *Corr.* iii.vii). He further states it "is printed from the same typesetting as the 'Extrait', but with fresh page-headlines, pagination, and signatures (the imposition is the same throughout, A1 corresponding to C1, and p. 1 to p.49). The upper part of the first page had to be changed for the 'Extrait', and at the end the 'Extrait' adds a paragraph (pp. 140-2) on Locke's thoughts about printing the *Essay*." (*ibid.*)

A copy at the Library Company of Philadelphia, though lacking the first two leaves, contains corrections to the text on pp. 79 and 88 in Locke's handwriting. It came to the library in the 1880s from the heirs of James Logan, the Philadelphia bookseller who purchased several books from the Churchills in 1700 (see no. 61, n.3). It is possibly Locke's own copy. For more details see my note in the *British Journal for the History of Philosophy* 4 (1966): 149–51.

Signature positions:
  A3 ſimpₐles
  A4 Ainſi ₐ j'appelle
  C5 *&* ſaₐns
  C6 *néa*ₐnmoins
  D3 qu'ellₐes

References: Attig 39; Christophersen p.12; L.L. 1802a.
Copies examined: O (Arch.B.f.56) L (526.s.42) PPL (Sev.Loc/Log2370.D4)

275. Extract of the Essay. English trans. (anon.) in *The Young Students-Library*, 1692.

Caption title: An *Extract* of a Book, *Entituled*, A | Philoſophical Eſſay upon Human | Underſtanding, *wherein is ſhewn the* | *Extenſion of certain Knowledge, and* | *the manner of attaining to it: By* | *Mr. Lock.*

IN (within a double rule, inner 286 × 147 mm, outer 296 × 157 mm): THE | 𝔜oung = 𝔖tudents = 𝔏ibrary, | CONTAINING, | EXTRACTS and ABRIDGMENTS | OF THE | Moſt Valuable Books | PRINTED | In *England*, and in the Forreign Journals, | FROM THE | Year Sixty Five, to This Time. | To which is Added, | *A New Eſſay upon all ſorts of Learning*; | WHEREIN | The USE of the SCIENCES | is Diſtinctly Treated on. | [rule 144 mm] | 𝔅y the 𝔄thenian 𝔖ociety. | [rule 144 mm] | ALSO, | A Large ALPHABETICAL TABLE, | COMPREHENDING | *The CONTENTS of this Volume.* [swash Ts] | And of All | The *Athenian Mercuries* and *Supplements*, &c. | Printed in the YEAR 1691. | [rule 144 mm] | LONDON, | Printed for 𝔍ohn 𝔇unton, at the *Raven* in the *Poultry. Where is* | *to be had the* 𝔍ntire 𝔖ett *of Athenian Gazettes, and the Sup-* [faint hyphen]

| *plements to 'em for the Year, 1691. bound up all together,* | *(with the Alphabetical Table to the Whole Year)* or elſe in Sepa- | rate Volumes, (Or ſingle Mercuries to this Time.) 1692.

Collation of the whole: folio (340 × 218 mm cut) A² a² (-a2) [a]-[d]² [e]² (-[e]2) A-U² 2A-2U² 3A-3U² χ1 4A-4M² 4N² (-4N2) 4O-4U² 5A-5V² 6A-6U² 7A-7D² [$ half signed]; 260 leaves; pp. *1-6* i-xviii 1-69 66-67 72-152 159 154-240 *i-ii* 241-289 288-316 321-479 *480-496* [= 520]. Pages 70-71 and 153 called '67-68' and '159' respectively; 288-9 repeated; 317-320 omitted.

Locke's text: 3A1ᵛ-3E2ʳ (pp. 162 mid first col.-179 top of 2d col.)

Contents: A1ʳ title (verso blank), A2ʳ-a1ᵛ (*3-6*) preface (set ital.), [a]1ʳ-[e]1ᵛ (i-xviii) 'An Essay upon all sorts of learning, written by the Athenian Society, A1ʳ-3U2ᵛ (1-240) selected texts, χ1ʳ title-page (verso blank) for [Hebrew title] 'Seu, De Punctorum Origine, Antiquitate & Authoritate: or, A Discourse concerning the Antiquity, Divine Original and Authority of the Points, Vowels and Accents that are placed to the Hebrew Bible . . . By a Member of the Athenian Society' (with imprint: *LONDON,* | Printed for *John Dunton*, at the *Raven* in the *Poultrey*, M DC XCII. [swash J, D, R, P]), 4A1ʳ-4N1ᵛ (241-288ᵇⁱˢ) text of 'De Punctorum Origine . . .', 4O1ʳ-6U2ʳ (289-479) rest of text selections, 6U2ᵛ blank, 7A1ʳ-7D2ᵛ (*481-496*) 'An Alphabetical Table, comprehending the Five First Volumes of the *Athenian Gazette*', their supplements, this work and 'The History of the Athenian Society'.

Illustration: front. is an engraving compartmentalized in 6 layers: (1) scholars seated at a table, (2) seal of Athenian Society above, (3) several scholars standing below; (4) below them a row of ordinary persons; (5) small landscape scene with carriages, and the inscription 'F. H. van Hove sculp.'; in the four external corners of these five layers taken as a block there are stylised views of Athens and Rome in upper corners, Oxford and Cambridge in lower; beneath is (6) a poem in 4 cols. italic; the whole subscribed 'London Printed For John Dunton at ẞ Rauen in ẞ Poultrey', 314 × 205 mm on plate 327 × 208 mm.

Text (3B1ʳ): 70 lines, in double cols., each 71 mm wide; 283 (299) × 145 mm; 81 R. Fair to very poor-quality laid paper.

Headlines, from verso to recto, for Locke's text: *Lock's Philoſophical Eſſay* | *on Human Underſtanding.* [swash U]

CW: Page. 3A2ᵛ 14. Al- [14. Although] 3C1ʳ (More-) over, 3E1ʳ be- [believe]

Note: An anonymous translation of the extract ('abrégé'), probably using no. 273, since the dedication to Pembroke is omitted. An English version is printed in King's *Life of John Locke* (1829, pp.362-98; 2d ed., 1830, ii.231-93; cf. no. 328-9 below). It is undoubtedly Locke's own (as copied by Sylvester Brounower), but varies in terminology from the extract printed here. That version is Bodleian Library's MS Locke c.28 ff. 52ʳ-82ᵛ. The edition published here does not use the same terms as the manuscript copy, and was obviously translated back into English from the French.

This edition was entered in the *Transcript* for 12 Oct. 1691 (p. 393).
References: Attig 40; Christophersen p. 12.
Copies examined: Y O (Hope Essays fol. 90; lacks front.) PU (AC4.A7)

276. Barometric observations, in Boyle's *General History of the Air* (1692)
Caption title: [rule 100 mm] | *A Regifter kept by Mr. Locke in Oxford.* | [rule 100 mm]
In (within a double rule, inner 157 × 101 mm, outer 166 × 108 mm): THE | *General Hiftory* | OF THE | AIR, | Defigned and Begun | BY THE | Honble *ROBERT BOYLE* Efq; | [rule 96 mm] | IMPRIMATUR. | *Robert Southwell*, | *June* 29. 1692. P.R.S. | [rule 96 mm] | *LONDON*, | Printed for *Awnfham* and *John* [swash J] *Churchill*, at the Black | Swan in *Pater-nofter-Row*, near *Amen-Corner*. | MDCXCII.
Collation of the whole: 4° (196 × 155 mm cut) A^4 a^2 B–2K^4 2L^2 [$ half signed]; 136 leaves; pp. *i–ii* iii–xii 1–259 260 [= 272].
Locke's texts: Register: pp. 104–32 (O4^v–S2^v); accompanying note headed "A Letter to the Author.", dated 'Ch. Ch. 5° May, 1666': pp. 137–41 (T1^r–T3^r).
Contents of the whole: A1^r title (verso blank), A2^r–A3^r (iii–v) note from publisher to the reader, A3^v–A4^v (vi–viii) contents, a1^r–a2^v (ix–xii) preface, B1^r–2L2^r (1–259) text, 2L2^v advt. in 2 cols. for 53 books (including *Two Treatises*, Locke's 3 letters on toleration, and *Some Considerations*, all without mentioning their author).
Boyle's text (E3^v): 34 lines; 157 (168) × 100 (121) mm; 93 R. Notes, set roman, at outer margins. Page no. centered within parentheses as headlines. Good-quality laid paper; orb surmounted by a cross with decorated finials as watermark (on 1st and 4th leaves at inner margin).
Headlines, for Locke's register, same as caption title. For Boyle's text there are page numbers centered within parentheses.
CW: Page. B1^v (ob-) ferve, G3^r (ne-) ver N2^r (Counter-) poife T1^r whilft T1^v ftink T2^r defired T2^v on T3^v (re-) turn, X8^r (vifio-) ne 2C1^r (Pil-) lar, 2E1^r TI- [TITLE] No CW for weather register.
Notes: This work of Boyle's was edited for publication by Locke, as attested by his letter to Boyle on 21 October 1691 (*Corr.* 1422; iv. 320–2 and n.). There is also some unpublished manuscript material in Bodleian Library MS. Locke c.37 and b.l.[1] An agreement with the Churchills relating to the copyright, dated 25 July 1692, is MS. Locke b.1 fol. 164. The series of barometric observations covers the period June 1666 to June 1683. Observations from 1692 to 1704 kept at Oates (Sir Francis Masham's residence in Essex) were published in *The Philosophical Transactions* of the Royal Society in 1705 (*see* no.262). The register is arranged in columns for year, month, day, hour, 'thermoscope' (temperature), 'baroscope', 'hygroscope', wind and weather at Oxford.

[1] Noted by M. A. Stewart in "Locke's Professional Contacts with Robert Boyle", *The Locke Newsletter*, 12 (1981): 19–44, espec. 36–8.

The letter from Locke to Boyle relating to the barometer on pp.137–41 is reprinted as *Corr.* 197 (i.273–76) and in Boyle's *Works* (1744), v.157–58. Boyle's work was entered in the Registers of the Stationers' Company on 16 July 1692 (*Transcript* p.485).

A microprint copy (on 3 opaque microcards) of this work is in the scientific set, *Landmarks of Science*.

References: Attig 521; Christophersen p. 13; Fulton 194 and p. 134 n.; L.L. 460 (interleaved; now in Bodleian Lib.); T.C.II.467; Wing[2] B3981.

Copies examined: O[1] (F.1.24 Linc.)   L (1651/1033)   O[2] (Ashm.c.40)

Very few items in this chapter were ever exposed to print after their initial appearance, before or after 1800, with the exception of the first two poems and the 'New Method of Making Common-place Books'. The poems in *Musarum Oxoniensium Helaiophoria* were reprinted in the *Remains of John Locke* (1714; no. 315) together with the introductory Latin poem to Sydenham's work (no. 256–7); the two poems from *Musarum Oxoniensium* were also printed in Fox Bourne's *Life of John Locke* (1876), i. 50–52 (no. 330). The 'New Method' is found not only in Locke's *Posthumous Works* (1706; no. 299), but also in the *Works* editions (Chap. XI).

There were several so-called 'adaptations' of his 'method' following his principles in the eighteenth century. *The Commonplace Book to the Holy Bible*, attributed to Locke in the nineteenth century, in its original manifestation of 1676 predates Locke's publication of his 'method'. Later editions capitalized on his name and the fact that the 1697 edition was issued by the Churchills, Locke's publisher, to attribute it to him; but even its being based on his 'method' is a wholly false statement. (See Chap. XIII: False Attributions.)

CHAPTER IX
Posthumous Publications from Manuscripts (nos. 277–345)

This chapter encompasses the posthumous appearance of materials written by Locke whenever they appeared, beginning with his 'Paraphrases' of the Epistles of St. Paul, in 1705, to the recent publications from his manuscripts, the early drafts of the *Essay*, and transcriptions of his journals, even when they have appeared after 1800. Separate chapters for collections of his correspondence, and collected and selected works editions follow.

In a letter dated 4 October 1704 to his nephew and executor Peter King (later, Baron King of Ockham), Locke sent some instructions "not fit to be put into so solemn and publique a writing" as his will (*Corr.* 3647; viii. 412-17). In the letter he mentions several papers "layd down in suddain and imperfect draughts" which he thought might be published, if his "judicious freinds" so decided; nor did he absolutely forbid their publication. He listed and made comments about his 'Paraphrases', his 'Examination of P. Malebranche's Opinion', the 'Discourse on Miracles', the 'Conduct of the Understanding', some papers inscribed '*Physica*' (perhaps a medical notebook, according to E. S. de Beer) and "two or three sheets of Memoires" among other miscellany. The 'Paraphrases' were the first to appear, beginning in 1705. A collection of most other posthumous papers mentioned was put together by Peter King, with part of that letter serving as a preface, and appeared shortly after, in 1706 (no. 299).

Locke's interest in Biblical texts dates from at least 1660–61, the date of the manuscripts later published as *Two Tracts on Government*.[1] As he grew older he spent more and more time on Scriptural studies, especially on the Epistles, as though their study would show him the way to salvation. According to A. P. Wainwright[2] Locke had the preparatory work done by 1703. A letter sent to him on August 17, 1704 (*Corr.* 3615; viii. 380) indicates he had received proofs of his paraphrase of the Epistle to the Galatians. It is curious that the *Paraphrases* were published without his name on the title-page, even after his death, when his authorship of the letters on toleration and of *Two Treatises*

---

[1] Edited with an introduction, notes and translation by Philip Abrams (Cambridge University Press, 1967; see no. 342). Transcribed from Bodleian Library MS. Locke c. 7 and c.28, ff. 3 et seq.
[2] *A Paraphrase and Notes on the Epistles of St. Paul to the Galatians, 1 and 2 Corinthians, Romans, Ephesians*. Edited by Arthur P. Wainwright (Oxford: Clarendon Press, 1987; 2 vols.)

of Government was revealed. His authorship was certainly known after the Churchills' advertisement in the paraphrase of the 'Epistle to the Galatians' (no. 277), reinforced by the publication of his *Posthumous Works* (1706; no.299). The Churchills preserved his anonymity in the editions of the *Paraphrases* as did succeeding publishers until the fourth edition of 1742 (no. 292). Wainwright suggests it was perhaps in case his views would be judged heretical that he might have preferred the safety of anonymity.

The early editions of all the paraphrases begin with a textual 'Synopsis' before the exegesis, section by section. Each section begins with the 'Contents' and is then followed by the Biblical text and matching paraphrase set in parallel columns, the latter twice the width of the text, with voluminous notes across the width of the rest of the page. Not until the octavo issues do the Biblical text, paraphrase and notes occupy the width of the page. Most copies located are bound as a set, the most usual set being copies of the first printings of each paraphrase, with the collective title leaves and the 'Essay on Understanding St. Paul' bound first (no. 286-7). Other copies bound in sets may include later editions of the first two paraphrases and a 'second edition' set of preliminary title leaves.

By his will (copy in *Corr.* viii.419-27) Locke bequeathed half his library to Francis Cudworth Masham, son of his friend Lady Masham. His papers and the other half of his library he left to his nephew, later Lord King (whose descendants became Earls of Lovelace). Francis Masham's moiety has more or less disappeared, though the odd book turns up occasionally; he squandered much of his inheritance in bits and pieces. All the interleaved books and the manuscripts went to Peter King, a large portion of which survive and are now housed as the Lovelace Collection in the Bodleian Library. For further information on the book collection and its survivors, see Jack Harrison and Peter Laslett's *The Library of John Locke* (no.343-4). For a description and catalogue of the manuscripts, see Philip Long's a *Summary Catalogue of the Lovelace Collection of the Papers of John Locke in the Bodleian Library* (Oxford: For the Library at the University Press, 1959). Further useful information on the surviving philosophical manuscripts is to be found in H. A. S. Schankula's articles in the *Bodleian Library Record*, 9 (1973): 24-35 and 81-82.

277. Paraphrases. Galatians. 1705. 4°
A | PARAPHRASE | AND | NOTES | ON THE | EPISTLE of St. *PAUL* | TO THE | *GALATIANS*. | [rule 124 mm] | LONDON, | Printed for *Awnſham* and *John* [swash J] *Churchill*, at the | *Black-Swan* [swash k] in *Paternoſter-Row*, 1705.

Coll: 4° (254 × 206 mm uncut) A^2 B–F^4 G^2 [$ half signed]; 24 leaves; pp. *i–iv* 1–42 *43–44* [=48].

Contents: A1^r (*i*) title (verso blank), A2^r (*iii*) 'The Publisher to the Reader' (14 lines), A2^v blank, B1^r–G1^v (1–42) text, G2^{r,v} (*43–44*) advt. for books sold by Churchills.

Text (C3ᵛ): 40 lines; 185 (198) × 125 (139) mm; 'paraphrase' set 93 R, biblical text and 'notes' set 67 R. Good quality laid paper, without watermarks. Marginal notes and verse number citations set roman.
HT: [double rule 122/126 mm] | THE | EPISTLE of St. *PAUL* | TO THE | *GALATIANS*. | [rule 123 mm]
RT: *GALATIANS*.
CW: Page (to the 'paraphrase' text). B3ᵛ pleaſe [had] C2ᵛ I E1ᵛ or E2ᵛ (con-) tinuing F3ʳ Spirit [Spirit.]
Press figures: none.
Notes: The first posthumous work to be published (anonymously), it is usually found as part of the set of paraphrases, with 'Essay' and title leaves (no. 286 and 287 or 288). The Biblical text is a transcription of the Authorised Version. The Churchills' advertisement in double cols. begins with the contemporary edition of all works covered in Chap. I–VII, followed by a note: "All these above writ by Mr. *Lock*." This is the first announcement Locke wrote the letters on 'Toleration' and the *Two Treatises*.

A microfilm of a British Library copy (L¹: 696.k.19 (2)) of 'Galatians' alone is in the collection, *The Eighteenth Century*, reel 3194 no. 18; another copy (L²: 690.f.26) is on reel 1349 no.4; as part of the set of 'paraphrases' (from the Harvard College Library copy) is on reel 1261 no. 14.
References: Attig 694; Christophersen p.75; ESTC t155204.
Copies examined. A: When part of set; see no. 287 and 288 for shelf marks.
  Y [Berlin]   C¹   Ck¹ (Keynes)   MH (Phil.2115.62.2*)   O¹   Oj (B10.17, gift of Jonathan Edwards)
  B: Other copies. DFo (B1268.P4G2 1705, unbound & untrimmed)   L¹ (696.k19 (2))   L² (690.f.26)   O² (4° W.48 Th (2))   O³ (4° B.76 Th.BS)

278. Paraphrases. Galatians. 2d ed., 1706. 4°
A | PARAPHRASE | ... [as in no. 277 until:] *GALATIANS*. | [rule 129 mm] | 𝕿𝖍𝖊 𝕾𝖊𝖈𝖔𝖓𝖉 𝕰𝖉𝖎𝖙𝖎𝖔𝖓. | [rule 128 mm] | LONDON, | Printed for *Awnſham* and *John Churchill*, [swash J] at the | *Black-Swan* in *Pater-noſter-Row*, 1706.
Coll: 4° (242 × 192 mm cut) A² B–F⁴ G² [$ half signed]; 24 leaves; pp. *i–iv* 1–43 44 [= 48].
Contents: A1ʳ (*i*) title (verso blank), A2ʳ (*iii*) introd. note to reader (14 lines set ital.), A2ᵛ (*iv*) 2-col. advt. of books by Churchills, B1ʳ–G2ʳ (1–43) text, G2ᵛ (44) blank.
Text: 40 lines; 183 (198) × 127 (146) mm; 93 R (Biblical text & notes 66 R).
Headlines: *GALATIANS*.
CW: Page (from introd. note, 'contents' or paraphrase). B1ʳ *Firſt*, C2ᵛ (communi-) cates E1ʳ SECT. E1ᵛ Woman, F3ʳ (Con-) duct G1ᵛ was
Press figures: none.
Notes: A new typesetting of 277, unchanged. Good-quality laid paper, without watermark.
References: Attig 695; ESTC t160511.

Copies examined. A: Part of sets; for shelfmark see no. 287–8.   C³ CaOTU Ck² (Keynes) CLaslett CtY O⁵ Oo PPL ViU
  B: Other copies. [GOT (8° TH.bibl.998/2)]

279. Paraphrases. Galatians. 3d ed., 1708. 4°
A | PARAPHRASE ... [&c. as in no. 277 until:] *GALATIANS.* | [rule 125 mm] | 𝕿𝖍𝖊 𝕿𝖍𝖎𝖗𝖉 𝕰𝖉𝖎𝖙𝖎𝖔𝖓. | [rule 123 mm] | *LONDON,* | Printed for *Awnſham* and *John* [swash J] *Churchill*, at the | *Black-Swan* in *Paternoſter-Row*, 1708.
Coll: 4° (236 × 186 mm cut) A^2 B–F^4 G^2 [$ half signed]; 24 leaves; pp. *i–iv* 1–43 44 [=48].
Contents: same as no. 278.
Text: 40 lines; 181 (200) × 127 (145) mm; 94 R. Biblical text & notes 66 R. Good-quality laid paper, without watermark.
RT: *GALATIANS*.
CW: Page (to 'paraphrase'). $C2^v$ (communi-) cates $E1^v$ Woman, $F3^r$ was $G1^v$ was
Press figures: none.
Notes: A new typesetting of no. 277, reprinting no. 278 line by line. The edition statement on the t.p. is in type 3 mm tall. Microfilm copies are in the collection, *The Eighteenth Century*, reel 3123, no. 6, and for the set (1st editions of all 'paraphrases' except this one) in reel 661, no. 4.
References: Attig 696; Christophersen p.75; ESTC t124322.
Copy examined: O^4 (CC 25. Th) C^2 (4.27.31, in set) L^2 (3268.d.11, in set)   PPL (A Lock (bw)/12594.Q3, in set)

280. Paraphrases. Galatians. '3d' [=4th] ed., 1718. 4°
A | PARAPHRASE | AND | NOTES | ON THE | *EPISTLE of St.* PAUL | TO THE | GALATIANS. | [rule 130 mm] | 𝕿𝖍𝖊 𝕿𝖍𝖎𝖗𝖉 𝕰𝖉𝖎𝖙𝖎𝖔𝖓. | [rule 129 mm] | *LONDON:* | Printed for *William Churchill*, at the *Black* | *Swan* in *Pater-noſter-row*. 1718.
Coll: 4° (242 × 192 mm cut) A–F^4 [$ half signed]; 24 leaves; pp. *1–4 5–47 48*.
Contents: $A1^r$ (*1*) title (verso blank), $A2^r$ (*3*) publisher's note to reader (14¼ lines), $A3^r$–$F4^r$ (*5–47*) text, $F4^v$ blank.
Text: 40 lines; 185 (200) × 127 (145) mm; 93 R. Biblical text & notes 66 R). Good-quality laid paper, without watermarks.
RT: *GALATIANS*.
CW: Page (to 'paraphrase'). $B1^r$ (devi-) ate $C2^v$ from $E1^r$ (bare-) ly $E1^v$ there $F3^r$ SECT.
Press figures: none.
Notes: A new typesetting of no. 278, unchanged textually. The edition statement for this truly 4th edition, is set in gothic type 5 mm high. Not in ESTC.
References: Attig 697; Christophersen p. 75.
Copies examined: O^6 (Vet. A4 d.118, in set)   Exeter Cathedral (in set)

281. Paraphrases. 1 Corinthians. 1706. 4°
A | PARAPHRASE | AND | NOTES | ON THE | Firſt Epiſtle of St. PAUL | TO THE | CORINTHIANS. | [rule 123 mm] | LONDON, | Printed for *Awnſham* and *John* [swash J] *Churchill*, at | the Black Swan in *Pater-noſter-Row*, 1706.

Coll: 4° (242 × 192 mm cut) A² B-O⁴ P² [$ half signed]; 56 leaves; pp. *i-iv* 1-107 *108* [=112].

Contents: A1ʳ blank, A1ᵛ 3-line 'ADVERTISEMENT' for *Galatians*, A2ʳ (*iii*) title (verso blank), B1ʳ-P2ʳ (1-107) text, P2ᵛ blank.

Text (E3ᵛ): 40 lines; 184 (200) × 125 (139) mm; 93 R. Biblical text & notes 66 R. Good-quality laid paper, without visible watermarks.

HT: [double rule 123 mm] | THE | Firſt EPISTLE of St. *PAUL* | TO THE | CORINTHIANS. | [rule 124 mm]

Headlines: I CORINTHIANS.

CW: Page (to the 'paraphrase' text; long footnotes also have CW). B1ᵛ SEC-[SECTION] C2ʳ SECT. C4ʳ World, [World (*e*),] E1ᵛ (wander-) ing G1ᵛ (look-) ing K1ᵛ (him-) ſelf, N2ᵛ (know-) ing O1ʳ be; [be:]

Press figures: none.

Notes: The Biblical text is in the Authorised Version. A microfilm copy of this edition is in the collection, *The Eighteenth Century*, reel 3123, no. 4; as part of British Library set (L³) in reel 661, and in reel 1261 no. 14.

References: Attig 698; Christophersen p.75; ESTC t124324.

Copies examined (part of set unless shelfmark given): Y [Berlin] C (sets 1-3) Ck (Keynes, both sets) CLaslett DFo (B1268.P4C8 1706, unbound) [GOT] L¹ (696.k.19 (3)) L³ MH (A1 lacking) O (sets 1, 5) O⁴ (CC.25Th) Oj Oo PPL ViU

282. Paraphrases. 1 Corinthians. [2nd ed.], 1718. 4°
A | PARAPHRASE | AND | NOTES | ON THE | Firſt EPISTLE of St. PAUL | TO THE | CORINTHIANS. | [rule 122 mm] | LONDON: | Printed for WILLIAM CHURCHILL at | the Black Swan in *Pater Noſter Row*, 1718.

Coll: 4° (242 × 185 mm cut) A-N⁴ O² [$ half signed]; 54 leaves; pp. *1-2* 3-108.

Contents: A1ʳ (*1*) title (verso blank), A2ʳ-O2ᵛ (3-108) text.

Text: 40 lines; 176 (198) × 125 (143) mm; 93 R. Biblical text & notes 66 R. Good-quality laid paper without watermarks.

RT: I CORINTHIANS.

CW: Page (to 'paraphrase' and to notes when carry over to next page). B1ᵛ the C2ʳ glorying C4ʳ diſtin- [diſtinguiſhed] E1ᵛ the G1ᵛ ſake, K1ᵛ above- [above-mentioned:] N2ᵛ be; [be:] O1ʳ come.

Press figures: none.

Notes: A new typesetting of no. 282. Not in ESTC.

Reference: Attig 699; Christophersen p. 75.

Copies examined: O⁶ (Vet. A4 d.118, in set) Exeter Cathedral (in set)

283. Paraphrases. 2 Corinthians. 1706. 4°
A | PARAPHRASE | AND | NOTES | ON THE | Second Epiftle of St. PAUL | TO THE | *CORINTHIANS*. | [rule 130 mm] | *LONDON,* | Printed for *Awnfham* and *John* [swash J] *Churchill*, at the | *Black Swan* in *Pater-nofter-Row*, 1706.

Coll: 4° (242 × 192 mm cut) A–G⁴ H² [$ half signed]; 30 leaves; pp. *1-2* 3-58 *59-60*.

Contents: A1ʳ (*1*) title (verso blank), A2ʳ–H1ᵛ (*3-58*) text, H2ʳ,ᵛ (*59-60*) advt. for books sold by Churchills (2 cols. per page).

Text (A2ᵛ): 40 lines; 182 (198) × 127 (143) mm; 93 R. Biblical text and notes 67 R. Good-quality laid paper, without watermarks.

HT: [double rule 124 mm] | THE | Epiftle of St. Paul | TO THE | ROMANS. | [rule 125 mm]

Headlines: II *CORINTHIANS.*

CW: Page (to 'paraphrase' and to notes when carry over). B1ʳ (ear-) neft C3ʳ (prea-) ching E1ᵛ Mu- [Munificence] F3ʳ HAVE [HAve] G3ᵛ (hum-) ble

Press figures: none.

Notes: The Biblical text, as in all these paraphrases, is the Authorised Version. A microfilm copy is in the collection, *The Eighteenth Century*, reel 3123, no. 5; as part of set, in reel 661 no. 4 and reel 1261 no.14.

References: Attig 700; Christophersen p. 75; ESTC t124323.

Copies examined (part of set unless shelfmark given): Y [Berlin] C (sets 1-3) CaOTU Ck (Keynes, both sets) CLaslett DFo (B1268.P4C85 1706 unbound) Exeter Cathedral [GOT] L¹ (696.k19 (3)) L³ MH O (sets 1, 4-6) Oj Oo (H2 bound before H1) PPL ViU

284. Paraphrases. Romans. 1707. 4°
A | PARAPHRASE | AND | NOTES | ON THE | Epiftle of St. Paul | TO THE | ROMANS. | [rule 125 mm] | *LONDON,* | Printed for *Awnfham* and *John* [swash J] *Churchill*, at | the *Black Swan* in *Pater-nofter-Row*, 1707.

Coll: 4° (242 × 192 mm cut) A–S⁴ [$ half signed; H1 signed 'G']; 72 leaves; pp. *1-2* 3-142 *143-144*.

Contents: A1ʳ (*1*) title (verso blank), A2ʳ–S3ᵛ (*3-142*) text, S4ʳ,ᵛ (*143-144*) advt. for Churchills' books (2 cols. per page).

Text (A2ᵛ): 40 lines; 185 (200) × 126 (140) mm; 93 R. Biblical text & notes set 66R. Good-quality laid paper without watermarks.

HT: [double rule 124/125 mm] THE | Epiftle of St. Paul | TO THE | ROMANS. | [rule 125 mm]

Headlines: ROMANS.

CW: Page (to 'paraphrase' and to notes when carry over). A2ᵛ (rai-) fing C1ʳ art, [art (*m*),] E3ᵛ There- [Therefore] K1ᵛ (car-) nal M2ʳ exter- [exterminate] Q1ᵛ (Pow-) er

Press figures: none.

Note: A microfilm copy of this work is in the collection, *The Eighteenth*

Century, reel 3123, no. 3; as part of set in reel 661 no.4 and reel 1261 no. 14.
References: Attig 701; Christophersen p.75; ESTC t124325.
Copies examined (part of set unless shelfmark given): Y [Berlin] C (sets 1-3) C⁴ (Ely c.252; closely trimmed) CaOTU Ck (Keynes, both sets) CLaslett DFo (B1268.P4R6 1707, not bound) Exeter Cathedral [GOT] L¹ (696.k19 (4)) L³ MH (S4 lacking) O (sets 1, 4-6) Oj Oo PPL

285. Paraphrases. Ephesians. 1707. 4°
A | PARAPHRASE | AND | NOTES | ON THE | Epiſtle of St. Paul | TO THE | EPHESIANS. | [rule 124 mm] | LONDON, | Printed for *Awnſham* and *John* [swash J] *Churchill*, at | the *Black Swan* in *Pater-noſter-Row*, 1707.
Coll: 4° (242 × 192 mm cut) A-G⁴ H² [$ half signed]; 30 leaves; pp. *1-2* 3-60.
Contents: A1ʳ (*1*) title (verso blank), A2ʳ-H2ᵛ (3-60) text.
Text (A2ᵛ): 40 lines; 182 (198) × 127 (142) mm; 93 R. Biblical text & notes 66 R. Good-quality laid paper, with flower (tulip?) watermark.
HT: [double rule 125 mm] | THE | Epiſtle of St. Paul | TO THE | EPHESIANS. | [rule 125 mm]
Headlines: EPHESIANS.
CW: Page (to 'paraphrase' and to notes when carry over). A2ᵛ par- [particular] B3ᵛ (Great-) neſs C3ᵛ World, [World (*o*),] E2ᵛ (Pro-) phets H1ᵛ Breaſt- [Breaſt-plate]
Press figures: none.
Notes: The biblical text is from the Authorised version. A microfilm copy is included in the sets in *The Eighteenth Century*, reel 661 no. 4 and reel 1261, no. 14.
References: Attig 702; Christophersen p. 75; ESTC t124328.
Copies examined (part of set unless shelfmark given): Y [Berlin] C (sets 1-3) CaOTU Ck (Keynes, both sets) CLaslett DFo (B1268.P4E7 1707, unbound) Exeter Cathedral EXu [GOT] L¹ (696.k19 (5)) L³ MH O (sets 1, 4-6) Oj Oo PPL ViU

286. Paraphrases. Essay. 1707. 4°
AN | ESSAY | FOR THE | UNDERSTANDING [E, S smaller font] | OF | Sᵀ. PAUL'S | EPISTLES, | By Conſulting | St. Paul himſelf. | [rule 127 mm] | LONDON, | Printed for *Awnſham* and *John* [swash J] *Churchill*, at | the *Black Swan* in *Pater-noſter-Row*, 1707.
Coll: 4° (242 × 192 mm cut) A⁴ a-b⁴ [$ half signed]; 12 leaves; pp. *i-ii* iii-xxiv.
Contents: A1ʳ (*i*) title (verso blank), A2ʳ-b4ᵛ (iii-xxiv) text.
Text (b3ᵛ): 32 lines; 184 (199) × 132 mm; 116 ital. Poor (browning)-quality paper without watermark.

HT: [double rule 127 mm] | THE | PREFACE.
Headlines: The PREFACE.
CW: Page. a2ʳ (*Epi-*) *piſtles* b3ʳ *Wri-* [*Writers*]
Press figures: none.
Notes: This 'Essay' is not mentioned in Locke's letter of instructions to Peter King (*Corr.* 3647; viii.412–7) though Locke did there specify the order in which he wished the 'paraphrases' published. It serves as an introduction to the collected 'paraphrases'.

There are copies as part of a set in the collection *The Eighteenth Century*, reel 661 no. 4 and reel 1261 no. 14.

References: Attig 703; Christophersen p. 75; ESTC t124326.
Copies examined: Y [Berlin] C (sets 1–3) CaOTU Ck (Keynes, both sets) Exeter Cathedral [GOT] L¹ (696.k.19 (1)) L³ MH O (sets 1, 4–6) O (4° W.48Th(1)) Oj Oo PPL (A Lock (bw)/12594.Q2) ViU

287. Paraphrases. Collective title-page. 1707. 4°
Within a double rule, inner 194 × 132 mm, outer 200 × 138 mm: A | PARAPHRASE | AND | NOTES | ON THE | Epiſtles of St. Paul | TO THE |

I & { Galatians, Corinthians, } { Romans, Epheſians. }
II

To which is Prefix'd, An | ESSAY | FOR THE | Underſtanding of St. *Paul*'s EPISTLES, by | Conſulting St. *Paul* Himſelf. | [rule 127 mm] | LONDON, | Printed by *J. H.* for *Awnſham* and *John* [swash J] *Churchill*, at the | *Black Swan* [swash k] in *Pater-noſter-Row*. 1707.

Coll: 4° (242 × 192 mm cut) π²; 2 leaves; pp. *i–iv*.
Contents: π1ʳ (*i*) title (verso blank), π2ʳ (*iii*) 'Books Written by Mr. John Lock.' (28 lines), π2ᵛ blank.
Notes: The collective title-page issued for the preliminary 'Essay' and the Paraphrases, in bound vols. usually found in the order listed on the title-page. In some copies the 2 leaves are found in reverse order; alternatively the 2nd leaf may be wanting. The list of Locke's writings includes those published anonymously in his lifetime (e.g. *Toleration* letters, *Two Treatises of Government*). Some copies of the collection contain 2nd or 3rd edition of 'Galatians' and/or 2nd edition of 'I Corinthians', with the second edition title leaves (no. 288). A copy of the set, including first editions of each 'paraphrase', is in the microfilm set, *The Eighteenth Century*, reel 1261, no. 14.
References: Attig 708; Christophersen p. 75; ESTC n011234 (collected set).
Notice: *Bibliothèque choisie* 13 (1707): 137–78 (of the collected set).
Copies examined. The ideal and most usual set has, in order, 286, 277, 281, 283–5. Some sets are bound in a different order (given below) and/or include a later edition of 'Galatians' or '1 Corinthians'.

The British Library's set (shelfmark 696.k19) is the usual set but lacks the title leaves, as does my own. O⁴ has no. 286 and 279 only.
[Berlin]
C¹ (4.27.30; usual set)
CaOTU (Locke L63.P37 1707; with 286, 284, 281, 283, 278, 285)
Ck¹ (Keynes A.12.39; with 286, 277, 280, 283)
Ck² (Keynes A.12.38; with 286, 278, 281, 283-5)
CLaslett (with 286, 278, 281, 283-5)
CtY (M*lz*755/707*l*; with 286, 278, 281, 283-5)
Exeter Cathedral (with 286, 280, 282-5)
[GOT]
MH (*Phil.2115.62.2; leaf c2 bd. after 'Essay'; usual set)
O¹ (Vet.M3 d.2; with 286, 284, 285, 281, 283, 277, in order)
O⁵ (Vet.A4 d.117; with 286, 278, 281, 283-5)
O⁶ (Vet.A4 d.118; with 286, 280, 282-5)
Oj (B10.17; with 284, 281, 283, 277; Jonathan Edwards' copy)
Oo (2Ug5; with 286, 278, 281, 283-5)

288. Paraphrases. Collective t.p., 2d ed. 1709.
Within a double rule, inner 197×131 mm, outer 205×138 mm: A | PARAPHRASE | ... [&c. as in 287, except: rule 126 mm] | 𝕴𝖍𝖊 𝕾𝖊𝖈𝖔𝖓𝖉 𝕰𝖉𝖎𝖙𝖎𝖔𝖓. | [rule 126 mm] | *LONDON,* | Printed by *J. H.* for *Awnſham* and *John Churchill,* [swash Js] at the *Black Swan* [swash k] in *Pater-noſter-Row.* 1709.
Coll: 4° (236×186 mm cut) π² (π1 blank or wanting); π2ʳ title (verso blank).
Notes: Collective title-page only, to accompany 2d or 3d ed. of *Galatians,* 1st or 2nd ed. of *1 Corinthians,* and first editions of the other 'paraphrases.' As a collective work it was advertised for sale on Sept. 8, 1708 in the *Bibliotheca Annua.* The 'conger' of booksellers headed by Thomas Bennet and Henry Clements (see no. 64, *Notes*) purchased 390 copies for their pool, paying 5 shillings each copy, and wholesaled them to the trade for 6/6d.

A microfilm copy of the set (L3) is in *The Eighteenth Century,* reel 661 no. 4.
References: Attig 709; Christophersen p. 75; ESTC t124327 (collective set).
Copies examined: C² (4.27.31; with 286, 279, 281, 283-5)
 C³ (Peterborough R.2.12; with 286, 278, 281, 283-5)
 L³ (3268 d.11; with 286, 284, 281, 283, 279, 285)
 O⁴ (CC.25 Th; with 279, 281, 281, 283-4, 286, 285)
 PPL (12584.Q; with 286, 279, 281, 283-5)
 ViU (with 286, 278, 281, 283-5)

289. Paraphrases. 3d ed., 1733. 4°
A | PARAPHRASE | AND | NOTES | ON THE | EPISTLES OF St. PAUL | TO THE |

     Galatians, | | *Romans,* and
           | |
I & ⎫ *Corinthians,* | | *Epheſians.*
II ⎭

To which is Prefix'd, An | ESSAY | FOR THE | Underſtanding of St. PAUL's EPISTLES, BY | Conſulting St. PAUL Himſelf. | [rule 124 mm] The THIRD EDITION. | [rule 126 mm] | *LONDON:* | Printed for A. BETTESWORTH, and C. HITCH, in *Pater-* | *noſter Row*; J. PEMBERTON, in *Fleetſtreet*; and E. SYMON, | in *Cornhill.* M.DCC.XXXIII.

Coll: 4° (223 × 172 mm cut) A⁴ a⁴ b² B–3E⁴ 3F² [$ half signed]; 212 leaves; pp. *i–ii* iii–xx 1–219 20 221–404 [= 424]. Page no. 220 has lost initial '2'.

Contents: A1ʳ (*i*) title (verso blank), A2ʳ–b2ᵛ (iii–xx) text of 'Essay for Understanding', B1ʳ–G2ʳ (1–43) text of paraphrase of Galatians, G2ᵛ–U3ᵛ (44–150) 1 Corinthians, U4ʳ–2D3ᵛ (151–206) 2 Corinthians, 2D4ʳ–2Y1ᵛ (207–346) Romans, 2Y2ʳ–3F2ᵛ (347–404) Ephesians.

Text (C3ᵛ): 187 (200) × 128 (146) mm. Set 40 lines 92 R in 'Essay' and introductory synopses. Biblical text & notes set 67 R. Good-quality laid paper, with inverted Y over GW as watermark. Page 346 (2Y1ᵛ) has orn. tailpiece of peacock-like feather swirls & flowers, 39 × 56 mm.

HT, A2ʳ: [double rule 127/125 mm] | AN | ESSAY | For the UNDERSTANDING | St. *Paul's* Epiſtles, *&c.*

Head titles, for each paraphrase, e.g.: [double rule 127 mm approx.] | A | PARAPHRASE *and* NOTES | ON THE | EPISTLE of St. *PAUL* | TO THE | *GALATIANS.* | [rule 127 mm approx.]

RT for 'Essay', from verso to recto: *An* ESSAY *for the Underſtanding* | St. PAUL's EPISTLES, *&c.*

Headlines, '*GALATIANS.*', 'II *CORINTHIANS.*', etc.

CW: Page (to paraphrase and to notes when carry over). C3ʳ (com-) mitted F3ᵛ (Mem-) bers, I1ᵛ World, [Worldᵉ,] N3ʳ Con- [Conſcience] S2ᵛ Law [Lawᑫ,] Z2ʳ (im-) mediate 2C2ᵛ Mini- [Miniſter] 2I1ᵛ There- [Therefore] 2N3ᵛ (car-) nal 2S1ᵛ eſtabliſhed 2X3ʳ I com- [I Commend] 3B3ʳ Deli- [Deliverance]

Press figures: vii (A4ʳ)-I xv (a4ʳ)-I xix (b2ʳ)-I 7 (B4ʳ)-I 8 (B4ᵛ)-I 15 (C4ʳ)-2 16 (C4ᵛ)-2 20 (D2ᵛ)-I 23 (D4ʳ)-I 29 (E3ʳ)-2 30 (E3ᵛ)-2 37 (F3ʳ)-I 38 (F3ᵛ)-I 46 (G3ᵛ)-I 48 (G4ᵛ)-I 50 (H1ᵛ)-2 53 (H3ʳ)-2 60 (I2ᵛ)-2 62 (I3ᵛ)-2 66 (K1ᵛ)-I 68 (K2ᵛ)-I 85 (M3ʳ)-I 87 (M4ʳ)-I 93 (N3ʳ)-2 94 (N3ᵛ)-2 100 (O2ᵛ)-I 103 (O4ʳ)-I 107 (P2ʳ)-I 108 (P2ᵛ)-I 114 (Q1ᵛ)-I 120 (Q4ᵛ)-2 122 (R1ᵛ)-I 125 (R3ʳ)-2 134 (S3ᵛ)-2 138 (T1ᵛ)-2 140 (T2ᵛ)-2 149 (U3ʳ)-I 150 (U3ᵛ)-I 158 (X3ᵛ)-I 160 (X4ʳ)-I 167 (Y4ʳ)-2 172 (Z2ᵛ)-I 175 (Z4ʳ)-2 180 (2A2ᵛ)-I 183 (2A4ʳ)-I 190 (2B3ᵛ)-2 196 (2C2ᵛ)-2 204 (2D2ᵛ)-3 214 (2E3ᵛ)-2 231 (2G4ʳ)-3 238 (2H3ʳ)-2 240 (2H4ʳ)-2 242 (2I1ᵛ)-2 248 (2I4ᵛ)-3 263 (2L4ʳ)-2 264 (2L4ᵛ)-inverted 3 269 (2M3ʳ)-3 276 (2N2ᵛ)-3 283 (2O2ʳ)-4 296 (2P4ᵛ)-3 304 (2Q4ᵛ)-I 309 (2R3ʳ)-3 319 (2S4ʳ)-2 325 (2T3ʳ)-3 333 (2U3ʳ)-3 338 (2X1ʳ)-3 348 (2Y2ᵛ)-4 359 (2Z4ʳ)-3 364 (3A2ᵛ)-2 367 (3A4ʳ)-I 370 (3B1ᵛ)-I

372 (3B2ᵛ)-1 380 (3C2ᵛ)-1 382 (3C3ᵛ)-1 388 (3D2ᵛ)-inverted 3 390 (3D3ᵛ)-1 398 (3E3ᵛ)-4 402 (3F1ᵛ)-inverted 3. No figures in sheets L, 2F, 2K; one figure each in S, Y, 2B-2E, 2G, 2M-2Z and 3E. O copy without figs. on p.30, 149 & 283; '2' on p.20, and 'I' on p. 214. Ob copy has '4' on p. 402.
Notes: A reprint of no. 286, 280, 282-5 with continuous paging. A microfilm copy is in *The Eighteenth Century*, reel 782 no. 9.
References: Attig 710; ESTC t123131.
Copies examined: Y C (7100.c.353) C(Keynes) L (3053 m.6) O (Vet.A4 d.159) Oa (SR76 b.12) Ob (Arch.E.VIII.8)

290. Paraphrases. '4th ed.', Dublin, 1738. 8° in 4s.
A | PARAPHRASE | . . .[&c. as no. 289, except: rule 84 mm] | The FOURTH EDITION. | [rule 85 mm] | *DUBLIN:* [swash D, U] | Printed by S. POWELL, | For EDWARD EXSHAW, at the *Bible*, over- | againſt the *Old-Exchange* on *Cork-Hill*, Bookſeller, | MDCCXXXVIII.
Coll: 8° in 4s (190 × 120 mm cut) A⁸ B-3N⁴ [$ half signed]; 240 leaves; pp. *i-iii* iv-xix 20-374 575 376-477 478-480. Page 375 called '575'.
Contents: A1ʳ (*i*) title (verso blank), A2ʳ-B2ʳ (*iii*-xix) 'Essay for understanding', B2ᵛ-H2ᵛ (20-68) paraphrase text of Galatians, H3ʳ-Y4ᵛ (69-184) 1 Corinthians, Z1ʳ-2G4ᵛ (185-248) 2 Corinthians, 2H1ʳ-3D3ᵛ (249-406) Romans, 3D4ʳ-3N3ʳ (407-477) Ephesians (bottom 4/5 of page is advt. of books sold by Exshaw), 3N3ᵛ (*478*) proposal with conditions, for printing works of John Tillotson, 3N4ʳ,ᵛ (*479-480*) 'The Subscribers Names' (68 names, including 3 copies for James Coulter, bookseller in Londonderry).
Text (A7ᵛ): 46 lines; 165 (173) × 88 (102) mm; 71 R. Biblical text & notes 66 R. Marginal notes 67 ital. Good-quality laid paper, without watermarks. Page no. in external corners of headlines; chapter no. in internal (e.g. 'Chap. V.')
Caption title, for each paraphrase, e.g. [double rule 87 mm] | A | PARAPHRASE *and* NOTES | ON THE | Second EPISTLE of St. *PAUL* [swash U] | TO THE | *CORINTHIANS.* [swash T] | [rule 89 mm].
Headlines, e.g.: *GALATIANS.* [swash T]
CW: Page (to 'paraphrase' and to notes when carry over). B8ᵛ (e-) ven H1ᵛ (cru-) cified R4ʳ (drink-) ing 2C1ᵛ where- [wherewithal] 2R2ᵛ *i* [*i.e.*] 3B1ʳ (over-) ruling 3L3ʳ (accord-) ing CW for note only on 2B2ʳ (p.203): Τὴν
Press figures: xvi (A8ᵛ)-3 87 (K4ʳ)-3
Notes: Reprint of 3rd ed. (1733, no. 289), following its format, with 'paraphrase' text in external column of 55 mm wide, and Biblical text in internal column 30 mm wide; 'notes' across bottom of page. Since the same typesetting is used for no. 291, with the same press figures, I suspect this was printed in England, not Ireland. ESTC also reports two copies at the National Library in Dublin.
References: Attig 711; ESTC t175047.
Copy examined: O (Vet.A4 e.2667)

291. Paraphrases. 4th ed., 1742 (Beecroft). 8° in 4s
A | PARAPHRASE | . . . [&c. as in no. 289 until 15th line:] Conſulting St.
PAUL Himſelf. | [rule 86 mm] | The FOURTH EDITION. | [rule 86 mm] |
LONDON: | Printed for JOHN BEECROFT, at the *Bible*, over-againſt |
New Church in *Lumbard-ſtreet.* M,DCC,XLII.
Coll: 8° in 4s (202 × 120 mm cut) A⁸ (±A1) B-3N⁴ [$ half signed]; 240 leaves; pp. *i-iii* iv-xix 20-374 575 376-477 *478-480*. Page 375 misnumbered '575'.
Contents: same as no. 290, except bottom of p. 477 and p. *478-480* are blank.
Text (A7ᵛ) 46 lines; 165 (173) × 88 (102) mm; 71 R. Biblical text & notes 66 R. Poor-quality laid paper, with vertical chainlines, without watermark. Page no. at outer ends of headlines, with chapter numbers (e.g. 'Chap. VIII.') at inner margins.
Caption titles, e.g. [double rule 87 mm] | A | PARAPHRASE *and* NOTES | ON THE | Second EPISTLE of St. *PAUL* [swash U] | TO THE | CORINTHIANS. [swash T] | [rule 89 mm]
Headlines, e.g. '*GALATIANS.*', '*I CORINTHIANS.*' [swash Ts]
CW: Page. Identical with those in no. 290.
Press figures: xvi (A8ᵛ)-3 87 (K4ʳ)-3
Notes: A reissue, on larger paper, of sheets A-3M of no. 290, with a new setting of the title leaf and gathering 3N. I cannot determine if it was issued prior to or after no. 292, but probably before it, in view of the fact that Locke's name is here omitted from the title. Beecroft was later one of the many booksellers joining together to publish Locke's works.
References: Attig 712 n. (as another issue of no. 292, 'unverified'); ESTC n034317 (NjP as sole loc.)
Copy examined: NjP (Wit.5271.177; ex libris John Witherspoon; also inscribed on title: 'James Gourlay 1755')

292. Paraphrases. 4th ed., 1742. 4°.
A | PARAPHRASE | AND | NOTES | ON THE | EPISTLES of St. PAUL | TO THE |

	Galatians,	*Romans,* and
I & II }	*Corinthians,*	*Epheſians.*

To which is Prefix'd, An | ESSAY | FOR THE | Underſtanding of St. PAUL's EPISTLES, by | Conſulting St. PAUL Himſelf. | [rule 125 mm] | *By* JOHN [swash J] LOCKE *Eſq*; | [rule 125 mm] | The FOURTH EDITION. | [double rule 125/126 mm] | LONDON: | Printed for A. WARD, S. BIRT, T. OSBORN, C. HITCH, | J. OSWALD, A. MILLAR, J.HODGES, J. PEMBERTON, | F. GOSLING, and T. COOPER. MDCCXLII.

Coll: 4° (234 × 185 mm cut) A⁴ a⁴ b² B–3E⁴ 3F² [$ half signed]; 212 leaves; pp. *i–ii* iii–xx 1–400 402–404 401 [= 424]. Pages 401–403 called '402-4'; 404 called '401'.

Contents: Same as no. 289, including paraphrase to Ephesians, pp. 347–401 (*rectē* 404).

Text: 40 lines; 175 (196) × 126 (139) mm; 91 R. Biblical text & notes 64 R. Good-quality laid paper without watermark. Orn. tailpiece on p.346: dove in flight with sunrayed circle on sconce, above is bowl of flowers, 42 × 46 mm.

Caption title, e.g.: [double rule 126/125 mm] | A | PARAPHRASE *and* NOTES | ON THE | EPISTLE of St. *PAUL* | TO THE | *GALATIANS*. [swash T] | [rule 125 mm]

Headlines, e.g. I *CORINTHIANS*.

CW: Page. C2ᵛ (communi-) cates F3ᵛ (Con-) duct M1ᵛ Con- [Concerning] X3ʳ (Ear-) nest 2N3ᵛ (car-) nal 2U3ᵛ (self-con-) demned, 3B3ʳ Deli- [Deliverance]

Press figures: x(a1ᵛ)-I   xiii (a3ʳ)-I   179 (2A2ʳ)-I   189 (2B3ʳ)-I   191 (2B4ʳ)-I   197 (2C3ʳ)-I   199 (2C4ʳ)-I   204 (2D2ᵛ)-I   207 (2D4ʳ)-I   212 (2E2ᵛ)-3   214 (2E3ᵛ)-3   220 (2F2ᵛ)-2   222 (2F3ᵛ)-2   228 (2G2ᵛ)-I   230 (2G3ᵛ)-I   234 (2H1ᵛ)-3   240 (2H4ᵛ)-3   242 (2I1ᵛ)-I   248 (2I4ᵛ)-I   252 (2K2ᵛ)-4   255 (2K4ʳ)-4   263 (2L4ʳ)-4   264 (2L4ᵛ)-4   266 (2M1ᵛ)-4   276 (2N2ᵛ)-4   285 (2O3ʳ)-2   286 (2O3ᵛ)-2   293 (2P3ʳ)-3   295 (2P4ᵛ)-3   303 (2Q4ʳ)-3   304 (2Q4ᵛ)-3   310 (2R3ᵛ)-3   312 (2R4ᵛ)-4   314 (2S1ᵛ)-I   316 (2S2ᵛ)-I   325 (2T3ʳ)-I   327 (2T4ʳ)-I   332 (2U2ᵛ)-3   334 (2U3ᵛ)-3   342 (2X3ᵛ)-3   344 (2X4ᵛ)-3   348 (2Y2ᵛ)-3   350 (2Y3ᵛ)-3   356 (2Z2ᵛ)-2   362 (3A1ᵛ)-4   368 (3A4ᵛ)-4   370 (3B1ᵛ)-4   376 (3B4ᵛ)-4   381 (3C3ʳ)-4   382 (3C3ᵛ)-4   386 (3D1ᵛ)-3   388 (3D2ᵛ)-3   394 (3E1ᵛ)-I   397 (3E3ʳ)-I   '403' (3F1ᵛ)-2.

Note: No CW in Paraphrase to I Corinthians, and first part of 2 Corinthians.

Notes: A new typesetting, without textual changes, following no. 289. The first time the author's name appears on the title-page. A microfilm copy of this edition is in the collection, *The Eighteenth Century*, reel 2983, no. 3.

References: Attig 712; ESTC n019456.

Copies examined: O (Vet.A4 d.281; ex libris John Nourse)   CaOTU (Locke L63.P37 1742)   CtY (WD3148)

293. Paraphrases. 5th ed., 1751. 4°

A | PARAPHRASE | . . . [&c. as in no. 292, until:] The FIFTH EDITION. | [double rule 125 mm] | *LONDON:* | Printed for S. BIRT, J. WALTHOE, T. LONGMAN, T. OSBORN, | C. HITCH and L. HAWES J. OSWALD, A. MILLAR, J. HODGES, | J. and J. RIVINGTON, J. WARD, and M. COOPER. | [rule 20 mm] | MDCCLI.

Coll: 4° (237 × 186 mm cut) A⁴ a–b⁴ B–F⁴ H⁴ ²H⁴ I–3E⁴ [$ half signed]; 212 leaves; pp. *i–ii* iii–xx 1–48 94 50–169 158 171–192 195 194–404 [= 424]. Signature G omitted, H repeated. Page 49 called '94', 170 called '158', 193 called '195'.

Contents: A1ʳ (*i*) title (verso blank), A2ʳ–b2ᵛ (iii–xx) 'Essay for the Understanding', b3ʳ–F4ʳ (1–43) text of paraphrase of Galatians, F4ᵛ–U1ᵛ (44–150) 1 Corinthians, U2ʳ–2D1ᵛ (151–206) 2 Corinthians, 2D2ʳ–2X3ᵛ (207–346) Romans, 2X4ʳ–3E4ᵛ (347–404) Ephesians.

Text: 40 lines; 173 (197) × 126 (143) mm; 93 R; Biblical text & notes 66 R. Good-quality laid paper, without watermarks. Page no. at outer ends of headlines.

Caption title, e.g.: [double rule 129/128 mm] | A | PARAPHRASE *and* NOTES | ON THE | Firſt EPISTLE of St. *PAUL* | TO THE | *CORINTHIANS*. [swash T] | [rule 128 mm]

Headlines, e.g.: I *CORINTHIANS*.

CW: Page (to 'paraphrase' and to notes when carry over). B4ᵛ (communi-) cates G1ʳ (Con-) duct L3ᵛ Con- [Concerning] X1ʳ (Ear-) neſt 2N1ᵛ (car-) nal 2U1ᵛ (self-con-) demned, 3B1ʳ Deli- [Deliverance] 3C4ʳ I there- [I Therefore]

Press figures: vi (A3ᵛ)-2 viii (A4ᵛ)-2 xiv (a3ᵛ)-2 xvi (a4ᵛ)-3 1 (b1ʳ)-1 6 (B1ᵛ)-3 8 (B2ᵛ)-3 16 (C2ᵛ)-3 19 (C4ʳ)-3 22 (D1ᵛ)-3 24 (D2ᵛ)-1 30 (E1ᵛ)-1 36 (E4ᵛ)-1 44 (F4ᵛ)-1 46 (H1ᵛ)-1 48 (H2ᵛ)-1 57 (2H3ʳ)-1 59 (2H4ʳ)-1 62 (I1ᵛ)-1 68 (I4ᵛ)-1 70 (K1ᵛ)-1 76 (K4ᵛ)-1 78 (L1ᵛ)-1 80 (L2ᵛ)-3 91 (M4ʳ)-1 92 (M4ᵛ)-1 98 (N3ᵛ)-3 100 (N4ᵛ)-3 102 (O1ᵛ)-1 108 (O4ᵛ)-1 115 (P4ʳ)-1 116 (P4ᵛ)-1 120 (Q2ᵛ)-3 123 (Q4ᵛ)-3 131 (R4ʳ)-3 137 (S3ʳ)-3 138 (S3ᵛ)-3 144 (T2ᵛ)-3 146 (T3ᵛ)-3 154 (U3ᵛ)-3 156 (U4ᵛ)-3 160 (X2ᵛ)-3 162 (X3ᵛ)-1 166 (Y1ᵛ)-3 168 (Y2ᵛ)-3 178 (Z3ᵛ)-1 180 (Z4ᵛ)-1 182 (2A1ᵛ)-1 185 (2A3ʳ)-1 192 (2B2ᵛ)-3 194 (2B3ᵛ)-3 204 (2C4ᵛ)-3 209 (2D3ʳ)-1 211 (2D4ʳ)-1 216 (2E2ᵛ)-3 218 (2E3ᵛ)-1 226 (2F3ᵛ)-3 228 (2F4ᵛ)-3 232 (2G2ᵛ)-3 235 (2G4ʳ)-1 241 (2H3ʳ)-1 242 (2H3ᵛ)-3 254 (2K1ᵛ)-1 257 (2K3ʳ)-1 262 (2L1ᵛ)-1 272 (2M2ᵛ)-2 282 (2N3ᵛ)-3 284 (2N4ᵛ)-1 291 (2O4ʳ)-2 292 (2O4ᵛ)-2 296 (2P2ᵛ)-1 298 (2P3ᵛ)-1 306 (2Q3ᵛ)-2 308 (2Q4ᵛ)-inverted 2 315 (2R4ʳ)-1 316 (2R4ᵛ)-1 320 (2S2ᵛ)-3 322 (2S3ᵛ)-3 326 (2T1ᵛ)-1 328 (2T2ᵛ)-1 334 (2U1ᵛ)-2 336 (2U2ᵛ)-2 344 (2X2ᵛ)-3 347 (2X4ʳ)-1 350 (2Y1ᵛ)-3 356 (2Y4ᵛ)-3 358 (2Z1ᵛ)-3 364 (2Z4ᵛ)-3 369 (3A3ʳ)-3 371 (3A4ʳ)-3 374 (3B1ᵛ)-1 377 (3B3ʳ)-1 382 (3C1ᵛ)-1 384 (3C2ᵛ)-1 390 (3D1ᵛ)-3 396 (3D4ᵛ)-2 398 (3E1ᵛ)-2 400 (3E2ᵛ)-2. None in sheet 2I.

Notes: A new typesetting of no. 292. Sheets have been rearranged so first page of text commences on b3ʳ; p. 5 on B1ʳ. Subheading on p. 87 (M2ʳ) reads 'ARPAPHRASE.' A microfilm copy of this edition is in *The Eighteenth Century*, reel 3337 no.3.

Reference: Attig 713; ESTC t170482.

Copies examined: O (Vet. A5 d.711) MH-AH (572.6)

294. Paraphrases. 6th ed., 1763. 4°

A | PARAPHRASE | . . . [&c. as no. 292, until 13th line:] Underſtanding of St. PAUL'S EPISTLES, by conſulting | St. PAUL Himſelf. | [rule 129 mm] | By *JOHN* [swash J] *LOCKE*, Eſq; | [rule 128 mm] | THE SIXTH EDITION. | [double rule 128/127 mm] | *LONDON:* | Printed for A.

Millar, H. Woodfall, J. Whiston and B. White, J. Rivington | L. Davis and C. Reymers, R. Baldwin; Hawes, Clarke, and Collins; W. John- | ston, W. Owen, J. Richardson, S. Crowder, T. Longman, B. Law, C. Ri- | vington, E. Dilly, R. Withy, C. and R. Ware, S. Baker, T. Payne, A. Shuck- | burgh, and J. Hinxman. | MDCCLXIII.

Coll: 4° (248 × 185 mm cut) A⁴ a–b⁴ B–3E⁴ [$ half signed]; 212 leaves; pp. *i–ii* iii–xx 1–404 [=424].

Contents, *Text* and *Headlines*: same as no. 293. Good-quality laid paper with fleur-de-lys watermark. Page no. at outer ends of headlines. Page 346 has tailpiece, bird on lyre, similar to Woodfall 293, 23 × 37 mm.

Caption title, A2ʳ: [double rule 127 mm] | AN | ESSAY | For the Understanding | St. *Paul*'s Epinles, *&c.*

Headlines, from verso to recto A2ᵛ–b2ʳ: *An* Essay *for the Underſanding* | St. Paul's Epistles, *&c.* (b2ᵛ: *An* Essay *for the Underſanding*, &c.) For body of text, e.g. 'I *Corinthians*.

CW: Page. B4ᵛ (communi-) cates C2ᵛ from F1ᵛ (Mem-) bers F3ʳ SECT. G1ʳ SEC- [SECTION] H3ᵛ World I3ᵛ Con- [COncerning] R4ᵛ Law, X1ʳ (Ear-) neſt 2B4ᵛ Mini- [Miniſter] 2N1ᵛ (car-) nal 2U1ᵛ (ſelf-con-) demned, 3B1ʳ Deli- [Deliverance] 3C4ʳ I there- [I therefore]

Press figures: x (a1ᵛ)-2 1 (b3ʳ)-4 3 (b4ʳ)-4 9 (B3ᵛ)-1 32 (E2ᵛ)-4 38 (F1ᵛ)-5 66 (I3ᵛ)-4 84 (L4ᵛ)-5 86 (M1ᵛ)-4 113 (P3ʳ)-4 122 (Q3ᵛ)-4 146 (T3ᵛ)-5 178 (Z3ᵛ)-4 182 (2A1ᵛ)-4 192 (2B2ᵛ)-1 209 (2D3ʳ)-1 214 (2E1ᵛ)-5 243 (2H4ʳ)-5 252 (2I4ᵛ)-1 256 (2K2ᵛ)-5 298 (2P3ᵛ)-1 326 (2T1ᵛ)-inverted 4 337 (2U3ʳ)-4 345 (2X3ʳ)-4 347 (2X4ʳ)-4 353 (2Y3ʳ)-5 354 (2Y3ᵛ)-5 362 (2Z3ᵛ)-5 364 (2Z4ᵛ)-5 366 (3A1ᵛ)-4 369 (3A3ʳ)-4 374 (3B1ᵛ)-5 385 (3C3ʳ)-4 386 (3C3ᵛ)-4 390 (3D1ᵛ)-4 392 (3D2ᵛ)-4 401 (3E3ʳ)-4 402 (3E3ᵛ)-4

Notes: Line-for-line reprint of no. 293, but signature and pagination errors and subheading on p. 87 corrected.

References: Attig 714; ESTC t170483.

Copies examined: Y CaOTU (Locke L63.P37 1763) MH-AH O (Vet.A5 d.432)

295. Paraphrases. 1794. 8°

A | PARAPHRASE | AND | NOTES | ON THE | EPISTLES OF ST. PAUL | TO THE | GALATIANS, CORINTHIANS, | ROMANS AND EPHESIANS. | TO WHICH IS PREFIX'D AN | ESSAY | FOR THE | UNDERSTANDING OF ST. PAUL'S EPISTLES, | BY CONSULTING ST. PAUL HIMSELF. | [double rule 96 mm] | BY JOHN [swash J] LOCKE, ESQ. | [double rule 96 mm] | LONDON: | PRINTED FOR T. LONGMAN, B. LAW AND SON, J. JOHNSON, | C. DILLY, G. G. AND J. ROBINSON, T. CADELL, J. SEWELL, | W. OTRDIGE, [sic] W. RICHARDSON, F. AND C. RIVINGTON, | W. GOLDSMITH, T. PAYNE, LEIGH AND SOTHEBY, | S. HAYES, R. FAULDER, B. AND

J. WHITE, | W. LOWNDES, G. AND T. WILKIE, | AND J. WALKER. | [double rule 8 mm] | 1794.

Coll: 8° (224 × 130 mm cut) A^2 (-A1; ±A2) B-2F^8 2G^4 [$ half signed]; 229 leaves; pp. *I-II i-iii* iv-xxiii *xxiv* 25-26 27-72 73-74 75-181 *182-184* 185-216 21 218-243 *244-246* 247-385 *386-388* 389-449 *450-456* [=458]. First page in each gathering also signed 'VOL. VII.' in direction line.

Contents: A2^r (*I*) title (verso blank), B1^r (*i*) section title (verso blank), B2^r-C4^r (*iii*-xxiii) 'Essay for Understanding', C4^v blank, C5^r (*25*) section title to 'Galatians', C5^v note from publisher, C6^r-F4^v (*27-72*) text of 'Galatians', F5^r (*73*) section title to I Corinthians (verso blank), F6^r-N3^r (*75-181*) text of I Corinthians (verso blank), N4^r (*183*) section title to 2 Corinthians (verso blank), N5^r-R2^r (*185-243*) text of 2 Corinthians, R2^v blank, R3^r (*245*) section title to Romans (verso blank), R4^r-2C1^r (*247-385*) text of Romans, 2C1^v blank, 2C2^r (*387*) section title to Ephesians (verso blank), 2C3^r-2G1^r (*389-449*) text of Ephesians, 2G1^v-2G3^v (*450-454*) 'Index to the seventh volume', 2G4 blank.

Text: 41 lines; 171 (184) × 96 mm; 84 R. Biblical text & notes 66 R. Wove paper, without watermarks. Page no. at outer ends of headlines with chap. no. at inner margins, e.g. 'CHAP. IV.'

Section title, e.g., (p. 73): A | PARAPHRASE | AND | NOTES | ON THE | FIRST EPISTLE OF ST. PAUL | TO THE | CORINTHIANS.

Headlines, pp. iv-xxiii: PREFACE.

pp. 75-181, e.g.: I. CORINTHIANS.

CW: Page, to 'paraphrase' text (and to notes when carry over). B4^v (inde-)pendent D2^r (Ci-) licia G6^v (them-) ſelves I6^r Where- [Wherefore,] M7^v 46 How- [46 Howbeit,] Q6^r (over-) much T1^v obedi- [obedience] X2^v (ſer-)vants 2B4^r (pati-) ence, 2E6^v 11 Ac- [11 According]

Press figures: xii (B6^v)-inverted 5 xv (B8^r)-3 xx (C2^v)-8 31 (C8^r)-I 45 (D7^r)-9 50 (E1^v)-4 78 (F7^v)-9 94 (G7^v)-5 107 (H6^v)-5 125 (I7^r)-horizontal I 127 (I8^r)-4 143 (K8^r)-I 153 (L5^r)-2 174 (M7^v)-4 180 (N2^v)-7 190 (N7^v)-6 194 (O1^v)-I 212 (P2^v)-8 214 (P3^v)-7 228 (Q2^v)-inverted 3 242 (R1^v)-7 262 (S3^v)-5 282 (T5^v)-4 303 (U8^r)-7 317 (X7^r)-6 318 (X7^v)-8 334 (Y7^v)-9 345 (Z5^v)-8 368 (2A8^v)-9 384 (2B8^v)-6 399 (2C8^r)-5 400 (2C8^v)-I [very small] 409 (2D5^v)-2 429 (2E7^r)-4 430 (3E7^v)-8 438 (2F3^v)-2 440 (2F4^v)-9 450 (2G1^v)-5. Figs. on inner and outer formes of sheets C I N P X and 2E.

Notes: A re-issue, with cancellans title leaf, of vol. 7 of the 9th ed. of the *Works*, 1794 (no. 371; leaf A1 = title leaf for *Works* set). 'Text', 'Paraphrase' and 'Notes' in sections each across width of the page. The press figures for this separate edition and that issued as part of the *Works* edition are the same. A microfilm copy of the *Works* edition printing, with its title leaves, is included in *The Eighteenth Century*, reel 1042 no. 1.

References: Attig 715; ESTC t180974.

Copies examined: O (Vet.A5 e.3724; without figs on pp.413-4) MH-AH (572.6) Om

296*. Paraphrase. Romans. Dutch trans. Amsterdam, 1768. 4°
"[Locke (J)] over den brief van Paulus aan de Romeinen / 1768, Amsterdam / A. van der Kroe, 4. 1 [florin] 6 [stuivers]".

Citation from Abkoude, p. 320, for a Dutch translation of Locke's *Paraphrase and Notes on the Epistle to the Romans*, published in quarto. No library is reported to own this in the union catalogue of Dutch libraries at the Royal Library in the Hague, nor have I found a record of it elsewhere.

297. Paraphrases. German trans. (Hofmann). Frankfurt a.M., 1768–69. 2 vols. in-4°.
Collective title: Johann Locks | Paraphrastische Erklärung | und | Anmerkungen | über | S. Pauli Briefe | an die | Galater Korinther Römer und Epheser | Zwei Bände | aus dem Englischen übersetzt | und mit Anmerkungen zur Erläuterung Beurtheilung und Widerlegung | versehen | von | D. Johann Georg Hofmann | der Theologie ausserordentl. der orientalischen Sprachen ordentl. Lehrer zu Giessen | [orn., 2 angels holding shield with letter 'A' within, 37 × 38 mm] | [rule 125 mm] | Frankfurt am Mayn | in der Andreäischen Buchhandlung 1769
Vol. 1: Johann Locks | Paraphrastische Erklärung | und | Anmerkungen | über | S. Pauli Briefe | an | die Galater, Korinther, Römer und Epheser. | Erster Band, | worinnen enthalten sind | der Brief Pauli an die Galater und die beyden an die Korinther, | nebst vorgesetztem Versuche | wie nach S. Pauli eigener Anleitung zum Verstand der paulinischen Briefe | zu gelangen sey. | Aus dem Englischen übersetzt | und mit Anmerkungen zur Erläuterung, Beurtheilung, und Widerlegung, | versehen | von D. Johann Georg Hofmann, | der Theologie ausserordentlichem, der orientalischen Sprachen ordentlichem Lehrer | zu Giessen. | Nebst einer Vorrede | von | Johann David Michaelis. | [rule 127 mm] | Frankfurt am Mayn, | in der Andreäischen Buchhandlung, 1768.
Vol. 2, as vol. 1 until 9th line:] Zweeter Band, | worinnen enthalten sind | die Briefe Pauli an die Römer, und Epheser. | Aus dem Englischen übersetzt | ... [&c. as in vol. 1 until 19th line:] Nebst einer Vorrede | den genauen historischen Verstand der Briefe Pauli, | und der heiligen Schrift überhaupt betreffend. | [rule 125 mm] | Frankfurt am Mayn, | in der Andreäischen Buchhandlung, 1769.
Coll: 4° (230 × 174 mm). Vol. 1: π1 a–c⁴ A–2Y⁴ [$3 (–2Y3) signed]; 193 leaves; pp. *i–ii I–III* IV–XII [*I*] [II]–[XII] 1 2–360 [= 386].
Vol. 2: a–c⁴ d² A–3M⁴ [$3 (–d2) signed]; 246 leaves; pp. *I–III* IV–XXVIII 1 2–464 [= 492].
Contents. Vol. 1: π1ʳ collective title (verso blank), a1ʳ (*I*) title (verso blank), a2ʳ–b2ᵛ (*III–XII*) 'Vorrede' (signed 'Göttingen, den 19. Martii 1768. Johann David Michaelis'), b3ʳ–c4ᵛ ([I]–[XII]) 'Vorrede des Uebersetzers', A1ʳ–C4ᵛ (*1–24*) 'Versuch, wie S. Pauli eigener Anleitung zum Verstande der paulinischen Briefe zu gelangen sey' (text of 'Essay for Understanding St. Paul'), D1ʳ–N1ᵛ (25–98) text of paraphrase of Galatians, N2ʳ–2L4ᵛ (99–272) of I Corinthians, 2M1ʳ–2Y4ᵛ (273–360 top 4/5 of page) of 2

Corinthians, 2Y4ᵛ (360 bottom fifth) 'Verbesserungen' (errata, 7 items in 2 cols. of 5 lines each).

Vol. 2: a1ʳ (*I*) title (verso blank), a2ʳ-d2ᵛ (*III-XXVIII*) 'Vorrede von der Briefe Pauli genauem historischem Verstande.', A1ʳ-2T4ᵛ (*1-336*) text of paraphrase of Romans, 2U1ʳ-3M4ᵛ (*337-464*) of Ephesians.

Text (v.1 D3ᵛ): 41 lines; 171 (182) × 122 mm; 83 fraktur. Biblical text & notes 71 fraktur. Display types (as in title-pages and section headings) not ligatured. Fair-quality laid paper, without watermarks. Page layout has biblical text in narrow column at inner edge (approx. 40 mm wide), headed 'Text'; paraphrase at outer margin headed 'Paraphrastische Erklärung' (approx. 76 mm wide); and notes across bottom of page, in mixed fonts 71 fraktur, with bolder type for emphasis.

Orn. headpieces in vol. 1: a2ʳ (scenic view with scrolls, 42 × 99 mm); b3ʳ (scenic view with seated lions, 33 × 85 mm); A1ʳ (standing cupid with leaves, rectangular, 43 × 122 mm). Tailpieces on C4ᵛ (cupid with bows near pedestal, 30 × 35 mm); 2Y4ᵛ (shell & leaves, 18 × 32 mm). Vol. 2 has headpieces on a2ʳ (spreading swan with leaves, 42 × 117 mm); A1ʳ (dolphin with peacock against scenic background, 33 × 115 mm); tailpieces on 2L4ᵛ (flying cupid with book and scrolls, 47 × 88 mm) and 2T4ᵛ (bird as fountain, with leaves, 31 × 41 mm).

Section title, e.g. D1ʳ: [orn. rule, leaves coiled about a rod, 5 × 67 mm] | Paraphraſtiſche Erklärung | und | Anmerkungen | über | die Epiſtel S. Pauli an die Galater | welche | im Jahre Chriſti, 57, und im 3ten Jahre der Regierung des Kaiſers Nero | zu Epheſus geſchrieben worden. | [orn. rule 3 × 111 mm]

Headlines, e.g.: 'Cap. XVI. Epiſtel an die Römer.', that is, chap. no. at inner margins, and page no. at outer ends.

CW: Page, to each part of text (paraphrase, Biblical text and notes). Paraphrase CW. Vol. 1: A3ʳ Er = [Erkenntniß] J1ᵛ 28. Hie P4ᵛ ge = [gehen:] X1ʳ 13. unge = [13. ungeacht] 2S1ᵛ (ge =) ſchrieben: 2R2ʳ angeneh = [angenehmen] 2Y1ᵛ Ohren = [Ohrenbläſereyen,]

Vol. 2: A1ʳ (die =) ſem E3ᵛ Iſrae = [Iſraeliten] O4ᵛ 18. Dero = [18. Derohalben] Y1ʳ Verder = [Verderbens] 2B2ᵛ 5. Denn, 2K4ᵛ (aufgenom =) men, 2X3ᵛ 4. nach = [4. nachdem] 3G1ʳ (Geheim =) niß

Note: The presswork for this German translation of the 'Paraphrases' by Johann George Hofmann is rather elegant, with numerous head- and tailpieces. Attig reports it was reprinted in 1773. I have found no such exemplars, nor is it listed in the GV (*Gesamtverzeichnis*, 1700-1910). Dr. Marie-Luise Spieckermann, of the English Seminar at the University of Münster, informs me that none with that imprint is listed in German libraries.

References: Attig 721; Christophersen p. 76

Copy examined: O (Vet.D5.e.563) [Berlin] Mun (4. Exeg. 464ᵐ; lacks collective title)

298. 'Memoirs relating to the Life of Anthony first Earl of Shaftesbury'. French trans. in *Bibliothèque choisie*, 1705.

Caption title: ARTICLE III. | *Mémoires pour servir à la Vie* d'AN- | TOINE ASHLEY, *Comte de Shaftes-* | *bury, & Grand Chancellier d'An-* | *gleterre, sous Charles* II.
IN: *Bibliothèque choisie*, 7 (1705): 146–191.
Notes: The first appearance of this memoir, published as a sequel to the 'Eloge de feu Mr. Locke' which appeared in vol. 6 (1705; no. C1705-5) of the same journal. It includes Le Clerc's one and one-half page introductory note and a similar endnote. The MS of the original English text is now in the Bodleian Library's Lovelace Collection, MS. Locke b. 4, ff. 109 et seq. It was first published in Locke's *Posthumous Works* of 1706 (no. 299).
References: Attig 782; Christophersen p. 73.
Copies examined: Y O

299. Posthumous Works. 1706. 8°
Within a double rule, inner 146 × 83 mm, outer 154 × 91 mm: POSTHUMOUS | WORKS | OF | Mr. *JOHN LOCKE:* [swash J] | VIZ. |
   I. Of the Conduct of the Underſtanding.
   II. An Examination of *P. Malebranche*'s Opi- | nion of *Seeing all things in God.*
   III. A Difcourſe [*sic*] of Miracles.
   IV. Part of a Fourth Letter for Toleration.
   V. Memoirs relating to the Life of *Anthony* | firſt Earl of *Shaftſbury.* |
To which is added, | VI. His New Method of a Common-Place- | Book, written originally in *French*, and | now tranſlated into *Engliſh.* | [rule 80 mm] | *LONDON,* | Printed by W. B. for A. and *J. Churchill* [swash J] at the | *Black Swan* in *Pater-Noſter-Row.* 1706.
Coll: 8° (190 × 120 mm cut) A^2 B–O^8 P^8 (±P8) Q–Y^8 [$ half signed]; 170 leaves; pp. *i–iv 1-2* 3-137 *138-140* 141-213 *214-216* 217-231 *232-234* 235-277 *278-280* 281-310 *311* 312-336 [= 340].
Contents: A1^r (*i*) title (verso blank), A2^{r,v} (*iii–iv*) 'Advertisement to the Reader.' ending with 5-line errata, B1^r (*1*) section title (verso blank), B2^r–K5^r (3-137) text of 'Conduct' (in §§ 43), K5^v blank, K6^r (*139*) section title (verso blank), K7^r–P3^r (141-213) text of 'Examination of Malebranche', P3^v blank, P4^r (*215*) section title (verso blank), P5^r–Q4^r (217-231) text of 'Discourse of Miracles', Q4^v blank, Q5^r (*233*) section title (verso blank), Q6^r–T3^r (235-277) text of 'Part of a' 4th letter on toleration, T3^v blank, T4^r (*279*) section title (verso blank), T5^r–X3^v (281-307) text of 'Memoirs' on Shaftesbury, X4^r (*311*) section title for 'New Method', X4^v–X5^r (*312-313*) diagram for an index, X5^v–Y8^v (314-336) text of 'New Method of a Common-Place-Book.
Illustration: the two facing pages *312-3* are each divided by rules into 2 columns vertically (each 39 mm wide), including a short inner column at left for capital letters, the first column for letters A B C D E, 2d for F G H I L, 3d for M N O P R, and 4th for S T U X Z and Q (same as in no. 266).

Each letter's area is further subdivided by horizontal red lines for the first occurring vowels (a e i o and u), to follow the inital capital letter, except Q has only one line, u, as part of vowels assigned to Z. As examples Locke has also entered page numbers: '4' under A | e, '18.24' under C | o, '2.14' under E | i, and '16.20' under H | a.

Text (B6ᵛ): 31 lines; 148 (158) × 78 (91) mm; 93 R. Good-quality laid paper, with letters BS over L in a circle as watermark. Topical headings or references in ital. in external margins. Page no. at external ends of headlines. Leaf P8 (pp. 223-4) is a cancellans, possibly from an accident at the press. (I have found no copies with original leaf.)

Section title, p.1: [rule 91 mm] | OF THE | CONDUCT | OF THE | UNDERSTANDING. | [rule 91 mm] | *Quid tam temerarium tamque indignum ſapientis gravitate atque* | *conſtantiâ, quam aut falſum ſentire, aut quod non ſatis explorate perceptum* | *ſit & cognitum ſine ullâ dubitatione defendere?* Cic. de Naturâ Deorum, | lib. I.

(Translation: What is so ill-considered or so unworthy of the dignity of a philosopher as either to hold an opinion that is not true or to maintain with unhesitating certainty a proposition not based on adequate examination, comprehension and knowledge, without any doubting?)

p. *139*: [rule 91 mm] | AN | EXAMINATION | OF | P. MALEBRANCHE's | OPINION | OF | *Seeing all things in GOD.* | [rule 91 mm]

p. *215*: [rule 91 mm] | A DISCOURSE | OF | MIRACLES. | [rule 91 mm]

p. *233*: [broken rule 91 mm] | Part of a | FOURTH LETTER | FOR | TOLERATION, *&c.* | [rule 89 mm]

p. *279*: [rule 91 mm] | MEMOIRS | Relating to the LIFE of | ANTHONY | Firſt EARL of | SHAFTSBURY. | To which are added, | Three Letters writ by the E. of SHAFTSBURY | while Priſoner in the Tower; one to | King CHARLES II. another to the Duke of | YORK, and a third to a noble Lord; found | with Mr. LOCKE's MEMOIRS, *&c.* | [rule 91 mm] (Note: 7th line in Oo copy reads: 'To which is added,'.)

p. *311*: [rule 92 mm] | A NEW | METHOD | OF A | Common-Place-Book. | [rule 90 mm] | Tranſlated out of *French* from the Second | Volume of the *Bibliotheque Univerſelle.* | [rule 90 mm]

RT (from verso to recto): pp.4-137: *Of the* CONDUCT *of* | *the* UNDERSTANDING.

pp. 142-213: *An* EXAMINATION *of* | *P.* MALEBRANCHE's *Opinion*, &c.

pp. 219-231: *A* DISCOURSE | *of* MIRACLES.

pp. 236-277: *A Fourth* LETTER | *for* TOLERATION, *&c.* [pp. 245 & 277 have a period preceding '*&c.*'

Headlines, pp. 282-307: MEMOIRS.

pp. 309-10: LETTERS.

RT, pp. 312-335: *A New* METHOD *of* | *a* COMMON-PLACE-BOOK.

CW: Page. B3ᵛ § 3. Be- [§ 3. Beſides] C5ʳ parti- [Particulars,] E2ʳ them [them.] E6ʳ § 17. This [§ 19. This *rectē*] H6ᵛ § 36. The [§ 35. This *rectē*] H8ᵛ a Mat- [a matter] N1ᵛ (Mo-) difica- [difications] P8ᵛ So Q4ʳ J. LOCKE. [Part *rectē*] R3ᵛ them, [them] S8ʳ (Magi-) ſtrates [ſtrate's] X6ʳ vende [4. I take (CW part of text)]

Press figures: none.

Notes: As detailed in the Introduction to this chapter, this collection was put together by Peter King following Locke's letter of 4 Oct. 1704 (*Corr.* 3647; viii.412-17). The 'Fourth Letter' for toleration is incomplete, and lacks two 'lost or mislaid' pages of the manuscript; another draft of that missing material later turned up in the Lovelace papers and is included by Peter King, the 7th Baron King, in his *Life of John Locke* (1829; no. 328).

The text was printed by William Bowyer; see *Bowyer Ledgers*, D704.

The translation from the French into the English of 'A New Method of a Common-place-book' is anonymously done. Its first, French appearance was in the *Bibliothèque universelle* in 1686 (no. 266). The original Latin and English manuscript sent to Nicolas Toinard is now British Library MS. Add. 28728, fols. 54–63.

The 'Conduct' was written as part of "some additions to my book [the *Essay*], against the next edition, and within these few days have fallen upon a subject that I know not how far it will lead me . . . but the matter, the farther I go, opens the more upon me, and I cannot yet get sight of any end of it. The title of the chapter will be Of the Conduct of the Understanding, which, if I shall pursue, as far as I imagine it will reach, and as it deserves, will, I conclude, make the largest chapter of my Essay." (*Corr.* 2243, vi. 87: letter to William Molyneux, dated 10 April 1697.) Locke did not complete his revisions or incorporate it in the *Essay*. In this collection is its first published appearance.

The 'Conduct' proved especially popular and was separately reprinted at least nine times before 1800, and translated as well into Dutch, German, and Italian, and with other material into French.

The 'Memoirs' of the first Earl of Shaftesbury first appeared in French in the *Bibliothèque choisie* in 1705 (no. 298).

These 'posthumous' materials are included in all *Works* editions (Chap. XI).

This vol. was reviewed in the *Acta eruditorum* for 1708. Abstracts appear in the *History of the Works of the Learned*, 8 no. 6 (June 1706): 366-76. The review in the *Bibliothèque choisie*, 12 (1707): 123-70, contains an extensive summary of the 'Conduct' (pp. 123-56) and of the 'Discourse of Miracles' (pp. 156-69). It follows a review of the fifth edition of the *Essay* (pp. 80-123).

From the *Notebook of Thomas Bennet and Henry Clements (1686-1719)* edited by Norma Hodgson and Cyprian Blagden (p. 159) we learn that this work was published in Trinity Term 1706, and on July 3rd, 510 copies were pooled, for which two shillings were paid, and sold to the trade for 3 s. 4 d.

A microfilm copy of this work is in the collection, *The Eighteenth Century*, reel 3300, no. 4.

References: Attig 724; Christophersen p. 12, 31, 71; ESTC t148785.
Copies examined: Y   C   C (Keynes)   CaOHM (shelf B0396)   CaOTU (Locke L63.A105 1706)   Ck (Keynes A13.8))   CLaslett   DFo (acc.140203)   [GOT]   DLC (B1255.1706)   L (2 cops.)   MH   NjP (Ex.6106.1706)   NjR (X B1253.B3Po)   O (Godw.Subt.302)   Ob (525.a.8)   Oo (2T.d.4)   PPL (Ia Lock/Log365.O)   PU (B1255 1706) ViU (B1253.1706)

300. Conduct. (London?) 1741. 12° in 6s
SOME | THOUGHTS | On the CONDUCT of the | UNDERSTANDING | In the Search of TRUTH. | [rule 75 mm] | PARTICULARLY, Of |

Parts, Reaſoning,	Partiality, Haſte,
Practice, Habits,	Anticipation,
Ideas, Principles,	Reſignation, Practice,
Mathematicks,	Words, Wandering,
Religion, Ideas,	Diſtinctions, Similies,
Prejudices, Indifferency,	Aſſent, Indifferency,
Examination,	Perſeverance,
Obſervation, Biaſs,	Preſumption,
Arguments, Haſte,	Deſpondency,
Deſultory, Smattering,	Analogy, Aſſociation,
Univerſality, Reading,	Fallacies,
Intermediate Principles,	Fundamental Verities,
Partiality, Theology,	Transferring of Thoughts.

[rule 75 mm] | By *JOHN LOCKE* [swash J] Eſq; | [rule 76 mm] | *Quid* [swash Q] *tam temerarium tamque indignum ſapientis gravitate* | *atque conſtantiâ quam aut falſum ſentire, aut quod non* | *ſatis explorate perceptum ſit & cognitum ſine ûlla dubita-* | *tione defendere?* Cic. de Natura Deorum, lib. I. | [double rule 77 mm] | Printed in the YEAR M DCC XLI.

Coll: 12° in 6s (162 × 98 mm cut) π^2 A–I^6 K^6 (– K3.4 = π^2) [$ half signed]; 60 leaves; pp. *i–iv* 1–2 *3–115* 116 [= 120].

Contents: π1–π2^r blank, π2^v (*iv*) 'Advertisement to the Reader', A1^r (*1*) title (verso blank), A2^r–K4^r (*3–115*) text, K4^v blank.

Text (C3^r): 34 lines; 139 (146) × 77 mm; 82 R. Later pages (e.g. G3^r): 35 lines, 143 (151) × 77 mm. Prefatory 'advertisement' set 23 lines ital. Good-quality laid paper with horizontal chainlines, and fleur-de-lys watermark (Heawood 1547). Page no. within parentheses at head of page as headlines.

CW: Page. A5^v never- [nevertheleſs] B6^v at- [attaining] E6^r diſtin- [diſtinguiſh] H5^r nearer [nearer,] E5^v has text on line with CW.

Press figures: none.

Notes: First separate issue of the 'Conduct', reprinted from the *Posthumous Works* and undoubtedly not authorised. The booksellers' label in the

Bodleian Library copy (bought from Falkner, Greirson, Dublin) suggests Belfast as the place of printing, ESTC 'London', and Attig suggests Glasgow. Princeton University Library attributes the publication to the Foulis brothers in Glasgow. The double-column list of topics on the title is taken from the marginal headings printed in *Posthumous Works*.
References: Attig 726; ESTC n023702.
Copies examined: O (Vet. A4 f.827) CLaslett NjP (6106.332.121) PPH (D1812) PPL (3630.D Mackenzie)

301. Conduct. Glasgow, 1754. 12° in 6s.
SOME | THOUGHTS | On the CONDUCT Of the | UNDERSTANDING | In the ſearch of TRUTH. | By *JOHN LOCKE* [swash J] Eſq; | *Quid tam temerarium tamque indignum ſapientis gravitate* | *atque conſtantia, quam aut falſum ſentire, aut quod non* | *ſatis explorate perceptum ſit, et cognitum, ſine ulla dubita-* | *tione defendere?* Cic. de natura deorum, lib. I. | GLASGOW: | Printed by R. URIE, MDCCLIV.
Coll: 12° in 6s (156 × 93 mm) A-P⁶ [$ half signed]; 90 leaves; pp. *1-2* 3-178 *179-180*.
Contents: A1ʳ (*1*) title (verso blank), A2ʳ-P5ᵛ (3-178) text, P6ʳ,ᵛ (*179-180*) contents of 45 numbered sections (by page no.).
Text (E2ᵛ): 25 lines; 122 (133) × 63 mm; 97 R with 1 mm leading between. Good-quality laid paper without watermark. Horizontal chainlines. Page no. in outer ends of headlines.
RT, from verso to recto: *Of the* CONDUCT | *of the* UNDERSTANDING.
CW: none.
Note: Reprint of 1741 edition. A microfilm copy of this edition is in the collection, *The Eighteenth Century*, reel 2807, no. 8.
References: Attig 727; Christophersen p.71; ESTC t100210.
Copies examined: Y L¹ (1509/603) L² (1509/1374) O (265.k.104; P6 bound after A1)

302. Conduct. 1762. 12° in 6s.
SOME | THOUGHTS | On the CONDUCT of the | UNDERSTANDING | In the ſearch of TRUTH. | By *JOHN LOCKE*, Eſq; | *Quid . . . gravitate at-* | *que . . . ſatis ex-* | *plorate . . . defen-* | *dere?* Cic. de natura deorum, lib. I. | LONDON, | Printed and Sold by all the Bookſellers. 1762.
Coll: 12° in 6s (163 × 93 mm closely cut) A-P⁶ [$ half signed]; 90 leaves; pp. *1-2* 3-178 *179-180*.
Contents: A1ʳ (*1*) title (verso blank), A2ʳ-P5ᵛ (3-178) text, P6ʳ,ᵛ (*179-80*) contents of 45 §§.
Illustration: front. is poor quality portrait of Locke by T. Phinn after Kneller.
Text (B1ᵛ): 25 lines 137 (149) × 64 (79) mm; 109 R with 2 mm leading between lines. Fair laid paper without watermarks. Page no. at outer ends

of headlines. Full line space between sections, which are numbered in roman, with topical marginal headings in roman.
RT, from verso to recto: *Of the* CONDUCT | of the UNDERSTANDING.
CW: none.
Press figures: none.
Note: Standard reprint, possibly a piracy, in view of the imprint statement. Phinn's portrait of Locke is usually found in Scottish editions, suggesting a Scottish origin for this printing (cf. no. 75, 182, etc.).
References: Attig 728; Christophersen p.71; ESTC t147107.
Copies examined: L (8463.bb.l8 (2)) CaOHM (B1756; lacks port.) NjP (6106.333.122)

303. Conduct. Glasgow, 1763. 12° in 8s.
SOME | THOUGHTS | ON THE | CONDUCT | OF THE | UNDERSTANDING | IN THE | SEARCH OF TRUTH. | *By* JOHN [swash J] LOCKE, E*f*q; | *Quid tam . . . gravi- | tate atque . . . aut | quod non . . . cognitum, | sine . . . defendere?* CIC. de natura deorum, lib. I. | GLASGOW: | PRINTED FOR THE BOOKSELLERS. | MDCCLXIII.
Coll: 12° in 8s (143 × 83 mm cut) A^8 C–M^8 N^4 [$ half (–A3) signed]; 92 leaves; pp. *1-2* 3–159 *190* 161–183 *184*. Page 160 called '190'.
Contents: A1^r (*1*) title (verso blank), A2^r–N4^r (*3–183*) text, N4^v (*184*) contents by section and page no.
Text (B1^v): 25 lines; 117 (128) × 70 mm; 93 R. Fair-quality paper, with horizontal chainlines, without watermarks. Page no. in outer corners of running titles.
RT, from verso to recto: OF THE CONDUCT | OF THE UNDERSTANDING.
CW: Page. A7^v with- [within] C7^r per- [permitted] F4^r multi- [multiplying] H3^v know- [knowledge,] K2^v (co-) lours, M3^v expe- [experiment]
Note: Standard reprint. A microfilm copy of the British Library's copy is in the collection, *The Eighteenth Century*, reel 508, no. 9.
References: Attig 729; Christophersen p.71; ESTC t108837.
Copies examined: O (Vet.A5.f.2411 (1)) DLC (B1270 1763) L (8409.a.31)

304. Conduct. Cambridge, 1781. 8°. With: Gilbert's *Abstract*. Two issues.
THE | CONDUCT | OF THE | UNDERSTANDING. | BY | JOHN LOCKE, [swash J] ESQ. | TO WHICH IS ADDED, AN | ABSTRACT | OF | Mr. LOCKE's ESSAY | ON | HUMAN UNDERSTANDING. | CAMBRIDGE, | Printed by J. ARCHDEACON Printer to the UNIVERSITY; | For J. NICHOLSON, Book*f*eller, in Cambridge, | and *f*old by T. & J. MERRILL; J. C. & F. RIV- | INGTON, S. CROWDER, H. GARDNER, and S. HAYES, in London; | and W. NICHOLSON, | Wi*f*beach. | MDCCLXXXI.

Coll: 8°. First issue 172 × 112 mm cut; second, large paper issue 240 × 150 mm uncut; a⁴ B–T⁸ U⁴ [$ half signed; a2 signed 'a']; 152 leaves; pp. *i–viii* 1 2–238 *239–241* 242–292 *1* 2–4 [= 304].

Contents: a1ʳ (*i*) title (verso blank), a2ʳ–a4ʳ (*iii–vii*) 'SUBSCRIBERS.', a4ᵛ (*viii*) contents of 'Conduct', B1ʳ–Q7ᵛ (*1–238*) text of 'Conduct', Q8ʳ (*239*) section title (verso blank), R1ʳ–U2ᵛ (*241–292*) Gilbert's 'Abstract' of the Essay, U3ʳ–U4ʳ (*1–3*) advt. of books sold by Nicholson in Cambridge, U4ᵛ (*4*) advt. for his circulating library.

Text (N3ʳ): 22 lines (pp.242–292: 23 lines); 113 (129) × 67 mm; 103 R. Good-quality laid paper with watermark similar to Heawood 1829 or 1837, initials LVG. Large-paper issue on heavy laid paper without watermark. Page no. in outer corners of headlines. Line space between each paragraph.

HT, B1ʳ: [orn. quadruple rule 7 × 64 mm] | THE | CONDUCT | OF THE | UNDERSTANDING. | [orn. rule 3 × 63 mm]

R1ʳ: [orn. rule 7 × 64 mm] | AN | ABSTRACT | OF | MR. LOCKE's ESSAY, &c.

Section title, Q8ʳ: [orn. rule 8 × 65 mm] | AN | ABSTRACT | OF | MR. LOCKE's ESSAY | ON | HUMAN UNDERSTANDING. | [orn. rule inverted 8 × 65 mm]

RT, from verso to recto, pp.2–237: 'THE CONDUCT OF | THE UNDERSTANDING.', with section titles on second, following line, e.g. 'IDEAS.'

pp.242–291: AN ABSTRACT OF | MR. LOCKE'S ESSAY, &c.

CW: Page. B6ᵛ re- [relations.] E1ᵛ argu- [argument] F2ʳ hood- [hoodwinks] I5ᵛ (com-) mon L4ʳ in- [indeed] N7ᵛ (ap-) ply Q4ʳ (an-) other [other;] R8ᵛ vege- [vegetables] T8ᵛ Ift. Ori- [Ift. Original]

Press figures (1 mm high). 11 (B6ʳ)-a   32 (C8ᵛ)-i   48 (D8ᵛ)-a   58 (E5ᵛ)-u   66 (F1ᵛ)-u   82 (G1ᵛ)-a   98 (H1ᵛ)-u   126 (I7ᵛ)-i   134 (K3ᵛ)-a   159 (L8ʳ)-i   162 (M1ᵛ)-u   186 (N5ᵛ)-a   206 (O7ᵛ)-i   224 (P8ᵛ)-u   234 (Q5ᵛ)-a   251 (R6ʳ)-a   266 (S5ᵛ)-u   285 (T7ʳ)-a

Large-paper issues I have seen lack figure on p. 251.

Note: The two issues are distinguished by paper size, but are from the same typesetting. The 'Abstract' is that made by Baron Gilbert (see no. 147 et seq.). A microfilm copy of this edition is in the collection, *The Eighteenth Century,* reel 317, no. 13.

References: Attig 730; Christophersen p.71; ESTC t109720.

Copies examined. Usual issue: CLU-C   Ct   DFo (acc.174990)   L (8464.aa.26)   MH (*Phil.2115.50.10)   O (Buchanan e.113)

Large paper issue: Y (lacks U4)   C (Cam.c.781; uncut)   CaOTU (Locke L63.C65 1781)

305. Conduct. Dublin, 1782. 12° in 6s.
THE | CONDUCT | OF THE | UNDERSTANDING. | [orn. rule 26 mm] | BY | JOHN LOCKE. [swash J] | [French rule 39 mm] |

DUBLIN: | Printed for W. WILSON, No. 6, DAME-STREET, | [rule 17 mm] | M D CC LXXXII.
Coll: 12° in 6s (173 × 104 mm cut) A^2 B–K^6 L^2 [$ half signed]; 58 leaves; pp. *i–iv* 1 2–111 *112* [= 116].
Contents: A1^r (*i*) title (verso blank), A2^r (*iii*) publisher's advt. for 'this cheap EDITION', A2^v (*iv*) contents of sections in order of appearance (not numbered), B1^r–L2^r (*1–111*) text with 43 sections numbered internally in roman, L2^v blank.
Text (E5^v): 36 lines; 132 (143) × 73 mm; 73 R. Fair-quality laid paper, without watermarks. Page no. in outer corners of RTs. Line space between each paragraph.
HT: [orn. double rule 73 mm] | THE | CONDUCT | OF THE | UNDERSTANDING. | [orn. rule 38 mm]
RT, from verso to recto: 'THE CONDUCT OF | THE UNDERSTAND-ING.' A second headline immediately beneath RT gives topic of numbered section, e.g. 'INTERMEDIATE PRINCIPLES.'
CW: none.
Note: A standard reprint.
References: Attig 731; ESTC t162332.
Copies examined: Y   C (Hib.7.782.42)   O (Vet.A5 e.4087)

306. Conduct. 'New' ed., 1794. 12° in 6s
THE | CONDUCT | OF THE | UNDERSTANDING. | [French rule 23 mm] | BY JOHN LOCKE, ESQ. [swash J, Q] | [Oxford rule 49 mm] | A NEW EDITION, | DIVIDED UNDER HEADS. | DEDICATED | TO THE RIGHT HON. | EARL SPENCER. | [French rule 17 mm] | LONDON: | PRINTED FOR DANIEL ELZEVIR, JUN. [swash J] | M.DCC.XCIV.
Coll: 12° in 6s (136 × 84 mm cut) a^6 b^2 A–P^6 Q–R^4 [$ half signed]; 106 leaves; pp. *i–v* vi–vii *viii* ix–xv *xvi* 1–4 *5* 6–130 13 132–195 *196* [= 212]. Page no. 131 has lost its last digit.
Contents: a1^r (*i*) half-title (verso blank), a2^r (*iii*) title (verso blank), a3^r–a4^r (*v–vii*) dedication by 'The Editor.', a4^v blank, a5^r–b2^r (ix–xv) contents of 45 sections, b2^v blank, A1^r–R4^r (*1–195*) text, R4^v blank.
Text (D3^r): 24 lines; 94 (103) × 51 mm; 79 R with 1 mm leading. Wove paper without watermarks. Page no. in outer corners of headlines.
Half-title: THE | CONDUCT | OF THE | UNDERSTANDING. | [French rule 17 mm] | (Price Three Shillings ſewed.)
RT, from verso to recto: OF THE CONDUCT OF | THE UNDERSTANDING.
CW: Page. a3^v in- [intended] A2^r opera- [operative] C4^v (be-) fore E5^r deter- [determine;] G6^v I anſwer [I anſwer,] K6^r mean- [meaning] O1^v a mat- [a matter] P6^v (whe-) ther Q6^v (im-) pertinent
Press figures: none.

Note: According to John Stephens, "a Scottish piracy: a typical witty use of a false imprint." Standard reprint. A microfilm of the British Library's copy is in the collection, *The Eighteenth Century*, reel 3263, no. 6.
References: Attig 732; ESTC t162333.
Copies examined: C (7180 e.33) L (8475.a.36) O (Vet.A5 f.1924)

307. Conduct. 'New' ed., 1800. 16mo in 8s.
THE | CONDUCT | OF THE | UNDERSTANDING. | [French rule 14 mm] | BY JOHN LOCKE, ESQ. | [rule 13 mm] | For a man to underſtand fully the buſineſs of his par- | ticular calling, and of his religion, is uſually enough | to take up his whole time. See SECT. XIX. | [rule 13 mm] | A NEW EDITION. | *DIVIDED UNDER HEADS.* | DEDICATED | TO THE RIGHT HON. | EARL SPENCER. | [double rule 45 mm] | LONDON: | *Printed by W. Blackader, 10, Took's Court, Chancery Lane,* | For E. JEFFERY, 11, PALL-MALL. | 1800.
Coll: 16° in 8s (140 × 76 mm uncut) a^8 (–a8) B–K^8 L^2 [$ half signed; a2-3 both signed 'a3']; 81 leaves; pp. *I–V* VI–VIII IX X–XIV *1* 2–145 *146–148* [= 162].
Contents: a1^r (*I*) half title (verso blank), 'a3^r' [i.e. a2^r] (*III*) title (verso blank), a3^r–a4^v (*V–VIII*) dedication to Spencer, 'First Lord of the Admirality', a5^r–a7^v (*IX–XIV*) contents of 45 sections, B1^r–L1^r (*1–145*) text, L1^v–L2 blank.
Illustration: front. is port. after Kneller, oval-shaped, 'Le Coeur Sculp.', the whole subscribed '*John Locke Esq*'. | Publiſh'd Jany 1800.'
Text: 24 lines; 69 (76) × 46 mm; 55 R with 1 mm leading between lines. Fair laid paper without watermarks. Page no. centered at head of page (without headlines).
HT: [double rule 44 mm] | THE | CONDUCT | OF THE | UNDERSTANDING. | [double rule 45 mm]
CW and press figures: none.
Notes: Textually a reprint of no. 306. A minature edition (for the pocket?). Attig records the bookseller's name as 'Jeffrey': a variant issue or misprint? A microfilm copy of this edition is in the collection, *The Eighteenth Century*, reel 3263, no. 7.
References: Attig 733; Christophersen p.71; ESTC t108833.
Copies examined: O (Vet.A5 g.130; lacks leaf a1) L (8410.aa.8; uncut)

308*. Conduct. Dutch trans. (anon.) 1766.
"Korte inhoud van een werk genaamt, Wysgeerige proeven; aangaande het mensche lyk verstand. Antwerpen, W. Jugla, 1766. (-IV-).140. 51 × 105."

The above citation, with a shelfmark: 'vak 14 No 220' is from a slip in the Centrale Catalogus Boeken, kept in the Royal Library at the Hague. The copy recorded had belonged to a Catholic library, there abbreviated as 'O.F.M. 37'. Since the record was made, the library has been dispersed, and the books divided between the University of Tilburg, the University of Nijmegen, and the

Stadsbibliotheek Maastricht. None of these three libraries now reports owning the book. Nor are copies to be found in the Bibliothèque Royale Albert 1ᵉʳ in Brussels, the library at the University of Ghent, or the Stadsbibliotheek in Antwerp. I have found no other record of this edition, nor any other libraries in Belgium or the Netherlands (through their union catalogue) reporting it.

309. Conduct. German trans. (Kypke). Koenigsberg, 1755. 8°. With: Miracles.

Johann Lodens | Anleitung | des | menschlichen | Verstandes [ornamental V] | zur | Erkäntniß der Wahrheit | nebst desselben | Abhandlung | von den | Wunderwerken. | aus dem Englischen übersetzt | von | George David Kypke. | der Weltweisheit und der morgenländischen | Sprachen Professore. | [rule 86 mm] | Königsberg, | bey Johann Heinrich Hartung. 1755.

Coll: 8° (177 × 114 mm cut))(⁸ A–L⁸ a⁸ [$ 5 (–)(2; –a1) signed; L3 and 5 both signed 'L3']; 104 leaves; pp. *i–xvi 1* 2–165 196 167–173 175–176 176 *1–3* 4–16 [= 208]. Page 166 called '196'; 174–5 called 175–6.

Contents:)(1ʳ (*i*) title (verso blank),)(2ʳ (*iii*) ornamental page of dedication to Jacob Friedrich, Freyherr von Bielefeld (verso blank),)(3ʳ–)(4ᵛ (*v–viii*) translator's dedicatory letter dated '20 Merz 1755',)(5ʳ–)(8ᵛ (*ix–xvi*) 'Vorrede', A1ʳ–L8ᵛ (*1–176*) trans. of 'Conduct' in 103 §§, a1ʳ (*1*) section title (verso blank), a2ʳ–8ᵛ (*3–16*) trans. of 'Miracles' (signed at end 'Joh. Locke.').

Text (B3ʳ) 30 lines; 143 (154) × 77 (91) mm; 95 fraktur. Marginal notes set in smaller fraktur. Poor-quality laid paper with torch-like watermark. Page no. at external ends of headlines. Headpieces on)(5ʳ (shell-like scroll, 26 × 78 mm) and a2ʳ (vase with leafy scrolls, 30 × 86 mm).

Section title, a1ʳ: Eine | Abhandlung | von den | Wunderwerken. [orn. W]

RT, from verso to recto: Von der Leitung | des Verstandes. | [broken rule, 76 mm]

pp.4–16 at end: Eine Abhandlung | von dem Wunderwerken. | [broken rule, 76mm]

CW: Page. a3ʳ Wun = [Wunderwerke] A7ʳ (ge =) wiß C2ʳ (fa =) gen; E4ʳ (Ge =) walt G2ᵛ (Nachden =) ten J4ᵛ (Erfor =) schung

Notes: H. R. Fox Bourne, in his *Life of John Locke* (ii.441 n.2; no. 330) confused this translation of the 'Conduct' with the first German translation of the *Essay* (no. 108): the Latin translation of the *Essay* "was reprinted at Leipsig in 1709 . . . The first German translation appeared at Königsberg in 1755." The titles were similar, the *Essay*'s translation is entitled *Versuch vom menschlichen Verstande* (1757). This translation of the 'Conduct' includes a translation of the 'Discourse of Miracles', also taken from the *Posthumous Works*.

References: Attig 768; Christophersen p. 72.

Copies examined: O (Vet.A5.e.4835) [Berlin] [Berlin (Potsd.)] Thoemmes (in stock 1990)

310. Conduct. Italian trans. (Soave). Milan, 1776. 8°
GUIDA | DELL' | [hollow type:] INTELLETTO | NELLA RICERCA | DELLA VERITA' | OPERA POSTUMA | [garlanded hollow type:] DI GIO. LOCKE | Tradotta, e commentata | DA FRANCESCO SOAVE C. R. S. | *Prof. di Filoſ. Mor. nel R. Ginnaſio di Brera.* | [orn.: open book, quill & leaves 15 × 49 mm] | IN MILANO. | [Oxford rule 77 mm] | Per GAETANO MOTTA. | *Con Licenza de' Superiori.* | MDCCLXXVI.
Coll: 8° (182 × 115 mm cut) A–M⁸ N¹⁰ (N4 + 2 leaves) [$ half (–A3) signed]; 106 leaves; pp. *i–viii* 1–200 *201–204* [= 212].
Contents: A1ʳ (*i*) half-title (verso blank), A2ʳ (*iii*) title (verso blank), A3ʳ (*v*) dedication to Carlo, 'Conte e Signore di Firmian', (17 lines), A3ᵛ blank, A4ʳ,ᵛ (*vii–viii*) dedicatory letter signed F. Soave, A5ʳ–N1ʳ (1–185) text in 39 articles, N1ᵛ–N8ᵛ (186–200) 'APPENDICE', N9ʳ–N10ʳ (*201–203*) contents of 39 articles and 'Appendice', N10ᵛ blank.
Text (G4ʳ): 28 lines; 128 (138) × 77 mm; 92 R. Good-quality laid paper without watermark. Footnotes and appendix set 86 R with 1 mm leading.
Half title: same as lines 1–3 of title.
Caption title, p. 186: APPENDICE. | DEL METODO | *Che dee tenerſi per trovare la verità,* | *e per inſegnarla ad altrui.*
Headlines, on verso pages, pp. 2–184: 'GUIDA DELL'INTELL.' Recto pages show article no., e.g. ARTICOLO VI.
  Versos, pp. 188–200: APPENDICE. Rectos, pp.187–199: SUL MET. ANAL. E SINT.
CW: none.
Notes: This is the first appearance of Locke's 'Conduct' in Italian. It appeared in 1790 and in 1794 as the third vol. to Soave's translation of Wynne's abridgement of the *Essay* (no. 145–6), called 'SECONDA' and 'TERZE EDIZIONE VENETA.' It was also reprinted in 1801 and 1807.
Reference: Attig 772.
Copy examined: O (Vet.F5 e.133)

311. Conduct. Abstract. In: Miscellaneous Tracts (ed. Simm), 1753.
Caption title: Of the Conduct of the Underſtanding in the | Search of Truth. | Containing the Subſtance of the moſt material Things | Writ by Mr *Locke* on that Subject. | Compendized by *Alexander Simm*, M.A. ſome time | Maſter of the Grammar-ſchool of *Bathgate.*
In: MISCELLANEOUS TRACTS; | OR, | SELECT PASSAGES, HISTORICAL, | CHRONOLOGICAL, MORAL, *&c.* | Extracted from eminent Authors, ancient and | modern. | CONTAINING | An Abſtract of Mr *Locke*'s Conduct of the Under- | ſtanding. | *For the Benefit of younger Scholars.* | By Mr *ALEXANDER SIMM*, late School- | maſter at *Bathgate.* | *Quædam breviare permittitur.* Quintil. | EDINBURGH: | Printed by WILLIAM GRAY, and ſold at his | Printing-houſe at *Magdalen's Chapel*, in the *Cow-* | *gate*; and by the Bookſellers in Town and Country. | MDCCLIII.

Collation of the whole: 8° in 4s (161 × 100 mm cut) a^4 b^2 A–2N^4 2O^2 [$ half signed]; 152 leaves; pp. *i–iv* v–vii *viii* ix–xii *1* 2–291 *292* [= 304].
Locke's text on pp. 125–146 line 8 (Q3^r–T1^v). Another work begins on 9th line of p. 146.
Contents of the whole: a1^r (*i*) title (verso blank), a2^r (*iii*) dedication, a2^v–a4^r (*iv*–vii) preface, a4^v–b2^v (*viii*–xii) contents, A1^r–O2^r (*1*–291) texts, O2^v blank.
Text (Q3^v): 38 lines (144) × 75 mm; 72 R. Poor-quality laid paper without watermarks. No headlines; page no. within parentheses centered at head of page.
CW: Page. Q4^v (Be-) nefit R3^v (Mul-) titude, S3^r (Con-) fiftency.
Notes: The whole work is composed of brief summaries on various topics from many writers. A microfilm copy of this edition is in the collection, *The Eighteenth Century*, reel 2594, no. 12.
References: Attig 761; ESTC t119426.
Copies examined: O (3987 f.489)   L (1607/3922)

312. Discourse of Miracles. Glasgow, 1743. 12° in 6s. With: G. Burnet's *Treatise concerning the Truth* . . .
A SHORT | TREATISE | ON | MIRACLES. | [rule 61 mm] | By JOHN LOCKE [swash J] Efq; | [rule 60 mm] | JOHN III. 2. THOU art a Teacher come from | GOD, for no man can do thefe miracles, that | THOU doft, except GOD be with him. | [orn., fruit, 23 × 31 mm] | [rule 59 mm] | Printed, M.DCC.XLIII.
Issued with: A | TREATISE | Concerning the TRUTH of the | CHRISTIAN RELIGION. | [rule 60 mm] | By GILBERT BURNET D.D. [swash Ds] | Sometime Profeffor of Divinity in the Univerfity | of *Glafgow*, afterwards Bifhop of *Sarum*. | [rule 61 mm] | To which is added, A DISCOURSE on | MIRACLES, by JOHN [swash J] LOCKE Efq; | [rule 60 mm] | GLASGOW, | Printed by ROBERT FOULIS and fold by him | there, and at *Edinburgh* by Meff. G. HA- | MILTON and J. BALFOUR. MDCCXLIII.
Collation of the whole: 12° in 6s (157 × 101 mm uncut) π1 A–G^6 H^4 χ1 A^2 B^6 C^4 [$ half signed]; 60 leaves; pp. *i–ii* 1–91 *92 i–ii* 1–21 *22–24* [= 120].
Locke's text (sheets signed in ital.): χ1 (*i*) title (verso blank), A1^r–C3^r (1–21) text of 'Miracles', C3^v–4^v (*22–24*) advertisements for books sold by Foulis.
Text (B3^v): 26 lines; 108 (116) × 60 mm; 83 R. Medium quality paper, with fleur-de-lys watermark. Page no. at outer ends of headlines.
HT, A1^r: [double rule 60/59 mm] | A | TREATISE | OF | MIRACLES.
RT for Locke's text, from verso to recto: A TREATISE | *of* MIRACLES.
CW: Page. A1^r (pe-) tulant C1^v (Im-) poftors D3^v (ei-) ther A1^r (hifto-) ry B3^v (fupe-) rior C2^v Such
Notes: First published in the *Posthumous Works* (no. 299) this 'Discourse' was written "on occasion of Mr Fleetwoods book on that subject [*An Essay upon Miracles*, 1701] and an anonymous answer [by Benjamin Hoadley, *A*

Letter to Mr. Fleetwood, occasion'd by his late Essay on Miracles, 1702] published to it." (*Corr.* 3647; viii.413)

Gaskell states it was issued 28 February 1743, in 2 states: on crown paper priced at 1 s. sewed or 1/6d bound and titled; or on ordinary, poor small crown paper ("size of sheet 18 × 14 in.") at 6d sewed in blue paper or bound for 10d.

References: Attig 780; ESTC n024007; Gaskell 28.
Copies examined: DFo (acc. 159482, barely trimmed, detached, unbound; Burnet's work separately shelved, acc. 159471)   O (Godw. Pamph. 2707 (1*))

313. Discourses by Pierre Nicole, translated by Locke. 1712. 12°

Within a double rule, inner 121 × 60 mm, outer 129 × 66 mm: DISCOURSES | ON THE | *Being of a God,* | AND THE | Immortality of the SOUL; | OF THE | Weakneſs of Man; | And concerning the Way of | *Preſerving Peace* [swash v, 2d P swash] *with Men:* [swash M] | Being ſome of the ESSAYS | written in *French* by Meſſieurs | du PORT ROYAL. | [rule 57 mm] | Render'd into *Engliſh* by the late | JOHN LOCK, *Gent.* | [rule 57 mm] | LONDON: | Printed and Sold by *J.* [swash J] *Downing* in Bartho- | lomew-Cloſe near Weſt-Smithfield, 1712.

Coll: 12° (152 × 89 mm cut) A² B–L¹² M⁶ [$5 signed]; 128 leaves; pp. i–iv 1–252 [= 256].

Contents: A1ʳ (*i*) title (verso blank), A2ʳ (*iii–iv*) 'Advertisement.', B1ʳ–C1ᵛ (1–26) text of 'Discourse I, Containing in short the natural proof of the existence of a god and the immortality of the soul', C2ʳ–F3ᵛ (27–102) text of 'Discourse II, Of the weakness of man', F4ʳ–M6ᵛ (103–252) text of 'Discourse III, Concerning the way of preserving peace with men' (in two parts).

Text (B2ᵛ): 30 lines; 121 (130) × 63 mm; 80 R. Medium-quality paper without watermark. Page no. at outer ends of headlines.

RT, from verso to recto, e.g. '*Diſcourſe* II. | *Man's Weakneſſ.*'

CW: Page. B3ʳ ex- [extreamly] C12ʳ wil- [wilfully] E3ʳ form- [formed] G5ᵛ (o-) thers I1ʳ (min-) gle L8ʳ Ac- [Acknowledgments] M4ʳ (An-) ger

Press figures: none.

Notes: The unknown editor's 'advertisement' states Locke had "once intended to have rendred into *English* all the *Port Royal Essays*; but when he had Translated these, he was inform'd that they were done by another hand, so he desisted, and presented and dedicated what he had done in *Manuscript* to the late Countess of *Shaftsbury*; who transcrib'd them with her own Hand, and gave them to a Friend, as a Token of the great Esteem she had for her. From this *Copy* it is that they are now *printed*, but the Countess's great Humility would not suffer her to transcribe the *Dedication*, which is the Reason why that is not publish'd with them. . . ." This edition did not come to light until 1979. The Bodleian Library's copy is the only one known.

Locke had run across Nicole's *Essais de morale* when visiting France in the 1670s and probably translated these essays in the autumn of 1676 (cf. *Corr.* i.xcviii). He owned several editions published 1671-79 (L.L. 2040, 2040a, 2040b). Locke's translation is rather free and impressionistic; some of Nicole's examples have been changed so as to quote more familiar English authors. The extreme accuracy of Lady Shaftesbury's transcription is shown by a comparison with Locke's original manuscript, now in the collection of the Pierpont Morgan Library, New York. Fuller information about this work is to be found in two articles by M. R. Ayers and me in the *Locke Newsletter*, 11 (1980); 101-3, 104-7.
References: Attig 784; E5TC t198758.
Copy examined: O (Vet. A4 f.1770)

314. Discourses by Pierre Nicole, translated by Locke. 1828. 12°
DISCOURSES: | TRANSLATED FROM NICOLE'S ESSAYS, | BY JOHN LOCKE, | WITH IMPORTANT VARIATIONS FROM THE | ORIGINAL FRENCH. | 1. ON THE EXISTENCE OF GOD. | 2. ON THE WEAKNESS OF MAN. | 3. ON THE WAY OF PRESERVING PEACE. | [rule 23 mm] | *Dedicated to the Countess of Shaftesbury.* | [rule 23 mm] | Now first printed from the Autograph of the Translator, | in the possession of | THOMAS HANCOCK, M.D. | [rule with diamond at center, 18 mm] | 𝕷𝖔𝖓𝖉𝖔𝖓: | PRINTED FOR HARVEY AND DARTON, | GRACECHURCH STREET. | [rule 7 mm] | 1828.
Colophon, p. 239: [rule 31 mm] | Harvey, Darton, and Co. Printers, | Gracechurch-street, London. | [rule 31 mm]
Binding, *Trade*: Boards covered in greyish beige paper with white-paper label: [Oxford rule] | "LOCKE'S | TRANSLATION | from | *Nicole's Essays* | [rule 6 mm] | Price 5 s. boards".
Coll: 12° (164 × 100 mm cut) A^{12} a^2 B–L^{12} [$ 1-2 and 5 (–a2) signed]; 134 leaves; pp. *i–iii* iv–xxi *xxii* xxiii–xxvii *xxviii* 1-239 *240* [= 268].
Contents: A1^r (*i*) title (verso blank), A2^r-11^r (*iii*–xxi) 'PREFACE BY THE EDITOR.' (signed 'Thomas Hancock. London, 1828.'), A11^v blank, A12^r–a2^r (*xxiii*–xxvii) Locke's dedication, a2^v blank, B1^r–L12^r (*1*–239) text, L12^v blank.
Illustration: mounted leaf following title reproduces the dedicatory heading and the final paragraph and signature of the dedication in a close imitation (by engraving) of Locke's handwriting.
Text (C7^r): 26 lines (some with 25 or 27); 117 (127) × 68 mm; 90 R (with 1.5 mm leading between lines). Good-quality wove paper, without watermarks. Page no. in outer corners of headlines. No catchwords.
RT, from verso to recto, e.g. 'FIRST DISCOURSE. | OF THE EXISTENCE OF A GOD.'
Notes: The notice in the *English Catalogue of Books* states it is a foolscap octavo, published in March 1828.

A transcription made from Locke's manuscript now in the Pierpont Morgan Library, New York, this edition differs little from the 1712 edition, although Hancock modernised the spelling and punctuation. He has included the dedicatory letter to the countess which prefaces the original manuscript; it is undated and it is not included in de Beer's edition of the *Correspondence*. Until the recent surfacing of the 1712 edition this was long thought to be the first and only edition.
References: Attig 785; Christophersen p. 79.
Copies examined: Y CaOTU (Locke N52.E88E5 1828) L (528.e.8) NjP (Ex.6135.672.331.79) O (28.63) Thoemmes (as of III.1995)

315. Remains. 1714. 2°
Within a double rule, inner 255 × 139 mm, outer 262 × 146 mm: THE | REMAINS | OF | *JOHN LOCKE* [swash J, K] Eſq; | VIZ. | I. Some MEMOIRS of the Life and Character | of Dr. EDWARD POCOCKE. | II. Inſtructions for the Conduct of a young | Gentleman, as to Religion and Government, *&c.* | III. The beſt Method of Studying, and Inter- | preting the Scriptures. | IV. Sentiments concerning the Society for Promo- | ting *Chriſtian Knowledg.* | [rule 136 mm] | *Publiſh'd* [swash P] *from his Original Manuſcripts.* | [rule 136 mm] | To which are added, | Three Copies of VERSES formerly Written. | [rule 135 mm] | [orn., bowl of flowers surrounded by leafy branches, 37 × 50 mm] | [rule 137 mm] | LONDON, | Printed for E. CURLL at the Dial and Bible againſt *St. Dunſtan's* | Church in *Fleetſtreet*. M.DCC.XIV. Price 1 s. | Where may be had, An Account of the Life and Writings of | JOHN LOCKE, *Eſq*; Price 1 s.
Coll: 2° (333 × 195 mm) A–F² [$1 (+ A2) signed]; 12 leaves; pp. *i–ii* iii–iv 1–20 [= 24].
Contents: A1ʳ (*ii*) title, A1ᵛ (*i*) note to Curll dated 'Exon, July 10. 1714', signed R.K. (Rev. Richard King), A2ʳ,ᵛ (iii–iv) preface, B1ʳ–E2ᵛ (1–16) 'FIVE LETTERS Written by' Locke, F1ʳ–F2ᵛ (17–20) Locke's verses (see *Notes* below).
Text (B1ᵛ): 44 lines; 252 (267) × 131 mm, 114 R. Pref. set 115 ital. Chainlines vertical on laid paper, without watermarks. Page no. at outer ends of headlines. Orn. on title is similar to Bowyer 128; repeated on C2ᵛ and E2ᵛ. Orn. of bird within shield beneath a lion head, 42 × 42 mm, on A2ᵛ and F2ᵛ. Pref. (A2ʳ) begins with a 4-line T very close to Bowyer 187T2.
Section title, p. 1: [orn. rectangle of repeated fleurons, 20 × 130 mm] | FIVE | LETTERS | Written by | *JOHN LOCKE* [swash J, K] Eſq; | [rule 131 mm]
Headlines are ital. summaries of page contents, sometimes mixed with small caps, e.g., pp.18–20: '*Verſes on ſeveral Occaſions.*'; '*Some Memoirs of the Life and Character | of* DR. EDWARD POCOCKE.'
CW: Page. B2ʳ innocent D2ᵛ LETTER F2ʳ *Nec*
Press figures: none.

Notes: The five letters by Locke are (1) one to Humfry Smith concerning Edward Pococke sent through Richard King (pp. 1-6; *Corr*. 3321; viii.37-42) dated 23 July 1703, in reply to Smith's request of 19 June (?) 1703 (*Corr*. 3303); (2) letter also dated 23 July, to King (p. 7, *Corr*. 3322); page 8 gives the inscription on Pococke's monument in the cathedral at Christ Church, Oxford; (3) pp. 9-12 print Locke's letter of 25 August 1703 (*Corr*. 3328; viii. 56-9) giving King 'Instructions for the Conduct of a Young Gentleman as to Religion and Government, &c.'; (4) pp. 13-14 has Locke's letter of 27 September 1703 (*Corr*. 3339; viii.69-70) headed 'The best method of Studying and Interpreting the Scriptures'; and (5) a letter to King dated 20 January 1703/4 (*Corr*. 2846; E. S. de Beer dates it 20 January 1701; see vii.225 n.). The verses on pp. 17-20 are the 'Pax regit Augusti . . .' (see no. 251), 'Crowns, Scepters, Thrones . . .' (from no. 255), and the introductory poem, 'Febriles, aetus, victumque . . .' for Sydenham's work (no. 256).

Curll's reputation was not high; Alexander Pope called him 'an emetic potion'. H.R. Plomer says he "was troubled by few scruples." The introductory note by R. K. (Richard King) offers Curll these five letters for publication. Curll was quick to seize upon the popularity of Locke at this time, and padded out his publication with the verses and the monument inscription for Pococke. The work was published July 22, 1714.

Bound with the Bodleian Library copy (O¹) is Locke's 'Last Will and Testament' detached from Curll's folio edition of Le Clerc's life of Locke, pp. 29-34 (see no. C1714-1).

The five letters are reprinted in Desmaizeaux's *Collection of Several Pieces* (1720; no. 316) and in *Works* editions, beginning with the 2nd (1722).

A copy of this work is in *The Eighteenth Century* microfilm set, reel 5637 no. 4.

References: Attig 810; Christophersen p. 8, 9, 77; ESTC t112897.
Copies examined: [Berlin] CaQMMO CLU-C CtY (in Folio Pamph.22) DFo (acc.181736) L (715.k.8 (1)) O¹ (Vet. A4.c.150 (3); with 'Last Will') O² (G. Pamph. 1680 (34))

316. Collection. (ed. Desmaizeaux) 1720. 8° Two issues.
316A. First issue: A | COLLECTION | OF SEVERAL | PIECES | OF | Mʳ. JOHN [swash J] LOCKE, | Never before printed, or not extant in | his Works. | *Publiſh'd by the Author of the* LIFE *of the ever-* | *memorable Mr*. John HALES, &c. | [vignette.: seated muse with cherubs in leafy round frame 51 × 67 mm] | LONDON: | Printed by J. [swash J] BETTENHAM for R. FRANCKLIN, | at the Sun in Fleetſtreet. M.DCC.XX. Pr. 5 s.

Coll: 8° (195 × 120 mm cut) A⁸ ᵖ2A⁸ ᵖ2B² a⁸ b⁴ c² (-c2 = E7 cancellans) B-D⁸ E⁸ (±E7) F-2B⁸ [$ half (-E4, L4, N1, R4) signed]; 223 leaves; pp. *I-XXXVI* i-xxiv *xxv-xxvi* 1-53 *54-56* 57-149 *150-152* 153-176 *177-178* 179-245 *246-248* 249-362 *363-384* [=446]. Some copies have 3 in signature 'E3' inverted.

316B. Second issue: Same as first issue, except title page vignette is winged angel, with books, on a cloud 38 × 62 mm on plate 46 × 65 mm.
 Coll: same as first issue except A^8 (± A1).
States: In all copies the dedication is dated and subscribed: "Your moſt obedient | and moſt humble Servant." In some copies the subscript is followed by 'P. DES MAIZEAUX.', regardless of issue (a stop-press addition), thus achieving a second state of sheet $^{\pi}$2B.
Contents: A1^a (I) title (verso blank), A2^r-$^{\pi}$2B2^r (III–XXXV) dedicatory pref. to 'HUGH WROTTESLEY ESQUIRE' dated 'March 23, 1719-20.', $^{\pi}$2B2^v blank, a1^r–a2^r anon. letter (dated Feb. 4, 1720) to the compiler enclosing translation of Coste's 'Eloge' dated Feb. 4, 1720, a2^v–b4^v (iv–xxiv) 'The Character of Mr. Locke' by Pierre Coste (trans. from *Nouvelles de la republique des lettres*, Feb. 1705), c1^{r,v} (*xxv–xxvi*) contents of vol., B1^r–E3^r (1–53) 'The Fundamental Constitutions of Carolina', E3^v blank, E4^r (*55*) section title (verso blank), E5^r–L3^r (57–149) 'A Letter from a Person of Quality', L3^v blank, L4^r (*151*) section title (verso blank), L5^r–M8^v (153–176) 'Remarks upon Some of Mr. Norris's Books', N1^r (*177*) section title (verso blank), N2^r–Q3^v (179–230) 'Elements of Natural Philosophy', Q4^r–R3^r (231–245) 'Some Thoughts concerning Reading and Study for a Gentleman', R3^v blank, R4^r (*247*) section title (verso blank), R5^r–2A3^r (249–357) letters to Collins, Oldenburg, Lady Calverley, Richard King, &c., 2A3^v–5^v (358–362) 'Rules of a Society', 2A4^r–6^v (*363–380*) alphabetical index, 2B7^r (*381*) errata (9½-line paragraph), 2B7^v–8^v (*382–384*) advt. of 12 books printed for and sold by R. Francklin.
Illustration: leaf facing p. 187 (N6^r) has engraving, 'The Solar System.' giving a diagram of the orbits of planets and of a comet, on a plate 159 × 102 mm.
Text (B6^v): 31 lines; 146 (158) × 78 (89) mm; 107 R with 1.5 mm leading. Pref. set 22 lines, 130 R with leading; pp. v–xxiv set 30 lines, 96 R. Good-quality laid paper without watermarks. Many pages have marginal topics in italics. Page no. at external end of headlines.
Ornaments: Most of the various items making up this collection have framed headpieces, and tailpieces. Headpieces are on (a) p. *xxv*: framed bowl of flowers a perched bird on each side (similar to Bowyer 36), 21 × 77 mm, repeated on pp. 153 & 358; (b) p. 1: framed perched bird between seated angels, 27 × 69 mm; (c) pp. 57 & 249: 2 rows of small fleurons, the lower inverted, 17 × 77 mm; (d) p. 179: framed Aldus-like anchor on shell, 20 × 77 mm; (e) p. 231: framed headpiece, turk's head on oval frame, between cherubs, 21 × 76 mm; and (f) p. 363: double orn. rule, similar to that on p. 57, 17 x77 mm. Tailpieces are on (1) pp. xxiv: bowl of flowers 29 × 34 mm (similar to Bowyer 185); (2) *xxvi*: hearts aflame above a pedestal 37 × 39 mm; (3) p. 149: bird perched on a shield, cornucopia on each side, 39 × 52 mm; (4) p. 230: dove on a branch (similar to Bowyer 182), 53 × 61 mm; (5) p. 245: inverted-triangle ornament, with birds & leaves, 24 × 46 mm; (6) p. 251: a cupid atop a sconce, 36 × 55 mm; and (7)

p. *380*: open book within a frame, 26 × 44 mm. Most parts begin with 3- or 4-line factotum initials. Both title vignettes signed 'C. *Gardner Sculp.*'

Section title, p.*55*: A | LETTER | FROM A | PERSON of QUALITY, | TO HIS | FRIEND in the COUNTRY. | GIVING | An Account of the Debates and | Refolutions of the Houfe of LORDS, | in April and May, 1675, concerning a | Bill, entitled, *An Act to prevent the* | *Dangers* [swash D] *which may arife from Perfons* [swash P] | *difaffected to the Government.*

p. *151*: REMARKS | Upon fome of | MR. NORRIS's | BOOKS, | Wherein he afferts | F. MALEBRANCHE's | OPINION | OF | *Our feeing all things in God.*

p. *177*: ELEMENTS | OF | NATURAL | PHILOSOPHY.

p. *247*: SEVERAL | LETTERS | TO | ANTH. COLLINS Efq; | and | Other Perfons.

Headlines, from verso to recto, in roman caps. to match content, e.g. 'THE LAWS OF | CAROLINA.', 'REMARKS UPON | M^R. NORRIS'S BOOKS, &c.'

CW: Page. $^\pi$2A1^v what- [whatever] c1^v THE FUN- [THE FUNDAMENTAL] C4^r (Opi-) nions G5^v "Where- ["Whereas] I6^v (ta-) ken, O5^v com- [commonly] Q7^v (an-) cient S8^v (a-) way U4^r re- [reform'd] Z1^v How- [However,] 2B3^v Per- [*Perfius*]

No CW on $^\pi$2B2^r, b4^v, Q3^v, or section title pages.

Press figures: IV (A2^v)-I   XIV (A7^v)-I   *xxvi* (c1^v)-I   369 (2B1^r)-I

Notes: This collection was put together from ms. papers in the hands of Anthony Collins, Samuel Bold, and others, with the help of Locke's nephew Peter King. Cancellans leaf E7 (pp. 61–62) was conjugate with leaf c2 (pp. *xxv–xxvi*) shown by a copy in the Bodleian Library (Vet.A4 e.781) where both cancellandum and cancellans are present. The variation is a change in the footnote on p. 62: in both the first sentence refers to an act for public prayers on the feast of St. Bartholomew (dated 19 May 1662). In the cancellandum, the second & final sentence reads: "As to the number of Ministers *thrown out* by that Act, see Dr. Calamy's *Preface* to the second edition of his *Account of the Ministers, Lecturers, Masters and Fellows of Colleges, and School-masters who were ejected or silenced after the Restoration in 1660; by, or before the Act for Uniformity*, &c." The second sentence of the footnote in the cancellans reads: "And it is certain, that *the Common-Prayer-Book with the Alterations and Amendments . . . . made by the Convocation, did not come out of the Press till a few days before the 24th of August.* See Dr. CALAMY's *Abridgment of Mr.* BAXTER's *History of his Life and Times*, ubi supra, p. 201."

'The Fundamental Constitutions of Carolina' ('sealed 1 March 1670') is now thought to be chiefly the work of Anthony Ashley Cooper, the first Earl of Shaftesbury, though Locke may have helped draft it while a member of his household (see Chap. XII, no. D8). It had been in circulation since the early 1670s, and is listed in Wing^2 with a query, under Locke as L2743A and

L2744 (1682 reprint). Further information can be found in Peter Laslett's editions of the *Two Treatises of Government* (1960, 1971), pp. 29-30. An extensive review of Locke's part in its composition is J. R. Milton's recent article, "John Locke and the Fundamental Constitutions of Carolina" in *The Locke Newsletter*, 21 (1990): 111-33. He questions whether much of the manuscript (PRO 30/24/47/3) is truly in Locke's hand, and posits an initial publication date of 1672.

'A Letter from a Person of Quality, to His Friend in the Country', first published in 1675, is also thought to be Shaftesbury's work despite Desmaizeaux's statement here that Locke wrote it under Shaftesbury's 'inspection' or dictation. "Desmaizeaux gives no authority for his statement; there is no stylistic or external evidence to substantiate it" (E.S. de Beer, *Corr.* ii. 664 n.3; see no. D9). In a letter to Thomas Herbert, Earl of Pembroke, dated 28 November 1684, Locke emphatically stated "I here solemnly protest in the presence of god, that I am not the author, not only of any libell, but not of any pamphlet or treatise whatsoever in print good bad or indifferent", the exception being some verses published with his name on them (*Corr.* 797; ii. 664). The 'Letter' is listed in Wing^2 under Shaftesbury's name as S2879.

The 'Remarks' on John Norris, or a draft of them written in 1693, is in the Bodleian Library, Lovelace Collection (MS. Locke d.3, pp. 89-109) headed 'Some other loose thoughts [on] some of Mr Norris's writings . . .' An earlier draft answer to Norris's 'Cursory Reflections upon a Book Called, An Essay . . .' (appended to Norris's *Christian Blessedness*; no. C1690-2) and headed 'JL to Mr Norris' (now MS Locke c. 28, ff. 107^r-122^v) was published by Richard Acworth in *The Locke Newsletter*, 2 (1971): 7-11.

The 'Elements of Natural Philosophy' is supposed to have been written at Oates, shortly after Locke took up residence there, for the benefit of 'young Frank' Masham (cf. Fox Bourne, ii.449). In § 194 of the *Education* Locke had counselled that a young gentleman ought to acquaint himself with some of the systems of natural philosophy (physics). J. Axtell^3 suggests that Locke used material in the first four (of seven) chapters supplied by his friend Isaac Newton. We do not have a manuscript copy, it was presumably part of his inheritance from Locke dispersed by 'young Frank'.

'Some Thoughts on Reading and Study' is printed from the British Library MS. Sloane 4290, fols. 11-14. Headed 'Mr Locke's Extempore Advice &c.', the ms. is in Samuel Bold's scraggly hand, recorded from Locke's dictation. Transcriptions of the manuscript are to be found in Axtell's *The Educational Writings of John Locke* (1968) and in the Clarendon Edition of *Some Thoughts concerning Education* (1989).

The 'Several Letters' here are chiefly those to Anthony Collins, with the first four (out of five) letters to Richard King and Humphry Smith (Smith's on the character of Edward Pococke) already printed in the *Remains* (no. 315, q.v.).

---

[3] Axtell, J. L., 'Locke, Newton, and the Elements of Natural Philosophy', *Paedagogica Europaea*, 1 (1965): 235-45.

The first letter is that sent to Oldenburg, with its letter of transmittal, published in the *Philosophical Transactions* of the Royal Society in 1675, but written by Richard Lilburne (see no. 258). The letters to Collins are in chronological sequence, interrupted in October 1703 to include a copy of an undated letter to Lady Calverley; E. S. de Beer gives early May 1689 (?) as the date (*Corr.*, 1133; iii. 613-5). Locke's letters to Collins, with some omissions, are those printed in full as no. 3278 (*Corr.* vii. 776) and as no. 3293 et seq. in *Corr.* viii, excluding no. 3387, 3530, 3573A, 3619 and 3640. Collins's letters to Locke are not included.

The materials printed in *The Remains* (no. 315) but omitting the poems are included here, together with the 'Rules of a Society' which I judge to be 'the printed Paper (Richard King) sent me . . . for the Support and Enlargement of Religion'. I do not think they are Locke's work, but were found with his papers (see *Corr.* 2846, to King, dated 20 January 1703/4 [i.e. 1701]; vii.225).

In sum, only the 'Remarks' on Norris, the 'Elements', 'Some Thoughts on Reading and Study' and the 'Several Letters' can truly be said to be Locke's. However, all the pieces in this collection are reprinted in *Works* editions, beginning with the 5th (1751; no. 367).[4]

A microfilm copy of the first issue of this edition is in the collection, *The Eighteenth Century*, reel 2085, no. 6.

References: Attig 787; Christophersen pp. 9, 10, 78; ESTC t117306.
Notice: *Bibliothèque ancienne et moderne* 13 (1720): 444-59.
Copies examined:
First issue: C (N.3.70)   CaOHM (B6193)   CaOTU¹ (Locke L63A105 1720a)   CLU-C   DFo (B1255.A2; without fig. on p.369)   DLC (B1255.A5 1720)   MH (TP2115.25*)   NjR (X B1253.B3Co; dedic. not signed)   NNPM (W22.G)   O¹ (Vet.A4 e.781; dedic. not signed)   Ob (525.a.7)   PPL¹ (Am1720Loc/Aa720.L63)   PPL² (Am1720 Loc/330.O; gift of Benj. Franklin)   PU (B1255.A5 1720)   ViU¹ (B1255.A5 1720a; dedic.not signed)   ViU² (B1255.A5 1720; lacks A2-7)   ViU³ (McGregor coll. *E172.L62; dedic. signed)   ViW
Second issue: Y (without figs. on pp.XIV and 369)   CaOTU² (Locke L63.A105 1730b; dedic. not signed)   CtY (K8.L79/a720; dedic. not signed)   L (1134.d.3; dedic. signed)   O² (12.i.1633; dedic. not signed)   PPL³ (Am1720/Af.422)

317. Collection. 2d ed., 1724. 8°
A | COLLECTION | OF SEVERAL | PIECES | OF | Mr. JOHN [swash J] LOCKE, | Never before printed, or not extant in his | WORKS. | [rule 79 mm] | *Publiſh'd by the Author of the* LIFE *of the ever* | *memorable Mr.* JOHN HALES, &c. | [rule 82 mm] | The SECOND

---

[4] Concerning 'The Fundamental Constitutions of Carolina' and 'A Letter from a Person of Quality', Laslett incorrectly states that "Both pieces are reprinted in collected Lockes from the 4th, 1740" (*op. cit.* p. 29 n. §).

EDITION. | [rule 80 mm] | [engr. vignette as on first issue of no. 316] | [rule 81 mm] | LONDON: | Printed for R. FRANCKLIN, under *Tom*'s [swash T] | Coffee-houſe *in Ruſſel Street Covent-Garden*. | MDCCXXIV. [*Price* 5 s.]

Collation, Contents and *Text*: same as no. 316, except A^8 ($\pm A1$): with cancellans title and E7 leaves. Same press figures. A re-issue of the sheets of no. 316. The only copy I have seen has the dedication unsigned.

References: Attig *787A; ESTC t188561.

Copy examined: O (Vet.A4 e.2262; lacks leaf A8)

318. Collection. '2d', [i.e. 3d] 1739. 2°

A | COLLECTION | OF | SEVERAL PIECES | OF | M^r. JOHN [swash J] LOCKE. | [rule 137 mm] | Publiſh'd by Mr. DESMAIZEAUX, under the Direction of | ANTHONY COLLINS, *Eſq;* | [rule 138 mm] | THE SECOND EDITION. | [rule 138 mm] | [orn. bowl of fruit in frame 47 × 52 mm] | [double rule 141/139 mm] | LONDON: | Printed for R. FRANCKLIN, in *Ruſſel-ſtreet, Covent-Garden*; 1739.

Coll: folio (375 × 237 mm uncut) A^2 B–$2M^2$ [$1 signed]; 70 leaves; pp. *I–X* i–x 1-2 3-16 17-18 19-44 45-46 47-54 55-56 57-78 79-80 81-118 119-120 [= 140].

Contents: A1^r (*I*) title (verso blank), A2^r–C1^v (*III–X*) dedication by Desmaizeaux to Hugh Wrottesley (signed '*March* 23, 1719. ... DES MAIZEAUX.'), C2^r–E2^v (i–x) 'The Character' of Locke by Coste, F1^r (*1*) section title (verso blank), F2^r–I2^v (3-16) constitutions of Carolina, K1^r (*17*) section title (verso blank), K2^r–Q2^v (19-44) 'Letter from a Person of Quality', R1^r (*45*) section title (verso blank), R2^r–T1^v (47-54) 'Remarks' on Norris, T2^r (*55*) section title (verso blank), U1^r–2A1^r (57-73) 'Elements', 2A1^v–2B1^v (74-78) 'Reading and Study', 2B2^r (*79*) section title (verso blank), 2C1^r–2L1^r (81-113) 'Several Letters' to Collins & others, 2L1^{r,v} (113 lower half–114) 'Rules of a society', 2L2^r–2M1^v (115-118) index, 2M2^r (*119*) 'Table of pieces contained in this collection.', 2M2^v blank.

Text: 55 lines; 257 (270) × 138 mm; 93 R. Medium-quality laid paper, with petalled flower as watermark. Index entries in itals., further information set in roman, 67 mm. Page no. at outer ends of headlines. Factotum initials at beginning of each section. The orn. on title-page is repeated as a tailpiece on E2^v, Q2^v, T1^v, and 2A1^r. Tailpiece of a face within a sunburst on a pedestal, between peacocks, 38 × 48 mm, on C2^v, 2B1^v and 2M2^r.

Section titles, F1^r: [headpiece, 6 lines of fleurons, 138 × 32 mm] | THE | FUNDAMENTAL CONSTITUTIONS | OF | CAROLINA.

K1^r: [rule 141 mm] | A | LETTER | FROM A | PERSON of QUALITY, | TO HIS | FRIEND in the COUNTRY. | GIVING | An Account of the Debates and Reſolutions in the Houſe of LORDS, in | April and May 1675, concerning a Bill, entitled, *An Act to prevent the* | *Dangers which may ariſe from Perſons diſaffected to the Government*. | [rule 140 mm]

R1^r: [rule 139 mm] | REMARKS | Upon ſome of | Mr. Norris's Books, | wherein he aſſerts | F. Malebranche's Opinion | Of | *Our ſeeing all things in God.* | [rule 139 mm]

T2^r: [rule 139 mm] | ELEMENTS | OF | NATURAL PHILOSOPHY. | [rule 138 mm]

2B2^r: [rule 138 mm] | SEVERAL | LETTERS | TO | ANTH. COLLINS Eſq; | AND | Other Persons. | [rule 138 mm]

Head or caption titles are each preceded by rectangular headpiece (6 rows of small fleurons repeated, 4th row as inversion of 3d, 33 × 139 mm), on A2^r, F2^r, K2^r, R2^r, U1^r, 2A1^v and 2M2^r.

Headlines, from verso to recto, in mixed styles, to match text, e.g., pp. 75–77: Some Thoughts | concerning Reading. (p.78: 'Some Thoughts, &c.'); pp. 82–114: 'The Laws of | Carolina.'

CW: Page. B2^r into F1^v Land- [Landgraves,] K2^r after- [afterwards] Q2^r (bot-) tom Y2^v That [That,] 2H1^v nicely 2I1^v oppo- [oppoſition]

Press figures: none.

Notes: A new setting of the text of 1720 (no.316), uniform with the 4th edition of the *Works* (1740), and a beautiful production. A microfilm of the British Library's copy of this edition is in the collection, *The Eighteenth Century*, reel 3194, no. 17.

References: Attig 788; Christophersen p. 78; ESTC t112895.

Copies examined: O^1 (fol. Godw. 223, uncut) C(Keynes) CLU-C (leaf 2M2 bd.between E2 and F1) CtY (Franklin coll. 720/ +L72) L (715.k.8 (2)) NjP (Ex.6106.1739q) O^2 (Vet.A4.c.94 bound in *Works* (1740) vol.1 between leaves g1 and B1 = after p. xxxii)

319. Elements of Natural Philosophy. [1750?] 12° in 6s. With: Reading and Study.

ELEMENTS | OF | Natural Philoſophy. | By JOHN LOCKE, Eſquire. | To which are added, | SOME THOUGHTS | CONCERNING | READING AND STUDY | For a Gentleman. | BY THE SAME AUTHOR. | LONDON, | Printed for J. Thomſon and S. Dampier in the Strand.

Coll: 12° in 6s (170 × 97 mm cut) A–G^6 [$ half signed]; 42 leaves; pp. *I–II i–ii iii–x 1* 2–56 *57* 58–72 [= 84].

Contents: A1^r blank, A1^v (*II*) frontispiece (see *Illustration* below), A2^r (*i*) title (verso blank), A3^r–6^v (*iii–x*) selected statement from Desmaizeaux's dedication to 'Collection' (no. 316–8) concerning these texts, B1^r–F4^v (*1–56*) text of 'Elements', F5^r–G6^v (*57–72*) text of 'Reading and Study.'

Illustration: front. is a very poorly engraved portrait of '*Johannes Locke.*' in oval frame, facing right, subscribed '*G. Kneller pin*: *T. Phinn sculp.*', 137 × 86 mm on plate 155 × 98 mm.

Text (E3^v): 23 lines; 138 (145) × 69 mm; 121R with 2 mm leading. Very poor-quality paper with horizontal chainlines, not watermarked. Page no. at external ends of headlines.

HT: ELEMENTS | OF | Natural Philoſophy.
Headlines, from verso to recto, pp. 2–55: ELEMENTS OF | NATURAL PHILOSOPHY.
  pp. 58–71; THOUGHTS | CONCERNING READING.
CW and press figures: none.
Notes: First reprint of the 'Elements' as a separate publication, by pirates (?), using the text from *A Collection* (no. 316). Publication date estimated; booksellers' names do not occur in Plomer. Since Phinn's portraits are usually found in editions printed in Scotland, I suspect this was printed there. A copy of this edition is in *The Eighteenth Century*, reel 4028 no.12.
References: Attig 793; Christophersen p. 78; ESTC n009118.
Copies examined: C (White d.146) CaOTU (Locke L63E43 175-; lacks port.) CLU-C

320. Elements [1750?] 12°. With: Reading and Study.
ELEMENTS | OF | NATURAL PHILOSOPHY. | By JOHN [swash J] LOCKE, Eſquire. | To which are added | SOME THOUGHTS | CONCERNING | READING AND STUDY | FOR A GENTLEMAN. | BY THE SAME AUTHOR. | [rule 79 mm] | [orn., vase with leaves 20 × 26 mm] | [double rule 77/74 mm] | LONDON: | Sold by J. THOMSON, S. DAMPIER, | and R. BLAND.
Coll: 12° (174 × 115 mm cut) A–C^{12} [$ half signed]; 36 leaves; pp. *i–ii* iii–vii *viii* 1 *2–48 49–51 62–64* [=72].
Contents: A1^r (*i*) title (verso blank), A2^r–4^r (iii–vii) selected statement from Desmaizeaux's dedication to 'A Collection' (as in no. 319), A4^v blank, A5^r–C4^v (*1–48*) text of 'Elements', C5^r (*49*) section title (verso blank), C6^r–12^v (*51–64*) text of 'Reading and Study'.
Illustration: front. is poorly done engraved portrait of Locke, after Kneller by T. Phinn (same as in no. 319).
Text (B3^r): 28 lines; 132 (143) × 78 mm; 94 R with 1 mm leading. Some pages have 29 lines: 137 (148) × 78 mm, e.g. B6^r. Fair-quality laid paper with fleur-de-lys watermark. Page no. for p. iii–vi centered at head of page within square brackets; the rest are at outer ends of headlines.
HT: [rectangle of small irons, 7 × 75 mm] | ELEMENTS | OF | NATURAL PHILOSOPHY. | [rule 78 mm]
Section title, p. 49: [orn. rule 7 × 75 mm] | SOME THOUGHTS | CONCERNING | READING AND STUDY | FOR A | GENTLEMAN. | [orn. rule, as 1st rule inverted, 7 × 75 mm]
Headlines, from verso to recto: p. 2–47: ELEMENTS of | NATURAL PHILOSOPHY.
  p. 52–63: THOUGHTS | Concerning READING.
CW: Page. A2^v (deter-) mined B1^v (feve-) ral B6^r vege- [vegetables;] C4^r (probabili-) ty, C8^v (lat-) ter
Press figures: none.
Notes: A different setting of the 'Elements', taken from 'A Collection' (no.

316). Again the date of publication is an estimate. Because of the addition of R. Bland as bookseller (not in Plomer), I judge this edition to be later than no. 319. The frontispiece is still terrible, but the paper is here much better quality. Again, like no. 319, probably printed in Scotland. A microfilm copy of this printing is in the collection, *The Eighteenth Century*, reel 318, no.2.
References: Attig 792; Christophersen p. 78; ESTC t109474.
Copies examined: O (198 g.71) C (7340 d.1) CaOTU (Locke L63E43 1750; lacks port.) DFo (B1280 1750) PU (B1280 1754)

321. Elements. Glasgow, 1751. 8° in 4s. With: Reading and study.
ELEMENTS | OF | NATURAL | PHILOSOPHY. | BY | JOHN LOCKE Esq; | TO WHICH IS ADDED | SOME THOUGHTS | CONCERNING | READING AND STUDY, | FOR A | GENTLEMAN, | BY THE SAME AUTHOR. | GLASGOW, | PRINTED AND SOLD BY R. AND A. FOULIS | M DCC LI.
Coll: 8° in 4s (163 × 98 mm cut) a⁴ A-I⁴ [$ 2 signed; a2 signed '2a']; 40 leaves; pp. *1–2* [3]–[8] *1* 2–54 *55* 56–70 *71–72* [= 80].
Contents: a1ʳ (*1*) title (verso blank), a2r–4v ([3]–[8]) selected statement from Desmaizeaux's *Collection* (no. 316), A1ʳ–G3ᵛ (*1–54*) text of 'Elements', G4ʳ–I3ᵛ (*55–70*) text of 'Reading and study', I4 blank.
Text: 27 lines; 126 (133) × 79 mm; 93 R. Medium-quality laid paper, with vertical chainlines, 'foolscap'. Page no. at external ends of headlines.
Caption title, G4ʳ: SOME THOUGHTS | CONCERNING | READING AND STUDY | FOR A | GENTLEMAN.
Headlines, from verso to recto, pp. 2–53: ELEMENTS OF | NATURAL PHILOSOPHY.
  pp. 56–69: THOUGHTS | CONCERNING READING.
CW: none.
Notes: Reprint of the text first published in *A Collection of Several Pieces*. Gaskell states it was published "by February 1751 (GC)."
References: Attig 794; Christophersen p. 78; Gaskell 195; ESTC t112248.
Copies examined: Ck (Keynes) L (8705.aa.7) O (Rigaud f.25 (3)) PPL (Ia Lock/Log1858.D8; lacks leaf a1)

322. Elements. Berwick, 1754. 8° in 4s. With: 'Reading and study'.
ELEMENTS | OF | NATURAL | PHILOSOPHY. | BY | JOHN LOCKE, Esq; [swash J, Q] | To which is added, | SOME THOUGHTS | CONCERNING | READING AND STUDY | FOR A | GENTLEMAN, | BY THE SAME AUTHOR. | BERWICK UPON TWEED: | PRINTED AND SOLD BY R. TAYLOR. | M.DCC.LIV.
Coll: 8° in 4s (155 × 94 mm cut) A⁴ B-K⁴ [$1 signed]; 40 leaves; pp. *i–ii* [iii]–[viii] *1* 2–56 *57* 58–72 [= 80].
Contents: A1ʳ (*i*) title (verso blank), A2ʳ–4ᵛ ([iii]–[viii]) selections from Desmaizeaux's pref. to the *Collection* (no. 316-8), B1ʳ–H4ᵛ (*1–56*) text of 'Elements', I1ʳ–K4ᵛ (*57–72*) text of 'Reading and Study'.

Text (B1ᵛ): 21 lines; 108 (119) × 64 mm; 102 R with 2 mm leading. Medium-quality laid paper with 'Propatria' watermark. Page no. at outer ends of headlines.
HT, B1ʳ: ELEMENTS | OF | NATURAL | PHILOSOPHY.
  I1ʳ: SOME THOUGHTS | CONCERNING | READING AND STUDY | FOR A | GENTLEMAN.
RT, from verso to recto, pp.2–55: ELEMENTS OF | NATURAL PHILOSOPHY. (p.56: 'ELEMENTS OF'.)
  pp.58–71: THOUGHTS | CONCERNING READING. (p. 72: 'THOUGHTS, &c.')
CW: Page. B1ᵛ (quan-) tity C2ʳ (be-) tween E3ᵛ cor- [cornelians,] G3ᵛ (propagat-) ed I3ᵛ (profi-) tably
Notes: A close reprint of the Foulis edition (no. 321). A microfilm copy is in the collection, *The Eighteenth Century*, reel 7038 no. 6.
References: Attig 795; Christophersen p. 78; ESTC t112155.
Copies examined: Y O (Vet.A5 f.374)

323. Elements. Glasgow, 1758. 12° in 6s
ELEMENTS | OF | NATURAL | PHILOSOPHY. | BY | JOHN [swash J] LOCKE, Eſq; | *GLASGOW:* | Printed by R. URIE, M D CC LVIII.
Coll: 12° in 6s (172 × 100 mm cut) A^4 B–H^6 I^6 (I3 + χ1) K^6; 59 leaves; pp. *I–II i–ii iii–v vi 1* 2–110 [= 118].
Contents: A1ʳ (*I*) half title (verso blank), A2ʳ (*i*) title (verso blank), A3ʳ–A4ʳ (*iii–v*) 'Advertisement' (selected quotation from Desmaizeaux's *Collection*, signed 'MAIZEAUX.'), A4ᵛ (*vi*) contents of 12 chap., B1ʳ–K6ᵛ (*1–110*) text. Illustration: frontispiece is a diagram of the solar system on a folded plate, 258 × 225 mm on sheet 305 × 246 mm, headed 'LOCKE's ELEMENTS of NATURAL PHILOSOPHY Chap. III.'
Text (E1ʳ): 18 lines; 99 (112) × 60 mm; 113 R with 1 mm leading. Good-quality laid paper with fleur-de-lys watermark, horizontal chainlines. Page no. at outer ends of headlines. Full line space between paragraphs.
Half title and HT: same as first 4 lines of title.
RT, from verso to recto: ELEMENTS OF | NATURAL PHILOSOPHY.
CW: none.
Note: Straight-forward reprint, but an excellent-quality production. Copies are also reported at the National Library of Scotland, and at the University of Glasgow Library.
References: Attig 796; Christophersen p. 78; ESTC t112642.
Copy examined: L (8709.b.3 (1))

324. Elements. Whitehaven, 1764. 8° in 4s. With 'Reading and Study'.
ELEMENTS | OF | NATURAL PHILOSOPHY. | BY | JOHN LOCKE, ESQ; | To which is added, | SOME THOUGHTS | CONCERNING | READING AND STUDY | FOR A | GENTLEMAN, | BY THE SAME

AUTHOR. | WHITEHAVEN: | PRINTED AND SOLD BY W. SHEPERD. | M,DCC,LXIV.
Coll: 8° in 4s (150 × 86 mm cut) A^4 B-K^4 [$1 signed]; 40 leaves; pp. *i–ii* iii–vii *viii* 1 2-55 56 57-72 [= 80].
Contents: A1^r title (verso blank), A2^r-4^r (iii–vii) selected quotation from Desmaizeaux's introd. to *Collection* (no.316), A4^v blank, B1^r-H4^r (*1-55*) text of 'Elements', H4^v-K4^v (*56-72*) text of 'Reading and Study'.
Text (G1^r): 27 lines; 126 (134) × 67 mm; 94 R. Medium-quality laid paper without watermarks. Headlines same as no. 322. Page no. at outer ends of headlines.
Headlines, from verso to recto, pp.2–55: ELEMENTS OF | PHILOSOPHY. pp. 57-71: THOUGHTS | CONCERNING READING. (p.72: 'THOUGHTS')
CW: none.
Notes: Reprint, probably unauthorized, following the Foulis or Taylor edition (no. 321-22). Perhaps the bookseller Sheperd felt close enough to the Scots border to escape detection of infringement laws. He is not listed in Plomer. ESTC records an M. Sheperd at Ramsey on the Isle of Man in the 1760s.
References: Attig 797; Christophersen p. 78; ESTC t147286.
Copies examined: C (7340.d.87) CtY (K8.L79/s764) L^1(8707.a.13) L^2 (8707.a.32) O (1994 f.8)

325. Elements. French trans. (anon.) Amsterdam & Leipzig, 1757. 8°
ELEMENS | DE | PHYSIQUE, | *Par JEAN* [swash J] *LOCKE*, | Avec les Pense'es du Meme Auteur | Sur la Lecture & les Etudes qui con- | viennent à un Gentilhomme; | Ouvrages nouvellement tra- | duits de l'Anglois. | [orn., vase 32 × 43 mm] | *A AMSTERDAM ET A LEIPZIG.* | Chez J. SCHREUDER, et | PIERRE MORTIER, le jeune. [swash J] | M.DCC.LVII.
Coll: small 8° (156 × 97 mm cut) *^{8} (– 2 leaves = G) A-F^8 G^2 [$ 5 (-G2) signed]; 56 leaves; pp. *I-III* IV-X XI-XII 1 2-72 73 74-98 99-100 [= 112].
Contents: *1^r (*I*) title (verso blank), *2^r-*5^v (*III-X*) 'Avertissement du libraire', *6^{r,v} (*XI-XII*) contents for 12 chapters of 'Elements', A1^r-E6^v (*1-72*) text of French trans. of 'Elements', E7^r-G1^r (*73-98*) text of French trans. of 'Reading and Study', G2 blank.
Illustration: engr. plate, 136 × 94 mm, showing orbit of the planets inserted between A6 & 7 or, alternatively, A5 & 6 (similar to that in *A Collection*, no. 316), on a plate 136 × 94 mm.
Text (A2^v): 25 lines; 118 (129) × 63 mm; 95 R. Good-quality laid paper with coat-of-arms watermark. Page no. at outer ends of headlines. Tailpieces on p. *xii* (facing birds, 21 × 39 mm) and p. 98 (vase, 33 × 47 mm).
HT, p. *1*: [framed headpiece, vase, 20 × 60 mm] | ELEMENS | DE | PHYSIQUE. | [orn. rule, 3 × 61 mm]

p. 79: [framed headpiece as on p.1] | PENSEES | Sur la Lecture & ſur les E- | tudes, à l'uſage d'un | GENTILHOMME.
Headlines, from verso to recto, pp. 2–71: ELEMENS | DE PHYSIQUE. pp. 74–97: PENSEES SUR LA | LECTURE ET LES ETUDES.
CW: Page. A2^v vingt- [vingt-ſix] B3^r par- [partent] C4^v mer- [mercure] D3^v ver- [verres] E6^r (joig-) nent F6^v (gouverne-) ment
Notes: This is the only French translation of the 'Elements'. According to Rochedieu, the translator is Salvemini de Castilhon.
References: Attig 798; Rochedieu p. 193.
Copies examined: O (Vet.B5 f.65; plate inserted after A6) [BBR] Vat (Ferraioli V3267; plate inserted after A5)

326*. Elements. Russian trans. (anon.) St. Petersburg, 1774. 12°
Первоначальныя основания физики сочиненныя г. Локом переведено с французскаго языка. Спб., [тип. Сухопутн. кад. корпуса], 1774.
Title romanized: Pervonachal'nyia osnovaniia fiziki sochinennyia g. Lokom perevedeno s frantsuzskago iazyka. Spb., [tip. Sukhoputn. kad. korpusa], 1774.
Title translated: Elementary Foundations of Physics. Translated from the French language. St. Petersburg, [Infantry Cadet Corps Press], 1774.
Coll: [2], 60 pp. 1 engraved plate. 12°
Note: Information from *Svodnyi katalog* 3722. I have not seen a copy.
Reference: Attig *799 ('not verified'); source "*Eighteenth-Century Russian publications* ; 3722."

327. Observations upon the Growth and Culture of Vines. 1766. 8°
OBSERVATIONS UPON | THE GROWTH AND CULTURE | OF VINES AND OLIVES: | THE PRODUCTION OF SILK: | THE PRESERVATION OF FRUITS. | WRITTEN AT THE REQUEST OF | THE EARL OF SHAFTESBURY: | TO WHOM IT IS INSCRIBED: | BY M^R. JOHN [swash J] LOCKE. | NOW FIRST PRINTED FROM | THE ORIGINAL MANUSCRIPT IN | THE POSSESSION OF THE | PRESENT EARL OF | SHAFTESBURY. | LONDON: | PRINTED FOR W. SANDBY, IN FLEET STREET. | M DCC LXVI.
Colophon, G1^v (74): [rule 64 mm] | PRINTED BY RICHARDSON AND CLARK, | IN FLEET STREET, LONDON. | [rule 64 mm]
Coll: small 8° (155 × 95 mm cut) A^8 (-A1 = G1) B-E^8 F^4 G^1 [$ half signed]; 44 leaves; pp. *iii–v* vi–xii *xiii* xiv–xv *xvi* 1 2–23 24–25 26–51 *52–53* 54–62 63 64–73 74 [=88].
Contents: A2^r (*iii*) title (verso blank), A3^r–A6^v (*v*–xii) 'THE EDITOR | TO THE READER.' (signed 'G.S. Temple, March 1766.'), A7^r–A8^r (*xiii*–xv) note 'TO THE RIGHT HONORABLE | ANTHONY | EARL OF SHAFTESBURY.' (signed: 'Ch. Ch. | 1 Feb. 1679. | JOHN LOCKE'), A8^v blank, B1^r–C4^r (*1–23*) text on wine, C4^v blank, C5^r–E2^r (*25–51*) on oil, E2^v blank, E3^r–E7^v (*53–62*) on fruit, E8^r–G1^r (*63–73*) on silk.

Text (B3ʳ): 20 lines; 112 (127) × 63 mm; 112 R with 2 mm leading (type-size approx. 72 R). Editor's note set 17 lines, 93 R-sized type with 2 mm leading. Good-quality laid paper with 'propatria' watermark (similar to Heawood 3708) and letters G & R with a bell between, also 'IV' within a crowned circle. Page no. within square brackets at head of page. Full line space between each paragraph. Caption titles, e.g. 'WINE.', set beneath 2 double rules (on pp. *1, 25, 53, 63*)

CW: Page. A4ʳ (confe-) quently B3ʳ (vine-) yards C8ʳ fucceffion, D3ʳ (circum-) ference, E7ᵛ SILK. No CW when a paragraph ends at bottom of page.

Binding: beige diapered (Russian) cloth with red morocco corners and spine in quarter binding. Spine label, reading vertically from head to foot: LOCKE. CULTURE OF VINES & OLIVES. (This appears to be a trade binding.)

Note: The manuscript copy is with the first Earl of Shaftesbury's papers at the Public Record Office. The text was probably written in the period November 1675 to March 1677 when Locke was residing chiefly at Montpellier, and probably completed while in Paris (May 1677 to May 1679). It reappears for the first time in the Hollis edition of the *Works*, 7th edition (1768; no. 369) at the end of the 4th vol.; it is reprinted in subsequent *Works* editions. All copies seen have been rebound except that in the Bodleian.

References: Attig 803; Christophersen p. 78-9; ESTC t098146.

Copies examined: O (Douce L.37) CaQMMO CtY (Z697.110) DFo (SB393.L6 1766; inscribed 'Ex Dono Comitis de Shaftesbury') [GOT] L¹ (1651/1128) L² (234.b.13)

328. 'Extracts from his correspondence, journals, & common-place books' (ed. King) 1829. 4°

The Life of John Locke, with Extracts from His Correspondence, Journals, and Common-place Books. By Lord King. Literis innutritus, eousque tantum profeci ut veritati unicè litarem. London: Henry Colburn, New Burlington Street, 1829.

xi, 407 pp.: 2 plates. large 4° (270 × 215 mm cut). Signatures: a⁴ b² B-3F⁴ [$ half signed]. Index: pp. 405-7; errata (7 lines): p.*408*. Listed price: 42 s. Colophon (on verso of half title): London: Printed by S. and R. Bentley, Dorset Street, Fleet Street.

Note: The preface is signed 'Ockham, April 24th, 1829', the residence of Peter King, seventh Baron King, the great-grandson of Locke's executor (and son of his nephew Jeremy King). The collection, published in June 1829, was compiled from the King moiety of the Locke inheritance. The biography occupies the first forty pages. It is followed by extracts from Locke's journals, correspondence, commonplace book and miscellaneous papers. The two missing pages from the fourth 'Letter for Toleration' have been supplied from an original draft (pp. 360-61); that 'letter', with the omission, was first published in the *Posthumous Works* of 1706 (no. 299). There are some 40 letters or excerpts of letters from Locke and "40 letters and 10 excerpts to him. The latter are accurately printed, the texts being modernized. With [Locke's letters] King took great liberties, omitting passages without indication, sometimes combining parts of two or more letters to form a single letter." (*Corr.* i. xlv)

The two plates are (1) a portrait of Locke by Worthington after Greenhill, as frontispiece, and (2) facsimiles of the handwriting of Locke, Sir Isaac Newton, and the first Earl of Shaftesbury (facing p. 1).

The Barons King of Ockham were created Earls of Lovelace in 1838.
References: Attig 895; Christophersen p.80.

329. 'Extracts from his correspondence . . ., &c.' (ed. King). New ed., 1830. 2 vols. 8°

The Life of John Locke, with Extracts from His Correspondence, Journals, and Common-place Books. By Lord King. Literis innutritus, eousque tantum profeci ut veritati unicè litarem. New Edition, with Considerable Additions. In Two Volumes . . . London: Henry Colburn and Richard Bentley, New Burlington Street. 1830.

2 vols. in-8° (225 × 140 mm cut). Vol. 1: viii, 447 pp.: 2 plates (as in 1829 ed.; A^4 $B-2E^8$ $2F^4$ [\$2 signed]). Vol. 2: [4], 375, iv, iv, 144 pp. (A^2 $B-2B^8$ $a-i^8$ [\$2 signed]). Binding: dark green cloth with horizontal ribs; spine with mounted beige paper label. Listed price: 28 s. Published in July 1830.

Contents: Vol. 1 contains pref., 'Life' (pp. 1–85) and text from 1st ed. through p. 241 (pp. 81–447). Vol.2 has rest of text of 1st ed. (pp. 1–305), with the addition of letters between Locke and Limborch, and excerpts from five others (pp. 305–75); and "Notes of Domestic and Foreign Affairs during the Last Years of the Reign of George I and the Early Part of the Reign of George II" by Peter King, Locke's cousin and executor, covering 1 June 1725 to October 1732 (iv, iv, 1–132 pp. at end). Index to the 'Life of Locke': pp. 133–40; to King's notes: pp. 141–4.

Note: According to E. S. de Beer, this new edition "retains all the defects of the first but has an important addition. . . . King appended nine letters from van Limborch to Locke and the passage omitted from [Limborch's letter in] *Some Familiar Letters* narrating his discussion with the young woman who preferred Judaism to Christianity, and one letter from Locke to van Limborch . . . King added also excerpts from five letters to Locke." (*Corr.* i.xlvi) King also appended a transcription of Peter King's notes made while he was Lord Chancellor.

First leaf of each gathering also signed 'VOL. I.' [–'II.'] in direction line.
Reference: Attig 895 n.

330. Extracts (comp. Fox Bourne). 1876. 2 vols. 8°

The Life of John Locke. By H. R. Fox Bourne. In Two Volumes. Volume I. [–II.] Henry S. King & Co., London, 1876. 2 vols. in 8° (220 × 140 mm). Vol. 1: xvi, 488 pp. Vol. 2: xii, 574 pp.; includes index, pp. 562–74. List price: 28 s.

Note: Many texts of Locke are incorporated in the biographical narrative, including letters or parts of them, from materials in the Public Record Office (the Shaftesbury papers), the British Library (from the recently acquired papers of Nicolas Toinard); Limborch's papers in Amsterdam; "Esther Masham's letter book; and what he could find in the Bodleian Library [and] the Lambeth Palace Library" (*Corr.* i. xlvii). He also made use of materials published in Lord King's *Life* (no. 328-9) but did not have access to the Lovelace Collection.

There was a facsim. reprint of this edition by Scientia Verlag (Aalen, Ger.) in 1969.

References: Attig 898; Christophersen pp.9, 81, 86.

331. Drafts of the Essay. Draft B (ed. Rand) 1931. 8°
An Essay concerning the Understanding, Knowledge, Opinion, and Assent. By John Locke. Edited with an introduction by Benjamin Rand, Ph.D., LL.D., Harvard University. Cambridge [Mass.]: Harvard University Press, 1931.
   lix, [1], 306, [1] pp. : 2 plates. 8° (210 × 148 mm cut). List price (*Eng.cat. books*): $3.50; 15 s.

   Locke's text: pp.15-307. First plate is front.: port. of Locke after Greenhill; the second plate, between pp. 14 and 15, contains facsim. of manuscripts: cover page, 'Intellectus 1671 J. L.' and 'De Intellectu humano 1671 An Essay'; plate verso is facsim. of first textual page of ms.
Note: The text transcribed by Rand is from the Lovelace Collection, and is now in the Bodleian Library (MS Locke f.26). It is wholly in Locke's hand. Because Aaron and Gibb thought this manuscript was written prior to *An Early Draft* . . . (no. 332, q.v.), they called it 'Draft B'. Rand dedicated his work "to the memory of the Right Honourable Lionel Fortescue, Third Earl of Lovelace."
Reference: Attig 936.

332. Drafts of the Essay, Draft A (ed. Aaron & Gibb) 1936. 8°
An Early Draft of Locke's Essay, together with Excerpts from His Journals. Edited by R.I. Aaron, Professor of Philosophy, University of Wales, Aberystwyth, and Jocelyn Gibb. Oxford: At the Clarendon Press, 1936.
   xxviii, 132 p. 8° (222 × 135 mm cut) List price: 12 s. 6 d.
Note: This manuscript was transcribed from a folio-sized commonplace-book in the collection of the fourth Earl of Lovelace. It was subsequently sold privately by him to Mr. A.A. Houghton, Jr. of New York in 1947; it was again sold at auction in 1979 to Mr. Haven O'More for his 'Collection of the Garden, Ltd.' This part of that collection (as lot no. 123) was sold at auction at Sotheby's, New York, November 9-10, 1989, to an unnamed French private collector. Because this manuscript was thought to be written a few months prior to the draft transcribed by Rand, Aaron and Gibb named this

one 'Draft A' and the one transcribed by Rand 'B'. There is also a partial copy of Draft A among the Shaftesbury Papers in the Public Record Office (shelfmark PRO 30/24/47/7). Some of the excerpts from Locke's Journals, in the Lovelace Collection, "are an important source for some positions which Locke takes in the *Essay*" (no.334, p. xix).
Reference: Attig 932.

333. Drafts of the Essay, Draft A (ed. Nidditch) 1980.
Draft A of Locke's *Essay concerning Human Understanding*; the Earliest Extant Autograph Version. Transcribed with critical apparatus by Peter H. Nidditch, Professor of Philosophy, University of Sheffield. [Sheffield]: Department of Philosophy, University of Sheffield, 1980.
   200 p. ; facsims. of ms. (on pp. 15-19). 'Perfect' binding in grey cardboard covers (210 × 140 mm). Cover title and title-page typeset; rest of vol. reproduced from typewritten copy.
Note: A preliminary edition of the text being prepared for the Clarendon Edition of the Works of John Locke, "more accurate in the transcription" than Aaron and Gibb's (no. 332), and with errors corrected and ms. alterations noted (pp. 7-8). Last page signed: Grindleford, Derbyshire, 29th May 1980.
Reference: Attig 933.

334. Drafts of the Essay, Draft B (ed. Nidditch). 1982.
Draft B of Locke's *Essay concerning Human Understanding*: the Fullest [cover: Earliest] Extant Autograph Version. *Transcribed with Critical Apparatus* by Peter H. Nidditch, Professor of Philosophy, University of Sheffield. [Sheffield]: Department of Philosophy, University of Sheffield, 1982.
   360 pp. (facsims. of ms. on pp. 355-60). 'Perfect' binding with yellow cardboard cover, typeset (206 × 146 mm). Text reproduced from typewritten copy. Available when published from the Philosophy Dept. for £8.50.
Notes: A preliminary edition, or 'preprint' of the text for the Clarendon Edition of the Works of John Locke, transcribed from the Bodleian Library MS. Locke f. 26. The 'contents' portion is a transcription of MS. Locke c.28, f.33. The introduction is signed from 'Grindleford, Derbyshire, May 1982'.
Reference: Attig 937.

335. Drafts for the Essay . . . (ed. Nidditch & Rogers) 1990.
Drafts for the *Essay concerning Human Understanding*, and Other Philosophical Writings / John Locke. Edited by Peter H. Nidditch and G. A. J. Rogers. In Three Volumes. Oxford: Clarendon Press, 1990. Series: Clarendon Edition of the Works of John Locke.
   Vol. 1: xxvi, [2], 299 pp. ; front. (port. by Greenhill), 12 facsims. of mss. from both drafts; 8° (217 × 135 mm). ISBN 0-19-824545-9; price £50.

Colophon, vol. 1 p. *iv*: "*Set by Joshua Associates Limited, Oxford   Printed in Great Britain by Biddles Ltd.   Guildford and King's Lynn Britain*".

Contents. Vol. 1: pref. & introd.; Draft A, pp. 1-83; contents of Draft B, pp. 87-98; Draft B, pp, 99-270; Appendices, pp. 271-295; 'Glossary of recurring Greek and Latin expressions', pp. 296; index, pp. 297-9.

Note: The definitive edition of the Drafts, for which Peter Nidditch did the preliminary editions (no. 333-4), completed by John Rogers. Vol. 2 will contain Draft C along with the epitome of the *Essay* in French (cf. no. 273) with an English translation, and other philosophical papers. The third vol. will contain the *Conduct* (cf. no. 299), "other projected additions . . . [and] other papers relating to Locke's philosophical thought, in particular his papers on Norris and Malebranche" (v. 1, p. xv).

336. Draft of 'Education' (ed. Kenyon) 1933.

In red & black: Directions concerning Education / John Locke: Being the First Draft of His *Thoughts concerning Education*, Now Printed from Additional MS. 38771 in the British Museum. With an Introduction by Frederic George Kenyon. Oxford: Printed for Presentation to the Members of the Roxburghe Club, MCMXXXIII.

[8], 84 pp. ; plate (front.) in 4° (Signatures: A^4 B-K^4 L^6 [$1 (+L2) signed]); 285 × 223 mm.

Contents (by page no.): *1* title, *2* note ('Printed in Great Britain'), *3* dedication to members of Roxburghe Club, *5* lists of club members, 1-27 Kenyon's introduction, 28-29 tables showing 'Correspondence of Sections in the Several Editions' with the manuscript, 33-84 transcription of the manuscript.

Note: The frontispiece is a facsim. reproduction of fols. 2^r, 51^v and 52^v of the ms. in Locke's hand. The bulk of the manuscript is the work of his amanuensis Sylvester Brounower, with some corrections by Locke. The edition was of limited distribution, chiefly to the members listed by name on p. 5. Kenyon took some liberties with the manuscript, changing capitalisation and punctuation and expanding contractions.

Reference: Attig 943.

337. 'De arte medica' (ed. Gibson). 1933.

Caption title: DE ARTE MEDICA | 1669.

In: The Physician's Art: an Attempt to Expand John Locke's Fragment, De Arte Medica : By Alexander George Gibson. Oxford: At the Clarendon Press, 1933.

[8], 237 pp. (8° in 4s: A^4 B-$2G^4$ $2H^2$; 189 × 130 mm). Binding: beige linen cloth, with spine stamped in gold, Oxford Univ. seal at foot. Price: $3.00; 12 s. 6 d.

Colophon, *p. 238*: Printed in Great Britain at the University Press, Oxford, by John Johnson, Printer to the University.

Locke's text: pp. 13-26.

Note: Gibson's transcription of the manuscript in Locke's hand in the Shaftesbury papers at the Public Record Office (no.30/24/47/2). Gibson notes Locke has recorded a Latin quotation from Cicero's 'De Oratore,' I. 146, on the verso of the first leaf. The text is printed on laid paper, with '4028' in direction line of first page of each gathering. The original manuscript is said to be six leaves "two of which are larger than the others, folded once so as to make twelve small quarto pages. It is written in Locke's neat, close, and legible hand writing, and bears evidence of some but no careful emendation or correction." (p.11) Kenneth Dewhurst, in his biography of Thomas Sydenham (London, 1966; p. 73) attributes the authorship to Sydenham, whose assistant Locke was.
Reference: Attig 906.

338. Journals. Selections (ed. Lough) 1953.
Locke's Travels in France, 1675-1679, as Related in His Journals, Correspondence and Other Papers. Edited with an Introduction and Notes by John Lough, Professor of French in the Durham Colleges, University of Durham. Cambridge: At the University Press, 1953.
lxvi, 308, [1] pp. : 3 illus. 8° (a^{10} b-d^8 1-19^8 20^4 [$2 (-20/2) signed; 20/4 blank leaf]; 220 × 138 mm). Binding: light blue linen cloth, spine stamped in gold, with Cambridge Univ. seal at foot. Dust wrapper, compartmentalized, in light blue and cream. Price: 80 s. (£4.00).
Colophon, p.iv: *Printed in Great Britain at the University Press, Cambridge (Brooke Crutchley, University Printer)*
Note: A transcription of those parts of Locke's journals relating to his stay in France (pp.1-275), supplemented by the draft of a letter to an unknown correspondent, dated 1 March 1675/6 (*Corr.* 310; i.439-44) and other relevant materials. Locke went to France 12 November 1675 and returned to London in April 1679. The journals contain large portions written in his own version of Jeremiah Rich's shorthand. Except for the vol. for 1679 in the British Library (Add. MS. 15642) all the ms. vols. are part of the Lovelace Collection in the Bodleian Libray (MS. Locke f.1-3). The illustrations are (1) portrait of Locke by Greenhill as front.; (2) map of France showing Locke's tours 1675-9, facing p. lxvi; and (3) on its verso, facsim. of p. 1 of vol. for 1675, chiefly in shorthand (MS. Locke f.1). Contains bibliographical abbreviations (pp. xi-xiii) and index (pp. 289-309).
First page of each sheet signed 'LLJ' in direction line.
Reference: Attig 900.

339. Writings on the Law of Nature (ed. & trans. von Leyden) 1954.
Essays on the Law of Nature / John Locke; the Latin Text, with a Translation, Introduction and Notes, Together with Transcripts of Locke's Shorthand in His Journal for 1676. Edited by W. von Leyden, Lecturer in Philosophy in the University of Durham. Oxford: At the Clarendon Press, 1954.

xi, 292 pp. : 2 illus. 8° (A^6 B–S^8 T^{10} [$2 signed]; 218 × 138 mm).
Binding: dark blue linen cloth, spine stamped in gold, Oxford Univ. seal at foot. Dust jacket grey paper printed in dark blue. '*Price (in U.K. only) 35 s. net*'.
Contents: Preface & Contents. Introduction (pp. 1–92). Locke's texts in Latin with facing translation, each preceded by an 'analytical summary' (pp. 95–243). 'Philosophical Shorthand Writings': pp. 246–281. Index: pp. 284–92.
Note: Consists chiefly of transcriptions of the Latin mss. in the Lovelace Collection of eight essays, and draft notes for them, with related material from the collection (MS. Locke f. 31 with additions from MS. Locke e.6 and f.30); translations and notes.
Reference: Attig 944.

340. Writings on the Law of Nature (ed. & trans. Horwitz/Clay) 1990.
Questions concerning the Law of Nature / John Locke. With an Introduction, Text, and Translation by Robert Horwitz, Jenny Strauss Clay, and Diskin Clay. Ithaca and London: Cornell University Press, 1990.

x, [2], 260 p. front. (port.) 8° (228 × 147 mm). Price: $29.95. ISBN: 0-8014-2348-1.

Front. is Locke's port. by John Greenhill. Illus. on pp. *170–1*: facing pages of Bodleian Lib. MS. Locke f. 31, fols. 61^v–62^r (text of question, 'An lex n[atur]a cognosci potest ex hominum consensu?').
Note: Using von Leyden's terminology to distinguish MS. A (MS. Locke e.6, verso side of fols. 64–17 inverted; in Locke's hand), B (MS Locke f. 31 fols. 9–119, transcribed by an unknown secretary, with Locke's corrections) and C (MS. Locke f.30, fols. 122–173^v, in Brounower's hand), the editors have made a "diplomatic edition [and] collation of MSS A and B. MS. C . . . has no value for the establishment of the text" (p. 69). Introd. by Horwitz (pp. 1–62), 'The Manuscripts' by Jenny S. Clay (pp. 63–72), and 'Translator's Introduction' by D. Clay (pp. 73–89) precede Latin text with facing translation. Bibliography, pp. 253–6; index, pp.257–60.

341. Manuscripts on toleration (ed. Viano). 1961.
Scritti editi e inediti sulla tolleranza / John Locke. A cura di Carlo Augusto Viano. Torino: Taylor, editore, 1961. Series: Documenti e ricerche: Biblioteca di cultura contemporanea.

255, [5] pp. in-8° (239 × 165 mm paperbound). Initial price 3600 lire; in 1962 at 4000 lire.
Note: A miscellaneous collection of manuscript and published works on toleration, with Italian translations. The contents are as follows:
1) Pref. to the following item from MS. Locke c.28, ff. 1–2 (pp. 14–19; part printed in King, no. 329). Written in 1661.
2) 'Question: whether the Civil Magistrate . . .' from MS. Locke e.7 ff. 1–36 (pp. 20–61). Written in 1660.

3) 'An magistratus civilis . . .' from MS. Locke c. 28, ff. 3-20r (pp. 62-80). Written 1660-63.
4) 'An Essay concerning Toleration' from the copy in the Henry E. Huntington Library, San Marino, Calif., HM584, written 1667 (pp. 81-103). There are four copies, some briefer than others: in the Bodleian Library (MS. Locke c. 28 ff. 21-32r); in the Public Record Office (Shaftesbury Papers, 30/24/47/1); and a third headed 'Adversaria 1661' in the commonplace book, pp. 106-25 and 270-1, formerly owned by A. A. Houghton, Jr. (for its present location see no. 332). This essay was previously printed by Fox Bourne (i. 174-94; no. 330) and a part by King (no. 329). The editor gives references to variants in the Bodleian Library and PRO copies.
5) Italian translation of *A Letter concerning Toleration* (pp. 108-51), with title: 'Epistola su la tolleranza'. A copy of the translation made by Dr. Francesco A. Ferrari in 1920 (Attig 79).
6) Italian translations by Viano of the first three items above (pp. 152-239; notes: pp. 240-55).
7) Contents ('Indice'), p. 257.

Reference: Attig 949.

342. Drafts on toleration (ed. Abrams) 1967.
Two Tracts on Government / John Locke. Edited with an introduction, notes and translation by Philip Abrams, Fellow of Peterhouse and Lecturer in Economics and Politics in the University of Cambridge. Cambridge: At the University Press, 1967.

ix, [1], 263, [1] pp. 8° (π^5 1-16^{12} 17^8 [$2 signed]; 217 × 138 mm). Binding: light blue linen cloth, mounted black spine label printed in gold, with 'CAMBRIDGE' stamped at foot of spine. Dust jacket printed gold paper with black typeface. Price: '$7.50 in *U.S.A.* | 40s. *net in U.K.*'

Contents (by page no.): *i* half title, *iii* title, *iv* publisher's & printer's notes, *v* dedication to Peter Laslett, *vii* contents, ix-x foreword, *1* section title, 3-111 introduction (4 chap. with notes at end of each), 112-14 editorial pref., 115-181 'first tract on government' (MS. Locke e.7, 'Question: Whether the Civil Magistrate . . .') preceded by the preface (MS. Locke c. 28 ff. 1-2), *183*-209 text of second tract, in Latin ('An magistratus civilis . . .', from MS. Locke c. 28 ff. 3-20), 210-41, translation of Latin tract, 242-60 bibliographical appendices, 261-264 index.

Note: A critical edition of the two tracts written in 1660 and 1661 respectively, preceded by an introduction discussing 'Locke as a conservative' and the political setting.

First page of each gathering signed 'AJL' in direction line.

Reference: Attig 950.

343. Library catalogue (ed. Harrison & Laslett) 1965.
The Library of John Locke, by John Harrison and Peter Laslett. [Oxford]: Published for the Oxford Bibliographical Society by the Oxford University

Press, 1965. Series: Oxford Bibliographical Society Publications, New Series Volume XIII.

 viii, [3], 292, [2], pp. : front. (port.) & 9 illus. in-4° (A^6 B-S^8 T^{10} [$1 signed]; 247 × 203 mm). First page of each sheet also reads 'C1584' in direction line. List price: 60 s.

Colophon: PRINTED IN GREAT BRITAIN AT THE UNIVERSITY PRESS, OXFORD, BY VIVIAN RIDLER, PRINTER TO THE UNIVERSITY.

Binding: dark blue boards, with quarter binding of beige linen; spined titled in black (title | author | series | date). Dust jacket in purple and white coated paper with portrait from frontispiece on front.

Note: Locke's interleaved copy of *Catalogus impressorum librorum Bibliothecae Bodlejanae in Academia Oxoniensi*, compiled by Thomas Hyde (1647) is the basis for this record of books known to have been owned by Locke (formerly in Paul Mellon's collection at Oak Spring, Virginia; now in the Bodleian Library). The catalogue records the present location of each book where known. "[T]he most remarkable thing about the way Locke chose to enter up his holdings is that he succeeded in concealing the fact that he himself had written any books other than the *Essay concerning Human Understanding*, the work on *Education*, and the works on *Money*." The introductory essay, 'John Locke and his Books' is by Peter Laslett (pp. 1-61). The frontispiece reproduces Kneller's sketch for a portrait of Locke; the plates distributed in the introduction include facsimile pages from the catalogue, and of manuscripts from various sources. 'List of Authorities': p. *288*; index: pp. *289-92*.

Reference: Attig 956.

344. Library catalogue (ed. Harrison & Laslett). 2d ed., 1971.

The Library of John Locke, by John Harrison and Peter Laslett. Second Edition. Oxford: At the Clarendon Press, 1971.

 xiii, [4], 313 pp. : front. (port.), illustrative plates 2-9 on 5 leaves (between pp. 66 & 67). 4° (A^8 [A1 blank] B-T^8 U^4 X^8 [$1 signed]; 247 × 185 mm). Binding: black linen cloth; spine stamped with title, compilers' names, and edition, with Oxford Univ. seal at foot. Dust jacket in green and white, with front. port. on front cover. "Price: £4.00 *net* IN UK."

Note: Includes minor corrections and additions to the previous edition, and incorporates newly discovered present locations of a few items. 'List of Authorities': p. *309*; index: pp. *310-13*. First page of each gathering also signed '818139' in direction line.

Reference: Attig 956 n.

345. Medical notes (ed. Dewhurst) 1963.

Caption titles: Journals (1675-[1698]).

In: John Locke (1632-1704), Physician and Philosopher: a Medical Biography, with an Edition of the Medical Notes in his Journals, by

Kenneth Dewhurst, Wellcome Research Fellow in Medicine, Corpus Christi College, Oxford. London: The Wellcome Historical Medical Library, 1963.
 xii, 331 p. : front. (port.), 14 plates on 10 leaves. 8° (221 × 142 mm). Series: Publications of the Wellcome Historical Medical Library, New series, vol. II. Binding: dark blue simulated cloth, with gold stamping on spine. Dust jacket: light grey paper, printed in black. 'Price 42s.'
Note: The medical content from Locke's journals from 1675-1679 (pp. 62-151); 1679-1683 (pp. 165-223), 1683-1688 (pp. 236-281) and 1689-1698 (pp. 290-4). They are transcribed from Locke's journals in the Bodleian Library, MS. Locke f.1-3, British Library Add. MS. 15642, and Bodley's MS. Locke f. 4-10 respectively, with translation of the Latin and French passages, and decipherment of Locke's shorthand adaptation of Jeremiah Rich's system. The portrait is by John Greenhill; the other plates, scattered throughout, are chiefly portraits and manuscript facsimiles. Marginal notes cite pages of the manuscripts and whether the passages are translations. There are bibliographical footnotes, and an index (pp. 313-31).
Reference: Attig 925.

Of the many miscellaneous works included in this chapter, the *Paraphrases* and the 'Conduct of the Understanding' have received the most attention since 1800. The *Paraphrases* were reprinted in 1801, 1812, 1823; and in Cambridge, Mass., in 1832. The definitive edition for the Clarendon Edition of the Works of John Locke was prepared by Arthur Wainwright and published in two vols. in 1989.

The 'Conduct' has been reprinted in 1801, 1802, 1807 (Edinburgh), 1812, 1818, 1820, 1823, 1832, 1833, 1849, 1851, 1881 (ed. by Thomas Fowler; new editions in 1882, 1890, 1892 and 1901), 1891 (ed. by J.A. St. John), 1901, and 1966 (ed. by F. W. Garforth). It was also issued with Francis Bacon's political essays in 1813, 1822, 1823, 1825, 1828, 1832, 1837, 1838, 1841 and 1885. An 1829 reprint also included 'Reading and Study for a Gentleman' and the 'Elements of Natural Philosophy'. Additionally there have been numerous selections and abridgements published, many in collections of readings and in periodicals.

A new Dutch translation of the 'Conduct' was published in 1979, a new French in 1975, and three different German translations in 1857, 1883 and 1920. Soave's Italian edition (cf. no. 145-6 and 310) was reprinted in 1926. A Spanish translation, with the misleading title *Del Gobierno Civil*, published in 1827, contains the 'Conduct' and the first Spanish translation of the *Letter concerning Toleration*.

An Italian translation of Draft A, entitled *La Conoscenza umana*, by Armando Carlini appeared in 1948; it was revised by C.A. Viano and reprinted in 1968 under the title: *Saggio sull'intelligenza, Secondo abbozzo*. A French translation of no. 332, Draft A: *Première esquisse de l'Essai philosophique concernant l'entendement humain*, was translated with introd. and notes by Marylène Delbourg-Delphis, and published by Vrin in their series, Bibliothèque des textes philosophiques, in 1974, whether from the original ms. or from Aaron & Gibb's edition (no.332) is not stated (cf. Attig 934). An Italian translation by Armando Carlini with the title: *Il Primo abbozzo del Saggio*, and notes by Vittorio Sainati was published in 1951 (Laterza, at Bari. See Attig 935). An Italian version of Draft B made by Armando Carlini, with the title *La Conoscenza umana*, appeared in 1948; it was revised and reprinted by C. A. Viano in 1968 under the title: *Saggio sull'intelligenza, Secondo abbozzo*.

CHAPTER X
Correspondence (nos. 346-362)

Shortly after Locke's death, correspondents began publishing Locke's letters. The first authorised collection was *Some Familiar Letters*, printed for the Churchills in 1706. Other letters were thereafter published singly or from small collections, chiefly in periodicals or miscellaneous works. This chapter includes records of all letters wherever published up to 1800, and all collections published since that date. It does not include random reprints of single letters after 1800.

Locke's dedicatory letter to Margaret, Countess of Shaftesbury, is included in the 1828 edition of Locke's translation of three of Nicole's moral essays (no.314). It was not published elsewhere.

Five letters by Locke to Humfry Smith and Richard King were first printed in *The Remains* (no. 315, q.v.); they were reprinted in Desmaizeaux's *Collection of Several Pieces* (no. 316), and in the second and later editions of the *Works* (no. 364 et seq.). Letters to Collins, Oldenburg, Lady Calverley and others were also printed in Desmaizeaux's *Collection*.

Some of Locke's correspondence was printed in King's *Life of John Locke* (no. 328-9) and in Fox Bourne's biography (no. 330).

All letters (except the dedication to the Countess of Shaftesbury) appear in Dr. E. S. de Beer's definitive edition of the *Correspondence* (cited throughout as *Corr.*) with his full notes as to their prior publication and the present location of the manuscript where known.

346. 'Familiar Letters'. 1708. 8°
Within a double rule, inner 146 × 79 mm, outer 155 × 87 mm: SOME | Familiar Letters | BETWEEN | Mr. *LOCKE*, [swash K] | AND | Several of his Friends. | [rule 74 mm] | [orn., 6 vase-like fleurons, 14 × 50 mm] | [rule 77 mm] | *LONDON:* | Printed for A. and J. [swash J] CHURCHILL at the | *Black Swan* in *Pater-nofter Row.* 1708.

Coll: 8° (190 × 116 mm cut) A^2 B–2L^8 2M^8 (−2 leaves = A^2) [\$ half (−2M4) signed]; L3 signed 'K3'; 272 leaves; pp. *i–iv* 1–369 470 371–540 [= 544]. Page 370 called '470'.

Contents: A1^r (*i*) title (verso blank), A2^{r,v} (*iii–iv*) pref. 'To the Reader.' (*iv* has 11 lines of text, 5.2 lines of errata, followed by note: "These Books following were writ by Mr. Locke." and 12-line list), B1^r–2M6^v (1–540) text.

Text (F8ᵛ): 31 lines; 147 (158) × 78 mm; 95 R. Laid paper, watermark fleur-de-lys with letters 'PC'. Page no. within parentheses centered at top of page as headlines.

CW: Page. A2ʳ publiſh- [publiſhing] C1ʳ endea- [endeavouring] F7ᵛ (recei-) ved K8ᵛ reference P4ʳ (propa-) gating, S6ʳ (con-) cern'd Y1ᵛ (Cui-) dam 2C6ᵛ (trou-) ver 2I6ʳ conten- [contendis] 2M5ʳ (conſo-) nant

Press figures: 22 (C3ᵛ)-* 25 (C5ʳ)-5 55 (E4ʳ)-5 60 (E6ᵛ)-5 70 (F3ᵛ)-5 84 (G2ᵛ)-5 86 (G3ᵛ)-4 109 (H7ʳ)-* 116 (I2ᵛ)-* 148 (L2ᵛ)-5 162 (M1ᵛ)-* 164 (M2ᵛ)-4 185 (N5ʳ)-4 186 (N5ᵛ)-4 198 (O3ᵛ)-4 200 (O4ᵛ)-4 214 (P3ᵛ)-4 224 (P8ᵛ)-† 239 (Q8ʳ)-5 242 (R1ᵛ)-5 248 (R4ᵛ)-4 262 (S3ᵛ)-4 269 (S7ʳ)-4 290 (U1ᵛ)-4 301 (U7ʳ)-4 310 (X3ᵛ)-4 313 (X5ʳ)-4 322 (Y1ᵛ)-† 324 (Y2ᵛ)-† 342 (Z3ᵛ)-4 349 (Z7ʳ)-4 363 (2A6ᵛ)-5 365 (2A7ʳ)-5 374 (2B3ᵛ)-† 386 (2C1ᵛ)-† 413 (2D7ʳ)-5 415 (2D8ʳ)-5 418 (2E1ᵛ)-5 429 (2E7ʳ)-5 444 (2F6ᵛ)-* 463 (2G8ʳ)-5 464 (2G8ᵛ)-5 466 (2H1ᵛ)-* 472 (2H4ᵛ)-4 489 (2I5ʳ)-4 495 (2I8ᵛ)-5 509 (2K7ʳ)-5 511 (2K8ʳ)-5 524 (2L6ᵛ)-* 530 (2M1ᵛ)-† 532 (2M2ᵛ)-†. Note: The obeli on pp. 224, 374 and 386 are of a fancier font.

Notes: "There is nothing to show who projected" this collection; "it was perhaps Locke's principal heir Peter King . . . in conjunction with the Churchills. . . . The letters in the first part must have been contributed principally by Peter King and Samuel Molyneux, William Molyneux's son. . . . The second part was the work of van Limborch." (E.S. de Beer's Introd., *Corr.* i.xliii.) King inherited half of Locke's books and all his manuscripts and put together the *Posthumous Works* (no.299). The readers' preface begins: "The following Letters offer'd to your perusal are the genuin productions of those Gentlemen to whom they are attributed."

This collection contains, first, letters to and from William Molyneux, from July 1692 until 29 September 1698 (*Corr.* 1515, et seq.; iv.479–80, etc.) including as inclosures a copy of a letter from William King (later Archbishop of Dublin) and a copy of Leibniz's comments on the *Essay*. These are followed by one letter to Ezekiel Burridge (Irish translator for the Latin edition of the *Essay*), and by eight letters to and from William's brother, Dr. Thomas Molyneux; these are a thin filling for the other half of the vol. which is the Latin correspondence with Philippus van Limborch, beginning with a letter dated 26 September 1685, continuing until Locke's death (*Corr.* 834; ii.746–51; et seq.).

A microfilm copy is in the collection, *The Eighteenth Century*, reel 1913, no. 4.

References: Attig 806; Christophersen p. 81; ESTC t117287.

Notice: Bibliothèque choisie 17 (1709): 234–41.

Copies examined: Y CaOTU (Locke L63.A175 1708; no fig. p. 463; ex lib. Robert Gathorne Hardy) CaQMMO (L814s 1708) Ck (Keynes A13.10; no fig. p. 532) CLU-C (*PR3541.L5S5; no. fig. p.413) CtY (K8.L79/t708) DFo (B1296.A3 1708; no fig. pp. 466 & 532) [GhU (BL3410)] Han (P-A 986; no fig. p.413) L (1085.k.19; no fig. p.415) MH (Phil.2115.74.50; no fig. pp. 466, 530, 532) NjP (Ex.6106.386)

O (Godw.Subt. 8° 431; no fig. p.530)   Ob (525.a.9; no fig. p.415)   Oc (a.1.105)   Oq   PPL (Ia Lock 66774.0)   PU (B1296.A3 1708)

347. 'Familiar Letters'. 3d ed., 1737. 8°
SOME | FAMILIAR LETTERS | BETWEEN | Mr. LOCKE, | AND | Several of his FRIENDS. | [rule 82 mm] | The THIRD EDITION. | [rule 82 mm] | [diamond-shaped vase orn. 36 × 48 mm] | [double rule 82 mm] | LONDON: | Printed for A. BETTESWORTH and C. HITCH at the | *Red Lyon* in *Pater-Noſter-Row*; J. PEMBERTON, at the | *Golden Buck* in *Fleetſtreet*; and E. SYMON, over againſt | the *Royal Exchange*, in *Cornhill*. | M.DCC.XXXVII.
Coll: 8° (195 × 124 mm cut) A–2C⁸ 2D⁴ [$ half signed]; 212 leaves; pp. *I–III* IV 5 6–424.
Contents: A1ʳ (*I*) title (verso blank), A2ʳ,ᵛ (*III*–IV) 'TO THE | READER.', A3ʳ–2D4ᵛ (*5–424*) text.
Text: 37 lines; 155 (165) × 79 mm; 83 R. Medium-quality laid paper without watermarks. Page no. at external ends of headlines. Framed headpiece on pp. *III* (eagle, 24 × 81 mm), p. *5* (flowers in vase, 26 × 80 mm); and tailpiece on p.424 (flowers in vase on a pedestal, 36 × 47 mm).
RT, from verso to recto: *Familiar* LETTERS, *between* | *Mr.* Locke *and ſeveral of his* Friends.
CW: Page. A7ᵛ (cu-) rious D8ᵛ (Maſ-) ter I4ʳ (pur-) poſe R6ᵛ magni- [magnifice,] X2ʳ plu- [pluralité] 2A7ʳ (cu-) jus
Press figures: 14 (A7ᵛ)-I   29 (B7ʳ)-I   48 (C8ᵛ)-2   54 (D3ᵛ)-2   64 (D8ᵛ)-I   70 (E3ᵛ)-2   94 (F7ᵛ)-2   96 (F8ᵛ)-I   111 (G8ᵛ)-2   143 (I8ʳ)-I   144 (I8ᵛ)-2   146 (K1ᵛ)-2   176 (L8ᵛ)-2   186 (M5ᵛ)-I   188 (M6ᵛ)-2   194 (N1ᵛ)-2   220 (O6ᵛ)-I   223 (O8ʳ)-2   230 (P3ᵛ)-2   256 (Q8ᵛ)-2   267 (R6ʳ)-I   276 (S2ᵛ)-2   290 (T1ᵛ)-I   318 (U7ᵛ)-I   334 (X7ᵛ)-I   350 (Y7ᵛ)-I   365 (Z7ʳ)-2   367 (Z8ᵛ)-I   380 (2A6ᵛ)-2   390 (2B3ᵛ)-2   414 (2C7ᵛ)-2   421 (2D3ʳ)-2
Note: Reprint of 1708 edition (no. 346) without textual change. I have found no record of a second edition. A microfilm copy of this edition is in the collection, *The Eighteenth Century*, reel 3123, no. 2.
References: Attig 807; Christophersen p. 81–2; ESTC t116553.
Copies examined: O (Vet.A4 e.1281; no fig. p. 223)   CaOTU (Locke L63.A175 1737)   L (1086.h.6)   NR (no fig. p.380)   PPH (Gff.292)

348. 'Familiar Letters'. 4th ed., 1742. 8°
FAMILIAR LETTERS | BETWEEN | Mr. *John Locke*, | AND | Several of his FRIENDS. | In which are EXPLAIN'D, | His NOTIONS in his ESSAY concerning | Human Underſtanding, and in ſome of his | other Works. | [rule 77 mm] | The FOURTH EDITION. | [rule 78 mm] | To which is added, | The LIFE and CHARACTER of | Mr. *JOHN LOCKE*. | [double rule 77 mm] | LONDON: | Printed for F. NOBLE, at *Otway's Head* in St. Mar- | tin's Court, near *Leiceſter-Fields*; T. WRIGHT, | at the *Bible* in

Exeter-Exchange, Strand; and J. DUNCAN, in St. Martin's Court, near Leicefter- | Fields. MDCCXLII.

Coll: 8° (195 × 118 mm cut) A^8 (±A1) ^{2}A^8 (-^{2}A1; A1 + ^{2}A2-8) B-2C^8 2D^4 [$ half signed]; 219 leaves; pp. I-II 1 2-13 14 III IV 5 6-424 [=438].

Contents: A1^r (I) title (verso blank), ^{2}A2^r-8^r (1-13) abridgement of English trans. of Le Clerc's 'Eloge' (no. C1705-5), ^{2}A8^v (14) advt. for books sold by H. Slater, Wright & Duncan, A2^{r,v} (III-IV) 'TO THE | READER.', A3^r-2D4^v (5-424) text.

Illustration: front. is a portrait of Locke by G. Vertue, after Kneller, in oval frame.

Text, CW and press figures: same as no. 343.

Notes: The title leaf is a cancellans. Le Clerc's 'Eloge' in the 2d A quire (without its first leaf) has been inserted after the title page. It is possible the GOT copy has the leaf ^{2}A1 which could contain the list of subscribers mentioned in Jefcoate ('The name of H. Slater added to list of subscribers p.14.') The advertisement on p. 14 (^{2}A8^v) lists 6 titles and reads: 'Just Published, Printed for H. Slater . . . T. Wright . . . and J. Duncan . . .' The rest of the volume uses the same sheets and contents as the 1737 ed. (no. 347). The 'Eloge' first appeared in the Bibliothèque choisie, 6 (1705): 342-411 (cf. no. C1705-5. English translation no. C1706-3). A microfilm copy is in The Eighteenth Century, reel 3258, no. 18.

References: Attig 809; Christophersen p. 82; ESTC t130566; Jefcoate.

Copies examined: O (Vet.A4.e.1144; no fig. p. 146)   C (7180.d.162) [GOT]   L (1508/1456)   MH^1 (*Phil.2115.75)   MH^2 (Phil.2115.75.2) ViU (B1294.L6)

349. 'Familiar Letters': Selections (Limborch). In: Gretton, 1726.

Caption title: [double rule 75 mm] | EXTRACTS | FROM THE | Familiar Letters | BETWEEN | Mr. Locke and his Friends. | Relating to | A Debate concerning the ARGUMENT | à Priori, with refpect to the Divine | Unity.

In: A | REVIEW | OF THE | ARGUMENT | A PRIORI | In Relation to the | BEING and ATTRIBUTES of GOD: | In Reply to Dr. CLARKE's Anfwer to a Seventh | Letter concerning that Argument, printed at the | end of the laft Edition of his Boyleian Lectures. | [rule 83 mm] | With fome EXTRACTS from the Letters | of Mr. LOCKE, concerning the fame. | [rule 82 mm] | [7 lines of ital. quotation from 'Bafil. Hom. 29.'] | [rule 84 mm] | By PHILLIPS GRETTON, [swash Ps, Ts] M. A. | Sometime Fellow of Trinity-College [swash T] in Cambridge, | and now Rector of Springfield in Effex. | [rule 81 mm] | LONDON, | Printed for BERNARD LINTOT, at the Crofs-Keys, | between the Temple-Gates in Fleetftreet. | M.DCC.XXVI.

Collation of the whole: 8° (188 × 123 mm cut) A-H^8 [$ half signed]; 64 leaves; pp. i-iii iv-xv xvi 1-112 [=128].

Locke's text: H1^v-H8^v (pp. 98-112) set in double cols., Latin or French in left col., English translation in right col., separated by vertical rule.

Contents: A1ʳ (*i*) title (verso blank), A2ʳ-7ʳ (iii-xiii) pref., A7ᵛ-8ʳ (xiv-xv) contents of 24 chap. & the 'Extracts', A8ᵛ (xvi) advt. with prices of books by Lintot, B1ʳ-H1ʳ (1-97) Gretton's text in 25 chap., H1ᵛ-8ᵛ (98-112) correspondence of Locke and Limborch, H8ᵛ (112 last 12 lines) advt. for Gretton's *Vindication of the Doctrines of the Church of England*.

Text, pp.1-97: 33 lines; 154 (169)×77 (91) mm; 93 R. Pages 98-112: 38 lines, 152 (166)×77 mm, 93 R; columns 35 mm wide in left, 39 mm (English text) in right. Medium-quality paper. Page no. at outer end of headlines.

RT, pp. 98-111, from verso to recto: EXTRACTS, *from the* | *Letters of Mr.* LOCKE. Page 112: EXTRACTS, *&c*.

CW: Page (*to both cols*). H2ᵛ *left col*: (Qua-) re *right*: there- [therefore] H7ᵛ *left*: (pof-) fum, *right*: (with-) out

Note: Text of Locke material in 33 numbered sections, comprising selected sentences from Locke and Limborch's correspondence relating to Gretton's argument. The quotation on the title is from St. Basil's homiletic advice to the young. A microfilm copy of this work is in *The Eighteenth Century*, reel 2758, no. 8.

Reference: ESTC t065228.

Copies examined: O (1243.e.153 (3)) C (Cam.d.726.5) L (859.c.4 (3))

350. Correspondence with Limborch, et al. '3d' ed., 1739. 2°
TWENTY YEARS | *LITERARY CORRESPONDENCE* | BETWEEN | JOHN [swash J] LOCKE, E*ſq*; | MESSIEURS | LIMBORCH, LEIBNITZ, and the Reverend | Mr. KING of *Exeter*, from 1685 to 1705. | WHEREIN | *Some of the moſt Important* Theological *and* | Philoſophical Points *are clearly Diſcuſſed*. | WITH | Impartial Characters of MEN and BOOKS, SECTS, | PARTIES and OPINIONS. | [rule 139 mm] | TO WHICH ARE SUBJOINED, [swash J] | Monſieur LE CLERC's Hiſtorical Account of Mr. LOCKE's | Life and Writings; with His Laſt-Will and Teſtament. | THE THIRD EDITION. | [rule 138 mm] | [tailpiece, bird-bath with flame above, and leaves, 36×51 mm] | LONDON: | Printed for THOMAS GARDNER, at COWLEY's Head without *Temple-Bar*. [swash T] | E. CURLL in *Roſe-ſtreet, Covent-Garden*. J. HODGES upon *London-Bridge*. | J. JAMES under the *Royal-Exchange*; and J. JACKSON nearSt. [sic] *James's-Palace*. [swash J] | MDCCXXXIX. | [Price of the Whole 4 *s*. Without Mr. *Locke*'s Life and Remains 1 *s*. 6.]

Coll: 2° (336×190 mm cut) a² B-E² F² [$1 signed; a2 called 'a']; 12 leaves; pp. *i-iii iv 1* 2-17 *18* 19-20 [=24].

Contents: a1ʳ (*i*) title (verso blank), a2ʳ·ᵛ (*iii-iv*) 'PREFACE.' (signed: "EASTER-EVE. *April*, 1739. J. [swash J] Bancks.", B1ʳ-F1ʳ (*1-17*) text, F1ᵛ-2ᵛ (*18-20*) advertisement in double cols. ("BOOKS printed for E. CURLL at POPE's Head, in *Roſe-Street Covent-Garden*.")

Text (B1ᵛ): 53 lines; 277 (295)×157 mm; 104 R. Page no. at outer ends of headlines. Pref. set 116 R.

HT, p.1: [double rule 137/138 mm] | EXTRACTS | OF THE | *Literary Correſpondence* | WHICH PASSED BETWEEN | Mr. LOCKE *and Monſieur* LIMBORCH. | From the 28*th* of *Sept.* 1685, to the 4*th* of *Aug.* 1704.

RT, from verso to recto, B1ᵛ-F1ʳ: EXTRACTS *of the* | LITERARY CORRESPONDENCE, *&c.* (The second T in 'Extracts' is swash except on B-E2ᵛ; F1ʳ reads 'CRRESPONDENCE'.)

CW: Page. B2ᵛ (*Lon-*) *don*, E1ʳ (Indiffe-) rence

Press figures: none.

Notes: I am indebted to the Abteilung Historische Drucke, of the Staatsbibliothek zu Berlin, for a microfilm copy of this work (shelfmark Aw 10.534 fol., 3d item) from which all the above information is taken. The measurements are accurate within 3 per cent.; they have been made from the film enlargement.

The preface by John Banks (or Bancks, '1709-1751 . . . miscellaneous writer' - DNB) explains that since the letters were mainly of compliments and of domestic matters, "it was thought needless to give an entire Translation of them . . . we have only given a Narrative, as it were, of this Correspondence, including a Version of such Passages as may now be of public Use . . ." The material consists of an isolated sentence or several sentences translated from various letters (reprinted as *Corr.* 831 (ii.740), 868 (iii.49) et seq.). Further, the compiler has added a translation of Leibnitz's 'Remarks' on the *Essay* in "Deference to the great Name of Mr. *Leibnitz*, and for no other Reason . . ." The original 'Réflexions' were first published in *Some Familiar Letters* (no. 346, pp. 196–205) from the version sent by to William Molyneux; they are reproduced in *Corr.* 2243 (vi.88–93).

Of correspondence with Richard King, Le Clerc's 'Account of Mr. Locke's Life . . .' and his last will and testament there is no sign.

This is another production of the 'unspeakable Mr. Curll' (cf. no. 315). The booksellers probably avoided charges of unauthorised publication by printing translations of materials whose copy was owned by successors to the Churchills.

Attig (808) states the work is a "prospectus consisting of the preface and extracts."; the collation as '17,[1]p.'

351. Letter to Collins, 23 August 1704. In Le Clerc, 1714.
In: *An Account of the Life and Writings of Mr. John Locke, Author of the* Essay concerning Humane Understanding [by Jean Le Clerc]. The Third Edition. London: Printed for J. Clarke and E. Curll, 1714. 34 pp. in-folio.

The letter from Locke at Oates, to be delivered after Locke's death, was "printed in the postscript . . . p. 28." (*Corr.* 3648; viii. 417). Part was printed in Desmaizeaux's *Collection of Several Pieces* (1720; no. 316), pp. 328-9; "the whole, from a copy, B. M. Add. MS. 4290, ff. 1-2, in Fox Bourne [no. 330] ii. 550-1" (ibid.). The letter is reprinted in full as *Corr.* 3648; viii. 417-19. The original manuscript is in the Carl H. Pforzheimer Library, New

York. Pages 29–34 contain Locke's 'Last Will and Testament'. For more information about this inflated piracy of Le Clerc's *Life and Character of Mr. John Locke*, see no. C1714–1.

For Locke's correspondence with Humfry Smith and Richard King, published in 1714, see *The Remains* (no. 315).
Reference: ESTC t128626.
Copies examined: CaOTU (Locke coll.pamphlet fL42 1714) L (12272.m.5) O¹ (G. Pamph. 1680 (35) pp.1–28 only) O² (Vet.A4.c.150 (2); no. 315 intervenes after p. 28)

352. Letters to Boyle, 1665–91. In Boyle, 1744.
Letters from Locke to Boyle, from 12 December 1665 to 21 October 1691.
In: THE | WORKS | OF THE HONOURABLE | *ROBERT BOYLE.* | In FIVE VOLUMES. | To which is prefixed | The Life of the AUTHOR. | VOLUME I.[–V.] | [engr. vignette] | LONDON: Printed for A. MILLAR, opposite *Catharine-Street*, in the Strand. | MDCCXLIV.
This collection was edited by Thomas Birch.
Locke's letters to Boyle are in the fifth vol., pp. 565–71. This vol. also contains a reprint of Locke's weather record, 'A Register Kept by Mr Locke in Oxford' (pp. 157–8) first published in Boyle's *General History of the Air*, (1692; no. 276). The letters are those printed in *Corr.* i–iv, no. 175, 197, 223, 228, 335, 397, 478, 1001 and 1422. The letters are also included in vol.6 of the second, 'New Edition' of Boyle's *Works* edited by Birch published in 1772. See John F. Fulton's *A Bibliography of the Honourable Robert Boyle*, Second Edition (Oxford: Clarendon Press, 1961), no. 240–1.

A microfilm copy of the 1744 edition is in *The Eighteenth Century*, reel 5351, no.1.
References: Attig 813; Christophersen p.83; ESTC (Boyle's Works) t004460.
Copies examined: O (D.2.4–8 Art.) L¹ (96.h.1–5; large paper copy) L² (535.k.15–19)

353. Letter to Bold, 1699. In *The Museum*, 1746.
Caption title: An ORIGINAL LETTER *from Mr.* John Locke, | *to Mr.* Samuel Bold, *at* Steeple.
In: The MUSEUM: OR, THE Literary and Historical REGISTER. NUMB. XX, *Saturday* December 20. [1746]. [London: Printed for R. Dodsley . . ., 1746].
Locke's letter, dated '*Oats, May* 16, 1699.' is on pp. 205–9 (2H1ʳ–3ʳ). It was included for the first time in the 7th edition of Locke's *Works* (1768), i. xv n.; reprinted in the 8th edition (1777), iv. *645–*649. It was later reprinted by Robert Goadby in *The Moral and Entertaining Magazine*, 2 (1778); reprinted as *Corr.* 2590 (vi. 626–30). The original ms. does not survive.
Reference: Attig 814; Christophersen p.83.
Copy examined: O (Hope 8° 699)

354. Letters to Mapletoft, 1670-79. In *The European Magazine*, 1788.
Title from contents: Original Letters from Mr. Locke, Algernon Sidney, and Lady R. Russell, to Dr. Mapletoft.
In: The European Magazine, and London Review . . . By the Philological Society of London. Vol. XIV.[-XV.] for 1788. [-1789.] London: Printed for J. Sewell, Cornhill, 1788 [-89].
Letters from Locke to Dr. John Mapletoft are printed as follows:
  Corr. 243, 260: i. 338-40, 362-3, in vol. 14 (Nov. 1788), pp. 321-3;
  ibid. 259: i.360-62, in 14 (Dec. 1788), pp. 401-3;
  ibid. 265, 339, 348, 360-62, 364, 417, 450: i.369 et seq., passim, in vol.15 (1789), pp. 9-11, 89-91, 185-6, 273-4, and 353-4.
The letters range from 10 July 1670 to ca. 1 March 1679; they were published in chronological order except *Corr.* 417 which was printed after no. 348 (pp. 89-90 and 90-91 respectively). The originals do not survive, and were printed in the *Correspondence* from their publication here. The other letters from Algernon Sidney and Lady Rachel Russell, and from Dr. Simon Patrick, all to Dr. Mapletoft, are scattered through successive issues of *The European Magazine*.
References: Attig 817; Christophersen p.83.
Copy examined: O (Hope Adds.745-6)

355. 'Original Letters' (ed. Forster). 1830. 12°
ORIGINAL LETTERS | OF | LOCKE; | ALGERNON SIDNEY; | AND | ANTHONY LORD SHAFTESBURY, | AUTHOR OF THE "CHAR-ACTERISTICS." | [rule 11 mm] | WITH AN ANALYTICAL SKETCH OF | THE WRITINGS AND OPINIONS OF LOCKE | AND OTHER METAPHYSICIANS, | BY | T. FORSTER, M.B. F.L.S. M.A.S. | CORR. MEMB. OF THE ACAD. OF N. SCIENCE AT PHILADEL-PHIA, &c. | [rule 30 mm] | LONDON: | J.B. NICHOLS AND SON, PARLIAMENT STREET. | 1830.
Coll: 12° (200 × 122 mm uncut) a-e^{12} B-M^{12} N^6 O^2 [$1 2 & 5 (+N3; -N5, -O2) signed]; 200 leaves; pp.*i-iii* iv-cxx *1-3* 4-49 *50* 51-65 *66* 67-75 *76-79* 80-98 *99-101* 102-274 *275* 276-279 *280* [= 400].
Contents: a1^r (*i*) title, a1^v (*ii*) Nichols' address ('J.B. NICHOLS AND SON, 25, Parliament Street, London.'), a2^r-e12^v (*iii*-cxx) preface (signed 'Boreham, March 31, 1830.'), B1^r (*1*) section title (verso blank), B2^r-D1^r (*3-49*) Locke's letters chiefly to B. Furly, D1^v-D9^r (*50-65*) letters to Edw. Clarke, D9^v-E2^r (*66-75*) letters to Hans Sloane, E2^v blank, E3^r (*77*) section title (verso blank), E4^r-F1^v (*79-98*) letters of Sidney to B. Furley, F2^r (*99*) section title (verso blank), F3^r-N5^v (*101-274*) letters of 3d Earl of Shaftesbury to Furly and others (June 1691-Feb. 1713), N6^r-O2^r (*275-279*) index of names and topics, O2^v (*280*) advt. for 6 books published by Nichols.
Illustrations: 1. facing p. 38 is fold. engr. plate 199 × 144 mm on leaf 218 × 171 mm, tipped in, captioned 'Page 38. COPY FOR WRITING DESIGNED BY LOCKE', signed '*Joh. de Broen. Scul.*'

2. within text on p. xiii (a7ʳ) is picture of Locke's birthplace at Wrington, Somerset, 55 × 75 mm (without heading).
3. within text on p. cxvi (e10ᵛ) is picture of a silver goblet, the gift of Sidney to Furly, 51 × 41 mm, subscribed 'THE GIFT OF COLONEL ALGERNON SIDNEY.'.

Section title, p. 1: LETTERS | OF | JOHN LOCKE.
p. 77: LETTERS | OF | ALGERNON SYDNEY.
p. 99: LETTERS | OF | ANTHONY | EARL OF SHAFTESBURY, | AUTHOR OF "THE CHARACTERISTICS."

Text: 24 lines; 127 (139) × 76 mm; 105 R with 1.8 mm leading. Good wove paper without watermarks. Page no. at upper external corners. No catchwords. Probably issued in boards, and (according to D. Neill) with spine label: [Oxford rule] | LETTERS | OF | LOCKE, | A. SIDNEY, | AND | SHAFTESBURY.

Notes: Benjamin Furley (rather, Furly)'s letters were inherited by Thomas Forster through Dorothy, Benjamin's daughter who married Edward Forster, Thomas Forster's (the editor) grandfather. Locke's, Sidney's and Shaftesbury's letters were part of that inheritance. The correspondence between Locke and the others is printed in *Corr.* iii et seq.: "the dates of some of those from Locke are wrong" (ibid. iii. 40 n.). The originals are now in the Bodleian Library.

This work was listed in the *English Catalogue of Books* under Forster as a post octavo, priced at 10 s. 6 d.; published May 1830.

I am indebted to Desmond Neill for corrections, and information about the uncut size and the spine label.

Reference: Attig 819; Christophersen p.82.
Copies examined: L (10921 cc.3) MH (*AC9.R1523.Zz830f, Benj. Rand's copy) O (30.162) PPH (Gff.29) PPL (Ia.Lock/66774.O PU (DA430.F73)

356. 'Original Letters' (ed. Forster). 2d ed., 1847. 8°
Original Letters of John Locke, Alg. Sidney, and Lord Shaftesbury, with an Analytical Sketch of the Writings and Opinions of Locke and Other Metaphysicians, by T. Forster, M.B. F.L.S. M.A.S. Corr. Memb. of the Acad. of N. Science at Philadelphia, &c. The Second Edition. London: Privately Printed. 1847.
 i–vii x–lxxx, 1–3 4–211, *212–214* pp. : ill. (on p. ii: Sidney's goblet & Locke's birthplace at Wrington) 8° (215 × 135 mm cut)

Note: The publisher's preface to this edition (dated 'Dec. 1, 1847.') states that he "has added several others written by the same eminent men, and procured from the same source, namely the MSS. collection of the Forster family." The letters have been numbered I–CII, followed by "Letter I* [omitted at page 4.]" For this edition they have been rearranged in chronological order, beginning with Letter I: Algern. Sidney to B. Furley, dated Nov. 29, 1677; the collection ends at no. 102: W. Forster to his brothers, dated 9 Feb. 1749/50. The prefatory pages have signatures and collate as a^8 (–a1) b–i^4 [$ 1 signed]. Pages 212–4 contain the index.

This edition was listed in the *English Catalogue of Books* as an octavo, priced at 7 s. 6 d.; available through Bell and Daldy in 1848.

A facsimile reprint of this edition was published by Thoemmes, Bristol, in 1990.

References: Attig 820; Christophersen p. 82.
Copies examined: L (10920.g.16) Y

357. Letters to Toinard, 1678–81 (ed. Ollion). 1908. 8°
Notes sur la Correspondance de John Locke, suivies de trente-deux lettres inédites de Locke à Thoynard (1678–1681) / H. Ollion, Docteur ès lettres, Maître de conférences à la Faculté libre des lettres de Lyon. Paris: Alphonse Picard & fils, éditeurs, 82, rue Bonaparte, 82. 1908.

144 pp. large 8° (254 × 165 mm uncut). Gatherings 1 2–9, $1 signed. Listed price: 2 fr., 50 c. (Lorenz)

Half-title: Lettres inédites de Locke à Thoynard.

Note: The thirty-one letters from Locke to Nicolas Toinard (pp. 28–144) were acquired by the British Library in 1868 from an auction by E. Charavay of the collection of J.-C. Brunet. The bulk of Toinard's letters is now in the Bibliothèque nationale, MSS. Nouvelles acquisitions françaises, no 560-3. Locke's letters follow a detailed calendar of Locke's correspondence (by writer or recipient), date written, present locations, and (if published) details of publication (pp. 9–24). They are included in de Beer's edition of the *Correspondence*, vols. iii et seq. (see note, iii. 579–82).

Issued with light grey paper covers; the back cover lists other books for sale by Picard.

References: Attig 813; Christophersen p. 82.

358. Letters to Toinard, et al. (ed. Ollion) 1912. 8°
Lettres inédites de John Locke à ses amis Nicolas Thoynard, Philippe van Limborch et Edward Clarke. Publiées avec une introduction et des notes explicatives par M. Henri Ollion, docteur ès lettres, professeur à la Faculté libre des lettres de Lyon, avec la collaboration de M. le professeur Dr. T. J. de Boer, de l'Université d'Amsterdam. La Haye: Martinus Nijhoff, 1912.

x, 258 pp., large 8° (250 × 165 mm uncut). Gatherings for pp. 1–258 numbered 1–15^8 16^{10} [$1 signed] (bifolium signed 16*, inserted as 2nd and 9th leaves of 16th gathering; 10th leaf blank). Index of proper names on p. 254–8. Listed price: 7.50 guilders.

Note: This collection includes the 32 letters published in the 1908 work (no. 357), and a further 27 "all except one apparently from originals or copies in the [British Library's] holding." (*Corr.* iii.581). The letters are in various languages (Latin, French, English).

References: Attig 833; Christophersen p. 82.

359. Correspondence with Clarke (ed. Rand). 1927. 8°
The Correspondence of John Locke and Edward Clarke. Edited, with a Biographical Study, by Benjamin Rand, Ph.D., LL.D., Harvard University. Cambridge, Mass.: Harvard University Press; London: Humphrey Milford, Oxford University Press, 1927.
   xvi, 607 pp. : plates (incl. front.); 8° (220 × 150 mm cut). Correspondence: pp. 77–602; index: pp. 603–7. Listed price: 30 s.
Colophon, on verso of title: Printed in Great Britain by Robert Maclehose and Co., Ltd. The University Press, Glasgow.
Note: The letters on pp. 77–602 were transcribed from the Lovelace Collection (now in the Bodleian Library), the Nynehead Collection of Col. E.C.A. Sanford of Chipley (now also in the Bodleian), and some from the British Library. They are all included in de Beer's edition of the *Correspondence*. The four plates are (1) a portrait of Locke by John Greenhill as frontispiece; (2) portrait of Edward Clarke, facing p. 75; (3) of Mrs. Clarke, facing p. 247; and (4) a portrait of their daughter Elizabeth, facing p. 581. Half-title (p. *i*) reads: Locke and Clarke.
   This edition was published in July 1927. It is printed on machine-made laid-style paper with vertical chainlines; bound in dark ('Harvard') green linen, with spine stamped in gold, Harvard University Press seal at foot. A facsim. reprint was issued in 1975 by Books for Libraries Press, Plainview, N.Y.
References: Attig 834; Christophersen p. 82.

360. Correspondence with Le Clerc (ed. Bonno). 1959. 8°
Lettres inédites de Le Clerc à Locke. Edited, with an introduction and notes, by Gabriel Bonno. Berkeley and Los Angeles; University of California Press, 1959.
   [6], 135 pp. in-8° (234 × 153 mm, paperbound), Series: University of California Publications in Modern Philology, Volume 52.
Note: Transcription of 65 previously unpublished letters from Jean Le Clerc to Locke from Bodleian Lib. MS. Locke f. 13 (pp. 28–130), and two letters from Locke to Le Clerc translated into French, from the library of the Remonstrants' Church in Amsterdam (now in Amsterdam University Library: MS. R.K. J.53b and MS. R.K. Ba 258u). Locke's first letter is dated 2 October 1686 (22 September 1686 N.S.), and the English text is reprinted on p. 131 (reprinted *Corr*. 866; iii. 38–9). The second letter dated 30 July 1688 (20 July N.S.) was first published in Fox Bourne (ii. 76–9; see no. 346) and here appears only in French translation (English reprinted *Corr*. 1069; iii. 489–92). All these and three further letters from Le Clerc and two more from Locke are printed in *Corr*. iii–viii. Bonno's edition is preceded by an introduction (pp. 1–25) and followed by index (pp. 133–35).
   Verso of the title-page reads "Submitted by editors May 21, 1958. Issued November 30, 1959. Price, $4.00."
Reference: Attig 842.

361. Correspondence with Le Clerc (ed. Sina). In Sina, 1987-date (in progress).
Epistolario / Jean Le Clerc . . . A cura di Mario Sina. Firenze: Leo S. Olschki, editore, 1987-date. 8° (255 x 176 mm uncut; cream card covers) Series: Le Corrispondenze letterarie, scientifiche ed erudite, dal Riniascimento all'età moderna, 1-
Vol. 1: 1679-1689. 1987 (xxxiii, 564 pp.) ISBN: 88-222-3495-2. Price: 96,000 lire.
Vol. 2, 'a cura di Maria Grazia e Mario Sina': 1690-1705. [1991] (xv, [2], 636 pp.) ISBN: 88-222-3872-9. Price: 120,000 lire.
Vol.3: 'a cura di Maria Grazia e Mario Sina': 1706-1718. 1994. (xx, [2], 638 pp.) ISBN: 88-222-4211-4. Price: 130,000 lire.
Note: A definitive edition of all Le Clerc's correspondence from materials in the Bodleian Library, the University of Amsterdam Library, Bibliothèque nationale in Paris, Royal Library in the Hague, and elsewhere. The letters are chiefly in Latin or French, with some in English. Locke's correspondence in the first vol. dates from 22 September 1686 to December 1689 (here numbered 116, 141, 144-7, 148-50, 154, 157 and 161).

Vol. 2 includes Locke's correspondence from 21 Jan. 1690 to 24 June 1704 (no. 162-365 passim); more than half of pp. 1-449 are their letters. The citations include present location of manuscripts, details of prior publication including citations to Corr. 866 (iii. 38-9) and following vols.

Vol.3 contains letters dated Feb. 19, 1706 to Nov. 17, 1718. Correspondents include Henry Dodwell, A. A. Cooper (3d Lord Shaftesbury), Jean Barbeyrac, Josph Addison, Jacques Basnage, Berkeley, Crousaz, Fontenelle, Hutchinson, Spanheim and Tyrrell. Le Clerc was a correspondent of Phillppus van Limborch, Pierre Bayle, Gilbert Burnet, Robert Boyle, and many others. He died in January 1736.

362. Correspondence (ed. de Beer). 1976-date
The Correspondence of John Locke. Edited by E. S. de Beer. In Eight Volumes. Oxford: At the Clarendon Press, 1976-date. Issued in the series: The Clarendon Edition of the Works of John Locke. Black buckram binding, with spine stamped in gold; the press's seal at the foot. Prices of individual vols. given below.
Notes: The complete, definitive edition, it includes all known letters to and from Locke, and notes spurious attributions. It is replete with concise informative scholarly notes. Dates of composition, where previously published, are corrected. De Beer records present location of the manuscripts, and gives details of prior publication. Each volume contains, in addition to the text, a preliminary 'Locke's Life; Principal Dates for This Volume', 'An Index of Correspondents', and (from vol. ii) 'Recurrent Designations Other than Proper Names'. The are also several genealogical charts (some folded). The contents of each vol. are as follows:

i (1976). Preface & Introduction (pp. v–lxxix). Bibliography ('Finding-List . . .', pp. lxxx–xcv). Genealogical tables (pp. xcx–xcxi). Letters 1–461 (c. 1650–1652 to 31 March 1679). ISBN 0-19-824396-0. Price £25.

ii (1976). Letters 462–848 (About April 1679 to 8 April 1686). ISBN 0-19-824550-0. Price £25.

iii (1978). Letters 849–1241 (24 April 1686–28 January 1690). ISBN 0-19-824560-2. Price £30.

iv (1979). Letters 1242–1701 (2 February 1690–27 January 1694). ISBN 0-19-824561-0. Price £30.

v (1979). Letters 1702–2198 (30 January 1694–c. 18 February 1697). Appendix: Documents relating to the termination of the Licensing Act, 1695 (pp. 785–96). ISBN 0-19-824562-9. Price £30 in 1979; raised to £35 in 1980 (*BNB*).

vi (1981). Letters 2199–2664 (19 February 1697–27 January 1700). Appendix I: Leibniz's 'Quelques Remarques' (on the *Essay*, pp. 777–82). Appendix II: The Drafts of Locke's Letters to van Limborch on the Unity of God (pp. 783–93). ISBN 0-19-824563-7. Price £35.

vii (1982). Letters 2665–3286 (27 January 1700–14 May 1703). ISBN 0-19-824564-5. Price £45.

viii (1989). Letters 3287–3648 (15 May 1703–25 October 1704). Includes a copy of Locke's will (pp.419–427) and additional letters omitted from previous vols. Appendix I: Locke's Portraits (pp. 444–8). Appendix II: Distribution Lists for Copies of Locke's Books (pp. 449–58). Appendix III: Information on 'Unprinted Items in the Bodleian Library Mss. Locke c. 3–23' (chiefly legal documents, scraps & irrelevant materials: pp. 459–60). ISBN 0-19-824565-3. Price £50.

A ninth and final volume containing the index is in progress.

Reference: Attig 847.

CHAPTER XI
Works, Collected and Selected (nos. 363–373)

The Churchill brothers, Awnsham and John, had published most of Locke's acknowledged and unacknowledged publications, and owned the right to republish them. The first collected edition bears the publication date of 1714, ten years after Locke's death. To justify their including such anonymously issued works as the 'Toleration' letters, *Two Treatises of Government*, *The Reasonableness of Christianity* and its two *Vindications*, they prefaced their edition with a note 'To the Reader' quoting that part of the codicil to Locke's will wherein he acknowledged his authorship of them. That part had also served as the preface to his *Posthumous Works* (1706; no. 299).

Locke's will, with its codicil, is printed in full in *Corr.* viii. 419–27. It was first published in full in Curll's folio edition of Le Clerc's *Account of the Life and Writings . . . of . . . Mr. John Locke* (no. C1714-1, below).

Until the Hollis edition of Locke's *Works* in 1768 (no. 369), all subsequent editions were mere reprints of the 1714 collection without editorial attention, although Desmaizeaux's *Collection* (no. 316–18) was incorporated into the *Works* beginning with the 5th edition of 1751 (no. 367), together with the English translation of Le Clerc's 'Eloge' (from no. C1706-3). The 1794 edition (no. 371), an expansion of Bishop Law's revision of Hollis's edition, set the pattern for all subsequent English *Works* editions until the present time.

363. Works. 1714. 3 vols. 2° in 2s and 4s.
Vol. 1. Within a double rule, inner 258 × 139 mm, outer 264 × 147 mm: THE | WORKS [S inverted] | OF | *JOHN LOCKE* [swash J, K] Eſq. | [rule 134 mm] | In Three Volumes. | [rule 135 mm] | The CONTENTS of which follow in the next Leaf. | [rule 135 mm] | With ALPHABETICAL TABLES. | [rule 134 mm] | VOL. I. | [rule 134 mm] | [orn., bird within bower, 47 × 50 mm] | [rule 134 mm] | *LONDON*, [swash Ns, D] | Printed for JOHN CHURCHILL at the Black Swan in | *Pater-noſter-Row*, [swash P, R] and SAM. MANSHIP at the Ship in | *Cornhil.* M.DCC.XIV.
Vol. 2, within a double rule, inner 258 × 141 mm, outer 265 × 148 mm: . . . [1st 4 lines as vol. 1] | [rule 136 mm] | VOL. II. | [rule 135 mm] | CONTAINING, | . . . [10 titles in 2 cols., 19 & 18 lines each, separated by vertical rule 92 mm] | [rule 135 mm] | *LONDON*, [swash Ns, D] | Printed for JOHN [swash J] CHURCHILL at the Black Swan in | *Pater-noſter-Row.* [swash P, R] M.DCC.XIV.

Vol. 3, within a double rule, inner 252 × 149 mm, outer 261 × 159 mm: THE | WORKS | OF | *JOHN LOCKE* [swash J, K] Efq; | [rule 145 mm] | VOL. III. | [rule 143 mm] | CONTAINING, | . . . [2 cols. divided by vertical rule 77 mm; left col. of 6 titles in 13 lines; right col. in 15 lines headed 'POSTHUMOUS WORKS, *Viz.*' listing contents numbered I–VI, concluding:] Familiar Letters between Mr. *Locke* and | feveral of his Friends. | [rule 145 mm] | *LONDON*; [sic] | Printed for JOHN CHURCHILL, at the *Black* | *Swan*, in *Pater-Nofter-Row*. MDCCXIV.

Coll: 2o in 4s (320 × 200 mm cut). Vol. 1: A² [a]² a–g² B–4D 4E–4H² [$ half signed]; 314 leaves; pp. *I–VIII i–ii* iii–xxviii 1–*575* 576–592 [=628].

Vol.2: π1 A–4P⁴ 4Q–4T² [$ half (–2K1) signed]; 345 leaves; pp. *i–ii* 1–2 *3–14* 17 *16–62* 63–66 *67–97* 98–*101* 102–227 *228–230* 231–256 *257–258* 259–291 *292–294* 295–470 *471–472* 473–532 353 *543*–541 *542–544* *545*–553 *554–556* *557*–671 *672–688* [=690]. Page 15 called '17'; 533 called '353'.

Vol. 3: π1 A–R² S–3Z⁴ 4A² 4B–5A⁴ 5B–5E² [$ half signed]; 345 leaves; pp. *i–vi* 1–98 *99–100* 101–113 *114* 115–143 *144* 145–307 230 309–341 *342* 343–384 *385–388* 389–455 *456* 457–469 *470* 471–480 *481* 482–494 509 496–500 *501*–668 *669–684* [=690]. Page 308 called '230'; 495 called '509' (MH copy has '495').

Each page with a signature is also signed in direction line 'Vol. I.' 'II.', or 'III.' except vol. 3 p. 217 which is only signed 'Oo'.

Illustrations: 1. Vol. 1 has engr. port. reading '*G. Kneller Eques pinxit 1697. Geo. Vertue Sculp. 1713.*', 243 × 152 mm on plate 255 × 160, the whole subscribed: '*Effigies Iohannis Locke* | *Ex Archetypo, quod in Musæo Alexandri Geekie Chirurgi adservatur exprefsa.*'

2. Vol. 1 also has engraved plate of Locke's Latin epitaph, styled after the tablet in the church at High Laver, Essex, 287 × 178 mm on plate 302 × 190 mm. It is often found bound after leaf [a]1; sometimes facing frontispiece.

Contents. Vol. 1: A1ʳ (*I*) title (verso blank), A2ʳ˒ᵛ (*III–IV*) contents of 3 vols., [a]1ʳ˒ᵛ (*V–VI*) preface 'To the Reader' (includes quoting that part of Locke's will concerning his authorship of the 'Toleration' letters, *Two Treatises*, and the *Reasonableness of Christianity*), [a]2ʳ˒ᵛ (*VII–VIII*) advt. of books sold by J. Churchill (in double cols., listed by size),

Essay concerning Human Understanding: a1ʳ (*i*) section title to *Essay* (verso blank), a2ʳ–b1ʳ (iii–v) dedication, b1ᵛ–c2ᵛ (vi–xii) reader's epistle, d1ʳ–g2ᵛ (xiii–xxvii) contents by book, chap. & sections, B1ʳ–2X3ᵛ (1–342) text;

Letter to . . . [Stillingfleet]: 2X4ʳ–3D2ʳ (343–387) text;

Mr. Locke's Reply to [Stillingfleet]: 3D2ᵛ–3I3ʳ (388–431) text;

Mr. Locke's Second Reply to [Stillingfleet]: 3I3ᵛ–4D4ʳ (432–575) text; 4D4ᵛ (*576*) errata & addenda to the 'Second Reply' (19 lines);

Index to vol.: 4E1ʳ–4H2ᵛ (577–592; last page upper half is text, bottom is 5-line errata).

Vol. 2: π1^r (*i*) title (verso blank),

Some Considerations of the ... Lowering of Interest ...: A1^r (*1*) section title (verso blank), A2^r-G4^r (*3-55*) text;

Short Observations ...: G4^v-H3^v (*56-62*) text;

Further Considerations ...: H4^r (*63*) section title (verso blank), I1^r-N1^r (*65-97*) text, N1^v (*98*) value table;

Two Treatises of Government: N2^r (*99*) section title (verso blank), N3^r-2F2^r (*101-227*) text, 2F2^v (*228*) contents;

A Letter concerning Toleration: 2F3^r (*229*) section title (verso blank), 2F4^r-2I4^v (*231-256*) text;

A Second Letter concerning Toleration: 2K1^r (*257*) section title (verso blank), 2K2^r-2O2^r (*259-291*) text, 2O2^v blank;

A Third Letter for Toleration: 2O3^r (*293*) section title, 2O3^v (*294*) abbreviations explained, 2O4^r-3N3^v (*295-470*) text;

The Reasonableness of Christianity: 3N4^r (*471*) section title (verso blank), 3O1^r (*473*) preface, 3O1^v-3Y3^r (*474-541*) text, 3Y3^v blank;

Vindication: 3Y4^r (*543*) section title (verso blank), 3Z1^r-4A1^r (*545-553*) text, 4A1^v blank;

Second Vindication: 4A2^r (*555*) section title (verso blank), 4A3^r-4^v (*557-560*) preface, 4B1^r-4P4^r (*561-671*) text, 4P4^v blank;

Index to vol.: 4Q1^r-4T2^r (*673-687*) text, 4T2^v (*688*) blank.

Vol. 3: π1^r (*i*) title (verso blank), A1^r (*iii*) section title to *Some Thoughts* (verso blank),

Some Thoughts concerning Education: A2^{r,v} (*v-vi*) dedicatory letter, B1^r-Y1^v (*1-98*) text;

A Paraphrase and Notes on the Epistles of St. Paul: Y2^r (*99*) section title (verso blank), Y3^r-Z4^v (*101-112*) Essay for the Understanding, 2A1^r (*113*) section title to the Galatians, with publisher's note (verso blank), 2A2^r-2D4^r (*115-143*) text of Galatians, 2D4^v blank, 2E1^r-2N2^v (*145-212*) 1 Corinthians, 2N3^r-2S1^v (*213-250*) 2 Corinthians, 2S2^r-3F3^r (*251-341*) Romans, 3F3^v blank, 3F4^r-3L4^v (*343-384*) Ephesians;

Posthumous Works: 3M1^r (*385*) section title, with contents (verso blank), 3M2^r-3Z4^v (*387-480*) text as in no. 299, 4A1^r (*481*) section title, 4A1^v-4C2^r (*482-509* [*495 rectē*]) text of 'New Method of a Common-Place-Book', 4C2^v blank;

Some Familiar Letters: 4C3^r (*497*) section title (verso blank), 4C4^r-5A4^v (*499-668*) text;

Index to vol. 3: 5B1^r-5E2^r (*669-683*); 5E2^v (*684*) blank.

Text (v.1 C1^v): 61 lines (varies slightly); 248 (260) × 132 (155) mm (varies); 82 R. Good-quality laid paper with watermark similar to Heawood 414. Page no. at external ends of headlines. Marginal notes chiefly set 67 italic; in 'Letters' to Stillingfleet set roman. Footnotes set 67R.

Ornaments and initials. Vol. 1: tailpiece on title-page (bird in a bower) also appears on c2^v (xii), 3D2^r (*387*), 3I3^r (*429*) and 4D4^v (*576*). Framed 6-line initials of figures supporting a letter (21 × 22 mm, similar to

Bowyer 187 series) are found on a2ʳ, b1ᵛ, B1ʳ, E4ᵛ, 2A3ʳ, 2I2ʳ, 3D2ᵛ and 3I4ᵛ.

Vol. 2 has Bowyer tailpieces 131–2, 122 and 124. Initials are chiefly from the 187 series except for I2ʳ and N3ᵛ which are 184 series. Page 671 (4P3ʳ) has same 'bird in bower' tailpiece as found in vol. 1.

Vol. 3 has no tailpieces. Framed initial As, 5-line, with scrolls and the bar of the 'A' V-shaped (21 × 21 mm) occur on 4A2ᵛ and 5B1ʳ; a 7-line unframed A (with oak leaves, 28 × 27 mm) on B1ʳ and 3X1ʳ. Other framed initials (5-line, 20 × 21 mm) are on Y2ʳ, 3Y4ʳ, 4D1ʳ; and a 7-line (floral, 25 × 25 mm) on 3M3ʳ, 3R3ʳ and 4C4ʳ. A 7-line unframed floral A (27 × 27 mm) is on A2ʳ and 2A2ʳ.

Headlines or RTs are chap. titles, printed in italics, with roman for emphasis; book no. at inner margin of headline on versos, chap. numbers on rectos, e.g. 'Of Clear and Obſcure Ideas. Book II. | Chap. 29. *Of Clear and Obſcure* Ideas.'

CW: Page. Vol. 1: [a]1ᵛ A [*Books*] b1ᵛ This [This,] E1ᵛ Im- [Impreſſions,]
Vol. 2: A2ʳ SIR, [SIR,] B1ᵛ A King- [A Kingdom] C4ʳ Acci- [Accidents]
Vol. 3: F1ʳ §.55. Re- [§.55. Rewards,] H1ʳ Maſter's [Maſters] M3ʳ §.102. Be- [§.102. Begin] 3B4ᵛ (diſ-) honour [nour (*rectē* honour)]

Press figures. Vol. 1 has inverted obelus or dagger (†) as figure throughout on all gatherings except 2B 2F 2O 2S 2U 3B–C and 3R–S. Gatherings have each from one to four figures per gathering; most have two; gatherings 2R, 3D, 3M, 3P, 3T and 3X have four. The multiplicity of daggers and the vol. numbering on each signed page indicate each quire was separately printed, and the 2d and 3d leaves were tucked in between the first and 4th when a gathering is in 4s.

Vol. 2: none.

Vol. 3 has asterisks as press figures throughout, but none in sheets A C G I L N–O 2C 2M 2Y 3D 3G 3I 3O–T and 4B–5E. There are 4 asterisks in 2B 2P 2T and 3X; 3 in 2K and 2S; all the rest have one or 2 per gathering. Beginning with 2O1ʳ the asterisks are smaller, 5-point figures, before that they were 8-point; but this does not indicate a different printer since a line of type on p. 478 (3Z3ᵛ) uses both styles of asterisk.

Notes: The first collected edition of Locke's work and the earliest to put his name to the letters of 'Toleration' and to *The Reasonableness of Christianity*. The texts generally follow the readings of the most recently published editions (except for minor spelling variants and typographical errors). The fifth edition of the *Essay* (1706; no. 65) is that followed here with the addition of ten words omitted from the 'Epistle to the Reader' in the 1706 and 1710 editions (see Nidditch's edition, p. 12 lines 5–6 n.); the long quotations from the 'Letters' to Bishop Edward Stillingfleet are also omitted, since the 'Letters' themselves are included in this collecion.

This edition was put together by Peter King, Locke's nephew and executor, and John Churchill, brother of Awnsham (John is thought to have died in 1714. Cf. Plomer). The vols. were issued sequentially, vol. 1 published late in 1713.

Manship is not generally known to have published after 1713 (ibid.), hence his omission from the imprint of the second and third vols., but he reappears in the imprint of vol. 1 of the 1722 edition. Awnsham Churchill was giving more attention to politics at this time, but resurfaced as the publisher of the 1722 *Works* (no. 364); he lived until 1728.

J. Nichols, in his *Literary Anecdotes* (i. 67) reports this edition was printed under William Bowyer's "superintendance more immediate" in 1713. The decorative initials and the ornaments show that there were three different printers for this edition: those used in vol. 1 differ from those in vol. 3, and those in vol. 2 (except gatherings 4C-4H) differ from both. The ornaments and initials in vol. 2 gatherings A-4B are those known to be used by William Bowyer. The style of the swash letters R and C in the italicized headlines from 4C on (pp. 569 et seq.) in vol. 2 are different from those preceding; the tailpiece on p. 671 is the same as that on the title-page of vol.1. I therefore think printer 'A' printed vol. 1 and gathering 4C to the end of vol. 2; Bowyer printed gatherings A-4B of vol. 2; and third printer, 'C' printed vol. 3.

A microfilm copy of this edition is in the collection, *The Eighteenth Century*, reel 1081, no. 1.

References: Alston 7:112; Attig 848; Christophersen pp.87-8; ESTC t128627.

Copies examined: Y C CaOHM CLU-C Ct DFo (B1253.1714; ex lib. Joseph Laing) Dm EXu (ex lib. Arthur Tremayne) [GhU (Ph20)] L (12272.m.5; ex lib. John Elliott; v.1 bound with no.C1714-1) MH (Phil.2115.1F) [MnU] NR O (H1.4-6 Th; lacks front.) Oba (JL5.h2-4; v.1 lacks ill.; 'Ex libris Benj. Jowett') Oc Occ (fol.VI.9-12) Om PU (Founders 103.F) ViU WaU (192.2.AAc)

364. Works. 2d ed., 1722. 3 vols. 2° in 2s and 4s. Two states of vol. 2.
364:1. Vol. 1. Within a double rule, inner 260 × 140 mm, outer 268 × 150 mm: THE | WORKS | OF | *JOHN LOCKE* [swash J, K] Efq; | [rule 135 mm] | . . . [&c. as no. 363, until 12th line:] VOL. I. | [rule 135 mm] | 𝕿𝖍𝖊 𝕾𝖊𝖈𝖔𝖓𝖉 𝕰𝖉𝖎𝖙𝖎𝖔𝖓. | [rule 136 mm] | [orn., 2 cherubs with cornucopia, 50 × 60 mm] | [rule 135 mm] | *LONDON*, | Printed for A. CHURCHILL, and A. MANSHIP, and fold | by W. TAYLOR in *Pater-nofter-Row*. M.DCC.XXII.
364:2A. Vol. 2, first state. Within a double rule, inner 262 × 138 mm, outer 271 × 148 mm: THE | WORKS | OF | *JOHN LOCKE*, [swash J, K] Efq; | [rule 136 mm] | VOL. II. | [rule] | The SECOND EDITION. | [rule 136 mm] | CONTAINING, | . . . | [contents of 10 titles in 2 cols., of 19 and 18 lines, as in no. 363] | [rule 136 mm] | *LONDON:* | Printed by *Samuel Negus*, for A. CHURCHILL. M.DCC.XXII.
364:2B. Vol. 2, second state. Within a double rule, same as first state, until imprint: *LONDON:* | Printed for AWNSHAM CHURCHILL. M.DCC.XXII.
364:3. Vol. 3. Within a double rule: . . . [first 4 lines as vol. 1] | [rule 141 mm] | VOL. III. | [rule 140 mm] | CONTAINING, | . . . [contents as

in no. 363, left column: 6 titles in 12 lines; right col.: 'Posthumous Works' and 'Familiar Letters' in 14 lines] | [rule 141 mm] | LONDON: | Printed for AWNSHAM CHURCHILL; and Sold | by WILLIAM TAYLOR, at the *Ship and* | *Black Swan* in *Pater-Nofter-Row*. MDCCXXII. [Xs a point larger than other small caps.]

Coll: 2° in 4s (340 × 220 mm cut). Vol. 1: A^2 [a]^2 (-[a]2) a-g^2 B-4D^4 4E-4H^2 [half signed]; 313 leaves; pp. *I–VI i–iii* iv–xxviii *1* 2–575 576–592 [= 626]. (MnU reports in their copy page 531 is unnumbered.)

Vol. 2: π1 A^4 B-4P^4 4Q-4S^2 4T^2 (-4T2) [$ half signed; leaves 2R1 and 2R2 both signed 'Rr']; 344 leaves. *First state*: pp. *i–ii* 1–2 3–14 *17* 16–62 *63*–66 67–97 *98*–102 103–227 *228*–230 231–249 *250* 251–256 257–258 259–291 292–294 295–314 *115* 316–399 *409* 401–470 471–472 473–532 *353* 534–541 542–544 545–553 554–556 557–656 *659* 658–663 *662* 665–671 672–686 [= 688]. Pages 15, 250, 315, 400, 657 and 664 numbered in error as 17, 025, 115, 409, 659 and 662 respectively.

Vol. 2 *second state* has all pagination errors but one corrected, page 657 still called '659'. In some copies p. 533 is called '353'.

Vol. 3: π1 A^2 B-R^2 S-3Z^4 4A^2 4B-5A^4 5B-5E^2 [$ half signed]; 343 leaves; pp. *i–vi* 1–98 *99*–100 101–113 *114* 115–143 *144* 145–341 *342* 343–384 *385*–388 389–455 *456* 457–469 *470* 471–480 *481* 482–495 496–500 501–668 669–684 [= 686].

Each page with a signature is also signed 'Vol. I.', 'II.' or 'III.' respectively in direction line.

Contents: Vol. 1: same contents as vol. 1 of 1714 edition (no. 363), except [a]2 leaf at front with advts. for books sold by J. Churchill is absent; and last page of index (4H2^v) has no errata.

Vol. 2: same as no. 363, vol. 2 except index ends on p. 685 (4T1^r).

Vol. 3: same as no. 363, vol. 3.

Illustrations: Vol. 1 has. front. portrait and epitaph plates as in no. 363.

Text: 61 lines; 252 (265) × 132 (152) mm; 82 R. Good-quality laid paper watermarked with a hollow letter C or D. Page no. at external ends of headlines. RTs reflect contents, set ital., with roman for emphasis.

Ornaments and initials: Each vol. contains many ornaments, different from those in 1714 edition; no ornament used in any one vol. appears in the others, indicating a different printer for each vol. Some identifiable ornaments are noticed here. Vol. 1 has the framed headpiece of a landscape scene on a2^r, 135 × 60 mm, signed 'FH' for Francis Hoffman (cf. Acker, p.10; Woodfall, p. ix). Bowyer 113 occurs on c2^v. Vol.2 has the same tailpiece on H3^v, N1^r, 3O1^r and 4A4^v, very similar to Woodfall 219, but without birds at upper corners. Vol. 3 includes a headpiece on A2^r, very similar to Bowyer 3 but not framed, 34 × 142 mm; headpiece Bowyer 132 on 3U4^r; and a tailpiece very similar to Bowyer 133 on 3U1^v, 64 × 68 mm

CW: Page. Vol. 1: [a]1^v A [AN] b1^v *This* [This,] E1^v Im- [Impreffions,]

Vol. 2: A2^r SIR, [SIR,] B1^v A King- [A Kingdom] C4^r Acci- [Accidents] Q2^r (*Mo-*) *ther* [ther:] 2A1^v (uni-) ting

Vol. 3: F1ʳ §.55. Re- [§.55. Rewards,] H1ᵛ Educa- [Education] X4ᵛ (Free-) dom? 2H3ʳ (bet-) ter 2Y4ᵛ (Domi-) nion 3O3ᵛ unque- [unqueſtionable] 4K3ʳ Gentle- [Gentleman,] 4T2ʳ pro- [probetur] 5B4ᵛ Igno- [Ignorance]
Press figures. Vol. 2: 263 (2K4ʳ)-* (Found in Oo copy only.)
Notes: A line-for line reprint of 1714 ed. (no.363). Third vol. lacks edition statement on the title. Some copies lack vol. 1 front., some have epitaph tablet facing front. in vol. 1 or elsewhere, even in a different vol.

There are two states of vol. 2, the first state in the library of the University of Minnesota. The title of both states is from the identical typesetting, only a 'stop-press' correction has changed the wording in the last line of the imprint. I assume the incorrect page numbers in this vol. to be accidental errors, all but one of which was caught and corrected by 'stop-press' procedures. I know of no other copy of this first state, and am indebted to John R. Jenson of the University of Minnesota Library for this information.

In view of the ornaments, Bowyer may have printed the preliminary matter in vol. 1 and part of vol. 3.

According to Plomer, Manship's name ceased appearing in imprints after 1713. However there are more than a dozen works listed in ESTC published up to 1719, but this *Works* is the only item there listed after 1719. Also, according to Plomer, William Taylor died in 1723.

A microfilm copy of the British Library copy is in the microfilm collection, *The Eighteenth Century*, reel 3123, no. 1.

References: Alston 7:113; Attig 849; Christophersen p. 88; ESTC t128551 (only reference to v.2, 1st state: ESTC n031845)
Copies examined, all with v.2 in 2d state: O (26782.c.1-3) C (Bassingbourn 29) CtY (K8.L79/ +A722) L (12268.i.7) MH (Phil.2115.1.1F) NjP (6106.1722q) OCin (RA192.fL81xb; v. 3 only) Oo (Vd.5-6, vols. 1, 3 only; ex lib. J. Cook Wilson) Oq (FF.g.620) PU (B1253.1722)

365. Works. 3d ed., 1727. 3 vols. 2° in 2s and 4s. Two issues.
365A.1 (First issue). Vol. 1. Within a double rule, inner 261 × 144 mm, outer 265 × 149 mm: THE | WORKS | OF | JOHN LOCKE [swash J, K] Eſq; | [rule 134 mm] | . . . [&c. as in 1714 ed. until 12th line:] VOL.I. | [rule 138 mm] | The THIRD EDITION. | [rule 137 mm] | [orn. tailpiece, Woodfall 246, 25 × 27 mm] | [rule 134 mm] | *LONDON*, [swash D] | Printed for ARTHUR BETTESWORTH, at the *Red Lion*, in *Pater-* [swash P] | *noſter-Row*; EDMUND PARKER, at the *Bible and Crown*, in | *Lombard-ſtreet*; JOHN PEMBERTON, at the *Buck*, in *Fleet-ſtreet*; and | EDWARD SYMON, againſt the *Royal-Exchange*, in *Cornhill*. | [rule 26 mm] | M.DCC.XXVII.
365A.2. Vol. 2. Within a double rule, inner 252 × 138 mm, outer 263 × 148 mm: . . . [1st 4 lines as v. 1] | [rule 134 mm] | VOL. II. | [rule 133 mm] | CONTAINING, | [contents as in 1714 ed., 10 titles in 2 cols., 18 & 15 lines, line space between each title] | [rule 134 mm] | 𝕿𝔥𝔢 𝕿𝔥𝔦𝔯𝔡 𝔈𝔡𝔦𝔱𝔦𝔬𝔫 𝕮𝔬𝔯𝔯𝔢𝔠𝔱𝔢𝔡. | [rule 133 mm] | *LONDON*: [roman colon] | Printed for

ARTHUR BETTESWORTH in *Pater-noſter-Row*, | JOHN PEMBERTON in *Fleetſtreet*, and EDWARD SYMON | in *Cornhill*. M DCC XXVII.

365A.3. Vol. 3. Within a double rule, inner 250 × 143 mm, outer 260 × 154 mm: . . . [1st 4 lines as v.1] | [rule 140 mm] | VOL. III. | [rule 141 mm] | CONTAINING, | [contents as in 1714 ed., 6 titles in left col. of 12 lines; right col. of 14 lines, with line space between each item] | [rule 136 mm] | LONDON: [swash D, roman colon] | Printed for ARTHUR BETTESWORTH in *Pater-noſter-* | *Row*, JOHN PEMBERTON in *Fleetſtreet*, and EDWARD | SYMON in *Cornhil*. MDCCXXVII.

Coll: 2· in 4s (330 × 216 mm; 315 × 205 mm cut). Vol. 1: A^2 [a]^2 (-[a]2) a-g^2 B-4F^4 [$ half (+ A2) signed]; 313 leaves; pp. *I-VI i-iii* iv-v *vi* vii-xxviii *1* 2-277 178 279-293 296 295-356 349 358-575 576-592 [= 626]. Page 278 called '178'; 294 called '296'; 357 called '349'. Each signed page also signed 'Vol. I.' in direction line.

Vol. 2: π1 A-4Q^4 4R^2 [$ half signed]; 343 leaves; pp. *i-ii 1-2* 3-35 26 37-62 *63-66* 67-97 98-102 103-158 *159* 160-227 228-230 231-256 *257-258 259-291 292-294* 295-398 317 400-470 471-472 473-541 542-544 545-553 554-556 557-671 672-684 [= 686]. Page 36 called '26'; 399 called '317'. Each signed page of quires A-2O signed 'VOL.II.' in direction line; 2P-4R signed 'Vol.II.'

Vol. 3: π1 A^2 B-R^2 S-5C^4 [$ half signed]; 345 leaves; pp. *i-vi* 1-98 *99-100* 101-143 *144* 145-277 178 279-341 *342* 343-384 *385-387* 388-455 *456* 457-469 470 471-480 *481* 482-495 496-500 501-575 586-587 578-668 669-684 [= 690]. Page 278 called '178' and 576-577 called '586-587'. Some signed pages read 'VOL.III' in direction line (B E-F I-K Q T2 U2 Y2, &c.); most of the others read 'Vol.III.'

365B.1. Second issue, vol.1: THE | WORKS | . . . [&c., as in first issue until 16th line: orn. of crown above a book, framed, between flowers & leaves, 31 × 63 mm] | LONDON, [swash D] | Printed for EDMUND PARKER, at the *Bible* and *Crown*, | over againſt the New Church in *Lombard-ſtreet*. | M.DCC.XXVII.

365B.2. Second issue, vol. 2: same as 1st issue until last 6 lines:] The THIRD EDITION. | [rule 133 mm] | LONDON, [swash D] | Printed for EDMUND PARKER, at the *Bible* and *Crown*, | over againſt the New Church in, *Lombard-ſtreet*. | M.DCC.XXVII.

365B.3. Second issue, vol. 3: same as 1st issue through contents in 2 columns, until broken rule 128 mm] | The THIRD EDITION. | [broken rule 131 mm] | LONDON, [swash D] | Printed for EDMUND PARKER, at the *Bible* and *Crown*, | over againſt the New Church in *Lombard-ſtreet*. | M.DCC.XXVII.

Coll: Vols. 1-2: same as 1st issue.

Vol. 3: same as 1st issue except with a different π1.

Contents: Vol. 1: same as 1722 ed. (no. 364) but pp. *i-575* occupy signatures a1^r-4D4^r; 4D4^v blank; index on 4E1^r-4F4^v (pp. *577-592*).

Vol. 2: same as no. 364 but pp. *i-575* occupy signatures π1^r-4P4^r; index on 4P4^v-4R2^v (pp.*672-684*).

Vol. 3: same as no. 364 but pp. *i*–668 occupy signatures π1ʳ–5A4ᵛ; index on 5B1ʳ–5C4ᵛ (pp. 669–684).

Illustrations: Vol. 1 has front. portrait of Locke by Vertue after Kneller, as in 1714 ed. The epitaph plate is also bound with preliminary matter, usually after leaf [a]1.

Text: 61 lines; 250 (263) × 131 (151) mm; 82 R. Good-quality laid paper without visible watermark. Page no. at external end of headlines. Text occasionally in direction line, e.g. vol. 1, 3P1ᵛ.

Ornaments and initials: First issue of vol. 1, as well as Woodfall 246 on title, has headpiece Woodfall 1 on [a]1ʳ and 5-line initial Woodfall 381T2; a framed headpiece, Woodfall 6 on a2ʳ; Woodfall 2 on b1ᵛ; and an unframed headpiece, Woodfall 78, on d1ʳ. Tailpieces are Woodfall 249 on A2ᵛ; Woodfall 229 on [a]1ᵛ and c2ᵛ; on 3D2ʳ there is a tailpiece very similar to Woodfall 234, but bird facing left.

Vol. 2 has an 8-line factotum very similar to Bowyer 216 on A2ʳ but with vertical shading, 32 × 32 mm. A tailpiece very similar to Ackers 89 (used by Samuel Palmer?) but with screen-type shading, occurs on 2I4ᵛ.

Vol. 3: Bowyer ornaments occur only in the later end of the vol.: headpieces are Bowyer 15 on 4C4ʳ (together with initial series 188T) and Bowyer 19 on 4D1ʳ; tailpieces are Bowyer 140 on 3Z4ᵛ and 137 on 4C4ᵛ. Kissing doves as an unidentified tailpiece, 29 × 46 mm, occurs on A2ᵛ; facing peacocks above a winged angel's face, 39 × 71 mm, on 3M2ᵛ; bowl of fruit with flowers above a sconce, 57 × 70 mm, on 3R2ᵛ and 3U1ᵛ; pair of peacocks surrounding a flower vase, 36 × 58 mm, on Y1ᵛ, repeated on 3U4ʳ (same as found in no. 33). Decorative initials through sheet 3X are all factotums.

CW: Page. Vol. 1: b2ʳ (*dif-*) *ferent* E1ᵛ Im- [Impreffions,] M2ʳ Com- [Combinations] U2ʳ (*Socra-*) *tes* 2K2ʳ (hard-) ly 3D1ʳ Lord- [Lordſhip] 3T1ʳ (un-) derſtood

Vol. 2. B1ᵛ A King- [A Kingdom] S1ᵛ fore- [foregoing] 2N3ᵛ (dif-) fers 3D2ᵛ (*ve-*) *ry* 3T2ᵛ *Meaffiah,* [*Meffiah,*] 4I4ᵛ ſearching [Searching]

Vol. 3: F1ʳ § 55. Re- [§ 55. Rewards,] H1ʳ Maſter's T2ᵛ (there-) fore 2Y4ᵛ (Domi-) nion 4N3ʳ (*ter-*) *minus*

Press figures. Vol. 1: 461 (3N3ʳ)-† 462 (3N3ᵛ)-† 488 (3Q4ᵛ)-† 497 (3S1ʳ)-I 508 (3T2ᵛ)-† 521 (3X1ʳ)-I 565 (4C3ʳ)-I 572 (4D2ᵛ)-† 583 (4E4ʳ)-† 584 (4E4ᵛ)†

Vol. 2 has figures 1, 2, 3, 4 and 5 in both inner and outer formes, chiefly on leaf versos. From gathering 4G on, there are only daggers (†). Quires H, 2L, 2M, 2U, 3O, 3U, 4A and 4E lack figures entirely.

Vol. 3 uses figures 1, 2 and 3 most commonly; 4 additionally in 3M–3X gatherings; and 8 in 4D–4Z. Again figures in both inner and outer formes.

Notes: A line-by-line reprint of the 1722 ed., with the only exceptions being the organization of contents on the titles of vols. 2 and 3, and of the index to vol. 2. The title of the first issue of vol.3 still lacks an edition statement.

The second issue title leaves of vols. 1-2 probably embody 'stop-press' changes: they are from the same typesetting as first issue, with the same rules and spacing except for the imprint. The only set I have seen (at CaOTU) is fragile, and the title leaves have separated from the rest of the vol. The title-page of vol. 3 however is a completely new typesetting and is a cancellans.

Vol. 1 has Woodfall ornaments in the preliminary matter, indicating Henry Woodfall was the printer of those pages. Vol. 2 between 2F2 and 2O4 has Charles Ackers' ornaments: "Changes in typographical style suggest [Samuel] Palmer printed sheets Ff to Kkk." (Ackers, p.82.) Also gatherings 3L to the end show a larger type for the page numbers, indicating a different printer for the rest of the vol. Vol. 3 seems largely to have been printed by an unidentified printer, with Bowyer's ornaments only in the last 200 pages; the different ways of identifying the vol. number in the signed pages could also point to different printers. Nichols, in his *Literary Anecdotes* (i. 387) reports William Bowyer was the printer of the third vol. of this edition.

ESTC also reports copies of the second issue at the Cathedral Library at Canterbury, Hatfield Broadoak Parish Library and Northwestern University Library (Evanston, Ill.). A microfilm of the British Library's copy of the first issue is in the collection, *The Eighteenth Century*, reels 2562-3, no. 1.

References: Alston 7:114; Attig 850; Christophersen p. 88; ESTC 1st state t115711; 2d n036061.

Copies examined. 365A: O (Vet.A4.c.101-3) C (7180.b.3) CLU-C CtY (K8.L79/ + a727) L (832.m.7-9) MH (Phil.2115.1.2) MH-AH OCin (RA192/fL81xb, v.1-2 only) Oj Osj PPL (*IaLock/Log833.F (Mackenzie), v.2-3 only) PU (B1253.1727) Wol (Va4o 5)
365B: CaOTU (Locke L63.A1.1727a)

366. Works. 4th ed., 1740. 3 vols. in-2°
Vol. 1: THE | WORKS | OF | JOHN LOCKE, Eſq; | [rule 142 mm] | In Three Volumes. | [rule 141 mm] | The CONTENTS of which follow in the next Leaf. | [rule 146 mm] | With ALPHABETICAL TABLES. | [rule 143 mm] | VOL. I. | [rule 142 mm] | The FOURTH EDITION. | [rule 142 mm] | [tailpiece, seated Justice in scroll frame, 35 × 51 mm] | [double rule 140 mm] | LONDON, | Printed for EDMUND PARKER, at the Bible and Crown, in Lombard- | Street; EDWARD SYMON, againſt the Royal- Exchange, in Cornhill; | CHARLES HITCH, at the Red-Lion, in Paternoſter-Row; and | JOHN PEMBERTON, at the Golden-Buck, in Fleetſtreet. | [rule 30 mm] | M. DCC. XL.
Vol. 2: . . . [1st 4 lines as v.1] | [rule 138 mm] | VOL. II. | [rule 138 mm] | CONTAINING, | [contents as in 1714 ed., in 2 cols., 18 & 15 lines, roman type, 1st word in each entry in large & small caps] | [rule 138 mm] | The FOURTH EDITION. | [double rule 137 mm] | . . . [imprint as v.1 except small rule 35 mm]
Vol. 3: . . . [1st 4 lines as v. 1] | [rule 140 mm] | VOL. III. | [rule 139 mm] | The FOURTH EDITION. | [rule 139 mm] | CONTAINING | [contents

as in 1714 ed., in 2 cols. 13 & 15 lines, roman type] | [double rule 139 mm] | . . . [imprint as v. 1 except 'Pater-noſter Row;']

Coll: 2° (350 × 218 mm cut). Vol. 1: A^2 a–g^2 B–7T^2 [$ half signed; 7P called '6P']; 328 leaves; pp. *i–v* vi *vii–ix* x–xi *xii* xiii–xvi *xvii* xviii–xxxii *1* 2–405 *406* 407–450 *451* 452 *453* 454–477 *748* 479–608 *609–624* [= 656]. Page 478 called '748'.

Vol. 2: π1 A–6L^2 *6M–*6P^2 6M–8Z^2 [$ half signed]; 377 leaves; pp. *i–ii 1-2* 3–66 *67–68* 69–105 *106–108* 109–245 *246–248* 249–276 *277–278* 279–316 *317–318* 319–504 *505–*519 *504 505 506–585 *586–588* 589–598 *599–600* 601–724 *725–736* [= 754]. Quires *6M–*6P correct the omission of the text of the 'Third Letter for Toleration', shown by pp. *505–19, and *504.

Vol. 3: π1 A–3R^2 3S^2 (–3S2) 3T–7X^2 7Z–8N^2 [$ half signed; 5B called 'Bbbb']; 346 leaves; pp. *i–vi* 1–98 *99–100* 101–111 *112* 113 *114* 115–143 *144* 145–339 *340* 341–380 *381–382* 383–430 451–473 *474* 475–487 *488* 489–513 *514* 515 *516* 517 *518* 519–586 583–687 *688–702* [= 692]. No 7Y gathering; page no. 431–450 omitted; 583–586 repeated. First page of each gathering also signed, e.g., 'VOL. II.' in direction line.

Contents. **Vol. 1**: A1^r (*i*) title (verso blank), A2^{r,v} (*iii–iv*) contents of 3 vols., a1^{r,v} (*v*–vi) 'To the Reader' (partial quotation from Locke's will, as in no. 363),

Essay concerning Human Understanding: a2^r (*vii*) section title (verso blank), b1^r–2^r (*ix*–xi) dedication, b2^v–c2^v (*xii*–xvi) preface ('To the Reader'), d1^r–g2^v (*xvii*–xxxii) contents by book, chap. and sections, B1^r–4Y1^v (pp.*1*–358) text;

Letter to Stillingfleet: 4Y2^r–5L1^r (*359–405*) text;

Mr. Locke's Reply: 5L1^v–5Y2^v (*406–452*) text;

Mr. Locke's Second Reply: 5Z1^r–7Q2^v (*453–608*) text;

Index: 7R1^r = 7T2^r (*609–623*); advt. of booksellers, 7T2^v (*624*).

Vol. 2: π1^r (*i*) title (verso blank),

Some Considerations: A1^r section title (verso blank), A2^r–P2^r (*3–59*) text;

Short Observations: P2^v–R1^v (*60–66*) text;

Further Considerations: R2^r (*67*) section title (verso blank), S1^r–2D1^r (*69–105*) text, 2D1^v (*106*) value table;

Two Treatises: 2D2^r (*107*) section title (verso blank), 2E1^r–3Q1^r (*109–245*) text, 3Q1^v (*246*) contents;

A Letter concerning Toleration: 3Q2^r (*247*) section title (verso blank), 3R1^r–3Z2^v (*249–276*) text;

A Second Letter concerning Toleration: 4A1^r (*277*) section title (verso blank), 4A2^r–4K2^v (*279–316*) text;

A Third Letter for Toleration: 4L1^r (*317*) section title (verso blank), 4L2^r–*6P2^v (*319*–*519*, *504) text;

The Reasonableness of Christianity: 6M1^r (*505*) section title, 6M1^v (*506*) pref., 6M2^r–7I1^r (*507–585*) text, 7I1^v blank;

Vindication: 7I2^r (*587*) section title (verso blank), 7K1^r–7M1^v (*569–598*) text;

Second Vindication: 7M2ʳ (599) section title (verso blank), 7N1ʳ-8U2ᵛ (601-724) text;
  Index of vol.: 8X1ʳ-8Z2ʳ (725-735), 8Z2ᵛ blank.
Vol. 3: π1ʳ (i) title (verso blank),
  Some Thoughts concerning Education: A1ʳ (iii) section title (verso blank), A2ʳ-2C1ᵛ (v-98) text;
  A Paraphrase and Notes on the Epistles of St. Paul: 2C2ʳ (99) section title (verso blank), 2D1ʳ-2F2ʳ (101-111) Essay for Understanding St. Paul's Epistles, 2F2ᵛ blank, 2G1ʳ (113) section title (verso blank), 2G2ʳ-2O2ʳ (115-143) Galatians, 2O2ᵛ blank, 2P1ʳ-3H2ᵛ (145-212) 1. Corinthians, 3I1ʳ-3S1ʳ (213-250) 2. Corinthians, 3T1ʳ-4S1ʳ (251-339) Romans, 4S1ᵛ blank, 4S2ʳ-5E1ᵛ (341-380) Ephesians;
  Posthumous Works: 5E2ᵛ (381) section title (verso blank), 5F1ʳ-6K2ʳ (383-513) text, 6K2ᵛ blank;
  Some Familiar Letters: 6L1ʳ (515) section title (verso blank), 6L2ʳ-8K1ʳ (517-687) text, 8K1ᵛ blank;
  Index of vol.: 8K2ʳ-8N2ʳ (689-701), 8N2ᵛ blank.
Illustrations: Vol. 1 has front. portrait facing title page, and epitaph plate, as in previous editions (no. 363-5) usually bound after leaf c2.
Text: 58 lines; 274 (280) × 141 (160) mm; 94 R. Good-quality laid paper but mixed sheets, without visible watermarks.
CW: Page.
Press figures. Vol. 1: 12 (D2ᵛ)-1 40 (L2ᵛ)-2 47 (N2ʳ)-2 75 (U2ʳ)-2 79 (X2ʳ)-2 80 (X2ᵛ)-2 83 (Y2ʳ)-2 84 (Y2ᵛ)-2 90 (2A1ᵛ)-2 94 (2B1ᵛ)-2 238 (3P1ᵛ)-1 340 (4R2ᵛ)-1 555 (7B2ᵛ)-1 572 (7F2ᵛ)-1 612 (7Q2ᵛ)-1 628 (7S2ᵛ)-1
  Vol. 2: in order of frequency: 1 2 4 3 and 5, one per sheet. No figures in sheets A, I, M-2F, 3F, 3P, 4I, 6G, 6K, *6L, *6O, *6P, 6N, 7I, 7M, 7Q, 8T and 8Z. Figures chiefly on recto of leaf.
  Vol. 3: in order of frequency: 4 2 3 1 and 5, one per sheet. No figures in sheets A, F, I-L, N-O, Q-R, T-U, Y, 2A, 2C, 2E-2G, 2I-2L, 2N-2Q, 2S, 2X, 3D, 3I-3L, 3N, 3P-3Q, 3S, 4N, 5B, 5E, 6G, 6L, 7Y and 8M. Figures about equally on rectos and versos, frequently on inner and outer formes.
Notes: A newly-set reprint of the 1714 ed., without new material. Some copies lack the epitaph plate in vol. 1 or have it bound before p. *xvii* ('Essay' contents).
References: Alston 7:115; Attig 851; Christophersen p. 88; ESTC t128552.
Copies examined: O¹ (Vet. A4.c.94-6; Desmaizeaux's Collection, no. 318, bound in vol.1 preceding leaf B1) CaNSHDa (RB B1253.1740) CaOTU (Locke L63.A1.1740) CLU-C (*fPR3541.l57 1740) L (12295.l.1) MH (*71-70F) O² (Don.c.91-3) Om PPL (*IaLock/7547.F)

367. Works. 5th ed., 1751. 3 vols. in-2°. Two issues of v.1-2, 2 states of 2d issue.
367A.1. First issue, vol. 1: THE | WORKS | OF | JOHN LOCKE, Eſq; | [rule 145 mm] | In THREE VOLUMES. | [rule 146 mm] | The

CONTENTS of which follow in the next Leaf. | [rule 146 mm] | With ALPHABETICAL TABLES. | [rule 146 mm] | VOL. I. | The FIFTH EDITION. | [rule 144 mm] | [tailpiece: seated Minerva, 36 × 53 mm] | [double rule 145 mm] | LONDON: | Printed for S. BIRT, D. BROWNE, T. LONGMAN, J. SHUCKBURGH, | C. HITCH and L. HAWES, J. HODGES, J. OSWALD, A. MILLAR, | J. and J. RIVINGTON, J. WARD, and M. COOPER. | [rule 24 mm] | M. DCC. LI.

367A.2. First issue, vol. 2: . . . [1st 4 lines as vol. 1] | [rule 142 mm] | VOL. II. | [rule 142 mm] | CONTAINING, | [contents in 2 columns, as in 1714 ed., 18 & 15 lines respectively, in roman type, first word of each title printed in large & small capitals] | [rule 142 mm] | The FIFTH EDITION. | [double rule 142 mm] | LONDON: | . . . [imprint as in vol. 1, 1st issue]

367a.3. Only issue, first state of vol. 3: . . . [1st 4 lines as vol. 1, first issue] | [rule 142 mm] | In THREE VOLUMES. | [rule 141 mm] | The FIFTH EDITION. | [rule 142 mm] | To which is now firſt added, | The LIFE of the AUTHOR; | AND | A COLLECTION of ſeveral of his PIECES publiſhed | by Mr. DESMAIZEAUX. | [rule 142 mm] | VOL. III. | [rule 140 mm] | [tailpiece: 3 hawks & vase with flower garlands, 26 × 40 mm] | [double rule 139/140 mm] | LONDON: | . . . [imprint as in vol. 1, first issue]

Coll: 2° (335 × 227 mm cut). Vol. 1: A^2 a–k^2 B–$7O^2$ [$ half signed]; 324 leaves; pp. *i–iii* iv *v* vi–xv xvi *1–12* xvii xviii–xxxii *1* 2–392 *393* 394–587 *588*–604 [= 648]. Some copies have 2 title leaves: A1 cancellandum and A1 cancellans; see *Notes*.

Vol. 2: $\pi 1$ A–$8Y^2$ [$ half signed]; 367 leaves; pp. *i–ii 1–2* 3–64 *65–66* 67–102 *103–104* 105–239 *240* 241–267 *268–270* 271–307 *308–310* 313 *312*–508 *509* 510–586 *587–588* 589–590 *599–600* 601–719 *720*–732 [= 734]. Page 311 called '313'. Some copies have 2 title leaves (π^2); see *Notes*.

Vol. 3: $\pi 1$ A–$4X^2$ $4Y^2$ (–4Y2) 5B–$9K^2$ [$ half signed; 4Y1 (p.357) signed 'Yyyy-5A']; 385 leaves; pp. *i–vi* 1–96 *97–98* 99–357 *358–360* 369–458 *459* 460–473 *474* 473 474 475 478 479–648 *649–650* 651–757 *758*–770 [= 770]. Page no. 361-8 omitted; 473-4 repeated; 477 called '475'.

First page of each gathering also signed 'VOL. II.', e.g., in direction line.

367.Ba.1-2. Second issue, first state of vols. 1–2: same as first state of vol.3, except 'VOL. I.', 'VOL. II.'

Coll. Vol. 1: same as first issue of vol. 1 except A^2 (±A1).

Vol. 2: same as first issue of vol. 2 except with a different $\pi 1$ (original $\pi 1$ is cancellandum).

367.Bb.1-2 and 367.b3. Second issue, 2d state of vols. 1–2, and 2d state of vol. 3: same as second issue first state of vols. 1–2 and first state of vol. 3 except 'J. Beecroft' is added to penultimate line of names of booksellers: J. BEECROFT, J. and J. RIVINGTON, J. WARD, and M. COOPER. | . . . [&c.]

The change is a 'stop-press' correction.

Contents. **Vol. 1**: A1ʳ (*i*) title (verso blank), A2ʳ·ᵛ (*iii–iv*) contents of vols.1–3, a1ʳ–c2ʳ (*v–xv*) Le Clerc's 'Life of the Author' (abstracted), c2ᵛ blank, d1ʳ (*1*) prefatory note to *Works* (verso blank),

Essay concerning Human Understanding: d2ʳ (*3*) section title (verso blank), e1ʳ–e2ʳ (*5–7*) dedication, e2ᵛ–f2ᵛ (*8–12*) preface to *Essay*, g1ʳ–k2ᵛ (*xvii–xxxii*) contents by book, chap. & §§, B1ʳ–4T1ᵛ (*1–346*);

Letter to Bishop Stillingfleet: 4T2ʳ–5G2ᵛ (*347–392*);

Locke's Reply to Bishop Stillingfleet: 5H1ʳ–5T1ʳ (*393–437*);

Locke's Reply to the Bishop's Second Letter: 5T1ᵛ–7K2ʳ (*438–587*), 7K2ᵛ blank;

Index of vol.: 7L1ʳ–7O2ʳ (*589–603*), 7O2ᵛ blank.

Vol. 2: π1ʳ title (verso blank),

Some Considerations: A1ʳ (*1*) section title (verso blank), A2ʳ–P1ʳ (*3–57*) text;

Short Observations: P1ᵛ–Q2ᵛ (*58–64*) text;

Further Considerations: R1ʳ (*65*) section title (verso blank), R2ʳ–2C1ᵛ (*67–102*) text;

Two Treatises: 2C2ʳ (*103*) section title (verso blank), 2D1ʳ–2T1ᵛ (*105–166*) text of 1st Treatise, 2T2ʳ–3O1ʳ (*167–237*) text of 2nd, 3O1ᵛ (*238*) contents;

A Letter concerning Toleration: 3O2ʳ (*239*) section title (verso blank), 3P1ʳ–3X2ʳ (*241–267*) text, 3X2ᵛ blank;

A Second Letter concerning Toleration: 3Y1ʳ (*269*) section title (verso blank), 3Y2ʳ–4H2ʳ (*271–307*) text, 4H2ᵛ blank;

A Third Letter for Toleration: 4I1ʳ (*309*) section title, 4I1ᵛ (*310*) note of abbrevs., 4I2r–6M2ᵛ ('*313*', *312–508*) text;

The Reasonableness of Christianity: 6N1ʳ (*509*) section title, 6N1ᵛ (*510*) pref., 6N2ʳ–7I1ᵛ (*511–586*) text;

Vindication: 7I2ʳ (*587*) section title (verso blank), 7K1ʳ–7M1ᵛ (*589–598*) text;

Second Vindication: 7M2ʳ (*599*) section title (verso blank), 7N1ʳ–8T2ʳ (*601–719*) text, 8T2ᵛ blank;

Index of vol.: 8U1ʳ–8Y2ʳ (*721–731*), 8Y1ᵛ blank.

Vol. 3: π1ʳ (*i*) title (verso blank),

Some Thoughts concerning Education: A1ʳ (*iii*) section title (verso blank), A2ʳ·ᵛ (*v–vi*) dedication, B1ʳ–2B2ᵛ (*1–96*) text;

A Paraphrase and Notes on the Epistles of St.Paul: 2C1ʳ (*97*) section title (verso blank), 2C2ʳ–4Y1ʳ (*99–357*) text, 4Y1ᵛ blank;

Posthumous Works: 5B1ʳ (*359*) section title (verso blank), 5B2ʳ–6E2ʳ (*369–473*) text, 6E2ᵛ blank;

Some Familiar Letters: 6F1ʳ (*473 bis*) section title (verso blank), 6F2ʳ ('*475*') pref. (verso blank), 6G1ʳ–8C1ᵛ (*479–648*) text;

Collection of Several Pieces, ed. Desmaizeaux: 8C2ʳ (*649*) section title (verso blank), 8D1ʳ–9G2ʳ (*651–757*) text;

Index of vol.: 9G2ᵛ–9K2ʳ (*758–769*), 9K2ᵛ blank.

Illustrations: (1) front. port. by G. Vertue after Kneller, as in previous editions; (2) epitaph plate, usually bound after leaf c2 (L copy has it bound between c1 and c2).
Text: 59 lines; 270 (280) × 146 (165) mm; 93 R. Medium-quality laid paper without watermarks. All vols. have a mixture of sheets, chiefly with vertical chainlines, but many sheets or groups of sheets have horizontal chainlines derived from using half broadsheets (Gaskell's '1°'). The British Library copy is almost solely printed on half broad sheets except as follows: vol.1 sheets a–c and 3G on folios; vol.2 sheets 8C–Y are the only folio sheets; vol. 3, 7H–9H on folios. Page no. at external ends of headlines.
CW: Page.
Press figures. Vol. 1: viii (a2^v)-5 6 (e1^v)-4 11 (f2^r)-1 xx (g2^v)-3 xxiii (h2^r)-2 xxvi (i1^v)-1 3 (B2^r)-1 4 (B2^v)-2

Vol. 2: figures 2 and 3, at least one on every sheet, A through 8T, chiefly on inner *or* outer forme only. On both formes in 4L, 6Q, 6S and 7T; no figures in 2C.

Vol. 3: 1, 2, 3, 4, 5 and 6, frequently on both formes; a dagger (†) on F2^{r,v} (pp. 19–20).

Notes: A new typesetting based on the 4th (1740) edition, and the first *Works* edition to include the English translation of Le Clerc's 'Eloge de feu Mr. Locke' from the *Bibliothèque choisie* (see ch. XIII, C1705-5; C1706-3) and to incorporate Desmaizeaux's *Collection* (no. 316-8). Stylistically it is a transitional edition, in that the earlier issue (A) follows the pattern of previous editions, in indicating each volume's contents on the title page. The second issue, with a cancellans title leaf, uses the same wording for all three volumes, the only variant being a vol. number. The pattern of the title-pages for the second (B) issue is the model for all later *Works* editions.

I would suppose John Beecroft was added to the group of booksellers later, since his name is not included in the first issue. He was also one of the booksellers involved in the distribution of the 1759 and 1768 *Works* editions (no. 368-9). According to Plomer Beecroft was engaged in business from 1740 to 1769 and '[h]eld shares in most of the important publications of his day.' The name of a possible relative or inheritor, T. Beecroft, occurs in the 1777 edition imprint.

Some copies of this edition have both first- and second-issue title leaves of vol. 1 and 2; see table below. It is possible that there was a first-issue appearance of vol. 3, but I have not found any.
References: Alston 7:116; Attig 852; Christophersen p. 88; ESTC t179724.
Copies examined: O (Vet.A5.e.115-7; vol.1 lacks A2 and sheets a–k) CtY (K8.L79/ + A751) L (Cup.504.de.23) MH-AH (Codman fL814) NjP (Ex6106.1751q) NjR (X Folio B1253 1751; v.3 has epitaph plate as front.) PU^1 (B1253.1751; v.1 lacks front. but has fold. plate bound after leaf c2, headed 'An Analysis of Mr. Locke's Ideas in his Essay on Human Understanding', 458 × 543 mm, 'grangerised'? from another *Works* ed.,

see no. 370 below; v.2 has epitaph plate as front.) PU^2 (B1253.1751b) WaU (192.2.AAb)

Distribution of Issues and States			
	A (1st issue)	B (2d issue) 1st state (lacks Beecroft)	B 2nd state (with Beecroft)
vol. 1	CtY L* PU^1 WaU*	NjP NjR PU^2	L* MH-AH O
vol. 2	O* PU^{1*} WaU*	CtY L NjP NjR O* PU^{1*} PU^2 WaU*	MH-AH
vol. 3	–	CtY L NjP NjR O PU^1 PU^2 WaU	MH-AH
* indicates has two title leaves			

368. Works. 6th ed., 1759. 3 vols. in-2°
Vol. 1: THE | WORKS | OF | JOHN LOCKE, Efq; | [rule 142 mm] | In THREE VOLUMES. | [rule 144 mm] | The SIXTH EDITION. | [rule 146 mm] | To which is added, | The LIFE of the AUTHOR; | AND | A COLLECTION of feveral of his PIECES publifhed | by Mr. DESMAIZEAUX. | [rule 149 mm] | VOL. I. | [rule 139 mm] | [tailpiece, Woodfall 296, 27 × 37 mm] | [double rule 142/144 mm] | LONDON: | Printed for D. BROWNE, C. HITCH and L. HAWES, J. SHUCKBURGH, | A. MILLAR, J. BEECROFT, JOHN RIVINGTON, JAMES RIVINGTON | and J. FLETCHER, J. WARD, R. BALDWIN, J. RICHARDSON, S. CROWDER, | P. DAVEY and B. LAW, T. LONGMAN, E. DILLY, R. WITHY, T. PAYNE, | and M. COOPER. | [rule 30 mm] | M. DCC. LIX.
Vol. 2, as vol. 1 except 'VOL. II.' and tailpiece before imprint is flowered wall sconce, 20 × 38 mm.
Vol. 3, as vol. 1 except 'VOL. III.' and tailpiece is angel with trumpet, seated amid scrolls, 22 × 34 mm.
Coll: 2° (376 × 244 mm uncut). Vol. 1: A^2 a-k^2 B-7O^2 [$ half signed]; 324 leaves; pp. *i-v* vi-xv *xvi* 1-12 *xvii* xviii-xxxii 1 2-392 393 394-587 588-604 [= 648].
Vol. 2: π1 A-8Y^2 [$ signed half; in some copies first leaf of 2P signed 'Oo']; 367 leaves; pagination same as 1751 ed., including p. 311 called '313'.
Vol. 3: π1 A-4X^2 4Y^2 (-4Y2) 5B-9K^2 [$ half signed; 4Y1 (p.357) signed 'Yyyy-5A']; 385 leaves; pagination same as 1751 ed., including page no. 361-8 omitted; 473-4 repeated, and 477 called '475'.

First page of each gathering also signed 'VOL. III.', e.g., in direction line.
Contents: same as 1751 edition.
Illustrations: (1) Vol.1 has front. port. of Locke by Vertue after Kneller, as in previous editions; (2) epitaph plate, usually bound in vol. 1 after leaf c2.
Text: 59 lines; 93 R. Print block of v. 1-2 measures 270 (290) × 146 (165) mm; of v. 3, 276 (292) × 146 (160) mm. Medium-quality laid paper without watermarks. Page no. at external ends of headlines. Again printed from mixed sheets, some with vertical, some with horizontal chainlines (employing half broadsheets (Gaskell's '1°'). In my copy, vol. 1 has horizontal chainlines in quires G-I, M-N, P, R, U, 2A-2B, 2D, 2G, 2K-2L, 2P and 2U. Vol. 2, similarly, in quires D-E, G-K, Q, 2D, 2H-2I; and vol. 3 only in quire M. Some copies have various combinations. Throughout all vols. the first word of each paragraph is printed in large and small caps, except in the *Paraphrases*.
Ornaments. Vol. 1 has ornamental initials (some factotums); tailpiece of a seated Minerva on 4T1^v, 35 × 51 mm; a bowl of flowers on a wall sconce on 4G2^v, 47 × 60 mm; a square-shaped vase of flowers, 39 × 54 mm, on 5S2r; and a vase of flowers on a pedestal, 46 × 61 mm, on 7O2^r. Vol. 2 has no head- or tailpieces; it has one ornamental initial, the rest are factotums. Identifiable orn. in vol. 3 are Woodfall 298 (tailpiece) on 5T1^v; and a tailpiece similar to Woodfall 240 with top and bottom cut away, on 8Q2^v, 20 × 50 mm.
CW: Page. Vol. 1: b1^r (im-) mortal, d1^r AN g2^r 16. Ap- [16. A*ppeal*] B1^r FIRST M1^r (re-) moves 2H2^v (in-) finitely
Vol. 2: I1^v IF Q2^r (fhil-) lings 2E1^v "tole- [tolerable] 3B2^r legi- [legiflative] 3R2^v accord- [according] 5I1^r contain- [containing]
Vol. 3: A2^r *I am* c1^r (fto-) machs N1^v (ob-) viate 2D1^r (indepen-) dent 3B1^r (pro-) phets, 4R1^r (crea-) ted
Press figures. Vol. 1 has one or two figures on every quire, from 1 to 8, except c-d, X, 2D, 3A, 3C, 3H, 3Y, 4C-D, 5G, 5R and 7N.
Vol. 2 has fewer figures, 1-5; only 10 sheets with figures on inner and outer formes. No figures in quires H-K, M, P, R, Y-Z, 2A-2L, 2N-2R, 2T-2X 2Z, 3A-3D, 3F, Eh, 3K-3P, 3R-3S, 3X-3Y, 4C-4F, 4H-4K, 4O-4Q, 4S-4T, 5B, 5F, 5Q, 5S, 5Y, 6C-6E, 6H-6K, 6N, 6P-6Q, 6S, 7E, 7G, 7K, 7L-7M, 7R-7S, 8B, 8E, 8G, 8P-8Q, 8Y.
Vol. 3 has numerous marks, very frequently on the inner and outer formes of each sheet, except leaf 'Yyyy-5A' (p.357), and range from no. 1 to 8.
Notes: A careful reprint of the 1751 edition, with an increasing number of typographical errors from earlier editions corrected; the last folio edition. The presence of Woodfall ornaments on the title-page of vol. 1 and another in vol. 3 may indicate these were printed by the younger Henry Woodfall (1737-1764?; cf. Plomer). I suspect he inherited some of his father's fonts and ornaments.
A microfilm copy of this edition is in the collection, *The Eighteenth Century*, reel 3158, no. 1.

References: Alston 7:117; Attig 853; Christophersen p. 88; ESTC t113384.
Copies examined: Y L (524.m.11-13) MH (TP2115.1.5F) MH-AH (f17.45) O (Vet.A5.c.48-50) Oa (SR15.b.2.1-3) Oc (E1.1.4) Omc (f1759.3) Oq Wol (Va.2°; v.1 only, uncut)

369. Works. 7th ed. (ed.Hollis), 1768. 4 vols. in-4°. Two issues.

369A.1-4. First issue: THE WORKS OF IOHN LOCKE | IN FOUR VOLUMES | THE SEVENTH EDITION | VOLUME I ['II', 'III', 'IIII'] | LONDON, PRINTED FOR H. WOODFALL, A. MILLAR, | I. BEECROFT, I. AND F. RIVINGTON, I. WHISTON, | S. BAKER, T. PAYNE, L. DAVIS AND CO. R. BALDWIN, | HAWES CLARKE AND COLLINS, B. WHITE, | W. IOHNSTON, W. OWEN, T. CASLON, S. CROWDER, | T. LONGMAN, B. LAW, C. RIVINGTON, E. AND C. DILLY, | T. DAVIES, ROBINSON AND ROBERTS, I. SHUCKBURGH, | AND T. CADELL. MDCCLVIII.

Coll: 4° (280 × 230 mm cut). **Vol. 1**: A^2 a^4 (-a1) b-g^4 B-5G^4 5H^2 [$ half signed]; 424 leaves; pp. I-II i-ii iii-xxii *xxiii-xxv* xxvi-xxvii *xxviii-xxix* xxx-xxxv *xxxvi* xxxvii-lvi *1* 2-517 *518* 519-600 *599-606* 609-774 *775-788* [=848]. Page no. 599-600 repeated, 607-8 omitted.

Vol. 2: A^2 (-A2) B-4Y^4 4Z^2 [$ half signed]; 363 leaves; pp. *i-iv* 1-2 3-84 *85-86* 87-134 *135-136* 137-313 *314-316* 317-343 *344-346* 347-382 *383-384* 385-432 *433-434* 435-593 *694-696* 697-713 *714-724* [=726].

Vol. 3: A^2 (-A2) B-4$1^4$ 4K^2 (-4K2) [$ half signed]; 310 leaves; pp. *i-ii* 1 2-99 *100* 101 *102* 103-115 *116-118* 119-123 *124-125* 126-152 145-161 170-194 196 196-272 *273-274* 275-287 *288-290* 291-408 *409* 410-561 *562* 563-610 *611-618* [=620]. Page no. 145-152 repeated; 162-169 omitted; 195 & 196 both called '196'.

Vol. 4: A^2 (-A2) B-4R^4 [$ half (-2K2, -2L2) signed]; 343 leaves; pp. *i-vi* 1 2-135 *136-141* 142-194 *195* 196-231 *232-233* 234-245 *246-247* 248-261 *262-267* 268-496 *497-499* 500-506 *507-509* 510-518 *519* 520-538 *539* 540-570 *571* 572-579 *580* 581-599 *600* 601-605 *606* 607-644 *645-647* 648 *649-651* 652-670 *671-680* [=686].

First page of each gathering of vol. 1 signed 'VOL.I.' in direction line; each gathering in vols. 2-4 signed, e.g., 'VOL. IV.'

369B.1, 4. Second issue. Vols. 1 & 4: THE | WORKS | OF | JOHN LOCKE, | IN FOUR VOLUMES. | THE SEVENTH EDITION. | VOLUME THE FIRST. ['THE FOURTH.'] | [double rule, thick/thin; v.1 140/138 mm; v.4 135/129 mm] | LONDON, | Printed for H. WOODFALL, A. MILLAR, J. BEECROFT, J. and F. RIVINGTON, | J. WHISTON, S. BAKER, T. PAYNE, L. DAVIS and Co. R. BALDWIN, HAWES, | CLARKE, and COLLINS, B. WHITE, W. JOHNSTON, W. OWEN, T. CASLON, | S. CROWDER, T. LONGMAN, B. LAW, C. RIVINGTON, E. and C. DILLY, | T. DAVIES, ROBINSON and ROBERTS, A. and J. SHUCKBURGH, and T. CADELL. | [rule, v.1 27 mm; v.4 30 mm] | MDCCLXVIII.

369B.2. Second issue. Vol. 2: as in v. 1 & 4 until 7th line: VOLUME THE SECOND. | [double rule 140 mm] | . . . [&c. until 11th line:] J. WHISTON, S. BAKER, T. PAYNE, L. DAVIS and Co. R. BALDWIN, L. HAWES | and W. CLARKE and R. COLLINS, B. WHITE, W. JOHNSTON, W. OWEN, | T. CASLON, S. CROWDER, T. LONGMAN, B. LAW, C. RIVINGTON, E. and | C. DILLY, T. DAVIES, ROBINSON and ROBERTS, A. and J. SHUCKBURGH, and | T. CADELL. | [rule 33 mm] | MDCCLXVIII.

369B.3. Second issue. Vol. 3: as in v. 2 until 7th line: VOLUME THE THIRD. | [triple rule, thin/thick/thin 138 mm] | . . . [&c. until 11th line:] J. WHISTON, S. BAKER, T. PAYNE, L. DAVIS and Co. R. BALDWIN, HAWES | CLARKE and COLLINS, B. WHITE, W. JOHNSTON, W. OWEN, T. CASLON, | S. CROWDER, T. LONGMAN, B. LAW, C. RIVINGTON, E. and C. DILLY, | T. DAVIES, ROBINSON and ROBERTS, A. & J. SHUCKBURGH, and T. CADELL. | [broken rule 36 mm] | MDCCLXVIII.

Coll: Vol. 1: a–g^4 B–5G^4 5H^2; 423 leaves; [846 pp.] That is, a1 present, but not A^2.

Vols. 2–4: same as 1st issue except A^2 (–A1). (A2 is title leaf.)

Contents: **Vol. 1**: A1 blank, A2^r 1st issue title (verso blank) {or a1^r (*i*) 2nd issue title (verso blank)}, a2^{r,v} (iii–iv) 'To the Reader' note (as in previous editions, with note of additional material, dated 'April 14, 1768.'), a3^{r,v} (v–vi) contents of 4 vols., a4^r–c3^v (vii–xxii) 'The Life of the Author' from Le Clerc (with letter as note; see *Notes*),

Essay concerning Human Understanding: c4^r section title (verso blank), d1^r–d2^r (*xxv*–xxvii) dedication, d2^v blank, d3^r–e2^r (*xxix*–xxxv) 'Epistle to the Reader', e2^v blank, e3^r–g4^v (xxxvii–lvi) contents by book, chap. & sections, B1^r–3N1^r (*1–457*) text;

Letter to [Stillingfleet]: 3N1^v–3U3^r (*458–517*);

Mr. Locke's Reply to [Stillingfleet]: 3U3^v–4E1^r (*518–577*);

Mr. Locke's Second Reply to [Stillingfleet]: 4E1^v–5F3^v (*578–774*);

Index to 1st vol.: 5F4^r–5H2^v (*775–788*).

Vol. 2: A1^r 1st issue title (verso blank) or A2^r 2nd issue title (verso blank),

Some Considerations of the . . . Lowering of Interest: B1^r (*1*) section title (verso blank), B2^r–L2^r (*3–75*) text;

Short Observations: L2^v–M2^v (*76–84*);

Further Observations: M3^r (*85*) section title (verso blank), M4^r–S3^r (*87–133*) text, S3^v (*134*) value table;

Two Treatises of Government: S4^r (*135*) section title (verso blank), T1^r–2R4^v(*137–312*) text, 2S1^r (*313*) contents (verso blank);

Epistola de tolerantia: 2S2^r (*315*) section title (verso blank), 2S3^r–2X4^r (*317–343*) text (in Latin), 2X4^v blank;

Letter concerning Toleration: 2Y1^r (*345*) section title (verso blank), 2Y2^r–3C3^v (*347–382*) text;

Second Letter concerning Toleration: 3C4^r (*383*) section title (verso blank), 3D1^r–3I4^v (*385–432*) text;

Third Letter for Toleration: 3K1^r (*433*) section title (verso blank), 3K2^r–4T3^r (*435-693*) text, 4T3^v blank;

Fourth Letter for Toleration: 4T4^r (*695*) section title (verso blank), 4U1^r–4Y1^r (*691-713*) text, 4Y1^v blank;

Index of vol.: 4Y2^r–4Z2^v (*715-724*).

Vol. 3: A1^r 1st issue title (verso blank) or A2^r 2nd issue title (verso blank), Reasonableness of Christianity: B^{1}r (*1*) section title, B1^v (*2*) preface, B2^r–O2^r (*3-99*) text, O2^v blank;

Vindication: O3^r (*101*) section title (verso blank), O4^r–Q2^r (*103-115*) text, Q2^v blank;

Second Vindication: Q3^r (*117*) section title (verso blank), Q4^r–R2^r (*119-123*) preface, R2^v blank, R3^r–2M4^v (*125-272*) text;

A Paraphrase and Notes on the Epistles of St. Paul: 2N1^r (*273*) section title (verso blank), 2N2^r–2O4^r (*275-287*) Essay for the Understanding, 2O4^v blank, 2P1^r (*289*) section title, 2P1^v (*290*) publisher's note, 2P2^r–2T3^v (*291-326*) text for Galatians, 2T4^r–3F4^v (*327-408*) of I Corinthians, 3G1^r–3M2^v (*409-452*) 2 Corinthians, 3M3^r–4C1^r (*453-561*) Romans, 4C1^v blank, 4C2^r–4I1^v (*563-610*) Ephesians;

Index of vol.: 4I2^r–4K1^r (*611-617*), 4K1^v blank.

Vol. 4: A1^r 1st issue title (verso blank) or A2^r 2nd issue title (verso blank), Some Thoughts concerning Education: A3^r (*iii*) section title (verso blank), A4^{r,v} (*v-vi*) dedication, B1^r–S4^r (*1-135*) text, S4^v blank;

Posthumous Works: T1^r (*137*) section title (verso blank), T2^{r,v} (*139-140*) advertisement 'to the Reader', T3^r–2L3^r (*141-261*) text, 2L3^v blank;

Some Familiar Letters: 2L4^r (*263*) section title (verso blank), 2M1^r–3R4^v (*265-496*) text;

Collection of Several Pieces: 3S1^r (*497*) section title (verso blank), 3S2^r–4N2^v (*499-644*) text;

Observations on the Growth and Culture of Vines . . .: 4N3^r (*645*) section title (verso blank), 3N4^r–4Q3^v (*647-670*) text;

Index of vol.: 4Q4^r–4R4^v (*671-680*).

Illustration: Vol. 1 has engr. oval port. of Locke after Kneller, by Cipriani and Basire, 119 × 104 mm, with liberty cap at bottom of portrait, subscribed 'IOHN LOCKE'.

Ornaments: Vol. 1 has a liberty cap also on c3^v. Tailpieces are (1) of two seated female figures amid flowers, 28 × 41 mm, on 4D3^v; and a bird in a bower, very similar to Bowyer 147, 33 × 39 mm, on 4E1^r. There are no ornaments in the other vols.

Text (v.1 3I4^v): 46 lines (varies); 216 (230) × 141 (160) mm; 95 R. Good-quality laid paper with fleur-de-lys watermark and letters 'GR' similar to Heawood 113. Page no. at external ends of headlines. Headlines frequently in large & small capitals, some in upper & lower case.

Vol. 3 appears to be from a different printer, is of mixed sheets, some watermarked with the initials 'LVG' and a smaller fleur-de-lys, similar to Heawood 115. The diagrammatic table for the 'New Method for Making a

Common-place Book' in the *Posthumous Works* text in vol. 4 is printed solely in black ink.

CW: Page. Vol. 1: b2^r power [power:] d1^r (appear-) ance: E3^v (worm-) wood Q3^r § 7. THOUGH 2M4^v (concep-) tions 3E1^r § 15. SE- [§ 15. SECONDLY,]
Vol. 2: D1^r (can-) not E1^v (Eng-) land, L4^v (im-) mediately 2A4^r (govern-) ment 2S1^r LET- [EPISTOLA] 2X4^r A LET- [A LETTER] 3L2^v (wor-) ſhip
Vol. 3: B2^v (te-) ſtament D3^v ("Af-) "ter I1r (a-) gain 2B3^v (Who-) ever 2D2^v us 2E2^v "pro- ["pounded (CW part of text)] 2S4^v [in Notes] (are) the [are the ('are' repeated)] 2X4^v (writ-) ten, 3I3^v (accept-) able 3M4^v Of [which number (CW part of text)]
Vol. 4: B4^r (gor-) mands C2^v (volun-) tary, C3^v ſome [time (CW part of text)] I1^r (advan-) tage X1^v (fre-) quent 2I1^v (prin-) ciples, 3B1^v (diſ-) agree- [agreement] 4B3^v pro- [proteſtants,]

Press figures. Vol. 1 has figures 1 through 9 distributed on the inner and outer forme of each quire. Vol. 2 has fewer, frequently only on one forme of a sheet, figures 2, 4 and 6 only. Vol. 3, similarly, has figures 1 through 6. Vol. 4 also has few quires with figures on both formes of a quire, and uses figures 1–2, 4, and 6–8.

Notes: One of "The books [Thomas Hollis] published, or procured to be published", according to Francis Blackburne, in his *Memoirs of Thomas Hollis, Esq.* (London, 1780, 2 vols. in-4°). Blackburne further states that Hollis had little or no share in preparing this edition, "He only revised and corrected the Life of Locke" by Le Clerc (i. 386). The edition was edited by John Noorthouck after a proposal to do so made by Hollis (ibid. i.375–6, 386–8). It is the first quarto edition, and the first to include the Latin text of the first 'Toleration' letter, and the *Observations on the Growth and Culture of Vines*.

The title-page of the first issue follows the pattern of other Hollis editions, in being sparing of punctuation and in using 'I's in place of 'J's; compare his editions of the *Letters concerning Toleration* (no. 28), and *Two Treatises of Government* (no. 35).

I have found the Hollis-type title-pages at the British Library and in the late Robert Shackleton's copy (now in John Rylands Library, Manchester); each of his vols. has two title-pages, the first- and second-issue style.

The group of 'Toleration' letters follows the text of the 1765 Hollis edition (no. 28) but is here newly typeset.

A long footnote in vol. 1, pp. xv–xvii reprints a letter from Locke to Samuel Bold dated 16 May 1699 (no. 353; reprinted in all future *Works* editions, and as *Corr.* 2590, vi. 626–30).

A microfilm of the British Library's copy of the first issue is in the collection, *The Eighteenth Century*, reels 3191–3.

References: Alston 7:118; Attig 854; Christophersen p. 88; ESTC 1st issue: t114397, 2d issue: n025684.

Copies examined. 1st issue: L (526.n.15) R.Shackleton's copy (now at MRu)

2d issue: Y   C (Acton b.51.69-72)   CtY (K8.L79/A768)   NjP (Ex6106.1768q)   NN   O (Vet.A5.d.369-72)   PPL (*IaLock/7Q)   Vat

370. Works. 8th ed. (ed. Hollis & Law), 1777. 4 vols. in 4-°
THE | WORKS | OF | JOHN LOCKE, | IN FOUR VOLUMES. | THE EIGHTH EDITION. | VOLUME THE FIRST. ['THE SECOND.', 'THE THIRD.', 'THE FOURTH.'] | [double rule 150 mm] | LONDON: | Printed for W. STRAHAN, J. F. and C. RIVINGTON, L. DAVIS, W. OWEN, S. BAKER | and G. LEIGH, T. PAYNE and Son, T. CASLON, S. CROWDER, T. LONGMAN, B. LAW, | C. RIVINGTON, E. and C. DILLY, J. WILKIE, T. CADELL, N. CONANT, T. BEECROFT, | T. LOWNDES, G. ROBINSON, JOS. JOHNSON, J. ROBSON, J. KNOX, T. BECKET, and | T. EVANS. | MDCCLXXVII.

Coll: 4° (290 × 238 mm cut). Vol. 1: A^2 (-A1 blank or wanting) a-e^4 *e^4 (-*e4) f-g^4 B-$5I^4$ $5K^2$ [$ half signed]; 434 leaves; pp. *i-ii* iii-xiii *xiv* xv-xxviii v xxx *xxxi-xxxiii* xxxiv-xxxv *xxxvi* xxxvii-xl *xli-*xliii *xliv* *xlv-*xlviii xli-lvi 1 2-517 *518* 519-788 *789-804* [= 868]. Page xxix called 'v'. Pages numbered with asterisks occur on e4 as well as *e1-3.

Vol. 2: A^4 (-A4 blank or wanting; -A2.3 = $4T^2$) B-$4S^4$ $4T^2$ [$ half signed]; 347 leaves; pp. *i-ii* 1-2 3-84 *85-86* 87-134 *135-136* 137-312 *313-314* 315-350 *351-352* 353-400 *401-402* 406-661 *662-664* 665-681 *682-692* [= 694].

Vol. 3: A^2 (-A2 = 4K1) B-$4I^4$ 4K1 [$ half signed]; 310 leaves; pp. *i-ii* 1 2-99 *100* 101 *102* 103-115 *116-118* 119-123 *124* 125-272 *273-275* 276-287 *288-290* 291-408 *409* 410-561 *562* 563-610 *611-618* [= 620].

Vol. 4: A^4 (-A4) B-$4M^4$ $4N^4$ (4N2 + *4) 4O-$4R^4$ [$ half (-2I2) signed]; 347 leaves; pp. *i-vi* 1 2-135 *136-141* 142-171 127 173-194 *195* 196-209 201 211-231 *232-233* 234-245 *246-247* 248-261 *262-266* 267-496 *497-498* 499-506 *507-508* 509-644 *645-*651 *652 645-646 647-648 649-650 651-670 *671-680* [= 694]. Page 172 called '127', 210 called '201'. Asterisked pages (quire *4) inserted after 4N2 = p. 644).

Contents. **Vol. 1**: A1 blank or wanting, A2^r (*i*) title (verso blank), a1^r-b2^r (iii-xiii) editor's pref. (by Edmund Law), b2^v blank, b3^r-d1^v (xv-xxviii) 'Life of the Author' from Le Clerc, d2^{r,v} ('v', xxx) contents of set of 4 vols.,

Essay concerning Human Understanding: d3^r (*xxxi*) section title (verso blank), d4^r-e1^r (*xxxiii*-xxxv) dedication, e1^v blank, e2^r-*e1^r (xxxvii-xl, *xli-*xliii) 'Epistle to the Reader', *e1^v blank, *e2^r-*e3^v and f1r-g4v (*xlv-*xlviii, xli-lvi) contents of the *Essay* by book, chap. and sections, B1^r-5F3^v (*1-774*) same as 1768 ed. (no. 369);

'A DEFENCE of Mr. LOCKE's OPINION' by Edmund Law: 5F4^r-5H1^v (775-786);

'APPENDIX' on Locke's use of 'Person' by Law: 5H2^{r,v} (787-788);

Index of vol.: 5H3^r-5K1^v (*789-802*) index of vol.

Vol. 2: A1^r (*i*) title (verso blank), B1^r-2R4^v (*1-312*) same as 1768 ed. (no. 369);

A Letter concerning Toleration: 2S1^r (*313*) section title (verso blank), 2S2^r–2Y3^v (*315–350*) text;

Second Letter concerning Toleration: 2Y4^r (*351*) section title (verso blank), 2Z1^r–3E4^v (*353–400*) text;

Third Letter for Toleration: 3F1^r (*401*) section title (verso blank), 3F2^r–4P3^r (*403–661*) text, 4P3^v blank;

Fourth Letter: 4P4^r (*663*) section title (verso blank), 4Q1^r–4S1^r (*665–681*) text, 4S1^v blank;

Index of vol.: 4S2^r–4T2^v (*683–692*).

Vol. 3: A1^r (*i*) title (verso blank), B1^r–4K1^r (*i–617*) same as 1768 ed. (no.369), 4K1^v blank.

Vol. 4: A1^r (*i*) title (verso blank),

Some Thoughts concerning Education: A2^r (*iii*) section title (verso blank), A3^{r,v} (*v–vi*) dedication, B1^r–S4^r (*1–135*) text, S4^v blank;

T1^r–4N2^v (*137–644*) same as 1768 ed. (no. 369);

'Several Letters': *1^r–*4^r (**645*–*651*): (1) to Mrs. Cockburn dated 30 Dec. 1702; (2) to Samuel Bold, 16 May 1699; (3) to 'Dear Coll' dated 24 April 1696, (4) from 'Lord Ashley' to Dr. Fell dated 8 Dec. 1670; and (5) a brief note from Peter King to the 3rd Earl of Shaftesbury dated 9 Dec. 1704 (1–3 reprinted as *Corr.* 3234, 2590 and 2073 respectively);

4N3^r–4R4^v (*645–680*) same as 1768 ed.

Illustrations: (1) Vol. 1 has front. port. of Locke signed 'F.B. CIPRIANI', copied from 1768 edition but of lesser quality, with liberty cap and subscription 'IOHN LOCKE'. (2) Vol. 1 also has a folded broadside usually bound after leaf g4, 435 × 528 mm, captioned: '*An* ANALYSIS *of* Mr. LOCKE's Doctrine *of* IDEAS, *in his* ESSAY on HUMAN UNDERSTANDING.'

Text: 93 R. Other technical details vary, 46 or 47 lines; in v.2, for example, 2Z1^r: 46 lines, 216 (231 × 141 (160); in v.3 3B1^v: 47 lines 219 (236) × 144 (164) mm. Medium-quality laid paper with fleur-de-lys watermark and initials 'GR'. Page no. at external ends of headlines.

CW: Page. Vol. 1: b2^r THE d1^v CON- [CONTENTS] E3^v (worm-) wood Q3^r § 7. THOUGH 2M4^v (concep-) tions 3E1^r § 15. SE- [§ 15. SECONDLY,]

Vol. 2: D1^r, E1^v, L4^v, 2A4^v identical with those in 1768 ed. 2S1^r A LET- [A LETTER] 2X4^r opinion 3L2^v of

Vol. 3: same as those in 1768 ed. except: 2D2^v su [us]

Vol. 4 identical with those in 1768 ed.

Press figures. Vol. 1: 1 2 3 5 or 7 on inner and outer form of each quire, except 2G which has '5' on 1st leaf verso (p. 226).

Vol. 2: 1, 3, 5 or 7 on average on inner and outer form of each quire.

Vol. 3, similarly but with figures 1, 2, 3, 5 and 7.

Vol. 4: figures 1, 3, 5 and 7 on inner and outer form of each quire, except 3C (pp. 377–84) and 4N (pp. 641–8): p. 382 has 3, p. 642 has 1.

Notes: A reprint, chiefly line-for-line and word-for-word, of the Hollis edition, with some editing and additions by Bishop Edmund Law. The 'Defence' and its appendix in vol. 1 were written by him. Though he omits the Latin text of the first 'toleration' letter, he does include some additional letters (v.4, pp.*645–51), all except the letter to Bold here published for the first time. In the editor's preface, he also discusses some works "written or supposed to be written" by Locke, and his reasons for excluding them from this edition. For details see chap. XII, 'Doubtful and Spurious Works'.

Bishop Law mentions the broadside diagrammatic chart, 'An Analysis', in his Preface to this edition. John Stephens informs me the chart was designed by Law, but an ESTC entry (t209505) reports an anonymous broadside with the same title, and with an imprint: 'Cambridge, printed by J. Bentham, sold by T. & J. Merrill, 1766' (found at Cambridge Univ. Library, Broadsides A.76.2; cf. no. C1766–1 below). Law had many connections with Cambridge, at one time he was Master of Peterhouse, and in 1760 was appointed librarian of the university, before becoming Bishop of Carlisle (cf. DNB). The chart here is without imprint.

A microfilm of the British Library's copy of this edition is to be found in the collection, *The Eighteenth Century*, reel 3589–90.

References: Alston 7:119; Attig 855; Christophersen pp. 88–9; ESTC t147728.

Copies examined: O (4° BS.362-5) C (Yorke b.41-44) EXu (gift of Jas. B. Baillie) L (684.i.18) MH (TP2115.1.8F) Om PPL (*IaLock/ 1025.Q) TxDaM-P

371. Works. 9th ed., 1794. 9 vols. in-8°
THE | WORKS | OF | [hollow type:] JOHN LOCKE, | IN NINE VOLUMES. | [rule 97 mm] | THE NINTH EDITION. | [double rule 97 mm] | VOLUME THE FIRST. ['SECOND.', &c.] | [double rule 97 mm] | *LONDON:* | PRINTED FOR T. LONGMAN, B. LAW AND SON, J. JOHNSON, | C. DILLY, G. G. AND J. ROBINSON, T. CADELL, J. SEWELL, | W. OTRIDGE, W. RICHARDSON, F AND C. RIVINGTON, | W. GOLDSMITH, T. PAYNE, LEIGH AND SOTHEBY, | S. HAYES, R. FAULDER, B. AND J. WHITE, | W. LOWNDES, G. AND T. WILKIE, | AND J. WALKER. | [double rule 8 mm] | 1794.

Coll: 8° (220 × 125 mm cut). Vol. 1: A^8 (– A2-8) a–b^8 c^4 *a–*b^2 A2-8 $^2a^8$ B–$2K^8$ [$ half signed]; 296 leaves; pp. *I–II* i–xxxix *xl–lxxviii* 1 2–510 *511–512* [= 592]. Gatherings a–*b (pp. i–*xlviii*) inserted between A1 and A2. Second 'a' gathering, preceding leaf B1, is a smaller 'a'.

Vol. 2: A^2 a^4 b^2 B–$2G^8$ $2H$–$2I^4$ $2K^4$ (–2K4) [$ half signed; A2 signed 'a3']; 251 leaves; pp. *i–xvi* 1 2–298 *299–300* 301–320 *321–322* 323–401 *402–404* 405–412 *413–414* 415–440 *441* 442–459 *460–486* [= 502].

Vol. 3: A^2 B–$2I^8$ $2K^2$ [$ half signed; A2 signed 'a']; 252 leaves; pp. *i–iv* 1–3 4–96 *97–98* 99–189 *190–192* 193–498 *499–500* [= 504].

Vol. 4: A^2 B–$2I^8$ [$ half signed; A2 signed 'a']; 250 leaves; pp. *i–iv* 1–3

4-130 *131-133* 134-135 *136* 137-206 *207-209* 210-211 *212* 213-337 338 339-485 *486-496* [=500].

Vol. 5: A^2 B-2O^8 2P^4 [$ half signed; A2 signed 'a']; 294 leaves; pp. *i-iv 1-2* 3-58 *59-60* 61-137 *138-140* 141-546 *547-548* 549-574 *575-584* [=588].

Vol. 6: A^2 B-2E^8 [$ half (-N3) signed; A2 signed 'a']; 218 leaves; pp. *i-iv 1-2* 3-158 *159-160* 161-180 *181-182* 183-424 *425-432* [=436].

Vol. 7: A^2 B-2P^8 2G^4 [$ half (-N4, R3, 2C2) signed; A2 signed 'a']; 230 leaves; pp. I-IV *i-iii* iv-xxiii *xxiv-xxvi* 27-72 *73-74* 75-181 *182-184* 185-243 *244-246* 247-385 *386-388* 389-449 *450-456* [=560].

Vol. 8: A^2 B-2H^8 [$ half signed; A2 signed 'a']; 242 leaves; pp. I-IV *i-iii* iv-v 6 7-205 *206-211* 212-255 *256* 257-265 *266* 267-284 *285-289* 290-472 *473-480* [=484].

Vol. 9: A^2 B-2N^8 2O^8 (-2O4.5 = A^2) [$ half signed; A2 signed 'a'; 2O5 signed 'Oo3')]; 288 leaves; pp. *i-iv 1-2* 3-145 *146-149* 150-158 *159-160* 161-246 *247* 248-259 *260* 261-322 *323-325* 326-327 *328-329* 330-356 *357-360* 361-512 *513* 514-564 *565-572* [=576].

First page of each gathering also signed in direction line, e.g. 'VOL. VI.'

Contents. **Vol. 1:** A1^r (*I*) title (verso blank), a1^r-b1^v (*i-xviii*) 'Preface by the Editor.', b2^r-c4^r (*xix-xxxix*) 'The Life of the Author' (from Le Clerc), c4^v blank, *a1^r-*a2^v (*xli-xliv*) contents of 9 vols., *b1^r (*xlv*) contents of vol. 1 (verso blank),

Essay concerning Human Understanding: *b2^r (*xlvii*) section title (verso blank), A2^r-A3^v (*xlix-lii*) dedication, A4^r-2a1^r (*liii-lxiii*) reader's epistle, ^{2}a1^v-^{2}a8^v (*lxiv-lxxii*) contents by book, chap. and sections, B1^r-2K7^v (1-510) text of Books I-III, ch. 6, 2K8 blank.

Vol. 2: A1^r title (verso blank), 'a3^r (*iii*) contents of vol. 2 (verso blank), a1^r-b1^v (*v-xiv*) contents of *Essay* by book, chap. & sections, b2 (*xv-xvi*) blank, B1^r-U5^v (*1-298*) text of Books III, ch. 7-IV.

Bishop Law's 'Defence of Mr. Locke's Opinion concerning Personal Identity': U6^r section title (verso blank), U7^r-X8^v (301-320) text;

Conduct of the Understanding: Y1^r section title (verso blank), Y2^r-2D1^r (323-401) text, 2D1^v blank;

Some Thoughts upon Reading and Study for a Gentleman: 2D2^r section title (verso blank), 2D3^r-2D6^v (405-412) text;

Elements of Natural Philosophy: 2D7^r section title (verso blank), 2D8^r-2F4^v (415-440) text;

New Method of a Common-place-book: 2F5^r section title (verso blank), 2F5^v-2F6^r (442-3) diagrammatic table (printed in black ink), 2F6^v-2G6^r (444-459) text, 2G6^v blank;

Index to vol.: 2^r-2K1^v (461-482); 'Index to the additional pieces in the Second Volume': 2K2^r-2K3^v (483-486).

Vol. 3: A1^r title (verso blank), 'a'1^r contents of vol. (verso blank),

Letter to the Bishop of Worcester: B1^r section title (verso blank), B2^r-G8^v (*3-96*) text;

Locke's Reply: H1ʳ section title (verso blank), H2ʳ–N7ʳ (99–189) text, N7ᵛ blank;
Locke's Second Reply: N8ʳ section title (verso blank), O1ʳ–2K1ᵛ (193–498) text;
Index to vol.: 2K2ʳ,ᵛ (499–500).

Vol. 4: A1ʳ title (verso blank), 'a'1ʳ contents of vol. (verso blank),
Several Papers Relating to Money: B1ʳ section title (verso blank),
    Some Considerations: B2ʳ–I2ᵛ (3–116);
    Short Observations: I3ʳ–K1ᵛ (117–130);
    Further Considerations: K2ʳ section title (verso blank), K3ʳ–O7ʳ (133–205) O7ᵛ (206) value table;
Two Treatises of Government: O8ʳ section title (verso blank), P1ʳ–2I3ʳ (209–485) text, 2I3ᵛ (486) contents of both treatises;
Index of vol.: 2I4ʳ–2I7ᵛ (487–494) text, 2I8 blank.

Vol. 5: A1ʳ title (verso blank), 'a'1ʳ contents (verso blank),
Letters concerning Toleration: B1ʳ section title (verso blank),
    A Letter concerning Toleration, B2ʳ–E5ᵛ (3–58);
    Second Letter: E6ʳ section title (verso blank), E7ʳ–K5ʳ (61–137) text, K5ᵛ blank;
    Third Letter: K6ʳ section title (verso blank), K7ʳ–2N1ᵛ (141–546) text;
    Part of fourth letter: 2N2ʳ section title (verso blank), 2N3ʳ–2O7ᵛ (549–574) text;
Index of vol.: 2O8ʳ–2P3ᵛ (575–582), 2P4 blank.

Vol. 6: A1ʳ title (verso blank), 'a'1ʳ contents (verso blank),
The Reasonableness of Christianity: B1ʳ section title (verso blank), B2ʳ–L7ᵛ (3–158) text;
Vindication: L8ʳ section title (verso blank), M1ʳ–N2ᵛ (161–180) text;
Second Vindication: N3ʳ section title (verso blank), N4ʳ–N7ᵛ (183–190) preface, N8ʳ–2E4ᵛ (191–424) text;
Index of vol.: 2E5ʳ–2E7ᵛ (425–430); 2E8 blank.

Vol. 7: A1ʳ (I) title (verso blank), 'a'1ʳ (III) contents (verso blank),
A Paraphrase and Notes on St. Paul's Epistles: B1ʳ (i) section title (verso blank),
    Essay for the Understanding: B2ʳ–C4ʳ (*iii*–xxiii) text, C4ᵛ blank;
    Galatians: C5ʳ section title, C5ᵛ publisher's note to reader, C6ʳ–F4ᵛ (27–72) text;
    I. Corinthians: F5ʳ section title (verso blank), F6ʳ–N3ʳ (75–181) text, N3ᵛ blank;
    II. Corinthians: N4ʳ section title (verso blank), N5ʳ–R2ʳ (185–243) text, R2ᵛ blank;
    Romans: R3ʳ section title (verso blank), R4ʳ–2C1ʳ (247–385) text, 2C2ᵛ blank;
    Ephesians: 2C2ʳ section title (verso blank), 2C3ʳ–2G1ʳ (389–449) text;
Index of vol.: 2G1ᵛ–2G3ᵛ (450–454), 2G⁴ blank.

Vol. 8: A1ʳ (I) title (verso blank), 'a'1ʳ (III) contents (verso blank),

Some Thoughts concerning Education: B1^r section title (verso blank), B2^r–B3^r (*iii*–v) dedication, B3^v–O7^r (6–205) text, O7^v blank;
Posthumous Works: O8^r section title (verso blank), with note that the 'Conduct' and the fourth letter for toleration are printed in vols.2 and 5 respectively (verso blank),
Examination of Malebranche's Opinion: P1^r–R8^r (209–255);
Discourse of Miracles: R8^v–S5^r (256–265);
Memoirs of the Earl of Shaftesbury: S5^v–T6^v (266–284);
Familiar Letters: T7^r section title (verso blank), T8^r introductory note (verso blank), U1^r–2H4^v (289–472) text;
Index of vol.: 2H5^r–2H8^v (473–480).

Vol. 9: A1^r title (verso blank), 'a'1^r (*iii*) contents (verso blank),
Some Familiar Letters (remaining part): B1^r section title (verso blank) B2^r–L1^r (3–145) text, L1^v blank;
Collection of Several Pieces (ed. Desmaizeaux): L2^r section title (verso blank), L3^r–L7^v (149–158) dedication, L8^r (159) contents (verso blank), M1^r–Y1^v (161–322) text;
Observations on the Growth and Culture of Vines: Y2^r section title (verso blank), Y3^r–2A2^v (325–356) text;
The Whole History of Navigation (from Churchill's *Collection of Voyages*): 2A3^r section title (verso blank), 2A4^r–2K8^v (359–512) text;
'A Catalogue and Character of Most Books of Voyages and Travels' (contents of the Churchill *Collection*?): 2L1^r–2O2^v (513–564);
Index of vol.: 2O3^r–2O6^v (565–572).

Illustrations. Vol. 1 has front. portrait of Locke facing right, in oval frame 112 × 98 mm, after Kneller, '*Cook Sculp.*', the whole subscribed: 'JOHN LOCKE, ESQ^R | *born 1632, died 1704.*' A folded plate, 421 × 537 mm, containing the 'Analysis of Mr. Locke's Doctrine of Ideas . . .' (no. C1766-1; cf. no. 370, *Notes*) is included in vol. 1, usually bound before B1.

Text (v.1 F4^v): 41 lines; 171 (181) × 95 mm; 84 R. Wove paper without watermark. Page no. centered in headlines within square brackets, where a new work begins; otherwise at outer ends of headlines.

*HT*s or headlines are individual chap. titles or titles of works set in italics.

CW: Page.

Press figures: 1 through 9 in all vols., one figure per sheet, usually on verso pages. Vol.1 and 2 have same figures as in no. 87; vol. 7 same as in no. 295.

Notes: The first octavo edition, based on the text of the previous edition, with the contents rearranged so as to place all the correspondence together, and the non-correspondence items in Desmaizeaux's *Collection* (no. 316-8) repositioned to follow relevant works (e.g. the *Elements of Natural Philosophy* repositioned with other miscellaneous pieces relating to the *Essay*). The first edition also to include 'The Whole History of Navigation' (not by Locke. Cf. Chap.XII: Doubtful and Spurious Works).

The Bodleian Library's copy of vol. 1 has 'J. WALKE.' as the final name of the booksellers given on the title-page; I assume it was changed to 'J. WALKER.' by a 'stop-press' procedure.

The text of the *Essay* in vols. 1–2 is identical with that of the 1793 edition of the *Essay* (no. 87); only the preliminary matter in both vols. has been reset.

A microfilm of the British Library's copy of this edition is in the collection, *The Eighteenth Century*, reels 1042-3. This edition was reprinted by Routledge/Thoemmes Press, London, in 1997.

References: Alston 7:120; Attig 856; Christophersen p. 89; ESTC t136838.

Copies examined: O (Vet.A5.e.2378-86; v.2 lacks b2 leaf) CaOTU (Locke L63.A1 1794) CtY (K8.L79/a794) L (12269.e.1) NjR (X B1253.1794, v.6-7 only) Omc

372. Selected Works. French trans. (ed. Bernard) Rotterdam, 1710. 12°

In red & black: [red line:] OEUVRES | *DIVERSES* | DE | MONSIEUR | [red:] JEAN [swash J] LOCKE. | [tailpiece: seated Minerva with books & press, scroll above: 'PRESARE SURGET', monogram initials F, B below, 43 × 42 mm] | [red:] *A ROTTERDAM,* [swash Ts] | Chez FRITSCH et BÖHM, | MDCCX.

Coll: 12° (160 × 98 mm cut) *⁴ a–c¹² d¹⁴ A–T¹² V⁶ [$ half + 1 (+ d9) signed]; 288 leaves; pp. *i–viii* I–XCIX C 1–372 373 374–468 [= 576].

Contents: *1ʳ (*i*) title (verso blank), *2ʳ–*4ᵛ (*iii–viii*) 'AVERTISSEMENT', a1ʳ–d12ʳ (I–XCIX) Le Clerc's 'Eloge', d14ᵛ (C) Locke's Latin epitaph, A1ʳ–F10ᵛ (1–140) 'Lettre sur la tolerance' (French trans. of 'Epistola de tolerantia'), F11ʳ–P6ᵛ (141–348) trans. of the 'Conduct of the Understanding', P7ʳ–Q6ᵛ (349–372) 'Discours sur les miracles', Q7ʳ (*373*) section title, Q7ᵛ–Q8ʳ (374–5) diagrammatic box in red & black (repr. from no. 266, q.v.), Q8ᵛ–R11ᵛ (376–406) 'Méthode nouvelle de dresser des recueils', R12ʳ–V6ᵛ (407–468) 'Mémoires pour servir à la vie d'Antoine Ashley, Comte de Shaftesbury'.

Text (B5ᵛ): 24 lines; 121 (133) × 66 mm; 101 R; pp. 1–XCIX set 102 ital. Good-quality laid paper with coat-of-arms watermark. Page no. at outer ends of headlines. The 'Avertissement', 'Eloge', Toleration and the 'Memoires' begin each with an orn. 5-line initial. Pages a1ʳ, A1ʳ, F11ʳ, P7ʳ and R12ʳ called 'Pag.I', 'Pag.I', 'Pag.141', 'Pag.349' and 'Pag.407' respectively. The only ornaments are unframed 5-line leafy initials, 22 × 23 mm: L on *2r, and P on A1ʳ and R12ʳ.

Section title, p. 373: METHODE | NOUVELLE | *De dreſſer des* | RECUEILS.

HT, a1ʳ: ELOGE | HISTORIQUE | DE FEU | Mr. LOCKE, | PAR | Mr. Jean [swash J] le Clerc.

A1ʳ: LETTRE | SUR LA | TOLERANCE.

F11r: DE LA | CONDUITE | DE | L'ESPRIT | DANS LA | RECHERCHE | DE LA | VERITÉ.

P7ʳ: DISCOURS | SUR | LES | MIRACLES.

R11^r: MEMOIRES | pour fervir à la VIE | D'ANTOINE ASHLEY, | *Comte de Shaftesbury, & Grand* | *Chancelier d'Angleterre, fous* | CHARLES II. | Tirées des Papiers de feu | MR. JEAN LOCKE, | & redigées par | Mr. JEAN LE CLERC.
Headlines are titles of the different contents, with occasional large & small capitals for emphasis, frequently as running titles (chiefly in italics), e.g. 'Eloge hiftorique | de Mr. LOCKE.' '*Difcours* | *fur les Miracles.*'
CW: Page. a6^r *nean-* [*neanmoins,*] c6^v *veuil-* [*veuillent*] A4^r (pu-) bli- [bliques] D9^v (D'a-) bord H12^v (entrai-) nent P10^r po- [pofer] V1^r ,,vou- [,,voulut]
Notes: Modelled after the *Posthumous Works* of 1706 (no. 299) but printing the first French translation of the 'toleration' letter from the Latin edition (instead of the incomplete fourth letter), and omitting the 'Examination of P. Malebranche's Opinion'. The 'Eloge' is reprinted from the *Bibliothèque choisie*, 6 (1705), as is the Shaftesbury memoir (ibid. 7 (1705), pp. 146–91; see no. 298). The preface to this collection indicates that this is the first French edition of the 'toleration' letter: 'qui n'avoit pas encore paru en nôtre Langue' (p. *iv*), thus contradicting Popple's statement in the preface to his English translation that it had already been translated into Dutch and French (cf. no.3). Unlike Popple, the anonymous editor correctly translates Locke's list of religious groups which should also be allowed religious freedom (Remonstrants, Anti-remonstrants, Lutherans, Anabaptists and Socinians (cf. Klibansky-Gough ed., p.145; 162 n.64.) Most of the translations are by Jean Le Clerc.

The British Library catalogue attributes the new edition of 1732 (no. 372) to Jean Frédéric Bernard, its publisher; he was a friend of Pierre Bayle. He was probably the editor of this edition too. Neither Cioranescu nor the *Dictionnaire des journalistes* credits Bernard with these editions. The 'Avertissement' to this edition, reprinted in the next, speaks disparagingly of Le Clerc, saying he acted as if Locke had never understood the question of freedom; "it is difficult to understand how such a man [Le Clerc] could ignore the state of the controversy [with Limborch] which concerned him for a good part of his life." Certainly this collection was *not* put together by Le Clerc.

This is also the first French translation of the 'Conduct'. A notice of Locke's *Posthumous Works* (no. 299) appeared in the *Bibliothèque choisie*, 7 (1707): 123–70. As was usual, it contains French-language abstracts of its contents, pp. 124–156 alone being devoted to the 'Conduct'. Christophersen (p.73) mistakenly states that was the first French appearance of the 'Conduct'.
References: Attig 868; Christophersen p. 73, 90; Rochedieu p. 192.
Copies examined: Y [GhU] Han (PA 987) MH (TP2115.20) NjP (Ex.6106.2710) P (D2.4933) Utr (Utenhove oct.440) Wol (Va 261)

373. Selected Works. French trans. (ed. Bernard) New ed., Amsterdam, 1732. 2 vols. 12°
Vol. 1: OEUVRES | *DIVERSES* | DE | MONSIEUR | LOCKE. | Nouvelle edition confidérablement augmentée. | TOME PREMIER. |

[ornament: monogram-like interlaced branches, 24 × 51 mm] | A AMSTERDAM, | Chez JEAN [swash J] FREDERIC BERNARD. | M. DCC. XXXII.

Vol. 2, as vol. 1 except:] TOME SECOND. | [tailpiece: Indian head with headdress, 39 × 46 mm] . . . [&c. as in vol. 1 until imprint, where 'RD' in 'BERNARD' are slightly above the line].

Coll: 12° (179 × 105 mm uncut) Vol. 1: *^{8} (± *1; *5 + ^{2}*5) 2*–4*^{12} 5*^{6} A–N^{12} O^8 P^2 [$ half + 1 (–P2) signed; leaf inserted after *5 also signed '*5']; 217 leaves; pp. *I–III* IV–X X X–XCII CXIII XCIV–XCVII CXIX C *1* 2–329 *330–332* [= 434]. Leaf ^{2}*5 also paged X–X, that is, 3 pages numbered X; page no. xciii called 'CXIII', xcix called 'CXIX'. For further details, see *Notes*.

Vol. 2: A^4 (± A1) B–S^{12} T^8 [$ half + 1 signed]; 216 leaves; pp. *1–3* 4–91 *92* 93–145 *146* 147–176 167–255 *256* 257–420 *421–422* [= 432]. Page no. 167–176 (on leaves I1–I5) repeated.

Contents: Vol. 1: *1^r (*I*) title (verso blank), *2^r–5^v (*III–X*) 'Avertissement' (by editor), ^{2}*5^r–5*6^r (^{2}X–^{3}X XI–'CXIX') Le Clerc's 'Eloge'(from the *Bibliothèque choisie*), 5*6^v (*C*) Locke's Latin epitaph, A1^r–F2^r (*1–123*) 'Lettre sur la tolérance', F2^v–N10^v (*124–308*) 'De la conduite de l'esprit', N11^r–P1^r (*309–329*) 'Discours sur les miracles'.

Vol. 2: A1^r title (verso blank), A2^r (*3*) section title, A2^v–A3^r (*4–5*) diagrammatic table, A3^v–C2^v (*6–36*) text of 'Méthode nouvelle de dresser des recueils', C3^r–E6^r (*37–91*) 'Mémoires sur la vie de' Shaftesbury, E6^v–G9^r (*92–145*) 'Essai sur la nécessité d'expliquer les Epitres de S. Paul meme', G9^v–M9^r (*146–255*) 'Examen du sentiment du P. Mallebranche, qu'on vit toutes choses en Dieu', M9^v–T7^v (*256–420*) 23 letters between Locke and Limborch trans. from the Latin concerning the unity of God and man's liberty, beginning with one from Limborch dated Oct. 8, 1697 (*Corr.* 2318, vi.206–10) and continuing to Limborch's letter of Jan. 3, 1702 (*ibid.* 3055, vii.518–21).

Text (v.1 A3^v): 26 lines; 120 (130) × 69 mm; 93 R. Fair-quality laid paper without watermarks. Page no. at external ends of headlines.

Section title: v. 2, A2^r: MÉTHODE | NOUVELLE | *De dreſſer des* | RECUEILS.

*R T*s or headlines are titles of individual works in capitals, e.g. 'DE LA CONDUITE | DE L'ESPRIT &c.'

Ornaments: tailpiece of a portrait medallion, 39 × 44 mm, in v. 1 F2^r, N10^v and v.2 E6^r; a vase of flowers, 24 × 34 mm, in v.2 G10^r. Unframed decorative initials with leafy surrounds occur: 5-line L on v.1 *2^r; 5-line C on v.1 *5^r, P on v.1 A1^r and v.2 C3^r.

CW: Page. Vol. 1: *2^v LIM- [LIMBURGIUM] 3*6^v *d'ail*- [*d'ailleurs*] A5^r Sol- [Soldats] C4^r (don-) niez F10^v (at-) tri- [tribue,] I3^r el- [elles] M4^r cha- [chacun] P1^r ME- [in v.2 A2^r: MÉTHODE]

Vol. 2: B6^v qu'el- [qu'elle] E6^r ES- [ESSAI] H12^v *el*- [*elles*] L10^r(l'au-) tre O7^v (con-) trai- [traire] R11^v (Traduc-) tion

Notes: A new edition of no. 372, expanded by the inclusion of the 'Essay for the Understanding of St. Paul's Epistles', the 'Examination of P. Malebranche's Opinion', and selected correspondence with Philippus van Limborch (trans. from *Some Familiar Letters*). The British Library catalogue states this edition was edited by Jean Frédéric Bernard, its publisher (see *Notes* to previous entry).

The title leaves of both vols. are cancellantia. The complicated arrangement of the preliminary pages testifies perhaps to a change of booksellers during production. My copy is loosely sewn, so it is possible to determine that *3 is conjugate with *6, and that a cancellandum (shown by a stub) is conjugate with $^{2*}5$; that is, conjugate leaves are as follows: cancellandum *1.8, *2.7, *3.6, stub. $^{2*}5$, *4.5.

References: Attig 869; Christophersen p. 90; Rochedieu p. 192.

Copies examined: Y (uncut) [BBR] CtY (K8.L79/ah732) [GhU] L (528.e.6-7; v.1 lacks pp.313 to the end, but has bound duplicate pp.287-420 from v.2) O (Vet.B4.f.184-5) P^1 (8° Z.18336) P^2 (R.42165, v.1 only)

Nineteenth-century editions of the *Works* were reprints of the 1794 collection (no. 373): the 10th edition in 1801 and the 11th in 1812 divided the *Essay* into 3 vols., thus achieving 10-vol. octavo sets. Thomas Tegg's 'new' edition of 1823 followed the same pattern; his is the text used for the facsimile reprint by Scientia Verlag (in Aalen, Ger.) in 1963. The 12th *Works* edition of 1824, with some rearrangement of contents, reverted to the 9-vol. format; it was reprinted in 1826 and 1854.

There were English-language selections published with the title, *Philosophical Beauties*, in 1802, 1828, 1829 and 1844. A *Philosophical Works* in a small folio-sized format printed in double columns with a preface by J. A. St. John was published in 1843, reissued in 2-vols. as 'Bohn's Standard Library' in 1854, 1872, 1882 and 1892. Ward Lock published a 4-vol. *Works* in the 1890's (without imprint date) containing only the 'toleration' letters, the *Essay* and the first paper on money (no. 155).

None of these reprints of *Works* or selections received editorial attention. We have had to wait 165 years for serious attention to texts, which began with Peter Laslett's edition of the *Two Treatises of Government* in 1963, and is being continued with the 'Clarendon Edition of the Works of John Locke', in progress since 1975.

French readers had to wait until the 1820s to see any 'works' editions: François Thurot edited a 7-vol. *Oeuvres philosophiques*, published 1821-25. Vol. 1 contains the *Education*, vols. 2-6 the *Essay*, and the 7th vol. is a miscellany (the 'Conduct', the 'Examination of P. Malebranche's Opinion', 'Remarks on Norris's Books', 'New Method of Making Common-place Books' and the memoir of the first Earl of Shaftesbury).

For Italian readers, in 1979 Mario Sina's edition, *Scritti filosofici e religiosi*, was published, with his Italian translations. It contains (1) Le Clerc's 'Eloge',

(2) the extract, or 'Abregé' of the *Essay*, from the *Bibliothèque universelle* (no. 273); (3) *The Reasonableness of Christianity*, and its vindications as rearranged and summarized by Pierre Coste (no. 240-1 et seq.); (4) the first letter to Bishop Edward Stillingfleet, (5) the 'Essay for the Understanding St. Paul's Epistles'; and (6) the 'Conduct', with some brief description of the manuscripts in the Lovelace Collection in the Bodleian Library.

A two-vol. Russian translation of J. A. St. John's *Philosophical Works* was published in Moscow in 1960.

CHAPTER XII
Doubtful and Spurious Works

Several works were attributed to Locke, even in his lifetime, for various reasons, association with the first Earl of Shaftesbury (Locke helped him draft some papers), publication by the Churchills, his publishers; criticism masked as being 'from his own words'. Some spurious letters can be included: one on masonry supposedly written to the Earl of Pembroke, dated 6 May 1696; another in support of the Quakers, to Rebecca Collier on November 21, 1696. Details of the letters can be found in Esmond S. de Beer's edition of the *Correspondence*. For contributions to the *Philosophical Transactions* of the Royal Society not by Locke, see Chap. VIII, no. 258-9, 272. For reviews doubtfully attributed to him in Le Clerc's journal, the *Bibliothèque universelle*, see introductory note to Chap. VIII, Part B. More serious are published books or pamphlets attributed to him because they can be found in many library catalogues under Locke's name.

Bishop Edmund Law at the end of his editor's preface to the *Works* edition of 1777 (no. 370) listed ten works "written or supposed to be written, by Mr. Locke" including three "Pieces groundlessly ascribed, or of doubtful authority" and two "Spurious ones", all of which he therefore omits from the collected edition.

E. S. de Beer, in an article, "Bishop Law's List of Books Attributed to Locke" (*Locke Newletter* 7, 1976: 47-54) reorders and examines items in Law's list, the attributions and Law's remarks; the numbers given within parentheses are De Beer's. A brief listing and summary of his statements about these works is given. For ease of citation to this bibliography, I have assigned 'D' numbering (for 'doubtful'). Following discussion of these ten items, other works falsely attributed are given in chronological order.

(1) Epistola de Tolerantia. [1689]
Law has omitted this, "as we have it translated by Mr. Popple to the author's entire satisfaction, and as there is nothing extraordinary in the language of the original, it was judged unnecessary to repeat so many things over again by inserting it." De Beer comments he is ignorant of the source of the statement of Locke's approval. But in Locke's *Second Letter concerning Toleration* (p. 10; no. 25) Locke writes in answer to Proast that "the Translator [of the Latin original] is not to be blamed, if he chose to express the Sense of the Author, in words that very lively represented" the concepts of his work. For details, see *supra*, no. 3.

(2) **D-1.** 'The History of our Saviour Jesus Christ . . .' [London, 1721, 1724]
The Churchills published an anonymous edition of this in 1705; Locke's name appeared on the title of the 1721 and 1724 editions. Law mistakenly thought Locke "compiled this Harmony, the History of Christ, for his own immediate use, as the basis of his Reasonableness of Christianity" (*Works* i.vi). For the chronology of events in Christ's life in the *Reasonableness* Locke relied on "Toinard's 1678 version of his *Evangeliorum Graeco-Latina*", sheets of which Toinard sent him. Jean Le Clerc's *Harmonia Evangelica cui subjecta est Historia Christi ex Quatuor Evangeliis concinnata* (Amsterdam, 1699) and its English translation, The *Harmony of the Evangelists* (London, 1701) were reworked to create this *History of Our Saviour*. De Beer concludes there is no evidence "that Locke had anything to do with the translation of the *History*." A French translation, *Petite paraphrase de tous les passages remarquables . . . dans les quatre Evangiles . . . par le savant Lock*, was published in 1730 with the imprint "Suivant la copie imprimée a Amsterdam".
References: Attig A29–32; Christophersen p. 74; ESTC t130296 (1705 ed.), t107844 (1721 ed.).

(3) **D-2.** 'Select Moral Books of the Old Testament and Apocrypha paraphras'd . . .' [London: A. & J. Churchill, 1706]
A work assigned to Locke possibly because he paraphrased St. Paul's Epistles (no. 277 et seq.) and his publishers were the publishers of this work. Law describes the work, and states "This useful work is given by tradition to Mr. Locke, and his name often written before it". He made no further statement as to its authorship. The British Library credits it to Philip Bedingfield; de Beer is content with this attribution.
References: Attig A35; ESTC t123137.

(4) **D-3.** 'His Introductory Discourse to Churchill's Collection of Voyages . . . containing the whole History of Navigation . . . with a Catalogue and Character of most Books of Travels.' (Preface to *A Collection of Voyages and Travels* . . . [London: A. and J. Churchill, 1704, vol.1. pp. ix–c].)
The attribution to Locke first appeared in the third edition of the *Collection of Voyages* (1744–46). The text is included in the ninth edition of Locke's *Works* (1794; no. 371) and in later editions. Locke's correspondence contains no mention either of the 'whole History' or of the 'Catalogue'. His library catalogue (L.L. 343-4) indicates he owned some but not all of the works listed, and according to De Beer could not have compiled the 'Catalogue' (See also *Corr*. vii. 172–3 n.1). Locke is known to have been very interested in travel literature, witness the many citations in his *Essay*. De Beer suggests Edward Wells (1667–1727) as a candidate for the authorship, two of whose works were also published by the Churchills (cf. DNB). A French translation, anonymous as to author and translator, was published in Amsterdam in 1722 with the title: *Histoire de la*

navigation. An 'Account of Navigation', translated from the French edition was included in vol. 1 of a 2-vol. Russian work, *Skazanie o moreplavanii* printed at Moscow University in 1782-83 (cf. *Svodnii katalog* no. 6492).
References: Attig 24-28; Christophersen p. 74; ESTC t097848 (for 4-vol. Collection)

(5) 'The Exceptions of Mr. Edwards, in His Causes of Atheism, against The Reasonableness of Christianity . . . Examin'd, and Found Unreasonable, Unscriptural, and Injurious . . .' [London, 1695]
Addressed to Locke, perhaps "on purpose to conceal [Locke as] the true author" Bishop Law had no doubt this work was Locke's. Dr. de Beer states that the "attribution conflicts with everything that is known about Locke." It was included in a Unitarian *Collection of Tracts, Proving the God and Father of Our Lord Jesus Christ the Only True God* (1695). See also no. C1695-2.
References: Attig 670; Christophersen pp. 59-60; Wing² E3840.

(6) **D-4. Occasional Thoughts in Reference to a Vertuous or Christian Life.** [London: A. and J. Churchill, 1705]
Bishop Law correctly states this was written by Damaris Cudworth, Lady Masham. It was attributed to Locke by Abel Boyer in his *The History of the Reign of Queen Anne*, Year the Third (1705), p. 241. A reprint with title, *Thoughts on a Christian Life, by John Locke, Esq*; was published in 1747 (ESTC n047814). Again I feel sure this is another instance of a book on a topic congenial to Locke being published by Locke's publishers.
References: Attig A33; Christophersen p. 32; ESTC t115727.

(7) **D-5. A Discourse concerning the Love of God.** [London: A. and J. Churchill, 1696]
Bishop Law tells us Lady Masham "was generally believed (as Le Clerc tells us) to be the author of" this discourse. The attribution to Locke "was perhaps due to its containing an attack on Malebranche's opinion of seeing all things in God" (De Beer, in *Locke Newsletter* 7, 1976, p. 52). A French translation by Pierre Coste, entitled *Discours sur l'amour divin* appeared in 1715.
References: Attig 438; Christophersen p. 32; Wing² M905.

(8) Locke's '*Right Method of searching after Truth*, which Le Clerc mentions, is hardly to be met with' - Law.
Law says "we have good ground to believe that he wrote" this tract, going by what Le Clerc said in his 'Eloge': "il a laissé un Ecrit, touchant la Maniere de se conduire dans la recherche de la Verité". The tract is in fact 'Of the Conduct of the Understanding', first published in Locke's *Posthumous Works* (no. 299, q.v.) The French translation was first published in his *Oeuvres diverses* (1710; no. 372) with the title: De la

conduite de l'esprit dans la recherche de la verité.
Reference: Christophersen p. 90.

(9) **D-6**. A Common-place Book to the Holy Bible. [London: Printed by Edw. Jones, for A. & J. Churchil, 1697]

First published in 1676 under the title: ΓΡΑΦΑΥΤΑΡΚΕΙΑ, *or The Scriptures Sufficiency Practically Demonstrated* (London: Printed for S. Evans; Wing² G1563. Reprinted in 1684, Wing² G1564), this work according to Law "was first published in 1693 [sic], and afterwards swelled out with a great deal of matter, ill digested, and all declared to be Mr. Locke's . . . but it is plain he had [no hand] in the preface, which is neither sense nor English." Later editions were published in 1725 and 1738; the 'fifth' edition of 1766 revised by William Dodd attributes the preface to Locke. Locke's name as author appears on editions of 1805, 1828, and later. De Beer finds it "impossible to believe that Locke could have been in any way concerned with the edition."
References: Attig A1–A14; Christophersen p.10; ESTC r019113; Wing² L2737 (1697 ed.), L2746B (1676 ed.), L2746C (1684 ed.)

(10) **D-7**. "Æsop's Fables in English and Latin, interlineary, for the Benefit of those who, not having a Master, would learn either of those Tongues. The Second Edition, with Sculptures. By John Locke, gent. Printed for A. Bettesworth, 1723."

Law's transcription of the title (above) obscures the fact that the first edition lacked Locke's name and was published in 1703 by A. & J. Churchill. He correctly hazards that his name is on the second edition and "was in all probability ascribed to him for no better reason than the frequent mention made of that book in his Thoughts on Education" (p. vii). The full details of the book's history and its preparation by William Grigg, son of Mrs. Anne Grigg, friend and correspondent of Locke, are covered in "Locke's Aesop's Fables", *The Locke Newsletter*, 6 (Summer 1975): 71–88, written by Robert H. Horwitz and Judith B. Finn. In turn, Grigg's text appears to derive from Charles Hoole's *Æsopi Phrygis fabulae* (1621 and 1629), according to Horwitz and Finn. Locke had some interest in its publication as shown in correspondence with his publishers the Churchills, and with William Grigg.
References: Attig 686–7; Christophersen p.74; ESTC t084704, t084705.

D-8. 'The Fundamental Constitutions of Carolina.' "Sealed 1 March 1670." [1672?]

Now attributed to the first Earl of Shaftesbury, although the *Encyclopedia Americana*, 1980 ed., states it was drawn up by Locke. It was reissued together with 'The First Charter' in 1698 under the title, *The Two Charters Granted by King Charles IId to the Proprietors of Carolina* (ESTC r004148; Wing² C3622). For more details see no. 316, *Notes*.

References: Attig 7; Christophersen p.10; ESTC r012486; Wing² L2743A, L2744.

D-9. *A Letter from a Person of Quality to His Friend in the Country.* [London:] Printed in Year 1675.
Thought to be written by the first Earl of Shaftesbury. Two different editions were published in 1675. For details see no. 316, *Notes*.
References: Attig 15-18; Christophersen p.9; ESTC r003320, r024837; Wing² S2897, S2897aA.

D-10. *Five Letters concerning the Inspiration of the Holy Scriptures.* Translated out of French. [London?] Printed in the Year 1690.
Contains selected translations from two works by Jean Le Clerc: *Sentimens de quelques théologiens de Holland sur L'histoire critique du Vieux Testament* [by Richard Simon] (1685) and his *Défense des Sentimens de quelque théologiens . . .* (1686). It is sometimes thought to have been translated by Locke; there is no evidence for that supposition in any manuscript collections, including the Bodleian Library's Lovelace Collection.
References: Attig A20; ESTC r022740; Wing² L815.

D-11. *Political Aphorisms, or The True Maxims of Government Displayed . . .* London: Printed for Tho. Harrison, 1690.
Text consists largely of material plagarised or adapted from *Two Treatises of Government* and from Hubert Languet's *Vindicia contra tyrannos*. It has been additionally attributed to Daniel Defoe, Robert Ferguson, and to its printer Thomas Harrison. A 'third edition' was published in 1691. For a discussion see the article by Richard Ashcraft and M. M. Goldsmith: 'Locke, Revolution Principles, and the Formation of Whig Ideology', *The Historical Journal* 26 (1983): 773-800. See also Chap. II, End note. Microfilm copies in EEB reel 1189 no. 4, 1672 no. 21; 1691 ed. in reel 1926 no.5.
References: ESTC r035445, Wing² H917C; 1691 ed.: ESTC r216382, Wing² H917E.

D-12. *A Gentleman's Religion, with the Grounds and Reasons of It . . . By a Private Gentleman.* [London: A. and J. Churchil, 1693]
According to Christophersen, this tract "has also been attributed to Locke, but is known to be written by Edward Synge."
References: Attig A21; Christophersen p. 70; Wing² S6378.

D-13. *Reason and Religion, in Some Useful Reflections on the Most Eminent Hypotheses concerning the First Principles and Nature of Things . . .* London: Printed for W. Rogers, 1694.
Though Locke might share the sentiments here expressed, the linguistic

style is not his, nor is there any evidence whatsoever that he wrote it. Arber, in his transcription of the *Term Catalogues*, II.498 (probably from a misreading) states it is by Locke. A microfilm copy is in EEB, reel 111 no. 9.
References: ESTC r019663; Wing² R460A.

D-14. *A Ladies' Religion. In a Letter to the Honourable Lady Howard. By a Divine of the Church of England* . . . [London: Printed by T. Warren for R. Baldwin, 1697]
According to Christophersen, this work has been attributed to Locke. For details of it, and its French translation by Pierre Coste, with the title 'La Religion des dames', and his attribution of it to an Anglican divine named 'Mr. Stephens', see no. 242, *Notes*.
References: Attig A23; Christophersen p. 70; Wing² L159.

D-15. *An Account of Mr. Lock's Religion, Out of His Own Writings, and in His Own Words*. [By John Milner. London: Printed and Sold by J. Nutt, 1700]
An anonymously published compilation, to bolster pejorative criticism. For details see Chap. XIII, no. C1700-2.
References: Attig 460; Christophersen p. 69-70; ESTC r000548; Wing₂ M2075.

D-16. *The Rights of Protestant Dissenters* . . . [London: s.n., 1704]
Sometimes attributed to Locke, its author is now thought to be John Shute Barrington. A second edition, in two parts, was published in 1705. For details see Chap. XIII, no. C1704-3.
References: Attig 91; Christophersen p. 19, 70; ESTC t065657 (1704 ed.), t065661 (1705 ed.)

D-17. 'Rules of a Society, which met once a week, for their improvement in useful knowledge, and for the promoting of truth and Christian charity.' [1720]
Desmaizeaux includes this piece in his *Collection of Several Pieces* (no. 316). It was sent to Locke by Richard King. For details see no. 316, *Notes*.
References: Attig 802; Christophersen p. 78.

D-18. *Dialogues on the Uses of Foreign Travel, Considered as Part of an English Gentleman's Education, between Lord Shaftesbury and Mr. Locke.* (London: Printed by W[illiam] B[owyer] for A. Millar, 1764).
Written by Richard Hurd, Bishop of Worcester, it is a dialogue constructed from unidentifiable passages in Locke's writings. A German translation by C. H. Wilken was published at Breslau in 1765 with the title: *Von dem Nutzen der Reisen in fremde Länder . . . zwischen dem Lord Schaftesbury und M. Johann Locken, in einer Unterredung gehandelt*. Also in 1765

there was a French translation published at Yverdon under the title: *Dialogues entre Lord Shaftesbury et M. Locke, sur quelques points essentiels à l'éducation de la jeunesse, pour servir de suite au traité du dernier sur l'éducation des enfans.* Another 1765 edition published 'A Londres et se trouve à Paris' bore the title: *Dialogues sur les moeurs des Anglois, et sur les voyages.* Both these French editions Barbier has attributed to Jean Bernard Le Blanc. Cioranescu includes the latter title in a list of works by Le Blanc, but I would think Le Blanc the translator, not the author.
References: Cioranescu 38000; ESTC t067492.

A recently published article by John R. Milton in the *British Journal for the History of Philosophy*[1] examines in some detail several of the manuscripts in the Shaftesbury collection of papers in the Public Record Office (P.R.O. 30/24) which have been attributed to Locke, chiefly falsely, by Noel Sainsbury the office clerk who catalogued them, by Fox Bourne, Maurice Cranston, Richard Ashcraft and others. Most are **not** in Locke's hand, and in content and style Milton does not consider them Locke's. They range from single sheets to a 5000-word manuscript, and chiefly concern political topics.

[1] Vol. 4 no. 2 (Sept. 1996): 247–66.

CHAPTER XIII
Contemporary Criticism

A detailed record of critical works about Locke with abstracts of their contents has been published elsewhere.[1] What follows is a checklist of all known works published in response to or criticism of his publications, through 1800. Works are listed in chronological order, subarranged alphabetically by author (where known), alternatively by title. Notices of publications and textual summaries (without criticism) in scholarly journals are given in chapters I–XI. Excluded here are materials from standard early reference compilations, such as biographical dictionaries and encyclopaedias, and books of a more general subject content, for example, such as Mary Astell's *The Christian Religion* (1705), where Locke is mentioned on two pages out of a 418-page work.

At the end of each entry is a note of existing modern reprints, microfilm copies, and brief citations to other sources, e.g. Attig, Wing[2], etc.

Locke was aware of the criticism directed to his publications, though he may not have chosen to reply. That several critical works were in his library does not imply his ignorance of others. Those in his library are noted in these entries of criticism, by L.L. numbers.

C1689-1. Long, Thomas. *The Letter for Toleration Decipher'd, and the Absurdity and Impiety of an Absolute Toleration Demonstrated, by the Judgment of the Presbyterians, Independents, and by Mr. Calvin, Mr. Baxter, and the Parliament* (London: Printed by F. Collins. 30 pp.)
  Microfilm: EEB 1530 no. 2. Attig 85; Christophersen p.16; Wing[2] L2973.

C1690-1. A[twood], W[illiam]. *The Fundamental Constitution of the English Government, Proving King William and Queen Mary Our Lawful and Rightful King and Queen* (London: Printed by J. D. xxxiv, 107, 35, 19 pp.)
  The first mention of *Two Treatises*, in the author's discussion of monarchism vs. patriarchalism. Microfilm: EEB 1375 no.28. Attig 217; Christophersen p. 21; L.L.147; Wing[2] A4171.

---

[1] Yolton, Jean S. and John W., *John Locke, a Reference Guide* (Boston, Mass.: G. K. Hall, 1985).

C1690-2. Norris, John. 'Cursory Reflections upon a Book Call'd, *An Essay concerning Human Understanding.*' In his: *Christian Blessedness, or Discourses upon the Beatitudes of Our Lord and Saviour Jesus Christ* (London: Printed for S. Manship. 44 pp. at end.)
   Reprint by Augustan Reprint Society (UCLA, Clark Library) 1961, publication no. 93. Christophersen p. 29; L.L. 2094; Wing^2 N1246.

C1690-3. [Proast, Jonas]. *The Argument of the* Letter concerning Toleration *Briefly Consider'd and Answer'd* (Oxford: Printed at the Theatre for H. West and A. Clements. 28 pp.)
   A biography of Proast, written by Mark Goldie, is contained in the 'Missing Persons' vol. of the DNB (1993). Microfilm: EEB 507 no.7; facsim. reprint by Garland Pub. Co., NY, 1984 (includes C1691-1, C1704-1). Attig 86; Christophersen pp. 16-17; L.L. 2944; T.C. II, 323; Wing^2 3538.

C1691-1. [———]. *A Third Letter concerning Toleration: in Defence of the* Argument of the *Letter concerning Toleration* Briefly Consider'd and Answer'd: *Being a Reply to the Second Letter* [concerning Toleration] . . . (Oxford: Printed by H. Lichfield for G. West & H. Clements. 79 pp.)
   Microfilm: EEB 1338 no. 10; facsim. reprint with C1690-3. Attig 88; Christophersen p. 18; L.L. 2946; Wing^2 P3539.

C1692-1. Norris, John. *Cursory Reflections upon a Book Call'd* An Essay Concerning Human Understanding . . . *In a Letter to a Friend* (London: Printed for S. Manship. 65 pp.)
   Separately issued republication of C1690-1. Thereafter frequently reprinted with his *Christian Blessedness*, and in its later guise under title, *Practical Discourses upon the Beatitudes of Our Lord and Saviour Jesus Christ* (15th ed. published in 1728). Microfilm of 1694 ed.: EEB 1640 no. 21. Attig 435; Christophersen pp. 29-31; L.L. 2094 (1692 ed.); Wing^2 N1247.

C1694-1. Lowde, James. *A Discourse concerning the Nature of Man, Both in His Natural and Political Capacity, Both as He Is a Rational Creature, and Member of a Civil Society. With an Examination of Some of Mr. Hobbs's Opinions relating Hereunto* (London: Printed by T. Warren for W. Kittilby. 243 pp.)
   Microfilm: EEB 1152 no. 56. Attig 436; Christophersen pp. 32-3; L.L. 1813; Wing^2 L3299.

C1695-1. Edwards, John. *Some Thoughts concerning the Several Causes and Occasions of Atheism, Especially in the Present Age; With Some Brief Reflections on Socinianism, and on a Late Book Entituled,* The

Reasonableness of Christianity, as Deliver'd in the Scriptures (London: Printed for J. Robinson & J. Wyatt. 126 pp.)

Microfilm: EEB 182 no. 13; facsim reprint by Garland Pub. Co., 1984 (includes C1696-2). Attig 668; Christophersen pp. 58–9; L.L. 1024; Wing^2 E215.

C1695-2. *The Exceptions of Mr. Edwards, in His* Causes of Atheism, *against* The Reasonableness of Christianity, as Deliver'd in the Scriptures, *Examin'd, and Found Unreasonable, Unscriptural, and Injurious* . . . (London: s.n. 47 pp.)

Microfilm: EEB 379 no. 22. Attig 670; Christophersen pp. 59–60; L.L. 1025; Wing^2 E3840. Also published as one item in *A Third Collection of Tracts Proving the God and Father of Our Lord Jesus Christ the Only True God* (microfilm: EEB 1537 no. 40). See also Chap. XII, no. (5).

C1695-3. [Lowndes, William]. *A Report Containing an Essay for the Amendment of the Silver Coins* (London: Printed by C. Bill. 159 pp.)

Published at government expense to explain monetary changes. Microfilm: EEB 1127 no. 19. Attig 501A; Christophersen pp. 23–4; L.L. 1816; Wing^2 L3323.

C1696-1. Barbon, Nicholas. *A Discourse concerning Coining the New Money Lighter. In Answer to Mr. Locke's Considerations about Raising the Value of Money* (London: Printed for R. Chiswell. 96 pp.)

Locke's annotated copy (L.L. 205) is in the New York Public Library. Attig 512; Christophersen pp. 24–5; Goldsmiths'-Kress Lib. 3248 (also on microfilm); Wing^2 B706.

C1696-2. Edwards, John. *Socinianism Unmask'd: A Discourse Shewing the Unreasonableness of a Late Writer's* [Locke] *Opinion concerning the Necessity of Only One Article of Christian Faith, and of His Other Assertions in His Book Entituled,* The Reasonableness of Christianity as Deliver'd in the Scriptures, *and in His Vindication of It. With a Brief Reply to Another (Professed) Socinian Writer* (London: Printed for J. Robinson and J. Wyat. 142 pp.)

Microfilm: EEB 491 no. 13; facsim. reprint with C1695-1. Attig 671; Christophersen p. 60; L.L. 1026; Wing^2 E214.

C1696-3. *A Letter Humbly Offer'd to the Consideration of All Gentlemen, Yeomen, Citizens, Freeholders, &c. That Have Right to Elect Members to Serve in Parliament* (London: Printed for E. Whitlock. 31 pp.)

Views about currency devaluation, including Locke's. Attig 509; Goldsmiths'-Kress Lib. 3309 (also on microfilm); L.L.2219; Wing^2 L1552.

C1696-4. *A Review of the Universal Remedy for All Diseases Incident to Coin, with Application to Our Present Circumstances; in a Letter to Mr. Locke* (London: Printed for A. and J. Churchill. 61 pp.)
'Sometimes attributed to W. Paterson.' Microfilm: EEB 474 no. 8. Attig 510; Christophersen p. 25; L.L. 800; Wing² R1200.

C1696-5. *Some Considerations about the Raising of Coin: in a Second Letter to Mr. Locke* (London: Printed for A. and J. Churchill. 52 pp.)
Attig 511; Christophersen p. 25; Goldsmiths'-Kress Lib. 3271 (also on microfilm); L.L. 801; Wing² S4481.

C1696-6. Stillingfleet, Edward, Bishop of Worcester. *A Discourse in Vindication of the Doctrine of the Trinity. With an Answer to the Late Socinian Objections against It from Scripture, Antiquity and Reason . . .* (London: Printed by J. H. for H. Mortlock. 292 pp.)
The first salvo in the Locke-Stillingfleet debate. Facsim. reprint of pp. 230–292 of 2d ed. (1697), pp.230–92 containing criticism of Locke, published by G. Olms Verlag (Hildesheim, 1987) under the title *Three Criticisms of Locke*; includes C1697-13 and C1698-4. Microfilm of 2d ed. (1697): EEB 751 no. 44. Attig 439; Christophersen pp. 35–7; L.L. 2787; Wing² S5585.

C1696-7. Temple, Sir Richard. *Some Short Remarks upon Mr. Lock's Book, in Answer to Mr. Lounds* [i.e. Lowndes] *. . . concerning Coin* (London: Printed for R. Baldwin. 12 pp.)
Attig 513; Christophersen p. 25; Goldsmiths'-Kress Lib. 3350 (also on microfilm); L.L. 2846; Wing² T633.

C1696-8. [Toland John]. *Christianity Not Mysterious, or A Treatise Shewing That There Is Nothing in the Gospel Contrary to Reason Nor Above It, and That No Christian Doctrine Can Be Properly Call'd a Mystery* (London: s.n. xxxii, 176 pp.)
Facsim. reprint by Garland Pub Co., 1984. Attig 674; Christophersen p. 35; L.L. 2935; Wing² T1762.

C1697-1. *Animadversions on a Late Book Entituled* The Reasonableness of Christianity, As Delivered in the Scriptures (Oxford: Printed by L. Lichfield for G. West and A. Piesley. 103 pp.)
Sometimes attributed to Richard West, D.D. Attig 683; Christophersen pp. 66–8; L.L. 702; Wing² A3191.

C1697-2. Bold, Samuel. *Some Passages* in The Reasonableness of Christianity, *&c. and Its Vindication* (London: Printed for A. and J. Churchill. 52 pp.)

Usually issued with his *A Short Discourse of the True Knowledge of Jesus Christ*. Microfilm copy with C1706-1. Attig 676; Christophersen p. 61; L.L. 374; Wing² B3495.

C1697-3. Browne, Peter. *A Letter in Answer to a Book Entituled* Christianity Not Mysterious [by John Toland], *As Also to All Those Who Set up for Reason and Evidence in Opposition to Revelation and Mysteries* (London: Printed for R. Clavell. 180 pp.)
Attig 675; L.L.500; Wing² B5135.

C1697-4. [Burnet, Thomas]. *Remarks upon* An Essay concerning Human Understanding, *in a Letter Address'd to the Author* (London: Printed for M. Wotton. 15 pp.)
First of his three 'remarks'. Locke's answer was included at the end of his *Reply* to the Bishop of Worcester; see no. 249. Facsim. reprint by Garland Pub. Co., 1984 (includes his 'Second' and 'Third Remarks'). Attig 448; Christophersen pp. 44–5; L.L. 1794; Wing² B5944.

C1697-5. ———. *Second Remarks upon* An Essay concerning Human Understanding, *In a Letter Address'd to the Author; Being a Vindication of the First Remarks against the Answer of Mr. Locke at the End of His Reply to the Bishop of Worcester* (London: Printed for W. Wotton. 30 pp.)
Facsim. reprint with C1697-4. Attig 449; Christophersen pp. 45–6; L.L. 1795; Wing² B5946.

C1697-6. Edwards, John. *A Brief Vindication of the Fundamental Articles of the Christian Faith, As Also of the Clergy, Universities and Publick Schools, from Mr. Locke's Reflections upon Them in His Book of Education, &c., with Some Animadversions on Two Late Pamphlets, viz. of Mr. Bold and a Nameless Socinian Writer* (London: Printed for J. Robinson and J. Wyat. [8], 125 pp.)
Microfilm: EEB 182 no. 12. Attig 682; Christophersen pp. 57–8, 66; L.L. 1028; Wing² E198.

C1697-7. ———. *The Socinian Creed, or A Brief Account of the Professed Tenets and Doctrines of the Foreign and English Socinians, Wherein Is Shew'd the Tendency of Them to Irreligion and Atheism; with Proper Antidotes against Them* (London: Printed for J. Robinson. 264 pp.)
Microfilm: EEB 787 no. 23. Attig 677; Christophersen p. 62; L.L. 1027; Wing² E212.

C1697-8. Elys, Edmund. *A Refutation of Some of the False Conceits in Mr. Locke's* Essay concerning Human Understanding, *Together with a Brief Answer (in Latine) to the Argumentation of Gerardus de Vries against the*

Innate Idea of God (London: Printed for and Sold by W. and J. Marshall. 30 pp.)
Attig 450; L.L. 1038; Wing² E692A.

C1697-9. *The Occasional Paper*, no. 1. *Containing an Account of the Author's Design, Together with Some Reflections on a Book Entituled*, A Letter to the Deists [by Humphrey Prideaux]; *in a Letter to a Friend* (London: Printed for W. Wotton. 34 pp.)
Attributed to Richard Willis. Includes comments on the *Reasonableness*. Attig 679; Christophersen p. 64; L.L. 2118 (for issues 1-6).

C1697-10. *The Occasional Paper*, no. 3. *Being Reflexions upon Mr. Toland's Book, Called* Christianity Not Mysterious; *with Some Considerations about the Use of Reason in Matters of Religion* (London: Printed for W. Wotton. 34 pp.)
Christophersen p. 64.

C1697-11. *The Occasional Paper*, no. 5. *Containing a Defence of the Ministry and Ministers of the Gospel; against the Suggestion of Some Late Writers. In a Letter to a Friend, with a Post-Script Relating to the Author of* The Reasonableness of Christianity (London: Printed for W. Wotton. 42 pp.)
The 'post-script' (pp. 37-42) replies to charges in the *Second Vindication*. Christophersen p. 66.

C1697-12. S[ergeant], J[ohn]. *Solid Philosophy Asserted, against the Fancies of the Ideists, or The Method to Science Farther Illustrated. With Reflexions on Mr. Locke's* Essay concerning Human Understanding (London: Printed for R. Clavel, A. Roper and T. Metcalf. [52], 460, [24] pp.)
Locke's own copy (L.L.2626) is in the library of St. John's College, Cambridge; its marginal notes were published by John Yolton, 'Locke's Unpublished Marginal Replies to John Sergeant', *Journal of the History of Ideas* 12 (Oct. 1951): 528-59. Microfilm: EEB 990 no. 15; facsim. reprint by Garland Pub. Co., 1984. Attig 451; Christophersen p. 43; Wing² S2594.

C1697-13. Stillingfleet, Edward. *The Bishop of Worcester's Answer to Mr. Locke's Letter, concerning Some Passages Relating to His Essay of Humane Understanding, Mention'd in the Late Discourse in Vindication of the Trinity; With a Postscript in Answer to Some Reflections Made on That Treatise in a Late Socinian Pamphlet* (London: Printed by J.J. for H. Mortlock. 154 pp.)
Facsim. reprint by G. Olms Verlag (Hildesheim, 1987) included with selection from C1696-6 and with C1698-4. Microfilm: EEB 515 no. 30. Attig 442; Christophersen p. 38; L.L. 2789; Wing² S5557.

C1697-14. *A Vindication of the Epistles* [and other essays] (s.l.: s. n. 102, [2] pp. 4°) Publication date supplied by internal reference to the *Second Vindication* 'just published'; with criticism of the *Reasonableness*. The British Library copy (shelfmark: 690.f.10 (1).) is the only one known; it lacks title leaf and prelim. pages (all before quire B). Not in Wing.

C1698-1. B., F. *A Free but Modest Censure of the Late Controversial Writings and Debates of the Lord Bishop of Worcester and Mr. Locke; Mr. Edwards and Mr. Locke; the Honble Charles Boyle, Esq; and Dr. Bentley. Together with Brief Remarks on Monsieur Le Clerc's* Ars Critica. By F. B., M.A. of Cambridge (London: Printed for A. Baldwin. 31 pp.)
Microfilm: EEB 163 no. 20. Attig 452; Christophersen p. 42; L.L. 159a; Wing² B59.

C1698-2. Becconsall, Thomas. *The Grounds and Foundation of Natural Religion Discovered, in the Principal Branches of It, in Opposition to the Prevailing Notions of the Modern Scepticks and Latitudinarians. With an Introduction concerning the Necessity of Revealed Religion* (London: Printed by W. O. for A. Roper. xi, vi, [45], 256 pp.)
Microfilm: EEB 1348 no. 4. Attig 453; Christophersen pp. 49–50; L.L. 251a; Wing² B1657.

C1698-3. Bold, Samuel. *Observations on the Animadversions (Lately Printed at Oxford) on a Late Book, Entituled* The Reasonableness of Christianity . . . (London: Printed for A. and J. Churchill. 124 pp.)
Microfilm copy with C1706-1. Attig 684; Christophersen p. 69; L.L. 376; Wing² B3483.

C1698-4. Stillingfleet, Edward. *The Bishop of Worcester's Answer to Mr. Locke's Second Letter; Wherein His Notion of Ideas Is Prov'd to Be Inconsistent with It Self and with the Articles of the Christian Faith* (London: Printed by J. H. for H. Mortlock. 178 pp.)
Facsim. reprint by G. Olms Verlag (Hildesheim, 1987) included with selection from C1696-6 and with C1697-13. Attig 444; Christophersen pp. 40–41; L.L. 2790; Wing² S5558.

C1699-1. Bold, Samuel. *Some Considerations on the Principal Objections and Arguments Which Have Been Publish'd against Mr. Lock's Essay of Humane Understanding.* (London: Printed for A. and J. Churchill. 60 pp.)
Microfilm copy with C1706-1. Attig 455; Christophersen p. 50; L.L. 384; Wing² B3494.

C1699-2. [Burnet, Thomas]. *Third Remarks upon An Essay concerning Humane Understanding; in a Letter Address'd to the Author* (London: Printed for M. Wotton, 30 pp.)

Locke's copy (L.L. 1799) with his marginal notes is in Yale University Library. Noah Porter published the marginalia in the *New Englander and Yale Review*, new ser. 11 (July 1887): 33-49. For facsim. reprint see C1697-4. Attig 456; Christophersen pp. 46-7; Wing^2 B5955.

C1699-3. Lowde, James. *Moral Essays, Wherein Some of Mr. Lock's and Mons' Malbranch's Opinions Are Briefly Examin'd. Together with an Answer to Some Chapters in the* Oracles of Reason [by Charles Blount] *concerning Deism* (York: Printed by J. White for F. Hildyard. [15], 179 pp.)
  Microfilm: EEB 1014 no. 10. Attig 458; Christophersen pp. 33-4, 50; L.L. 1814; Wing^2 L3301.

C1700-1. Leibniz, Gottfried Wilhelm. Review of Coste's translation of the *Essay* (no. 89), *Monatlicher Auszug*, Sept.: 611-36.
  Attig 482 n.

C1700-2. [Milner, John]. *An Account of Mr Lock's Religion, Out of His Own Writings, and in His Own Words, Together with Some Observations upon It, and a Twofold Appendix*: I. *A Specimen of Mr Lock's Way of Answering Authors, Out of His Essay* l. I. c. 3, *Where He Takes upon Him to Examine Some of Lord Herbert's Principles.* II. *A Brief Enquiry Whether Socinianism Be Justly Charged upon Mr. Lock* (London: Printed for J. Nutt. 188 pp.)
  Attig 460; Christophersen pp. 69-70; L.L. 1802b; Wing^2 M2075. See also Chap. XII, no. D-15.

C1701-1. Norris, John. *An Essay towards the Theory of the Ideal or Intelligible World, Part I. Design'd for Two Parts. The First Considering It Absolutely in It Self, and the Second in Relation to Human Understanding* (London: Printed for S. Manship. xvi, 452, [10]; [32], 574 pp.)
  Part II published in 1704. Microfilm: *The Eighteenth Century* 3609 no. 2. Attig 462; Christophersen p. 30; ESTC t076546.

C1702-1. [Cockburn, Catharine Trotter]. *A Defence of the* Essay of Human Understanding, *Written by Mr. Locke, Wherein Its Principles with Reference to Morality, Reveal'd Religion, and the Immortality of the Soul Are Consider'd and Justify'd; in Answer to Some Remarks on That Essay* [by Thomas Burnet] (London: Printed for W. Turner. 70 pp.)
  For Burnet's *Remarks*, see C1697-4, et seq. Microfilm: *The Eighteenth Century* 5638 no. 26. Attig 463; Christophersen pp. 48-9; ESTC t105423; L.L. 1801.

C1702-2. Lee, Henry. *Anti-Scepticism, or Notes upon Each Chapter of . . . Mr. Lock's* Essay concerning Human Understanding; *with an Explication*

of All the Particulars of Which He Treats, and in the Same Order. In Four Books (London: Printed for R. Clavel and C. Harper. 140, 201-342 pp.)
Facsim. reprint by Garland Pub. Co., 1984. Attig 464; Christophersen pp. 53-4; ESTC n015708.

C1702-3. Parker, Samuel. *Essays on Divers Weighty and Curious Subjects, Particularly on Mr. Lock's and Sir William Temple's Notions . . .* (London: Printed and Sold by Nic. Cox. [8] 270 pp.)
'Letter I' (pp. 1-46) is a defence of Locke against Stillingfleet; 'Letter VIII, Of the Soul' is a further defence. References to Locke throughout. Attig 465; ESTC t137336.

C1703-1. Broughton, John. *Psychologia, or An Account of the Nature of the Rational Soul. In Two Parts. The First, An Essay concerning the Nature of the Human Soul* (London: Printed by W[illiam] B[owyer] for T. Bennet. [23], 418 pp.)
The second part, paged continuously with the first, is entitled 'A Vindication of the Human Soul, &c.' Microfilm: *The Eighteenth Century* 2674 no.4. Attig 467; Christophersen p. 53; ESTC t115365; L.L. 495.

C1704-1. [Proast, Jonas]. *A Second Letter to the Author of the Three Letters for Toleration, from the Author of* The Argument of the Letter concerning Toleration, Briefly Consider'd and Answer'd, *and of the Defence of It. With a Postscript, Taking Notice of Two Passages in* The Rights of the Protestant Dissenters [by J. S. Barrington] (Oxford: Printed by L. Lichfield for H. Clements. 24 pp.)
For Proast's earlier criticism, see C1690-3 and C1691-1. Imprimatur dated 19 June 1704; possibly not issued until after Locke's death. Facsim. reprint included with C1690-1. Attig 90; Christophersen pp. 18-19; ESTC n021801.

C1704-2. [Barrington, John Shute]. *The Rights of Protestant Dissenters. In Two Parts; the First Being the Case of the Dissenter Review'd. The Second, a Vindication of Their Right to an Absolute Toleration from the Objections of Sir H. Mackworth, in His Treatise Intituled* Peace at Home. Part I (London: s.n. 103 pp.)
The Postscript (pp. 83-103) discusses the 'toleration' letters. A second edition was printed in 1705, still without a second part. Microfilm: *The Eighteenth Century* 6441 no. 7; Christophersen pp. 19, 70; ESTC t065657.

C1704-3. Sherlock, William. 'A Digression concerning Connate Ideas, or Inbred Knowledge.' In his: *A Discourse concerning the Happiness of Good Men,* Part 1. (London; Printed for W. Rogers. pp. 124-64).
Microfilm: *The Eighteenth Century* 2765 no. 11. Attig 471; Christophersen p. 43; ESTC t079380.

C1705-1. [Bold, Samuel]. *A Discourse concerning the Resurrection of the Same Body; with Two Letters concerning the Necessary Immateriality of Created Thinking Substance* (London: Printed by S. Holt for A. and J. Churchill. 206 pp.)
   Microfilm copy with C1706-1. Attig 474; Christophersen pp. 52, 70; ESTC t117683.

C1705-2. Carroll, William. *Remarks upon Mr. Clarke's Sermons, Preached at St. Paul's against Hobbs, Spinoza, and Other Atheists* . . . (London: Printed for J. Robinson. 42 pp.)
   Attig 476; ESTC t046868.

C1705-3. Coste, Pierre. 'Lettre de Mr. Coste à l'auteur des ces Nouvelles, à l'occasion de la mort de M.Locke', *Nouvelles de la république des lettres*, Feb. 1705: 154–77.
   Brief 'éloge' and obituary (cf. no. 316); translations incorporated in French editions of the *Essay*, 1729–1799 (no. 94–105); included in the first German edition of the *Essay*, 1757 (no. 108). Attig 688; Christophersen p. 85.

C1705-4. *An Essay upon Government: Wherein the Republican Schemes Reviv'd by Mr. Lock, Dr. Blackal, &c., Are Fairly Consider'd and Refuted* . . . (London: Printed for G. Sawbridge. 69 pp.)
   Microfilm: *The Eighteenth Century* 410 no. 12. Attig 225; ESTC t094344 (2d ed. corr.: t166892).

C1705-5. [Le Clerc, Jean]. 'Eloge du feu Mr. Locke', *Bibliothèque choisie* 6: 342–411.
   Basic biographical sketch, including information from Damaris, Lady Masham. A Latin translation included in no. 112–14. Attig 691; Christophersen p. 83.

C1705-6. *A Philosophick Essay concerning Ideas, According to Dr. Sherlock's Principles. Wherein His Notion of Them Is Stated, and His Reasonings Thereupon Examin'd. In a Letter to a Friend* (London: Printed for B. Bragg. 24 pp.)
   Attig 473; ESTC t010633.

C1706-1. Bold, Samuel. *A Collection of Tracts Publish'd in Vindication of Mr. Lock's* Reasonableness of Christianity . . . *and of his* Essay concerning Human Understanding (London: Printed for A. and J. Churchill. 6 parts).
   Reprints C1697-2, C1698-3, C1699-1, C1705-1 and two other tracts. Microfilm: *The Eighteenth Century* 3045 no. 4. Attig 685; Christophersen p. 50; ESTC t117722.

C1706-2. Carroll, William. *A Dissertation upon the Tenth Chapter of the Fourth Book of Mr. Locke's Essay . . . Wherein the Author's Endeavours to Establish Spinoza's Atheistical Hypothesis Especially in That Tenth Chapter Are Discover'd and Confuted* (London: Printed for J. Matthews. xv, 592 pp.)
  Microfilm: *The Eighteenth Century* 320 no. 1; facsim. reprint by Thoemmes Press, Bristol, 1991. Attig 477; Christophersen p. 106; ESTC t101291.

C1706-3. Le Clerc, Jean. *The Life and Character of Mr. John Locke . . . Written in French by Mr. Le Clerc, and Done into English by T. F. P., Gent.* (London: Printed for John Clark. 31 pp.)
  Translation of C1705-5. Included in no. 367. Lady Masham's letter included therein reprinted in *A Locke Miscellany*. Microfilm: *The Eighteenth Century* 949 no. 16. Attig 691 n.; Christophersen p. 84; ESTC t138884.

C1707-1. Carroll, William. *A Letter to the Reverend Dr. Benjamin Prat . . . Wherein the Dangerous Errors in a Late Book, Intituled* An Essay concerning the Use of Reason in Propositions [by Anthony Collins] *Are Detected, Confuted, and Gradually Deduc'd from the Very Basis of All Atheism, upon Which Alone They Are Bottom'd* (London: Printed for R. Sare. 24 pp.)
  Microfilm: *The Eighteenth Century* 3081 no. 7. Attig 479; ESTC n037313, t038335.

C1707-2. Le Clerc, Jean. Review of the *Essay*, 5th ed. (no. 65) and of the *Posthumous Works* (no. 299): *Bibliothèque choisie* 12: 80–170.
  The coverage of the *Essay* is chiefly a defence of Locke's account of substance. The second part of the article (pp.123–70) has extended summaries of the 'Conduct' and the 'Discourse of Miracles'. Attig 724 n.; Christophersen p. 71.

C1708-1. Culpeper, Sir Thomas. *Sir Thomas Colepeper's Tracts concerning Usury Reprinted, Shewing Its Biting Quality on the Private and Publick; with Some Animadversions on the Writings of Dr. Lock on That Subject* (London: Printed for J. Morphew. 27, 5 pp.)
  Originally published 1623–40. Christophersen p. 25 n.; ESTC t141104. Reprint of 1709 (with added postscript): Goldsmiths'-Kress Lib. no. 4196 (also on microfilm), ESTC t141105.

C1708-2. *A Dissertation on Deistical and Arian Corruption, or Plain Proof That the Principles and Practices of Arians and Deists Are Founded upon Spiritual Blindness, and Resolve into Atheism . . . Where Mr. Jack--n's Dissertation on Matter and Spirit, Mr. Locke's Essay, &c., Are*

Particularly Examined, &c. (London: Printed for G. Strahan. 69 pp.)
Christophersen p. 129; ESTC t192575.

C1708-3. Jaeger, Johann Wolfgang. *Judicium, sine affectu, de duobus adversariis, J. Lookio* [sic] *et Petro Poireto, eorumque pugna de ratione et fide, pro materia disputationis propositum* [Judgment, without issue, of the two adversaries Locke and Poiret and on their argument about faith and reason, proposed as a disputation] (Frankfurt & Leipzig: G. V. Kuhnen. 56 pp.)
Attig 484; Christophersen p. 127.

C1708-4. Leibniz, Gottfried Wihelm. 'Réflexions de Mr. L------sur l'*Essay de l'entendement humain* de Monsieur Locke.' In: *Some Familiar Letters* (no. 346), pp. 196-205.
This is the version sent to Locke by William Molyneux (*Corr.* 2243; vi. 88-93). Another version printed *ibid.*, Appendix I, vi. 777-87. Attig 482; Christophersen pp. 54-6.

C1708-5. [Metternich, Wolf von, Baron]. *Fides et ratio collatae, ac suo utraque loco redditae, adversus principia Joannis Lockii . . . Cum accessione triplici*, 1. *De fide implicita, sive nuda.* 2. *De SS. Scripturarum certitudine ac sensu.* 3. *De perfectione et felicitate in hac vita.* Edidit et praefatus est P. Poiret (Amsterdam: Officina Wetsteniana. 61, [19], 471 [104] pp.)
Attig 483; Christophersen p. 127.

C1709-1. [Carroll, William] *Spinoza Reviv'd, or A Treatise Proving the Book Entitled,* The Rights of the Christian Church [by Matthew Tindal] *&c. (in the Most Notorius Parts of It) to Be the Same with Spinoza's* Rights of the Christian Clergy, *&c. And That Both of Them Are Grounded upon Downright Atheism.* To which is added, A Preliminary Discourse . . . by Rev. Dr. George Hicks (London: Printed for J. Morphew. [72], 179 pp.)
Pages [3]-[59] are Hickes's pref. Microfilm: *The Eighteenth Century* 4761 no. 15. Attig 485; ESTC t100265.

C1709-2. Jenkin, Robert. *Remarks on Some Books Lately Publish'd*, viz. Mr. *Basnage's* History of the Jews, *Mr. Whiston's* Eight Sermons, *Mr. Lock's* Paraphrase and Notes on St. Paul's Epistles, *Mr. Le Clerc's* Bibliothèque Choisie (London: Printed by W. B. for R. Sare. 205 pp.)
The 'Paraphrases' are dealt with on pp. 117-73. Microfilm: *The Eighteenth Century* 1477 no.12. Attig 722; Christophersen p. 77; ESTC n012648.

C1711-1. Carroll, William. *Spinoza Reviv'd, Part the Second, or A Letter to*

M. Le Clerc, Occasion'd by his Bibliotheque Choisie, Tom. 21 (London: Printed and Sold by J. Morphew. 76 pp.)
   Vol. 21 contained a review of the first part, C1709-1. Attig 485 n.; ESTC n036640.

C1711-2. Hampton, Benjamin. *The Existence of Human Soul after Death Proved from Scripture, Reason, and Philosophy; Wherein Mr. Locke's Notion That Understanding May Be Given to Matter . . . and All Other Such . . . Opinions Are Briefly and Plainly Confuted* (London: Printed for S. Popping. ii, 44 pp.)
   Attig 487; Christophersen p. 128; ESTC t033802.

C1711-3. [Leslie, Charles]. *The Finishing Stroke, Being a Vindication of the Patriarchal Scheme of Government . . .* (London: Printed and Sold by All the Booksellers of London and Westminster. [16], 239 pp.).
   Anonymous. Chiefly an attack on Benjamin Hoadley. Microfilm: *The Eighteenth Century* 2174 no. 16. ESTC t035536.

C1711-4. Lupton, Will. *The Resurrection of the Same Body; a Sermon Preach'd before the University of Oxford, at St. Mary's on Easter-Monday, Apr. 2. 1711* (Oxford: Printed at the Theatre for John Wilmot. 30, [2] pp.)
   Microfilm: *The Eighteenth Century* 1398 no. 28. Attig 488; Christophersen p. 128; ESTC t141282.

C1711-5. *Reflections upon Some Passages in Mr. Le Clerc's* Life of Mr. John Locke: *in a Letter to a Friend. With a Preface, Containing Some Remarks on Two Large Volumes of Libels . . .* (London: Printed for J. Morphew. 34 pp. 4)
   Criticizes Le Clerc, 'a *foreigner*', for misunderstanding English politics in Shaftesbury's time. Attig 691 n.; ESTC t138886.

C1712-1. Ditton, Humphry. *A Discourse concerning the Resurrection of Jesus Christ; in Three Parts* (London: Printed for J. Darby, and Sold by A. Bell and B. Lintott. xvi, 568 pp.)
   Microfilm: *The Eighteenth Century* 3296 no. 5. Attig 489; ESTC t145308.

C1712-2. Greene, Robert. *The Principles of Natural Philosophy, in which is shewn the Insufficiency of the Present Systems, to give us any just Account of that Science . . .* (Cambridge: Printed at the University-Press for Edm. Jeffery, and are to be sold by J. Knapton and B. Took, London. [70], 391, [9], 38, [2] pp.)
   Microfilm: *The Eighteenth Century* reel 5485 no.3. ESTC t112866.

C1712-3. Schramm, Jonas Conrad. *De haeresi per libros symbolicos, contra Lokki huiusque interpretis Germani accusationes iniquissimas: programma* [Concerning the heresy through Scripture against vile accusations of Locke and his German interpreter] (Helmstadt: Litteris Hammianis. 35 pp.)

C1713-1. Le Clerc, Jean. *An Account of the Life and Writings of Mr. John Locke.* The Second Edition Enlarged (London: Printed for John Clarke and E. Curll. 63 pp.)
   Reprint of C1706-3. Microfilm: *The Eighteenth Century* 5575 no. 26. Attig 691 n.; ESTC t137407.

C1713-2. [Metternich, Wolf von, Baron]. *Faith and Reason Compared: Shewing That Divine Faith and Natural Reason Proceed from Two Different and Distinct Principles in Man, against the Notions and Errors of the Modern Rationalists. Written Originally in Latin by a Person of Quality in Answer to Certain Theses (Drawn from Lock's Principles) concerning Faith and Reason.* With a New Preface. Translated and Edited by D. C. H[ungerford] (London: Printed for B. Cowse. lxxvi, 259 pp.)
   Translation of C1708-5. Attig 483 n.; Christophersen p. 127; ESTC t103411.

C1714-1. Le Clerc, Jean. *An Account of the Life and Writings of John Locke Esq;.* The Third Edition Enlarged (London: Printed for J. Clarke and E. Curll. 34 pp. 2°)
   A reprint of C1706-3 in folio format to match the size of the *Works* of 1714 (no. 363) with which it is occasionally found bound, e.g. the British Library copy (pp.1-28 only). The enlargement consists of 'The Last Will and Testament of John Locke, Esq;' printed on pp. 29-34, copied from an unidentified source. (Both p. 28 and p. 34 end '*FINIS.*') This is the only appearance of the full text of the will until E.S. de Beer transcribed a manuscript copy from the Lovelace Collection in the Bodleian Library (MS Locke b.5, item no. 14) for publication in 1989 (*Corr.* viii. 419-27). That part of the codicil alone wherein Locke acknowledges authorship of the 'Toleration' letters, *Two Treatises of Government*, *The Reasonableness of Christianity*, and its 'Vindications', is printed as a prefatory note to the collected *Works* of 1714 and in subsequent *Works* editions. Lord King included the codicil in the second edition of his *Life of John Locke* (1830, ii.51-53; no.329). Fox Bourne, in his *Life* (1876, ii.540-41; no. 330) gave a brief summary of the main provisions of the will.
   The bookseller, 'the unspeakable Curll'[2] was notorious for his publishing adventures, among other things, seeking out relatives and acquaintances of the newly deceased to find any manuscript remains (cf. no. 315).

---

[2] Straus, Ralph: *The Unspeakable Curll, being Some Account of Edmund Curll, Bookseller* (London: Chapman and Hall, 1927).

I included a reprint of Locke's will from this edition of Le Clerc's *Account* in the collection, *A Locke Miscellany*, pp. 353-62.
Attig 691 n.; ESTC t128626.

C1714-2. Schueler, Johann Gottfried. *Io. Locki Sublestas de ratione sententias . . .* [Trivial opinions of Locke on reason] (Wittenberg: Formes S. Kreusii. 8 leaves)
Thesis, Dresden. Christophersen p. 107.

C1716-1. Boulton, Richard. 'A Full Confutation of All the Arguments That Have Ever Been Produced against the Belief of Apparitions, Witches, &c. With a Judgment concerning Spirits, by the Late Learned Mr. John Locke.' In his: *The Compleat History of Magic, Sorcery and Witchcraft* (London: Printed for E. Curll, J. Pemberton, and W. Taylor. 4th section of vol. 2)
Vol. 1 published 1715. Microfilm: *The Eighteenth Century* 5389 no. 5. Christophersen p.127; ESTC t061245.

C1716-2. [Coole, Benjamin]. *Some Brief Observations on the Paraphrase and Notes of the Judicious John Locke, Relating to Women's Exercising Their Spiritual Gifts in the Church* (London: Printed and Sold by P. Gwillim. [6], 28 pp.)
First ed. possibly published in 1714. ESTC lists only this 2d ed. (1716): n023052. Attig 723 n.

C1716-3. Martin, Josiah. *A Letter to the Author of* Some Brief Observations on the Paraphrase and Notes of the Judicious John Locke, Relating to Women's Exercising Their Spiritual Gifts in the Church [by Benjamin Coole] (London: s.n. 32 pp.)
Microfilm: *The Eighteenth Century* 2786 no.6. ESTC t014248.

C1717-1. Coole, Benjamin. *Reflections on* A Letter to the Author of Some Brief Observations on the Paraphrase and Notes of the Judicious John Lock, &c. [by Josiah Martin] (London: Printed by P. Gwillim. 80 pp.)
Microfilm: *The Eighteenth Century* 2786 no.7. ESTC t014236.

C1717-2. Martin, Josiah. *A Vindication of Women's Preaching, As Well from Holy Scripture . . . as from the Paraphrase and Notes of the Judicious John Locke, on I Cor. xi., Wherein the Brief Observations of B[enjamin] C[oole] on the Said Paraphrase and Notes, and the Arguments in His Book, Intitled* Reflections, &c., *Are Fully Consider'd* (London: Printed and Sold by the Assigns of J. Sowle. 128 pp.)
Pages 1-58 concern Locke. ESTC t093891.

C1717-3. Reinbathius, Johannes. *Dissertatio philosophico-rationalis de spatio vacuo ideam Lockii examinans* [Philosophical-rational dissertation

examining Locke's idea of empty space] (Altorf Noric.: I. G.Kohlesius. 32 pp.)
Thesis, Nuremberg.

C1717-4. *A Vindication of Mankind, or Free-Will Asserted. In Answer to* A Philosophical Inquiry concerning Human Liberty [by Anthony Collins]. *To Which Is Added, An Examination of Mr. Locke's Scheme of Freedom* (London: Sold by S. Popping. 31 pp.)
'Sometimes attributed to Solomon Lowe.' – ESTC t017790.

C1720-1. Coste, Pierre. 'The Character of Mr. Locke . . . With a Letter Relating to That Character and to the Author of It.' In: *A Collection of Several Pieces* . . . (London: Printed by J. Bettenham for R. Francklin. pp. i–xxiv)
In no. 316-8. Translation of C1705-3. Included in *Works* editions beginning with 1751 (no. 367). Reprinted in my *Locke Miscellany*.

C1720-2. Holdsworth, Winch. *A Sermon* [on John 5. 28-9] *Preached before the University of Oxford at St. Mary's on Easter Monday, 1719, in Which the Cavils, False Reasonings, and False Interpretations of Scripture of Mr. Lock and Others, against the Resurrection of the Same Body, Are Examin'd and Answered* (Oxford: Printed at the Theatre for R. Wilkin, London. 27 pp.)
Microfilm: *The Eighteenth Century* 5647 no. 12. Christophersen p. 128; ESTC t047843.

C1723-1. Janus [i.e. Jan], Johann Wilhelm. *Principia innata, adversus Ioannis Lockii obiectiones, vindicabunt.* Praeses M. Io. Guilelmus Ianus . . . et respondens Io. Christianus Hampe . . . 23 Nov. 1709 [Innate principles vindicated, against Locke's objections] (Wittenberg. 32 pp.)

C1725-1. Felton, Henry. *The Resurrection of the Same Numerical Body, and Its Reunion to the Same Soul, Asserted in a Sermon . . . In Which Mr. Locke's Notions of Personality and Identity Are Confuted, and the Author of* The Naked Gospel *Is Answered. Preached before the University of Oxford on Easter-Monday 1725* (Oxford: At the Theatre. 26 pp.)
Christophersen p. 129; ESTC t044842.

C1725-2. Review of *An Account of Mr. Lock's Religion* [by John Milner: C1700-2], *Mémoires pour l'histoire des sciences et des beaux-arts* [known as *Journal de Trévoux*], Sept. 1725, Art. 88, pp. 1680-95.

C1726-1. [Cockburn, Catharine Trotter]. *A Letter to Dr. Holdsworth, Occasioned by His Sermon Preached before the University of Oxford on Easter-Monday, concerning the Resurrection of the Same Body. In Which* the Passages That Concern Mr. Lock are Chiefly Considered. By the Author of A Defence of Mr. Lock's Essay . . . in Answer to Some Remarks on That Essay [by Thomas Burnet] (London: Printed for B. Motte. 70 pp.)

Reply to C1720-1. Cf. C1702-1. Christophersen p. 128; ESTC t142637.

C1727-1. Greene, Robert. *The Principles of the Philosophy of the Expansive and Contractive Forces, or An Enquiry into the Principles of Modern Philosophy* . . . (Cambridge: C. Crownfield at the University Press. 981 pp. 2°).

Book V, pp. 599–722: 'Concerning the Metaphysics and Logick, or the System of Ideas, of Mr. Locke.' Microfilm: *The Eighteenth Century* 3177 no. 1. ESTC t113292.

C1727-2. Holdsworth, Winch. *A Defence of the Doctrine of the Resurrection of the Same Body: in . . . Which the Character, Writings, and Religious Principles of Mr. Lock Are . . . Considered, and the Doctrine . . . Is Defended against the Notions . . . of That Gentleman* (London: Printed for C. Rivington. 276 pp.)

Reply to Mrs. Cockburn, C1726-1. Microfilm: *The Eighteenth Century* 2764 no.10. Christophersen p. 128; ESTC t103781.

C1728-1. [Browne, Peter]. *The Procedure, Extent and Limits of Human Understanding* (London: Printed [by James Bettenham] for W. Innys. 477 pp.)

Microfilm: *The Eighteenth Century* 2106 no. 1. Christophersen p. 107; ESTC t130658.

C1728-2. D'Oyly, Robert. 'Of the Resurrection of the Same Body.' In his: *Four Dissertations* (London: Printed for R. Gosling. pp. 425–75.)

Microfilm: *The Eighteenth Century* 2674 no. 3. Christophersen p. 129; ESTC t115172.

C1729-1. Nicéron, Jean-Pierre. 'John Locke.' In his: *Mémoires pour servir à l'histoire des hommes illustres dans la république des lettres* (Paris: Briasson. i: 35–49).

C1730-1. Strutt, Samuel. *A Defence of the Late Learned Dr. Clarke's Notion of Natural Liberty: in Answer to Three Letters Wrote to Him by a Gentleman at the University of Cambridge, on the Side of Necessity; together with Some Remarks on Mr. Locke's Chapter of Power* (London: Printed for T. Green, and Sold by A. Dodd. 68 pp.)

Microfilm: *The Eighteenth Century* 5431 no. 21. Christophersen p. 107; ESTC t026534.

C1731-1. *The Infidel Convicted, or A Brief Defence of the Christian Religion: In Which the Excellency of the Christian Morality Is Fully Shewn, and the Consistency of Revelation with Human Reason is Proved; Corroborated by Unanswerable Arguments from Mr. Locke, on Whose Writings Many Persons Causelessly Profess to Build Their Sceptical Notions, &c.* (London: Printed for J. Roberts. 62 pp.)
 Microfilm: *The Eighteenth Century* 2709 no. 17. Christophersen p. 129; ESTC t017485.

C1732-1. Burnet, Thomas. *The Judgment of Dr. Thomas Burnet ... concerning the Doctrine of the Trinity, etc.; with a Preface concerning Mr. Locke, Sir Isaac Newton and Mr. Wollaston* (London: Printed for J. Roberts. xx, 43 pp.)
 Microfilm: *The Eighteenth Century* 3301 no. 3. Christophersen p. 129; ESTC t103692.

C1732-2. Conybeare, John. *A Defence of Reveal'd Religion against the Exceptions of a Late Writer* [Matthew Tindal], *in His Book Intituled,* Christianity as Old as the Creation, &c. (London: Printed for S. Wilmot in Oxford, and Sold by J. and J. Knapton [et al.]. 467 pp.)
 Criticism of Locke on demonstrative morality and on probability: pp. 231-9, 319-21. Microfilm: *The Eighteenth Century* 2874 no. 7. Christophersen p. 130; ESTC t135208.

C1732-3. Doria, Paolo Mattia. *Difesa della metafisica degli antichi filosofi contro . . . G. Locke, ed alcuni altri moderni autori* (Venice: s.n. 2 vols.)
 Vol. 1 (270 pp.) on Locke passim. Christophersen p. 109.

C1733-1. [Baxter, Andrew]. *An Enquiry into the Nature of the Human Soul: Wherein the Immateriality of the Soul Is Evinced from the Principles of Reason and Philosophy* (London: Printed for J. Bettenham, and Sold by G. Strahan [et al.]. 376 pp.)
 Microfilm: *The Eighteenth Century* 5081 no. 6. Second ed., 1737; third, 1745. Christophersen p. 107; ESTC t032759.

C1733-2. [Voltaire, François Marie Arouet de]. *Letters concerning the English Nation* (London: Printed for C. Davis and A. Lyon. 253 pp.)
 The French edition, entitled *Lettres sur les Anglois,* was published in 1734. Letter XIII is on Locke. 'The ornaments are those used by William Bowyer . . . Translated by John Lockman.'–ESTC t137614. Chap. XIII reprinted in *A Locke Miscellany*. Microfilm of complete text: *The Eighteenth Century* 4216 no. 15. Christophersen p. 109.

C1733-3. W[atts], I[saac]. *Philosophical Essays on Various Subjects, viz. Space, Substance, Body, Spirit . . . With Some Remarks on Mr. Locke's*

Essay on the Human Understanding. *To which is subjoined, A Brief Scheme of Ontology* (London: Printed for R. Ford and Richard Hett. xii, 403 pp.)
Microfilm: *The Eighteenth Century* 318 no. 15; facsim. reprint of the 1742 ed. by Thoemmes Press, Bristol, 1991. Christophersen p. 108; ESTC t095980.

C1734-1. *Characteristicks, or A Specimen of the Worth and Integrity of Some of the Most Favourite Authors of the Present Age.* Number I (London: Printed for J. Wilford. ix, 31 pp.)
No more numbers published. Pages 1-20 are on Bayle and his Dictionary; pp. 21-31, 'Of Mr. Lock, and His Essay . . .' ESTC t030441.

C1734-2. Gottsched, Johann Christoph. *Iniquitatem externorum in ferendo de eruditis nostratibus iudicio illustrium virorum Io. Lockii et Wilh. Molynaei exemplis confirmatam, sistit et ad audiendam oratio* . . . [Speech indicating the wickedness of foreigners judging our native scholars by examples from Locke and Molyneux] (Lipsiae: Breitkoff. [23] pp.)
Chiefly explains Locke's criticism of Leibniz.

C1735-1. 'Réflexions sur quelques principes de la philosophie de Mr. Locke, à l'occasion des *Lettres philosophiques* de Mr. de Voltaire', *Bibliothèque françoise: Histoire littéraire de la France*, 20, pt. 2: 189-214.
'Lettres philosophiques' is the later title of *Lettres sur les Anglois* (cf. C1733-2).

C1735-2. Perronet, Vincent. *A Vindication of Mr. Locke . . . Wherein Is Likewise Enquired, Whether Mr. Locke's . . . Opinion of the Soul's Immateriality Was Not Mistaken by . . . Leibnitz* (London: Printed for J. J. and P. Knapton. 124 pp.)
Microfilm: *The Eighteenth Century* 259 no. 7. ESTC t004944.

C1737-1. *Some Reflections concerning the Reduction of Gold Coin in Ireland, upon the Principles of the Dean of St. Patrick's and Mr. Lock . . .* (Dublin, 1737).
ESTC t160235; Goldsmith's-Kress Lib. 7526 (also on microfilm).

C1738-1. Perronet, Vincent. *A Second Vindication of Mr. Locke: Wherein His Sentiments Relating to Personal Identity Are Clear'd up from Some Mistakes of the Rev. Dr. Butler, in His Dissertation on That Subject . . .* (London: Printed for F. Gyles, and Sold by J. Roberts [et al.]. 132 pp.)
"(Price two Shillings.)" (Most copies have price carefully erased.) Facsim. reprint by Thoemmes Press, Bristol, 1991. ESTC t080742.

C1741-1. Richardson, Samuel. *Pamela, or Virtue Rewarded* (London: Printed for C. Rivington and J. Osborn. Vol. 2, pp. 248-324)
Includes comments on Locke's *Education*, education for women, and travel. The beginning pages are a parody of *Education*, §§ 1-2.

C1742-1. [Cuentz (or Künz), Caspar]. *Essai d'un système nouveau concernant la nature des êtres spirituels, fondé en partie sur les principes du célèbre M. Locke, philosophe anglois, dont l'auteur fait l'apologie* (Neufchatel: De l'imprimerie des éditeurs du Journal helvétique. 4 vols.)
Christophersen p. 130.

C1742-2. Edelmann, Johann Christian. 'Anhang: Bestehend in einer kurtzen Beleuchtung des Viten Cap. derjenigen Schrifft, so Anno 1719, zu Berlin unter folgenden Titul gedruckt worden: Der Socinianische Glaube . . . Worgegen ein dienliches Gegen-Gifft zugerichtet Johann Edwards . . . Worinnen: Die Vernunfftmässigkeit des Christentums.' In his: *Die Göttlichkeit der Vernunfft* . . . (Berlenburg: s.n. pp. 423-607).

C1742-3. *Memoirs of the Life and Character of Mr. John Locke* (London: Printed for F. Noble [et al.]. 15 pp.)
Microfilm: *The Eighteenth Century* 949 no. 17. Christophersen p. 85; ESTC t110275.

C1743-1. [Ellis, John]. *Some Brief Considerations upon Mr. Locke's Hypothesis, That the Knowledge of God Is Attainable by Ideas of Reflexion. Wherein Is Demonstrated, upon His Own Principles, That the Knowledge of God Is Not Attainable by Ideas of Reflexion* . . . (London: Printed by J. Watts, and Sold by B. Dod [et al.] 51 pp.)
Microfilm: *The Eighteenth Century* 317 no. 14. Christophersen p. 110; ESTC t097818.

C1743-2. *An Enquiry How Far It Might Be Expedient and Seasonable to Permit the Importation of Irish Cattle, upon Conditions of Advantage and Security to the Woollen Trade of Great Britain. The Several Judgments of Sir W. Temple and Mr. Locke in Reference Thereto* . . . (London: Printed for J. Roberts. 47 pp.)
Microfilm: *The Eighteenth Century*: 2925 no. 7. Christophersen p. 120; ESTC t032724.

C1743-3. [Fontenelle, Bernard Le Bovier de]. 'Réflexions sur l'argument de Monsieur Pascal et de Monsieur Locke concernant la possibilité d'une autre vie à venir.' In: *Nouvelles libertés de penser* . . . ('Amsterdam' [i.e. Paris: Piget] pp. 3-61.)

A clandestine publication of 205 pages; for fuller information see Jørn Schøsler's bibliography.[3] Christophersen p. 130.

C1744-1. Bayle, Pierre. 'An Account of the Life of John Locke, Esq;, Extracted from Mr. Bayle's Historical and Critical Dictionary', *American Magazine* 2 (Sept.): 540-44.

C1746-1. Böldicke, Joachim. *Methodus Lockio-Barateriana, das ist Ein Vorschlag, durch Hilfe des Spielens, der Musik, Poesie und anderer Ergötzlichkeiten; abermaliger Versuch einer Theodicee, darin von dem Ursprunge des Bösen in der besten Welt*... (Berlin & Leipzig, 1746-51. 4 parts).
Christophersen p. 123.

C1747-1. Ellis, John. *The Knowledge of Divine Things from Revelation, Not from Reason or Nature*. ... The Second Edition. *With Some Additional Considerations upon Mr. Locke's* Essay on the Human Understanding ... (London: Printed by J. Watts, and Sold by B. Dod [et al.]. xxiv, 132; 51; 133-440 pp.)
Chap. III (51 pp.) reprints C1743-1; also issued separately. ESTC t145561.

C1747-2. Gerdil, Giacinto Sigismondo (Père Barnabite). *L'Immatérialité de l'âme démontrée contre Locke* (Torino: Imprimerie royale. 283 pp.)
Christophersen p. 109.

C1748-1. *Confutationis specimen in Lokii metaphisicen, caput* I[-V]. (Neapoli: Typis Raymundi & Viventii. [20], 84 pp.)
Written 'a Sacerdote Neapolitano'.

C1748-2. Gerdil, Giacinto Sigismondo (Père Barnabite). *Défense du sentiment du P. Malebranche, sur la nature & l'origine des idées contre l'examen de M. Locke* (Torino: Impr. royale. 246 pp.)
Christophersen p. 109.

C1750-1. Chaufepié, Jacques-Georges. 'Locke (Jean).' In his: *Nouveau dictionaire historique et critique, pour servir de Supplément ... au* Dictionaire historique et critique *de Mr. Pierre Bayle* (Amsterdam: Chez Z. Chatelain [et al.] Vol. 3, pp. 100-106).
Based on C1705-5, and other sources.

---

[3] *Bibliographie des éditions et traductions d'ouvrages philosophiques français et particulièrement des écrivains obscurs, 1680-1800.* Études romanes de l'Université d'Odense, vol. 22 (Odense University Press, 1986). Especially p. 226.

C1750-2. [Massie, Joseph]. *An Essay on the Governing Causes of the Natural Rate of Interest; Wherein the Sentiments of Sir William Petty and Mr. Locke on That Head Are Considered* (London: Printed for W. Owen. 62 pp.)
   Microfilm: *The Eighteenth Century* 4111 no. 17. Christophersen p. 120; ESTC t056744.

C1751-1. Cockburn, Catharine Trotter. 'A Vindication of Mr. Locke's Christian Principles, from the Injurious Imputations of Dr. Holdsworth. Part I' [–II]. In her: *Works* (London: Printed for J. and P. Knapton. Vol. 1, pp. 155–378)
   Part II entitled: 'A Vindication of Mr. Locke, in the Controversy concerning the Resurrection of the Same Body.' Microfilm: *The Eighteenth Century* 2641 no. 3. Christophersen p. 128; ESTC t139309.

C1751-2. [Flemyng, Malcolm]. *A New Critical Examination of an Important Passage in Mr. Locke's Essay on Human Understanding; in a Familiar Letter to a Friend. To which is added an Extract from* . . . Anti-Lucretius [by Cardinal Polignac] *concerning the Same Subject* (London: Printed for J. Robinson. 57 pp.)
   Christophersen p. 110; ESTC t114237.

C1751-3. *The Real Presence, As It Is Held by the Roman Catholicks, Demonstrated to be Neither Contrary to Reason, nor the Evidence of the Senses upon Any Principles of Knowledge; with the Notions of Mr. Locke Thereon Considered and Confuted* (Dublin. 31 pp.).
   ESTC t179986.

C1753-1. Preface to *The Evidences of the Christian Religion*, by Joseph Addison . . . *With a Preface Containing the Sentiments of Mr. Boyle, Mr. Lock, and Sir Isaac Newton concerning the Gospel-Revelation.* The Fourth Edition (London: Printed for J. and R. Tonson and S. Draper. pp. xii–xx)
   Addison's work first published in 1730. The preface is new to this edition. Microfilm: *The Eighteenth Century* 2253 no. 6. Christophersen p. 129; ESTC t126796.

C1753-2. *The Jews Advocate, Containing Mr. Locke's Sentiments in Respect to the Treatment of Jews by Christians* . . . (London: Printed for M. Cooper [et al.] ii, 54 [i.e. 58] pp.)
   ESTC t014647.

C1759-1. 'O razumienii cheloviecheskom po Mnieniiu Lokka' [On human understanding, according to Locke's view], *Trudoliubivaia pchela* May 1759: 259–63.
   A brief paraphrase, unsigned. Text in old Cyrillic (pre-reform) orthography. Neustroev, p. 349.

C1759-2. [Roche, Antoine-Martin]. *Traité de la nature de l'âme et de l'origine de ses connoissances; contre le système de M. Locke & de ses partisans* (Paris: Chez la Veuve Lottin & J. J. Butard. 2 vols.)
Christophersen p. 109.

C1760-1. Massie, Joseph. *Observations Relating to the Coin of Great Britain; Consisting Partly of Extracts from Mr. Locke's Treatise concerning Money, but Chiefly of Such Additions thereto, as Are Thought to Be Very Necessary* . . . (London: Printed for T. Payne; Sold by W. Owen and C. Henderson. 40 pp. 4°)
Christophersen p. 120; ESTC t088146.

C1760-2. Ploucquet, Gottfried. *Examen meletematum celeberrimi Anglorum philosophi Lockii, de personalitate* . . . [Favourable examination of the very famous English philosopher Locke, on personality] (Tübingen: Bauhof & Franckianis. 36 pp.)
Thesis, Tübingen.

C1764-1. [Hurd, Richard, Bishop of Worcester]. *Dialogues on the Uses of Foreign Travel, Considered as Part of an English Gentleman's Education; between Lord Shaftesbury and Mr. Locke* . . . (London: Printed for W. B. and A. Millar. 201 pp.)
Frequently attributed to Locke; see ch. XII, D-16. Microfilm: *The Eighteenth Century* 1299 no. 4. ESTC t067492.

C1764-2. Reid, Thomas. *An Inquiry into the Human Mind, on the Principles of Common Sense* (Edinburgh: Printed for A. Millar; London: Printed for A. Kincaid and J. Bell. xvi, 541 pp.)
Microfilm: *The Eighteenth Century* 258 no. 3. ESTC t110558.

C1765-1. [Diderot, Denis]. 'Locke, Philosophie de'. In: *Encyclopédie, ou Dictionnaire raisonné des arts, des sciences, et des métiers.* Edited by D. Diderot and Jean d'Alembert (Neufchâtel: Chez S. Faulché [et al.] Vol. 9, pp. 625-7)
Translation printed in *A Locke Miscellany*.

C1765-2. [Hurd, Richard.] *Dialogues entre Lord Shaftesbury et M. Locke sur quelques points essentiels à l'éducation de la jeunesse, pour servir de suite au traité du dernier sur l'éducation des enfans.* Traduits de l'anglois (Yverdon. xxviij, 172 pp.)
Translation of C1764-1.

C1765-3. [———] *Dialogues sur les moeurs des Anglois, et sur les voyages, considérés comme faisant partie de l'éducation de la jeunesse.* Traduits de l'anglois (À Londres et se trouve à Paris: Chez B. Hochereau. xxxvi, 149 pp.)

Translation of C1764-1; authorship (better, translation) attributed to the Abbé Jean Bernard Le Blanc (cf. Cioranescu 38000). Microfilm: *The Eighteenth Century* 3043 no. 12. ESTC n032683.

C1765-4. Leibniz, Gottfried Wilhelm. 'Nouveaux essais sur l'entendement humain, par l'auteur du Systeme de l'harmonie pré-établie.' In his: *Oeuvres philosophiques latines et françoises . . . tirées de ses manuscrites qui se conservent dans la Bibliothèque royale à Hanovre*. Edited by Rud. Eric Raspe (Amsterdam: Chez G. Schreuder. pp.1–496).
Posthumous publication; written 1706–7. Attig 482 n.

C1765-5. ———. 'Remarques sur le sentiment de P. Malebranche, qui porte, que nous voyons tout en Dieu; concernans l'examen que M. Locke en a fait.' *Ibid.*, pp. 496–504.

C1765-6. *The Morality of the New Testament, Digested under Various Heads . . . By a Rational Christian. And Some Observations on the Arguments of Mr. Locke and Dr. Leland* (London: Printed for J. Johnson. xxxv, 404 pp.)
British Lib. attributes to Francis Webb; the *National Union Catalog* to Peter Annet. Christophersen p. 130; ESTC t153582; Goldsmiths'-Kress Lib. 7526 (also on microfilm).

C1766-1. *An Analysis of Mr. Locke's Doctrine of Ideas, in his Essay on Human Understanding* (Cambridge: Printed by J. Bentham, Sold by T. & J. Merrill).
The first publication of the broadside, a diagrammatic chart later published without imprint in vol. 1 of Bishop Law's edition of Locke's *Works* (no. 370). ESTC t209505.

C1766-2. [Oswald, James]. *Appeal to Common Sense in Behalf of Religion* (Edinburgh: Printed for A. Kincaid and J. Bell. 2 vols.)
The second vol. was published in 1772. Microfilm: *The Eighteenth Century* 351 no. 6. Christophersen p. 130; ESTC t088013.

C1768-1. [Tucker, Abraham]. *The Light of Nature Pursued*, by Edward Search, Esq; (London: Printed by T. Jones and Sold by T. Payne. 2 vols. in 5 parts)
'Edward Search' is a pseudonym. Vol. 1, pp. 1–384 on various topics, frequently mentioning Locke. Microfilm: *The Eighteenth Century* 319 no. 1. Christophersen p. 110; ESTC t109651.

C1769-1. Law, Edmund, Bishop of Carlisle. *A Defence of Mr. Locke's Opinion concerning Personal Identity, in Answer to the First Part of a Late Essay on that Subject* (Cambridge: Printed for J. Archdeacon. 41 pp.)

Reprinted in editions of Locke's *Works*, beginning with 1777 ed. (no. 370). Microfilm: *The Eighteenth Century* 258 no. 20. Christophersen p. 109; ESTC t094346.

C1770-1. Castillon, Jean-Louis. 'Descartes et Locke conciliés.' In: *Nouveaux mémoires de l'Académie royale des sciences et belles-lettres* (Berlin), pp. 277–82.

C1774-1. Williams, David. *A Treatise on Education, in which the General Method Pursued in the Public Institutions of Europe, that of Milton, Locke, Rousseau and Helvetius Are Considered* . . . (London: Printed for T. Payne [et al.] viii, 261 pp.)
ESTC t078140.

C1774-2. Wood, John. *Considerations of the Great Mr. Locke, on Raising the Value of Money; in order to prove the legislative wisdom and expediency of the late GOLD ACT, by which our Current Gold Money was ordered to pass by weight. In these Considerations we have the arguments on both side [sic] of the question, as they were urged by Mr. Locke, and the learned Lawyer Mr. Lowndes . . . These Considerations are published with a design to justify the Parliament, and satisfy the subject. To which are added, Some Introductory Observations . . . To this are added also, The different Gold and Silver Coins made use of in the different States of Europe* . . . (Exeter: Printed for the Author, by R. Trewman; and sold by Bedwell Law . . . London; E. Score, in Exeter; and P. Parkhouse in Tiverton.)

The above information is from an advertisement in *The London Chronicle* for Dec. 29–31, 1774 (p. 628), headed '*This Day were published*, Price 1s. 6d.' I am grateful to John Stephens for bringing this notice to my attention. To date there is no record of a surviving copy.

C1776-1. [Applegarth, Robert]. *A Theological Survey of the Human Understanding: Intended as an Antidote against Modern Deism* (Salisbury: Printed for the Author by J. Hodson, and Sold by Wallis and Stonehouse, London. 276 pp.)
Anonymous; the 1779 ed. states 'By Robert Applegarth'. Microfilm: *The Eighteenth Century* 320 no. 3. ESTC t004987.

C1776-2. [Mortimer, Thomas]. 'The Life of John Locke.' In: *The British Plutarch, Containing the Lives of the Most Eminent Statesmen, Patriots* . . . Edited [i.e. written] by Thomas Mortimer. (London: Printed for E. and C. Dilly. Vol. 5, pp. 216–30).

The first edition appeared anonymously in 1762. Chiefly copied from other sources by Mortimer. Microfilm: *The Eighteenth Century* 1824 no.1. ESTC t107370.

C1776-3. 'Stikhi. pisan. odnim' Oksfordsk. studentom smotria na L[ocke]-v portret' " [Verses written by an Oxford student on contemplating a portrait of Locke.], *Opyt trudov Vol'nago rossiiskago sobraniia* (Imp. Moskovskii universitet), ch. 3 (1776): 72-4.

Not seen. I am grateful to J. S. G. Simmons for supplying this information. Neustroev, p. 349.

C1776-4. [Coste, Pierre]. 'Svoistva Lokka, izobrazhenie v' pis'mie k' avtoru *Novostei uchenoi respubliki*', [The character of Locke, portrayed in a letter to the editor of the *Nouvelles de la république des lettres*], *Sobranie raznykh sochinenii i novostei* (later called *Sobranie novostei*), June 1776: 3-18.

Selective translation of C1705-3. In old-style Russian orthography. Neustroev, p. 349.

C1778-1. [Cajot, Jean-Joseph]. *Les plagiats de J. J. Rousseau de Genève sur l'éducation*, par D.J.C.B. [pseud.] (La Haye: Chez Durand. xxii, 378 pp.)
Argues Rousseau plagiarized from Locke. Christophersen p. 126.

C1778-2. Tucker, Josiah. *The Notions of Mr. Locke, and His Followers, That All Civil Governments Whatever, Not Founded on the Personal Choice of the Governed, Are So Many Usurpations on the Unalienable Rights of Mankind, Considered and Examined* (Gloucester: s.n. 113 pp.)
Reprinted in C1781-1. Not listed in ESTC.

C1779-1. [Barwis, Jackson]. *Dialogues concerning Innate Principles; Containing an Examination of Mr. Locke's Doctrine on That Subject*. By the Author of *Three Dialogues concerning Liberty* (London: Printed for J. Dodsley. 99 pp.)
Microfilm: *The Eighteenth Century* 351 no. 3. Christophersen p. 110; ESTC t109266.

C1781-1. Tucker, Josiah. *A Treatise concerning Civil Government: in Three Parts* (London: Printed for T. Cadell. vi, 428 pp.)
Part I reprints C1778-2. Christophersen p. 121; ESTC t051616; Goldsmiths'-Kress Lib. 12237 (also on microfilm).

C1782-1. 'Razsuzhdenie o bytīi Boga, vyvedennoe iz razsmatrivaniia prirody' [Thoughts about the existence of God, deduced from a consideration of nature], *Vecherniaia zaria* (Moscow), ch. 3 (Sept. 1782): 1-18.
Text in old Cyrillic (pre-reform) orthography. Neustroev, p. 349.

C1782-2. Towers, Joseph. *A Vindication of the Political Principles of Mr.*

Locke, in Answer to the Objections of . . . Dr. Tucker (London: Printed for G. Robinson. 113 pp.)
   Microfilm: *The Eighteenth Century* 621 no. 14. Christophersen p. 121; ESTC t050874.

C1782-3. Turner, Baptist Noel. *Candid Suggestions; in Eight Letters to Soame Jenyns, Esq; on the Respective Subjects of His Disquisitions, Lately Published; With Some Remarks on the Answerer of His Seventh Disquisition* [Richard Watson], *Respecting the Principles of Mr. Locke* (London: Printed by W. Harrod for T. Lowndes. 194 pp.)
   Microfilm: *The Eighteenth Century* 6356 no. 10. Christophersen p. 122; ESTC t145200.

C1783-1. Dawes, Manasseh. *The Nature and Extent of Supreme Power, in a Letter to the Rev. David Williams . . . Showing the Ultimate End of All Human Power, and of a Free Government under God. And in Which Mr. Locke's Theory of Government Is Examined and Explained, Contrary to the General Construction of That Writer's Particular Sentiments on the Supremacy of the People* (London: Printed for J. Stockdale, iv, 34 pp.)
   Microfilm: *The Eighteenth Century* 410 no. 17. Christophersen p. 122; ESTC t135143.

C1783-2. Tucker, Josiah. 'Letter IV: The Evil Consequences Arising from the Propagation of Mr. Locke's Democratical Principles.' In his: *Four Letters on Important National Subjects* . . . (Glocester: Printed by R. Raikes. pp. 89–113)
   ESTC t087839.

C1785-1. Reid, Thomas. *Essays on the Intellectual Powers of Man* (Edinburgh: Printed for J. Bell. xii, 766 pp.)
   Microfilm: *The Eighteenth Century* 2825 no. 3. ESTC t109176.

C1786-1. Tooke, John Horne. 'Some Considerations of Mr. Locke's Essay.' In his ΈΠΕΑ ΠΤΕΡΟΕΝΤΑ, *or The Diversions of Purley*. Part I (London: Printed for J. Johnson. 519 pp.)
   Romanized title: Epea pteroenta. Material on Locke: pp. 30–43.
   Microfilm: *The Eighteenth Century* 4843 no. 7. Christophersen p. 110; ESTC t032790.

C1789-1. Coste, Pierre. 'John Locke, Esqr.: The Character of Mr. Locke', *The Christian's, Scholar's, and Farmer's Magazine*, 1 no. 5 and 6 (Dec./Jan., Feb./Mar.): 515–9, 735–8.
   Summary of C1705-3.

C1790-1. Costa, Francisco José da. 'Discurso sobre o punto se à materia repugnar o pensar?' [Discourse on whether thinking is repugnant to matter], *Sessões literarias dos alumnos de Academia dos obsequiosos do Lugar de Sacavem*, 2: 175–83.

C1790-2. Ludlam, Thomas. *Logical Tracts, Comprising Observations and Essays Illustrative of Mr. Locke's Treatise upon the Human Understanding; with Occasional Remarks on the Writings of . . . Reid and Stewart upon the Same Subject; and a Preface in Vindication of Mr. Locke, against the Mistakes and Misrepresentations of . . . Mr. Milner . . . Dr. Horne . . . Mr. Kett . . . and Dr. Napleton . . .* (Cambridge: Printed by M. Watson, for J. Nicholson, Cambridge; Sold also by Rivingtons [et al.]. 31, 77 pp.)
  Facsim. reprint by Thoemmes Press, Bristol, 1991. Christophersen pp. 110, 130; ESTC n056029.

C1790-3. *Remarks on the Religious Sentiments of Learned and Eminent Laymen, viz. Sir Isaac Newton, Hon. Robert Boyle, Locke, Sir Matthew Hale, Addison . . . With Occasional Reflections on Incredulity* (London: Sold by Messrs. Robinson [et al.]. 157 pp.)
  Especially pp. 33–44. Microfilm: *The Eighteenth Century* 3528 no. 2. ESTC t143252.

C1793-1. 'Mnienie Lokka o zhivotnykh' [Locke's views on animals], *Prokhladnye chasy*, ch. 1 (Mar.): 184–7.
  In old Russian (pre-reform) orthography. Neustroev, p. 349.

C1794-1. Morell, Thomas. *Notes and Annotations on Locke on the Human Understanding. Written by Order of the Queen . . .* (London: Printed for G. Sael. iv, 125 pp.)
  Microfilm: *The Eighteenth Century* 5088 no. 12; facsim. reprint by Thoemmes Press, Bristol, 1991. Christophersen p. 111; ESTC t098207.

C1794-2. Whiter, Walter. *A Specimen of a Commentary on Shakspeare, Containing, I. Notes on As You Like It. II. An Attempt to Explain and Illustrate Various Passages, on a New Principle of Criticism Derived from Mr. Locke's Doctrine of the Association of Ideas* (London: Printed for T. Cadell. vii, 258 pp.)
  Microfilm: *The Eighteenth Century* 2916 no. 5. ESTC t092969.

C1795-1. Horne, George, Bishop of Norwich. 'Some Considerations on Mr. Locke's Scheme of Deriving Government from an Original Compact.' In: *The Scholar Armed against the Errors of the Times, or A Collection of Tracts on the Principles and Evidences of Christianity . . .* [Edited by William Jones] (London: Printed for F. and C. Rivington. 2 vols.)

Vol. 2 pp. 342–52, about Locke. Microfilm: *The Eighteenth Century* 4768 no. 21. ESTC t101689.

C1795-2. Napleton, John. *Advice to a Student in the University concerning the Qualifications and Duties of a Minister of the Gospel in the Church of England* (Oxford: Printed for Fletcher and Hanwell. vi, 147 pp.)
Microfilm: *The Eighteenth Century* 5226 no. 2. ESTC t062742.

C1796-1. 'Remarks on Mr. Locke's *Paraphrase and Notes on St. Paul's Epistles.*' In: *A Discourse concerning Faith as the Condition of the Gospel Covenant, and as the Instrument Whereby Salvation Is Wrought in the Heart by Divine Power. With an Appendix Containing Some Remarks on Mr. Locke's* Paraphrase and Notes . . . (George-Town [D.C.]: From the Press of Green, English, & Co. 60 pp.)
ESTC w025180; Evans 32050 (facsim. also on micro-opaque cards).

C1798-1. Bowles, John. *The Retrospect, or A Collection of Tracts, Published at Various Periods of the War, Including Some Reflections on the Influence of Mr. Locke's Theories on Government* . . . (London: Printed for T. N. Longman, and Sold by J. Hatchard; and by L'Homme).
Microfilm: *The Eighteenth Century* 441 no. 2. ESTC t084407.

INDEXES

Contents

Entries 1–373 in Chap. I–XI are covered in indices A–F; index G Part I additionally includes Chap. XII (doubtful attributions), shown by D numbers.

A. Editors and Translators	470
B. Illustrators and Engravers	472
C. Recipients of Dedications	474
D. Booksellers and Printers	
I. By Name	475
II. By Location	484
E. Names on titles/title-pages other than Locke, dedicatees, editors, illustrators and engravers, printers, booksellers and translators	487
F. Languages of Text	489
G. Titles	
I. Under which or within which Locke's writings were published	490
II. Works of Criticism (Chap. XIII)	497
H. Provenance (former owners)	503
GENERAL INDEX	505

A. Index of Editors and Translators

Aaron, R. I. 332
Abrams, Philip 342
Antonskii, Mikhail 153
'Author of the Life of . . . John Hales' *see* Desmaizeaux, P.
Bancks, John 350
Baron, Richard 28
Becelli, Giulio Cesare 219
Bernard, Jean Frédéric 372–3
Boer, T. J. de 358
Bonno, Gabriel 360
Bosset, J. P. 133–41
Bourne, H. R. Fox 330
Burridge, Ezekiel 110–14
Campe, J. H. 215
Castilhon, Salvemini 325
Clay, Jenny Strauss 340
Clay, Diskin 340
Cockin, J. 14
Collins, Anthony 318
Coste, Pierre 91–105, 114, 192–210, 239–45
Cyankiewicz, Andrej 114.1
De Beer, E. S. 362
Delbourg-Delphis, Marylène 332 n.
Desmaizeaux, Pierre 316–18
Dewhurst, Kenneth 345
Elrington, Thomas 43–4
Ferrari, Francesco A. 341
Forster, T. 355–6
G. 58
Gibb, Jocelyn 332
Gibson, Alexander George 337
Gilbert, Sir Jeffrey 147–52
Grazia, Marcia 361
Gretton, Phillips 349
Hancock, Thomas 314
Harmens, Hans 60
Harrison, John 343–4
Hofmann, Johann Georg 297
Hollis, Sir Thomas 28, 35–6, 369–70
Horwitz, Robert 340
Kenyon, Sir Frederic G. 336
King, Peter, (1st) Lord King 299, 372
King, Peter, (7th) Baron King 328–9

Kypke, Georg David 309
L.C.R.D.M.A.D.P. 50-51, 56; *see also* Mazel, David
Laslett, Peter 343-4
Law, Edmund 369-70
LeClerc, Jean 372-3
Lough, John 338
Marchini, Fabio 217, 220
Marugi, Giovanni Leonardo 114
Mazel, David 46-56, 58-60
Meinigen, Johann Christoph 246
Nidditch, P. H. 333-5
Noorthouck, John 369-70
Olearius, Gottfried 21-23, 212-13
Ollion, Henri 357-8
Ouvrier, Carl Siegmund 215
Pagnini, Giovanni Francesco 164
Poleyen, Heinrich Engelhard 108
Popovskii, Nikolai 224-6
Popple, William 3-15
Rand, Benjamin 331, 359
Rogers, G.A.J. 335
Rossi, Giuseppe 222-3
Rousset de Missy, Jean 50-51, 56
Rudolphi, L. 215
Sainati, Vittorio 332 n.
Schwabe, Johann Joachim 214
Shaftesbury, Earl of (4th or 5th, in 1766) 327
Simm, Alexander 311
Sina, Mario 361
Soave, Francesco 114, 143-6, 310
Starck, Sebastian Gottfried 211
Tennemann, Wilhelm Gottlieb 109
Thiele, Gotthelf Heinrich 112-14
Tittel, Gottlob August 142
Truskolawski, Edmund 223.1
V., V. D. 19
Verwer, Pieter Adriaen 191
Viano, Carlo Augusto 341
Von Leyden, Wolfgang 339
Watson, Richard 237-8
Wynne, John 115-32
Wynne, Richard 228
Yorke, Henry 41

B. Index of Illustrators and Engravers of Portraits and Vignettes

Fuller information about portraits of Locke and their present locations are to be found in *Corr.* viii, Appendix I (pp. 444–8).

Amman, Joh. 198
Baratti, Antonio 113
Basire, James 369–70
Beale, Maria (or Mary) 257
Blooteling, A. 257
Bosch, B. de 191
Broen, Joh. de 355–6
Brounower, Sylvester 62–4, 66–7, 110, 189
C. 52
Cattini, Giovanni 218, 222–3
Cipriani, F. B. 28, 35, 369
Cook 371
Dahl, Michael (port. of Sir J. Gilbert) 152
Duflos, Claude 99, 135, 137–8
Fehr, P. 93
Fokke, S. 98
Gardner, C. 316–17
Greenhill, John 91–94, 111, 328–9, 335, 338, 345, 359
Gunst, P. 91–94
Holloway, T. 152
Kneller, Sir Godfrey 28, 35, 68–75, 77, 79, 81, 84, 96, 98–9, 108, 135, 137–8, 175, 177, 179, 182, 184, 194, 197, 199–201, 204, 206, 209, 221–22, 242, 245–6, 302, 307, 319–20, 338, 343, 348, 363–9, 371
L.F.D.B. 50
Le Coeur 307
M. 52
Morellon la Cavé, F. 50, 96
Nutting, T. 66–7
Papillon 205
Philips, J. C. 191
Phinn, T. 75, 182, 184, 302, 319–20
Picart, B. 94, 197, 199, 204, 245
Putter, C. d. 245
Scaphu-- (?) 198
Schoonebeek, A. 190
Scotin, J. B. 194, 200–201
Simms, P. 175, 177, 179
Sveicart, A. 164
Sysang, I. C. 108
Tanjé, P. 98

Vanderbanck (or Vanderbank), P. 62-4, 110
Van Hove, F. H. 275
Verelst, Herman 112-13
Vertue, George 68-74, 77, 79, 81, 84, 348, 363-8
Worthington, ---- 328-9

C. Recipients of Dedications

Italicized citations are to works (by others) within which a composition by Locke is included. For works dedicated to Locke, see Introduction, p. xiv.

Bielefeld, Jacob Friedrich, Freiherr von 309
Boyle, Robert *256*
Charles II, King of England *255*
Chittenden, Thomas 12
Clarke, Edward 165-89, 190, 211-14
Cooper, Anthony Ashley, 1st Earl of Shaftesbury 327
Cooper, Margaret (Coventry), Countess of Shaftesbury 314
Cromwell, Oliver *251*
Dom-Vrobst Dechant (Brandenburg) 211
Durazzo, Girolamo 59
Episcopal Society, Brandenburg 211
Fénelon (de la Mothe-Salignac) 197-9, 204-207, 209-10, 218, 221
Firmian, Carlo, Conte di 144, 310
Friedrich Christian, Prince of Saxony 108
George III, King *150*
Grimani, Antonio 219
Herbert, Thomas, Earl of Pembroke 61-93, 110, 274
Hermes, ---- 24
Hilmer, ---- 24
Keene, Edmund *150*
La Fontaine, (Mme.) Anne Wolfgang de 192
La Motte, M. de *see* Fénelon
Lovelace, Henry Fortescue, Earl of 331
Mapletoft, John *257*
Northey, Edward, of Hackney 267
Parensi, Sra. Chiara Guinigi 217
Pembroke, Earl of *see* Herbert, Thomas
Richecourt, Emanuele di 164
Shaftesbury *see under* Cooper
Sheffield, Edmund, Duke of Buckinghamshire 94-6, 98
Somers, Sir John 160-62, 164
Spencer, George John, Earl 306-307
Wolfgang, Mlle. Anne *see* La Fontaine
Woltersdorf, ---- 24
Wrottesley, Hugh 316-18
Wynne, John 133-5, 137-8

D. Index of Booksellers and Printers

This index covers bibliographic entries by citation numbers (1–372) described in Chapters I–XI, including those mentioned in Notes. Works without names of printers or booksellers and those reading 'For a Company of Stationers', 'Aux dépens de la Compagnie', etc., are omitted.

I. By Names

Abel, J., Northampton 154
Ackers, Charles, London 365
Adams, James, Wilmington, Del. 9
Adolphi, Georg Heinrich, Greiffswald 211
Akademische Leseinstitut, Jena 109
Allen & West, London 88
André, Paris 56
Andreaeische Buchhandlung, Frankfurt a.M. 297
Andrews, Loring, Stockbridge, Mass. 13
Archdeacon, John, Cambridge 237, 304
Astley, Thomas, London 119, 121
Baalde, S.J., Amsterdam 271
Baglioni, Venice 145-6
Baker, J., London 171, 294
Baker, Samuel, London 28, 35, 37, 77, 79, 81, 84, 183, 185, 236, 294, 369-70
Baldwin, Robert, London 28, 35, 77, 79, 84, 183, 236, 294, 368-9
Balfour, John, Edinburgh 312
Barry, John, Glasgow 150
Barth, Johann Ambrosius, Jena & Leipzig 109
Basset, Thomas, London 61
Bathurst, Charles, London 88
Baynes, W., London 189
Becket, Thomas, London 37, 81, 185, 370
Beecroft, John, London 72-74, 77, 79, 81, 84, 291, 367-8
Beecroft, T., London 369-70
Bell and Daldy, London 356
Bentham, John, Cambridge 150
Bentley, Richard, London 328-9
Bentley, S., London 328
Bernard, Jean Frédéric, Amsterdam 373
Bettenham, J., London 316
Bettesworth, Arthur, London 33, 70-71, 119, 121, 176, 178, 232, 234, 289, 292, 347, 365
Biddles Ltd., Guildford & King's Lynn 335
Birt, Samuel, London 73-4, 180-81, 292-3, 367-8

Blackader, W., London 307
Blake, William Pynson, Boston, Mass. 132 n.
Bland, R., London 320
Boag, D. [Glasgow?] 42
Bonducci, Andrea, Florence 164
Bonham, George, Dublin 43-4
Bos, Barent, Rotterdam 190
Bossange, Masson et Besson, Paris 105
Bousquet, Marc-Michel, Lausanne 205, 207
Bowyer, William, London 32, 66, 117, 299, 365
Brandmüller, Basel 93
Brook, J., Huddersfield 14
Brotherton, R., London 88
Brown, J., Edinburgh 182
Browne, D., London 73-4, 77, 181, 367-8
Buisson, Paris 53
C., A. (Andrew Clark?) London 257
C., A. (Awnsham Churchill?) London 174
Cadell, Thomas, London 37, 79, 81, 84, 86-7, 89 (with T. Davies), 185, 295, 369-71
Cambridge University Press 338, 342
Carnan, T., London 88
Caslon, T., London 37, 79, 81, 84, 185, 369
Castle, Edward, London 115, 233, 248-50
Cater, R., London 88
Chamberlaine, D., Dublin 82, 85
Chatelain, Zacharie, Amsterdam 242 (with L'Honoré), 244-5
Churchill, Awnsham, London 3-4, 24-5, 27-31, 62-69, 110, 115-17, 155-6, 158-63, 165-70, 172-3, 174 (?), 229-31, 233, 248-50, 276-9, 281-88, 299, 346, 364
Churchill, John, London 3-4, 24-5, 28-32, 62-7, 110, 115-16, 155-6, 158-63, 165-70, 172, 229-31, 233, 248-50, 276-9, 281-88, 299, 346, 363
Churchill, William, London 157, 280, 282
Clarendon Press, Oxford 332, 335, 337, 339, 344, 362
Clark, H., London 248-50 ('H.C.' in 250)
Clarke, J., London 351
Clarke, W. & Son, London 152, 369
Coke, William, Edinburgh 78
Colburn, Henry, London 328-9
Collins, R., London 369
Conant, N., London 86, 88, 370
Conder, T., London 154
Cooper, M., London 73-4, 77, 180-81, 293, 367-8
Cooper, T., London 292

Cornell University Press 340
Cost, Sipkes, Groningen 45
Cotter, Sarah, Dublin 36
Crook, J., London 256
Crowder, J., London 15
Crowder, S., London 28, 35, 37, 77, 79, 81, 84, 86, 183, 185, 236, 294, 304, 368–70
Crusius, Siegfried Lebrecht, Leipzig 216
Crutchley, Brooke, Cambridge 338
Curll, E., London 315, 350–51
Dampier, S., London 319–20
Davey, P., London 77, 368
David le jeune, Paris 206
Davies, L., London 88
Davies, T., London 37, 79, 81, 84, 88–9, 185, 369
Davis, Lockyer, London 28, 35, 37, 77, 79, 81, 84, 86, 183, 185, 236, 294, 360–70
Deighton, J., Cambridge 154
Desveux, Paris 54–5
Dickson, J., Edinburgh 83
Dilly, C., London 37, 79, 81, 84, 86–7, 89, 152, 295, 369–71
Dilly, E., London 28, 35, 37, 77, 79, 81, 84, 183, 185, 236, 295, 368–70
Dobson, E., Dublin 118
Dod, B., London 150
Dodsley, Robert, London 353
Dóll, Jan, Amsterdam 19
Donaldson, Alexander, Edinburgh (also shops in London) 78, 125, 127, 129
Downing, J., London 313
Dring, Thomas, London 62
Du Villard, Geneva 47
Duncan, J., London 348
Duncan, J. & A., Glasgow 88
Dunton, John, London 275
Eaton, D. I., London 41
Edes and Gill, Boston, Mass. 38
Edman, Jean Fr. (widow of), Upsala 141
Elliot, C., Edinburgh 83
Elzevir, Daniel, jun., London 306
Evans, Thomas, London 81, 237–8, 370
Ewing, George, Dublin 175, 177, 179
Exshaw, Edward, Dublin 290
Exshaw, John, Dublin 123, 126
Faulder, R., London 87, 89, 295, 371
Faulkner, George, Dublin 148
Fenwick, H., London 186

Fickweiler, Johann Wolffgang, Greiffswald 211
Fletcher, J., London 368
Fletcher, J., Oxford 150, 238; J. & J., 227
Flower, Benjamin, Cambridge 154
Foerster, Nicolaus & Sohn, Hanover 213
Forrest, Will., Dublin 175
Foulis, Andrew, Glasgow 124, 321
Foulis, Robert, Glasgow 122, 124, 312, 321
Fowle, Boston, Mass. 6
Francklin, R., London 316-18
Fritsch & Böhm, Rotterdam 372
Fritschen, Thomas, Leipzig 212
Gales, J., Sheffield 41
Gardner, H., London 304
Gardner, Thomas, London 350
Georg, Theophilus (Gottlieb?), Leipzig 111-13
Glichi, Nicolò, Venice 143
Goldsmith, W., London 86-7, 295, 371
Gosling, F., London 292
Gosse, Henri-Albert, Geneva 136
Gosse, The Hague 243
Graesser, Rudolph & Co., Vienna & Wolfenbüttel 215
Gray, William, Edinburgh 311
Greenwood, J., London 267
Griffin, T., London 10
Guenther, Christian Friedrich, Glogau 247
H., J., London (John Humphrys?) 287-8
Hamilton, G., Edinburgh 312
Hansy, --- de, le jeune, Paris 99
Harrison, Thomas, London: ch.2 end n.
Hartung, Johann Bernhardt, Frankfurt a.M. 58
Hartung, Johann Heinrich, Koenigsberg 309
Harvard University Press 331, 359
Harvey and Darton, London 314
Hawes, L., London 77, 88, 181, 293, 367-9
Hawes, Clarke & Collins, London 28, 35, 37, 79, 71, 84, 183, 185, 236, 294, 369
Hayes, S., London 86-8, 89, 295, 304, 371
Hemingway and Crook, Blackburn 189
Heybruch, Heinrich, Dessau 216
Hickey, Ben., Dublin 175
Hildyard, John, York 151
Hill, P., Edinburgh 238
Hills, H., London 66
Hinxman, J., London 35, 183, 236, 294

Index of Booksellers and Printers

Hitch, Charles, London 70–74, 77, 119, 121, 176, 178, 180–81, 232, 234, 289, 292–3, 347, 366–8
Hodges, J., London 73–4, 180–81, 292–3, 367
Hoeve, Justus ab, Gouda 1
Hoey, James, Dublin 148–9
Holt, Elizabeth, London 61
Hooper, S., London 128
Houttuin, F., Amsterdam 191
Husson, Pierre, The Hague 92
Hyde, J., Dublin 118, 120
Infantry Cadet Corps Press, St. Petersburg 326
Innys, William, London 147.1
J., M., London 69
Jackson, J., London 350
James, J., London 350
Janssonio-Waisbergius, Amsterdam 2
Jaquier, Geneva 47
Jeffery, E., London 87 ('Jefferey'), 89, 307
Johnson, J., London 15, 86–7, 89, 295, 370 ('Jos.'), 371
Johnston, E., London 81
Johnston, W., London 28, 35, 37, 77, 79, 84, 88, 183, 185, 236, 294, 369
Joshua Associates, Oxford 335
Jugla, W., Antwerp 308
Keith, G., London 88
Kent, John, London 172
Kettilby, Walter, London 257
Kiernan, J., Dublin 187
Kincaid, A., Edinburgh 150
King, Henry S., London 330
Knapton, J. and J. London 119
Knapton, J. and P., London 121
Knox, J., London 370
Kompanii tipograficheskoi, Moscow 226
Kongl. Tryckeriet, Stockholm 60
Korten, Jonas, Hamburg & Leipzig 23
Krauss, Johann Paul, Vienna 214
Larkin, E., Boston 132
Law, B., London 28, 35, 37, 77, 79, 81, 84, 86–7, 89, 183, 185, 236, 293–5, 368–71
Le Breton, Paris 206
Leigh, George, London 86–7, 89, 295, 370–71 (with J. Sotheby 1780–1815)
Letellier, Paris 1042
L'Honoré & Chatelain, Amsterdam 242
Lichfield, Anne, Oxford 255
Lichfield, Leonard, Oxford 251, 255

Lintot, Bernard, London 349
Logan, James, Philadelphia 64
Longman, Thomas, London 28, 35, 37, 74 (with nephew Thomas), 77, 79, 81, 84, 86-7, 89, 152, 174, 181, 183, 236, 293-5, 367-71
Lowndes, Thomas, London 370
Lowndes, W., London 86-7, 89, 295, 371
Lunn, W. H., Cambridge 154
M'Kenzie (McKenzie), William, Dublin 40, 238
Maclehose, Robert, Glasgow 359
Manfredius, Vincentius, Naples 114
Manning & Loring, Boston, Mass. 132
Manship, Samuel, London 62-86, 363-4
March, J., Norwich 154
Marescandoli, Giandomenico, Lucca 217, 220
Marescandoli, Salvatore, Lucca 217, 220
Matthiae, Julius G., Stockholm 227
Mawman, York 11
Menassion, Jaques, 'Amsterdam' (i.e. Geneva) 193
Merkus, widow of, Amsterdam 208
Merrill, John, Cambridge 237-8 (with Joseph), 304
Merrill, Thomas, Cambridge 150, 304
Millar, A., London 28, 35, 73-4, 77, 79, 84, 88, 180-81, 183, 236, 292-4, 352, 367-9
Mortier, Pierre, Amsterdam 94-7
Mortier, Pierre le jeune, Amsterdam 50; Amsterdam & Leipzig 98, 325
Mory, Edward, London 61
Moscow University, Moscow 224-6
Motta, Gaetano, Milan 144, 310
Moutardier, Paris 210
Mozley, J., Gainsborough 10, 88
Mundell, J., Edinburgh 88
Mundell, J., Glasgow 90
Mundell & Son, Edinburgh 90
Musier, Jean, Paris 195
Neaulme, J., The Hague 243
Negus, Samuel, London 364
Newbery, F., London 88
Nichols, John, London 86, 237
Nichols, J. B. and Son, London 355
Nicholson, J., Cambridge 130-31, 304
Nicholson, W., Wisbeach 304
Nijhoff, Martinus, The Hague 358
Noble, F., London 348
Nourse, C., London 88
Nourse, John, London 135, 137-8

Nugent, G., Dublin 39
Ogilvie and Speare, London 89
Olschki (Leo S.), Florence 351
Osborn, John, London 174, 235
Osborn, T., London 292-3
Osborne, J., London 10
Osborne, Thomas, London 180
Oswald, J., London 73-4, 180-81, 292-3, 367
Otridge, W., London 86-7, 89, 152, 295, 371
Owen, W., London 28, 35, 37, 77, 79, 81, 84, 88, 183, 185, 236, 294, 369-70
Oxford Bibliographical Society 343
Oxford University Press (H. Milford) 359
P., H., London 174
Palmer, Samuel, London 365
Parker, Edmund, London 69-71, 365-6
Paton, W., Glasgow 42
Payne, Thomas, London 28, 35, 37, 77, 79, 81, 82, 86 (with son Thomas), 87, 89, 183, 185, 236, 294, 368-71
Pellissari & Co., Geneva 134
Pemberton, Henry, London 180; Executors of 73
Pemberton, J., in Fleet Street, London 33, 119, 121, 176, 178, 232, 234, 289, 292
Pemberton, John, at the (Golden) Buck, London 70-72, 119, 121, 178, 347, 365-6
Picard, Alphonse & fils, Paris 357
Pitteri, Francesco, Venice 218, 221-22
Plowman, Henry, 174
Pottischer Buchhandlung, Leipzig 23
Potts, J., Dublin 82, 85
Powell, S., Dublin 175, 290
Prince and Cooke, Oxford 238
Ramazini, Dionigi, Verona 219
Reid, J., Edinburgh 78
Reilly, R., Dublin 177, 179
Renger, Braunschweig (Brunswick) 246
Reymers, C., London 28, 35, 183, 236, 294
Richards, R., London 8
Richardson, J., London 35, 77, 183, 294, 368
Richardson, M., London 28, 236
Richardson, William, London 81, 86-7, 89, 295, 371
Richardson & Clark, London 327
Richter, Altenburg 108
Ridler, Vivian, Oxford 343
Risk, George, Dublin 175, 177, 179

Rivington, Charles, London 28, 35, 37, 79, 81, 84, 86-7, 152, 183, 185, 236, 294-5, 304, 369-71
Rivington, Francis, London 79, 81, 84, 86, 89, 152, 185, 295, 304, 369-71
Rivington, James (with John) London 74, 181, 185, 293, 367-70
Rivington, John, London 28, 35, 37, 74, 77, 79, 81, 84, 86, 152, 181, 183, 185, 236, 293-5, 304, 367-8
Roberts, John (with George Robinson) London 79, 84, 369
Robinson, George, London 37, 79, 81, 84, 86-7, 89, 154, 185, 295, 367-71
Robinson, George, son of George (with other Robinsons) London 86-7, 89, 154, 295, 371
Robinson, J. ('G. G. J. and J.', with George father & son & John), London 86-7, 89
Robinson, John, brother of George ('G. G. and J.', 'G. G. J. and J.') London 86-7, 89, 154, 295, 370-71
Robson, James, London 37, 81, 86, 185, 370
Rogers, Boston, Mass. 6
Rossi, Giuseppe qu. Bortolo, Venice 223
Roxburghe Club, London 336
Royal Society, London 258-62
Royer, Paris 54-5
Ryan, R., London 86-7
Sandby, William, London 151, 327
Saunders, Henry, Dublin 80, 82
Savoye, Paris 102
Scatcherd and Whitaker, London 86-7, 89
Schelte, Antoine, Amsterdam 192
Schelte, Henri, Amsterdam 91, 93 ('après la copie'), 194, 241
Schreuder, J., Amsterdam 50; Amsterdam & Leipzig 98, 325
Schwann und Goetz, Mannheim 142
Servière, Paris 52, 102, 209
Sewell, J., London 86-7, 89, 295, 354, 371
Shand, Francis, Edinburgh 78
Sheffield, University of (Philosophy Dept.) 333-4
Sheperd, W., Whitehaven 324
Sheppard, J., Dublin 36, 39
Shuckburgh, A., London 28, 35, 79, 84, 183, 294, 369
Shuckburgh, J., London 73-4, 77, 79, 84, 181, 236, 367-9
Slater, H., London 348 (advt. only)
Sleater, W., Dublin 82, 85
Smith, R., Paisley 42
Smith, William, Dublin 175, 177, 179
Sotheby, John 86-7, 89, 295, 371
Spence, R., York 11
Spooner, Alden, Windsor, Vt. 12
Steenhouwer & Uytwerf (*see also* Uytwerf) Amsterdam 197

Strahan, A., London 152
Strahan, William, London 28, 81, 185, 370
Symon, Edward, London 33, 70-71, 176, 178, 232, 234, 289, 347, 365-6
Symon, S., London 72
Symonds and Ridgeway, London 41
Taylor, Robert, Berwick 75, 322
Taylor, William, at the Ship, London 68, 117, 173-4, 364
Taylor, Turin 341
ter Beek, Jacob, Amsterdam 18
Thomas & Andrews, Boston 132
Thomson, J., London 319-20
Thomson, Joseph, Windsor, Vt. 12
Thurlbourn, William, Cambridge 150
Tirion, Isaak, Amsterdam 18
Tongerlo, K. van, Amsterdam 191
Tonson, J., London 184, 188, 228
Tonson, R., London 88, 184, 188, 228
University of California Press 360
University of Glasgow Press 359
Urie, Robert, Glasgow 7, 76, 301, 323
Uytwerf, Herman, Amsterdam 197, 199-201
Uytwerf, Maynard, Amsterdam 203-4
Valliant, P., London 88
Vander Kloot, Amsterdam 202
van der Kroe, A., Amsterdam 296
van der Plaats, F., Harlingen 17
Vernor and Hood, London 89
Visscher, Evert, Amsterdam 239
Vlam, Barthelemi, Amsterdam 51
W., T., London 69
Walker, J., London 295, 371
Walker, T., Dublin 187
Walther, C. & F., Dresden 131.1, 140
Walthoe, J., London 292
Ward, A., London 180, 292
Ward, J., London 73-4, 77, 181, 293, 367-8
Ware, C. and R., London 28, 35, 183, 236, 294
Watts, John, London 133
Wellcome Historical Medical Library, London 345
West, D., Boston 132
West, J., Boston 132
Wetstein, Henri, Amsterdam 240
Whiston, J., London 28, 35, 37, 77, 79, 81, 84, 183, 185, 236, 294, 369
White, B., London 28, 35, 37, 79, 81, 84, 86 (with B. White), 87, 183, 185, 236, 294-5 369, 371

White, J. ('B. & J.') London 87, 89, 295, 371
White, J., Boston, Mass. 132
Wiering, Johan von, Frankfurt and Leipzig 272
Wilkie, G. and T., London 86-7, 89, 295, 371
Wilkie, J., London 37, 81, 185, 370
Wilson, T., York 11
Wilson, W., Dublin 305
Wit, Kornelis de, Amsterdam 268-70
Withy, R., London 28, 35, 77, 183, 236, 294, 368
Wolfgang, Abraham, Amsterdam 46
Woodfall, H., London 28, 35, 79, 84, 183, 236, 294, 369
Woodfall, W., London 152
Wright, T., London 348

II. By Place

1) British Isles (except London)

Berwick on Tweed: R. Taylor
Blackburn: Hemingway & Crook
Cambridge: Archdeacon, Bentham, Cambridge University Press, Brooke Crutchley, Deighton, Flower, Lunn, Merrill, J. Nicholson, Thurlbourn
Dublin: Bonham, Camberlaine, Cotter, Dobson, Ewing, Exshaw, Faulkner, Forrest, Hickey, Hoey, Hyde, Kiernan, McKenzie, Nugent, Potts, Powell, Reilly, Risk, Saunders, Sheppard, Sleater, W. Smith, T. Walker, W. Wilson
Edinburgh: Balfour, Brown, Coke, Dickson, Donaldson;, Elliot, Gray, Hamilton, Hill, Kincaid, Mundell, Reid, Shand
Gainsborough: Mozley
Glasgow: Barry, Boag (?), Duncan, Foulis, Maclehose, Mundell, Paton, University Press, Urie
Guildford: Biddles Ltd.
Huddersfield: Brook
King's Lynn: Biddles Ltd.
Norwich: March
Oxford: Clarendon Press, Joshua Associates, Lichfield, Oxford Bibliographical Society, Oxford University Press, Prince & Cooke, Ridler
Paisley: R. Smith
Sheffield: Gales, University of Sheffield
Whitehaven: Sheperd
Wisbeach: W. Nicholson
York: Hildyard, Mawman, Spence, T. Wilson

2) North America

Berkeley, Calif.: University of California Press
Boston, Mass.: Edes & Gill, Fowle, Larkin, Manning & Loring, Rogers, Thomas & Andrews, W. P. Blake
Ithaca, N. Y.: Cornell University Press
Philadelphia: Logan
Stockbridge, Mass.: Andrews
Wilmington, Del.: Adams
Windsor, Vt.: Spooner, Jos. Thomson

3) Continental Europe

Altenburg: Richter
Amsterdam: Baalde, Bernard, Chatelain, Dóll, Houttuin, Janssonio-Waesbergios, L'Honoré, Merkus, Mortier, Schelte, Schreuder, Steenhouwer, ter Beek, Tirion, Tongerlo, Uytwerf, Vander Kloot, van der Kroe, Vischer, Vlam, Wetstein, Wit, Wolfgang
Antwerp: Jugla
Basel: Brandmüller
Brunswick: Renger
Dessau: Heybruch
Dresden: Walther
Florence: Bonducci, Olschki
Frankfurt and Leipzig: Wiering
Geneva: Du Villard, Gosse, Jaquier, Menassion, Pellissari
Glogau: Guenther
Gouda: Hoeve
Greifswald: Adolphi, Fickweiler
Groningen: Cost
Hague (The): Gosse, Husson, Neaulme, Nijhoff
Hamburg: Korten
Hanover: Foerster
Harlingen: van der Plaats
Jena: Akademische Leseinstitut, Barth
Koenigsberg: J. H. Hartung
Lausanne: Bousquet
Leipzig: Barth, Crusius, Fritschen, Georg, Korten, Pottischer Buchhandlung, Schreuder, Wiering
Lucca: Marescandoli
Mannheim: Schwann & Goetz
Milan: Motta
Moscow: Kompanii tipograficheskoi, Moscow University Press
Naples: Manfredius
Paris: André; Bossange, Masson & Besson; Buisson, David le jeune, Desveux, Hansy, Le Breton, Letellier, Moutardier, Musier, Picard, Royer,

Savoye, Servière
Rotterdam: Bos, Fritsch & Böhm
St. Petersburg: Infantry Cadet Corps Press (Sukhoputn. Kad. Korpusa)
Stockholm: Kongl. Tryckeriet, Matthiae
Tergow ('Ter Gouw') see Gouda
Turin: Taylor
Upsala: Edman
Venice: Baglioni, Glichi, Pitteri, Rossi
Verona: Ramazini
Vienna: Graesser, Krauss
Wolfenbüttel: Graesser

E. Index of Proper Names Appearing in Titles, Title-pages

The names of Locke, the dedicatees, editors, translators, printers and booksellers are excluded. Authors of quotations are included. Anonymous 'Authors of . . .' when identifiable, are listed by name.

Athenian Society 275
'Author of the Third Letter concerning Toleration' [Proast] 27
Ayloffe, Mr. 252.1
Bahama Islands 260
Barbeyrac, J. 19
Basil (Basilius), Saint 349
Bold, Samuel 353
Böhmer, Justus Henning 23–24
Boyle, Robert 263, 276, 352
Burnet, Bishop Gilbert 312
Busby, Mr. 252–3
Catharine of Braganza, Queen of England 255
Charles II, King of England 298
Churchill, A. & J. 240
Cicero, M. T. 61–87, 91–104, 110–11, 257, 300–303
Clarke, Edward 358–9
Clarke, Samuel 150, 349
Condorcet, Marquis de 53
Constitutional Society of Sheffield 41
Cooper, A. A., 1st Earl of Shaftesbury 298, 299, 327
Cooper, A. A., 3rd Earl of Shaftesbury 355–6
Coste, Pierre 114
Crew, Dr. 252–3
Cromwell, Oliver 251–52
Desmaizeaux, Pierre 88, 90, 367–8
Drieberge, J. 19
Ecclesiastes (Bible) 64–87, 110
Edwards, John 231–2, 234–5
Ephesians (Epistle of St. Paul) 239
Fénelon, Bishop of Cambrai 212–13
Filmer, Sir Robert 29–33, 35–6, 39–40, 42
Formentin (?) 208
G—n, Sir W. 252–3
Grotius, Hugo 150
Hancock, Thomas 314
Hoadley, B. 19
Horace 154, 167–78, 180–89, 227
John (N.T. Gospel of) 312
King, Richard 350

Le Chapelier, M. de 53
Le Clerc, Jean 88, 90, 267, 350, 360–61
Leibnitz, G. W. 350
Limborch, Philippus van 1–2, 350, 358–9
Livy 32–33, 42
Lofft, Capel 152
Lowndes, William 160–62
Malebranche, P. 299
Mapletoft, John 354
'A Member of Parliament' see Somers, Sir John
'Messieurs de Port-Royal' 313
Michaelis, Johann David 297
Milton, John 28, 228, 252.1
Molyneux, Thomas 259
Newton, Isaac 265
Nicole, Pierre 314
Noodt, G. 19, 23
P.A.P.O.I.L.A. see Limborch, Philippus van
Paul, Saint 287–97
Peysonel, M. de 53
Plato 43–4
Pococke, Dr. Edward 315
'Port-Royal, Messieurs de' 313
Price, Dr. (Richard) 12
Prior, Mr. 252
Quintilian 311
Rochester, Lord 252.1
Rollin, Charles 179, 222–3
Russell, Lady Rachel 354
Seneca 256
Sidney, Algernon 354–6
Soave, F. 114
Somers, Sir John 155–6
South, Dr. 252–3
Southwell, Robert 276
'Spectator, The Authors of the' 228
Stepney, Mr. 252.1
Stillingfleet, Edward, Bishop of Worcester 248–50
Strimesius, Samuel 2
Sydenham, Thomas 256–7, 264
Thiele, G. H. 114
Toinard (Thoynard), Nicolas 266, 357–8
Wallis, John 267
Worcester, Bishop of see Stillingfleet, E.
Wynne, Richard 228

F. (other than English)

Dutch 16-19, 26, 45, 190-91, 239, 268-71, 296, 308
French 20, 46-56, 91-106, 133-41, 192-210, 240-45, 263-6, 273-4, 298, 325, 357-8, 360-61, 372-3
German 21-24, 57-8, 107-109, 142, 211-216, 246-7, 272, 297, 309
Greek 143
Italian 59, 144-6, 164, 217-23, 310, 341
Latin 1-2, 110-14, 251-53, 255-6, 339-42
Polish 114.1, 223.1
Russian 153, 224-6, 326
Swedish 60, 227

G. Title Index

Part I.

Titles of works in Chap. I–XI (entries 1–373) and Chap. XII (D numbers for doubtful attributions) under which and with or within which Locke's writings have appeared are indexed here. Titles in non-roman alphabets have been transliterated. Italicized citation numbers refer to internal contents of a bibliographic entry. For titles of works not by Locke, the author's, editor's or compiler's name is given within parentheses; authors of doubtful attributions are given within square brackets. Titles of works of criticism in Chap. XIII (C numbers) are indexed separately in Part II, below.

Abbrégé de l'Essay de Monsieur Locke sur l'ent. hum. (Bosset) 138, 141
Abdruck eines Christlichens Bedenckens (Seitz) 23
Abhandlung über den Empirismus in der Philosophie (Tennemann) 109
Abregé d'un ouvrage intitulé Essai philosophique . . . 274
Abrégé de l'Essai de Monsieur Locke sur l'ent. hum. (Bosset) 134, 136, 137, 139–40
Abrégé de l'Essay de Mr. Locke sur l'entendement humain (Bosset) 133, 135, 137
Abridgment of Mr. Locke's Essay . . . (Wynne) 115–32
Abstract of Mr. Locke's Essay on Human Understanding (Gilbert) 150–52, 304
Abstract of the Essay of Human Understanding (Gilbert) 147–9
'Account of a not yet Described Scolopendra Marina, by Thomas Molyneux' 259
Account of Mr. Locke's Religion, A [Milner] D-15; C1700-2.
'Account of one who had horny excrescencies . . .' 260
Account of the Life and Writings of Mr. John Locke (Le Clerc) 315, 351
Æsop's Fables in English and Latin, Interlineary . . . [Grigg] D-7
Allgemeine Revision des gesammten Schul- und Erziehungswesens . . . (Campe) 215
'An magistratus civilis' 341–2
'Analyse de l'oeuvre (ouvrage) suivant . . .' (after Gilbert) 136, 139
Analysis of Mr. Locke's Doctrine of Ideas (anon.) 87, 89, 370–71; see also C1766-1
Anleitung des menschlichen Verstandes 309
Answer to *Remarks upon an Essay concerning Humane Understanding*, An 249
Arte dell'educare i fanciulli 219
Auszug aus dem Versuche von menschlichem Verstande (Gilbert) 108
'Authori in tractatum ejus de febribus' 256
Bedencken von Erziehung der Kinder (Fénelon) 212–3
Berühmten Engländers Johann Locke Vernunftmässiges Christenthum . . . 247

'Best Method of Studying, and Interpreting the Scriptures, The' *315*
Bibliothèque choisie (Le Clerc) *298*
Bibliothèque de l'homme public (Condorcet) *53*
Bibliothèque universelle et historique (Le Clerc) *263–6, 273*
Breve considerazioni . . . *164*
Brief aangaande de verdraagzaamheit, Een *18*
Brief over de verdraagszaamheit *17*
'Catalogue and Character of Most Books of Voyages . . .' *371*
'Character of Mr. Locke, The' (P. Coste) *316–18*
Christianisme raisonnable, Le *242–5*
Collection of Several Pieces . . ., A *316–18, 367–71*
Collection of Theological Tracts, A (Watson) *237–8*
Common-place Book to the Holy Bible, A D-6
Conduct of the Understanding, (The, Of the, Some Thoughts on the) *87–90, 300–307, 311*
Correspondence of John Locke (ed. de Beer) *362*
Correspondence of John Locke and Edward Clarke (ed. Rand) *359*
'Crowns, Scepters, Thrones . . .' *255, 315*
De arte medica *337*
De intellectu humano *110*
De l'éducation des enfans *192–94, 196–205, 207–10*
'De la conduite de l'esprit' *372–3*
De pace ecclesiastica (Strimesius) *2*
De specificorum remediorum . . . (R. Boyle), *review 263*
Defence of Mr. Locke's Opinion concerning Personal Identity,' (B. Law) *87, 89, 370–71*
Del Gobierno Civil ch.I & IX end n.
Del modo che dee tenersi . . . (Soave) *146*
Della educazione dei fanciulli *218, 221*
Dialogues on the Uses of Foreign Travel [Hurd] D-18; C1764-1
Directions concerning Education *336*
'Discours sur les miracles' *372–3*
Discourse concerning the Love of God, A [Masham] D-5
Discourse of *or* on Miracles, A *299, 312*
Discourses on the Being of a God. . . (P. Nicole) *313*
Discourses translated from Nicole's Essays *314*
Dissertation sur la réunion des Chrétiens (Coste) *242, 244–5*
Domiduca oxoniensis (ed. Baylie) *255*
Draft A of Locke's Essay . . . *333*
Draft B of Locke's Essay . . . *334*
Drafts for the Essay . . . *335*
Du gouvernement civil *46–53, 56*
Early Draft of Locke's Essay *332*
Education des enfans *206*
Educational Writings of John Locke ch. V end n.

Educazione de' figliuoli, L' 217, 220, 222
Educazione dei fanciulli, L' 218, 223-4
Eerste brief over de verdraagzaamheid 19
Einzige wahre Mittel des Vernunftmässigen Christenthums (Coste) 247
Elémens de physique 325
Elementary Foundations of Physics (in Russian) 326
Elements of Natural Philosophy 87, 89, 316-24
'Eloge de feu Mr. Locke' (Le Clerc) 372-35 (see also Index, part II)
'Eloge de M. Locke' (Coste) 94-105
Encheiridion metaphysiko-dialektikon 143
Epistola de tolerantia 1-2, 28, 369
'Epistola/Lettre de Monsieur J. L. . . . contenant une méthode nouvelle . . .', 266
Epistola su la tolleranza 341
Epistolario (Le Clerc) 361
Erläuterung des Vernunftmässigen Christenthums 247
Essai philosophique concernant l'entendement humain 91-106
'Essai sur la necessité d'expliquer les Epitres' 373
Essay concerning Human Understanding, An 66-90, 363-71
Essay concerning Human Understanding, Abridged 131.1
Essay concerning Humane Understanding, An 61-65
Essay concerning the True Original Extent and End of Civil Govt., An 38, 43-4
Essay concerning the Understanding, Knowledge, Opinion . . . 331
'Essay concerning Toleration' 341
Essay for the Understanding of St. Paul's Epistles . . . 286, 287-95, 363-71
Essays on Education (R. Wynne) 228
Essays on the Law of Nature 339
European Magazine, and London Review (Philological Society) 354
'Examen du sentiment du P. Mallebranche' 373
Examination of P. Malebranche's Opinion . . ., An 299
Extract of a Book, Entituled, A Philosophical Essay . . . 275
'Extract of a Letter .. about poisonous Fish in . . . Bahama Islands' (Lilburne) 258
Extract from Mr. Locke's Thoughts concerning Education 228
Extracts from the Familiar Letters 349
'Extrait d'un Livre Anglois . . . intitulé Essai philosophique . . .' 133-41, 273
Familiar Letters 348
'Febriles, aetus, victumque . . .' 256, 315
Five Letters concerning the Inspiration of the Holy Scriptures [Le Clerc] D-10
Fourth Letter for Toleration (Part of a) 299, 369-71
'Fundamental Constitutions of Carolina, The' 316-18; D-8
Further Considerations concerning Raising the Value of Money 160-62, 363-71
Gedencken von Erziehung der Kinder 214

Gedencken von Erziehung der Tochter (Fénelon) *212–13*
Gedencken von Erziehung junger Edelleute 211
Gelehrte Rede von der Freiheit des Gewissens (Noodt) *23*
General History of the Air (R. Boyle) 276
Gentleman's Religion, A [Synge] D-12
Giusto pregio delle cose . . . *164*
Gouvernement civil, Le, oder Die Kunst wohl zu regieren *58*
Governo civile, Il *59*
Gründlicher Beweiss dass die Christliche Religion . . . 246
Guida dell'intelletto nella ricerca della verità *145–6, 310*
Handbuch der Erziehung 216
Handbuch für Eltern und Erzieher 215
'Historical Account of Mr. Locke's Life . . . (Le Clerc) *350*
History of our Saviour Jesus Christ, The [Le Clerc] D-1
How to Bring up Your Children ch.V end n.
'If Greece with so much mirth . . .' *251–54, 315*
'In tractatum de febribus D. D. Sydenham . . .' *256, 315*
Instructions for the Conduct of a Young Gentleman *315*
'Introductory Discourse' to Churchills' Collection of Voyages [Wells?] D-3
Istruzione de' fanciulli e giovanette, L' (Rollin) *222*
Istruzione per la buona educazione . . . (Rollin) *223*
J. Locke over de Opvoeding der Kinderen 191
J. Locke über Duldung 24
John Locke on Toleration and the Unity of God ch.I end n.
John Locke . . . Physician and Philosopher (ed. Dewhurst) *345*
Journals (1675–98) *345*
Korte inhoud van een werk . . . *308*
Ksiażka o edukacji dezieci J. Lock'a 223.1
Kunst wohl zu regieren, Die *58*
Kurtze und deutliche in natürlich- und Göttl. Rechten . . . Vorstellung (Seitz) *23*
'Kurze Nachricht von Lockes's Leben . . .' (Le Clerc) *142*
Lady's Religion, A [Stephens?] 242 n.; D-14
'Last Will and Testament' *362*; see also C1714-1
Law of Evidence, The (Gilbert) *152*
Letter concerning Toleration, A *3–15, 28, 363–72*
Letter from a Person of Quality, A (Earl of Shaftesbury) *316–18*; D-9
Letter to Edward Lord Bishop of Worcester, A 248A
Letter to the Right Reverend Edward Lord Bishop of Worcester, A 248B, *363–71*
Letters concerning Toleration 28
Lettre de Jean Locke sur la tolérance *20*
'Lettre sur la tolérance' *354*
Lettres inédites de John Locke (ed. Ollion) *358*
Lettres inédites de Le Clerc à Locke (ed. Bonno) *360*

Leven van den Heere Johan Locke, Het (Le Clerc) *191*
Library of John Locke, The 343-4
Libri IV de intellectu humano 111-14
Life and Character of Mr. John Locke (Le Clerc) *348*
'Life of the Author' [John Locke] (Le Clerc) *88, 90, 367-71*
Life of John Locke (Bourne) *330*
Life of John Locke (King) *328-9*
Lobschrift auf den Herrn Locke (Coste) *108*
Locke vom menschlichen Verstande 142
Locke's Travels in France (ed. Lough) *338*
Logika czyli myśli z Lokko o rozumie ludzkim wyjęte 114.1
'Loix pour une société . . .' *136, 139*
'Mémoires pour servir à la vie d'Antoine Ashley . . .' *298, 372-35*
'Memoirs relating to the Life of Anthony first Earl of Shaftsbury' *299*
'Méthode nouvelle de dresser des recueuils' *266, 372-3*
Méthode (nouvelle) observée en France pour l'éducation des enfans (anon.) 209-10
Methodus curandi febres (Sydenham) *256*
Miracles, Discourse of (on, Short Treatise of or on) *299, 312*
Miscellaneous Tracts (ed. A. Simm) *311*
Mr. Locke's Reply to the . . . Bishop of Worcester's Answer to His Letter *249, 363-71*
Mr. Locke's Reply to the [Bishop's] Answer to His Second Letter *250, 363-71*
Musarum oxoniensium helaiophoria (ed. J. Owen) *251*
Museum, or The Literary and Historical Register (anon.) *353*
Neuerfundene Manier Excerpta . . . *272*
New Collection of Poems . . . *254*
New Essay upon All Sorts of Learning (Athenian Society) *275*
New Method of a Common-place Book *87, 89, 299, 363-71*
New Method of Making Common-Place-Books, A *267*
New Thoughts concerning Education (by Rollin) *179*
Nieuwe Manier om Verzaamelingen of Aantekeningen te maaken, Eene 269-71
Notes sur la correspondance de John Locke (ed. Ollion) *357*
'Nouveau système des idées' (Bosset?) *133-5, 137-8, 141*
Nouvelles instructions pour l'éducation des enfans 193
Nuove considerazioni . . . *164*
Nutzbarkeit der Toleranz . . . (Seitz) *23*
O poznanii, Bozhiia bytiia 153
O vospitanii detiei 224-6
Observationes medicae circa morborum acutorum historiam . . . (Sydenham) *257*
Observations on the Growth and Culture of Vines . . . *327, 369-71*
Occasional Thoughts in Reference to a Vertuous or Christian Life [Masham] D-4

Oeuvres diverses de Monsieur (Jean) Locke 372-3
Of Civil Polity 34
Of the Conduct of the Understanding 87-90, 299, 311
Ofoergripelige Tankar om Werldslig Regerings 60
Original Letters from Mr. Locke . . . 353
Original Letters of Locke, Algernon Sidney, and . . . Shaftesbury 355-6
Over de Burgerlyke Regering 45
Over de Opvoeding der Kinderen 191
Over den Brief van Paulus aan de Romeinen 296
Paraphrase and Notes on the Epistle of St. Paul to the Ephesians 285, 287-95
Paraphrase and Notes on the Epistle of St. Paul to the Galatians 277-80, 287-95
Paraphrase and Notes on the Epistle of St. Paul to the Romans 284, 287-95
Paraphrase and Notes on the First Epistle of St. Paul to the Corinthians 281-2, 287-95
Paraphrase and Notes on the Second Epistle of St. Paul to the Corinthians 283, 287-95
Paraphrase and Notes on the Epistles of St. Paul 287-95, 363-71
Paraphrastische Erklärung und Anmerkungen über S. Pauli Briefe . . . 297
Part of a Fourth Letter for Toleration 299, 369-71
'Part of a Letter, giving an Account . . .' (B. Furly) 261
'Pax regit Augusti . . .' 251-3, 315
'A Peaceful Sway the Great Augustus bore . . .' 252.1-2
Pensées sur la lecture & les études à l'usage d'un Gentilhomme 325
Pervonachal'nyia osnovaniia fiziki 326
Philosophia naturalis principia mathematica (I. Newton), *review* 265
Philosophical Transactions of the Royal Society 258-62
Physician's Art, The (Gibson) 337
Poems on Affairs of State 252.1-2
Political Aphorisms (anon) ch.II end n.
Posthumous Works of Mr. John Locke 299, 363-71
Present State of the Republick of Letters 148
Que la religion chrétienne est très-raisonnable 240-41
Quelques pensées sur l'éducation *ch. V end n.*
'Question: Whether the Civil Magistrate' 341-2
Questions concerning the Law of Nature 340
Ragionamenti sopra la moneta, l'interesse del danaro . . . 164
Reason and Religion D-13
Reasonableness of Christianity, The 229-32, 234-8, 363-71
Rechtmässigkeit, Nothwendigkeit u. Nutzbarkeit der Toleranz . . ., Die 23
Rede von der Freiheit . . . (Noodt) 23
'Register kept by Mr Locke, In Oxford' 276
'Register of the Weather for the Year 1692 . . .' 263
Religion des dames, La [Stephens?] 242, 244
Remains of John Locke, The 315

Remarks upon Some of Mr. Norris's Books 316–18
Reply to the . . . Bishop of Worcester's Answer to His Letter 249
Reply to the . . . Bishop of Worcester's Answer to His Second Letter 250
Review of the Argument A Priori . . . (Gretton) 349
'Right Method of Searching after Truth' (Ch.XII, Law's no.8) see Conduct of the Understanding
Rights of Protestant Dissenters, The [Barrington] D-16; C1704-3
'Rules of a Society . . . for the Promoting of Truth and Christian Charity' 316–18; D-17
Saggio filosofico di Gio.Locke su l'umano intelletto 144–61
Saggio sopra il giusto pregio . . . (Pagnini & Tavanti) 164
Schedula monitoria . . . (T. Sydenham), review 264
Schriftmatige Redelykheyt van 't Christendom, De 239
Scripta et Vita J. Lockii (Le Clerc) 112–14
Scritti editi e inediti sulla tolleranza (ed. Viano) 341
Second Letter concerning Toleration, A 25, 27–28, 363–71
Second Vindication of the Reasonableness of Christianity, A 233–5, 363–71
Select Moral Books of the Old Testament and Apocrypha, Paraphras'd [Bedingfield] D-2
Sendschreiben von der Toleranz 21–23
'Sentiments concerning the Society for Promoting Christian Knowledg' 315
'Several Letters' 315–16
Several Papers relating to Money, Interest and Trade, &c. 163
Short Observations on a Printed Paper . . . 158–9, 363–71
Short Treatise on Miracles, A 312
Some Considerations of the Consequences of the Lowering of Interest . . . 155–6, 363–71
Some Familiar Letters 346–7, 363–71
'Some Memoirs of the Life and Character of Dr. Edward Pococke' 315
Some Thoughts concerning Education 165–89, 363–71
Some Thoughts concerning Reading and Study for a Gentleman 87, 89, 316–18, 319–22, 324
Some Thoughts on the Conduct of the Understanding 300–303
Spirit of John Locke on Civil Government, The 41
State Poems continued . . . (ed. anon.) 252–3
Syllabus of Locke's Essay on the Human Understanding, A 154
Synopsis compendiaria librorum (Grotius et al.) 150
Tankar och Anmärkningar . . . 227
Third Letter concerning Toleration, A (Proast) 27 n.
Third Letter for Toleration, A 27, 28, 363–71
Thoughts on the Conduct of the Understanding 88, 90
Traité de bonheur [Formentin?] 200–201, 208
Traité du gouvernement civil 54–5
Traité sur la tolérance (Voltaire) 20
Travels in France, Locke's (ed. Lough) 338

Treatise concerning the Truth of the Christian Religion (Gilbert Burnet) *312*
Treatise of Raising Our Coin, A *157*
Treatise on the Conduct of the Understanding *87, 89*
Tweede brief over de verdraagzaamheid *19*
Twenty Years Literary Correspondence *350*
Two Tracts on Government (ed. Abrams) *342*
Two Treatises of Government *29-33, 35-7, 39-40, 42, 363-71*
Über die Erziehung der Jugend unter den hoeheren Volksklassen *215*
Über Duldung *24*
Unterricht von Erziehung der Kinder *212-13*
Verhandeling over de Opvoeding der Kinderen *190*
Vernünfftige und Schrifftmässige Untersuchung . . . (anon.) *23*
Vernunftmässiges Christenthum . . . *247*
Versuch vom menschlichen Verstande *108*
Versuch über den menschlichen Verstand *109*
Verzameling van eenige verhandelingen over de verdraagzaamheid *18*
Vindication of the Reasonableness of Christianity, A *230-31, 234-5, 363-71*
Vita et scripta J. Lockii (Le Clerc) *112-14*
Vom menschlichen Verstande *142*
Vorstellung von dem Recht . . . (Seitz) *23*
Vox Populi Vox Dei *ch.II end n.*
Vryheid van Godsdienst in de burgerlijke Maatschappy, De *19*
'Whether the Civil Magistrate . . .' *341-2*
Whole History of Navigation *371*
Works of John Locke, Esq., The *363-71*
Works of . . . Robert Boyle *352*
Young-Students-Library, The (Athenian Society) *275*

Part II. Index to Chapter XIII: Titles of Works of Criticism

Authors of works published anonymously are supplied in square brackets.

Account of Mr. Lock's Religion, An [Milner] C1700-2
Account of the Life and Writings of Mr. John Locke, An (Le Clerc) C1706-3, C1713-1, C1714-1
Account of the Life of John Locke, Esq; (Bayle) C1744-1
Advice to a Student in the University (Napleton) C1795-2
American Magazine (article by Bayle) C1744-1
Analysis of Mr. Locke's Doctrine of Ideas . . . C1766-1
Animadversions on a Late Book . . . *The Reasonableness* . . . [West?] C1697-1
Anti-Scepticism (Lee) C1702-2
Appeal to Common Sense in Behalf of Religion [Oswald] C1766-2
Argument of the *Letter concerning Toleration* Briefly Consider'd . . . [Proast] C1690-3

'Bestehend in einer kurtzen Beleuchtung' (Edelmann) C1742-2
Bibliothèque choisie (Le Clerc's 'Eloge' & review in) C1705-5, C1707-2
Bibliothèque françoise (article on Locke) C1735-1
Biographia Britannica (article on Locke) C1760-1
Bishop of Worcester's Answer to Mr. Locke's Letter, The (Stillingfleet) C1697-13
Bishop of Worcester's Answer to Mr.Locke's Second Letter (Stillingfleet) C1698-4
Brief Vindication of the Fundamental Articles . . . Christian Faith (Edwards) C1697-6
British Plutarch (article on Locke) C1776-2
Candid Suggestions (Turner) C1782-2
'Character of Mr. Locke, The' (Coste) C1720-1
Characteristicks, or A Specimen . . . C1734-1
Christian Blessedness (Norris) C1690-2
Christian's, Scholar's and Farmer's Magazine, The (article by Coste) C1789-1
Christianity Not Mysterious [Toland] C1696-8
Collection of Tracts . . ., A (Bold) C1706-1
Compleat History of Magic, Sorcery and Witchcraft, A (Boulton) C1715-1
Confutationis specimen in Lokii metaphisicen caput I[-V] C1748-1
Considerations of the Great Mr. Locke . . . (Wood) C1774-2
'Cursory Reflections' (Norris) C1690-2, C1692-1
De haeresi per libros symbolicos (Schramm) C1712-3
Defence of Mr. Locke's Opinion (Law) C1769-1
Defence of Reveal'd Religion . . . (Conybeare) C1732-2
Defence of the Doctrine of the Resurrection . . ., A (Holdsworth) C1727-2
Defence of the *Essay of Human Understanding* [Cockburn] C1702-1
Defence of the late Learned Dr. Clarke's Notion . . ., A (Strutt) C1730-1
Défense du sentiment du P. Malebranche (Gerdil) C1748-2
'Descartes et Locke conciliés' (Castillon) C1770-1
Dialogue on the Uses of Foreign Travel [Hurd] C1764-1
Dialogues concerning Innate Principles [Barwis] C1779-1
Dialogues entre Lord Shaftesbury et M. Locke . . . [Hurd] C1765-2
Dialogues sur les moeurs des Anglois [Hurd] C1765-2
Difesa della metafisica (Doria) C1732-2
'Digression concerning Connate Ideas, A' (Sherlock) C1704-2
Discourse concerning Coining the New Money Lighter, A (Barbon) C1696-1
Discourse concerning Faith as the Condition . . . Gospel Covenant, A C1796-1
Discourse concerning the Happiness of Good Men, A (Sherlock) C1704-3
Discourse concerning the Nature of Man, A (Lowde) C1694-1
Discourse concerning the Resurrection of Jesus Christ (Ditton) C1712-1
Discourse concerning the Resurrection of the Same Body [Bold] C1705-1
Discourse in Vindication of the Doctrine of the Trinity (Stillingfleet) C1696-6

'Discurso sobre o punte se à materia repugnar o pensar?' (Costa) C1790-1
Dissertatio philosophico-rationalis de spatio vacuo . . . (Reinbathius) C1717-3
Dissertation on Deistical and Arian Corruption, A C1708-2
Dissertation upon the Tenth Chap. of the Fourth Book of . . . *Essay* (Carroll) C1706-2
'Eloge du feu Mr. Locke' (Le Clerc) C1705-5
Encyclopédie, ou Dictionnaire raisonné des arts . . . (article on Locke) C1765-3
Enquiry How Far It Might Be Expedient . . . Importation of Irish Cattle C1743-2
Enquiry into the Nature of the Human Soul, An [Baxter] C1733-1
Epea Ptepoenta (Tooke) C1786-1
Essai d'un système nouveau [Cuentz] C1742-1
Essay on the Governing Causes of the Natural Rate of Interest [Massie] C1750-1
Essay towards the Theory of the Ideal . . . World (Norris) C1701-1
Essay upon Government, An C1705-4
Essays on Divers Weighty and Curious Subjects (Parker) C1702-3
Essays on the Intellectual Powers of Man (Reid) C1785-1
Evidences of the Christian Religion, The: Preface (Addison) C1753-2
'Evil Consequences Arising from . . . Locke's Democratic Principles, The' (Tucker) C1783-2
Examen meletematum . . . philosophi Lockii de personalitate (Ploucquet) C1760-3
Exceptions of Mr. Edwards, The C1695-2
Existence of the Human Soul after Death . . ., The (Hampton) C1711-2
Faith and Reason Compared [Metternich] C1713-2
Fides et ratio collatae [Metternich] C1708-5
Finishing Stroke, The [Leslie] C1711-3
Four Dissertations (D'Oyly) C1728-2
Four Dissertations on Important National Subjects (Tucker) C1783-2
Free but Modest Censure . . ., A (F. B.) C1698-1
'Full Confutation of All the Arguments . . ., A' (Boulton) C1715-1
Fundamental Constitution of the English Government, The [Atwood] C1690-1
Gentleman's Magazine (article on Locke) C1792-1
Göttlichkeit der Vernunfft, Die (Edelmann) C1742-2
Grounds and Foundation of Natural Religion Discovered, The (Becconsall) C1698-2
Immatérialité de l'âme demontrée contre M. Locke, L' (Gerdil) C1747-1
Infidel Convicted, The C1731-1
Iniquitatem exterorum in ferendo . . . sistit . . . oratio (Gottsched) C1734-2
Inquiry into the Human Mind, An (Reid) C1764-2
Io. Locki Sublestas de ratione sententias (Schueler) C1714-2

Jews Advocate, The C1753-2
'John Locke' (Nicéron) C1729-1
Judgment of Dr. Thomas Burnet . . . (Burnet) C1732-1
Judicium, sine affectu, de duobus adversariis (Jaeger) C1708-3
Knowledge of Divine Things from Revelation, The (Ellis) C1747-1
Letter for Toleration Decipher'd (Long), A C1689-1
Letter Humbly Offer'd to the Consideration . . ., A C1696-3
Letter in Answer to . . . *Christianity Not Mysterious* (Browne) C1697-3
Letter to Dr. Holdsworth . . ., [Cockburn] C1726-1
Letter to the Author of *Some Brief Observations* . . . Paraphrase . . . (Martin) C1716-2
Letter to the Reverend Dr. Benjamin Prat (Carroll) C1707-1
Letters concerning the English Nation [Voltaire] C1733-2
Lettre de Mr. Coste . . . à l'occasion de la mort de M. Locke' (Coste) C1705-3
Lettres sur les Anglois [Voltaire] C1733-2 n.
Life and Character of Mr. John Locke, The (Le Clerc) C1706-3
'Life of John Locke' (article in the British Plutarch) C1776-2
Light of Nature Pursued, The (Tucker) C1768-1
'Locke (Jean)' (Chaufepié) C1753-1
'Locke, Philosophie de' [Diderot] C1765-3
Logical Tracts (Ludlam) C1790-2
Mémoires pour l'histoire des sciences . . . (Trévoux; review of C1700-2) C1725-2
Mémoires pour servir à l'histoire des hommes illustres (Nicéron) C1729-1
Memoirs of the Life and Character of Mr. John Locke C1742-3
Methodus Lockio-Baratieriana (Böldicke) C1746-1
'Mnienie Lokka o zhivotnykh' C1793-1
Monatlicher Auszug (review in, by Leibniz) C1700-1
Moral Essays (Lowde) C1699-3
Morality of the New Testament . . ., The [Webb?] C1765-6
Nature and Extent of Supreme Power, The (Dawes) C1783-1
New Critical Examination of an Important Passage in . . . *Essay* [Fleming] C1751-2
Notes and Annotations on Locke on the Human Understanding (Morell) C1794-1
Notions of Mr. Locke, and His Followers, The (Tucker) C1778-2
Nouveau dictionnaire historique et critique (Chaufepié) C1753-1
'Nouveaux essais sur l'entendement humain' (Leibniz) C1765-4
Nouveaux mémoires de l'Académie royale [à Berlin] (article by Castillon) C1770-1
Nouvelles de la république des lettres (Coste's letter in) C1705-3
Nouvelles libertés de penser C1743-3
'O razumienii cheloviecheskom po Mnieniiu Lokka' C1759-1
Observations on the Animadversions . . . (Bold) C1698-3

Observations Relating to the Coin of Great Britain (Massie) C1760-2
Occasional Paper, no. 1, 3, 5 C1697-9, -10, -11
'Of the Resurrection of the Same Body' (D'Oyly) C1728-2
Pamela, or Virtue Rewarded (Richardson) C1741-1
Philosophical Essays on Various Subjects [Watts] C1733-3
Philosophick Essay concerning Ideas, A C1705-6
Plagiats de J.J. Rousseau . . . sur l'éducation, Les (Cajot) C1778-1
Practical Discourses upon the Beatitudes . . . (Norris) C1692-1 n.
Principia innata (Jan) C1723-1
Principles of Natural Philosophy, The (Greene) C1712-2
Principles of the Philosophy of the Expansive & Contractive Forces (Greene) C1727-1
Procedure, Extent and Limits of Human Understanding, The (Browne) C1728-1
Psychologia (Broughton) C1703-1
'Razsuzhdenie o bytii Boga . . .' C1782-1
Real Presence, The C1751-3
Reflections on *A Letter to the Author of Some Brief Observations* . . . (Coole) C1717-1
Reflections upon Some Passages in Mr. Le Clerc's *Life of Mr. John Locke* . . . C1711-5
'Réflexions de Mr. L—- sur l'*Essay sur l'entendement humain*' (Leibniz) C1708-4
'Réflexions sur l'argument de Monsieur Pascal [et Locke]' [Fontenelle] C1743-3
'Réflexions sur quelques principes . . . de Mr. Locke' C1735-1
Refutation of Some of the False Conceits, A (Elys) C1697-8
'Remarks on Mr. Locke's Paraphrase and Notes . . .' C1796-1
Remarks on Some Books Lately Published (Jenkin) C1709-2
Remarks on the Religious Sentiments of Learned . . . Laymen C1790-3
Remarks upon *An Essay concerning Human Understanding* [Burnet] C1697-4
Remarks upon Mr. Clarke's Sermons (Carroll) C1705-2
'Remarques sur le sentiment de P. Malebranche' (Leibniz) C1765-5
Report Containing an Essay for the Amendments of . . . Coins, A [Lowndes] C1695-3
Resurrection of the Same Body, The (Lupton) C1711-4
Resurrection of the Same Numerical Body, The (Felton) C1725-1
Retrospect, The (Bowles) C1798-1
Review of the Universal Remedy . . . [Paterson?] C1696-4
Rights of Protestant Dissenters, The [Barrington] C1704-2
Scholar Armed, The (Horne) C1795-1
Second Letter to the Author of . . . Letters for Toleration [Proast] C1704-1
Second Remarks upon *An Essay concerning Human Understanding* [Burnet] C1697-5
Second Vindication of Mr. Locke, A (Perronet) C1738-1

Sermon Preached . . . Easter Monday, 1719 (Holdworth) C1720-2
Sessoes literarias . . . de Academia dos obsequiosos . . . (article by Costa) C1790-1
Short Discourse of the True Knowledge of Jesus Christ, A (Bold) C1697-2 n.
Sir Thomas Colepeper's Tracts concerning Usury reprinted (Culpeper) C1708-1
Socinian Creed, The (Edwards) C1697-7
Socianism Unmask'd (Edwards) C1696-2
Solid Philosophy Asserted . . . [Sergeant] C1697-12
Some Brief Considerations upon Mr. Locke's Hypothesis [Ellis] C1743-1
Some Brief Observations on the Paraphrase and Notes . . . [Coole] C1716-1
Some Considerations about the Raising of Coin C1696-5
'Some Considerations of Mr. Locke's Essay' (Tooke) C1786-1
'Some Considerations on Mr. Locke's Scheme . . .' (Horne) C1795-1
Some Considerations on the Principal Objections . . . (Bold) C1699-1
Some Passages in *The Reasonableness* . . . (Bold) C1697-2
Some Reflections concerning the Reduction of Gold in Ireland (C1737-1
Some Short Remarks upon Mr. Lock's Book (Temple) C1696-7
Some Thoughts concerning the Several Causes . . . of Atheism (Edwards) C1695-1
Specimen of a Commentary on Shakespeare (Whiter) C1794-2
Spinoza Reviv'd [Carroll] C1709-1, C1711-1
'Stikhi. pisan. odnim' Oksfordsk. studentom . . .' C1776-3
'Svoistva Lokka . . .' [Coste] C1776-4
Theological Survey of the Human Understanding, A [Applegarth] C1776-1
Third Collection of Tracts, A C1695-2 n.
Third Remarks upon *An Essay conc. Humane Understanding* [Burnet] C1699-2
Third Letter concerning Toleration [Proast], The C1691-1
Tracts concerning Usury reprinted (Culpeper) C1708-1
Traité de la nature de l'âme . . . [Roche] C1759-2
Treatise concerning Civil Government, A (Tucker) C1781-1
Treatise on Education, A (Williams) C1774-1
Vindication of Mankind, A [S. Lowe?] C1717-4
Vindication of Mr. Locke, A (Perronet) C1736-2
'Vindication of Mr. Locke's Christian Principles, A' (Cockburn) C1751-1
Vindication of the Epistles . . . C1697-14
Vindication of the Political Principles of Mr. Locke, A (Towers) C1782-2
Vindication of Women's Preaching, A (Martin) C1717-2

H. Provenance (former owners)

N.B. Former owners very infrequently recorded. Indexed by page numbers.

Alcott, Amos Bronson, 231
Antonelli, Angelo, 261
Arnold, Rev. T., 79
Baillie, James B., 422
Ben Damph Forest Library, 273
Blemus, Chr., Rosano, 153
Calverley, Lady Mary, 70
Carlyle, Thomas, 79
Codrington, Christopher, 82
Cooper, Anthony Ashley, 3d Earl of Shaftesbury, 374
Cooper, David, 9
Crediton Parish Library, 276
Disney, John, 2
Dodgson, Edward Spencer, 234
Duke, Mrs. Isabella, 72
Edwards, Jonathan, 84, 203, 278, 331, 337
Elliott, John, 403
Franklin, Benjamin, 366
Fretwell, Thomas, 234
Gourlay, James, 340
Guenellon, Peter, 72–3
Hardy, Robert Gathorne, 386
Hollis, Thomas, 2, 24, 36, 44, 185
Holmes (O. W.) family, 106
Jones, Edward Powis, 274
Jowett, Benjamin, 403
Laing, Joseph, 403
Lamprecht, S. P., 79, 82, 303
Laslett, Peter, 9
Leibniz, Gottfried Wilhelm, 73, 123, 194, 205
Liancourt, Duc de, 247
Locke, John, 36, 211, 214, 273–4, 324(?)
MacEune, Dan., 73
Map...t, Lord (Cambridge), 167
Mitchell, Joseph, 26
Molyneux, William, 72–3, 211
Nourse, John, 341
Osler, Sir William, 300
Philosophisches Seminar, Heidelberg, 18
Pierce, John, Jr., 48
Pratt, F. Alcott, 231

Rand, Benjamin, 393
Rush, Benjamin & Richard, 106
Rush, William, 227
St George's Chapel, Windsor, 298
Schick, Karl, 72
Schiff, Mortimer, L., 72
Schoenborn-Buchheim Library, 170
Shackleton, Robert, 419
Smith, Joseph, 26
Somers, John, Baron Somers, 72
Spry, R., 73
Tooke, J. Horne, 102
Tremayne, Arthur, 403
Turnour, Francis, 79
Tyrrell, James, 70, 73
Valtravers (or Vautravers), Giovanni Ridolfo, 2
Warner, H. H., 300
Wilson, J. Cook, 405
Witherspoon, John, 38, 340
Wolf, Edwin, 2nd, 219
Wynne, John, 156
Wynne, John (1796), 161
Yeatman, H. I., 165
Yonge, Sir Walter, 211
Yorke, Philip, Earl of Hardwicke, 72
Zabriskie, Christian A., 274

GENERAL INDEX

Citations, by page number, cover persons and topics other than those in Special Indexes.

Aaron, Richard I., 69 n.
Abrams, Philip, 329
Acworth, Richard, 365
Adamson, J.W., 269
Addison, Joseph, 396, 460
Alden, John Eliot, 211
Alston, R.C., 158
Annet, Peter, 462
Antwerp Stadsbibliotheek, 355-6
Aristotle, 58
arrangement of this bibliography, xi-xiii
Ashcraft, Richard, 29, 66, 435, 437
Ashley, Lord, see Cooper, A. A., 3d Earl of Shaftesbury
Ashley, Maurice, see Cooper, Maurice Ashley
Ashurst, ——, 76
Astell, Mary, 439
Astley, T. (bookseller), 159
Atwood, William, 71
Axtell, James L., 212, 222, 269, 317, 365
Ayer, A.J., 189
Ayers, Michael R., 360

Bacon, Francis, 383
Banks (or Bancks), J., 389-90
Barbagallo, Mario, 269
Barbeyrac, Jean de, 15, 127, 396
Baron, Richard, 25
Barrington, John Shute, Viscount, 2, 282, 436
Barsov, Anton, 187

Basnage, Jacques, 396
Baxter, Richard, 364
Bayle, Pierre, 314, 396, 427, 457
Bedingfield, Philip, 432
Beecroft, T., bookseller, 413
Bell and Daldy, firm, London, 394
Bellamont, Richard Coote, Earl of, 71-72
Bennet, Thomas, see under Hodgson, N.
Benson, George, 282
Bentinck van Rhoon, Willem, 56
Bentley, Richard, 297, 300, 302
Berkeley, Elizabeth (later, Mrs. Burnet), 297, 300, 301
Berkeley, George, 396
Berlin Staatsbibliothek, 322, 355-6, 390
Bernard, Dr. Fr., 76
Bernard, Jean Frédéric, 127, 427
Bernier, François, 314
Berst, Karin, 293
Bible, 118
bibliographical sources, xxiii-xxix
Bibliotheca Annua, 149, 337
Bibliothèque royale Albert 1er, Brussels, 321, 355-6
Bibliothèque universelle & historique, 169, 318, 322
Birch, Thomas, 315, 391
Blackburne, Francis, 3, 25-6, 36, 40, 44, 419
Blagden, Cyprian, see under Hodgson, N.
Blake, William Pynson, 169

Blasselle, B., 131
Blathwaite, William, 198
Bodin, Jean, 58
Boehmer, Justus (Jobst) Henning, 21
Bold, Samuel, 81, 278, 300, 302, 363, 365, 419
Bond, W.H., 25, 44 n.
Bonville, John, 212
Bosset, J.P., 84
Boulton, Richard, 79
Bourne, H.R. Fox, 145, 315–16, 327, 356, 365, 381, 385, 437, 452
Bowers, Fredson, 31
Bowyer, William, 86, 171, 403, 456
Boyer, Abel, 433
Boyle, Robert, xiv, 71–72, 313–15, 326–7, 396
Boyle Lectures, 184, 349
Bridges, Brook, 71–72, 77, 212, 216
Bridgewater, John Egerton, Earl of, 198
British Library, 394
The British Plutarch, 259
Bromley, J.S., 313
Brounower, Sylvester, x, 2, 71–72, 209, 298, 323, 325, 378, 380
Brunet, Jacques-Charles, 319
Buckinghamshire, Duke of, *see* Sheffield, Edmund, Duke of Buckinghamshire
Burgermaster of Amsterdam, 123
Burlington, Richard Boyle, Earl of, 75
Burnet, Gilbert, 65, 314, 396
Burnet, Thomas, 300
Burridge, Ezechiel, 149, 297, 300, 302, 386
Burthogge, Richard, xiv, 297, 300
Busby, Richard, 306

Caglioni, G., 269

Calamy, Edmund, 364
Calas, 'l'affaire', 17
Calkins, Mary Whiton, 189
Calverley, Lady Mary, 70, 71–72, 300, 363, 366, 385
Campe, J.H., 258–9, 260
Canada Council, xv
Capper, Louisa, 189
Cappiello, Ida, 293
Carbery, John Vaughan, 3d Earl of, 71–72, 302
Carlini, Armando, 269, 383–4
Carvalho, Joaquim de, 189
Catherine of Braganza, Queen, 305, 310
Chadwick, James, 198, 204, 297
Chadwick, Mary (nee Tillotson), 198 n.
Chamberlen, Dr. Hugh, 198
Charles II, King, 305, 310
Charleton (Courten), William, 71–72
Chicheley, —— (? Sir John), 216
Chicheley, Sir John, 71–72
Child, Sir Josiah, 191, 198
Christ Church, Oxford, 71–72, 306, 310
Christ's College, Cambridge, 36, 37, 44
Christophersen, H.O., viii, 145
Churchill, Awnsham, ix–xi, 40, 193, 210, 215, 217, 220, 272, 316, 326–7, 330, 399, 401–402, 431
Churchill, John, ix–xi, 193, 210, 215, 217, 220, 272, 326–7, 330, 399, 402, 431
Churchill, William, 195
Churchills' *Collection of Voyages*, 432
Clark, H., printer, 302
Clarke, Edward, x–xi, 71–72, 76–7, 192, 198, 209, 212, 216, 297, 300, 302, 392
Clarke, Mary (née Jepp), 209

Clarke, Samuel, 127, 282
Clarke, Samuel, commissioner of Customs, 198
Cleary, Robert, 189
Clements, Henry, *see under* Hodgson, N.
Cockburn, Mrs. Catharine, 455
Cockin, J., 12
Codrington, Col. Christopher, 81
Coimbra University Library, 189
Colie, Rosalie, 313-14
Collins, Anthony, vii, xi, 363-6, 385
Commissaire de la Marre, 272
Common Prayer Book, 118
Compayré, Gabriel, 269
Condillac, Etienne Bonnot de, 180
contracts to publish, 69, 75, 80, 158, 181, 215, 272, 326
Conyers, John, 199, 216
Cooper, Anthony Ashley, Earl of Shaftesbury, 71, 76-7, 198, 212, 216, 364-5, 374, 431, 434-5
Cooper, Anthony Ashley, 3d Earl of Shaftesbury, 297, 299, 300, 393, 396
Cooper, Maurice Ashley, 198, 216, 297, 300, 302
copy (or copies), sales of to booksellers (or 'congers'), 82, 83, 217, 218, 298, 308, 337, 349
copyright agreements, 193, 326
Coste, Pierre, 36, 37, 44, 78, 81, 122, 128, 129, 146, 147, 154, 170, 216, 239, 240, 272, 283-7, 298, 302, 363, 433, 436
Coulter, James, bookseller, 339
Covel, John, Master of Trinity College, Cambridge, 302
Coxe, Dr. Daniel, 76
Cranston, Maurice, 189, 191, 437
Crediton Parish Library, 276

Crell, Mr. (? Samuel Crellius), 217, 302
Crellius, Samuel, 298
Crewe, Nathaniel, 306
Croft, Herbert, 276
Cromwell, Oliver, 305
Crousaz, Jean-Pierre de, 396
Cudworth, Ralph, vii
Cumberland, Richard, 15
Cunningham, Alexander, 81
Curll, Edmund, 320, 362, 390, 399, 452

D'Allone, Abel Tassin, 71-72
Daniel, Evan, 269
D'Aranda, Paul, 71-72, 212
Davys, Ferdinando, 223
De Beer, Edmund S., vii, xvii, xxii, 209, 324, 329, 365, 374-75, 385, 431-33
dedications of Locke's works, 474
dedications to Locke, xiv-xv, 155
Deermann, Johann Bernhard, 269
Defoe, Daniel, 435
del Boca, S. Drago, 269
Del Gobierno Civil, 383
Delbourg-Delphis, Marylène, 384
Descartes, René, 128
Desmaizeaux, Pierre, 173, 365, 399, 413
Devonshire, William Cavendish, Duke of, 199
Dewhurst, Kenneth, 378-9
Dickinson, Dr. Edmund, 76
Dodd, William, 184, 229, 434
Dodwell, Henry, 396
Dorset, Charles Sackville, Earl of, 199, 216
Drieberge, J., 15
Du Bos, Jean-Baptiste, Abbé, 217, 302
Duke, Mrs. Isabella, 71-72, 212
Dunton, John, xiv
Dutch culture & politics, 57, 237

Eccles, Lady Mary (formerly Mrs. Mary Hyde), 209
Edwards, John, 271-2, 278, 285, 295, 433
epitaph (Locke's), 151, 153, 145, 236-7; (in *Works*, 1st-6th edns.): 400, 404, 407, 410, 413, 415; 426, 428
Ewing, George, 293
The Exceptions of Mr. Edwards . . . , 273
Eyre, Sir Samuel, 198-9

F., M.J., 314
Fabian, Dr. Bernhard, xv, 18, 21, 62, 125, 133, 145, 258
Fagiani, Francisco, 208
Fatio (or Faccio) de Duillier, Nicolas, 71-72
Feather, John, 100
Fénelon, François S. de la Motte-, 256
Ferguson, Robert, 65, 435
Ferrari, Francesco A., 381
Ferris, J.A., 293
Filmer, Sir Robert, 29
Finn, Judith B., 434
Firmin, Thomas, 71-72, 76, 212, 297, 300
Fleetwood, William, 358
Fletcher, Andrew, 77, 216
Fontenelle, Bernard le Bovier de, 396, 458
Forfar, Robina Douglas, Countess of, 71-72, 212, 216
Formentin, M., 246, 252
Forster, Thomas, 393
Forster, W., 393
Foulis (Robert & Andrew), publishers, Glasgow, 351
Fowler, Dr. Edward, Bp. of Gloucester, 199, 298, 302
Fowler, Thomas, 383
Fox, S. Jean de Bruggs, 314
Fox, Sir Stephen, 199

France: despotic government of (1795), 60
Franklin, Benjamin, 39 n.
Fraser, Alexander Campbell, 122, 189
Fraser, James, 'divine', 298, 300
Fraser, James, licenser, 32, 192-3
Freke, John, 'the bachelor', ix, 71-72, 76-7, 81, 198, 199, 212, 297, 300, 302
Freke, Thomas, 72
Fuhrmann, Karl Heinrich, 21
Fulton, John F., xiv, 314, 391
Furly (or Furley), Benjamin, 71-72, 76-7, 198-9, 212, 216, 298, 300, 302, 392-3
Furly, Arent, 315

Gallitto, A., 269
Gantz, Harold, 258
Garforth, F.W., 269, 383
Gaskell, Philip, xiii, 162, 163, 359, 370, 413
Gastrell, Francis (later, Bp. of Chester), 302
Gay, Peter, 269
Gerritsen, Johann, 31-32
Ghent University Library, 321, 355-6
Gibson, W.T., 156
Gilbert, Sir Jeffrey, 173, 353
Glanville, William, 76-7
Goadby, Robert, 391
Godolphin, Sidney Godolphin, Earl of, 199
Goldie, Mark, 440
Goldsmith, Maurice M., 66, 435
Gollop, Mike, 52
Gonzalez-Puertas, L., 293
Goodall, Dr. Charles, 71-72
Gottsched, Johann Christoph, 258
Gough, J.W., 26-7
Goulden, R.J., 161 n.
Graves, John, 71
Gresham College, 76

Grigg, Mrs. Anne, 71-72, 434
Grigg, William, 434
Grotius (de Groot), Hugo, 15
Gualdini, C., 269
The Guardian, 268
Guenellon, Dr. Peter, 71-72, 76-7, 212, 216, 298, 300, 302
Guise, Lady Elizabeth *or* Sir John, 71-72

Halifax, Charles Montagu, Earl of, 199
Halle (Ger.) University Library, 21
Hampden, John *or* Richard, 71-72
Hardwicke, Mary (Cocks), 72
Hardwicke, Philip Yorke, Earl of, 72
Harley, Robert (later, Earl of Oxford), 216
Harley, Sir Edward, 199
Harrison, John, vii, 330
Harrison, Thomas, 65
Harrison, Thomas, printer, London, 435
Harvard Classics, 269
Helmont, Baron F.M. van, 71-72, 212
Henning, B.D., 198 n.
Higgins-Biddle, John, 272-4, 294
Hill, Abraham, 298, 300, 302
Hills, Henry, 86
Histoire des ouvrages des savans (sçavans), 239
The History of the Works of the Learned, 80
Hoadley, Benjamin, 15, 358-9, 451
Hodgson, Norma, 82 n., 211, 217, 298, 302, 337, 349
Hoffman, Francis, 404
Hollis, Thomas, 25, 36, 44, 374, 399, 419
Holt, Sir John, 199, 297, 300, 301

Holy Office (Vatican), 272; Inquisitor General at Venice, 178
Hoole, Charles, 434
Horwitz, Robert H., 434
Houghton, A.A., Jr., 376, 381
Hudson, Dr. John, ix
Hume, David, 59
Hunt, Mrs. Frances, 71-72
Hurd, Richard, Bp. of Worcester, 436
Hussel, Luba, xv
Husson, Pierre, 123-4
Hutchinson, Francis, 396
Hutton, Dr. John, 71-72
Huygens, Konstantijn, the younger, 71-72
Huygens van Zuylichem, Christian, 71-72
Hyde, Mrs. Mary, *see* Lady Mary Eccles
Hyde, Thomas, 382

Imperial Moscow University Student Seminar, 187
Inzodda, F., 269
Israel, Jonathan I., 15 n., 56-7, 127

Jefcoate, G., 388
Jenson, John R., 405
John Rylands Library, Manchester, 419
Johnston, Charlotte S. (Ware), 69
Johnstoun, James, 71-72, 77, 198-9, 212, 297, 300, 302
Jones, G.P., 50
Journal de Trevoux, 240

Kelley, A.M., publisher, New York, 194, 196, 204, 205
Kelly, Patrick Hyde, Chap. IV passim
Kenyon, Sir Frederic G., 209, 211
Keynes (Geoffrey) Collection, xx, 31

Keynes (John Maynard) Collection, xx
Kidder, Richard, Bp. of Bath and Wells, 77
King, Jeremy, 374
King, Peter (Locke's nephew; later, Baron King), vii, 2, 81, 83, 300, 302, 329, 330, 336, 349, 363-4, 375, 386, 402
King, Peter, 7th Baron King (later, 1st Earl of Lovelace), 26, 325, 349, 374-5, 385, 452
King, Richard, 173, 362-6, 385, 389-90, 436
King, William, Archbp. of Dublin, 386
Kleerkooper, M.M., 124
Klibansky, Raymond, 4, 26
Kneller, Sir Godfrey, 298, 302
Kołłątaj, Hugo, 155
Kossmann, E.H., 313

La Bruyère, Jean de, 217-18
La Fontaine, Jean de, 239
La Vega, Garcilaso de, 32
Labussière, ——, 319
A Lady's Religion, 287
Landon, Richard, xv
Languet, Hubert, 434
Laslett, Peter, vii n.; ch. II passim; 330, 365, 366 n., 382, 429
last will & testament (Locke's), 5, 271, 330, 389, 390-91, 399, 452
Law, Edmund, Bp., 116, 399, 422, 431-34, 462
Le Blanc, Jean Bernard, Abbé, 437, 462
Le Cène, Charles, 1
Le Clerc, Jean, viii, xiv, 2, 54, 57-8, 61, 71-72, 76-7, 78, 81, 83, 122, 149, 151, 169-70, 212, 236, 256-7, 271, 284, 286, 298, 300, 302, 313, 318-19, 323, 388, 390, 395,

399, 413, 427, 432, 435, 451
Leers, Reinier, 298
Leibniz, Gottfried Wilhelm, 123, 180, 204, 297, 300, 386, 389-90, 397, 457
Leijoncrona, Christopher, 199
Leipzig Fair Catalogue, 125
Lemaire, Paul, 189
A Letter to a Friend concerning Usury, 193, 207
Lewine, J., 133
Li, Ming Hsun, 191
Library Company of Philadelphia, 324
library locations, xx-xxii
licences to publish, 32, 187, 192-3
Licensing Act (1695), 220
Liddell, Robert, 199
Lidell, Ecbert, 216
Lilburne, Richard, 315, 366
Limborch, Francis, 212
Limborch, Philipp van, 1, 4-5, 14, 127, 271, 314, 375-6, 386, 389-90, 396, 397, 427-9
Lindenbaum, Peter, 69 n.
The Literary Magazine, 182
Liverpool University Library, 222-3
Livy, 59
Locker, John, 313
Lockhart, Martha, 71-72
Lockman, John, 456
Loeb Classical Library, 38, 118
Lofft, Capel, 186
Logan, James, 70 n., 82, 217, 324
The London Chronicle, 26, 106, 463
The London Gazette, xiii-xiv, 69, 75, 80, 156, 210, 215, 271, 273
Long, P.A., vii n.
Long, Thomas, 1
Lovelace, Earl of, *see* Peter King, 7th Baron King

Lovelace Collection, vii, ix, 330, 395, 430
Lowe, Solomon, 454
Lowndes, William, 191, 199
Lyde, Cornelius, 198-9
Lytton, Edward Bulwer, Baron Lytton, 215

McCarthy, Denis, 189
McCulloch, J.R., 208
Machiavelli, Niccolò, 59
Malebranche, Nicolas, 127, 378, 433
Marchesi, Tullio, 269
Marchesini, G., 269
Marcuzzi, Antonio, 269
Marlow, Mr., 216
Masham, Damaris Cudworth, Lady, vii, 3, 71-72, 76-7, 81, 198-9, 204, 216, 298, 300, 301, 314, 433, 448, 449
Masham, (Mrs.) Esther, 302, 376
Masham, Sir Francis, vii, 76, 199
Masham, Francis Cudworth, vii, 78, 122, 240, 286, 330, 365
Mazel, David, 63-5
Meadows, Sir Philip, 199
Mellon, Paul, vii, 382
Memoirs of Literature, 182
Migne, J.P., 293
Millar, Andrew, 25
The Millenial Harbinger, 26
Milner, John, x
Milton, John (1608-1674), 69, 268
Milton, John R., 72 n., 365, 437
Minnesota University Library, 405
Mitchell, William Andrew, xiv
Molesworth, Robert (later, Viscount Molesworth), 76-7, 199
Molyneux, Samuel, 386
Molyneux, Thomas, 79-81, 212, 217, 302, 315, 386

Molyneux, William, xiv, 72, 76-7, 149, 198-9, 212, 216, 297, 299, 300, 315, 386, 390, 450
Monmouth, Charles Mordaunt, Earl of (later, Earl of Peterborough), 71-72, 199, 212, 298, 301
Montague, Charles (later, Earl of Halifax), 77
Montaigne, Michel de, 127, 242, 244, 258
Montanari, P., 269
Montuori, Mario, 3, 26
The Moral and Entertaining Magazine, 391
Mordaunt, Col. Lewis, 199
Murray, John, 189

Naert, Emilienne, 189
The Naked Truth, 276
Nantes, Edict of, 1
National Library of Scotland, 70
Neill, Desmond, xv, 104, 234, 296, 393
The New Palgrave, 191
Newton, Isaac, 71-72, 76, 206, 298, 300, 302, 313-15, 365
Nichols, J., 403
Nidditch, Peter H., xiii; ch. III passim; 210, 295
Noodt, Gerard, 15, 20
Noorthouck, John, 419
Norris, John, 91, 93-5, 97, 363, 365, 378
Northey, Sir Edward, 319-20
Norton, Roger, printing house, 38
Nourse, John, 172
Nynehead Collection (at Bodleian Library), 395
Nynehead version of *Some Thoughts*, 209

Oates (Masham residence), 122, 301, 326

Oldenburg, Henry, 315, 363, 366, 385
O'Moore, Haven, 376
Otago, University of (New Zealand), xxii
Ouvrier, Siegmund, 259, 269
Owen, John, Oxford Vice-Chancellor, 305–306
Oxoniensia, 156

Palmer, Samuel, printer, 39 n., 408
Pascal, Blaise, 127
Paterson, W., 442
Patrick, Dr. Simon, 392
Pawling, Robert, 212
Pelt, Susanna, 123
Pembroke, Thomas Herbert, Earl of, 71–72, 77, 81, 199, 212, 216, 297, 300, 301, 365
Penn, William, 21
Pepys, Samuel, 76–7, 216
Pforzheimer (Carl H.) Library, New York, 390–91
Philosophical Transactions of the Royal Society, viii, 318, 326, 366, 431
Picart, Bernard, 127
Picinelli, Lauro Maria, 262
Pierpont Morgan Library, New York, 359–61
Pilgrim Trust, vii
Pitt, Mrs., 216
Pivano, Fernanda, 269
Plomer, H.R., 86
Pococke, Edward, 71–72, 362, 365
Poems on Affairs of State, 305–309
Pogliaghi, O., 269
Polish culture, 266
Political Aphorisms (1691), 65
Pollexfen, John, 199
Pope, Alexander, 362

Popple, William, 4–5, 18, 27, 71–72, 76–7, 199, 212, 300, 302, 427, 431
Porter, Noah, 446
The Post-Boy, xiv, 198, 202
Powys, Sir Littleton, 298, 301
presentation copy lists, 70–72, 75–7, 78, 81, 198, 204–205, 212, 215–16, 297–8, 300, 301–302 (For separate list, see also *Corr.* viii. 454–8)
Price, Richard, 11
Princeton University Library, 351
Pringle-Pattison, Andrew Seth, 189
Proast, Jonas, x, 1–2, 5, 22–4, 431
Probyn, C.T., 303
Public Record Office, 374, 376–7
Pufendorf, Samuel von, 15, 314

Quick, R.H., 269

Ramsey, Ian, 293
Rawlins, John or William, printing house, 38
Ray, John, 314
Raynard (Reynard) the Fox, 239
Reed, Sarah, 232
Remonstrants' Church Library, Amsterdam, 3, 395
Rhodes, Dennis E., 3
Rich, Jeremiah, 379, 383
Richardson, Thomas, 298, 300
Rogers, G.A.J., xiii, 155, 266
Rollin, Charles, 225–6, 264–5
Rosicka, Janina, 155, 266
Rousseau, Jean-Jacques, 251, 252, 464
Rousset de Missy, Jean, 56
Roxburghe Club, 209
Royal Library at the Hague, 14, 31, 322, 345, 355
Royal Society, viii, xiv, 313
Rush, Benjamin & Richard, 106
Russell, Lady Rachel, 392

Sächsische Landesbibliothek, Dresden, 168
Sainati, Vittorio, 384
Sainsbury, Noel, 437
St. John, J.A., 303, 383, 429–30
Sallwürk, Ernst von, 269
Sanford, Col.E.C., 395
Sare, Richard, 86
Sauvy, Anne, 272
Schankula, H.A.S., 330
Schelte, Henri, 122
Schick, Karl, 72
Schiff, John M., 72
Schiff, Mortimer L., 72
Schøsler, Jørn, 123, 127–8, 459
Schuster, Moritz, 269
Scolar Press, Menston, Yorks., 211
Seitz, Johann Christian, 20–21
Seneca, 177
Shackleton, Robert, xv, 419
Shaftesbury, Earls of, *see under* Cooper, A. A.
Shaftesbury, Margaret Cooper, Countess of, 71–72, 359–61, 385
Shanafelt, Gary W., xv
Sheffield, Edmund, Duke of Buckinghamshire, 127
Sheffield University Library, 211
Sheppard, Sir Fleetwood, 79, 199, 216
Shrewsbury, Charles Talbot, Duke of, 199
Sibelius, Dr. Caspar, 71–72
Sidney, Algernon, 392
Simmons, J.S.G., xv, 187 n., 464
Simon, Richard, 435
Sina, Mario, 293, 303, 429
Slater, H., bookseller, 388
Sloane, Dr. Hans (later, Sir Hans), 76–7, 81, 298, 300, 302, 316–17, 392
Smith, Humfry, 362, 365, 385
Smith, John, 282
Smith, John (commissioner of the Treasury), 199
Smith, Mrs., 212
Soave, Francesco, 383
Social Sciences and Humanities Research Council of Canada, xv
Soldania, 32
Somers, John Somers, Baron, 71–72, 76–7, 81, 199, 213, 297, 301
Souchai, ——, 251
South, Dr. Robert, 81, 298, 300, 302, 306
Spanheim, Ezechiel, 396
The Spectator, 268
Spencer, Charles, Lord Spencer (later, Earl of Sunderland), 199, 300, 301
Spieckermann, Marie-Louise, 145, 293, 346
Stamford, Thomas Grey, Earl of, 199
Stationers' Company, London, 23, 24, 75
Stephens, John, xv, 12, 26, 44, 230, 355, 422, 463
Stephens, William, 286, 436
Stepney, George, 205, 300
Stewart, M.A., 303, 326
Stillingfleet, Edward, Bp. of Worcester, ix, 83, 116, 118–19; ch. VII; 447
Strahan, William, 25
Straus, Ralph, 452 n.
Stringer, Thomas, 75
subscribers' lists, 50, 223, 339, 353, 388
Sully, Maximilien de Béthune, Duc de, 59
Swift, Jonathan, 303
Sydenham, Thomas, viii, 71, 305, 311, 314–15, 327, 362, 379
Synge, Edward, 435

The Tatler, 268

Taylor, Jeremy, Bp., 276
Tegg, Thomas, publisher, London, 429
Tenison, Dr. Thomas, Archbp. of Canterbury, 199, 297, 300, 301
Tennemann, Wilhelm Gottlieb, 147-8
Terence, 127
Teut (Marcus Antonius or Willem), Mr., 216
Thoemmes Antiquarian Books/ Press, Bristol, 19, 136, 160, 394, 426
Thomas, Dr. David, 67, 69, 71-72
Thomas, Dr., Master of Christ's College, Cambridge, 36
Thomson, Ann, 247
Thurot, François, 429
Tilladet, La Marque, 241
Tillotson, John, Archbp. of Canterbury, 198 n., 213, 339
Tindall, Matthew, 297, 300, 302
Toinard, Nicolas, 318, 320, 349, 375, 432
Toland, John, 298
Tonson, Jacob, 230
Tooke, J. Horne, 102
Traister, Daniel, 247
Trapp, Ernst Christian, 259
Treby, Sir George, 76-7
Treby, Sir John, 199, 213, 216, 297, 300-301
Trevor, Sir William, 199
Trumbull, Sir William, 77, 199, 298, 300
Turner, Dr. Francis, Bp. of Ely, 71-72
Tyrrell, James, 67, 71-72, 76, 216, 297, 300, 302, 396

Valpy, A.J., 189
Vergil, 127
Vernon, —— (James?), 199
Viano, C.A., 27, 381, 383-4

Vincent, ——, 251
Vox Populi, Vox Dei (1709), 65

Wainwright, Arthur P., 329-30, 383
Wall, John, 306
Walls, George, 71-72, 76, 298, 300
Warrington, Henry Booth, Earl of 76
Wattendorf, Ludwig, 269
Watts, John, 170
Webb, Francis, 462
Wehmeyer, Annette, xx n.
Weiz, Friedrich A., 258
Weller, E.O., 125
Wells, Edward, 432
West, Richard, D.D., 442
Wetstein, firm, publishers, Amsterdam, 124, 272, 284
Wheeler, Marcus C.C., 187 n.
Wilburn, Raymond, 189
Wilken, C.H., 436
will & codicil (Locke's) see last will & testament
Willis, Richard, 444
Winckler, Carl, 293
Wnorowski, F., 270
Wohlers, Heinz, 269
Wolf, Edwin, 2d: 36, 70 n., 217
Woodward, John, 302
Woozley, A.D., 189
Wright, William, Alderman (?), 7
Wynne, John, xiv, 84, 297, 300, 302

Yard, —— (Robert?), 199
Yolton, John W., xv, 189, 209, 212, 269, 439, 444
Yonge, Sir Walter, 71-72, 199, 21
York University Library, North York, Ont., xiv n.
Yorke, Henry, 50

Znosko, Jan, 270

Portrait of Locke from no. 35 (1765).

Reproduced by courtesy of the
Thomas Fisher Rare Books Library, University of Toronto.

EPISTOLA
de
TOLERANTIA
ad
Clariſſimum Virum
T. A. R. P. T. O. L. A.
Scripta à
P. A. P. O. I. L. A.

GOUDÆ,
Apud JUSTUM AB HOEVE.
cIɔ Iɔc Lxxxix.

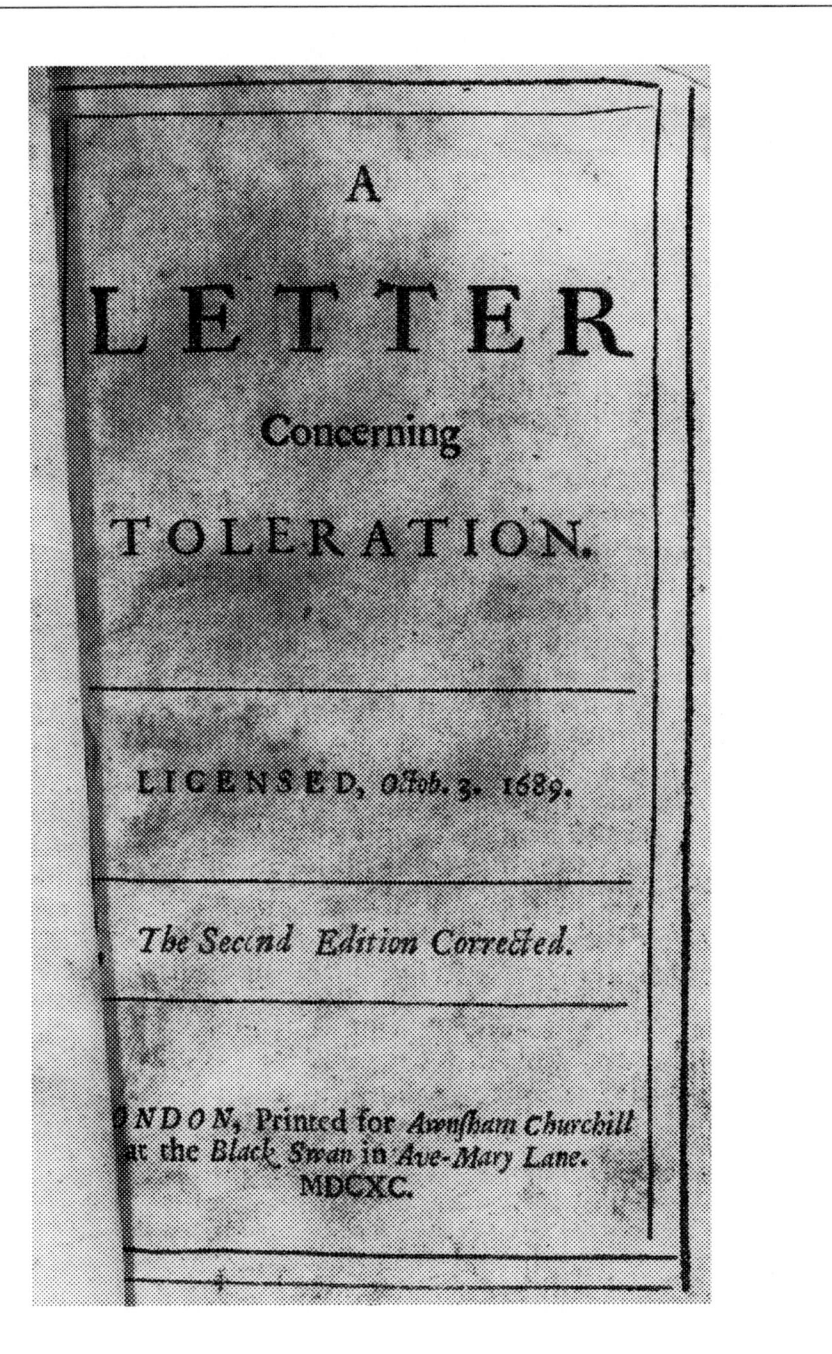

No. 4.

Reproduced by courtesy of the
Thomas Fisher Rare Books Library, University of Toronto.

LETTERS CONCERNING TOLERATION

BY IOHN LOCKE

LONDON, PRINTED FOR A. MILLAR, H. WOODFALL, I. WHISTON AND B. WHITE, I. RIVINGTON, L. DAVIS AND C. REYMERS, R. BALDWIN, HAWES CLARKE AND COLLINS, W. IOHNSTON, W. OWEN, S. CROWDER, T. LONGMAN, B. LAW, C. RIVINGTON, E. DILLY, R. WITHY, C. AND R. WARE, S. BAKER, T. PAYNE, A. SHUCKBURGH, M. RICHARDSON

MDCCLXV

—— FOR ON EARTH,
WHO AGAINST FAITH AND CONSCIENCE CAN BE HEARD
INFALLIBLE? YET MANY WILL PRESUME:
WHENCE HEAVIE PERSECUTION ——

TWO TREATISES OF Government:

In the former,
The *falſe Principles*, and *Foundation*
OF
Sir *ROBERT FILMER*,
And his FOLLOWERS,
ARE
Detected and **Overthrown**.
The latter is an
ESSAY
CONCERNING THE
True Original, Extent, and End
OF
Civil Government.

LONDON,
Printed for *Awnſham Churchill*, at the *Black Swan* in *Ave-Mary-Lane*, by *Amen-Corner*, 1690.

No. 29.

Reproduced by courtesy of the
Thomas Fisher Rare Books Library, University of Toronto.

(205)

Freedom, without being subjected to the Will or Authority of any other Man.

55. Children, I confess are not born in this full state of Equality, though they are born to it. Their Parents have a sort of Rule and Jurisdiction over them when they come into the World, and for some time after; but 'tis but a temporary one. The Bonds of this Subjection are like the Swadling Cloths they are wrapt up in, and supported by in the weakness of their Infancy. Age and Reason as they grow up, loosen them till at length they drop quite off, and leave a Man at his own free Disposal.

56. *Adam* was created a perfect Man, his Body and Mind in full possession of their Strength and Reason, and so was capable from the first Instant of his being to provide for his own Support and Preservation, and govern his Actions according to the Dictates of the Law of Reason which God had implanted in him. From him the World is peopled with his Descendants, who are all born Infants, weak and helpless, without Knowledge or Understanding. But to supply the Defects of this imperfect State, till the Improvement of Growth and Age hath removed them, *Adam* and *Eve*, and after them all Parents were by the Law of Nature, under an obligation to preserve, nourish, and educate the Children they had begotten, not as their own Workmanship, but the Workmanship of their own Maker, the Almighty, to whom they were to be accountable for them.

57. The Law that was to govern *Adam*, was the same that was to govern all his Posterity, the Law of Reason. But his Off-spring having ano- ther

(206)

ther way of entrance into the World, different from him, by a natural Birth, that produced them ignorant and without the use of Reason, they were not presently under that Law; for no Body can be under a Law, which is not promulgated to him, and this Law being promulgated or made known by Reason only, he that is not come to the Use of his Reason, cannot be said to be under this Law; and *Adam*'s Children being not presently as soon as born under this Law of Reason were not presently free. For Law, in its true Notion, is not so much the Limitation as the direction of a free and intelligent Agent to his proper Interest, and prescribes no farther than is for the general Good of those under that Law. Could they be happier without it, the Law, as an useless thing, would of it self vanish, and that ill deserves the Name of Confinement which hedges us in only from Bogs and Precipices. So that, however it may be mistaken, the end of Law is not to abolish or restrain, but to preserve and enlarge Freedom; for in all the states of created beings capable of Laws, where there is no Law, there is no Freedom. For Liberty is to be free from restraint and violence from others which cannot be, where there is no Law: not, as we are told, *A Liberty for every Man to do what he lists*. (For who could be free, when every other Man's Humour might domineer over him?) But a Liberty to dispose, and order, as he lists, his Person, Actions, Possessions, and his whole Property, within the Allowance of those Laws under which he is, and therein not to be subject to the arbitrary Will of another, but freely follow his own.

Pages from Locke's copy of no. 31, showing some of his corrections.

Reproduced by courtesy of Christ's College, Cambridge.

AN
ESSAY
CONCERNING
𝔥𝔲𝔪𝔞𝔫𝔢 𝔘𝔫𝔡𝔢𝔯𝔰𝔱𝔞𝔫𝔡𝔦𝔫𝔤.

In Four BOOKS.

Writtten by *JOHN LOCKE*, Gent.

The Second Edition, with large Additions.

Quam bellum est velle confiteri potius nescire quod nescias, quam ista effutientem nauseare, atque ipsum sibi displicere! Cic. de Natur. Deor. *l.* 1.

LONDON,

Printed for **Thomas Dring**, at the *Harrow*, over-against the *Inner-Temple Gate* in *Fleet-street*; and **Samuel Manship**, at the *Black Bull* in *Cornhill*, near the *Royal Exchange*, MDCXCIV.

Ashley Atwood

Boyle Bellamont Bridge

Clark le Clerc Carlyn Calverly Charleton
Chickley Clutterbuck
Duke Delme Taranta

E β!

Freke Tuly Freis Forfar Fermin

Grig Goodall Guenellon Guise

Hauden Huggens Helmont Mr Houl Hutton

J Johnson

K

L Mr Lockart

Monmouth Masham

Newton

O

Pembroke pople Ed Pocock
Queen
R
Stephen Somers Syl C Shaftsbury Silchey
Tilotson Tyrrell Thomas
U
W Wally
X
Yonge

A distribution list for no. 62.

Reproduced by permission of the
Bodleian Library, University of Oxford, shelfmark MS Locke c.25 fol. 50ᵛ.

ESSAI PHILOSOPHIQUE
CONCERNANT
L'ENTENDEMENT
HUMAIN,

Où l'on montre quelle est l'Etenduë de nos Connoissances certaines, & la Maniere dont nous y parvenons.

Traduit de l'Anglois de Mr. LOCKE,
Par PIERRE COSTE,
Nouvelle Edition, revûë, corrigée, & augmentée par l'Auteur.

Quàm bellum est velle confiteri potius nescire quod nescias, quàm ista effutientem nauseare, atque ipsum sibi displicere!
Cic. de Nat. Deor. Lib. I.

Suivant la Copie imprimée
A AMSTERDAM,
Chez HENRI SCHELTE.
M DCC XXIII.

FURTHER Considerations

Concerning

Raising the Value
OF
MONEY.

WHEREIN

Mr. *Lowndes*'s Arguments for it in his late Report concerning *An Essay for the Amendment of the Silver Coins*, are particularly Examined.

The Second Edition Corrected.

LONDON,
Printed for *A.* and *J. Churchil* at the *Black Swan* in *Pater-Noster-Row*, MDCXCV.

SEVERAL PAPERS

Relating to

Money, Intereſt and *Trade*, &c.

Writ upon ſeveral Occaſions, and Publiſhed at different Times.

By Mr. *JOHN LOCKE*,

LONDON:

Printed for *A.* and *J. Churchill*, at the *Black-Swan* in *Pater-Noſter-Row*, 1696.

SOME THOUGHTS CONCERNING Education.

Doctrina vires promovet insitas,
Rectiq; cultus pectora roborant :
Utcunq; defecere mores,
Dedecorant bene nata culpæ.

Hor. L. IV. Od. 4.

The Fourth Edition Enlarged.

LONDON,
Printed for *A.* and *J. Churchill*, at the
Black Swan in *Pater-noster-row*, 1699.

No. 168.

Reproduced from a personal copy.

THE
REASONABLENESS
OF
Christianity,

As delivered in the
SCRIPTURES.

LONDON:

Printed for *Awnsham* and *John Churchil*, at the *Black Swan* in *Pater-Noster-Row*. 1695.

London 12 June 1695. Wee agree and Covenant with mr John Locke, his Executrs Administratrs and assignes that wee will pay to him the said John Locke his Executrs Administratrs, or Assignes, Six shillings p sheet for as many sheets as a booke Intitulod The Reasonableness of Christianity as delivered in the holy Scriptures, shall amount onto, to be printed of the same page and Letter as his booke of Education — for every Impression wee shall print of the said booke dureing his Life, this first Impression not to exceed fourtxix hundred, & no Impression afterwards to be above one thousand bookes, & no Edition to be made dureing his Life without his knowledge & Consent, and if it shall happen that he the said Jn Locke shall dy before a second Impression of the said booke, then wee promise and Covenant to pay to his Excecutrs Adminrs or assignes, six sheets more of sheet in full Consideration for the said Copy

Awnsham & Jn Churchill

W allso promise to deliver mr Lok Twenty two: bookes bound of every Impression of the above mentioned booke

A & Jn Churchill

Contract for no. 229; cf. p. 272.

Reproduced by permission of the Bodleian Library, University of Oxford, shelfmark MS. Locke b.1 fol. 178.

QUE
LA RELIGION
CHRETIENNE
EST
TRES-RAISONNABLE,

Telle qu'elle nous est representée dans

L'ECRITURE SAINTE.

Traduit de l'Anglois, imprimé à Londres, chez A. & J. Churchill.

A AMSTERDAM,
Chez Henri Wetstein. 1696.

A LETTER TO *Edward* Ld Bishop of *Worcester*,

Concerning some

PASSAGES

RELATING TO

Mr. LOCKE's Essay

OF

Humane Understanding:

IN A LATE

Discourse of his Lordships,

IN

Vindication of the Trinity.

By *JOHN LOCKE*, Gent.

LONDON: Printed for *A.* and *J. Churchill*, at the *Black Swan* in *Paternoster-Row*. 1697.

ΕΛΑΙΟΦΟΡΙΑ.   45

Quem nunc invenies titulum, quæ nomina finges?
Hæretici eripinus jam tua Templa Tibi.
　　　　　　N. HODGES *A. B. ex Æd. Ch.*

PAX regit Augusti, quem vicit Julius, Orbem:
　Ille fago factus clarior, ille togâ.
Hos sua Roma vocat magnos, & numina credit,
　Hic quod iit mundi victor, & ille quies.
Tu bellum ut pacem popalis das, unus utrisq;
　Major es; ipse orbem vincis, & ipse regis.
Non hominem è Cœlo missum Te credimus, unus
　Sic poteras binos qui superare Deos!
　　　　　　　　　　J. LOCKE *ex Æd.Christ.*

PAX peregrina diu binas nunc uniet oras,
　Surget ab armato funere viva falus:
Undiq; lætantes animantur lædere Belgæ
　E Iano Anglorum corpore corpus habent:
Unde furius medici fimul & medicamina, vulnus
　Quod bellum infixit fanat amica quies:
Dum nimiùm gestiunt de falfo flumine Belgæ,
　Dicunt, plus aloes quam falis æquor habet.

Ad PROTECTOREM.

Magne Leo, qui Marte poces; Germania vires,
　At placidam victrix Anglia fentit opem:
Victorum princeps, arctoq; voluminis victos
　Cingis; Tu centrum, circulus orbis erit.
Uni cæterna duas gentes conplectitur, ipsâm
　Et terram & pontum continet una manus:
Sedata est populi rabies nec Belgica classis,
　Nec loquitur pelagi sævior ira ruinas:
Pace silent hostes, bello, formidine languent,
　Sollicitat mentes terror amorq; suas:

G　　　　　　　　　　　　　　　　　　Quid

MUSARUM
OXONIENSIUM
ΕΛΑΙΟΦΟΡΙΑ.
SIVE,
Ob Fœdera, Auspiciis
SERENISSIMI
OLIVERI
Reipub. Ang. Scot. & Hiber.
DOMINI PROTECTORIS,
Inter Rempub. Britannicam & *Ordines*
Fœderatos Belgii Feliciter
STABILITA,

Gentis Togatæ ad vada Isidis
Celeusma Metricum.

OXONIÆ,
Excudebat *Leonardus Lichfield* Academiæ
Typographus 1654.

No. 251.

Reproduced by permission of the
Bodleian Library, University of Oxford, shelfmark B. 13.4 Linc (10).

Musarum OXONIENSIUM

COme see what Peace can doe, beyond th'successe
Of Nature, we are joyn'd to th'Continent,
Olive's of Peace, of Triumph Palme's the signe,
Lets build our ships with those, no more with Pine.
Come Traveller, save thy voyage now that wee
Short of the Line have a Pacifick Sea.

EDWARD CAMPION
ex Æde Ch.

IF Greece with so much mirth did entertaine
Her *Arg* comming, laden home againe:
With what loud mirth, and triumph shall we greet
The with't approaches of our welcome Fleet:
When of that prize our ships doe us possesse,
Whereof their Fleece was but an emblem, *Peace*?
Then the loud musick of the warbling Spheare,
Whose welcome voice found sweeter in our eare,
And ravishing more then those, doth plainly show
That sweetest harmony we to discord owe.
Each Sea-mans voice pronouncing Peace doth charme
And seems a Siren, but that 't hath lesse harme
And dangerin't, and yet like them doth please
Above all other and make us love the Sea.
W'have Heaven in this Peace, like soules above,
W'have nought to doe now, but admire and love.
Glory of *Warre* is victory, but here
Both glorious be, 'cause neither's conquerer.
T'had been lesse honour if it might be sed
They fought with those that could be conquered.
Our reunited Seas, like streams that grow
Into one River doe the smoother flow:
Where Ships no longer grapple, but like those,
The loving Seamen in embraces close,
We need no Fire-ships now, a nobler flame
Of love doth us Proceed, whereby our name

ΕΥΧΟΦΟΡΙΑ

Shall shine more glorious, a flame as pure
As those of Heaven, and shall as long endure:
This shall direct our ships, and he that steers
Shall not consult heavens fires, but those he beares
In his own breast. Let *Lilly* threaten Warrs:
While this Conjunction lasts wee'l feare no starrs.
Our ships are now must beneficiall growne,
Since they bring home no spoiles but what's their owne,
Unto these branchlesse *Pines* our forward spring
Owes better fruit, then Autumn's wont to bring:
Which give not only gemms and Indian ore,
But adde at once whole Nations to our shore:
Nay if to make a World's but to compose
The difference of things, and make them close
In mutuall amitie, and cause Peace to creep
Out of the jarring Chaos of the deep:
Our ships doe this, so that while others take
Their course about the World, Ours a World make.

J. LOCKE *Student of Ch.Ch.*

COme now Philosophers, that by the line
Of art have found the depth of natures mine:
And learne this famous Paradox from hence
Three Spheares are turned by one Intelligence:
Now may *Pythagoras*'s conceit revive,
For by one Happy Soule all bodyes thrive.

JOS. STRETCH *of Ball. Coll.*

SHould I but ranke thy Honours here alone
Each letter must curse *Polysyllabon*:
No Bounds, no Prison honour knowes in Thee,
Charging through Fame unto Eternity.

DISCOURSES
ON THE
Being of a God,
AND THE
Immortality of the Soul;
OF THE
Weakneſs of Man;
And concerning the Way of
Preſerving Peace with Men:

Being ſome of the ESSAYS written in *French* by Meſſieurs du PORT ROYAL.

Render'd into *Engliſh* by the late JOHN LOCK, *Gent.*

LONDON:
Printed and Sold by *J. Downing* in *Bartholomew-Cloſe* near *Weſt-Smithfield*, 1712.

No. 313.

Reproduced by permission of the
Bodleian Library, University of Oxford, shelfmark Vet.A.4.f.1770.

OBSERVATIONS UPON
THE GROWTH AND CULTURE
OF VINES AND OLIVES:
THE PRODUCTION OF SILK:
THE PRESERVATION OF FRUITS.

WRITTEN AT THE REQUEST OF
THE EARL OF SHAFTESBURY,
TO WHOM IT IS INSCRIBED:
BY MR. JOHN LOCKE.

NOW FIRST PRINTED FROM THE
ORIGINAL MANUSCRIPT IN
THE POSSESSION OF THE
PRESENT EARL OF
SHAFTESBURY.

LONDON:
PRINTED FOR W. SANDBY, IN FLEET STREET.
M DCC LXVI.

No. 327.

Reproduced by permission of the
Osler Memorial Library, McGill University, Montreal.

SOME
Familiar Letters
BETWEEN
Mr. *LOCKE,*
AND
Several of his Friends.

LONDON:

Printed for A. and J. CHURCHILL at the
Black Swan in *Pater-noster Row.* 1708.

No. 346.

Reproduced by courtesy of the
Thomas Fisher Rare Books Library, University of Toronto.

THE
WORKS
OF
JOHN LOCKE Esq;

VOL. II.

CONTAINING,

Some Confiderations of the Confequences of the lowering of Intereft, and raifing the Value of Money. In a Letter fent to a Member of Parliament. 1691.

Short Obfervations on a printed Paper, entitled, *For encouraging the coining Silver Money in England, and after for keeping it here.*

Further Obfervations concerning raifing the Value of Money. Wherein Mr. *Lowndes*'s Arguments for it, in his late Report concerning *An Effay for the Amendment of the Silver Coin*, are particularly examined.

Two Treatifes of Government. In the Former, the falfe Principles and Foundation of Sir Robert *Filmer*, and his Followers, are detected and overthrown. The Latter is an Effay concerning the true Original, Extent, and End of Civil Government.

A Letter concerning Toleration.

A Second Letter concerning Toleration.

A Third Letter for Toleration: To the Author of the Third Letter concerning Toleration.

The Reafonablenefs of Chriftianity, as deliver'd in the Scriptures.

A Vindication of *The Reafonablenefs of Chriftianity*, from Mr. *Edwards*'s Reflections.

A Second Vindication of *The Reafonablenefs of Chriftianity*.

LONDON,
Printed for JOHN CHURCHILL at the Black Swan in *Pater-nofter-Row.* M.DCC.XIV.

No. 363.

Reproduced by courtesy of the
Thomas Fisher Rare Books Library, University of Toronto.

THE
WORKS
OF
JOHN LOCKE Esq;

VOL. III.

CONTAINING,

Some Thoughts concerning Education.

An Essay for the Understanding St. *Paul's* Epistles, by consulting St. *Paul* himself.

A Paraphrase and Notes on the Epistle of St. *Paul* to the *Galatians*.

A Paraphrase and Notes on St. *Paul's* First and Second Epistle to the *Corinthians*.

A Paraphrase and Notes on his Epistle to the *Romans*.

A Paraphrase and Notes on his Epistle to the *Ephesians*.

POSTHUMOUS WORKS, *Viz.*
I. Of the Conduct of the Understanding.
II. An Examination of P. *Malebranche's* Opinion, of *Seeing all Things in God.*
III. A Discourse of Miracles.
IV. Part of a Fourth Letter for Toleration.
V. Memoirs relating to the Life of *Anthony* first Earl of *Shaftsbury*.
VI. His new Method of a Common-Place-Book, written originally in *French*, and now translated into *English*.
Familiar Letters between Mr. *Locke* and several of his Friends.

LONDON;

Printed for JOHN CHURCHILL, at the *Black Swan*, in *Pater-Noster-Row*. MDCCXIV.

OEUVRES
DIVERSES
DE
MONSIEUR
JEAN LOCKE.

A ROTTERDAM,
Chez FRITSCH ET BÖHM,
MDCCX.

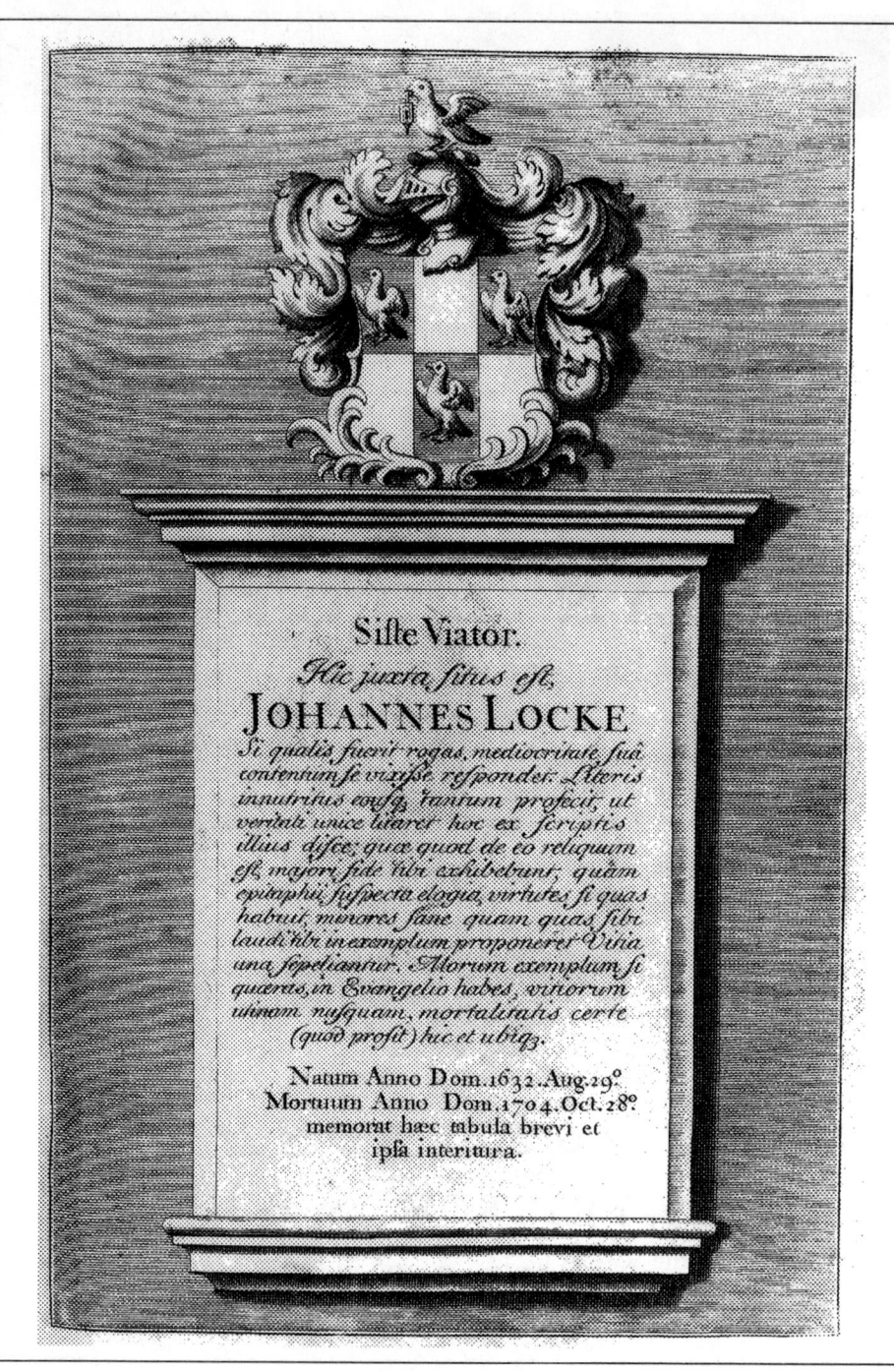

Epitaph, copied from his monument in the church at High Laver, Essex; printed in *Works* (1714), no. 363.

Reproduced from a personal copy.

Also Available from Thoemmes Press

John LOCKE
Of the Conduct of the Understanding
(From the *Posthumous Works*)

New introduction by **John W. Yolton,** Rutgers University

ISBN 1 85506 225 9 : 160pp : Pb : 1706 edition : £12.99 / $19.95

John LOCKE
The Reasonableness of Christianity
As Delivered in the Scriptures

New introduction by **Victor Nuovo,** Middlebury College, Vermont

ISBN 1 85506 522 3 : 440pp : Pb : 1794 edition : £17.99 / $29.95

Victor NUOVO (Edited with an Introduction)
John Locke and Christianity
Contemporary Responses to the Reasonableness of Christianity

ISBN 1 85506 540 1 : 328pp : Pb : 1997 : £14.95 / $24.95
ISBN 1 85506 539 8 : 328pp : Hb : 1997 : £45.00 / $72.00

Jean S. YOLTON (Editor)
A Locke Miscellany

ISBN 1 85506 009 4 : 392pp : Hb : 1990 : £37.50 / $48.00

John W. YOLTON
Locke and the Way of Ideas

ISBN 1 85506 226 7 : 248pp : Pb : 1956 edition : £15.99 / $28.95

To order any of these titles, please contact Thoemmes Press either at our UK or US address listed at the front of this book.